PHILIP'S

WORLD ATLAS
& GAZETTEER

The Gazetteer of Nations
Text
Keith Lye

The World in Focus
Cartography by Philip's

Picture Acknowledgements
Page 14
Science Photo Library/NOAA

Illustrations
Stefan Chabluk

CONSULTANTS
Philip's are grateful to the following people for acting as specialist geography consultants on '*The World in Focus*' front section:

Professor D. Brunsden, Kings College, University of London, UK
Dr C. Clarke, Oxford University, UK
Dr I. S. Evans, Durham University, UK
Professor P. Haggett, University of Bristol, UK
Professor K. McLachlan, University of London, UK
Professor M. Monmonier, Syracuse University, New York, USA
Professor M-L. Hsu, University of Minnesota, Minnesota, USA
Professor M. J. Tooley, University of St Andrews, UK
Dr T. Unwin, Royal Holloway, University of London, UK

Published in Great Britain in 1998
by George Philip Limited,
an imprint of Reed Consumer Books Limited,
Michelin House, 81 Fulham Road, London SW3 6RB,
and Auckland and Melbourne

Cartography by Philip's

ISBN 0–540–07559–0

A CIP catalogue record for this book is available
from the British Library.

Printed in China

PHILIP'S

WORLD ATLAS
& GAZETTEER

SIXTH EDITION

IN ASSOCIATION WITH
THE ROYAL GEOGRAPHICAL SOCIETY
WITH THE INSTITUTE OF BRITISH GEOGRAPHERS

Contents

v

World Statistics: Countries

This alphabetical list includes all the countries and territories of the world. If a territory is not completely independent, then the country it is associated with is named. The area figures give the total area of land, inland water and ice. The population figures are 1997 estimates. The annual income is the Gross National Product per capita in US dollars. The figures are the latest available, usually 1995.

Country/Territory	Area km² Thousands	Area miles² Thousands	Population Thousands	Capital	Annual Income US $
Adélie Land (France)	432	167	0.03	–	–
Afghanistan	652	252	23,000	Kabul	300
Albania	28.8	11.1	3,600	Tirana	670
Algeria	2,382	920	29,300	Algiers	1,600
American Samoa (US)	0.20	0.08	62	Pago Pago	2,600
Andorra	0.45	0.17	75	Andorra-la-Vella	14,000
Angola	1,247	481	11,200	Luanda	410
Anguilla (UK)	0.1	0.04	10	The Valley	6,800
Antigua & Barbuda	0.44	0.17	66	St John's	6,390
Argentina	2,767	1,068	35,400	Buenos Aires	8,030
Armenia	29.8	11.5	3,800	Yerevan	730
Aruba (Netherlands)	0.19	0.07	70	Oranjestad	17,500
Ascension Is. (UK)	0.09	0.03	1.5	Georgetown	–
Australia	7,687	2,968	18,400	Canberra	18,720
Austria	83.9	32.4	8,200	Vienna	26,890
Azerbaijan	86.6	33.4	7,700	Baku	480
Azores (Portugal)	2.2	0.87	238	Ponta Delgada	–
Bahamas	13.9	5.4	280	Nassau	11,940
Bahrain	0.68	0.26	605	Manama	7,840
Bangladesh	144	56	124,000	Dhaka	240
Barbados	0.43	0.17	265	Bridgetown	6,560
Belarus	207.6	80.1	10,500	Minsk	2,070
Belgium	30.5	11.8	10,200	Brussels	24,710
Belize	23	8.9	228	Belmopan	2,630
Benin	113	43	5,800	Porto-Novo	370
Bermuda (UK)	0.05	0.02	65	Hamilton	27,000
Bhutan	47	18.1	1,790	Thimphu	420
Bolivia	1,099	424	7,700	La Paz/Sucre	800
Bosnia-Herzegovina	51	20	3,600	Sarajevo	2,600
Botswana	582	225	1,500	Gaborone	3,020
Brazil	8,512	3,286	159,500	Brasília	3,640
British Indian Ocean Terr. (UK)	0.08	0.03	0	–	–
Brunei	5.8	2.2	300	Bandar Seri Begawan	14,500
Bulgaria	111	43	8,600	Sofia	1,330
Burkina Faso	274	106	10,900	Ouagadougou	230
Burma (= Myanmar)	677	261	47,500	Rangoon	1,000
Burundi	27.8	10.7	6,300	Bujumbura	160
Cambodia	181	70	10,500	Phnom Penh	270
Cameroon	176	101	13,900	Yaoundé	650
Canada	9,976	3,852	30,200	Ottawa	19,380
Canary Is. (Spain)	7.3	2.8	1,494	Las Palmas/Santa Cruz	–
Cape Verde Is.	4	1.6	410	Praia	960
Cayman Is. (UK)	0.26	0.10	35	George Town	20,000
Central African Republic	623	241	3,400	Bangui	340
Chad	1,284	496	6,800	Ndjaména	180
Chatham Is. (NZ)	0.96	0.37	0.05	Waitangi	——
Chile	757	292	14,700	Santiago	4,160
China	9,597	3,705	1,210,000	Beijing	620
Christmas Is. (Australia)	0.14	0.05	2	The Settlement	–
Cocos (Keeling) Is. (Australia)	0.01	0.005	1	West Island	–
Colombia	1,139	440	35,900	Bogotá	1,910
Comoros	2.2	0.86	630	Moroni	470
Congo	342	132	2,700	Brazzaville	680
Congo (= Zaïre)	2,345	905	47,200	Kinshasa	120
Cook Is. (NZ)	0.24	0.09	20	Avarua	900
Costa Rica	51.1	19.7	3,500	San José	2,610
Croatia	56.5	21.8	4,900	Zagreb	3,250
Cuba	111	43	11,300	Havana	1,250
Cyprus	9.3	3.6	800	Nicosia	11,500
Czech Republic	78.9	30.4	10,500	Prague	3,870
Denmark	43.1	16.6	5,400	Copenhagen	29,890
Djibouti	23.2	9	650	Djibouti	1,000
Dominica	0.75	0.29	78	Roseau	2,990
Dominican Republic	48.7	18.8	8,200	Santo Domingo	1,460
Ecuador	284	109	11,800	Quito	1,390
Egypt	1,001	387	63,000	Cairo	790
El Salvador	21	8.1	6,000	San Salvador	1,610
Equatorial Guinea	28.1	10.8	420	Malabo	380
Eritrea	94	36	3,500	Asmara	500
Estonia	44.7	17.3	1,500	Tallinn	2,860
Ethiopia	1,128	436	58,500	Addis Ababa	100
Falkland Is. (UK)	12.2	4.7	2	Stanley	–
Faroe Is. (Denmark)	1.4	0.54	45	Tórshavn	23,660
Fiji	18.3	7.1	800	Suva	2,440
Finland	338	131	5,200	Helsinki	20,580
France	552	213	58,800	Paris	24,990
French Guiana (France)	90	34.7	155	Cayenne	6,500
French Polynesia (France)	4	1.5	226	Papeete	7,500
Gabon	268	103	1,200	Libreville	3,490
Gambia, The	11.3	4.4	1,200	Banjul	320
Georgia	69.7	26.9	5,500	Tbilisi	440
Germany	357	138	82,300	Berlin/Bonn	27,510
Ghana	239	92	18,100	Accra	390
Gibraltar (UK)	0.007	0.003	28	Gibraltar Town	5,000
Greece	132	51	10,600	Athens	8,210
Greenland (Denmark)	2,176	840	57	Nuuk (Godthåb)	9,000
Grenada	0.34	0.13	99	St George's	2,980
Guadeloupe (France)	1.7	0.66	440	Basse-Terre	9,500
Guam (US)	0.55	0.21	161	Agana	6,000
Guatemala	109	42	11,300	Guatemala City	1,340
Guinea	246	95	7,500	Conakry	550
Guinea-Bissau	36.1	13.9	1,200	Bissau	250
Guyana	215	83	820	Georgetown	590
Haiti	27.8	10.7	7,400	Port-au-Prince	250
Honduras	112	43	6,300	Tegucigalpa	600
Hong Kong (China)	1.1	0.40	6,500	–	22,990
Hungary	93	35.9	10,200	Budapest	4,120
Iceland	103	40	275	Reykjavik	24,950
India	3,288	1,269	980,000	New Delhi	340
Indonesia	1,905	735	203,500	Jakarta	980
Iran	1,648	636	69,500	Tehran	4,800
Iraq	438	169	22,500	Baghdad	1,800
Ireland	70.3	27.1	3,600	Dublin	14,710
Israel	27	10.3	5,900	Jerusalem	15,920
Italy	301	116	57,800	Rome	19,020
Ivory Coast	322	125	15,100	Yamoussoukro	660
Jamaica	11	4.2	2,600	Kingston	1,510
Jan Mayen Is. (Norway)	0.38	0.15	0.06	–	–
Japan	378	146	125,900	Tokyo	39,640
Johnston Is. (US)	0.002	0.0009	1	–	–
Jordan	89.2	34.4	5,600	Amman	1,510
Kazakhstan	2,717	1,049	17,000	Aqmola	1,330
Kenya	580	224	31,900	Nairobi	280
Kerguelen Is. (France)	7.2	2.8	0.7	–	–
Kermadec Is. (NZ)	0.03	0.01	0.1	–	–
Kiribati	0.72	0.28	85	Tarawa	710
Korea, North	121	47	24,500	Pyŏngyang	1,000
Korea, South	99	38.2	46,100	Seoul	9,700
Kuwait	17.8	6.9	2,050	Kuwait City	17,390
Kyrgyzstan	198.5	76.6	4,700	Bishkek	700
Laos	237	91	5,200	Vientiane	350
Latvia	65	25	2,500	Riga	2,270
Lebanon	10.4	4	3,200	Beirut	2,660
Lesotho	30.4	11.7	2,100	Maseru	770
Liberia	111	43	3,000	Monrovia	850
Libya	1,760	679	5,500	Tripoli	7,000
Liechtenstein	0.16	0.06	32	Vaduz	33,500
Lithuania	65.2	25.2	3,700	Vilnius	1,900
Luxembourg	2.6	1	400	Luxembourg	41,210
Macau (Portugal)	0.02	0.006	450	Macau	7,500
Macedonia	25.7	9.9	2,200	Skopje	860
Madagascar	587	227	15,500	Antananarivo	230
Madeira (Portugal)	0.81	0.31	253	Funchal	–
Malawi	118	46	10,300	Lilongwe	170
Malaysia	330	127	20,900	Kuala Lumpur	3,890
Maldives	0.30	0.12	275	Malé	990
Mali	1,240	479	11,000	Bamako	250
Malta	0.32	0.12	400	Valletta	11,000
Marshall Is.	0.18	0.07	60	Dalap-Uliga-Darrit	1,500
Martinique (France)	1.1	0.42	405	Fort-de-France	10,000
Mauritania	1,030	412	2,400	Nouakchott	460
Mauritius	2.0	0.72	1,200	Port Louis	3,380
Mayotte (France)	0.37	0.14	105	Mamoundzou	1,430
Mexico	1,958	756	97,400	Mexico City	3,320
Micronesia, Fed. States of	0.70	0.27	127	Palikir	1,560
Midway Is. (US)	0.005	0.002	2	–	–
Moldova	33.7	13	4,500	Chişinău	920
Monaco	0.002	0.0001	33	Monaco	16,000
Mongolia	1,567	605	2,500	Ulan Bator	310
Montserrat (UK)	0.10	0.04	12	Plymouth	4,500
Morocco	447	172	28,100	Rabat	1,110
Mozambique	802	309	19,100	Maputo	80
Namibia	825	318	1,700	Windhoek	2,000
Nauru	0.02	0.008	12	Yaren District	10,000
Nepal	141	54	22,100	Katmandu	200
Netherlands	41.5	16	15,900	Amsterdam/The Hague	24,000
Netherlands Antilles (Neths)	0.99	0.38	210	Willemstad	10,500
New Caledonia (France)	18.6	7.2	192	Nouméa	16,000
New Zealand	269	104	3,700	Wellington	14,340
Nicaragua	130	50	4,600	Managua	380
Niger	1,267	489	9,700	Niamey	220
Nigeria	924	357	119,000	Abuja	260
Niue (NZ)	0.26	0.10	2	Alofi	–
Norfolk Is. (Australia)	0.03	0.01	2	Kingston	–
Northern Mariana Is. (US)	0.48	0.18	50	Saipan	11,500
Norway	324	125	4,400	Oslo	31,250
Oman	212	82	2,400	Muscat	4,820
Pakistan	796	307	136,000	Islamabad	460
Palau	0.46	0.18	17	Koror	2,260
Panama	77.1	29.8	2,700	Panama City	2,750
Papua New Guinea	463	179	4,400	Port Moresby	1,160
Paraguay	407	157	5,200	Asunción	1,690
Peru	1,285	496	24,500	Lima	2,310
Philippines	300	116	73,500	Manila	1,050
Pitcairn Is. (UK)	0.03	0.01	0.05	Adamstown	–
Poland	313	121	38,800	Warsaw	2,790
Portugal	92.4	35.7	10,100	Lisbon	9,740
Puerto Rico (US)	9	3.5	3,800	San Juan	7,500
Qatar	11	4.2	620	Doha	11,600
Queen Maud Land (Norway)	2,800	1,081	0	–	–
Réunion (France)	2.5	0.97	680	Saint-Denis	4,500
Romania	238	92	22,600	Bucharest	1,480
Russia	17,075	6,592	147,800	Moscow	2,240
Rwanda	26.3	10.2	7,000	Kigali	180
St Helena (UK)	0.12	0.05	6	Jamestown	–
St Kitts & Nevis	0.36	0.14	42	Basseterre	4,470
St Lucia	0.62	0.24	150	Castries	3,370
St Pierre & Miquelon (France)	0.24	0.09	7	Saint Pierre	–
St Vincent & Grenadines	0.39	0.15	114	Kingstown	2,280
San Marino	0.06	0.02	26	San Marino	20,000
São Tomé & Príncipe	0.96	0.37	135	São Tomé	350
Saudi Arabia	2,150	830	19,100	Riyadh	7,040
Senegal	197	76	8,900	Dakar	600
Seychelles	0.46	0.18	78	Victoria	6,370
Sierra Leone	71.7	27.7	4,600	Freetown	180
Singapore	0.62	0.24	3,200	Singapore	26,730
Slovak Republic	49	18.9	5,400	Bratislava	2,950
Slovenia	20.3	7.8	2,000	Ljubljana	8,200
Solomon Is.	28.9	11.2	410	Honiara	910
Somalia	638	246	9,900	Mogadishu	500
South Africa	1,220	471	42,300	C. Town/Pretoria/Bloem.	3,160
South Georgia (UK)	3.8	1.4	0.05	–	–
Spain	505	195	39,300	Madrid	13,580
Sri Lanka	65.6	25.3	18,700	Colombo	700
Sudan	2,506	967	31,000	Khartoum	750
Surinam	163	63	500	Paramaribo	880
Svalbard (Norway)	62.9	24.3	4	Longyearbyen	–
Swaziland	17.4	6.7	1,000	Mbabane	1,170
Sweden	450	174	8,900	Stockholm	23,750
Switzerland	41.3	15.9	7,100	Bern	40,630
Syria	185	71	15,300	Damascus	1,120
Taiwan	36	13.9	21,700	Taipei	12,000
Tajikistan	143.1	55.2	6,000	Dushanbe	340
Tanzania	945	365	31,200	Dodoma	120
Thailand	513	198	60,800	Bangkok	2,740
Togo	56.8	21.9	4,500	Lomé	310
Tokelau (NZ)	0.01	0.005	2	Nukunonu	–
Tonga	0.75	0.29	107	Nuku'alofa	1,610
Trinidad & Tobago	5.1	2	1,300	Port of Spain	3,770
Tristan da Cunha (UK)	0.11	0.04	0.33	Edinburgh	–
Tunisia	164	63	9,200	Tunis	1,820
Turkey	779	301	63,500	Ankara	2,780
Turkmenistan	488.1	188.5	4,800	Ashkhabad	920
Turks & Caicos Is. (UK)	0.43	0.17	15	Cockburn Town	5,000
Tuvalu	0.03	0.01	10	Fongafale	600
Uganda	236	91	20,800	Kampala	240
Ukraine	603.7	233.1	51,500	Kiev	1,630
United Arab Emirates	83.6	32.3	2,400	Abu Dhabi	17,400
United Kingdom	243.3	94	58,600	London	18,700
United States of America	9,373	3,619	268,000	Washington, DC	26,980
Uruguay	177	68	3,300	Montevideo	5,170
Uzbekistan	447.4	172.7	23,800	Tashkent	970
Vanuatu	12.2	4.7	175	Port-Vila	1,200
Vatican City	0.0004	0.0002	1	–	–
Venezuela	912	352	22,500	Caracas	3,020
Vietnam	332	127	77,100	Hanoi	240
Virgin Is. (UK)	0.15	0.06	13	Road Town	–
Virgin Is. (US)	0.34	0.13	105	Charlotte Amalie	12,000
Wake Is. (US)	0.008	0.003	0.30	–	–
Wallis & Futuna Is. (France)	0.20	0.08	15	Mata-Utu	–
Western Sahara	266	103	280	El Aaiún	980
Western Samoa	2.8	1.1	175	Apia	1,120
Yemen	528	204	16,500	Sana	260
Yugoslavia	102.3	39.5	10,500	Belgrade	1,400
Zambia	753	291	9,500	Lusaka	400
Zimbabwe	391	151	12,100	Harare	540

At the time of going to press, the government of Kazakhstan planned to rename the capital Aqmola to Astana.

World Statistics: Physical Dimensions

Each topic list is divided into continents and within a continent the items are listed in order of size. The bottom part of many of the lists is selective in order to give examples from as many different countries as possible. The order of the continents is the same as in the atlas, beginning with Europe and ending with South America. The figures are rounded as appropriate.

World, Continents, Oceans

	km²	miles²	%
The World	509,450,000	196,672,000	–
Land	149,450,000	57,688,000	29.3
Water	360,000,000	138,984,000	70.7
Asia	44,500,000	17,177,000	29.8
Africa	30,302,000	11,697,000	20.3
North America	24,241,000	9,357,000	16.2
South America	17,793,000	6,868,000	11.9
Antarctica	14,100,000	5,443,000	9.4
Europe	9,957,000	3,843,000	6.7
Australia & Oceania	8,557,000	3,303,000	5.7
Pacific Ocean	179,679,000	69,356,000	49.9
Atlantic Ocean	92,373,000	35,657,000	25.7
Indian Ocean	73,917,000	28,532,000	20.5
Arctic Ocean	14,090,000	5,439,000	3.9

Ocean Depths

Atlantic Ocean		m	ft
Puerto Rico (Milwaukee) Deep		9,220	30,249
Cayman Trench		7,680	25,197
Gulf of Mexico		5,203	17,070
Mediterranean Sea		5,121	16,801
Black Sea		2,211	7,254
North Sea		660	2,165
Indian Ocean		**m**	**ft**
Java Trench		7,450	24,442
Red Sea		2,635	8,454
Pacific Ocean		**m**	**ft**
Mariana Trench		11,022	36,161
Tonga Trench		10,882	35,702
Japan Trench		10,554	34,626
Kuril Trench		10,542	34,587
Arctic Ocean		**m**	**ft**
Molloy Deep		5,608	18,399

Mountains

Europe		m	ft
Mont Blanc	France/Italy	4,807	15,771
Monte Rosa	Italy/Switzerland	4,634	15,203
Dom	Switzerland	4,545	14,911
Liskamm	Switzerland	4,527	14,852
Weisshorn	Switzerland	4,505	14,780
Taschorn	Switzerland	4,490	14,730
Matterhorn/Cervino	Italy/Switzerland	4,478	14,691
Mont Maudit	France/Italy	4,465	14,649
Dent Blanche	Switzerland	4,356	14,291
Nadelhorn	Switzerland	4,327	14,196
Grandes Jorasses	France/Italy	4,208	13,806
Jungfrau	Switzerland	4,158	13,642
Grossglockner	Austria	3,797	12,457
Mulhacén	Spain	3,478	11,411
Zugspitze	Germany	2,962	9,718
Olympus	Greece	2,917	9,570
Triglav	Slovenia	2,863	9,393
Gerlachovka	Slovak Republic	2,655	8,711
Galdhöpiggen	Norway	2,468	8,100
Kebnekaise	Sweden	2,117	6,946
Ben Nevis	UK	1,343	4,406
Asia		**m**	**ft**
Everest	China/Nepal	8,848	29,029
K2 (Godwin Austen)	China/Kashmir	8,611	28,251
Kanchenjunga	India/Nepal	8,598	28,208
Lhotse	China/Nepal	8,516	27,939
Makalu	China/Nepal	8,481	27,824
Cho Oyu	China/Nepal	8,201	26,906
Dhaulagiri	Nepal	8,172	26,811
Manaslu	Nepal	8,156	26,758
Nanga Parbat	Kashmir	8,126	26,660
Annapurna	Nepal	8,078	26,502
Gasherbrum	China/Kashmir	8,068	26,469
Broad Peak	China/Kashmir	8,051	26,414
Xixabangma	China	8,012	26,286
Kangbachen	India/Nepal	7,902	25,925
Trivor	Pakistan	7,720	25,328
Pik Kommunizma	Tajikistan	7,495	24,590
Elbrus	Russia	5,642	18,510
Demavend	Iran	5,604	18,386
Ararat	Turkey	5,165	16,945
Gunong Kinabalu	Malaysia (Borneo)	4,101	13,455
Fuji-San	Japan	3,776	12,388
Africa		**m**	**ft**
Kilimanjaro	Tanzania	5,895	19,340
Mt Kenya	Kenya	5,199	17,057
Ruwenzori (Margherita)	Ug./Congo (Z.)	5,109	16,762
Ras Dashan	Ethiopia	4,620	15,157
Meru	Tanzania	4,565	14,977
Karisimbi	Rwanda/Congo (Zaïre)	4,507	14,787
Mt Elgon	Kenya/Uganda	4,321	14,176
Batu	Ethiopia	4,307	14,130
Toubkal	Morocco	4,165	13,665
Mt Cameroon	Cameroon	4,070	13,353
Oceania		**m**	**ft**
Puncak Jaya	Indonesia	5,029	16,499
Puncak Trikora	Indonesia	4,750	15,584
Puncak Mandala	Indonesia	4,702	15,427
Mt Wilhelm	Papua New Guinea	4,508	14,790
Mauna Kea	USA (Hawaii)	4,205	13,796
Mauna Loa	USA (Hawaii)	4,170	13,681
Mt Cook (Aoraki)	New Zealand	3,753	12,313
Mt Kosciuszko	Australia	2,237	7,339
North America		**m**	**ft**
Mt McKinley (Denali)	USA (Alaska)	6,194	20,321
Mt Logan	Canada	5,959	19,551
Citlaltepetl	Mexico	5,700	18,701
Mt St Elias	USA/Canada	5,489	18,008
Popocatepetl	Mexico	5,452	17,887
Mt Foraker	USA (Alaska)	5,304	17,401
Ixtaccihuatl	Mexico	5,286	17,342
Lucania	Canada	5,227	17,149
Mt Steele	Canada	5,073	16,644
Mt Bona	USA (Alaska)	5,005	16,420
Mt Whitney	USA	4,418	14,495
Tajumulco	Guatemala	4,220	13,845
Chirripó Grande	Costa Rica	3,837	12,589
Pico Duarte	Dominican Rep.	3,175	10,417
South America		**m**	**ft**
Aconcagua	Argentina	6,960	22,834
Bonete	Argentina	6,872	22,546
Ojos del Salado	Argentina/Chile	6,863	22,516
Pissis	Argentina	6,779	22,241
Mercedario	Argentina/Chile	6,770	22,211
Huascaran	Peru	6,768	22,204
Llullaillaco	Argentina/Chile	6,723	22,057
Nudo de Cachi	Argentina	6,720	22,047
Yerupaja	Peru	6,632	21,758
Sajama	Bolivia	6,542	21,463
Chimborazo	Ecuador	6,267	20,561
Pico Colon	Colombia	5,800	19,029
Pico Bolivar	Venezuela	5,007	16,427
Antarctica		**m**	**ft**
Vinson Massif		4,897	16,066
Mt Kirkpatrick		4,528	14,855

Rivers

Europe		km	miles
Volga	Caspian Sea	3,700	2,300
Danube	Black Sea	2,850	1,770
Ural	Caspian Sea	2,535	1,575
Dnepr (Dnipro)	Black Sea	2,285	1,420
Kama	Volga	2,030	1,260
Don	Black Sea	1,990	1,240
Petchora	Arctic Ocean	1,790	1,110
Oka	Volga	1,480	920
Dnister (Dniester)	Black Sea	1,400	870
Vyatka	Kama	1,370	850
Rhine	North Sea	1,320	820
N. Dvina	Arctic Ocean	1,290	800
Elbe	North Sea	1,145	710
Asia		**km**	**miles**
Yangtze	Pacific Ocean	6,380	3,960
Yenisey–Angara	Arctic Ocean	5,550	3,445
Huang He	Pacific Ocean	5,464	3,395
Ob–Irtysh	Arctic Ocean	5,410	3,360
Mekong	Pacific Ocean	4,500	2,795
Amur	Pacific Ocean	4,400	2,730
Lena	Arctic Ocean	4,400	2,730
Irtysh	Ob	4,250	2,640
Yenisey	Arctic Ocean	4,090	2,540
Ob	Arctic Ocean	3,680	2,285
Indus	Indian Ocean	3,100	1,925
Brahmaputra	Indian Ocean	2,900	1,800
Syrdarya	Aral Sea	2,860	1,775
Salween	Indian Ocean	2,800	1,740
Euphrates	Indian Ocean	2,700	1,675
Amudarya	Aral Sea	2,540	1,575
Africa		**km**	**miles**
Nile	Mediterranean	6,670	4,140
Congo	Atlantic Ocean	4,670	2,900
Niger	Atlantic Ocean	4,180	2,595
Zambezi	Indian Ocean	3,540	2,200
Oubangi/Uele	Congo (Zaïre)	2,250	1,400
Kasai	Congo (Zaïre)	1,950	1,210
Shaballe	Indian Ocean	1,930	1,200
Orange	Atlantic Ocean	1,860	1,155
Cubango	Okavango Swamps	1,800	1,120
Limpopo	Indian Ocean	1,600	995
Senegal	Atlantic Ocean	1,600	995
Australia		**km**	**miles**
Murray–Darling	Indian Ocean	3,750	2,330
Darling	Murray	3,070	1,905
Murray	Indian Ocean	2,575	1,600
Murrumbidgee	Murray	1,690	1,050
North America		**km**	**miles**
Mississippi–Missouri	Gulf of Mexico	6,020	3,740
Mackenzie	Arctic Ocean	4,240	2,630
Mississippi	Gulf of Mexico	3,780	2,350
Missouri	Mississippi	3,780	2,350
Yukon	Pacific Ocean	3,185	1,980
Rio Grande	Gulf of Mexico	3,030	1,880
Arkansas	Mississippi	2,340	1,450
Colorado	Pacific Ocean	2,330	1,445
Red	Mississippi	2,040	1,270
Columbia	Pacific Ocean	1,950	1,210
Saskatchewan	Lake Winnipeg	1,940	1,205
South America		**km**	**miles**
Amazon	Atlantic Ocean	6,450	4,010
Paraná–Plate	Atlantic Ocean	4,500	2,800
Purus	Amazon	3,350	2,080
Madeira	Amazon	3,200	1,990
São Francisco	Atlantic Ocean	2,900	1,800
Paraná	Plate	2,800	1,740
Tocantins	Atlantic Ocean	2,750	1,710
Paraguay	Paraná	2,550	1,580
Orinoco	Atlantic Ocean	2,500	1,550
Pilcomayo	Paraná	2,500	1,550
Araguaia	Tocantins	2,250	1,400

Lakes

Europe		km²	miles²
Lake Ladoga	Russia	17,700	6,800
Lake Onega	Russia	9,700	3,700
Saimaa system	Finland	8,000	3,100
Vänern	Sweden	5,500	2,100
Asia		**km²**	**miles²**
Caspian Sea	Asia	371,800	143,550
Aral Sea	Kazakstan/Uzbekistan	33,640	13,000
Lake Baykal	Russia	30,500	11,780
Tonlé Sap	Cambodia	20,000	7,700
Lake Balqash	Kazakstan	18,500	7,100
Africa		**km²**	**miles²**
Lake Victoria	East Africa	68,000	26,000
Lake Tanganyika	Central Africa	33,000	13,000
Lake Malawi/Nyasa	East Africa	29,600	11,430
Lake Chad	Central Africa	25,000	9,700
Lake Turkana	Ethiopia/Kenya	8,500	3,300
Lake Volta	Ghana	8,500	3,300
Australia		**km²**	**miles²**
Lake Eyre	Australia	8,900	3,400
Lake Torrens	Australia	5,800	2,200
Lake Gairdner	Australia	4,800	1,900
North America		**km²**	**miles²**
Lake Superior	Canada/USA	82,350	31,800
Lake Huron	Canada/USA	59,600	23,010
Lake Michigan	USA	58,000	22,400
Great Bear Lake	Canada	31,800	12,280
Great Slave Lake	Canada	28,500	11,000
Lake Erie	Canada/USA	25,700	9,900
Lake Winnipeg	Canada	24,400	9,400
Lake Ontario	Canada/USA	19,500	7,500
Lake Nicaragua	Nicaragua	8,200	3,200
South America		**km²**	**miles²**
Lake Titicaca	Bolivia/Peru	8,300	3,200
Lake Poopo	Peru	2,800	1,100

Islands

Europe		km²	miles²
Great Britain	UK	229,880	88,700
Iceland	Atlantic Ocean	103,000	39,800
Ireland	Ireland/UK	84,400	32,600
Novaya Zemlya (N.)	Russia	48,200	18,600
Sicily	Italy	25,500	9,800
Corsica	France	8,700	3,400
Asia		**km²**	**miles²**
Borneo	Southeast Asia	744,360	287,400
Sumatra	Indonesia	473,600	182,860
Honshu	Japan	230,500	88,980
Sulawesi (Celebes)	Indonesia	189,000	73,000
Java	Indonesia	126,700	48,900
Luzon	Philippines	104,700	40,400
Hokkaido	Japan	78,400	30,300
Africa		**km²**	**miles²**
Madagascar	Indian Ocean	587,040	226,660
Socotra	Indian Ocean	3,600	1,400
Réunion	Indian Ocean	2,500	965
Oceania		**km²**	**miles²**
New Guinea	Indonesia/Papua NG	821,030	317,000
New Zealand (S.)	Pacific Ocean	150,500	58,100
New Zealand (N.)	Pacific Ocean	114,700	44,300
Tasmania	Australia	67,800	26,200
Hawaii	Pacific Ocean	10,450	4,000
North America		**km²**	**miles²**
Greenland	Atlantic Ocean	2,175,600	839,800
Baffin Is.	Canada	508,000	196,100
Victoria Is.	Canada	212,200	81,900
Ellesmere Is.	Canada	212,000	81,800
Cuba	Caribbean Sea	110,860	42,800
Hispaniola	Dominican Rep./Haiti	76,200	29,400
Jamaica	Caribbean Sea	11,400	4,400
Puerto Rico	Atlantic Ocean	8,900	3,400
South America		**km²**	**miles²**
Tierra del Fuego	Argentina/Chile	47,000	18,100
Falkland Is. (E.)	Atlantic Ocean	6,800	2,600

Philip's World Maps

The reference maps which form the main body of this atlas have been prepared in accordance with the highest standards of international cartography to provide an accurate and detailed representation of the Earth. The scales and projections used have been carefully chosen to give balanced coverage of the world, while emphasizing the most densely populated and economically significant regions. A hallmark of Philip's mapping is the use of hill shading and relief colouring to create a graphic impression of landforms: this makes the maps exceptionally easy to read. However, knowledge of the key features employed in the construction and presentation of the maps will enable the reader to derive the fullest benefit from the atlas.

Map sequence

The atlas covers the Earth continent by continent: first Europe; then its land neighbour Asia (mapped north before south, in a clockwise sequence), then Africa, Australia and Oceania, North America and South America. This is the classic arrangement adopted by most cartographers since the 16th century. For each continent, there are maps at a variety of scales. First, physical relief and political maps of the whole continent; then a series of larger-scale maps of the regions within the continent, each followed, where required, by still larger-scale maps of the most important or densely populated areas. The governing principle is that by turning the pages of the atlas, the reader moves steadily from north to south through each continent, with each map overlapping its neighbours. A key map showing this sequence, and the area covered by each map, can be found on the endpapers of the atlas.

Map presentation

With very few exceptions (e.g. for the Arctic and Antarctica), the maps are drawn with north at the top, regardless of whether they are presented upright or sideways on the page. In the borders will be found the map title; a locator diagram showing the area covered and the page numbers for maps of adjacent areas; the scale; the projection used; the degrees of latitude and longitude; and the letters and figures used in the index for locating place names and geographical features. Physical relief maps also have a height reference panel identifying the colours used for each layer of contouring.

Map symbols

Each map contains a vast amount of detail which can only be conveyed clearly and accurately by the use of symbols. Points and circles of varying sizes locate and identify the relative importance of towns and cities; different styles of type are employed for administrative, geographical and regional place names. A variety of pictorial symbols denote features such as glaciers and marshes, as well as man-

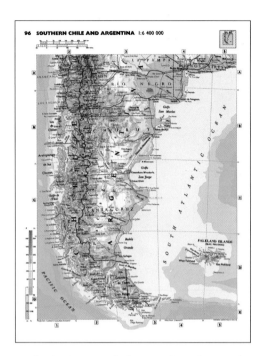

made structures including roads, railways, airports and canals. International borders are shown by red lines. Where neighbouring countries are in dispute, for example in the Middle East, the maps show the *de facto* boundary between nations, regardless of the legal or historical situation. The symbols are explained on the first page of the World Maps section of the atlas.

Map scales

The scale of each map is given in the numerical form known as the 'representative fraction'. The first figure is always one, signifying one unit of distance on the map; the second figure, usually in millions, is the number by which the map unit must be multiplied to give the equivalent distance on the Earth's surface. Calculations can easily be made in centimetres and kilometres, by dividing the Earth units figure by 100 000 (i.e. deleting the last five 0s). Thus 1:1 000 000 means 1 cm = 10 km. The calculation for inches and miles is more laborious, but 1 000 000 divided by 63 360 (the number of inches in a mile) shows that the ratio 1:1 000 000 means approximately 1 inch = 16 miles. The table below provides distance equivalents for scales down to 1:50 000 000.

LARGE SCALE		
1:1 000 000	1 cm = 10 km	1 inch = 16 miles
1:2 500 000	1 cm = 25 km	1 inch = 39.5 miles
1:5 000 000	1 cm = 50 km	1 inch = 79 miles
1:6 000 000	1 cm = 60 km	1 inch = 95 miles
1:8 000 000	1 cm = 80 km	1 inch = 126 miles
1:10 000 000	1 cm = 100 km	1 inch = 158 miles
1:15 000 000	1 cm = 150 km	1 inch = 237 miles
1:20 000 000	1 cm = 200 km	1 inch = 316 miles
1:50 000 000	1 cm = 500 km	1 inch = 790 miles
SMALL SCALE		

Measuring distances

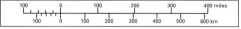

Although each map is accompanied by a scale bar, distances cannot always be measured with confidence because of the distortions involved in portraying the curved surface of the Earth on a flat page. As a general rule, the larger the map scale (i.e. the lower the number of Earth units in the representative fraction), the more accurate and reliable will be the distance measured. On small-scale maps such as those of the world and of entire continents, measurement may only be accurate along the 'standard parallels', or central axes, and should not be attempted without considering the map projection.

Latitude and longitude

Accurate positioning of individual points on the Earth's surface is made possible by reference to the geometrical system of latitude and longitude. Latitude *parallels* are drawn west–east around the Earth and numbered by degrees north and south of the Equator, which is designated 0° of latitude. Longitude *meridians* are drawn north–south and numbered by degrees east and west of the *prime meridian*, 0° of longitude, which passes through Greenwich in England. By referring to these co-ordinates and their subdivisions of minutes ($^1/60$th of a degree) and seconds ($^1/60$th of a minute), any place on Earth can be located to within a few hundred metres. Latitude and longitude are indicated by blue lines on the maps; they are straight or curved according to the projection employed. Reference to these lines is the easiest way of determining the relative positions of places on different maps, and for plotting compass directions.

Name forms

For ease of reference, both English and local name forms appear in the atlas. Oceans, seas and countries are shown in English throughout the atlas; country names may be abbreviated to their commonly accepted form (e.g. Germany, not The Federal Republic of Germany). Conventional English forms are also used for place names on the smaller-scale maps of the continents. However, local name forms are used on all large-scale and regional maps, with the English form given in brackets only for important cities – the large-scale map of Russia and Central Asia thus shows Moskva (Moscow). For countries which do not use a Roman script, place names have been transcribed according to the systems adopted by the British and US Geographic Names Authorities. For China, the Pin Yin system has been used, with some more widely known forms appearing in brackets, as with Beijing (Peking). Both English and local names appear in the index, the English form being cross-referenced to the local form.

The
GAZETTEER
OF NATIONS

Index to Countries

Notes

The countries are arranged alphabetically, with Afghanistan as the first entry and Zimbabwe as the last. Information is given for all countries and territories, except for some of the smallest and near uninhabited islands. The form of names for all the countries follows the conventions used in all Philip's world atlases.

The statistical data is the latest available, usually for 1997. In the statistics' boxes: Country area includes inland water and land areas covered in ice, as in Greenland and Canada, for example. City populations are usually those of the 'urban agglomerations' rather than within the legal city boundaries.

AFGHANISTAN

GEOGRAPHY The Republic of Afghanistan is a landlocked, mountainous country in southern Asia. The central highlands reach a height of more than 7,000 m [22,966 ft] in the east and make up nearly three-quarters of Afghanistan. The main range is the Hindu Kush, which is cut by deep, fertile valleys.

The height of the land and the country's remote position have a great effect on the climate. In winter, northerly winds bring cold, snowy weather to the mountains, but summers are hot and dry.

POLITICS & ECONOMY The modern history of Afghanistan began in 1747, when the various tribes in the area united for the first time. In the 19th century, Russia and Britain struggled for control of the country. Following Britain's withdrawal in 1919, Afghanistan became fully independent. Soviet troops invaded Afghanistan in 1979 to support a socialist regime in Kabul, but, facing fierce opposition from Muslim groups, they withdrew in 1989. But Muslim factions continued to fight each other. By early 1998 a group called Taliban ('Islamic students') controlled most of the country apart from the north.

Afghanistan is one of the world's poorest countries. About 60% of the people live by farming. Many people are semi-nomadic herders. Natural gas is produced, together with some coal, copper, gold, precious stones and salt.

AREA 652,090 sq km [251,772 sq mls]
POPULATION 23,000,000
CAPITAL (POPULATION) Kabul (1,565,000)
GOVERNMENT Islamic republic
ETHNIC GROUPS Pashtun ('Pathan') 52%, Tajik 20%, Uzbek 9%, Hazara 9%, Chahar 3%, Turkmen 2%, Baluchi 1%
LANGUAGES Pashto, Dari / Persian (both official), Uzbek
RELIGIONS Islam (Sunni Muslim 74%, Shiite Muslim 25%)
CURRENCY Afghani = 100 puls

ALBANIA

GEOGRAPHY The Republic of Albania lies in the Balkan peninsula, facing the Adriatic Sea. About 70% of the land is mountainous, but most Albanians live in the west on the coastal lowlands.

The coastal areas of Albania have a typical Mediterranean climate, with fairly dry, sunny summers and cool, moist winters. The mountains have a severe climate, with heavy winter snowfalls.

POLITICS & ECONOMY Albania is Europe's poorest country. Formerly an independent Communist regime, unaligned to either the Soviet Union or China, Albania introduced a multiparty system in the early 1990s. The transition from Communism to a market economy has been traumatic and, by 1997, a state of near anarchy existed in the south. Following elections, a socialist government committed to the market system took office.

In the early 1990s, agriculture employed 56% of the people. The land was divided into large collective and state farms, but private ownership has been encouraged since 1991. Albania has some minerals and chromite, copper and nickel are exported.

AREA 28,750 sq km [11,100 sq mls]
POPULATION 3,600,000
CAPITAL (POPULATION) Tirana (251,000)
GOVERNMENT Multiparty republic
ETHNIC GROUPS Albanian 98%, Greek 1.8%, Macedonian, Montenegrin, Gypsy
LANGUAGES Albanian (official)
RELIGIONS Many people say they are non-believers; of the believers, 65% follow Islam and 33% follow Christianity (Orthodox 20%, Roman Catholic 13%)
CURRENCY Lek = 100 qindars

ALGERIA

GEOGRAPHY The People's Democratic Republic of Algeria is Africa's second largest country after Sudan. Most Algerians live in the north, on the fertile coastal plains and hill country bordering the Mediterranean Sea. Four-fifths of Algeria is in the Sahara, the world's largest desert.

Algiers has a Mediterranean climate; summers here are warm and dry, and winters are mild and moist. The Sahara is hot by day, but cool at night.

POLITICS & ECONOMY France ruled Algeria from 1830 until 1962, when the socialist FLN (National Liberation Front) formed a one-party government. Following the recognition of opposition parties in 1989, a Muslim group, the FIS (Islamic Salvation Front) won an election in 1991. The FLN cancelled the elections and civil conflict broke out. About 75,000 people were killed between 1991 and 1997 and, by 1998, the conflict had attracted international attention, though opinions differed on who was responsible for the massacres.

Algeria is a developing country, whose chief resources are oil and natural gas. The natural gas reserves are among the world's largest, and gas and oil account for 90% of Algeria's exports. Cement, iron and steel, textiles and vehicles are manufactured.

AREA 2,381,740 sq km [919,590 sq mls]
POPULATION 29,300,000
CAPITAL (POPULATION) Algiers (1,722,000)
GOVERNMENT Socialist republic
ETHNIC GROUPS Arab 83%, Berber 16%
LANGUAGES Arabic (official), Berber, French
RELIGIONS Sunni Muslim 98%
CURRENCY Algerian dinar = 100 centimes

AMERICAN SAMOA

An 'unincorporated territory' of the United States, American Samoa lies in the south-central Pacific Ocean. **AREA** 200 sq km [77 sq mls]; **POPULATION** 62,000; **CAPITAL** Pago Pago.

ANDORRA

A mini-state situated in the Pyrenees Mountains, Andorra is a co-principality whose main activity is tourism. Most Andorrans live in the six valleys (the Valls) that drain into the River Valira. **AREA** 453 sq km [175 sq mls]; **POPULATION** 75,000; **CAPITAL** Andorra la Vella.

ANGOLA

GEOGRAPHY The Republic of Angola is a large country in south-western Africa. Most of the country is part of the plateau that forms most of southern Africa, with a narrow coastal plain in the west.

Angola has a tropical climate, with temperatures of over 20°C [68°F] throughout the year, though the highest areas are cooler. The coastal regions are dry, but the rainfall increases to the north and east.

POLITICS & ECONOMY A former Portuguese colony, Angola gained its independence in 1975, after which rival nationalist forces began a struggle for power. A long-running civil war developed, finally ending with a peace treaty in 1994, which led to a coalition government in 1997. Angola is a developing country where more than 70% of the people make a meagre living by farming. The main food crops are cassava and maize, while coffee is exported.

Angola has much economic potential. It has oil reserves near Luanda and in the Cabinda enclave, which is separated from Angola by a strip of land belonging to Congo (Zaïre). Oil is the leading export. Angola also produces diamonds and has reserves of copper, manganese and phosphates. The country has a growing manufacturing sector.

AREA 1,246,700 sq km [481,351 sq mls]
POPULATION 11,200,000
CAPITAL (POPULATION) Luanda (2,250,000)
GOVERNMENT Multiparty republic
ETHNIC GROUPS Ovimbundu 37%, Mbundu 22%, Kongo 13%, Luimbe-Nganguela 5%, Nyaneka-Humbe 5%, Chokwe, Luvale, Luchazi
LANGUAGES Portuguese (official), many others
RELIGIONS Christianity (Roman Catholic 69%, Protestant 20%), traditional beliefs 10%
CURRENCY Kwanza = 100 lwei

ANGUILLA

Formerly part of St Kitts and Nevis, Anguilla became a British dependency (now a British overseas territory) in 1980. The main source of revenue is now tourism, although lobster still accounts for half the island's exports. **AREA** 96 sq km [37 sq mls]; **POPULATION** 10,000; **CAPITAL** The Valley

ANTIGUA AND BARBUDA

A former British dependency in the Caribbean, Antigua and Barbuda became independent in 1981. Tourism is the main industry. **AREA** 440 sq km [170 sq mls]; **POPULATION** 66,000; **CAPITAL** St John's.

ARGENTINA

GEOGRAPHY The Argentine Republic is South America's second largest and the world's eighth largest country. The high Andes range in the west contains Mount Aconcagua, the highest peak in the Americas. In southern Argentina, the Andes Mountains overlook Patagonia, a plateau region. In east-central Argentina lies a fertile plain called the *pampas*.

The climate varies from subtropical in the north to temperate in the south. Rainfall is abundant in the north-east, but is lower to the west and south. Patagonia is a dry region, crossed by rivers that rise in the Andes.

POLITICS & ECONOMY Argentina became independent from Spain in the early 19th century, but it later suffered from instability and periods of military rule. In 1982, Argentina invaded the Falkland (Malvinas) islands, but Britain regained the islands later in the year. Elections were held in 1983 and constitutional government was restored.

According to the World Bank, Argentina is an 'upper-middle-income' developing country. Large areas are fertile and the main agricultural products are beef, maize and wheat. But about 87% of the people live in cities and towns, where many work in factories that process farm products. Other industries include the manufacture of cars, electrical equipment and textiles. Oil is the leading mineral resource. The leading exports include meat, wheat, maize, vegetable oils, hides and skins, and wool. In 1991, Argentina, Brazil, Paraguay and Uruguay set up Mercosur, an alliance aimed at creating a common market.

AREA 2,766,890 sq km [1,068,296 sq mls]
POPULATION 35,400,000
CAPITAL (POPULATION) Buenos Aires (10,990,000)
GOVERNMENT Federal republic
ETHNIC GROUPS European 85%, Mestizo, Amerindian
LANGUAGES Spanish (official)
RELIGIONS Christianity (Roman Catholic 92%)
CURRENCY Peso = 10,000 australs

ARMENIA

GEOGRAPHY The Republic of Armenia is a landlocked country in south-western Asia. Most of Armenia consists of a rugged plateau, criss-crossed by long faults (cracks). Movements along the faults cause earthquakes. The highest point is Mount Aragats, at 4,090 m [13,419 ft] above sea level.

The height of the land, which averages 1,500 m [4,920 ft] above sea level gives rise to severe winters and cool summers. The highest peaks are snow-capped, but the total yearly rainfall is generally low.

POLITICS & ECONOMY In 1920, Armenia became a Communist republic and, in 1922, it became, with Azerbaijan and Georgia, part of the Transcaucasian Republic within the Soviet Union. But the three territories became separate Soviet Socialist Republics in 1936. After the break-up of the Soviet Union in 1991, Armenia became an independent republic. Fighting broke out over Nagorno-Karabakh, an area enclosed by Azerbaijan where the majority of the people are Armenians. In 1992, Armenia occupied the territory between it and Nagorno-Karabakh. A cease-fire agreed in 1994 left Armenia in control of about 20% of Azerbaijan's land area.

The World Bank classifies Armenia as a 'lower-middle-income economy'. The conflict has badly damaged the economy, but the government has encouraged free enterprise, selling farmland and government-owned businesses.

AREA 29,800 sq km [11,506 sq mls]
POPULATION 3,800,000
CAPITAL (POPULATION) Yerevan (1,226,000)
GOVERNMENT Multiparty republic
ETHNIC GROUPS Armenian 93%, Azerbaijani 3%, Russian, Kurd
LANGUAGES Armenian (official)
RELIGIONS Christianity (Armenian Apostolic)
CURRENCY Dram = 100 couma

ARUBA

Formerly part of the Netherlands Antilles, Aruba became a separate self-governing Dutch territory in 1986. **AREA** 193 sq km [75 sq mls]; **POPULATION** 70,000; **CAPITAL** Oranjestad.

AUSTRALIA

GEOGRAPHY The Commonwealth of Australia, the world's sixth largest country, is also a continent. Australia is the flattest of the continents and the main highland area is in the east. Here the Great Dividing Range separates the eastern coastal plains from the Central Plains. This range extends from the Cape York Peninsula to Victoria in the far south. The longest rivers, the Murray and Darling, drain the south-eastern part of the Central Plains. The Western Plateau makes up two-thirds of Australia. A few mountain ranges break the monotony of the generally flat landscape.

Only 10% of Australia has an average yearly rainfall of more than 1,000 mm [39 in]. These areas include the tropical north, where Darwin is situated, the north-east coast, and the south-east, where Sydney is located. The interior is dry, and water is quickly evaporated in the heat.

POLITICS & ECONOMY The Aboriginal people of Australia entered the continent from South-east Asia more than 50,000 years ago. The first European explorers were Dutch in the 17th century, but they did not settle. In 1770, the British Captain Cook explored the east coast and, in 1788, the first British settlement was established for convicts on the site of what is now Sydney. Australia has strong ties with the British Isles. But in the last 50 years, people from other parts of Europe and, most recently, from Asia have settled in Australia. Ties with Britain were also weakened by Britain's membership of the European Union. Many Australians now believe that they should become more involved with the nations of eastern Asia and the Americas rather than with Europe. By the late 1990s, many people thought that Australia should become a republic, with a president replacing the British monarch as head of state.

Australia is a prosperous country. Crops can be grown on only 6% of the land, though dry pasture covers another 58%. Yet the country remains a major producer and exporter of farm products, particularly cattle, wheat and wool. Grapes grown for wine-making are also important. The country is also rich in natural resources. It is a major producer of minerals, including bauxite, coal, copper, diamonds, gold, iron ore, manganese, nickel, silver, tin, tungsten and zinc. Australia also produces some oil and natural gas. Metals, minerals and farm products account for the bulk of exports. Australia's imports are mostly manufactured products, although the country makes many factory products, especially consumer goods, such as foods and household articles. Major imports include machinery and other goods used by factories.

AREA 7,686,850 sq km [2,967,893 sq mls]
POPULATION 18,400,000
CAPITAL (POPULATION) Canberra (325,000)
GOVERNMENT Federal constitutional monarchy
ETHNIC GROUPS White 95%, Aboriginal 1.5%, Asian 1.3%
LANGUAGES English (official)
RELIGIONS Christianity (Roman Catholic 26%, Anglican 24%, others 20%), Islam, Buddhism, Judaism
CURRENCY Australian dollar = 100 cents

AUSTRIA

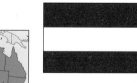

GEOGRAPHY The Republic of Austria is a landlocked country in the heart of Europe. Northern Austria contains the valley of the River Danube, which flows from Germany to the Black Sea, and the Vienna basin – Austria's main farming regions. Southern Austria contains ranges of the Alps, which reach their highest point at Grossglockner, at 3,797 m [12,457 ft] above sea level.

The climate of Austria is influenced both by westerly and easterly winds. The moist westerly winds bring rain and snow. They also moderate the temperatures. But dry easterly winds bring cold weather in winter and hot weather in summer.

POLITICS & ECONOMY Formerly part of the powerful monarchy of Austria-Hungary, which collapsed in 1918, Austria was annexed by Germany in 1938. After World War II, the Allies partitioned and occupied the country until 1955, when Austria became a neutral federal republic. Austria joined the European Union on 1 January 1995.

Austria is a prosperous country. It has plenty of hydroelectric power, as well as some oil, gas and coal reserves. The country's leading economic activity is manufacturing metals and metal products. Crops are grown on 18% of the land and another 24% is pasture. Dairy and livestock farming are the leading activities. Major crops include barley, potatoes, rye, sugar beet and wheat. Tourism is a major activity in this scenic country.

AREA 83,850 sq km [32,374 sq mls]
POPULATION 8,200,000
CAPITAL (POPULATION) Vienna (1,560,000)
GOVERNMENT Federal republic
ETHNIC GROUPS Austrian 93%, Yugoslav 2%, Turkish, German
LANGUAGES German (official)
RELIGIONS Christianity (Roman Catholic 78%, Protestant 6%), Islam
CURRENCY Schilling = 100 Groschen

AZERBAIJAN

GEOGRAPHY The Azerbaijani Republic is a country in the south-west of Asia, facing the Caspian Sea to the east. It includes an area called the Naxçivan Autonomous Republic, which is completely cut off from the rest of Azerbaijan by Armenian territory. The Caucasus Mountains border Russia in the north.

Azerbaijan has hot summers and cool winters, with low rainfall on the plains and much higher rainfall in the highlands.
POLITICS & ECONOMY After the Russian Revolution of 1917, attempts were made to form a Transcaucasian Federation made up of Armenia, Azerbaijan and Georgia. When this failed, Azerbaijanis set up an independent state. But Russian forces occupied the area in 1920. In 1922, the Communists set up a Transcaucasian Republic consisting of Armenia, Azerbaijan and Georgia under Russian control. In 1936, the three areas became separate Soviet Socialist Republics within the Soviet Union. In 1991, following the break-up of the Soviet Union, Azerbaijan became an independent nation. After independence, the country's economic progress was slow, partly because of the conflict with Armenia over the enclave of Nagorno-Karabakh, a region in Azerbaijan where the majority of people are Armenians. A cease-fire in 1994 left Armenia in control of about 20% of Azerbaijan's area, including Nagorno-Karabakh.

In the mid-1990s, the World Bank classified Azerbaijan as a 'lower-middle-income' economy. Yet by the late 1990s, the enormous oil reserves in the Baku area, on the Caspian Sea and in the sea itself, held out great promise for the future. Oil extraction and manufacturing, including oil refining and the production of chemicals, machinery and textiles, are now the most valuable activities.

AREA 86,600 sq km [33,436 sq mls]
POPULATION 7,650,000
CAPITAL (POPULATION) Baku (1,081,000)
GOVERNMENT Federal multiparty republic
ETHNIC GROUPS Azerbaijani 83%, Russian 6%, Armenian 6%, Lezgin, Avar, Ukrainian, Tatar
LANGUAGES Azerbaijani (official)
RELIGIONS Islam
CURRENCY Manat = 100 gopik

BAHAMAS

A coral-limestone archipelago off the coast of Florida, the Bahamas became independent from Britain in 1973, since when it has developed strong ties with the United States. Tourism and banking are major activities. **AREA** 13,880 sq km [5,359 sq mls]; **POPULATION** 190,000; **CAPITAL** Nassau.

BAHRAIN

The Emirate of Bahrain, an island nation in the Gulf, became independent from the UK in 1971. Oil accounts for 80% of the country's exports. **AREA** 678 sq km [262 sq mls]; **POPULATION** 605,000; **CAPITAL** Manama.

BANGLADESH

GEOGRAPHY The People's Republic of Bangladesh is one of the world's most densely populated countries. Apart from hilly regions in the far north-east and south-east, most of the land is flat and covered by fertile alluvium spread over the land by the Ganges, Brahmaputra and Meghna rivers. These rivers overflow when they are swollen by the annual monsoon rains. Floods also occur along the coast, 575 km [357 mls] long, when cyclones (hurricanes) drive sea-water inland. These periodic storms cause great human suffering.

Bangladesh has a tropical monsoon climate. In the winter, dry winds blow from the north. But in the spring, the land heats up and moist winds blow from the south, bringing heavy rain.
POLITICS & ECONOMY In 1947, British India was partitioned between the mainly Hindu India and the Muslim Pakistan. Pakistan consisted of two parts, West and East Pakistan, which were separated by about 1,600 km [1,000 mls] of Indian territory. Differences developed between West and East Pakistan. In 1971, the East Pakistanis rebelled. After a nine-month civil war, they declared East Pakistan to be a separate nation named Bangladesh.

Bangladesh is one of the world's poorest countries. Its economy depends mainly on agriculture, which employs over half the population. Bangladesh is the world's fourth largest producer of rice.

AREA 144,000 sq km [55,598 sq mls]
POPULATION 124,000,000
CAPITAL (POPULATION) Dhaka (6,105,000)
GOVERNMENT Multiparty republic
ETHNIC GROUPS Bengali 98%, tribal groups
LANGUAGES Bengali, English (both official)
RELIGIONS Islam 87%, Hinduism 12%, Buddhism, Christianity
CURRENCY Taka = 100 paisas

BARBADOS

The most easterly Caribbean country, Barbados became independent from the UK in 1960. A densely populated island, Barbados is prosperous by comparison with most Caribbean countries. **AREA** 430 sq km [166 sq mls]; **POPULATION** 263,000; **CAPITAL** Bridgetown.

BELARUS

GEOGRAPHY The Republic of Belarus is a landlocked country in Eastern Europe. The land is low-lying and mostly flat. In the south, much of the land is marshy and this area contains Europe's largest marsh and peat bog, the Pripet Marshes.

The climate of Belarus is affected by both the moderating influence of the Baltic Sea and continental conditions to the east. The winters are cold and the summers warm.
POLITICS & ECONOMY In 1918, Belarus (White Russia) became an independent republic, but Russia invaded the country and, in 1919, a Communist state was set up. In 1922, Belarus became a founder republic of the Soviet Union. In 1991, after the break-up of the Soviet Union, Belarus again became an independent republic, though it retained ties with Russia through an organization called the Commonwealth of Independent States. In 1996, Belarus moved even closer to Russia with the creation of an inner-core within the CIS. A full reunion is possible, but has its opponents on both sides.

The World Bank classifies Belarus as an 'upper-middle-income' economy. Like other former republics of the Soviet Union, it faces many problems in working to turn a government-run economy into a free-market one.

AREA 297,600 sq km [80,154 sq mls]
POPULATION 10,500,000
CAPITAL (POPULATION) Minsk (1,700,000)
GOVERNMENT Multiparty republic
ETHNIC GROUPS Belarussian 80%, Russian, Polish
LANGUAGES Belarussian, Russian (both official)
RELIGIONS Christianity (mainly Belarussian Orthodox, with Roman Catholics in the west)
CURRENCY Belarussian rouble = 100 kopecks

BELGIUM

GEOGRAPHY The Kingdom of Belgium is a densely populated country in western Europe. Behind the coastline on the North Sea, which is 63 km [39 mls] long, lie coastal plains. Central Belgium consists of low plateaux and the only highland region is the Ardennes in the south-east.

Belgium has a cool, temperate climate. Moist winds from the Atlantic Ocean bring fairly heavy rain, especially in the Ardennes. In January and February much snow falls on the Ardennes.

POLITICS & ECONOMY In 1815, Belgium and the Netherlands united as the 'low countries', but Belgium became independent in 1830. Belgium's economy was weakened by the two World Wars, but, from 1945, the country recovered quickly, first through collaboration with the Netherlands and Luxembourg, which formed a customs union called Benelux, and later through its membership of the European Union.

A central political problem in Belgium has been the tension between the Dutch-speaking Flemings and the French-speaking Walloons. In the 1970s, the government divided the country into three economic regions: Dutch-speaking Flanders, French-speaking Wallonia and bilingual Brussels. In 1993, Belgium adopted a federal system of government. Each of the regions now has its own parliament, which is responsible for local matters. Elections under this new system were held in 1995.

Belgium is a major trading nation, with a highly developed economy. Its main products include chemicals, processed food and steel. The textile industry is also important and has existed since medieval times in the Belgium province of Flanders.

Agriculture employs only 3% of the people, but Belgian farmers produce most of the food needed by the people. Barley and wheat are the chief crops, followed by flax, hops, potatoes and sugar beet, but the most valuable activities are dairy farming and livestock rearing.

AREA 30,510 sq km [11,780 sq mls]
POPULATION 10,225,000
CAPITAL (POPULATION) Brussels (952,000)
GOVERNMENT Federal constitutional monarchy
ETHNIC GROUPS Belgian 91% (Fleming 55%, Walloon 32%), Italian, French, Dutch, Turkish, Moroccan
LANGUAGES Dutch, French, German (all official)
RELIGIONS Christianity (Roman Catholic 90%), Islam
CURRENCY Belgian franc = 100 centimes

BELIZE

GEOGRAPHY Behind the swampy coastal plain in the south, the land rises to the low Maya Mountains, which reach a height of 1,120 m [3,674 ft] at Victoria Peak. The north is mostly low-lying and swampy.

Belize has a tropical, humid climate. Temperatures are high throughout the year and the average yearly rainfall ranges from 1,300 mm [51 in] in the north to over 3,800 mm [150 in] in the south.

POLITICS & ECONOMY From 1862, Belize (then called British Honduras) was a British colony. Full independence was achieved in 1981, but Guatemala, which had claimed the area since the early 19th century, opposed Belize's independence and British troops remained to prevent a possible invasion. In 1983, Guatemala reduced its claim to the southern fifth of Belize. Improved relations in the early 1990s led Guatemala to recognize Belize's independence and, in 1992, Britain agreed to withdraw its troops from the country.

The World Bank classifies Belize as a 'lower-middle-income' developing country. Its economy is based on agriculture and sugar cane is the chief commercial crop and export. Other crops include bananas, beans, citrus fruits, maize and rice. Forestry, fishing and tourism are other important activities.

AREA 22,960 sq km [8,865 sq mls]
POPULATION 228,000
CAPITAL (POPULATION) Belmopan (44,000)
GOVERNMENT Constitutional monarchy
ETHNIC GROUPS Mestizo (Spanish-Indian) 44%, Creole (mainly African American) 30%, Mayan Indian 11%, Garifuna (Black-Carib Indian) 7%, White 4%, East Indian 3%
LANGUAGES English (official), Creole, Spanish
RELIGIONS Christianity (Roman Catholic 58%, Protestant 29%), Hinduism 2%
CURRENCY Belize dollar = 100 cents

BENIN

GEOGRAPHY The Republic of Benin is one of Africa's smallest countries. It extends north–south for about 620 km [390 mls]. Lagoons line the short coastline, and the country has no natural harbours.

Benin has a hot, wet climate. The average annual temperature on the coast is about 25°C [77°F], and the average rainfall is about 1,330 mm [52 in]. The inland plains are wetter than the coast.

POLITICS & ECONOMY After slavery was ended in the 19th century, the French began to gain influence in the area. Benin became self-governing in 1958 and fully independent in 1960. After much instability and many changes of government, a military group took over in 1972. The country, renamed Benin in 1975, became a one-party socialist state. Socialism was abandoned in 1989, and multiparty elections were held in 1991 and 1996.

Benin is a developing country. About 70% of the people earn their living by farming, though many remain at subsistence level. The chief exports include cotton, petroleum and palm products.

AREA 112,620 sq km [43,483 sq mls]
POPULATION 5,800,000
CAPITAL (POPULATION) Porto-Novo (179,000)
GOVERNMENT Multiparty republic
ETHNIC GROUPS Fon, Adja, Bariba, Yoruba, Fulani
LANGUAGES French (official), Fon, Adja, Yoruba
RELIGIONS Traditional beliefs 60%, Christianity 23%, Islam 15%
CURRENCY CFA franc = 100 centimes

BERMUDA

A group of about 150 small islands situated 920 km [570 mls] east of the USA. Bermuda remains Britain's oldest overseas territory, but it has a long tradition of self-government. **AREA** 53 sq km [20 sq mls]; **POPULATION** 65,000; **CAPITAL** Hamilton.

BHUTAN

GEOGRAPHY A mountainous, isolated Himalayan country located between India and Tibet. The climate is similar to that of Nepal, being dependent on altitude and affected by monsoonal winds.

POLITICS & ECONOMY The monarch of Bhutan is head of both state and government and this predominantly Buddhist country remains, even in the Asian context, both conservative and poor. Bhutan is the world's most 'rural' country, with over 90% of the population dependent on agriculture and only 6% living in towns.

AREA 47,000 sq km [18,147 sq mls]
POPULATION 1,790,000
CAPITAL (POPULATION) Thimphu [30,000]
GOVERNMENT Constitutional monarchy
ETHNIC GROUPS Bhutanese, Nepali
LANGUAGES Dzongkha (official)
RELIGIONS Buddhism 75%, Hindu
CURRENCY Ngultrum = 100 chetrum

BOLIVIA

GEOGRAPHY The Republic of Bolivia is a land-locked country which straddles the Andes Mountains in central South America. The Andes rise to a height of 6,542 m [21,464 ft] at Nevado Sajama in the west.

About 40% of Bolivians live on a high plateau called the Altiplano in the Andean region, while the sparsely populated east is essentially a vast lowland plain.

The Bolivian climate is greatly affected by altitude, with the Andean peaks permanently snow-covered, while the eastern plains remain hot and humid.

POLITICS & ECONOMY American Indians have lived in Bolivia for at least 10,000 years. The main groups today are the Aymara and Quechua people.

In the last 50 years, Bolivia, an independent country since 1825, has been ruled by a succession of civilian and military governments, which violated human rights. Constitutional government was restored in 1982, but Bolivia faced many problems, including high inflation and poverty.

Bolivia is one of the poorest countries in South America. It has several natural resources, including tin, silver and natural gas, but the chief activity is agriculture, which employs 47% of the people. But experts believe that the main export may be coca, which is used to make the drug cocaine. Coca is exported illegally. The government is trying to stamp out this growing industry.

AREA 1,098,580 sq km [424,162 sq mls]
POPULATION 7,650,000
CAPITAL (POPULATION) La Paz (1,126,000)
GOVERNMENT Multiparty republic
ETHNIC GROUPS Mestizo 31%, Quechua 25%, Aymara 17%, White 15%
LANGUAGES Spanish, Aymara, Quechua (all official)
RELIGIONS Christianity (Roman Catholic 94%)
CURRENCY Boliviano = 100 centavos

BOSNIA-HERZEGOVINA

GEOGRAPHY The Republic of Bosnia-Herzegovina is one of the five republics to emerge from the former Federal People's Republic of Yugoslavia. Much of the country is mountainous or hilly, with an arid limestone plateau in the south-west. The River Sava, which forms most of the northern border with Croatia, is a tributary of the River Danube. Because of the country's odd shape, the coastline is limited to a short stretch of 20 km [13 mls] on the Adriatic coast.

A Mediterranean climate, with dry, sunny summers and moist, mild winters, prevails only near the coast. Inland, the weather becomes more severe, with hot, dry summers and bitterly cold, snowy winters.

POLITICS & ECONOMY In 1918, Bosnia-Herzegovina became part of the Kingdom of the Serbs, Croats and Slovenes, which was renamed Yugoslavia in 1929. Germany occupied the area during World War II (1939–45). From 1945, Communist governments ruled Yugoslavia as a federation containing six republics, one of which was Bosnia-Herzegovina. In the 1980s, the country faced problems as Communist policies proved unsuccessful and differences arose between ethnic groups.

In 1990, free elections were held in Bosnia-Herzegovina and the non-Communists won a majority. A Muslim, Alija Izetbegovic, was elected president. In 1991, Croatia and Slovenia, other parts of the former Yugoslavia, declared themselves independent. In 1992, Bosnia-Herzegovina held a vote on independence. Most Bosnian Serbs boycotted the vote, while the Muslims and Bosnian Croats voted in favour. Many Bosnian Serbs, opposed to independence, started a war against the non-Serbs. They soon occupied more than two-thirds of the land. The Bosnian Serbs were accused of 'ethnic cleansing' – that is, the killing or expulsion of other ethnic groups from Serb-occupied areas. The war was later extended when Croat forces seized other parts of the country.

In 1995, the warring parties agreed to a solution to the conflict. This involved keeping the present boundaries of Bosnia-Herzegovina, but dividing it into two self-governing provinces, one Bosnian Serb and the other Muslim-Croat, under a central, unified, multi-ethnic government. Elections were held in 1996 under this new arrangement.

The economy of Bosnia-Herzegovina, the least developed of the six republics of the former Yugoslavia apart from Macedonia, was shattered by the war in the early 1990s. Before the war, manufactures were the main exports, including electrical equipment, machinery and transport equipment, and textiles. Farm products include fruits, maize, tobacco, vegetables and wheat, but the country has to import food.

AREA 51,129 sq km [19,745 sq mls]
POPULATION 3,600,000
CAPITAL (POPULATION) Sarajevo (526,000)
GOVERNMENT Transitional
ETHNIC GROUPS Muslim 49%, Serb 31%, Croat 17%
LANGUAGES Serbo-Croatian
RELIGIONS Islam 40%, Christianity (Serbian Orthodox 31%, Roman Catholic 15%, Protestant 4%)
CURRENCY Dinar = 100 paras

BOTSWANA

GEOGRAPHY The Republic of Botswana is a landlocked country in southern Africa. The Kalahari, a semi-desert area covered mostly by grasses and thorn scrub, covers much of the country. Most of the south has no permanent streams. But large depressions in the north are inland drainage basins. In one of them, the Okavango River, which rises in Angola, forms a large, swampy delta.

Temperatures are high in the summer months (October to April), but the winter months are much cooler. In winter, night-time temperatures sometimes drop below freezing point. The average annual rainfall ranges from over 400 mm [16 in] in the east to less than 200 mm [8 in] in the south-west.

POLITICS & ECONOMY The earliest inhabitants of the region were the San, who are also called Bushmen. They had a nomadic way of life, hunting wild animals and collecting wild plant foods.

Britain ruled the area as the Bechuanaland Protectorate between 1885 and 1966. When the country became independent, it adopted the name of Botswana. Since then, unlike many African countries, Botswana has been a stable multiparty democracy.

In 1966, Botswana was one of Africa's poorest countries, depending on meat and live cattle for its exports. But the discovery of minerals, including coal, cobalt, copper, diamonds and nickel, has boosted the economy. However, more than 40% of the people still work as farmers, raising cattle and growing crops, such as millet, maize, beans and vegetables. Botswana also has some food-processing plants and factories producing such things as soap and textiles.

AREA 581,730 sq km [224,606 sq mls]
POPULATION 1,510,000
CAPITAL (POPULATION) Gaborone (133,000)
GOVERNMENT Multiparty republic
ETHNIC GROUPS Tswana 75%, Shona 12%, San (Bushmen) 3%
LANGUAGES English (official), Setswana
RELIGIONS Traditional beliefs 49%, Christianity 50%
CURRENCY Pula = 100 thebe

BRAZIL

GEOGRAPHY The Federative Republic of Brazil is the world's fifth largest country. It contains three main regions. The Amazon basin in the north covers more than half of Brazil. The Amazon, the world's second longest river, has a far greater volume than any other river. The second region, the north-east, consists of a coastal plain and the *sertão*, which is the name for the inland plateaux and hill country. The main river in this region is the São Francisco.

The third region is made up of the plateaux in the south-east. This region, which covers about a quarter of the country, is the most developed and densely populated part of Brazil. Its main river is the Paraná, which flows south through Argentina.

Manaus has high temperatures all through the year. The rainfall is heavy, though the period from June to September is drier than the rest of the year. The capital, Brasília, and the city Rio de Janeiro also have tropical climates, with much more marked dry seasons than Manaus. The far south has a temperate climate. The north-eastern interior is the driest region, with an average annual rainfall of only 250 mm [10 in] in places. The rainfall is also unreliable and severe droughts are common in this region.

POLITICS & ECONOMY The Portuguese explorer Pedro Alvarez Cabral claimed Brazil for Portugal in 1500. With Spain occupied in western South America, the Portuguese began to develop their colony, which was more than 90 times as big as Portugal. To do this, they enslaved many local Amerindian people and introduced about 4 million African slaves to work on their plantations and in the mines. Brazil declared itself an independent empire in 1822 and a republic in 1889. From the 1930s, Brazil faced many problems, including corruption and spells of dictatorial military government. Civilian government was restored in 1985 and Brazil adopted a new constitution in 1988.

The United Nations has described Brazil as a 'Rapidly Industrializing Country', or RIC. Its total volume of production is one of the largest in the world. But many people, including poor farmers and residents of the *favelas* (city slums), do not share in the country's fast economic growth. Widespread poverty, together with high inflation and unemployment, cause political problems.

By the early 1990s, industry was the most valuable activity, employing 25% of the people. Brazil is among the world's top producers of bauxite, chrome, diamonds, gold, iron ore, manganese and tin. It is also a major manufacturing country. Its products include aircraft, cars, chemicals, processed food, including raw sugar, iron and steel, paper and textiles.

Brazil is one of the world's leading farming countries and agriculture employs 28% of the people. Coffee is a major export. Other leading products include bananas, citrus fruits, cocoa, maize, rice, soya beans and sugar cane. Brazil is also the top producer of eggs, meat and milk in South America.

Forestry is a major industry, though many people fear that the exploitation of the rainforests, with 1.5% to 4% of Brazil's forest being destroyed every year, is a disaster for the entire world.

AREA 8,511,970 sq km [3,286,472 sq mls]
POPULATION 159,500,000
CAPITAL (POPULATION) Brasília (1,596,000)
GOVERNMENT Federal republic
ETHNIC GROUPS White 53%, Mulatto 22%, Mestizo 12%, African American 11%, Japanese 1%, Amerindian 0.1%
LANGUAGES Portuguese (official)
RELIGIONS Christianity (Roman Catholic 88%)
CURRENCY Real = 100 centavos

BRUNEI

The Islamic Sultanate of Brunei, a British protectorate until 1984, lies on the north coast of Borneo. The climate is tropical and rainforests cover large areas. Brunei is a prosperous country because of its oil and natural gas production, and the Sultan is said to be the world's richest man. **AREA** 5,770 sq km [2,228 sq mls]; **POPULATION** 300,000; **CAPITAL** Bandar Seri Begawan

BULGARIA

GEOGRAPHY The Republic of Bulgaria is a country in the Balkan peninsula, facing the Black Sea in the east. The heart of Bulgaria is mountainous. The main ranges are the Balkan Mountains in the centre and the Rhodope (or Rhodopi) Mountains in the south.

Summers are hot and winters are cold, though seldom severe. The rainfall is moderate throughout the year.

POLITICS & ECONOMY Ottoman Turks ruled Bulgaria from 1396 and ethnic Turks still form a sizeable minority in the country. In 1879, Bulgaria became a monarchy, and in 1908 it became fully independent. Bulgaria was an ally of Germany in World War I (1914–18) and again in World War II (1939–45). In 1944, Soviet troops invaded Bulgaria and, after the war, the monarchy was abolished and the country became a Communist ally of the Soviet Union. In the late 1980s, reforms in the Soviet Union led Bulgaria's government to introduce a multiparty system in 1990. A non-Communist government was elected in 1991, the first free elections in 44 years. Since 1991, Bulgaria has faced problems in trying to transform the old Communist economy into a new one based on private enterprise.

According to the World Bank, Bulgaria in the 1990s was a 'lower-middle-income' developing country. Bulgaria has some deposits of minerals, including brown coal, manganese and iron ore. But manufacturing is the leading economic activity, though problems arose in the early 1990s, because much industrial technology is outdated. The main products are chemicals, processed foods, metal products, machinery and textiles. Manufactures are the leading exports. Bulgaria trades mainly with countries in Eastern Europe.

AREA 110,910 sq km [42,822 sq mls]
POPULATION 8,560,000
CAPITAL (POPULATION) Sofia (1,117,000)
GOVERNMENT Multiparty republic
ETHNIC GROUPS Bulgarian 86%, Turkish 10%, Gypsy 3%, Macedonian, Armenian, Romanian, Greek
LANGUAGES Bulgarian (official), Turkish
RELIGIONS Christianity (Eastern Orthodox 87%), Islam 13%
CURRENCY Lev = 100 stotinki

BURKINA FASO

GEOGRAPHY The Democratic People's Republic of Burkina Faso is a landlocked country, a little larger than the United Kingdom, in West Africa. But Burkina Faso has only one-sixth of the population of the UK. The country consists of a plateau, between about 300 m and 700 m [650 ft to 2,300 ft] above sea level. The plateau is cut by several rivers.

The capital city, Ouagadougou, in central Burkina Faso, has high temperatures throughout the year. Most of the rain falls between May and September, but the rainfall is erratic and droughts are common.

POLITICS & ECONOMY The people of Burkina Faso are divided into two main groups. The Voltaic group includes the Mossi, who form the largest single group, and the Bobo. The French conquered the Mossi capital of Ouagadougou in 1897 and they made the area a protectorate. In 1919, the area became a French colony called Upper Volta. After independence in 1960, Upper Volta became a one-party state. But it was unstable – military groups seized power several times and a number of political killings took place.

In 1984, the country's name was changed to Burkina Faso. Elections were held in 1991 – for the first time in more than ten years – but the military kept an important role in the government.

Burkina Faso is one of the world's 20 poorest countries and has become very dependent on foreign aid. Most of Burkina Faso is dry with thin soils. The country's main food crops are beans, maize, millet, rice and sorghum. Cotton, groundnuts and shea nuts, whose seeds produce a fat used to make cooking oil and soap, are grown for sale abroad. Livestock are also an important export.

The country has few resources and manufacturing is on a small scale. There are some deposits of manganese, zinc, lead and nickel in the north of the country, but there is not yet a good enough transport system there. Many young men seek jobs abroad in Ghana and Ivory Coast. The money they send home to their families is important to the country's economy.

AREA 274,200 sq km [105,869 sq mls]
POPULATION 10,900,000
CAPITAL (POPULATION) Ouagadougou (690,000)
GOVERNMENT Multiparty republic
ETHNIC GROUPS Mossi 48%, Mande 9%, Fulani 8%, Bobo 7%
LANGUAGES French (official), Mossi, Fulani
RELIGIONS Traditional beliefs 45%, Islam 43%, Christianity 12%
CURRENCY CFA franc = 100 centimes

BURMA (MYANMAR)

GEOGRAPHY The Union of Burma is now officially known as the Union of Myanmar; its name was changed in 1989. Mountains border the country in the east and west, with the highest mountains in the north. Burma's highest mountain is Hkakabo Razi, which is 5,881 m [19,294 ft] high. Between these ranges is central Burma, which contains the fertile valleys of the Irrawaddy and Sittang rivers. The Irrawaddy delta on the Bay of Bengal is one of the world's leading rice-growing areas. Burma also includes the long Tenasserim coast in the south-east.

Burma has a tropical monsoon climate. There are three seasons. The rainy season runs from late May to mid-October. A cool, dry season follows, between late October and the middle part of February. The hot season lasts from late February to mid-May, though temperatures remain high during the humid rainy season.

POLITICS & ECONOMY Many groups settled in Burma in ancient times. Some, called the hill peoples, live in remote mountain areas where they have retained their own cultures. The ancestors of the country's main ethnic group today, the Burmese, arrived in the 9th century AD.

Britain conquered Burma in the 19th century and made it a province of British India. But, in 1937, the British granted Burma limited self-government. Japan conquered Burma in 1942, but the Japanese were driven out in 1945. Burma became a fully independent country in 1948.

Revolts by Communists and various hill people led to instability in the 1950s. In 1962, Burma became a military dictatorship and, in 1974, a one-party state. Attempts to control minority liberation movements and the opium trade led to repressive rule. The National League for Democracy led by Aung San Suu Kyi won the elections in 1990, but the military ignored the result and continued their repressive rule. They earned Burma the reputation for having one of the world's worst records on human rights. Burma's internal political problems have helped to make it one of the world's poorest countries. Its admission to ASEAN (Association of South-east Asian Nations) in 1997 may have implied regional recognition of the regime, but the European Union continues to voice its concern over human rights abuses.

Agriculture is the main activity, employing 64% of the people. The chief crop is rice. Maize, pulses, oilseeds and sugar cane are other major products. Forestry is important. Teak and rice together make up about two-thirds of the total value of the exports. Burma has many mineral resources, though they are mostly undeveloped, but the country is famous for its precious stones, especially rubies. Manufacturing is mostly on a small scale.

AREA 676,577 sq km [261,228 sq mls]
POPULATION 47,500,000
CAPITAL (POPULATION) Rangoon (2,513,000)
GOVERNMENT Military regime
ETHNIC GROUPS Burman 69%, Shan 9%, Karen 6%, Rakhine 5%, Mon 2%, Kachin 1%
LANGUAGES Burmese (official), Shan, Karen, Rakhine, Mon, Kachin, English, Chin
RELIGIONS Buddhism 89%, Christianity, Islam
CURRENCY Kyat = 100 pyas

BURUNDI

GEOGRAPHY The Republic of Burundi is the fifth smallest country in mainland Africa. It is also the second most densely populated after its northern neighbour, Rwanda. Part of the Great African Rift Valley, which runs throughout eastern Africa into south-western Asia, lies in western Burundi. It includes part of Lake Tanganyika.

Bujumbura, the capital city, lies on the shore of Lake Tanganyika. It has a warm climate. A dry season occurs from June to September, but the other months are fairly rainy. The mountains and plateaux to the east are cooler and wetter, but the rainfall generally decreases to the east.

POLITICS & ECONOMY The Twa, a pygmy people, were the first known inhabitants of Burundi. About 1,000 years ago, the Hutu, a people who speak a Bantu language, gradually began to settle the area, pushing the Twa into remote areas.

From the 15th century, the Tutsi, a cattle-owning people from the north-east, gradually took over the country. The Hutu, although greatly outnumbering the Tutsi, were forced to serve the Tutsi overlords.

Germany conquered the area that is now Burundi and Rwanda in the late 1890s. The area, called

Ruanda-Urundi, was taken by Belgium during World War I (1914–18). In 1961, the people of Urundi voted to become a monarchy, while the people of Ruanda voted to become a republic. The two territories became fully independent as Burundi and Rwanda in 1962. After 1962, the rivalries between the Hutu and Tutsi led to periodic outbreaks of fighting. The Tutsi monarchy was ended in 1966 and Burundi became a republic. Instability continued with coups in 1976, 1987, 1993 and 1996, with periodic massacres of thousands of people as Tutsis and Hutus fought for power.

Burundi is one of the world's ten poorest countries. About 92% of the people are farmers, who mostly grow little more than they need to feed their own families. The main food crops are beans, cassava, maize and sweet potatoes. Cattle, goats and sheep are raised, while fish are an important supplement to people's diets. However, Burundi has to import food.

AREA 27,830 sq km [10,745 sq mls]
POPULATION 6,250,000
CAPITAL (POPULATION) Bujumbura (300,000)
GOVERNMENT Republic
ETHNIC GROUPS Hutu 85%, Tutsi 14%, Twa (pygmy) 1%
LANGUAGES French and Kirundi (both official)
RELIGIONS Christianity 85% (Roman Catholic 78%), traditional beliefs 13%
CURRENCY Burundi franc = 100 centimes

CAMBODIA

GEOGRAPHY The Kingdom of Cambodia is a country in South-east Asia. Low mountains border the country except in the south-east. But most of Cambodia consists of plains drained by the River Mekong, which enters Cambodia from Laos in the north and exits through Vietnam in the south-east. The north-west contains Tonlé Sap (or Great Lake). In the dry season, this lake drains into the River Mekong. But in the wet season, the level of the Mekong rises and water flows in the opposite direction from the river into Tonlé Sap – the lake then becomes the largest freshwater lake in Asia.

Cambodia has a tropical monsoon climate, with high temperatures all through the year. The dry season, when winds blow from the north or north-east, runs from November to April. During the rainy season, from May to October, moist winds blow from the south or south-east. The high humidity and heat often make conditions unpleasant. The rainfall is heaviest near the coast, and rather lower inland.

POLITICS & ECONOMY From 802 to 1432, the Khmer people ruled a great empire, which reached its peak in the 12th century. The Khmer capital was at Angkor. The Hindu stone temples built there and at nearby Angkor Wat form the world's largest group of religious buildings. France ruled the country between 1863 and 1954, when the country became an independent monarchy. But the monarchy was abolished in 1970 and Cambodia became a republic.

In 1970, US and South Vietnamese troops entered Cambodia but left after destroying North Vietnamese Communist camps in the east. The country became involved in the Vietnamese War, and then in a civil war as Cambodian Communists of the Khmer Rouge organization fought for power. The Khmer Rouge took over Cambodia in 1975 and launched a reign of

terror in which between 1 million and 2.5 million people were killed. In 1979, Vietnamese and Cambodian troops overthrew the Khmer Rouge government. But fighting continued between several factions. Vietnam withdrew in 1989, and in 1991 Prince Sihanouk was recognized as head of state. Elections were held in May 1993, and in September 1993 the monarchy was restored. Sihanouk again became king. In 1997, the prime minister, Prince Norodom Ranariddh, was deposed, so ending four years of democratic rule. This led to Cambodia's application to join the Association of South-east Asian Nations to be put on hold.

Cambodia is a poor country whose economy has been wrecked by war. Until the 1970s, the country's farmers produced most of the food needed by the people. But by 1986, it was only able to supply 80% of its needs. Farming is the main activity and rice, rubber and maize are major products. Manufacturing is almost non-existent, apart from rubber processing and a few factories producing items for sale in Cambodia.

AREA 181,040 sq km [69,900 sq mls]
POPULATION 10,500,000
CAPITAL (POPULATION) Phnom Penh (920,000)
GOVERNMENT Constitutional monarchy
ETHNIC GROUPS Khmer 94%, Chinese 3%, Cham 2%, Thai, Lao, Kola, Vietnamese
LANGUAGES Khmer (official)
RELIGIONS Buddhism 88%, Islam 2%
CURRENCY Riel = 100 sen

CAMEROON

GEOGRAPHY The Republic of Cameroon in West Africa got its name from the Portuguese word *camarões*, or prawns. This name was used by Portuguese explorers who fished for prawns along the coast. Behind the narrow coastal plains on the Gulf of Guinea, the land rises to a series of plateaux, with a mountainous region in the south-west where the volcano Mount Cameroon is situated. In the north, the land slopes down towards the Lake Chad basin.

The rainfall is heavy, especially in the highlands. The rainiest months near the coast are June to September. The rainfall decreases to the north and the far north has a hot, dry climate. Temperatures are high on the coast, whereas the inland plateaux are cooler.

POLITICS & ECONOMY Germany lost Cameroon during World War I (1914–18). The country was then divided into two parts, one ruled by Britain and the other by France. In 1960, French Cameroon became the independent Cameroon Republic. In 1961, after a vote in British Cameroon, part of the territory joined the Cameroon Republic to become the Federal Republic of Cameroon. The other part joined Nigeria. In 1972, Cameroon became a unitary state called the United Republic of Cameroon. It adopted the name Republic of Cameroon in 1984, but the country had two official languages. In 1995, partly to placate English-speaking people, Cameroon became the 52nd member of the Commonwealth.

Like most countries in tropical Africa, Cameroon's economy is based on agriculture, which employs 73% of the people. The chief food crops include cassava, maize, millet, sweet potatoes and yams. The country also has plantations to produce such crops as cocoa and coffee for export.

Cameroon is fortunate in having some oil, the country's chief export, and bauxite. Although Cameroon has few manufacturing and processing industries, its mineral exports and its self-sufficiency in food production make it one of the better-off countries in tropical Africa.

AREA 475,440 sq km [183,567 sq mls]
POPULATION 13,800,000
CAPITAL (POPULATION) Yaoundé (750,000)
GOVERNMENT Multiparty republic
ETHNIC GROUPS Fang 20%, Bamileke and Bamum 19%, Duala, Luanda and Basa 15%, Fulani 10%
LANGUAGES French and English (both official)
RELIGIONS Christianity 53%, traditional beliefs 25%, Islam 22%
CURRENCY CFA franc = 100 centimes

CANADA

GEOGRAPHY Canada is the world's second largest country after Russia. It is thinly populated, however, with much of the land too cold or too mountainous for human settlement. Most Canadians live within 300 km [186 mls] of the southern border.

Western Canada is rugged. It includes the Pacific ranges and the mighty Rocky Mountains. East of the Rockies are the interior plains. In the north lie the bleak Arctic islands, while to the south lie the densely populated lowlands around lakes Erie and Ontario and in the St Lawrence River valley.

Canada has a cold climate. In winter, temperatures fall below freezing point throughout most of Canada. But Vancouver, on the west coast, has a relatively mild climate. In the north, along the Arctic Circle, mean temperatures are below freezing for seven months per year.

Western and south-eastern Canada experience high rainfall, but the prairies are dry with 250 mm to 500 mm [10 in to 20 in] of rain every year.

POLITICS & ECONOMY Canada's first people, the ancestors of the Native Americans, or Indians, arrived in North America from Asia around 40,000 years ago. Later arrivals were the Inuit (Eskimos), who also came from Asia. European explorers reached the Canadian coast in 1497 and soon a race began between France and Britain for the riches in this new land.

France gained an initial advantage, and the French founded Québec in 1608. But the British later occupied eastern Canada. In 1867, Britain passed the British North America Act, which set up the Dominion of Canada, which was made up of Québec, Ontario, Nova Scotia and New Brunswick. Other areas were added, the last being Newfoundland in 1949.

Canada fought alongside Britain in both World Wars and many Canadians feel close ties with Britain. Canada is a constitutional monarchy. The head of state is Queen Elizabeth II, though the country is governed by a prime minister, a cabinet and an elected, two-chamber parliament.

Rivalries between French- and English-speaking Canadians continue. In 1995, Québeckers voted against a move to make Québec a sovereign state. The majority was less than 1% and this issue seems unlikely to disappear. Another problem concerns the future of the Native Americans, who would like to have more say in running their own affairs.

Canada is a highly developed and prosperous country. Although farmland covers only 8% of the country, Canadian farms are highly productive. Canada is one of the world's leading producers of barley, wheat, meat and milk. Forestry and fishing are other important industries. It is rich in natural resources, especially oil and natural gas, and is a major exporter of minerals. The country also produces copper, gold, iron ore, uranium and zinc. Manufacturing is highly developed, especially in the cities where 77% of the people live. Canada has many factories that process farm and mineral products. It also produces cars, chemicals, electronic goods, machinery, paper and timber products.

AREA 9,976,140 sq km [3,851,788 sq mls]
POPULATION 30,200,000
CAPITAL (POPULATION) Ottawa (1,010,000)
GOVERNMENT Federal multiparty constitutional monarchy
ETHNIC GROUPS British 34%, French 26%, German 4%, Italian 3%, Ukrainian 2%, Native American (Amerindian/Inuit) 1.5%, Chinese
LANGUAGES English and French (both official)
RELIGIONS Christianity (Roman Catholic 47%, Protestant 41%), Judaism, Islam, Hinduism
CURRENCY Canadian dollar = 100 cents

CAPE VERDE

Cape Verde consists of ten large and five small islands, and is situated 560 km [350 mls] west of Dakar in Senegal. The islands have a tropical climate, with high temperatures all year round. Cape Verde became independent from Portugal in 1975 and is rated as a 'low-income' developing country by the World Bank. AREA 4,030 sq km [1,556 sq mls]; POPULATION 410,000; CAPITAL Praia.

CAYMAN ISLANDS

The Cayman Islands are an overseas territory of the UK, consisting of three low-lying islands. Financial services are the main economic activity and the islands offer a secret tax haven to many companies and banks. AREA 259 sq km [100 sq mls]; POPULATION 35,000; CAPITAL George Town.

CENTRAL AFRICAN REPUBLIC

GEOGRAPHY The Central African Republic is a remote, landlocked country in the heart of Africa. It consists mostly of a plateau lying between 600 m and 800 m [1,970 ft to 2,620 ft] above sea level. The Ubangi drains the south, while the Chari (or Shari)

River flows from the north to the Lake Chad basin.

Bangui, the capital, lies in the south-west of the country on the Ubangi River. The climate is warm throughout the year, with average yearly rainfall totalling 1,574 mm [62 in]. The north is drier, with an average yearly rainfall of about 800 mm [31 in].
POLITICS & ECONOMY France set up an outpost at Bangui in 1899 and ruled the country as a colony from 1894. Known as Ubangi-Shari, the country was ruled by France as part of French Equatorial Africa until it gained independence in 1960.

Central African Republic became a one-party state in 1962, but army officers seized power in 1966. The head of the army, Jean-Bedel Bokassa, made himself emperor in 1976. The country was renamed the Central African Empire, but after a brutal and tyrannical reign, Bokassa was overthrown by a military group in 1979. As a result, the monarchy was abolished and the country again became a republic.

The country adopted a new, multiparty constitution in 1991. Elections were held in 1993. An army rebellion was put down in 1996 with help from French troops.

The World Bank classifies Central African Republic as a 'low-income' developing country. Over 80% of the people are farmers, and most of them produce little more than they need to feed their families. The main crops are bananas, maize, manioc, millet and yams. Coffee, cotton, timber and tobacco are produced for export, mainly on commercial plantations. The country's development has been impeded by its remote position, its poor transport system and its untrained workforce. The country depends heavily on aid, especially from France.

AREA 622,980 sq km [240,533 sq mls]
POPULATION 3,400,000
CAPITAL (POPULATION) Bangui (706,000)
GOVERNMENT Multiparty republic
ETHNIC GROUPS Banda 29%, Baya 25%, Ngbandi 11%, Azande 10%, Sara 7%, Mbaka 4%
LANGUAGES French and Sango (both official)
RELIGIONS Traditional beliefs 57%, Christianity 35%, Islam 8%
CURRENCY CFA franc = 100 centimes

CHAD

GEOGRAPHY The Republic of Chad is a landlocked country in north-central Africa. It is Africa's fifth largest country and is more than twice as big as France, the country which once ruled it as a colony.

Ndjamena in central Chad has a hot, tropical climate, with a marked dry season from November to April. The south of the country is wetter, with an average yearly rainfall of around 1,000 mm [39 in]. The burning-hot desert in the north has an average yearly rainfall of less than 130 mm [5 in].
POLITICS & ECONOMY Chad straddles two worlds. The north is populated by Muslim Arab and Berber peoples, while black Africans, who follow traditional beliefs or who have converted to Christianity, live in the south.

French explorers were active in the area in the late 19th century. France finally made Chad a colony in 1902. After becoming independent in 1960, Chad has been hit by ethnic conflict. In the 1970s, civil war, frequent coups and intervention in the north by Libya retarded the country's economic development. Chad

and Libya agreed a truce in 1987 and, in 1994, the International Court of Justice ruled that Libya had no claim on the Aozou Strip in the far north.

Hit by drought and civil war, Chad is one of the world's poorest countries. Farming, fishing and livestock raising employ 83% of the people. Groundnuts, millet, rice and sorghum are major food crops in the wetter south, but the most valuable crop in export terms is cotton. The country has few natural resources and very few manufacturing industries.

AREA 1,284,000 sq km [495,752 sq mls]
POPULATION 6,750,000
CAPITAL (POPULATION) Ndjaména (530,000)
GOVERNMENT Transitional
ETHNIC GROUPS Bagirmi, Kreish and Sara 31%, Sudanic Arab 26%, Teda 7%, Mbum 6%
LANGUAGES French and Arabic (both official)
RELIGIONS Islam 40%, Christianity 33%, traditional beliefs 27%
CURRENCY CFA franc = 100 centimes

CHILE

GEOGRAPHY The Republic of Chile stretches about 4,260 km [2,650 mls] from north to south, although the maximum east–west distance is only about 430 km [267 mls]. The high Andes Mountains form Chile's eastern borders with Argentina and Bolivia. To the west are basins and valleys, with coastal uplands overlooking the shore. Most people live in the central valley, where Santiago is situated.

Santiago, Chile's capital, has a Mediterranean climate, with hot, dry summers from November to March and mild, moist winters from April to October. However, the Atacama Desert in the north is one of the world's driest places, while southern Chile is cold and stormy.
POLITICS & ECONOMY Amerindian people reached the southern tip of South America at least 8,000 years ago. In 1520, the Portuguese navigator Ferdinand Magellan became the first European to sight Chile, but the country became a Spanish colony in the 1540s. Chile became independent in 1818 and, during a war (1879–83), it gained mineral-rich areas from Peru and Bolivia.

In 1970, Salvador Allende became the first Communist leader ever to be elected democratically. He was overthrown in 1973 by army officers, who were supported by the CIA. General Augusto Pinochet then ruled as a dictator. A new constitution was introduced in 1981 and elections were held in 1989.

The World Bank classifies Chile as a 'lower-middle-income' developing country. Mining is important, especially copper production. Minerals dominate Chile's exports. But the most valuable activity is manufacturing; products include processed foods, metals, iron and steel, wood products, transport equipment and textiles.

AREA 756,950 sq km [292,258 sq mls]
POPULATION 14,700,000
CAPITAL (POPULATION) Santiago (5,077,000)
GOVERNMENT Multiparty republic
ETHNIC GROUPS Mestizo 92%, Amerindian 7%
LANGUAGES Spanish (official)
RELIGIONS Christianity (Roman Catholic 81%)
CURRENCY Peso = 100 centavos

CHINA

GEOGRAPHY The People's Republic of China is the world's third largest country. It is also the only country with more than 1,000 million people. Most people live in the east – on the coastal plains or in the fertile valleys of the Huang He (Hwang Ho or Yellow River), the Chang Jiang (Yangtze Kiang), which is Asia's longest river at 6,380 km [3,960 mls], and the Xi Jiang (Si Kiang).

Western China is thinly populated. It includes the bleak Tibetan plateau which is bounded by the Himalaya, the world's highest mountain range. Other ranges include the Kunlun Shan, the Altun Shan and the Tian Shan. Deserts include the Gobi desert along the Mongolian border and the Taklimakan desert in the far west.

Beijing in north-eastern China has cold winters and warm summers, with a moderate rainfall. Shanghai, in the east-central region of China, has milder winters and more rain. The south-east has a wet, subtropical climate. In the west, the climate is severe. Lhasa has very cold winters and a low rainfall.

POLITICS & ECONOMY China is one of the world's oldest civilizations, going back 3,500 years. Under the Han dynasty (202 BC to AD 220), the Chinese empire was as large as the Roman empire. Mongols conquered China in the 13th century, but Chinese rule was restored in 1368. The Manchu people of Mongolia ruled the country from 1644 to 1912, when the country became a republic.

War with Japan (1937–45) was followed by civil war between the nationalists and the Communists. The Communists triumphed in 1949, setting up the People's Republic of China.

In the 1980s, following the death of the revolutionary leader Mao Tse-tung in 1976, China introduced reforms. It encouraged private enterprise and foreign investment, policies forbidden under Mao's rule. But China's Communist leaders have not permitted political freedoms. Opponents of the regime continue to be harshly treated.

China's economy, which is one of the world's largest, has expanded rapidly since the late 1970s. This is partly the result of the gradual abandonment of some fundamental Communist policies, including the setting up of many private manufacturing industries in the east. China's sheer size, combined with its rapid economic growth, have led to predictions that China will soon become a superpower. It was forecast in 1996 that China would become the world's biggest economy 'within a generation'. This was only made more likely by the return of Hong Kong in July 1997, although by the end of the year, the crash in several other Asian economies led some to make pessimistic predictions about China's future growth.

In the early 1990s, agriculture employed about 70% of the people, although only 10% of the land is used for crops. Major products include rice, sweet potatoes, tea and wheat, together with many fruits and vegetables. Livestock farming is also important. Pork is a popular meat and China has more than a third of the world's pigs.

China's resources include coal, oil, iron ore and various other metals. China has huge steel industries and manufactures include cement, chemicals, fertilizers, machinery, telecommunications and recording equipment, and textiles. Consumer goods, such as bicycles and radios, are becoming increasingly important.

AREA 9,596,960 sq km [3,705,386 sq mls]
POPULATION 1,210,000,000
CAPITAL (POPULATION) Beijing (12,362,000)
GOVERNMENT Single-party Communist republic
ETHNIC GROUPS Han Chinese 92%, 55 minority groups
LANGUAGES Mandarin Chinese (official)
RELIGIONS Atheist 50%, Confucian 20%
CURRENCY Renminbi yuan = 10 jiao = 100 fen

COLOMBIA

GEOGRAPHY The Republic of Colombia, in north-eastern South America, is the only country in the continent to have coastlines on both the Pacific and the Caribbean Sea. Colombia also contains the northernmost ranges of the Andes Mountains.

There is a tropical climate in the lowlands. But the altitude greatly affects the climate of the Andes. The capital, Bogotá, which stands on a plateau in the eastern Andes at about 2,800 m [9,200 ft] above sea level, has mild temperatures throughout the year. The rainfall is heavy, especially on the Pacific coast

POLITICS & ECONOMY Amerindian people have lived in Colombia for thousands of years. But today, only a small proportion of the people are of unmixed Amerindian ancestry. Mestizos (people of mixed white and Amerindian ancestry) form the largest group, followed by whites and mulattos (people of mixed European and African ancestry).

Spaniards opened up the area in the early 16th century and they set up a territory known as the Viceroyalty of the New Kingdom of Granada, which included Colombia, Ecuador, Panama and Venezuela. In 1819, the area became independent, but Ecuador and Venezuela soon split away, followed by Panama in 1903. Colombia's recent history has been very unstable. Rivalries between the main political parties led to civil wars in 1899–1902 and 1949–57, when the parties agreed to form a coalition. The coalition government ended in 1986 when the Liberal Party was elected. Colombia faces many economic problems, as well as the difficulty of controlling a large illicit drug industry run by violent dealers. Colombia exports coal and oil, and it also produces emeralds and gold.

AREA 1,138,910 sq km [439,733 sq mls]
POPULATION 35,900,000
CAPITAL (POPULATION) Bogotá (5,026,000)
GOVERNMENT Multiparty republic
ETHNIC GROUPS Mestizo 58%, White 20%, Mulatto 14%, Black 4%
LANGUAGES Spanish (official)
RELIGIONS Christianity (Roman Catholic 93%)
CURRENCY Peso = 100 centavos

COMOROS

The Federal Islamic Republic of the Comoros consists of three large islands and some smaller ones, lying at the north end of the Mozambique Channel in the Indian Ocean. The country became independent from France in 1974, but the people on a fourth island, Mayotte, voted to remain French. In 1997, secessionists on the island of Anjouan, who favoured a return to French rule, defeated forces from Grand Comore and, in 1998, they voted overwhelmingly to break away from the Comoros. Most people are subsistence farmers, although cash crops such as coconuts, coffee, cocoa and spices are also produced. The main exports are cloves, perfume oils and vanilla. **AREA** 2,230 sq km [115 sq mls]; **POPULATION** 630,000; **CAPITAL** Moroni.

CONGO

GEOGRAPHY The Republic of Congo is a country on the River Congo in west-central Africa. The Equator runs through the centre of the country. Congo has a narrow coastal plain on which its main port, Pointe Noire, stands. Behind the plain are uplands through which the River Niari has carved a fertile valley. Central Congo consists of high plains. The north contains large swampy areas in the valleys of rivers that flow into the River Congo and its large tributary, the Oubangi.

Congo has a hot, wet equatorial climate. Brazzaville and its environs experience a dry season between June and September. The coastal plain is drier and cooler than the rest of the country because a cold ocean current, the Benguela, flows northwards along the coast.

POLITICS & ECONOMY Part of the huge Kongo kingdom between the 15th and 18th centuries, the coast of the Congo later became a centre of the European slave trade. The area came under French protection in 1880. It was later governed as part of a larger region called French Equatorial Africa. The country remained under French control until 1960.

Congo became a one-party state in 1964 and a military group took over the government in 1968. In 1970, Congo declared itself a Communist country, though it continued to seek aid from Western countries. The government officially abandoned its Communist policies in 1990. Multiparty elections were held in 1992, but the elected president, Pascal Lissouba, was overthrown in 1997 by former president, Denis Sassou-Nguesso.

The World Bank classifies Congo as a 'lower-middle-income' developing country. Agriculture is the most important activity, employing more than 60% of the people. But many farmers produce little more than they need to feed their families. Major food crops include bananas, cassava, maize and rice, while the leading cash crops are coffee and cocoa. Congo's main exports are oil (which makes up 70% of the total) and timber. Manufacturing is relatively unimportant at the moment, still hampered by poor transport links, but it is gradually being developed.

AREA 342,000 sq km [132,046 sq mls]
POPULATION 2,730,000
CAPITAL (POPULATION) Brazzaville (938,000)
GOVERNMENT Multiparty republic
ETHNIC GROUPS Kongo 52%, Teke 17%, Mboshi 12%, Mbete 5%
LANGUAGES French (official), Kongo, Teke
RELIGIONS Christianity (Roman Catholic 54%, Protestant 25%, African Christians 14%
CURRENCY CFA franc = 100 centimes

CONGO (ZAÏRE)

GEOGRAPHY The Democratic Republic of the Congo, formerly known as Zaïre, is the world's 12th largest country. Much of the country lies within the drainage basin of the huge River Congo. The river reaches the sea along the country's coastline, which is 40 km [25 mls] long. Mountains rise in the east, where the country's borders run through lakes Tanganyika, Kivu, Edward and Albert. These lakes lie on the floor of an arm of the Great Rift Valley.

The equatorial region has high temperatures and heavy rainfall throughout the year. In the subtropical south, where the town of Lubumbashi is situated, there is a marked wet and dry season.

POLITICS & ECONOMY Pygmies were the first inhabitants of the region, with Portuguese navigators not reaching the coast until 1482, but the interior was not explored until the late 19th century. In 1885, the country, called Congo Free State, became the personal property of King Léopold II of Belgium. In 1908, the country became a Belgian colony.

The Belgian Congo became independent in 1960 and was renamed Zaïre in 1971. Ethnic rivalries caused instability until 1965, when the country became a one-party state, ruled by President Mobutu. The government allowed the formation of political parties in 1990, but elections were repeatedly postponed. In 1996, fighting broke out in eastern Zaïre, as the Tutsi–Hutu conflict in Burundi and Rwanda spilled over. A rebel leader, Laurent Kabila, took advantage and eventually seized power after an eight-month march through the country. One of his first acts was to rename the country, and to change the flag.

The World Bank classifies the Democratic Republic of the Congo as a 'low-income' developing country, despite its reserves of copper, the main export, and other minerals. Agriculture employs 71% of the people, though many farmers grow barely enough to feed their own families.

AREA 2,344,885 sq km [905,365 sq mls]
POPULATION 47,200,000
CAPITAL (POPULATION) Kinshasa (3,804,000)
GOVERNMENT Single-party republic
ETHNIC GROUPS Luba 18%, Kongo 16%, Mongo 14%, Rwanda 10%, Azande 6%, Bandi and Ngale 6%, Rundi 4%, Teke, Boa, Chokwe, Lugbara, Banda
LANGUAGES French (official), tribal languages
RELIGIONS Christianity (Roman Catholic 48%, Protestant 29%, indigenous Christian churches 17%), traditional beliefs 3%, Islam 1%
CURRENCY Congolese franc

COSTA RICA

GEOGRAPHY The Republic of Costa Rica in Central America has coastlines on both the Pacific Ocean and also on the Caribbean Sea. Central Costa Rica consists of mountain ranges and plateaux with many volcanoes.

The coolest months are December and January. The north-east trade winds bring heavy rain to the Caribbean coast. There is less rainfall in the highlands and on the Pacific coastlands.

POLITICS & ECONOMY Christopher Columbus reached the Caribbean coast in 1502 and rumours of treasure soon attracted many Spaniards to settle in the country. Spain ruled the country until 1821, when Spain's Central American colonies broke away to join Mexico in 1822. In 1823, the Central American states broke with Mexico and set up the Central American Federation. Later, this large union broke up and Costa Rica became fully independent in 1838. From the late 19th century, Costa Rica experienced a number of revolutions, with periods of dictatorship and periods of democracy. In 1948, following a revolt, the armed forces were abolished. Since 1948, Costa Rica has enjoyed a long period of stable democracy, which many in Latin America admire and envy.

Costa Rica is classified by the World Bank as a 'lower-middle-income' developing country and one of the most prosperous countries in Central America. There are high educational standards and a high life expectancy (to an average of 73.5 years). Agriculture employs 24% of the people.

The country's resources include its forests, but it lacks minerals apart from some bauxite and manganese. Manufacturing is increasing. The United States is Costa Rica's chief trading partner. Tourism is a growing industry.

AREA 51,100 sq km [19,730 sq mls]
POPULATION 3,500,000
CAPITAL (POPULATION) San José (1,186,000)
GOVERNMENT Multiparty republic
ETHNIC GROUPS White 85%, Mestizo 8%, Black and Mulatto 3%, East Asian (mostly Chinese) 3%
LANGUAGES Spanish (official)
RELIGIONS Christianity (Roman Catholic 81%)
CURRENCY Colón = 100 céntimos

CROATIA

GEOGRAPHY The Republic of Croatia was one of the six republics that made up the former Communist country of Yugoslavia until it became independent in 1991. The region bordering the Adriatic Sea is called Dalmatia. It includes the coastal ranges, which contain large areas of bare limestone. Most of the rest of the country consists of the fertile Pannonian plains.

The coastal area has a typical Mediterranean climate, with hot, dry summers and mild, moist winters. Inland, the climate becomes more continental. Winters are cold, while temperatures often soar to 38°C [100°F] in the summer months.

POLITICS & ECONOMY Slav people settled in the area around 1,400 years ago. In 803, Croatia became part of the Holy Roman Empire and the Croats soon adopted Christianity. Croatia was an independent kingdom in the 10th and 11th centuries. In 1102, the king of Hungary also became king of Croatia, creating a union that lasted 800 years. In 1526, part of Croatia came under the Turkish Ottoman empire, while the rest came under the Austrian Habsburgs.

After Austria-Hungary was defeated in World War I (1914–18), Croatia became part of the new Kingdom of the Serbs, Croats and Slovenes. This kingdom was renamed Yugoslavia in 1929. Germany occupied Yugoslavia during World War II (1939–45). Croatia was proclaimed independent, but it was really ruled by the invaders.

After the war, Communists took power with Josip Broz Tito aş the country's leader. Despite ethnic differences between the people, Tito held Yugoslavia together until his death in 1980. In the 1980s, economic and ethnic problems, including a deterioration in relations with Serbia, threatened stability. In the 1990s, Yugoslavia split into five nations, one of which was Croatia, which declared itself independent in 1991.

After Serbia supplied arms to Serbs living in Croatia, war broke out between the two republics, causing great damage. Croatia lost more than 30% of its territory. But in 1992, the United Nations sent a peacekeeping force to Croatia, which effectively ended the war with Serbia.

In 1992, when war broke out in Bosnia-Herzegovina, Bosnian Croats occupied parts of the country. But in 1994, Croatia helped to end Croat–Muslim conflict in Bosnia-Herzegovina and, in 1995, after retaking some areas occupied by Serbs, it helped to draw up the Dayton Peace Accord which ended the civil war there.

The wars of the early 1990s disrupted Croatia's economy, which had been quite prosperous before the disturbances. Tourism on the Dalmatian coast had been a major industry. Croatia also had major manufacturing industries, and manufactures remain the chief exports.

AREA 56,538 sq km [21,824 sq mls]
POPULATION 4,850,000
CAPITAL (POPULATION) Zagreb (931,000)
GOVERNMENT Multiparty republic
ETHNIC GROUPS Croat 78%, Serb 12%, Bosnian
LANGUAGES Serbo-Croatian
RELIGIONS Christianity (Roman Catholic 77%, Eastern Orthodox 11%), Islam 1%
CURRENCY Kuna = 100 lipas

CUBA

GEOGRAPHY The Republic of Cuba is the largest island country in the Caribbean Sea. It consists of one large island, Cuba, the Isle of Youth (Isla de la Juventud) and about 1,600 small islets. Mountains and hills cover about a quarter of Cuba. The highest mountain range, the Sierra Maestra in the south-east, reaches 2,000 m [6,562 ft] above sea level. The rest of the land consists of gently rolling country or coastal plains, crossed by fertile valleys carved by the short, mostly shallow and narrow rivers.

Cuba lies in the tropics. But sea breezes moderate the temperature, warming the land in winter and cooling it in summer.

POLITICS & ECONOMY Christopher Columbus discovered the island in 1492 and Spaniards began to settle there from 1511. Spanish rule ended in 1898, when the United States defeated Spain in the Spanish-American War. American influence in Cuba remained strong until 1959, when revolutionary forces under Fidel Castro overthrew the dictatorial government of Fulgencio Batista.

The United States opposed Castro's policies, when he turned to the Soviet Union for assistance. In 1961, Cuban exiles attempting an invasion were defeated. In 1962, the US learned that nuclear missile bases armed by the Soviet Union had been established in Cuba. The US ordered the Soviet Union to remove the missiles and bases and, after a few days, when many people feared that a world war might break out, the Soviet Union agreed to the American demands.

Cuba's relations with the Soviet Union remained strong until 1991, when the Soviet Union was broken up. The loss of Soviet aid greatly damaged Cuba's economy, but Castro continued the country's left-wing policies. Elections in February 1993 showed a continuing high level of support from the people for Castro.

The government runs Cuba's economy and owns 70% of the farmland. Agriculture is important and sugar is the chief export, followed by refined nickel ore. Other exports include cigars, citrus fruits, fish, medical products and rum.

Before 1959, US companies owned most of Cuba's manufacturing industries. But under Fidel Castro, they became government property. After the collapse of Communist governments in the Soviet Union and its allies, Cuba worked to increase its trade with Latin America and China.

AREA 110,860 sq km [42,803 sq mls]
POPULATION 11,250,000
CCAPITAL (POPULATION) Havana (2,241,000)
GOVERNMENT Socialist republic
ETHNIC GROUPS White 66%, Mulatto 22%, Black 12%
LANGUAGES Spanish (official)
RELIGIONS Christianity (Roman Catholic 40%, Protestant 3%)
CURRENCY Cuban peso = 100 centavos

CYPRUS

GEOGRAPHY The Republic of Cyprus is an island nation in the north-eastern Mediterranean Sea. Geographers regard it as part of Asia, but it resembles southern Europe in many ways.

Cyprus has scenic mountain ranges, including the Kyrenia range in the north and the Troodos Mountains in the south, which rise to 1,951 m [6,401 ft] at Mount Olympus. The island also contains several fertile lowlands, including the broad Mesaoria plain between the Kyrenia and Troodos mountains.

Cyprus has a Mediterranean climate, with hot, dry summers and mild, moist winters. But the summers are hotter than in the western Mediterranean lands; this is because Cyprus lies close to the hot mainland of south-western Asia.

POLITICS & ECONOMY Greeks settled on Cyprus around 3,200 years ago. From AD 330, the island was part of the Byzantine empire. In the 1570s, Cyprus became part of the Turkish Ottoman empire. Turkish rule continued until 1878 when Cyprus was leased to Britain. Britain annexed the island in 1914 and proclaimed it a colony in 1925.

In the 1950s, Greek Cypriots, who made up four-fifths of the population, began a campaign for enosis (union) with Greece. Their leader was the Greek Orthodox Archbishop Makarios. A secret guerrilla force called EOKA attacked the British, who exiled Makarios. Cyprus became an independent country in 1960, although Britain retained two military bases. Independent Cyprus had a constitution which provided for power-sharing between the Greek and Turkish Cypriots. But the constitution

proved unworkable and fighting broke out between the two communities. In 1964, the United Nations sent in a peacekeeping force. Communal clashes recurred in 1967.

In 1974, Cypriot forces led by Greek officers overthrew Makarios. This led Turkey to invade northern Cyprus, a territory occupying about 40% of the island. Many Greek Cypriots fled from the Turkish-occupied area, which, in 1979, was proclaimed to be a self-governing region. In 1983, the Turkish Cypriots declared the north to be an independent state called the Turkish Republic of Northern Cyprus. But only Turkey recognizes this state. The UN regards Cyprus as a single nation under the Greek Cypriot government in the south.

Cyprus got its name from the Greek word *kypros*, meaning copper. But little copper remains and the chief minerals today are asbestos and chromium. However, the most valuable activity in Cyprus is tourism. In the early 1990s, the United Nations reclassified Cyprus as a developed rather than a developing country. But the economy of the Turkish-Cypriot north lags behind that of the more prosperous Greek-Cypriot south.

AREA 9,250 sq km [3,571 sq mls]
POPULATION 770,000
CAPITAL (POPULATION) Nicosia (189,000)
GOVERNMENT Multiparty republic
ETHNIC GROUPS Greek Cypriot 81%, Turkish Cypriot 19%
LANGUAGES Greek and Turkish (both official)
RELIGIONS Christianity (Greek Orthodox), Islam
CURRENCY Cyprus pound = 100 cents

CZECH REPUBLIC

GEOGRAPHY The Czech Republic is the western three-fifths of the former country of Czechoslovakia. It contains two regions: Bohemia in the west and Moravia in the east. Mountains border much of the country in the west. The Bohemian basin in the north-centre is a fertile lowland region, with Prague, the capital city, as its main centre. Highlands cover much of the centre of the country, with lowlands in the south-east.

The climate is influenced by its landlocked position in east-central Europe. Prague has warm, sunny summers and cold winters. The average rainfall is moderate, with 500 mm to 750 mm [20 in to 30 in] every year in lowland areas.

POLITICS & ECONOMY After World War I (1914–18), Czechoslovakia was created. Germany seized the country in World War II (1939–45). In 1948, Communist leaders took power and Czechoslovakia was allied to the Soviet Union. When democratic reforms were introduced in the Soviet Union in the late 1980s, the Czechs also demanded reforms. Free elections were held in 1990, but differences between the Czechs and Slovaks and a resurgence of Slovak nationalism led the government to agree in 1992 to the partitioning of the country on 1 January 1993. The break was peaceful and the two new nations retained many ties.

Under Communist rule the Czech Republic became one of the most industrialized parts of Eastern Europe. The country has deposits of coal, uranium, iron ore, magnesite, tin and zinc. Manufacturing employs about 40% of the Czech Republic's entire

workforce. Farming is also important. Under Communism, the government owned the land, but private ownership is now being restored. The country was admitted into the OECD in 1995.

AREA 78,864 sq km [30,449 sq mls]
POPULATION 10,500,000
CAPITAL (POPULATION) Prague (1,213,000)
GOVERNMENT Multiparty republic
ETHNIC GROUPS Czech 81%, Moravian 13%, Slovak 3%, Polish, German, Silesian, Gypsy, Hungarian, Ukrainian
LANGUAGES Czech (official), Moravian
RELIGIONS Christianity (Roman Catholic 39%, Protestant 4%)
CURRENCY Czech koruna = 100 haler

DENMARK

GEOGRAPHY The Kingdom of Denmark is the smallest country in Scandinavia. It consists of a peninsula, called Jutland (or Jylland), which is joined to Germany, and more than 400 islands, 89 of which are inhabited.

The land is flat and mostly covered by rocks dropped there by huge ice-sheets during the last Ice Age. The highest point in Denmark is on Jutland. It is only 173 m [568 ft] above sea level.

Denmark has a cool but pleasant climate, except during cold spells in the winter when The Sound between Sjælland and Sweden may freeze over. Summers are warm. Rainfall occurs all through the year.

POLITICS & ECONOMY Danish Vikings terrorized much of Western Europe for about 300 years after AD 800. Danish kings ruled England in the 11th century. In the late 14th century, Denmark formed a union with Norway and Sweden (which included Finland). Sweden broke away in 1523, while Denmark lost Norway to Sweden in 1814.

After 1945, Denmark played an important part in European affairs, becoming a member of the North Atlantic Treaty Organization (NATO). In 1973, Denmark joined the European Union, although it remains one of its least enthusiastic members. The Danes now enjoy some of the world's highest living standards, although the extensive social welfare provisions exert a considerable cost.

Denmark has few natural resources apart from some oil and gas from wells deep under the North Sea. But the economy is highly developed. Manufacturing industries, which employ about 27% of all workers, produce a wide variety of products, including furniture, processed food, machinery, television sets and textiles. Farms cover about three-quarters of the land. Farming employs only 4% of the workers, but it is highly scientific and productive. Meat and dairy farming are the chief activities.

AREA 43,070 sq km [16,629 sq mls]
POPULATION 5,350,000
CAPITAL (POPULATION) Copenhagen (1,353,000)
GOVERNMENT Parliamentary monarchy
ETHNIC GROUPS Danish 97%
LANGUAGES Danish (official)
RELIGIONS Christianity (Lutheran 91%, Roman Catholic 1%)
CURRENCY Krone = 100 øre

DJIBOUTI

GEOGRAPHY The Republic of Djibouti is a small country in eastern Africa which occupies a strategic position where the Red Sea meets the Gulf of Aden. Behind the coastal plain on the northern side of the Gulf of Tadjoura is a highland region, the Mabla Mountains, rising to 1,783 m [5,850 ft] above sea level. Djibouti also contains Lake Assal, the lowest point on land in Africa.

Djibouti has one of the world's hottest and driest climates. Summer days are very hot with recorded temperatures of more than 44°C [112°F]. On average, it rains on only 26 days every year.

POLITICS & ECONOMY Islam was introduced into the area which is now Djibouti in the 9th century AD. The conversion of the Afars led to conflict between them and the Christian Ethiopians who lived in the interior. By the 19th century, the Issas, who are Somalis, had moved north and occupied much of the traditional grazing land of the Afars. France gained influence in the area in the second half of the 19th century and, in 1888, they set up a territory called French Somaliland. The capital of the territory, Djibouti, became important when the Ethiopian emperor, Menelik II, decided to build a railway to it from Addis Ababa, thus making it the main port handling Ethiopian trade.

In 1967, the people voted to retain their links with France, though most of the Issas favoured independence. The country was renamed the French Territory of the Afars and Issas, but it was named Djibouti when it became fully independent in 1977.

Djibouti became a one-party state in 1981, but a new constitution was introduced in 1992, permitting four parties which must maintain a balance between the ethnic groups in the country. However, in 1992 and 1993, tensions between the Afars and Issas flared up when Afars launched an uprising which was put down by government troops.

Djibouti is a poor country. Its economy is based mainly on money it gets for use of its port and the railway that links it to Addis Ababa. Most of the food the country needs has to be imported.

AREA 23,200 sq km [8,958 sq mls]
POPULATION 650,000
CAPITAL (POPULATION) Djibouti (383,000)
GOVERNMENT Multiparty republic
ETHNIC GROUPS Issa 47%, Afar 37%, Arab 6%
LANGUAGES Arabic and French (both official)
RELIGIONS Islam 96%, Christianity 4%
CURRENCY Djibouti franc = 100 centimes

DOMINICA

The Commonwealth of Dominica, a former British colony, became independent in 1978. The island has a mountainous spine and less than 10% of the land is cultivated. Yet agriculture employs more than 60% of the people. Manufacturing, mining and tourism are other minor activities. **AREA** 751 sq km [290 sq mls]; **POPULATION** 78,000; **CAPITAL** Roseau.

DOMINICAN REPUBLIC

GEOGRAPHY Second largest of the Caribbean nations in both area and population, the Dominican Republic shares the island of Hispaniola with Haiti. The country is mountainous, and the generally hot and humid climate eases with altitude.

POLITICS & ECONOMY The Dominican Republic has chaotic origins, having been held by Spain, France, Haiti and the USA at various times. Civil war broke out in 1966 but soon ended after US intervention. Joaquín Balaguer, elected president in 1966 under a new constitution, stood down in 1996 and was replaced by Leonel Fernández.

AREA 48,730 sq km [18,815 sq mls]
POPULATION 8,150,000
CAPITAL (POPULATION) Santo Domingo (2,135,000)
GOVERNMENT Multiparty republic
ETHNIC GROUPS Mulatto 73%, White 16%, Black 11%
LANGUAGES Spanish (official)
RELIGIONS Roman Catholic 93%
CURRENCY Peso = 100 centavos

ECUADOR

GEOGRAPHY The Republic of Ecuador straddles the Equator on the west coast of South America. Three ranges of the high Andes Mountains form the backbone of the country. Between the towering, snow-capped peaks of the mountains, some of which are volcanoes, lie a series of high plateaux, or basins. Nearly half of Ecuador's population lives on these plateaux.

The climate in Ecuador depends on the height above sea level. Though the coastline is cooled by the cold Peruvian Current, temperatures are between 23°C and 25°C [73°F to 77°F] all through the year. In Quito, at 2,500 m [8,200 ft] above sea level, temperatures are 14°C to 15°C [57°F to 59°F], though the city is just south of the Equator.

POLITICS & ECONOMY The Inca people of Peru conquered much of what is now Ecuador in the late 15th century. They introduced their language, Quechua, which is widely spoken today. Spanish forces defeated the Incas in 1533 and took control of Ecuador. The country became independent in 1822, following the defeat of a Spanish force in a battle near Quito. In the 19th and 20th centuries, Ecuador suffered from political instability, while successive governments failed to tackle the country's social and economic problems. A war with Peru in 1941 led to a loss of territory, and border disputes continued, with the most recent conflict occurring in 1995. An agreement was eventually signed in January 1998. Civilian governments have ruled Ecuador since multiparty elections took place in 1979.

The World Bank classifies Ecuador as a 'lower-middle-income' developing country. Agriculture employs 30% of the people and bananas, cocoa and coffee are all important crops. Fishing, forestry, mining and manufacturing are other activities.

AREA 283,560 sq km [109,483 sq mls]
POPULATION 11,800,000
CAPITAL (POPULATION) Quito (1,101,000)
GOVERNMENT Multiparty republic
ETHNIC GROUPS Mestizo (mixed White and Amerindian) 40%, Amerindian 40%, White 15%, Black 5%
LANGUAGES Spanish (official), Quechua
RELIGIONS Christianity (Roman Catholic 92%)
CURRENCY Sucre = 100 centavos

EGYPT

GEOGRAPHY The Arab Republic of Egypt is Africa's second largest country by population after Nigeria, though it ranks 13th in area. Most of Egypt is desert. Almost all the people live either in the Nile Valley and its fertile delta or along the Suez Canal, the artificial waterway between the Mediterranean and Red seas. This canal shortens the sea journey between the United Kingdom and India by 9,700 km [6,027 mls]. Recent attempts have been made to irrigate parts of the western desert and thus redistribute the rapidly growing Egyptian population into previously uninhabited regions.

Apart from the Nile Valley, Egypt has three other main regions. The Western and Eastern deserts are parts of the Sahara. The Sinai peninsula (Es Sina), to the east of the Suez Canal, is a mountainous desert region, geographically within Asia. It contains Egypt's highest peak, Gebel Katherina (2,637 m [8,650 ft]); few people live in this area.

Egypt is a dry country. The low rainfall occurs, if at all, in winter and the country is one of the sunniest places on Earth.

POLITICS & ECONOMY Ancient Egypt, which was founded about 5,000 years ago, was one of the great early civilizations. Throughout the country, pyramids, temples and richly decorated tombs are memorials to its great achievements.

After Ancient Egypt declined, the country came under successive foreign rulers. Arabs occupied Egypt in AD 639–42. They introduced the Arabic language and Islam. Their influence was so great that most Egyptians now regard themselves as Arabs.

Egypt came under British rule in 1882, but it gained partial independence in 1922, becoming a monarchy. The monarchy was abolished in 1952, when Egypt became a republic. The creation of Israel in 1948 led Egypt into a series of wars in 1948–9, 1956, 1967 and 1973. Since the late 1970s, Egypt has sought for peace. In 1979, Egypt signed a peace treaty with Israel and regained the Sinai region which it had lost in a war in 1967. Extremists opposed contacts with Israel and, in 1981, President Sadat, who had signed the treaty, was assassinated.

While Egypt is important in foreign affairs, most people are poor. Some groups within the country dislike Western influences on their way of life and favour a return to the fundamental principles of Islam. In the 1990s, attacks on foreign visitors caused a decline in the valuable tourist industry. In 1997, 62 people, mostly foreign tourists, were killed by Islamic terrorists near Luxor.

Egypt is Africa's second most industrialized country after South Africa, but it remains a developing country and income levels remain low for the vast majority of Egyptian people. Oil and textiles are the chief exports.

AREA 1,001,450 sq km [386,660 sq mls]
POPULATION 63,000,000
CAPITAL (POPULATION) Cairo (9,656,000)
GOVERNMENT Republic
ETHNIC GROUPS Egyptian 99%
LANGUAGES Arabic (official), French, English
RELIGIONS Islam (Sunni Muslim 94%), Christianity (mainly Coptic Christian 6%)
CURRENCY Pound = 100 piastres

EL SALVADOR

GEOGRAPHY The Republic of El Salvador is the only country in Central America which does not have a coast on the Caribbean Sea. El Salvador has a narrow coastal plain along the Pacific Ocean. Behind the coastal plain, the coastal range is a zone of rugged mountains, including volcanoes, which overlooks a densely populated inland plateau. Beyond the plateau, the land rises to the sparsely populated interior highlands.

The coast has a hot, tropical climate. Inland, the climate is moderated by the altitude. Rain falls on practically every afternoon between May and October.

POLITICS & ECONOMY Amerindians have lived in El Salvador for thousands of years. The ruins of Mayan pyramids built between AD 100 and 1000 are still found in the western part of the country. Spanish soldiers conquered the area in 1524 and 1525, and Spain ruled until 1821. In 1823, all the Central American countries, except for Panama, set up a Central American Federation. But El Salvador withdrew in 1840 and declared its independence in 1841. El Salvador suffered from instability throughout the 19th century. The 20th century saw more stable government, but from 1931 military dictatorships alternated with elected governments and the country remained poor.

In the 1970s, El Salvador was plagued by conflict as protesters demanded that the government introduce reforms to help the poor. Kidnappings and murders committed by left- and right-wing groups caused instability. A civil war broke out in 1979 between the US-backed, right-wing government forces and left-wing guerrillas in the FMLN (Farabundo Marti National Liberation Front). In the 12 years that followed, more than 75,000 people were killed and hundreds of thousands were made homeless. A cease-fire came into effect on 1 February 1992. But the country's economy was shattered.

According to the World Bank, El Salvador is a 'lower-middle-income' economy. Farmland and pasture cover about three-quarters of the country. Coffee, grown in the highlands, is the main export, followed by sugar and cotton, which grow on the coastal lowlands. Fishing for lobsters and shrimps is important, but manufacturing is on a small scale.

AREA 21,040 sq km [8,124 sq mls]
POPULATION 5,950,000
CAPITAL (POPULATION) San Salvador (1,522,000)
GOVERNMENT Republic
ETHNIC GROUPS Mestizo (mixed White and Amerindian) 89%, Amerindian 10%, White 1%
LANGUAGES Spanish (official)
RELIGIONS Christianity (Roman Catholic 94%)
CURRENCY Colón = 100 centavos

EQUATORIAL GUINEA

GEOGRAPHY The Republic of Equatorial Guinea is a small republic in west-central Africa. It consists of a mainland territory which makes up 90% of the land area, called Mbini (or Rio Muni), between Cameroon and Gabon, and five offshore islands in the Bight of Bonny, the largest of which is Bioko. The island of Annobon lies 560 km [350 mls] south-west of Mbini. Mbini consists mainly of hills and plateaux behind the coastal plains.

The climate is hot and humid. Bioko is mountainous, with the land rising to 3,008 m [9,869 ft], and hence it is particularly rainy. But there is a marked dry season between the months of December and February. Mainland Mbini has a similar climate, though the rainfall diminishes inland.

POLITICS & ECONOMY Portuguese navigators reached the area in 1471. In 1778, Portugal granted Bioko, together with rights over Mbini, to Spain.

In 1959, Spain made Bioko and Mbini provinces of overseas Spain and, in 1963, it gave the provinces a degree of self-government. Equatorial Guinea became independent in 1968.

The first president of Equatorial Guinea, Francisco Macias Nguema, proved to be a tyrant. He was overthrown in 1979 and a group of officers, led by Lt.-Col. Teodoro Obiang Nguema Mbasogo, set up a Supreme Military Council to rule the country. In 1991, the people voted to set up a multiparty democracy. Elections were held in 1993 and 1996, amid many allegations of intimidation and fraud.

Equatorial Guinea is a poor country. Agriculture employs up to 66% of the people. The main food crops are bananas, cassava and sweet potatoes, but the most valuable crop is cocoa, grown on Bioko.

AREA 28,050 sq km [10,830 sq mls]
POPULATION 420,000
CAPITAL (POPULATION) Malabo (35,000)
GOVERNMENT Multiparty republic (transitional)
ETHNIC GROUPS Fang 83%, Bubi 10%, Ndowe 4%
LANGUAGES Spanish (official), Fang, Bubi
RELIGIONS Christianity 89%, traditional beliefs 5%
CURRENCY CFA franc = 100 centimes

ERITREA

GEOGRAPHY The State of Eritrea consists of a hot, dry coastal plain facing the Red Sea, with a fairly mountainous area in the centre. Most people live in the cooler highland area.

POLITICS & ECONOMY Eritrea, which was an Italian colony from the 1880s, was part of Ethiopia from 1952 until 1993, when it became a fully independent nation. Independence came at a price, however, and the guerrilla campaign lasted 40 years, resulting in many deaths and a devastated infrastructure.

Farming and nomadic livestock rearing are the main activities in this poor, war-ravaged territory. Eritrea has a few manufacturing industries, based mainly in Asmara.

AREA 94,000 sq km [36,293 sq mls]
POPULATION 3,500,000
CAPITAL (POPULATION) Asmara (367,500)
GOVERNMENT Transitional government
ETHNIC GROUPS Tigrinya 49%, Tigre 32%, Afar 4%, Beja 3%, Saho 3%, Kunama 3%, Nara 2%
LANGUAGES Arabic, English, Tigrinya, Tigre, Saho
RELIGIONS Coptic Christian 50%, Muslim 50%
CURRENCY Nacfa

ESTONIA

GEOGRAPHY The Republic of Estonia is the smallest of the three states on the Baltic Sea, which were formerly part of the Soviet Union, but which became independent in the early 1990s. Estonia consists of a generally flat plain which was covered by ice-sheets during the Ice Age. The land is strewn with moraine (rocks deposited by the ice).

The country is dotted with more than 1,500 small lakes, and water, including the large Lake Peipus (Chudskoye Ozero) and the River Narva, makes up much of Estonia's eastern border with Russia. Estonia has more than 800 islands, which together make up about a tenth of the country. The largest island is Saaremaa (Sarema).

Despite its northerly position, Estonia has a fairly mild climate because of its nearness to the sea. This is because sea winds tend to warm the land in winter and cool it in summer.

POLITICS & ECONOMY The ancestors of the Estonians, who are related to the Finns, settled in the area several thousand years ago. German crusaders, known as the Teutonic Knights, introduced Christianity in the early 13th century. By the 16th century, German noblemen owned much of the land in Estonia. In 1561, Sweden took the northern part of the country and Poland the south. From 1625, Sweden controlled the entire country until Sweden handed it over to Russia in 1721.

Estonian nationalists campaigned for their independence from around the mid-19th century. Finally, Estonia was proclaimed independent in 1918. In 1919, the government began to break up the large estates and distribute land among the peasants.

In 1939, Germany and the Soviet Union agreed to take over parts of Eastern Europe. In 1940, Soviet forces occupied Estonia, but they were driven out by the Germans in 1941. Soviet troops returned in 1944 and Estonia became one of the 15 Soviet Socialist Republics of the Soviet Union. The Estonians strongly opposed Soviet rule. Many of them were deported to Siberia.

Political changes in the Soviet Union in the late 1980s led to renewed demands for freedom. In 1990, the Estonian government declared the country independent and, finally, the Soviet Union recognized this act in September 1991, shortly before the Soviet Union was dissolved. Estonia adopted a new constitution in 1992, when multiparty elections were held for a new national assembly. In 1993, Estonia negotiated an agreement with Russia to withdraw its troops.

Under Soviet rule, Estonia was the most prosperous of the three Baltic states. Since 1988, Estonia has begun to change its government-dominated economy to one based on private enterprise, and the country has started to strengthen its links with the rest of Europe. Estonia's resources include oil shale and its forests. Industries produce fertilizers, machinery, petrochemical products, machinery, processed food, wood products and textiles. Agriculture and fishing are also important.

AREA 44,700 sq km [17,300 sq mls]
POPULATION 1,460,000
CAPITAL (POPULATION) Tallinn (435,000)
GOVERNMENT Multiparty republic
ETHNIC GROUPS Estonian 62%, Russian 30%, Ukrainian 3%, Belarussian 2%, Finnish 1%
LANGUAGES Estonian (official), Russian
RELIGIONS Christianity (Lutheran, with Orthodox and Baptist minorities)
CURRENCY Kroon = 100 sents

ETHIOPIA

GEOGRAPHY Ethiopia is a landlocked country in north-eastern Africa. The land is mainly mountainous, though there are extensive plains in the east, bordering southern Eritrea, and in the south, bordering Somalia. The highlands are divided into two blocks by an arm of the Great Rift Valley which runs throughout eastern Africa. North of the Rift Valley, the land is especially rugged, rising to 4,620 m [15,157 ft] at Ras Dashen. South-east of Ras Dashen is Lake Tana, source of the River Abay (Blue Nile).

The climate in Ethiopia is greatly affected by the altitude. Addis Ababa, at 2,450 m [8,000 ft], has an average yearly temperature of 20°C [68°F]. The rainfall is generally more than 1,000 mm [39 in]. But the lowlands bordering the Eritrean coast are hot.

POLITICS & ECONOMY Ethiopia was the home of an ancient monarchy, which became Christian in the 4th century. In the 7th century, Muslims gained control of the lowlands, but Christianity survived in the highlands. In the 19th century, Ethiopia resisted attempts to colonize it. Italy invaded Ethiopia in 1935, but Ethiopian and British troops defeated the Italians in 1941.

In 1952, Eritrea, on the Red Sea coast, was federated with Ethiopia. But in 1961, Eritrean nationalists demanded their freedom and began a struggle that ended in their independence in 1993. The ethnic diversity within the country led to civil wars in several areas besides Eritrea, as a number of minorities demanded self-government. The military regime collapsed in 1991. In 1995 Ethiopia was divided into nine provinces, each with its own regional assembly.

Ethiopia is one of the world's poorest countries, particularly in the 1970s and 1980s when it was plagued by civil war and famine caused partly by long droughts. Many richer countries have sent aid (money and food) to help the Ethiopian people. Agriculture remains the leading activity.

AREA 1,128,000 sq km [435,521 sq mls]
POPULATION 58,500,000
CAPITAL (POPULATION) Addis Ababa (2,316,000)
GOVERNMENT Federation of nine provinces
ETHNIC GROUPS Amharic 38%, Galla 35%, Tigrinya 9%, Guage 3%, 60 others
LANGUAGES Amharic (official), 280 others
RELIGIONS Ethiopian Orthodox 53%, Sunni Muslim 31%, animist beliefs 11%
CURRENCY Birr = 100 cents

FALKLAND ISLANDS

Comprising two main islands and over 200 small islands, the Falkland Islands lie 480 km [300 mls] from South America. Sheep farming is the main activity, though the search for oil and diamonds holds out hope for the future of this harsh and virtually treeless environment. **AREA** 12,170 sq km [4,699 sq mls]; **POPULATION** 2,000; **CAPITAL** Stanley.

FAROE ISLANDS

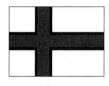

The Faroe Islands are a group of 18 volcanic islands and some reefs in the North Atlantic Ocean between the Shetland Islands and Iceland. Denmark has ruled the islands since the 1380s, but the islands secured a large degree of self-government in 1948. **AREA** 1,400 sq km [541 sq mls]; **POPULATION** 45,000; **CAPITAL** Torshávn.

FIJI

The Republic of Fiji comprises more than 800 Melanesian islands, the biggest being Viti Levu and Vanua Levu. The climate is tropical, with south-east trade winds blowing throughout the year. A former British colony, Fiji became independent in 1970. Its membership of the Commonwealth lapsed in 1987 after the enactment of discriminatory legislation against the country's Indian population. Fiji rejoined the Commonwealth in 1997 following changes in the constitution. **AREA** 18,270 sq km [7,054 sq mls]; **POPULATION** 800,000; **CAPITAL** Suva.

FINLAND

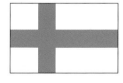

GEOGRAPHY The Republic of Finland is a beautiful country in northern Europe. In the south, behind the coastal lowlands where most Finns live, lies a region of sparkling lakes worn out by ice-sheets in the Ice Age. The thinly populated northern uplands cover about two-fifths of the country.

Helsinki, the capital city, has warm summers, but the average temperatures between the months of December and March are below freezing point. Snow covers the land in winter. The north has less precipitation than the south, but it is much colder.

POLITICS & ECONOMY Between 1150 and 1809, Finland was under Swedish rule. The close links between the countries continue today. Swedish

remains an official language in Finland and many towns have Swedish as well as Finnish names.

In 1809, Finland became a grand duchy of the Russian empire. It finally declared itself independent in 1917, after the Russian Revolution and the collapse of the Russian empire. But during World War II (1939–45), the Soviet Union declared war on Finland and took part of Finland's territory. Finland allied itself with Germany, but it lost more land to the Soviet Union at the end of the war.

After World War II, Finland became a neutral country and negotiated peace treaties with the Soviet Union. Finland also strengthened its relations with other northern European countries and became an associate member of the European Free Trade Association (EFTA) in 1961. Finland became a full member of EFTA in 1986, but in 1992, along with most of its fellow EFTA members, it applied for membership of the European Union. In 1994, the Finnish people voted in favour of membership of the EU. Finland officially joined on 1 January 1995.

Forests are Finland's most valuable resource, and forestry accounts for about 35% of the country's exports. The chief manufactures are wood products, pulp and paper. Since World War II, Finland has set up many other industries, producing such things as machinery and transport equipment. Its economy has expanded rapidly, but there has been a large increase in the number of unemployed people.

AREA 338,130 sq km [130,552 sq mls]
POPULATION 5,180,000
CAPITAL (POPULATION) Helsinki (525,000)
GOVERNMENT Multiparty republic
ETHNIC GROUPS Finnish 93%, Swedish 6%
LANGUAGES Finnish and Swedish (both official)
RELIGIONS Christianity (Evangelical Lutheran 88%)
CURRENCY Markka = 100 penniä

FRANCE

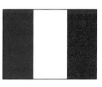

GEOGRAPHY The Republic of France is the largest country in Western Europe. The scenery is extremely varied. The Vosges Mountains overlook the Rhine valley in the north-east, the Jura Mountains and the Alps form the borders with Switzerland and Italy in the south-east, while the Pyrenees straddle France's border with Spain. The only large highland area entirely within France is the Massif Central in southern France.

Brittany (Bretagne) and Normandy (Normande) form a scenic hill region. Fertile lowlands cover most of northern France, including the densely populated Paris basin. Another major lowland area, the Aquitanian basin, is in the south-west, while the Rhône-Saône valley and the Mediterranean lowlands are in the south-east.

The climate of France varies from west to east and from north to south. The west comes under the moderating influence of the Atlantic Ocean, giving generally mild weather. To the east, summers are warmer and winters colder. The climate also becomes warmer as one travels from north to south. The Mediterranean Sea coast has hot, dry summers and mild, moist winters. The Alps, Jura and Pyrenees mountains have snowy winters. Winter sports centres are found in all three areas. Large glaciers occupy high valleys in the Alps.

FRANCE

POLITICS & ECONOMY The Romans conquered France (then called Gaul) in the 50s BC. Roman rule began to decline in the fifth century AD and, in 486, the Frankish realm (as France was called) became independent under a Christian king, Clovis. In 800, Charlemagne, who had been king since 768, became emperor of the Romans. He extended France's boundaries, but, in 843, his empire was divided into three parts and the area of France contracted. After the Norman invasion of England in 1066, large areas of France came under English rule, but this was finally ended in 1453.

France later became a powerful monarchy. But the French Revolution (1789–99) ended absolute rule by French kings. In 1799, Napoleon Bonaparte took power and fought a series of brilliant military campaigns before his final defeat in 1815. The monarchy was restored until 1848, when the Second Republic was founded. In 1852, Napoleon's nephew became Napoleon III, but the Third Republic was established in 1875. France was the scene of much fighting during World War I (1914–18) and World War II (1939–45), causing great loss of life and much damage to the economy.

In 1946, France adopted a new constitution, establishing the Fourth Republic. But political instability and costly colonial wars slowed France's post-war recovery. In 1958, Charles de Gaulle was elected president and he introduced a new constitution, giving the president extra powers and inaugurating the Fifth Republic.

Since the 1960s, France has made rapid economic progress, becoming one of the most prosperous nations in the European Union. But France's government faced a number of problems, including unemployment, pollution and the growing number of elderly people, who find it difficult to live when inflation rates are high. One social problem concerns the presence in France of large numbers of immigrants from Africa and southern Europe, many of whom live in poor areas.

A socialist government under Lionel Jospin was elected in June 1997. Jospin pledged to take France into the European single currency, but also increased the minimum wage and shortened the working week. The French system of high social security taxes and inflexible labour laws seems set to continue, although the economy continues to develop, with exports booming and inflation negligible.

France is one of the world's most developed countries. Its natural resources include its fertile soil, together with deposits of bauxite, coal, iron ore, oil and natural gas, and potash. France is also one of the world's top manufacturing nations, and it has often innovated in bold and imaginative ways. The TGV, Concorde and hypermarkets are all typical examples. Paris is a world centre of fashion industries, but France has many other industrial towns and cities. Major manufactures include aircraft, cars, chemicals, electronic products, machinery, metal products, processed food, steel and textiles.

Agriculture employs about 7% of the people, but France is the largest producer of farm products in Western Europe, producing most of the food it needs. Wheat is the leading crop and livestock farming is of major importance. Fishing and forestry are leading industries, while tourism is a major activity.

AREA 551,500 sq km [212,934 sq mls]
POPULATION 58,800,000
CAPITAL (POPULATION) Paris (9,469,000)
GOVERNMENT Multiparty republic
ETHNIC GROUPS French 93%, Arab, German
LANGUAGES French (official), Breton, Occitan
RELIGIONS Roman Catholic 86%, Islam 3%
CURRENCY Franc = 100 centimes

FRENCH GUIANA

GEOGRAPHY French Guiana is the smallest country in mainland South America. The coastal plain is swampy in places, but some dry areas are cultivated. Inland lies a plateau, with the low Tumachumac Mountains in the south. Most of the rivers run north towards the Atlantic Ocean.

French Guiana has a hot, equatorial climate, with high temperatures throughout the year. The rainfall is heavy, especially between December and June, but it is dry between August and October. The north-east trade winds blow constantly across the country.

POLITICS & ECONOMY The first people to live in what is now French Guiana were Amerindians. Today, only a few of them survive in the interior. The first Europeans to explore the coast arrived in 1500, and they were followed by adventurers seeking El Dorado, the mythical city of gold. Cayenne was founded in 1637 by a group of French merchants. The area became a French colony in the late 17th century.

France used the colony as a penal settlement for political prisoners from the times of the French Revolution in the 1790s. From the 1850s to 1945, the country became notorious as a place where prisoners were harshly treated. Many of them died, unable to survive in the tropical conditions.

In 1946, French Guiana became an overseas department of France, and in 1974 it also became an administrative region. An independence movement developed in the 1980s, but most people want to retain their links with France and continue to obtain financial aid to develop their territory.

Although it has rich forest and mineral resources, such as bauxite (aluminium ore), French Guiana is a developing country. It depends greatly on France for money to run its services and the government is the country's biggest employer. Since 1968, Kourou in French Guiana, the European Space Agency's rocket-launching site, has earned money for France by sending communications satellites into space.

AREA 90,000 sq km [34,749 sq mls]
POPULATION 155,000
CAPITAL (POPULATION) Cayenne (42,000)
GOVERNMENT Overseas department of France
ETHNIC GROUPS Creole 42%, Chinese 14%, French 10%, Haitian 7%
LANGUAGES French (official)
RELIGIONS Christianity (Roman Catholic 80%, Protestant 4%)
CURRENCY French franc = 100 centimes

FRENCH POLYNESIA

French Polynesia consists of 130 islands, scattered over 4 million sq km [1.5 million sq mls] of the Pacific Ocean. Tribal chiefs in the area agreed to a French protectorate in 1843. They gained increased autonomy in 1984, but the links with France ensure a high standard of living. **AREA** 3,941 sq km [1,520 sq mls]; **POPULATION** 226,000; **CAPITAL** Papeete.

GABON

GEOGRAPHY The Gabonese Republic lies on the Equator in west-central Africa. In area, it is a little larger than the United Kingdom, with a coastline 800 km [500 mls] long. Behind the narrow, partly lagoon-lined coastal plain, the land rises to hills, plateaux and mountains divided by deep valleys carved by the River Ogooué and its tributaries.

Most of Gabon has an equatorial climate, with high temperatures and humidity throughout the year. The rainfall is heavy and the skies are often cloudy.

POLITICS & ECONOMY Gabon became a French colony in the 1880s, but it achieved full independence in 1960. In 1964, an attempted coup was put down when French troops intervened and crushed the revolt. Gabon became a one-party state in 1968. Opposition parties were legalized in 1990 and elections took place amid allegations of fraud. The Gabonese Democratic Party, formerly the only party, won a majority in the National Assembly.

Gabon's abundant natural resources include its forests, oil and gas deposits near Port Gentil, together with manganese and uranium. These mineral deposits make Gabon one of Africa's better-off countries. But agriculture still employs about 75% of the population and many farmers produce little more than they need to support their families.

AREA 267,670 sq km [103,347 sq mls]
POPULATION 1,200,000
CAPITAL (POPULATION) Libreville (418,000)
GOVERNMENT Multiparty republic
ETHNIC GROUPS Fang 36%, Mpongwe 15%, Mbete 14%, Punu 12%
LANGUAGES French (official), Bantu languages
RELIGIONS Christianity (Roman Catholic 65%, Protestant 19%, African churches 12%), traditional beliefs 3%, Islam 2%
CURRENCY CFA franc = 100 centimes

GAMBIA, THE

GEOGRAPHY The Republic of The Gambia is the smallest country in mainland Africa. It consists of a narrow strip of land bordering the River Gambia. The Gambia is almost entirely enclosed by Senegal, except along the short Atlantic coastline.

The Gambia has hot and humid summers, but the winter temperatures (November to May) drop to around 16°C [61°F]. In the summer, moist south-westerlies bring rain, which is heaviest on the coast.

POLITICS & ECONOMY English traders bought rights to trade on the River Gambia in 1588, and in 1664 the English established a settlement on an island in the river estuary. In 1765, the British founded a colony called Senegambia, which included parts of The Gambia and Senegal. In 1783, Britain handed this colony over to France.

In the 1860s and 1870s, Britain and France discussed the exchange of The Gambia for some other French territory. But no agreement was reached and Britain made The Gambia a British colony in 1888. It remained under British rule until it achieved full independence in 1965. In 1970, The Gambia became a republic. Relations between the English-speaking Gambians and the French-speaking Senegalese form a major political issue. In 1981, an attempted coup in The Gambia was put down with the help of Senegalese troops. In 1982, The Gambia and Senegal set up a defence alliance, called the Confederation of Senegambia. But this alliance was dissolved in 1989. In July 1994, a military group overthrew the president, Sir Dawda Jawara, who fled into exile. Captain Yahya Jammeh, who took power, was elected president in 1996.

Agriculture employs more than 80% of the people. The main food crops include cassava, millet and sorghum, but groundnuts and groundnut products are the chief exports. Tourism is a growing industry.

AREA 11,300 sq km [4,363 sq mls]
POPULATION 1,200,000
CAPITAL (POPULATION) Banjul (171,000)
GOVERNMENT Military regime
ETHNIC GROUPS Mandinka (also called Mandingo or Malinke) 40%, Fulani (also called Peul) 19%, Wolof 15%, Dyola 10%, Soninke 8%
LANGUAGES English (official), Mandinka, Fula
RELIGIONS Islam 95%, Christianity 4%, traditional beliefs 1%
CURRENCY Dalasi = 100 butut

GEORGIA

GEOGRAPHY Georgia is a country on the borders of Europe and Asia, facing the Black Sea. The land is rugged with the Caucasus Mountains forming its northern border. The highest mountain in this range, Mount Elbrus (5,633 m [18,481 ft]), lies over the border in Russia.

The Black Sea plains have hot summers and mild winters, when the temperatures seldom drop below freezing point. The rainfall is heavy, but inland Tbilisi has moderate rainfall, with the heaviest rains in the spring and early summer.

POLITICS & ECONOMY The first Georgian state was set up nearly 2,500 years ago. But for much of its history, the area was ruled by various conquerors. Christianity was introduced in AD 330. Georgia freed itself of foreign rule in the 11th and 12th centuries, but Mongol armies attacked in the 13th century. From the 16th to the 18th centuries, Iran and the Turkish Ottoman empire struggled for control of the area, and in the late 18th century Georgia sought the protection of Russia and, by the early 19th century, Georgia was part of the Russian empire. After the Russian Revolution of 1917, Georgia declared itself independent and was recognized by the League of Nations. But Russian troops invaded and made Georgia part of the Soviet regime.

In 1991, following reforms in the Soviet Union, Georgia declared itself independent. It became a separate country when the Soviet Union was dissolved in December 1991.

Georgia contains three regions containing minority peoples: Abkhazia in the north-west, South Ossetia in north-central Georgia, and Adjaria (also spelled Adzharia) in the south-west. Communal conflict in the early 1990s led to outbreaks of civil war in South Ossetia and Abkhazia, where the people expressed

the wish to set up their own independent countries.

Georgia is a developing country. Agriculture is important. Major products include barley, citrus fruits, grapes for wine-making, maize, tea, tobacco and vegetables. Food processing and silk and perfume-making are other important activities. Sheep and cattle are reared.

AREA 69,700 sq km [26,910 sq mls]
POPULATION 5,450,000
CAPITAL (POPULATION) Tbilisi (1,279,000)
GOVERNMENT Multiparty republic
ETHNIC GROUPS Georgian 70%, Armenian 8%, Russian 6%, Azerbaijani 6%, Ossetes 3%, Greek 2%, Abkhazian 2%, others 3%
LANGUAGES Georgian (official)
RELIGIONS Christianity (Georgian Orthodox 65%, Russian Orthodox 10%, Armenian Orthodox 8%), Islam 11%
CURRENCY Lari

GERMANY

GEOGRAPHY The Federal Republic of Germany is the fourth largest country in Western Europe, after France, Spain and Sweden. The North German plain borders the North Sea in the north-west and the Baltic Sea in the north-east. Major rivers draining the plain include the Weser, Elbe and Oder.

The central highlands contain plateaux and highlands, including the Harz Mountains, the Thuringian Forest (Thüringer Wald), the Ore Mountains (Erzgebirge), and the Bohemian Forest (Böhmerwald) on the Czech border. South Germany is largely hilly, but the land rises in the south to the Bavarian Alps, which contain Germany's highest peak, Zugspitze, at 2,963 m [9,721 ft] above sea level. The scenic Black Forest (Schwarzwald) overlooks the River Rhine, which flows through a rift valley in the south-west. The Black Forest contains the source of the River Danube.

Germany has a mild climate. The north-west is influenced by the warm waters of the North Sea, but the Baltic coastlands in the north-east are cooler. To the south, the climate becomes more continental, especially in the highlands. The precipitation is greatest on the hills and mountains, many of which are snow-capped in winter.

POLITICS & ECONOMY Germany and its allies were defeated in World War I (1914–18) and the country became a republic. Adolf Hitler came to power in 1933 and ruled as a dictator. His order to invade Poland led to the start of World War II (1939–45), which ended with Germany in ruins.

In 1945, Germany was divided into four military zones. In 1949, the American, British and French zones were amalgamated to form the Federal Republic of Germany (West Germany), while the Soviet zone became the German Democratic Republic (East Germany), a Communist state. Berlin, which had also been partitioned, became a divided city. West Berlin was part of West Germany, while East Berlin became the capital of East Germany. Bonn was the capital of West Germany.

Tension between East and West mounted during the Cold War, but West Germany rebuilt its economy quickly. In East Germany, the recovery was less rapid. In the late 1980s, reforms in the Soviet Union led to unrest in East Germany. Free elections were

held in East Germany in 1990 and, on 3 October 1990, Germany was reunited.

The united Germany adopted West Germany's official name, the Federal Republic of Germany. Elections in December 1990 returned Helmut Kohl, West Germany's Chancellor (head of government) since 1982, to power. His government faced many problems, especially the restructuring of the economy of the former East Germany.

West Germany's 'economic miracle' after the destruction of World War II was greatly helped by foreign aid. Today, despite all the problems caused by reunification, Germany is one of the world's greatest economic and trading nations.

Manufacturing is the most valuable part of Germany's economy and manufactured goods make up the bulk of the country's exports. Cars and other vehicles, cement, chemicals, computers, electrical equipment, processed food, machinery, scientific instruments, ships, steel, textiles and tools are among the leading manufactures. Germany has some coal, lignite, potash and rock salt deposits. But it imports many of the raw materials needed by its industries.

Germany also imports food. Major agricultural products include fruits, grapes for wine-making, potatoes, sugar beet and vegetables. Beef and dairy cattle are raised, together with many other livestock. In the east, the government has begun to break up the large state-owned farms and collectives.

AREA 356,910 sq km [137,803 sq mls]
POPULATION 82,300,000
CAPITAL (POPULATION) Berlin (3,472,000) / Bonn (293,000)
GOVERNMENT Federal multiparty republic
ETHNIC GROUPS German 93%, Turkish 2%, Yugoslav 1%, Italian 1%, Greek, Polish, Spanish
LANGUAGES German (official)
RELIGIONS Christianity (Protestant, mainly Lutheran 45%, Roman Catholic 37%), Islam 2%
CURRENCY Deutschmark = 100 Pfennig

GHANA

GEOGRAPHY The Republic of Ghana faces the Gulf of Guinea in West Africa. This hot country, just north of the Equator, was formerly called the Gold Coast. Behind the thickly populated southern coastal plains, which are lined with lagoons, lies a plateau region in the south-west.

Accra has a hot, tropical climate. Rain occurs all through the year, though Accra is drier than areas inland.

POLITICS & ECONOMY Portuguese explorers reached the area in 1471 and named it the Gold Coast. The area became a centre of the slave trade in the 17th century. The slave trade was ended in the 1860s and, gradually, the British took control of the area. After independence in 1957, attempts were made to develop the economy by creating large state-owned manufacturing industries. But debt and corruption, together with falls in the price of cocoa, the chief export, caused economic problems. This led to instability and frequent coups. In 1981, power was invested in a Provisional National Defence Council, led by Flight-Lieutenant Jerry Rawlings.

The government steadied the economy and introduced several new policies, including the relaxation of government controls. In 1992, the

GIBRALTAR

government introduced a new constitution, which allowed for multiparty election, and Rawlings was re-elected later that year.

The World Bank classifies Ghana as a 'low-income' developing country. Most people are poor and farming employs 59% of the population.

AREA 238,540 sq km [92,100 sq mls]
POPULATION 18,100,000
CAPITAL (POPULATION) Accra (1,781,000)
GOVERNMENT Republic
ETHNIC GROUPS Akan 54%, Mossi 16%, Ewe 12%, Ga-Adangame 8%, Gurma 3%
LANGUAGES English (official), Akan, Mossi
RELIGIONS Christianity 62%, traditional beliefs 21%, Islam 16%
CURRENCY Cedi = 100 pesewas

GIBRALTAR

Gibraltar occupies a strategic position on the south coast of Spain where the Mediterranean meets the Atlantic. It was recognized as a British possession in 1713 and, despite Spanish claims, its population has consistently voted to retain its contacts with Britain. **AREA** 6.5 sq km [2.5 sq mls]; **POPULATION** 28,000; **CAPITAL** Gibraltar Town.

GREECE

GEOGRAPHY The Hellenic Republic, as Greece is officially called, is a rugged country situated at the southern end of the Balkan peninsula. Olympus, at 2,917 m [9,570 ft] is the highest peak. Islands make up about a fifth of the land.

Low-lying areas in Greece have mild, moist winters and hot, dry summers. The east coast has more than 2,700 hours of sunshine a year and only about half of the rainfall of the west. The mountains have a much more severe climate, with snow on the higher slopes in winter.

POLITICS & ECONOMY After World War II (1939–45), when Germany had occupied Greece, a civil war broke out between Communist and nationalist forces. This war ended in 1949. A military dictatorship took power in 1967. The monarchy was abolished in 1973 and democratic government was restored in 1974. Greece joined the European Community in 1981. But despite efforts to develop the economy, Greece remains one of the poorest nations in the European Union.

Manufacturing is important. Products include processed food, cement, chemicals, metal products, textiles and tobacco. Greece also mines lignite (brown coal), bauxite and chromite.

Farmland covers about a third of the country, and grazing land another 40%. Major crops include barley, grapes for wine-making, dried fruits, olives, potatoes, sugar beet and wheat. Poultry, sheep, goats, pigs and cattle are raised. Tourism is a major activity. Attractions include the beaches and the ruins of ancient Greece.

AREA 131,990 sq km [50,961 sq mls]
POPULATION 10,600,000
CAPITAL (POPULATION) Athens (3,097,000)
GOVERNMENT Multiparty republic
ETHNIC GROUPS Greek 96%, Macedonian 2%, Turkish 1%, Albanian, Slav
LANGUAGES Greek (official)
RELIGIONS Christianity (Eastern Orthodox 97%)
CURRENCY Drachma = 100 lepta

GREENLAND

Greenland is the world's largest island. Settlements are confined to the coast, because an ice-sheet covers four-fifths of the land. Greenland became a Danish possession in 1380. Full internal self-government was granted in 1981 and, in 1997, Danish place names were superseded by Inuit forms. However, Greenland remains heavily dependent on Danish subsidies. **AREA** 2,175,600 sq km [838,999 sq mls]; **POPULATION** 57,000; **CAPITAL** Nuuk (Godthaab).

GRENADA

The most southerly of the Windward Islands in the Caribbean Sea, Grenada became independent from the UK in 1974. A military group seized power in 1983, when the prime minister was killed. US troops intervened and restored order and constitutional government. **AREA** 344 sq km [133 sq mls]; **POPULATION** 99,000; **CAPITAL** St George's.

GUADELOUPE

Guadeloupe is a French overseas department which includes seven Caribbean islands, the largest of which is Basse-Terre. French aid has helped to mantain a reasonable standard of living for the people. **AREA** 1,710 sq km [660 sq mls]; **POPULATION** 440,000; **CAPITAL** Basse-Terre.

GUAM

Guam, a strategically important 'unincorporated territory' of the USA, is the largest of the Mariana Islands in the Pacific Ocean. It is composed of a coralline limestone plateau. **AREA** 541 sq km [209 sq mls]; **POPULATION** 161,000; **CAPITAL** Agana.

GUATEMALA

GEOGRAPHY The Republic of Guatemala in Central America contains a thickly populated mountain region, with fertile soils. The mountains, which run in an east–west direction, contain many volcanoes, some of which are active. Volcanic eruptions and earthquakes are common in the highlands. South of the mountains lie the thinly populated Pacific coastlands, while a large inland plain occupies the north.

Guatemala lies in the tropics. The lowlands are hot and rainy. But the central mountain region is cooler and drier. Guatemala City, at about 1,500 m [5,000 ft] above sea level, has a pleasant, warm climate, with a marked dry season between November and April.

POLITICS & ECONOMY In 1823, Guatemala joined the Central American Federation. But it became fully independent in 1839. Since independence, Guatemala has been plagued by instability and periodic violence.

Guatemala has a long-standing claim over Belize, but this was reduced in 1983 to the southern fifth of the country. Violence became widespread in Guatemala from the early 1960s, because of conflict between left-wing groups, including many Amerindians, and government forces. Talks were held to end the war in 1993, but by then the conflict had claimed an estimated 100,000 lives.

The World Bank classifies Guatemala as a 'lower-middle-income' developing country. Agriculture employs nearly half of the population and coffee, sugar, bananas and beef are the leading exports. Other important crops include the spice cardamom and cotton, while maize is the chief food crop. But Guatemala still has to import food to feed the people.

AREA 108,890 sq km [42,042 sq mls]
POPULATION 11,250,000
CAPITAL (POPULATION) Guatemala City (1,814,000)
GOVERNMENT Republic
ETHNIC GROUPS Amerindian 45%, Ladino (mixed Hispanic and Amerindian) 45%, White 5%, Black 2%, others including Chinese 3%
LANGUAGES Spanish (official), Mayan languages
RELIGIONS Christianity (Roman Catholic 75%, Protestant 25%)
CURRENCY Guatemalan quetzal = 100 centavos

GUINEA

GEOGRAPHY The Republic of Guinea faces the Atlantic Ocean in West Africa. A flat, swampy plain borders the coast. Behind this plain, the land rises to a plateau region called Fouta Djalon. The Upper Niger plains, named after one of Africa's longest rivers, the Niger, which rises there, are in the north-east.

Guinea has a tropical climate and Conakry, on the coast, has heavy rains between May and November. This is also the coolest period in the year. During the dry season, hot, dry harmattan winds blow south-westwards from the Sahara Desert.

POLITICS & ECONOMY Guinea became independent in 1958. The first president, Sékou Touré, followed socialist policies, but most people remained poor and Touré had to introduce repressive policies to hold on to power. After his death in 1984, military leaders took over. Colonel Lansana Conté became president and his government introduced free enterprise policies. In 1993, Conté won a presidential election.

The World Bank classifies Guinea as a 'low-income' developing country. It has several natural resources, including bauxite (aluminium ore), diamonds, gold, iron ore and uranium. Bauxite and alumina (processed bauxite) account for 90% of the value of the exports. Agriculture, however, employs 78% of the people, many of whom produce little more than they need for their own families. Guinea has some manufacturing industries. Products include alumina, processed food and textiles.

AREA 245,860 sq km [94,927 sq mls]
POPULATION 7,450,000
CAPITAL (POPULATION) Conakry (1,508,000)
GOVERNMENT Multiparty republic
ETHNIC GROUPS Fulani 40%, Malinke 26%, Susu 11%, Kissi 7%, Kpelle 5%
LANGUAGES French (official), Fulani, Malinke
RELIGIONS Islam 85%, traditional beliefs 5%
CURRENCY Guinean franc = 100 cauris

GUINEA-BISSAU

GEOGRAPHY The Republic of Guinea-Bissau, formerly known as Portuguese Guinea, is a small country in West Africa. The land is mostly low-lying, with a broad, swampy coastal plain and many flat offshore islands, including the Bijagós Archipelago.

The country has a tropical climate, with one dry season (December to May) and a rainy season from June to November.

POLITICS & ECONOMY Portugal appointed a governor to administer Guinea-Bissau and the Cape Verde Islands in 1836, but in 1879 the two territories were separated and Guinea-Bissau became a colony, then called Portuguese Guinea. But development was slow, partly because the territory did not attract settlers on the same scale as Portugal's much healthier African colonies of Angola and Mozambique.

In 1956, African nationalists in Portuguese Guinea and Cape Verde founded the African Party for the Independence of Guinea and Cape Verde (PAIGC). Because Portugal seemed determined to hang on to its overseas territories, the PAIGC began a guerrilla war in 1963. By 1968, it held two-thirds of the country. In 1972, a rebel National Assembly, elected by the people in the PAIGC-controlled area, voted to make the country independent as Guinea-Bissau.

In 1974, newly independent Guinea-Bissau faced many problems arising from its under-developed economy and its lack of trained people to work in the administration. One objective of the leaders of Guinea-Bissau was to unite their country with Cape Verde. But, in 1980, army leaders overthrew Guinea-Bissau's government. The Revolutionary Council, which took over, did not favour unification with Cape Verde and instead concentrated on national policies. In 1991, the country abolished the law making the PAIGC the country's only political party. Multiparty elections were held in 1994.

Guinea-Bissau is a poor country. Agriculture employs more than 80% of the people, but most farming is at subsistence level. Major crops include beans, coconuts, groundnuts, maize, palm kernels and rice, the staple food.

AREA 36,120 sq km [13,946 sq mls]
POPULATION 1,150,000
CAPITAL (POPULATION) Bissau (145,000)
GOVERNMENT Multiparty republic
ETHNIC GROUPS Balante 27%, Fulani (or Peul) 23%, Malinke 12%, Mandyako 11%, Pepel 10%
LANGUAGES Portuguese (official), Crioulo
RELIGIONS Traditional beliefs 54%, Islam 38%
CURRENCY Guinea-Bissau peso = 100 centavos

GUYANA

GEOGRAPHY The Co-operative Republic of Guyana is a country facing the Atlantic Ocean in north-eastern South America. The coastal plain is flat and much of it is below sea level.

The climate is hot and humid, though the interior highlands are cooler than the coast. The rainfall is heavy, occurring on more than 200 days a year.

POLITICS & ECONOMY British Guiana became independent in 1966. A black lawyer, Forbes Burnham, became the first prime minister. Under a new constitution adopted in 1980, the powers of the president were increased. Burnham became president until his death in 1985. He was succeeded by Hugh Desmond Hoyte. Hoyte was defeated in presidential elections in 1993 by Cheddli Jagan. Following Jagan's death in 1997, his wife Janet was elected president.

Guyana is a poor, developing country. Its resources include gold, bauxite (aluminium ore) and other minerals, and its forests and fertile soils. Agriculture employs 27% of the people. Sugar cane and rice are the leading crops. Electric power is in short supply, although the country has great potential for producing hydroelectricity from its many rivers.

AREA 214,970 sq km [83,000 sq mls]
POPULATION 820,000
CAPITAL (POPULATION) Georgetown (200,000)
GOVERNMENT Multiparty republic
ETHNIC GROUPS Asian Indian 49%, Black 36%, Mixed 7%, Amerindian 7%, Portuguese, Chinese
LANGUAGES English (official)
RELIGIONS Christianity (Protestant 34%, Roman Catholic 18%), Hinduism 34%, Islam 9%
CURRENCY Guyana dollar = 100 cents

HAITI

GEOGRAPHY The Republic of Haiti occupies the western third of Hispaniola in the Caribbean. The land is mainly mountainous. The climate is hot and humid, though the northern highlands, with about 200 mm [79 in], have more than twice as much rainfall as the southern coast.

POLITICS & ECONOMY Visited by Christopher Columbus in 1492, Haiti was later developed by the French to become the richest territory in the Caribbean region. The African slaves revolted in 1791 and the country became independent in 1804. Since independence, Haiti has suffered from instability, violence and dictatorial governments. Elections in 1990 returned Jean-Bertrand Aristide as president. But he was overthrown in 1991. Following US intervention, Aristide returned in 1994. In 1995, René Preval was elected president.

AREA 27,750 sq km [10,714 sq mls]
POPULATION 7,400,000
CAPITAL (POPULATION) Port-au-Prince (1,402,000)
GOVERNMENT Multiparty republic
ETHNIC GROUPS Black 95%, Mulatto 5%
LANGUAGES French (official), Creole
RELIGIONS Roman Catholic 80%, Voodoo
CURRENCY Gourde = 100 centimes

HONDURAS

GEOGRAPHY The Republic of Honduras is the second largest country in Central America. The northern coast on the Caribbean Sea extends more than 600 km [373 mls], but the Pacific coast in the south-east is only about 80 km [50 mls] long.

Honduras has a tropical climate, but the highlands, where the capital Tegucigalpa is situated, have a cooler climate than the hot coastal plains. The months between May and November are the rainiest and the north coast is sometimes hit by fierce hurricanes that cause great damage.

POLITICS & ECONOMY In the 1890s, American companies developed plantations in Honduras to grow bananas, which soon became the country's chief source of income. The companies exerted great political influence in Honduras and the country became known as a 'banana republic', a name that was later applied to several other Latin American nations. Instability has continued to mar the country's progress. In 1969, Honduras fought the short 'Soccer War' with El Salvador. The war was sparked off by the treatment of fans during a World Cup soccer series. But the real reason was that Honduras had forced Salvadoreans in Honduras to give up their land. In 1980, the countries signed a peace agreement.

Honduras is a developing country – one of the poorest in the Americas. It has few resources besides some silver, lead and zinc, and agriculture dominates the economy. Bananas and coffee are the leading exports, and maize is the main food crop.

Honduras is the least industrialized country in Central America. Manufactures include processed food, textiles, and a wide variety of wood products.

AREA 112,090 sq km [43,278 sq mls]
POPULATION 6,300,000
CAPITAL (POPULATION) Tegucigalpa (739,000)
GOVERNMENT Republic
ETHNIC GROUPS Mestizo 90%, Amerindian 7%, Black (including Black Carib) 2%, White 1%
LANGUAGES Spanish (official)
RELIGIONS Christianity (Roman Catholic 85%)
CURRENCY Honduran lempira = 100 centavos

HONG KONG

Hong Kong, or Xianggang as it is known in Chinese, was a British dependency until 1 July 1997. It is now a Special Administrative Region of China. It consists of 236 islands, part of the mainland, and is home to over six million people. Hong Kong is a major financial and industrial centre, the world's biggest container port, and a major producer of textiles. **AREA** 1,071 sq km [413 sq mls]; **POPULATION** 6,205,000.

HUNGARY

GEOGRAPHY The Hungarian Republic is a land-locked country in central Europe. The land is mostly low-lying and drained by the Danube (Duna) and its tributary, the Tisza. Most of the land east of the Danube belongs to a region called the Great Plain (Nagyalföld), which covers about half of Hungary.

Hungary lies far from the moderating influence of the sea. As a result, summers are warmer and sunnier, and the winters colder than in Western Europe.
POLITICS & ECONOMY Hungary entered World War II (1939–45) in 1941, as an ally of Germany, but the Germans occupied the country in 1944. The Soviet Union invaded Hungary in 1944 and, in 1946, the country became a republic. The Communists gradually took over the government, taking complete control in 1949. From 1949, Hungary was an ally of the Soviet Union. In 1956, Soviet troops crushed an anti-Communist revolt. But in the 1980s, reforms in the Soviet Union led to the growth of anti-Communist groups in Hungary.

In 1989, Hungary adopted a new constitution making it a multiparty state. Elections held in 1990 led to a victory for the non-Communist Democratic Forum. In 1994, the Hungarian Socialist Party, composed of ex-Communists who had renounced Communism, won a majority in new elections.

Before World War II, Hungary's economy was based mainly on agriculture. But the Communists set up many manufacturing industries. The new factories were owned by the government, as also was most of the land. However, from the late 1980s, the government has worked to increase private ownership. This change of policy caused many problems, including inflation and high rates of unemployment. Manufacturing is the most valuable activity. The major products include aluminium made from local bauxite, chemicals, electrical and electronic goods.

AREA 93,030 sq km [35,919 sq mls]
POPULATION 10,150,000
CAPITAL (POPULATION) Budapest (1,909,000)
GOVERNMENT Multiparty republic
ETHNIC GROUPS Magyar (Hungarian) 98%, Gypsy, German, Croat, Romanian, Slovak
LANGUAGES Hungarian (official)
RELIGIONS Christianity (Roman Catholic 64%, Protestant 23%, Orthodox 1%), Judaism 1%
CURRENCY Forint = 100 fillér

ICELAND

GEOGRAPHY The Republic of Iceland, in the North Atlantic Ocean, is closer to Greenland than Scotland. Iceland sits astride the Mid-Atlantic Ridge. It is slowly getting wider as the ocean is being stretched apart by continental drift.

Iceland has around 200 volcanoes and eruptions are frequent. An eruption under the Vatnajökull ice-cap in 1996 created a subglacial lake which sub-sequently burst, causing severe flooding. Geysers and hot springs are other common volcanic features. Ice-caps and glaciers cover about an eighth of the land. The only habitable regions are the coastal lowlands.

Although it lies far to the north, Iceland's climate is moderated by the warm waters of the Gulf Stream. The port of Reykjavik is ice-free all the year round.
POLITICS & ECONOMY Norwegian Vikings colonized Iceland in AD 874, and in 930 the settlers founded the world's oldest parliament, the Althing.

Iceland united with Norway in 1262. But when Norway united with Denmark in 1380, Iceland came under Danish rule. Iceland became a self-governing kingdom, united with Denmark, in 1918. It became a fully independent republic in 1944, following a referendum in which 97% of the people voted to break their country's ties with Denmark.

Iceland has played an important part in European affairs. It is a member of the North Atlantic Treaty Organization, though it has been involved in disputes with the United Kingdom over fishing rights. In 1977, the UK agreed not to fish within Iceland's 370 km [200 nautical mls] fishing limits.

Iceland has few resources besides the fishing grounds which surround it. Fishing and fish processing are major industries which dominate Iceland's overseas trade. Barely 1% of the land is used to grow crops, mainly root vegetables and fodder for livestock. But 23% of the country is used for grazing sheep and cattle.

AREA 103,000 sq km [39,768 sq mls]
POPULATION 275,000
CAPITAL (POPULATION) Reykjavik (103,000)
GOVERNMENT Multiparty republic
ETHNIC GROUPS Icelandic 97%, Danish 1%
LANGUAGES Icelandic (official)
RELIGIONS Christianity (Evangelical Lutheran 92%, other Lutheran 3%, Roman Catholic 1%)
CURRENCY Króna = 100 aurar

INDIA

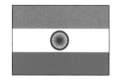

GEOGRAPHY The Republic of India is the world's seventh largest country. In population, it ranks second only to China. The north is mountainous, with mountains and foothills of the Himalayan range. Rivers, such as the Brahmaputra and Ganges (Ganga), rise in the Himalaya and flow across the fertile northern plains. Southern India consists of a large plateau, called the Deccan. The Deccan is bordered by two mountain ranges, the Western Ghats and the Eastern Ghats.

India has three main seasons. The cool season runs from October to February. The hot season runs from March to June. The rainy monsoon season starts in the middle of June and continues into September. Delhi has a moderate rainfall, with about 640 mm [25 in] a year. The south-western coast and the north-east have far more rain. Darjeeling in the north-east has an average annual rainfall of 3,040 mm [120 in]. But parts of the Thar Desert in the north-west have only 50 mm [2 in] of rain per year.
POLITICS & ECONOMY In southern India, most people are descendants of the dark-skinned Dravidians, who were among India's earliest people. In the north, most people are descendants of the lighter-skinned Indo-Aryans who arrived around 3,500 years ago.

India was the birthplace of several major religions, including Hinduism, Buddhism and Sikhism. Islam was introduced from about AD 1000. The Muslim Mughal empire was founded in 1526. From the 17th century, Britain began to gain influence. From 1858 to 1947, India was ruled as part of the British Empire. Independence in 1947 led to the break-up of British India into India and Muslim Pakistan.

Although India has 15 major languages and hundreds of minor ones, together with many religions, the country has remained united as the world's largest democracy. It has faced many problems, especially with Pakistan over the disputed territory of Jammu and Kashmir, and with China.

Economic development has been a major problem and, according to the World Bank, India is a 'low-income' developing country. Socialist policies have failed to raise the living standards of the poor and, in the early 1990s, the government introduced private enterprise policies to stimulate growth.

Farming employs more than 60% of the people. The main food crops are rice, wheat, millet and sorghum, together with beans and peas. India has more cattle than any other country. These animals provide milk, but Hindus do not eat beef. India's large mineral reserves include coal, iron ore and oil, and manufacturing has expanded greatly since 1947. Products include iron and steel, machinery, refined petroleum, textiles and transport equipment.

AREA 3,287,590 sq km [1,269,338 sq mls]
POPULATION 980,000,000
CAPITAL (POPULATION) New Delhi (part of Delhi, 301,000)
GOVERNMENT Multiparty federal republic
ETHNIC GROUPS Indo-Aryan (Caucasoid) 72%, Dravidian (Aboriginal) 25%, other (mainly Mongoloid) 3%
LANGUAGES Hindi 30% and English (both official), Telugu 8%, Bengali 8%, Marati 8%, Urdu 5%, Tamil, many local languages
RELIGIONS Hinduism 83%, Islam (Sunni Muslim) 11%, Christianity 2%, Sikhism 2%, Buddhism 1%
CURRENCY Rupee = 100 paisa

INDONESIA

GEOGRAPHY The Republic of Indonesia is an island nation in South-east Asia. In all, Indonesia contains about 13,600 islands, less than 6,000 of which are inhabited. Three-quarters of the country is made up of five main areas: the islands of Sumatra, Java and Sulawesi (Celebes), together with

Kalimantan (southern Borneo) and Irian Jaya (western New Guinea). The islands are generally mountainous and Indonesia has more active volcanoes than any other country. The larger islands have extensive coastal lowlands.

Indonesia lies on the Equator and temperatures are high throughout the year. The climate is also humid. The rainfall is generally heavy, and only Java and the Sunda Islands have a relatively dry season. The highlands are cooler than the lowlands.

POLITICS & ECONOMY Indonesia is the world's most populous Muslim nation, though Islam was introduced as recently as the 15th century. The Dutch became active in the area in the early 17th century and Indonesia became a Dutch colony in 1799. After a long struggle, the Netherlands recognized Indonesia's independence in 1949. Despite instability, the economy has expanded, although a general depression hit the economies of most nations in eastern Asia in 1997. One controversial issue concerns East (formerly Portuguese) Timor, which Indonesia took over in 1976. Many Timorese want independence and Indonesia has been accused of violations of human rights in suppressing Timorese nationalists.

Indonesia is a developing country. Its resources include oil, natural gas, tin and other minerals, its fertile volcanic soils and its forests. Oil and gas are major exports. Timber, textiles, rubber, coffee and tea are also exported. The chief food crop is rice. Manufacturing is increasing, especially on Java.

AREA 1,904,570 sq km [735,354 sq mls]
POPULATION 203,500,000
CAPITAL (POPULATION) Jakarta (11,500,000)
GOVERNMENT Multiparty republic
ETHNIC GROUPS Javanese 39%, Sundanese 16%, Indonesian (Malay) 12%, Madurese 4%, more than 300 others
LANGUAGES Bahasa Indonesian (official), others
RELIGIONS Islam 87%, Christianity 10% (Roman Catholic 6%), Hinduism 2%, Buddhism 1%
CURRENCY Indonesian rupiah = 100 sen

IRAN

GEOGRAPHY The Republic of Iran contains a barren central plateau which covers about half of the country. It includes the Dasht-e-Kavir (Great Salt Desert) and the Dasht-e-Lut (Great Sand Desert). The Elburz Mountains north of the plateau contain Iran's highest peak, Damavand, while narrow lowlands lie between the mountains and the Caspian Sea. West of the plateau are the Zagros Mountains, beyond which the land descends to the plains bordering the Gulf.

Much of Iran has a severe, dry climate, with hot summers and cold winters. In Tehran, rain falls on only about 30 days in the year and the annual temperature range is more than 25°C [45°F]. The climate in the lowlands, however, is generally milder.
POLITICS & ECONOMY Iran was called Persia until 1935. The empire of Ancient Persia flourished between 550 and 350 BC, when it fell to Alexander the Great. Islam was introduced in AD 641.

Britain and Russia competed for influence in the area in the 19th century, and in the early 20th century the British began to develop the country's oil resources. In 1925, the Pahlavi family took power.

Reza Khan became shah (king) and worked to modernize the country. The Pahlavi dynasty was ended in 1979 when a religious leader, Ayatollah Ruhollah Khomeini, made Iran an Islamic republic. In 1980–8, Iran and Iraq fought a war over disputed borders. Khomeini died in 1989, but his fundamentalist views and anti-Western attitudes continued to influence many Muslims around the world. In 1995, Iran's alleged support for such terrorist groups as the Palestinian Hamas led the United States to impose trade sanctions.

Iran's prosperity is based on its oil production and oil accounts for 95% of the country's exports. However, the economy was severely damaged by the Iran–Iraq war in the 1980s. Oil revenues have been used to develop a growing manufacturing sector. Agriculture is important even though farms cover only a tenth of the land. The main crops are wheat and barley. Livestock farming and fishing are other important activities, although Iran has to import much of the food it needs.

AREA 1,648,000 sq km [636,293 sq mls]
POPULATION 69,500,000
CAPITAL (POPULATION) Tehran (6,750,000)
GOVERNMENT Islamic republic
ETHNIC GROUPS Persian 46%, Azerbaijani 17%, Kurdish 9%, Gilaki 5%, Luri, Mazandarani, Baluchi, Arab
LANGUAGES Farsi/Persian (official), Kurdish
RELIGIONS Islam 99%
CURRENCY Rial = 100 dinars

IRAQ

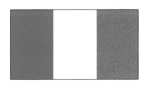

GEOGRAPHY The Republic of Iraq is a south-west Asian country at the head of The Gulf. Rolling deserts cover western and south-western Iraq, with mountains in the north-east. The northern plains, across which flow the rivers Euphrates (Nahr al Furat) and Tigris (Nahr Dijlah), are dry. But the southern plains, including Mesopotamia, and the delta of the Shatt al Arab, the river formed south of Al Qurnah by the combined Euphrates and Tigris, contain irrigated farmland, together with marshes.

The climate of Iraq varies from temperate in the north to subtropical in the south and east. Baghdad, in central Iraq, has cool winters, with occasional frosts, and hot summers. The rainfall is generally low.
POLITICS & ECONOMY Mesopotamia was the home of several great civilizations, including Sumer, Babylon and Assyria. It later became part of the Persian empire. Islam was introduced in AD 637 and Baghdad became the brilliant capital of the powerful Arab empire. But Mesopotamia declined after the Mongols invaded it in 1258. From 1534, Mesopotamia became part of the Turkish Ottoman empire. Britain invaded the area in 1916. In 1921, Britain renamed the country Iraq and set up an Arab monarchy. Iraq finally became independent in 1932.

By the 1950s, oil dominated Iraq's economy. In 1952, Iraq agreed to take 50% of the profits of the foreign oil companies. This revenue enabled the government to pay for welfare services and development projects. But many Iraqis felt that they should benefit more from their oil.

Since 1958, when army officers killed the king and made Iraq a republic, the country has undergone turbulent times. In the 1960s, the Kurds, who live in

northern Iraq and also in Iran, Turkey, Syria and Armenia, asked for self-rule. The government rejected their demands and war broke out. A peace treaty was signed in 1975, but conflict has continued.

In 1979, Saddam Hussein became Iraq's president. Under his leadership, Iraq invaded Iran in 1980, starting an eight-year war. During this war, Iraqi Kurds supported Iran and the Iraqi government attacked Kurdish villages with poison gas.

In 1990, Iraqi troops occupied Kuwait but an international force drove them out in 1991. Since 1991, Iraqi troops have attacked Shiite Marsh Arabs and Kurds. In 1996, the government aided the forces of the Kurdish Democratic Party in an offensive against the Patriotic Union of Kurdistan, a rival Kurdish faction. An international crisis was averted in 1998 when Kofi Annan, the UN secretary-general, negotiated an agreement whereby certain strategic sites in Iraq were opened up to UN inspection.

Civil war, war damage, UN sanctions and economic mismanagement have all contributed to economic chaos in the 1990s. Oil remains Iraq's main resource, but a UN trade embargo in 1990 halted oil exports. Farmland, including pasture, covers about a fifth of the land. Products include barley, cotton, dates, fruit, livestock, wheat and wool, but Iraq still has to import food. Industries include oil refining and the manufacture of petrochemicals and consumer goods.

AREA 438,320 sq km [169,235 sq mls]
POPULATION 22,500,000
CAPITAL (POPULATION) Baghdad (3,841,000)
GOVERNMENT Republic
ETHNIC GROUPS Arab 77%, Kurdish 19%, Turkmen, Persian, Assyrian
LANGUAGES Arabic (official), Kurdish (official in Kurdish areas)
RELIGIONS Islam 96%, Christianity 4%
CURRENCY Iraqi dinar = 20 dirhams = 1,000 fils

IRELAND

GEOGRAPHY The Republic of Ireland occupies five-sixths of the island of Ireland. The country consists of a large lowland region surrounded by a broken rim of low mountains. The uplands include the Mountains of Kerry where Carrauntoohill, Ireland's highest peak at 1,041 m [3,415 ft], is situated. The River Shannon is the longest in the British Isles. It flows through three large lakes, loughs Allen, Ree and Derg.

Ireland has a mild, damp climate greatly influenced by the warm Gulf Stream current that washes its shores. The effects of the Gulf Stream are greatest in the west. Dublin in the east is cooler than places on the west coast. Rain occurs throughout the year.
POLITICS & ECONOMY In 1801, the Act of Union created the United Kingdom of Great Britain and Ireland. But Irish discontent intensified in the 1840s when a potato blight caused a famine in which a million people died and nearly a million emigrated. Britain was blamed for not having done enough to help. In 1916, an uprising in Dublin was crushed, but between 1919 and 1922 civil war occurred. In 1922, the Irish Free State was created as a Dominion in the British Commonwealth. But Northern Ireland remained part of the UK.

Ireland became a republic in 1949. Since then, Irish governments have sought to develop the economy, and it was for this reason that Ireland joined the European Community in 1973. Irish reunification remains a major issue, supported by all of the country's political parties. But Ireland opposes the terrorist tactics of the IRA (Irish Republican Army).

Major farm products in Ireland include barley, cattle and dairy products, pigs, potatoes, poultry, sheep, sugar beet and wheat, while fishing provides another valuable source of food. Farming is now a prosperous activity, aided by grants from the European Union, but manufacturing is now the most valuable economic sector. Many factories use farm products to make beverages and processed food. Others produce chemicals and pharmaceuticals, electronic equipment, machinery, paper and textiles.

AREA 70,280 sq km [27,135 sq mls]
POPULATION 3,625,000
CAPITAL (POPULATION) Dublin (1,024,000)
GOVERNMENT Multiparty republic
ETHNIC GROUPS Irish 94%
LANGUAGES Irish and English (both official)
RELIGIONS Christianity (Roman Catholic 93%, Protestant 3%)
CURRENCY Irish pound = 100 new pence

ISRAEL

GEOGRAPHY The State of Israel is a small country in the eastern Mediterranean. It includes a fertile coastal plain, where Israel's main industrial cities, Haifa (Hefa) and Tel Aviv–Jaffa are situated. Inland lie the Judaeo-Galilean highlands, which run from northern Israel to the northern tip of the Negev Desert in the south. To the east lies part of the Great Rift Valley which runs through East Africa into Asia. In Israel, the Rift Valley contains the River Jordan, the Sea of Galilee and the Dead Sea.

Israel has hot, dry, sunny summers. Winters are mild and moist on the coast, but the total rainfall decreases from west to east and also from north to south, where the Dead Sea region has only 70 mm [2.5 in] a year.

POLITICS & ECONOMY Israel is part of a region called Palestine. Some Jews have always lived in the area, though most modern Israelis are descendants of immigrants who began to settle there from the 1880s. Britain ruled Palestine from 1917. Large numbers of Jews escaping Nazi persecution arrived in the 1930s, provoking an Arab uprising against British rule. In 1947, the UN agreed to partition Palestine into an Arab and a Jewish state. Fighting broke out after Arabs rejected the plan. The State of Israel came into being in May 1948, but fighting continued into 1949. Other Arab–Israeli wars in 1956, 1967 and 1973 led to land gains for Israel.

In 1978, Israel signed a treaty with Egypt which led to the return of the occupied Sinai peninsula to Egypt in 1979. But conflict continued between Israel and the PLO (Palestine Liberation Organization). In 1993, the PLO and Israel agreed to establish Palestinian self-rule in two areas: the occupied Gaza Strip, and in the town of Jericho in the occupied West Bank. The agreement was extended in 1995 to include more than 30% of the West Bank. Israel's prime minister, Yitzhak Rabin, was assassinated in 1995 and his successor, Simon Peres, was narrowly defeated in elections in 1996. His right-wing successor, Benjamin Netanyahu, favoured a more

hardline policy towards Palestinians and the peace process became stalled.

Israel is a prosperous country. The most valuable activity is manufacturing and the country's products include chemicals, electronic equipment, fertilizers, jewellery, military equipment, plastics, processed food, scientific instruments and textiles. Farming is highly scientific and fruits and vegetables are leading exports. Tourism is also important.

AREA 26,650 sq km [10,290 sq mls]
POPULATION 5,900,000
CAPITAL (POPULATION) Jerusalem (591,000)
GOVERNMENT Multiparty republic
ETHNIC GROUPS Jewish 82%, Arab and others 18%
LANGUAGES Hebrew and Arabic (both official)
RELIGIONS Judaism 82%, Islam 14%, Christianity 2%, Druse and others 2%
CURRENCY New Israeli sheqel = 100 agorat

ITALY

GEOGRAPHY The Republic of Italy is famous for its history and traditions, its art and culture, and its beautiful scenery. Northern Italy is bordered in the north by the high Alps, with their many climbing and skiing resorts. The Alps overlook the northern plains – Italy's most fertile and densely populated region – drained by the River Po. The rugged Apennines form the backbone of southern Italy. Bordering the range are scenic hilly areas and coastal plains.

Southern Italy contains a string of volcanoes, stretching from Vesuvius, near Naples (Nápoli), through the Lipari Islands, to Mount Etna on Sicily. Sicily is the largest island in the Mediterranean. Sardinia is also part of Italy.

Milan (Milano), in the north, has cold, often snowy winters. But the summer months are warm and sunny. Rainfall is plentiful, with brief but powerful thunderstorms in summer. Southern Italy has mild, moist winters and warm, dry summers.

POLITICS & ECONOMY Magnificent ruins throughout Italy testify to the glories of the ancient Roman Empire, which was founded, according to legend, in 753 BC. It reached its peak in the AD 100s. It finally collapsed in the 400s, although the Eastern Roman Empire, also called the Byzantine Empire, survived for another 1,000 years.

In the Middle Ages, Italy was split into many tiny states. But they made a great contribution to the revival of art and learning, called the Renaissance, in the 14th to 16th centuries. Beautiful cities, such as Florence (Firenze) and Venice (Venézia), testify to the artistic achievements of this period.

Italy finally became a united kingdom in 1861, although the Papal Territories (a large area ruled by the Roman Catholic Church) was not added until 1870. The Pope and his successors disputed the take-over of the Papal Territories. The dispute was finally resolved in 1929, when the Vatican City was set up in Rome as a fully independent state.

Italy fought in World War I (1914–18) alongside the Allies – Britain, France and Russia. In 1922, the dictator Benito Mussolini, leader of the Fascist party, took power. Under Mussolini, Italy conquered Ethiopia. During World War II (1939–45), Italy at first fought on Germany's side against the Allies. But in late 1943, Italy declared war on Germany. Italy became a republic in 1946. It has played an

important part in European affairs. It was a founder member of the North Atlantic Treaty Organization (NATO) in 1949 and also of what has now become the European Union in 1958.

After the setting up of the European Union, Italy's economy developed quickly. But the country faced many problems. For example, much of the economic development was in the north. This forced many people to leave the poor south to find jobs in the north or abroad. Social problems, corruption at high levels of society, and a succession of weak coalition governments all contributed to instability. Elections in 1996 were won by the left-wing Olive Tree alliance led by Romano Prodi.

Only 50 years ago, Italy was a mainly agricultural society. But today it is a leading industrial power. The country lacks mineral resources, and most raw materials used in industry, including oil, are imported. Leading manufactures include textiles and clothing, processed foods, machinery, cars and chemicals. The main industrial region is in the north-west, in the area bounded by Milan (Milano), Turin (Torino) and Genoa (Génova).

Farmland covers around 42% of the land, pasture 17%, and forest and woodland 22%. Major crops include citrus fruits, grapes which are used to make wine, olive oil, sugar beet and vegetables. Livestock farming is important, though meat is imported.

AREA 301,270 sq km [116,320 sq mls]
POPULATION 57,750,000
CAPITAL (POPULATION) Rome (2,688,000)
GOVERNMENT Multiparty republic
ETHNIC GROUPS Italian 94%, German, French, Albanian, Ladino, Slovenian, Greek
LANGUAGES Italian 94% (official)
RELIGIONS Christianity (Roman Catholic) 83%
CURRENCY Lira = 100 centesimi

IVORY COAST

GEOGRAPHY The Republic of the Ivory Coast, in West Africa, is officially known as Côte d'Ivoire. The south-east coast is bordered by sand bars that enclose lagoons, on one of which the former capital and chief port of Abidjan is situated. But the south-western coast is lined by rocky cliffs.

Ivory Coast has a hot and humid tropical climate, with high temperatures throughout the year. The south of the country has two distinct rainy seasons: between May and July, and from October to November. Inland, the rainfall decreases and the north has one dry and one rainy season.

POLITICS & ECONOMY From 1895, Ivory Coast was governed as part of French West Africa, a massive union which also included what are now Benin, Burkina Faso, Guinea, Mali, Mauritania, Niger and Senegal. In 1946, Ivory Coast became a territory in the French Union.

Ivory Coast became fully independent in 1960 and its first president, Félix Houphouët-Boigny, became the longest serving head of state in Africa with an uninterrupted period in office which ended with his death in 1993. Houphouët-Boigny was a paternalistic, pro-Western leader, who made his country a one-party state. In 1983, the National Assembly agreed to move the capital from Abidjan to Yamoussoukro, the president's birthplace.

Agriculture employs about two-thirds of the people,

and farm products, notably cocoa beans, coffee, cotton and cotton cloth, make up nearly half of the value of the exports. Manufacturing has grown in importance since 1960; products include fertilizers, processed food, refined oil, textiles and timber.

AREA 322,460 sq km [124,502 sq mls]
POPULATION 15,100,000
CAPITAL (POPULATION) Yamoussoukro (120,000)
GOVERNMENT Multiparty republic
ETHNIC GROUPS Akan 41%, Kru 17%, Voltaic 16%, Malinke 15%, Southern Mande 10%
LANGUAGES French (official), Akan, Voltaic
RELIGIONS Islam 38%, Christianity 28%, traditional beliefs 17%
CURRENCY CFA franc = 100 centimes

JAMAICA

GEOGRAPHY Third largest of the Caribbean islands, half of Jamaica lies above 300 m [1,000 ft] and moist south-east trade winds bring rain to the central mountain range.

The 'cockpit country' in the north-west of the island is an inaccessible limestone area of steep broken ridges and isolated basins.

POLITICS & ECONOMY Britain took Jamaica from Spain in the 17th century, and the island did not gain its independence until 1962. Some economic progress was made by the socialist government in the 1980s, but migration and unemployment remain high. Farming is the leading activity and sugar cane is the main crop, though bauxite production provides much of the country's income. Jamaica has some industries and tourism is a major industry.

AREA 10,990 sq km [4,243 sq mls]
POPULATION 2,600,000
CAPITAL (POPULATION) Kingston (644,000)
GOVERNMENT Constitutional monarchy
ETHNIC GROUPS Black 76%, Afro-European 15%, East Indian 3%, White 3%
LANGUAGES English (official), Creole, Hindi, Spanish, Chinese
RELIGIONS Protestant 70%, Roman Catholic 8%
CURRENCY Dollar = 100 cents

JAPAN

GEOGRAPHY Japan's four largest islands – Honshu, Hokkaido, Kyushu and Shikoku – make up 98% of the country. But Japan contains thousands of small islands. The four largest islands are mainly mountainous, while many of the small islands are the tips of volcanoes. Japan has more than 150 volcanoes, about 60 of which are active. Volcanic eruptions, earthquakes and tsunamis (destructive sea waves triggered by underwater earthquakes and eruptions) are common because the islands lie in an unstable part of our planet, where continental plates are always on the move. One powerful recent earthquake

killed more than 5,000 people in Kobe in 1995.

The climate of Japan varies greatly from north to south. Hokkaido in the north has cold, snowy winters. At Sapporo, temperatures below –20°C [4°F] have been recorded between December and March. But summers are warm, with temperatures sometimes exceeding 30°C [86°F]. Rain falls throughout the year, though Hokkaido is one of the driest parts of Japan.

Tokyo has higher rainfall and temperatures, though frosts may occur as late as April when north-westerly winds are blowing. The southern islands of Shikoku and Kyushu have warm temperate climates. Summers are long and hot. Winters are mild.

POLITICS & ECONOMY In the late 19th century, Japan began a programme of modernization. Under its new imperial leaders, it began to look for lands to conquer. In 1894–5, it fought a war with China and, in 1904–5, it defeated Russia. Soon its overseas empire included Korea and Taiwan. In 1930, Japan invaded Manchuria (north-east China) and, in 1937, it began a war against China. In 1941, Japan launched an attack on the US base at Pearl Harbor in Hawaii. This drew both Japan and the United States into World War II.

Japan surrendered in 1945 when the Americans dropped atomic bombs on two cities, Hiroshima and Nagasaki. The United States occupied Japan until 1952. During this period, Japan adopted a democratic constitution. The emperor, who had previously been regarded as a god, became a constitutional monarch. Power was vested in the prime minister and cabinet, who are chosen from the Diet (elected parliament).

From the 1960s, Japan experienced many changes as the country rapidly built up new industries. By the early 1990s, Japan had become the world's second richest economic power after the US. But economic success has brought problems. For example, the rapid growth of cities has led to housing shortages and pollution. Another problem is that the proportion of people over 65 years of age is steadily increasing.

Japan has the world's second highest gross domestic product (GDP) after the United States. [The GDP is the total value of all goods and services produced in a country in one year.] The most important sector of the economy is industry. Yet Japan has to import most of the raw materials and fuels it needs for its industries. Its success is based on its use of the latest technology, its skilled and hard-working labour force, its vigorous export policies and its comparatively small government spending on defence. Manufactures dominate its exports, which include machinery, electrical and electronic equipment, vehicles and transport equipment, iron and steel, chemicals, textiles and ships.

Japan is one of the world's top fishing nations and fish is an important source of protein. Because the land is so rugged, only 15% of the country can be farmed. Yet Japan produces about 70% of the food it needs. Rice is the chief crop, taking up about half of the total farmland. Other major products include fruits, sugar beet, tea and vegetables. Livestock farming has increased since the 1950s.

AREA 377,800 sq km [145,869 sq mls]
POPULATION 125,900,000
CAPITAL (POPULATION) Tokyo (26,836,000)
GOVERNMENT Constitutional monarchy
ETHNIC GROUPS Japanese 99%, Chinese, Korean, Ainu
LANGUAGES Japanese (official)
RELIGIONS Shintoism 93%, Buddhism 74%, Christianity 1% (most Japanese consider themselves to be both Shinto and Buddhist)
CURRENCY Yen = 100 sen

JORDAN

GEOGRAPHY The Hashemite Kingdom of Jordan is an Arab country in south-western Asia. The Great Rift Valley in the west contains the River Jordan and the Dead Sea, which Jordan shares with Israel. East of the Rift Valley is the Transjordan plateau, where most Jordanians live. To the east and south lie vast areas of desert.

Amman has a much lower rainfall and longer dry season than the Mediterranean lands to the west. The Transjordan plateau, on which Amman stands, is a transition zone between the Mediterranean climate zone to the west and the desert climate to the east.

POLITICS & ECONOMY In 1921, Britain created a territory called Transjordan east of the River Jordan. In 1923, Transjordan became self-governing, but Britain retained control of its defences, finances and foreign affairs. This territory became fully independent as Jordan in 1946.

Jordan has suffered from instability arising from the Arab–Israeli conflict since the creation of the State of Israel in 1948. After the first Arab–Israeli War in 1948–9, Jordan acquired East Jerusalem and a fertile area called the West Bank. In 1967, Israel occupied this area. In Jordan, the presence of Palestinian refugees led to civil war in 1970–1.

In 1974, Arab leaders declared that the PLO (Palestine Liberation Organization) was the sole representative of the Palestinian people. In 1988, King Hussein of Jordan renounced his country's claims to the West Bank and passed responsibility for it to the PLO. In 1991, opposition parties were legalized and multiparty elections were held in 1993.

In October 1994, Jordan and Israel signed a peace treaty ending a state of war which had been going on for over 40 years. The treaty restored some land in the south to Jordan.

Jordan lacks natural resources, apart from phosphates and potash, and the country's economy depends substantially on aid. The World Bank classifies Jordan as a 'lower-middle-income' developing country. Because of the dry climate, under 6% of the land is farmed or used as pasture.

Jordan has an oil refinery and manufactures include cement, pharmaceuticals, processed food, fertilizers and textiles.

AREA 89,210 sq km [34,444 sq mls]
POPULATION 5,600,000
CAPITAL (POPULATION) Amman (1,300,000)
GOVERNMENT Constitutional monarchy
ETHNIC GROUPS Arab 99%, of which Palestinians make up roughly half
LANGUAGES Arabic (official)
RELIGIONS Islam 93%, Christianity 5%
CURRENCY Jordan dinar = 1,000 fils

KAZAKSTAN

GEOGRAPHY Kazakstan is a large country in west-central Asia. In the west, the Caspian Sea lowlands include the Karagiye depression, which reaches 132 m [433 ft] below sea level. The lowlands extend eastwards through the Aral Sea area. The north contains high plains, but the highest land is along the eastern and southern borders. These areas include parts of the Altai and Tian Shan mountain ranges.

Eastern Kazakstan contains several freshwater lakes, the largest of which is Lake Balkhash. The water in the rivers has been used for irrigation, causing ecological problems. For example, the Aral Sea, deprived of water, shrank from 66,900 sq km [25,830 sq mls] in 1960 to 33,642 sq km [12,989 sq mls] in 1993. Areas which once provided fish have dried up and are now barren desert.

The climate reflects Kazakstan's position in the heart of Asia, far from the moderating influence of the oceans. Winters are cold and snow covers the land for about 100 days, on average, at Almaty. The rainfall is generally low.

POLITICS & ECONOMY After the Russian Revolution of 1917, many Kazaks wanted to make their country independent. But the Communists prevailed and in 1936 Kazakstan became a republic of the Soviet Union, called the Kazak Soviet Socialist Republic. During World War II and also after the war, the Soviet government moved many people from the west into Kazakstan. From the 1950s, people were encouraged to work on a 'Virgin Lands' project, which involved bringing large areas of grassland under cultivation.

Reforms in the Soviet Union in the 1980s led to the break-up of the country in December 1991. Kazakstan kept contacts with Russia and most of the other republics in the former Soviet Union by joining the Commonwealth of Independent States (CIS), and in 1995 Kazakstan announced that its army would unite with that of Russia. In December 1997, the Kazak government moved their capital from Almaty to Aqmola, a town in the Russian-dominated north. It was hoped that this move would bring some Kazak identity to the area.

The World Bank classifies Kazakstan as a 'lower-middle-income' developing country. Livestock farming, especially sheep and cattle, is an important activity, and major crops include barley, cotton, rice and wheat. The country is rich in mineral resources, including coal and oil reserves, together with bauxite, copper, lead, tungsten and zinc. Manufactures include chemicals, food products, machinery and textiles. Oil is exported via a pipeline through Russia, though, to reduce dependence on Russia, Kazakstan signed an agreement in 1997 to build a new pipeline to China. Other exports include metals, chemicals, grain, wool and meat.

AREA 2,717,300 sq km [1,049,150 sq mls]
POPULATION 17,000,000
CAPITAL (POPULATION) Aqmola (280,000)
GOVERNMENT Multiparty republic
ETHNIC GROUPS Kazak 40%, Russian 38%, German 6%, Ukrainian 5%, Uzbek, Tatar
LANGUAGES Kazak (official); Russian, the former official language, is widely spoken
RELIGIONS Mainly Islam, with a Christian minority
CURRENCY Tenge

KENYA

GEOGRAPHY The Republic of Kenya is a country in East Africa which straddles the Equator. It is slightly larger in area than France. Behind the narrow coastal plain on the Indian Ocean, the land rises to high plains and highlands, broken by volcanic mountains, including Mount Kenya, the country's highest peak at 5,199 m [17,057 ft]. Crossing the country is an arm of the Great Rift Valley, on the floor of which are several lakes, including Baringo, Magadi, Naivasha, Nakuru and, on the northern frontier, Lake Turkana (formerly Lake Rudolf).

Mombasa on the coast is hot and humid. But inland, the climate is moderated by the height of the land. As a result, Nairobi, in the thickly populated south-western highlands, has summer temperatures which are 10°C [18°F] lower than Mombasa. Nights can be cool, but temperatures do not fall below freezing. Nairobi's main rainy season is from April to May, with 'little rains' in November and December. However, only about 15% of the country has a reliable rainfall of 800 mm [31 in].

POLITICS & ECONOMY The Kenyan coast has been a trading centre for more than 2,000 years. Britain took over the coast in 1895 and soon extended its influence inland. In the 1950s, a secret movement, called Mau Mau, launched an armed struggle against British rule. Although Mau Mau was eventually defeated, Kenya became independent in 1963.

Many Kenyan leaders felt that the division of the population into 40 ethnic groups might lead to instability. They argued that Kenya should have a strong central government and it was a one-party state for much of the time since independence. Multiparty democracy was restored in the early 1990s and elections were held in 1992 and 1997, each resulting in a victory for the ruling president Daniel Arap Moi.

According to the United Nations, Kenya is a 'low-income' developing country. Agriculture employs about 80% of the people, but many Kenyans are subsistence farmers, growing little more than they need to support their families. The chief food crop is maize. The main cash crops and leading exports are coffee and tea. Manufactures include chemicals, leather and footwear, processed food, petroleum products and textiles.

AREA 580,370 sq km [224,081 sq mls]
POPULATION 31,900,000
CAPITAL (POPULATION) Nairobi (2,000,000)
GOVERNMENT Multiparty republic
ETHNIC GROUPS Kikuyu 21%, Luhya 14%, Luo 13%, Kamba 11%, Kalenjin 11%
LANGUAGES Swahili and English (both official)
RELIGIONS Christianity (Roman Catholic 27%, Protestant 19%, others 27%), traditional beliefs 19%, Islam 6%
CURRENCY Kenya shilling = 100 cents

KIRIBATI

The Republic of Kiribati comprises three groups of coral atolls scattered over about 5 million sq km [2 million sq mls]. Kiribati straddles the equator and temperatures are high and the rainfall is abundant.

Formerly part of the British Gilbert and Ellice Islands, Kiribati became independent in 1979. The main export is copra and the country depends heavily on foreign aid. **AREA** 728 sq km [281 sq mls]; **POPULATION** 85,000; **CAPITAL** Tarawa.

KOREA, NORTH

GEOGRAPHY The Democratic People's Republic of Korea occupies the northern part of the Korean peninsula which extends south from north-eastern China. Mountains form the heart of the country, with the highest peak, Paektu-san, reaching 2,744 m [9,003 ft] on the northern border.

North Korea has a fairly severe climate, with bitterly cold winters when winds blow from across central Asia, bringing snow and freezing conditions. In summer, moist winds from the oceans bring rain.

POLITICS & ECONOMY North Korea was created in 1945, when the peninsula, a Japanese colony since 1910, was divided into two parts. Soviet forces occupied the north, with US forces in the south. Soviet occupation led to a Communist government being established in 1948 under the leadership of Kim Il Sung. He initiated a Stalinist regime in which he assumed the role of dictator, and a personality cult developed around him. He was to become the world's most durable Communist leader.

The Korean War began in June 1950 when North Korean troops invaded the south. North Korea, aided by China and the Soviet Union, fought with South Korea, which was supported by troops from the United States and other UN members. The war ended in July 1953. An armistice was signed but no permanent peace treaty was agreed. After the war, North Korea adopted a hostile policy towards South Korea in pursuit of its policy of reunification. At times, the situation grew so tense that it became a matter of international concern.

The ending of the Cold War in the late 1980s eased the situation and both North and South Korea joined the United Nations in 1991. The two countries made several agreements, including one in which they agreed not to use force against each other.

As Communism collapsed in the Soviet Union, however, North Korea remained as isolated as ever, pursuing the overriding principle of self-reliance.

In 1993, North Korea began a new international crisis by announcing that it was withdrawing from the Nuclear Non-Proliferation Treaty. This led to suspicions that North Korea, which had signed the Treaty in 1985, was developing its own nuclear weapons. Kim Il Sung, who had ruled as a virtual dictator from 1948 until his death in 1994, was succeeded by his son, Kim Jong Il.

North Korea has considerable resources, including coal, copper, iron ore, lead, tin, tungsten and zinc. Under Communism, North Korea has concentrated on developing heavy, state-owned industries. Manufactures include chemicals, iron and steel, machinery, processed food and textiles. Agriculture employs about a third of the people of North Korea and rice is the leading crop. Economic decline and mismanagement, aggravated by three successive crop failures caused by floods in 1995 and 1996 and a drought in 1997, led to famine on a large scale.

AREA 120,540 sq km [46,540 sq mls]
POPULATION 24,500,000
CAPITAL (POPULATION) Pyongyang (2,639,000)
GOVERNMENT Single-party people's republic
ETHNIC GROUPS Korean 99%
LANGUAGES Korean (official)
RELIGIONS Traditional beliefs 16%, Chondogyo 14%, Buddhism 2%, Christianity 1%
CURRENCY North Korean won = 100 chon

KOREA, SOUTH

GEOGRAPHY The Republic of Korea, as South Korea is officially known, occupies the southern part of the Korean peninsula. Mountains cover much of the country. The southern and western coasts are major farming regions. Many islands are found along the west and south coasts. The largest is Cheju-do, which contains South Korea's highest peak, which rises to 1,950 m [6,398 ft].

Like North Korea, South Korea is chilled in winter by cold, dry winds blowing from central Asia. Snow often covers the mountains in the east. The summers are hot and wet, especially in July and August.

POLITICS & ECONOMY After Japan's defeat in World War II (1939–45), North Korea was occupied by troops from the Soviet Union, while South Korea was occupied by United States forces. Attempts to reunify Korea failed and, in 1948, a National Assembly was elected in South Korea. This Assembly created the Republic of Korea, while North Korea became a Communist state. North Korean troops invaded the South in June 1950, sparking off the Korean War (1950–3).

In the 1950s, South Korea had a weak economy, which had been further damaged by the destruction caused by the Korean War. From the 1960s to the 1980s, South Korean governments worked to industrialize the economy. The governments were dominated by military leaders, who often used authoritarian methods, imprisoning opponents and restricting freedom of speech. In 1987, a new constitution was approved, enabling presidential elections to be held every five years.

In 1991, both South and North Korea became members of the United Nations. The two countries signed several agreements, including one in which they agreed not to use force against each other. But tensions between them continued.

The World Bank classifies South Korea as an 'upper-middle-income' developing country. It is also one of the world's fastest growing industrial economies. The country's resources include coal and tungsten, and its main manufactures are processed food and textiles. Since partition, heavy industries have been built up, making chemicals, fertilizers, iron and steel, and ships. South Korea has also developed the production of such things as computers, cars and television sets. In late 1997, however, the dramatic expansion of the economy was halted by a market crash which affected many of the booming economies of Asia. In an effort to negate the economic and social turmoil that resulted, tough reforms were demanded by the International Monetary Fund and an agreement was reached to restructure much of the short-term debt faced by the government.

Farming remains important in South Korea. Rice is the chief crop, together with fruit, grains and vegetables, while fishing provides a major source of protein.

AREA 99,020 sq km [38,232 sq mls]
POPULATION 46,050,000
CAPITAL (POPULATION) Seoul (11,641,000)
GOVERNMENT Multiparty republic
ETHNIC GROUPS Korean 99%
LANGUAGES Korean (official)
RELIGIONS Buddhism 28%, Christianity (Protestant 19%, Roman Catholic 6%)
CURRENCY South Korean won = 100 chon

KUWAIT

The State of Kuwait at the north end of the Gulf is largely made up of desert. Temperatures are high and the rainfall low. Kuwait became independent from Britain in 1961 and revenues from its oil wells have made it highly prosperous. Iraq invaded Kuwait in 1990 and much damage was inflicted in the ensuing conflict in 1991 when Kuwait was liberated. **AREA** 17,820 sq km [6,880 sq mls]; **POPULATION** 2,050,000; **CAPITAL** Kuwait City.

KYRGYZSTAN

GEOGRAPHY The Republic of Kyrgyzstan is a landlocked country between China, Tajikistan, Uzbekistan and Kazakstan. The country is mountainous, with spectacular scenery. The highest mountain, Pik Pobedy in the Tian Shan range, reaches 7,439 m [24,406 ft] in the east.

The lowlands of Kyrgyzstan have warm summers and cold winters. But the altitude influences the climate in the mountains, where the January temperatures plummet to –28°C [–18°F]. Far from any sea, Kyrgyzstan has a low annual rainfall.

POLITICS & ECONOMY In 1876, Kyrgyzstan became a province of Russia and Russian settlement in the area began. In 1916, Russia crushed a rebellion among the Kyrgyz, and many subsequently fled to China. In 1922, the area became an autonomous *oblast* (self-governing region) of the newly formed Soviet Union but, in 1936, it became one of the Soviet Socialist Republics. Under Communist rule, nomads were forced to work on government-run farms, while local customs and religious worship were suppressed. However, there were concurrent improvements in education and health.

In 1991, Kyrgyzstan became an independent country following the break-up of the Soviet Union. The Communist party was dissolved, but the country maintained ties with Russia through an organization called the Commonwealth of Independent States. Kyrgyzstan adopted a new constitution in 1994 and parliamentary elections were held in 1995.

In the early 1990s, when Kyrgyzstan was working to reform its economy, the World Bank classified it as a 'lower-middle-income' developing country. Agriculture, especially livestock rearing, is the chief activity. The chief products include cotton, eggs, fruits, grain, tobacco, vegetables and wool. But food must be imported. Industries are mainly concentrated around the capital Bishkek.

AREA 198,500 sq km [76,640 sq mls]
POPULATION 4,650,000
CAPITAL (POPULATION) Bishkek (584,000)
GOVERNMENT Multiparty republic
ETHNIC GROUPS Kyrgyz 52%, Russian 22%, Uzbek 13%, Ukrainian 3%, German 2%, Tatar 2%
LANGUAGES Kyrgyz (official), Russian, Uzbek
RELIGIONS Islam
CURRENCY Som = 100 tyiyn

LAOS

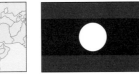

GEOGRAPHY The Lao People's Democratic Republic is a landlocked country in South-east Asia. Mountains and plateaux cover much of the country.

Most people live on the plains bordering the River Mekong and its tributaries. This river, one of Asia's longest, forms much of the country's north-western and south-western borders.

Laos has a tropical monsoon climate. Winters are dry and sunny, with winds blowing in from the north-east. The temperatures rise until April, when the wind directions are reversed and moist south-westerly winds reach Laos, heralding the start of the wet monsoon season.

POLITICS & ECONOMY France made Laos a protectorate in the late 19th century and ruled it as part of French Indo-China, a region which also included Cambodia and Vietnam. Laos became a member of the French Union in 1948 and an independent kingdom in 1954.

After independence, Laos suffered from instability caused by a long power struggle between royalist government forces and a pro-Communist group called the Pathet Lao. A civil war broke out in 1960 and continued into the 1970s. The Pathet Lao took control in 1975 and the king abdicated. Laos then came under the influence of Communist Vietnam, which had used Laos as a supply base during the Vietnam War (1957–75). However, from the late 1980s, Laos began to introduce economic reforms, including the encouragement of private enterprise.

Laos is one of the world's poorest countries. Agriculture employs about 76% of the people, as compared with 7% in industry and 17% in services. Rice is the main crop, and timber and coffee are both exported. But the most valuable export is electricity, which is produced at hydroelectric power stations on the River Mekong and is exported to Thailand. Laos also produces opium. In the early 1990s, Laos was thought to be the world's third biggest source of this illegal drug.

AREA 236,800 sq km [91,428 sq mls]
POPULATION 5,200,000
CAPITAL (POPULATION) Vientiane (449,000)
GOVERNMENT Single-party republic
ETHNIC GROUPS Lao 67%, Mon-Khmer 17%, Tai 8%
LANGUAGES Lao (official), Khmer, Tai, Miao
RELIGIONS Buddhism 58%, traditional beliefs 34%, Christianity 2%, Islam 1%
CURRENCY Kip = 100 at

LATVIA

GEOGRAPHY The Republic of Latvia is one of three states on the south-eastern corner of the Baltic Sea which were ruled as parts of the Soviet Union between 1940 and 1991. Latvia consists mainly of flat plains separated by low hills, composed of moraine (ice-worn rocks).

Riga has warm summers, but the winter months

(from December to March) are subzero. In the winter, the sea often freezes over. The rainfall is moderate and it occurs throughout the year, with light snow in winter.

POLITICS & ECONOMY In 1800, Russia was in control of Latvia, but Latvians declared their independence after World War I. In 1940, under a German-Soviet pact, Soviet troops occupied Latvia, but they were driven out by the Germans in 1941. Soviet troops returned in 1944 and Latvia became part of the Soviet Union. Under Soviet rule, many Russian immigrants settled in Latvia and many Latvians feared that the Russians would become the dominant ethnic group.

In the late 1980s, when reforms were being introduced in the Soviet Union, Latvia's government ended absolute Communist rule and made Latvian the official language. In 1990, it declared the country to be independent, an act which was finally recognized by the Soviet Union in September 1991.

Latvia held its first free elections to its parliament (the Saeima) in 1993. Voting was limited only to citizens of Latvia on 17 June 1940 and their descendents. This meant that about 34% of Latvian residents were unable to vote. In 1994, Latvia adopted a law restricting the naturalization of non-Latvians, including many Russian settlers, who were not allowed to vote or to own land. Latvia formally applied to join the European Union in 1995.

The World Bank classifies Latvia as a 'lower-middle-income' country and, in the 1990s, it faced many problems in transforming its government-run economy into a free-market one.

Its industries cover a wide range, with products including electronic goods, farm machinery, fertilizers, processed food, plastics, radios, washing machines and vehicles. But Latvia produces only about a tenth of the electricity it needs. The rest has to be imported from Belarus, Russia and Ukraine.

AREA 64,589 sq km [24,938 sq mls]
POPULATION 2,450,000
CAPITAL (POPULATION) Riga (840,000)
GOVERNMENT Multiparty republic
ETHNIC GROUPS Latvian 53%, Russian 34%, Belarussian 4%, Ukrainian 3%, Polish 2%, Lithuanian, Jewish
LANGUAGES Latvian (official), Russian
RELIGIONS Christianity (including Lutheran, Russian Orthodox and Roman Catholic)
CURRENCY Lats = 10 santimi

LEBANON

GEOGRAPHY The Republic of Lebanon is a country on the eastern shores of the Mediterranean Sea. Behind the coastal plain are the rugged Lebanon Mountains (Jabal Lubnan), which rise to 3,088 m [10,131 ft]. Another range, the Anti-Lebanon Mountains (Al Jabal Ash Sharqi), form the eastern border with Syria. Between the two ranges is the Bekaa (Beqaa) Valley, a fertile farming region.

The Lebanese coast has the hot, dry summers and mild, wet winters that are typical of many Mediterranean lands. Inland, onshore winds bring heavy rain to the western slopes of the mountains in the winter months, with snow at the higher altitudes.

POLITICS & ECONOMY Lebanon was ruled by Turkey from 1516 until World War I. France ruled

the country from 1923, but Lebanon became independent in 1946. After independence, the Muslims and Christians agreed to share power, and Lebanon made rapid economic progress. But from the late 1950s, development was slowed by periodic conflict between Sunni and Shia Muslims, Druze and Christians. The situation was further complicated by the presence of Palestinian refugees who used bases in Lebanon to attack Israel.

In 1975, civil war broke out as private armies representing the many factions struggled for power. This led to intervention by Israel in the south and Syria in the north. UN peacekeeping forces arrived in 1978, but bombings, assassinations and kidnappings became almost everyday events in the 1980s. From 1991, Lebanon enjoyed an uneasy peace. However, Israel continued to occupy an area in the south and, periodically, Israel launched attacks on pro-Iranian (Shia) Hezbollah guerrilla bases in Lebanon.

Lebanon's civil war almost destroyed the valuable trade and financial services which had been Lebanon's chief source of income, together with tourism. The manufacturing industry, formerly another major activity, was also badly hit and many factories were damaged.

AREA 10,400 sq km [4,015 sq mls]
POPULATION 3,200,000
CAPITAL (POPULATION) Beirut (1,500,000)
GOVERNMENT Multiparty republic
ETHNIC GROUPS Arab (Lebanese 80%, Palestinian 12%), Armenian 5%, Syrian, Kurdish
LANGUAGES Arabic (official)
RELIGIONS Islam 58%, Christianity 27%, Druze
CURRENCY Lebanese pound = 100 piastres

LESOTHO

GEOGRAPHY The Kingdom of Lesotho is a landlocked country, completely enclosed by South Africa. The land is mountainous, rising to 3,482 m [11,424 ft] on the north-eastern border. The Drakensberg range covers most of the country, giving Lesotho some spectacular scenery.

The climate of Lesotho is greatly affected by the altitude, because most of the country lies above 1,500 m [4,921 ft]. Maseru has warm summers, but the temperatures fall below freezing in the winter. The mountains are colder. The rainfall varies, averaging around 700 mm [28 in].

POLITICS & ECONOMY The Basotho nation was founded in the 1820s by King Moshoeshoe I, who united various groups fleeing from tribal wars in southern Africa. Britain made the area a protectorate in 1868 and, in 1971, placed it under the British Cape Colony in South Africa. But in 1884, Basutoland, as the area was called, was reconstituted as a British protectorate, where whites were not allowed to own land.

The country finally became independent in 1966 as the Kingdom of Lesotho, with Moshoeshoe II, great-grandson of Moshoeshoe I, as its king. Since independence, Lesotho has suffered instability. The military seized power in 1986 and stripped Moshoeshoe II of his powers in 1990, installing his son, Letsie III, as the monarch.

Multiparty elections in 1993 were won by the Basotho Congress Party led by Ntsu Mokhele and, in January 1995, Moshoeshoe II was restored to the

throne. However, when Moshoeshoe died in a car crash in 1996, Letsie III again became king.

The World Bank classifies Lesotho as a 'low-income' developing country. Lesotho lacks natural resources apart from water. Agriculture, mainly at subsistence level, light manufacturing, and money sent home by Basotho working mainly in the mines of South Africa are the main sources of income.

AREA 30,350 sq km [11,718 sq mls]
POPULATION 2,100,000
CAPITAL (POPULATION) Maseru (130,000)
GOVERNMENT Constitutional monarchy
ETHNIC GROUPS Sotho 99%
LANGUAGES Sesotho and English (both official)
RELIGIONS Christianity 93% (Roman Catholic 44%), traditional beliefs 6%
CURRENCY Loti = 100 lisente

LIBERIA

GEOGRAPHY The Republic of Liberia is a country in West Africa. Behind the coastline, 500 km [311 mls] long, lies a narrow coastal plain. Beyond, the land rises to a plateau region, with the highest land along the border with Guinea.

Liberia has a tropical climate with high temperatures and high humidity all through the year. The rainfall is abundant all year round, but there is a particularly wet period from June to November. The rainfall generally increases from east to west.

POLITICS & ECONOMY In the late 18th century, some white Americans in the United States wanted to help freed black slaves to return to Africa. In 1816, they set up the American Colonization Society, which bought land in what is now Liberia.

In 1822, the Society landed former slaves at a settlement on the coast which they named Monrovia. In 1847, Liberia became a fully independent republic with a constitution much like that of the United States. For many years, the Americo-Liberians controlled the country's government. US influence remained strong and the American Firestone Company, which ran Liberia's rubber plantations, was especially influential. Foreign companies were also involved in exploiting Liberia's mineral resources, including its huge iron-ore deposits.

In 1980, a military group composed of people from the local population killed the Americo-Liberian president, William R. Tolbert. An army sergeant, Samuel K. Doe, was made president of Liberia. Elections held in 1985 resulted in victory for Doe.

From 1989, the country was plunged into civil war between various ethnic groups. Doe was assassinated in 1990, but his successor, Amos Sawyer, continued to struggle with rebel groups. Peacekeeping forces from other West African countries arrived in Liberia, but the fighting continued. In 1995, a cease-fire was agreed and a council of state, composed of former warlords, was set up. In 1997, one of the warlords, Charles Taylor, was elected president.

Liberia's civil war devastated its economy. Three out of every four people depend on agriculture, though many of them grow little more than they need to feed their families. The chief food crops include cassava, rice and sugar cane, while rubber, cocoa and coffee are grown for export. But the most valuable export is iron ore.

Liberia also obtains revenue from its 'flag of

convenience', which is used by about one-sixth of the world's commercial shipping, exploiting low taxes.

AREA 111,370 sq km [43,000 sq mls]
POPULATION 2,950,000
CAPITAL (POPULATION) Monrovia (490,000)
GOVERNMENT Multiparty republic
ETHNIC GROUPS Kpelle 19%, Bassa 14%,
Grebo 9%, Gio 8%, Kru 7%, Mano 7%
LANGUAGES English (official), Mande, Mel, Kwa
RELIGIONS Christianity 68%, Islam 14%,
traditional beliefs and others 18%
CURRENCY Liberian dollar = 100 cents

LIBYA

GEOGRAPHY The Socialist People's Libyan Arab Jamahiriya, as Libya is officially called, is a large country in North Africa. Most people live on the coastal plains in the north-east and north-west. The Sahara, the world's largest desert which occupies 95% of Libya, reaches the Mediterranean coast along the Gulf of Sidra (Khalij Surt).

The coastal plains in the north-east and north-west of the country have Mediterranean climates, with hot, dry summers and mild winters, with some rain in the winter months. Inland, the average yearly rainfall drops to 100 mm [4 in] or less.

POLITICS & ECONOMY Italy took over Libya in 1911, but lost it during World War II. Britain and France then jointly ruled Libya until 1951, when the country became an independent kingdom.

In 1969, a military group headed by Colonel Muammar Gaddafi deposed the king and set up a military government. Under Gaddafi, the government took control of the economy and used money from oil exports to finance welfare services and development projects. Gaddafi has attracted international criticism for his support for radical movements, such as the PLO (Palestine Liberation Organization) and various terrorist groups. In 1986, his policies led the United States to bomb installations in the capital. Libya has disputes with its neighbours, including Chad, where it sent troops to intervene in a civil war. In 1994, the International Court of Justice ruled against Libya's claim for territory in the Aozou Strip in northern Chad.

The discovery of oil and natural gas in 1959 led to the transformation of Libya's economy. Formerly one of the world's poorest countries, it has become Africa's richest in terms of its per capita income. But it remains a developing country because of its dependence on oil, which accounts for nearly all of its export revenues.

Agriculture is important, although Libya has to import food. Crops include barley, citrus fruits, dates, olives, potatoes and wheat. Cattle, sheep and poultry are raised. Libya has oil refineries and petrochemical plants. Other manufactures include cement and steel.

AREA 1,759,540 sq km [679,358 sq mls]
POPULATION 5,500,000
CAPITAL (POPULATION) Tripoli (960,000)
GOVERNMENT Single-party socialist state
ETHNIC GROUPS Libyan Arab and Berber 89%
LANGUAGES Arabic (official), Berber
RELIGIONS Islam
CURRENCY Libyan dinar = 1,000 dirhams

LIECHTENSTEIN

The tiny Principality of Liechtenstein is sandwiched between Switzerland and Austria. The River Rhine flows along its western border, while Alpine peaks rise in the east and south. The climate is relatively mild. Since 1924, Liechtenstein has been in a customs union with Switzerland and, like its neighbour, it is extremely prosperous. Taxation is low and, as a result, the country has become a haven for international companies. AREA 157 sq km [61 sq mls]; POPULATION 32,000; CAPITAL Vaduz.

LITHUANIA

GEOGRAPHY The Republic of Lithuania is the southernmost of the three Baltic states which were ruled as part of the Soviet Union between 1940 and 1991. Much of the land is flat or gently rolling, with the highest land in the south-east.

Winters are cold. January's temperatures average –3°C [27°F] in the west and –6°C [21°F] in the east. Summers are warm, with average temperatures in July of 17°C [63°F]. The average rainfall in the west is about 630 mm [25 in]. Inland areas are drier.

POLITICS & ECONOMY The Lithuanian people were united into a single nation in the 12th century, and later joined a union with Poland. In 1795, Lithuania came under Russian rule. After World War I (1914–18), Lithuania declared itself independent, and in 1920 it signed a peace treaty with the Russians, though Poland held Vilnius until 1939. In 1940, the Soviet Union occupied Lithuania, but the Germans invaded in 1941. Soviet forces returned in 1944, and Lithuania was integrated into the Soviet Union. In 1988, when the Soviet Union was introducing reforms, the Lithuanians demanded independence. Their language is one of the oldest in the world, and the country was always the most homogenous of the Baltic states, staunchly Catholic and resistant of attempts to suppress their culture. Pro-independence groups won the national elections in 1990 and, in 1991, the Soviet Union recognized Lithuania's independence.

After independence, Lithuania faced many problems as it sought to reform its economy and introduce a private enterprise system. In 1998, Valdas Adamkus, a Lithuanian-American who had fled the country in 1944, was elected president.

The World Bank classifies Lithuania as a 'lower-middle-income' developing country. Lithuania lacks natural resources, but manufacturing, based on imported materials, is the most valuable activity.

AREA 65,200 sq km [25,200 sq mls]
POPULATION 3,710,000
CAPITAL (POPULATION) Vilnius (576,000)
GOVERNMENT Multiparty republic
ETHNIC GROUPS Lithuanian 80%, Russian 9%,
Polish 7%, Belarussian 2%
LANGUAGES Lithuanian (official), Russian, Polish
RELIGIONS Christianity (mainly Roman Catholic)
CURRENCY Litas = 100 centai

LUXEMBOURG

GEOGRAPHY The Grand Duchy of Luxembourg is one of the smallest and oldest countries in Europe. The north belongs to an upland region which includes the Ardenne in Belgium and Luxembourg, and the Eifel highlands in Germany.

Luxembourg has a temperate climate. The south has warm summers and autumns, when grapes ripen in sheltered south-eastern valleys. Winters are sometimes severe, especially in upland areas.

POLITICS & ECONOMY Germany occupied Luxembourg in World Wars I and II. In 1944–5, northern Luxembourg was the scene of the famous Battle of the Bulge. In 1948, Luxembourg joined Belgium and the Netherlands in a union called Benelux and, in the 1950s, it was one of the six founders of what is now the European Union. Luxembourg has played a major role in Europe. Its capital contains the headquarters of several international agencies, including the European Coal and Steel Community and the European Court of Justice. The city is also a major financial centre.

Luxembourg has iron-ore reserves and is a major steel producer. It also has many high-technology industries, producing electronic goods and computers. Steel and other manufactures, including chemicals, rubber products, glass and aluminium, dominate the country's exports. Other major activities include tourism and financial services.

AREA 2,590 sq km [1,000 sq mls]
POPULATION 425,000
CAPITAL (POPULATION) Luxembourg (76,000)
GOVERNMENT Constitutional monarchy (Grand Duchy)
ETHNIC GROUPS Luxembourger 71%, Portuguese 10%, Italian 5%, French 3%, Belgian 3%
LANGUAGES Letzeburgish/Luxembourgian (official), French, German
RELIGIONS Christianity (Roman Catholic 95%)
CURRENCY Luxembourg franc = 100 centimes

MACAU

Macau is a small peninsula at the head of the Zhu Jiang (Pearl) River, west of Hong Kong. A Portuguese colony since 1557, Macau will return to China in 1999. Its main industries are textiles, gambling and tourism. AREA 16 sq km [6 sq mls]; POPULATION 450,000; CAPITAL Macau.

MACEDONIA

GEOGRAPHY The Republic of Macedonia is a country in south-eastern Europe, which was once one

MADAGASCAR

of the six republics that made up the former Federal People's Republic of Yugoslavia. This landlocked country is largely mountainous or hilly.

Macedonia has hot summers, though highland areas are cooler. Winters are cold and snowfalls are often heavy. The climate is fairly continental in character and rain occurs throughout the year.

POLITICS & ECONOMY Between 1912 and 1913, the area called Macedonia was divided between Serbia, Bulgaria, which took a small area in the east, and Greece, which gained the south. At the end of World War I, Serbian Macedonia became part of the Kingdom of the Serbs, Croats and Slovenes, which was renamed Yugoslavia in 1929. After World War II, a Communist government under Josip Broz Tito took power in Yugoslavia.

Tito died in 1980 and, in the early 1990s, the country broke up into five separate republics. Macedonia declared its independence in September 1991. Greece objected to this territory using the name Macedonia, which it considered to be a Greek name. It also objected to a symbol on Macedonia's flag and a reference in the constitution to the desire to reunite the three parts of the old Macedonia.

Macedonia adopted a new clause in its constitution rejecting any Macedonian claims on Greek territory and, in 1993, the United Nations accepted the new republic as a member under the name of The Former Yugoslav Republic of Macedonia (FYROM).

By the end of 1993, all the countries of the European Union, except Greece, were establishing diplomatic relations with the FYROM. Greece barred Macedonian trade in 1994, but lifted the ban in 1995 when Macedonia agreed to redesign its flag and remove all territorial claims from its constitution.

According to the World Bank, Macedonia ranks as a 'lower-middle-income' developing country. The leading sector of the economy is manufacturing, and manufactures dominate the country's exports. Macedonia mines coal, but it has to import all its oil and natural gas. The country's farmers produce Macedonia's basic food needs.

AREA 25,710 sq km [9,927 sq mls]
POPULATION 2,150,000
CAPITAL (POPULATION) Skopje (541,000)
GOVERNMENT Multiparty republic
ETHNIC GROUPS Macedonian 65%, Albanian 21%, Turkish 5%, Romanian 3%, Serb 2%
LANGUAGES Macedonian (official), Albanian
RELIGIONS Christianity (mainly Eastern Orthodox, with Macedonian Orthodox and Roman Catholic communities), Islam
CURRENCY Dinar = 100 paras

MADAGASCAR

GEOGRAPHY The Democratic Republic of Madagascar, in south-eastern Africa, is an island nation, which has a larger area than France. Behind the narrow coastal plains in the east lies a highland zone, mostly between 610 m and 1,220 m [2,000 ft to 4,000 ft] above sea level. Broad plains border the Mozambique Channel in the west.

Temperatures in the highlands are moderated by the altitude. The winters (from April to September) are dry, but heavy rains occur in summer. The eastern coastlands are warm and humid. The west is drier and the south and south-west are hot and dry.

POLITICS & ECONOMY People from South-east Asia began to settle on Madagascar around 2,000 years ago. Subsequent influxes from Africa and Arabia added to the island's diverse heritage, culture and language.

French troops defeated a Malagasy army in 1895 and Madagascar became a French colony. In 1960, it achieved full independence as the Malagasy Republic. In 1972, army officers seized control and, in 1975, under the leadership of Lt-Commander Didier Ratsiraka, the country was renamed Madagascar. Parliamentary elections were held in 1977, but Ratsiraka remained president of a one-party socialist state. The government resigned in 1991 following huge demonstrations. In 1992–3, Ratsiraka was defeated by opposition leader, Albert Zafy. But Ratsiraka returned to power following presidential elections in 1996.

Madagascar is one of the world's poorest countries. The land has been badly eroded because of the cutting down of the forests and overgrazing of the grasslands. Farming, fishing and forestry employ about 80% of the people. The country's food crops include bananas, cassava, rice and sweet potatoes. Coffee is the leading export.

AREA 587,040 sq km [226,656 sq mls]
POPULATION 15,500,000
CAPITAL (POPULATION) Antananarivo (1,053,000)
GOVERNMENT Republic
ETHNIC GROUPS Merina 27%, Betsimisaraka 15%, Betsileo 11%, Tsimihety 7%, Sakalava 6%
LANGUAGES Malagasy, French (both official)
RELIGIONS Christianity 51%, traditional beliefs 47%, Islam 2%
CURRENCY Malagasy franc = 100 centimes

MALAWI

GEOGRAPHY The Republic of Malawi includes part of Lake Malawi, which is drained by the River Shire, a tributary of the River Zambezi. The land is mostly mountainous. The highest peak, Mulanje, reaches 3,000 m [9,843 ft] in the south-east.

While the low-lying areas of Malawi are hot and humid all year round, the uplands have a pleasant climate. Lilongwe, at about 1,100 m [3,609 ft] above sea level, has a warm and sunny climate. Frosts sometimes occur in July and August, in the middle of the long dry season.

POLITICS & ECONOMY Malawi, then called Nyasaland, became a British protectorate in 1891. In 1953, Britain established the Federation of Rhodesia and Nyasaland, which also included what are now Zambia and Zimbabwe. Black African opposition, led in Nyasaland by Dr Hastings Kamuzu Banda, led to the dissolution of the federation in 1963. In 1964, Nyasaland became independent as Malawi, with Banda as prime minister. Banda became president when the country became a republic in 1966 and, in 1971, he was made president for life. Banda ruled autocratically through the only party, the Malawi Congress Party. However, a multiparty system was restored in 1993, and in elections in 1994, Banda and his party were defeated and Bakili Muluzi became president. Banda died in 1997.

Malawi is one of the world's poorest countries. More than 80% of the people are farmers, but many grow little more than they need to feed their families.

AREA 118,480 sq km [45,745 sq mls]
POPULATION 10,250,000
CAPITAL (POPULATION) Lilongwe (395,000)
GOVERNMENT Multiparty republic
ETHNIC GROUPS Maravi (Chewa, Nyanja, Tonga, Tumbuka) 58%, Lomwe 18%, Yao 13%, Ngoni 7%
LANGUAGES Chichewa and English (both official)
RELIGIONS Christianity (Protestant 34%, Roman Catholic 28%), traditional beliefs 21%, Islam 16%
CURRENCY Kwacha = 100 tambala

MALAYSIA

GEOGRAPHY The Federation of Malaysia consists of two main parts. Peninsular Malaysia, which is joined to mainland Asia, contains about 80% of the population. The other main regions, Sabah and Sarawak, are in northern Borneo, an island which Malaysia shares with Indonesia. Much of the land is mountainous, with coastal lowlands bordering the rugged interior. The highest peak, Kinabalu, reaches 4,101 m [13,455 ft] in Sabah.

Malaysia has a hot equatorial climate. The temperatures are high all through the year, though the mountains are much cooler than the lowland areas. The rainfall is heavy throughout the year.

POLITICS & ECONOMY Japan occupied what is now Malaysia during World War II, but British rule was re-established in 1945. In the 1940s and 1950s, British troops fought a war against Communist guerrillas, but Peninsular Malaysia (then called Malaya) became independent in 1957. Malaysia was created in 1963, when Malaya, Singapore, Sabah and Sarawak agreed to unite, but Singapore withdrew in 1965.

From the 1970s, Malaysia achieved rapid economic progress and, by the mid-1990s, it was playing a major part in regional affairs, especially through its membership of ASEAN (Association of South-east Asian Nations). However, together with several other countries in eastern Asia, Malaysia was hit by economic recession in 1997, including a major fall in stock market values. In response to the crisis, the government ordered the repatriation of many temporary foreign workers and initiated a series of austerity measures aimed at restoring confidence and avoiding the chronic debt problems affecting some other Asian countries.

The World Bank classifies Malaysia as an 'upper-middle-income' developing country. Malaysia is a leading producer of palm oil, rubber and tin.

Manufacturing now plays a major part in the economy. Manufactures are diverse, including cars, chemicals, a wide range of electronic goods, plastics, textiles, rubber and wood products.

AREA 329,750 sq km [127,316 sq mls]
POPULATION 20,900,000
CAPITAL (POPULATION) Kuala Lumpur (1,145,000)
GOVERNMENT Federal constitutional monarchy
ETHNIC GROUPS Malay and other indigenous groups 62%, Chinese 30%, Indian 8%
LANGUAGES Malay (official), Chinese, Iban
RELIGIONS Islam 53%, Buddhism 17%, Chinese folk religionist 12%, Hinduism 7%, Christianity 6%
CURRENCY Ringgit (Malaysian dollar) = 100 cents

MALDIVES

The Republic of the Maldives consists of about 1,200 low-lying coral islands, south of India. The highest point is 24 m [79 ft], but most of the land is only 1.8 m [6 ft] above sea level. The islands became a British territory in 1887 and independence was achieved in 1965. Tourism and fishing are the main industries. **AREA** 298 sq km [115 sq mls]; **POPULATION** 275,000; **CAPITAL** Malé.

MALI

GEOGRAPHY The Republic of Mali is a landlocked country in northern Africa. The land is generally flat, with the highest land in the Adrar des Iforhas on the border with Algeria.

Northern Mali is part of the Sahara, with a hot, practically rainless climate. But the south has enough rain for farming.

POLITICS & ECONOMY France ruled the area, then known as French Sudan, from 1893 until the country became independent as Mali in 1960.

The first socialist government was overthrown in 1968 by an army group led by Moussa Traoré, but he was ousted in 1991. Multiparty democracy was restored in 1992 and Alpha Oumar Konaré was elected president. The new government agreed a pact providing for a special administration for the Tuareg minority in the north.

Mali is one of the world's poorest countries and 70% of the land is desert or semi-desert. Only about 2% of the land is used for growing crops, while 25% is used for grazing animals. Despite this, agriculture employs more than 80% of the people, many of whom still subsist by nomadic livestock rearing.

AREA 1,240,190 sq km [478,837 sq mls]
POPULATION 11,000,000
CAPITAL (POPULATION) Bamako (746,000)
GOVERNMENT Multiparty republic
ETHNIC GROUPS Bambara 32%, Fulani (or Peul) 14%, Senufo 12%, Soninke 9%, Tuareg 7%, Songhai 7%, Malinke (Mandingo or Mandinke) 7%
LANGUAGES French (official), Voltaic languages
RELIGIONS Islam 90%, traditional beliefs 9%, Christianity 1%
CURRENCY CFA franc = 100 centimes

MALTA

GEOGRAPHY The Republic of Malta consists of two main islands, Malta and Gozo, a third, much smaller island called Comino lying between the two large islands, and two tiny islets.

Malta's climate is typically Mediterranean, with hot and dry summers and mild and wet winters. The sirocco, a hot wind that blows from North Africa, may raise temperatures considerably during the spring.

POLITICS & ECONOMY During World War I (1914–18) Malta was an important naval base. In World War II (1939–45), Italian and German aircraft bombed the islands. In recognition of the bravery of the Maltese, the British King George VI awarded the George Cross to Malta in 1942. In 1953, Malta became a base for NATO (North Atlantic Treaty Organization). Malta became independent in 1964, and in 1974 it became a republic. In 1979, Britain's military agreement with Malta expired, and Malta ceased to be a military base when all the British forces withdrew. In the 1980s, the people declared Malta a neutral country. In the 1990s, Malta applied to join the European Union, but the application was scrapped when the Labour Party won the elections in 1996.

The World Bank classifies Malta as an 'upper-middle-income' developing country. It lacks natural resources, and most people work in the former naval dockyards, which are now used for commercial shipbuilding and repair, in manufacturing industries and in the tourist industry.

Manufactures include chemicals, processed food and chemicals. Farming is difficult, because of the rocky soils. The main crops are barley, fruits, potatoes and wheat. Malta also has a small fishing industry.

AREA 316 sq km [122 sq mls]
POPULATION 375,000
CAPITAL (POPULATION) Valletta (102,000)
GOVERNMENT Multiparty republic
ETHNIC GROUPS Maltese 96%, British 2%
LANGUAGES Maltese and English (both official)
RELIGIONS Christianity (Roman Catholic 99%)
CURRENCY Maltese lira = 100 cents

MARSHALL ISLANDS

The Republic of the Marshall Islands, a former US territory, became fully independent in 1991. This island nation, lying north of Kiribati in a region known as Micronesia, is heavily dependent on US aid. The main activities are agriculture and tourism. **AREA** 181 sq km [70 sq mls]; **POPULATION** 60,000; **CAPITAL** Dalap-Uliga-Darrit, on Majuro island.

MARTINIQUE

Martinique, a volcanic island nation in the Caribbean, was colonized by France in 1635. It became a French overseas department in 1946. Tourism and agriculture are major activities. About 70% of Martinique's Gross Domestic Product is provided by the French government, allowing for a good standard of living. **AREA** 1,100 sq km [425 sq mls]; **POPULATION** 405,000; **CAPITAL** Fort-de-France.

MAURITANIA

GEOGRAPHY The Islamic Republic of Mauritania in north-western Africa is nearly twice the size of France. But France has more than 26 times as many people. Part of the world's largest desert, the Sahara, covers northern Mauritania and most Mauritanians live in the south-west.

The amount of rainfall and the length of the rainy season increase from north to south. Much of the land is desert, with dry north-east and easterly winds throughout the year. But south-westerly winds bring summer rain to the south.

POLITICS & ECONOMY Originally part of the great African empires of Ghana and Mali, France set up a protectorate in Mauritania in 1903, attempting to exploit the trade in gum arabic. The country became a territory of French West Africa and a French colony in 1920. French West Africa was a huge territory, which included present-day Benin, Burkina Faso, Guinea, Ivory Coast, Mali, Niger and Senegal, as well as Mauritania. In 1958, Mauritania became a self-governing territory in the French Union and it became fully independent in 1960.

In 1976, Spain withdrew from Spanish (now Western) Sahara, a territory bordering Mauritania to the north. Morocco occupied the northern two-thirds of this territory, while Mauritania took the rest. But Saharan guerrillas belonging to POLISARIO (the Popular Front for the Liberation of Saharan Territories) began an armed struggle for independence. In 1979, Mauritania withdrew from the southern part of Western Sahara, which was then occupied by Morocco. In 1991, the country adopted a new constitution when the people voted to create a multiparty government. Multiparty elections were held in 1992.

The World Bank classifies Mauritania as a 'low-income' developing country. Agriculture employs 69% of the people. Some are herders who move around with herds of cattle and sheep, though recent droughts forced many farmers to seek aid in the cities.

AREA 1,030,700 sq km [397,953 sq mls]
POPULATION 2,400,000
CAPITAL (POPULATION) Nouakchott (600,000)
GOVERNMENT Multiparty Islamic republic
ETHNIC GROUPS Moor (Arab-Berber) 70%, Wolof 7%, Tukulor 5%, Soninke 3%, Fulani 1%
LANGUAGES Arabic (official), Wolof, French
RELIGIONS Islam 99%
CURRENCY Ouguiya = 5 khoums

MAURITIUS

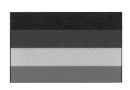

The Republic of Mauritius, an Indian Ocean nation lying east of Madagascar, was previously ruled by France and Britain until it achieved independence in 1968. It became a republic in 1992. Sugar is the main export, but tourism is now vital to the economy. **AREA** 1,860 sq km [718 sq mls]; **POPULATION** 1,155,000; **CAPITAL** Port Louis.

MEXICO

GEOGRAPHY The United Mexican States, as Mexico is officially named, is the world's most populous Spanish-speaking country. Much of the land is mountainous, although most people live on the central plateau. Mexico contains two large peninsulas, Lower (or Baja) California in the north-west and the flat Yucatán peninsula in the south-east.

The climate varies according to the altitude. The resort of Acapulco on the south-west coast has a dry and sunny climate. Mexico City, at about 2,300 m [7,546 ft] above sea level, is much cooler. Most rain occurs between June and September. The rainfall decreases north of Mexico City and northern Mexico is mainly arid.

POLITICS & ECONOMY In the mid-19th century, Mexico lost land to the United States, and between 1910 and 1921 violent revolutions created chaos.

Reforms were introduced in the 1920s and, in 1929, the Institutional Revolutionary Party (PRI) was formed. The PRI dominated Mexican politics, though it lost its overall majority in the Chamber of Deputies in 1997. Mexico faces many problems, including unemployment and rapid urbanization especially around Mexico City, demands for indigenous rights by Amerindian groups, and illegal emigration to the USA.

The World Bank classifies Mexico as an 'upper-middle-income' developing country. Agriculture is important. Food crops include beans, maize, rice and wheat, while cash crops include coffee, cotton, fruits and vegetables. Beef cattle, dairy cattle and other livestock are raised and fishing is also important.

But oil and oil products are the chief exports, while manufacturing is the most valuable activity. Many factories near the northern border assemble goods, such as car parts and electrical products, for US companies. These factories are called *maquiladoras*. Hope for the future lies in increasing economic co-operation with the USA and Canada through NAFTA (North American Free Trade Association), which came into being on 1 January 1994.

AREA 1,958,200 sq km [756,061 sq mls]
POPULATION 97,400,000
CAPITAL (POPULATION) Mexico City (15,643,000)
GOVERNMENT Federal republic
ETHNIC GROUPS Mestizo 60%, Amerindian 30%, European 9%
LANGUAGES Spanish (official)
RELIGIONS Christianity (Roman Catholic 90%, Protestant 5%)
CURRENCY New peso = 100 centavos

MICRONESIA

The Federated States of Micronesia, a former US territory covering a vast area in the western Pacific Ocean, became fully independent in 1991. The main export is copra. Fishing and tourism are also important. **AREA** 705 sq km [272 sq mls]; **POPULATION** 127,000; **CAPITAL** Palikir.

MOLDOVA

GEOGRAPHY The Republic of Moldova is a small country sandwiched between Ukraine and Romania. It was formerly one of the 15 republics that made up the Soviet Union. Much of the land is hilly and the highest areas are near the centre of the country.

Moldova has a moderately continental climate, with warm summers and fairly cold winters when temperatures dip below freezing point. Most of the rain comes in the warmer months.

POLITICS & ECONOMY In the 14th century, the Moldavians formed a state called Moldavia. It included part of Romania and Bessarabia (now the modern country of Moldova). The Ottoman Turks took the area in the 16th century, but in 1812 Russia took over Bessarabia. In 1861, Moldavia and Walachia united to form Romania. Russia retook southern Bessarabia in 1878.

After World War I (1914–18), all of Bessarabia was returned to Romania, but the Soviet Union did not recognize this act. From 1944, the Moldovan Soviet Socialist Republic was part of the Soviet Union.

In 1989, the Moldovans asserted their independence and ethnicity by making Romanian the official language and, at the end of 1991, Moldova became an independent country. In 1992, fighting occurred between Moldovans and Russians in Trans-Dniester, a mainly Russian-speaking area east of the River Dniester. This region was given a special status within Moldova in 1996. The first multiparty elections were held in 1994, when a proposal to unite with Romania was decisively rejected.

Moldova is a fertile country in which agriculture remains central to the economy. Major products include fruits, maize, tobacco and wine.

There are few natural resources within Moldova, and the government imports materials and fuels for its industries. Light industries, such as food processing and the manufacturing of household appliances, are gradually expanding.

AREA 33,700 sq km [13,010 sq mls]
POPULATION 4,450,000
CAPITAL (POPULATION) Chisinau (700,000)
GOVERNMENT Multiparty republic
ETHNIC GROUPS Moldovan 65%, Ukrainian 14%, Russian 13%, Gagauz 4%, Jewish 2%, Bulgarian
LANGUAGES Moldovan/Romanian (official)
RELIGIONS Christianity (Eastern Orthodox)
CURRENCY Leu = 100 bani

MONACO

The tiny Principality of Monaco consists of a narrow strip of coastline and a rocky peninsula on the French Riviera. Its considerable wealth is derived largely from banking, finance, gambling and tourism. Monaco's citizens do not pay any state tax. Its attractions include the Monte Carlo casino and such sporting events as the Monte Carlo Rally and the Monaco Grand Prix. **AREA** 1.5 sq km [0.6 sq mls]; **POPULATION** 30,000; **CAPITAL** Monaco.

MONGOLIA

GEOGRAPHY The State of Mongolia is the world's largest landlocked country. It consists mainly of high plateaux, with the Gobi desert in the south-east.

Ulan Bator lies on the northern edge of a desert plateau in the heart of Asia. It has bitterly cold winters. In the summer months, the temperatures are moderated by the height of the land.

POLITICS & ECONOMY In the 13th century, Genghis Khan united the Mongolian peoples and built up a great empire. Under his grandson, Kublai Khan, the Mongol empire extended from Korea and China to eastern Europe and present-day Iraq.

The Mongol empire broke up in the late 14th century. In the early 17th century, Inner Mongolia came under Chinese control, and by the late 17th century Outer Mongolia had become a Chinese province. In 1911, the Mongolians drove the Chinese out of Outer Mongolia and made the area a Buddhist kingdom. But in 1924, under Russian influence, the Communist Mongolian People's Republic was set up. From the 1950s, Mongolia supported the Soviet Union in its disputes with China. In 1990, the people demonstrated for more freedom and free elections in June 1990 resulted in victory for the Mongolian People's Revolutionary Party, which was composed of Communists. But Communist rule finally ended in 1996 when the elections were won by the opposition Democratic Union coalition.

The World Bank classifies Mongolia as a 'lower-middle-income' developing country. Most people were once nomads, who moved around with their herds of sheep, cattle, goats and horses. Under Communist rule, most people were moved into permanent homes on government-owned farms. But livestock and animal products remain leading exports. The Communists also developed industry, especially the mining of coal, copper, gold, molybdenum, tin and tungsten, and manufacturing. Minerals and fuels now account for around half of Mongolia's exports.

AREA 1,566,500 sq km [604,826 sq mls]
POPULATION 2,500,000
CAPITAL (POPULATION) Ulan Bator (619,000)
GOVERNMENT Multiparty republic
ETHNIC GROUPS Khalkha Mongol 79%, Kazak 6%
LANGUAGES Khalkha Mongolian (official), Kazak
RELIGIONS Tibetan Buddhist (Lamaist)
CURRENCY Tugrik = 100 möngös

MONTSERRAT

Monserrat is a British overseas territory in the Caribbean Sea. The climate is tropical and hurricanes often cause much damage. Intermittent eruptions of the Soufrière Hills volcano between 1995 and 1998 led to the emigration of many of the inhabitants and the virtual destruction of Plymouth, the capital, in the southern part of the island. **AREA** 1,100 sq km [39 sq mls]; **POPULATION** (prior to the volcanic activity) 12,000; **CAPITAL** Plymouth.

MOROCCO

GEOGRAPHY The Kingdom of Morocco lies in north-western Africa. Its name comes from the Arabic Maghreb-el-Aksa, meaning 'the farthest west'. Behind the western coastal plain the land rises to a broad plateau and ranges of the Atlas Mountains. The High (Haut) Atlas contains the highest peak, Djebel Toubkal, at 4,165 m [13,665 ft]. East of the mountains, the land descends to the arid Sahara.

The Atlantic coast of Morocco is cooled by the Canaries Current. Inland, summers are hot and dry. The winters are mild. In winter, between October and April, south-westerly winds from the Atlantic Ocean bring moderate rainfall, and snow often falls on the High Atlas Mountains.

POLITICS & ECONOMY The original people of Morocco were the Berbers. But in the 680s, Arab invaders introduced Islam and the Arabic language. By the early 20th century, France and Spain controlled Morocco, but Morocco became an independent kingdom in 1956. Although Morocco is a constitutional monarchy, King Hassan II has ruled the country in a generally authoritarian way since coming to the throne in 1961. He pressed Morocco's claims for Western Sahara, but the cost of the struggle to contain the Saharan nationalist guerrillas has drained the country's resources.

The United Nations classifies the Kingdom of Morocco as a 'lower-middle-income' developing country. Morocco's main resource is phosphate rock, which is used to make fertilizers. Morocco is the world's third largest producer. One of the reasons why Morocco wants to keep Western Sahara is that it, too, has large phosphate reserves. Farming employs 46% of the people, and tourism is also important.

AREA 446,550 sq km [172,413 sq mls]
POPULATION 28,100,000
CAPITAL (POPULATION) Rabat (1,220,000)
GOVERNMENT Constitutional monarchy
ETHNIC GROUPS Arab 70%, Berber 30%
LANGUAGES Arabic (official), Berber, French
RELIGIONS Islam 99%, Christianity 1%
CURRENCY Moroccan dirham = 100 centimes

MOZAMBIQUE

GEOGRAPHY The Republic of Mozambique borders the Indian Ocean in south-eastern Africa. The coastal plains are narrow in the north but broaden in the south. Inland lie plateaux and hills, which make up another two-fifths of Mozambique.

Mozambique has a mostly tropical climate. The capital Maputo, which lies outside the tropics, has hot and humid summers, though the winters are mild and fairly dry.

POLITICS & ECONOMY In 1885, when the European powers divided Africa, Mozambique was recognized as a Portuguese colony. But black African opposition to European rule gradually increased. In 1961, the Front for the Liberation of Mozambique (FRELIMO) was founded to oppose Portuguese rule.

In 1964, FRELIMO launched a guerrilla war, which continued for ten years. Mozambique became independent in 1975.

After independence, Mozambique became a one-party state. Its government aided African nationalists in Rhodesia (now Zimbabwe) and South Africa. But the white governments of these countries helped an opposition group, the Mozambique National Resistance Movement (RENAMO) to lead an armed struggle against Mozambique's government. The civil war, combined with severe droughts, caused much human suffering in the 1980s. In 1989, FRELIMO declared that it had dropped its Communist policies and ended one-party rule. The war officially ended in 1992 and multiparty elections in 1994 heralded more stable conditions. In 1995 Mozambique became the 53rd member of the Commonwealth, joining its English-speaking allies in southern Africa.

According to the World Bank, Mozambique is one of the world's five poorest countries. Agriculture employs 85% of the people, though many farmers grow little more than they need to feed their families. Crops include cassava, cotton, cashew nuts, fruits, maize, rice, sugar cane and tea.

AREA 801,590 sq km [309,494 sq mls]
POPULATION 19,100,000
CAPITAL (POPULATION) Maputo (2,000,000)
GOVERNMENT Multiparty republic
ETHNIC GROUPS Makua 47%, Tsonga 23%, Malawi 12%, Shona 11%, Yao 4%, Swahili 1%, Makonde 1%
LANGUAGES Portuguese (official), many others
RELIGIONS Traditional beliefs 48%, Christianity (Roman Catholic 31%, others 9%), Islam 13%
CURRENCY Metical = 100 centavos

NAMIBIA

GEOGRAPHY The Republic of Namibia was formerly ruled by South Africa, who called it South West Africa. The country became independent in 1990. The coastal region contains the arid Namib Desert, which is virtually uninhabited. Inland is a central plateau, bordered by a rugged spine of mountains stretching north–south. Eastern Namibia contains part of the Kalahari desert.

Namibia is a warm and mostly arid country. Lying at 1,700 m [5,500 ft] above sea level, Windhoek has an average annual rainfall of about 370 mm [15 in], often occurring during thunderstorms in the hot summer months.

POLITICS & ECONOMY During World War I, South African troops defeated the Germans who ruled what is now Namibia. After World War II, many people challenged South Africa's right to govern the territory and a civil war began in the 1960s between African guerrillas and South African troops. A cease-fire was agreed in 1989 and the country became independent in 1990. After winning independence, the government pursued a successful policy of 'national reconciliation'. A small area on Namibia's coast, called Walvis Bay (Walvisbaai), remained part of South Africa until 1994, when South Africa transferred it to Namibia.

Namibia is rich in mineral reserves, including diamonds, uranium, zinc and copper. Minerals make up 90% of the exports. But farming employs about two out of every five Namibians. Sea fishing is also important, though overfishing has reduced the yields of the country's fishing fleet. The country has few industries, but tourism is increasing.

AREA 825,414 sq km [318,434 sq mls], including Walvis Bay, a former South African territory
POPULATION 1,650,000
CAPITAL (POPULATION) Windhoek (126,000)
GOVERNMENT Multiparty republic
ETHNIC GROUPS Ovambo 50%, Kavango 9%, Herero 7%, Damara 7%, White 6%, Nama 5%
LANGUAGES English (official), Ovambo
RELIGIONS Christianity 90% (Lutheran 51%)
CURRENCY Namibian dollar = 100 cents

NAURU

Nauru is the world's smallest republic, located in the western Pacific Ocean, close to the equator. Independent since 1968, Nauru's prosperity is based on phosphate mining, but the reserves are running out. **AREA** 21 sq km [8 sq mls]; **POPULATION** 12,000; **CAPITAL** Yaren.

NEPAL

GEOGRAPHY Over three-quarters of Nepal lies in the Himalayan mountain heartland, culminating in the world's highest peak (Mount Everest, or Chomolongma in Nepali) at 8,848 m [29,029 ft]. The far lower Siwalik Range overlooks the Ganges plain.

As a result, there is a wide range of climatic conditions from tropical forest to the permanently glaciated landscape of the high Himalaya.

POLITICS & ECONOMY Nepal was united in the late 18th century, although its complex topography has ensured that it remains a diverse patchwork of peoples. From the mid-19th century to 1951, power was held by the royal Rana family. Attempts to introduce a democratic system in the 1950s failed and political parties were banned in 1962. The first democratic elections for 32 years were held in 1991.

Agriculture remains the chief activity in this overwhelmingly rural country and the government is heavily dependent on aid. Tourism, centred around the high Himalaya, grows in importance year by year, although Nepal was closed to foreigners until 1951. There are also ambitious plans to exploit the hydroelectric potential offered by the ferocious Himalayan rivers.

AREA 140,880 sq km [54,363 sq mls]
POPULATION 22,100,000
CAPITAL (POPULATION) Katmandu (535,000)
GOVERNMENT Constitutional monarchy
ETHNIC GROUPS Nepalese 53%, Bihari 18%, Tharu 5%, Tamang 5%, Newar 3%
LANGUAGES Nepali (official), local languages
RELIGIONS Hindu 86%, Buddhist 8%, Muslim 4%
CURRENCY Nepalese rupee = 100 paisa

NETHERLANDS

GEOGRAPHY The Netherlands lies at the western end of the North European Plain, which extends to the Ural Mountains in Russia. Except for the far south-eastern corner, the Netherlands is flat and about 40% lies below sea level at high tide. To prevent flooding, the Dutch have built dykes (sea walls) to hold back the waves. Large areas which were once under the sea, but which have been reclaimed, are called polders.

Because of its position on the North Sea, the Netherlands has a temperate climate. The winters are mild, with rain coming from the Atlantic depressions which pass over the country.

POLITICS & ECONOMY Before the 16th century, the area that is now the Netherlands was under a succession of foreign rulers, including the Romans, the Germanic Franks, the French and the Spanish. The Dutch declared their independence from Spain in 1581 and their status was finally recognized by Spain in 1648. In the 17th century, the Dutch built up a great overseas empire, especially in South-east Asia. But in the early 18th century, the Dutch lost control of the seas to England.

France controlled the Netherlands from 1795 to 1813. In 1815, the Netherlands, then containing Belgium and Luxembourg, became an independent kingdom. Belgium broke away in 1830 and Luxembourg followed in 1890.

The Netherlands was neutral in World War I (1914–18), but was occupied by Germany in World War II (1939–45). After the war, the Netherlands Indies became independent as Indonesia. The Netherlands became active in West European affairs. With Belgium and Luxembourg, it formed a customs union called Benelux in 1948. In 1949, it joined NATO (the North Atlantic Treaty Organization), and the European Coal and Steel Community (ECSC) in 1953. In 1957, it became a founder member of the European Economic Community (now the European Union), and its economy prospered. Although the economy was based on private enterprise, the government introduced many social welfare programmes.

The Netherlands is a highly industrialized country and industry and commerce are the most valuable activities. Its resources include natural gas, some oil, salt and china clay. But the Netherlands imports many of the materials needed by its industries and it is, therefore, a major trading country. Industrial products are wide-ranging, including aircraft, chemicals, electronic equipment, machinery, textiles and vehicles. Agriculture employs only 5% of the people, but scientific methods are used and yields are high. Dairy farming is the leading farming activity. Major products include barley, flowers and bulbs, potatoes, sugar beet and wheat.

AREA 41,526 sq km [16,033 sq mls]
POPULATION 15,900,000
CAPITAL (POPULATION) Amsterdam (1,100,000)
GOVERNMENT Constitutional monarchy
ETHNIC GROUPS Netherlander 95%, Indonesian, Turkish, Moroccan, German
LANGUAGES Dutch (official), Frisian
RELIGIONS Christianity (Roman Catholic 34%, Dutch Reformed Church 17%, Calvinist 8%), Islam 3%
CURRENCY Guilder = 100 cents

NETHERLANDS ANTILLES

The Netherlands Antilles consists of two different island groups; one off the coast of Venezuela, and the other at the northern end of the Leeward Islands, some 800 km [500 mls] away. They remain a self-governing Dutch territory. The island of Aruba was once part of the territory, but it broke away in 1986. Oil refining and tourism are important activities. **AREA** 993 sq km [383 sq mls]; **POPULATION** 210,000; **CAPITAL** Willemstad.

NEW CALEDONIA

New Caledonia is the most southerly of the Melanesian countries in the Pacific. A French possession since 1853 and an Overseas Territory since 1958, there is now a fundamental split over the question of independence between the indigenous Melanesians and the French settlers. The country is rich in mineral resources, especially nickel. **AREA** 18,580 sq km [7,174 sq mls]; **POPULATION** 192,000; **CAPITAL** Nouméa.

NEW ZEALAND

GEOGRAPHY New Zealand lies about 1,600 km [994 mls] south-east of Australia. It consists of two main islands and several other small ones. Much of North Island is volcanic. Active volcanoes include Ngauruhoe and Ruapehu. Hot springs and geysers are common, and steam from the ground is used to produce electricity. The Southern Alps, which contain the country's highest peak Mount Cook (Aoraki), at 3,753 m [12,313 ft] form the backbone of South Island. The island also has some large, fertile plains.

Auckland in the north has a warm, humid climate throughout the year. Wellington has cooler summers, while in Dunedin, in the south-east, temperatures sometimes dip below freezing in winter. The rainfall is heaviest on the western highlands.

POLITICS & ECONOMY Evidence suggests that early Maori settlers arrived in New Zealand more than 1,000 years ago. The Dutch navigator Abel Tasman reached New Zealand in 1642, but his discovery was not followed up. In 1769, the British Captain James Cook rediscovered the islands. In the early 19th century, British settlers arrived and, in 1840, under the Treaty of Waitangi, Britain took possession of the islands. Clashes occurred with the Maoris in the 1860s but, from the 1870s, the Maoris were gradually integrated into society.

In 1907, New Zealand became a self-governing dominion in the British Commonwealth. The country's economy developed quickly and the people became increasingly prosperous. However, after Britain joined the European Economic Community in 1973, New Zealand's exports to Britain shrank and the country had to reassess its economic and defence strategies and seek new markets. The world economic recession also led the government to cut back on its spending on welfare services in the 1990s. Maori rights and the preservation of Maori culture are other major political issues.

New Zealand's economy has traditionally depended on agriculture, but manufacturing now employs twice as many people as agriculture. Meat and dairy products are the most valuable items produced on farms. The country has more than 48 million sheep, 4 million dairy cattle and 5 million beef cattle.

AREA 268,680 sq km [103,737 sq mls]
POPULATION 3,650,000
CAPITAL (POPULATION) Wellington (329,000)
GOVERNMENT Constitutional monarchy
ETHNIC GROUPS New Zealand European 74%, New Zealand Maori 10%, Polynesian 4%
LANGUAGES English and Maori (both official)
RELIGIONS Christianity (Anglican 21%, Presbyterian 16%, Roman Catholic 15%)
CURRENCY New Zealand dollar = 100 cents

NICARAGUA

GEOGRAPHY The Republic of Nicaragua is the second largest country in Central America. In the east is a broad plain bordering the Caribbean Sea. The plain is drained by rivers that flow from the Central Highlands. The fertile western Pacific region contains about 40 volcanoes, many of which are active, and earthquakes are common.

Nicaragua has a tropical climate. Managua is hot throughout the year and there is a marked rainy season from May to October. The Central Highlands and Caribbean region are cooler and wetter. The wettest region is the humid Caribbean plain.

POLITICS & ECONOMY In 1502, Christopher Columbus claimed the area for Spain, which ruled Nicaragua until 1821. By the early 20th century, the United States had considerable influence in the country and, in 1912, US forces entered Nicaragua to protect US interests. From 1927 to 1933, rebels under General Augusto César Sandino, tried to drive US forces out of the country. In 1933, US marines set up a Nicaraguan army, the National Guard, to help to defeat the rebels. Its leader, Anastasio Somoza Garcia, had Sandino murdered in 1934 and, from 1937, Somoza ruled as a dictator.

In the mid-1970s, many people began to protest against Somoza's rule. Many joined a guerrilla force, called the Sandinista National Liberation Front, named after General Sandino. The rebels defeated the Somoza regime in 1979. In the 1980s, the US-supported forces, called the 'Contras', launched a campaign against the Sandinista government. The US government opposed the Sandinista regime, under Daniel José Ortega Saavedra, claiming that it was a Communist dictatorship. A coalition, the National Opposition Union, defeated the Sandinistas in elections in 1990. In 1996, the Sandinistas were again defeated and Arnoldo Alemán, leader of the Liberal Alliance Party, became president.

In the early 1990s, Nicaragua faced many problems in rebuilding its shattered economy. Agriculture is the main activity, employing nearly half of the people.

Coffee, cotton, sugar and bananas are grown for export, while rice is the main food crop.

AREA 130,000 sq km [50,193 sq mls]
POPULATION 4,544,000
CAPITAL (POPULATION) Managua (974,000)
GOVERNMENT Multiparty republic
ETHNIC GROUPS Mestizo 77%, White 10%, Black 9%, Amerindian 4%
LANGUAGES Spanish (official), Misumalpan
RELIGIONS Christianity (Roman Catholic 91%, others 9%)
CURRENCY Córdoba oro (gold córdoba) = 100 centavos

NIGER

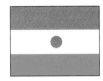

GEOGRAPHY The Republic of Niger is a landlocked nation in north-central Africa. The northern plateaux lie in the Sahara Desert, while Central Niger contains the rugged Aïr Mountains, but the most fertile and densely populated region is the narrow Niger valley in the south-west.

Niger has a tropical climate and the south has a rainy season between June and September. The hot harmattan wind blows from the Sahara between March and May. The north is practically rainless.

POLITICS & ECONOMY Since independence in 1960, Niger, a French territory from 1900, has suffered severe droughts. Food shortages and the collapse of the traditional nomadic way of life of some of Niger's people have caused political instability. After a period of military rule, a multiparty constitution was adopted in 1992, but the military again seized power in 1996. Later that year, the coup leader Col. Ibrahim Barre Mainassara, was elected president.

Niger's chief resource is uranium and it is the fourth largest producer in the world. Some tin and tungsten are also mined, though other mineral resources are largely untouched.

Despite its resources, Niger is one of the world's poorest countries. Farming employs 85% of the population, though only 3% of the land can be used for crops and 7% for grazing.

AREA 1,267,000 sq km [489,189 sq mls]
POPULATION 9,149,000
CAPITAL (POPULATION) Niamey (398,000)
GOVERNMENT Multiparty republic
ETHNIC GROUPS Hausa 53%, Zerma-Songhai 21%, Tuareg 11%, Fulani (or Peul) 10%
LANGUAGES French (official), Hausa, Songhai
RELIGIONS Islam 98%
CURRENCY CFA franc = 100 centimes

NIGERIA

GEOGRAPHY The Federal Republic of Nigeria is the most populous nation in Africa. The country's main rivers are the Niger and Benue, which meet in central

Nigeria. North of the two river valleys are high plains and plateaux. The Lake Chad basin is in the north-east, with the Sokoto plains in the north-west. Southern Nigeria contains hilly uplands and broad coastal plains, including the swampy Niger delta.

Lagos has a tropical climate, with high temperatures and rain throughout the year. The north of the country is drier and often hotter than the south, though the highlands are cooler.

POLITICS & ECONOMY Nigeria has a long artistic tradition. Major cultures include the Nok (500 BC to AD 200), Ife, which developed about 1,000 years ago, and Benin, which flourished between the 15th and 17th centuries. Britain gradually extended its influence over the area in the second half of the 19th century. Nigeria became independent in 1960 and a federal republic in 1963. A federal constitution dividing the country into regions was necessary because Nigeria contains more than 250 ethnic and linguistic groups, as well as several religious ones. Local rivalries have long been a threat to national unity, and six new states were created in 1996 in an attempt to overcome this. Civil war occurred between 1967 and 1970, when the people in the south-east fought unsuccessfully to make their area a separate country called Biafra. Since 1970, instability has continued and, between 1960 and 1998, Nigeria has enjoyed only nine years of civilian government. It remains politically unstable.

Nigeria is a developing country, with great economic potential. Its greatest natural resource is oil, which accounts for the bulk of its exports. But agriculture employs 43% of the people. The country is a major producer of cocoa, palm oil and palm kernels, groundnuts and rubber.

AREA 923,770 sq km [356,668 sq mls]
POPULATION 88,515,000
CAPITAL (POPULATION) Abuja (339,000)
GOVERNMENT Federal republic
ETHNIC GROUPS Hausa 21%, Yoruba 21%, Ibo (or Igbo) 19%, Fulani 11%, Ibibio 6%
LANGUAGES English (official), Hausa, Yoruba, Ibo
RELIGIONS Christianity (Protestant 26%, Roman Catholic 12%, others 11%), Islam 45%
CURRENCY Naira = 100 kobo

NORTHERN MARIANA ISLANDS

The Commonwealth of the Northern Mariana Islands contains 16 mountainous islands north of Guam in the western Pacific Ocean. In a 1975 plebiscite, the islanders voted for Commonwealth status in union with the USA and, in 1986, they were granted US citizenship. **AREA** 477 sq km [184 sq mls]; **POPULATION** 50,000; **CAPITAL** Saipan.

NORWAY

GEOGRAPHY The Kingdom of Norway forms the western part of the rugged Scandinavian peninsula. The deep inlets along the highly indented coastline

were worn out by glaciers during the Ice Age.

The warm North Atlantic Drift off the coast of Norway moderates the climate, with mild winters and cool summers. Nearly all the ports are ice-free throughout the year. Inland, winters are colder and snow cover lasts for at least three months a year.

POLITICS & ECONOMY Under a treaty in 1814, Denmark handed Norway over to Sweden, but it kept Norway's colonies – Greenland, Iceland and the Faroe Islands. Norway briefly became independent, but Swedish forces defeated the Norwegians and Norway had to accept Sweden's king as its ruler.

The union between Norway and Sweden ended in 1903. During World War II (1939–45), Germany occupied Norway. Norway's economy developed quickly after the war and the country now enjoys one of the world's highest standards of living. In 1960, Norway, together with six other countries, formed the European Free Trade Association (EFTA). In 1994, the Norwegians voted against joining the EU.

Norway's chief resources and exports are oil and natural gas which come from wells under the North Sea. Farmland covers only 3% of the land. Dairy farming and meat production are important, but Norway has to import food. Norway has many industries powered by cheap hydroelectricity.

AREA 323,900 sq km [125,050 sq mls]
POPULATION 4,361,000
CAPITAL (POPULATION) Oslo (714,000)
GOVERNMENT Constitutional monarchy
ETHNIC GROUPS Norwegian 97%
LANGUAGES Norwegian (official), Lappish, Finnish
RELIGIONS Christianity (Lutheran 88%)
CURRENCY Krone = 100 ore

OMAN

GEOGRAPHY The Sultanate of Oman occupies the south-eastern corner of the Arabian peninsula. It also includes the tip of the Musandam peninsula, overlooking the strategic Strait of Hormuz.

Oman has a hot tropical climate. In Muscat, temperatures may reach 47°C [117°F] in summer.

POLITICS & ECONOMY British influence in Oman dates back to the end of the 18th century, but the country became fully independent in 1971. Since then, using revenue from oil, which was discovered in 1964, the government has sought to modernize and develop the country.

The World Bank classifies Oman as an 'upper-middle-income' developing country. Its economy is based on oil production and oil accounts for more than 90% of Oman's export revenues. But agriculture still provides a living for half of the people. Major crops include alfalfa, bananas, coconuts, dates, limes, tobacco, vegetables and wheat. Some farmers raise cattle, and fishing, especially for sardines, is also important, though Oman still has to import food.

AREA 212,460 sq km [82,031 sq mls]
POPULATION 2,252,000
CAPITAL (POPULATION) Muscat (350,000)
GOVERNMENT Monarchy with consultative council
ETHNIC GROUPS Omani Arab 74%, Pakistani 21%
LANGUAGES Arabic (official), Baluchi, English
RELIGIONS Islam (Ibadiyah) 86%, Hinduism 13%
CURRENCY Omani rial = 100 baizas

PAKISTAN

GEOGRAPHY The Islamic Republic of Pakistan contains high mountains, fertile plains and rocky deserts. The Karakoram range, which contains K2, the world's second highest peak, lies in the northern part of Jammu and Kashmir, which is occupied by Pakistan but claimed by India. Other mountains rise in the west. Plains, drained by the River Indus and its tributaries, occupy much of eastern Pakistan. The Thar Desert is in the south-east and the dry Baluchistan plateau is in the south-west.

The mountains have cold, snowy winters. But most of Pakistan has hot summers and cool winters. The rainfall is sparse throughout much of the country. Most of it comes between July and September, when south-west monsoon winds blow.

POLITICS & ECONOMY Pakistan was the site of the Indus Valley civilization which developed about 4,500 years ago. But Pakistan's modern history dates from 1947, when British India was divided into India and Pakistan. Muslim Pakistan was divided into two parts: East and West Pakistan, but East Pakistan broke away in 1971 to become Bangladesh. In 1948–9, 1965 and 1971, Pakistan and India clashed over the disputed territory of Kashmir. In 1998, Pakistan responded in kind to a series of Indian nuclear weapon tests, provoking global controversy.

Pakistan has been subject to several periods of military rule, but elections held in 1988 led to Benazir Bhutto, daughter of a former prime minister and president, Zulfikar Ali Bhutto, becoming prime minister. Benazir Bhutto was removed from office in 1990 but she again became prime minister in 1993, until she was dismissed in 1996. Following elections in 1997, Nawaz Sharif became prime minister.

According to the World Bank, Pakistan is a 'low-income' developing country. The economy is based on farming or rearing goats and sheep. Agriculture employs nearly half the people. Major crops, grown mainly on irrigated land, include cotton, fruits, rice, sugar cane and, most important of all, wheat.

AREA 796,100 sq km [307,374 sq mls]
POPULATION 143,595,000
CAPITAL (POPULATION) Islamabad (204,000)
GOVERNMENT Federal republic
ETHNIC GROUPS Punjabi 60%, Sindhi 12%, Pushtun 13%, Baluch, Muhajir
LANGUAGES Urdu (official), many others
RELIGIONS Islam 97%, Christianity, Hinduism
CURRENCY Pakistan rupee = 100 paisa

PALAU

The Republic of Palau became fully independent in 1994, after the USA refused to accede to a 1979 referendum that declared this island nation a nuclear-free zone. The economy relies on US aid, tourism, fishing and subsistence agriculture. The main crops include cassava, coconuts and copra.
AREA 458 sq km [177 sq mls]; **POPULATION** 18,000; **CAPITAL** Koror.

PANAMA

GEOGRAPHY The Republic of Panama forms an isthmus linking Central America to South America. The Panama Canal, which is 81.6 km [50.7 mls] long, cuts across the isthmus. It has made the country a major transport centre.

Panama has a tropical climate. Temperatures are high, though the mountains are much cooler than the coastal plains. The main rainy season is between May and December.

POLITICS & ECONOMY Christopher Columbus landed in Panama in 1502 and Spain soon took control of the area. In 1821, Panama became independent from Spain and a province of Colombia.

In 1903, Colombia refused a request by the United States to build a canal. Panama then revolted against Colombia, and became independent. The United States then began to build the canal, which was opened in 1914. The United States administered the Panama Canal Zone, a strip of land along the canal. But many Panamanians resented US influence and, in 1979, the Canal Zone was returned to Panama. The USA also agreed to hand over control of the Canal to Panama on 31 December 1999.

Panama's government has changed many times since independence, and there have been periods of military dictatorships. In 1983, General Manuel Antonio Noriega became Panama's leader. In 1988, two US grand juries in Florida indicted Noriega on charges of drug trafficking. In 1989, Noriega was apparently defeated in a presidential election, but the government declared the election invalid. After the killing of a US marine, US troops entered Panama and arrested Noriega, who was convicted by a Miami court of drug offences in 1992. Elections in 1994 were won the Democratic Revolutionary Party, led by Ernesto Pérez Balladares.

The World Bank classifies Panama as a 'lower-middle-income' developing country. The Panama Canal is an important source of revenue and it generates many jobs in commerce, trade, manufacturing and transport. Away from the Canal, the main activity is agriculture, which employs 27% of the people.

AREA 77,080 sq km [29,761 sq mls]
POPULATION 2,629,000
CAPITAL (POPULATION) Panama City (452,000)
GOVERNMENT Multiparty republic
ETHNIC GROUPS Mestizo 60%, Black and Mulatto 20%, White 10%, Amerindian 8%, Asian 2%
LANGUAGES Spanish (official)
RELIGIONS Christianity (Roman Catholic 84%, Protestant 5%), Islam 5%
CURRENCY Balboa = 100 centésimos

PAPUA NEW GUINEA

GEOGRAPHY Papua New Guinea is an independent country in the Pacific Ocean, north of Australia. It is part of a Pacific island region called Melanesia. Papua New Guinea includes the eastern part of New Guinea, the Bismarck Archipelago, the northern Solomon Islands, the D'Entrecasteaux Islands and the Louisiade Archipelago. The land is largely mountainous.

Papua New Guinea has a tropical climate, with high temperatures throughout the year. Most of the rain occurs during the monsoon season (from December to April), when the north-westerly winds blow. Winds blow from the south-east during the dry season.

POLITICS & ECONOMY The Dutch took western New Guinea (now part of Indonesia) in 1828, but it was not until 1884 that Germany took north-eastern New Guinea and Britain the south-east. In 1906, Britain handed the south-east over to Australia. It then became known as the Territory of Papua. When World War I broke out in 1914, Australia took German New Guinea and, in 1921, the League of Nations gave Australia a mandate to rule the area, which was named the Territory of New Guinea.

Japan invaded New Guinea in 1942, but the Allies reconquered the area in 1944. In 1949, Papua and New Guinea were combined into the Territory of Papua and New Guinea. Papua New Guinea became fully independent in 1975.

Since independence, the government of Papua New Guinea has worked to develop its mineral reserves. One of the most valuable mines was on Bougainville, in the northern Solomon Islands. But the people of Bougainville demanded a larger share in the profits of the mine. Conflict broke out, the mine was closed and the Bougainville Revolutionary Army proclaimed the island independent. But their attempted secession was not recognized internationally. An agreement to end the conflict was finally signed in New Zealand in January 1998.

The World Bank classifies Papua New Guinea as a 'lower-middle-income' developing country. Agriculture employs three out of every four people, many of whom produce little more than they need to feed their families. But minerals, notably copper and gold, are the most valuable exports.

AREA 462,840 sq km [178,703 sq mls]
POPULATION 4,292,000
CAPITAL (POPULATION) Port Moresby (174,000)
GOVERNMENT Constitutional monarchy
ETHNIC GROUPS Papuan 84%, Melanesian 1%
LANGUAGES English (official), about 800 others
RELIGIONS Christianity (Protestant 58%, Roman Catholic 33%, Anglican 5%), traditional beliefs 3%
CURRENCY Kina = 100 toea

PARAGUAY

GEOGRAPHY The Republic of Paraguay is a land-locked country and rivers, notably the Paraná, Pilcomayo (Brazo Sur) and Paraguay, form most of its borders. A flat region called the Gran Chaco lies in the north-west, while the south-east contains plains, hills and plateaux.

Northern Paraguay lies in the tropics, while the south is subtropical. Most of the country has a warm, humid climate.

POLITICS & ECONOMY In 1776, Paraguay became part of a large colony called the Vice-royalty of La Plata, with Buenos Aires as the capital. Paraguayans opposed this move and the country declared its independence in 1811.

For many years, Paraguay was torn by internal strife and conflict with its neighbours. A war against Brazil, Argentina and Uruguay (1865–70) led to the deaths of more than half of Paraguay's population, and a great loss of territory.

General Alfredo Stroessner took power in 1954 and ruled as a dictator. His government imprisoned many opponents. Stroessner was overthrown in 1989. Free multiparty elections held in 1993 resulted in the instalment of Juan Carlos Wasmosy, leader of the Colorado Party. Wasmosy was Paraguay's first civilian president since 1954.

The World Bank classifies Paraguay as a 'lower-middle-income' developing country. Agriculture and forestry are the leading activities, employing 48% of the population. The country has abundant hydroelectricity and it exports power to Argentina and Brazil.

AREA 406,750 sq km [157,046 sq mls]
POPULATION 4,979,000
CAPITAL (POPULATION) Asunción (945,000)
GOVERNMENT Multiparty republic
ETHNIC GROUPS Mestizo 90%, Amerindian 3%
LANGUAGES Spanish and Guaraní (both official)
RELIGIONS Christianity (Roman Catholic 96%, Protestant 2%)
CURRENCY Guaraní = 100 céntimos

PERU

GEOGRAPHY The Republic of Peru lies in the tropics in western South America. A narrow coastal plain borders the Pacific Ocean in the west. Inland are ranges of the Andes Mountains, which rise to 6,768 m [22,205 ft] at Mount Huascarán, an extinct volcano. East of the Andes, the land descends to the Amazon basin.

Lima, on the coastal plain, has an arid climate. The coastal region is chilled by the cold, offshore Humboldt Current. The rainfall increases inland and many mountains in the high Andes are snow-capped.

POLITICS & ECONOMY Spanish conquistadors conquered Peru in the 1530s. In 1820, an Argentinian, José de San Martín, led an army into Peru and declared it independent. But Spain still held large areas. In 1823, the Venezuelan Simon Bolívar led another army into Peru and, in 1824, one of his generals defeated the Spaniards at Ayacucho. The Spaniards surrendered in 1826. Peru suffered much instability throughout the 19th century.

Instability continued in the 20th century. In 1980, when civilian rule was restored, a left-wing group called the Sendero Luminoso, or the 'Shining Path', began guerrilla warfare against the government. In 1990, Alberto Fujimori, son of Japanese immigrants, became president. In 1992, he suspended the constitution and dismissed the legislature. The guerrilla leader, Abimael Guzmán, was arrested in 1992, but instability continued. A new constitution was introduced in 1993, giving increased power to the president, who faced many problems in rebuilding the shattered economy.

The World Bank classifies Peru as a 'lower-middle-income' developing country. Agriculture employs 35% of the people and major food crops include beans, maize, potatoes and rice. Fish products are exported, but the most valuable export is copper. Peru also produces lead, silver, zinc and iron ore.

AREA 1,285,220 sq km [496,223 sq mls]
POPULATION 25,588,000
CAPITAL (POPULATION) Lima (Lima-Callao, 6,601,000)
GOVERNMENT Transitional republic
ETHNIC GROUPS Quechua 47%, Mestizo 32%, White 12%, Aymara 5%
LANGUAGES Spanish and Quechua (both official), Aymara
RELIGIONS Christianity (Roman Catholic 93%, Protestant 6%)
CURRENCY New sol = 100 centavos

PHILIPPINES

GEOGRAPHY The Republic of the Philippines is an island country in south-eastern Asia. It includes about 7,100 islands, of which 2,770 are named and about 1,000 are inhabited. Luzon and Mindanao, the two largest islands, make up more than two-thirds of the country. The land is mainly mountainous and lacks large lowlands.

The country has a tropical climate, with high temperatures all through the year. The dry season runs from December to April. The rest of the year is wet. The high rainfall is associated with typhoons which periodically strike the east coast.

POLITICS & ECONOMY The first European to reach the Philippines was the Portuguese navigator Ferdinand Magellan in 1521. Spanish explorers claimed the region in 1565 when they established a settlement on Cebu. The Spaniards ruled the country until 1898, when the United States took over at the end of the Spanish–American War. Japan invaded the Philippines in 1941, but US forces returned in 1944. The country became fully independent as the Republic of the Philippines in 1946.

Since independence, the country's problems have included armed uprisings by left-wing guerrillas demanding land reform, and Muslim separatist groups, crime, corruption and unemployment. The dominant figure in recent times was Ferdinand Marcos, who ruled in a dictatorial manner from 1965 to 1986. His successor was Corazon Aquino, widow of an assassinated opponent of Marcos. Aquino did not stand in the presidential elections in 1992. Her successor was General Fidel Ramos.

The Philippines is a developing country with a lower-middle-income economy. Agriculture employs 45% of the people. The main foods are rice and maize, while such crops as bananas, cocoa, coconuts, coffee, sugar cane and tobacco are grown commercially. Manufacturing now plays an increasingly important role in the economy.

AREA 300,000 sq km [115,300 sq mls]
POPULATION 67,167,000
CAPITAL (POPULATION) Manila (Metro Manila, 9,280,000)
GOVERNMENT Multiparty republic
ETHNIC GROUPS Tagalog 30%, Cebuano 24%, Ilocano 10%, Hiligaynon Ilongo 9%, Bicol 6%
LANGUAGES Pilipino (Tagalog) and English (both official), Spanish, many others
RELIGIONS Christianity (Roman Catholic 84%, Philippine Independent Church or Aglipayan 6%, Protestant 4%), Islam 4%
CURRENCY Philippine peso = 100 centavos

PITCAIRN ISLANDS

Pitcairn Island is a British overseas territory in the Pacific Ocean. Its inhabitants are descendants of the original settlers – nine mutineers from *HMS Bounty* and 18 Tahitians who arrived in 1790. **AREA** 48 sq km [19 sq mls]; **POPULATION** 60; **CAPITAL** Adamstown.

POLAND

GEOGRAPHY The Republic of Poland faces the Baltic Sea and, behind its lagoon-fringed coast, lies a broad plain. The land rises to a plateau region in the south-east, while the Sudeten Highlands straddle part of the border with the Czech Republic. Part of the Carpathian range (the Tatra) lies on the south-eastern border with the Slovak Republic.

Poland's climate is influenced by its position in Europe. Warm, moist air masses come from the west, while cold air masses come from the north and east. Summers are warm, but winters are cold and snowy.

POLITICS & ECONOMY Poland's boundaries have changed several times in the last 200 years, partly as a result of its geographical location between the powers of Germany and Russia. It disappeared from the map in the late 18th century, when a Polish state called the Grand Duchy of Warsaw was set up. But in 1815, the country was partitioned, between Austria, Prussia and Russia. Poland became independent in 1918, but in 1939 it was divided between Germany and the Soviet Union. The country again became independent in 1945, when it lost land to Russia but gained some from Germany. Communists took power in 1948, but opposition mounted and eventually became focused through an organization called Solidarity.

Solidarity was led by a trade unionist, Lech Walesa. A coalition government was formed between Solidarity and the Communists in 1989. In 1990, the Communist party was dissolved and Walesa became president. But Walesa faced many problems in turning Poland towards a market economy. In presidential elections in 1995, Walesa was defeated by ex-Communist Aleksander Kwasniewski. However, Kwasniewski continued to follow westward-looking policies and, in 1996, Poland joined the OECD. It is likely to be among the first countries to enter an expanded EU.

Poland has large reserves of coal and deposits of various minerals which are used in its factories. Manufactures include chemicals, processed food, machinery, ships, steel and textiles.

AREA 312,680 sq km [120,726 sq mls]
POPULATION 38,587,000
CAPITAL (POPULATION) Warsaw (1,638,000)
GOVERNMENT Multiparty republic
ETHNIC GROUPS Polish 98%, Ukrainian 1%, German 1%
LANGUAGES Polish (official)
RELIGIONS Christianity (Roman Catholic 94%, Orthodox 2%)
CURRENCY Zloty = 100 groszy

PORTUGAL

GEOGRAPHY The Republic of Portugal is the most westerly of Europe's mainland countries. The land rises from the coastal plains on the Atlantic Ocean to the western edge of the huge plateau, or Meseta, which occupies most of the Iberian peninsula. Portugal also contains two autonomous regions, the Azores and Madeira island groups.

The climate is moderated by winds blowing from the Atlantic Ocean. Summers are cooler and winters are milder than in other Mediterranean lands.

POLITICS & ECONOMY Portugal became a separate country, independent of Spain, in 1143. In the 15th century, Portugal led the 'Age of European Exploration'. This led to the growth of a large Portuguese empire, with colonies in Africa, Asia and, most valuable of all, Brazil in South America. Portuguese power began to decline in the 16th century and, between 1580 and 1640, Portugal was ruled by Spain. Portugal lost Brazil in 1822 and, in 1910, Portugal became a republic. Instability hampered progress and army officers seized power in 1926. In 1928, they chose Antonio de Salazar to be minister of finance. He became prime minister in 1932 and ruled as a dictator from 1933.

Salazar ruled until 1968, but his successor, Marcello Caetano, was overthrown in 1974 by a group of army officers. The new government made most of Portugal's remaining colonies independent. Free elections were held in 1978. Portugal joined the European Community (now the European Union) in 1986. But despite great efforts to increase economic growth, Portugal remains one of its poorest members.

Agriculture and fishing were the mainstays of the economy until the mid-20th century. But manufacturing is now the most valuable sector.

AREA 92,390 sq km [35,670 sq mls]
POPULATION 10,600,000
CAPITAL (POPULATION) Lisbon (2,561,000)
GOVERNMENT Multiparty republic
ETHNIC GROUPS Portuguese 99%, Cape Verdean, Brazilian, Spanish, British
LANGUAGES Portuguese (official)
RELIGIONS Christianity (Roman Catholic 95%, other Christians 2%)
CURRENCY Escudo = 100 centavos

PUERTO RICO

The Commonwealth of Puerto Rico, a mainly mountainous island, is the easternmost of the Greater Antilles chain. The climate is hot and wet. Puerto Rico is a dependent territory of the USA and the people are US citizens. Migration to the USA is common, though the island is the most industrialized in the Caribbean. US companies are attracted by tax exemptions to invest in the island, and the manufacturing sector is expanding. Debate continues as to whether Puerto Rico should eventually become the 51st state. **AREA** 8,900 sq km [3,436 sq km]; **POPULATION** 3,689,000; **CAPITAL** San Juan.

QATAR

The State of Qatar occupies a low, barren peninsula that extends northwards from the Arabian peninsula into the Gulf. The climate is hot and dry. Qatar became a British protectorate in 1916, but it became fully independent in 1971. Oil, first discovered in 1939, is the mainstay of the economy of this prosperous nation. **AREA** 11,000 sq km [4,247 sq mls]; **POPULATION** 594,000; **CAPITAL** Doha.

RÉUNION

Réunion is a French overseas department in the Indian Ocean. The land is mainly mountainous, though the lowlands are intensely cultivated. Sugar and sugar products are the main exports, but French aid, given to the island in return for its use as a military base, is important to the economy. **AREA** 2,510 sq km [969 sq mls]; **POPULATION** 655,000; **CAPITAL** Saint-Denis.

ROMANIA

GEOGRAPHY Romania is a country on the Black Sea in eastern Europe. Eastern and southern Romania form part of the Danube river basin. The delta region, near the mouths of the Danube, where the river flows into the Black Sea, is one of Europe's finest wetlands. The southern part of the coast contains several resorts. The heart of the country is called Transylvania. It is ringed in the east, south and west by scenic mountains which are part of the Carpathian mountain system.

Romania has hot summers and cold winters. The rainfall is heaviest in spring and early summer, when thundery showers are common.

POLITICS & ECONOMY From the late 18th century, the Turkish empire began to break up. The modern history of Romania began in 1861 when Walachia and Moldavia united. After World War I (1914–18), Romania, which had fought on the side of the victorious Allies, obtained large areas, including Transylvania, where most people were Romanians. This almost doubled the country's size and population. In 1939, Romania lost territory to Bulgaria, Hungary and the Soviet Union. Romania fought alongside Germany in World War II, and Soviet troops occupied the country in 1944. Hungary returned northern Transylvania to Romania in 1945, but Bulgaria and the Soviet Union kept former Romanian territory. In 1947, Romania officially became a Communist country.

In 1990, Romania held its first free elections since the end of World War II. The National Salvation Front, led by Ion Iliescu and containing many former Communist leaders, won a large majority. A new constitution, approved in 1991, made the country a democratic republic. Elections held under this constitution in 1992 again resulted in victory for Ion Iliescu, whose party was renamed the Party of Social Democracy (PDSR) in 1993. But the government faced many problems as it tried to reform the economy. In 1996, the PDSR was defeated in elections by the centre-right Democratic Convention led by Emil Constantinescu.

According to the World Bank, Romania is a 'lower-middle-income' economy. Under Communist rule, industry, including mining and manufacturing, became more important than agriculture.

AREA 237,500 sq km [91,699 sq mls]
POPULATION 22,863,000
CAPITAL (POPULATION) Bucharest (2,061,000)
GOVERNMENT Multiparty republic
ETHNIC GROUPS Romanian 89%, Hungarian 7%, Gypsy 2%
LANGUAGES Romanian (official), Hungarian
RELIGIONS Christianity (Romanian Orthodox 87%, Roman Catholic 5%, Greek Orthodox 4%)
CURRENCY Romanian leu = 100 bani

RUSSIA

GEOGRAPHY Russia is the world's largest country. About 25% lies west of the Ural Mountains in European Russia, where 80% of the population lives. It is mostly flat or undulating, but the land rises to the Caucasus Mountains in the south, where Russia's highest peak, Elbrus, at 5,633 m [18,481 ft], is found. Asian Russia, or Siberia, contains vast plains and plateaux, with mountains in the east and south. The Kamchatka peninsula in the far east has many active volcanoes. Russia contains many of the world's longest rivers, including the Yenisey-Angara and the Ob-Irtysh. It also includes part of the world's largest inland body of water, the Caspian Sea, and Lake Baikal, the world's deepest lake.

Moscow has a continental climate with cold and snowy winters and warm summers. Krasnoyarsk in south-central Siberia has a harsher, drier climate, but it is not as severe as parts of northern Siberia.

POLITICS & ECONOMY In the 9th century AD, a state called Kievan Rus was formed by a group of people called the East Slavs. Kiev, now capital of Ukraine, became a major trading centre, but, in 1237, Mongol armies conquered Russia and destroyed Kiev. Russia was part of the Mongol empire until the late 15th century. Under Mongol rule, Moscow became the leading Russian city.

In the 16th century, Moscow's grand prince was retitled 'tsar'. The first tsar, Ivan the Terrible, expanded Russian territory. In 1613, after a period of civil war, Michael Romanov became tsar, founding a dynasty which ruled until 1917. In the early 18th century, Tsar Peter the Great began to westernize Russia and, by 1812, when Napoleon failed to conquer the country, Russia was a major European power. But during the 19th century, many Russians demanded reforms and discontent was widespread.

In World War I (1914–18), the Russian people suffered great hardships and, in 1917, Tsar Nicholas II was forced to abdicate. In November 1917, the Bolsheviks seized power under Vladimir Lenin. In 1922, the Bolsheviks set up a new nation, the Union of Soviet Socialist Republics (also called the USSR or the Soviet Union).

From 1924, Joseph Stalin introduced a socialist economic programme, suppressing all opposition. In 1939, the Soviet Union and Germany signed a non-aggression pact, but Germany invaded the Soviet Union in 1941. Soviet forces pushed the Germans back, occupying eastern Europe. They reached Berlin in May 1945. From the late 1940s, tension between the Soviet Union and its allies and Western nations developed into a 'Cold War'. This continued until 1991, when the Soviet Union was dissolved.

The Soviet Union collapsed because of the failure of its economic policies. From 1991, its new leader, Boris Yeltsin, worked to develop democratic systems, reform the economy and increase private ownership. Russia kept contacts with 11 of the republics in the former Soviet Union through the Commonwealth of Independent States. But fighting in Chechenia in the mid-1990s showed that Russia's diverse population makes national unity difficult to achieve.

Russia's economy was thrown into disarray after the collapse of the Soviet Union, and in the early 1990s the World Bank described Russia as a 'lower-middle-income' economy. Russia was admitted to the Council of Europe in 1997, essentially to discourage instability in the Caucasus. More significantly still, Boris Yeltsin was invited to attend the G7 summit in Denver in 1997. The summit became known as 'the Summit of the Eight' and it appeared that Russia will now be included in future meetings of the world's most powerful economies. Industry is the most valuable activity, though, under Communist rule, manufacturing was less efficient than in the West and the emphasis was on heavy industry. Today, light industries producing consumer goods are becoming important. Russia's abundant resources include oil and natural gas, coal, timber, metal ores and hydroelectric power.

Most farmland is still government-owned or run as collectives. Russia is a major producer of farm products, though it imports grains. Major crops include barley, flax, fruits, oats, rye, potatoes, sugar beet, sunflower seeds, vegetables and wheat. Livestock farming is also important.

AREA 17,075,000 sq km [6,592,800 sq mls]
POPULATION 148,385,000
CAPITAL (POPULATION) Moscow (9,233,000)
GOVERNMENT Federal multiparty republic
ETHNIC GROUPS Russian 82%, Tatar 4%, Ukrainian 3%, Chuvash 1%, more than 100 other nationalities
LANGUAGES Russian (official), many others
RELIGIONS Christianity (mainly Russian Orthodox, with Roman Catholic and Protestant minorities), Islam, Judaism
CURRENCY Russian rouble = 100 kopeks

RWANDA

GEOGRAPHY The Republic of Rwanda is a small, landlocked country in east-central Africa. Lake Kivu and the River Ruzizi in the Great African Rift Valley form the country's western border.

Kigali stands on the central plateau of Rwanda. Here, temperatures are moderated by the altitude. The rainfall is abundant, but much heavier rain falls on the western mountains.

POLITICS & ECONOMY Germany conquered the area, called Ruanda-Urundi, in the 1890s. But Belgium occupied the region during World War I (1914–18) and ruled it until 1961, when the people of Ruanda voted for their country to become a republic, called Rwanda. This decision followed a rebellion by the majority Hutu people against the Tutsi monarchy. About 150,000 deaths resulted from this conflict. Many Tutsis fled to Uganda, where they formed a rebel army. Burundi became independent as a monarchy, though it became a republic in 1966. Relations between Hutus and Tutsis continued to cause friction. Civil war broke out in 1994 and in 1996 the conflict spilled over into Congo (then Zaïre), where Tutsis clashes with government troops.

According to the World Bank, Rwanda is a 'low-income' developing country. Most people are poor farmers, who produce little more than they need to feed their families. Food crops include bananas, beans, cassava and sorghum. Some cattle are raised.

AREA 26,340 sq km [10,170 sq mls]
POPULATION 7,899,000
CAPITAL (POPULATION) Kigali (235,000)
GOVERNMENT Republic
ETHNIC GROUPS Hutu 90%, Tutsi 9%, Twa 1%
LANGUAGES French, English and Kinyarwanda (all official)
RELIGIONS Christianity 74% (Roman Catholic 65%), traditional beliefs 17%, Islam 9%
CURRENCY Rwanda franc = 100 centimes

ST HELENA

St Helena, which became a British colony in 1834, is an isolated volcanic island in the south Atlantic Ocean. Now a British overseas territory, it is also the administrative centre of Ascension and Tristan da Cunha. **AREA** 122 sq km [47 sq mls]; **POPULATION** 8,200; **CAPITAL** Jamestown.

ST KITTS AND NEVIS

The Federation of St Kitts and Nevis became independent from Britain in 1983. A movement to separate Nevis from the union gained strength in 1997. **AREA** 360 sq km [139 sq mls]; **POPULATION** 45,000; **CAPITAL** Basseterre.

ST LUCIA

St Lucia, which became independent from Britain in 1979, is a mountainous, forested island of extinct volcanoes. It exports bananas and coconuts, and now attracts many tourists. **AREA** 610 sq km [236 sq mls]; **POPULATION** 147,000; **CAPITAL** Castries.

ST VINCENT AND THE GRENADINES

St Vincent and the Grenadines achieved its independence from Britain in 1979. Tourism is growing, but the territory is less prosperous than its neighbours. **AREA** 388 sq km [150 sq mls]; **POPULATION** 111,000; **CAPITAL** Kingstown.

SAN MARINO

The 'Most Serene Republic of San Marino', as this tiny state in northern Italy is officially called, has been independent since 885 and a republic since the 14th century. This makes it the world's oldest republic. **AREA** 61 sq km [24 sq mls]; **POPULATION** 26,000; **CAPITAL** San Marino

SÃO TOMÉ AND PRÍNCIPE

The Democratic Republic of São Tomé and Príncipe, a mountainous island territory west of Gabon, became a Portuguese colony in 1522. Following independence in 1975, the islands became a one-party Marxist state, but multiparty elections were held in 1991. Cocoa is the main product. **AREA** 964 sq km [372 sq mls]; **POPULATION** 133,000; **CAPITAL** Sao Tome.

SAUDI ARABIA

GEOGRAPHY The Kingdom of Saudi Arabia occupies about three-quarters of the Arabian peninsula in south-west Asia. Deserts cover most of the land. Mountains border the Red Sea plains in the west. In the north is the sandy Nafud Desert (An Nafud). In the south is the Rub' al Khali (the 'Empty Quarter'), one of the world's bleakest deserts.

Saudi Arabia has a hot, dry climate. In the summer months, the temperatures in Riyadh often exceed 40°C [104°F], though the nights are cool.

POLITICS & ECONOMY Saudi Arabia contains the two holiest places in Islam – Mecca (or Makka), the birthplace of the Prophet Muhammad in AD 570, and Medina (Al Madinah) where Muhammad went in 622. These places are visited by many pilgrims.

Saudi Arabia was poor until the oil industry began to operate on the eastern plains in 1933. Oil revenues have been used to develop the country and Saudi Arabia has given aid to poorer Arab nations. The monarch has supreme authority and Saudi Arabia

SENEGAL

has no formal constitution. In the first Gulf War (1980-88), Saudi Arabia supported Iraq against Iran. But when Iraq invaded Kuwait in 1990, it joined the international alliance to drive Iraq's forces out of Kuwait in 1991.

Saudi Arabia has about 25% of the world's known oil reserves, and oil and oil products make up 85% of its exports. But agriculture still employs 48% of the people, including nomadic herders who rear cattle, goats, sheep, and other animals. Crops grown in the south-western highlands and at oases include dates and other fruits, vegetables and wheat. Modern irrigation and desalination schemes have greatly increased crop production in recent years. The government continues to encourage the development of modern agriculture and new industries as a method of diversifying the economy.

AREA 2,149,690 sq km [829,995 sq mls]
POPULATION 18,395,000
CAPITAL (POPULATION) Riyadh (2,000,000)
GOVERNMENT Absolute monarchy with consultative assembly
ETHNIC GROUPS Arab (Saudi 82%, Yemeni 10%, other Arab 3%)
LANGUAGES Arabic (official)
RELIGIONS Islam 99%, Christianity 1%
CURRENCY Saudi riyal = 100 halalas

SENEGAL

GEOGRAPHY The Republic of Senegal is on the north-west coast of Africa. The volcanic Cape Verde (Cap Vert), on which Dakar stands, is the most westerly point in Africa. Plains cover most of Senegal, though the land rises gently in the south-east.

Dakar has a tropical climate, with a short rainy season between July and October when moist winds blow from the south-west.

POLITICS & ECONOMY In 1882, Senegal became a French colony, and from 1895 it was ruled as part of French West Africa, the capital of which, Dakar, developed as a major port and city.

In 1959, Senegal joined French Sudan (now Mali) to form the Federation of Mali. But Senegal withdrew in 1960 and became the separate Republic of Senegal. Its first president, Léopold Sédar Senghor, was a noted African poet. He continued in office until 1981, when he was succeeded by the prime minister, Abdou Diouf.

Senegal and The Gambia have always enjoyed close relations despite their differing French and British traditions. In 1981, Senegalese troops put down an attempted coup in The Gambia and, in 1982, the two countries set up a defence alliance, called the Confederation of Senegambia. But this confederation was dissolved in 1989.

According to the World Bank, Senegal is a 'lower-middle-income' developing country. It was badly hit in the 1960s and 1970s by droughts, which caused starvation. Agriculture still employs 81% of the population though many farmers produce little more than they need to feed their families. Food crops include groundnuts, millet and rice. Phosphates are the country's chief resource, but Senegal also refines oil which it imports from Gabon and Nigeria. Dakar is a busy port and has many industries.

Senegal exports fish products, groundnuts, oil products and phosphates.

AREA 196,720 sq km [75,954 sq mls]
POPULATION 8,308,000
CAPITAL (POPULATION) Dakar (1,729,000)
GOVERNMENT Multiparty republic
ETHNIC GROUPS Wolof 44%, Fulani-Tukulor 24%, Serer 15%
LANGUAGES French (official), tribal languages
RELIGIONS Islam 94%, Christianity (mainly Roman Catholic) 5%, traditional beliefs and others 1%
CURRENCY CFA franc = 100 centimes

SEYCHELLES

The Republic of Seychelles in the western Indian Ocean achieved independence from Britain in 1976. Coconuts are the main cash crop and fishing and tourism are important. AREA 455 sq km [176 sq mls]; POPULATION 75,000; CAPITAL Victoria.

SIERRA LEONE

GEOGRAPHY The Republic of Sierra Leone in West Africa is about the same size as the Republic of Ireland. The coast contains several deep estuaries in the north, with lagoons in the south. The most prominent feature is the mountainous Freetown (or Sierra Leone) peninsula. North of the peninsula is the River Rokel estuary, West Africa's best natural harbour.

Sierra Leone has a tropical climate, with heavy rainfall between April and November.

POLITICS & ECONOMY After independence, Sierra Leone became a monarchy. Its head of state was the British monarch, who was represented in the country by a governor-general. But after a military government took power in 1968, Sierra Leone became a republic in 1971 and a one-party state in 1978. In 1991, a majority of the people voted for the restoration of democracy but, in 1992, a military group seized power. In 1994 and 1995, civil war caused a collapse of law and order in some areas. Multiparty elections were held in 1996, but another military coup occurred in 1997. In 1998, the West African peace force drove the military junta from Freetown, paving the way for a return to democracy.

The World Bank classifies Sierra Leone among the 'low-income' economies. Agriculture provides a living for 70% of the people, though farming is mainly at subsistence level. The most valuable exports are minerals, including diamonds, bauxite and rutile (titanium ore). The country has few manufacturing industries.

AREA 71,740 sq km [27,699 sq mls]
POPULATION 4,467,000
CAPITAL (POPULATION) Freetown (505,000)
GOVERNMENT Single-party republic
ETHNIC GROUPS Mende 35%, Temne 37%
LANGUAGES English (official), Mande, Temne
RELIGIONS Traditional beliefs 51%, Islam 39%
CURRENCY Leone = 100 cents

SINGAPORE

GEOGRAPHY The Republic of Singapore is an island country at the southern tip of the Malay peninsula. It consists of the large Singapore Island and 58 small islands, 20 of which are inhabited.

Singapore has a hot and humid climate, typical of places near the Equator. The temperatures are high and the rainfall is heavy throughout the year.

POLITICS & ECONOMY Singapore's modern history began in 1819 when Sir Thomas Stamford Raffles (1781–1826), agent of the British East India Company, made a treaty with the Sultan of Johor. This treaty allowed the British to build a settlement on Singapore Island. Singapore soon became the leading British trading centre in South-east Asia and it later became a naval base. Japanese forces seized the island in 1942, but British rule was restored in 1945.

In 1963, Singapore became part of the Federation of Malaysia, which also included Malaya and the territories of Sabah and Sarawak on the island of Borneo. But, in 1965, Singapore broke away from the Federation and became an independent country.

The People's Action Party (PAP) has ruled Singapore since 1959. Its leader, Lee Kuan Yew, served as prime minister from 1959 until 1990, when he resigned and was succeeded by Goh Chok Tong. Under the PAP, the economy has expanded rapidly, though some people consider that the PAP's rule has been rather dictatorial and oversensitive to criticism.

The World Bank classifies Singapore as a 'high-income' economy. Its highly skilled workforce has created one of the world's fastest growing economies, though the recession in East Asia in 1997–8 was a setback. Trade and finance are leading activities and manufactures include chemicals, electronic products, machinery, metal products, paper, scientific instruments, ships and textiles. Singapore has a large oil refinery and petroleum products and manufactures are the main exports.

AREA 618 sq km [239 sq mls]
POPULATION 2,990,000
CAPITAL (POPULATION) Singapore City (2,874,000)
GOVERNMENT Multiparty republic
ETHNIC GROUPS Chinese 78%, Malay 14%, Indian 7%
LANGUAGES Chinese, Malay, Tamil and English (all official)
RELIGIONS Buddhism, Taoism and other traditional beliefs 54%, Islam 15%, Christianity 13%, Hinduism 4%
CURRENCY Singapore dollar = 100 cents

SLOVAK REPUBLIC

GEOGRAPHY The Slovak Republic is a predominantly mountainous country, consisting of part of the Carpathian range. The highest peak is Gerlachovka in the Tatra Mountains, which reaches 2,655 m [8,711 ft]. The south is a fertile lowland drained by the River Danube.

The Slovak Republic has cold winters and warm summers. Kosice, in the east, has average temperatures ranging from –3°C [27°F] in January to 20°C [68°F] in July. The highland areas are much colder. Snow or rain falls throughout the year. Kosice has an average annual rainfall of 600 mm [24 in], the wettest months being July and August.

POLITICS & ECONOMY Slavic peoples settled in the region in the 5th century AD. They were subsequently conquered by Hungary; the beginning of a millennium of Hungarian rule and concurrent suppression of Slovak culture.

In 1867, Hungary and Austria united to form Austria-Hungary, of which the present-day Slovak Republic was a part. Austria-Hungary collapsed at the end of World War I (1914–18). The Czech and Slovak people then united to form a new nation, Czechoslovakia, but Czech domination of the union led to resentment by many Slovaks. In 1939, the Slovak Republic declared itself independent, but Germany occupied the entire country. At the end of World War II, the Slovak Republic again became part of Czechoslovakia.

The Communist party took control in 1948. In the 1960s, many Czechs and Slovaks sought to reform the Communist system, but the Russians crushed the reformers. However, in the late 1980s, demands for democracy mounted as Soviet reformers began to question Communist policies. Elections in Czechoslovakia in 1992 led to victory for the Movement for a Democratic Slovakia, led by a former Communist and nationalist, Vladimir Meciar. In September 1992, the Slovak National Council voted to create a separate, independent Slovak Republic on 1 January 1994.

After independence, the Slovaks maintained close relations with the Czech Republic, although occasional diplomatic spats occurred. Relations with Hungary were damaged in 1996 when the Slovak government initiated eight new administrative regions which the Hungarian minority claimed underrepresented them politically. In addition, a law was convened to make Slovak the only official language.

Before 1948, the Slovak Republic's economy was based on farming, but Communist governments developed manufacturing industries, producing such things as chemicals, machinery, steel and weapons. Since the late 1980s, many state-run businesses have been handed over to private owners.

AREA 49,035 sq km [18,932 sq mls]
POPULATION 5,400,000
CAPITAL (POPULATION) Bratislava (451,000)
GOVERNMENT Multiparty republic
ETHNIC GROUPS Slovak, Hungarian, with small groups of Czechs, Germans, Gypsies, Poles, Russians and Ukrainians
LANGUAGES Slovak (official), Hungarian
RELIGIONS Christianity (Roman Catholic 60%, Protestant 6%, Orthodox 3%)
CURRENCY Koruna = 100 halierov

SLOVENIA

GEOGRAPHY The Republic of Slovenia was one of the six republics which made up the former Yugoslavia. Much of the land is mountainous, rising to 2,863 m [9,393 ft] at Mount Triglav in the Julian Alps (Julijske Alpe) in the north-west. Central

Slovenia contains the limestone Karst region. The Postojna caves near Ljubljana are among the largest in Europe.

The coast has a mild Mediterranean climate, but inland the climate is more continental. The mountains are snow-capped in winter.

POLITICS & ECONOMY In the last 2,000 years, the Slovene people have been independent as a nation for less than 50 years. The Austrian Habsburgs ruled over the region from the 13th century until World War I. Slovenia became part of the Kingdom of the Serbs, Croats and Slovenes (later called Yugoslavia) in 1918. During World War II, Slovenia was invaded and partitioned between Italy, Germany and Hungary but, after the war, Slovenia again became part of Yugoslavia.

From the late 1960s, some Slovenes demanded independence, but the central government opposed the break-up of the country. In 1990, when Communist governments had collapsed throughout Eastern Europe, elections were held and a non-Communist coalition government was set up. Slovenia then declared itself independent. This led to fighting between Slovenes and the federal army, but Slovenia did not become a battlefield like other parts of the former Yugoslavia. The European Community recognized Slovenia's independence in 1992 and elections were held. A coalition government led by the Liberal Democrats was set up.

The reform of the economy, formerly run by the government, and the fighting in areas to the south have caused problems for Slovenia, although it remains one of the fastest growing economies in Europe. In 1992, the World Bank classified Slovenia as an 'upper-middle-income' developing country, and it is expected to be among the first countries to join an expanded European Union.

Manufacturing is the leading activity and manufactures are the principal exports. Manufactures include chemicals, machinery and transport equipment, metal goods and textiles. Agriculture employs 8% of the people. Fruits, maize, potatoes and wheat are major crops, while many farmers raise cattle, pigs and sheep.

AREA 20,251 sq km [7,817 sq mls]
POPULATION 2,000,000
CAPITAL (POPULATION) Ljubljana (280,000)
GOVERNMENT Multiparty republic
ETHNIC GROUPS Slovene 88%, Croat 3%, Serb 2%, Bosnian 1%
LANGUAGES Slovene (official), Serbo-Croat
RELIGIONS Christianity (mainly Roman Catholic)
CURRENCY Tolar = 100 stotin

SOLOMON ISLANDS

The Solomon Islands, a chain of mainly volcanic islands south of the equator in the Pacific Ocean, were a British territory territory between 1893 and 1978. The chain extends for some 2,250 km [1,400 mls]. They were the scene of fierce fighting during World War II. Most people are Melanesians, and the islands have a very young population profile, with half the people aged under 20. Fish, coconuts and cocoa are leading products, although development is hampered by the mountainous, densely forested terrain. **AREA** 29,900 sq km [11,158 sq mls]; **POPULATION** 378,000; **CAPITAL** Honiara.

SOMALIA

GEOGRAPHY The Somali Democratic Republic, or Somalia, is in a region known as the 'Horn of Africa'. It is more than twice the size of Italy, the country which once ruled the southern part of Somalia. The most mountainous part of the country is in the north, behind the narrow coastal plains that border the Gulf of Aden.

Rainfall is light throughout Somalia. The wettest regions are the south and the northern mountains, but droughts often occur. Temperatures are high on the low plateaux and plains.

POLITICS & ECONOMY European powers became interested in the Horn of Africa in the 19th century. In 1884, Britain made the northern part of what is now Somalia a protectorate, while Italy took the south in 1905. The new boundaries divided the Somalis into five areas: the two Somalilands, Djibouti (which was taken by France in the 1880s), Ethiopia and Kenya. Since then, many Somalis have longed for reunification in a Greater Somalia.

Italy entered World War II in 1940 and invaded British Somaliland. But British forces conquered the region in 1941 and ruled both Somalilands until 1950, when the United Nations asked Italy to take over the former Italian Somaliland for ten years. In 1960, both Somalilands became independent and united to become Somalia.

Somalia has faced many problems since independence. Economic problems led a military group to seize power in 1969. In the 1970s, Somalia supported an uprising of Somali-speaking people in the Ogaden region of Ethiopia. But Ethiopian forces prevailed and, in 1988, Somalia signed a peace treaty with Ethiopia. The cost of the fighting weakened Somalia's economy.

Further problems occurred when people in the north fought to secede from Somalia. In 1991, they set up the 'Somaliland Republic', with its capital at Hargeisa. But the new state was recognized neither internationally nor by Somalia's government. Fighting continued and US troops sent by the UN in 1993 had to withdraw by 1994. By 1995, Somalia was divided into three main regions – the north, the north-east and the south. The country had no effective national government.

Somalia is a developing country, whose economy has been shattered by drought and war. Catastrophic flooding in late 1997 displaced tens of thousands of people, further damaging the country's infrastrucure and destroying the slender hope of an economic recovery.

Many Somalis are nomads who raise livestock. Live animals, meat and hides and skins are major exports, followed by bananas grown in the wetter south. Other crops include citrus fruits, cotton, maize and sugar cane. Mining and manufacturing remain relatively unimportant in the economy.

AREA 637,660 sq km [246,201 sq mls]
POPULATION 9,180,000
CAPITAL (POPULATION) Mogadishu (1,000,000)
GOVERNMENT Single-party republic, military dominated
ETHNIC GROUPS Somali 98%, Arab 1%
LANGUAGES Somali and Arabic (both official), English, Italian
RELIGIONS Islam 99%
CURRENCY Somali shilling = 100 cents

SOUTH AFRICA

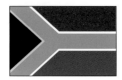

GEOGRAPHY The Republic of South Africa is made up largely of the southern part of the huge plateau which makes up most of southern Africa. The highest peaks are in the Drakensberg range, which is formed by the uptilted rim of the plateau. In the south-west lie the folded Cape Mountain ranges. The coastal plains are mostly narrow. The Namib Desert is in the north-west.

Most of South Africa has a mild, sunny climate. Much of the coastal strip, including the city of Cape Town, has warm, dry summers and mild, rainy winters, just like the Mediterranean lands in northern Africa. Inland, large areas are arid.

POLITICS & ECONOMY Early inhabitants in South Africa were the Khoisan. In the last 2,000 years, Bantu-speaking people moved into the area. Their descendants include the Zulu, Xhosa, Sotho and Tswana. The Dutch founded a settlement at the Cape in 1652, but Britain took over in the early 19th century, making the area a colony. The Dutch, called Boers or Afrikaners, resented British rule and moved inland. Rivalry between the groups led to Anglo-Boer Wars in 1880–1 and 1899–1902.

In 1910, the country was united as the Union of South Africa. In 1948, the National Party won power and introduced a policy known as apartheid, under which non-whites had no votes and their human rights were strictly limited. In 1990, Nelson Mandela, leader of the banned African National Congress (ANC), was released after serving 28 years as a political prisoner. Under a new constitution, multi-racial elections were held in 1994. They resulted in victory for the ANC and Mandela became president. A new constitution was adopted in 1996.

South Africa is Africa's most developed country. But most of the black people are poor, with low standards of living. Natural resources include diamonds, gold and many other metals. Mining and manufacturing are the most valuable activities.

AREA 1,219,916 sq km [470,566 sq mls]
POPULATION 44,000,000
CAPITAL (POPULATION) Cape Town (legislative, 2,350,000); Pretoria (administrative, 1,080,000); Bloemfontein (judiciary, 300,000)
GOVERNMENT Multiparty republic
ETHNIC GROUPS Black 76%, White 13%, Coloured 9%, Asian 2%
LANGUAGES Afrikaans, English, Ndebele, North Sotho, South Sotho, Swazi, Tsonga, Tswana, Venda, Xhosa, Zulu (all official)
RELIGIONS Christianity 68%, Hinduism 1%, Islam 1%
CURRENCY Rand = 100 cents

SPAIN

GEOGRAPHY The Kingdom of Spain is the second largest country in Western Europe after France. It shares the Iberian peninsula with Portugal. A large plateau, called the Meseta, covers most of Spain.

Much of the Meseta is flat, but it is crossed by several mountain ranges, called sierras.

The northern highlands include the Cantabrian Mountains (Cordillera Cantabrica) and the high Pyrenees, which form Spain's border with France. But Mulhacén, the highest peak on the Spanish mainland, is in the Sierra Nevada in the south-east. Spain also contains fertile coastal plains. Other major lowlands are the Ebro river basin in the north-east and the Guadalquivir river basin in the south-west. Spain also includes the Balearic Islands in the Mediterranean Sea and the Canary Islands off the north-west coast of Africa.

The Meseta has a continental climate, with hot summers and cold winters, when temperatures often fall below freezing point. Snow often covers the mountain ranges on the Meseta. The Mediterranean coastal regions also have hot, dry summers, but the winters are mild.

POLITICS & ECONOMY In the 16th century, Spain became a world power. At its peak, it controlled much of Central and South America, parts of Africa and the Philippines in Asia. Spain began to decline in the late 16th century. Its sea power was destroyed by a British fleet in the Battle of Trafalgar (1805). By the 20th century, it was a poor country.

Spain became a republic in 1931, but the republicans were defeated in the Spanish Civil War (1936–9). General Francisco Franco (1892–1975) became the country's dictator, though, technically, it was a monarchy. When Franco died, the monarchy was restored. Prince Juan Carlos became king.

Spain has several groups with their own languages and cultures. Some of these people want to run their own regional affairs. In the northern Basque region, some Basque nationalists continue to wage a terrorist campaign for complete independence.

Since the late 1970s, a regional parliament with a considerable degree of autonomy has been set up in the Basque Country (called Euskadi in the indigenous tongue and Pais Vasco in Spanish). Similar parliaments have been initiated in Catalonia in the north-east and Galicia in the north-west. All these regions have their own languages.

The revival of Spain's economy, which was shattered by the Civil War, began in the 1950s and 1960s, especially through the growth of tourism and manufacturing. Since the 1950s, Spain has changed from a poor country, dependent on agriculture, to a fairly prosperous industrial nation.

By the early 1990s, agriculture employed 10% of the people, as compared with industry 35% and services, including tourism, 55%. Farmland, including pasture, makes up about two-thirds of the land, with forest making up most of the rest. Major crops include barley, citrus fruits, grapes for winemaking, olives, potatoes and wheat. Sheep are the leading livestock.

Spain has some high-grade iron ore in the north, though otherwise it lacks natural resources. But it has many manufacturing industries. Manufactures include cars, chemicals, clothing, electronics, processed food, metal goods, steel and textiles. The leading manufacturing centres are Barcelona, Bilbao and Madrid.

AREA 504,780 sq km [194,896 sq mls]
POPULATION 39,664,000
CAPITAL (POPULATION) Madrid (3,041,000)
GOVERNMENT Constitutional monarchy
ETHNIC GROUPS Castilian Spanish 72%, Catalan 16%, Galician 8%, Basque 2%
LANGUAGES Castilian Spanish (official), Catalan, Galician, Basque
RELIGIONS Christianity (Roman Catholic 97%)
CURRENCY Peseta = 100 céntimos

SRI LANKA

GEOGRAPHY The Democratic Socialist Republic of Sri Lanka is an island nation, separated from the south-east coast of India by the Palk Strait. The land is mostly low-lying, but a mountain region dominates the south-central part of the country.

The western part of Sri Lanka has a wet equatorial climate. Temperatures are high and the rainfall is heavy. Eastern Sri Lanka is drier than the west.

POLITICS & ECONOMY From the early 16th century, Ceylon (as Sri Lanka was then known) was ruled successively by the Portuguese, Dutch and British. Independence was achieved in 1948 and the country was renamed Sri Lanka in 1972.

After independence, rivalries between the two main ethnic groups, the Sinhalese and Tamils, marred progress. In the 1950s, the government made Sinhala the official language. Following protests, the prime minister made provisions for Tamil to be used in some areas. In 1959, the prime minister was assassinated by a Sinhalese extremist and he was succeeded by Sirimavo Bandanaraike, who became the world's first woman prime minister.

Conflict between Tamils and Sinhalese continued in the 1970s and 1980s. In 1987, India helped to engineer a cease-fire. Indian troops arrived to enforce the agreement, but withdrew in 1990 after failing to subdue the main guerrilla group, the Tamil Tigers, who wanted to set up an independent Tamil homeland in northern Sri Lanka. In 1993, the country's president was assassinated by a suspected Tamil separatist. Offensives against the Tamil Tigers continued through the 1990s.

The World Bank classifies Sri Lanka as a 'low-income' developing country. Agriculture employs half of the workforce and coconuts, rubber and tea are exported.

AREA 65,610 sq km [25,332 sq mls]
POPULATION 18,359,000
CAPITAL (POPULATION) Colombo (1,863,000)
GOVERNMENT Multiparty republic
ETHNIC GROUPS Sinhalese 74%, Tamil 18%, Sri Lankan Moor 7%
LANGUAGES Sinhala and Tamil (both official)
RELIGIONS Buddhism 69%, Hinduism 16%, Islam 8%, Christianity 7%
CURRENCY Sri Lankan rupee = 100 cents

SUDAN

GEOGRAPHY The Republic of Sudan is the largest country in Africa. From north to south, it spans a vast area extending from the arid Sahara in the north to the wet equatorial region in the south. The land is mostly flat, with the highest mountains in the far south. The main physical feature is the River Nile.

The climate of Khartoum represents a transition between the virtually rainless northern deserts and the equatorial lands in the south. Some rain falls in Khartoum in summer.

POLITICS & ECONOMY In the 19th century, Egypt

gradually took over Sudan. In 1881, a Muslim religious teacher, the Mahdi ('divinely appointed guide'), led an uprising. Britain and Egypt put the rebellion down in 1898. In 1899, they agreed to rule Sudan jointly as a condominium.

After independence in 1952, the black Africans in the south, who were either Christians or followers of traditional beliefs, feared domination by the Muslim northerners. For example, they objected to the government declaring that Arabic was the only official language. In 1964, civil war broke out and continued until 1972, when the south was given regional self-government, though executive power was still vested in the military government in Khartoum.

In 1983, the government established Islamic law throughout the country. This sparked off further conflict when the Sudan People's Liberation Army in the south launched attacks on government installations. Despite attempts to restore order, the fighting continued into the late 1990s. The problems of food shortages and the displacement of people who became refugees added to Sudan's difficulties. By 1998, the situation had become critical. Widespread famine in southern Sudan attracted global attention and humanitarian aid.

AREA 2,505,810 sq km [967,493 sq mls]
POPULATION 29,980,000
CAPITAL (POPULATION) Khartoum (925,000)
GOVERNMENT Military regime
ETHNIC GROUPS Sudanese Arab 49%, Dinka 12%, Nuba 8%, Beja 6%, Nuer 5%, Azande 3%
LANGUAGES Arabic (official), Nubian, Dinka
RELIGIONS Islam 73%, traditional beliefs 17%, Christianity (Roman Catholic 4%, Protestant 2%)
CURRENCY Dinar = 10 Sudanese pounds

SURINAM

GEOGRAPHY The Republic of Surinam is sandwiched between French Guiana and Guyana in north-eastern South America. The narrow coastal plain was once swampy, but it has been drained and now consists mainly of farmland. Inland lie hills and low mountains, which rise to 1,280 m [4,199 ft].

Surinam has a hot, wet and humid climate. Temperatures are high throughout the year.

POLITICS & ECONOMY In 1667, the British handed Surinam to the Dutch in return for New Amsterdam, an area that is now the state of New York. Slave revolts and Dutch neglect hampered development. In the early 19th century, Britain and the Netherlands disputed the ownership of the area. The British gave up their claims in 1813. Slavery was abolished in 1863 and, soon afterwards, Indian and Indonesian labourers were introduced to work on the plantations. Surinam became fully independent in 1975, but the economy was weakened when thousands of skilled people emigrated from Surinam to the Netherlands.

In 1992, the government negotiated a peace agreement with the *boschneger*, descendants of African slaves, who had launched a struggle against the government in 1986. This rebellion had disrupted the area where bauxite, the main export, was mined. But instability continued, especially among the military. In 1993, the Netherlands stopped financial aid after an EC report stated that Surinam had failed to reform the economy and control inflation.

The World Bank classifies Surinam as an 'upper-middle-income' developing country. Its economy is based on mining and metal processing. Surinam is a leading producer of bauxite, from which the metal aluminium is made.

AREA 163,270 sq km [63,039 sq mls]
POPULATION 421,000
CAPITAL (POPULATION) Paramaribo (201,000)
GOVERNMENT Multiparty republic
ETHNIC GROUPS Asian Indian 37%, Creole (mixed White and Black), 31%, Indonesian 14%, Black 9%, Amerindian 3%, Chinese 3%, Dutch 1%
LANGUAGES Dutch (official), Sranantonga
RELIGIONS Christianity (Roman Catholic 23%, Protestant 19%), Hinduism 27%, Islam 20%
CURRENCY Surinam guilder = 100 cents

SWAZILAND

GEOGRAPHY The Kingdom of Swaziland is a small, landlocked country in southern Africa. The country has four regions which run north-south. In the west, the Highveld, with an average height of 1,200 m [3,937 ft], makes up 30% of Swaziland. The Middleveld, between 350 m and 1,000 m [1,148 ft to 3,281 ft], covers 28% of the country. The Lowveld, with an average height of 270 m [886 ft], covers another 33%. Finally, the Lebombo Mountains reach 800 m [2,600 ft] along the eastern border.

The Lowveld is almost tropical, with an average temperature of 22°C [72°F] and low rainfall. The altitude moderates the climate in the west of the country. Mbabane has a climate typical of the Highveld with warm summers and cool winters.

POLITICS & ECONOMY In 1894, Britain and the Boers of South Africa agreed to put Swaziland under the control of the South African Republic (the Transvaal). But at the end of the Anglo-Boer War (1899–1902), Britain took control of the country. In 1968, when Swaziland became fully independent as a constitutional monarchy, the head of state was King Sobhuza II. Sobhuza died in 1982 after a reign of 82 years. In 1983, one of his sons, Prince Makhosetive (born 1968), was chosen as his heir. In 1986, he was installed as King Mswati III. In 1993, Swaziland held its first-ever multiparty elections.

The World Bank classifies Swaziland as a 'lower-middle-income' developing country. Agriculture employs 74% of the people, and farm products and processed foods, including soft drink concentrates, sugar, wood pulp, citrus fruits and canned fruit, are the leading exports. Many farmers live at subsistence level, producing little more than they need to feed their own families. Swaziland is heavily dependent on South Africa and the two countries are linked through a customs union.

AREA 17,360 sq km [6,703 sq mls]
POPULATION 849,000
CAPITAL (POPULATION) Mbabane (42,000)
GOVERNMENT Monarchy
ETHNIC GROUPS Swazi 84%, Zulu 10%, Tsonga 2%
LANGUAGES Siswati and English (both official)
RELIGIONS Christianity 77%, traditional beliefs
CURRENCY Lilangeni = 100 cents

SWEDEN

GEOGRAPHY The Kingdom of Sweden is the largest of the countries of Scandinavia in both area and population. It shares the Scandinavian peninsula with Norway. The western part of the country, along the border with Norway, is mountainous. The highest point is Kebnekaise, which reaches 2,117 m [6,946 ft] in the north-west.

The climate of Sweden becomes more severe from south to north. Stockholm has cold winters and cool summers. The far south is much milder.

POLITICS & ECONOMY Swedish Vikings plundered areas to the south and east between the 9th and 11th centuries. Sweden, Denmark and Norway were united in 1397, but Sweden regained its independence in 1523. In 1809, Sweden lost Finland to Russia, but, in 1814, it gained Norway from Denmark. The union between Sweden and Norway was dissolved in 1905. Sweden was neutral in World Wars I and II. Since 1945, Sweden has become a prosperous country. It was a founder member of the European Free Trade Association, but in 1994 the people voted to join the European Union on 1 January 1995.

Sweden has wide-ranging welfare services. But many people are concerned about the high cost of these services and the high taxes they must pay. In 1991, the Social Democrats, who had built up the welfare state, were defeated by a coalition of centre and right-wing parties, though a minority Social Democrat government took office in 1994.

Sweden is a highly developed industrial country. Major products include steel and steel goods. Steel is used in the engineering industry to manufacture aircraft, cars, machinery and ships. Sweden has some of the world's richest iron ore deposits. They are located near Kiruna in the far north. But most of this ore is exported, and Sweden imports most of the materials needed by its industries. In 1996, a decision was taken to decommission all of Sweden's nuclear power stations. This is said to be one of the boldest and most expensive environmental pledges ever made by a government.

AREA 449,960 sq km [173,730 sq mls]
POPULATION 8,893,000
CAPITAL (POPULATION) Stockholm (1,553,000)
GOVERNMENT Constitutional monarchy
ETHNIC GROUPS Swedish 91%, Finnish 3%
LANGUAGES Swedish (official), Finnish
RELIGIONS Christianity (Lutheran 89%, Roman Catholic 2%)
CURRENCY Swedish krona = 100 öre

SWITZERLAND

GEOGRAPHY The Swiss Confederation is a landlocked country in Western Europe. Much of the land is mountainous. The Jura Mountains lie along Switzerland's western border with France, while the Swiss Alps make up about 60% of the country in the south and east. Four-fifths of the people of

Switzerland live on the fertile Swiss plateau, which contains most of Switzerland's large cities.

The climate of Switzerland varies greatly according to the height of the land. The plateau region has a central European climate with warm summers, but cold and snowy winters. Rain occurs all through the year. The rainiest months are in summer.

POLITICS & ECONOMY In 1291, three small cantons (states) united to defend their freedom against the Habsburg rulers of the Holy Roman Empire. They were Schwyz, Uri and Unterwalden, and they called the confederation they formed 'Switzerland'. Switzerland expanded and, in the 14th century, defeated Austria in three wars of independence. After a defeat by the French in 1515, the Swiss adopted a policy of neutrality, which they still follow. In 1815, the Congress of Vienna expanded Switzerland to 22 cantons and guaranteed its neutrality. Switzerland's 23rd canton, Jura, was created in 1979 from part of Bern. Neutrality combined with the vigour and independence of its people have made Switzerland prosperous. In 1993, the Swiss people voted against joining the European Union.

Although lacking in natural resources, Switzerland is a wealthy, industrialized country. Many workers are highly skilled. Major products include chemicals, electrical equipment, machinery and machine tools, precision instruments, processed food, watches and textiles. Farmers produce about three-fifths of the country's food – the rest is imported. Livestock raising, especially dairy farming, is the chief agricultural activity. Crops include fruits, potatoes and wheat. Tourism and banking are also important. Swiss banks attract investors from all over the world.

AREA 41,290 sq km [15,942 sq mls]
POPULATION 7,268,000
CAPITAL (POPULATION) Bern (324,000)
GOVERNMENT Federal republic
ETHNIC GROUPS German 64%, French 19%, Italian 8%, Yugoslav 3%, Spanish 2%, Romansch 1%
LANGUAGES French, German, Italian, Romansch (all official)
RELIGIONS Christianity (Roman Catholic 46%, Protestant 40%)
CURRENCY Swiss franc = 100 centimes

SYRIA

GEOGRAPHY The Syrian Arab Republic is a country in south-western Asia. The narrow coastal plain is overlooked by a low mountain range which runs north–south. Another range, the Jabal ash Sharqi, runs along the border with Lebanon. South of this range is the Golan Heights, which Israel has occupied since 1967.

The coast has a Mediterranean climate, with dry, warm summers and wet, mild winters. The low mountains cut off Damascus from the sea. It has less rainfall than the coastal areas. To the east, the land becomes drier.

POLITICS & ECONOMY After the collapse of the Turkish Ottoman empire in World War I, Syria was ruled by France. Since independence in 1946, Syria has been involved in the Arab–Israeli wars and, in 1967, it lost a strategic border area, the Golan Heights, to Israel. In 1970, Lieutenant-General

Hafez al-Assad took power, establishing a stable but repressive regime which attracted international criticism. In the mid-1990s, Syria had talks with Israel over the future of the Golan Heights, but the negotiations were suspended after the election of Benjamin Netanyahu's right-wing government in Israel in 1996.

The World Bank classifies Syria as a 'lower-middle-income' developing country. But it has great potential for development. Its main resources are oil, hydro-electricity from the dam at Lake Assad, and fertile land. Oil is the main export; farm products, textiles and phosphates are also important. Agriculture employs about 26% of the workforce.

AREA 185,180 sq km [71,498 sq mls]
POPULATION 14,614,000
CAPITAL (POPULATION) Damascus (2,230,000)
GOVERNMENT Multiparty republic
ETHNIC GROUPS Arab 89%, Kurd 6%
LANGUAGES Arabic (official)
RELIGIONS Islam 90%, Christianity 9%
CURRENCY Syrian pound = 100 piastres

TAIWAN

GEOGRAPHY High mountain ranges run down the length of the island, with dense forest in many areas.

The climate is warm, moist and suitable for agriculture.

POLITICS & ECONOMY Chinese settlers occupied Taiwan from the 7th century. In 1895, Japan seized the territory from the Portuguese, who had named it Isla Formosa, or 'beautiful island'. China regained the island after World War II. In 1949, it became the refuge of the Nationalists who had been driven out of China by the Communists. They set up the Republic of China, which, with US help, launched an ambitious programme of economic development. Today, it produces a wide range of manufactured goods. Mainland China regards Taiwan as one of its provinces, though reunification seems unlikely in the foreseeable future.

AREA 36,000 sq km [13,900 sq mls]
POPULATION 21,100,000
CAPITAL (population) Taipei (2,653,000)
GOVERNMENT Unitary multiparty republic
ETHNIC GROUPS Taiwanese (Han Chinese) 84%, mainland Chinese 14%
LANGUAGES Mandarin (official), Min, Hakka
RELIGIONS Buddhist 43%, Taoist & Confucian 49%
CURRENCY New Taiwan dollar = 100 cents

TAJIKISTAN

GEOGRAPHY The Republic of Tajikistan is one of the five central Asian republics that formed part of the former Soviet Union. Only 7% of the land is below 1,000 m [3,280 ft], while almost all of eastern

Tajikistan is above 3,000 m [9,840 ft]. The highest point is Communism Peak (Pik Kommunizma), which reaches 7,495 m [24,590 ft].

Tajikistan has a severe continental climate. Summers are hot and dry in the lower valleys, and winters are long and bitterly cold in the mountains.

POLITICS & ECONOMY Russia conquered parts of Tajikistan in the late 19th century and, by 1920, Russia took complete control. In 1924, Tajikistan became part of the Uzbek Soviet Socialist Republic, but, in 1929, it was expanded, taking in some areas populated by Uzbeks, becoming the Tajik Soviet Socialist Republic.

While the Soviet Union began to introduce reforms in the 1980s, many Tajiks demanded freedom. In 1989, the Tajik government made Tajik the official language instead of Russian and, in 1990, it stated that its local laws overruled Soviet laws. Tajikistan became fully independent in 1991, following the break-up of the Soviet Union. As the poorest of the ex-Soviet republics, Tajikistan faced many problems in trying to introduce a free-market system.

In 1992, civil war broke out between the government, which was run by former Communists, and an alliance of democrats and Islamic forces. The government maintained control, but it relied heavily on aid from the Commonwealth of Independent States, the organization through which most of the former republics of the Soviet Union kept in contact.

The World Bank classifies Tajikistan as a 'low-income' developing country. Agriculture, mainly on irrigated land, is the main activity and cotton is the chief product. Other crops include fruits, grains and vegetables. The country has large hydroelectric power resources and it produces aluminium.

AREA 143,100 sq km [55,520 sq mls]
POPULATION 6,102,000
CAPITAL (POPULATION) Dushanbe (524,000)
GOVERNMENT Transitional democracy
ETHNIC GROUPS Tajik 62%, Uzbek 24%, Russian 8%, Tatar, Kyrgyz, Ukrainian, German
LANGUAGES Tajik (official), Uzbek, Russian
RELIGIONS Islam
CURRENCY Tajik rouble = 100 tanga

TANZANIA

GEOGRAPHY The United Republic of Tanzania consists of the former mainland country of Tanganyika and the island nation of Zanzibar, which also includes the island of Pemba. Behind a narrow coastal plain, most of Tanzania is a plateau, which is broken by arms of the Great African Rift Valley. In the west, this valley contains lakes Nyasa and Tanganyika. The highest peak is Kilimanjaro, Africa's tallest mountain.

The coast has a hot and humid climate, with the greatest rainfall in April and May. The inland plateaux and mountains are cooler and less humid.

POLITICS & ECONOMY Mainland Tanganyika became a German territory in the 1880s, while Zanzibar and Pemba became a British protectorate in 1890. Following Germany's defeat in World War I, Britain took over Tanganyika, which remained a British territory until its independence in 1961. In 1964, Tanganyika and Zanzibar united to form the United Republic of Tanzania. The country's president, Julius Nyerere, pursued socialist policies of self-help (*ujamaa*) and egalitarianism. Many of its social reforms were successful, but the country failed to make economic progress. Nyerere resigned as president in 1985 and his successors introduced more liberal economic policies.

Tanzania is one of the world's poorest countries. Although crops are grown on only 5% of the land, agriculture employs 85% of the people. Most farmers grow only enough to feed their families. Food crops include bananas, cassava, maize, millet, rice and vegetables.

AREA 945,090 sq km [364,899 sq mls]
POPULATION 29,710,000
CAPITAL (POPULATION) Dodoma (204,000)
GOVERNMENT Multiparty republic
ETHNIC GROUPS Nyamwezi and Sukuma 21%, Swahili 9%, Hehet and Bena 7%, Makonde 6%, Haya 6%
LANGUAGES Swahili and English (both official)
RELIGIONS Christianity (mostly Roman Catholic) 34%, Islam 33% (99% in Zanzibar), traditional beliefs and others 33%
CURRENCY Tanzanian shilling = 100 cents

THAILAND

GEOGRAPHY The Kingdom of Thailand is one of the ten countries in South-east Asia. The highest land is in the north, where Doi Inthanon, the highest peak, reaches 2,595 m [8,514 ft]. The Khorat Plateau, in the north-east, makes up about 30% of the country and is the most heavily populated part of Thailand. In the south, Thailand shares the finger-like Malay Peninsula with Burma and Malaysia.

Thailand has a tropical climate. Monsoon winds from the south-west bring heavy rains between the months of May and October. The rainfall in Bangkok is lower than in many other parts of South-east Asia, because mountains shelter the central plains from the rain-bearing winds.

POLITICS & ECONOMY The first Thai state was set up in the 13th century. By 1350, it included most of what is now Thailand. European contact began in the early 16th century. But, in the late 17th century, the Thais, fearing interference in their affairs, forced all Europeans to leave. This policy continued for 150 years. In 1782, a Thai General, Chao Phraya Chakkri, became king, founding a dynasty which continues today. The country became known as Siam, and Bangkok became its capital. From the mid-19th century, contacts with the West were restored. In World War I, Siam supported the Allies against Germany and Austria-Hungary. But in 1941, the country was conquered by Japan and became its ally. But, after the end of World War II, it became an ally of the United States.

Since 1967, when Thailand became a member of ASEAN (the Association of South-east Asian Nations), its economy has grown, especially its manufacturing and service industries. However, in 1997, it suffered recession along with other eastern Asian countries. Despite its rapid progress, the World Bank classifies the country as a 'lower-middle-income' developing country. Manufactures, including food products, machinery, timber products and textiles, are ex-ported, but agriculture still employs two-thirds of the people. Rice is the main food, while other major crops include cassava, cotton, maize, pineapples, rubber, sugar cane and tobacco. Thailand also mines tin and other minerals, and tourism is a major source of income.

AREA 513,120 sq km [198,116 sq mls]
POPULATION 58,432,000
CAPITAL (POPULATION) Bangkok (5,876,000)
GOVERNMENT Constitutional monarchy
ETHNIC GROUPS Thai 80%, Chinese 12%, Malay 4%, Khmer 3%
LANGUAGES Thai (official), Chinese, Malay
RELIGIONS Buddhism 94%, Islam 4%, Christianity 1%
CURRENCY Thai baht = 100 satang

TOGO

GEOGRAPHY The Republic of Togo is a long, narrow country in West Africa. From north to south, it extends about 500 km [311 mls]. Its coastline on the Gulf of Guinea is only 64 km [40 mls] long and it is only 145 km [90 mls] at its widest point.

Togo has high temperatures all through the year. The main wet season is from March to July, with a minor wet season in October and November.

POLITICS & ECONOMY Togo became a German protectorate in 1884 but, in 1919, Britain took over the western third of the territory, while France took over the eastern two-thirds. In 1956, the people of British Togoland voted to join Ghana, while French Togoland became an independent republic in 1960.

Local rivalries, especially between the northerners and southerners, are important political factors, and, in 1963, a group of army officers from the north assassinated the president, a southerner. In 1967, Gnassingbé Eyadéma, one of the officers responsible for the 1963 coup, took power and suspended the constitution. Constitutional government was restored in 1980 and multiparty elections were held in 1994.

Togo is a poor developing country. Farming employs 65% of the people, but most farmers grow little more than they need to feed their families. Major food crops include cassava, maize, millet and yams. The leading export is phosphate rock, which is used to make fertilizers.

AREA 56,790 sq km [21,927 sq mls]
POPULATION 4,140,000
CAPITAL (POPULATION) Lomé (590,000)
CAPITAL Multiparty republic
ETHNIC GROUPS Ewe-Adja 43%, Tem-Kabre 26%, Gurma 16%
LANGUAGES French (official), Ewe, Kabiye
RELIGIONS Traditional beliefs 50%, Christianity 35%, Islam 15%
CURRENCY CFA franc = 100 centimes

TONGA

The Kingdom of Tonga, a former British protectorate, became independent in 1970. Situated in the South Pacific Ocean, it contains more than 170 islands, 36 of which are inhabited. Agriculture is the main activity; coconuts, copra, fruits and fish are leading products. **AREA** 75 sq km [290 sq mls]; **POPULATION** 107,000; **CAPITAL** Nuku'alofa.

TRINIDAD AND TOBAGO

The Republic of Trinidad and Tobago became independent from Britain in 1962. These tropical islands, populated by people of African, Asian (mainly Indian) and European origin, are hilly and forested, though there are some fertile plains. Oil production is the main sector of the economy. **AREA** 5,130 sq km [1,981 sq mls]; **POPULATION** 1,295,000; **CAPITAL** Port-of-Spain.

TUNISIA

GEOGRAPHY The Republic of Tunisia is the smallest country in North Africa. The mountains in the north are an eastwards and comparatively low extension of the Atlas Mountains. To the north and east of the mountains lie fertile plains, especially between Sfax, Tunis and Bizerte. In the south, low-lying regions contain a vast salt pan, called the Chott Djerid, and part of the Sahara Desert.

Northern Tunisia has a Mediterranean climate, with dry, sunny summers, and mild winters with a moderate rainfall. The average yearly rainfall decreases towards the south.

POLITICS & ECONOMY In 1881, France established a protectorate over Tunisia and ruled the country until 1956. The new parliament abolished the monarchy and declared Tunisia to be a republic in 1957, with the nationalist leader, Habib Bourguiba, as president. His government introduced many reforms, including votes for women, but various problems arose, including unemployment among the middle class and fears that Western values introduced by tourists might undermine Muslim values. In 1987, the prime minister Zine el Abidine Ben Ali removed Bourguiba from office and succeeded him as president. He was elected in 1989 and again in 1994.

The World Bank classifies Tunisia as a 'middle-income' developing country. The main resources and chief exports are phosphates and oil. Most industries are concerned with food processing. Agriculture employs 22% of the people; major crops being barley, dates, grapes, olives and wheat. Fishing is important, as is tourism. Almost four million tourists visited Tunisia in 1994.

AREA 163,610 sq km [63,170 sq mls]
POPULATION 8,906,000
CAPITAL (POPULATION) Tunis (1,827,000)
CAPITAL Multiparty republic
ETHNIC GROUPS Arab 98%, Berber 1%, French
LANGUAGES Arabic (official), French
RELIGIONS Islam 99%
CURRENCY Dinar = 1,000 millimes

TURKEY

GEOGRAPHY The Republic of Turkey lies in two continents. The European section lies west of a waterway between the Black and Mediterranean seas. European Turkey, also called Thrace, is a fertile, hilly region. Most of the Asian part of Turkey consists of plateaux and mountains, which rise to 5,165 m [16,945 ft] at Mount Ararat (Agri Dagi) near the border with Armenia.

Central Turkey has a dry climate, with hot, sunny summers and cold winters. The driest part of the central plateau lies south of the city of Ankara, around Lake Tuz. Western Turkey has a Mediterranean climate, while the Black Sea coast has cooler summers.

POLITICS & ECONOMY In AD 330, the Roman empire moved its capital to Byzantium, which it renamed Constantinople. Constantinople became capital of the East Roman (or Byzantine) empire in 395. Muslim Seljuk Turks from central Asia invaded Anatolia in the 11th century. In the 14th century, another group of Turks, the Ottomans, conquered the area. In 1435, the Ottoman Turks took Constantinople, which they called Istanbul.

The Ottoman Turks built up a large empire which finally collapsed during World War I (1914–18). In 1923, Turkey became a republic. Its leader Mustafa Kemal, who was called Atatürk ('father of the Turks'), launched policies to modernize and secularize the country.

Since the 1940s, Turkey has sought to strengthen its ties with Western powers. It joined NATO (North Atlantic Treaty Organization) in 1951 and it applied to join the European Economic Community in 1987. But Turkey's conflict with Greece, together with its invasion of northern Cyprus in 1974, have led many Europeans to treat Turkey's aspirations with caution. Political instability, military coups, conflict with Kurdish nationalists in eastern Turkey and concern about the country's record on human rights are other problems. Turkey has enjoyed democracy since 1983, though, in 1998, the government banned the Islamist Welfare Party, which it accused of violating secular principles. However, although Turkey no longer occupies a key strategic position as it did during the Cold War, it remains an important bridge between Europe and Asia.

The World Bank classifies Turkey as a 'lower-middle-income' developing country. Agriculture employs 47% of the people, and barley, cotton, fruits, maize, tobacco and wheat are major crops. Livestock farming is important and wool is a leading product.

Turkey is a major producer of chromium, but manufacturing is the most valuable activity. The chief manufactures are processed farm products and textiles. Also important are cars, fertilizers, iron and steel, machinery, metal products and paper products. Over six million tourists visited Turkey in 1994, and growth in this sector seems likely to continue.

> **AREA** 779,450 sq km [300,946 sq mls]
> **POPULATION** 61,303,000
> **CAPITAL (POPULATION)** Ankara (3,028,000)
> **GOVERNMENT** Multiparty republic
> **ETHNIC GROUPS** Turkish 86%, Kurdish 11%, Arab 2%
> **LANGUAGES** Turkish (official), Kurdish
> **RELIGIONS** Islam 99%
> **CURRENCY** Turkish lira = 100 kurus

TURKMENISTAN

GEOGRAPHY The Republic of Turkmenistan is one of the five central Asian republics which once formed part of the former Soviet Union. Most of the land is low-lying, with mountains lying on the southern and south-western borders. In the west lies the salty Caspian Sea. Most of Turkmenistan is arid and the Garagum, Asia's largest sand desert, covers about 80% of the country.

Turkmenistan has a continental climate. The average annual rainfall varies from 80 mm [3 in] in the desert to 300 mm [12 in] in the southern mountains. The summer months are hot. In the winter, temperatures sometimes drop well below freezing point.

POLITICS & ECONOMY Just over 1,000 years ago, Turkic people settled in the lands east of the Caspian Sea and the name 'Turkmen' comes from this time. Mongol armies conquered the area in the 13th century and Islam was introduced in the 14th century. Russia took over the area in the 1870s and 1880s. After the Russian Revolution of 1917, the area came under Communist rule and, in 1924, it became the Turkmen Soviet Socialist Republic. The Communists strictly controlled all aspects of life and, in particular, they discouraged religious worship. But they also improved such services as education, health, housing and transport.

In the 1980s, when the Soviet Union began to introduce reforms, the Turkmen began to demand more freedom. In 1990, the Turkmen government stated that its laws overruled Soviet laws. In 1991, Turkmenistan became fully independent after the break-up of the Soviet Union. But the country kept ties with Russia through the Commonwealth of Independent States (CIS).

In 1992, Turkmenistan adopted a new constitution, allowing for the setting up of political parties, providing that they are not ethnic or religious in character. But, effectively, Turkmenistan remained a one-party state and, in 1992, Saparmurad Niyazov, the former Communist and now Democratic party leader, was the only candidate.

Faced with many economic problems, Turkmenistan began to look south rather than to the CIS for support. As part of this policy, it joined the Economic Co-operation Organization which had been set up in 1985 by Iran, Pakistan and Turkey. In 1996, the completion of a rail link from Turkmenistan to the Iranian coast was seen both as a revival of the traditions of the ancient silk road, and as a highly significant step for the future economic development of Central Asia.

Turkmenistan's chief resources are oil and natural gas, but the main activity is agriculture, with cotton, grown on irrigated land, as the main crop. Grain and vegetables are also important. Manufactures include cement, glass, petrochemicals and textiles.

> **AREA** 488,100 sq km [188,450 sq mls]
> **POPULATION** 4,100,000
> **CAPITAL (POPULATION)** Ashgabat (407,000)
> **GOVERNMENT** Single-party republic
> **ETHNIC GROUPS** Turkmen 72%, Russian 10%, Uzbek 9%, Kazak 3%, Tatar
> **LANGUAGES** Turkmen (official), Russian, Uzbek, Kazak
> **RELIGIONS** Islam
> **CURRENCY** Manat = 100 tenesi

TURKS AND CAICOS ISLANDS

The Turks and Caicos Islands, a British territory in the Caribbean since 1776, are a group of about 30 islands. Fishing and tourism are major activities. **AREA** 430 sq km [166 sq mls]; **POPULATION** 15,000; **CAPITAL** Cockburn Town.

TUVALU

Tuvalu, formerly called the Ellice Islands, was a British territory from the 1890s until it became independent in 1978. It consists of nine low-lying coral atolls in the southern Pacific Ocean. Copra is the chief export. **AREA** 24 sq km [9 sq mls]; **POPULATION** 10,000; **CAPITAL** Fongafale.

UGANDA

GEOGRAPHY The Republic of Uganda is a land-locked country on the East African plateau. It contains part of Lake Victoria, Africa's largest lake and a source of the River Nile, which occupies a shallow depression in the plateau.

The equator runs through Uganda and the country is warm throughout the year, though the high altitude moderates the temperature. The wettest regions are the lands to the north of Lake Victoria, where Kampala is situated, and the western mountains, especially the high Ruwenzori range.

POLITICS & ECONOMY Little is known of the early history of Uganda. When Europeans first reached the area in the 19th century, many of the people were organized in kingdoms, the most powerful of which was Buganda, the home of the Baganda people. Britain took over the country between 1894 and 1914, and ruled it until independence in 1962.

In 1967, Uganda became a republic and Buganda's Kabaka (king), Sir Edward Mutesa II, was made president. But tensions between the Kabaka and the prime minister, Apollo Milton Obote, led to the dismissal of the Kabaka in 1966. Obote also abolished the traditional kingdoms, including Buganda. Obote was overthrown in 1971 by an army group led by General Idi Amin Dada. Amin ruled as a dictator. He forced most of the Asians who lived in Uganda to leave the country and had many of his opponents killed.

In 1978, a border dispute between Uganda and Tanzania led Tanzanian troops to enter Uganda. With help from Ugandan opponents of Amin, they overthrew Amin's government. In 1980, Obote led his party to victory in national elections. But after charges of fraud, Obote's opponents began guerrilla warfare. A military group overthrew Obote in 1985, but strife continued until 1986, when Yoweri

Museveni's National Resistance Movement seized power. In 1993, Museveni restored the traditional kingdoms, including Buganda where a new Kabaka was crowned. Museveni also held national elections in 1994 but political parties were not permitted. Museveni was elected president in 1996.

The strife in Uganda since the 1960s has greatly damaged the economy. By 1991 Uganda was, according to the World Bank, among the world's five poorest countries. Agriculture dominates the economy, employing 86% of the people. The chief export is coffee.

AREA 235,880 sq km [91,073 sq mls]
POPULATION 21,466,000
CAPITAL (POPULATION) Kampala (773,000)
GOVERNMENT Republic in transition
ETHNIC GROUPS Baganda 18%, Banyoro 14%, Teso 9%, Banyan 8%, Basoga 8%, Bagisu 7%, Bachiga 7%, Lango 6%, Acholi 5%
LANGUAGES English and Swahili (both official)
RELIGIONS Christianity (Roman Catholic 40%, Protestant 29%), traditional beliefs 18%, Islam 7%
CURRENCY Uganda shilling = 100 cent

UKRAINE

GEOGRAPHY Ukraine is the second largest country in Europe after Russia. It was formerly part of the Soviet Union, which split apart in 1991. This mostly flat country faces the Black Sea in the south. The Crimean peninsula includes a highland region overlooking Yalta.

Ukraine has warm summers, but the winters are cold, becoming more severe from west to east. In the summer, the east of the country is often warmer than the west. The heaviest rainfall occurs in the summer.

POLITICS & ECONOMY Kiev was the original capital of the early Slavic civilization known as Kievan Rus. In the 17th and 18th centuries, parts of Ukraine came under Polish and Russian rule. But Russia gained most of Ukraine in the late 18th century. In 1918, Ukraine became independent, but in 1922 it became part of the Soviet Union. Millions of people died in the 1930s as the result of Soviet policies, while millions more died during the Nazi occupation (1941–4).

In the 1980s, Ukrainian people demanded more say over their affairs. The country finally became independent when the Soviet Union broke up in 1991. Ukraine continued to work with Russia through an organization named the Commonwealth of Independent States. But Ukraine differed with Russia on several issues, including control over Crimea (which has a predominately Russian population) and the Soviet fleet.

The World Bank classifies Ukraine as a 'lower-middle-income' economy. Agriculture is important. Crops include wheat and sugar beet, which are the major exports, together with barley, maize, potatoes, sunflowers and tobacco. Livestock rearing and fishing are also important industries.

Manufacturing is the chief economic activity. Major manufactures include iron and steel, machinery and vehicles. The country has large coalfields. The country imports oil and natural gas, but it has hydro-electric and nuclear power stations. In 1986, an accident at the Chernobyl nuclear power plant caused widespread nuclear radiation.

AREA 603,700 sq km [233,100 sq mls]
POPULATION 52,027,000
CAPITAL (POPULATION) Kiev (2,630,000)
GOVERNMENT Multiparty republic
ETHNIC GROUPS Ukrainian 73%, Russian 22%, Jewish 1%, Belarussian 1%, Moldovan, Bulgarian, Polish
LANGUAGES Ukrainian (official), Russian
RELIGIONS Christianity (mostly Ukrainian Orthodox)
CURRENCY Hryvna

UNITED ARAB EMIRATES

The United Arab Emirates were formed in 1971 when the seven Trucial States of the Gulf (Abu Dhabi, Dubai, Sharjah, Ajman, Umm al Qawayn, Ra's al Khaymah and Al Fujayrah) opted to join together and form an independent country. The economy of this hot and dry country depends on oil production, and oil revenues give the United Arab Emirates one of the highest per capita GNPs in Asia.
AREA 83,600 sq km [32,278 sq mls]; **POPULATION** 2,800,000; **CAPITAL** Abu Dhabi.

UNITED KINGDOM

GEOGRAPHY The United Kingdom (or UK) is a union of four countries. Three of them – England, Scotland and Wales – make up Great Britain. The fourth country is Northern Ireland. The Isle of Man and the Channel Islands, including Jersey and Guernsey, are not part of the UK. They are self-governing British dependencies.

The land is highly varied. Much of Scotland and Wales is mountainous, and the highest peak is Scotland's Ben Nevis at 1,343 m [4,406 ft]. England has some highland areas, including the Cumbrian Mountains (or Lake District) and the Pennine range in the north. But England also has large areas of fertile lowland. Northern Ireland is also a mixture of lowlands and uplands. It contains the UK's largest lake, Lough Neagh.

The UK has a mild climate, influenced by the warm Gulf Stream which flows across the Atlantic from the Gulf of Mexico, then past the British Isles. Moist winds from the south-west bring rain, but the rainfall decreases from west to east. Winds from the east and north bring cold weather in winter.

POLITICS & ECONOMY In ancient times, Britain was invaded by many peoples, including Iberians, Celts, Romans, Angles, Saxons, Jutes, Norsemen, Danes, and Normans, who arrived in 1066. The evolution of the United Kingdom spanned hundreds of years. The Normans finally overcame Welsh resistance in 1282, when King Edward I annexed Wales and united it with England. Union with Scotland was achieved by the Act of Union of 1707. This created a country known as the United Kingdom of Great Britain.

Ireland came under Norman rule in the 11th century, and much of its later history was concerned with a struggle against English domination. In 1801, Ireland became part of the United Kingdom of Great Britain and Ireland. But in 1921, southern Ireland broke away to become the Irish Free State. Most of the people in the Irish Free State were Roman Catholics. In Northern Ireland, where the majority of the people were Protestants, most people wanted to remain citizens of the United Kingdom. As a result, the country's official name changed to the United Kingdom of Great Britain and Northern Ireland.

The modern history of the UK began in the 18th century when the British empire began to develop, despite the loss in 1783 of its 13 North American colonies which became the core of the modern United States. The other major event occurred in the late 18th century, when the UK became the first country to industrialize its economy.

The British empire broke up after World War II (1939–45), though the UK still administers many small, mainly island, territories around the world. The empire was transformed into the Commonwealth of Nations, a free association of independent countries which numbered 54 in 1998.

But while the UK retained a world role through the Commonwealth and the United Nations, it recognized that its economic future lay within Europe. As a result, it became a member of the European Economic Community (now the European Union) in 1973. In the 1990s, most people accepted the importance of the European Union to the UK's economic future. But some feared a loss of British identity should the European Union evolve into a political federation. In 1997, the UK itself began to decentralize power away from London, when the people of Scotland and Wales voted in referendums in favour of devolution plans.

The UK is a major industrial and trading nation. It lacks natural resources apart from coal, iron ore, oil and natural gas, and has to import most of the materials it needs for its industries. The UK also has to import food, because it produces only about two-thirds of the food it needs.

In the first half of the 20th century, the UK became known for exporting such products as cars, ships, steel and textiles. However, many traditional industries have suffered from increased competition from other countries, whose lower labour costs enable them to produce goods more cheaply. Today, a growing number of industries use sophisticated high-technology in order to compete on the world market.

The UK is one of the world's most urbanized countries, and agriculture employs only 2% of the people. Yet production is high because farms use scientific methods and modern machinery. Major crops include barley, potatoes, sugar beet and wheat. Sheep are the leading livestock, but beef cattle, dairy cattle, pigs and poultry are also important. Fishing is another major activity.

Service industries play a major part in the UK's economy. Financial and insurance services bring in much-needed foreign exchange, while tourism has become a major earner.

AREA 243,368 sq km [94,202 sq mls]
POPULATION 58,306,000
CAPITAL (POPULATION) London (8,089,000)
GOVERNMENT Constitutional monarchy
ETHNIC GROUPS White 94%, Asian Indian 1%, Pakistani 1%, West Indian 1%
LANGUAGES English (official), Welsh, Gaelic
RELIGIONS Christianity (Anglican 57%, Roman Catholic 13%, Presbyterian 7%, Methodist 4%, Baptist 1%), Islam 1%, Judaism, Hinduism, Sikhism
CURRENCY Pound sterling = 100 pence

UNITED STATES OF AMERICA

GEOGRAPHY The United States of America is the world's fourth largest country in area and the third largest in population. It contains 50 states, 48 of which lie between Canada and Mexico, plus Alaska in north-western North America, and Hawaii, a group of volcanic islands in the North Pacific Ocean. Densely populated coastal plains lie to the east and south of the Appalachian Mountains. The central lowlands drained by the Mississippi–Missouri rivers stretch from the Appalachians to the Rocky Mountains in the west. The Pacific region contains fertile valleys, separated by mountain ranges.

The climate varies greatly, ranging from the Arctic cold of Alaska to the intense heat of Death Valley, a bleak desert in California. Of the 48 states between Canada and Mexico, winters are cold and snowy in the north, but mild in the south, a region which is often called the 'Sun Belt'.

POLITICS & ECONOMY The first people in North America, the ancestors of the Native Americans (or American Indians) arrived perhaps 40,000 years ago from Asia. Although Vikings probably reached North America 1,000 years ago, European exploration proper did not begin until the late 15th century.

The first Europeans to settle in large numbers were the British, who founded settlements on the eastern coast in the early 17th century. British rule ended in the War of Independence (1775–83). The country expanded in 1803 when a vast territory in the south and west was acquired through the Louisiana Purchase, while the border with Mexico was fixed in the mid-19th century.

The Civil War (1861–5) ended the threat that the nation might split in two parts. It also ended slavery for the country's many African Americans. In the late 19th century, the West was opened up, while immigrants flooded in from Europe and elsewhere.

During the late 19th and early 20th centuries, industrialization led to the United States becoming the world's leading economic superpower and a pioneer in science and technology. Because of its economic strength, it has been able to take on the mantle of the champion of the Western world and of democratic government. The fall of Communism and the subsequent break-up of the Soviet Union left the US as the world's only real superpower. While this supremacy may well be challenged by China in time, the USA remains the most powerful voice in global politics.

The United States has the world's largest economy in terms of the total value of its production. Although agriculture employs only 2% of the people, farming is highly mechanized and scientific, and the United States leads the world in farm production. Major products include beef and dairy cattle, together with such crops as cotton, fruits, groundnuts, maize, potatoes, soya beans, tobacco and wheat.

The country's natural resources include oil, natural gas and coal. There are also a wide range of metal ores which are used in manufacturing industries, together with timber, especially from the forests of the Pacific north-west. Manufacturing is the single most important activity, employing about 17% of the population. Major products include vehicles, food products, chemicals, machinery, printed goods, metal products and scientific instruments. California is now the leading manufacturing state. Many southern states, petroleum rich and climatically favoured, have also become highly prosperous in recent years.

AREA 9,372,610 sq km [3,618,765 sq mls]
POPULATION 263,563,000
CAPITAL (POPULATION) Washington, D.C. (4,466,000)
GOVERNMENT Federal republic
ETHNIC GROUPS White 80%, African American 12%, other races 8%
LANGUAGES English (official), Spanish, more than 30 others
RELIGIONS Christianity (Protestant 53%, Roman Catholic 26%, other Christian 8%), Islam 2%, Judaism 2%
CURRENCY US dollar = 100 cents

URUGUAY

GEOGRAPHY Uruguay is South America's second smallest independent country after Surinam. The land consists mainly of flat plains and hills. The River Uruguay, which forms the country's western border, flows into the Río de la Plata, a large estuary which leads into the South Atlantic Ocean.

Uruguay has a mild climate, with rain in every month, though droughts sometimes occur. Summers are pleasantly warm, especially near the coast. The weather remains relatively mild throughout the winter.

POLITICS & ECONOMY In 1726, Spanish settlers founded Montevideo in order to halt the Portuguese gaining influence in the area. By the late 18th century, Spaniards had settled in most of the country. Uruguay became part of a colony called the Viceroyalty of La Plata, which also included Argentina, Paraguay, and parts of Bolivia, Brazil and Chile. In 1820 Brazil annexed Uruguay, ending Spanish rule. In 1825, Uruguayans, supported by Argentina, began a struggle for independence. Finally, in 1828, Brazil and Argentina recognized Uruguay as an independent republic. Social and economic developments were slow in the 19th century, but, from 1903, governments made Uruguay a democratic and stable country.

From the 1950s, economic problems caused unrest. Terrorist groups, notably the Tupumaros, carried out murders and kidnappings. The army crushed the Tupumaros in 1972, but the army took over the government in 1973. Military rule continued until 1984 when elections were held. Julio Maria Sanguinetti, who led Uruguay back to civilian rule, was re-elected president in 1994.

The World Bank classifies Uruguay as an 'upper-middle-income' developing country. Agriculture employs only 5% of the people, but farm products, notably hides and leather goods, beef and wool, are the leading exports, while the leading manufacturing industries process farm products. The main crops include maize, potatoes, wheat and sugar beet.

AREA 177,410 sq km [68,498 sq mls]
POPULATION 3,186,000
CAPITAL (POPULATION) Montevideo (1,326,000)
GOVERNMENT Multiparty republic
ETHNIC GROUPS White 86%, Mestizo 8%, Mulatto or Black 6%
LANGUAGES Spanish (official)
RELIGIONS Christianity (Roman Catholic 66%, Protestant 2%), Judaism 1%
CURRENCY Uruguay peso = 100 centésimos

UZBEKISTAN

GEOGRAPHY The Republic of Uzbekistan is one of the five republics in Central Asia which were once part of the Soviet Union. Plains cover most of western Uzbekistan, with highlands in the east. The main rivers, the Amu (or Amu Darya) and Syr (or Syr Darya), drain into the Aral Sea. So much water has been taken from these rivers to irrigate the land that the Aral Sea shrank from 66,900 sq km [25,830 sq mls] in 1960 to 33,642 sq km [12,989 sq mls] in 1993. The dried-up lake area has become desert, like much of the rest of the country.

Uzbekistan has a continental climate. The winters are cold, but the temperatures soar in the summer months. The west is extremely arid, with an average annual rainfall of about 200 mm [8 in].

POLITICS & ECONOMY Russia took the area in the 19th century. After the Russian Revolution of 1917, the Communists took over and, in 1924, they set up the Uzbek Soviet Socialist Republic. Under Communism, all aspects of Uzbek life were controlled and religious worship was discouraged. But education, health, housing and transport were improved. In the late 1980s, the people demanded more freedom and, in 1990, the government stated that its laws overruled those of the Soviet Union. Uzbekistan became independent in 1991 when the Soviet Union broke up, but it retained links with Russia through the Commonwealth of Independent States. Islam Karimov, leader of the People's Democratic Party (formerly the Communist Party), was elected president in December 1991. In 1992–3, many opposition leaders were arrested because the government said that they threatened national stability. In 1994–5, the PDP won sweeping victories in national elections and, in 1995, a referendum extended Karimov's term in office until 2000.

The World Bank classifies Uzbekistan as a 'lower-middle-income' developing country and the government still controls most economic activity. The country produces coal, copper, gold, oil and natural gas.

AREA 447,400 sq km [172,740 sq mls]
POPULATION 22,833,000
CAPITAL (POPULATION) Tashkent (2,106,000)
GOVERNMENT Socialist republic
ETHNIC GROUPS Uzbek 71%, Russian 8%, Tajik 5%, Kazak 4%, Tatar 2%, Kara-Kalpak 2%
LANGUAGES Uzbek (official), several others
RELIGIONS Islam
CURRENCY Som = 100 tyiyn

VANUATU

The Republic of Vanuatu, formerly the Anglo-French Condominium of the New Hebrides, became independent in 1980. It consists of a chain of 80 islands in the South Pacific Ocean. Its economy is based on agriculture and it exports copra, beef and veal, timber and cocoa. **AREA** 12,190 sq km [4,707 sq mls]; **POPULATION** 167,000; **CAPITAL** Port-Vila.

VATICAN CITY

Vatican City State, the world's smallest independent nation, is an enclave on the west bank of the River Tiber in Rome. It forms an independent base for the Holy See, the governing body of the Roman Catholic Church. **AREA** 0.44 sq km [0.17 sq mls]; **POPULATION** about 1,000.

VENEZUELA

GEOGRAPHY The Republic of Venezuela, in northern South America, contains the Maracaibo lowlands around the oil-rich Lake Maracaibo in the west. Andean ranges enclose the lowlands and extend across most of northern Venezuela. The Orinoco river basin, containing tropical grasslands called *llanos*, lies between the northern highlands and the Guiana Highlands in the south-east.

Venezuela has a tropical climate. Temperatures are high throughout the year on the lowlands, though the mountains are much cooler. The rainfall is heaviest in the mountains. But much of the country has a marked dry season between December and April.

POLITICS & ECONOMY In the early 19th century, Venezuelans, such as Simón Bolívar and Francisco de Miranda, began a struggle against Spanish rule. Venezuela declared its independence in 1811. But it only become truly independent in 1821, when the Spanish were defeated in a battle near Valencia.

The development of Venezuela in the 19th and the first half of the 20th centuries was marred by instability, violence and periods of harsh dictatorial rule. But the country has had elected governments since 1958. The country has greatly benefited from its oil resources which were first exploited in 1917. In 1960, Venezuela helped to form OPEC (the Organization of Petroleum Exporting Countries) and, in 1976, the government of Venezuela took control of the entire oil industry. Money from oil exports has helped Venezuela to raise living standards and diversify the economy.

The World Bank classifies Venezuela as an 'upper-middle-income' developing country. Oil accounts for 80% of the exports. Other exports include bauxite and aluminium, iron ore and farm products. Agriculture employs 13% of the people and cattle ranching is important. The chief industry is petroleum refining. Other manufactures include aluminium, cement, processed food, steel and textiles. The main manufacturing centres include Caracas, Ciudad Guayana (aluminium and steel) and Maracaibo (oil refineries).

AREA 912,050 sq km [352,143 sq mls]
POPULATION 21,810,000
CAPITAL (POPULATION) Caracas (2,784,000)
GOVERNMENT Federal republic
ETHNIC GROUPS Mestizo 67%, White 21%, Black 10%, Amerindian 2%
LANGUAGES Spanish (official), Goajiro
RELIGIONS Christianity (Roman Catholic 94%)
CURRENCY Bolívar = 100 céntimos

VIETNAM

GEOGRAPHY The Socialist Republic of Vietnam occupies an S-shaped strip of land facing the South China Sea in South-east Asia. The coastal plains include two densely populated, fertile delta regions: the Red (Hong) delta facing the Gulf of Tonkin in the north, and the Mekong delta in the south.

Vietnam has a tropical climate, though the driest months of January to March are a little cooler than the wet, hot summer months, when monsoon winds blow from the south-west. Typhoons (cyclones) sometimes hit the coast, causing much damage.

POLITICS & ECONOMY China dominated Vietnam for a thousand years before AD 939, when a Vietnamese state was founded. The French took over the area between the 1850s and 1880s. They ruled Vietnam as part of French Indo-China, which also included Cambodia and Laos.

Japan conquered Vietnam during World War II (1939–45). In 1946, war broke out between a nationalist group, called the Vietminh, and the French colonial government. France withdrew in 1954 and Vietnam was divided into a Communist North Vietnam, led by the Vietminh leader, Ho Chi Minh, and a non-Communist South.

A force called the Viet Cong rebelled against South Vietnam's government in 1957 and a war began, which gradually increased in intensity. The United States aided the South, but after it withdrew in 1975, South Vietnam surrendered. In 1976, the united Vietnam became a Socialist Republic.

Vietnamese troops intervened in Cambodia in 1978 to defeat the Communist Khmer Rouge government, but it withdrew its troops in 1989. In the 1990s, Vietnam began to introduce reforms. In 1995, relations with the US were normalized when the US opened an embassy in Hanoi.

The World Bank classifies Vietnam as a 'low-income' developing country and agriculture employs 67% of the population. The main food crop is rice. The country also produces chromium, oil (which was discovered off the south coast in 1986), phosphates and tin.

AREA 331,689 sq km [128,065 sq mls]
POPULATION 74,580,000
CAPITAL (POPULATION) Hanoi (3,056,000)
GOVERNMENT Socialist republic
ETHNIC GROUPS Vietnamese 87%, Tho (Tay), Chinese (Hoa), Tai, Khmer, Muong, Nung
LANGUAGES Vietnamese (official), Chinese
RELIGIONS Buddhism 55%, Christianity (Roman Catholic 7%)
CURRENCY Dong = 10 hao = 100 xu

VIRGIN ISLANDS, BRITISH

The British Virgin Islands, the most northerly of the Lesser Antilles, are a British overseas territory, with a substantial measure of self-government. **AREA** 153 sq km [59 sq mls]; **POPULATION** 20,000; **CAPITAL** Road Town.

VIRGIN ISLANDS, US

The Virgin Islands of the United States, a group of three islands and 65 small islets, are a self-governing US territory. Purchased from Denmark in 1917, its residents are US citizens and they elect a non-voting delegate to the US House of Representatives. **AREA** 340 sq km [130 sq mls]; **POPULATION** 105,000; **CAPITAL** Charlotte Amalie.

WALLIS AND FUTUNA

Wallis and Futuna, in the South Pacific Ocean, is the smallest and the poorest of France's overseas territories. **AREA** 200 sq km [77 sq mls]; **POPULATION** 13,000; **CAPITAL** Mata-Utu.

WESTERN SAMOA

The Independent State of Western Samoa comprises two islands in the South Pacific Ocean. Governed by New Zealand from 1920, the territory became independent in 1962. Exports include taro, coconut cream and beer. **AREA** 2,840 sq km [1,097 sq mls]; **POPULATION** 169,000; **CAPITAL** Apia.

YEMEN

GEOGRAPHY The Republic of Yemen faces the Red Sea and the Gulf of Aden in the south-western corner of the Arabian peninsula. Behind the narrow coastal plain along the Red Sea, the land rises to a mountain region called High Yemen.

The climate ranges from hot and often humid conditions on the coast to the cooler highlands. Most of the country is arid.

POLITICS & ECONOMY After World War I, northern Yemen, which had been ruled by Turkey, began to evolve into a separate state from the south, where Britain was in control. Britain withdrew in 1967 and a left-wing government took power in the south. In North Yemen, the monarchy was abolished in 1962 and the country became a republic.

Clashes occurred between the traditionalist Yemen Arab Republic in the north and the formerly British Marxist People's Democratic Republic of Yemen but, in 1990, the two Yemens merged to form a single country. Since then, the union has held together, despite a two-month civil war in 1994.

The World Bank classifies Yemen as a 'low-income'

developing country. Agriculture employs up to 63% of the people. Herders raise sheep and other animals, while farmers grow such crops as barley, fruits, wheat and vegetables in highland valleys and around oases. Cash crops include coffee and cotton.

Imported oil is refined at Aden and petroleum extraction began in the north-west in the 1980s. Handicrafts, leather goods and textiles are manufactured. Remittances from Yemenis abroad are a major source of revenue.

AREA 527,970 sq km [203,849 sq mls]
POPULATION 14,609,000
CAPITAL (POPULATION) San'a (972,000)
GOVERNMENT Multiparty republic
ETHNIC GROUPS Arab 96%, Somali 1%
LANGUAGES Arabic (official)
RELIGIONS Islam
CURRENCY Rial = 100 fils

YUGOSLAVIA

GEOGRAPHY The Federal Republic of Yugoslavia consists of Serbia and Montenegro, two of the six republics which made up the former country of Yugoslavia until it broke up in 1991 and 1992. Behind the short coastline along the Adriatic Sea lies a mountainous region, including the Dinaric Alps and part of the Balkan Mountains. The Pannonian Plains make up northern Yugoslavia.

The coast has a Mediterranean climate. The highlands have cold winters and cool summers.
POLITICS & ECONOMY People who became known as the South Slavs began to move into the region around 1,500 years ago. Each group, including the Serbs and Croats, founded its own state. But, by the 15th century, foreign countries controlled the region. Serbia and Montenegro were under the Turkish Ottoman empire.

In the 19th century, many Slavs worked for independence and Slavic unity. In 1914, Austria-Hungary declared war on Serbia, blaming it for the assassination of Archduke Francis Ferdinand of Austria-Hungary. This led to World War I and the defeat of Austria-Hungary. In 1918, the South Slavs united in the Kingdom of the Serbs, Croats and Slovenes, which consisted of Bosnia-Herzegovina, Croatia, Dalmatia, Montenegro, Serbia and Slovenia. The country was renamed Yugoslavia in 1929. Germany occupied Yugoslavia during World War II, but partisans, including a Communist force led by Josip Broz Tito, fought the invaders.

From 1945, the Communists controlled the country, which was called the Federal People's Republic of Yugoslavia. But after Tito's death in 1980, the country faced many problems. In 1990, non-Communist parties were permitted and non-Communists won majorities in elections in all but Serbia and Montenegro, where Socialists (former Communists) won control. In 1991–2, the six republics which formed Yugoslavia split apart. Bosnia-Herzegovina, Croatia, Macedonia and Slovenia proclaimed their independence. The fifth country, consisting of Serbia and Montenegro, took the name Yugoslavia.

Fighting broke out in Croatia and Bosnia-Herzegovina as rival groups struggled for power. In 1992, the United Nations withdrew recognition of Yugoslavia because of its failure to halt atrocities committed by Serbs living in Croatia and Bosnia. International sanctions were imposed, causing an economic crisis. In 1995, Yugoslavia played an important part in the talks that led to the Dayton Peace Accord, which brought peace to Bosnia-Herzegovina. As a result, the UN voted to lift sanctions. However, international criticism of Yugoslav repression of minorities flared up once again in 1998, when conflict occurred in Kosovo province, where the majority are ethnic Albanians.

Under Communist rule, manufacturing became increasingly important in Yugoslavia. But in the early 1990s, the World Bank classified Yugoslavia as a 'lower-middle-income' economy. Its resources include bauxite, coal, copper and other metals, together with oil and natural gas. Manufactures include aluminium, machinery, plastics, steel, textiles and vehicles. The chief exports are manufactures, but agriculture remains important. Crops include fruits, maize, potatoes, tobacco and wheat. Cattle, pigs and sheep are reared.

AREA 102,170 sq km [39,449 sq mls]
POPULATION 10,881,000
CAPITAL (POPULATION) Belgrade (1,137,000)
GOVERNMENT Federal republic
ETHNIC GROUPS Serb 62%, Albanian 17%, Montenegrin 5%, Hungarian, Muslim, Croat
LANGUAGES Serbo-Croat (official), Albanian
RELIGIONS Christianity (mainly Serbian Orthodox), Islam
CURRENCY Yugoslav new dinar = 100 paras

ZAMBIA

GEOGRAPHY The Republic of Zambia is a landlocked country in southern Africa. Zambia lies on the plateau that makes up most of southern Africa. Much of the land is between 900 m and 1,500 m [2,950 ft to 4,920 ft] above sea level. The Muchinga Mountains in the north-east rise above this flat land.

Zambia lies in the tropics, but temperatures are moderated by the altitude. The rainy season runs from November to March.
POLITICS & ECONOMY European contact with Zambia began in the 19th century, when the explorer David Livingstone crossed the River Zambezi. In the 1890s, the British South Africa Company, set up by Cecil Rhodes (1853–1902), the British financier and statesman, made treaties with local chiefs and gradually took over the area. In 1911, the Company named the area Northern Rhodesia. In 1924, Britain took over the government of the country.

In 1953, Britain formed a federation of Northern Rhodesia, Southern Rhodesia (now Zimbabwe) and Nyasaland (now Malawi). Because of African opposition, the federation was dissolved in 1963 and Northern Rhodesia became independent as Zambia in 1964. Kenneth Kaunda became president and one-party rule was introduced in 1972. However, a new constitution was adopted in 1990 and, in 1991, Kaunda's party was defeated and Frederick Chiluba became president.

Copper is the leading export, accounting for 90% of Zambia's total exports in 1990. Zambia also produces cobalt, lead, zinc and various gemstones. Agriculture accounts for 75% of the workers, as compared with 8% in industry, including mining. Maize is the chief crop. Other crops include cassava, coffee and millet.

AREA 752,614 sq km [290,586 sq mls]
POPULATION 9,500,000
CAPITAL (POPULATION) Lusaka (982,000)
GOVERNMENT Multiparty republic
ETHNIC GROUPS Bemba 36%, Maravi (Nyanja) 18%, Tonga 15%
LANGUAGES English (official), Bemba, Nyanja
RELIGIONS Christianity 68%, traditional beliefs 27%
CURRENCY Kwacha = 100 ngwee

ZIMBABWE

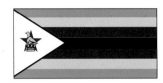

GEOGRAPHY The Republic of Zimbabwe is a landlocked country in southern Africa. Most of the country lies on a high plateau between the Zambezi and Limpopo rivers between 900 m and 1,500 m [2,950 ft to 4,920 ft] above sea level. The highest land is in the east near the Mozambique border.

In the summer, between October and March, the weather is hot and wet. But in the winter, daily temperatures can vary greatly. Frosts have been recorded between June and August. The climate varies according to the altitude.
POLITICS & ECONOMY The Shona people became dominant in the region about 1,000 years ago. They built the impressive Great Zimbabwe, a city of stone buildings. The British South Africa Company, under the statesman Cecil Rhodes (1853–1902), occupied the area in the 1890s, after obtaining mineral rights from local chiefs. The area was named Rhodesia and later Southern Rhodesia. It became a self-governing British colony in 1923. Between 1953 and 1963, Southern and Northern Rhodesia (now Zambia) were joined to Nyasaland (Malawi) in the Central African Federation.

In 1965, the European government of Southern Rhodesia (then called Rhodesia) declared their country independent. But Britain refused to accept Rhodesia's independence. Finally, after a civil war, the country became legally independent in 1980. After independence, rivalries between the Shona and Ndebele people threatened its stability. But order was restored when the Shona prime minister, Robert Mugabe, brought his Ndebele rivals into his government. In 1987, Mugabe became the country's executive president and, in 1991, the government renounced its Marxist ideology. Mugabe was re-elected president in 1990 and 1996.

The World Bank classifies Zimbabwe as a 'low-income' developing country. The country has valuable mineral resources and mining accounts for a fifth of the country's exports. Gold, asbestos, chromium and nickel are all mined. Zimbabwe also has some coal and iron ore, and some metal and food-processing industries. But agriculture employs 68% of working people. Maize is the chief food crop, while export crops include tobacco, cotton and sugar.

AREA 390,579 sq km [150,873 sq mls]
POPULATION 11,453,000
CAPITAL (POPULATION) Harare (1,189,000)
GOVERNMENT Multiparty republic
ETHNIC GROUPS Shona 71%, Ndebele 16%, other Bantu-speaking Africans 11%, White 2%
LANGUAGES English (official), Shona, Ndebele, Nyanja
RELIGIONS Christianity 45%, traditional beliefs 40%
CURRENCY Zimbabwe dollar = 100 cents

The
WORLD IN
FOCUS

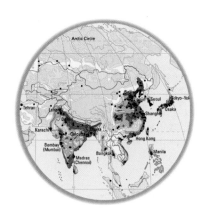

Planet Earth

Sun — Mercury — Mars — Saturn — Neptune

Venus — Earth — Jupiter — Uranus — Pluto

The Solar System

A minute part of one of the billions of galaxies (collections of stars) that comprises the Universe, the Solar System lies some 27,000 light-years from the centre of our own galaxy, the 'Milky Way'. Thought to be over 4,700 million years old, it consists of a central sun with nine planets and their moons revolving around it, attracted by its gravitational pull. The planets orbit the Sun in the same direction – anti-clockwise when viewed from the Northern Heavens – and almost in the same plane. Their orbital paths, however, vary enormously.

The Sun's diameter is 109 times that of Earth, and the temperature at its core – caused by continuous thermonuclear fusions of hydrogen into helium – is estimated to be 15 million degrees Celsius. It is the Solar System's only source of light and heat.

Profile of the Planets

	Mean distance from Sun (million km)	Mass (Earth = 1)	Period of orbit (Earth years)	Period of rotation (Earth days)	Equatorial diameter (km)	Number of known satellites
Mercury	57.9	0.055	0.24 years	58.67	4,878	0
Venus	108.2	0.815	0.62 years	243.00	12,104	0
Earth	149.6	1.0	1.00 years	1.00	12,756	1
Mars	227.9	0.107	1.88 years	1.03	6,787	2
Jupiter	778.3	317.8	11.86 years	0.41	142,800	16
Saturn	1,427	95.2	29.46 years	0.43	120,000	20
Uranus	2,871	14.5	84.01 years	0.75	51,118	15
Neptune	4,497	17.1	164.80 years	0.80	49,528	8
Pluto	5,914	0.002	248.50 years	6.39	2,320	1

All planetary orbits are elliptical in form, but only Pluto and Mercury follow paths that deviate noticeably from a circular one. Near perihelion – its closest approach to the Sun – Pluto actually passes inside the orbit of Neptune, an event that last occurred in 1983. Pluto will not regain its station as outermost planet until February 1999.

The Seasons

Seasons occur because the Earth's axis is tilted at a constant angle of 23½°. When the northern hemisphere is tilted to a maximum extent towards the Sun, on 21 June, the Sun is overhead at the Tropic of Cancer (latitude 23½° North). This is midsummer, or the summer solstice, in the northern hemisphere.

On 22 or 23 September, the Sun is overhead at the Equator, and day and night are of equal length throughout the world. This is the autumn equinox in the northern hemisphere. On 21 or 22 December, the Sun is overhead at the Tropic of Capricorn (23½° South), the winter solstice in the northern hemisphere. The overhead Sun then tracks north until, on 21 March, it is overhead at the Equator. This is the spring (vernal) equinox in the northern hemisphere.

In the southern hemisphere, the seasons are the reverse of those in the north.

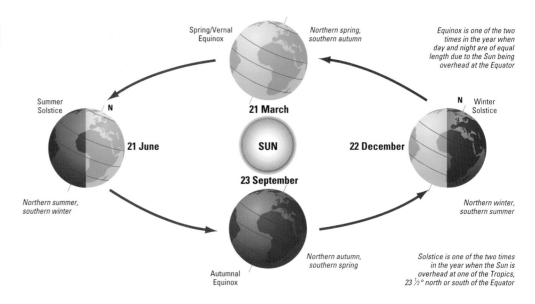

Spring/Vernal Equinox — Northern spring, southern autumn

Equinox is one of the two times in the year when day and night are of equal length due to the Sun being overhead at the Equator

Summer Solstice — 21 June — N — 21 March — SUN — 22 December — N — Winter Solstice

Northern summer, southern winter

23 September

Northern autumn, southern spring

Autumnal Equinox

Northern winter, southern summer

Solstice is one of the two times in the year when the Sun is overhead at one of the Tropics, 23 ½° north or south of the Equator

Day and Night

The Sun appears to rise in the east, reach its highest point at noon, and then set in the west, to be followed by night. In reality, it is not the Sun that is moving but the Earth rotating from west to east. The moment when the Sun's upper limb first appears above the horizon is termed sunrise; the moment when the Sun's upper limb disappears below the horizon is sunset.

At the summer solstice in the northern hemisphere (21 June), the Arctic has total daylight and the Antarctic total darkness. The opposite occurs at the winter solstice (21 or 22 December). At the Equator, the length of day and night are almost equal all year.

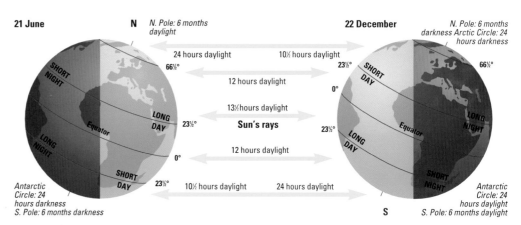

21 June — N — N. Pole: 6 months daylight

24 hours daylight — 10½ hours daylight
66½° — 23½°
12 hours daylight
13½ hours daylight
SHORT NIGHT — Sun's rays — SHORT DAY
LONG DAY — 23½° — 23½° — LONG NIGHT
0° — 12 hours daylight — 0°
LONG NIGHT — LONG DAY
SHORT DAY — 23½° — 10½ hours daylight — 24 hours daylight — SHORT NIGHT

22 December — N. Pole: 6 months darkness Arctic Circle: 24 hours darkness

66½°

Antarctic Circle: 24 hours darkness
S. Pole: 6 months darkness

Antarctic Circle: 24 hours daylight
S. Pole: 6 months daylight

S

Time

Year: The time taken by the Earth to revolve around the Sun, or 365.24 days.

Leap Year: A calendar year of 366 days, 29 February being the additional day. It offsets the difference between the calendar and the solar year.

Month: The approximate time taken by the Moon to revolve around the Earth. The 12 months of the year in fact vary from 28 (29 in a Leap Year) to 31 days.

Week: An artificial period of 7 days, not based on astronomical time.

Day: The time taken by the Earth to complete one rotation on its axis.

Hour: 24 hours make one day. Usually the day is divided into hours AM (ante meridiem or before noon) and PM (post meridiem or after noon), although most timetables now use the 24-hour system, from midnight to midnight.

Sunrise

Spring Equinox *Autumnal Equinox*

Hours AM — Latitude (60°N, 40°N, 20°N, 0°(Equator), 20°S, 40°S, 60°S)

Months of the year: J F M A M J J A S O N D

Sunset

Spring Equinox *Autumnal Equinox*

Hours PM — Latitude (60°S, 40°S, 20°S, 0°(Equator), 20°N, 40°N, 60°N)

Months of the year: J F M A M J J A S O N D

The Moon

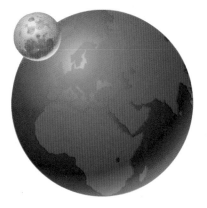

The Moon rotates more slowly than the Earth, making one complete turn on its axis in just over 27 days. Since this corresponds to its period of revolution around the Earth, the Moon always presents the same

Phases of the Moon

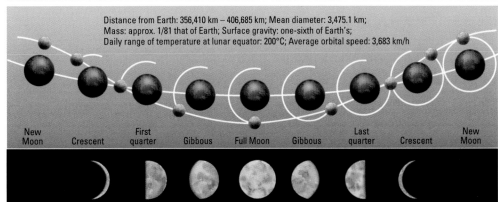

Distance from Earth: 356,410 km – 406,685 km; Mean diameter: 3,475.1 km; Mass: approx. 1/81 that of Earth; Surface gravity: one-sixth of Earth's; Daily range of temperature at lunar equator: 200°C; Average orbital speed: 3,683 km/h

New Moon — Crescent — First quarter — Gibbous — Full Moon — Gibbous — Last quarter — Crescent — New Moon

hemisphere or face to us, and we never see 'the dark side'. The interval between one full Moon and the next (and between new Moons) is about 29½ days – a lunar month. The apparent changes in the

shape of the Moon are caused by its changing position in relation to the Earth; like the planets, it produces no light of its own and shines only by reflecting the rays of the Sun.

Eclipses

When the Moon passes between the Sun and the Earth it causes a partial eclipse of the Sun (1) if the Earth passes through the Moon's outer shadow (P), or a total eclipse (2) if the inner cone shadow crosses the Earth's surface. In a lunar eclipse, the Earth's shadow crosses the Moon and, again, provides either a partial or total eclipse.

Eclipses of the Sun and the Moon do not occur every month because of the 5° difference between the plane of the Moon's orbit and the plane in which the Earth moves. In the 1990s only 14 lunar eclipses are possible, for example, seven partial and seven total; each is visible only from certain, and variable, parts of the world. The same period witnesses 13 solar eclipses – six partial (or annular) and seven total.

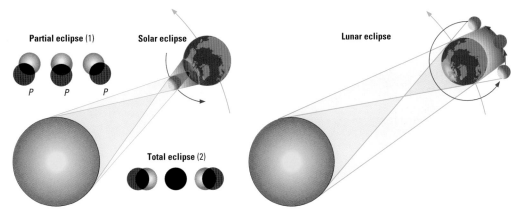

Partial eclipse (1) — Solar eclipse — Lunar eclipse — P P P — Total eclipse (2)

Tides

The daily rise and fall of the ocean's tides are the result of the gravitational pull of the Moon and that of the Sun, though the effect of the latter is only 46.6% as strong as that of the Moon. This effect is greatest on the hemisphere facing the Moon and causes a tidal 'bulge'. When the Sun, Earth and Moon are in line, tide-raising forces are at a maximum and Spring tides occur: high tide reaches the highest values, and low tide falls to low levels. When lunar and solar forces are least coincidental with the Sun and Moon at an angle (near the Moon's first and third quarters), Neap tides occur, which have a small tidal range.

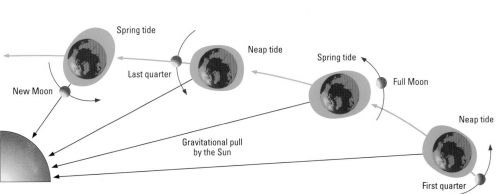

Spring tide — Neap tide — Spring tide — Last quarter — Full Moon — New Moon — Neap tide — Gravitational pull by the Sun — First quarter

Restless Earth

The Earth's Structure

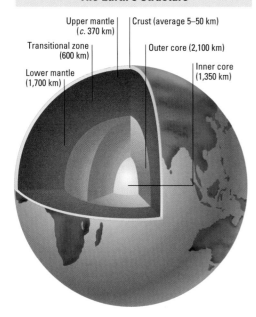

Upper mantle (c. 370 km)

Crust (average 5–50 km)

Transitional zone (600 km)

Outer core (2,100 km)

Lower mantle (1,700 km)

Inner core (1,350 km)

Continental Drift

About 200 million years ago the original Pangaea landmass began to split into two continental groups, which further separated over time to produce the present-day configuration.

180 million years ago

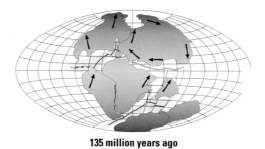

135 million years ago

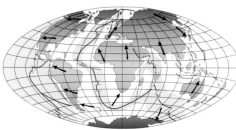

Present day

Trench
Rift
New ocean floor
Zones of slippage

Notable Earthquakes Since 1900

Year	Location	Richter Scale	Deaths
1906	San Francisco, USA	8.3	503
1906	Valparaiso, Chile	8.6	22,000
1908	Messina, Italy	7.5	83,000
1915	Avezzano, Italy	7.5	30,000
1920	Gansu (Kansu), China	8.6	180,000
1923	Yokohama, Japan	8.3	143,000
1927	Nan Shan, China	8.3	200,000
1932	Gansu (Kansu), China	7.6	70,000
1933	Sanriku, Japan	8.9	2,990
1934	Bihar, India/Nepal	8.4	10,700
1935	Quetta, India (now Pakistan)	7.5	60,000
1939	Chillan, Chile	8.3	28,000
1939	Erzincan, Turkey	7.9	30,000
1960	Agadir, Morocco	5.8	12,000
1962	Khorasan, Iran	7.1	12,230
1968	N.E. Iran	7.4	12,000
1970	N. Peru	7.7	66,794
1972	Managua, Nicaragua	6.2	5,000
1974	N. Pakistan	6.3	5,200
1976	Guatemala	7.5	22,778
1976	Tangshan, China	8.2	255,000
1978	Tabas, Iran	7.7	25,000
1980	El Asnam, Algeria	7.3	20,000
1980	S. Italy	7.2	4,800
1985	Mexico City, Mexico	8.1	4,200
1988	N.W. Armenia	6.8	55,000
1990	N. Iran	7.7	36,000
1993	Maharashtra, India	6.4	30,000
1994	Los Angeles, USA	6.6	61
1995	Kobe, Japan	7.2	5,000
1995	Sakhalin Is., Russia	7.5	2,000
1997	N.E. Iran	7.1	2,500
1998	Takhar, Afghanistan	6.1	4,200

The highest magnitude recorded on the Richter scale is 8.9 in Japan on 2 March 1933 which killed 2,990 people. The most devastating earthquake ever was at Shaanxi (Shenshi) province, central China, on 3 January 1556, when an estimated 830,000 people were killed.

Earthquakes

Earthquake magnitude is usually rated according to either the Richter or the Modified Mercalli scale, both devised by seismologists in the 1930s. The Richter scale measures absolute earthquake power with mathematical precision: each step upwards represents a tenfold increase in shockwave amplitude. Theoretically, there is no upper limit, but the largest earthquakes measured have been rated at between 8.8 and 8.9. The 12–point Mercalli scale, based on observed effects, is often more meaningful, ranging from I (earthquakes noticed only by seismographs) to XII (total destruction); intermediate points include V (people awakened at night; unstable objects overturned), VII (collapse of ordinary buildings; chimneys and monuments fall) and IX (conspicuous cracks in ground; serious damage to reservoirs).

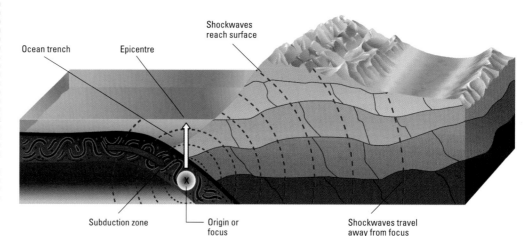

Ocean trench

Epicentre

Shockwaves reach surface

Subduction zone

Origin or focus

Shockwaves travel away from focus

Structure and Earthquakes

Mobile land areas
Submarine zones of mobile land areas
Stable land platforms
Submarine extensions of stable land platforms
Mid-oceanic volcanic ridges
Oceanic platforms

1976 Principal earthquakes and dates

Earthquakes are a series of rapid vibrations originating from the slipping or faulting of parts of the Earth's crust when stresses within build up to breaking point. They usually happen at depths varying from 8 km to 30 km. Severe earthquakes cause extensive damage when they take place in populated areas, destroying structures and severing communications. Most initial loss of life occurs due to secondary causes such as falling masonry, fires and flooding.

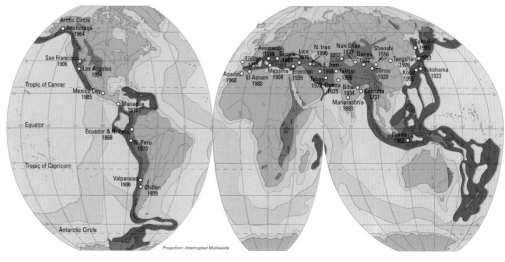

Projection: Interrupted Mollweide

4

Plate Tectonics

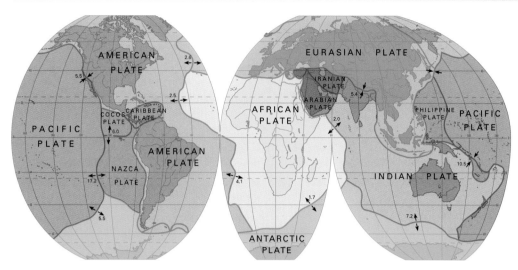

The drifting of the continents is a feature that is unique to Planet Earth. The complementary, almost jigsaw-puzzle fit of the coastlines on each side of the Atlantic Ocean inspired Alfred Wegener's theory of continental drift in 1915. The theory suggested that the ancient super-continent, which Wegener named Pangaea, incorporated all of the Earth's landmasses and gradually split up to form today's continents.

The original debate about continental drift was a prelude to a more radical idea: plate tectonics. The basic theory is that the Earth's crust is made up of a series of rigid plates which float on a soft layer of the mantle and are moved about by continental convection currents within the Earth's interior. These plates diverge and converge along margins marked by seismic activity. Plates diverge from mid-ocean ridges where molten lava pushes upwards and forces the plates apart at rates of up to 40 mm [1.6 in] a year.

The three diagrams, left, give some examples of plate boundaries from around the world. Diagram (a) shows sea-floor spreading at the Mid-Atlantic Ridge as the American and African plates slowly diverge. The same thing is happening in (b) where sea-floor spreading at the Mid-Indian Ocean Ridge is forcing the Indian plate to collide into the Eurasian plate. In (c) oceanic crust (sima) is being subducted beneath lighter continental crust (sial).

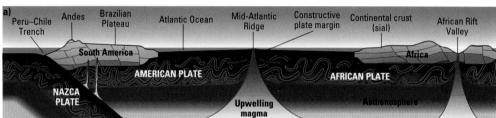

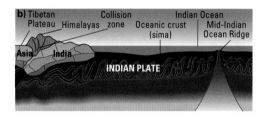

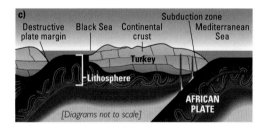

Volcanoes

Volcanoes occur when hot liquefied rock beneath the Earth's crust is pushed up by pressure to the surface as molten lava. Some volcanoes erupt in an explosive way, throwing out rocks and ash, whilst others are effusive and lava flows out of the vent. There are volcanoes which are both, such as Mount Fuji. An accumulation of lava and cinders creates cones of variable size and shape. As a result of many eruptions over centuries, Mount Etna in Sicily has a circumference of more than 120 km [75 miles].

Climatologists believe that volcanic ash, if ejected high into the atmosphere, can influence temperature and weather for several years afterwards. The 1991 eruption of Mount Pinatubo in the Philippines ejected more than 20 million tonnes of dust and ash 32 km [20 miles] into the atmosphere and is believed to have accelerated ozone depletion over a large part of the globe.

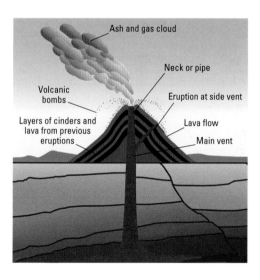

Distribution of Volcanoes

Volcanoes today may be the subject of considerable scientific study but they remain both dramatic and unpredictable: in 1991 Mount Pinatubo, 100 km [62 miles] north of the Philippines capital Manila, suddenly burst into life after lying dormant for more than six centuries. Most of the world's active volcanoes occur in a belt around the Pacific Ocean, on the edge of the Pacific plate, called the 'ring of fire'. Indonesia has the greatest concentration with 90 volcanoes, 12 of which are active. The most famous, Krakatoa, erupted in 1883 with such force that the resulting tidal wave killed 36,000 people and tremors were felt as far away as Australia.

- Submarine volcanoes

▲ Land volcanoes active since 1700

— Boundaries of tectonic plates

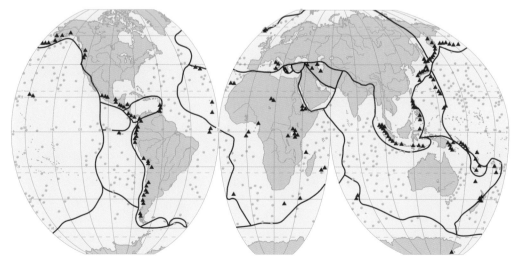

Landforms

The Rock Cycle

James Hutton first proposed the rock cycle in the late 1700s after he observed the slow but steady effects of erosion.

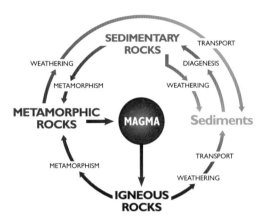

Above and below the surface of the oceans, the features of the Earth's crust are constantly changing. The phenomenal forces generated by convection currents in the molten core of our planet carry the vast segments or 'plates' of the crust across the globe in an endless cycle of creation and destruction. A continent may travel little more than 25 mm [1 in] per year, yet in the vast span of geological time this process throws up giant mountain ranges and creates new land.

Destruction of the landscape, however, begins as soon as it is formed. Wind, water, ice and sea, the main agents of erosion, mount a constant assault that even the most resistant rocks cannot withstand. Mountain peaks may dwindle by as little as a few millimetres each year, but if they are not uplifted by further movements of the crust they will eventually be reduced to rubble and transported away.

Water is the most powerful agent of erosion – it has been estimated that 100 billion tonnes of sediment are washed into the oceans every year. Three Asian rivers account for 20% of this total, the Huang He, in China, and the Brahmaputra and Ganges in Bangladesh.

Rivers and glaciers, like the sea itself, generate much of their effect through abrasion – pounding the land with the debris they carry with them. But as well as destroying they also create new landforms, many of them spectacular: vast deltas like those of the Mississippi and the Nile, or the deep fjords cut by glaciers in British Columbia, Norway and New Zealand.

Geologists once considered that landscapes evolved from 'young', newly uplifted mountainous areas, through a 'mature' hilly stage, to an 'old age' stage when the land was reduced to an almost flat plain, or peneplain. This theory, called the 'cycle of erosion', fell into disuse when it became evident that so many factors, including the effects of plate tectonics and climatic change, constantly interrupt the cycle, which takes no account of the highly complex interactions that shape the surface of our planet.

Mountain Building

Mountains are formed when pressures on the Earth's crust caused by continental drift become so intense that the surface buckles or cracks. This happens where oceanic crust is subducted by continental crust or, more dramatically, where two tectonic plates collide: the Rockies, Andes, Alps, Urals and Himalayas resulted from such impacts. These are all known as fold mountains because they were formed by the compression of the rocks, forcing the surface to bend and fold like a crumpled rug. The Himalayas are formed from the folded former sediments of the Tethys Sea which was trapped in the collision zone between the Indian and Eurasian plates.

The other main mountain-building process occurs when the crust fractures to create faults, allowing rock to be forced upwards in large blocks; or when the pressure of magma within the crust forces the surface to bulge into a dome, or erupts to form a volcano. Large mountain ranges may reveal a combination of those features; the Alps, for example, have been compressed so violently that the folds are fragmented by numerous faults and intrusions of molten igneous rock.

Over millions of years, even the greatest mountain ranges can be reduced by the agents of erosion (most notably rivers) to a low rugged landscape known as a peneplain.

Types of faults: Faults occur where the crust is being stretched or compressed so violently that the rock strata break in a horizontal or vertical movement. They are classified by the direction in which the blocks of rock have moved. A normal fault results when a vertical movement causes the surface to break apart; compression causes a reverse fault. Horizontal movement causes shearing, known as a strike-slip fault. When the rock breaks in two places, the central block may be pushed up in a horst fault, or sink (creating a rift valley) in a graben fault.

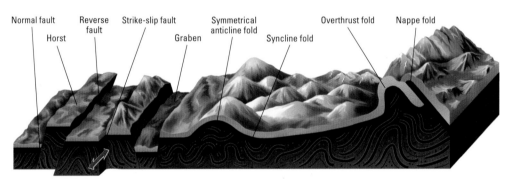

Types of fold: Folds occur when rock strata are squeezed and compressed. They are common therefore at destructive plate margins and where plates have collided, forcing the rocks to buckle into mountain ranges. Geographers give different names to the degrees of fold that result from continuing pressure on the rock. A simple fold may be symmetric, with even slopes on either side, but as the pressure builds up, one slope becomes steeper and the fold becomes asymmetric. Later, the ridge or 'anticline' at the top of the fold may slide over the lower ground or 'syncline' to form a recumbent fold. Eventually, the rock strata may break under the pressure to form an overthrust and finally a nappe fold.

Continental Glaciation

Ice sheets were at their greatest extent about 200,000 years ago. The maximum advance of the last Ice Age was about 18,000 years ago, when ice covered virtually all of Canada and reached as far south as the Bristol Channel in Britain.

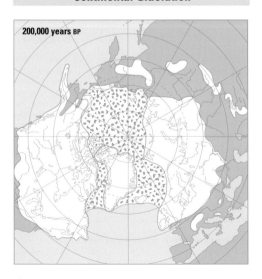

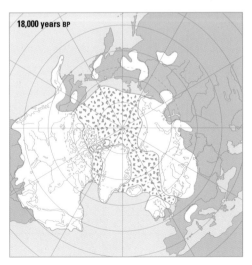

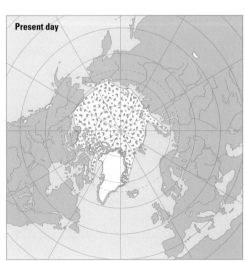

Natural Landforms

A stylized diagram to show a selection of landforms found in the mid-latitudes.

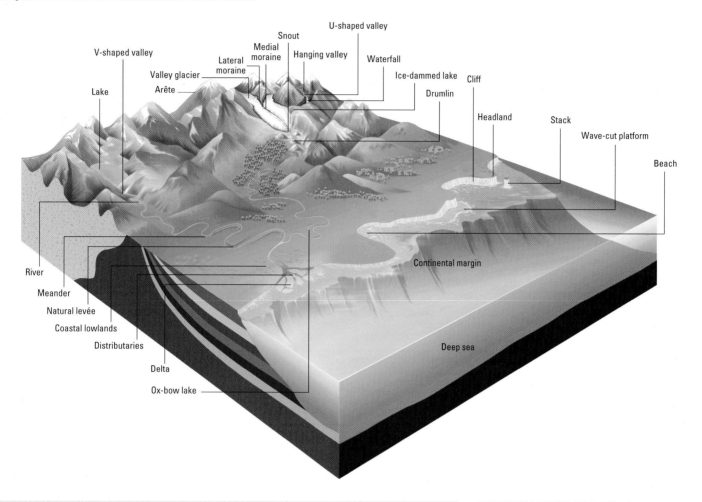

V-shaped valley

Lake

Valley glacier

Arête

Lateral moraine

Medial moraine

Snout

Hanging valley

U-shaped valley

Waterfall

Ice-dammed lake

Drumlin

Cliff

Headland

Stack

Wave-cut platform

Beach

Continental margin

River

Meander

Natural levée

Coastal lowlands

Distributaries

Delta

Ox-bow lake

Deep sea

Desert Landscapes

The popular image that deserts are all huge expanses of sand is wrong. Despite harsh conditions, deserts contain some of the most varied and interesting landscapes in the world. They are also one of the most extensive environments – the hot and cold deserts together cover almost 40% of the Earth's surface.

The three types of hot desert are known by their Arabic names: sand desert, called *erg*, covers only about one-fifth of the world's desert; the rest is divided between *hammada* (areas of bare rock) and *reg* (broad plains covered by loose gravel or pebbles).

In areas of *erg*, such as the Namib Desert, the shape of the dunes reflects the character of local winds. Where winds are constant in direction, crescent-shaped *barchan* dunes form. In areas of bare rock, wind-blown sand is a major agent of erosion. The erosion is mainly confined to within 2 m [6.5 ft] of the surface, producing characteristic, mushroom-shaped rocks.

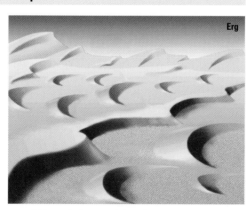

Erg

Hammada

Reg

Surface Processes

Catastrophic changes to natural landforms are periodically caused by such phenomena as avalanches, landslides and volcanic eruptions, but most of the processes that shape the Earth's surface operate extremely slowly in human terms. One estimate, based on a study in the United States, suggested that 1 m [3 ft] of land was removed from the entire surface of the country, on average, every 29,500 years. However, the time-scale varies from 1,300 years to 154,200 years depending on the terrain and climate.

In hot, dry climates, mechanical weathering, a result of rapid temperature changes, causes the outer layers of rock to peel away, while in cold mountainous regions, boulders are prised apart when water freezes in cracks in rocks. Chemical weathering, at its greatest in warm, humid regions, is responsible for hollowing out limestone caves and decomposing granites.

The erosion of soil and rock is greatest on sloping land and the steeper the slope, the greater the tendency for mass wasting – the movement of soil and rock downhill under the influence of gravity. The mechanisms of mass wasting (ranging from very slow to very rapid) vary with the type of material, but the presence of water as a lubricant is usually an important factor.

Running water is the world's leading agent of erosion and transportation. The energy of a river depends on several factors, including its velocity and volume, and its erosive power is at its peak when it is in full flood. Sea waves also exert tremendous erosive power during storms when they hurl pebbles against the shore, undercutting cliffs and hollowing out caves.

Glacier ice forms in mountain hollows and spills out to form valley glaciers, which transport rocks shattered by frost action. As glaciers move, rocks embedded into the ice erode steep-sided, U-shaped valleys. Evidence of glaciation in mountain regions includes cirques, knife-edged ridges, or arêtes, and pyramidal peaks.

Oceans

The Great Oceans

Relative sizes of the world's oceans

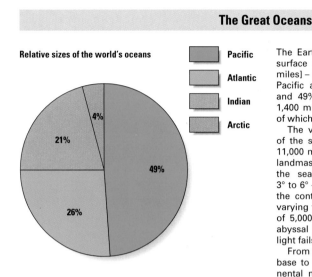

- Pacific
- Atlantic
- Indian
- Arctic

4%
21%
49%
26%

In a strict geographical sense there are only three true oceans – the Atlantic, Indian and Pacific. The legendary 'Seven Seas' would require these to be divided at the Equator and the addition of the Arctic Ocean – which accounts for less than 4% of the total sea area. The International Hydrographic Bureau does not recognize the Antarctic Ocean (even less the 'Southern Ocean') as a separate entity.

The Earth is a watery planet: more than 70% of its surface – over 360,000,000 sq km [140,000,000 sq miles] – is covered by the oceans and seas. The mighty Pacific alone accounts for nearly 36% of the total, and 49% of the sea area. Gravity holds in around 1,400 million cu. km [320 million cu. miles] of water, of which over 97% is saline.

The vast underwater world starts in the shallows of the seaside and plunges to depths of more than 11,000 m [36,000 ft]. The continental shelf, part of the landmass, drops gently to around 200 m [650 ft]; here the seabed falls away suddenly at an angle of 3° to 6° – the continental slope. The third stage, called the continental rise, is more gradual with gradients varying from 1 in 100 to 1 in 700. At an average depth of 5,000 m [16,500 ft] there begins the aptly-named abyssal plain – massive submarine depths where sunlight fails to penetrate and few creatures can survive.

From these plains rise volcanoes which, taken from base to top, rival and even surpass the tallest continental mountains in height. Mount Kea, on Hawaii, reaches a total of 10,203 m [33,400 ft], some 1,355 m [4,500 ft] more than Mount Everest, though scarcely 40% is visible above sea level.

In addition, there are underwater mountain chains up to 1,000 km [600 miles] across, whose peaks sometimes appear above sea level as islands such as Iceland and Tristan da Cunha.

The Ocean Depths

Average and maximum depths of the world's great oceans, in metres

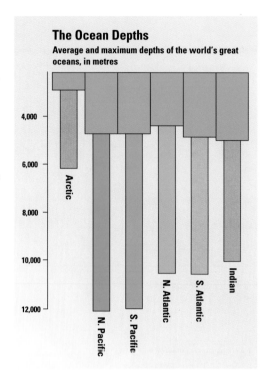

4,000
6,000
8,000
10,000
12,000

Arctic
N. Pacific
S. Pacific
N. Atlantic
S. Atlantic
Indian

Ocean Currents

January temperatures and ocean currents

ACTUAL SURFACE TEMPERATURE

°C
30
20
10
0
-10
-20
-30
-40

OCEAN CURRENTS
Cold   Warm   Speed (knots)
----   ----   Less than 0.5
----   ----   0.5 – 1.0
----   ----   Over 1.0

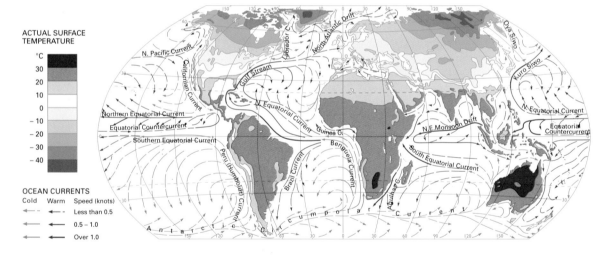

July temperatures and ocean currents

ACTUAL SURFACE TEMPERATURE

°C
30
20
10
0
-10

OCEAN CURRENTS
Cold   Warm   Speed (knots)
----   ----   Less than 0.5
----   ----   0.5 – 1.0
----   ----   Over 1.0

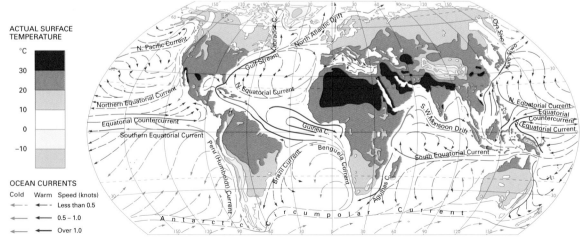

Moving immense quantities of energy as well as billions of tonnes of water every hour, the ocean currents are a vital part of the great heat engine that drives the Earth's climate. They themselves are produced by a twofold mechanism. At the surface, winds push huge masses of water before them; in the deep ocean, below an abrupt temperature gradient that separates the churning surface waters from the still depths, density variations cause slow vertical movements.

The pattern of circulation of the great surface currents is determined by the displacement known as the Coriolis effect. As the Earth turns beneath a moving object – whether it is a tennis ball or a vast mass of water – it appears to be deflected to one side. The deflection is most obvious near the Equator, where the Earth's surface is spinning eastwards at 1,700 km/h [1,050 mph]; currents moving polewards are curved clockwise in the northern hemisphere and anti-clockwise in the southern.

The result is a system of spinning circles known as gyres. The Coriolis effect piles up water on the left of each gyre, creating a narrow, fast-moving stream that is matched by a slower, broader returning current on the right. North and south of the Equator, the fastest currents are located in the west and in the east respectively. In each case, warm water moves from the Equator and cold water returns to it. Cold currents often bring an upwelling of nutrients with them, supporting the world's most economically important fisheries.

Depending on the prevailing winds, some currents on or near the Equator may reverse their direction in the course of the year – a seasonal variation on which Asian monsoon rains depend, and whose occasional failure can bring disaster to millions.

World Fishing Areas

Main commercial fishing areas (numbered FAO regions)

Catch by top marine fishing areas, thousand tonnes (1992)

1. Pacific, NW	[61]	24,199	29.3%
2. Pacific, SE	[87]	13,899	16.8%
3. Atlantic, NE	[27]	11,073	13.4%
4. Pacific, WC	[71]	7,710	9.3%
5. Indian, W	[51]	3,747	4.5%
6. Indian, E	[57]	3,262	4.0%
7. Atlantic, EC	[34]	3,259	3.9%
8. Pacific, NE	[67]	3,149	3.8%

Principal fishing areas

Leading fishing nations

China 17.3% Peru 8.3% Japan 8.0% Chile 5.9% U.S.A. 5.9% Russia 4.4% India 4.3% Indonesia 3.6%

World total (1993): 101,417,500 tonnes
(Marine catch 83.1% Inland catch 16.9%)

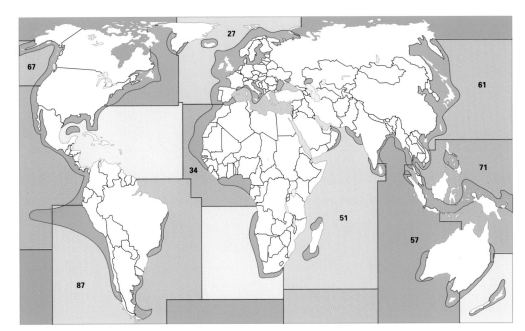

Marine Pollution

Sources of marine oil pollution (latest available year)

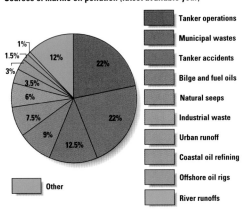

1% 1.5% 3% 3.5% 6% 7.5% 9% 12.5% 22% 22% 12%

- Tanker operations
- Municipal wastes
- Tanker accidents
- Bilge and fuel oils
- Natural seeps
- Industrial waste
- Urban runoff
- Coastal oil refining
- Offshore oil rigs
- River runoffs
- Other

Oil Spills

Major oil spills from tankers and combined carriers

Year	Vessel	Location	Spill (barrels)**	Cause
1979	Atlantic Empress	West Indies	1,890,000	collision
1983	Castillo De Bellver	South Africa	1,760,000	fire
1978	Amoco Cadiz	France	1,628,000	grounding
1991	Haven	Italy	1,029,000	explosion
1988	Odyssey	Canada	1,000,000	fire
1967	Torrey Canyon	UK	909,000	grounding
1972	Sea Star	Gulf of Oman	902,250	collision
1977	Hawaiian Patriot	Hawaiian Is.	742,500	fire
1979	Independenta	Turkey	696,350	collision
1993	Braer	UK	625,000	grounding
1996	Sea Empress	UK	515,000	grounding

Other sources of major oil spills

Year	Source	Location	Spill (barrels)	Cause
1983	Nowruz oilfield	The Gulf	4,250,000†	war
1979	Ixtoc 1 oilwell	Gulf of Mexico	4,200,000	blow-out
1991	Kuwait	The Gulf	2,500,000†	war

** 1 barrel = 0.136 tonnes/159 lit./35 Imperial gal./42 US gal. † estimated

River Pollution

Sources of river pollution, USA (latest available year)

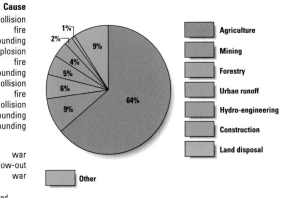

1% 2% 9% 4% 5% 6% 9% 64%

- Agriculture
- Mining
- Forestry
- Urban runoff
- Hydro-engineering
- Construction
- Land disposal
- Other

Water Pollution

- Severely polluted sea areas and lakes
- Polluted sea areas and lakes
- Areas of frequent oil pollution by shipping
- Major oil tanker spills
- Major oil rig blow-outs
- Offshore dumpsites for industrial and municipal waste
- Severely polluted rivers and estuaries

The most notorious tanker spillage of the 1980s occurred when the *Exxon Valdez* ran aground in Prince William Sound, Alaska, in 1989, spilling 267,000 barrels of crude oil close to shore in a sensitive ecological area. This rates as the world's 28th worst spill in terms of volume.

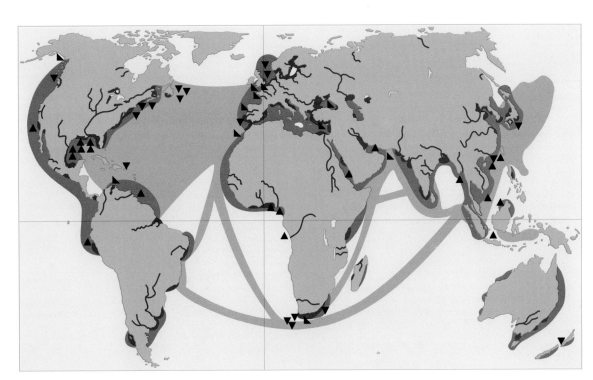

Climate

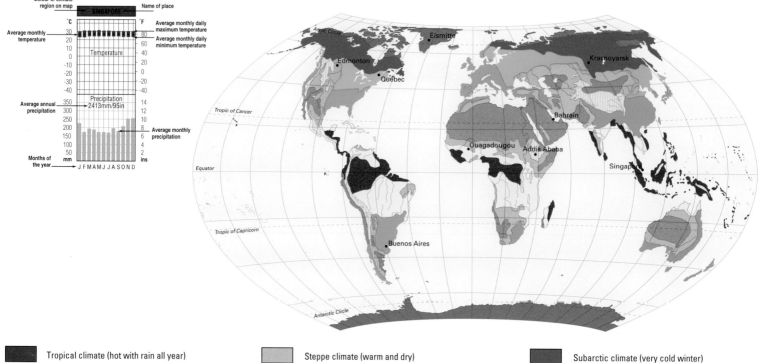

Legend

- Tropical climate (hot with rain all year)
- Desert climate (hot and very dry)
- Savanna climate (hot with dry season)
- Steppe climate (warm and dry)
- Mild climate (warm and wet)
- Continental climate (wet with cold winter)
- Subarctic climate (very cold winter)
- Polar climate (very cold and dry)
- Mountainous climate (altitude affects climate)

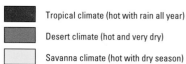

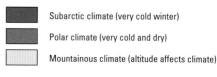
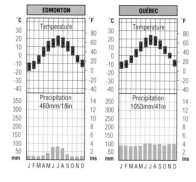
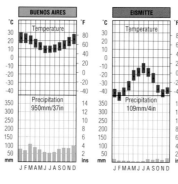
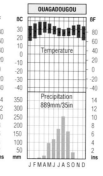
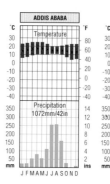
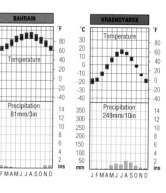

Climate graphs for: EDMONTON (460mm/18in), QUÉBEC (1053mm/41in), BUENOS AIRES (950mm/37in), EISMITTE (109mm/4in), OUAGADOUGOU (889mm/35in), ADDIS ABABA (1072mm/42in), BAHRAIN (81mm/3in), KRASNOYARSK (249mm/10in).

Climate Records

Temperature

Highest recorded shade temperature: Al Aziziyah, Libya, 58°C [136.4°F], 13 September 1922.

Highest mean annual temperature: Dallol, Ethiopia, 34.4°C [94°F], 1960–66.

Longest heatwave: Marble Bar, W. Australia, 162 days over 38°C [100°F], 23 October 1923 to 7 April 1924.

Lowest recorded temperature (outside poles): Verkhoyansk, Siberia, –68°C [–90°F], 6 February 1933.

Lowest mean annual temperature: Plateau Station, Antarctica, –56.6°C [–72.0°F]

Pressure

Longest drought: Calama, N. Chile, no recorded rainfall in 400 years to 1971.

Wettest place (12 months): Cherrapunji, Meghalaya, N. E. India, 26,470 mm [1,040 in], August 1860 to August 1861. Cherrapunji also holds the record for the most rainfall in one month: 2,930 mm [115 in], July 1861.

Wettest place (average): Mawsynram, India, mean annual rainfall 11,873 mm [467.4 in].

Wettest place (24 hours): Cilaos, Réunion, Indian Ocean, 1,870 mm [73.6 in], 15–16 March 1952.

Heaviest hailstones: Gopalganj, Bangladesh, up to 1.02 kg [2.25 lb], 14 April 1986 (killed 92 people).

Heaviest snowfall (continuous): Bessans, Savoie, France, 1,730 mm [68 in] in 19 hours, 5–6 April 1969.

Heaviest snowfall (season/year): Paradise Ranger Station, Mt Rainier, Washington, USA, 31,102 mm [1,224.5 in], 19 February 1971 to 18 February 1972.

Pressure and winds

Highest barometric pressure: Agata, Siberia (at 262 m [862 ft] altitude), 1,083.8 mb, 31 December 1968.

Lowest barometric pressure: Typhoon Tip, Guam, Pacific Ocean, 870 mb, 12 October 1979.

Highest recorded wind speed: Mt Washington, New Hampshire, USA, 371 km/h [231 mph], 12 April 1934. This is three times as strong as hurricane force on the Beaufort Scale.

Windiest place: Commonwealth Bay, Antarctica, where gales frequently reach over 320 km/h [200 mph].

Climate

Climate is weather in the long term: the seasonal pattern of hot and cold, wet and dry, averaged over time (usually 30 years). At the simplest level, it is caused by the uneven heating of the Earth. Surplus heat at the Equator passes towards the poles, levelling out the energy differential. Its passage is marked by a ceaseless churning of the atmosphere and the oceans, further agitated by the Earth's diurnal spin and the motion it imparts to moving air and water. The heat's means of transport – by winds and ocean currents, by the continual evaporation and recondensation of water molecules – is the weather itself. There are four basic types of climate, each of which can be further subdivided: tropical, desert (dry), temperate and polar.

Composition of Dry Air

Nitrogen	78.09%	Sulphur dioxide	trace
Oxygen	20.95%	Nitrogen oxide	trace
Argon	0.93%	Methane	trace
Water vapour	0.2–4.0%	Dust	trace
Carbon dioxide	0.03%	Helium	trace
Ozone	0.00006%	Neon	trace

El Niño

In a normal year, south-easterly trade winds drive surface waters westwards off the coast of South America, drawing cold, nutrient-rich water up from below. In an El Niño year (which occurs every 2–7 years), warm water from the west Pacific suppresses up-welling in the east, depriving the region of nutrients. The water is warmed by as much as 7°C [12°F], disturbing the tropical atmospheric circulation. During an intense El Niño, the south-east trade winds change direction and become equatorial westerlies, resulting in climatic extremes in many regions of the world, such as drought in parts of Australia and India, and heavy rainfall in south-eastern USA. An intense El Niño occurred in 1997–8, with resultant freak weather conditions across the entire Pacific region.

Normal year

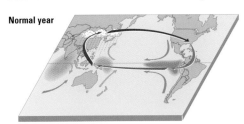

El Niño event

Beaufort Wind Scale

Named after the 19th-century British naval officer who devised it, the Beaufort Scale assesses wind speed according to its effects. It was originally designed as an aid for sailors, but has since been adapted for use on the land.

Scale	Wind speed km/h	mph	Effect
0	0–1	0–1	**Calm** Smoke rises vertically
1	1–5	1–3	**Light air** Wind direction shown only by smoke drift
2	6–11	4–7	**Light breeze** Wind felt on face; leaves rustle; vanes moved by wind
3	12–19	8–12	**Gentle breeze** Leaves and small twigs in constant motion; wind extends small flag
4	20–28	13–18	**Moderate** Raises dust and loose paper; small branches move
5	29–38	19–24	**Fresh** Small trees in leaf sway; wavelets on inland waters
6	39–49	25–31	**Strong** Large branches move; difficult to use umbrellas
7	50–61	32–38	**Near gale** Whole trees in motion; difficult to walk against wind
8	62–74	39–46	**Gale** Twigs break from trees; walking very difficult
9	75–88	47–54	**Strong gale** Slight structural damage
10	89–102	55–63	**Storm** Trees uprooted; serious structural damage
11	103–117	64–72	**Violent storm** Widespread damage
12	118+	73+	**Hurricane**

Conversions

°C = (°F − 32) × 5/9; °F = (°C × 9/5) + 32; 0°C = 32°F
1 in = 25.4 mm; 1 mm = 0.0394 in; 100 mm = 3.94 in

Temperature

Average temperature in January

Temperature
- 30°C
- 20°C
- 10°C
- 0°C
- −10°C
- −20°C
- −30°C
- −40°C

Average temperature in July

Temperature
- 30°C
- 20°C
- 10°C
- 0°C
- −10°C

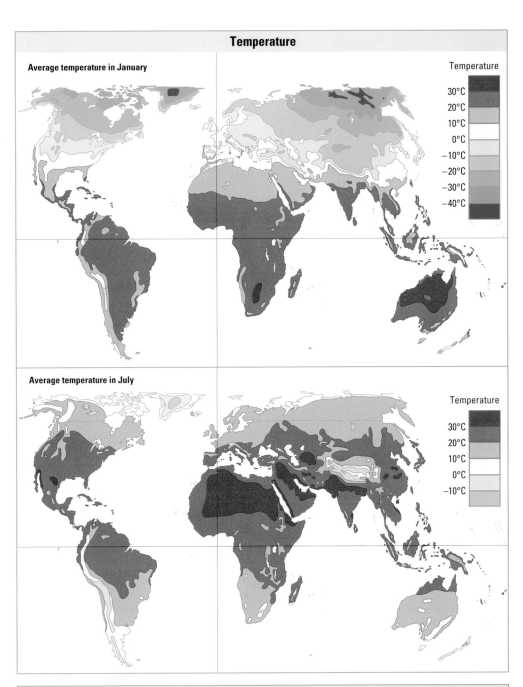

Precipitation

Average annual precipitation
- 3,000 mm
- 2,000 mm
- 1,000 mm
- 500 mm
- 250 mm

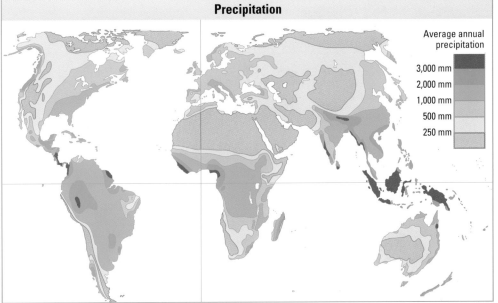

Water and Vegetation

The Hydrological Cycle

The world's water balance is regulated by the constant recycling of water between the oceans, atmosphere and land. The movement of water between these three reservoirs is known as the hydrological cycle. The oceans play a vital role in the hydrological cycle: 74% of the total precipitation falls over the oceans and 84% of the total evaporation comes from the oceans.

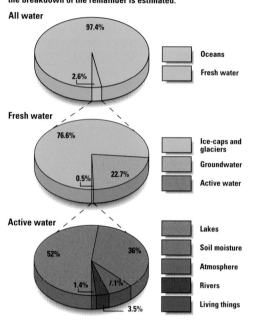

Water Distribution

The distribution of planetary water, by percentage. Oceans and ice-caps together account for more than 99% of the total; the breakdown of the remainder is estimated.

All water

- 97.4% Oceans
- 2.6% Fresh water

Fresh water

- 76.6% Ice-caps and glaciers
- 22.7% Groundwater
- 0.5% Active water

Active water

- 52% Lakes
- 36% Soil moisture
- 1.4% Atmosphere
- 1.1% Rivers
- 3.5% Living things

Water Utilization

| Domestic | Industrial | Agriculture |

The percentage breakdown of water usage by sector, selected countries (latest available year)

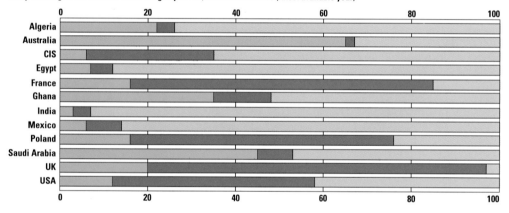

Algeria, Australia, CIS, Egypt, France, Ghana, India, Mexico, Poland, Saudi Arabia, UK, USA

Water Usage

Almost all the world's water is 3,000 million years old, and all of it cycles endlessly through the hydrosphere, though at different rates. Water vapour circulates over days, even hours, deep ocean water circulates over millennia, and ice-cap water remains solid for millions of years.

Fresh water is essential to all terrestrial life. Humans cannot survive more than a few days without it, and even the hardiest desert plants and animals could not exist without some water. Agriculture requires huge quantities of fresh water: without large-scale irrigation most of the world's people would starve. In the USA, agriculture uses 43% and industry 38% of all water withdrawals.

The United States is one of the heaviest users of water in the world. According to the latest figures the average American uses 380 litres a day and the average household uses 415,000 litres a year. This is two to four times more than in Western Europe.

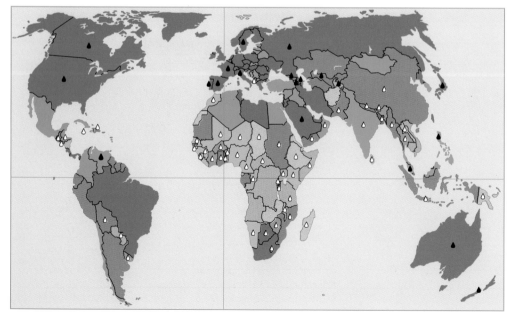

Water Supply

Percentage of total population with access to safe drinking water (average 1990–96)

- Over 90% with safe water
- 75 – 90% with safe water
- 60 – 75% with safe water
- 45 – 60% with safe water
- 30 – 45% with safe water
- Under 30% with safe water

- △ Under 80 litres per person per day domestic water consumption
- ▲ Over 320 litres per person per day domestic water consumption

NB: 80 litres of water a day is considered necessary for a reasonable quality of life.

Least well-provided countries

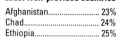

Afghanistan	23%	Papua New Guinea	28%
Chad	24%	Haiti	28%
Ethiopia	25%	Madagascar	29%

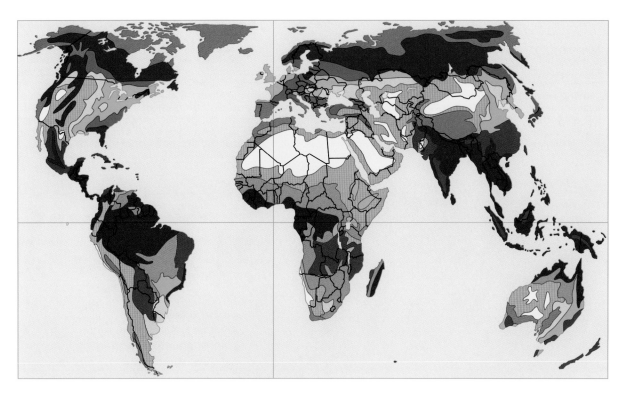

Regional variation in vegetation

Tundra and mountain vegetation

Needleleaf evergreen forest

Mixed needleleaf evergreen & broadleaf deciduous trees

Broadleaf deciduous woodland

Mid-latitude grassland

Evergreen broadleaf and deciduous trees & shrubs

Semi-desert scrub

Desert

Tropical grassland (savanna)

Tropical broadleaf rainforest and monsoon forest

Subtropical broadleaf and needleleaf forest

The map shows the natural 'climax vegetation' of regions, as dictated by climate and topography. In most cases, however, agricultural activity has drastically altered the vegetation pattern. Western Europe, for example, lost most of its broadleaf forest many centuries ago, while irrigation has turned some natural semi-desert into productive land.

Land Use by Continent

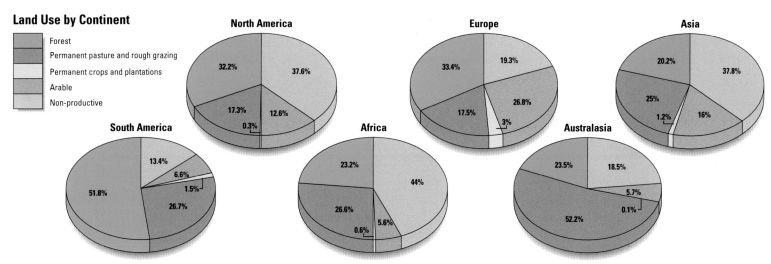

- Forest
- Permanent pasture and rough grazing
- Permanent crops and plantations
- Arable
- Non-productive

North America
37.6% 12.6% 0.3% 17.3% 32.2%

Europe
19.3% 26.8% 3% 17.5% 33.4%

Asia
37.8% 16% 1.2% 25% 20.2%

South America
13.4% 6.6% 1.5% 26.7% 51.8%

Africa
44% 5.6% 0.6% 26.6% 23.2%

Australasia
18.5% 5.7% 0.1% 52.2% 23.5%

Forestry: Production

Annual production (1993, million cubic metres)

	Forest and woodland (million hectares)	Fuelwood and charcoal	Industrial roundwood*
World	**3,987.9**	**1,875.8**	**1,528.5**
CIS	827.8	51.5	172.9
S. America	829.3	247.8	122.0
N. & C. America	709.8	156.7	586.7
Africa	684.6	493.6	59.5
Asia	490.2	866.4	278.1
Europe	157.3	50.9	272.2
Australasia	157.2	8.7	36.9

Paper and Board

Top producers (1993)**		Top exporters (1993)**	
USA	77,250	Canada	12,896
Japan	27,764	Finland	8,526
China	23,816	USA	7,146
Canada	17,557	Sweden	7,008
Germany	13,034	Germany	4,763

* roundwood is timber as it is felled

** in thousand tonnes

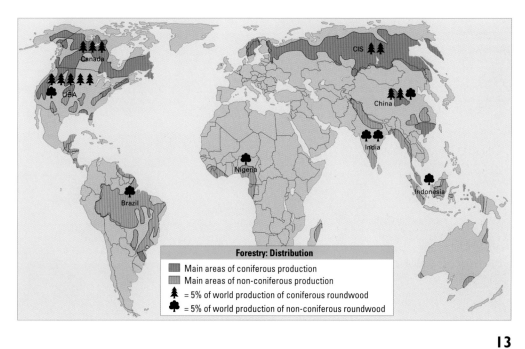

Forestry: Distribution

- Main areas of coniferous production
- Main areas of non-coniferous production
- ♣ = 5% of world production of coniferous roundwood
- ♣ = 5% of world production of non-coniferous roundwood

Environment

Humans have always had a dramatic effect on their environment, at least since the development of agriculture almost 10,000 years ago. Generally, the Earth has accepted human interference without obvious ill effects: the complex systems that regulate the global environment have been able to absorb substantial damage while maintaining a stable and comfortable home for the planet's trillions of lifeforms. But advancing human technology and the rapidly-expanding populations it supports are now threatening to overwhelm the Earth's ability to compensate.

Industrial wastes, acid rainfall, desertification and large-scale deforestation all combine to create environmental change at a rate far faster than the great slow cycles of planetary evolution can accommodate. As a result of overcultivation, overgrazing and overcutting of groundcover for firewood, desertification is affecting as much as 60% of the world's croplands. In addition, with fire and chain-saws, humans are destroying more forest in a day than their ancestors could have done in a century, upsetting the balance between plant and animal, carbon dioxide and oxygen, on which all life ultimately depends.

The fossil fuels that power industrial civilization have pumped enough carbon dioxide and other so-called greenhouse gases into the atmosphere to make climatic change a near-certainty. As a result of the combination of these factors, the Earth's average temperature has risen by approximately 0.5°C [1°F] since the beginning of the 20th century, and it is still rising.

Global Warming

Carbon dioxide emissions in tonnes per person per year (1992)

- Over 10 tonnes of CO_2
- 5 – 10 tonnes of CO_2
- 1 – 5 tonnes of CO_2
- Under 1 tonne of CO_2

Changes in CO_2 emissions 1980–90

- ▲ Over 100% increase in emissions
- ▲ 50–100% increase in emissions
- ▽ Reduction in emissions
- — Coastal areas in danger of flooding from rising sea levels caused by global warming

High atmospheric concentrations of heat-absorbing gases, especially carbon dioxide, appear to be causing a steady rise in average temperatures worldwide – up to 1.5°C [3°F] by the year 2020, according to some estimates. Global warming is likely to bring with it a rise in sea levels that may flood some of the Earth's most densely populated coastal areas.

Greenhouse Power

Relative contributions to the Greenhouse Effect by the major heat-absorbing gases in the atmosphere.

The chart combines greenhouse potency and volume. Carbon dioxide has a greenhouse potential of only 1, but its concentration of 350 parts per million makes it predominate. CFC 12, with 25,000 times the absorption capacity of CO_2, is present only as 0.00044 ppm.

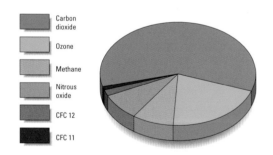

- Carbon dioxide
- Ozone
- Methane
- Nitrous oxide
- CFC 12
- CFC 11

Ozone Layer

The ozone 'hole' over the northern hemisphere on 12 March 1995.

The colours represent Dobson Units (DU). The ozone 'hole' is seen as the dark blue and purple patch in the centre, where ozone values are around 120 DU or lower. Normal levels are around 280 DU. The ozone 'hole' over Antarctica is much larger.

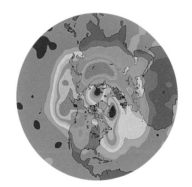

Carbon Dioxide

Carbon dioxide released in millions of tonnes (1992)

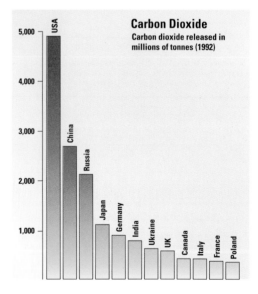

The Greenhouse Effect

Carbon dioxide is increased by burning fossil fuels and cutting forests

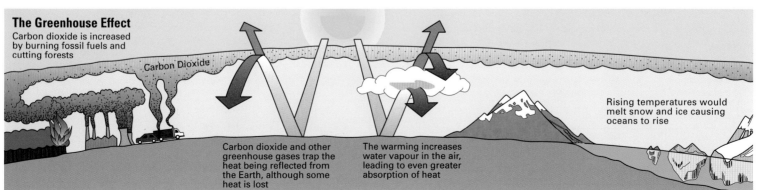

Carbon Dioxide

Carbon dioxide and other greenhouse gases trap the heat being reflected from the Earth, although some heat is lost

The warming increases water vapour in the air, leading to even greater absorption of heat

Rising temperatures would melt snow and ice causing oceans to rise

Desertification

- Existing deserts
- Areas with a high risk of desertification
- Areas with a moderate risk of desertification
- Former areas of rainforest
- Existing rainforest

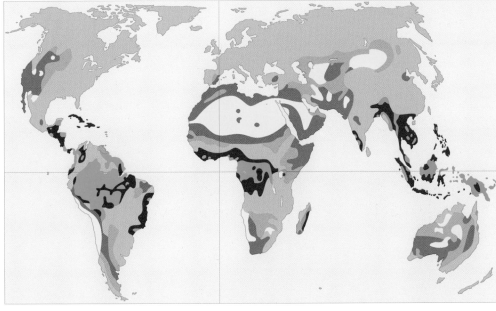

Forest Clearance

Thousands of hectares of forest cleared annually, tropical countries surveyed 1981–85 and 1987–90. Loss as a percentage of remaining stocks is shown in figures on each column.

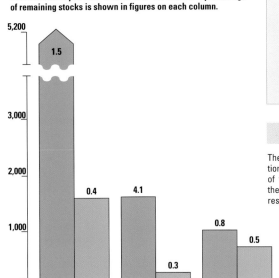

Deforestation

The Earth's remaining forests are under attack from three directions: expanding agriculture, logging, and growing consumption of fuelwood, often in combination. Sometimes deforestation is the direct result of government policy, as in the efforts made to resettle the urban poor in some parts of Brazil; just as often, it comes about despite state attempts at conservation. Loggers, licensed or unlicensed, blaze a trail into virgin forest, often destroying twice as many trees as they harvest. Landless farmers follow, burning away most of what remains to plant their crops, completing the destruction.

▨ 1987–90   ▨ 1981–85

	Brazil	India	Indonesia	Burma	Thailand	Vietnam	Philippines	Costa Rica	Cameroon
1987–90	1.5	4.1	0.8	2.1	2.5	2.0	1.5	7.6	0.6
1981–85	0.4	0.3	0.5	0.3	2.4	0.7	1.0	4.0	0.4

Ozone Depletion

The ozone layer, 25–30 km [15–18 miles] above sea level, acts as a barrier to most of the Sun's harmful ultra-violet radiation, protecting us from the ionizing radiation that can cause skin cancer and cataracts. In recent years, however, two holes in the ozone layer have been observed during winter: one over the Arctic and the other, the size of the USA, over Antarctica. By 1996, ozone had been reduced to around a half of its 1970 amount. The ozone (O_3) is broken down by chlorine released into the atmosphere as CFCs (chlorofluorocarbons) – chemicals used in refrigerators, packaging and aerosols.

Air Pollution

Sulphur dioxide is the main pollutant associated with industrial cities. According to the World Health Organization, at least 600 million people live in urban areas where sulphur dioxide concentrations regularly reach damaging levels. One of the world's most dangerously polluted urban areas is Mexico City, due to a combination of its enclosed valley location, three million cars and 60,000 factories. In May 1998, this lethal cocktail was added to by nearby forest fires and the resultant air pollution led to over 20% of the population (three million people) complaining of respiratory problems.

Acid Rain

Killing trees, poisoning lakes and rivers and eating away buildings, acid rain is mostly produced by sulphur dioxide emissions from industry and volcanic eruptions. By the mid 1990s, acid rain had sterilized 4,000 or more of Sweden's lakes and left 45% of Switzerland's alpine conifers dead or dying, while the monuments of Greece were dissolving in Athens' smog. Prevailing wind patterns mean that the acids often fall many hundred kilometres from where the original pollutants were discharged. In parts of Europe acid deposition has slightly decreased, following reductions in emissions, but not by enough.

World Pollution

Acid rain and sources of acidic emissions (latest available year)

Acid rain is caused by high levels of sulphur and nitrogen in the atmosphere. They combine with water vapour and oxygen to form acids (H_2SO_4 and HNO_3) which fall as precipitation.

 Regions where sulphur and nitrogen oxides are released in high concentrations, mainly from fossil fuel combustion

• Major cities with high levels of air pollution (including nitrogen and sulphur emissions)

Areas of heavy acid deposition

pH numbers indicate acidity, decreasing from a neutral 7. Normal rain, slightly acid from dissolved carbon dioxide, never exceeds a pH of 5.6.

- pH less than 4.0 (most acidic)
- pH 4.0 to 4.5
- pH 4.5 to 5.0

 Areas where acid rain is a potential problem

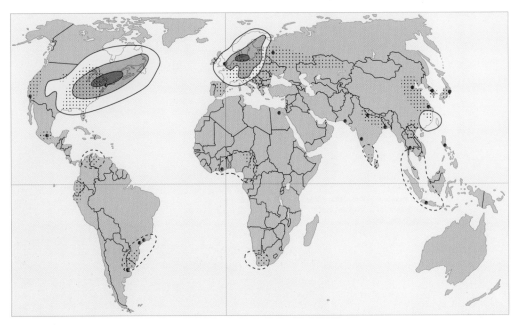

Population

Demographic Profiles

Developed nations such as the UK have populations evenly spread across the age groups and, usually, a growing proportion of elderly people. The great majority of the people in developing nations, however, are in the younger age groups, about to enter their most fertile years. In time, these population profiles should resemble the world profile (even Kenya has made recent progress with reducing its birth rate), but the transition will come about only after a few more generations of rapid population growth.

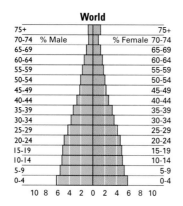

World

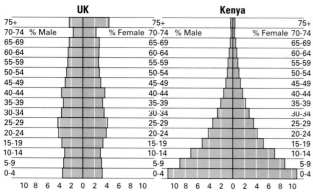

UK   **Kenya**

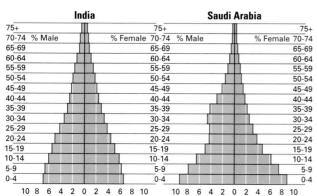

India   **Saudi Arabia**

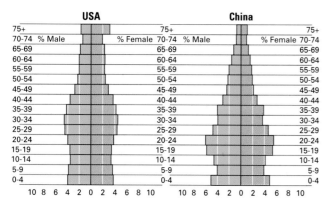

USA   **China**

Most Populous Nations [in millions (1997)]

1.	China	1,210	9. Bangladesh	124	17. Egypt	63
2.	India	980	10. Nigeria	118	18. Thailand	61
3.	USA	268	11. Mexico	97	19. France	59
4.	Indonesia	204	12. Germany	82	20. UK	59
5.	Brazil	160	13. Vietnam	77	21. Ethiopia	59
6.	Russia	148	14. Philippines	74	22. Italy	58
7.	Pakistan	136	15. Iran	70	23. Ukraine	52
8.	Japan	126	16. Turkey	64	24. Burma	48

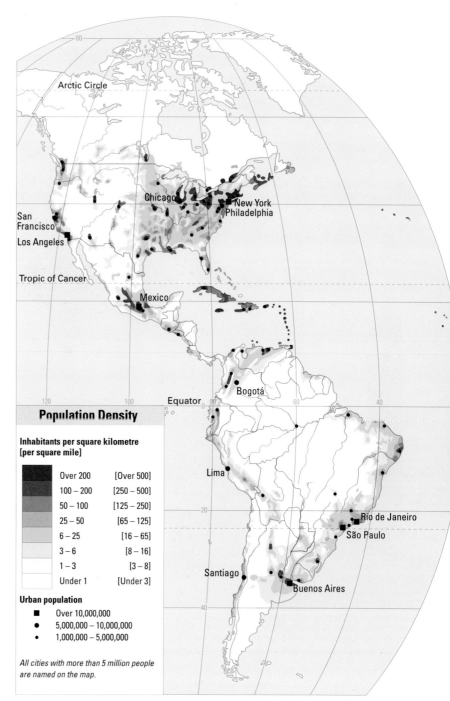

Population Density

Inhabitants per square kilometre [per square mile]

Over 200	[Over 500]
100 – 200	[250 – 500]
50 – 100	[125 – 250]
25 – 50	[65 – 125]
6 – 25	[16 – 65]
3 – 6	[8 – 16]
1 – 3	[3 – 8]
Under 1	[Under 3]

Urban population

- ■ Over 10,000,000
- ● 5,000,000 – 10,000,000
- • 1,000,000 – 5,000,000

All cities with more than 5 million people are named on the map.

Continental Comparisons

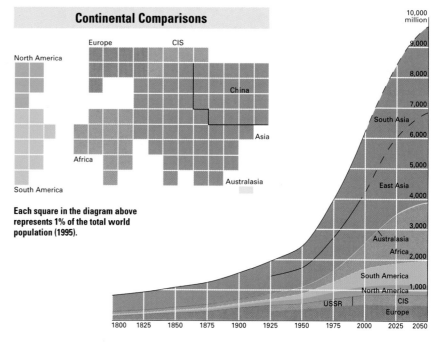

Each square in the diagram above represents 1% of the total world population (1995).

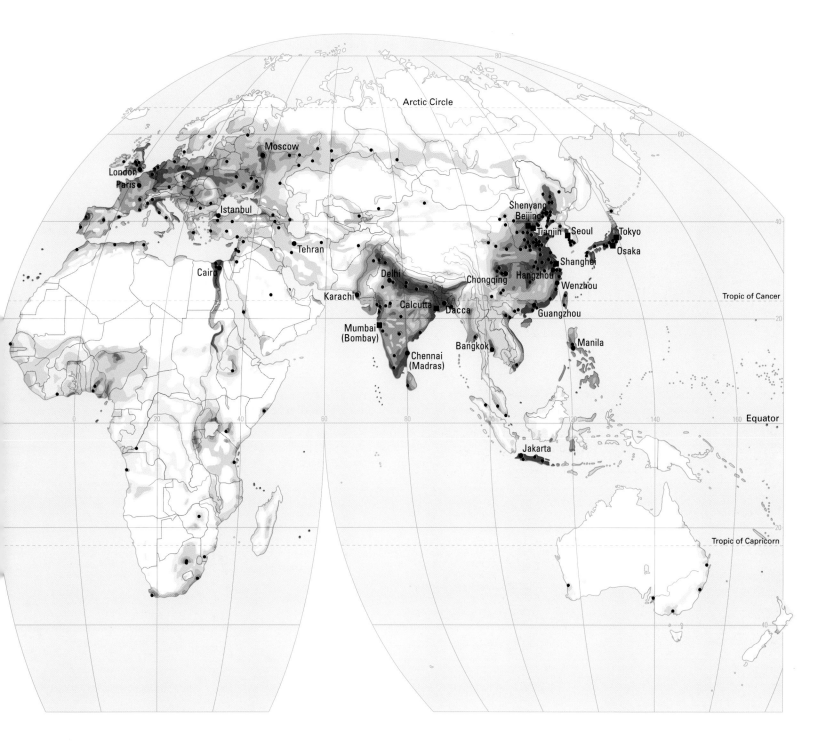

Arctic Circle

Moscow

London
Paris

Istanbul

Tehran

Cairo

Shenyang
Beijing
Tianjin Seoul Tokyo
Shanghai Osaka
Hangzhou
Chongqing Wenzhou

Delhi

Karachi

Calcutta Dacca

Guangzhou

Tropic of Cancer

Mumbai
(Bombay)

Bangkok

Manila

Chennai
(Madras)

Equator

Jakarta

Tropic of Capricorn

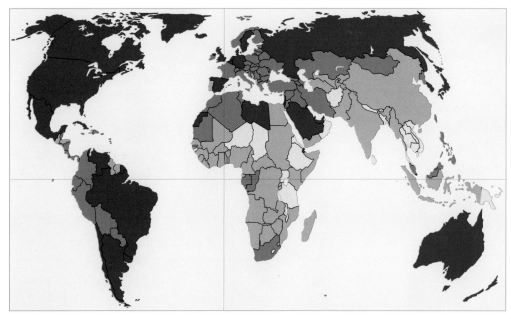

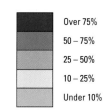

Urban Population

Percentage of total population living in towns and cities (1995)

- Over 75%
- 50 – 75%
- 25 – 50%
- 10 – 25%
- Under 10%

Most urbanized		Least urbanized	
Singapore	100%	Rwanda	6%
Belgium	97%	Bhutan	8%
Kuwait	95%	Burundi	9%
Iceland	93%	Nepal	12%
Venezuela	91%	Uganda	12%

[UK 89%]

The Human Family

Predominant Languages

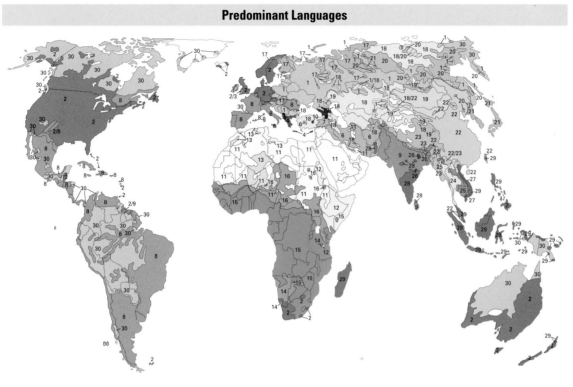

INDO-EUROPEAN FAMILY

1	Balto-Slavic group (incl. Russian, Ukrainian)
2	Germanic group (incl. English, German)
3	Celtic group
4	Greek
5	Albanian
6	Iranian group
7	Armenian
8	Romance group (incl. Spanish, Portuguese, French, Italian)
9	Indo-Aryan group (incl. Hindi, Bengali, Urdu, Punjabi, Marathi)
10	CAUCASIAN FAMILY

AFRO-ASIATIC FAMILY

11	Semitic group (incl. Arabic)
12	Kushitic group
13	Berber group
14	KHOISAN FAMILY
15	NIGER-CONGO FAMILY
16	NILO-SAHARAN FAMILY
17	URALIC FAMILY

ALTAIC FAMILY

18	Turkic group
19	Mongolian group
20	Tungus-Manchu group
21	Japanese and Korean

SINO-TIBETAN FAMILY

22	Sinitic (Chinese) languages
23	Tibetic-Burmic languages
24	TAI FAMILY

AUSTRO-ASIATIC FAMILY

25	Mon-Khmer group
26	Munda group
27	Vietnamese
28	DRAVIDIAN FAMILY (incl. Telugu, Tamil)
29	AUSTRONESIAN FAMILY (incl. Malay-Indonesian)
30	OTHER LANGUAGES

Predominant Religions

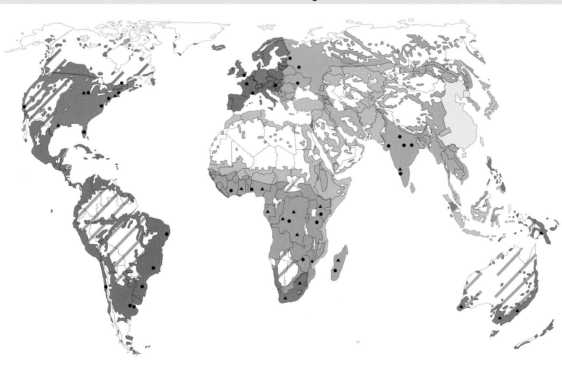

Religious Adherents

Religious adherents in millions:

Christian	1,669	Hindu	663
Roman Catholic	*952*	Buddhist	312
Protestant	*337*	Chinese Folk	172
Orthodox	*162*	Tribal	92
Anglican	*70*	Jewish	18
Other Christian	*148*	Sikhs	17
Muslim	966		
Sunni	*841*		
Shia	*125*		

- Roman Catholicism
- Orthodox and other Eastern Churches
- Protestantism
- Sunni Islam
- Shia Islam
- Buddhism
- Hinduism
- Confucianism
- Judaism
- Shintoism
- Tribal Religions

United Nations

Created in 1945 to promote peace and co-operation and based in New York, the United Nations is the world's largest international organization, with 185 members and an annual budget of US $2.6 billion (1996–97). Each member of the General Assembly has one vote, while the permanent members of the 15-nation Security Council – USA, Russia, China, UK and France – hold a veto. The Secretariat is the UN's principal administrative arm. The 54 members of the Economic and Social Council are responsible for economic, social, cultural, educational, health and related matters. The UN has 16 specialized agencies – based in Canada, France, Switzerland and Italy, as well as the USA – which help members in fields such as education (UNESCO), agriculture (FAO), medicine (WHO) and finance (IFC). By the end of 1994, all the original 11 trust territories of the Trusteeship Council had become independent.

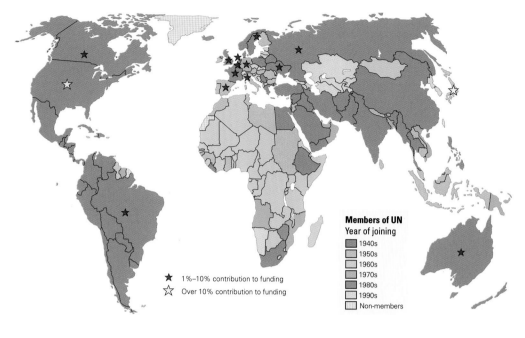

Members of UN
Year of joining
- 1940s
- 1950s
- 1960s
- 1970s
- 1980s
- 1990s
- Non-members

★ 1%–10% contribution to funding
☆ Over 10% contribution to funding

MEMBERSHIP OF THE UN In 1945 there were 51 members; by December 1994 membership had increased to 185 following the admission of Palau. There are 7 independent states which are not members of the UN – Kiribati, Nauru, Switzerland, Taiwan, Tonga, Tuvalu and the Vatican City. All the successor states of the former USSR had joined by the end of 1992. The official languages of the UN are Chinese, English, French, Russian, Spanish and Arabic.

FUNDING The UN budget for 1996–97 was US $2.6 billion. Contributions are assessed by the members' ability to pay, with the maximum 25% of the total, the minimum 0.01%. Contributions for 1996 were: USA 25.0%, Japan 15.4%, Germany 9.0%, France 6.4%, UK 5.3%, Italy 5.2%, Russia 4.5%, Canada 3.1%, Spain 2.4%, Brazil 1.6%, Netherlands 1.6%, Australia 1.5%, Sweden 1.2%, Ukraine 1.1%, Belgium 1.0%.

International Organizations

EU European Union (evolved from the European Community in 1993). The 15 members – Austria, Belgium, Denmark, Finland, France, Germany, Greece, Ireland, Italy, Luxembourg, Netherlands, Portugal, Spain, Sweden and the UK – aim to integrate economies, co-ordinate social developments and bring about political union. These members of what is now the world's biggest market share agricultural and industrial policies and tariffs on trade. The original body, the European Coal and Steel Community (ECSC), was created in 1951 following the signing of the Treaty of Paris.
EFTA European Free Trade Association (formed in 1960). Portugal left the original 'Seven' in 1989 to join what was then the EC, followed by Austria, Finland and Sweden in 1995. Only 4 members remain: Norway, Iceland, Switzerland and Liechtenstein.
ACP African-Caribbean-Pacific (formed in 1963). Members have economic ties with the EU.
NATO North Atlantic Treaty Organization (formed in 1949). It continues after 1991 despite the winding up of the Warsaw Pact. There are 16 member nations.
OAS Organization of American States (formed in 1948). It aims to promote social and economic co-operation between developed countries of North America and developing nations of Latin America.
ASEAN Association of South-east Asian Nations (formed in 1967). Burma and Laos joined in 1997.
OAU Organization of African Unity (formed in 1963). Its 53 members represent over 94% of Africa's population. Arabic, French, Portuguese and English are recognized as working languages.
LAIA Latin American Integration Association (1980). Its aim is to promote freer regional trade.
OECD Organization for Economic Co-operation and Development (formed in 1961). It comprises the 29 major Western free-market economies. Poland, Hungary and South Korea joined in 1996. 'G8' is its 'inner group' comprising Canada, France, Germany, Italy, Japan, Russia, the UK and the USA.
COMMONWEALTH The Commonwealth of Nations evolved from the British Empire; it comprises 16 Queen's realms, 32 republics and 5 indigenous monarchies, giving a total of 53.
OPEC Organization of Petroleum Exporting Countries (formed in 1960). It controls about three-quarters of the world's oil supply. Gabon left the organization in 1996.

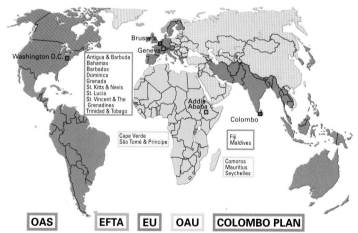

OAS — EFTA — EU — OAU — COLOMBO PLAN

ARAB LEAGUE (formed in 1945). The League's aim is to promote economic, social, political and military co-operation. There are 21 member nations.
COLOMBO PLAN (formed in 1951). Its 26 members aim to promote economic and social development in Asia and the Pacific.

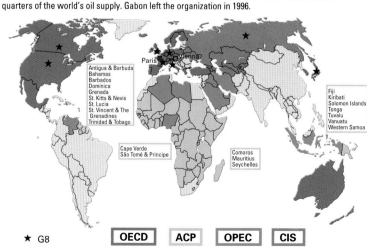

★ G8

OECD — ACP — OPEC — CIS

NATO — LAIA — ARAB LEAGUE — COMMONWEALTH — ASEAN

CARTOGRAPHY BY PHILIP'S. COPYRIGHT GEORGE PHILIP LTD

Wealth

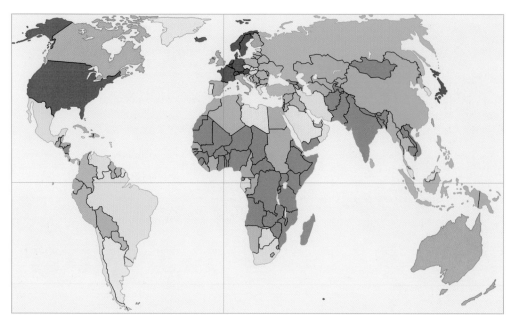

GNP per capita growth rate (%), selected countries, 1985–94

Thailand	8.2	Brazil	–0.4
Chile	6.9	Zimbabwe	–0.6
Japan	3.2	USA	–1.3
Germany	1.9	UK	–1.4
Australia	1.2	Armenia	–12.9

Wealth Creation

The Gross National Product (GNP) of the world's largest economies, US $ million (1995)

1.	USA	7,100,007	23.	Indonesia	190,105
2.	Japan	4,963,587	24.	Turkey	169,452
3.	Germany	2,252,343	25.	Thailand	159,630
4.	France	1,451,051	26.	Denmark	156,027
5.	UK	1,094,734	27.	Hong Kong	142,332
6.	Italy	1,088,085	28.	Norway	136,077
7.	China	744,890	29.	Saudi Arabia	133,540
8.	Brazil	579,787	30.	South Africa	130,918
9.	Canada	573,695	31.	Poland	107,829
10.	Spain	532,347	32.	Finland	105,174
11.	South Korea	435,137	33.	Portugal	96,689
12.	Netherlands	371,039	34.	Israel	87,875
13.	Australia	337,909	35.	Greece	85,885
14.	Russia	331,948	36.	Ukraine	84,084
15.	India	319,660	37.	Singapore	79,831
16.	Mexico	304,596	38.	Malaysia	78,321
17.	Switzerland	286,014	39.	Philippines	71,865
18.	Argentina	278,431	40.	Colombia	70,263
19.	Taiwan	256,300	41.	Venezuela	65,382
20.	Belgium	250,710	42.	Pakistan	59,991
21.	Austria	216,547	43.	Chile	59,151
22.	Sweden	209,720	44.	Peru	55,019

The Wealth Gap

The world's richest and poorest countries, by Gross National Product per capita in US $ (1995)

1.	Luxembourg	41,210	1.	Mozambique	80
2.	Switzerland	40,630	2.	Ethiopia	100
3.	Japan	39,640	3.	Congo (Zaïre)	120
4.	Liechtenstein	38,520	4.	Tanzania	120
5.	Norway	31,250	5.	Burundi	160
6.	Denmark	29,890	6.	Malawi	170
7.	Germany	27,510	7.	Sierra Leone	180
8.	USA	26,980	8.	Rwanda	180
9.	Austria	26,890	9.	Chad	180
10.	Singapore	26,730	10.	Nepal	200
11.	France	24,990	11.	Niger	220
12.	Iceland	24,950	12.	Madagascar	230
13.	Belgium	24,710	13.	Burkina Faso	230
14.	Sweden	23,750	14.	Vietnam	240
15.	Hong Kong	22,990	15.	Uganda	240
16.	Finland	20,580	16.	Bangladesh	240
17.	Canada	19,380	17.	Haiti	250
18.	Italy	19,020	18.	Guinea-Bissau	250
19.	Australia	18,720	19.	Yemen	250
20.	UK	18,700	20.	Nigeria	260

GNP per capita is calculated by dividing a country's Gross National Product by its total population.

Continental Shares

Shares of population and of wealth (GNP) by continent

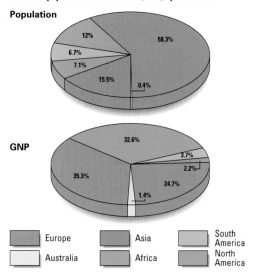

Population

GNP

Europe   Asia   South America

Australia   Africa   North America

Inflation

Average annual rate of inflation (1980–93)

Over 50%

20 – 50%

7.5 – 20%

1 – 7.5%

Negative inflation

No data available

Highest average inflation		Lowest average inflation	
Nicaragua	665%	Brunei	–5.1%
Brazil	423%	Oman	–2.3%
Argentina	374%	Saudi Arabia	–2.1%
Peru	316%	Equatorial Guinea	–0.6%
Bolivia	187%	Congo	–0.6%
Israel	70%	Bahrain	–0.3%
Poland	69%	Libya	0.2%

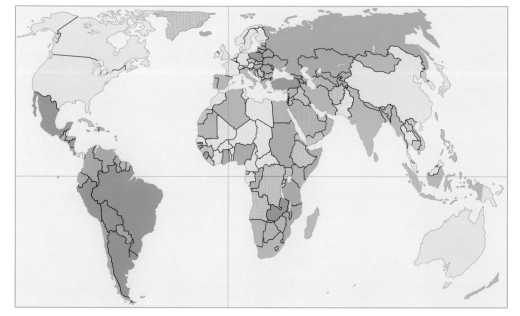

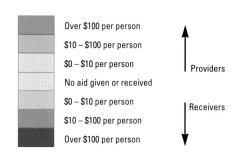

International Aid

Aid provided or received, divided by the total population, in US $ (1995)

Over $100 per person
$10 – $100 per person
$0 – $10 per person
No aid given or received
$0 – $10 per person
$10 – $100 per person
Over $100 per person

Providers
Receivers

Top 5 providers per capita (1994)		Top 5 receivers per capita (1994)	
France	$279	São Tomé & P.	$378
Denmark	$260	Cape Verde	$314
Norway	$247	Djibouti	$235
Sweden	$201	Surinam	$198
Germany	$166	Mauritania	$153

Debt and Aid

International debtors and the aid they receive (1993)

Although aid grants make a vital contribution to many of the world's poorer countries, they are usually dwarfed by the burden of debt that the developing economies are expected to repay. In 1992, they had to pay US $160,000 million in debt service charges alone – more than two and a half times the amount of Official Development Assistance (ODA) the developing countries were receiving, and US $60,000 million more than total private flows of aid in the same year. In 1990, the debts of Mozambique, one of the world's poorest countries, were estimated to be 75 times its entire earnings from exports.

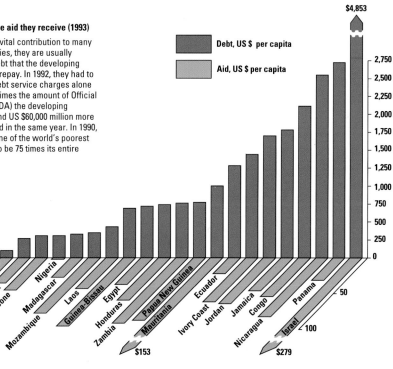

Debt, US $ per capita
Aid, US $ per capita

Distribution of Spending

Percentage share of household spending, selected countries

Food
Medicine & Education
Clothing
Transport
Energy & Housing
Other

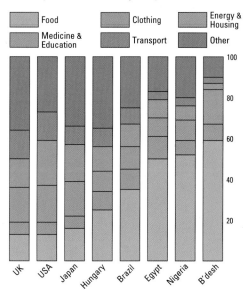

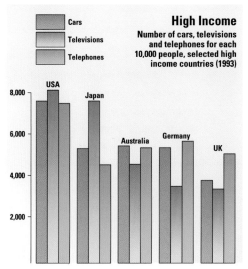

High Income

Cars
Televisions
Telephones

Number of cars, televisions and telephones for each 10,000 people, selected high income countries (1993)

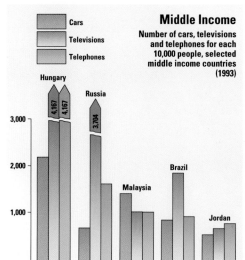

Middle Income

Cars
Televisions
Telephones

Number of cars, televisions and telephones for each 10,000 people, selected middle income countries (1993)

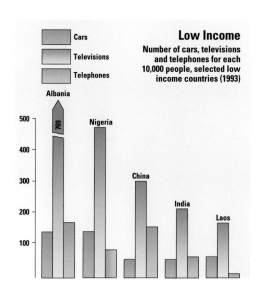

Low Income

Cars
Televisions
Telephones

Number of cars, televisions and telephones for each 10,000 people, selected low income countries (1993)

Quality of Life

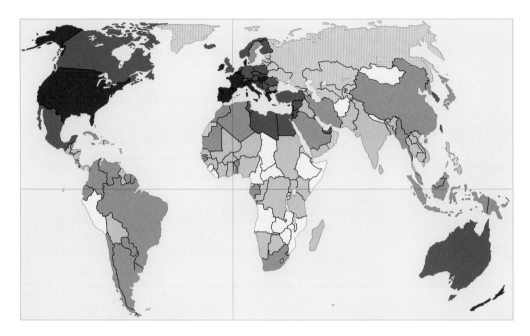

Hospital Capacity

Hospital beds available for each 1,000 people (1993)

Highest capacity		Lowest capacity	
Japan	13.6	Bangladesh	0.2
Kazakstan	13.5	Ethiopia	0.2
Ukraine	13.5	Nepal	0.3
Russia	13.5	Burkina Faso	0.4
Latvia	13.5	Afghanistan	0.5
North Korea	13.5	Pakistan	0.6
Moldova	12.8	Niger	0.6
Belarus	12.7	Mali	0.6
Finland	12.3	Indonesia	0.6
France	12.2	Guinea	0.6

[UK 6.4] [USA 4.6]

Although the ratio of people to hospital beds gives a good approximation of a country's health provision, it is not an absolute indicator. Raw numbers may mask inefficiency and other weaknesses: the high availability of beds in Kazakstan, for example, has not prevented infant mortality rates over three times as high as in the United Kingdom and the United States.

Life Expectancy

Years of life expectancy at birth, selected countries (1990–95)

The chart shows combined data for both sexes. On average, women live longer than men worldwide, even in developing countries with high maternal mortality rates. Overall, life expectancy is steadily rising, though the difference between rich and poor nations remains dramatic.

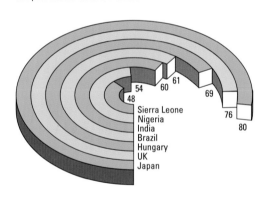

Sierra Leone 48
Nigeria 54
India 60
Brazil 61
Hungary 69
UK 76
Japan 80

Causes of Death

Causes of death for selected countries by % (1992–94)

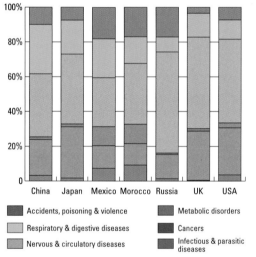

China Japan Mexico Morocco Russia UK USA

Accidents, poisoning & violence	Metabolic disorders
Respiratory & digestive diseases	Cancers
Nervous & circulatory diseases	Infectious & parasitic diseases

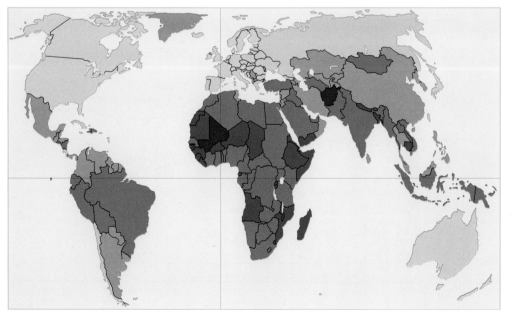

Child Mortality

Number of babies who will die under the age of one, per 1,000 births (average 1990–95)

	Over 150 deaths per 1,000 births
	100 – 150 deaths per 1,000 births
	50 – 100 deaths per 1,000 births
	20 – 50 deaths per 1,000 births
	10 – 20 deaths per 1,000 births
	Under 10 deaths per 1,000 births

Highest child mortality
Afghanistan 162
Mali..................................... 159
Sierra Leone....................... 143
Guinea-Bissau 140
Malawi 138

Lowest child mortality
Hong Kong 6
Denmark 6
Japan 5
Iceland 5
Finland 5

[UK 8 deaths]

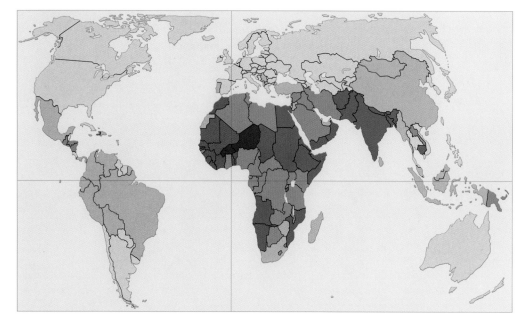

Percentage of the total population unable to read or write (latest available year)

- Over 75% of population illiterate
- 50 – 75% of population illiterate
- 25 – 50% of population illiterate
- 10 – 15% of population illiterate
- Under 10% of population illiterate

Educational expenditure per person (latest available year)

Top 5 countries		Bottom 5 countries	
Sweden	$997	Chad	$2
Qatar	$989	Bangladesh	$3
Canada	$983	Ethiopia	$3
Norway	$971	Nepal	$4
Switzerland	$796	Somalia	$4

Fertility and Education

Fertility rates compared with female education, selected countries (1992–95)

- Percentage of females aged 12–17 in secondary education
- Fertility rate: average number of children borne per woman

Denmark, Austria, France, Canada, Belgium, Switzerland, UK, Poland, Australia, Sri Lanka, Malaysia, Turkey, Saudi Arabia, Thailand, Bolivia, Nigeria, Sierra Leone, Niger

Living Standards

At first sight, most international contrasts in living standards are swamped by differences in wealth. The rich not only have more money, they have more of everything, including years of life. Those with only a little money are obliged to spend most of it on food and clothing, the basic maintenance costs of their existence; air travel and tourism are unlikely to feature on their expenditure lists. However, poverty and wealth are both relative: slum dwellers living on social security payments in an affluent industrial country have far more resources at their disposal than an average African peasant, but feel their own poverty nonetheless. A middle-class Indian lawyer cannot command a fraction of the earnings of a counterpart living in New York, London or Rome; nevertheless, he rightly sees himself as prosperous.

The rich not only live longer, on average, than the poor, they also die from different causes. Infectious and parasitic diseases, all but eliminated in the developed world, remain a scourge in the developing nations. On the other hand, more than two-thirds of the populations of OECD nations eventually succumb to cancer or circulatory disease.

Women in the Workforce

Women in paid employment as a percentage of the total workforce (latest available year)

- Over 50% are women
- 40 – 50% are women
- 30 – 40% are women
- 20 – 30% are women
- 10 – 20% are women
- Under 10% are women

Most women in the workforce		Fewest women in the workforce	
Cambodia	56%	Saudi Arabia	4%
Kazakstan	54%	Oman	6%
Burundi	53%	Afghanistan	8%
Mozambique	53%	Algeria	9%
Turkmenistan	52%	Libya	9%

[USA 45] [UK 44]

Energy

Production

North America

Europe

CIS

Middle East

Japan

Africa

Asia

South America

Australasia

Consumption

North America

Europe

CIS

Middle East

Japan

Africa

Asia

South America

Australasia

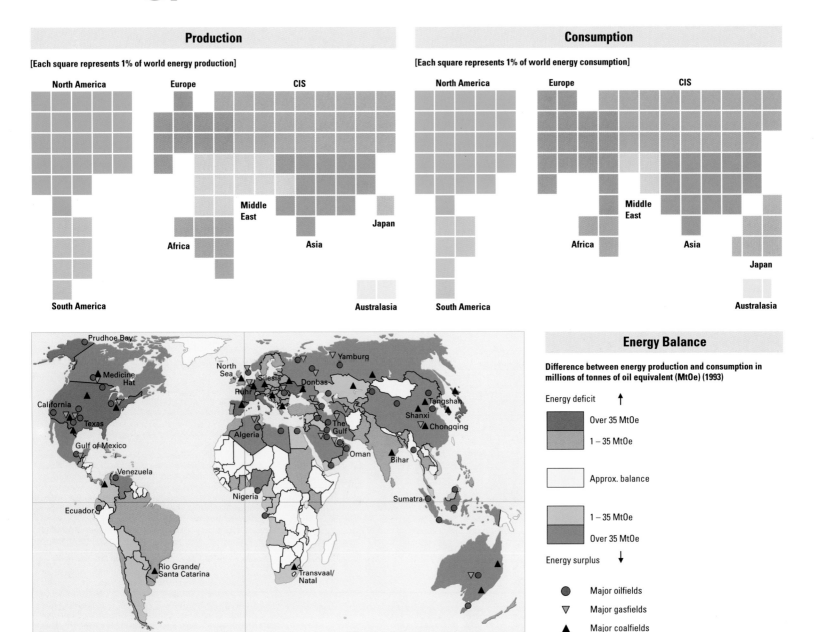

Prudhoe Bay

Medicine Hat

California

Texas

Gulf of Mexico

Venezuela

Ecuador

Rio Grande/
Santa Catarina

North Sea

Silesia

Ruhr

Algeria

Nigeria

Transvaal/
Natal

Yamburg

Donbas

The Gulf

Oman

Tangshan

Shanxi

Chongqing

Bihar

Sumatra

Energy Balance

Difference between energy production and consumption in millions of tonnes of oil equivalent (MtOe) (1993)

Energy deficit ↑

Over 35 MtOe

1 – 35 MtOe

Approx. balance

1 – 35 MtOe

Over 35 MtOe

Energy surplus ↓

● Major oilfields

▽ Major gasfields

▲ Major coalfields

World Energy Consumption

Energy consumed by world regions, measured in million tonnes of oil equivalent in 1993. Total world consumption was 7,804 MtOe. Only energy from oil, gas, coal, nuclear and hydroelectric sources are included. Excluded are fuels such as wood, peat, animal waste, wind, solar and geothermal which, though important in some countries, are unreliably documented in terms of consumption statistics.

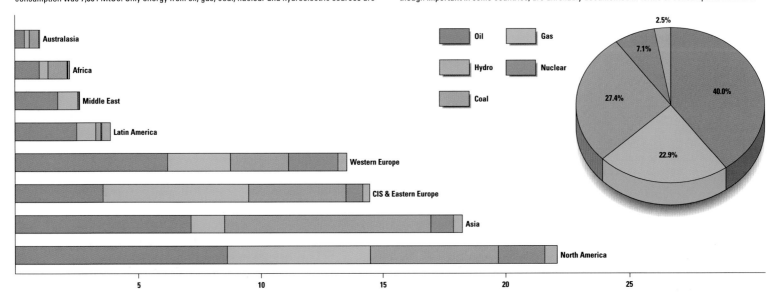

Australasia

Africa

Middle East

Latin America

Western Europe

CIS & Eastern Europe

Asia

North America

5   10   15   20   25

Oil   Gas

Hydro   Nuclear

Coal

2.5%

7.1%

40.0%

27.4%

22.9%

Energy

Energy is used to keep us warm or cool, fuel our industries and our transport systems, and even feed us; high-intensity agriculture, with its use of fertilizers, pesticides and machinery, is heavily energy-dependent. Although we live in a high-energy society, there are vast discrepancies between rich and poor; for example, a North American consumes 13 times as much energy as a Chinese person. But even developing nations have more power at their disposal than was imaginable a century ago.

The distribution of energy supplies, most importantly fossil fuels (coal, oil and natural gas), is very uneven. In addition, the diagrams and map opposite show that the largest producers of energy are not necessarily the largest consumers. The movement of energy supplies around the world is therefore an important component of international trade. In 1995, total world movements in oil amounted to 1,815 million tonnes.

As the finite reserves of fossil fuels are depleted, renewable energy sources, such as solar, hydro-thermal, wind, tidal and biomass, will become increasingly important around the world.

Nuclear Power

Percentage of electricity generated by nuclear power stations, leading nations (1995)

1. Lithuania..............85%	11. Spain....................33%
2. France.................77%	12. Finland................30%
3. Belgium...............56%	13. Germany............29%
4. Slovak Rep. 49%	14. Japan..................29%
5. Sweden................48%	15. UK.......................27%
6. Bulgaria..............41%	16. Ukraine...............27%
7. Hungary..............41%	17. Czech Rep. 22%
8. Switzerland........39%	18. Canada................19%
9. Slovenia..............38%	19. USA.....................18%
10. South Korea........33%	20. Russia................. 12%

Although the 1980s were a bad time for the nuclear power industry (major projects ran over budget, and fears of long-term environmental damage were heavily reinforced by the 1986 disaster at Chernobyl), the industry picked up in the early 1990s. However, whilst the number of reactors is still increasing, orders for new plants have shrunk. This is partly due to the increasingly difficult task of disposing of nuclear waste.

Hydroelectricity

Percentage of electricity generated by hydroelectric power stations, leading nations (1995)

1. Paraguay...........99.9%	11. Rwanda.............97.6%
2. Congo (Zaïre)....99.7%	12. Malawi..............97.6%
3. Bhutan.............99.6%	13. Cameroon..........96.9%
4. Zambia.............99.5%	14. Nepal.................96.7%
5. Norway.............99.4%	15. Laos...................95.3%
6. Ghana..............99.3%	16. Albania..............95.2%
7. Congo...............99.3%	17. Iceland...............94.0%
8. Uganda.............99.1%	17. Brazil 92.2%
9. Burundi.............98.3%	19. Honduras..........87.6%
10. Uruguay............98.0%	20. Tanzania............87.1%

Countries heavily reliant on hydroelectricity are usually small and non-industrial: a high proportion of hydroelectric power more often reflects a modest energy budget than vast hydroelectric resources. The USA, for instance, produces only 9% of power requirements from hydroelectricity; yet that 9% amounts to more than three times the hydropower generated by all of Africa.

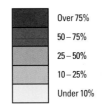

Fuel Exports

Fuels as a percentage of total value of exports (1990–94)

- Over 75%
- 50 – 75%
- 25 – 50%
- 10 – 25%
- Under 10%

Conversion Rates

1 barrel = 0.136 tonnes or 159 litres or 35 Imperial gallons or 42 US gallons

1 tonne = 7.33 barrels or 1,185 litres or 256 Imperial gallons or 261 US gallons

1 tonne oil = 1.5 tonnes hard coal or 3.0 tonnes lignite or 12,000 kWh

1 Imperial gallon = 1.201 US gallons or 4.546 litres or 277.4 cubic inches

Measurements
For historical reasons, oil is traded in 'barrels'. The weight and volume equivalents (shown right) are all based on average-density 'Arabian light' crude oil.

The energy equivalents given for a tonne of oil are also somewhat imprecise: oil and coal of different qualities will have varying energy contents, a fact usually reflected in their price on world markets.

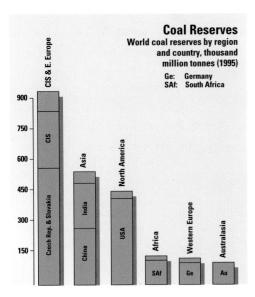

Coal Reserves
World coal reserves by region and country, thousand million tonnes (1995)

Ge: Germany
SAf: South Africa

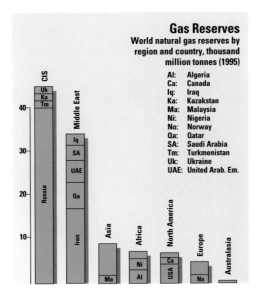

Gas Reserves
World natural gas reserves by region and country, thousand million tonnes (1995)

Al: Algeria
Ca: Canada
Iq: Iraq
Ka: Kazakstan
Ma: Malaysia
Ni: Nigeria
No: Norway
Qa: Qatar
SA: Saudi Arabia
Tm: Turkmenistan
Uk: Ukraine
UAE: United Arab. Em.

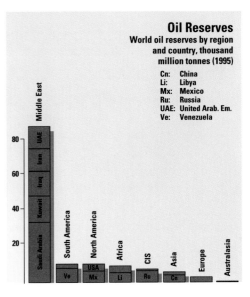

Oil Reserves
World oil reserves by region and country, thousand million tonnes (1995)

Cn: China
Li: Libya
Mx: Mexico
Ru: Russia
UAE: United Arab. Em.
Ve: Venezuela

Production

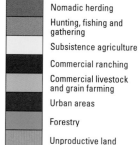

Agriculture

Predominant type of farming or land use.

- Nomadic herding
- Hunting, fishing and gathering
- Subsistence agriculture
- Commercial ranching
- Commercial livestock and grain farming
- Urban areas
- Forestry
- Unproductive land

The development of agriculture transformed human existence more than any other. The whole business of farming is constantly developing: due mainly to new varieties of rice and wheat, world grain production has increased by over 70% since 1965. New machinery and modern agricultural techniques enable relatively few farmers to produce enough food for the world's 5,800 million people.

Staple Crops

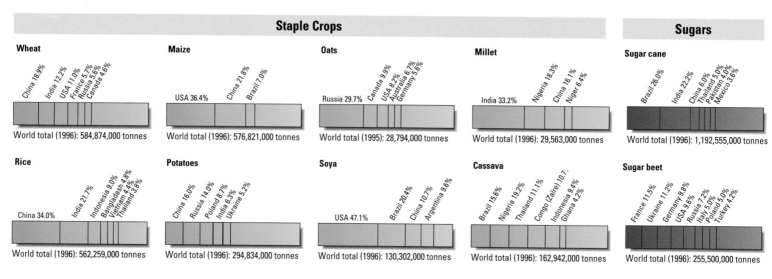

Wheat

China 18.9%
India 12.2%
USA 11.0%
France 5.7%
Russia 5.6%
Canada 4.6%

World total (1996): 584,874,000 tonnes

Maize

USA 36.4%
China 21.8%
Brazil 7.0%

World total (1996): 576,821,000 tonnes

Oats

Russia 29.7%
Canada 9.9%
USA 8.2%
Australia 6.7%
Germany 5.6%

World total (1995): 28,794,000 tonnes

Millet

India 33.2%
Nigeria 18.3%
China 16.1%
Niger 6.4%

World total (1996): 29,563,000 tonnes

Rice

China 34.0%
India 21.7%
Indonesia 9.0%
Bangladesh 4.8%
Vietnam 4.4%
Thailand 3.8%

World total (1996): 562,259,000 tonnes

Potatoes

China 16.0%
Russia 14.0%
Poland 8.7%
India 6.3%
Ukraine 5.2%

World total (1996): 294,834,000 tonnes

Soya

USA 47.1%
Brazil 20.4%
China 10.7%
Argentina 9.6%

World total (1996): 130,302,000 tonnes

Cassava

Brazil 15.6%
Nigeria 19.2%
Thailand 11.1%
Congo (Zaire) 10.7%
Indonesia 9.4%
Ghana 4.2%

World total (1996): 162,942,000 tonnes

Sugars

Sugar cane

Brazil 26.0%
India 22.2%
China 6.0%
Thailand 5.0%
Pakistan 4.0%
Mexico 3.6%

World total (1996): 1,192,555,000 tonnes

Sugar beet

France 11.5%
Ukraine 11.2%
Germany 9.8%
USA 8.6%
Russia 5.2%
Italy 5.0%
Poland 5.0%
Turkey 4.2%

World total (1996): 255,500,000 tonnes

Balance of Employment

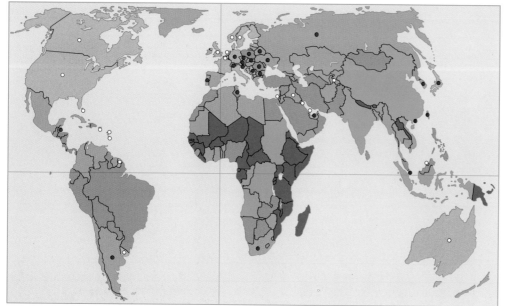

Percentage of total workforce employed in agriculture, including forestry and fishing (1990–92)

- Over 75% in agriculture
- 50 – 75% in agriculture
- 25 – 50% in agriculture
- 10 – 25% in agriculture
- Under 10% in agriculture

Employment in industry and services

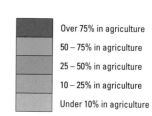

- ● Over a third of total workforce employed in manufacturing

- ○ Over two-thirds of total workforce employed in service industries (work in offices, shops, tourism, transport, construction and government)

Mineral Production

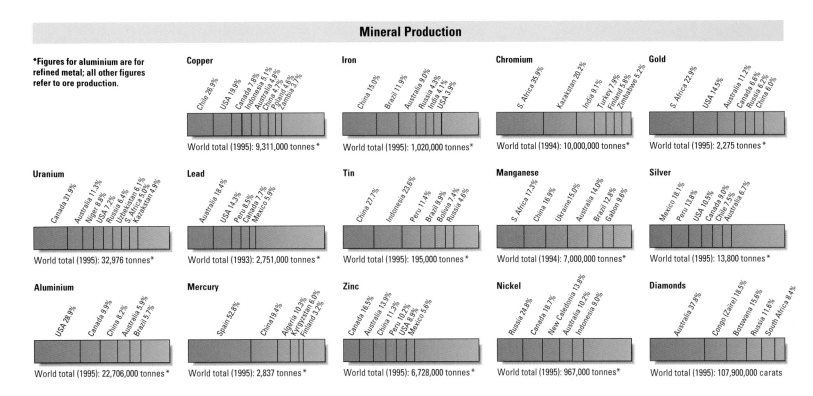

*Figures for aluminium are for refined metal; all other figures refer to ore production.

Copper
Chile 26.9% | USA 19.9% | Canada 7.8% | Indonesia 5.1% | Australia 4.8% | China 4.7% | Poland 4.6% | Zambia 3.7%
World total (1995): 9,311,000 tonnes *

Iron
China 15.0% | Brazil 11.9% | Australia 9.0% | Russia 4.3% | India 4.1% | USA 3.9%
World total (1995): 1,020,000 tonnes *

Chromium
S. Africa 35.9% | Kazakstan 20.2% | India 9.1% | Turkey 7.9% | Finland 5.8% | Zimbabwe 5.2%
World total (1994): 10,000,000 tonnes *

Gold
S. Africa 22.9% | USA 14.5% | Australia 11.2% | Canada 6.6% | Russia 6.2% | China 6.0%
World total (1995): 2,275 tonnes *

Uranium
Canada 31.9% | Australia 11.3% | Niger 8.8% | USA 7.2% | Russia 6.4% | Uzbekistan 6.1% | S Africa 5.0% | Kazakstan 4.9%
World total (1995): 32,976 tonnes *

Lead
Australia 18.4% | USA 14.3% | Peru 8.5% | Canada 7.7% | Mexico 5.9%
World total (1993): 2,751,000 tonnes *

Tin
China 27.7% | Indonesia 23.6% | Peru 11.4% | Brazil 9.9% | Bolivia 7.4% | Russia 4.6%
World total (1995): 195,000 tonnes *

Manganese
S. Africa 17.3% | China 16.9% | Ukraine 15.0% | Australia 14.0% | Brazil 12.8% | Gabon 9.6%
World total (1994): 7,000,000 tonnes *

Silver
Mexico 18.1% | Peru 13.9% | USA 10.5% | Canada 9.0% | Chile 7.5% | Australia 6.7%
World total (1995): 13,800 tonnes *

Aluminium
USA 28.9% | Canada 9.9% | China 8.2% | Australia 5.9% | Brazil 5.7%
World total (1995): 22,706,000 tonnes *

Mercury
Spain 52.8% | China 19.4% | Algeria 10.3% | Kyrgyzstan 6.0% | Finland 3.2%
World total (1995): 2,837 tonnes *

Zinc
Canada 16.5% | Australia 13.9% | China 11.3% | Peru 10.2% | USA 8.9% | Mexico 5.6%
World total (1995): 6,728,000 tonnes *

Nickel
Russia 24.8% | Canada 18.7% | New Caledonia 13.8% | Australia 10.2% | Indonesia 9.0%
World total (1995): 967,000 tonnes*

Diamonds
Australia 37.8% | Congo (Zaire) 18.5% | Botswana 15.6% | Russia 11.6% | South Africa 8.4%
World total (1995): 107,900,000 carats

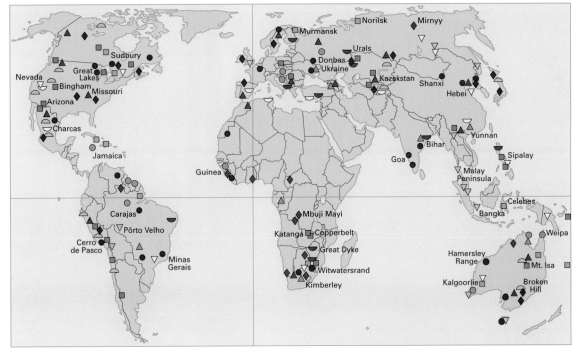

Mineral Distribution

The map shows the richest sources of the most important minerals. Major mineral locations are named.

Light metals
- Bauxite

Base metals
- Copper
- Lead
- Mercury
- Tin
- Zinc

Iron and ferro-alloys
- Iron
- Chrome
- Manganese
- Nickel

Precious metals
- Gold
- Silver

Precious stones
- Diamonds

The map does not show undersea deposits, most of which are considered inaccessible.

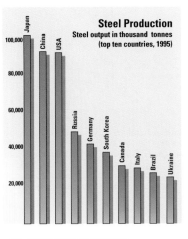

Steel Production
Steel output in thousand tonnes (top ten countries, 1995)

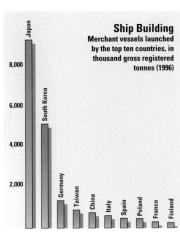

Ship Building
Merchant vessels launched by the top ten countries, in thousand gross registered tonnes (1996)

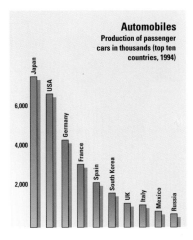

Automobiles
Production of passenger cars in thousands (top ten countries, 1994)

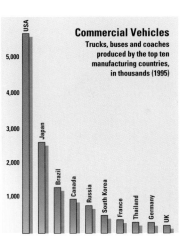

Commercial Vehicles
Trucks, buses and coaches produced by the top ten manufacturing countries, in thousands (1995)

Trade

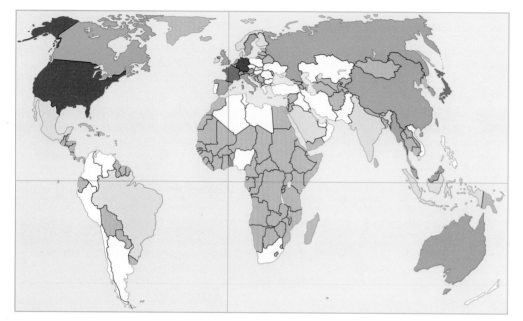

International trade is dominated by a handful of powerful maritime nations. The members of 'G8', the inner circle of OECD (see page 19), and the top seven countries listed in the diagram below, account for more than half the total. The majority of nations – including all but four in Africa – contribute less than one quarter of 1% to the worldwide total of exports; the EU countries account for 40%, the Pacific Rim nations over 35%.

The Main Trading Nations

The imports and exports of the top ten trading nations as a percentage of world trade (1994). Each country's trade in manufactured goods is shown in dark blue.

16 14 12 10 8 6 4 2 0		0 2 4 6 8 10 12 14
	USA	
	Japan	
	Germany	
	France	
	UK	
	Italy	
	Benelux	
	Netherlands	
	Canada	
	Switzerland	
	Taiwan	
	South Korea	

Imports   **Exports**

Patterns of Trade

Thriving international trade is the outward sign of a healthy world economy, the obvious indicator that some countries have goods to sell and others the means to buy them. Global exports expanded to an estimated US $3.92 trillion in 1994, an increase due partly to economic recovery in industrial nations but also to export-led growth strategies in many developing nations and lowered regional trade barriers. International trade remains dominated, however, by the rich, industrialized countries of the Organization for Economic Development: between them, OECD members account for almost 75% of world imports and exports in most years. However, continued rapid economic growth in some developing countries is altering global trade patterns. The 'tiger economies' of South-east Asia are particularly vibrant, averaging more than 8% growth between 1992 and 1994. The size of the largest trading economies means that imports and exports usually represent only a small percentage of their total wealth. In export-concious Japan, for example, trade in goods and services amounts to less than 18% of GDP. In poorer countries, trade – often in a single commodity – may amount to 50% of GDP.

Traded Products

Top ten manufactures traded, by value in billions of US $ (latest available year)

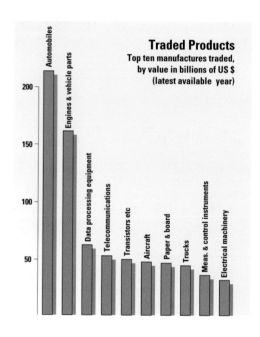

Balance of Trade

Value of exports in proportion to the value of imports (1995)

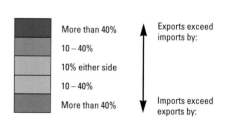

More than 40%   Exports exceed imports by:

10 – 40%

10% either side

10 – 40%

More than 40%   Imports exceed exports by:

The total world trade balance should amount to zero, since exports must equal imports on a global scale. In practice, at least $100 billion in exports go unrecorded, leaving the world with an apparent deficit and many countries in a better position than public accounting reveals. However, a favourable trade balance is not necessarily a sign of prosperity: many poorer countries must maintain a high surplus in order to service debts, and do so by restricting imports below the levels needed to sustain successful economies.

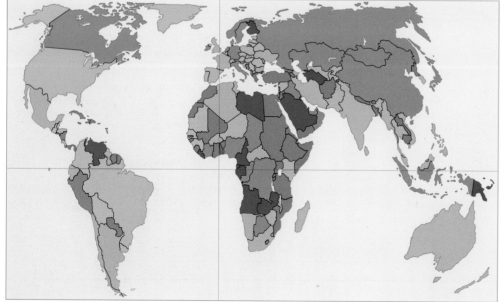

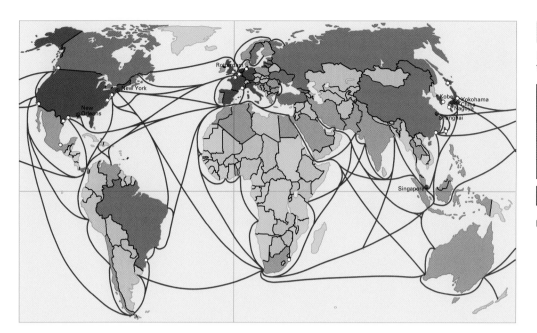

Seaborne Freight

Freight unloaded in millions of tonnes (latest available year)

- Over 100
- 50 – 100
- 10 – 50
- 5 – 10
- Under 5
- Landlocked countries

Major seaports

- ● Over 100 million tonnes per year
- ○ 50–100 million tonnes per year
- ── Major shipping routes

Cargoes

Type of seaborne freight

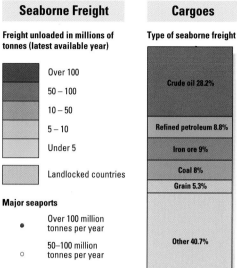

- Crude oil 28.2%
- Refined petroleum 8.8%
- Iron ore 9%
- Coal 8%
- Grain 5.3%
- Other 40.7%

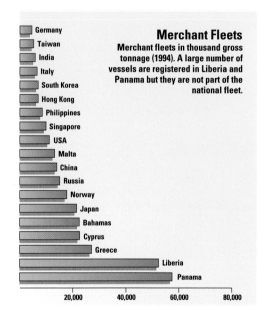

Merchant Fleets

Merchant fleets in thousand gross tonnage (1994). A large number of vessels are registered in Liberia and Panama but they are not part of the national fleet.

Germany, Taiwan, India, Italy, South Korea, Hong Kong, Philippines, Singapore, USA, Malta, China, Russia, Norway, Japan, Bahamas, Cyprus, Greece, Liberia, Panama

20,000 — 40,000 — 60,000 — 80,000

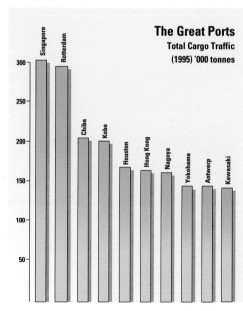

The Great Ports

Total Cargo Traffic (1995) '000 tonnes

Singapore, Rotterdam, Chiba, Kobe, Houston, Hong Kong, Nagoya, Yokohama, Antwerp, Kawasaki

World Shipping

World merchant fleet by type of vessel and deadweight tonnage (latest available year)

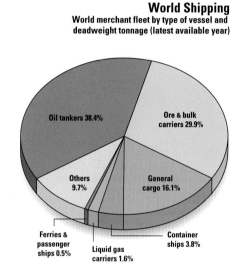

- Oil tankers 38.4%
- Ore & bulk carriers 29.9%
- Others 9.7%
- General cargo 16.1%
- Ferries & passenger ships 0.5%
- Liquid gas carriers 1.6%
- Container ships 3.8%

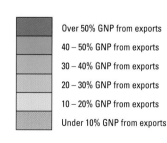

Dependence on Trade

Value of exports as a percentage of Gross National Product (1995)

- Over 50% GNP from exports
- 40 – 50% GNP from exports
- 30 – 40% GNP from exports
- 20 – 30% GNP from exports
- 10 – 20% GNP from exports
- Under 10% GNP from exports

- ● Most dependent on industrial exports (over 75% of total exports)
- ○ Most dependent on fuel exports (over 75% of total exports)
- ● Most dependent on mineral and metal exports (over 75% of total exports)

Travel and Tourism

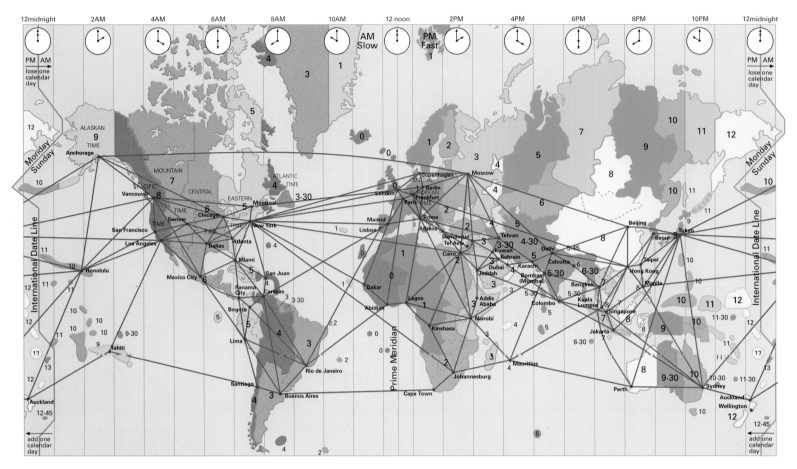

Time Zones

Zones using GMT	Zones fast of GMT	Certain time zones are affected by the incidence of 'summer time' in countries where it is adopted.
Zones slow of GMT	Half-hour zones	
International boundaries (dashed)	Time zone boundaries	Actual Solar Time, when it is noon at Greenwich, is shown along the top of the map.
10 — Hours slow or fast of GMT	International Date Line	
	Selected air routes	

The world is divided into 24 time zones, each centred on meridians at 15° intervals, which is the longitudinal distance the sun travels every hour. The meridian running through Greenwich, London, passes through the middle of the first zone.

Rail and Road: The Leading Nations

Total rail network ('000 km) (1995)	Passenger km per head per year	Total road network ('000 km)	Vehicle km per head per year	Number of vehicles per km of roads
1. USA 235.7	Japan 2,017	USA 6,277.9	USA...................12,505	Hong Kong 284
2. Russia 87.4	Belarus.............1,880	India 2,962.5	Luxembourg 7,989	Taiwan 211
3. India 62.7	Russia..............1,826	Brazil 1,824.4	Kuwait 7,251	Singapore 152
4. China...............54.6	Switzerland 1,769	Japan 1,130.9	France 7,142	Kuwait 140
5. Germany...........41.7	Ukraine.............1,456	China 1,041.1	Sweden 6,991	Brunei................96
6. Australia 35.8	Austria 1,168	Russia 884.0	Germany 6,806	Italy 91
7. Argentina 34.2	France 1,011	Canada..............849.4	Denmark 6,764	Israel 87
8. France.............31.9	Netherlands 994	France 811.6	Austria 6,518	Thailand 73
9. Mexico............26.5	Latvia................918	Australia 810.3	Netherlands 5,984	Ukraine................73
10. South Africa 26.3	Denmark 884	Germany 636.3	UK 5,738	UK 67
11. Poland.............24.9	Slovak Rep. 862	Romania.............461.9	Canada 5,493	Netherlands 66
12. Ukraine 22.6	Romania 851	Turkey 388.1	Italy 4,852	Germany 62

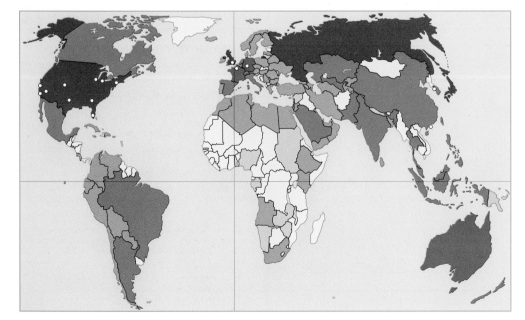

Air Travel

Passenger kilometres (the number of passengers – international and domestic – multiplied by the distance flown by each passenger from the airport of origin) (1994)

- Over 100,000 million
- 50,000 – 100,000 million
- 10,000 – 50,000 million
- 1,000 – 10,000 million
- 500 – 1,000 million
- Under 500 million

○ Major airports (handling over 25 million passengers in 1995)

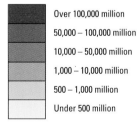

World's busiest airports (total passengers)	World's busiest airports (international passengers)
1. Chicago (O'Hare)	1. London (Heathrow)
2. Atlanta (Hatsfield)	2. London (Gatwick)
3. Dallas (Dallas/Ft Worth)	3. Frankfurt (International)
4. Los Angeles (Intern'l)	4. New York (Kennedy)
5. London (Heathrow)	5. Paris (De Gaulle)

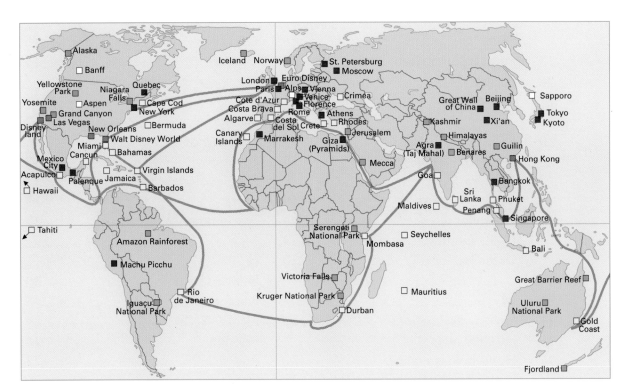

Destinations

- ■ Cultural and historical centres
- ▨ Coastal resorts
- □ Ski resorts
- ▦ Centres of entertainment
- ▨ Places of pilgrimage
- ▨ Places of great natural beauty
- — Popular holiday cruise routes

Visitors to the USA

Overseas travellers to the USA, thousands (1997 projections)

1.	Canada	13,900
2.	Mexico	12,370
3.	Japan	4,640
4.	UK	3,350
5.	Germany	1,990
6.	France	1,030
7.	Taiwan	885
8.	Venezuela	860
9.	South Korea	800
10.	Brazil	785

In 1996, the USA earned the most from tourism, with receipts of more than US $64 billion.

Tourist Spending

Countries spending the most on overseas tourism, US $ million (latest available year)

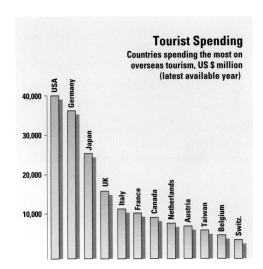

Importance of Tourism

		Arrivals from abroad (1995)	% of world total (1995)
1.	France	60,584,000	10.68%
2.	Spain	45,125,000	7.96%
3.	USA	44,730,000	7.89%
4.	Italy	29,184,000	5.15%
5.	China	23,368,000	4.12%
6.	UK	22,700,000	4.00%
7.	Hungary	22,087,000	3.90%
8.	Mexico	19,870,000	3.50%
9.	Poland	19,225,000	3.39%
10.	Austria	17,750,000	3.13%
11.	Canada	16,854,000	2.97%
12.	Czech Republic	16,600,000	2.93%

The latest figures reveal a 4.6% rise in the total number of people travelling abroad in 1996, to 593 million. Small economies in attractive areas are often completely dominated by tourism: in some West Indian islands, for example, tourist spending provides over 90% of total income.

Tourist Earning

Countries receiving the most from overseas tourism, US $ million (latest available year)

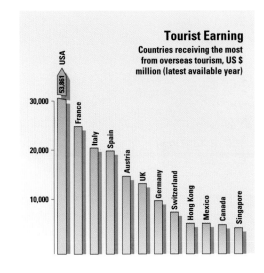

Tourism

Tourism receipts as a percentage of Gross National Product (1994)

- ■ Over 10% of GNP from tourism
- ▨ 5 – 10% of GNP from tourism
- ▨ 2.5 – 5% of GNP from tourism
- ▨ 1 – 2.5% of GNP from tourism
- ▨ 0.5 – 1% of GNP from tourism
- □ Under 0.5% of GNP from tourism

Countries spending the most on promoting tourism, millions of US $ (1996)

Australia	88
Spain	79
UK	79
France	73
Singapore	54

Fastest growing tourist destinations, % change in receipts (1994–5)

South Korea	49%
Czech Republic	27%
India	21%
Russia	19%
Philippines	18%

The World In Focus: Index

WORLD MAPS

SETTLEMENTS

⬡ **PARIS**   ■ **Berne**   ◉ **Livorno**   ● Brugge   ◎ Algeciras   ⊙ Fréjus   ○ Oberammergau   ○ Thira

Settlement symbols and type styles vary according to the scale of each map and indicate the importance of towns on the map rather than specific population figures

∴ Ruins or Archæological Sites   ˅ Wells in Desert

ADMINISTRATION

_____ International Boundaries

_ _ _ International Boundaries (Undefined or Disputed)

.... Internal Boundaries

⬭ National Parks

Country Names

NICARAGUA

Administrative Area Names

KENT

CALABRIA

International boundaries show the *de facto* situation where there are rival claims to territory

COMMUNICATIONS

_____ Principal Roads

⌒ Other Roads

-·-·- Trails and Seasonal Roads

≍ Passes

✿ Airfields

⌒ Principal Railroads

-·--·- Railroads Under Construction

⌒ Other Railroads

⊐---⊏ Railroad Tunnels

.... Principal Canals

PHYSICAL FEATURES

⌒ Perennial Streams

-·-·- Intermittent Streams

⬭ Perennial Lakes

⬭ Intermittent Lakes

Swamps and Marshes

Permanent Ice and Glaciers

▲ 8848 Elevations (m)

▼ 8050 Sea Depths (m)

1134 Height of Lake Surface Above Sea Level (m)

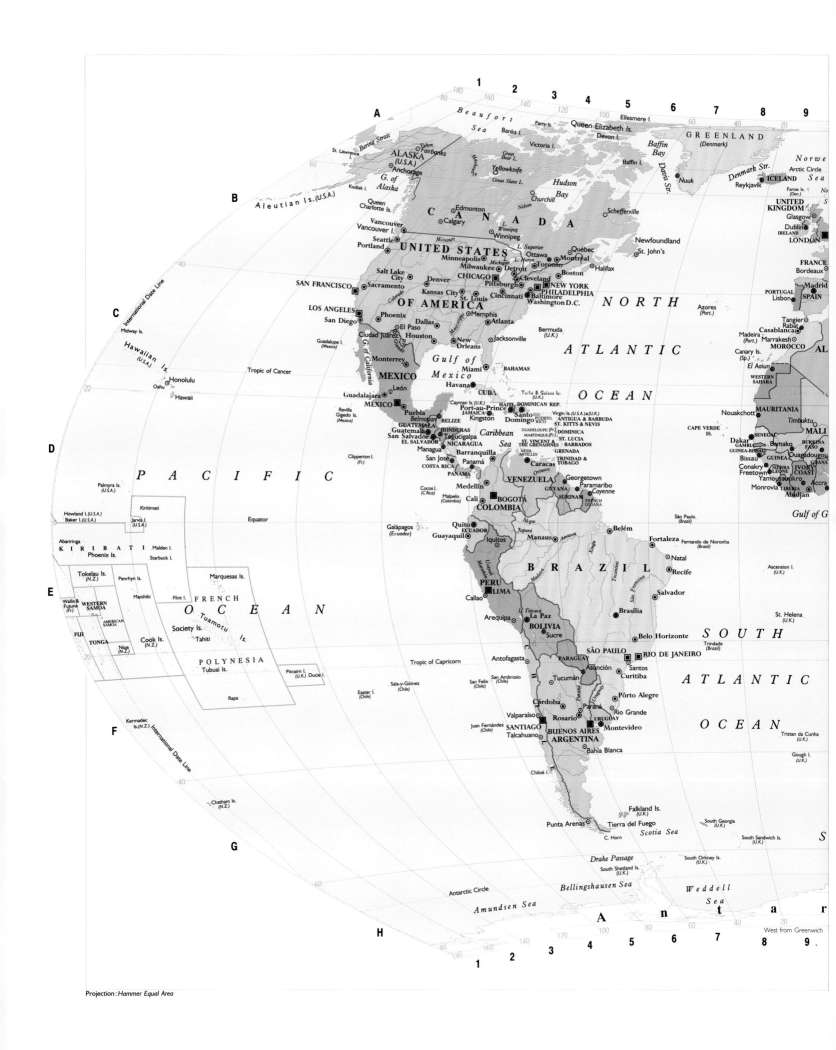

Projection: Hammer Equal Area

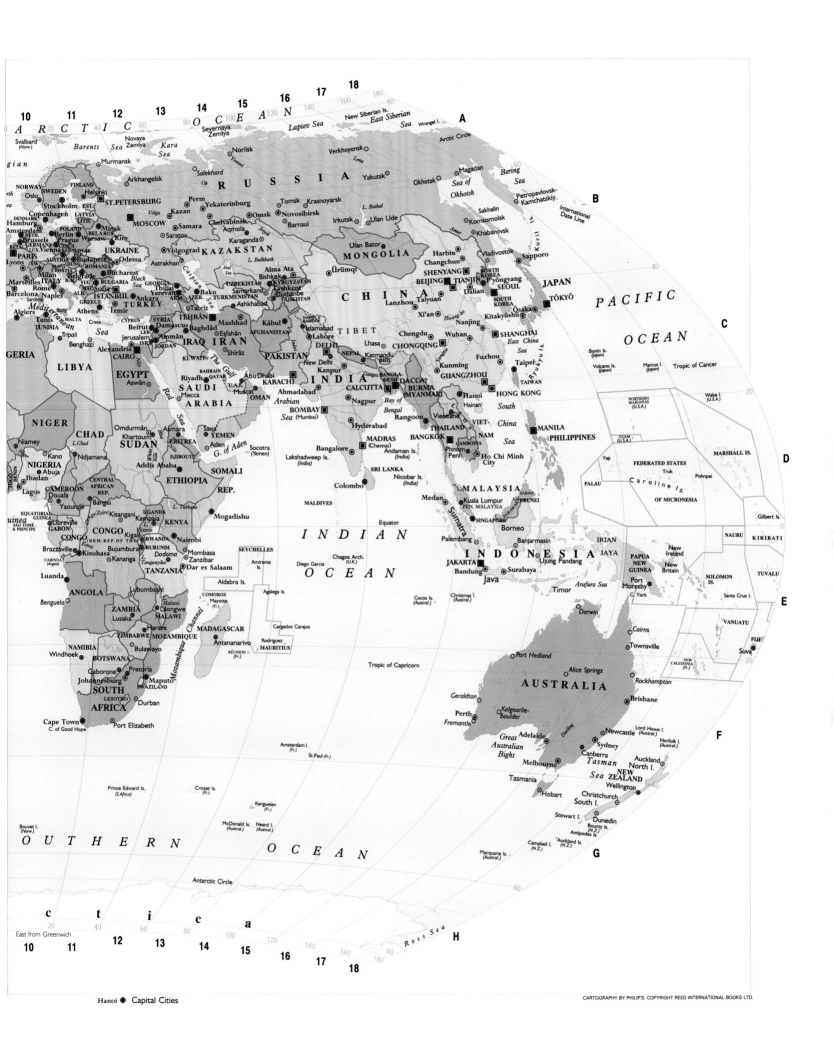

A R C T I C   O C E A N

Svalbard
(Nor.)

Barents   Sea   Novaya   Kara
Zemlya   Sea

gian

Norilsk

R U S S I A

New Siberian Is.
Laptev Sea   East Siberian
Sea   Wrangel I.

Arctic Circle

A

Murmansk

Arkhangelsk   Salekhard   Verkhoyansk   Yakutsk   Okhotsk   Sea of
Ob   Yenisey   Lena   Okhotsk

Magadan   Bering
Sea

Petropavlovsk-
Kamchatskiy

International
Date Line

B

NORWAY   FINLAND
SWEDEN   Helsinki
Oslo   Stockholm   EST.   ST.PETERSBURG
Copenhagen   LATVIA
DENMARK   LITH.
Hamburg   Perm   Yekaterinburg   Tomsk   Krasnoyarsk   L. Baikal   Ulan Ude   Sakhalin   Komsomolsk
Amsterdam   NETH.   Berlin   POLAND   BELARUS   MOSCOW   Kazan   Chelyabinsk   Omsk   Novosibirsk   Irkutsk   Khabarovsk
Brussels   GERMANY   Warsaw   Minsk   Volga   Samara   Barnaul   Amur   Vladivostok   Sapporo
LUX.   Vienna   CZECH REP.   Kiev   UKRAINE   Saratov   Aqmola   Ulan Bator   Harbin   JAPAN
Lyons   PARIS   SLOVAKIA   Volgograd   KAZAKSTAN   Karaganda   MONGOLIA   Changchun   NORTH   Sapporo
AUSTRIA   HUNG.   ROMANIA   Astrakhan   Aral   L. Balkhash   Ürümqi   BEIJING   TIANJIN   KOREA   PACIFIC
ITALY   Belgrade   Bucharest   Sea   Alma Ata   SHENYANG   SOUTH   P'yongyang   TŌKYŌ
Milan   CROATIA   YUG.   Black   GEORGIA   Caspian   Bishkek   KYRGYZSTAN   CHINA   Dalian   SEOUL   OCEAN
Marseilles   Rome   BULGARIA   Sea   Tbilisi   Baku   UZBEKISTAN   Tashkent   Lanzhou   Taiyuan   KOREA   Ōsaka   C
Barcelona   Naples   Sofia   ARM.   AZER.   Samarkand   TURKMENISTAN   Dushanbe   Xi'an   Nanjing   Kitakyūshū
Sardinia   ALB.   GREECE   Yerevan   TAJIKISTAN   Hwang Ho   Ryukyus
Mediterranean   Athens   ISTANBUL   Tabriz   Ashkhabad   Chengdu   Wuhan   SHANGHAI
Algiers   Sicily   Izmir   TURKEY   Ankara   TEHRĀN   Mashhad   Kābul   TIBET   Lhasa   CHONGQING   East China   Volcano Is.
Tunis   MALTA   Crete   SYRIA   Damascus   Baghdad   Eşfahān   AFGHANISTAN   Islamabad   Lahore   Kunming   Fuzhou   Sea   (Japan)
TUNISIA   Tripoli   CYPRUS   LEB.   Beirut   Amman   IRAQ   IRAN   Shīrāz   PAKISTAN   DELHI   NEPAL   Katmandu   GUANGZHOU   Taipei   TAIWAN   Bonin Is.
GERIA   Benghazi   Jerusalem   ISR.   JORDAN   KUWAIT   The Gulf   New Delhi   Ganges   BANGLA-   DACCA   HONG KONG   (Japan)
Alexandria   Riyadh   BAHRAIN   QATAR   Abu Dhabi   DESH   BURMA   Hanoi   Marcus I.   Tropic of Cancer
CAIRO   Aswān   U.A.E.   Muscat   KARACHI   INDIA   CALCUTTA   MYANMAR   Hainan   (Japan)
LIBYA   EGYPT   Nile   SAUDI   Mecca   OMAN   Ahmadabad   Nagpur   Bay of   Rangoon   VIET-   South
Red   ARABIA   Arabian   BOMBAY   Bengal   China
Sea   (Mumbai)   THAILAND   NAM   Sea
NIGER   Omdurman   Asmara   YEMEN   Sea   Hyderabad   MADRAS   BANGKOK   Volcano Is.   MANILA
CHAD   Khartoum   ERITREA   Aden   Socotra   Bangalore   (Chennai)   Andaman Is.   CAMBODIA   PHILIPPINES
Niamey   L. Chad   Blue Nile   DJIBOUTI   G. of Aden   (Yemen)   Lakshadweep Is.   (India)   Phnom   Ho Chi Minh
Kano   Addis Ababa   SOMALI   (India)   SRI LANKA   Penh   City
NIGERIA   Ndjamena   SUDAN   ETHIOPIA   REP.   Colombo   Nicobar Is.   MALAYSIA
Abuja   White Nile   Medan   Kuala Lumpur   SABAH
TOGO   Ibadan   CENTRAL   Nagpur   MALDIVES   PEN. MALAYSIA   BRUNEI
BENIN   Lagos   CAMEROON   AFRICAN   Equator   SINGAPORE   Borneo
uinea   Douala   Bangui   REP.   L. Turkana   INDIAN   Sumatra   Banjarmasin
EQUATORIAL   Yaoundé   Kisangani   UGANDA   KENYA   Mogadishu   Palembang   INDONESIA
SAO TOMÉ   Kampala   SEYCHELLES   OCEAN
& PRINCIPE   GABON   Libreville   Congo (Zaïre)   Victoria   JAKARTA
CONGO   Kigali   RWANDA   Nairobi   Bandung   Surabaya
Brazzaville   DEM. REP. OF THE   BURUNDI   Dodoma   Amirante   Java
CABINDA   Kinshasa   Bujumbura   Mombasa   Is.   Chagos Arch.   Diego Garcia
(Angola)   Kananga   Zanzibar   (U.K.)
Luanda   TANZANIA   Dar es Salaam   Aldabra Is.   COMOROS   Agalega Is.
Benguela   ANGOLA   Lubumbashi   Mayotte   Cocos Is.   Christmas I.
L. Tanganyika   (Fr.)   (Austral.)   (Austral.)
ZAMBIA   Malawi   Lilongwe   MADAGASCAR   Cargados Carajos   Timor
Lusaka   MALAWI   Antananarivo   Rodriguez
ZIMBABWE   MOZAMBIQUE   RÉUNION   MAURITIUS
NAMIBIA   Harare   (Fr.)
Windhoek   Bulawayo
BOTSWANA   Tropic of Capricorn   Port Hedland
Gaborone   Pretoria
Johannesburg   Maputo   SWAZILAND   Alice Springs
SOUTH   LESOTHO   Durban
AFRICA   Geraldton   AUSTRALIA   Rockhampton
Cape Town   Port Elizabeth   Amsterdam I.   Kalgoorlie-   Brisbane
C. of Good Hope   (Fr.)   Perth   Boulder
St.Paul (Fr.)   Fremantle   Great   Adelaide   Newcastle
Australian   Sydney
Bight   Canberra
Prince Edward Is.   Crozet Is.   Melbourne   Tasman
(S.Africa)   (Fr.)   Tasmania   Sea   Wellington
Kerguelen   Hobart   Christchurch
Bouvet I.   McDonald Is.   Heard I.   (Fr.)   South I.
(Norw.)   (Austral.)   (Austral.)   Stewart I.   Dunedin
OUTHERN   OCEAN   Campbell I.   Auckland Is.   Antipodes Is.
(N.Z.)   (N.Z.)
Antarctic Circle   Macquarie Is.   Ross Sea
(Austral.)

MARSHALL IS.   D

FEDERATED STATES   Truk   Pohnpei
PALAU   Yap   Caroline Is.
OF MICRONESIA   Gilbert Is.
NAURU   KIRIBATI   E
GUAM
(U.S.A.)
NORTHERN   Wake I.
MARIANAS   (U.S.A.)
(U.S.A.)   TUVALU
IRIAN   SOLOMON
JAYA   IS.   Santa Cruz I.
PAPUA   New   VANUATU   F
NEW   Ireland   FIJI
GUINEA   New   Suva
Port   Britain   NEW
Moresby   CALEDONIA
C York   (Fr.)   G
Darwin   Cairns   Lord Howe I.
Townsville   (Austral.)
Norfolk I.
(Austral.)
Auckland   H
NEW   North I.
ZEALAND

East from Greenwich

Hanoi ●   Capital Cities

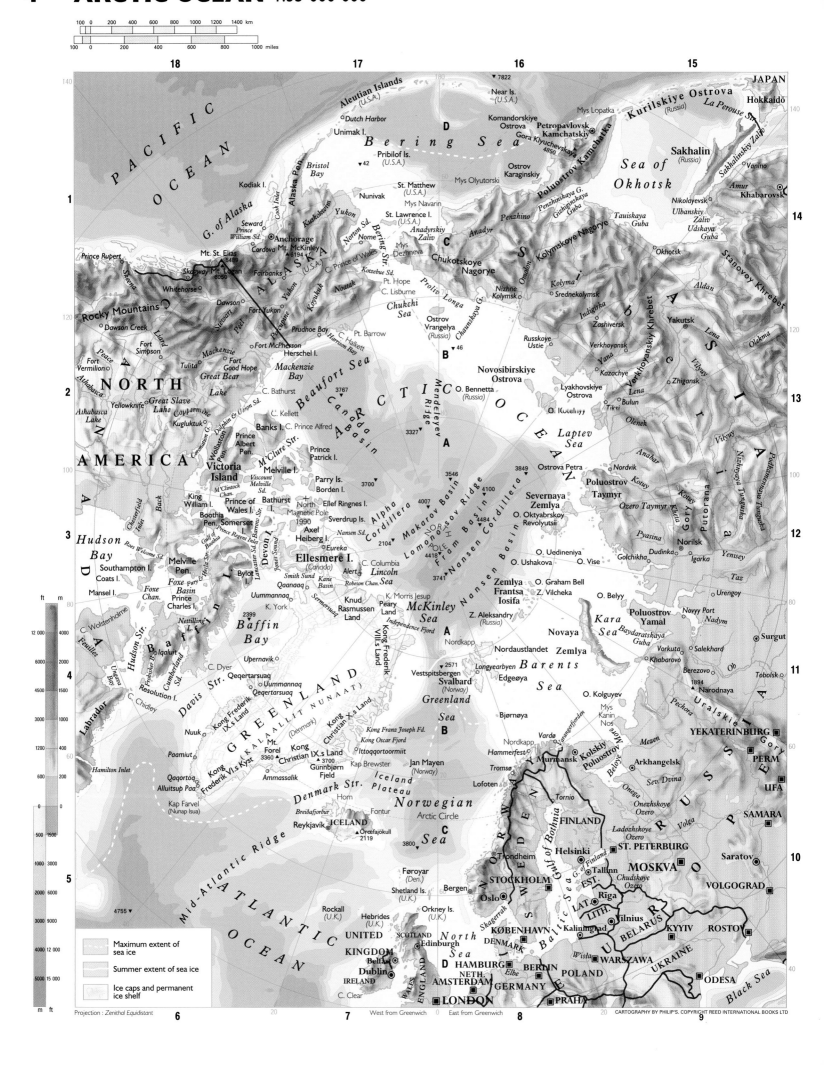

18   **17**   **16**   **15**

JAPAN

PACIFIC OCEAN

Aleutian Islands (U.S.A.)

Dutch Harbor

Unimak I.

7822

Near Is. (U.S.A.)

Kurilskiye Ostrova (Russia)

La Perouse Str.

Hokkaidō

D

Bering Sea

Komandorskiye Ostrova

Mys Lopatka

Petropavlovsk Kamchatskiy

Gora Klyuchevskaya 4850

Sakhalin (Russia)

Sea of Okhotsk

Sakhalinskiy Zaliv

Vanino

Pribilof Is. (U.S.A.)

42

St. Matthew (U.S.A.)

Ostrov Karaginskiy

Mys Olyutorski

Poluostrov Kamchatka

Penzhinskaya G.

Gizhiginskaya Guba

Amur

Nikolayevsk

Ulbanskiy Zaliv

Khabarovsk

Kodiak I.

Bristol Bay

Nunivak

Mys Navarin

Penzhino

Tauiskaya Guba

Udskaya Guba

G. of Alaska

Seward

Norton Sd.

St. Lawrence I. (U.S.A.)

Anadyrskiy Zaliv

Anadyr

Okhotsk

Stanovoy Khrebet

Prince William Sd.

Anchorage

Mt. McKinley 6194

Nome

Mys Deztneva

C

Kolymskoye Nagorye

1

Cordova

Mt. St. Elias 5489

ALASKA (U.S.A.)

C. Prince of Wales

Kotzebue Sd.

Chukotskoye Nagorye

Ondon

Omolon

Aldan

14

Prince Rupert

Skagway Mt. Logan 6050

Fairbanks

Yukon

Pt. Hope

C. Lisburne

Prolив Longa

Kolyma

Nizhne Kolymsk

Srednekolymsk

Indigirka

Zashiversk

Yakutsk

Lena

Olekma

Whitehorse

Dawson

Yukon

Koyukuk

Chukchi Sea

Russkoye Ustie

Verkhoyansk

Yana

Vilyuy

Rocky Mountains

Stewart

Pelly

Porcupine

Fort Yukon

Prudhoe Bay

C. Halkett

Harrison Bay

Pt. Barrow

Ostrov Vrangelya (Russia)

46

Chaunskaya G.

Kazachye

Zhigansk

120

Dawson Creek

Liard

Mackenzie

Fort McPherson

Herschel I.

B

Novosibirskiye Ostrova

Lyakhovskiye Ostrova

Bulun

120

Fort Simpson

Tulita

Fort Good Hope

Mackenzie Bay

Beaufort Sea

3767

O. Bennetta (Russia)

Tiksi

Olenek

Fort Vermilion

Peace

Great Bear Lake

C. Bathurst

C A N A D A

Mendeleyev Ridge

O. Kotelnyy

NORTH

2

Athabasca

Yellowknife

Great Slave Lake

Coppermine

C. Kellett

B A S I N

3327

Laptev Sea

Anabar

Nordvik

13

Athabasca Lake

Kugluktuk

Dolphin & Union Sd.

Banks I.

C. Prince Alfred

A R C T I C

O C E A N

Ostrova Petra

Khatanga

Olenek

AMERICA

C A N A D A

Coronation G.

Prince Albert Pen.

M'Clure Str.

Prince Patrick I.

3546

Norilsk

Putorana

Vilyuy

100

Victoria Island

Viscount Melville Sd.

Melville I.

Parry Is.

3700

Alpha Cordillera

4007

Makarov Basin

Lomonosov Ridge

3849

Severnaya Zemlya

Poluostrov Taymyr

Ozero Taymyr

Gory Byrranga

Nizhnyaya Tunguska

100

3

Hudson Bay

M'Clintock Chan.

King William I.

Prince of Wales I.

Bathurst I.

Borden I.

Ellef Ringnes I.

North Magnetic Pole 1990

Sverdrup I.

2104

Fram Basin

4418

POLE

4100

Nansen Cordillera

4484

O. Oktyabrskoy Revolyutsii

O. Uedineniya

O. Vise

Pyasina

Golchikha

Dudinka

Igarka

Yenisey

Taz

Urengoy

12

Chesterfield Inlet

Back

Boothia Pen.

Somerset I.

Axel Heiberg I.

Nansen Sd.

Nansen Basin

3741

O. Ushakova

O. Graham Bell

3

Roes Welcome Sd.

Fury & Hecla Str.

Gulf of Boothia

Prince Regent Inlet

Devon I.

Eureka

Ellesmere I. (Canada)

Alert

C. Columbia

Lincoln Sea

Zemlya Frantsa Iosifa

Z. Vilcheka

O. Belyy

Novyy Port

Nadym

Surgut

Southampton I.

Melville Pen.

Foxe Basin

Bylot I.

Jones Sd.

Lancaster Sd.

Smith Sund

Kane Basin

Robeson Chan.

K. Morris Jesup

McKinley Sea

A

Z. Aleksandry (Russia)

Kara Sea

Poluostrov Yamal

Ob

Tobolsk

11

Coats I.

Foxe Chan.

Prince Charles I.

2399

Qaanaaq

Uummannaq

Peary Land

Knud Rasmussen Land

Independence Fjord

Novaya

Baydaratskaya Guba

Berezovo

Mansel I.

C. Wolstenholme

Hudson Str.

Baffin Bay

K. York

Sermersuaq

Kong Frederik VIII.s Land

Nordkapp

Nordaustlandet

Zemlya

Vorkuta

Salekhard

Narodnaya

1894

Feuilles

Iqaluit

Upernavik

Baffin

Longyearbyen

Svalbard (Norway)

2571

Edgeøya

B a r e n t s

Khabarovo

O. Kolguyev

Pechora

Ural'skiye Gory

4

Frobisher Bay

C. Dyer

Qeqertarsuaq

Uummannaq

Qeqertarsuaq

Vestspitsbergen

Svalbard (Norway)

Greenland

Sea

Mys Kanin Nos

Mezen

YEKATERINBURG

Ungava Bay

Resolution I.

Davis Str.

Cumberland Sd.

GREENLAND

(KALAALLIT NUNAAT)

Kong Frederik IX.s Land

Kong Christian Xs Land

Jan Mayen (Norway)

Nordkapp

Vardø

Varangerfjord

Hammerfest

Bjørnøya

Mys Kanin Nos

Onega

Sev. Dvina

PERM

UFA

Labrador

C. Chidley

Nuuk

Kong Frederik VI.s Kyst

Kong Christian IX.s Land

3700

Kong Oscar Fjord

Kap Brewster

Ittoqqortoormiit

B

Tromsø

Lofoten

Murmansk

Kolskiy Poluostrov

Beloye More

Arkhangelsk

Onezhskoye Ozero

Dvina

SAMARA

Paamiut

Qaqortoq

Alluitsup Paa

Forel 3360

Gunnbjørn Fjeld 3700

Ammassalik

Iceland Plateau

Norwegian

Arctic Circle

Trondheim

Tornio

Ladozhskoye Ozero

Volga

60

Hamilton Inlet

Kap Farvel (Nunap Isua)

Breiðafjörður

Horn

Fontur

Sea

FINLAND

Helsinki

ST. PETERBURG

Chudskoye Ozero

MOSKVA

Saratov

10

5

Reykjavík

Öræfajökull 2119

3800

C

Føroyar (Den.)

Oslo

STOCKHOLM

Tallinn

G. of Finland

EST.

VOLGOGRAD

Mid-Atlantic Ridge

4755

ATLANTIC OCEAN

Rockall (U.K.)

Shetland Is. (U.K.)

Bergen

Skagerrak

Gulf of Bothnia

Baltic Sea

Rīga

LAT.

LITH.

Vilnius

KYYIV

ROSTOV

Hebrides (U.K.)

Orkney Is. (U.K.)

North Sea

KØBENHAVN

Kaliningrad

BELARUS

WARSZAWA

UKRAINE

ODESA

Black Sea

UNITED KINGDOM

SCOTLAND

Edinburgh

DENMARK

HAMBURG

BERLIN

Wisła

POLAND

Belfast

Dublin

IRELAND

ENGLAND

WALES

D

NETH.

AMSTERDAM

GERMANY

Elbe

PRAHA

40

C. Clear

LONDON

20

West from Greenwich

East from Greenwich

20

CARTOGRAPHY BY PHILIP'S. COPYRIGHT REED INTERNATIONAL BOOKS LTD

ft m

12 000 4000

6000 2000

4500 1500

3000 1000

1200 400

600 200

0 0

500 1500

1000 3000

2000 6000

3000 9000

4000 12 000

5000 15 000

m ft

Projection: Zenithal Equidistant

6   **7**   **8**   **9**

Maximum extent of sea ice

Summer extent of sea ice

Ice caps and permanent ice shelf

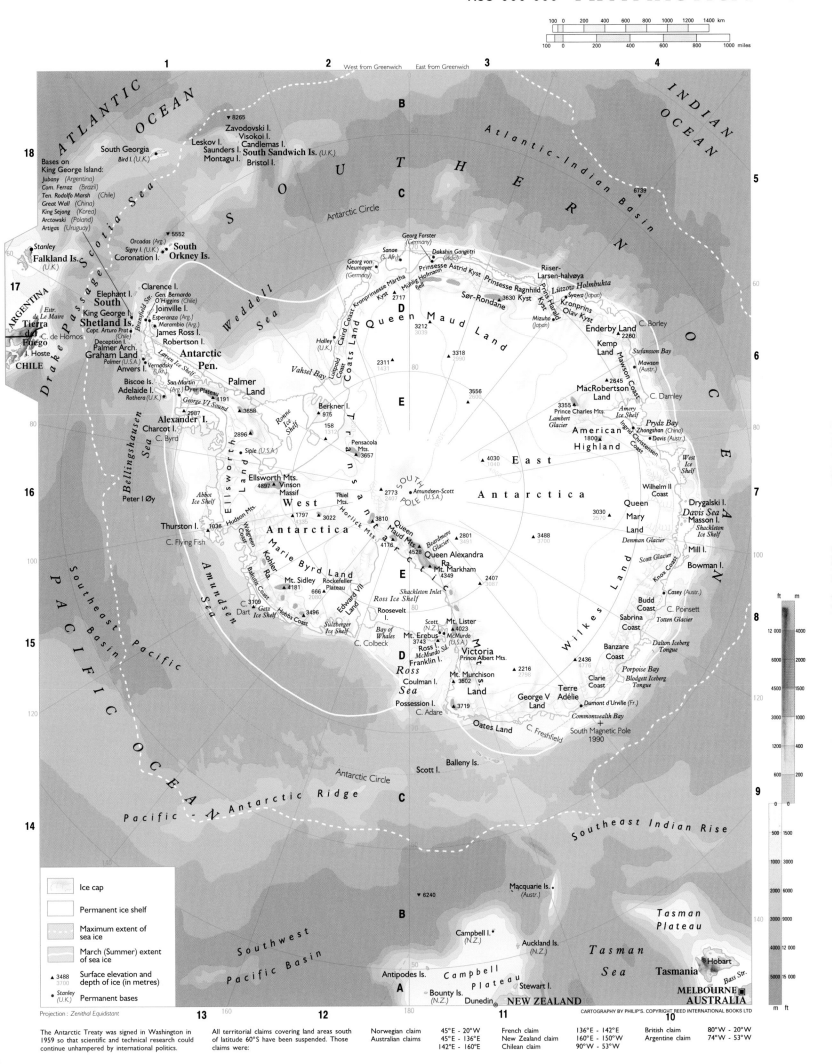

The Antarctic Treaty was signed in Washington in 1959 so that scientific and technical research could continue unhampered by international politics.

All territorial claims covering land areas south of latitude 60°S have been suspended. Those claims were:

Norwegian claim	45°E – 20°W	French claim	136°E – 142°E
Australian claims	45°E – 136°E	New Zealand claim	160°E – 150°W
	142°E – 160°E	Chilean claim	90°W – 53°W
British claim	80°W – 20°W		
Argentine claim	74°W – 53°W		

Projection: Zenithal Equidistant

CARTOGRAPHY BY PHILIP'S. COPYRIGHT REED INTERNATIONAL BOOKS LTD

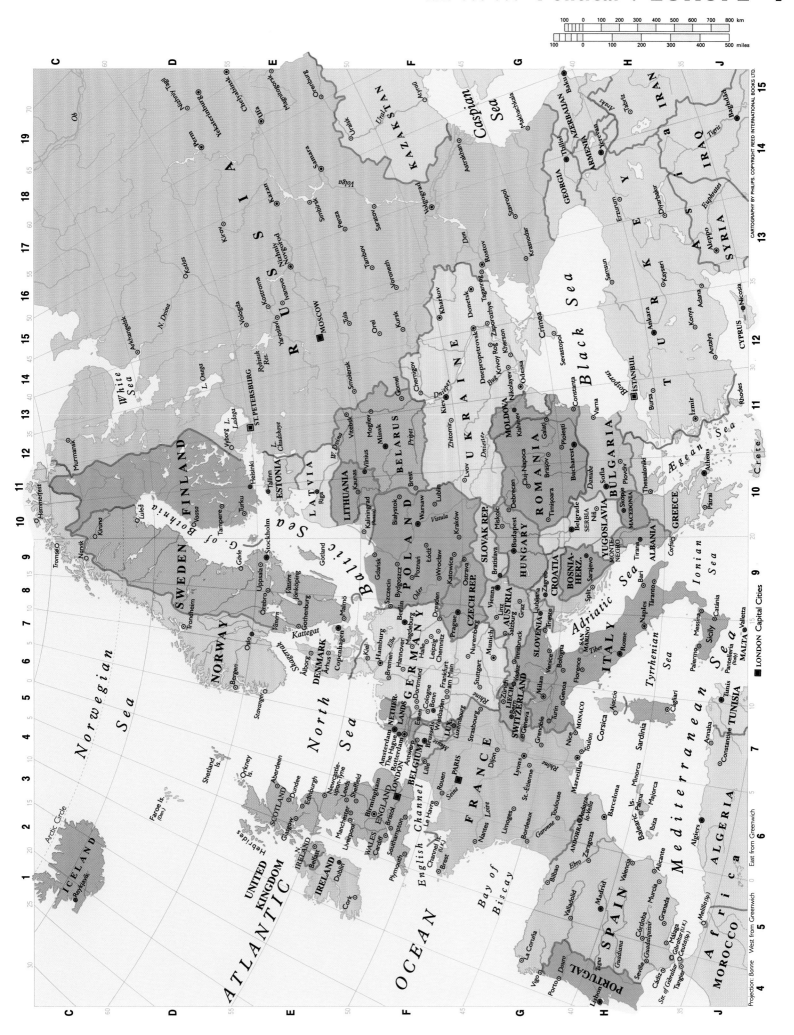

100 0 100 200 300 400 500 600 700 800 km
100 0 100 200 300 400 500 miles

■ LONDON Capital Cities

Projection: Bonne   West from Greenwich   East from Greenwich

SCANDINAVIA 1:5 000 000

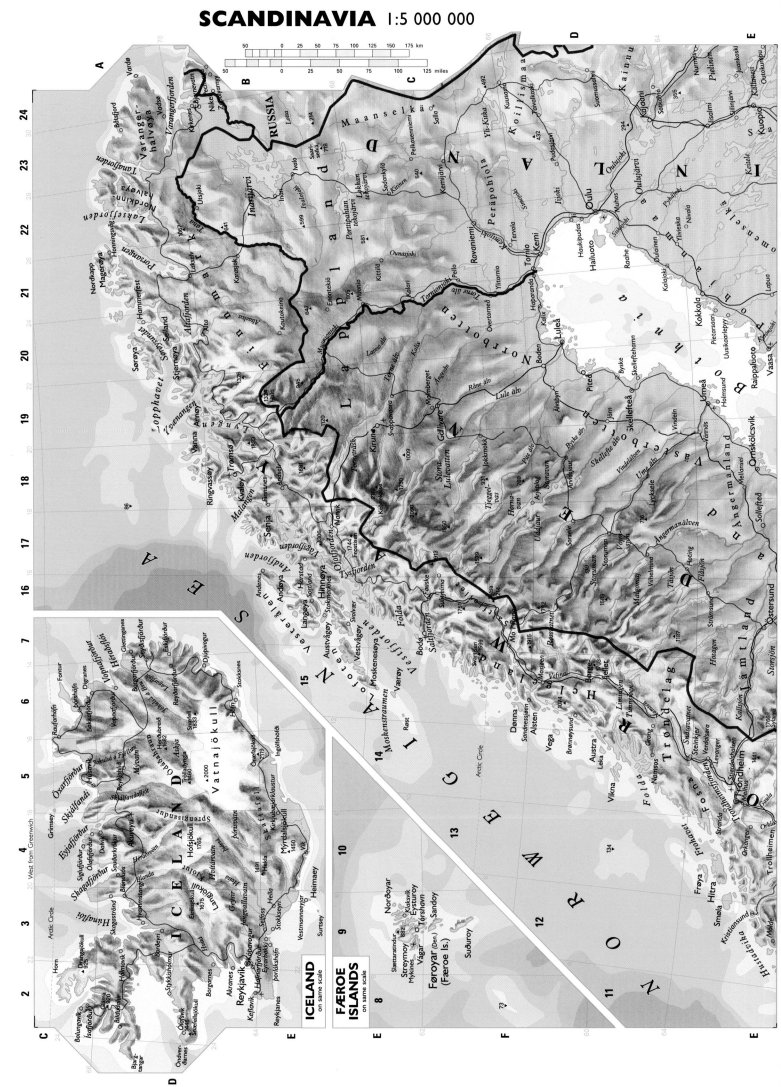

ICELAND
on same scale

**FÆROE
ISLANDS**
on same scale

Projection: Conical with two standard parallels

East from Greenwich

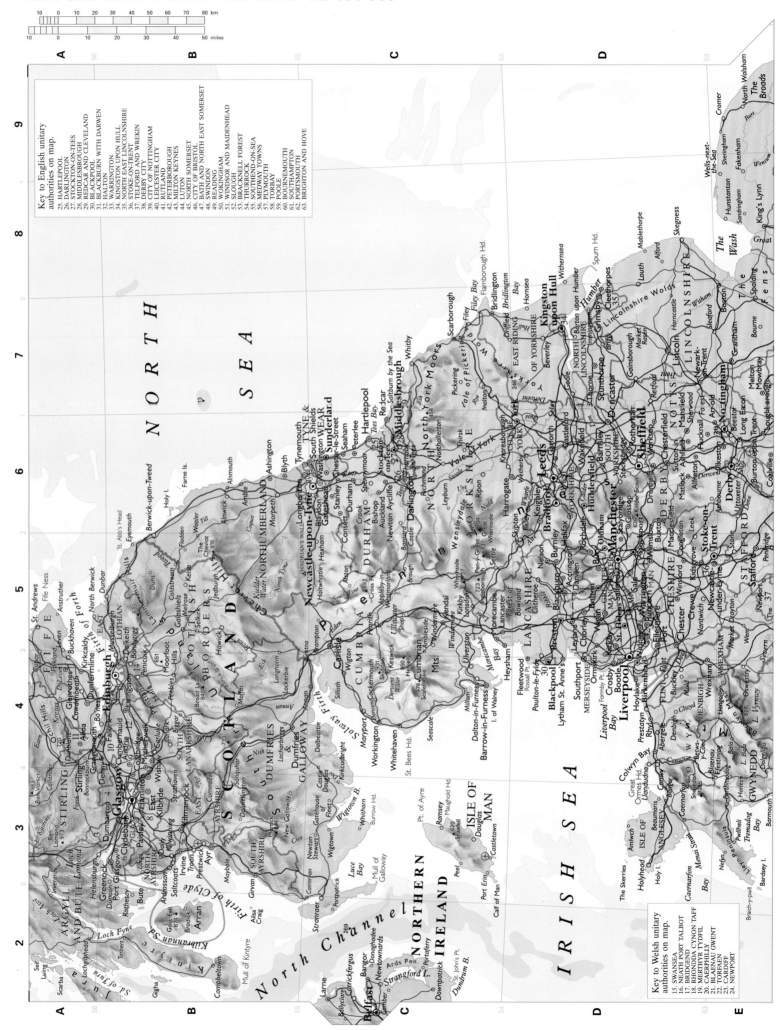

Key to English unitary
authorities on map.

25. HARTLEPOOL
26. DARLINGTON
27. STOCKTON-ON-TEES
28. MIDDLESBROUGH
29. REDCAR AND CLEVELAND
30. BLACKPOOL
31. BLACKBURN WITH DARWEN
32. HALTON
33. WARRINGTON
34. KINGSTON UPON HULL
35. NORTH EAST LINCOLNSHIRE
36. NORTH LINCOLNSHIRE
37. STOKE-ON-TRENT
38. TELFORD AND WREKIN
39. DERBY CITY
40. CITY OF NOTTINGHAM
41. LEICESTER CITY
42. RUTLAND
43. PETERBOROUGH
44. MILTON KEYNES
45. LUTON
46. NORTH SOMERSET
47. CITY OF BRISTOL
48. BATH AND NORTH EAST SOMERSET
49. SWINDON
50. READING
51. WOKINGHAM
52. WINDSOR AND MAIDENHEAD
53. SLOUGH
54. BRACKNELL FOREST
55. SOUTHEND-ON-SEA
56. THURROCK
57. MEDWAY TOWNS
58. PLYMOUTH
59. TORBAY
60. POOLE
61. BOURNEMOUTH
62. SOUTHAMPTON
63. PORTSMOUTH
64. BRIGHTON AND HOVE

Key to Welsh unitary
authorities on map.

15. SWANSEA
16. NEATH PORT TALBOT
17. BRIDGEND
18. RHONDDA CYNON TAFF
19. MERTHYR TYDFIL
20. CAERPHILLY
21. BLAENAU GWENT
22. TORFAEN
23. CARDIFF
24. NEWPORT

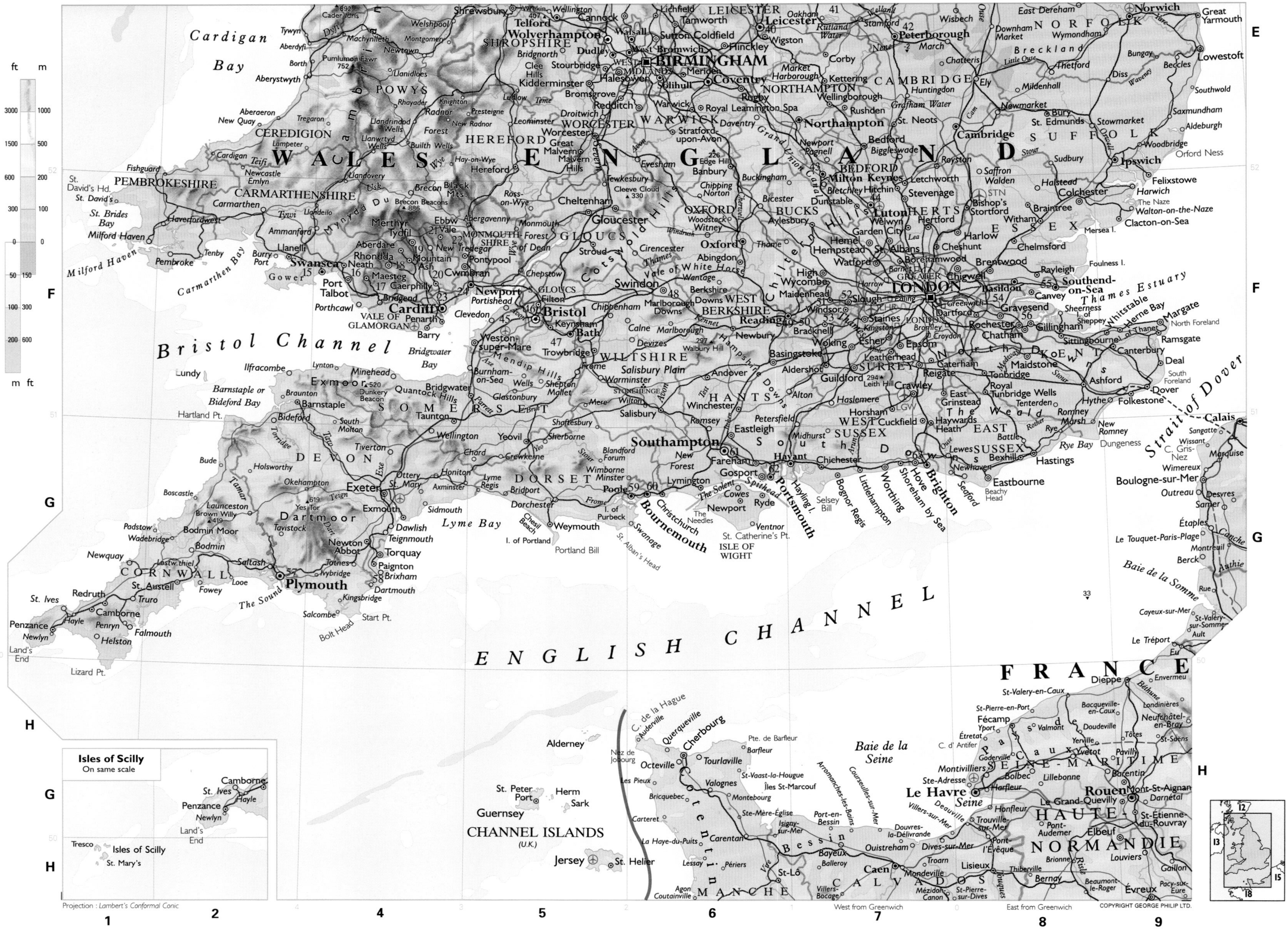
ENGLAND
WALES
FRANCE
ENGLISH CHANNEL
Bristol Channel
Cardigan Bay
Lyme Bay
Thames Estuary
Strait of Dover
Baie de la Seine
Baie de la Somme
CHANNEL ISLANDS (U.K.)
Alderney
Guernsey
St. Peter Port
Herm
Sark
Jersey
St. Helier
ISLE OF WIGHT
LONDON
BIRMINGHAM
Bristol
Cardiff
Southampton
Portsmouth
Bournemouth
Plymouth
Brighton
Exeter
Oxford
Cambridge
Norwich
Ipswich
Swansea
Newport
Gloucester
Coventry
Leicester
Peterborough
Northampton
Reading
Swindon
Bath
Dover
Calais
Boulogne-sur-Mer
Dieppe
Le Havre
Rouen
Caen
Cherbourg
CORNWALL
DEVON
DORSET
SOMERSET
WILTSHIRE
HANTS
SUSSEX
KENT
SURREY
ESSEX
SUFFOLK
NORFOLK
CAMBRIDGE
NORTHAMPTON
BEDFORD
BUCKS
HERTS
OXFORD
BERKSHIRE
GLOUCS
HEREFORD
WORCESTER
WARWICK
SHROPSHIRE
POWYS
CEREDIGION
PEMBROKESHIRE
CARMARTHENSHIRE
HAUTE-NORMANDIE
SEINE-MARITIME
CALVADOS
MANCHE
Isles of Scilly
On same scale
Projection : Lambert's Conformal Conic
West from Greenwich
East from Greenwich
COPYRIGHT GEORGE PHILIP LTD.

11

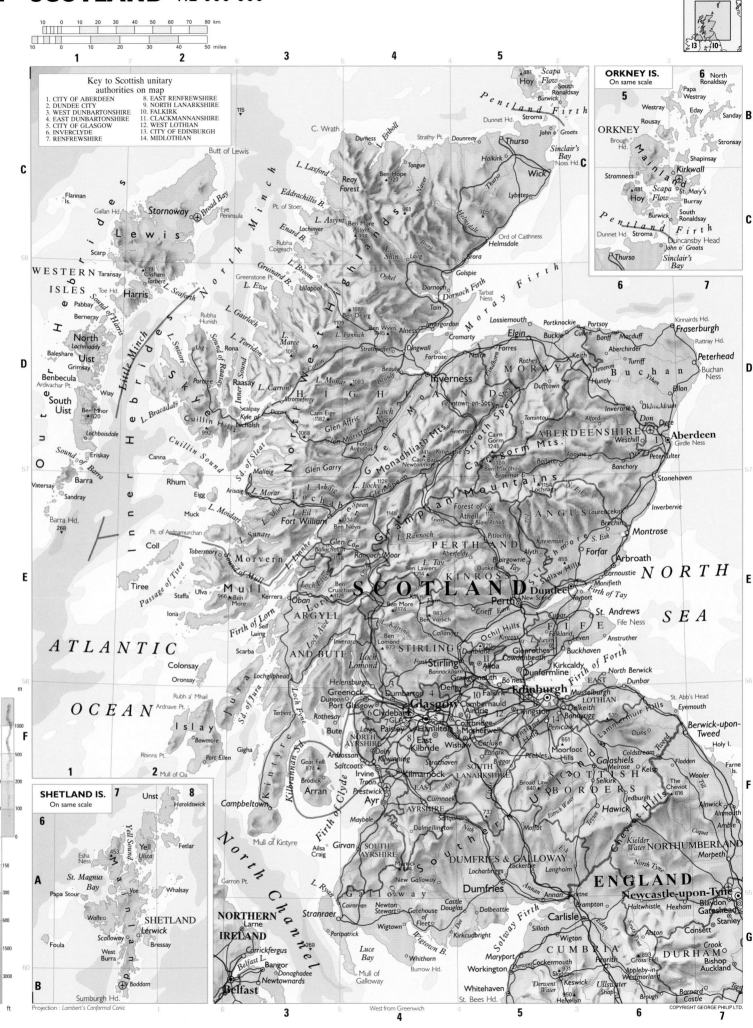

12 SCOTLAND 1:2 000 000

10 0 10 20 30 40 50 60 70 80 km
10 0 10 20 30 40 50 miles

Key to Scottish unitary authorities on map
1. CITY OF ABERDEEN
2. DUNDEE CITY
3. WEST DUNBARTONSHIRE
4. EAST DUNBARTONSHIRE
5. CITY OF GLASGOW
6. INVERCLYDE
7. RENFREWSHIRE
8. EAST RENFREWSHIRE
9. NORTH LANARKSHIRE
10. FALKIRK
11. CLACKMANNANSHIRE
12. WEST LOTHIAN
13. CITY OF EDINBURGH
14. MIDLOTHIAN

ORKNEY IS.
On same scale

ORKNEY

SHETLAND IS.
On same scale

SHETLAND

ATLANTIC OCEAN

WESTERN ISLES

Lewis

Harris

North Uist

South Uist

Barra

Skye

Cuillin Hills

HIGHLANDS

Inverness

MORAY

ABERDEENSHIRE

Aberdeen

Grampian Mountains

Cairngorm Mts.

Ben Nevis

Fort William

PERTH AND KINROSS

ANGUS

Dundee

Perth

SCOTLAND

ARGYLL AND BUTE

STIRLING

FIFE

St. Andrews

Glasgow

Edinburgh

Paisley

SOUTH LANARKSHIRE

EAST AYRSHIRE

SOUTH AYRSHIRE

NORTH AYRSHIRE

SCOTTISH BORDERS

DUMFRIES & GALLOWAY

NORTHUMBERLAND

ENGLAND

Newcastle-upon-Tyne

Carlisle

CUMBRIA

DURHAM

NORTHERN IRELAND

Belfast

North Channel

NORTH SEA

Pentland Firth

Thurso

Wick

John o' Groats

Projection : Lambert's Conformal Conic

West from Greenwich

COPYRIGHT GEORGE PHILIP LTD.

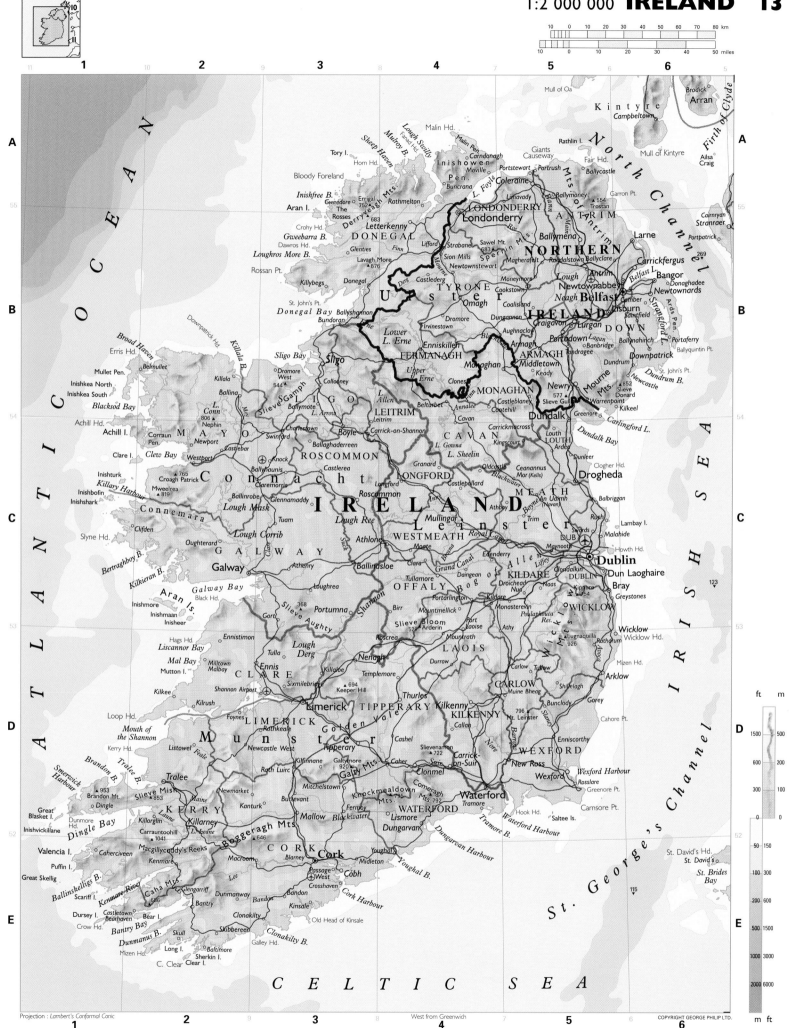

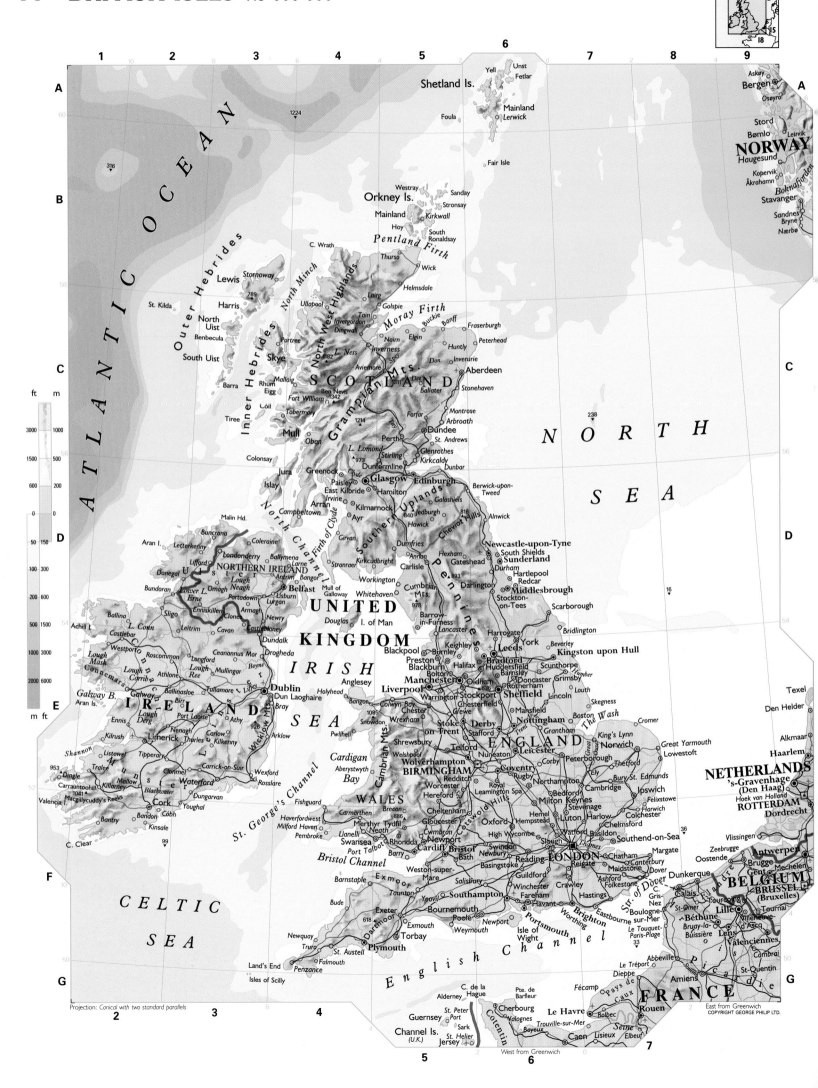

10 0 10 20 30 40 50 60 70 80 90 km
10 0 10 20 30 40 50 60 miles

NORTH SEA

UNITED KINGDOM

Waddeneilanden

Ostfriesische Inseln

Helgoland Düne
Scharhörn
Neuwerk
Alte Mellum

Cromer
North Walsham
The Broads
Norwich Great Yarmouth
Bungay
Beccles Lowestoft
Waveney Southwold
Saxmundham Aldeburgh
Woodbridge Orford Ness
Felixstowe

Terschelling West-Terschelling
Vlieland
Texel Den Burg
Den Helder Den Oever

Schiermonnikoog Ameland
Holwerd Dokkum Uithuizen Delfzijl
Leeuwarden Kollum Zoutkamp Bedum
Franeker Zuidhorn **Groningen** Weener
Harlingen Grouw Leek Hoogezand-Sappemeer
Bolsward Drachten Assen Stadskanaal
Sneek **FRIESLAND** Oosterwolde Ter Apel
Heerenveen Beilen Emmen
Workum Lemmer Borger Klazienaveen
Staveren Wolvega Hoogeveen **DRENTHE** Coevorden

Borkum Norddeich Esens Minsen
Rottumeroog Norden Wittmund Schortens **Bremerhaven**
Aurich Wiesmoor Varel Nordenham
Ostfriesland Emden Jade
Moormerland Westerstede Bad
Leer Zwischenahn Oldenburg
Papenburg Edewecht Friesoythe Hude
Aschendorf Sögel Löningen Vechta
Lathen Meppen Quakenbrück Lohne
Haselünne Bersenbrück Damme
Lingen Fürstenau
WESER-EMS Cloppenburg
Nordhorn Bramsche Wallenhorst
Rheine Ibbenbüren **Osnabrück**

Amsterdam Zaanstad Almere-Stad Harderwijk Ermelo
Haarlem Hilversum Nijkerk Epe Deventer Hengelo
Zandvoort Bussum Amersfoort Apeldoorn Enschede
Hillegom Soest Barneveld Zutphen Haaksbergen
Noordwijk **Utrecht** Ede Doesburg Winterswijk Ahaus
Katwijk Leiden Alphen a/d Rijn Wageningen Arnhem Doetinchem Coesfeld
's-Gravenhage (Den Haag) Zoetermeer Gouda Veenendaal Nijmegen Kleve Goch
Delft Lek **GELDERLAND** Emmerich
Hoek van Holland Europoort Waal 's-Hertogenbosch Uden Kevelaer **Münster**
Vlaardingen **Rotterdam** Gorinchem Oss Boxmeer Geldern Warendorf
Schiedam Maas Boxtel Venray Wesel Dorsten Dülmen Senden
Dordrecht Waalwijk Tilburg Helmond Venlo Kevelaer Recklinghausen
ZEELAND Bergen op Zoom Breda Eindhoven Deurne Oberhausen Gelsenkirchen Hamm
Middelburg Goes Roosendaal **NOORD-BRABANT** Weert Krefeld **Duisburg** **Essen** **Dortmund**
Vlissingen Oosterschelde Brecht Turnhout Roermond Neuss **Düsseldorf** Hagen
Zierikzee Schouwen Terneuzen **ANTWERPEN** **Antwerpen** Lier Mönchengladbach **Köln**
Knokke-Heist Brugge St-Niklaas Mechelen Diest Genk Jülich Bonn
Oostende Gent (Gand) Aalst Leuven Hasselt **Maastricht** Aachen Euskirchen
Dunkerque Roeselare Kortrijk Oudenaarde **Brussel (Bruxelles)** Tienen St-Truiden Liège Verviers
Calais Ieper Tournai Mons Charleroi Namur Dinant **LUXEMBOURG**
Boulogne-sur-Mer **NORD** **Lille** Valenciennes Maubeuge Philippeville Rochefort
PAS-DE-CALAIS Arras Cambrai Chimay Bouillon **RHEINLAND-PFALZ** **Wiesbaden** **Mainz**
Étaples Béthune Lens Douai **PICARDIE** Charleville-Mézières Bitburg Koblenz
Abbeville Amiens St-Quentin Laon **ARDENNES** **LUXEMBOURG** Trier **GERMANY**
Beauvais Compiègne Soissons Reims Verdun Metz **SAARLAND** Kaiserslautern
Reims Châlons-en-Champagne **LORRAINE** Nancy Strasbourg
PARIS Meaux **SEINE-ET-MARNE** **MARNE** **MEUSE** **MOSELLE** **BAS-RHIN**

FRANCE

Underlined towns give their name to the administrative area in which they stand.

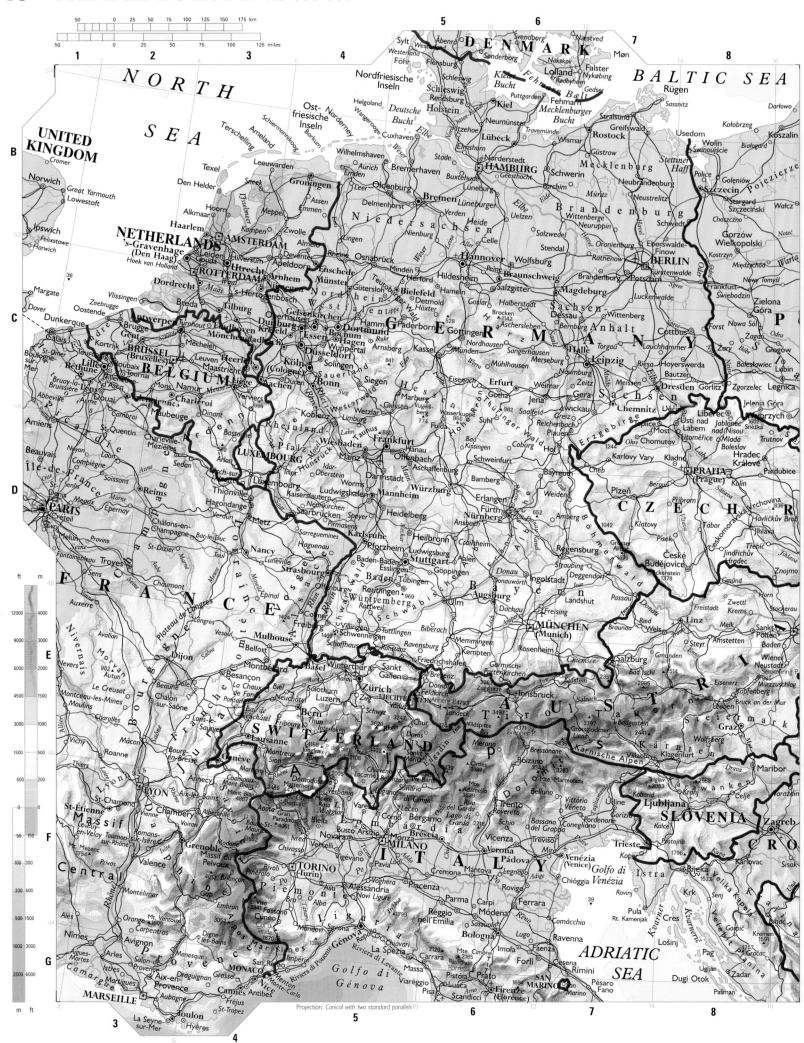

9 10 11 12 13 14 15 16

Słupsk Lębork Rumia *Gdańska* Polessk Prienai VILNIUS Ashmyany Smarhon Maladzyechna Barysaw Krupki Shklow Mstsislaw

Zatoka Wejherowo Gdynia *Baltiysk* Kaliningrad (Russia) Gusev Marijampolė Vileyka Zhodzina Cherven Cherykaw Krychaw

Wałcz Szczecinek Chojnice Świecie Grudziądz Brodnica Mława Ostrołęka Ciechanów Warszawa

LITHUANIA **BELARUS**

MINSK

POLAND **UKRAINE**

WARSZAWA
(Warsaw)

Łódź

Wrocław

Kraków

SLOVAK REP.

WIEN
Vienna

Bratislava

BUDAPEST

HUNGARY

ROMANIA

Transilvania

BUCUREȘTI
(Bucharest)

BOSNIA-
HERZEGOVINA

YUGOSLAVIA

BULGARIA

KYYIV
(Kiev)

Lviv
(Lvov)

Chernivtsi

Chișinău

MOLDOVA

B
C
D
E
F
G

East from Greenwich COPYRIGHT GEORGE PHILIP LTD.

9 10 11 12 13 14 15

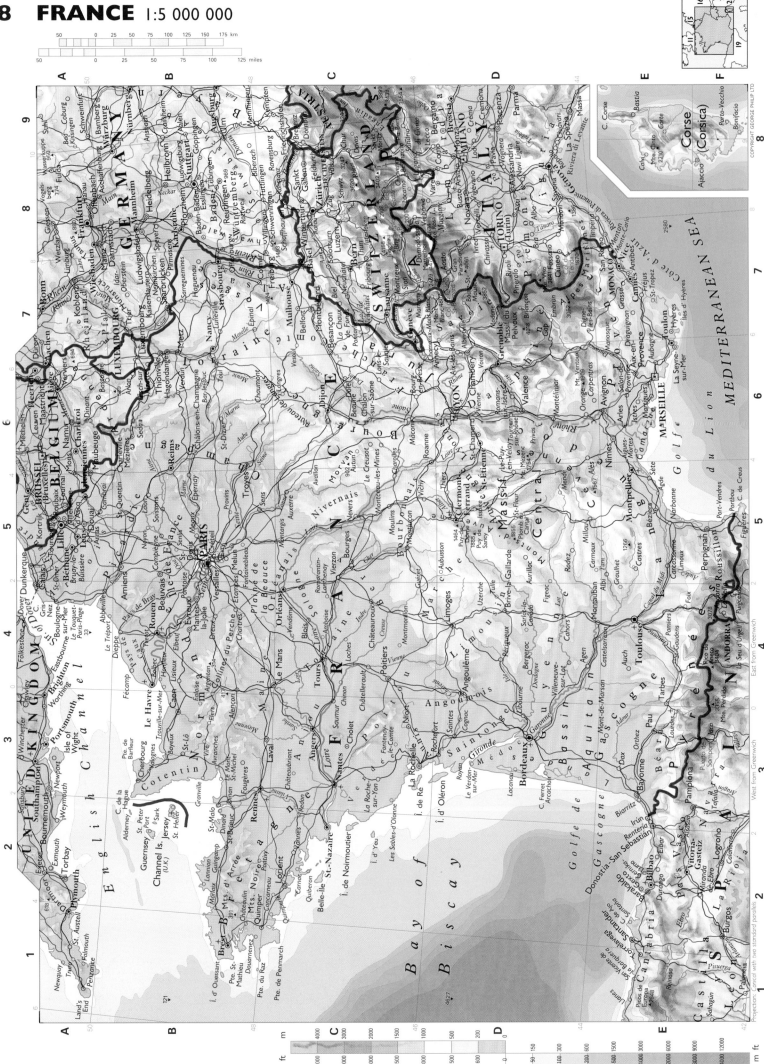

Corse (Corsica)

MEDITERRANEAN SEA

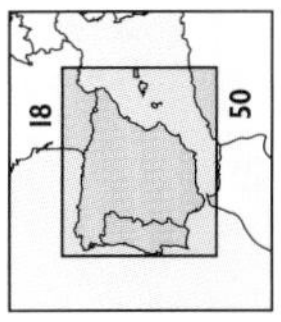

50 0 25 50 75 100 125 150 175 km
50 0 25 50 75 100 125 miles

FRANCE

Golfe du Lion

Montpellier · Sète · Agde · Béziers · Narbonne · Carcassonne · Limoux · Graulhet · Castres · Toulouse · Auch · Pamiers · Foix · St-Gaudens · Tarbes · Pau · Lourdes · Bayonne · Biarritz · Dax · Bordeaux

Gascogne y Luno · Bay of Biscay

ANDORRA

Perpignan · Port-Vendres · Portbou · C. de Creus · G. de Roses · Costa Brava · Figueres · Girona · Lloret de Mar · Sant Feliu de Guixols

BARCELONA · Badalona · Sabadell · Terrassa · Mataró · Santa Coloma de Gramenet · Hospitalet de Llobregat · El Prat de Llobregat · Manresa · Igualada · Vic · Berga

Costa Dorada · Sitges · Vilanova i la Geltrú · Tarragona · Reus · Valls · Tortosa · C. Tortosa · Vinaròs

PYRÉNÉES

Pic d'Aneto 3404 · 3078

Zaragoza · Huesca · Lleida · Barbastro · Monzón · Jaca · Pamplona · Tafalla · Tudela · Logroño · Calahorra · Vitoria-Gasteiz · Miranda de Ebro · San Sebastián · Donostia · Irún · Hendaye · Renteria · Eibar · Bilbao · Barakaldo

País Vasco · **Navarra** · **La Rioja**

Ebro · Soria · Calatayud · Almazán · Sigüenza · Guadalajara · Alcalá de Henares

SPAIN

MADRID · Getafe · Aranjuez · Alcázar · Torrejón · Segovia · Ávila · Sierra de Gredos

Castilla y León · Valladolid · Palencia · Burgos · Aranda de Duero · León · Zamora · Salamanca · Benavente · Ciudad Rodrigo

Castilla - La Mancha · Cuenca · Albacete · Toledo · Montes de Toledo · Ciudad Real · Valdepeñas · Manzanares · Tomelloso · Villarrobledo

Asturias · Oviedo · Gijón · Avilés · Mieres · Langreo · Cordillera Cantábrica · Picos de Europa

Galicia · A Coruña (La Coruña) · Santiago de Compostela · Ferrol · Lugo · Ourense (Orense) · Pontevedra · Vigo · Vila Nova de Gaia

PORTUGAL

LISBOA · Porto · Coimbra · Braga · Guimarães · Aveiro · Leiria · Santarém · Setúbal · Évora · Beja · Faro · Portimão · Sines · Sintra · Cascais

Algarve · C. de São Vicente · B. de Setúbal

Douro · Tejo · Guadiana

Bragança · Vila Real · Viseu · Guarda · Castelo Branco · Covilhã · Portalegre

Serra da Estrela

Mérida · Badajoz · Cáceres · Trujillo · Plasencia · Don Benito · Almendralejo · Zafra

Extremadura

Sevilla · Córdoba · Jaén · Úbeda · Linares · Andújar · Montilla · Écija · Carmona · Utrera · Dos Hermanas · Morón de la Frontera · Osuna · Lucena

Andalucía

Sierra Morena · Sierra Nevada · Mulhacén 3478

Granada · Guadix · Baza · Motril · Málaga · Marbella · Estepona · Torremolinos · Fuengirola · Ronda · Antequera · Loja · Costa del Sol

Huelva · Cádiz · Jerez de la Frontera · San Fernando · Sanlúcar de Barrameda · El Puerto de Santa María · Arcos de la Frontera · Algeciras · La Línea de la Concepción · Gibraltar (U.K.) · Pta. de Europa · Tarifa · C. Trafalgar

G. de Cádiz · Str. of Gibraltar

Ceuta (Sp.) · Melilla (Sp.)

MOROCCO · Tanger · Tétouan · Chefchaouen · Asilah · Larache · Ksar el Kebir

ALGERIA · Oran · Arzew · Mostaganem · Tiaret · Tlemcen

MEDITERRANEAN SEA

Valencia · L'Albufera · Sagunt · Sueca · Cullera · Gandia · Dénia · Xàtiva · Alcoy · Alicante · Elche · Elda · Villena · Benidorm · Villajoyosa · Torrevieja · C. de la Nao · Costa Blanca

Golfo de Valencia · Castelló de la Plana · Vila-real de los Infantes · Onda · Morella

Murcia · Cartagena · Lorca · Mazarrón · Águilas · Mar Menor · C. de Palos · Jumilla · Yecla · Cieza · Caravaca de la Cruz

Almería · Roquetas de Mar · C. de Gata · Vera · Berja · Adra

Islas Baleares

Mallorca · Palma de Mallorca · Inca · Manacor · Sóller · Calvià · Llucmajor · Cabrera

Menorca · Maó (Mahón) · C. Formentor

Eivissa (Ibiza) · Formentera · Sant Antoni Abat

Is. Columbretes

ATLANTIC OCEAN

Projection: Conical with two standard parallels

ft m
6000 2000
4500 1500
3000 1000
1500 500
200
0
−50 −150
100 300
200 600
500 1500
1000 3000
2000 6000
3000 9000
4000 12000
m ft

50   0   25   50   75   100 125 150 175 km
50   0   25   50   75   100 125 miles

Projection: Conical with two standard parallels

SWITZERLAND

AUSTRIA

SLOVENIA

CROATIA

HER

FRANCE

ALGERIA

TUNISIA

MALTA

LIGURIAN SEA

TYRRHENIAN SEA

ADRIATIC SEA

MEDITER

Corse

Sardegna

Sicilia

Golfo di Génova

Golfo dell' Asinara

Bouches de Bonifacio

Golfo di Venézia

Golfo di Táranto

Golfe de Tunis

Golfe de Hammamet

Str. di Messina

Ísole Eólie

Ísole Égadi

Ísole Pelagie (Italy)

LYON, Grenoble, Chambéry, Annecy, Valence, Montélimar, Avignon, Orange, Carpentras, MARSEILLE, Toulon, Aix-en-Provence, Cannes, Antibes, Nice, MONACO, Monte-Carlo, Menton, San Remo, Imperia, Savona, Génova, Rapallo, La Spezia, Carrara, Massa, Viaréggio, Pisa, Livorno

TORINO (Turin), Cuneo, Asti, Alessándria, Novara, Vercelli, Biella, Aosta, Ivrea, MILANO, Monza, Bérgamo, Bréscia, Cremona, Lodi, Pavia, Piacenza, Parma, Módena, Bologna, Ferrara, Ravenna, Rímini, Verona, Vicenza, Pádova, Venézia (Venice), Treviso, Udine, Trieste

Ljubljana, Zagreb, Maribor, Celje, Varaždin, Karlovac, Rijeka, Pula, Zadar, Šibenik, Split, Banja Luka

Firenze (Florence), Prato, Pistóia, Lucca, Arezzo, Siena, Grosseto, Perugia, Assisi, Terni, SAN MARINO, Pésaro, Fano, Ancona, Macerata, Fermo, Ascoli Piceno, Téramo, Pescara, Chieti, L'Aquila

ROMA, VATICAN CITY, Tivoli, Latina, Frosinone, Cassino, Terracina, Fórmia, NÁPOLI, Pozzuoli, Caserta, Benevento, Avellino, Salerno, Capri, Potenza, Matera, Táranto, Bari, Barletta, Trani, Molfetta, Andria, Foggia, Manfredónia, Cerignola, Altamura, Fasano, Monópoli

Catanzaro, Cosenza, Crotone, Rossano, Vibo Valéntia, Réggio di Calábria, Messina, Palermo, Trapani, Marsala, Mazara del Vallo, Sciacca, Agrigento, Gela, Ragusa, Siracusa, Catánia, Enna, Caltanissetta, Caltagirone, Módica, Vittória, Avola

ALGERIA — Annaba, Skikda, Constantine, El Khroub, El Milia, Collo

TUNISIA — Tunis, Bizerte, Ben Arous, Nabeul, Hammamet, Sousse, Kairouan, Mahdia, Monastir, Sfax (El Jem), Béja, Jendouba, El Kef, Kasserine

Pantelleria (Italy)

Lampedusa, Linosa

Valletta, Gozo, Rabat

ft m
12000 4000
9000 3000
6000 2000
4500 1500
3000 1000
1500 600
600   200
0
0
50   150
100   300
200   600
500   1500
1000 3000
2000 6000
3000 9000
4000 12000
m ft

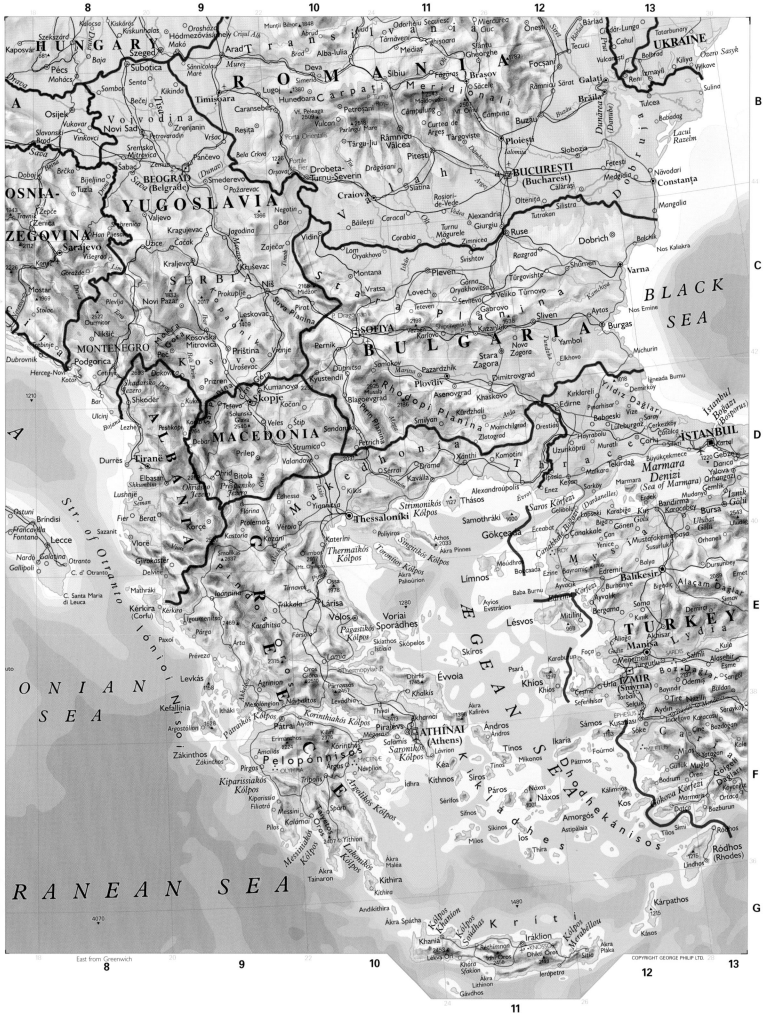

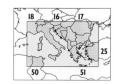
A

B

C

D

E

F

G

HUNGARY

Kaposvár
Szekszárd
681▲
Pécs
Mohács
Kalocsa
Kiskőrös
Kiskunhalas
Oroshája
Hódmezővásárhely
Makó
Crişul Alb
1848
Abrud

Baja
Szeged
Szentes
Sánnicolau Mare
Arad
Lugoj
1380
Muntii Bihor

Subotica
Senta
Kikinda
Mureş
T
r
a
n
s
Brad
Alba-Iulia

Sombor
Bečej
Zrenjanin
Timişoara
Caransebeş
Hunedoara
Deva
Simleria
Sibiu

Osijek
Novi Sad
Vojvodina
Vršac
Reşiţa
Vf. Peleaga
2509▲
Vulcan
2518▲
Petroşani
Fágáraş
Braşov

Slavonski Brod
Vukovar
Petrovaradin
Bela Crkva
Porta Orientalis
Parângul Mare
Câmpulung

OSNIA-
Doboj
Brčko
Sremska Mitrovica
Zemun
1226
Orşova
Drobeta-Turnu-Severin
Drágăsani
Piteşti
Târgovişte
Ploieşti

ZEGOVINA
2112
Bijeljina
Tuzla
BEOGRAD (Belgrade)
Smederevo
Požarevac
(Dunav)
Jiu
V l a h i a

Sarajevo
Han Pijesak
Srebrenica
Valjevo
Craiova

YUGOSLAVIA

ROMANIA

UKRAINE

BLACK SEA

BULGARIA

SOFIYA

MACEDONIA

ALBANIA

GREECE

TURKEY

ISTANBUL

ATHÍNAI (Athens)

IONIAN SEA

RANEAN SEA

East from Greenwich

COPYRIGHT GEORGE PHILIP LTD.

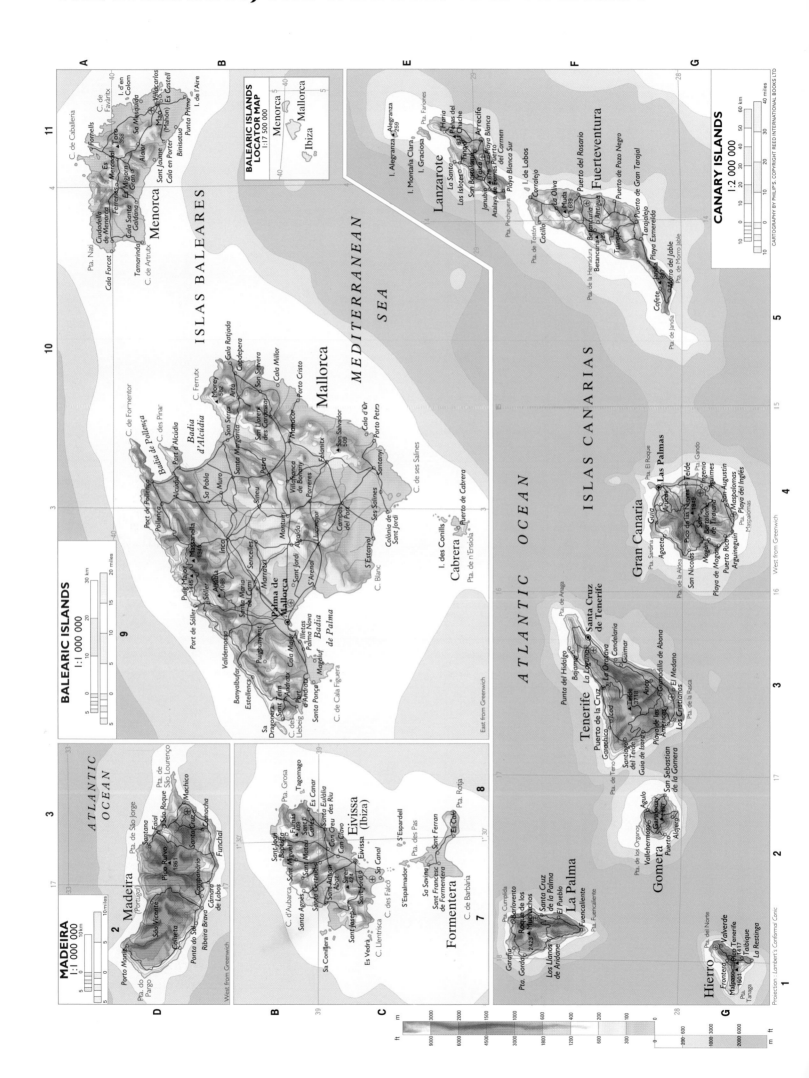

BALEARIC ISLANDS LOCATOR MAP
1:17 500 000

Menorca
Mallorca
Ibiza

BALEARIC ISLANDS
1:1 000 000

CANARY ISLANDS
1:2 000 000

CARTOGRAPHY BY PHILIP'S. COPYRIGHT REED INTERNATIONAL BOOKS LTD

MADEIRA
1:1 000 000

Projection: Lambert's Conformal Conic

ISLAS BALEARES

Menorca

Mallorca

MEDITERRANEAN SEA

ISLAS CANARIAS

ATLANTIC OCEAN

Lanzarote

Fuerteventura

Gran Canaria

Tenerife

La Palma

Gomera

Hierro

Madeira (Portugal)

Eivissa (Ibiza)

Formentera

Cabrera

West from Greenwich

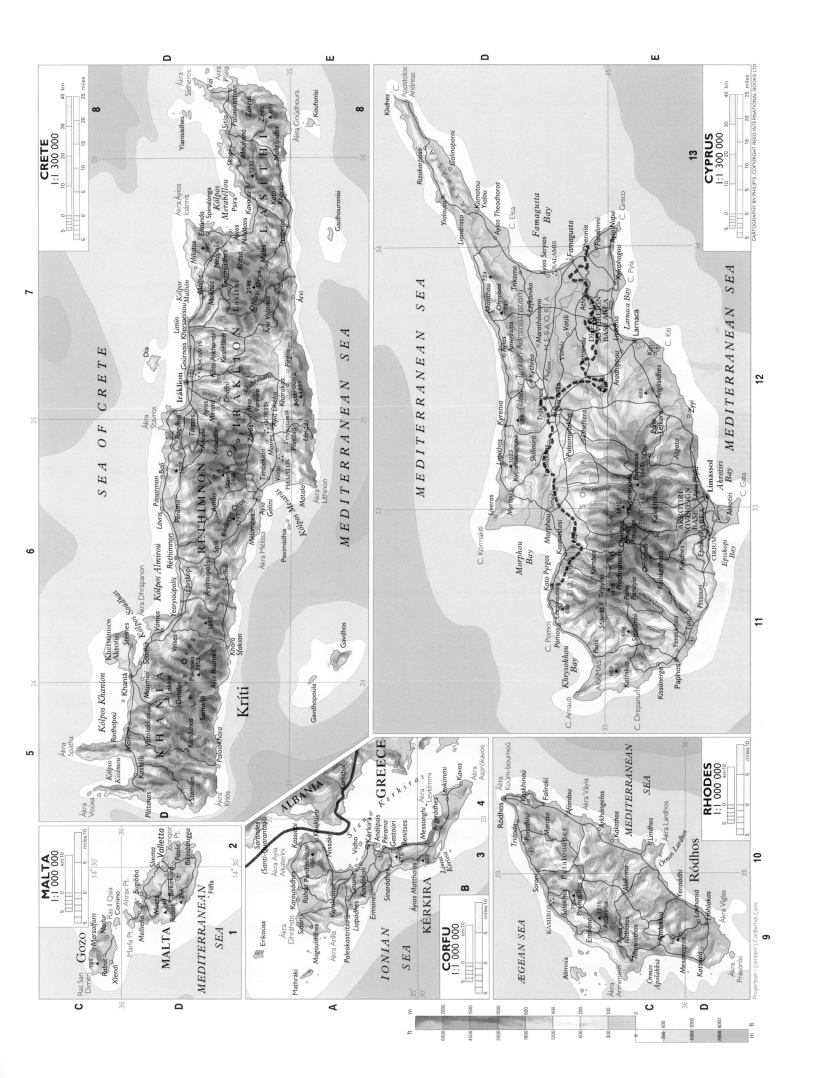

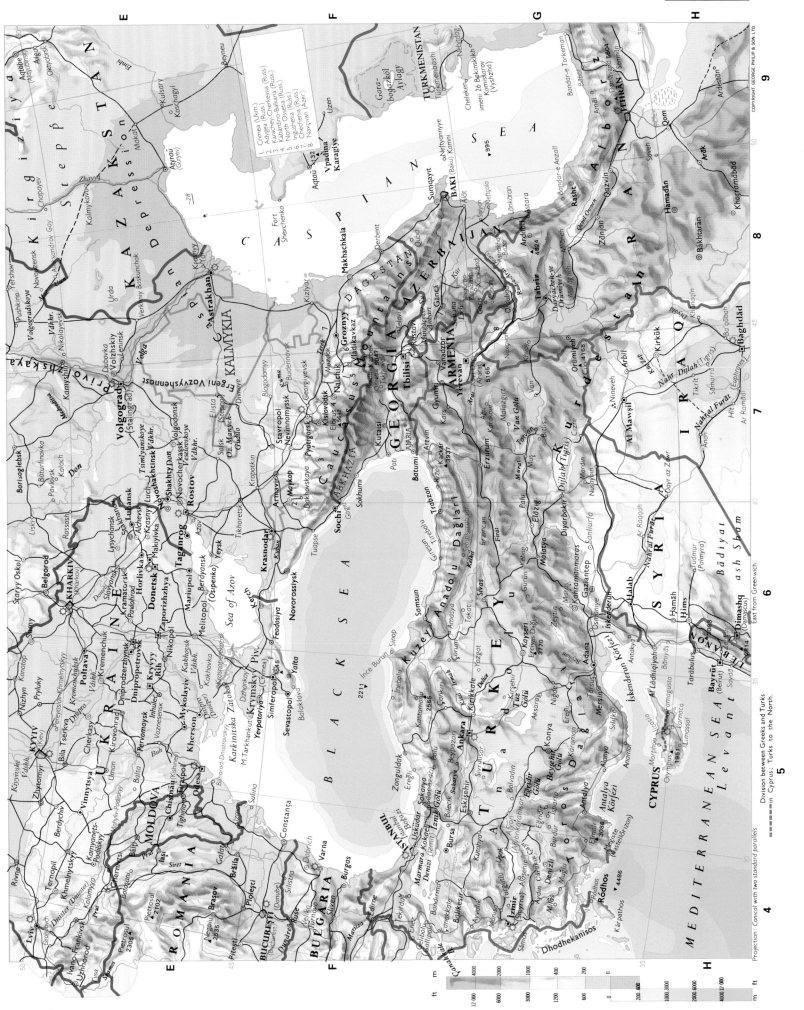

1. Crimea (Ukr.)
2. Adygea (Russ.)
3. Adhey-Cherkessia (Russ.)
4. Kabardino-Balkaria (Russ.)
5. North Ossetia (Russ.)
6. Ingushetia (Russ.)
7. Chechenia (Russ.)
8. Naxçıvan (Azer.)

Projection: Conical with two standard parallels

Division between Greeks and Turks
in Cyprus; Turks to the North.

East from Greenwich

100 0 100 200 300 400 500 600 700 800 km
100 0 100 200 300 400 500 miles

D   C   B   4 5 6 7

RUSSIA
1 Adygea
2 Karachey-Cherkessia
3 Kabardino-Balkaria
4 North Ossetia
5 Ingushetia
6 Chechenia
7 Dagestan
8 Mordvinia
9 Chuvashia
10 Mari El
11 Tatarstan
12 Udmurtia
13 Khakassia
AZERBAIJAN
14 Naxçivan
GEORGIA   **UKRAINE**
15 Ajaria   17 Crimea
16 Abkhazia

ft m
12 000   4000
6000   2000
3000   1000
1200   400
600   200
0   0
200   600
m ft

E

F

G

Projection: Conical Orthomorphic with two standard parallels

East from Greenwich

6   7   8   9

A   B   C

8   9   10   11   12   13   14   15   16   17   18   19

60

OCEAN

Mys Dezhneva
(East C.)
Uelen

Chukchi
Sea

St. Lawrence I.
(USA)

Ostrov
Shmidta

Mys Arkticheskiy

Ostrov
Komsomolets

Ostrov Oktyabrskoy
Revolyutsii

Ostrov
Pioner

965

Ostrov
Bolshevik

Severnaya
Zemlya

C

Proliv Vilkitskogo

Mys Chelyuskin

3800

Ostrov
Genryetty
Ostrov
Zhanetty

Ostrova Delonga

Ostrov
Bennetta
Novosibirskiye Ostrova

Ostrov Faddeyevskiy

Ostrov Zhokhova

Ostrov
Novaya Sibir

Laptev
Sea

East Siberian Sea

Ostrov Vrangelya

D

Chaun
Bay

Pevek
Ust Chaun

Chukotskoye Nagorye

Anadyr

Egvekinot

Beringovskiy

Anadyrskiy Zaliv

Provideniya

Bering
Sea

Poluostrov Byrranga

Gory

Taymyr

1146

Oz. Taymyr
Nordvik

Ostrov Bolshoy
Begichev

Mys Buorkhaya

Tiksi

Kazachye

Chokurdakh

Srednekolymsk

Nizhne Kolymsk

Ostrova
Medvezhi

Ostrov
Ayon

Bolshoy

Ust

Omolon

Markovo

Penzhino

Koryakskoye Nagorye

Ossora

Ostrov
Karaginskiy

Volochanka

Kheta

Khatanga

Novorybnoye

Khatanga

Zhilinda

Ust Olenek

Saskylakh

Bulun

Ust Kuyga

Druzhina

Zyryanka

Kolyma

Kironau

Pobeda
3147

Omsukchan

Onsukchan

Orotukan

Evensk

Gizhiga

Paren

Gizhiginskaya
Guba

Palana

Tigil

Uka

D

Poluostrov Kamchatka

Khrebet

50

Chernaya

Pyasina

Dudinka

Norilsk

Gory
Putorana
1701

Yessey

Kotuy

Anabar

Olenek

Tit-Ary

Verkhoyansk

Batagay

Yana

Ust-Nera

Gora Chen
2682

2389

Oymyakon

Oyagas

Sasuman

Yagodnoye

Magadan

Ola

Ratkha

Zaliv
Shelikhova

50

Igarka

Turukhansk

Noginsk

Nizhnyaya Tunguska

Tura

Yukta

Olenek

Zhigansk

Kystatyam

Sangar

Batamay

Khandyga

Okhotskiy
Perevoz

Okhotsk

Arka

Okhotsk

Gora Lopatina
1609

Sea   of   Okhotsk

1780

Ust Khayryuzov

3621

4570

Gora
Kyumbelsky

Ust-Kamchatsk

Kronotskaya

Petropavlovsk-
Kamchatskiy

2456

Kirovskiy

Ust-Bolsheretsk

Ostrov
Paramushir

Severo-Kurilsk

Ostrov
Onekotan

R   U   S   S   I   A

Arctic Circle

962

Vilyuy

Vilyuysk

Verkhnevilyuysk

Suntar

Nyurba

Namtsy

Pokrovsk

Yakutsk

Mayya

Amga

Ytyk Kyuyel

Ust-Mil

Aimo

Maya

Nelkan

Chumikan

Ayan

Khrebet Dzhugdzur

Ulya

Okha

Nikolayevsk-
na-Amure

Aleksandrovsk-
Sakhalinskiy

Sakhalin

Ostrova

Kurilskiye Ostrova

Chernyshevskiy

Mirnyy

Sinsk

Olekminsk

Tommot

Aldan

2246

Uchur

2246

Uda

Tugur

Poronaysk

Uglegorsk

Yuzhno-Sakhalinsk

Kholmsk

Korsakov

Ostrov Iturup

Ostrov Kunashir

Strelka

Yeniseysk

1104

Yartsevo

Severo-
Yeniseyskiy

Kuyumba

Mutoray

Vanavara

Angara

Boguchany

Podkamennaya Tunguska

Chuna

Kezhma

Korshunovo

Mama

Bodaybo

2999

Chara

Karalon

Vitim

Olema

Yenyuka

Neryungri

Nagornyy

Stanovoy Khrebet

Tynda

2840

Skovorodino

Zeya

Ushumun

Norsk

Selemdzha

Komsomolsk

Amgun

2078

Amursk

Vanino

2840

Khrebet Sikhote Alin

Sovetskaya
Gavan

Kholmsk

Ostrov Moneron

Achinsk

Kansk

Ilanskiy

Tayshet

Nizhneudinsk

Tulun

Zima

Cheremkhovo

Usolye Sibirskoye

Angarsk

1620

Bratsk

Ust-Ilimsk

Makarovo

Ust-Kut

Zheleznogorsk-
Ilimskiy

Magistralnyy

Lena

Kirensk

Kondratyevo

2840

Bagdarin

455

Barguzin

Vitim

Yablonovyy Khrebet

Mogocha

Chara

Kalakan

Ust-Nyukzha

Dzhalinda

Gulian

1054

Bukachacha

Chita

Sretensk

Nerchinsk

Shilka

Shilka

Amur

Shimanovsk

Svobodnyy

Belogorsk

Chernyakhovsk

Poyarkovo

Zavitinsk

Obluchye

Birobidzhan

Smidovich

Khabarovsk

Bikin

Vyazemskiy

Lesozavodsk

Spassk

Dalniy

Dalnegorsk

Terney

Amgu

Olga

Krasnoyarsk

Artemovsk

Chernogorsk

Minusinsk

Abakan

Zapadnyy Sayan

Turan

Toora-
Khem

Kyzyl

Chadan

Samagaltay

Uvs Nuur

Erzin

Vostochnyy Sayan

Munku-Sardyk
3491

Irkutsk

Slyudyanka

Ulan Ude

3491

Khilok

Petrovsk-
Zabaykalskiy

Aginskoye

Olovyannaya

Borzya

Zabaykalsk

Manzhouli

Hailar

Khapcheranga

Kyakhta

Zakamensk

Gusinoozersk

Darhan

Hentiyn
Nuruu

Choybalsan

Tamsagbulag

Hulun Nur

Ang'angxi

Qiqihar

Nenjiang

Jiamusi

Hegang

Dalnerechensk

Ussuriysk

Artem

Vladivostok

Nakhodka

Kraskino

E

Hovsgol
Nuur

Hatgal

Tsetserleg

Ulaanbaatar

Ondörhaan

2800

Tao'an

Changchun

Siping

Harbin

Dongbei

Mudanjiang

Jilin

Songhua Hu
2744

Yanji

Chongjin

Wonsan

Sea   of   Japan

Hokkaido

Otaru

Sapporo

Hakodate

Aomori

Hachinohe

Akita

Honshū

Niigata

Kanazawa

F

Har Us
Nuur

Hyargas Nuur

Hangayn
Nuruu

Döröö Nuur

Ulyasutay

Hova

4362

Altay

MONGOLIA

Luu

Xilinhot

1949

Linxi

Chifeng

Gobi

Dalandzadgad

Saynshand

3957

Erenhot

Baotou

Hohhot

Zhangjiakou

Chengde

Beijing

CHINA

Fushun

Shenyang

Anshan

Yingkou

Tonghua

Dandong

North Korea

Nampo

Pyongyang

Dalian

Wonsan

Kansong

Sŏul

Inch'ŏn

South Korea

Taejŏn

Taegu

Pusan

JAPAN

Osaka

Fuji-San
3776

4266

Hami

Gaxun Nur

10   100   11   110   12   120   13   130   14

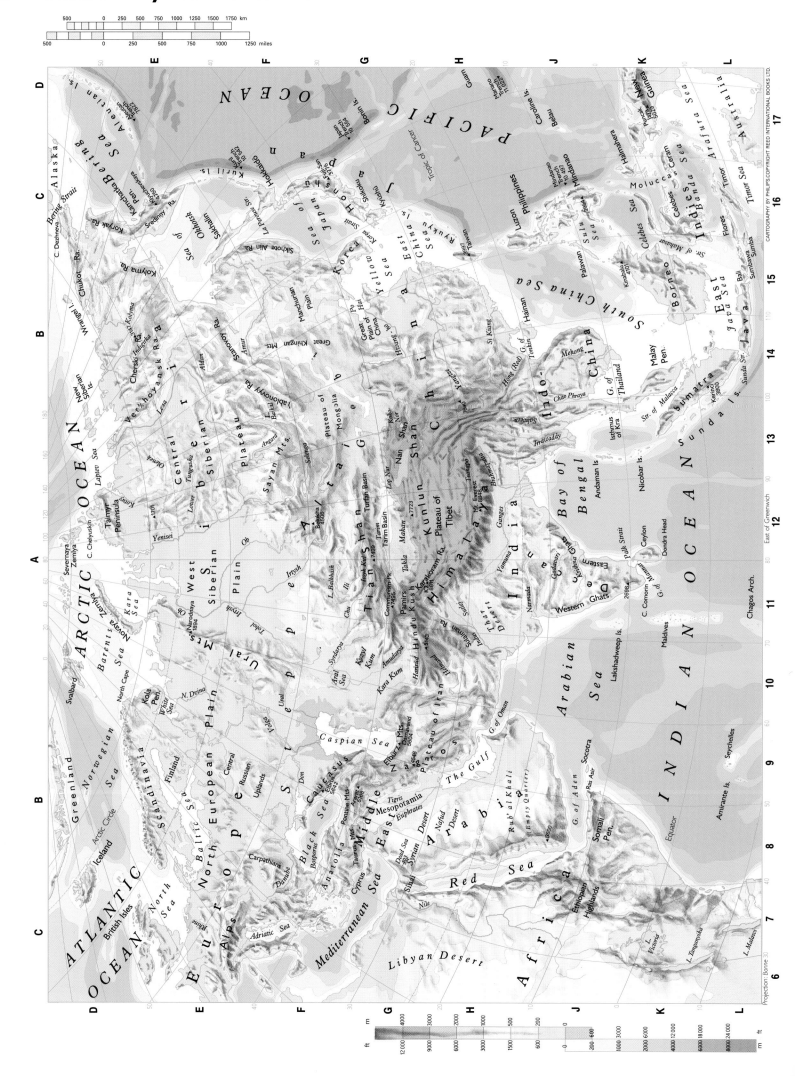

Projection: Bonne

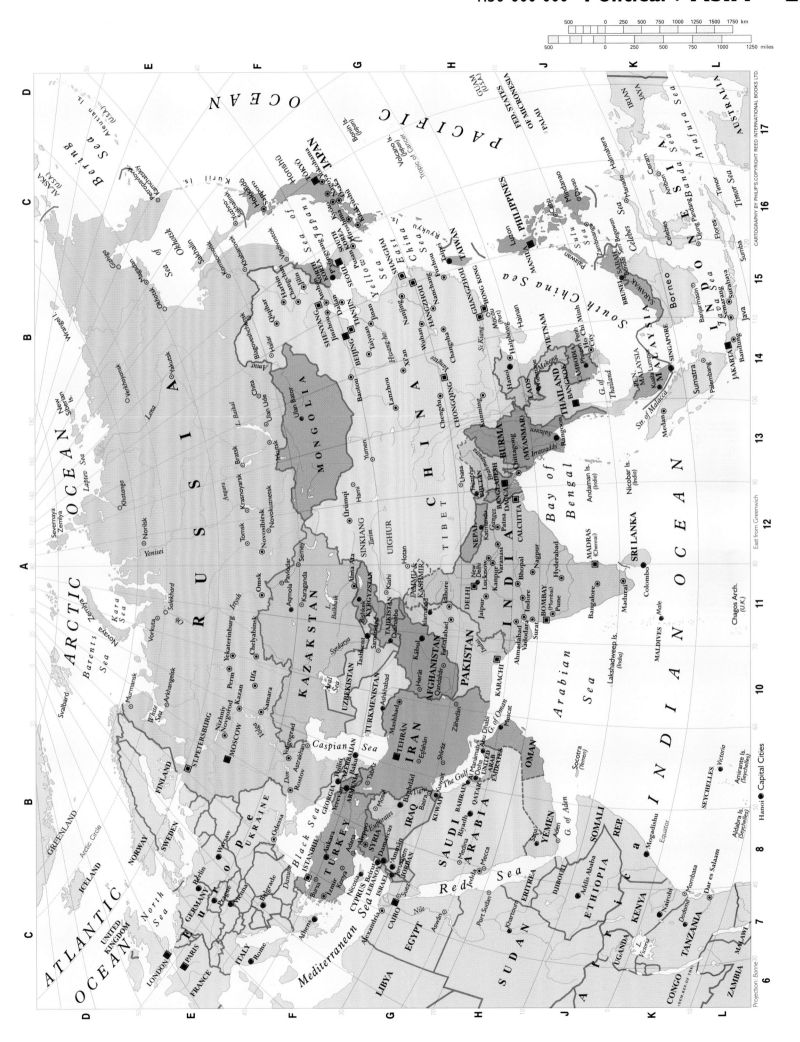

500   0   250   500   750   1000   1250   1500   1750 km
500   0   250   500   750   1000   1250 miles

D

ALASKA
(U.S.A.)

Bering
Sea

Aleutian Is.
(U.S.A.)

Wrangel I.

New
Siberian
Is.

ARCTIC   OCEAN

PACIFIC   OCEAN

GREENLAND

ATLANTIC
OCEAN

ICELAND

Svalbard

Barents
Sea

Novaya
Zemlya

Kara
Sea

Severnaya
Zemlya

Laptev
Sea

Lena

Khatanga

Yenisei

R   U   S   S   I   A

Sea of
Okhotsk

Kamchatka

Petropavlovsk

JAPAN
Honshu
TOKYO
Hokkaido
Sapporo

Sakhalin

Vladivostok

Yakutsk

Magadan

Kolyma

Kuril Is.

Bonin Is.
(Japan)

Volcano Is.
(Japan)

Tropic of Cancer

FED. STATES
OF MICRONESIA

PALAU

GUAM
(U.S.A.)

IRIAN
JAYA

NEW
GUINEA

AUSTRALIA

Celebes
Sea

Halmahera

Ceram

Banda
Sea

Arafura
Sea

Timor
Sea

Timor

I   N   D   O   N   E   S   I   A

CARTOGRAPHY BY PHILIP'S. COPYRIGHT REED INTERNATIONAL BOOKS LTD.

NORWAY

SWEDEN

FINLAND

Arctic Circle

White
Sea

Murmansk

Arkhangelsk

Vorkuta

Salekhard

Omsk

Novosibirsk

Tomsk

Krasnoyarsk

Bratsk

Irkutsk

L. Baikal

Chita

Ulan Ude

Angara

Ulan Bator

M   O   N   G   O   L   I   A

Harbin

Changchun

Shenyang

NORTH
KOREA
PYONGYANG

SOUTH
KOREA
SEOUL
Pusan

Sea of
Japan

Nagoya
Osaka
Kyoto

Kagoshima

Ryukyu
Is.

TAIWAN
Taipei

PHILIPPINES
Luzon
MANILA

Quezon

Cebu

Mindanao
Davao

Zamboanga

Sulu
Sea

Manado

Sabah

BRUNEI
SARAWAK

Borneo

Ujung Pandang

Flores

Sumba

Java

Semarang

Surabaya

Bandung

JAKARTA

Sumatra

Palembang

Banjarmasin

Java   Sea

MALAYSIA
Kuala Lumpur
SINGAPORE

Str. of Malacca

Medan

UNITED
KINGDOM
LONDON

FRANCE
PARIS

GERMANY
Berlin
Prague
Vienna

ITALY
Rome

Warsaw

Kiev

Belgrade

Athens

North
Sea

E   u   r   o   p   e

Danube

UKRAINE

Odessa

Black   Sea

Istanbul
Izmir
Bursa
Ankara

TURKEY

CYPRUS
Nicosia

LEBANON
Beirut
ISRAEL
Jerusalem
Amman
Damascus
SYRIA
Aleppo

JORDAN

Mediterranean   Sea

Alexandria
CAIRO

EGYPT

LIBYA

Nile

Aswân

Suez

Red
Sea

SUDAN

Khartoum

Port Sudan

ERITREA

ETHIOPIA
Addis Ababa

DJIBOUTI

SOMALI
REP.

Mogadishu

UGANDA
L. Victoria

KENYA
Nairobi

TANZANIA
Dodoma
Dar es Salaam
Mombasa

ZAMBIA

MALAWI

CONGO

A   f   r   i   c   a

Equator

Aldabra Is.
(Seychelles)

SEYCHELLES
Victoria

Amirante Is.
(Seychelles)

G. of Aden

YEMEN
Aden

Socotra
(Yemen)

OMAN
Muscat

G. of Oman

U.A.E.
Abu Dhabi

QATAR
Doha
BAHRAIN
Al Manāmah

KUWAIT

SAUDI
ARABIA
Riyadh

Mecca
Medina
Jedda

Baghdad
IRAQ
Basra

Tigris
Euphrates

Mosul

Tehran
IRAN
Esfahan
Shiraz
Zāhedān

TEHRĀN

Tabriz

AZERBAIJAN
Baku

ARMENIA
Yerevan

GEORGIA
Tbilisi

Rostov

Astrakhan

Volgograd

Don

Volga

Caspian   Sea

ST. PETERSBURG

MOSCOW

Nizhniy
Novgorod

Perm

Yekaterinburg

Chelyabinsk

Ufa

Kazan

Samara

Saratov

Aral
Sea

KAZAKSTAN

Agmola
Pavlodar

Karaganda

L.
Balkhash

Alma Ata

Semey

KYRGYZSTAN
Bishkek

TAJIKISTAN
Dushanbe

UZBEKISTAN
Tashkent

Samarkand

TURKMENISTAN
Ashkhabad

Mashhad

AFGHANISTAN
Kābul
Qandahār
Herāt

PAKISTAN
Islamabad
Faisalabad
Lahore
Multan

KARACHI

JAMMU &
KASHMIR

SINKIANG
UIGHUR

Kashi

Tarim

Hotan

Ürümqi

Hami

Yumen

Baotou

Lanzhou

C   H   I   N   A

T   I   B   E   T

Lhasa

Brahmaputra

Chengdu

Kunming

CHONGQING

Yangtze

Xi'an

Taiyuan

Huang-ho

BEIJING
TIANJIN
Jinzhou

Dalian

Qingdao

Yellow
Sea

Nanjing

SHANGHAI

HANGZHOU

Wuhan

Changsha

Nanchang

Fuzhou

Xiamen

GUANGZHOU
HONG KONG

East
China
Sea

Macau

Hainan

South   China   Sea

VIETNAM
Hanoi
Haiphong

LAOS
Vientiane

Mekong

THAILAND
BANGKOK

CAMBODIA
Phnom Penh

Ho Chi Minh
City

PEN.
MALAYSIA

G. of
Thailand

BURMA
(MYANMAR)
Rangoon

Irrawaddy

Salween

Chittagong

BANGLADESH
DACCA

NEPAL
Katmandu

Ganges

Patna
Varanasi

Lucknow

DELHI
New
Delhi

Jaipur

Kanpur

Bhopal

Indore

Nagpur

Hyderabad

Bangalore

MADRAS
(Chennai)

Madurai

Colombo
SRI LANKA

Bombay
(Mumbai)
Pune

Surat

Vadodara

Ahmadabad

Indus

I   N   D   I   A

Bay of
Bengal

Andaman Is.
(India)

Nicobar Is.
(India)

Lakshadweep Is.
(India)

MALDIVES
Male

Chagos Arch.
(U.K.)

CALCUTTA

A   r   a   b   i   a   n   S   e   a

I   N   D   I   A   N   O   C   E   A   N

East from Greenwich

Hanoi ● Capital Cities

Projection: Bonne

Tropic of Cancer

JAPAN 1:5 000 000

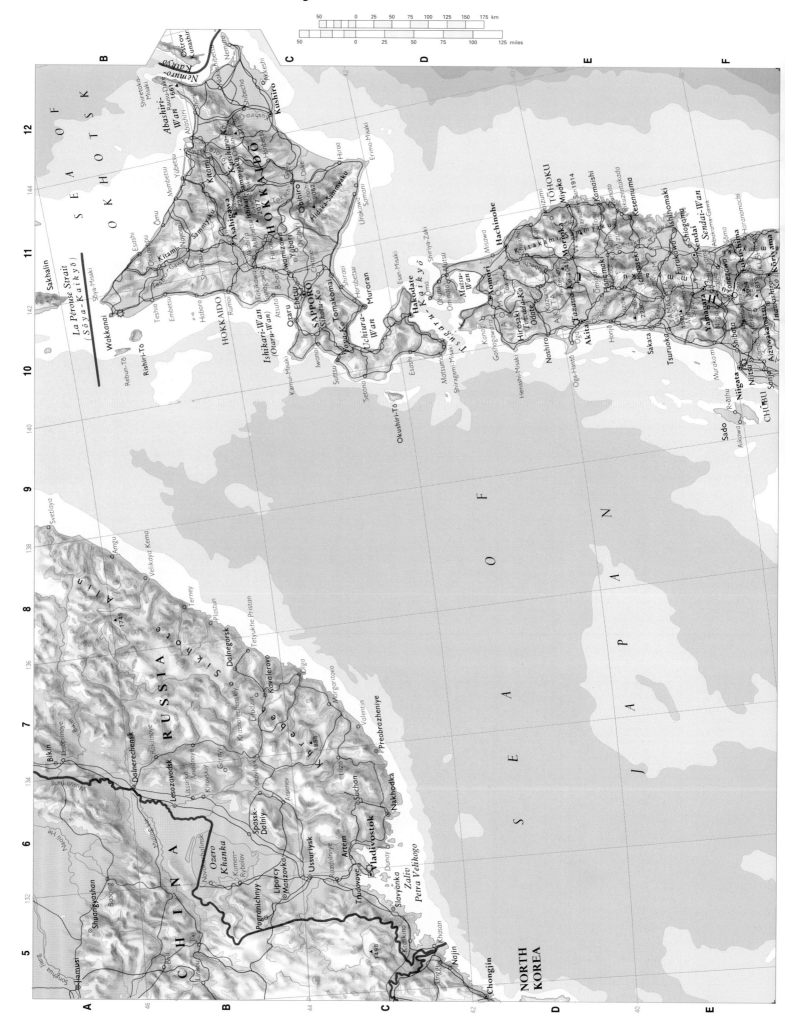

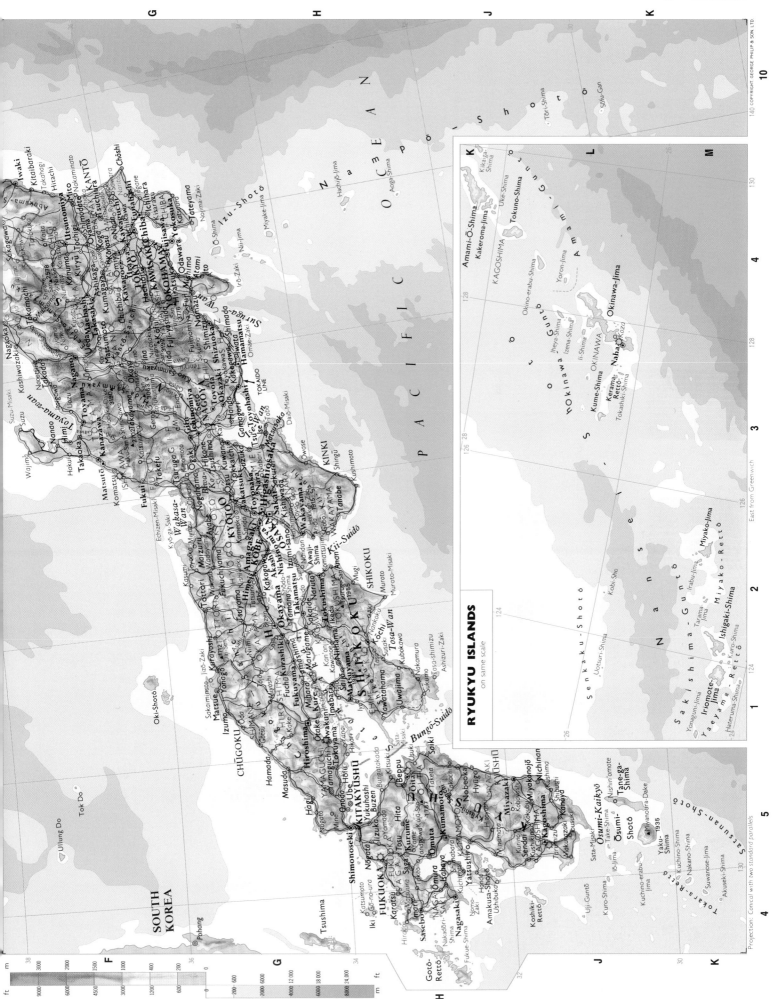

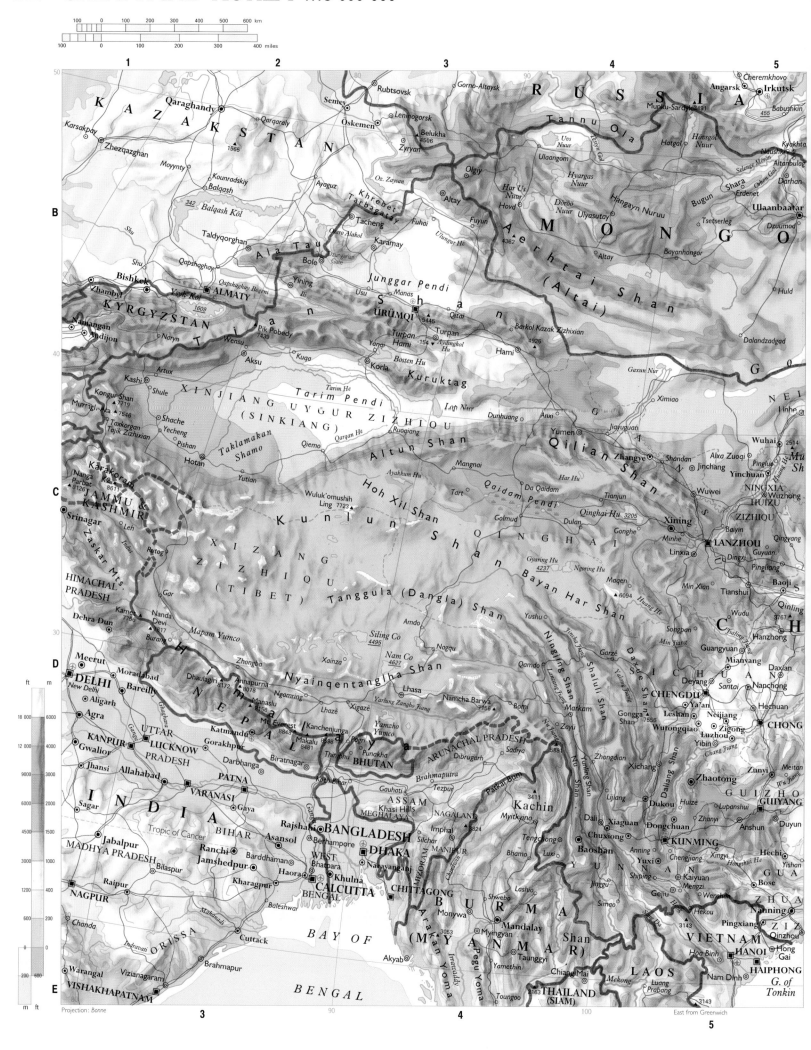

1 **2** **3** **4** **5**

RUSSIA

Cheremkhovo
Angarsk ⊙ Irkutsk

K A Z A K S T A N

Qaraghandy
Semey   Rubtsovsk
Qarqaraly   Gorno-Altaysk
Mupku-Sarojk   2491
Karsakpay   455   Babushkin
Zhezqazghan   Öskemen   Naushki   Kyakhta
Belukha   Selenge Mörön   Altanbulag
4506   Zyryan   Tannu Ola
Moyynty   Kounradskiy   Ulaangom
Balqash   Ayaguz   Olgiy   Hatgal   Hövsgöl Nuur   Darhan
342 Balqash Köl   Oz. Zaysan   Altay   Uvs   Shara   Erdenet   ⊙ Ulaanbaatar
Tacheng   Fuyun   Nuur   Hyargas   Erdenet   Tsetserleg   Dzuunmod
Ozero Alakol   Nuur   Döröö   Bugun
Taldyqorghan   4362   Dzuungarian   Nuur   Ulyasutay   Bayanhongor   Huld
Ala Tau   Gate   Hovd   A e r h t a i   S h a n   (A l t a i)
Qapshaghay   Bole   Dalandzadgad
Bishkek   ⊙ ALMATY   Yining   Junggar Pendi   Altay   M O N G O
Zhambyl   Qapshaghay Bögeni   Usu   Manas   Huld
Ysyk-Köl   Ili   T i a n   S h a n   Qitai   Barkol Kazak Zizhixian   G o
Namangan   1609   ÜRÜMQI   5445   Turpan   4925   O
Andijon   Naryn   Pik Pobedy   Hami -154   Hami   Gaxun Nur   NEI
7439   Wensu   Yangi   Aydingkol   Ximiao   Linhe
K Y R G Y Z S T A N   Aksu   Kuqa   Korla   Bosten Hu   Kuruktag   G   Dunhuang   Anxi   Jiayuguan
Kashi   Shule   Tarim He   Lop Nur   Yumen   Shandan   Wuhai   2514
Kongur Shan   Artux   XINJIANG UYGUR ZIZHIQU   Qarqan He   Ruoqiang   Jiuyuan   Alxa Zuoqi   Pingluo   Mu Sh
7719   Muztag-Ata   (SINKIANG)   Qiemo   Altun Shan   Qilian Shan   Zhangye   Jinchang   Yinchuan   NINGXIA
7546   Shache   Taklamakan   Mangnai   Da Qaidam   Tianjun   Wuwei   Wuzhong   HUIZU
Taxkorgan   Yecheng   Shamo   Yutian   Ayakkum Hu   Tart   Qaidam Pendi   Minhe   Baiyin   ZIZHIQU   Qingyang
Tajik Zizhixian   Pishan   Hotan   Wuluk'omushih   Hoh Xil Shan   Har Hu   Golmud   Qinghai Hu 3205   Xining   Linxia   ⊡ LANZHOU   Guyuan
Karakoram   Ling 7723   K u n l u n   S h a n   Dulan   Gonghe   Dingxi   Pingliang
JAMMU &   Nanga   K2 8611   Tart   Q I N G H A I   Maqen   Min Xian   Tianshui   Baoji
KASHMIR   Parbat 8126   X I Z A N G   Gyaring Hu   Ngoring Hu   6094   Huang He   C   H
⊙ Srinagar   Leh   Z I Z H I Q U   4237   Bayan Har Shan   Wudu   Qinling
Zaskar Mts.   Rutog   (T I B E T)   Yushu   Songpan   3767   Hanzhong
HIMACHAL   Gar   Tanggula (Dangla) Shan   Amdo   Jinsha Jiang   Garzê   Min Jiang   Guangyuan   Tianshui
PRADESH   Kamet 7756   Siling Co   Nagqu   Daxue Shan   Mianyang   Daxian
Dehra Dun   Nanda Mapam Yumco   4495   Qamdo   Shaluli Shan   CHENGDU   Nanchong
Meerut   Devi 7817   Burang   Zhongba   Nam Co   Ningjing Shan   Markam   S I C H U A N   Deyang   Santai   Hechuan
⊡ DELHI   Moradabad   H   Xainza   4627   Lhasa   Lancang Jiang   Zayu   Gongga   Ya'an   Neijiang   ⊡ CHONG
New Delhi   Bareilly   i   Ngamring   Nyainqentanglha Shan   Namcha Barwa   7556   Zigong   Luzhou   Chang Jiang
Aligarh   m   Zhongba   Xigazê   7756   Bomi   Shan   Wurongqiao   Zunyi   Meitan   Ww Jiang
Agra   a   Dhaulagiri Annapurna   Lhazê   Yarlung Zangbo Jiang   Xichang   Daliang Shan   Zhaotong   G U I Z H O
KANPUR   l   8172   8078   Yamzho   ARUNACHAL PRADESH   5881   Zhongdian   GUIYANG
UTTAR   a   Manaslu   Mt Everest   Yumco   Sadiya   Nu Jiang   Lijiang   Dukou   Zhanyi   Anshun   Duyun
LUCKNOW   y   7156   8848   Punakha   Dibrugarh   Patkai Bum   Dali   Xiaguan   GUIZHO
Gwalior   Katmandu   Makalu   Pogri   BHUTAN   Brahmaputra   Yunling Shan   Baoshan   Huize   Lupanshui
Jhansi   Gorakhpur   8481   Thimphu   Sadiya   3411   Chuxiong   Kachin   Tengchong   Anning   KUNMING   Hechi
Allahabad   Darbhanga   Koch Bihar   Gauhati   Tezpur   NAGALAND   Myitkyina   Luxi   Chengjiang   Yishan
Sagar   Biratnagar   Brahmaputra   ASSAM   3824   Imphal   Bhamo   Baoshan   Yuxi   Xingyi   G U A
I N D I A   PATNA   N E P A L   Gaya   Khasi Hills   MANIPUR   Silchar   Y U N N A N   Shiping   Kaiyuan   Bose
Jabalpur   BIHAR   Rajshahi   MEGHALAYA   Jinggu   Gejiu   Mengzi   Wenshan
MADHYA PRADESH   Asansol   BANGLADESH   Lashio   Simao   Hekou   Z H U A
Ranchi   Berhampore   DHAKA   MIZORAM   Shwebo   Hekou   Nanning   Z I Z
Raipur   Barddhaman   WEST   Monywa   Mandalay   Shan   Pingxiang   Qinzhou
NAGPUR   Jamshedpur   Bhatpara   Khulna   Haora   Myingyan   3143   VIETNAM   HANOI
Bilaspur   Kharagpur   CALCUTTA   CHITTAGONG   B U R M A   Taunggyi   Hoa Binh   Hong   HAIPHONG
Chanda   BENGAL   Baleshwar   (M Y A N M A R)   Pegu Yoma   Yamethin   Gai
ORISSA   Akyab   Arakan Yoma   3143   G. of
Raipur   Cuttack   BAY OF   Irrawaddy   Chiang Mai   LAOS   Tonkin
Warangal   Mahanadi   3053   THAILAND   Luang
Vizianagaram   Brahmapur   B E N G A L   Toungoo   1163   (SIAM)   Prabang   Nam Dinh
VISHAKHAPATNAM

27
40
38 37

50

B

N

40

C

J A P A N

30

D

E

20

Map labels (selected):

Oz. Baykal
Ulan Ude
Chita
Bukachacha
Sretensk
Nerchinsk
Gulian
Shimanovsk
Svobodnyy
Chegdomyn
Komsomolsk
Poronaysk
Mys Terpeniya

Petrovsk-Zabaykalskiy
Olovyannaya
Borzya
Priorgunsk
Orogen Zizhiqi
Blagoveshchensk
Aihui
Bureya
Birobidzhan
Aleksandrovsk-Sakhalinskiy
Sakhalin

Hentiyn Nuruu
Manzhouli
Hailar
Nenjiang
Bei'an
Qianjin
Khabarovsk
Vanino
Yuzhno-Sakhalinsk

Huhun Nur
Bei'an
Yichun
Hegang
Bikin
Hulin
Kholmsk

LIA
Choybalsan
Buir Nur
Butha Qi
Arxan
Solan
QIQIHAR
Anda
Daqing
Suihua
HARBIN
Jiamusi
Shuangyashan
Mishan
La Perouse Str.
Wakkanai
Kitami

Tamsagbulag
Horqin Youyi Qianqi
Shuangcheng
Fuyu
JILIN
Mudanjiang
L. Khanka
Ussuriysk
Asahigawa
2290
HOKKAIDO
SAPPORO
Otaru
Kushiro

Saynshand
Xilinhot
Huolin Gol
Tao'an
CHANGCHUN
Shuangliao
Dunhua
Vladivostok
Hunchun
Artern
Nakhodka
Hakodate
Muroran
Erimo-misaki

Dzamin Uud
Erenhot
Baicheng
Tongliao
Siping
Liaoyuan
Yanji
Changbei
Shan
Chongjin
Tsugaru-Kaikyō
Aomori
Hachinohe

Bayan Obo
Sonid Youqi
Duolun
Chifeng
Tieling
FUSHUN
SHENYANG
2744
Yingkou
North
Kimchaek
SEA OF
Akita
Morioka

Hohhot
Jining
Zhangjiakou
Xuanhua
Chaoyang
Liaoyang
Benxi
ANSHAN
Dandong
Hamhung
Hŭngnam
Wŏnsan
Sado
Niigata
Kōriyama
Sendai
Ishinomaki

Baotou
Datong
Baoding
Jinzhou
Qinhuangdao
Liaodong Bandao
P'YONGYANG
Nampo
Haeju
JAPAN
Wajima
Jōetsu
Yamagata
Fukushima

Yuanping
3058
BEIJING (PEKING)
BEIJING SHI
Anci
TANGSHAN
Liaodong Wan
Korea Bay
NORTH KOREA
Kaesŏng
Chunchon
Takaoka
Kanazawa
Toyama
Utsunomiya
Mito

Usamo
TAIYUAN
HEBEI
TIANJIN
TIANJIN SHI
DALIAN
Nampo
SŎUL (SEOUL)
Kangnŭng
Komatsu
TŌKYŌ
KAWASAKI
YOKOHAMA

GREAT WALL
SHIJIAZHUANG
Cangzhou
Bo Hai
Yantai
Weihai
INCH'ŎN
SOUTH KOREA
Chunchon
Matsue
NAGOYA
3776
Fuji-San
Shizuoka

Yangquan
Dezhou
Shandong
Bandao
TAEJŎN
TAEGU
Kanazawa
OSAKA
KYŌTO
KŌBE
Sakai
Hamamatsu

Yan'an
Yuci
Fenyang
JINAN
Weifang
Huang He (Hwang Ho)
Ye Xian
YELLOW SEA
Kunsan
Chŏnju
Masan
PUSAN
Okayama
HIROSHIMA
Kure
Shikoku
Wakayama

Changzhi
Handan
Tai'an
ZIBO
Jining
QINGDAO
Rizhao
KWANGJU
1815
Tsushima
Shimonoseki
Kōchi
Matsuyama

Linfen
Anyang
Jincheng
Xinxiang
Zaozhuang
Mokpo
KITAKYUSHU
FUKUOKA
Sasebo
Nagasaki

Tongchuan
Sanmenxia
Luoyang
Kaifeng
Lianyungang
Cheju Do
1950
Korea Strait
Kumamoto
Kyūshū
Miyazaki

Xianyang
XI'AN
Shangqiu
Huaibei
Xuzhou
Qingjiang
Yancheng
Nampō-Shotō

Shandi
ZHENGZHOU
HENAN
Shangshui
JIANGSU
Kagoshima

Pingdingshan
Nanyang
Fuyang
Bengbu
Yangzhou
Changzhou
Nantong

Han Shui
Zhumadian
Huainan
Taizhou
Wuxi
SHANGHAI

Ankang
Shiyan
Xinyang
HEFEI
Ma'anshan
Suzhou SHI
SHANGHAI

Daba Shan
Xiangfan
ANHUI
Tongling
Wuhu
Wuxing
Hangzhou

Fengjie
Dable Shan
Zhongxiang
WUHAN
Anqing
HANGZHOU
Hangzhou Wan

Wanxian
Yichang
HUBEI
Huangshi
Chang Jiang (Yangtze)
NINGBO

Enshi
Shashi
Jiujiang
Tunxi
Shaoxing
EAST CHINA SEA

QING
Changde
Dongting Hu
Jingdezhen
ZHEJIANG
Jinhua
LINHAI
Amami-Ō-Shima
Tokuno-Shima

Jishou
Yiyang
Poyang Hu
Shangrao
Quzhou
Wenzhou
Ryūkyū-rettō
Okinawa-Jima

2683
Huaihua
NANCHANG
CHANGSHA
HUNAN
Xiangtan
JIANGXI
Naha
7507

Shaoyang
Pingxiang
Ji'an
Nanping
FUZHOU
Ryūkyū Strait
PACIFIC

Hongjiang
Hengyang
FUJIAN
Sanming
Longyan
Chilung
Sakishima-Guntō
Miyako-Jima

Guilin
Xing'an
Ganzhou
Ruijin
Yong'an
Putian
Quanzhou
T'AIPEI
Tropic of Cancer
Ishigaki-Shima
Iriomote-Jima

Liuzhou
NGXI
Shaoguan
Zhangzhou
Hsinchu
T'aichung
Changhua

Wuzhou
GUANGDONG
Mei Xian
Chao'an
Xiamen
Yu Shan
3997
TAIWAN (FORMOSA)
T'aitung

Zhaoqing
Jiangmen
Foshan
Huizhou
Shantou
T'ainan
P'ingtung

HIQU
Yangjiang
Macau (Port.)
HONG KONG
KAOHSIUNG
Batan Is.

Beihai
Maoming
Zhanjiang

Leizhou Bandao
SOUTH CHINA SEA
PHILIPPINES
Babuyan Is.

Hainan Dao
1879
Haikou
HAINAN
OCEAN

Yacheng
Qiongzhou Haixia

6   7   120   7   130   8

110

COPYRIGHT GEORGE PHILIP LTD.

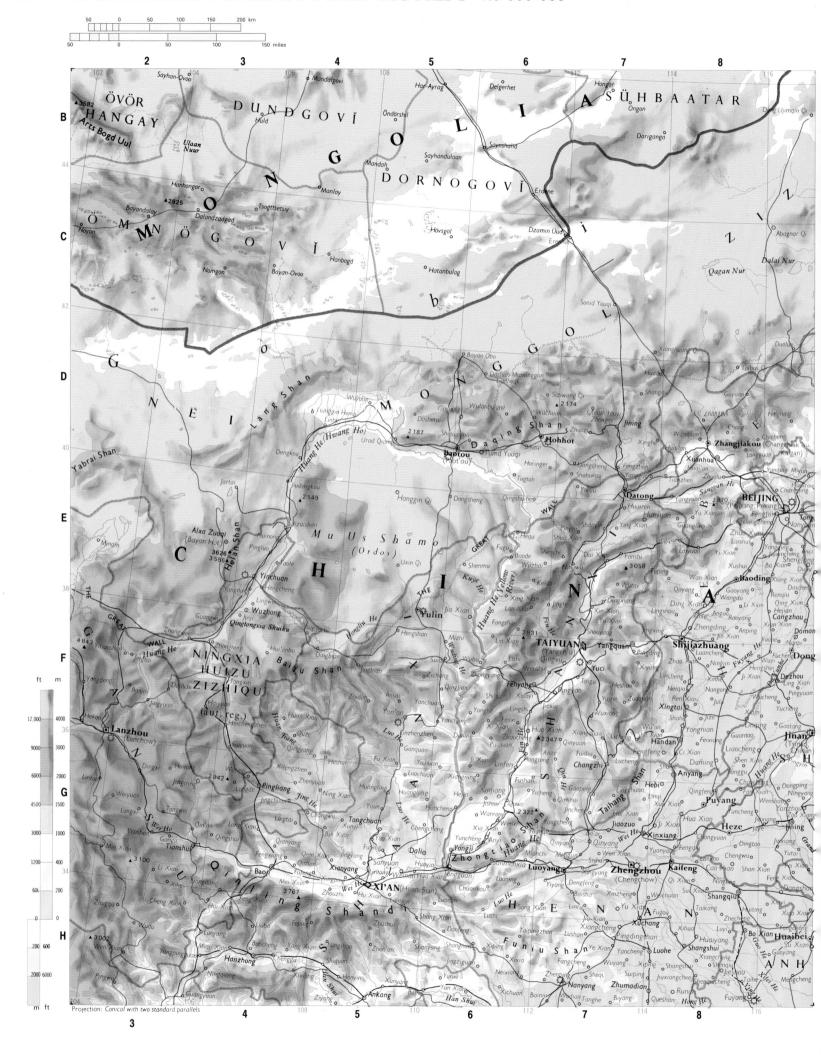

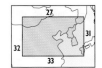

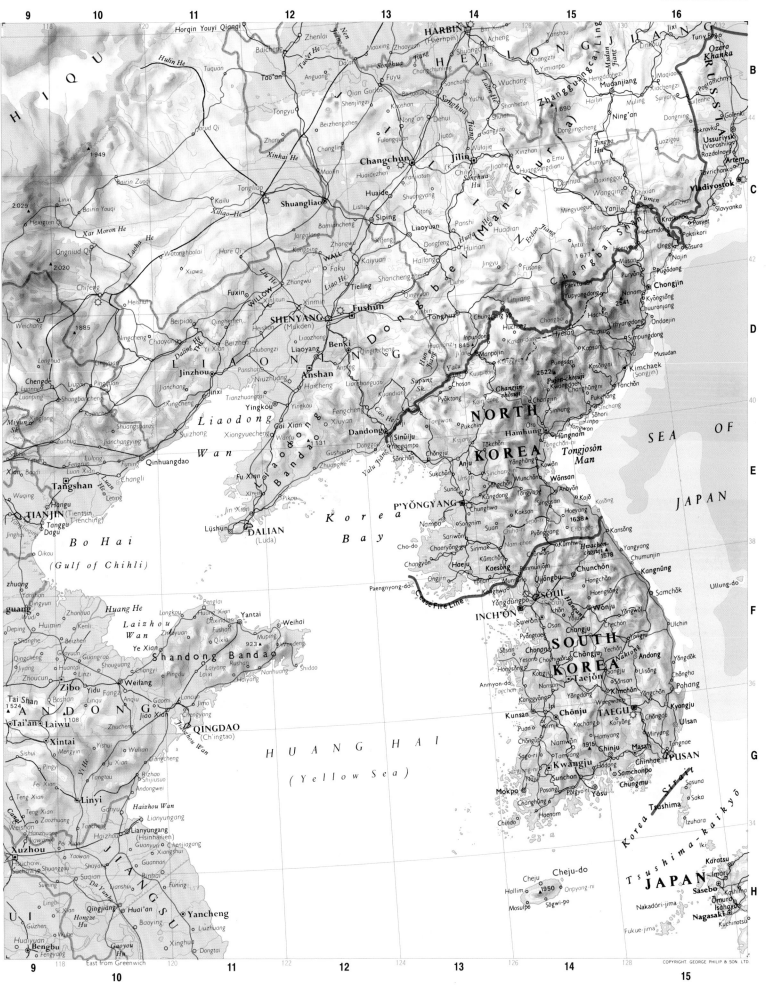

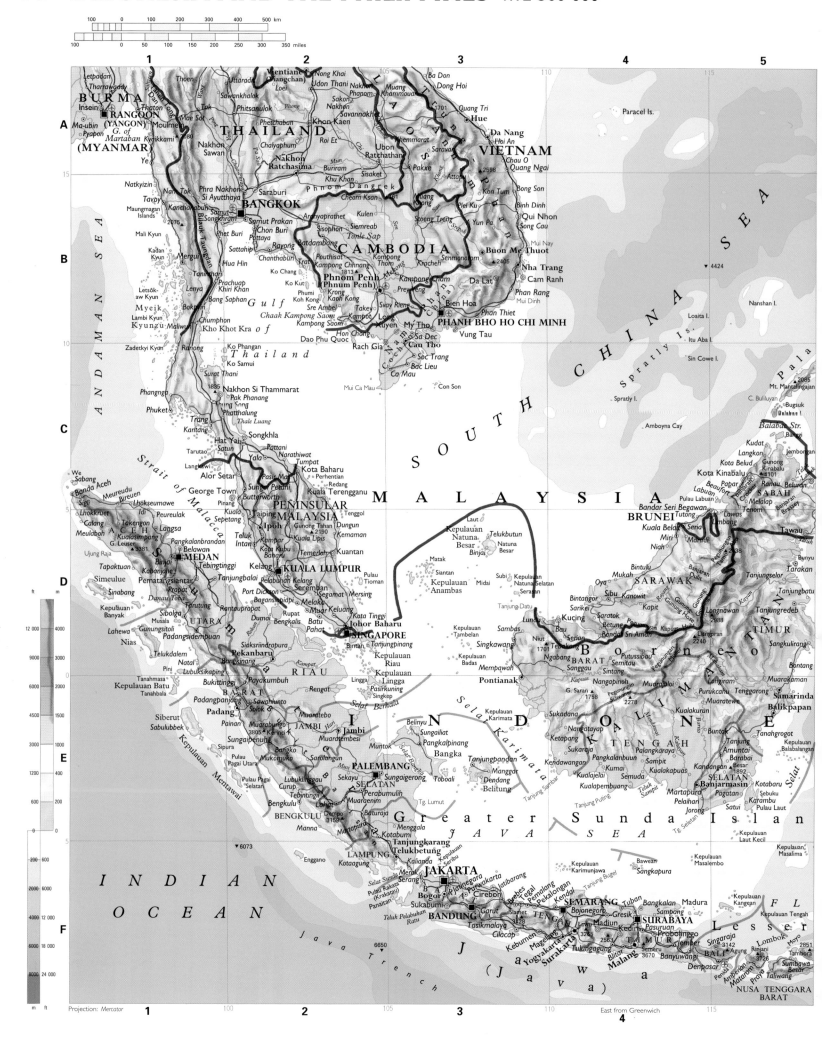

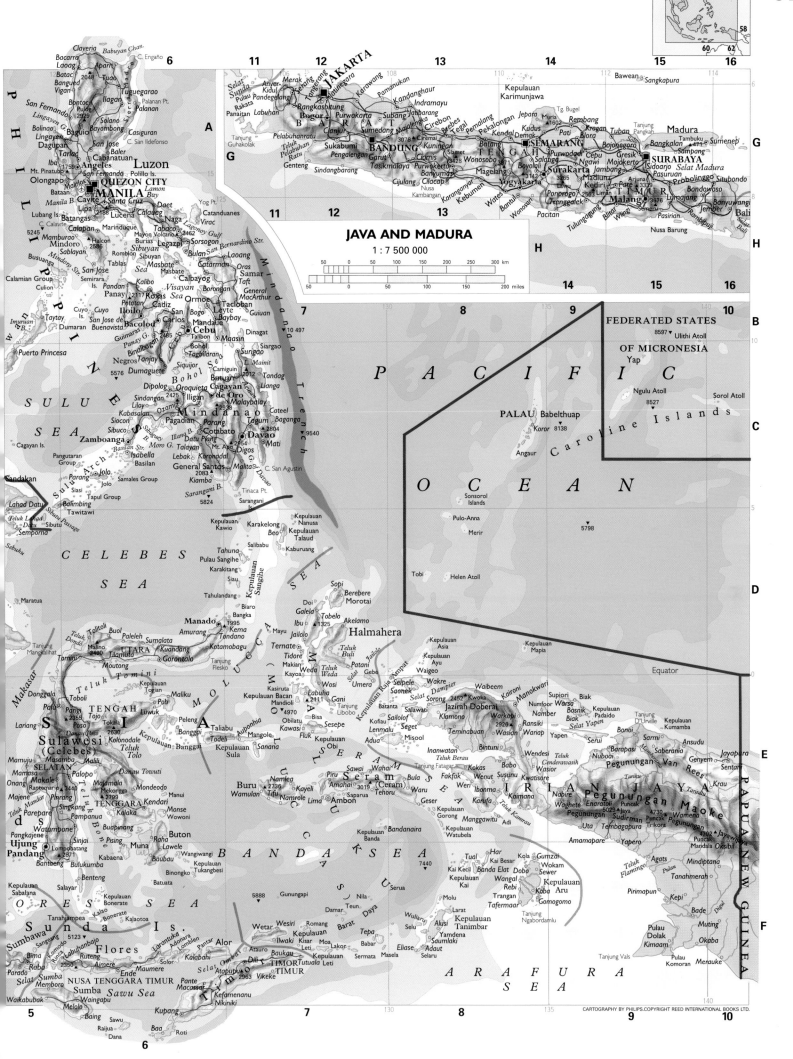

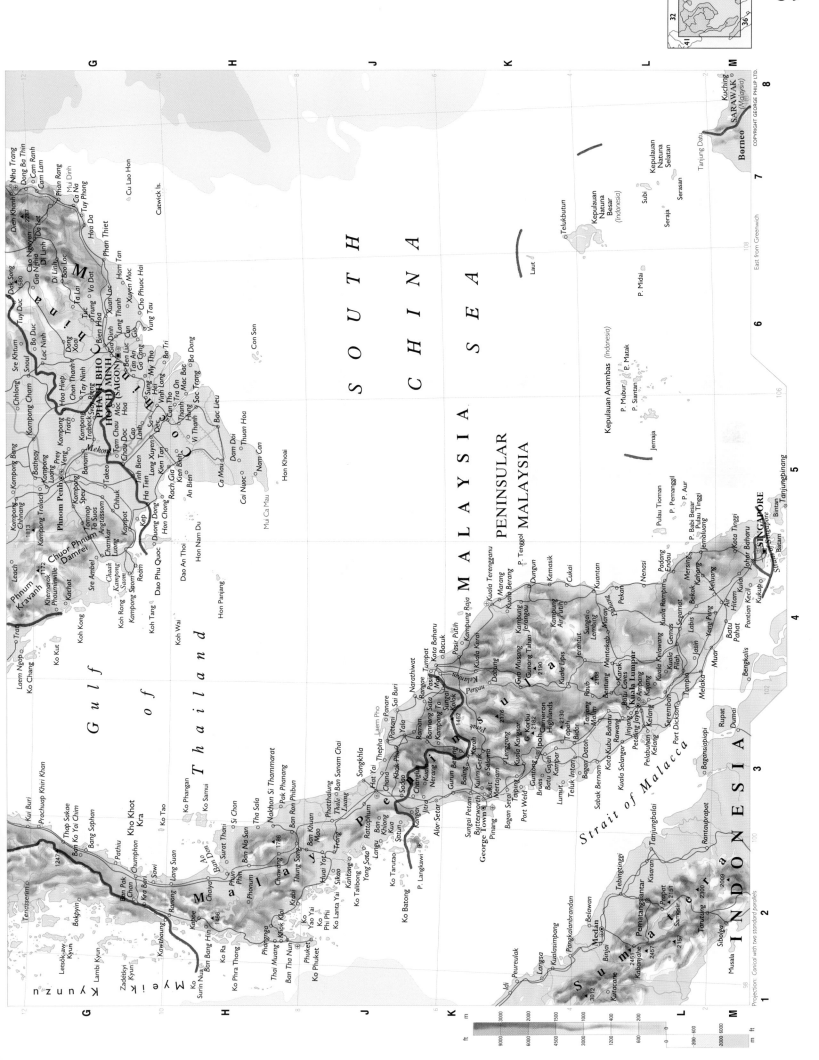

S O U T H   C H I N A   S E A

M A L A Y S I A

PENINSULAR MALAYSIA

I N D O N E S I A

Strait of Malacca

G u l f

o f

T h a i l a n d

Gulf of Thailand

SINGAPORE

Borneo

SARAWAK (Malaysia)

Kuching

Tanjung Datu

Kepulauan Natuna Selatan

Kepulauan Natuna Besar (Indonesia)

Telukbutun

Subi

Seraja

Serasan

P. Midai

Laut

Kepulauan Anambas (Indonesia)

P. Mubur   P. Matak

P. Siantan

Jemaja

Jemaja

East from Greenwich

COPYRIGHT GEORGE PHILIP LTD.

Projection: Conical with two standard parallels

ft   m
9000   3000
6000   2000
4500   1500
3000   1000
1200   400
600   200

m ft
2000 6000

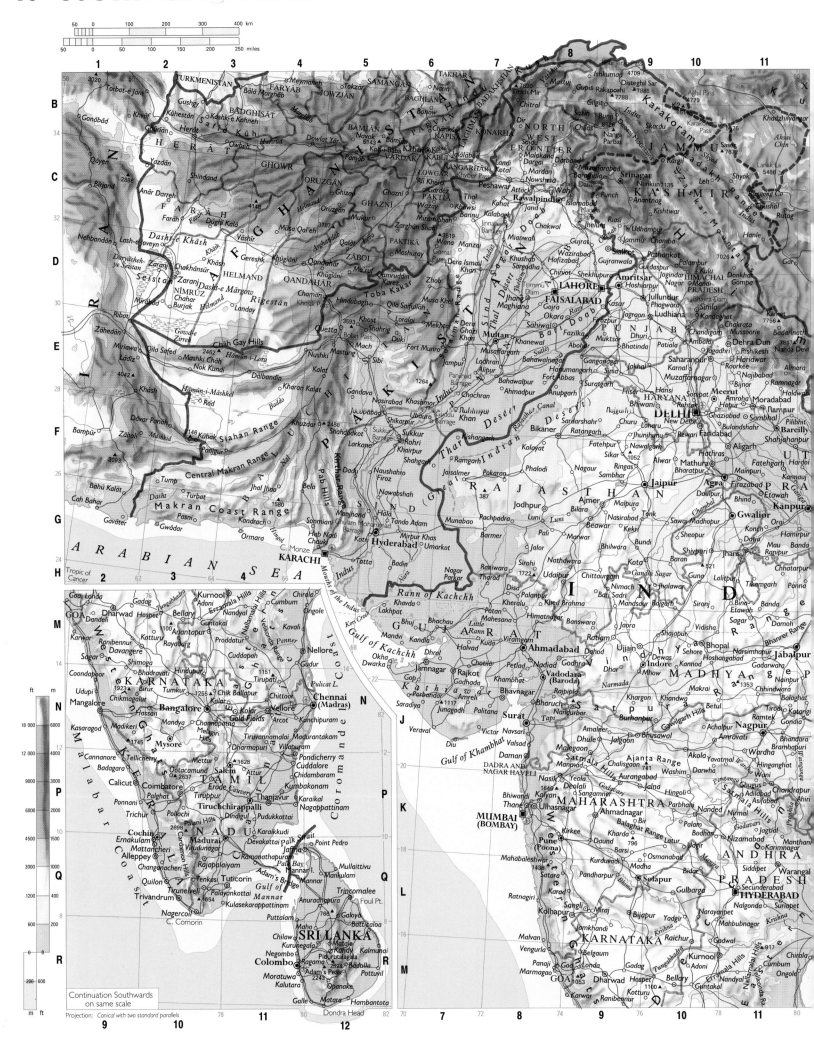

Continuation Southwards
on same scale

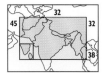

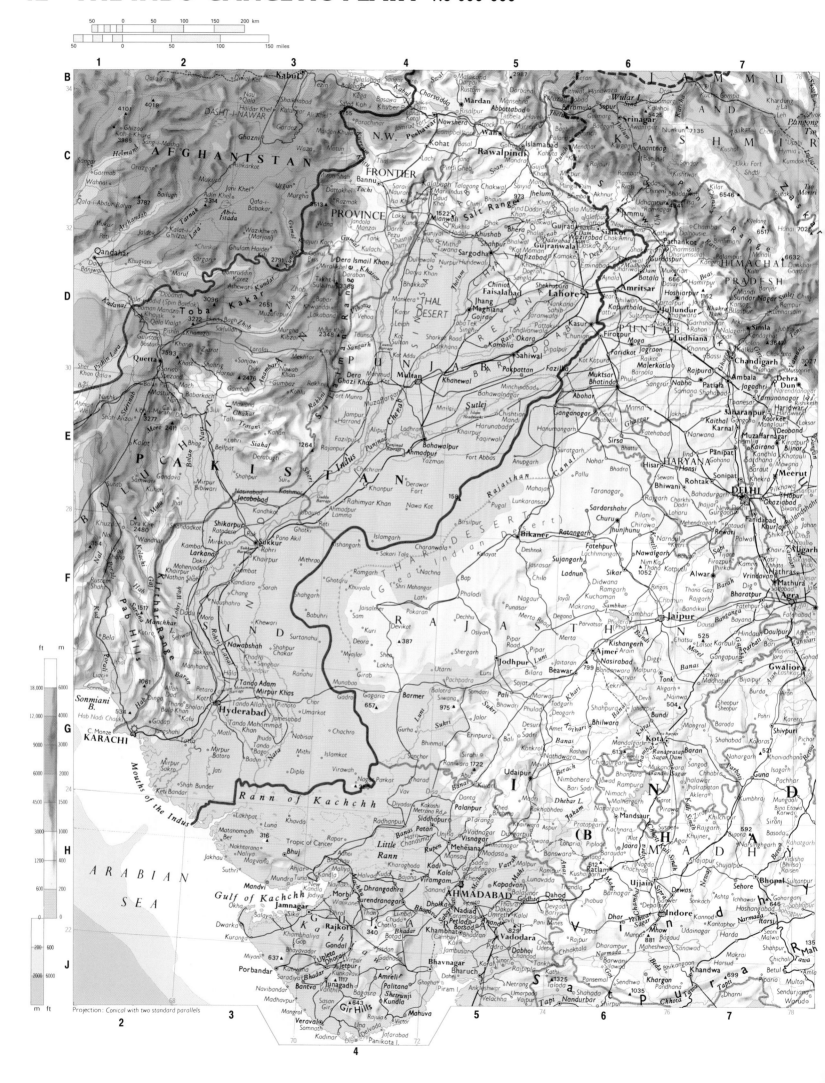

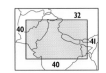

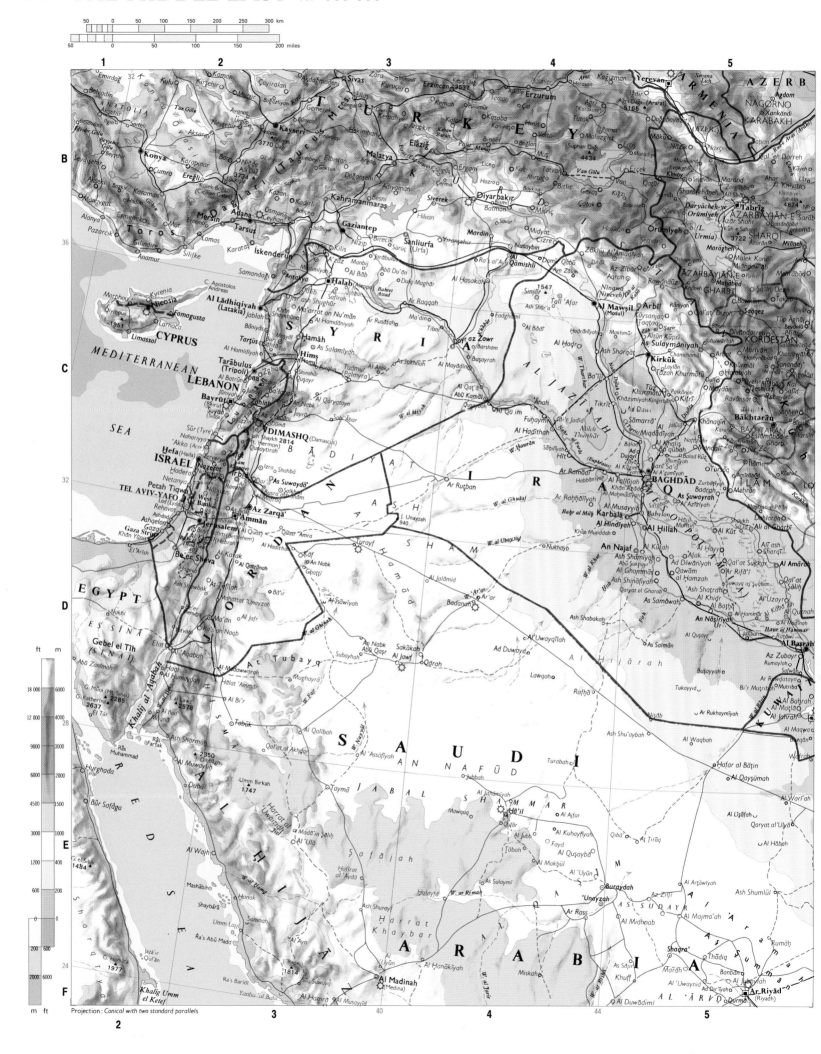

Projection: Conical with two standard parallels

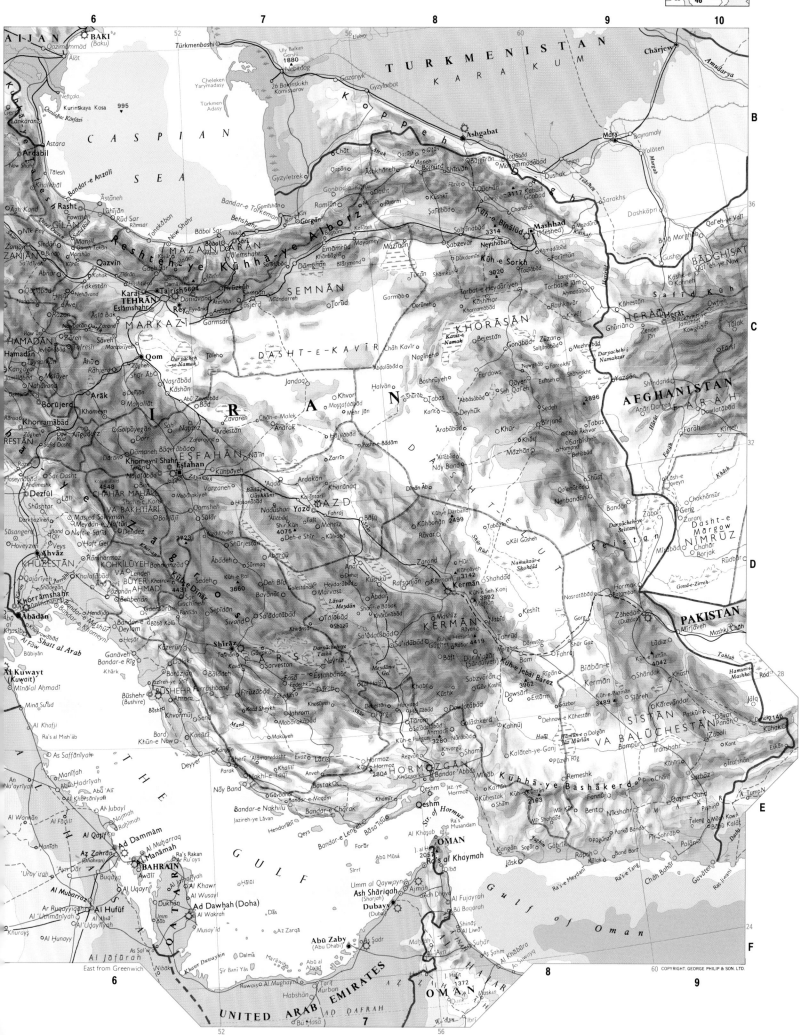

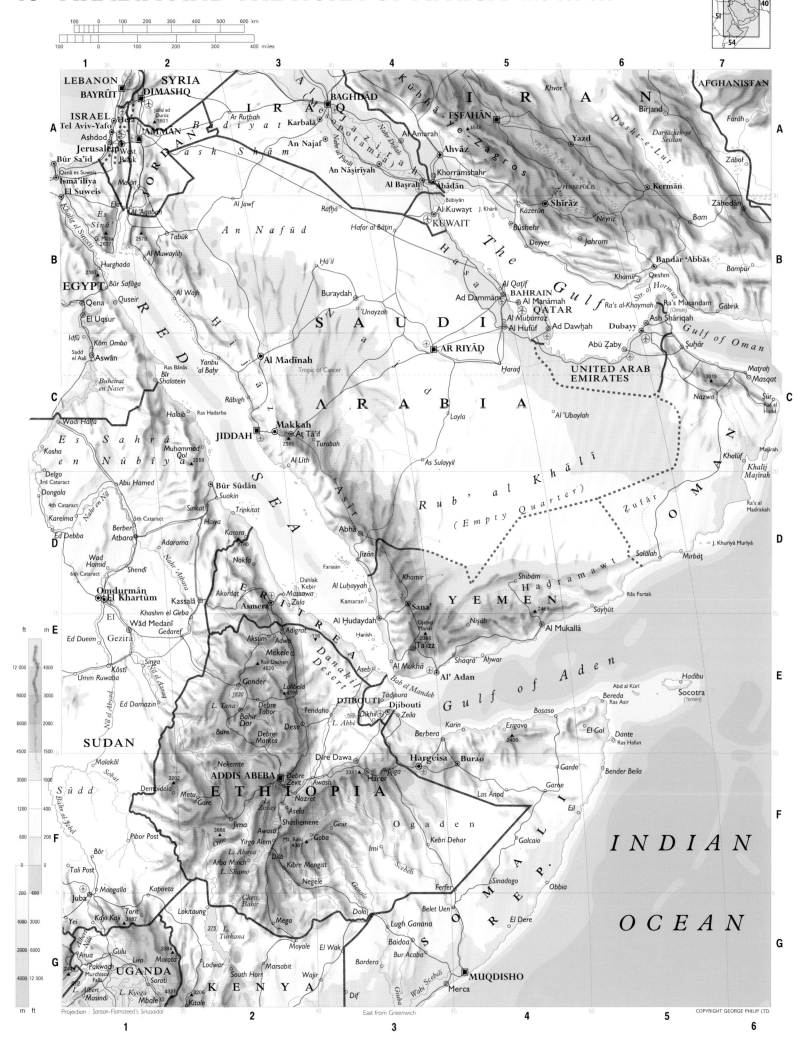

Projection : Sanson-Flamsteed's Sinusoidal

East from Greenwich

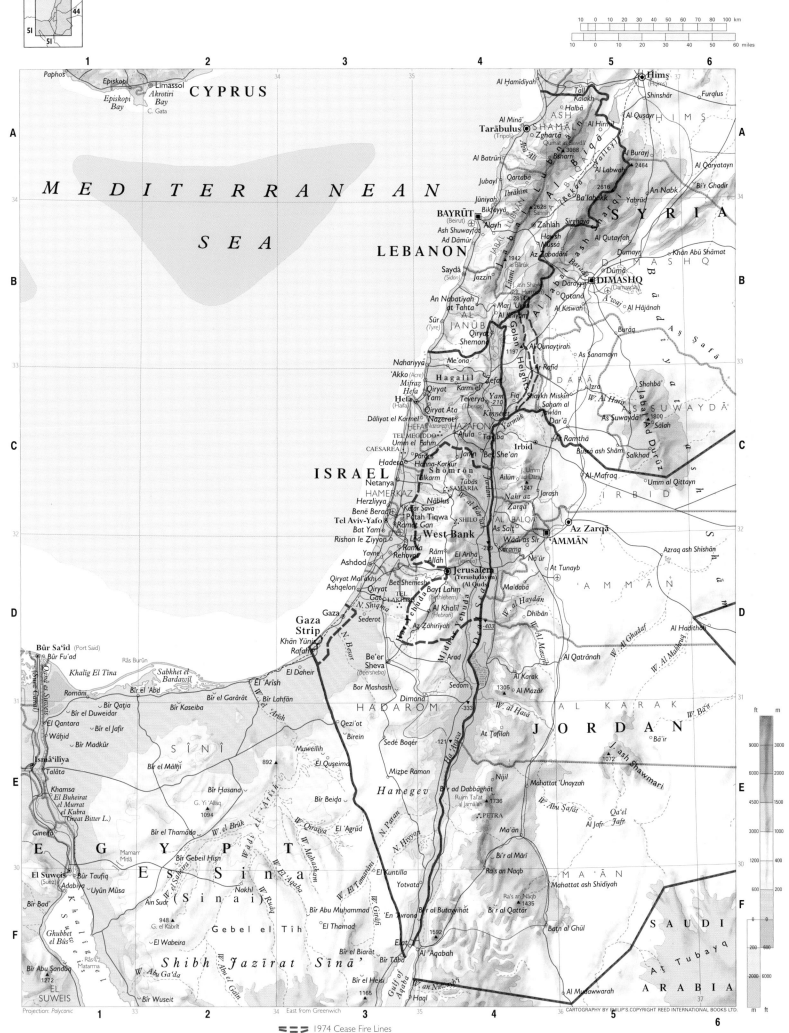

44
44
51
51

10 0 10 20 30 40 50 60 70 80 100 km
10 0 10 20 30 40 50 60 miles

1 **2** **3** **4** **5** **6**

Paphos
Episkopi
Limassol
Akrotiri
Bay
Episkopi
Bay
C. Gata

CYPRUS

34

Al Ḥamīdiyah
Al Mīnā'
Tarābulus
(Tripoli)
Tall
Kalakh
Halbā
Al Ḥirmil
Hims
(Homs)
Shinshār
Furqlus

ASH
SHAMĀL
Zgharta
Qumat as Sawdā'
3088
Bsharrī
Al Labwah
2464
Al Buraʿ
An Nabk
Bī'r Ghadīr
Al Qaryatayn

A

M E D I T E R R A N E A N

Al Batrūn
Jubayl
Qartaba
Ibrāhīm
Jūniyah
Bikfayyā
Zaḥlah
Ḥawsh
Mūssā
Baʿlabakk
2616
2628
Sannīn
Yabrūd
An Nabk

BAYRŪT
(Beirut)
Ash Shuwayfāt
SYRIA

34

S E A

Ad Dāmūr
Saydā
(Sidon)
ʿAlayh
Az Zabadānī
Al Quṭayfah
Dumayr
Khān Abū Shāmat
1942
al Bārūk

LEBANON

Jazzīn
An Nabaṭīyah
at Tahta
Marj ʿUyūn
Al Khiyām
2814
Mt. Hermon
DIMASHQ
(Damascus)
Dūmā
Darayyā
Qoṭana
Al Kiswah
Al Hājānah
Burāq

B

AL
JANUB
Ṣūr
(Tyre)
Qiryat
Shemona
Golan
Heights
1197
Al Qunayṭirah
Ar Rafīd
DIMASHQ
As Sanamayn

As Safā

B

Nahariyya
Me'ona
Zefat
Shaykh Miskīn
Izra
Shahbā
33

33

ʿAkko
(Acre)
Mifraz
Hefa
Qiryat
Yam
Hagalil
Karmi'el
Teverya
(Tiberias)
Yam
-210
Kinneret
Fiq
Sahamal
Jawlān
Darʿā
DARʿĀ
As Suwaydāʾ
Jabal
ad Durūz
1800
Ṣālah
SUWAYDĀ

Hefa
(Haifa)
Qiryat Ata
Dāliyat el Karmel
Nazerat
(Nazareth)
HAZAFON
Afula
Ṭamra
Yarmūk
ʿAt Ramthā
Bustā ash Shām
Salkhad

C

TEL MEGIDDO
Umm el Fahm
HEFA
Bet She'an
Aʿlūn
J. Umm
ad Daraj
Al-Mafraq

CAESAREA
Hadera
Hanna-Karkur
Jenīn
1247
Jarash
Umm al Qiṭṭayn

C

ISRAEL
Netanya
Pardes
Tulkarm
Shōmrōn
SAMARIA
Nablus
Nahr az
Zarqā
IRBID

Herzliyya
Kefar Sava
Benē Beraq
Petah Tiqwa
SHILO
AL BALQĀ
As Salt
Wādī as Sīr
AMMĀN
Az Zarqā
Azraq ash Shīshān

Tel Aviv-Yafo
Ramat Gan
Bat Yam
Rishon le Ziyyon
Lod
Ramla
Rehovot
Rām
Allāh
El Arīha
(Jericho)
-289
Karama
Naʿūr
At Tunayb
32

32

Yavne
West Bank
ʿAMMĀN

Ashdod
Qiryat Mal'akhi
Bet Shemesh
Jerusalem
(Yerushalayim)
(Al Quds)
Maʿdaba
Ashqelon
Qiryat
Gat
TEL
LAKHISH
Bayt Lahm
(Bethlehem)
Al Khalīl
(Hebron)
Dhībān
Al Ḥadīthah

N. Shiqma
Sederot
Az Zāhirīyah
-403
W. al Ḥaydān
Al Qaṭrānah
W. Al Ghadaf

D

**Gaza
Strip**
Khān Yūnis
Rafaḥ
Gaza
N. Besor
Be'er
Sheva
(Beersheba)
Arad
Sedom
1305
Al Karak
Al Mazār
AL KARAK

D

Bûr Saʿîd (Port Said)
Bûr Fu'ad
Râs Burûn
Sabkhet el
Bardawîl
El Daheir
El ʿArīsh
Bor Mashash
Dimona
333
W. al Ḥasā
W. Bāʾir

Khalîg El Tîna
Bîr el ʿAbd
HADAROM
Al Qaṭrānah
Bāʾir
31

Români
Bîr Qaṭia
Bîr el Duweidar
Bîr el Garārât
Bîr Lahfân
W. ʿArîsh
Bîr Kaseiba
Qezi'ot
Nijil
1072
31

El Qantara
Bîr el Jafir
Birein
Mahattat ʿUnayzah
Bî'r ad Dabbāghāt
Ruim Talʿat
al Jamāʾah
1736
W. Abū Ṣafāʾ
Qaʾel
Jafr

Wâhid
Bîr Madkûr
SÎNÎ
Muweilih
Sedé Boqér
JORDAN

E

Ismâ'ilîya
Talâta
892
El Quseima
Mizpe Ramon
PETRA
Al Jafr
MAʿĀN

E

Khamsa
El Buheirat
el Murrat
el Kubra
(Great Bitter L.)
Bîr Ḥasana
G. Yi ʿAllaq
1094
Bîr Beiḍa
El ʿAgrûd
Hanegev
Maʿān

Gineifra
W. Qiraiya
N. Paran
N. Ḥiyyon
E G Y P T
Mamarr
Mitla
W. el Brûk
SÎNI
(Sinai)
W. el Mahasham
El Kuntilla
En ʿAvrona
Yotvata
Raʾs an Naqb
Mahattat ash Shidīyah

El Suweis
(Suez)
Adabiya
Uyûn Mûsa
Ain Sudr
Nakhl
W. el Arîsh
W. el Giraîfi
Bî'r al Mārī
MAʿĀN
30

30

Bîr Badʿ
948
G. el Kabrît
El Thamad
Raʾs an Naqb
1435
Baṭn al Ghūl

F

Ghubbet
el Bûs
El Wabeira
Gebel el Tîh
Bîr Abu Muḥammad
En ʿAvrona
1592
Bî'r al Buṭayyiḥāt
Bī'r al Qaṭṭār
SAUDI

F

Bîr Abu Sandûq
1272
EL
SUWEIS
El Wabeira
W. Abu Gaʿda
Shibh Jazîrat Sînâ'
Bîr el Biarât
Elat
Al ʿAqaba
Al Mudawwarah
ARABIA

Râs
Matarma
W. an Nuwaybiʿ
At Tubayq

1165
Haql
Gulf of Aqaba
Bîr Ṭâba

ft m
9000 3000
6000 2000
4500 1500
3000 1000
1200 400
600 200
0
200 600
2000 6000
m ft

1 **2** **3** **4** **5** **6**

▬ ▬ ▬ 1974 Cease Fire Lines

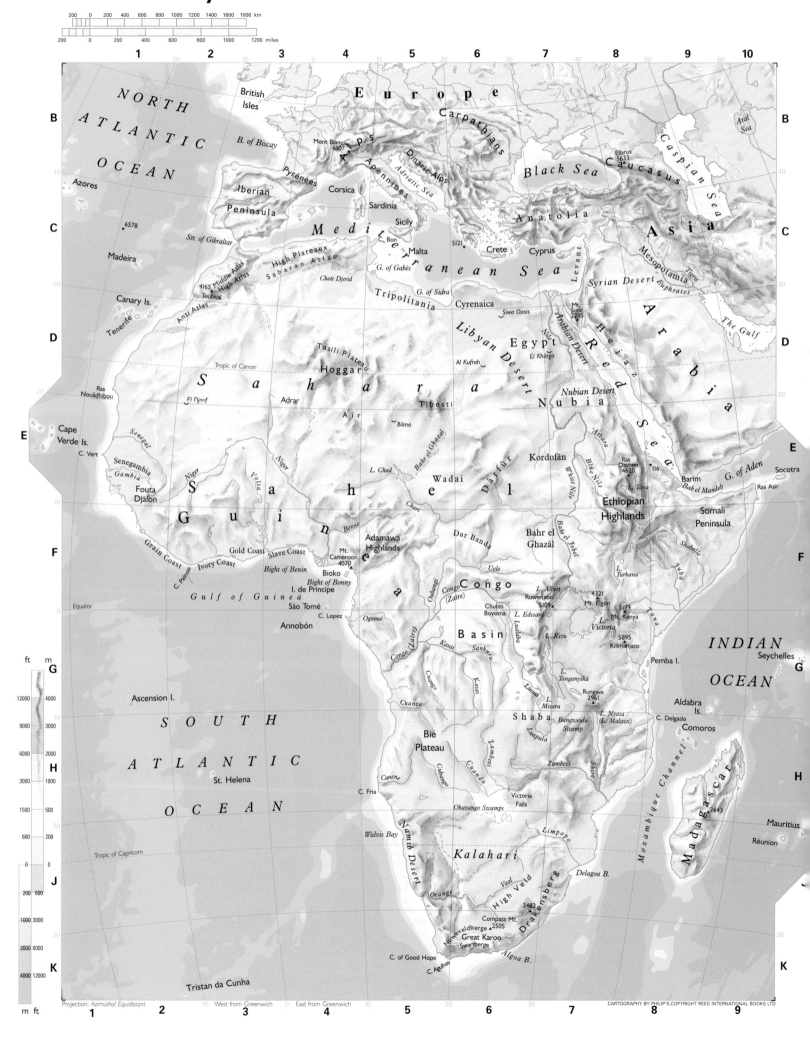

200 0 200 400 600 800 1000 1200 1400 1600 1800 km
200 0 200 400 600 800 1000 1200 miles

NORTH
ATLANTIC
OCEAN

British Isles
Europe
Carpathians
B. of Biscay
Mont Blanc 4807
Alps
Dinaric Alps
Adriatic Sea
Apennines
Elbrus 5633
Caucasus
Caspian Sea
Aral Sea
Black Sea

Azores
Iberian
Peninsula
Pyrénées
Corsica
Sardinia
Sicily
Anatolia
Asia

6578
Madeira
Str. of Gibraltar
Bon
Malta
5121
Crete
Cyprus
Mediterranean Sea
Levant
Mesopotamia
Tigris
Euphrates
The Gulf

Canary Is.
Tenerife
Anti Atlas
High Plateaux
Saharan Atlas
4165 Middle Atlas
High Atlas
Toubkal
Chott Djerid
G. of Gabès
G. of Sidra
Tripolitania
Cyrenaica
Siwa Oasis
Mt. Sinai 2285
Egypt
Libyan Desert
El Khârga
Al Kufrah
Syrian Desert
Arabian Desert
Hejaz
Arabia
Red Sea

Ras Nouâdhibou
Tropic of Cancer
Tasili Plateau
Hoggar
S a h a r a
Adrar
Air
Tibesti
Bilma
Nubian Desert
Nubia
Aibara
Ras Dashen 4620
116
Barim
Bab el Mandeb
G. of Aden
Socotra
Ras Asir

Cape Verde Is.
C. Vert
Senegambia
Gambia
Senegal
Fouta Djalon
S a h e l
Niger
Volta
Niger
L. Chad
Bahr el Ghazal
Wadai
Darfûr
Kordofân
White Nile
Blue Nile
L. Tana
Ethiopian Highlands
Somali Peninsula
Shabelle

Grain Coast
C. Palmas
Ivory Coast
Gold Coast
Slave Coast
Bight of Benin
G u i n e a
Mt. Cameroon 4070
Bioko
Bight of Bonny
I. de Principe
São Tomé
Benue
Adamawa Highlands
Dar Banda
Bahr el Ghazâl
Uele
Ubangi
Onbangi
Chari
L. Albert
Ruwenzori 5109
Mt. Elgon 5199
4321
Juba
L. Turkana

Gulf of Guinea
Equator
Annobón
C. Lopez
Ogooué
Congo (Zaïre)
Congo
Kasai
Sankuru
Lualaba
Chutes Boyoma
L. Edward
L. Kivu
L. Victoria
Mt. Kenya 5199
Kilimanjaro 5895
Pemba I.

INDIAN
OCEAN
Seychelles

Ascension I.
C o n g o
B a s i n
Cuango
Kasai
Cuanza
L. Tanganyika
Lucuga
Rungwe 2961
L. Mweru
Luapula
Bangweulu Swamp
L. Nyasa (L. Malawi)
Aldabra Is.
C. Delgado
Comoros

SOUTH
ATLANTIC
OCEAN
St. Helena

Bié Plateau
Shaba
Cubango
Zambezi
Cuando
Luangwa
Zambezi
Shire

Mozambique Channel
Madagascar
2643
Mauritius
Réunion

C. Fria
Cunene
Victoria Falls
Okavango Swamps
Tropic of Capricorn
Walvis Bay
Namib Desert
K a l a h a r i
Limpopo
Delagoa B.

Orange
Vaal
High Veld
Drakensberg
3482
Compass Mt. 2505
Nieuweldberge
Great Karoo
Swartberge
Algoa B.
C. of Good Hope
C. Agulhas

ft m
12000 4000
9000 3000
6000 2000
3000 1000
1500 500
600 200
0 0
200 600
1000 3000
2000 6000
4000 12000
m ft

Projection: Azimuthal Equidistant
West from Greenwich
East from Greenwich

200 0 200 400 600 800 1000 1200 1400 1600 1800 km

200 0 200 400 600 800 1000 1200 miles

NORTH

ATLANTIC

OCEAN

B. of Biscay

UNITED
KINGDOM
LONDON

NETH.
BELG.
PARIS
FRANCE
SWITZ.

GERMANY
Prague
CZECH REP.
Vienna
AUSTRIA
SLOVAK REP.
HUNGARY
CROATIA
BOS.-
HERZ.
YUG.
MAC.
ALB.

POLAND
Warsaw

Kiev
UKRAINE

RUSSIA

Volgograd

KAZAKSTAN

*Aral
Sea*

Azores
(Port.)

Madeira
(Port.)

Madrid

Lisbon
PORTUGAL
SPAIN

Corsica

Rome
ITALY
Sardinia

Sicily

ROMANIA

BULGARIA

GREECE
Athens

Crete
CYPRUS

Black Sea

Ankara

TURKEY

Odessa

GEORGIA
ARM.
AZER.
Baku

Caspian Sea

TURKMEN.

TEHRĀN

Canary Is.
(Sp.)

Rabat
Tetouan
Casablanca
Fès
MOROCCO
Marrakesh

Algiers
Annaba
Constantine
TUNISIA
Tunis

MALTA

Mediterranean Sea

Tripoli
Misrātah
Sfax

Benghazi

Aleppo
SYRIA
Tel Aviv
-Jaffa
ISRAEL
Damascus
JORDAN
Syrian Desert

Mosul
Tigris
Baghdād
Euphrates

IRAQ

Esfahān

IRAN

Mecca

Medina

SAUDI

ARABIA

Riyadh

BAHRAIN
QATAR
The Gulf

KUWAIT
Basra

Dakhla

WESTERN SAHARA
El Aaiún
Fdérik

ALGERIA

In Salah

Tropic of Cancer

Sahara

LIBYA

Marzūq

Al Jawf

EGYPT
CAIRO
El Faiyûm

Asyût
Aswān

Red Sea

Wâdi Halfa

Jedda
Mecca

Medina

Ras
Nouâdhibou

MAURITANIA
Nouakchott

Tombouctou
Niger

NIGER
Agades

CHAD

L. Chad
Abéché
Ndjamena

SUDAN

El Fâsher
El Obeid

Omdurmân
Khartoum
Atbara
Atbara

Port Sudan

Asmera
ERITREA
Mesewa

YEMEN

G. of Aden

Socotra
(Yemen)

Ras Asir

Berbera

CAPE VERDE IS.

Praia

St-Louis
C. Vert
Dakar
SENEGAL
GAMBIA
Banjul
GUINEA
BISSAU
Bissau
Senegal

MALI
Bámako

BURKINA
FASO
Ouagadougou
Bobo-
Didulasso

Niamey
Kano
Niger

NIGERIA
Abuja
Ibadan
Lagos
Enugu
Porto
Novo
Benin
Benue

BENIN

TOGO
GHANA
Kumasi
Accra

Maiduguri

Ndjamena
Chari

Wau
Bahr el Jebel
Malakâl
White Nile
Wâd Medani
Blue Nile

L. Tana

Addis Ababa
ETHIOPIA
Harer

DJIBOUTI
Djibouti

SOMALI REP.

Conakry
Freetown
SIERRA
LEONE
LIBERIA
Monrovia

GUINEA

IVORY
COAST
Yamoussoukro
Bouaké
Abidjan
Sekondi-
Takoradi

Lomé

CAMEROON
Douala
Malabo
Yaoundé

Bight of Benin
Port
Harcourt
EQUATORIAL
GUINEA

CENTRAL
AFRICAN REP.

Bangui
Oubangui
Mbandaka
Kisangani
*Congo
(Zaïre)*

UGANDA
Kampala
L. Albert
L. Edward
RWANDA
Kigali
L. Kivu
BURUNDI
Bujumbura

L. Turkana
Juba

KENYA
Nairobi
Kisumu
L. Victoria
Mombasa

Mogadishu

Gulf of Guinea

SÃO TOMÉ & PRINCIPE
C. Lopez
Annobón

GABON
Libreville

CONGO
Brazzaville
Pointe-Noire
CABINDA
(Angola)
Kinshasa
Matadi

CONGO
(DEM. REP. OF THE)
Kasai
Kananga

Dodoma
TANZANIA
Dar es Salaam
Zanzibar

L. Tanganyika

INDIAN

OCEAN

SEYCHELLES

Equator

Ascension I.
(U.K.)

SOUTH

ATLANTIC

St. Helena
(U.K.)

OCEAN

Luanda

Lobito
Namibe

ANGOLA
Huambo

Cubango
Cuando

Cunene

C. Fria

C. Frio

L. Mweru
Likasi
Lubumbashi

ZAMBIA
Ndola
Lusaka

L. Malawi
MALAWI
Lilongwe
Blantyre

Zambezi

MOZAMBIQUE
Moçambique

Aldabra
Is.

C. Delgado

COMOROS

Mayotte
(Fr.)

Antsiranana

Mahajanga

Toamasina

MADAGASCAR

MAURITIUS

Réunion
(Fr.)

Antananarivo

Fianarantsoa

Mozambique Channel

NAMIBIA
Windhoek

BOTSWANA
Gaborone

Livingstone
Harare
Bulawayo
ZIMBABWE

Beira

Limpopo

Tropic of Capricorn

Pretoria
Johannesburg
Vaal
Kimberley
Maseru
LESOTHO
Mbabane
SWAZ.
Maputo
Durban

SOUTH AFRICA
Orange

East
London

Cape Town
C. of Good Hope
C. Agulhas

Port
Elizabeth

Tristan da Cunha
(U.K.)

West from Greenwich   East from Greenwich

Projection: Azimuthal Equidistant

● Dakar Capital Cities

CARTOGRAPHY BY PHILIP'S. COPYRIGHT REED INTERNATIONAL BOOKS LTD

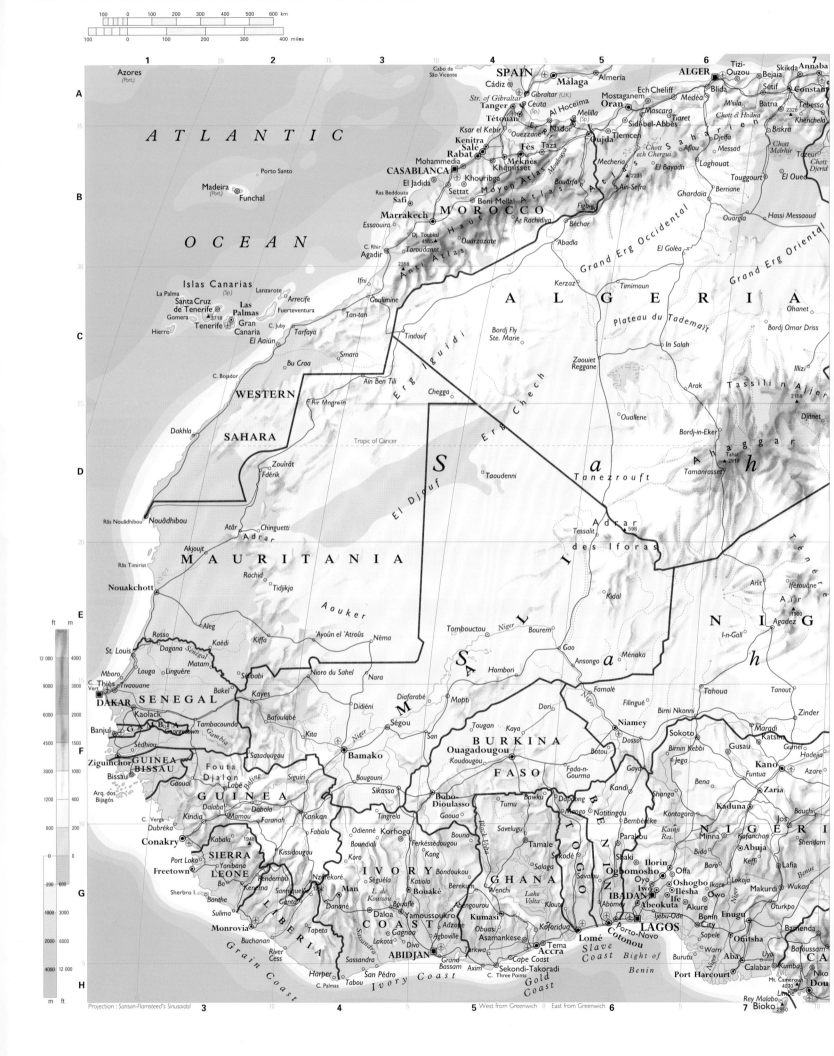

100 0 100 200 300 400 500 600 km
100 0 100 200 300 400 miles

ft m
12 000 4000
9000 3000
6000 2000
4500 1500
3000 1000
1200 400
600 200
0 0
200 600
1000 3000
2000 6000
4000 12 000
m ft

Projection : Sanson-Flamsteed's Sinusoidal
West from Greenwich East from Greenwich

ATLANTIC

OCEAN

Azores
(Port.)

Porto Santo

Madeira
(Port.)
Funchal

Islas Canarias
(Sp.)
La Palma
Santa Cruz
de Tenerife
Gomera 3718
Hierro
Tenerife
Gran
Canaria
Lanzarote
Arrecife
Fuerteventura
C. Juby

WESTERN

SAHARA

Dakhla
C. Bojador
Bu Craa
'Bir Mogreïn

Râs Nouâdhibou Nouâdhibou

MAURITANIA

Nouakchott

Ras Timirist

St. Louis
Rosso
Dagana Senegal
C. Thiès Louga Linguère
Vert Tivaouane
DAKAR Thiès
Kaolack
Banjul **SENEGAL**
Ziguinchor **GUINEA**
Bissau **BISSAU**
Arq. dos
Bijagós

SPAIN
Cabo de
São Vicente
Cádiz **MÁLAGA** Almería
Str. of Gibraltar
Gibraltar (UK)
Tanger Ceuta
Tétouan (Sp.)
Al Hoceïma
Melilla
(Sp.)
Kenitra Nador
Salé Fès Taza
Rabat
Mohammedia Meknès Khemisset
CASABLANCA Khouribga
El Jadida Settat
Ras Beddouza **MOROCCO**
Safi Beni Mellal
Essaouira
Marrakech
Figuig
C. Rhir Ar Rachidiya
Agadir Taroudannt
Ouarzazate
Dj. Toubkal Abadla
4165 Béchar
Ifni
Goulimine
Tan-tan
Tarfaya
El Aaiún
Smara
Aïn Ben Tili
Tindouf

ALGERIA

El Golea
Kerzaz
Timimoun
Bordj Fly
Ste. Marie
Zaouiet
Reggane
In Salah

Chegga

Tropic of Cancer

Taoudenni

Tessalit

Zouîrât
Fdérik
Atâr Chinguetti
Adrar
Akjoujt
Rachid
Tidjikja
Aleg
Kaédi Kiffa
'Ayoûn el 'Atroûs
Néma
Sélibabi
Nara
Nioro du Sahel

Tombouctou
Gao
Bourem

Ansongo
Hombori
Mopti

Kidal

Adrar
des Iforas

Tanezrouft

Tamanrasset
Tahat
2918

In Salah

Plateau du Tademaït

Ohanet
Bordj Omar Driss
Illizi
Tassili n'Ajjer
2158
Djanet
Bordj-in-Eker
Arak
Ouallene

MALI

Ségou
San
Bamako
Kita
Bafoulabé
Kayes
Bakel
Diafarabé
Didiéni
Koulikoro
Sikasso
Bougouni

Niger

Famalé
Dori
Filingué
Niamey
Dosso

NIGER

Agadez
1900
I-n-Gall
Tahoua
Birni Nkonni
Tanout
Zinder
Maradi
Katsina
Gumel

BURKINA
FASO
Ouagadougou
Koudougou
Bobo-
Dioulasso
Tumu
Gaoua

Kandi
Parakou

NIGERIA
Kano
Zaria
Kaduna
Bauchi
Gusau
Funtua
Azare
Hadejia
Jega
Birnin Kebbi
Sokoto
Shaki
Ilorin
Ogbomosho
 Offa
Oshogbo
Iwo Ilesha Ikare
IBADAN Ife Owo
Abeokuta Akure
Ijebu-Ode
LAGOS
Porto-Novo
Cotonou
Lomé

GHANA
Tamale
Salaga
Sekodé
Savalugu
Wenchi
Kumasi
Obuasi
Koforidua
Asamankese
Accra Tema
Cape Coast
Sekondi-Takoradi
C. Three Points

IVORY
COAST
Bouaké
Yamoussoukro
Daloa
Gagnoa
Divo
ABIDJAN
Grand
Bassam
Axim

GUINEA
Conakry
Kindia
Mamou
Dalaba
Faranah
Kankan
Siguiri
Labé
Dabola
Kissidougou
Nzérékoré
Man

SIERRA
LEONE
Freetown
Port Loko
Bo
Kenema

LIBERIA
Monrovia
Buchanan
Harper
Tabou
C. Palmas

Bioko

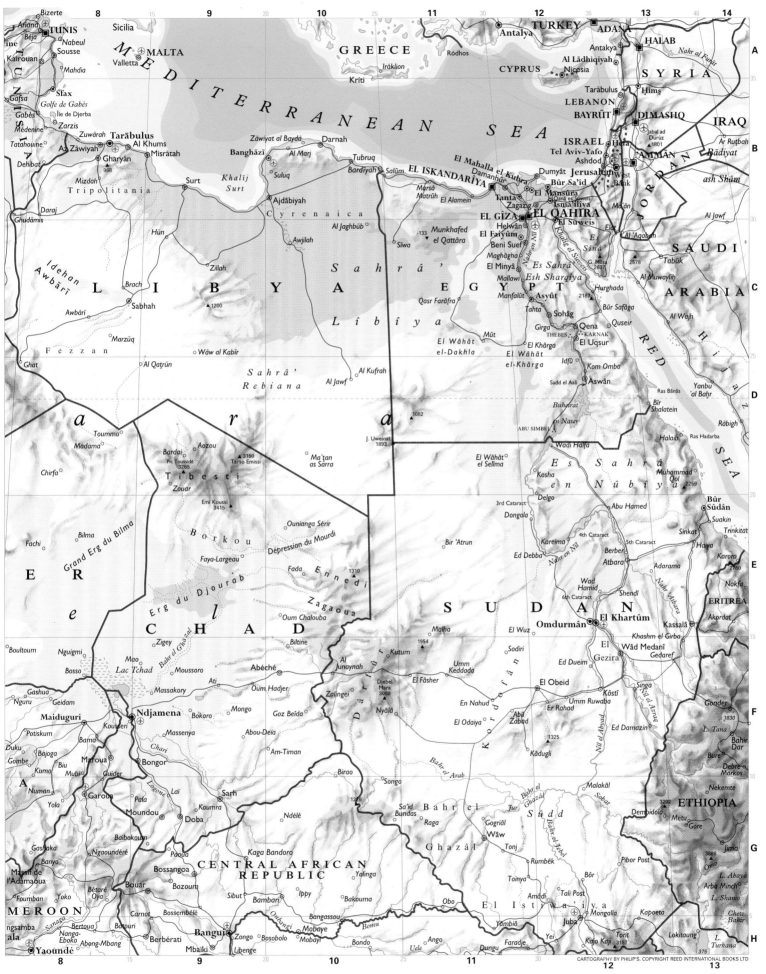

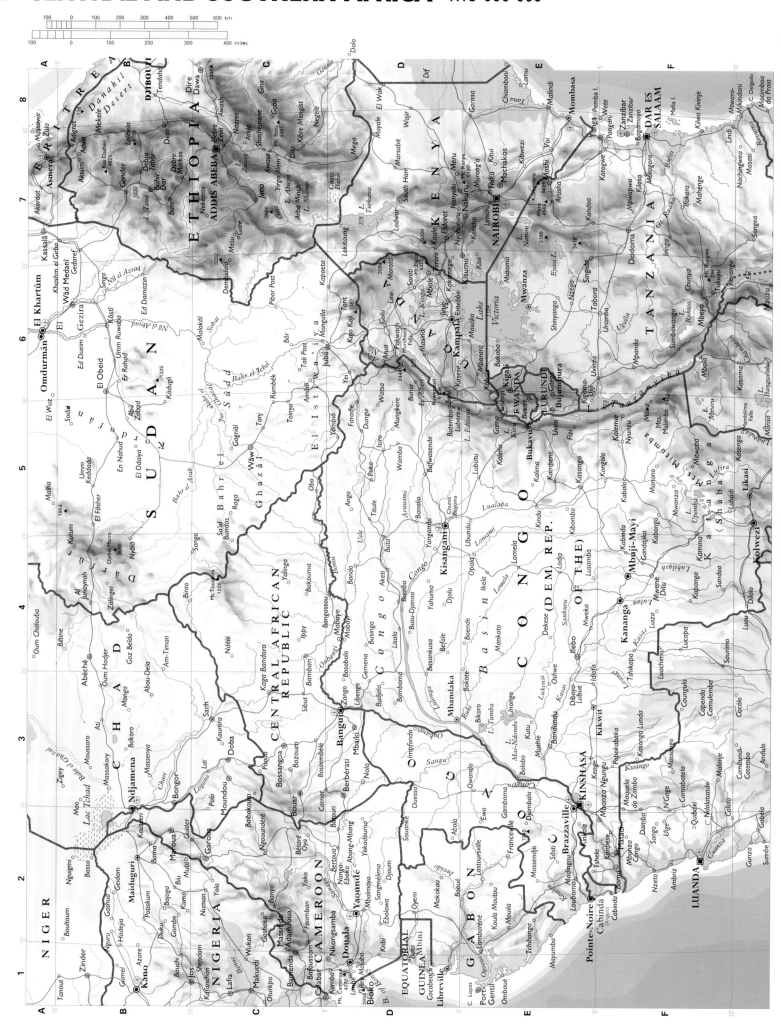

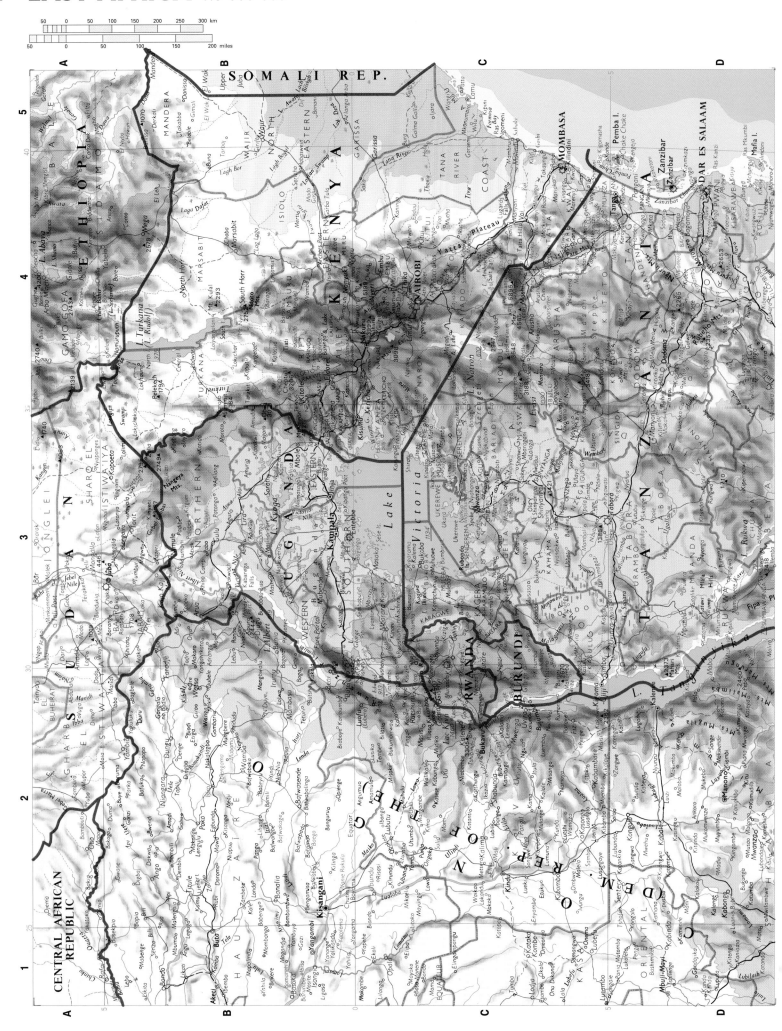

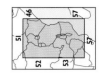

55

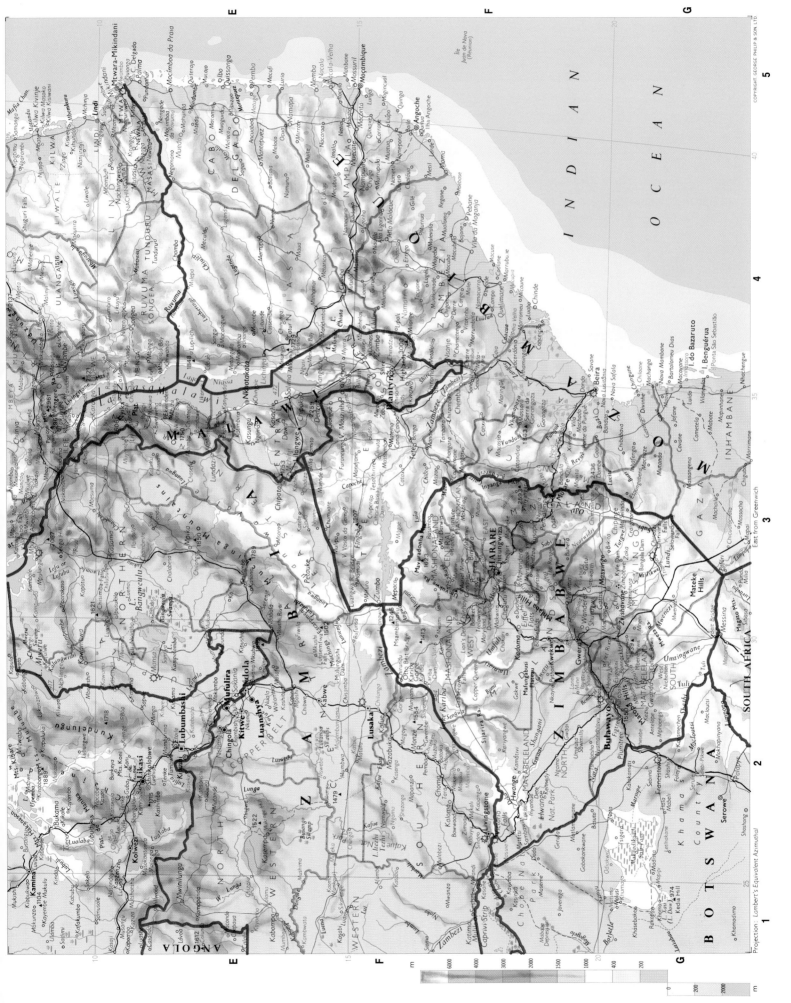

Projection: Lambert's Equivalent Azimuthal

East from Greenwich

COPYRIGHT GEORGE PHILIP & SON LTD

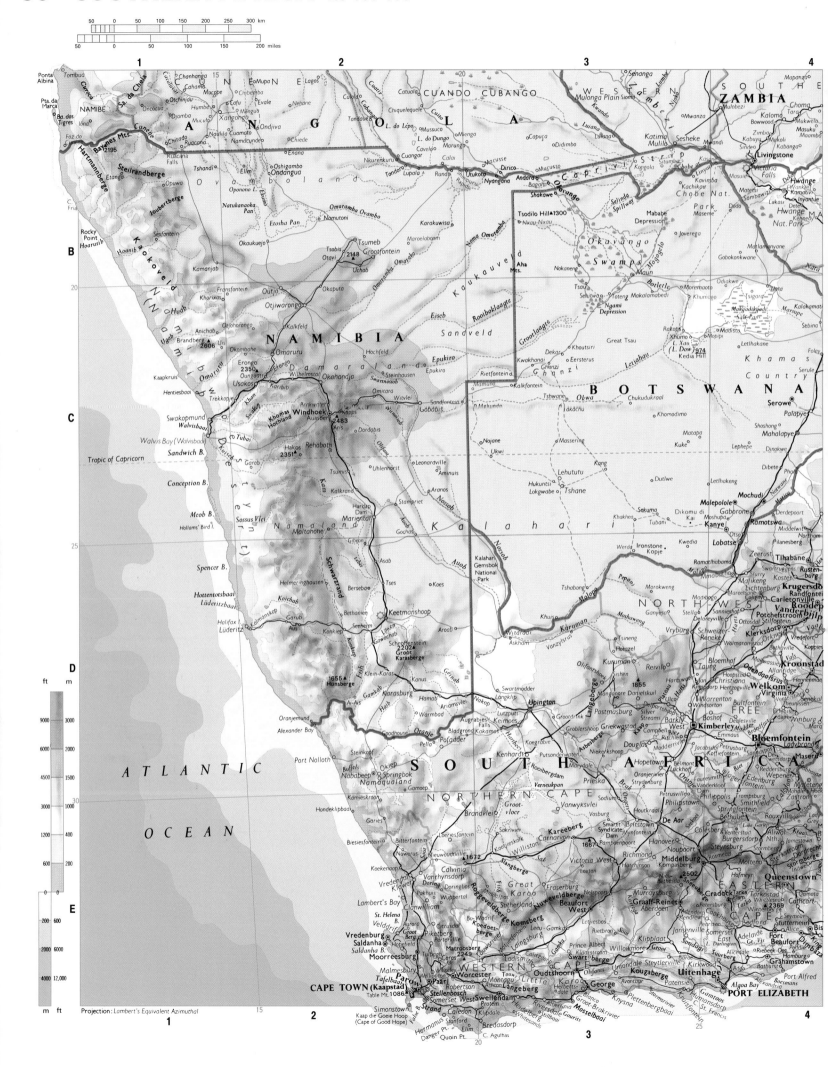

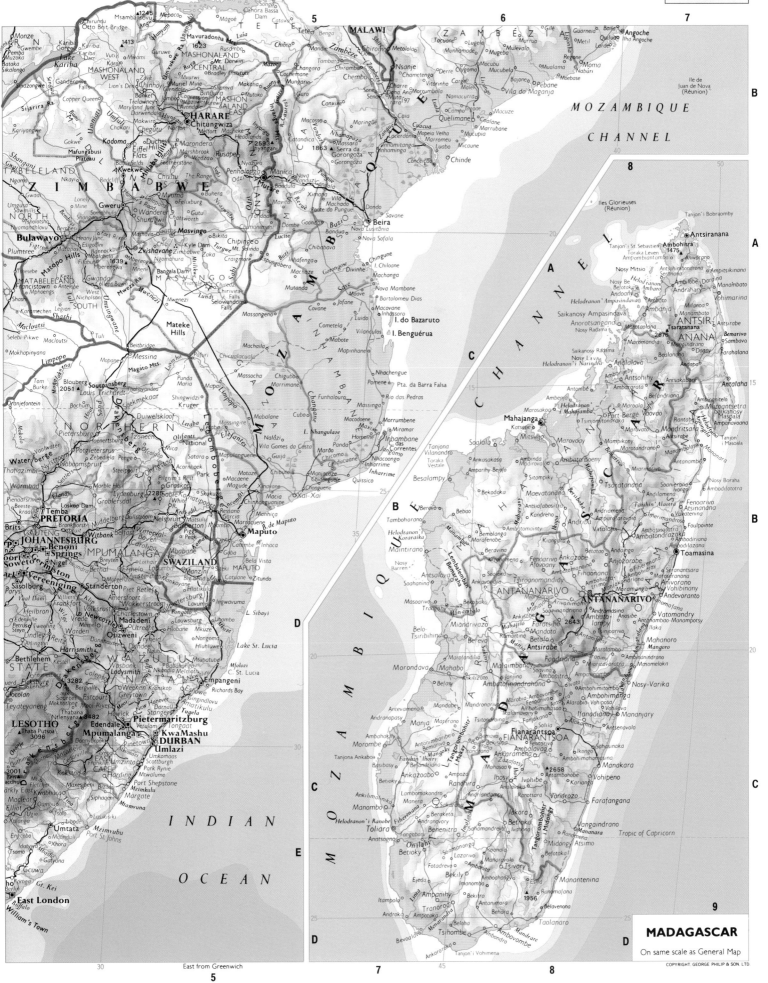

5 East from Greenwich

MADAGASCAR

On same scale as General Map

COPYRIGHT. GEORGE PHILIP & SON. LTD

MOZAMBIQUE CHANNEL

INDIAN OCEAN

ZIMBABWE

MOZAMBIQUE

MALAWI

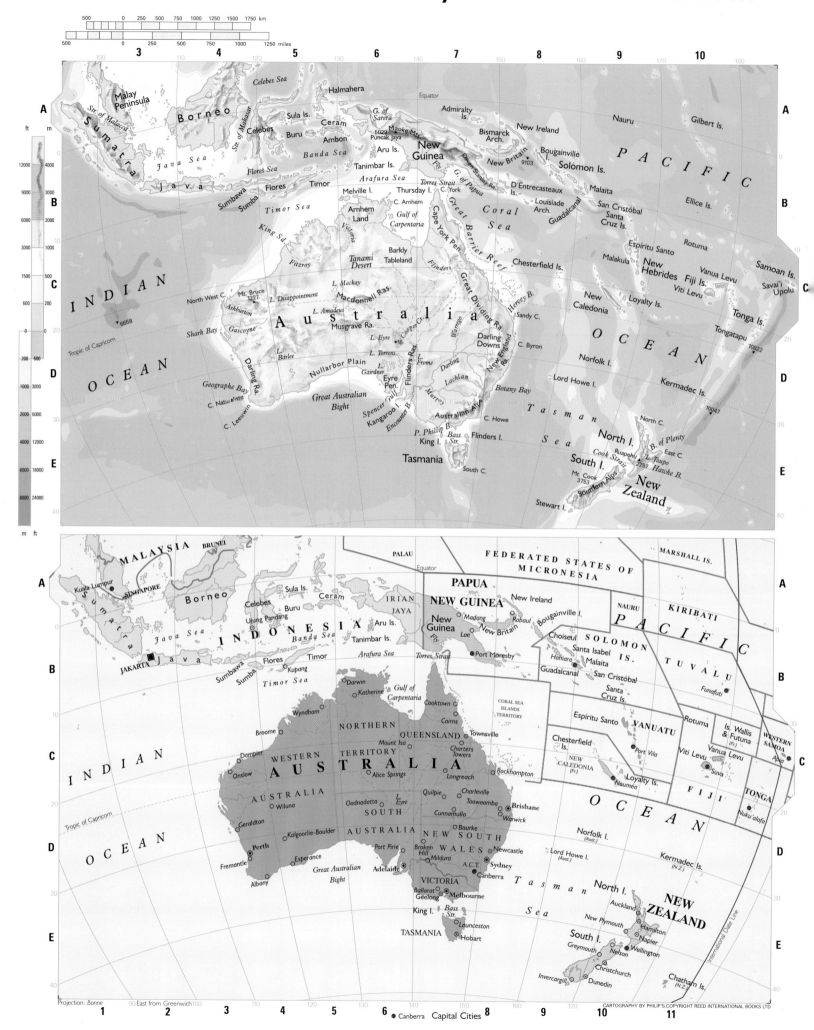

500 0 250 500 750 1000 1250 1500 1750 km
500 0 250 500 750 1000 1250 miles

Physical map labels:

Malay Peninsula, Str. of Malacca, Sumatra, Borneo, Celebes Sea, Halmahera, Equator, Admiralty Is., Nauru, Gilbert Is., Celebes, Sula Is., Ceram, G. of Sarera, Bismarck Arch., New Ireland, Buru, Ambon, Puncak Jaya 5029, Maoke Mts., New Guinea, New Britain, 9103, Bougainville I., Solomon Is., Aru Is., Tanimbar Is., Fly, Owen Stanley Ra., D'Entrecasteaux Is., Malaita, Ellice Is., Java Sea, Banda Sea, Arafura Sea, Torres Strait, G. of Papua, Louisiade Arch., Guadalcanal, San Cristobal, Santa Cruz Is., Java, Flores Sea, Flores, Timor, Melville I., Thursday I., C. York, Coral Sea, Espíritu Santo, Rotuma, Samoan Is., Sumbawa, Sumba, Timor Sea, C. Arnhem, Gulf of Carpentaria, Cape York Pen., Chesterfield Is., Malakula, New Hebrides, Fiji Is., Vanua Levu, Savai'i, Upolu, Arnhem Land, Victoria, Great Barrier Reef, Viti Levu, Loyalty Is., Tonga Is., INDIAN, King Sd., Barkly Tableland, Flinders, Great Dividing Ra., New Caledonia, North West C., Mt. Bruce 1227, L. Mackay, Macdonnell Ras., Hervey B., Sandy C., Tonga Is., Tongatapu, 10822, Fitzroy, Tanami Desert, Australia, Ashburton, L. Disappointment, L. Amadeus, Musgrave Ra., Cooper Cr., Warrego, Darling Downs, C. Byron, OCEAN, 6658, Gascoyne, Shark Bay, L. Eyre, 16, New England, Norfolk I., Tropic of Capricorn, L. Barlee, Nullarbor Plain, L. Torrens, L. Gairdner, Flinders Ra., L. Frome, Darling, C. Howe, Lord Howe I., Kermadec Is., Geographe Bay, Darling Ra., Eyre Pen., Lachlan, Murray, Botany Bay, 10047, C. Naturaliste, Great Australian Bight, Spencer Gulf, Kangaroo I., Encounter B., Australian Alps, Tasman Sea, C. Leeuwin, P. Phillip B., King I., Bass Str., Flinders I., North C., North I., B. of Plenty, East C., Tasmania, South C., South I., Mt. Cook 3753, Southern Alps, Ruapehu 2797, Taupo, Hawke B., New Zealand, Stewart I.

PACIFIC OCEAN

ft / m elevation scale:
12000 / 4000, 9000 / 3000, 6000 / 2000, 3000 / 1000, 1500 / 500, 600 / 200, 0 / 0, 200 / 600, 1000 / 3000, 2000 / 6000, 4000 / 12000, 6000 / 18000, 8000 / 24000 (m ft)

Political map labels:

MALAYSIA, BRUNEI, PALAU, FEDERATED STATES OF MICRONESIA, MARSHALL IS., Kuala Lumpur, SINGAPORE, Sumatra, Borneo, Celebes, Ujung Pandang, Sula Is., Ceram, IRIAN JAYA, PAPUA NEW GUINEA, New Ireland, NAURU, KIRIBATI, Buru, INDONESIA, Madang, New Guinea, Rabaul, Bougainville I., PACIFIC, Jakarta, Java, Java Sea, Banda Sea, Aru Is., Tanimbar Is., Lae, New Britain, Choiseul, SOLOMON IS., Santa Isabel, Malaita, TUVALU, Sumbawa, Sumba, Timor Sea, Kupang, Timor, Arafura Sea, Torres Strait, Port Moresby, Honiara, Guadalcanal, San Cristobal, Santa Cruz Is., Funafuti, Darwin, Katherine, Gulf of Carpentaria, Cooktown, CORAL SEA ISLANDS TERRITORY, Espíritu Santo, VANUATU, Rotuma, Is. Wallis & Futuna (Fr), WESTERN SAMOA, Wyndham, NORTHERN, Cairns, Townsville, Chesterfield Is., Port Vila, Viti Levu, Vanua Levu, Apia, Broome, QUEENSLAND, Mount Isa, Charters Towers, NEW CALEDONIA (Fr), Suva, Dampier, WESTERN, TERRITORY, Rockhampton, Loyalty Is., Nouméa, FIJI, Onslow, AUSTRALIA, Alice Springs, Longreach, INDIAN, AUSTRALIA, SOUTH, Oodnadatta, L. Eyre, Quilpie, Charleville, Toowoomba, Brisbane, Norfolk I. (Aust.), TONGA, Wiluna, Cunnamulla, Warwick, Nuku'alofa, Geraldton, Kalgoorlie-Boulder, AUSTRALIA, NEW SOUTH, Bourke, Norfolk I. (Aust.), OCEAN, Tropic of Capricorn, Perth, Port Pirie, Broken Hill, Mildura, WALES, Newcastle, Lord Howe I. (Aust.), Kermadec Is. (N.Z.), Fremantle, Esperance, Great Australian Bight, A.C.T., Sydney, Adelaide, VICTORIA, Canberra, North I., NEW ZEALAND, Ballarat, Melbourne, Tasman Sea, Auckland, Geelong, King I., Bass Str., New Plymouth, Hamilton, Napier, TASMANIA, Launceston, South I., Nelson, Wellington, Hobart, Greymouth, Invercargill, Dunedin, Christchurch, Chatham Is. (N.Z.), International Date Line

Projection: Bonne
90 East from Greenwich 100

● Canberra Capital Cities

CARTOGRAPHY BY PHILIP'S.COPYRIGHT REED INTERNATIONAL BOOKS LTD

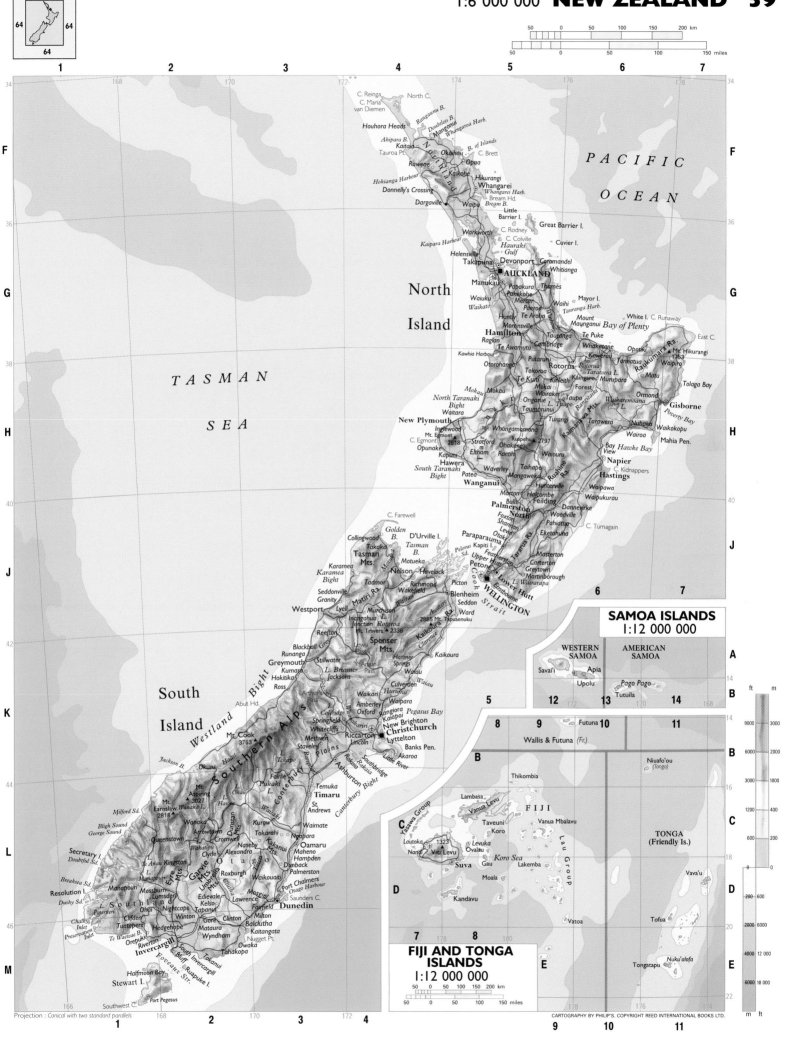

64

50 0 50 100 150 200 km
50 0 50 100 150 miles

F

C. Reinga
C. Maria
van Diemen
North C.
Houhora Heads
Rangaunu B.
Doubtless B.
Mangonui
Whangaroa Harb.
Ahipara B.
Kaitaia
Tauroa Pt.
Okaihau
B. of Islands
Rawene
Kaikohe
C. Brett
Hokianga Harbour
Opua
Hikurangi
Whangarei
Donnelly's Crossing
Whangarei Harb.
Bream Hd.
Bream B.
Dargaville
Waipu
Little
Barrier I.
Great Barrier I.

PACIFIC

OCEAN

F

G

Kaipara Harbour
Warkworth
Helensville
C. Rodney
C. Colville
Cuvier I.
Hauraki
Gulf
Coromandel
Whitianga
Takapuna
Devonport
AUCKLAND
Manukau
Papakura
Thames
Mayor I.
Pukekohe
Mercer
Paeroa
Waihi
Tauranga Harb.
Waiuku
Waikato
Mount
Maunganui
White I.
C. Runaway
Huntly
Te Aroha
Morrinsville
Bay of Plenty
Hamilton
Cambridge
Tauranga
Te Puke
Whakatane
Opotiki
East C.
Raglan
Te Awamutu
Rotorua
Kawerau
Raukumara Ra.
Mt. Hikurangi
1753
Kawhia Harbour
Otorohanga
Te Kuiti
Putaruru
Kinleith
Rotorua L.
Kaingaroa
Murupara
Taneatua
Waipiro
Motu
Tolaga Bay

North

Island

G

H

TASMAN

SEA

Mokau
Mokau
North Taranaki
Bight
Mokai
Wairakei
Taupo L.
Taupo
Taumarunui
Turangi
Rangitaiki
Waikaremoana
L.
Ormond
Gisborne
Poverty Bay
New Plymouth
Inglewood
Mt. Egmont
2518
Opunake
Kapuni
Hawera
South Taranaki
Bight
Patea
C. Egmont
Stratford
Ohakune
Eltham
Raetihi
Ruapehu 2797
Waiouru
Ohakenes
Kaimanawa Mts.
Tarawera
Nuhaka
Bay
View
Hawke Bay
Wairoa
Waikokopu
Mahia Pen.
Napier
C. Kidnappers
Hastings
Waipawa
Waverley
Wanganui
Taihape
Mangaweka
Ruahine
Ra.
Hunterville
Waipukurau
Marton
Morton
Halcombe
Bulls
Feilding
Danneivirke
Palmerston
Woodville
North
Foxton
Shannon
Pahiatua
Levin
Eketahuna
Otaki
C. Turnagain
Paraparaumu
Kapiti I.
Featherston
Tararua Ra.
Masterton
Carterton
Upper Hutt
Greytown
Martinborough

H

J

C. Farewell
Collingwood
Golden
B.
Takaka
D'Urville I.
Tasman
B.
Tasman
Mts.
Motueka
Nelson
Havelock
Richmond
Wakefield
Picton
Pelorus
Sd.
Blenheim
Seddon
Ward
Lower Hutt
Petone
WELLINGTON
Eastbourne
L. Wairarapa
Karamea
Karamea
Bight
Matiri Ra.
Seddonville
Granity
Westport
Lyell
Murchison
Inangahua
Junction
Rotoroa
Mt. Travers ▲ 2338
Reefton
Cook
2885 Mt. Tapuaenuku
Strait

6

7

J

K

South

Island

TASMAN

Blackball
Runanga
Greymouth
Kumara
Hokitika
Ross
Stillwater
Jacksons
Arthur's
Pass
L. Brunner
Lewis
Pass
Spenser
Mts.
Hanmer
Springs
Culverden
Waiau
Waikari
Hurunui
Waipara
Amberley
Oxford
Rangiora
Kaiapoi
Westland
Bight
Abut Hd.
Mt. Cook
3763
Jackson B.
Okuru
Haast
Arthur's
Pass
Coldstream
Whitecliffs
Methven
Springfield
Staveley
Kaikoura
Clarence
Waiau
Pegasus Bay
New Brighton
Christchurch
Riccarton
Lincoln
Lyttelton
Banks Pen.
Little River
Akaroa

SAMOA ISLANDS
1:12 000 000

**WESTERN
SAMOA**
**AMERICAN
SAMOA**
Savai'i
Apia
Upolu
Pago Pago
Tutuila

A

B

K

B

8
9
Futuna **10**
11
Wallis & Futuna (Fr.)

B

L

Southern Alps
Tekapo
Fairlie
Pukaki
L.
Mt. Aspiring
3027
Mt.
Earnslaw
2818
Wanaka L.
Wanaka
Hawea
L.
Ohau
Ashburton
Rangitata
Rakaia
Southbridge
Rakaia
Temuka
Timaru
St. Andrews
Canterbury Bight
Milford Sd.
Bligh Sound
George Sound
Queenstown
Arrowtown
Cromwell
Kurow
Waimate
Wakatipu
L.
Clyde
Naseby
Oamaru
Dunstan
Mts.
Alexandra
Maheno
Hampden
Dunback
Palmerston
Roxburgh
Waikouaiti
Port Chalmers
Secretary I.
Doubtful Sd.
Eyre
Mts.
Kingston
Garvie
Mts.
Umbrella
Mts.
Lawrence
Mosgiel
Saunders C.
Fairfield
Dunedin

Niuafo'ou
(Tonga)

C

C

L

Thikombia
Lambasa
Vanua Levu
FIJI
Yasawa Group
Taveuni
Koro
Vanua Mbalavu
Lau Group
TONGA
(Friendly Is.)
Vava'u

C

D

Breaksea Sd.
Resolution I.
Dusky Sd.
L. Manapouri
Mossburn
Lumsden
Manapouri
Ohai
Nightcaps
Winton
Clinton
Mataura
Southland
Edievale
Kelso
Tapanui
Gore
Waipahi
Balclutha
Kaitangata
Milton
Nugget Pt.
Lautoka
Nandi
Viti Levu
1323
Levuka
Ovalau
Gau
Suva
Moala
Kandavu
Koro Sea
Lakemba
Vatoa
Vava'u
Tofua

D

M

Chalky
Inlet
Preservation Inlet
Patereroa
Te Waewae B.
Orepuki
Clifden
Tuatapere
Hedgehope
Riverton
Wyndham
Wairio
Owaka
Tahakopa
South Invercargill
Invercargill
Bluff
Foveaux Str.
Ruapuke I.
Halfmoon Bay
Stewart I.
Southwest C.
Port Pegasus

**FIJI AND TONGA
ISLANDS**
1:12 000 000
50 0 50 100 150 200 km
50 0 50 100 150 miles

Tongatapu
Nuku'alofa

E

E

M

ft m
9000 3000
6000 2000
3000 1000
1200 400
600 200
0
200 600
2000 6000
4000 12 000
6000 18 000
m ft

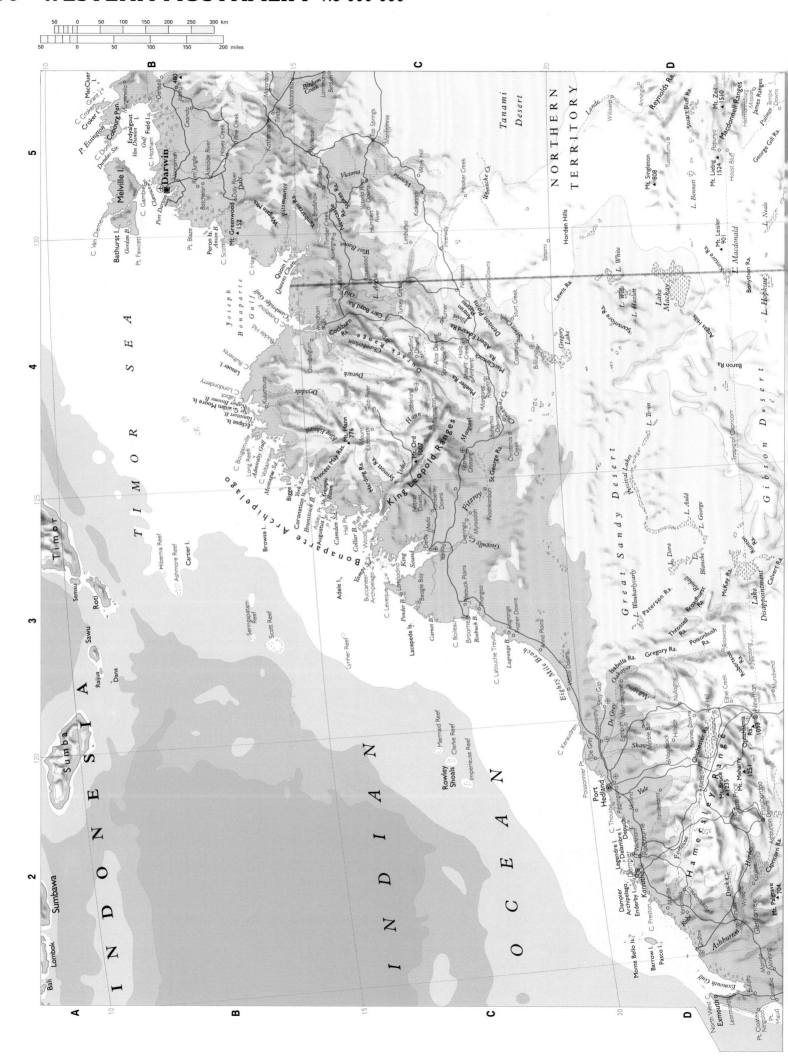

61

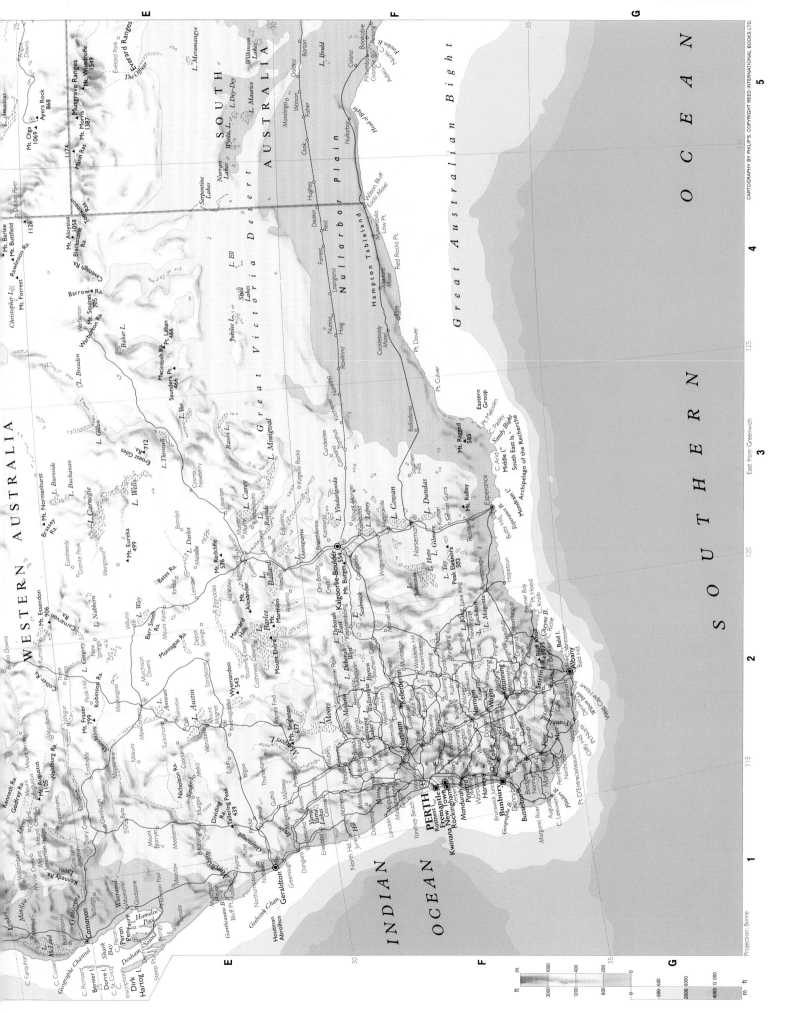

Projection: Bonne

CARTOGRAPHY BY PHILIPS. COPYRIGHT REED INTERNATIONAL BOOKS LTD.

East from Greenwich

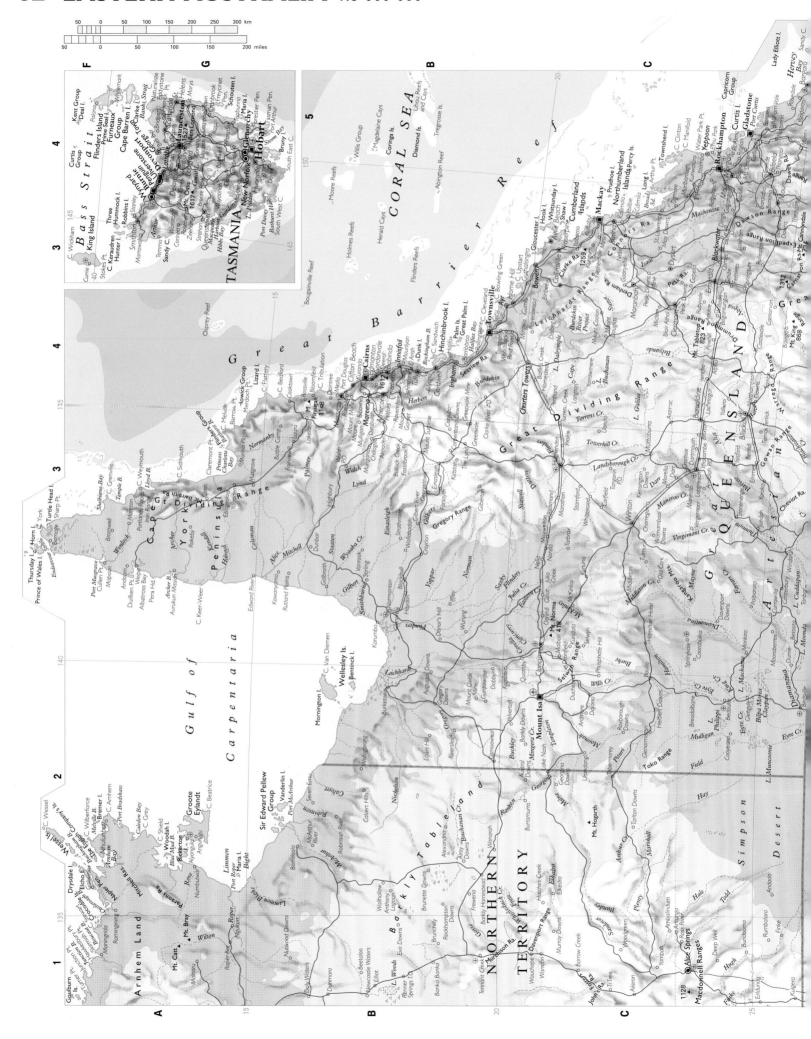

SOUTHERN OCEAN

TASMAN SEA

SOUTH AUSTRALIA

NEW SOUTH WALES

V I C T O R I A

BRISBANE

SYDNEY

CANBERRA

MELBOURNE

ADELAIDE

Newcastle

Wollongong

Bass Strait

King Island

Flinders Island

Furneaux Group

Cape Barren I.

CARTOGRAPHY BY PHILIP'S COPYRIGHT REED INTERNATIONAL BOOKS LTD.

Projection: Bonne

East from Greenwich

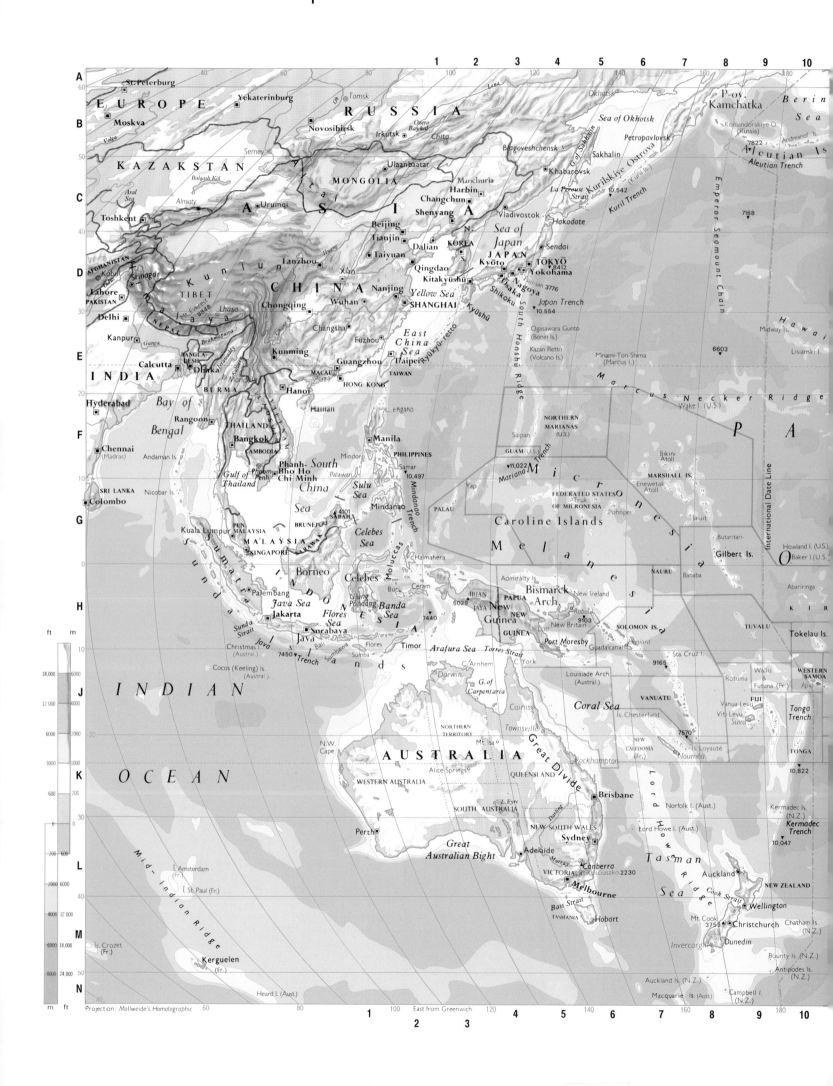

1 **2** **3** **4** **5** **6** **7** **8** **9** **10**

A

St. Peterburg

EUROPE   Yekaterinburg   RUSSIA   Tomsk   Lena   Okhotsk   P-ov.
Kamchatka   Berin
Sea

B

Moskva   Novosibirsk   Ozero   Irkutsk   Chita   Sea of Okhotsk   Petropavlovsk   Komandorskiye O.
(Russia)   Andreanof I.

KAZAKSTAN   Baykal   Blagoveshchensk   Sakhalin   7822   Aleutian   Is.
Aleutian Trench

Semey   Altai   Ulaanbaatar   Khabarovsk   Kurilskiye Ostrova   Emperor Seamount Chain

Balqash Köl   MONGOLIA   Manchuria   La Perouse   Kuril Trench   10.542   7168

Aral
Sea   Almaty   Urumqi   A   S   I   A   Harbin   Vladivostok   Hakodate

C

Toshkent   Beijing   Changchun   N.   Sea of
Japan   Sendai

AFGHANISTAN   Kabul   Tianjin   Dalian   KOREA   Kyōto   TOKYO   Midway Is.   Hawai

D

Srinagar   Lanzhou   Taiyuan   Qingdao   Nagoya   Yokohama   8412   Japan Trench   Lisianski I.

Lahore   Xian   CHINA   Nanjing   Yellow Sea   SHANGHAI   Shikoku   3776   10.554   6603   Minami-Toni-Shima
(Marcus I.)

PAKISTAN   TIBET   Chongqing   Wuhan   East
China
Sea   Kyūshū   Ogasawara Gunto
(Bonin Is.)   Necker Ridge

Delhi   Mt. Everest
8848   Lhasa   Changsha   Fuzhou   Taipei   Yūkyū-retto   Kazan Retto
(Volcano Is.)   Marcus   Wake I. (U.S)

E

Kanpur   Ganga   NEPAL   Brahmaputra   Kunming   Guangzhou   TAIWAN   Hawa

INDIA   BANGLA-
DESH   Dhaka   MACAU
(Port.)   HONG KONG   NORTHERN
MARIANAS
(U.S.)   PA

Calcutta   BURMA   Hainan   Saipan   Bikini
Atoll

Hyderabad   Rangoon   Engaño   GUAM (U.S.)   MARSHALL IS.

F

Chennai
(Madras)   THAILAND   Manila   11,022   Enewetak
Atoll

Bangkok   Andaman Is.   Mindoro   PHILIPPINES   Mariana Trench   Micronesia

CAMBODIA   Samar   FEDERATED STATES   Truk   Yap

Phanh-   South   10,497   OF MICRONESIA

Phnom   Bho Ho   China   Palawan   Mindanao   PALAU   Pohnpen   Jaluit

Gulf of
Thailand   Penh   Chi Minh   Sea   Sulu
Sea   4101   Caroline Islands

SRI LANKA   Nicobar Is.   SABAH   Mindanao   Butaritari

G

Colombo   Kuala Lumpur   PEN
MALAYSIA   BRUNEI   Celebes
Sea   Admiralty Is.   NAURU   Banaba   Gilbert Is.   Howland I. (U.S.)
Baker I. (U.S.)

MALAYSIA   SARAWAK   Halmahera   New Ireland   Abariringa

SINGAPORE   Borneo   Celebes   Moluccas   Buru   Ceram   IRIAN
JAYA   Bismarck
Arch.   New Britain   KIR

H

Palembang   Java Sea   Ujung
Pandang   Banda
Sea   5029   New
Guinea   Rabaul   9103   SOLOMON IS.   TUVALU

Jakarta   Flores
Sea   7440   PAPUA
NEW   Lae   SOLOMON IS.   Tokelau Is.

Sunda
Strait   Surabaya   Bali   Sumbawa   Flores   Timor   GUINEA   Port Moresby   Guadalcanal   Honiard

Christmas I.
(Aust.)   Java   Sumba   Arafura Sea   Torres Strait   Sta. Cruz I.   9165

J

Cocos (Keeling) Is.
(Aust.)   7450   Java
Trench   C. Arnhem   C. York   Louisiade Arch.
(Aust.)   Rotuma   WESTERN
SAMOA   Apia

INDIAN   Darwin   G. of
Carpentaria   Wallis &
Futuna (Fr.)

I. Amsterdam
(Fr.)   NORTHERN
TERRITORY   Cairns   Coral Sea   VANUATU   Vanua Levu   FIJI   Tonga
Trench

I. St. Paul (Fr.)   Townsville   Is. Chesterfield   Viti Levu   Suva

K

OCEAN   Mt. Isa   NEW
CALEDONIA
(Fr.)   Nouméa   7570   TONGA   10,822

AUSTRALIA   Alice Springs   QUEENSLAND   Great Divide   Rockhampton

WESTERN AUSTRALIA   L. Eyre   Brisbane   Norfolk I. (Aust.)   Kermadec Is.
(N.Z.)

SOUTH AUSTRALIA   Darling   Lord Howe I. (Aust.)   Kermadec
Trench

Perth   Great
Australian Bight   NEW SOUTH WALES   Sydney   Tasman   10,047

L

Mid-Indian Ridge   Murray   Canberra   Sea   Auckland Is.

VICTORIA   Mt. Kosciuszko 2230   NEW ZEALAND

Melbourne   Cook Strait   Wellington

M

Is. Crozet (Fr.)   Bass Strait   Mt. Cook
3753   Christchurch   Chatham Is.
(N.Z.)

TASMANIA   Hobart   Invercargill   Dunedin   Bounty Is. (N.Z.)

N

Kerguelen
(Fr.)   Heard I. (Aust.)   Auckland Is. (N.Z.)   Antipodes Is.
(N.Z.)

Macquarie Is. (Aust.)   Campbell I.
(N.Z.)

ft   m
18,000   6000
12 000   4000
6000   2000
3000   1000
600   200
0
200   600
2000   6000
4000   12 000
6000   18,000
8000   24,000
m   ft

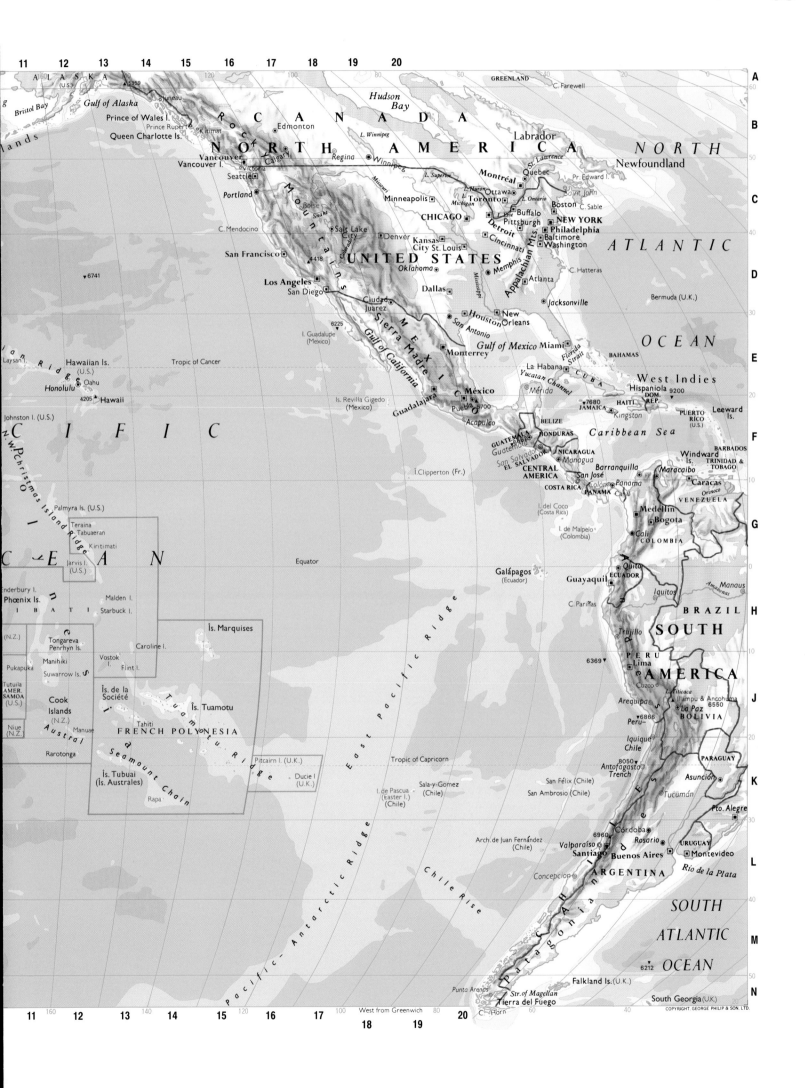

COPYRIGHT. GEORGE PHILIP & SON. LTD.

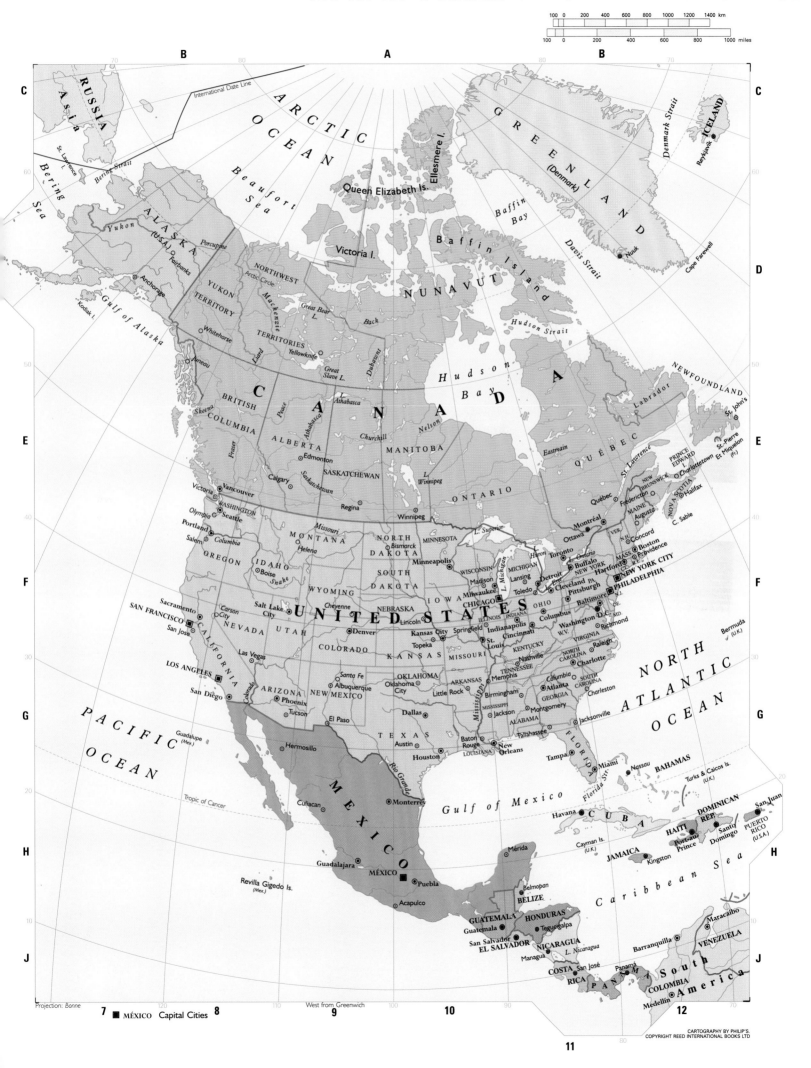

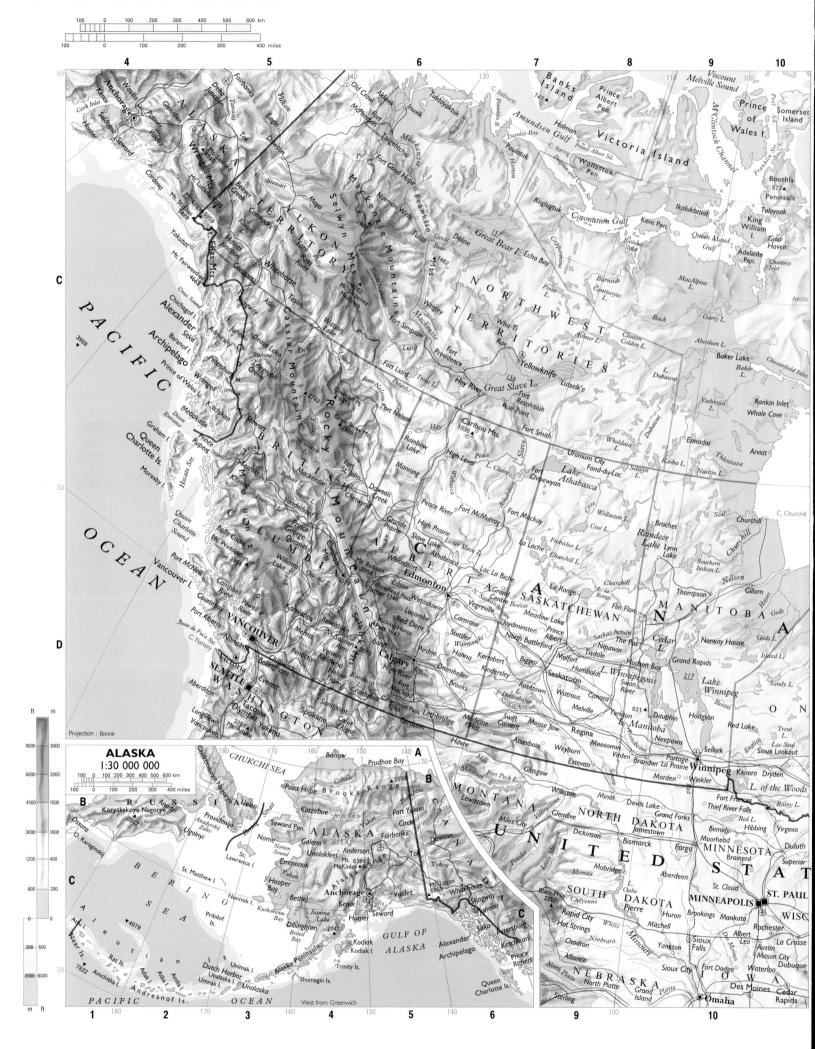

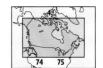

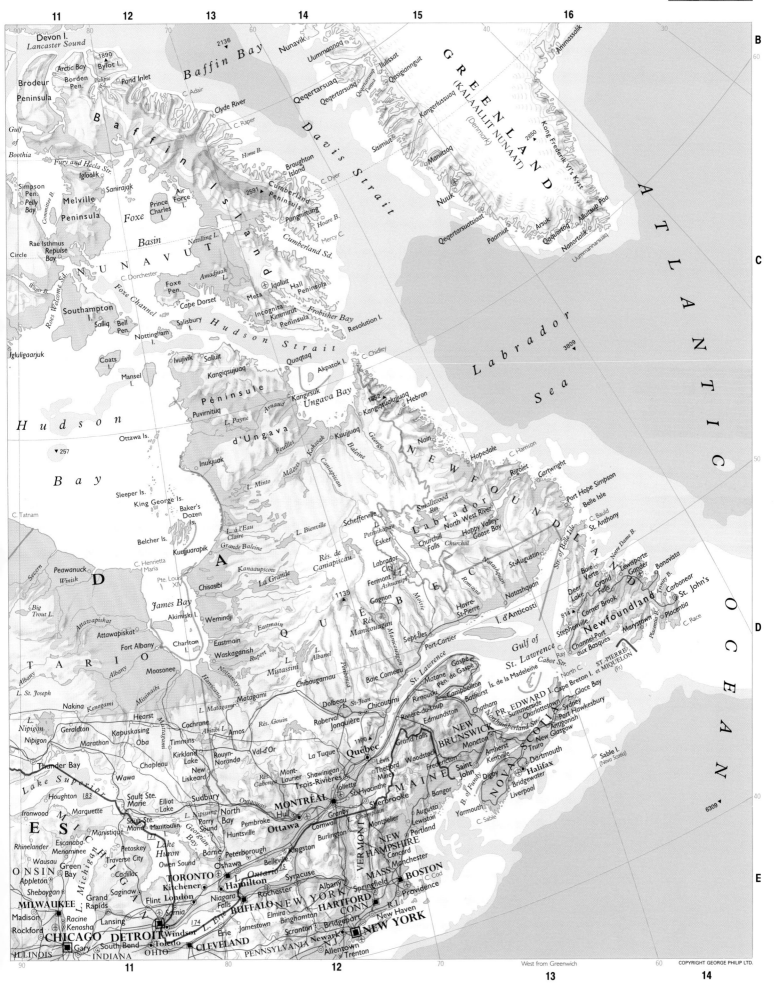

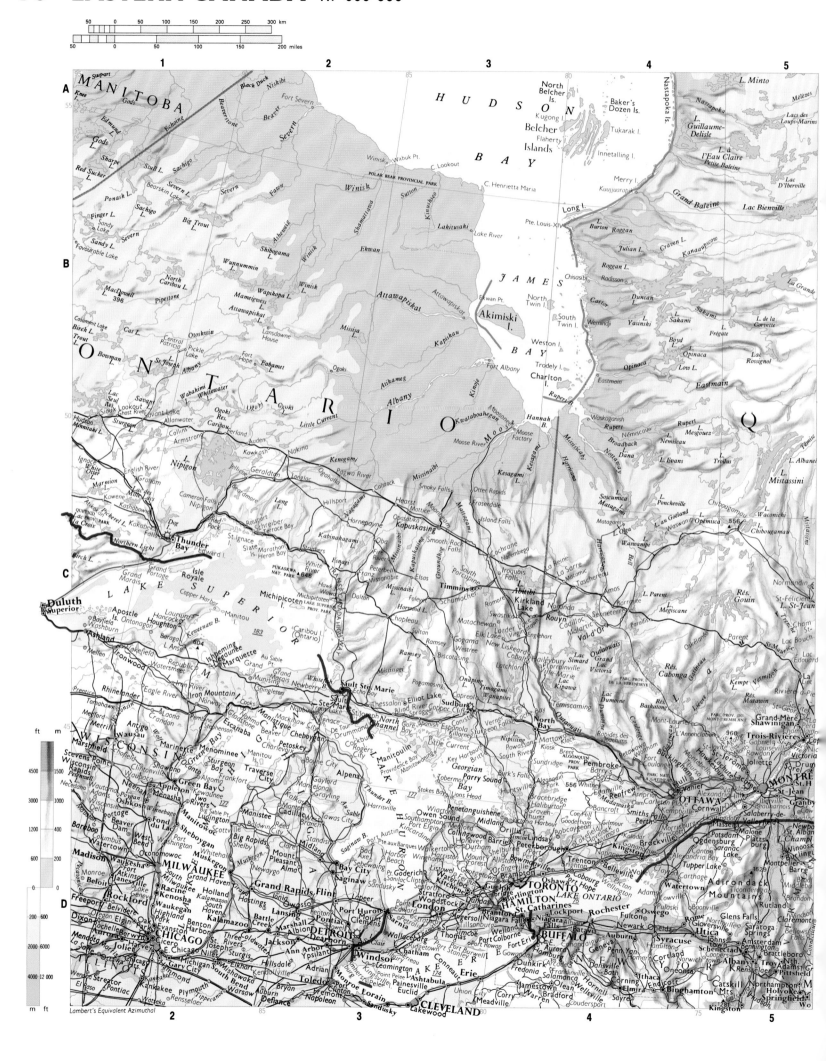

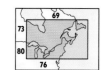

A

South Aulatsivik I.
High I.
Nain
Paul I.
Voisey's B.
Kogaluk
Tunungayualok I.
Davis Inlet
Nunaksaluk I.

Erlandson
Whale
George
Fraser
Du Gué
Fort
McKenzie
Nachicapau L.
Otelnuk L.
L. de la
Hutte
Sauvage

Big Bay
Hopedale
Kaipokok B.
Aillik
Makkovik
Adlavik I.
C. Harrison
Holton
Indian Harbour
Grosswater
B.

Chakonipau L.
Champdoré
L. Tudor
Whitegull
L.
610
Wakuach

Harp L.

Kanairiktok
Natkapi L.
Nipishish
Seal L.
Rigolet
Island of Ponds

Kamapiskau
Otelnuk L.
Petitsikapau L.
Woods
L.
Smallwood
Res.
North-West River
Grand
L. Melville
1128
Mealy Mts.
Separation
Point
Cartwright
Sandwich B.
Square Islands

Scheffeville
Goose
Happy Valley-
Goose Bay
Eagle
Paradise

B

L. Néret
Attikamagen L.
Churchill Falls
Ossokmanuan
Churchill
Alexis
St. Lewis

Menihek Lakes
Shabogamo
Opiskotish L.
Lac
Joseph
Winokapau L.
Minipi
L.
Red
Bay
Mary's
Harbour
Battle Harbour

L. Bermen
Opiscoteo L.
Labrador City
Wabush
Atikonak
L.
Little
Mecatina
St. Paul
Bradore Bay
St. Lunaire-
Griquet
Belle I.
St. Anthony
Hare B.

Nitchequon
Kaniapiskau
Lake
Ashuanipi
Burnt
L.
Labrador
St-Augustin
Anse-au-Loup
Lourdes-de-
Blanc-Sablon
Flower's
Cove
Str. of Belle Isle

L. Naocane
1128
Petit Lac
Manicouagan
St-Augustin-
Saguenay
Outer I.
Port
Saunders
Roddickton
Conche
Englee
Groais Is.
Bell I.

L. Plétipi
Gagnon
Res.
Manicouagan
1048
Natashquan
I. du
Petit Mécatina
Harrington Harbour
Daniel's
Harbour
Great
Harbour
Deep
White B.
Horse Is.
C. St. John

QUEBEC

Manouane
1268
Mt. Jacques-
Cartier
Manitou
L.
Lac
Allard
Kegaska
Gethsémoni
Etamamu
Trout River
Deer
Lake
Seal Cove
Sop's
Arm
La Scie
Baie
Verte
Notre Dame
Bay
Twillingate
Fogo I.

Péribonca
L.
Manouane
Sheldrake
Mingan
Aguanish
Natashquan
Musquaro
GROS MORNE
NAT. PARK
Howley
Springdale
Botwood
Lewisporte
Gander
Carmanville
C. Freels

C

Mistassini
Manicouagan
Clarke
City
Moisie
Havre-St-Pierre
Long Range Mts.
Bay of Islands
Corner Brook
814
Buchans
Grand
Falls
Glenwood
Westerville
Bonavista

Péribonca
Bersimites
Godbout
Port-Cartier
Rivière-Pentecôte
Long Pt.
Port au Port B.
Stephenville
Red Indian
L.
Windsor
Gander
Clovertown
C. Bonavista
Bonavista
Catalina

Dolbeau
Baie-
Comeau
Baie-Trinité
Pte. des Monts
Cap-Chat
Ste-Anne
Dét. de Jacques-Cartier
Jupiter
Heath Pt.
C. St. George
St. George's B.
Victoria
Res.
Grey Res.
Salmon
Res.
Terra Nova
Trinity
Boy de Verte

Alma
Forestville
Matane
Pte. Ouest
Port-Menier
Î. d'Anticosti
572
GULF OF
St. David's
South Branch
Long Range Mts.
Rose Blanche
White
Bear
Grand Falls
381
Clarenville
Content
Concention B.

Arvida
Chicoutimi
Sayabec
Grande-Vallée
Montmagny
Î. d'Anticosti
ST. LAWRENCE
C. Ray
Channel-Port
aux Basques
Burgeo
Ramea
François
Harbour Breton
Port Blandford
Carbonear
Bay
Torbay

Jonquière
Port Alfred
Mont-
Joli
Cap-Chat
Douglastown
Gaspé
Percé
St. Andrew Is.
Cabot Strait
Harbour
Grace
St.
John's

Saguenay
Rimouski
Amqui
Bonaventure
Grande-Rivière
Miscou I.
Grande-Entrée
St. Paul
Placentia
Argentia
Spaniard's
Bay

Trois-Pistoles
Causapscal
Matapédia
Chaleur Bay
Shippegan
Îs. de la
Madeleine
(Quebec)
Cap-aux-Meules
Placentia
Holyrood

Rivière-du-Loup
Dalhousie
Belledune
Lamèque
Tracadie
Havre-Aubert
C. Anguille
Fortune B.
Bulls

Cabano
Campbellton
Atholville
Bathurst
Miramichi R.
North Pt.
Tignish
Pleasant Bay
CAPE BRETON
NAT. PARK
Ingonish
Marystown
St. Lawrence
St. Mary's
C. Pine
Trepassey

Rivière-du-Loup
St-Pascal
Edmundston
Heath Steele
Negusec
Chatham
Alberton
Chéticamp
532
Ingonish
Miquelon
C. Race

Cacouna
St-Jean
Van Buren
St. Leonard 819
Grand Falls
Newcastle
Collette
Richibucto
PRINCE EDWARD
Summerside
East Pt.
Sydney Mines
New Waterford
Langlade
SAINT-PIERRE
ET MIQUELON
(Fr.)

QUÉBEC
Lauzon
Lévis
Montmagny
Pampie
St. Flavie
Van Buren
Caribou
Plaster
Rock
Chipman
ISLAND
Kensington
Borden
Charlottetown
Souris
N. Sydney
Glace Bay
St-Pierre

NEW
BRUNSWICK
Ashland
Presque Isle
Van Buren
Minto
Grand L.
Nashwaak
Georgetown
Montague
Sydney
Louisbourg
Cape Breton
Island

Deschaillons
Ste-Marie
Beauceville
St-Georges
Eagle L.
Island Falls
Chesuncook
Patten
Houlton
Hartland
Stanley
Fredericton
Gagetown
Shediac
Moncton
Amherst
Pictou
Antigonish
Mulgrave
Brasd'Or
Fourchu

Plessisville
Thetford Mines
Millinocket
1606
Woodstock
Petitcodiac
Springhill
New Glasgow
Stellarton
Joggins
Harbourville
Sherbrooke
Canso
Chedabucto B.

Asbestos
Lac-
Mégantic
Moosehead
L.
Lincoln
St. John
Fredericton
Junc.
Gagetown
Sussex
Chignecto
Truro
Upper
Musquodoboit
I. Madame

Sherbrooke
Jackman
Mooselook-
meguntic L.
Patten
Blacks
Hr.
Saint
John
Fundy
Gatetown
St. Martins
Minas
Basin
Stewiacke
Sheet Hr.

Magog
Coaticook
Bingham
Greenville
Old Town
Brewer
Calais
Machias
Eastport
Bay of
Fundy
Windsor
Kentville
Dartmouth
ATLANTIC

Rumford
Bethel
Waterville
Bangor
Ellsworth
Jonesport
Grand
Manan I.
Bridgetown
Middleton
Annapolis
Royal
Mahone Bay
Halifax
Musquodoboit Hr.

Berlin
Augusta
Belfast
Camden
Bar Harbor
Mt. Desert I.
Weymouth
Digby
NOVA SCOTIA
Lunenburg
Bridgewater

Littleton
1917
MAINE
Camden
Rockland
St. Mary's B.
Rossignol
Res.
Bridgewater
Liverpool
Port Mouton
Sable I.
(Nova Scotia)

Conway
Sebago
Brunswick
Bath
Yarmouth
Shelburne
OCEAN

D

Rochester
Sanford
Saco
Biddeford
Wedgeport
Lockeport

Concord
Dover
Portsmouth
Clark's Harbour
C. Sable

Keene
Manchester
Nashua
Haverhill
Lawrence
Lowell
Gloucester
Ann

Fitchburg
Greenfield
Lowell
Waltham
Lynn

BOSTON
Worcester
Brockton
Woonsocket

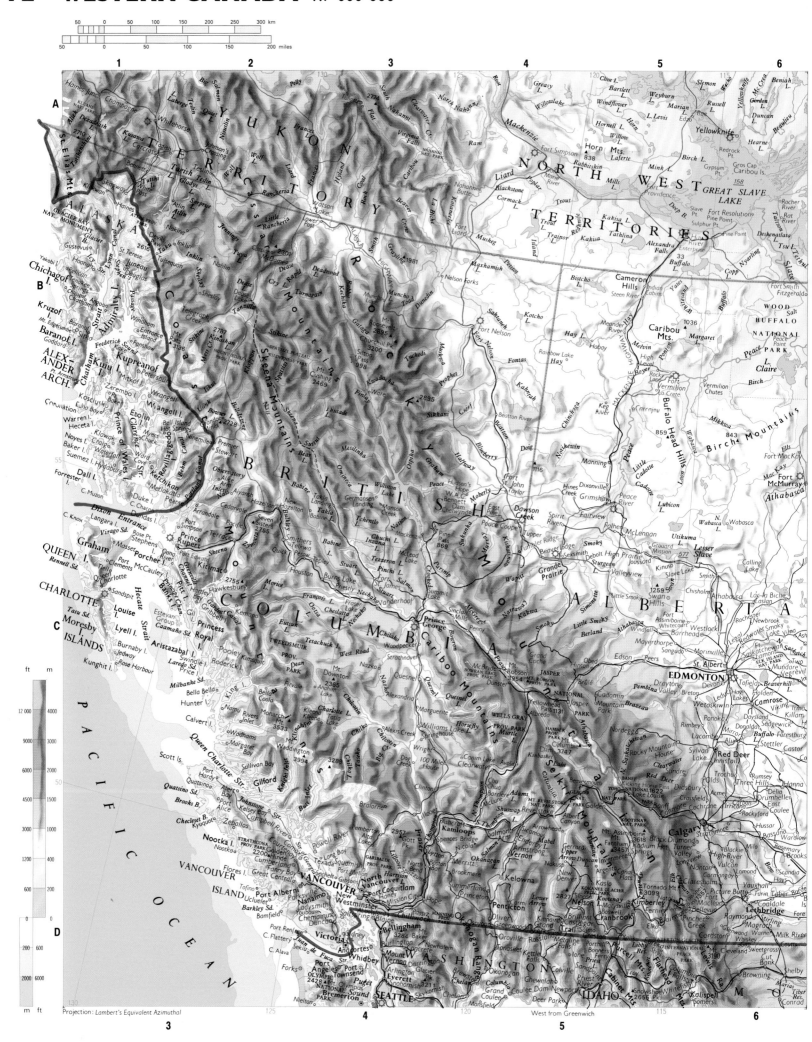

Projection: Lambert's Equivalent Azimuthal

West from Greenwich

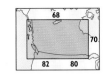

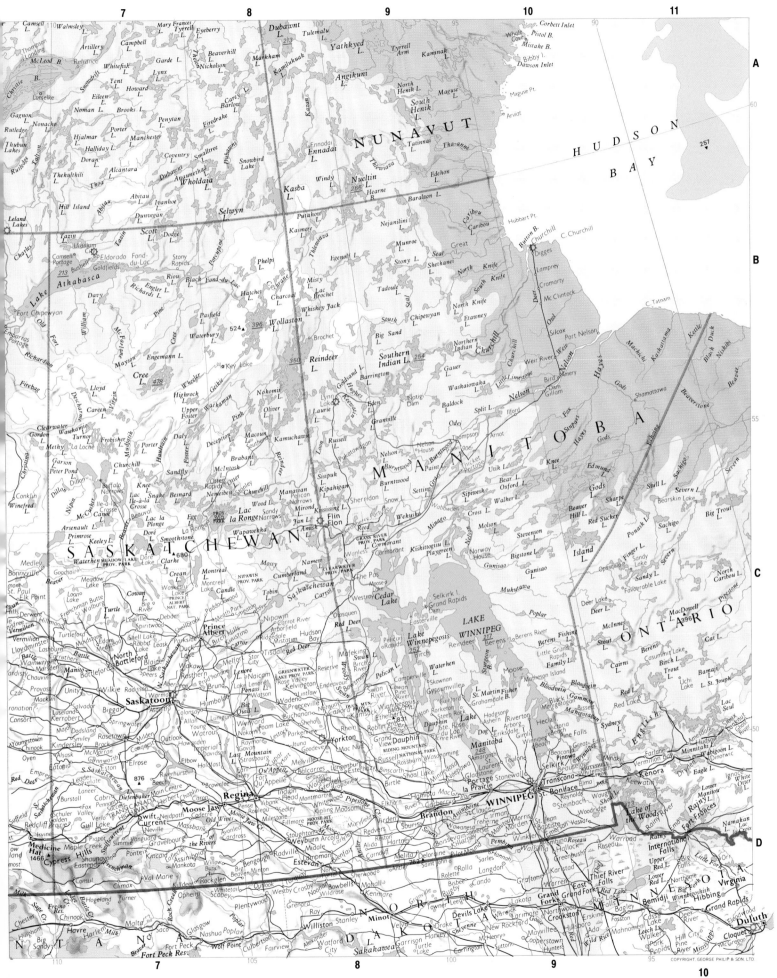

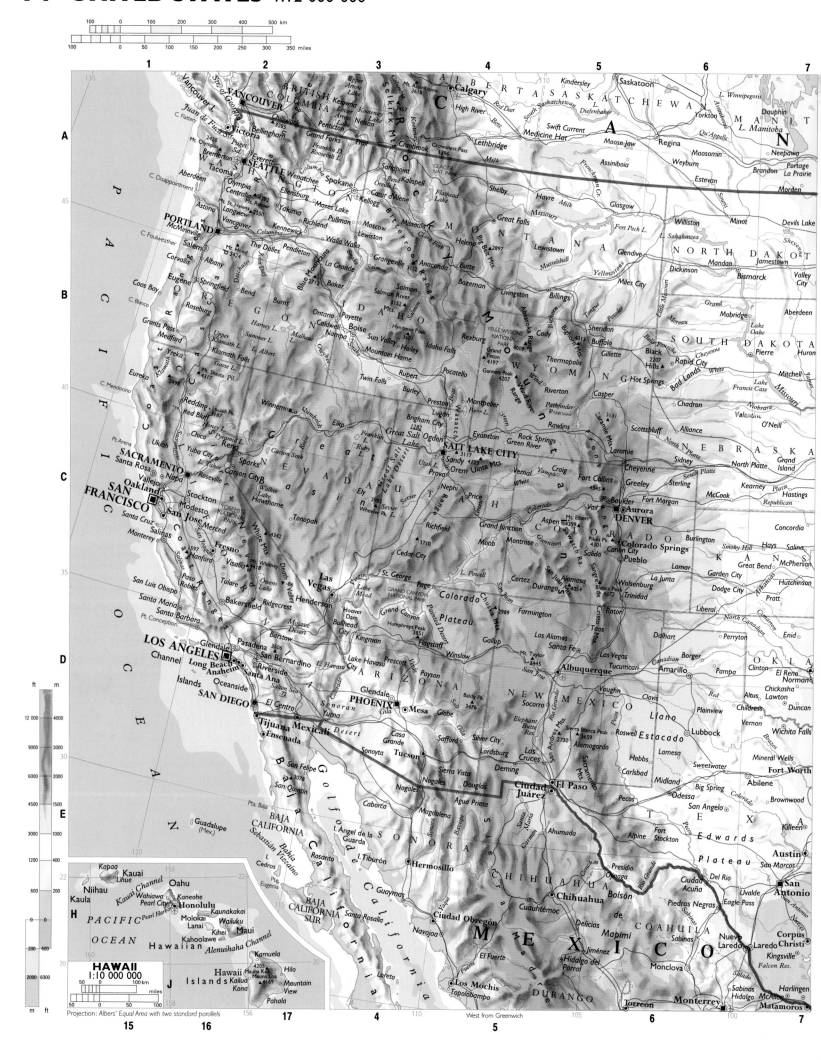

Projection: Albers' Equal Area with two standard parallels

HAWAII 1:10 000 000
50   0   100 km
miles

A B C D E H J

1 2 3 4 5 6 7
15 16 17 4 5 6 7

ft m
12 000   4000
9000   3000
6000   2000
4500   1500
3000   1000
1200   400
600   200
0   0
200   600
2000   6000
m ft

PACIFIC OCEAN

BRITISH COLUMBIA
ALBERTA
SASKATCHEWAN
MANITOBA

Vancouver I.
VANCOUVER
Victoria
SEATTLE
Tacoma
PORTLAND
Salem
WASHINGTON
OREGON
IDAHO
MONTANA
NORTH DAKOTA
SOUTH DAKOTA
WYOMING
NEBRASKA
NEVADA
UTAH
COLORADO
KANSAS
CALIFORNIA
SACRAMENTO
SAN FRANCISCO
Oakland
San Jose
Fresno
LOS ANGELES
SAN DIEGO
Las Vegas
ARIZONA
PHOENIX
NEW MEXICO
OKLA
SALT LAKE CITY
DENVER
Colorado Springs
Albuquerque
El Paso
Ciudad Juárez
TEXAS
San Antonio
Corpus Christi
Matamoros
Monterrey
MEXICO
BAJA CALIFORNIA
SONORA
CHIHUAHUA
COAHUILA
DURANGO
Tijuana
Mexicali
PACIFIC OCEAN
Hawaiian Islands
HAWAII
Kauai
Oahu
Honolulu
Maui
Hawaii
Hilo

West from Greenwich

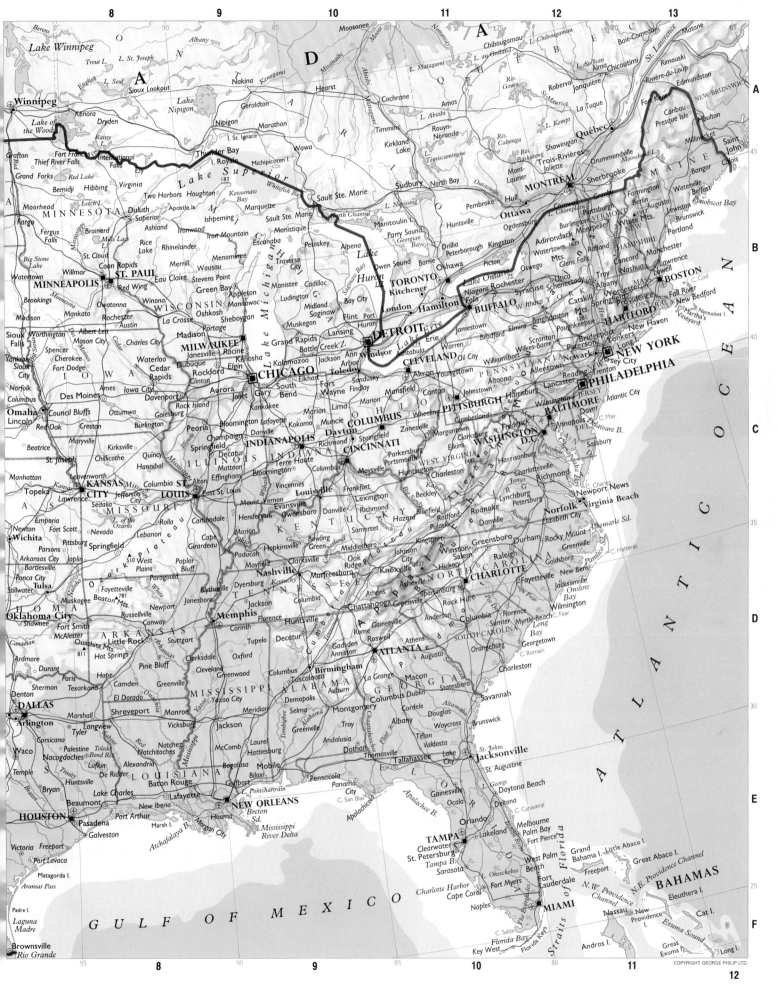

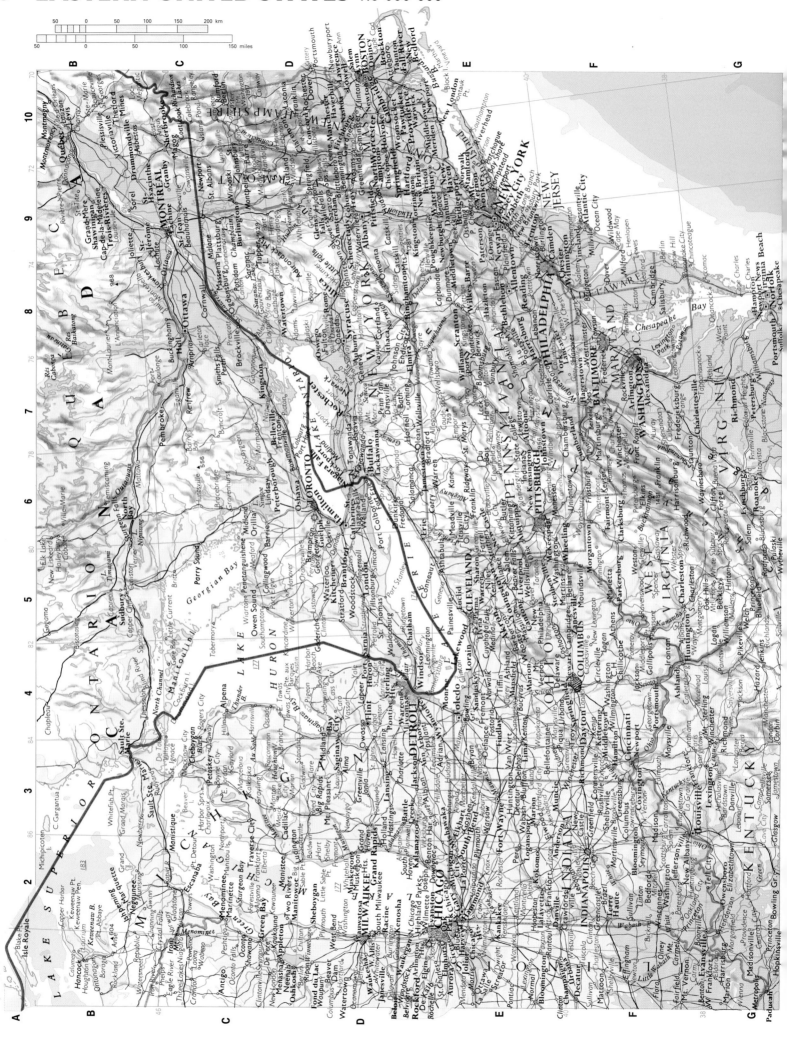

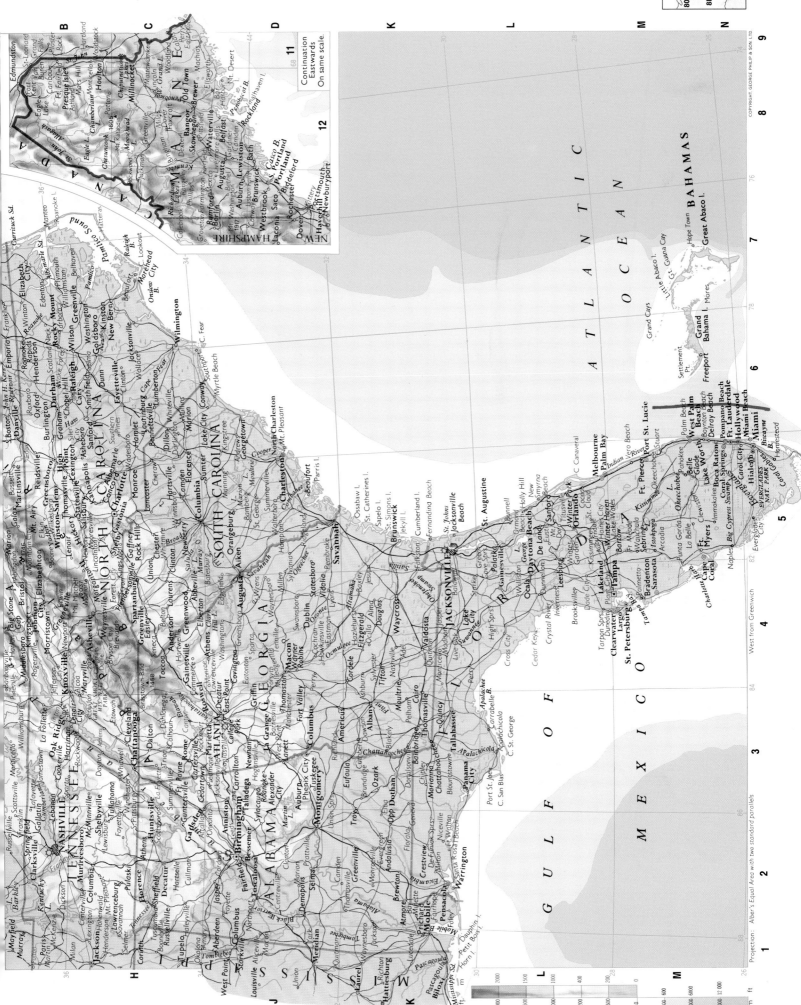

Projection: Alber's Equal Area with two standard parallels

West from Greenwich

COPYRIGHT GEORGE PHILIP & SON LTD.

Continuation
Eastwards
On same scale.

ATLANTIC OCEAN

GULF OF MEXICO

BAHAMAS

FLORIDA

GEORGIA

ALABAMA

SOUTH CAROLINA

NORTH CAROLINA

TENNESSEE

MAINE

NEW HAMPSHIRE

CANADA

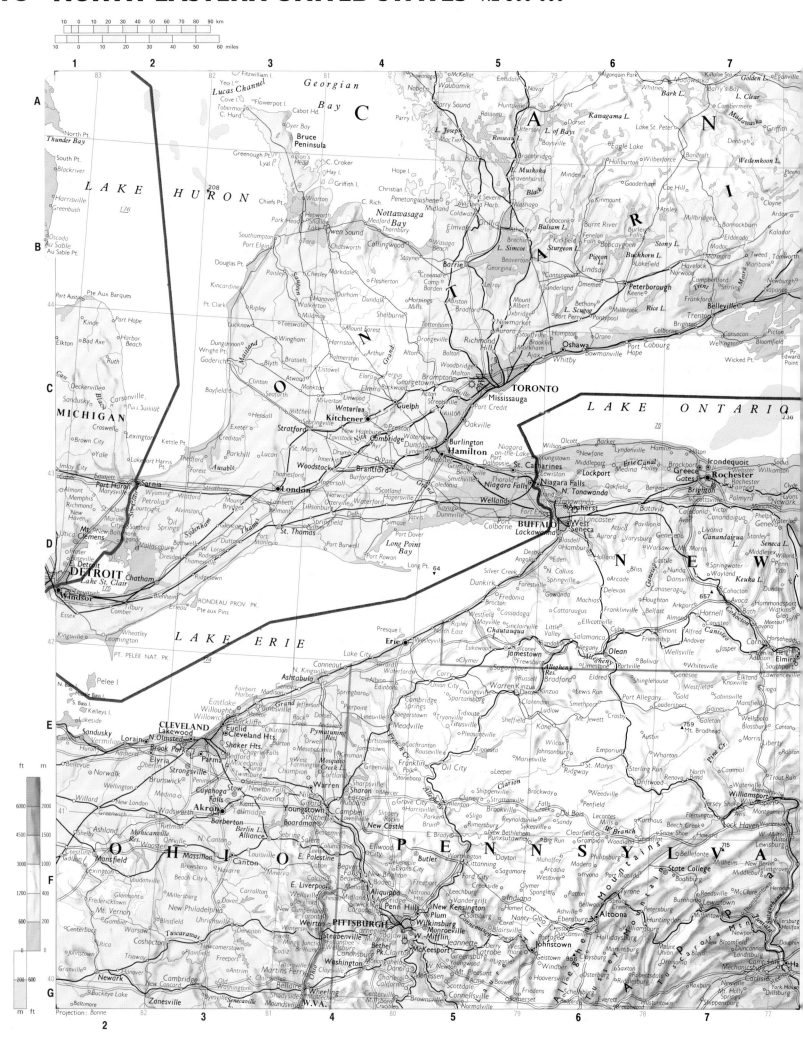

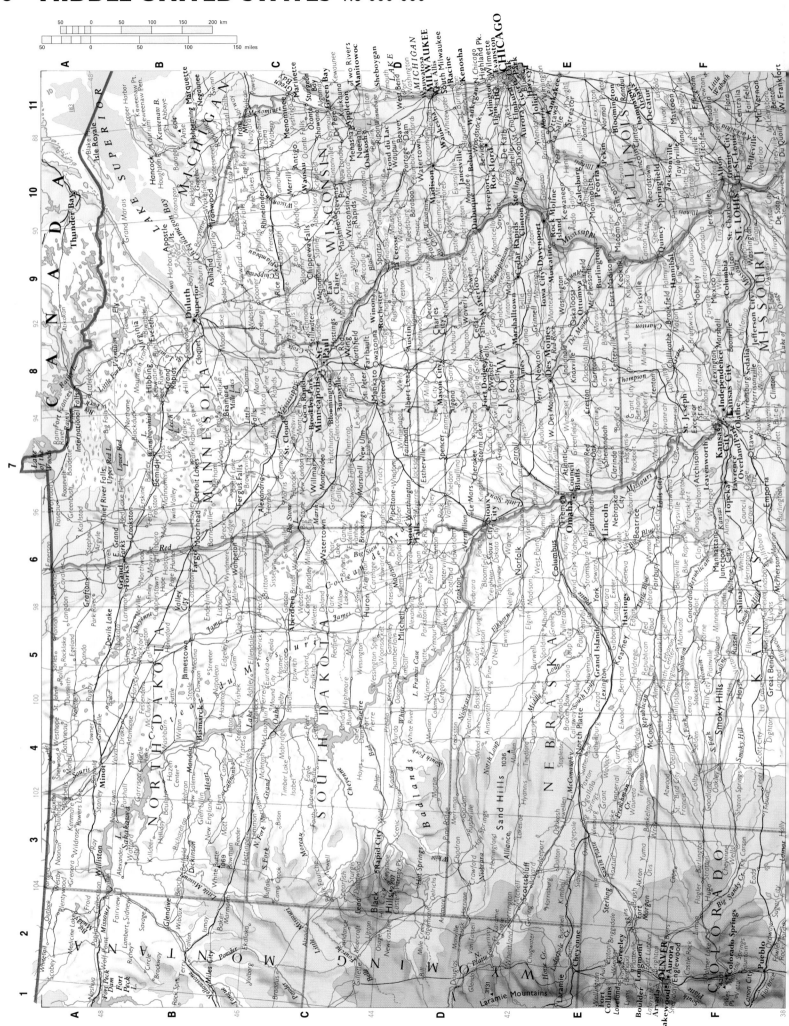

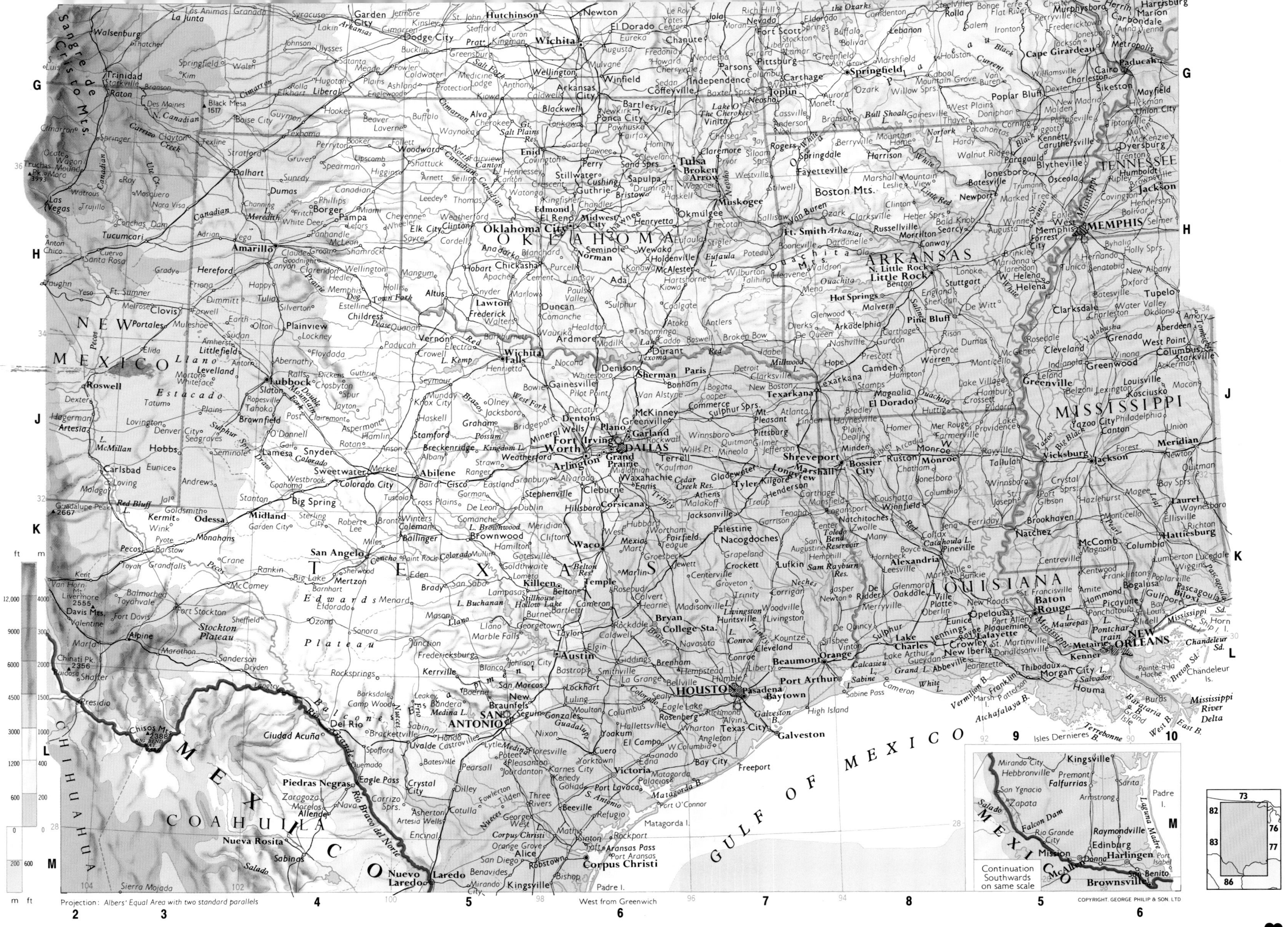

TENNESSEE

MISSISSIPPI

ARKANSAS

LOUISIANA

OKLAHOMA

TEXAS

NEW MEXICO

MEXICO

COAHUILA

CHIHUAHUA

GULF OF MEXICO

MEMPHIS

NEW ORLEANS

DALLAS

Fort Worth

HOUSTON

SAN ANTONIO

Austin

Corpus Christi

Laredo

Nuevo Laredo

Little Rock

Shreveport

Baton Rouge

Wichita

Oklahoma City

Tulsa

Amarillo

El Paso

Galveston

Brownsville

West from Greenwich

Projection: Albers' Equal Area with two standard parallels

COPYRIGHT GEORGE PHILIP & SON LTD

Continuation Southwards on same scale

Laguna Madre

Padre I.

Sangre de Cristo Mts.

Llano Estacado

Edwards Plateau

Stockton Plateau

Río Bravo del Norte

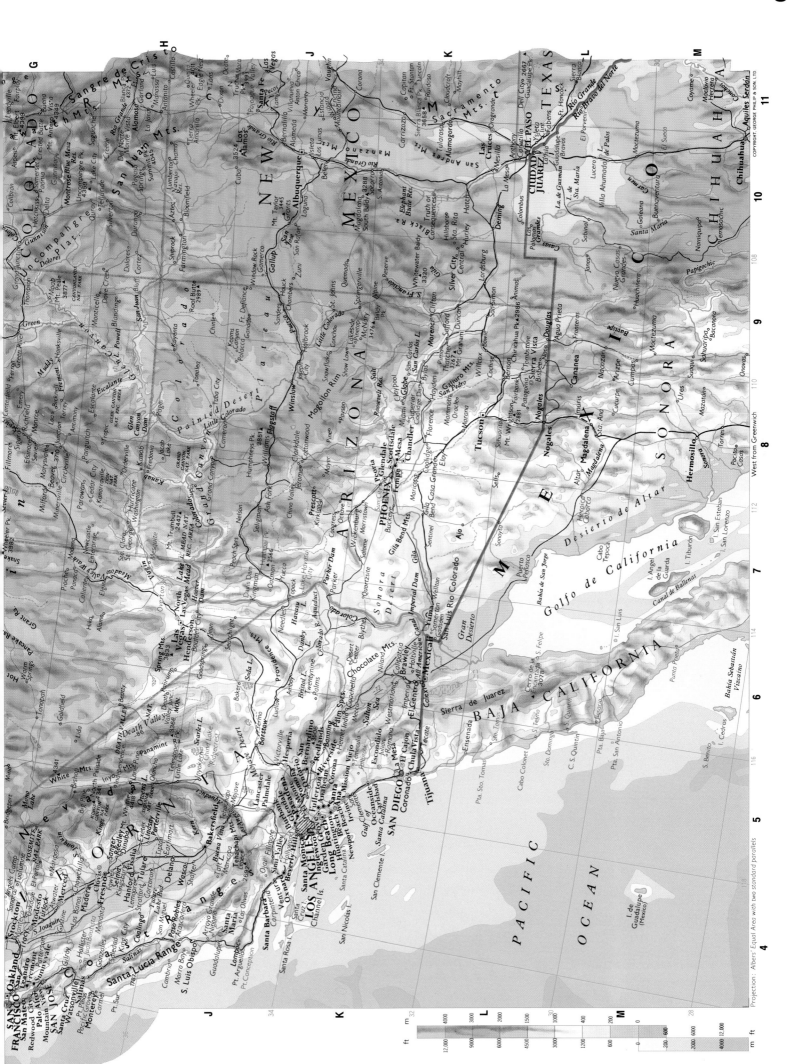

83

COPYRIGHT GEORGE PHILIP & SON, LTD.

Projection: Albers' Equal Area with two standard parallels

West from Greenwich

ft m
12,000 4000
9000 3000
6000 2000
4500 1500
3000 1000
1200 400
600 200
0
0
600 200
2000 6000
4000 12,000
m ft

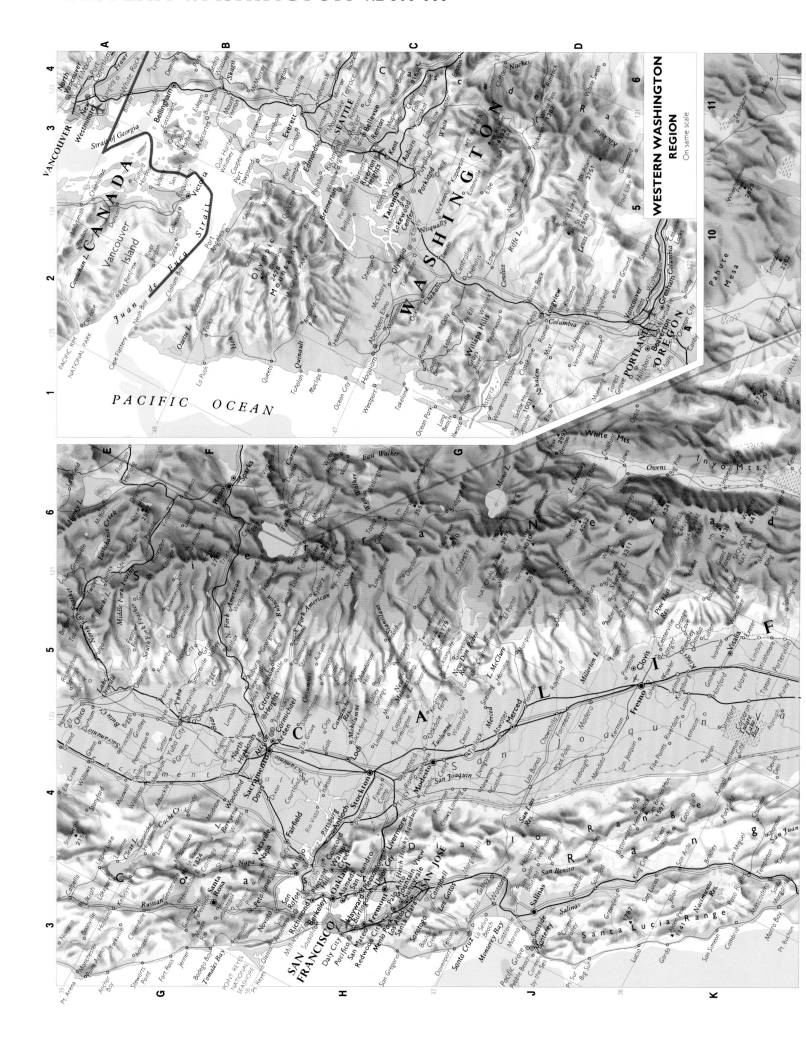

WESTERN WASHINGTON
REGION
On same scale

PACIFIC OCEAN

CANADA

VANCOUVER

Vancouver Island

Strait of Georgia

Juan de Fuca Strait

WASHINGTON

SEATTLE

Tacoma

Olympia

OREGON

PORTLAND

Olympic Mountains

CALIFORNIA

SAN FRANCISCO

SAN JOSE

Sacramento

Stockton

Modesto

Merced

Fresno

Clovis

Visalia

Santa Rosa

Napa

Fairfield

Reno

Sparks

Salinas

Monterey

Santa Cruz

Santa Lucia Range

Diablo Range

NEVADA

ARIZONA

C A L I F O R N I A

LOS ANGELES

San Bernardino

Las Vegas

North Las Vegas

Henderson

Lake Mead

LAKE MEAD
NATIONAL
RECREATION
AREA

Death Valley

Amargosa Range

Mojave Desert

Colorado Desert

Chocolate Mts.

MEXICO

San Diego

Tijuana

Mexicali

El Centro

Bakersfield

Santa Barbara

Oxnard

Ventura

Santa Monica

Long Beach

Santa Ana

Anaheim

Riverside

Pasadena

Glendale

Burbank

Palmdale

Lancaster

Apple Valley

Hesperia

Victorville

Barstow

Needles

Blythe

P A C I F I C   O C E A N

Santa Catalina I.

San Clemente I.

San Nicolas I.

Santa Cruz I.

San Miguel I.

Santa Rosa I.

San Pedro Channel

Santa Barbara Channel

Channel Islands

Salton Sea

Imperial Valley

Coachella Canal

Colorado R. Aqueduct

Sonora Desert

San Bernardino Mts.

San Gabriel Mts.

Tehachapi Mts.

San Rafael Mts.

Santa Ynez Mts.

Gulf of Santa Catalina

COPYRIGHT GEORGE PHILIP & SON, LTD.

Projection: Bonne

West from Greenwich

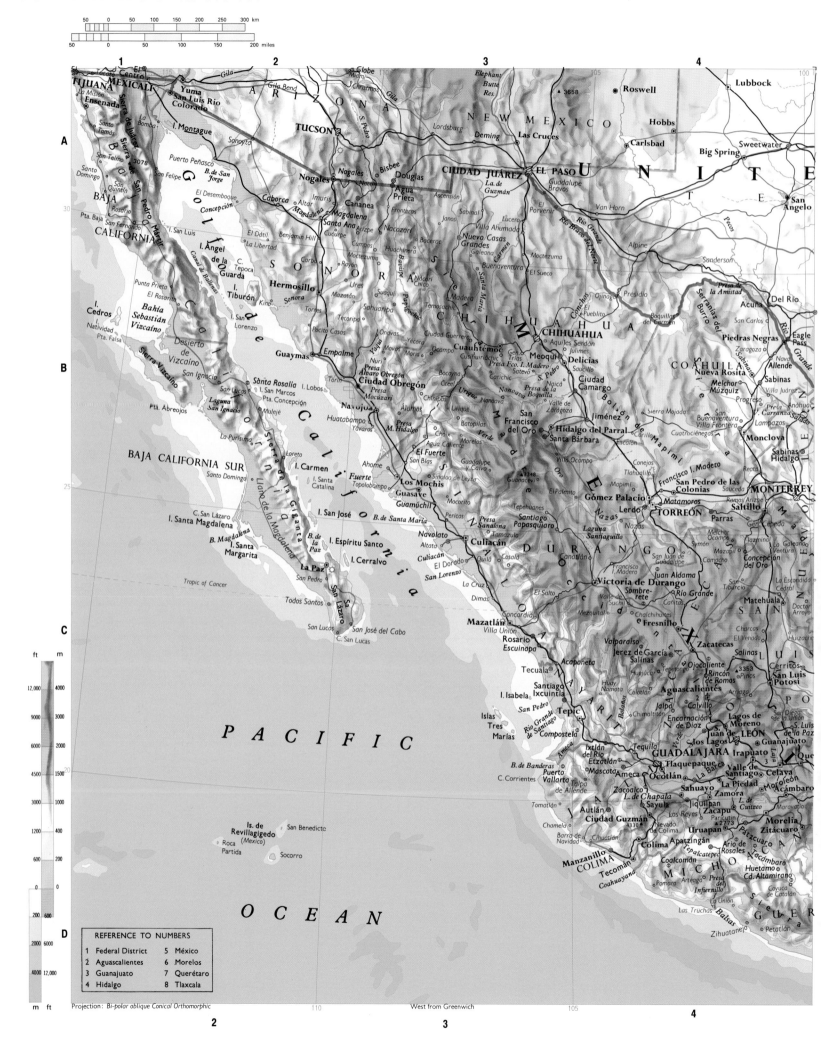

PACIFIC

OCEAN

REFERENCE TO NUMBERS
1 Federal District   5 México
2 Aguascalientes   6 Morelos
3 Guanajuato   7 Querétaro
4 Hidalgo   8 Tlaxcala

Projection: Bi-polar oblique Conical Orthomorphic   West from Greenwich

1:8 000 000

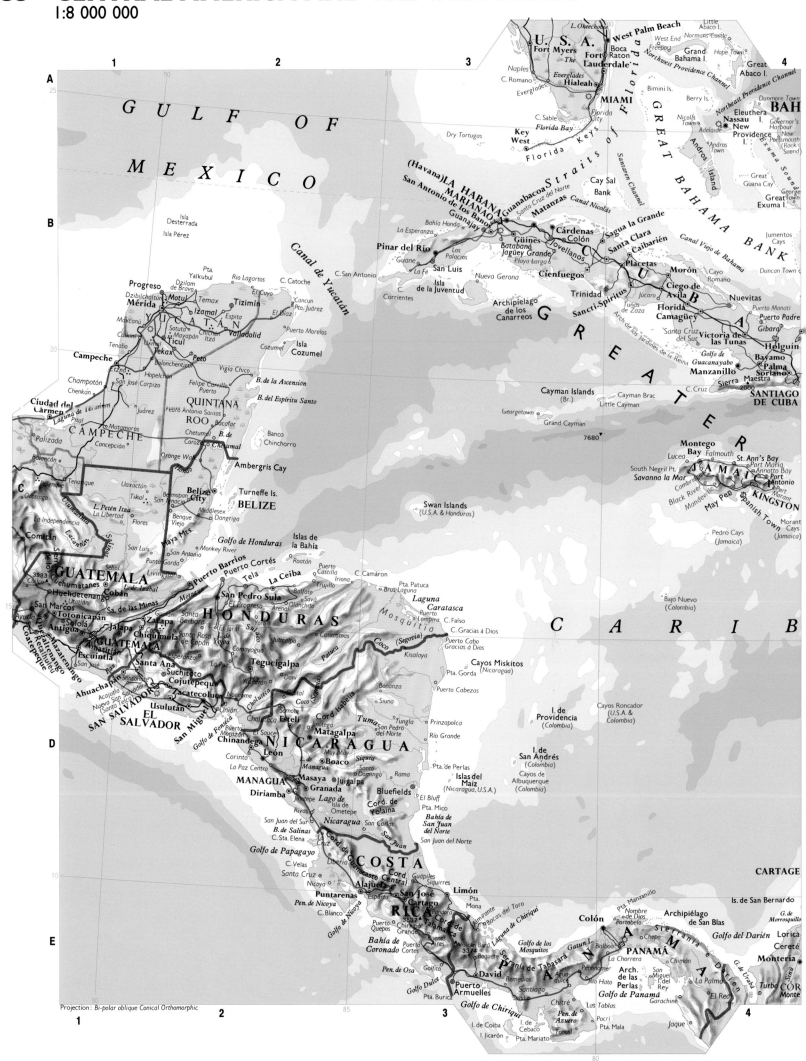

GULF OF MEXICO

U.S.A.

West Palm Beach
Fort Myers
Naples
C. Romano
Everglades
Hialeah
MIAMI
Key West
Dry Tortugas
Florida Bay
C. Sable
Florida Keys
Straits of Florida

Little Abaco I.
Grand Bahama I.
West End
Freeport
Hope Town
Great Abaco I.
BAH
Great Guana Cay
Great Abaco I.
Eleuthera
Nassau
New Providence I.
Andros I.
Dunmore Town
Governor's Harbour
George Town
Exuma I.
GREAT BAHAMA BANK

(Havana) LA HABANA
MARIANAO
San Antonio de los Baños
Guanabacoa
Guanajay
Bahía Honda
La Esperanza
Pinar del Río
Guane
La Fé
Los Palacios
San Luis
Batabanó
Jagüey Grande
Playa Larga
Nueva Gerona
Isla de la Juventud
Corrientes
C. San Antonio
Santa Cruz del Norte
Matanzas
Canal Nicolás
Cárdenas
Colón
Güines
Jovellanos
Santa Clara
Caibarién
Sagua la Grande
Placetas
Cienfuegos
Trinidad
Sancti Spíritus
Júcaro
Morón
Ciego de Ávila
Florida
Camagüey
Nuevitas
Puerto Manatí
Puerto Padre
Gibara
Victoria de las Tunas
Holguín
Bayamo
Palma Soriano
Manzanillo
Sierra Maestra
SANTIAGO DE CUBA
C. Cruz
CUBA
GREATER
Cayo Sal Bank
Canal Viejo de Bahama
Jumentos Cays
Duncan Town

Cay Sal Bank

Archipiélago de los Canarreos
Golfo de Guacanayabo
Golfo de Batabanó
Arch. de los Jardines de la Reina
2000

Cayman Islands (Br.)
Georgetown
Grand Cayman
Cayman Brac
Little Cayman
7680

Swan Islands (U.S.A. & Honduras)

Montego Bay
Lucea
Falmouth
St. Ann's Bay
Annotto Bay
Port Antonio
South Negril Pt.
Savanna la Mar
Black River
Mandeville
May Pen
Spanish Town
KINGSTON
Port Morant
JAMAICA
Pedro Cays (Jamaica)
Morant Cays (Jamaica)

CARIB

Isla Desterrada
Isla Pérez

Progreso
Pta. Yalkubul
Dzilam de Bravo
Río Lagartos
El Cuyo
C. Catoche
Mérida
Motul
Temax
Tizimín
Dzibilchaltún
Izamal
Cancún
Pto. Juárez
Maxcanú
Sotuta
Chichén Itzá
Espita
El Díaz
Campeche
Tekax
Ticul
Peto
Valladolid
Puerto Morelos
Calkini
Uxmal
Bolonchenticul
Vigía Chico
Isla Cozumel
Champotón
San José Carpizo
Felipe Carrillo Puerto
B. de la Ascensión
Chenkán
Hopelchén
Orange Walk
B. del Espíritu Santo
Palizada
YUCATÁN
QUINTANA ROO
CAMPECHE
Ciudad del Carmen
Laguna de Términos
Pital
Matamoros
Juárez
Chetumal
B. de Corozal
Chetumal
Banco Chinchorro
Tenosique
Concepción
Balancán
Ambergris Cay
Turneffe Is.
Middlesex
Belize City
BELIZE
Dangriga
Islas de la Bahía
Roatán
Ocosingo
Palenque
L. Petén Itzá
La Libertad
Flores
Benque Viejo
San Ignacio
Belmopan
San José
Tikal
Uaxactún
Sebol
Maya Mts.
Monkey River
Golfo de Honduras
Puerto Cortés
Puerto Barrios
Comitán
La Independencia
Lacantún
Usumacinta
Cobán
L. de Izabal
Livingston
Puerto Cortés
Tela
La Ceiba
Trujillo
Puerto Castilla
Iriona
C. Camarón
Pta. Patuca
Brus Laguna
Laguna Caratasca
C. Falso
3993
Cuchumatanes
Sa. de las Minas
Balfate
Olanchito
Sává
Olanchito
Catacamas
Mosquitia
Salamá
Sto.
Lempira
C. Gracias á Dios
Huehuetenango
GUATEMALA
San Pedro Sula
El Progreso
Santa Bárbara
Arenal
HONDURAS
San Marcos
Totonicapán
Zacapa
Chiquimula
Santa Rosa de Copán
L. de Yojoa
Comayagua
Juticalpa
Coco (Segovia)
Puerto Cabo Gracias á Dios
Kisalaya
Sololá
Quezaltenango
Jalapa
El Jaral
Esperanza
La Paz
TEGUCIGALPA
Dani
Patuca
Retalhuleu
Antigua
GUATEMALA
Chimaltenango
Copán
Santa Ana
Suchitoto
Comayagua
Choluteca
Danlí
Segovia
C. Gracias á Dios
Puerto Gracias á Dios
Coatepeque
Amatitlán
Escuintla
Zacatecoluca
Cojutepeque
Yuscarán
Totogalpa
Cayos Miskitos (Nicaragua)
Pta. Gorda
Mazatenango
San José
SAN SALVADOR
Usulután
Nacaome
Choluteca
Somoto
Cord. Isabella
Tuma
Bonanza
Ahuachapán
Sonsonate
Nueva San Salvador (Santa Tecla)
Acajutla
Unión
Coco
Estelí
Siuna
Puerto Cabezas
San Miguel
Puerto Morazán
El Sauce
Jinotega
San Pedro del Norte
Prinzapolca
EL SALVADOR
Golfo de Fonseca
La Unión
Chinandega
Matagalpa
Río Grande
Corinto
León
Boaco
Siquia
Rama
Pta. de Perlas
La Paz Centro
Managua
Santo Domingo
Bluefields
El Bluff
Masaya
Granada
Juigalpa
Pta. Mico
MANAGUA
Diriamba
Jinotepe
Lago de Nicaragua
Cord. de Yolaina
Bahía de San Juan del Norte
San Juan del Sur
B. de Salinas
Isla de Ometepe
San Carlos
San Juan
San Juan del Norte
Golfo de Papagayo
C. Velas
Sta. Elena
Liberia
Cord. de Guanacaste
NICARAGUA
I. de Providencia (Colombia)
Cayos Roncador (U.S.A. & Colombia)
San Juan
Santa Cruz
Cañas
Cord. Central
Guápiles
Siquirres
Puntarenas
Pen. de Nicoya
C. Blanco
Alajuela
San José
Cartago
Limón
Pta. Mona
COSTA RICA
3837
Cord. de Talamanca
Chirripó Grande
I. de San Andrés (Colombia)
Cayos de Albuquerque (Colombia)
Islas del Maíz (Nicaragua, U.S.A.)
CARTAGE
Quepos
Puerto Quepos
Buenos Aires
Volcán Barú
3337
Boquete
David
Puerto Armuelles
Golfo Dulce
Golfito
Pen. de Osa
Bahía de Coronado
Cortés
Pta. Burica
Golfo de Chiriquí
I. de Coiba
I. de Cebaco
I. Jicarón
Santiago
Chitré
Pocrí
Aguadulce
Río Hato
Pen. de Azuero
Pta. Mala
Las Tablas
Tonosí
Pta. Mariato
Laguna de Chiriquí
Bocas del Toro
Almirante
Pandora
Sierranía de Tabasará
Golfo de los Mosquitos
Nombre de Dios
Portobelo
Colón
Gatún
La Chorrera
Penonomé
Arch. de las Perlas
San Miguel
I. del Rey
PANAMÁ
Balboa
Chepo
Chimán
Serranía del Darién
Pta. Manzanillo
Is. de San Bernardo
Archipiélago de San Blas
Golfo del Darién
G. de Morrosquillo
Lorica
Cereté
Montería
COR
Turbo
Monte
El Real
La Palma
G. de Urabá
Sinú
Garachiné
Jaque

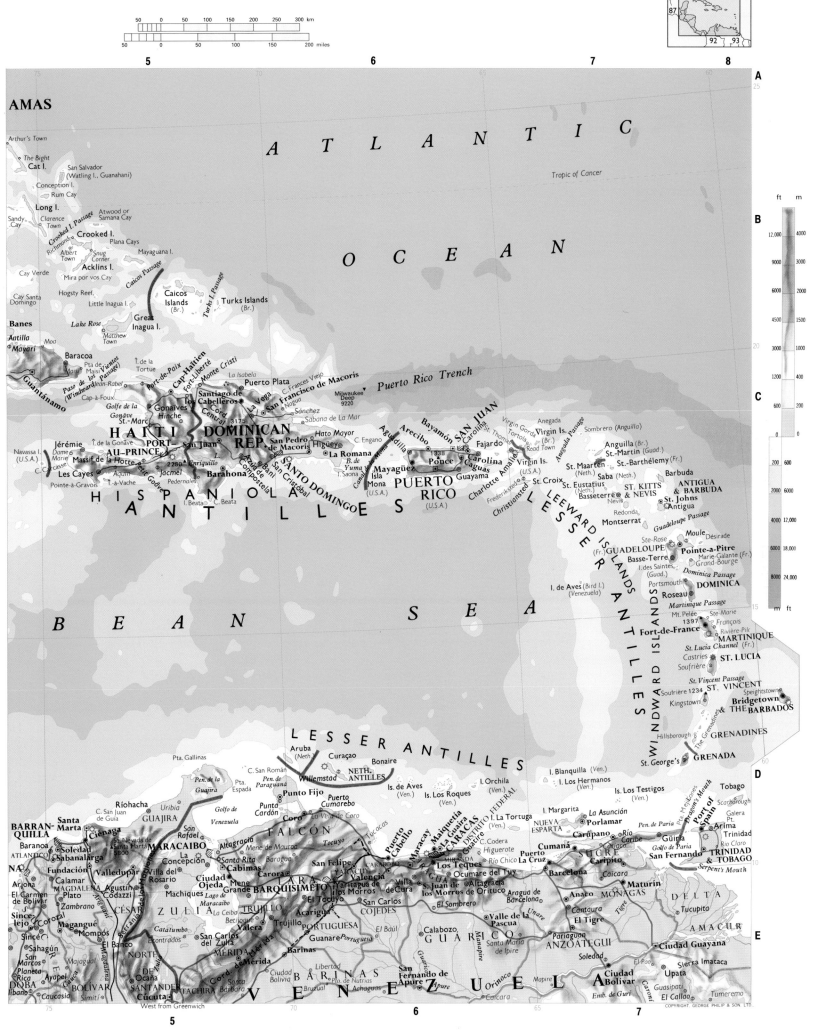

ATLANTIC

OCEAN

Tropic of Cancer

AMAS

Arthur's Town
The Bight
Cat I.
San Salvador
(Watling I., Guanahani)
Conception I.
Rum Cay
Long I.
Clarence Town
Sandy Cay
Crooked I. Passage
Crooked I.
Richmond
Albert Town
Snug Corner
Acklins I.
Cay Verde
Mira por vos Cay
Plana Cays
Mayaguana I.
Hogsty Reef
Little Inagua I.
Caicos Passage
Turks I. Passage
Caicos Islands (Br.)
Turks Islands (Br.)
Cay Santa Domingo
Banes
Lake Rose
Great Inagua I.
Matthew Town
Antilla
Mayarí
Moa
Baracoa
Pta. de los Maisí
Pta. de Maisí
Vientos
Port-de-Paix
Î. de la Tortue
Monte Cristi
La Isabela
Puerto Plata
C. Francés Viejo
Guantánamo
Cap-Haïtien
Fort-Liberté
Jean-Rabel
Santiago de los Caballeros
La Vega
San Francisco de Macoris
Milwaukee Deep 9220
Puerto Rico Trench
Paso de los Vientos (Windward Passage)
Cap-à-Foux
Gonaïves
Hinche
Cord. Central
Nagua
Sánchez
Sabana de la Mar
Golfe de la Gonâve
St.-Marc
3175
HAITI
DOMINICAN REP.
Hato Mayor
C. Engano
Virgin Gorda
Anegada
SAN JUAN
Sombrero (Anguilla)
Jérémie
Î. de la Gonâve
PORT-AU-PRINCE
San Juan
Azua de Compostela
B. de Yuma
Higüey
Aguadilla
Arecibo
Bayamón
Carolina
St. Thomas
Virgin Is.
Tortola (Br.)
Road Town
Anegada Passage
Anguilla (Br.)
St.-Martin (Guad.)
Navassa I. (U.S.A.)
Les Cayes
Dame Marie
Massif de la Hotte
Aquin
2280
Jácmel
Enriquillo
Bani
San Cristóbal
San Pedro de Macoris
La Romana
I. Saona
Mayagüez
Isla Mona (U.S.A.)
Ponce
1338
Caguas
Carolina
Guayama
PUERTO RICO (U.S.A.)
Virgin Is. (U.S.A.)
Charlotte Amalie
St. Croix
Frederiksted
Christiansted
St. Maarten (Neth.)
St.-Barthélemy (Fr.)
Saba (Neth.)
St. Eustatius (Neth.)
Basseterre
Nevis
ST. KITTS & NEVIS
Redonda
Montserrat
Barbuda
ANTIGUA & BARBUDA
St. Johns
Antigua
Pointe-à-Gravois
Î.-à-Vache
C. Carcasse
C. Beata
I. Beata
C. Beata
HISPANIOLA
SANTO DOMINGO
Pedernales
Barahona
ANTILLES
LESSER
Ste-Rose
Moule
Désirade
GUADELOUPE (Fr.)
Basse-Terre
Pointe-à-Pitre
Marie-Galante (Fr.)
Grand-Bourg
I. des Saintes (Guad.)
I. de Aves (Bird I.) (Venezuela)
Dominica Passage
Portsmouth
Roseau
DOMINICA
LEEWARD ISLANDS
Martinique Passage
Ste-Marie
Mt. Pelée
1397
François
Rivière-Pilote
Fort-de-France
MARTINIQUE
St. Lucia Channel (Fr.)
Castries
Soufrière
ST. LUCIA
St. Vincent Passage
Soufrière 1234
ST. VINCENT
Speightstown
Kingstown
Bridgetown
THE BARBADOS
Hillsborough
The Grenadines
GRENADINES
St. George's
GRENADA
WINDWARD ISLANDS

BEAN SEA

LESSER ANTILLES
Aruba (Neth.)
Curaçao
Bonaire
Willemstad
NETH. ANTILLES
Is. de Aves (Ven.)
I. Blanquilla (Ven.)
I. Los Hermanos (Ven.)
Tobago
Scarborough
Galera Pt.
Pta. Gallinas
C. San Román
Pen. de Paraguaná
Pta. Espada
Pen. de la Guajira
C. San Juan de Guia
Ríohacha
Uribia
GUAJIRA
Punto Fijo
Punta Cardón
Golfo de Venezuela
Puerto Cumarebo
Coro
La Vela de Coro
Is. Los Roques (Ven.)
I. Orchila (Ven.)
La Asunción
Porlamar
I. Margarita
NUEVA ESPARTA
I. La Tortuga (Ven.)
Is. Los Testigos (Ven.)
Pen. de Paria
Pta. Mejillones
Dragon's Mouth
Port of Spain
Arima
Trinidad
BARRANQUILLA
Santa Marta
Cienaga
Baranoa
Soledad
Sabanalarga
ATLANTICO
MARACAIBO
La Concepción
San Rafael
Altagracia
Santa Rita
Mene de Mauroa
Baragua
Tocuyo
Tucacas
FALCON
Puerto Cabello
Maracay
Maiquetía
La Guaira
CARACAS
DISTRITO FEDERAL
Guatire
Guatire
Carúpano
Río Caribe
Güiria
TRINIDAD & TOBAGO
San Fernando
Serpent's Mouth
NAÇ
San Planeta Rica
Arjona
Calamar
DOBA
El Carmen de Bolívar
Fundación
Agustín Codazzi
MAGDALENA
Plato
Zambrano
Valledupar
Villa del Rosario
Ciudad Ojeda
Machiques
Lago de Maracaibo
San Felipe
Carora
YARACUY
Barquisimeto
San Carlos
BARQUISIMETO
San Juan de los Morros
Villa de Cura
GUARICO
Higuerote
Río Chico
Ocumare del Tuy
Los Teques
San Juan de los Morros de Orituco
Aragua de Barcelona
Cumaná
La Cruz
Puerto La Cruz
Barcelona
Caicara
SUCRE
Carúpano
Caripito
MONAGAS
Maturín
Caigua
Anaco
Cantaura
El Tigre
Tucupita
DELTA
AMACUR
Sincé
Coveñas
Corozal
Sincelejo
Magangué
Mompós
Sahagún
San Marcos
Planeta Rica
Ayapel
Ciudad Bolivia
CESAR
ZULIA
Betijoque
TRUJILLO
Valera
Trujillo
MÉRIDA
BARINAS
Pto. de Nutrias
Libertad
San Fernando de Apure
El Baúl
Calabozo
Santa María de Ipire
Pariaguan
Valle de la Pascua
ANZOATEGUI
Soledad
Ciudad Guayana
Sierra Imataca
Upata
BOLÍVAR
SANTANDER
NORTE
Ocaña
Cúcuta
Simití
El Banco
TACHIRA
Santa Bárbara
Cord. de Mérida
PORTUGUESA
Guanare
Guanare
Barinas
El Callao
Emb. de Guri
Ciudad Bolívar
Guasipati
Tumeremo
VENEZUELA
Bruzual
Achaguas
Apure
Arauca
Orinoco
Cabruta
Caicara
Mapire
Soledad
El Pao
Río Claro
Caroni

West from Greenwich

100 0 200 400 600 800 1000 1200 1400 km
100 0 200 400 600 800 1000 miles

1   2   3   4   5   6   7

NORTH

ATLANTIC

OCEAN

Tropic of Cancer

Yucatán Channel
Cuba
Greater Antilles
Turks & Caicos Is.
Hispaniola
9200
Puerto Rico

Gulf of Campeche
Yucatán Peninsula

Isthmus of Tehuantepec
G. de Honduras
Jamaica

Guadeloupe
Dominica
Martinique
St. Lucia
Barbados
St. Vincent
Grenada
Tobago

Caribbean Sea

Lesser Antilles

C. Gracias a Dios

Guatemala Trench
Coco
L. Nicaragua

I. Margarita
Trinidad

C. de la Aguja
Sierra Nevada de Santa Marta 5800
L. Maracaibo

Panama Canal
G. of Darién

Cordillera Occidental
Cordillera Central
Cordillera Oriental
Cord. de Mérida

Orinoco
Llanos
Meta

Guiana Highlands
Mt. Roraima 2810
Sierra Pacaraima
C. Orange
Courantyne
Serra
Tumucumaque

Panama Canal
Gulf of Panamá

Guaviare

C. de San Francisco

Cotopaxi 6897
Chimborazo 6267

Caquetá

Putumayo
Napo
Marañón
Japurá
Negro
Branco
Essequibo

Amazon
Marajó I.
Equator

G. of Guayaquil
Pta. Parinas
Pta. Negra

Purus
Juruá
Amazon
Tapajós
Xingu
Tocantins
C. de São Roque

PACIFIC

Huascarán 6768

Ucayali
Madeira
Roosevelt
Araguaia
Parnaíba

S e l v a s

Madre de Dios
Guaporé
Araguaia
São Francisco
Plat. of Borborema

Chincha Alta
Mamoré
Arinos
Das Mortes

Nevada Ancohuma 6580

Bolivian Plateau
L. Titicaca
L. de Poopó

Plateau of Mato Grosso

Brazilian Highlands

OCEAN

Tropic of Capricorn
San Félix
San Ambrosio

8050
Atacama Desert
Cerro Ojos del Salado 6863

Salinas Grandes

Gran Chaco
Paraguay
Pilcomayo
Paraná
Salado
Paraná
Entre Ríos

Serra da Mantiqueira
Pico da Bandeira 2890
Abrolhos Bank
Serra do Mar
C. Frio

Iguaçu Falls
Uruguay
Paraná

Arch. de Juan Fernández

A n d e s

Mt. Aconcagua 6960
Sierra de Córdoba
L. Mar Chiquita

Río de la Plata
L. dos Patos

SOUTH

ATLANTIC

OCEAN

P a m p a s

Colorado
Bahía Blanca
Negro
G. San Matías
Valdés Peninsula 40

Argentine Basin

Chile Rise
Chiloé I.

Chubut

P a t a g o n i a

Chonos Archipelago
Mte. San Valentín 4058
Taitao Peninsula
Gulf of Penas

Gulf of San Jorge

6212

Wellington I.
Madre de Dios I.

West Falkland

Falkland Is.

Santa Inés I.
Magellan's Str.
Canal Cockburn
Canal Beagle
C. Horn

Tierra del Fuego
Staten I.

East Falkland

South Georgia

ft   m
12000   4000
9000   3000
6000   2000
3000   1000
1500   500
600   200
0   0
200   600
1000   3000
2000   6000
4000   12000
6000   18000
8000   24000
m   ft

100 0   200   400   600   800   1000 1200 1400 km

100 0   200   400   600   800   1000 miles

Projection: Lambert's Azimuthal Equal Area

■ LIMA Capital Cities

CARTOGRAPHY BY PHILIP'S.
COPYRIGHT REED INTERNATIONAL BOOKS LTD

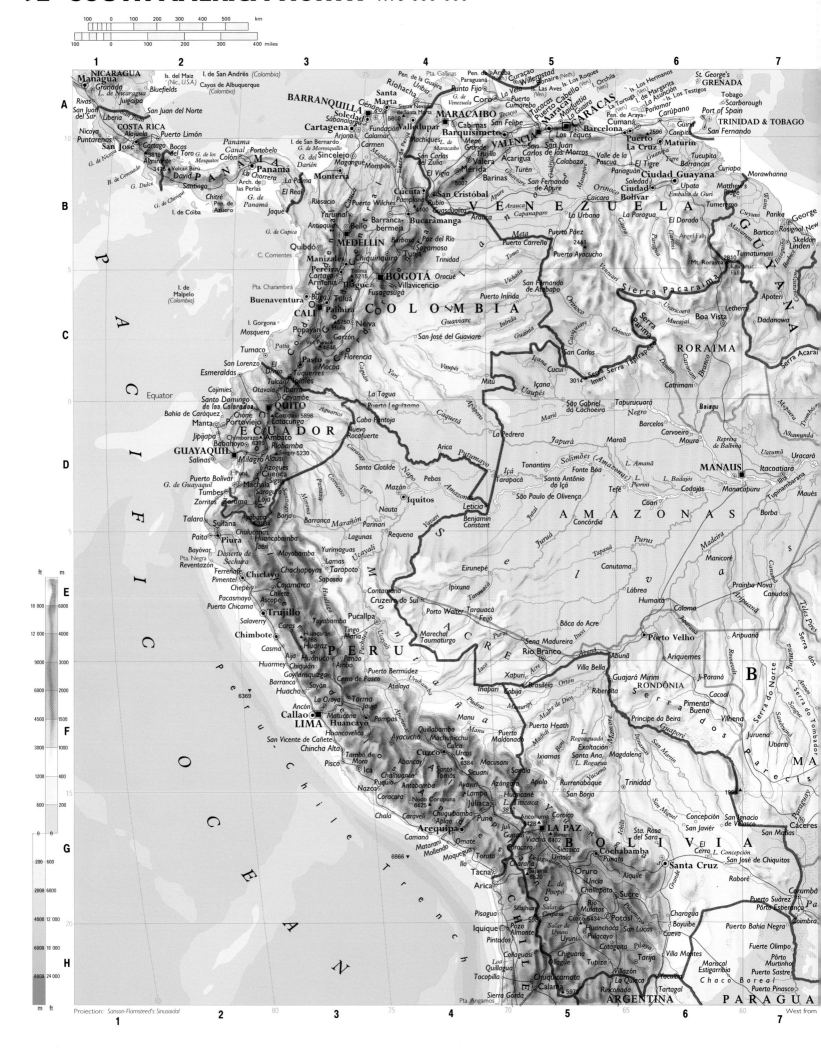

A

B

A T L A N T I C

O C E A N

C

São Paulo
(Braz.)

Equator

D

Rocas

Fernando de Noronha
(Braz.)

E

6059 ▾

F

G

Trindade
(Braz.)

H

COPYRIGHT GEORGE PHILIP LTD.

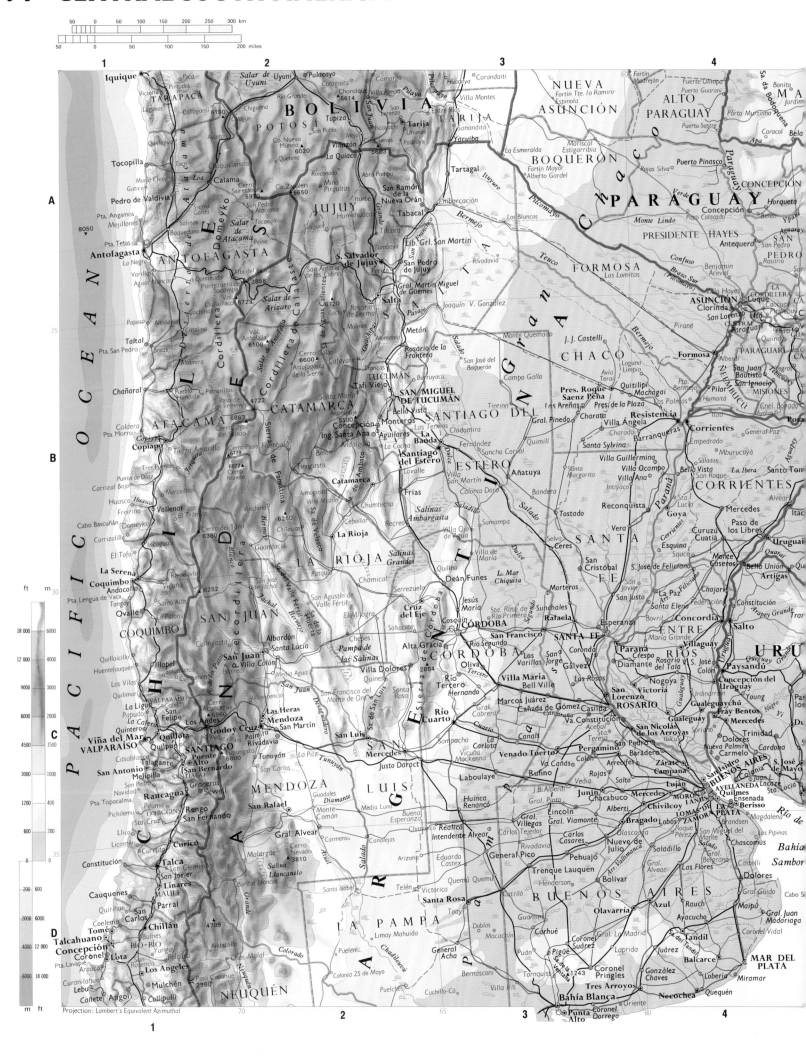

TO GROSSO
DO SUL
BRAZIL
PARANÁ
SÃO PAULO
RIO DE JANEIRO
BELO HORIZONTE
Vitória
Vila Velha
CAMPOS
NITERÓI
RIO DE JANEIRO
Tropic of Capricorn

SÃO PAULO
SANTO ANDRÉ
SANTOS
São Vicente
CURITIBA
Paranaguá
Joinville
São Francisco do Sul
BLUMENAU
Brusque
Itajaí
SANTA CATARINA
Florianópolis
Ilha de Santa Catarina

Lajes
Tubarão
Laguna
Criciúma
Araranguá
Caxias do Sul
Bento Gonçalves
RIO GRANDE
DO SUL
Santa Maria
Santa Cruz
do Sul
Novo Hamburgo
São Leopoldo
Canoas
Viamão
PORTO ALEGRE
Osório

São Gabriel
Bagé
Pelotas
Rio Grande
Lagoa dos Patos
Mostardas

GUAY
Melo
Jaguarão
Mirim
Lagoa Mangueira
Santa Vitória do Palmar

MONTEVIDEO
la Plata
ombón

Antonio

ATLANTIC

OCEAN

5304

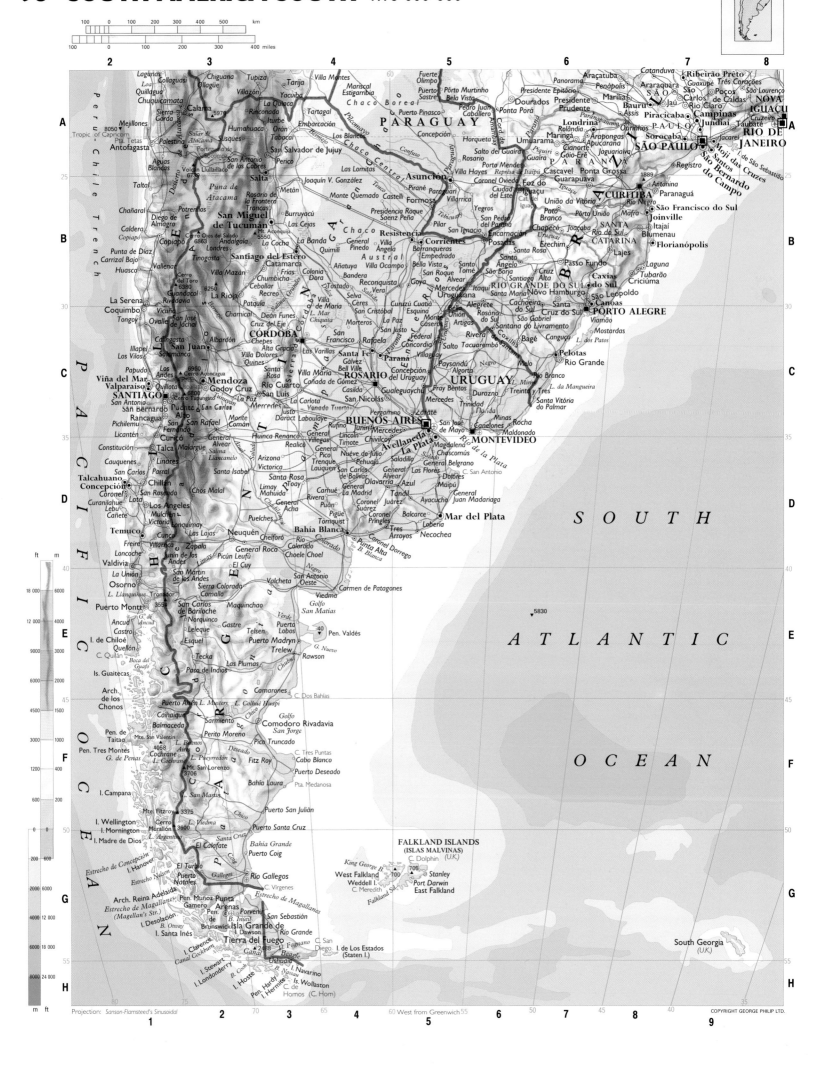

Projection: Sanson-Flamsteed's Sinusoidal

West from Greenwich

INDEX

The index contains the names of all the principal places and features shown on the World Maps. Each name is followed by an additional entry in italics giving the country or region within which it is located. The alphabetical order of names composed of two or more words is governed primarily by the first word and then by the second. This is an example of the rule:

Mīr Kūh, *Iran*	**45 E8**	26 22N	58 55 E
Mīr Shahdād, *Iran*	**45 E8**	26 15N	58 29 E
Mira, *Italy*	**20 B5**	45 26N	12 8 E
Mira por vos Cay, *Bahamas* .	**89 B5**	22 9N	74 30 W
Miraj, *India*	**40 L9**	16 50N	74 45 E

Physical features composed of a proper name (Erie) and a description (Lake) are positioned alphabetically by the proper name. The description is positioned after the proper name and is usually abbreviated:

Erie, L., *N. Amer.*	**78 D4**	42 15N	81 0 W

Where a description forms part of a settlement or administrative name however, it is always written in full and put in its true alphabetic position:

Mount Morris, *U.S.A.*	**78 D7**	42 44N	77 52 W

Names beginning with M' and Mc are indexed as if they were spelled Mac. Names beginning St. are alphabetised under Saint, but Sankt, Sint, Sant', Santa and San are all spelt in full and are alphabetised accordingly. If the same place name occurs two or more times in the index and all are in the same country, each is followed by the name of the administrative subdivision in which it is located. The names are placed in the alphabetical order of the subdivisions. For example:

Jackson, *Ky., U.S.A.*	**76 G4**	37 33N	83 23 W
Jackson, *Mich., U.S.A.*	**76 D3**	42 15N	84 24 W
Jackson, *Minn., U.S.A.*	**80 D7**	43 37N	95 1 W

The number in bold type which follows each name in the index refers to the number of the map page where that feature or place will be found. This is usually the largest scale at which the place or feature appears.

The letter and figure which are in bold type immediately after the page number give the grid square on the map page, within which the feature is situated. The letter represents the latitude and the figure the longitude.

In some cases the feature itself may fall within the specified square, while the name is outside. This is usually the case only with features which are larger than a grid square.

For a more precise location the geographical coordinates which follow the letter/figure references give the latitude and the longitude of each place. The first set of figures represent the latitude which is the distance north or south of the Equator measured as an angle at the centre of the earth. The Equator is latitude 0°, the North Pole is 90°N, and the South Pole 90°S.

The second set of figures represent the longitude, which is the distance East or West of the prime meridian, which runs through Greenwich, England. Longitude is also measured as an angle at the centre of the earth and is given East or West of the prime meridian, from 0° to 180° in either direction.

The unit of measurement for latitude and longitude is the degree, which is subdivided into 60 minutes. Each index entry states the position of a place in degrees and minutes, a space being left between the degrees and the minutes.

The latitude is followed by N(orth) or S(outh) and the longitude by E(ast) or W(est).

Rivers are indexed to their mouths or confluences, and carry the symbol → after their names. A solid square ■ follows the name of a country, while an open square □ refers to a first order administrative area.

Abbreviations used in the index

A.C.T. – Australian Capital Territory
Afghan. – Afghanistan
Ala. – Alabama
Alta. – Alberta
Amer. – America(n)
Arch. – Archipelago
Ariz. – Arizona
Ark. – Arkansas
Atl. Oc. – Atlantic Ocean
B. – Baie, Bahía, Bay, Bucht, Bugt
B.C. – British Columbia
Bangla. – Bangladesh
Barr. – Barrage
Bos.-H. – Bosnia-Herzegovina
C. – Cabo, Cap, Cape, Coast
C.A.R. – Central African Republic
C. Prov. – Cape Province
Calif. – California
Cent. – Central
Chan. – Channel
Colo. – Colorado
Conn. – Connecticut
Cord. – Cordillera
Cr. – Creek
Czech. – Czech Republic
D.C. – District of Columbia
Del. – Delaware
Dep. – Dependency
Des. – Desert
Dist. – District
Dj. – Djebel
Domin. – Dominica
Dom. Rep. – Dominican Republic
E. – East

E. Salv. – El Salvador
Eq. Guin. – Equatorial Guinea
Fla. – Florida
Falk. Is. – Falkland Is.
G. – Golfe, Golfo, Gulf, Guba, Gebel
Ga. – Georgia
Gt. – Great, Greater
Guinea-Biss. – Guinea-Bissau
H.K. – Hong Kong
H.P. – Himachal Pradesh
Hants. – Hampshire
Harb. – Harbor, Harbour
Hd. – Head
Hts. – Heights
I.(s). – Île, Ilha, Insel, Isla, Island, Isle
Ill. – Illinois
Ind. – Indiana
Ind. Oc. – Indian Ocean
Ivory C. – Ivory Coast
J. – Jabal, Jebel, Jazira
Junc. – Junction
K. – Kap, Kapp
Kans. – Kansas
Kep. – Kepulauan
Ky. – Kentucky
L. – Lac, Lacul, Lago, Lagoa, Lake, Limni, Loch, Lough
La. – Louisiana
Liech. – Liechtenstein
Lux. – Luxembourg
Mad. P. – Madhya Pradesh
Madag. – Madagascar
Man. – Manitoba
Mass. – Massachusetts

Md. – Maryland
Me. – Maine
Medit. S. – Mediterranean Sea
Mich. – Michigan
Minn. – Minnesota
Miss. – Mississippi
Mo. – Missouri
Mont. – Montana
Mozam. – Mozambique
Mt.(e) – Mont, Monte, Monti, Montaña, Mountain
N. – Nord, Norte, North, Northern, Nouveau
N.B. – New Brunswick
N.C. – North Carolina
N. Cal. – New Caledonia
N. Dak. – North Dakota
N.H. – New Hampshire
N.I. – North Island
N.J. – New Jersey
N. Mex. – New Mexico
N.S. – Nova Scotia
N.S.W. – New South Wales
N.W.T. – North West Territory
N.Y. – New York
N.Z. – New Zealand
Nebr. – Nebraska
Neths. – Netherlands
Nev. – Nevada
Nfld. – Newfoundland
Nic. – Nicaragua
O. – Oued, Ouadi
Occ. – Occidentale
Okla. – Oklahoma
Ont. – Ontario
Or. – Orientale

Oreg. – Oregon
Os. – Ostrov
Oz. – Ozero
P. – Pass, Passo, Pasul, Pulau
P.E.I. – Prince Edward Island
Pa. – Pennsylvania
Pac. Oc. – Pacific Ocean
Papua N.G. – Papua New Guinea
Pass. – Passage
Pen. – Peninsula, Péninsule
Phil. – Philippines
Pk. – Park, Peak
Plat. – Plateau
Prov. – Province, Provincial
Pt. – Point
Pta. – Ponta, Punta
Pte. – Pointe
Qué. – Québec
Queens. – Queensland
R. – Rio, River
R.I. – Rhode Island
Ra.(s). – Range(s)
Raj. – Rajasthan
Reg. – Region
Rep. – Republic
Res. – Reserve, Reservoir
S. – San, South, Sea
Si. Arabia – Saudi Arabia
S.C. – South Carolina
S. Dak. – South Dakota
S.I. – South Island
S. Leone – Sierra Leone
Sa. – Serra, Sierra
Sask. – Saskatchewan
Scot. – Scotland
Sd. – Sound

Sev. – Severnaya
Sib. – Siberia
Sprs. – Springs
St. – Saint
Sta. – Santa, Station
Ste. – Sainte
Sto. – Santo
Str. – Strait, Stretto
Switz. – Switzerland
Tas. – Tasmania
Tenn. – Tennessee
Tex. – Texas
Tg. – Tanjung
Trin. & Tob. – Trinidad & Tobago
U.A.E. – United Arab Emirates
U.K. – United Kingdom
U.S.A. – United States of America
Ut. P. – Uttar Pradesh
Va. – Virginia
Vdkhr. – Vodokhranilishche
Vf. – Vîrful
Vic. – Victoria
Vol. – Volcano
Vt. – Vermont
W. – Wadi, West
W. Va. – West Virginia
Wash. – Washington
Wis. – Wisconsin
Wlkp. – Wielkopolski
Wyo. – Wyoming
Yorks. – Yorkshire
Yug. – Yugoslavia

A Coruña

A

A Coruña, *Spain* **19 A1** 43 20N 8 25W
A Estrada, *Spain* **19 A1** 42 43N 8 27W
A Fonsagrada, *Spain* **19 A2** 43 8N 7 4W
Aachen, *Germany* **16 C4** 50 45N 6 6 E
Aalborg = Ålborg, *Denmark* **9 H13** 57 2N 9 54 E
Aalen, *Germany* **16 D6** 48 51N 10 6 E
Aalst, *Belgium* **15 D4** 50 56N 4 2 E
Aalten, *Neths.* **15 C6** 51 56N 6 35 E
Aalter, *Belgium* **15 C3** 51 5N 3 28 E
Äänekoski, *Finland* **9 E21** 62 36N 25 44 E
Aarau, *Switz.* **18 C8** 47 23N 8 4 E
Aare →, *Switz.* **18 C8** 47 33N 8 14 E
Aarhus = Århus, *Denmark* **9 H14** 56 8N 10 11 E
Aarschot, *Belgium* **15 D4** 50 59N 4 49 E
Aba, *Dem. Rep. of the Congo* **54 B3** 3 58N 30 17 E
Aba, *Nigeria* **50 G7** 5 10N 7 19 E
Ābādān, *Iran* **45 D6** 30 22N 48 20 E
Ābādeh, *Iran* **45 D7** 31 8N 52 40 E
Abadla, *Algeria* **50 B5** 31 2N 2 45W
Abaetetuba, *Brazil* **93 D9** 1 40S 48 50W
Abagnar Qi, *China* **34 C9** 43 52N 116 2 E
Abai, *Paraguay* **95 B4** 25 58S 55 54W
Abakan, *Russia* **27 D10** 53 40N 91 10 E
Abancay, *Peru* **92 F4** 13 35S 72 55W
Abariringa, *Kiribati* **64 H10** 2 50S 171 40W
Abarqū, *Iran* **45 D7** 31 10N 53 20 E
Abashiri, *Japan* **30 C12** 44 0N 144 15 E
Abashiri-Wan, *Japan* **30 C12** 44 0N 144 30 E
Abay, *Kazakstan* **26 E8** 49 38N 72 53 E
Abaya, L., *Ethiopia* **46 F2** 6 30N 37 50 E
Abaza, *Russia* **26 D10** 52 39N 90 6 E
'Abbāsābād, *Iran* **45 C8** 33 34N 58 23 E
Abbay = Nîl el Azraq →, *Sudan* **51 E12** 15 38N 32 31 E
Abbaye, Pt., *U.S.A.* **76 B1** 46 58N 88 8W
Abbeville, *France* **18 A4** 50 6N 1 49 E
Abbeville, *La., U.S.A.* **81 L8** 29 58N 92 8W
Abbeville, *S.C., U.S.A.* **77 H4** 34 11N 82 23W
Abbieglassie, *Australia* **63 D4** 27 15S 147 28 E
Abbot Ice Shelf, *Antarctica* **5 D16** 73 0S 92 0W
Abbotsford, *Canada* **72 D4** 49 5N 122 20W
Abbotsford, *U.S.A.* **80 C9** 44 57N 90 19W
Abbottabad, *Pakistan* **42 B5** 34 10N 73 15 E
Abd al Kūrī, *Ind. Oc.* **46 E5** 12 5N 52 20 E
Ābdar, *Iran* **45 D7** 30 16N 55 19 E
'Abdolābād, *Iran* **45 C8** 34 12N 56 30 E
Abéché, *Chad* **51 F10** 13 50N 20 35 E
Åbenrå, *Denmark* **9 J13** 55 3N 9 25 E
Abeokuta, *Nigeria* **50 G6** 7 3N 3 19 E
Aber, *Uganda* **54 B3** 2 12N 32 25 E
Aberaeron, *U.K.* **11 E3** 52 15N 4 15W
Aberayron = Aberaeron, *U.K.* **11 E3** 52 15N 4 15W
Aberchirder, *U.K.* **12 D6** 57 34N 2 37W
Abercorn = Mbala, *Zambia* **55 D3** 8 46S 31 24 E
Abercorn, *Australia* **63 D5** 25 12S 151 5 E
Aberdare, *U.K.* **11 F4** 51 43N 3 27W
Aberdare Ra., *Kenya* **54 C4** 0 15S 36 50 E
Aberdeen, *Australia* **63 E5** 32 9S 150 56 E
Aberdeen, *Canada* **73 C7** 52 20N 106 8W
Aberdeen, *S. Africa* **56 E3** 32 28S 24 2 E
Aberdeen, *U.K.* **12 D6** 57 9N 2 5W
Aberdeen, *Ala., U.S.A.* **77 J1** 33 49N 88 33W
Aberdeen, *Idaho, U.S.A.* **82 E7** 42 57N 112 50W
Aberdeen, *S. Dak., U.S.A.* **80 C5** 45 28N 98 29W
Aberdeen, *Wash., U.S.A.* **84 D3** 46 59N 123 50W
Aberdeen, City of □, *U.K.* **12 D6** 57 10N 2 10W
Aberdeenshire □, *U.K.* **12 D6** 57 17N 2 36W
Aberdovey = Aberdyfi, *U.K.* **11 E3** 52 33N 4 3W
Aberdyfi, *U.K.* **11 E3** 52 33N 4 3W
Aberfeldy, *U.K.* **12 E5** 56 37N 3 51W
Abergavenny, *U.K.* **11 F4** 51 49N 3 1W
Abergele, *U.K.* **10 D4** 53 17N 3 35W
Abernathy, *U.S.A.* **81 J4** 33 50N 101 51W
Abert, L., *U.S.A.* **82 E3** 42 38N 120 14W
Aberystwyth, *U.K.* **11 E3** 52 25N 4 5W
Abhar, *Iran* **45 B6** 36 9N 49 13 E
Abhayapuri, *India* **43 F14** 26 24N 90 38 E
Abidjan, *Ivory C.* **50 G5** 5 26N 3 58W
Abilene, *Kans., U.S.A.* **80 F6** 38 55N 97 13W
Abilene, *Tex., U.S.A.* **81 J5** 32 28N 99 43W
Abingdon, *U.K.* **11 F6** 51 40N 1 17W
Abingdon, *Ill., U.S.A.* **80 E9** 40 48N 90 24W
Abingdon, *Va., U.S.A.* **77 G5** 36 43N 81 59W
Abington Reef, *Australia* **62 B4** 18 0S 149 35 E
Abitau →, *Canada* **73 B7** 59 53N 109 3W
Abitau L., *Canada* **73 A7** 60 27N 107 15W
Abitibi L., *Canada* **70 C4** 48 40N 79 40W
Abkhaz Republic □ = Abkhazia □, *Georgia* **25 F7** 43 12N 41 5 E
Abkhazia □, *Georgia* **25 F7** 43 12N 41 5 E
Abminga, *Australia* **63 D1** 26 8S 134 51 E
Åbo = Turku, *Finland* **9 F20** 60 30N 22 19 E
Abohar, *India* **42 D6** 30 10N 74 10 E
Abomey, *Benin* **50 G6** 7 10N 2 5 E
Abong-Mbang, *Cameroon* **52 D2** 4 0N 13 8 E
Abou-Deïa, *Chad* **51 F9** 11 20N 19 20 E
Aboyne, *U.K.* **12 D6** 57 4N 2 47W
Abra Pampa, *Argentina* **94 A2** 22 43S 65 42W
Abreojos, Pta., *Mexico* **86 B2** 26 50N 113 40W
Abrud, *Romania* **17 E12** 46 19N 23 5 E
Absaroka Range, *U.S.A.* **82 D9** 44 45N 109 50W
Abū al Khaṣīb, *Iraq* **45 D6** 30 25N 48 0 E
Abū 'Alī, *Si. Arabia* **45 E6** 27 20N 49 27 E
Abū 'Alī →, *Lebanon* **47 A4** 34 25N 35 50 E
Abu Dhabi = Abū Ẓāby, *U.A.E.* **45 E7** 24 28N 54 22 E
Abū Du'ān, *Syria* **44 B3** 36 25N 38 15 E
Abu el Gairi, W. →, *Egypt* **47 F2** 29 35N 33 30 E
Abu Ga'da, W. →, *Egypt* **47 F1** 29 15N 32 53 E
Abū Ḥadrīyah, *Si. Arabia* **45 E6** 27 20N 48 58 E
Abu Hamed, *Sudan* **51 E12** 19 32N 33 13 E
Abū Kamāl, *Syria* **44 C4** 34 30N 41 0 E
Abū Madd, Ra's, *Si. Arabia* **44 E3** 24 50N 37 7 E
Abu Şafāt, W. →, *Jordan* **47 E5** 30 24N 36 7 E
Abū Şukhayr, *Iraq* **44 D5** 31 54N 44 30 E
Abû Zabad, *Sudan* **51 F11** 12 25N 29 10 E
Abū Ẓāby, *U.A.E.* **45 E7** 24 28N 54 22 E
Abū Zeydābād, *Iran* **45 C6** 33 54N 51 45 E
Abuja, *Nigeria* **50 G7** 9 16N 7 2 E
Abukuma-Gawa →, *Japan* **30 E10** 38 6N 140 52 E
Abukuma-Sammyaku, *Japan* **30 F10** 37 30N 140 45 E
Abunã, *Brazil* **92 E5** 9 40S 65 20W
Abunã →, *Brazil* **92 E5** 9 41S 65 20W
Aburo, *Dem. Rep. of the Congo* **54 B3** 2 4N 30 53 E
Abut Hd., *N.Z.* **59 K3** 43 7S 170 15 E
Açailândia, *Brazil* **93 D9** 4 57S 47 0W
Acajutla, *El Salv.* **88 D2** 13 36N 89 50W
Acámbaro, *Mexico* **86 D4** 20 0N 100 40W
Acaponeta, *Mexico* **86 C3** 22 30N 105 20W
Acapulco, *Mexico* **87 D5** 16 51N 99 56W
Acarai, Serra, *Brazil* **92 C7** 1 50N 57 50W
Acarigua, *Venezuela* **92 B5** 9 33N 69 12W
Acatlán, *Mexico* **87 D5** 18 10N 98 3W
Acayucan, *Mexico* **87 D6** 17 59N 94 58W
Accomac, *U.S.A.* **76 G8** 37 43N 75 40W
Accra, *Ghana* **50 G5** 5 35N 0 6W
Accrington, *U.K.* **10 D5** 53 45N 2 22W
Acebal, *Argentina* **94 C3** 33 20S 60 50W
Aceh □, *Indonesia* **36 D1** 4 15N 97 30 E
Achalpur, *India* **40 J10** 21 22N 77 32 E
Acheng, *China* **35 B14** 45 30N 126 58 E
Acher, *India* **42 H5** 23 10N 72 32 E
Achill Hd., *Ireland* **13 C1** 53 58N 10 15W
Achill I., *Ireland* **13 C1** 53 58N 10 1W
Achinsk, *Russia* **27 D10** 56 20N 90 20 E
Acireale, *Italy* **20 F6** 37 37N 15 10 E
Ackerman, *U.S.A.* **81 J10** 33 19N 89 11W
Acklins I., *Bahamas* **89 B5** 22 30N 74 0W
Acme, *Canada* **72 C6** 51 33N 113 30W
Aconcagua, Cerro, *Argentina* **94 C2** 32 39S 70 0W
Aconquija, Mt., *Argentina* **94 B2** 27 0S 66 0W
Açores, Is. dos = Azores, *Atl. Oc.* **48 C1** 38 44N 29 0W
Acraman, L., *Australia* **63 E2** 32 2S 135 23 E
Acre = 'Akko, *Israel* **47 C4** 32 55N 35 4 E
Acre □, *Brazil* **92 E4** 9 1S 71 0W
Acre →, *Brazil* **92 E5** 8 45S 67 22W
Acton, *Canada* **78 C4** 43 38N 80 3W
Ad Dammām, *Si. Arabia* **45 E6** 26 20N 50 5 E
Ad Dawḥah, *Qatar* **45 E6** 25 15N 51 35 E
Ad Dawr, *Iraq* **44 C4** 34 27N 43 47 E
Ad Dir'īyah, *Si. Arabia* **44 E5** 24 44N 46 35 E
Ad Dīwānīyah, *Iraq* **44 D5** 32 0N 45 0 E
Ad Dujayl, *Iraq* **44 C5** 33 51N 44 14 E
Ada, *Minn., U.S.A.* **80 B6** 47 18N 96 31W
Ada, *Okla., U.S.A.* **81 H6** 34 46N 96 41W
Adaja →, *Spain* **19 B3** 41 32N 4 52W
Adamaoua, Massif de l', *Cameroon* **52 C2** 7 20N 12 20 E
Adamawa Highlands = Adamaoua, Massif de l', *Cameroon* **52 C2** 7 20N 12 20 E
Adamello, Mte., *Italy* **18 C9** 46 9N 10 30 E
Adaminaby, *Australia* **63 F4** 36 0S 148 45 E
Adams, *Mass., U.S.A.* **79 D11** 42 38N 73 7W
Adams, *N.Y., U.S.A.* **79 C8** 43 49N 76 1W
Adams, *Wis., U.S.A.* **80 D10** 43 57N 89 49W
Adam's Bridge, *Sri Lanka* **40 Q11** 9 15N 79 40 E
Adams L., *Canada* **72 C5** 51 10N 119 40W
Adams Mt., *U.S.A.* **84 D5** 46 12N 121 30W
Adam's Peak, *Sri Lanka* **40 R12** 6 48N 80 30 E
Adana, *Turkey* **25 G6** 37 0N 35 16 E
Adapazarı, *Turkey* **25 F5** 40 48N 30 25 E
Adarama, *Sudan* **51 E12** 17 10N 34 52 E
Adare, C., *Antarctica* **5 D11** 71 0S 171 0 E
Adaut, *Indonesia* **37 F8** 8 8S 131 7 E
Adavale, *Australia* **63 D3** 25 52S 144 32 E
Adda →, *Italy* **18 D8** 45 8N 9 53 E
Addis Ababa = Addis Abeba, *Ethiopia* **46 F2** 9 2N 38 42 E
Addis Abeba, *Ethiopia* **46 F2** 9 2N 38 42 E
Addison, *U.S.A.* **78 D7** 42 1N 77 14W
Addo, *S. Africa* **56 E4** 33 32S 25 45 E
Ādeh, *Iran* **44 B5** 37 42N 45 11 E
Adel, *U.S.A.* **77 K4** 31 8N 83 25W
Adelaide, *Australia* **63 E2** 34 52S 138 30 E
Adelaide, *Bahamas* **88 A4** 25 4N 77 31W
Adelaide, *S. Africa* **56 E4** 32 42S 26 20 E
Adelaide I., *Antarctica* **5 C17** 67 15S 68 30W
Adelaide Pen., *Canada* **68 B10** 68 15N 97 30W
Adelaide River, *Australia* **60 B5** 13 15S 131 7 E
Adelanto, *U.S.A.* **85 L9** 34 35N 117 22W
Adele I., *Australia* **60 C3** 15 32S 123 9 E
Adélie, Terre, *Antarctica* **5 C10** 68 0S 140 0 E
Adélie Land = Adélie, Terre, *Antarctica* **5 C10** 68 0S 140 0 E
Aden = Al 'Adan, *Yemen* **46 E4** 12 45N 45 0 E
Aden, G. of, *Asia* **46 E4** 12 30N 47 30 E
Adendorp, *S. Africa* **56 E3** 32 15S 24 30 E
Adh Dhayd, *U.A.E.* **45 E7** 25 17N 55 53 E
Adhoi, *India* **42 H4** 23 26N 70 32 E
Adi, *Indonesia* **37 E8** 4 15S 133 30 E
Adieu, C., *Australia* **61 F5** 32 0S 132 10 E
Adieu Pt., *Australia* **60 C3** 15 14S 124 35 E
Adige →, *Italy* **20 B5** 45 9N 12 20 E
Adilabad, *India* **40 K11** 19 33N 78 20 E
Adin, *U.S.A.* **82 F3** 41 12N 120 57W
Adin Khel, *Afghan.* **40 C6** 32 45N 68 5 E
Adirondack Mts., *U.S.A.* **79 C10** 44 0N 74 0W
Adjumani, *Uganda* **54 B3** 3 20N 31 50 E
Adlavik Is., *Canada* **71 A8** 55 2N 57 45W
Admiralty G., *Australia* **60 B4** 14 20S 125 55 E
Admiralty I., *U.S.A.* **68 C6** 57 30N 134 30W
Admiralty Inlet, *U.S.A.* **82 C2** 48 8N 122 58W
Admiralty Is., *Papua N. G.* **64 H6** 2 0S 147 0 E
Adonara, *Indonesia* **37 F6** 8 15S 123 5 E
Adoni, *India* **40 M10** 15 33N 77 18 E
Adour →, *France* **18 E3** 43 32N 1 32W
Adra, *India* **43 H12** 23 30N 86 42 E
Adra, *Spain* **19 D4** 36 43N 3 3W
Adrano, *Italy* **20 F6** 37 40N 14 50 E
Adrar, *Algeria* **48 D4** 27 51N 0 11 E
Adrian, *Mich., U.S.A.* **76 E3** 41 54N 84 2W
Adrian, *Tex., U.S.A.* **81 H3** 35 16N 102 40W
Adriatic Sea, *Medit. S.* **20 C6** 43 0N 16 0 E
Adua, *Indonesia* **37 E7** 1 45S 129 50 E
Adwa, *Ethiopia* **46 E2** 14 15N 38 52 E
Adzhar Republic □ = Ajaria □, *Georgia* **25 F7** 41 30N 42 0 E
Ægean Sea, *Medit. S.* **21 E11** 38 30N 25 0 E
Aerhtai Shan, *Mongolia* **32 B4** 46 40N 92 45 E
'Afak, *Iraq* **44 C5** 32 4N 45 15 E
Afándou, *Greece* **23 C10** 36 18N 28 12 E
Afghanistan ■, *Asia* **40 C4** 33 0N 65 0 E
'Afrīn, *Syria* **44 B3** 36 32N 36 50 E
Afton, *U.S.A.* **79 D9** 42 14N 75 32W
Afuá, *Brazil* **93 D8** 0 15S 50 20W
'Afula, *Israel* **47 C4** 32 37N 35 17 E
Afyon, *Turkey* **25 G5** 38 45N 30 33 E
Afyonkarahisar = Afyon, *Turkey* **25 G5** 38 45N 30 33 E
Agadès = Agadez, *Niger* **50 E7** 16 58N 7 59 E
Agadez, *Niger* **50 E7** 16 58N 7 59 E
Agadir, *Morocco* **50 B4** 30 28N 9 55W
Agaete, *Canary Is.* **22 F4** 28 6N 15 43W
Agar, *India* **42 H7** 23 40N 76 2 E
Agartala, *India* **41 H17** 23 50N 91 23 E
Agassiz, *Canada* **72 D4** 49 14N 121 46W
Agats, *Indonesia* **37 F9** 5 33S 138 0 E
Agboville, *Ivory C.* **50 G5** 5 55N 4 15W
Agde, *France* **18 E5** 43 19N 3 28 E
Agen, *France* **18 D4** 44 12N 0 38 E
Āgh Kand, *Iran* **45 B6** 37 15N 48 4 E
Aginskoye, *Russia* **27 D12** 51 6N 114 32 E
Agra, *India* **42 F7** 27 17N 77 58 E
Agri →, *Italy* **20 D7** 40 13N 16 44 E
Ağrı Dağı, *Turkey* **25 G7** 39 50N 44 15 E
Ağrı Karakose, *Turkey* **25 G7** 39 44N 43 3 E
Agrigento, *Italy* **20 F5** 37 19N 13 34 E
Agrinion, *Greece* **21 E9** 38 37N 21 27 E
Agua Caliente, *Baja Calif., Mexico* **85 N10** 32 29N 116 59W
Agua Caliente, *Sinaloa, Mexico* **86 B3** 26 30N 108 20W
Agua Caliente Springs, *U.S.A.* **85 N10** 32 56N 116 19W
Água Clara, *Brazil* **93 H8** 20 25S 52 45W
Agua Hechicero, *Mexico* **85 N10** 32 26N 116 14W
Agua Prieta, *Mexico* **86 A3** 31 20N 109 32W
Aguadilla, *Puerto Rico* **89 C6** 18 26N 67 10W
Aguadulce, *Panama* **88 E3** 8 15N 80 32W
Aguanga, *U.S.A.* **85 M10** 33 27N 116 51W
Aguanish, *Canada* **71 B7** 50 14N 62 2W
Aguanus →, *Canada* **71 B7** 50 13N 62 5W
Aguapey →, *Argentina* **94 B4** 29 7S 56 36W
Aguaray Guazú →, *Paraguay* **94 A4** 24 47S 57 19W
Aguarico →, *Ecuador* **92 D3** 0 59S 75 11W
Aguas Blancas, *Chile* **94 A2** 24 15S 69 55W
Aguas Calientes, Sierra de, *Argentina* **94 B2** 25 26S 66 40W
Aguascalientes, *Mexico* **86 C4** 21 53N 102 12W
Aguascalientes □, *Mexico* **86 C4** 22 0N 102 20W
Aguilares, *Argentina* **94 B2** 27 26S 65 35W
Aguilas, *Spain* **19 D5** 37 23N 1 35W
Agüimes, *Canary Is.* **22 G4** 27 58N 15 27W
Aguja, C. de la, *Colombia* **90 B3** 11 18N 74 12W
Agulhas, C., *S. Africa* **56 E3** 34 52S 20 0 E
Agulo, *Canary Is.* **22 F2** 28 11N 17 12W
Agung, *Indonesia* **36 F5** 8 20S 115 28 E
Agur, *Uganda* **54 B3** 2 28N 32 55 E
Agusan →, *Phil.* **37 C7** 9 0N 125 30 E
Aha Mts., *Botswana* **56 B3** 19 45S 21 0 E
Ahaggar, *Algeria* **50 D7** 23 0N 6 30 E
Ahar, *Iran* **44 B5** 38 35N 47 0 E
Ahipara B., *N.Z.* **59 F4** 35 5S 173 5 E
Ahiri, *India* **40 K12** 19 30N 80 0 E
Ahmad Wal, *Pakistan* **42 E1** 29 18N 65 58 E
Ahmadabad, *India* **42 H5** 23 0N 72 40 E
Aḥmadābād, *Khorāsān, Iran* **45 C9** 35 3N 60 50 E
Aḥmadābād, *Khorāsān, Iran* **45 C8** 35 49N 59 42 E
Aḥmadī, *Iran* **45 E8** 27 56N 56 42 E
Ahmadnagar, *India* **40 K9** 19 7N 74 46 E
Ahmadpur, *Pakistan* **42 E4** 29 12N 71 10 E
Ahmedabad = Ahmadabad, *India* **42 H5** 23 0N 72 40 E
Ahmednagar = Ahmadnagar, *India* **40 K9** 19 7N 74 46 E
Ahome, *Mexico* **86 B3** 25 55N 109 11W
Ahram, *Iran* **45 D6** 28 52N 51 16 E
Ahrax Pt., *Malta* **23 D1** 35 59N 14 22 E
Āhū, *Iran* **45 C6** 34 33N 50 2 E
Ahuachapán, *El Salv.* **88 D2** 13 54N 89 52W
Ahvāz, *Iran* **45 D6** 31 20N 48 40 E
Ahvenanmaa = Åland, *Finland* **9 F19** 60 15N 20 0 E
Aḥwar, *Yemen* **46 E4** 13 30N 46 40 E
Aichi □, *Japan* **31 G8** 35 0N 137 15 E
Aigua, *Uruguay* **95 C5** 34 13S 54 46W
Aigues-Mortes, *France* **18 E6** 43 35N 4 12 E
Aihui, *China* **33 A7** 50 10N 127 30 E
Aija, *Peru* **92 E3** 9 50S 77 45W
Aikawa, *Japan* **30 E9** 38 2N 138 15 E
Aiken, *U.S.A.* **77 J5** 33 34N 81 43W
Aillik, *Canada* **71 A8** 55 11N 59 18W
Ailsa Craig, *U.K.* **12 F3** 55 15N 5 6W
'Ailūn, *Jordan* **47 C4** 32 18N 35 47 E
Aim, *Russia* **27 D14** 59 0N 133 55 E
Aimere, *Indonesia* **37 F6** 8 45S 121 3 E
Aimogasta, *Argentina* **94 B2** 28 33S 66 50W
Aïn Ben Tili, *Mauritania* **50 C4** 25 59N 9 27W
Aïn-Sefra, *Algeria* **50 B5** 32 47N 0 37W
'Ain Sudr, *Egypt* **47 F2** 29 50N 33 6 E
Ainaži, *Latvia* **9 H21** 57 50N 24 24 E
Ainsworth, *U.S.A.* **80 D5** 42 33N 99 52W
Aiquile, *Bolivia* **92 G5** 18 10S 65 10W
Aïr, *Niger* **50 E7** 18 30N 8 0 E
Air Hitam, *Malaysia* **39 M4** 1 55N 103 11 E
Airdrie, *U.K.* **12 F5** 55 52N 3 57W
Aire →, *U.K.* **10 D7** 53 43N 0 55W
Aire, I. de l', *Spain* **22 B11** 39 48N 4 16 E
Airlie Beach, *Australia* **62 C4** 20 16S 148 43 E
Aisne →, *France* **18 B5** 49 26N 2 50 E
Aitkin, *U.S.A.* **80 B8** 46 32N 93 42W
Aiud, *Romania* **17 E12** 46 19N 23 44 E
Aix-en-Provence, *France* **18 E6** 43 32N 5 27 E
Aix-la-Chapelle = Aachen, *Germany* **16 C4** 50 45N 6 6 E
Aix-les-Bains, *France* **18 D6** 45 41N 5 53 E
Aiyansh, *Canada* **72 B3** 55 17N 129 2W
Aiyion, *Greece* **21 E10** 38 15N 22 5 E
Aizawl, *India* **41 H18** 23 40N 92 44 E
Aizkraukle, *Latvia* **9 H21** 56 36N 25 11 E
Aizpute, *Latvia* **9 H19** 56 43N 21 40 E
Aizuwakamatsu, *Japan* **30 F9** 37 30N 139 56 E
Ajaccio, *France* **18 F8** 41 55N 8 40 E
Ajalpan, *Mexico* **87 D5** 18 22N 97 15W
Ajanta Ra., *India* **40 J9** 20 28N 75 50 E
Ajari Rep. = Ajaria □, *Georgia* **25 F7** 41 30N 42 0 E
Ajaria □, *Georgia* **25 F7** 41 30N 42 0 E
Ajax, *Canada* **78 C5** 43 50N 79 1W
Ajdâbiyah, *Libya* **51 B10** 30 54N 20 4 E
Ajka, *Hungary* **17 E9** 47 4N 17 31 E
'Ajmān, *U.A.E.* **45 E7** 25 25N 55 30 E
Ajmer, *India* **42 F6** 26 28N 74 37 E
Ajo, *U.S.A.* **83 K7** 32 22N 112 52W
Ajo, C. de, *Spain* **19 A4** 43 31N 3 35W
Akabira, *Japan* **30 C11** 43 33N 142 5 E
Akamas □, *Cyprus* **23 D11** 35 3N 32 18 E
Akanthou, *Cyprus* **23 D12** 35 22N 33 45 E
Akaroa, *N.Z.* **59 K4** 43 49S 172 59 E
Akashi, *Japan* **31 G7** 34 45N 134 58 E
Akelamo, *Indonesia* **37 D7** 1 35N 129 40 E
Aketi, *Dem. Rep. of the Congo* **52 D4** 2 38N 23 47 E
Akharnaí, *Greece* **21 E10** 38 5N 23 44 E
Akhelóös →, *Greece* **21 E9** 38 19N 21 7 E
Akhisar, *Turkey* **21 E12** 38 56N 27 48 E
Akhnur, *India* **43 C6** 32 52N 74 45 E
Aki, *Japan* **31 H6** 33 30N 133 54 E
Akimiski I., *Canada* **70 B3** 52 50N 81 30W
Akita, *Japan* **30 E10** 39 45N 140 7 E
Akita □, *Japan* **30 E10** 39 40N 140 30 E
Akjoujt, *Mauritania* **50 E3** 19 45N 14 15W
Akkeshi, *Japan* **30 C12** 43 2N 144 51 E
'Akko, *Israel* **47 C4** 32 55N 35 4 E
Aklavik, *Canada* **68 B6** 68 12N 135 0W
Akmolinsk = Aqmola, *Kazakstan* **26 D8** 51 10N 71 30 E
Akō, *Japan* **31 G7** 34 45N 134 24 E
Akola, *India* **40 J10** 20 42N 77 2 E
Akordat, *Eritrea* **46 D2** 15 30N 37 40 E
Akpatok I., *Canada* **69 B13** 60 25N 68 8W
Åkrahamn, *Norway* **9 G11** 59 15N 5 10 E
Akranes, *Iceland* **8 D2** 64 19N 22 5W
Akron, *Colo., U.S.A.* **80 E3** 40 10N 103 13W
Akron, *Ohio, U.S.A.* **78 E3** 41 5N 81 31W
Akrotiri, *Cyprus* **23 E11** 34 36N 32 57 E
Akrotiri Bay, *Cyprus* **23 E12** 34 35N 33 10 E
Aksai Chin, *India* **43 B8** 35 15N 79 55 E
Aksay, *Kazakstan* **24 D9** 51 11N 53 0 E
Aksu, *China* **32 B3** 41 5N 80 10 E
Aksum, *Ethiopia* **46 E2** 14 5N 38 40 E
Aktogay, *Kazakstan* **26 E8** 46 57N 79 40 E
Aktsyabrski, *Belarus* **17 B15** 52 38N 28 53 E
Aktyubinsk = Aqtöbe, *Kazakstan* **25 D10** 50 17N 57 10 E
Akure, *Nigeria* **50 G7** 7 15N 5 5 E
Akureyri, *Iceland* **8 D4** 65 40N 18 6W
Akuseki-Shima, *Japan* **31 K4** 29 27N 129 37 E
Akyab = Sittwe, *Burma* **41 J18** 20 18N 92 45 E
Al 'Adan, *Yemen* **46 E4** 12 45N 45 0 E
Al Aḥsā, *Si. Arabia* **45 E6** 25 50N 49 0 E
Al Ajfar, *Si. Arabia* **44 E4** 27 26N 43 0 E
Al Amādīyah, *Iraq* **44 B4** 37 5N 43 30 E
Al Amārah, *Iraq* **44 D5** 31 55N 47 15 E
Al 'Aqabah, *Jordan* **47 F4** 29 31N 35 0 E
Al Arak, *Syria* **44 C3** 34 38N 38 35 E
Al 'Aramah, *Si. Arabia* **44 E5** 25 30N 46 0 E
Al Arṭāwīyah, *Si. Arabia* **44 E5** 26 31N 45 20 E
Al 'Āşimah = 'Ammān □, *Jordan* **47 D5** 31 40N 36 30 E
Al 'Assāfīyah, *Si. Arabia* **44 D3** 28 17N 38 59 E
Al 'Ayn, *Oman* **45 E7** 24 15N 55 45 E
Al 'Ayn, *Si. Arabia* **44 E3** 25 4N 38 6 E
Al A'ẓamīyah, *Iraq* **44 C5** 33 22N 44 22 E
Al 'Azīzīyah, *Iraq* **44 C5** 32 54N 45 4 E
Al Bāb, *Syria* **44 B3** 36 23N 37 29 E
Al Bad', *Si. Arabia* **44 D2** 28 28N 35 1 E
Al Bādī, *Iraq* **44 C4** 35 56N 41 32 E
Al Baḥrah, *Kuwait* **44 D5** 29 40N 47 52 E
Al Baḥral Mayyit = Dead Sea, *Asia* **47 D4** 31 30N 35 30 E
Al Balqā' □, *Jordan* **47 C4** 32 5N 35 45 E
Al Bārūk, J., *Lebanon* **47 B4** 33 39N 35 40 E
Al Başrah, *Iraq* **44 D5** 30 30N 47 50 E
Al Baṭḥā, *Iraq* **44 D5** 31 6N 45 53 E
Al Batrūn, *Lebanon* **47 A4** 34 15N 35 40 E
Al Bayḍā, *Libya* **51 B10** 32 50N 21 44 E
Al Biqā □, *Lebanon* **47 A5** 34 10N 36 10 E
Al Bi'r, *Si. Arabia* **44 D3** 28 51N 36 16 E
Al Burayj, *Syria* **47 A5** 34 15N 36 46 E
Al Fallūjah, *Iraq* **44 C4** 33 20N 43 55 E
Al Fāw, *Iraq* **45 D6** 30 0N 48 30 E
Al Fujayrah, *U.A.E.* **45 E8** 25 7N 56 18 E
Al Ghadaf, W. →, *Jordan* **47 D5** 31 26N 36 43 E
Al Ghammās, *Iraq* **44 D5** 31 45N 44 37 E
Al Hābah, *Si. Arabia* **44 E5** 27 10N 47 0 E
Al Ḥadīthah, *Iraq* **44 C4** 34 0N 41 13 E
Al Ḥadīthah, *Si. Arabia* **44 D3** 31 28N 37 8 E
Al Ḥājānah, *Syria* **47 B5** 33 20N 36 33 E
Al Ḥāmad, *Si. Arabia* **44 D3** 31 30N 39 30 E
Al Hamdānīyah, *Syria* **44 C3** 35 25N 36 50 E
Al Ḥamīdīyah, *Syria* **47 A4** 34 42N 35 57 E
Al Ḥammār, *Iraq* **44 D5** 30 57N 46 51 E
Al Ḥarīr, W. →, *Syria* **47 C4** 32 44N 35 59 E
Al Ḥasā, W. →, *Jordan* **47 D4** 31 4N 35 29 E
Al Ḥasakah, *Syria* **44 B4** 36 35N 40 45 E
Al Haydān, W. →, *Jordan* **47 D4** 31 29N 35 34 E
Al Ḥayy, *Iraq* **44 C5** 32 5N 46 5 E
Al Ḥillah, *Iraq* **44 C5** 32 30N 44 25 E
Al Hirmil, *Lebanon* **47 A5** 34 26N 36 24 E
Al Hoceïma, *Morocco* **50 A5** 35 8N 3 58W

Amargosa Range

Al Ḩudaydah, *Yemen* **46 E3** 14 50N 43 0 E
Al Hufūf, *Si. Arabia* **45 E6** 25 25N 49 45 E
Al Ḩumaydah, *Si. Arabia* **44 D2** 29 14N 34 56 E
Al Ḩunayy, *Si. Arabia* **45 E6** 25 58N 48 45 E
Al 'Īsāwīyah, *Si. Arabia* **44 D3** 30 43N 37 59 E
Al Jafr, *Jordan* **47 E5** 30 18N 36 14 E
Al Jaghbūb, *Libya* **51 C10** 29 42N 24 38 E
Al Jahrah, *Kuwait* **44 D5** 29 25N 47 40 E
Al Jalāmīd, *Si. Arabia* **44 D3** 31 20N 39 45 E
Al Jamalīyah, *Qatar* **45 E6** 25 37N 51 5 E
Al Janūb □, *Lebanon* **47 B4** 33 20N 35 20 E
Al Jawf, *Libya* **51 D10** 24 10N 23 24 E
Al Jawf, *Si. Arabia* **44 D3** 29 55N 39 40 E
Al Jazirah, *Iraq* **44 C5** 33 30N 44 0 E
Al Jithāmīyah, *Si. Arabia* **44 E4** 27 41N 41 43 E
Al Jubayl, *Si. Arabia* **45 E6** 27 0N 49 50 E
Al Jubaylah, *Si. Arabia* **44 E5** 24 55N 46 25 E
Al Jubb, *Si. Arabia* **44 E4** 27 11N 42 17 E
Al Junaynah, *Sudan* **51 F10** 13 27N 22 45 E
Al Kabā'ish, *Iraq* **44 D5** 30 58N 47 0 E
Al Karak, *Jordan* **47 D4** 31 11N 35 42 E
Al Karak □, *Jordan* **47 E5** 31 0N 36 0 E
Al Kāzim Tyah, *Iraq* **44 C5** 33 22N 44 12 E
Al Khalīl, *West Bank* **47 D4** 31 32N 35 6 E
Al Khawr, *Qatar* **45 E6** 25 41N 51 30 E
Al Khiḑr, *Iraq* **44 D5** 31 12N 45 33 E
Al Khiyām, *Lebanon* **47 B4** 33 20N 35 36 E
Al Kiswah, *Syria* **47 B5** 33 23N 36 14 E
Al Kufrah, *Libya* **51 D10** 24 17N 23 15 E
Al Kuhayfiyah, *Si. Arabia* **44 E4** 27 12N 43 3 E
Al Kūt, *Iraq* **44 C5** 32 30N 46 0 E
Al Kuwayt, *Kuwait* **44 D5** 29 30N 48 0 E
Al Labwah, *Lebanon* **47 A5** 34 11N 36 20 E
Al Lādhiqīyah, *Syria* **44 C2** 35 30N 35 45 E
Al Liwā', *Oman* **45 E8** 24 31N 56 36 E
Al Luḩayyah, *Yemen* **46 D3** 15 45N 42 40 E
Al Madīnah, *Iraq* **44 D5** 30 57N 47 16 E
Al Madīnah, *Si. Arabia* **46 C2** 24 35N 39 52 E
Al Mafraq, *Jordan* **47 C5** 32 17N 36 14 E
Al Maḩmūdīyah, *Iraq* **44 C5** 33 3N 44 21 E
Al Majma'ah, *Si. Arabia* **44 E5** 25 57N 45 22 E
Al Makhruq, W. —▸, *Jordan* **47 D6** 31 28N 37 0 E
Al Makḩūl, *Si. Arabia* **44 E4** 26 37N 42 39 E
Al Manāmah, *Bahrain* **45 E6** 26 10N 50 30 E
Al Maqwa', *Kuwait* **44 D5** 29 10N 47 59 E
Al Marj, *Libya* **51 B10** 32 25N 20 30 E
Al Maţlā, *Kuwait* **44 D5** 29 24N 47 40 E
Al Mawjib, W. —▸, *Jordan* **47 D4** 31 28N 35 36 E
Al Mawşil, *Iraq* **44 B4** 36 15N 43 5 E
Al Mayādin, *Syria* **44 C4** 35 1N 40 27 E
Al Mazār, *Jordan* **47 D4** 31 4N 35 41 E
Al Midhnab, *Si. Arabia* **44 E5** 25 50N 44 18 E
Al Minā', *Lebanon* **47 A4** 34 24N 35 49 E
Al Miqdādīyah, *Iraq* **44 C5** 34 0N 45 0 E
Al Mubarraz, *Si. Arabia* **45 E6** 25 30N 49 40 E
Al Mughayrā', *U.A.E.* **45 E7** 24 5N 53 32 E
Al Muḩarraq, *Bahrain* **45 E6** 26 15N 50 40 E
Al Mukallā, *Yemen* **46 E4** 14 33N 49 2 E
Al Mukhā, *Yemen* **46 E3** 13 18N 43 15 E
Al Musayjīd, *Si. Arabia* **44 E3** 24 5N 39 5 E
Al Musayyib, *Iraq* **44 C5** 32 49N 44 20 E
Al Muwayliḩ, *Si. Arabia* **44 E2** 27 40N 35 30 E
Al Qā'im, *Iraq* **44 C4** 34 21N 41 7 E
Al Qalībah, *Si. Arabia* **44 D3** 28 24N 37 42 E
Al Qaryatayn, *Syria* **47 A6** 34 12N 37 13 E
Al Qaţ'ā, *Syria* **44 C4** 34 40N 40 48 E
Al Qaţīf, *Si. Arabia* **45 E6** 26 35N 50 0 E
Al Qatrānah, *Jordan* **47 D5** 31 12N 36 6 E
Al Qaţrūn, *Libya* **51 D9** 24 56N 15 3 E
Al Qayşūmah, *Si. Arabia* **44 D5** 28 20N 46 7 E
Al Quds = Jerusalem, *Israel* **47 D4** 31 47N 35 10 E
Al Qunayţirah, *Syria* **47 C4** 32 55N 35 45 E
Al Qurnah, *Iraq* **44 D5** 31 1N 47 25 E
Al Quşayr, *Iraq* **44 D5** 30 39N 45 50 E
Al Quşayr, *Syria* **47 A5** 34 31N 36 34 E
Al Qutayfah, *Syria* **47 B5** 33 44N 36 36 E
Al 'Uḑaylīyah, *Si. Arabia* **45 E6** 25 8N 49 18 E
Al 'Ulā, *Si. Arabia* **44 E3** 26 35N 38 0 E
Al Uqayr, *Si. Arabia* **45 E6** 25 40N 50 15 E
Al 'Uwaynid, *Si. Arabia* **44 E5** 24 50N 46 0 E
Al 'Uwayqīlah, *Si. Arabia* **44 D4** 30 30N 42 10 E
Al 'Uyūn, *Ḩijāz, Si. Arabia* **44 E3** 24 33N 39 35 E
Al 'Uyūn, *Najd, Si. Arabia* **44 E4** 26 30N 43 50 E
Al 'Uzayr, *Iraq* **44 D5** 31 19N 47 25 E
Al Wajh, *Si. Arabia* **44 E3** 26 10N 36 30 E
Al Wakrah, *Qatar* **45 E6** 25 10N 51 40 E
Al Wannān, *Si. Arabia* **45 E6** 26 55N 48 24 E
Al Waqbah, *Si. Arabia* **44 D5** 28 48N 45 33 E
Al Wari'āh, *Si. Arabia* **44 E5** 27 51N 47 25 E
Al Wusayl, *Qatar* **45 E6** 25 29N 51 29 E
Ala Tau Shankou = Dzungarian Gates, *Kazakstan* **32 B3** 45 0N 82 0 E
Alabama □, *U.S.A.* **77 J2** 33 0N 87 0W
Alabama —▸, *U.S.A.* **77 K2** 31 8N 87 57W
Alaçam Dağlan, *Turkey* **21 E13** 39 18N 28 49 E
Alaérma, *Greece* **23 C9** 36 9N 27 57 E
Alagoa Grande, *Brazil* **93 E11** 7 3S 35 35W
Alagoas □, *Brazil* **93 E11** 9 0S 36 0W
Alagoinhas, *Brazil* **93 F11** 12 7S 38 20W
Alaior, *Spain* **22 B11** 39 57N 4 8 E
Alajero, *Canary Is.* **22 F2** 28 3N 17 13W
Alajuela, *Costa Rica* **88 D3** 10 2N 84 8W
Alakamisy, *Madag.* **57 C8** 21 19S 47 14 E
Alakurtti, *Russia* **24 A5** 67 0N 30 30 E
Alameda, *Calif., U.S.A.* **84 H4** 37 46N 122 15W
Alameda, *N. Mex., U.S.A.* **83 J10** 35 11N 106 37W
Alamo, *U.S.A.* **85 J11** 36 21N 115 10W
Alamo Crossing, *U.S.A.* **85 L13** 34 16N 113 33W
Alamogordo, *U.S.A.* **83 K11** 32 54N 105 57W
Alamos, *Mexico* **86 B3** 27 0N 109 0W
Alamosa, *U.S.A.* **83 H11** 37 28N 105 52W
Åland, *Finland* **9 F19** 60 15N 20 0 E
Ålands hav, *Sweden* **9 F18** 60 0N 19 30 E
Alandur, *India* **40 N12** 13 0N 80 15 E
Alania = North Ossetia □, *Russia* **25 F7** 43 30N 44 30 E
Alanya, *Turkey* **25 G5** 36 38N 32 0 E
Alaotra, Farihin', *Madag.* **57 B8** 17 30S 48 30 E
Alapayevsk, *Russia* **26 D7** 57 52N 61 42 E
Alaşehir, *Turkey* **25 G4** 38 23N 28 30 E
Alaska □, *U.S.A.* **68 B5** 64 0N 154 0W
Alaska, G. of, *Pac. Oc.* **68 C5** 58 0N 145 0W
Alaska Peninsula, *U.S.A.* **68 C4** 56 0N 159 0W
Alaska Range, *U.S.A.* **68 B4** 62 50N 151 0W
Älät, *Azerbaijan* **25 G8** 39 58N 49 25 E
Alatyr, *Russia* **24 D8** 54 55N 46 35 E
Alausi, *Ecuador* **92 D3** 2 0S 78 50W
Alava, C., *U.S.A.* **82 B1** 48 10N 124 44W
Alavus, *Finland* **9 E20** 62 35N 23 36 E
Alawoona, *Australia* **63 E3** 34 45S 140 30 E
'Alayh, *Lebanon* **47 B4** 33 46N 35 33 E
Alba, *Italy* **18 D8** 44 42N 8 2 E
Alba-Iulia, *Romania* **17 E12** 46 8N 23 39 E
Albacete, *Spain* **19 C5** 39 0N 1 50W
Albacutya, L., *Australia* **63 F3** 35 45S 141 58 E
Albania ■, *Europe* **21 D9** 41 0N 20 0 E
Albany, *Australia* **61 G2** 35 1S 117 58 E
Albany, *Ga., U.S.A.* **77 K3** 31 35N 84 10W
Albany, *Minn., U.S.A.* **80 C7** 45 38N 94 34W
Albany, *N.Y., U.S.A.* **79 D11** 42 39N 73 45W
Albany, *Oreg., U.S.A.* **82 D2** 44 38N 123 6W
Albany, *Tex., U.S.A.* **81 J5** 32 44N 99 18W
Albany —▸, *Canada* **70 B3** 52 17N 81 31W
Albardón, *Argentina* **94 C2** 31 20S 68 30W
Albatross B., *Australia* **62 A3** 12 45S 141 30 E
Albemarle, *U.S.A.* **77 H5** 35 21N 80 11W
Albemarle Sd., *U.S.A.* **77 H7** 36 5N 76 0W
Alberche —▸, *Spain* **19 C3** 39 58N 4 46W
Alberdi, *Paraguay* **94 B4** 26 14S 58 20W
Albert, L., *Australia* **63 F2** 35 30S 139 10 E
Albert Canyon, *Canada* **72 C5** 51 8N 117 41W
Albert Edward Ra., *Australia* **60 C4** 18 17S 127 57 E
Albert L., *Africa* **54 B3** 1 30N 31 0 E
Albert Lea, *U.S.A.* **80 D8** 43 39N 93 22W
Albert Nile —▸, *Uganda* **54 B3** 3 36N 32 2 E
Albert Town, *Bahamas* **89 B5** 22 37N 74 33W
Alberta □, *Canada* **72 C6** 54 40N 115 0W
Alberti, *Argentina* **94 D3** 35 1S 60 16W
Albertinia, *S. Africa* **56 E3** 34 11S 21 34 E
Alberton, *Canada* **71 C7** 46 50N 64 0W
Albertville = Kalemie, *Dem. Rep. of the Congo* **54 D2** 5 55S 29 9 E
Albertville, *France* **18 D7** 45 40N 6 22 E
Albi, *France* **18 E5** 43 56N 2 9 E
Albia, *U.S.A.* **80 E8** 41 2N 92 48W
Albina, *Surinam* **93 B8** 5 37N 54 15W
Albina, Ponta, *Angola* **56 B1** 15 52S 11 44 E
Albion, *Idaho, U.S.A.* **82 E7** 42 25N 113 35W
Albion, *Mich., U.S.A.* **76 D3** 42 15N 84 45W
Albion, *Nebr., U.S.A.* **80 E6** 41 42N 98 0W
Albion, *Pa., U.S.A.* **78 E4** 41 53N 80 22W
Alborán, *Medit. S.* **19 E4** 35 57N 3 0W
Ålborg, *Denmark* **9 H13** 57 2N 9 54 E
Alborz, Reshteh-ye Kūhhā-ye, *Iran* **45 C7** 36 0N 52 0 E
Albreda, *Canada* **72 C5** 52 35N 119 10W
Albuquerque, *U.S.A.* **83 J10** 35 5N 106 39W
Albuquerque, Cayos de, *Caribbean* **88 D3** 12 10N 81 50W
Alburg, *U.S.A.* **79 B11** 44 59N 73 18W
Albury, *Australia* **63 F4** 36 3S 146 56 E
Alcalá de Henares, *Spain* **19 B4** 40 28N 3 22W
Alcalá la Real, *Spain* **19 D4** 37 27N 3 57W
Álcamo, *Italy* **20 F5** 37 59N 12 55 E
Alcañiz, *Spain* **19 B5** 41 2N 0 8W
Alcântara, *Brazil* **93 D10** 2 20S 44 30W
Alcántara, Embalse de, *Spain* **19 C2** 39 44N 6 50W
Alcantara L., *Canada* **73 A7** 60 57N 108 9W
Alcantarilla, *Spain* **19 D5** 37 59N 1 12W
Alcaraz, Sierra de, *Spain* **19 C4** 38 40N 2 20W
Alcaudete, *Spain* **19 D3** 37 35N 4 5W
Alcázar de San Juan, *Spain* **19 C4** 39 24N 3 12W
Alchevsk, *Ukraine* **25 E6** 48 30N 38 45 E
Alcira = Alzira, *Spain* **19 C5** 39 9N 0 30W
Alcoa, *U.S.A.* **77 H4** 35 48N 83 59W
Alcova, *U.S.A.* **82 E10** 42 34N 106 43W
Alcoy, *Spain* **19 C5** 38 43N 0 30W
Alcúdia, *Spain* **22 B10** 39 51N 3 7 E
Alcúdia, B. d', *Spain* **22 B10** 39 47N 3 15 E
Aldabra Is., *Seychelles* **49 G8** 9 22S 46 28 E
Aldama, *Mexico* **87 C5** 23 0N 98 4W
Aldan, *Russia* **27 D13** 58 40N 125 30 E
Aldan —▸, *Russia* **27 C13** 63 28N 129 35 E
Aldea, Pta. de la, *Canary Is.* **22 G4** 28 0N 15 50W
Aldeburgh, *U.K.* **11 E9** 52 10N 1 37 E
Alder, *U.S.A.* **82 D7** 45 19N 112 6W
Alder Pk., *U.S.A.* **84 K5** 35 53N 121 22W
Alderney, *U.K.* **11 H5** 49 42N 2 11W
Aldershot, *U.K.* **11 F7** 51 15N 0 44W
Aledo, *U.S.A.* **80 E9** 41 12N 90 45W
Aleg, *Mauritania* **50 E3** 17 3N 13 55W
Alegranza, *Canary Is.* **22 E6** 29 23N 13 32W
Alegranza, I., *Canary Is.* **22 E6** 29 23N 13 32W
Alegre, *Brazil* **95 A7** 20 50S 41 30W
Alegrete, *Brazil* **95 B4** 29 40S 56 0W
Aleisk, *Russia* **26 D9** 52 40N 83 0 E
Aleksandriya = Oleksandriya, *Ukraine* **17 C14** 50 37N 26 19 E
Aleksandrovsk-Sakhalinskiy, *Russia* **27 D15** 50 50N 142 20 E
Além Paraíba, *Brazil* **95 A7** 21 52S 42 41W
Alemania, *Argentina* **94 B2** 25 40S 65 30W
Alemania, *Chile* **94 B2** 25 10S 69 55W
Alençon, *France* **18 B4** 48 27N 0 4 E
Alenquer, *Brazil* **93 D8** 1 56S 54 46W
Alenuihaha Channel, *U.S.A.* **74 H17** 20 30N 156 0W
Aleppo = Ḩalab, *Syria* **44 B3** 36 10N 37 15 E
Alert Bay, *Canada* **72 C3** 50 30N 126 55W
Alès, *France* **18 D6** 44 9N 4 5 E
Alessándria, *Italy* **18 D8** 44 54N 8 37 E
Ålesund, *Norway* **9 E12** 62 28N 6 12 E
Aleutian Is., *Pac. Oc.* **68 C2** 52 0N 175 0W
Aleutian Trench, *Pac. Oc.* **64 C10** 48 0N 180 0 E
Alexander, *U.S.A.* **80 B3** 47 51N 103 39W
Alexander, Mt., *Australia* **61 E3** 28 58S 120 16 E
Alexander Arch., *U.S.A.* **72 B2** 56 0N 136 0W
Alexander Bay, *S. Africa* **56 D2** 28 40S 16 30 E
Alexander City, *U.S.A.* **77 J3** 32 56N 85 58W
Alexander I., *Antarctica* **5 C17** 69 0S 70 0W
Alexandra, *Australia* **63 F4** 37 8S 145 40 E
Alexandra, *N.Z.* **59 L2** 45 14S 169 25 E
Alexandra Falls, *Canada* **72 A5** 60 29N 116 18W
Alexandria = El Iskandarîya, *Egypt* **51 B11** 31 13N 29 58 E
Alexandria, *Australia* **62 B2** 19 5S 136 40 E
Alexandria, *B.C., Canada* **72 C4** 52 35N 122 27W
Alexandria, *Ont., Canada* **70 C5** 45 19N 74 38W
Alexandria, *Romania* **17 G13** 43 57N 25 24 E
Alexandria, *S. Africa* **56 E4** 33 38S 26 28 E
Alexandria, *U.K.* **12 F4** 55 59N 4 35W
Alexandria, *Ind., U.S.A.* **76 E3** 40 16N 85 41W
Alexandria, *La., U.S.A.* **81 K8** 31 18N 92 27W
Alexandria, *Minn., U.S.A.* **80 C7** 45 53N 95 22W
Alexandria, *S. Dak., U.S.A.* **80 D6** 43 39N 97 47W
Alexandria, *Va., U.S.A.* **76 F7** 38 48N 77 3W
Alexandria Bay, *U.S.A.* **79 B9** 44 20N 75 55W
Alexandrina, L., *Australia* **63 F2** 35 25S 139 10 E
Alexandroúpolis, *Greece* **21 D11** 40 50N 25 54 E
Alexis —▸, *Canada* **71 B8** 52 33N 56 8W
Alexis Creek, *Canada* **72 C4** 52 10N 123 20W
Alfabia, *Spain* **22 B9** 39 44N 2 44 E
Alfenas, *Brazil* **95 A6** 21 20S 46 10W
Alford, *Aberds., U.K.* **12 D6** 57 14N 2 41W
Alford, *Lincs., U.K.* **10 D8** 53 15N 0 10 E
Alfred, *Maine, U.S.A.* **79 C14** 43 29N 70 43W
Alfred, *N.Y., U.S.A.* **78 D7** 42 16N 77 48W
Alfreton, *U.K.* **10 D6** 53 6N 1 24W
Alga, *Kazakstan* **25 E10** 49 53N 57 20 E
Algaida, *Spain* **22 B9** 39 33N 2 53 E
Ålgård, *Norway* **9 G11** 58 46N 5 53 E
Algarve, *Portugal* **19 D1** 36 58N 8 20W
Algeciras, *Spain* **19 D3** 36 9N 5 28W
Algemesí, *Spain* **19 C5** 39 11N 0 27W
Alger, *Algeria* **50 A6** 36 42N 3 8 E
Algeria ■, *Africa* **50 C6** 28 30N 2 0 E
Alghero, *Italy* **20 D3** 40 33N 8 19 E
Algiers = Alger, *Algeria* **50 A6** 36 42N 3 8 E
Algoa B., *S. Africa* **56 E4** 33 50S 25 45 E
Algoma, *U.S.A.* **76 C2** 44 36N 87 26W
Algona, *U.S.A.* **80 D7** 43 4N 94 14W
Algonac, *U.S.A.* **78 D2** 42 37N 82 32W
Algorta, *Uruguay* **96 C5** 32 25S 57 23W
Alhambra, *U.S.A.* **85 L8** 34 8N 118 6W
Alhucemas = Al Hoceïma, *Morocco* **50 A5** 35 8N 3 58W
'Alī al Gharbī, *Iraq* **44 C5** 32 30N 46 45 E
'Alī ash Sharqī, *Iraq* **44 C5** 32 7N 46 44 E
'Alī Khēl, *Afghan.* **42 C3** 33 57N 69 43 E
Alī Shāh, *Iran* **44 B5** 38 9N 45 50 E
'Alīābād, *Khorāsān, Iran* **45 C8** 32 30N 57 30 E
'Alīābād, *Kordestān, Iran* **44 C5** 35 4N 46 58 E
'Alīābād, *Yazd, Iran* **45 D7** 31 41N 53 49 E
Aliağa, *Turkey* **21 E12** 38 47N 26 59 E
Aliákmon —▸, *Greece* **21 D10** 40 30N 22 36 E
Alicante, *Spain* **19 C5** 38 23N 0 30W
Alice, *S. Africa* **56 E4** 32 48S 26 55 E
Alice, *U.S.A.* **81 M5** 27 45N 98 5W
Alice —▸, *Queens., Australia* **62 C3** 24 2S 144 50 E
Alice —▸, *Queens., Australia* **62 B3** 15 35S 142 20 E
Alice Arm, *Canada* **72 B3** 55 29N 129 31W
Alice Downs, *Australia* **60 C4** 17 45S 127 56 E
Alice Springs, *Australia* **62 C1** 23 40S 133 50 E
Alicedale, *S. Africa* **56 E4** 33 15S 26 4 E
Aliceville, *U.S.A.* **77 J1** 33 8N 88 9W
Alick Cr. —▸, *Australia* **62 C3** 20 55S 142 20 E
Alida, *Canada* **73 D8** 49 25N 101 55W
Aligarh, *Raj., India* **42 G7** 25 55N 76 15 E
Aligarh, *Ut. P., India* **42 F8** 27 55N 78 10 E
Alīgūdarz, *Iran* **45 C6** 33 25N 49 45 E
Alimnía, *Greece* **23 C9** 36 16N 27 43 E
Alingsås, *Sweden* **9 H15** 57 56N 12 31 E
Alipur, *Pakistan* **42 E4** 29 25N 70 55 E
Alipur Duar, *India* **41 F16** 26 30N 89 35 E
Aliquippa, *U.S.A.* **78 F4** 40 37N 80 15W
Alitus = Alytus, *Lithuania* **9 J21** 54 24N 24 3 E
Aliwal North, *S. Africa* **56 E4** 30 45S 26 45 E
Alix, *Canada* **72 C6** 52 24N 113 11W
Aljustrel, *Portugal* **19 D1** 37 55N 8 10W
Alkmaar, *Neths.* **15 B4** 52 37N 4 45 E
All American Canal, *U.S.A.* **83 K6** 32 45N 115 15W
Allah Dad, *Pakistan* **42 G2** 25 38N 67 34 E
Allahabad, *India* **43 G9** 25 25N 81 58 E
Allan, *Canada* **73 C7** 51 53N 106 4W
Allanmyo, *Burma* **41 K19** 19 30N 95 17 E
Allanridge, *S. Africa* **56 D4** 27 45S 26 40 E
Allanwater, *Canada* **70 B1** 50 14N 90 10W
Allegan, *U.S.A.* **76 D3** 42 32N 85 51W
Allegany, *U.S.A.* **78 D6** 42 6N 78 30W
Allegheny —▸, *U.S.A.* **78 F5** 40 27N 80 1W
Allegheny Mts., *U.S.A.* **66 F11** 38 15N 80 10W
Allegheny Plateau, *U.S.A.* **76 G6** 38 0N 80 0W
Allegheny Reservoir, *U.S.A.* **78 E6** 41 50N 79 0W
Allen, Bog of, *Ireland* **13 C5** 53 15N 7 0W
Allen, L., *Ireland* **13 B3** 54 8N 8 4W
Allende, *Mexico* **86 B4** 28 20N 100 50W
Allentown, *U.S.A.* **79 F9** 40 37N 75 29W
Alleppey, *India* **40 Q10** 9 30N 76 28 E
Aller —▸, *Germany* **16 B5** 52 56N 9 12 E
Alliance, *Nebr., U.S.A.* **80 D3** 42 6N 102 52W
Alliance, *Ohio, U.S.A.* **78 F3** 40 55N 81 6W
Allier —▸, *France* **18 C5** 46 57N 3 4 E
Alliston, *Canada* **70 D4** 44 9N 79 52W
Alloa, *U.K.* **12 E5** 56 7N 3 47W
Allora, *Australia* **63 D5** 28 2S 152 0 E
Alma, *Canada* **71 C5** 48 35N 71 40W
Alma, *Ga., U.S.A.* **77 K4** 31 33N 82 28W
Alma, *Kans., U.S.A.* **80 F6** 39 1N 96 17W
Alma, *Mich., U.S.A.* **76 D3** 43 23N 84 39W
Alma, *Nebr., U.S.A.* **80 E5** 40 6N 99 22W
Alma, *Wis., U.S.A.* **80 C9** 44 20N 91 55W
Alma Ata = Almaty, *Kazakstan* **26 E8** 43 15N 76 57 E
Almada, *Portugal* **19 C1** 38 40N 9 9W
Almaden, *Australia* **62 B3** 17 22S 144 40 E
Almadén, *Spain* **19 C3** 38 49N 4 52W
Almanor, L., *U.S.A.* **82 F3** 40 14N 121 9W
Almansa, *Spain* **19 C5** 38 51N 1 5W
Almanzor, Pico, *Spain* **19 B3** 40 15N 5 18W
Almanzora —▸, *Spain* **19 D5** 37 14N 1 46W
Almaty, *Kazakstan* **26 E8** 43 15N 76 57 E
Almazán, *Spain* **19 B4** 41 30N 2 30W
Almeirim, *Brazil* **93 D8** 1 30S 52 34W
Almelo, *Neths.* **15 B6** 52 22N 6 42 E
Almendralejo, *Spain* **19 C2** 38 41N 6 26W
Almere-Stad, *Neths.* **15 B5** 52 20N 5 15 E
Almería, *Spain* **19 D4** 36 52N 2 27W
Almirante, *Panama* **88 E3** 9 10N 82 30W
Almiroú, Kólpos, *Greece* **23 D6** 35 23N 24 20 E
Almont, *U.S.A.* **78 D1** 42 55N 83 3W
Almonte, *Canada* **79 A8** 45 14N 76 12W
Almora, *India* **43 E8** 29 38N 79 40 E
Alness, *U.K.* **12 D4** 57 41N 4 16W
Alnmouth, *U.K.* **10 B6** 55 24N 1 37W
Alnwick, *U.K.* **10 B6** 55 24N 1 42W
Aloi, *Uganda* **54 B3** 2 16N 33 10 E
Alon, *Burma* **41 H19** 22 12N 95 5 E
Alor, *Indonesia* **37 F6** 8 15S 124 30 E
Alor Setar, *Malaysia* **39 J3** 6 7N 100 22 E
Aloysius, Mt., *Australia* **61 E4** 26 0S 128 38 E
Alpaugh, *U.S.A.* **84 K7** 35 53N 119 29W
Alpena, *U.S.A.* **76 C4** 45 4N 83 27W
Alpha, *Australia* **62 C4** 23 39S 146 37 E
Alphen aan den Rijn, *Neths.* **15 B4** 52 7N 4 40 E
Alpine, *Ariz., U.S.A.* **83 K9** 33 51N 109 9W
Alpine, *Calif., U.S.A.* **85 N10** 32 50N 116 46W
Alpine, *Tex., U.S.A.* **81 K3** 30 22N 103 40W
Alps, *Europe* **18 C8** 46 30N 9 30 E
Alroy Downs, *Australia* **62 B2** 19 20S 136 5 E
Alsace, *France* **18 B7** 48 15N 7 25 E
Alsask, *Canada* **73 C7** 51 21N 109 59W
Alsasua, *Spain* **19 A4** 42 54N 2 10W
Alsten, *Norway* **8 D15** 65 58N 12 40 E
Alston, *U.K.* **10 C5** 54 49N 2 25W
Alta, *Norway* **8 B20** 69 57N 23 10 E
Alta Gracia, *Argentina* **94 C3** 31 40S 64 30W
Alta Lake, *Canada* **72 C4** 50 10N 123 0W
Alta Sierra, *U.S.A.* **85 K8** 35 42N 118 33W
Altaelva —▸, *Norway* **8 B20** 69 54N 23 17 E
Altafjorden, *Norway* **8 A20** 70 5N 23 5 E
Altai = Aerhtai Shan, *Mongolia* **32 B4** 46 40N 92 45 E
Altamaha —▸, *U.S.A.* **77 K5** 31 20N 81 20W
Altamira, *Brazil* **93 D8** 3 12S 52 10W
Altamira, *Chile* **94 B2** 25 47S 69 51W
Altamira, *Mexico* **87 C5** 22 24N 97 55W
Altamont, *U.S.A.* **79 D10** 42 43N 74 3W
Altamura, *Italy* **20 D7** 40 49N 16 33 E
Altanbulag, *Mongolia* **32 A5** 50 16N 106 30 E
Altar, *Mexico* **86 A2** 30 40N 111 50W
Altata, *Mexico* **86 C3** 24 30N 108 0W
Altavista, *U.S.A.* **76 G6** 37 6N 79 17W
Altay, *China* **32 B3** 47 48N 88 10 E
Altea, *Spain* **19 C5** 38 38N 0 2W
Alto Araguaia, *Brazil* **93 G8** 17 15S 53 20W
Alto Cuchumatanes = Cuchumatanes, Sierra de los, *Guatemala* **88 C1** 15 35N 91 25W
Alto del Inca, *Chile* **94 A2** 24 10S 68 10W
Alto Ligonha, *Mozam.* **55 F4** 15 30S 38 11 E
Alto Molocue, *Mozam.* **55 F4** 15 50S 37 35 E
Alto Paraguay □, *Paraguay* **94 A4** 21 0S 58 30W
Alto Paraná □, *Paraguay* **95 B5** 25 30S 54 50W
Alton, *Canada* **78 C4** 43 54N 80 5W
Alton, *U.K.* **11 F7** 51 9N 0 59W
Alton, *U.S.A.* **80 F9** 38 53N 90 11W
Alton Downs, *Australia* **63 D2** 26 7S 138 57 E
Altoona, *U.S.A.* **78 F6** 40 31N 78 24W
Altūn Kūprī, *Iraq* **44 C5** 35 45N 44 9 E
Altun Shan, *China* **32 C3** 38 30N 88 0 E
Alturas, *U.S.A.* **82 F3** 41 29N 120 32W
Altus, *U.S.A.* **81 H5** 34 38N 99 20W
Alūksne, *Latvia* **9 H22** 57 24N 27 3 E
Alunite, *U.S.A.* **85 K12** 35 59N 114 55W
Alusi, *Indonesia* **37 F8** 7 35S 131 40 E
Alva, *U.S.A.* **81 G5** 36 48N 98 40W
Alvarado, *Mexico* **87 D5** 18 40N 95 50W
Alvarado, *U.S.A.* **81 J6** 32 24N 97 13W
Alvaro Obregón, Presa, *Mexico* **86 B3** 27 55N 109 52W
Alvear, *Argentina* **94 B4** 29 5S 56 30W
Alvesta, *Sweden* **9 H16** 56 54N 14 35 E
Alvie, *Australia* **63 F3** 38 14S 143 30 E
Alvin, *U.S.A.* **81 L7** 29 26N 95 15W
Alvinston, *Canada* **78 D3** 42 49N 81 52W
Älvkarleby, *Sweden* **9 F17** 60 34N 17 26 E
Älvsbyn, *Sweden* **8 D19** 65 40N 21 0 E
Alwar, *India* **42 F7** 27 38N 76 34 E
Alxa Zuoqi, *China* **34 E3** 38 50N 105 40 E
Alyata = Älät, *Azerbaijan* **25 G8** 39 58N 49 25 E
Alyth, *U.K.* **12 E5** 56 38N 3 13W
Alytus, *Lithuania* **9 J21** 54 24N 24 3 E
Alzada, *U.S.A.* **80 C2** 45 2N 104 25W
Alzira, *Spain* **19 C5** 39 9N 0 30W
Am-Timan, *Chad* **51 F10** 11 0N 20 10 E
Amadeus, L., *Australia* **61 D5** 24 54S 131 0 E
Amadi, *Dem. Rep. of the Congo* **54 B2** 3 40N 26 40 E
Amâdi, *Sudan* **51 G12** 5 29N 30 25 E
Amadjuak L., *Canada* **69 B12** 65 0N 71 8W
Amagasaki, *Japan* **31 G7** 34 42N 135 20 E
Amakusa-Shotō, *Japan* **31 H5** 32 15N 130 10 E
Åmål, *Sweden* **9 G15** 59 3N 12 42 E
Amaliás, *Greece* **21 F9** 37 47N 21 22 E
Amalner, *India* **40 J9** 21 5N 75 5 E
Amambaí, *Brazil* **95 A4** 23 5S 55 13W
Amambaí —▸, *Brazil* **95 A5** 23 22S 53 56W
Amambay □, *Paraguay* **95 A4** 23 0S 56 0W
Amambay, Cordillera de, *S. Amer.* **95 A4** 23 0S 55 45W
Amami-Guntō, *Japan* **31 L4** 27 16N 129 21 E
Amami-Ō-Shima, *Japan* **31 L4** 28 0N 129 0 E
Amaná, L., *Brazil* **92 D6** 2 35S 64 40W
Amanda Park, *U.S.A.* **84 C3** 47 28N 123 55W
Amangeldy, *Kazakstan* **26 D7** 50 10N 65 10 E
Amapá, *Brazil* **93 C8** 2 5N 50 50W
Amapá □, *Brazil* **93 C8** 1 40N 52 0W
Amarante, *Brazil* **93 E10** 6 14S 42 50W
Amaranth, *Canada* **73 C9** 50 36N 98 43W
Amargosa —▸, *U.S.A.* **85 J10** 36 14N 116 51W
Amargosa Range, *U.S.A.* **85 J10** 36 20N 116 45W

Amári

Amári, Greece 23 D6 35 13N 24 40 E
Amarillo, U.S.A. 81 H4 35 13N 101 50W
Amaro, Mte., Italy 20 C6 42 5N 14 5 E
Amarpur, India 43 G12 25 5N 87 0 E
Amatikulu, S. Africa 57 D5 29 3S 31 33 E
Amatitlán, Guatemala 88 D1 14 29N 90 38W
Amay, Belgium 15 D5 50 33N 5 19 E
Amazon = Amazonas →, S. Amer. 93 D9 0 5S 50 0W
Amazonas →, S. Amer. 93 D9 0 5S 50 0W
Ambahakily, Madag. 57 C7 21 36S 43 41 E
Ambala, India 42 D7 30 23N 76 56 E
Ambalavao, Madag. 57 C8 21 50S 46 56 E
Ambalindum, Australia 62 C2 23 23S 135 0 E
Ambanja, Madag. 57 A8 13 40S 48 27 E
Ambarchik, Russia 27 C17 69 40N 162 20 E
Ambarijeby, Madag. 57 A8 14 56S 47 41 E
Ambaro, Helodranon', Madag. 57 A8 13 23S 48 38 E
Ambato, Ecuador 92 D3 1 5S 78 42W
Ambato, Sierra de, Argentina 94 B2 28 25S 66 10W
Ambato Boeny, Madag. 57 B8 16 28S 46 43 E
Ambatofinandrahana, Madag. 57 C8 20 33S 46 48 E
Ambatolampy, Madag. 57 B8 19 20S 47 35 E
Ambatondrazaka, Madag. 57 B8 17 55S 48 28 E
Ambatosoratra, Madag. 57 B8 17 37S 48 31 E
Ambenja, Madag. 57 B8 15 17S 46 58 E
Amberg, Germany 16 D6 49 26N 11 52 E
Ambergris Cay, Belize 87 D7 18 0N 88 0W
Amberley, N.Z. 59 K4 43 9S 172 44 E
Ambikapur, India 43 H10 23 15N 83 15 E
Ambilobé, Madag. 57 A8 13 10S 49 3 E
Ambinanindrano, Madag. 57 C8 20 5S 48 23 E
Amble, U.K. 10 B6 55 20N 1 36W
Ambleside, U.K. 10 C5 54 26N 2 58W
Ambo, Peru 92 F3 10 5S 76 10W
Ambodifototra, Madag. 57 B8 16 59S 49 52 E
Ambodilazana, Madag. 57 B8 18 6S 49 10 E
Ambohimahasoa, Madag. 57 C8 21 7S 47 13 E
Ambohimanga, Madag. 57 C8 20 52S 47 36 E
Ambohitra, Madag. 57 A8 12 30S 49 10 E
Amboise, France 18 C4 47 24N 1 2 E
Amboseli, L., Kenya 54 C4 2 40S 37 10 E
Ambositra, Madag. 57 C8 20 31S 47 25 E
Ambovombé, Madag. 57 D8 25 11S 46 5 E
Amboy, U.S.A. 85 L11 34 33N 115 45W
Amboyna Cay, S. China Sea 36 C4 7 50N 112 50 E
Ambridge, U.S.A. 78 F4 40 36N 80 14W
Ambriz, Angola 52 F2 7 48S 13 8 E
Amby, Australia 63 D4 26 30S 148 11 E
Amchitka I., U.S.A. 68 C1 51 32N 179 0 E
Amderma, Russia 26 C7 69 45N 61 30 E
Ameca, Mexico 86 C4 20 30N 104 0W
Ameca →, Mexico 86 C3 20 40N 105 15W
Amecameca, Mexico 87 D5 19 7N 98 46W
Ameland, Neths. 15 A5 53 27N 5 45 E
American Falls, U.S.A. 82 E7 42 47N 112 51W
American Falls Reservoir, U.S.A. 82 E7 42 47N 112 52W
American Highland, Antarctica 5 D6 73 0S 75 0 E
American Samoa ■, Pac. Oc. 59 B13 14 20S 170 40W
Americana, Brazil 95 A6 22 45S 47 20W
Americus, U.S.A. 77 K3 32 4N 84 14W
Amersfoort, Neths. 15 B5 52 9N 5 23 E
Amersfoort, S. Africa 57 D4 26 59S 29 53 E
Amery, Australia 61 F2 31 9S 117 5 E
Amery, Canada 73 B10 56 34N 94 3W
Amery Ice Shelf, Antarctica 5 C6 69 30S 72 0 E
Ames, U.S.A. 80 E8 42 2N 93 37W
Amesbury, U.S.A. 79 D14 42 51N 70 56W
Amga, Russia 27 C14 60 50N 132 0 E
Amga →, Russia 27 C14 62 38N 134 32 E
Amgu, Russia 30 B8 45 45N 137 15 E
Amgun →, Russia 27 D14 52 56N 139 38 E
Amherst, Burma 41 L20 16 2N 97 20 E
Amherst, Canada 71 C7 45 48N 64 8W
Amherst, Mass., U.S.A. 79 D12 42 23N 72 31W
Amherst, N.Y., U.S.A. 78 D6 42 59N 78 48W
Amherst, Ohio, U.S.A. 78 E2 41 24N 82 14W
Amherst, Tex., U.S.A. 81 J3 34 1N 102 25W
Amherst I., Canada 79 B8 44 8N 76 43W
Amherstburg, Canada 70 D3 42 6N 83 6W
Amiata, Mte., Italy 20 C4 42 53N 11 37 E
Amiens, France 18 B5 49 54N 2 16 E
Amīrābād, Iran 44 C5 33 20N 46 16 E
Amirante Is., Seychelles 28 K9 6 0S 53 0 E
Amisk L., Canada 73 C8 54 35N 102 15W
Amistad, Presa de la, Mexico 86 B4 29 24N 101 0W
Amite, U.S.A. 81 K9 30 44N 90 30W
Amlwch, U.K. 10 D3 53 24N 4 20W
'Ammān, Jordan 47 D4 31 57N 35 52 E
'Ammān □, Jordan 47 D5 31 40N 36 30 E
Ammanford, U.K. 11 F4 51 48N 3 59W
Amnat Charoen, Thailand 38 E5 15 51N 104 38 E
Āmol, Iran 45 B7 36 23N 52 20 E
Amory, U.S.A. 77 J1 33 59N 88 29W
Amos, Canada 70 C4 48 35N 78 5W
Åmot, Norway 9 G13 59 57N 9 54 E
Amoy = Xiamen, China 33 D6 24 25N 118 4 E
Ampang, Malaysia 39 L3 3 8N 101 45 E
Ampanihy, Madag. 57 C7 24 40S 44 45 E
Ampasindava, Helodranon', Madag. 57 A8 13 40S 48 15 E
Ampasindava, Saikanosy, Madag. 57 A8 13 42S 47 55 E
Ampenan, Indonesia 36 F5 8 35S 116 13 E
Amper →, Germany 16 D6 48 29N 11 55 E
Ampotaka, Madag. 57 D7 25 3S 44 41 E
Ampoza, Madag. 57 C7 22 20S 44 44 E
Amqui, Canada 71 C6 48 28N 67 27W
Amravati, India 40 J10 20 55N 77 45 E
Amreli, India 42 J4 21 35N 71 17 E
Amritsar, India 42 D6 31 35N 74 57 E
Amroha, India 43 E8 28 53N 78 30 E
Amsterdam, Neths. 15 B4 52 23N 4 54 E
Amsterdam, U.S.A. 79 D10 42 56N 74 11W
Amsterdam, I., Ind. Oc. 3 F13 38 30S 77 30 E
Amstetten, Austria 16 D8 48 7N 14 51 E
Amudarya →, Uzbekistan 26 E6 43 58N 59 34 E
Amundsen Gulf, Canada 68 A7 71 0N 124 0W
Amundsen Sea, Antarctica 5 D15 72 0S 115 0W
Amuntai, Indonesia 36 E5 2 28S 115 25 E
Amur →, Russia 27 D15 52 56N 141 10 E
Amurang, Indonesia 37 D6 1 5N 124 40 E
Amuri Pass, N.Z. 59 K4 42 31S 172 11 E
Amursk, Russia 27 D14 50 14N 136 54 E
Amyderya = Amudarya →, Uzbekistan 26 E6 43 58N 59 34 E
An Bien, Vietnam 39 H5 9 45N 105 0 E
An Hoa, Vietnam 38 E7 15 40N 108 5 E
An Nabatīyah at Tahta, Lebanon 47 B4 33 23N 35 27 E
An Nabk, Si. Arabia 44 D3 31 20N 37 20 E
An Nabk, Syria 47 A5 34 2N 36 44 E
An Nabk Abū Qaşr, Si. Arabia 44 D3 30 21N 38 34 E
An Nafūd, Si. Arabia 44 D4 28 15N 41 0 E
An Najaf, Iraq 44 C5 32 3N 44 15 E
An Nāşirīyah, Iraq 44 D5 31 0N 46 15 E
An Nhon, Vietnam 38 F7 13 55N 109 7 E
An Nu'ayrīyah, Si. Arabia 45 E6 27 30N 48 30 E
An Nuwayb'ī, W. →, Si. Arabia 47 F3 29 18N 34 57 E
An Thoi, Dao, Vietnam 39 H5 9 58N 104 0 E
An Uaimh, Ireland 13 C5 53 39N 6 41W
Anabar →, Russia 27 B12 73 8N 113 36 E
'Anabtā, West Bank 47 C4 32 19N 35 7 E
Anaconda, U.S.A. 82 C7 46 8N 112 57W
Anacortes, U.S.A. 84 B4 48 30N 122 37W
Anadarko, U.S.A. 81 H5 35 4N 98 15W
Anadolu, Turkey 25 G5 39 0N 30 0 E
Anadyr, Russia 27 C18 64 35N 177 20 E
Anadyr →, Russia 27 C18 64 55N 176 5 E
Anadyrskiy Zaliv, Russia 27 C19 64 0N 180 0 E
Anaga, Pta. de, Canary Is. 22 F3 28 34N 16 9W
'Ānah, Iraq 44 C4 34 25N 42 0 E
Anaheim, U.S.A. 85 M9 33 50N 117 55W
Anahim Lake, Canada 72 C3 52 28N 125 18W
Anáhuac, Mexico 86 B4 27 14N 100 9W
Anakapalle, India 41 L13 17 42N 83 6 E
Anakie, Australia 62 C4 23 32S 147 45 E
Analalava, Madag. 57 A8 14 35S 48 0 E
Análipsis, Greece 23 A3 39 36N 19 55 E
Anambar →, Pakistan 42 D3 30 15N 68 50 E
Anambas, Kepulauan, Indonesia 39 L6 3 20N 106 30 E
Anambas Is. = Anambas, Kepulauan, Indonesia 39 L6 3 20N 106 30 E
Anamoose, U.S.A. 80 B4 47 53N 100 15W
Anamosa, U.S.A. 80 D9 42 7N 91 17W
Anamur, Turkey 25 G5 36 8N 32 58 E
Anan, Japan 31 H7 33 54N 134 40 E
Anand, India 42 H5 22 32N 72 59 E
Anantnag, India 43 C6 33 45N 75 10 E
Ananyiv, Ukraine 17 E15 47 44N 29 58 E
Anapodháris →, Greece 23 E7 34 59N 25 20 E
Anápolis, Brazil 93 G9 16 15S 48 50W
Anapu →, Brazil 93 D8 1 53S 50 53W
Anār, Iran 45 D7 30 55N 55 13 E
Anārak, Iran 45 C7 33 25N 53 40 E
Anatolia = Anadolu, Turkey 25 G5 39 0N 30 0 E
Anatone, U.S.A. 82 C5 46 8N 117 8W
Anatsogno, Madag. 57 C7 23 33S 43 46 E
Añatuya, Argentina 94 B3 28 20S 62 50W
Anaunethad L., Canada 73 A8 60 55N 104 25W
Anbyŏn, N. Korea 35 E14 39 1N 127 35 E
Anchor Bay, U.S.A. 84 G3 38 48N 123 34W
Anchorage, U.S.A. 68 B5 61 13N 149 54W
Anci, China 34 E9 39 20N 116 40 E
Ancohuma, Nevada, Bolivia 92 G5 16 0S 68 50W
Ancón, Peru 92 F3 11 50S 77 10W
Ancona, Italy 20 C5 43 38N 13 30 E
Ancud, Chile 96 E2 42 0S 73 50W
Ancud, G. de, Chile 96 E2 42 0S 73 0W
Anda, China 33 B7 46 24N 125 19 E
Andacollo, Argentina 94 D1 37 10S 70 42W
Andacollo, Chile 94 C1 30 5S 71 10W
Andado, Australia 62 D2 25 25S 135 15 E
Andalgalá, Argentina 94 B2 27 40S 66 30W
Åndalsnes, Norway 9 E12 62 35N 7 43 E
Andalucía □, Spain 19 D3 37 35N 5 0W
Andalusia, U.S.A. 77 K2 31 18N 86 29W
Andalusia □ = Andalucía □, Spain 19 D3 37 35N 5 0W
Andaman Is., Ind. Oc. 28 H13 12 30N 92 30 E
Andaman Sea, Ind. Oc. 36 B1 13 0N 96 0 E
Andara, Namibia 56 B3 18 2S 21 9 E
Andenes, Norway 8 B17 69 19N 16 18 E
Andenne, Belgium 15 D5 50 28N 5 5 E
Anderson, Calif., U.S.A. 82 F2 40 27N 122 18W
Anderson, Ind., U.S.A. 76 E3 40 10N 85 41W
Anderson, Mo., U.S.A. 81 G7 36 39N 94 27W
Anderson, S.C., U.S.A. 77 H4 34 31N 82 39W
Anderson →, Canada 68 B7 69 42N 129 0W
Andes, Cord. de los, S. Amer. 92 H5 20 0S 68 0W
Andfjorden, Norway 8 B17 69 10N 16 20 E
Andhra Pradesh □, India 40 L11 18 0N 79 0 E
Andijon, Uzbekistan 26 E8 41 10N 72 15 E
Andikíthira, Greece 21 G10 35 52N 23 15 E
Andīmeshk, Iran 45 C6 32 27N 48 21 E
Andizhan = Andijon, Uzbekistan 26 E8 41 10N 72 15 E
Andoany, Madag. 57 A8 13 25S 48 16 E
Andong, S. Korea 35 F15 36 40N 128 43 E
Andongwei, China 35 G10 35 6N 119 20 E
Andorra ■, Europe 18 E4 42 30N 1 30 E
Andorra La Vella, Andorra 18 E4 42 31N 1 32 E
Andover, U.K. 11 F6 51 12N 1 29W
Andover, Mass., U.S.A. 79 D13 42 40N 71 8W
Andover, N.Y., U.S.A. 78 D7 42 10N 77 48W
Andover, Ohio, U.S.A. 78 E4 41 36N 80 34W
Andøya, Norway 8 B16 69 10N 15 50 E
Andradina, Brazil 93 H8 20 54S 51 23W
Andrahary, Mt., Madag. 57 A8 13 37S 49 17 E
Andramasina, Madag. 57 B8 19 11S 47 35 E
Andranopasy, Madag. 57 C7 21 17S 43 44 E
Andratx, Spain 22 B9 39 39N 2 25 E
Andreanof Is., U.S.A. 68 C2 51 30N 176 0W
Andrewilla, Australia 63 D2 26 31S 139 17 E
Andrews, S.C., U.S.A. 77 J6 33 27N 79 34W
Andrews, Tex., U.S.A. 81 J3 32 19N 102 33W
Ándria, Italy 20 D7 41 13N 16 17 E
Andriba, Madag. 57 B8 17 30S 46 58 E
Androka, Madag. 57 C7 24 58S 44 2 E
Andropov = Rybinsk, Russia 24 C6 58 5N 38 50 E
Andros I., Bahamas 88 B4 24 30N 78 0W
Andros Town, Bahamas 88 B4 24 43N 77 47W
Andselv, Norway 8 B18 69 4N 18 34 E
Andújar, Spain 19 C3 38 3N 4 5W
Andulo, Angola 52 G3 11 25S 16 45 E
Anegada I., Virgin Is. 89 C7 18 45N 64 20W
Anegada Passage, W. Indies 89 C7 18 15N 63 45W
Aneto, Pico de, Spain 19 A6 42 37N 0 40 E
Ang Thong, Thailand 38 E3 14 35N 100 31 E
Angamos, Punta, Chile 94 A1 23 1S 70 32W
Angara →, Russia 27 D10 58 5N 94 20 E
Angarsk, Russia 27 D11 52 30N 104 0 E
Angas Downs, Australia 61 E5 25 2S 132 14 E
Angas Hills, Australia 60 D4 23 0S 127 50 E
Angaston, Australia 63 E2 34 30S 139 8 E
Ånge, Sweden 9 E16 62 31N 15 35 E
Ángel, Salto = Angel Falls, Venezuela 92 B6 5 57N 62 30W
Ángel de la Guarda, I., Mexico 86 B2 29 30N 113 30W
Angel Falls, Venezuela 92 B6 5 57N 62 30W
Angeles, Phil. 37 A6 15 9N 120 33 E
Ängelholm, Sweden 9 H15 56 15N 12 58 E
Angellala, Australia 63 D4 26 24S 146 54 E
Angels Camp, U.S.A. 84 G6 38 4N 120 32W
Ångermanälven →, Sweden 8 E17 62 40N 18 0 E
Ångermanland, Sweden 8 E18 63 36N 17 45 E
Angers, Canada 79 A9 45 31N 75 29W
Angers, France 18 C3 47 30N 0 35W
Ängesån →, Sweden 8 C20 66 16N 22 47 E
Angikuni L., Canada 73 A9 62 0N 100 0W
Angkor, Cambodia 38 F4 13 22N 103 50 E
Anglesey, U.K. 10 D3 53 17N 4 20W
Anglesey, Isle of □, U.K. 10 D3 53 16N 4 18W
Angleton, U.S.A. 81 L7 29 10N 95 26W
Anglisidhes, Cyprus 23 E12 34 51N 33 27 E
Ango, Dem. Rep. of the Congo 54 B2 4 10N 26 5 E
Angoche, Mozam. 55 F4 16 8S 39 55 E
Angoche, I., Mozam. 55 F4 16 20S 39 50 E
Angol, Chile 94 D1 37 56S 72 45W
Angola, Ind., U.S.A. 76 E3 41 38N 85 0W
Angola, N.Y., U.S.A. 78 D5 42 38N 79 2W
Angola ■, Africa 53 G3 12 0S 18 0 E
Angoon, U.S.A. 72 B2 57 30N 134 35W
Angoulême, France 18 D4 45 39N 0 10 E
Angoumois, France 18 D3 45 50N 0 25 E
Angra dos Reis, Brazil 95 A7 23 0S 44 10W
Angren, Uzbekistan 26 E8 41 1N 70 12 E
Angtassom, Cambodia 39 G5 11 1N 104 41 E
Angu, Dem. Rep. of the Congo 54 B1 3 25N 24 28 E
Anguang, China 35 B12 45 15N 123 45 E
Anguilla ■, W. Indies 89 C7 18 14N 63 5W
Anguo, China 34 E8 38 28N 115 15 E
Angurugu, Australia 62 A2 14 0S 136 25 E
Angus □, U.K. 12 E6 56 46N 2 56W
Anhanduí →, Brazil 95 A5 21 46S 52 9W
Anholt, Denmark 9 H14 56 42N 11 33 E
Anhui □, China 33 C6 32 0N 117 0 E
Anhwei □ = Anhui □, China 33 C6 32 0N 117 0 E
Anichab, Namibia 56 C1 21 0S 14 46 E
Animas, U.S.A. 83 L9 31 57N 108 48W
Anivorano, Madag. 57 B8 18 44S 48 58 E
Anjalankoski, Finland 9 F22 60 45N 26 51 E
Anjar, India 42 H4 23 6N 70 10 E
Anjidiv I., India 40 M9 14 40N 74 10 E
Anjou, France 18 C3 47 20N 0 15W
Anjozorobe, Madag. 57 B8 18 22S 47 52 E
Anju, N. Korea 35 E13 39 36N 125 40 E
Ankaboa, Tanjona, Madag. 57 C7 21 58S 43 20 E
Ankang, China 34 H5 32 40N 109 1 E
Ankara, Turkey 25 G5 39 57N 32 54 E
Ankaramena, Madag. 57 C8 21 57S 46 39 E
Ankazoabo, Madag. 57 C7 22 18S 44 31 E
Ankazobe, Madag. 57 B8 18 20S 47 10 E
Ankisabe, Madag. 57 B8 19 17S 46 29 E
Ankoro, Dem. Rep. of the Congo 54 D2 6 45S 26 55 E
Anmyŏn-do, S. Korea 35 F14 36 25N 126 25 E
Ann, C., U.S.A. 79 D14 42 38N 70 35W
Ann Arbor, U.S.A. 76 D4 42 17N 83 45W
Anna, U.S.A. 81 G10 37 28N 89 15W
Anna Plains, Australia 60 C3 19 17S 121 37 E
Annaba, Algeria 50 A7 36 50N 7 46 E
Annalee →, Ireland 13 B4 54 2N 7 24W
Annam, Vietnam 38 E7 16 0N 108 0 E
Annamitique, Chaîne, Asia 38 D6 17 0N 106 0 E
Annan, U.K. 12 G5 54 59N 3 16W
Annan →, U.K. 12 G5 54 58N 3 16W
Annapolis, U.S.A. 76 F7 38 59N 76 30W
Annapolis Royal, Canada 71 D6 44 44N 65 32W
Annapurna, Nepal 43 E10 28 34N 83 50 E
Annean, L., Australia 61 E2 26 54S 118 14 E
Annecy, France 18 D7 45 55N 6 8 E
Anning, China 32 D5 24 55N 102 26 E
Anningie, Australia 60 D5 21 50S 133 7 E
Anniston, U.S.A. 77 J3 33 39N 85 50W
Annobón, Atl. Oc. 49 G4 1 25S 5 36 E
Annotto Bay, Jamaica 88 C4 18 17N 76 45W
Annuello, Australia 63 E3 34 53S 142 55 E
Annville, U.S.A. 79 F8 40 20N 76 31W
Áno Viánnos, Greece 23 D7 35 2N 25 21 E
Anoka, U.S.A. 75 A8 45 12N 93 23W
Anorotsangana, Madag. 57 A8 13 56S 47 55 E
Anóyia, Greece 23 D6 35 16N 24 52 E
Anping, Hebei, China 34 E8 38 15N 115 30 E
Anping, Liaoning, China 35 D12 41 5N 123 30 E
Anqing, China 33 C6 30 30N 117 3 E
Anqiu, China 35 F10 36 25N 119 10 E
Ansai, China 34 F5 36 50N 109 20 E
Ansbach, Germany 16 D6 49 28N 10 34 E
Anshan, China 35 D12 41 5N 122 58 E
Anshun, China 32 D5 26 18N 105 57 E
Ansley, U.S.A. 80 E5 41 18N 99 23W
Anson, U.S.A. 81 J5 32 45N 99 54W
Anson B., Australia 60 B5 13 20S 130 6 E
Ansongo, Mali 50 E6 15 25N 0 35 E
Ansonia, U.S.A. 79 E11 41 21N 73 5W
Anstruther, U.K. 12 E6 56 14N 2 41W
Ansudu, Indonesia 37 E9 2 11S 139 22 E
Antabamba, Peru 92 F4 14 40S 73 0W
Antakya, Turkey 25 G6 36 14N 36 10 E
Antalaha, Madag. 57 A9 14 57S 50 20 E
Antalya, Turkey 25 G5 36 52N 30 45 E
Antalya Körfezi, Turkey 25 G5 36 15N 31 30 E
Antananarivo, Madag. 57 B8 18 55S 47 31 E
Antananarivo □, Madag. 57 B8 19 0S 47 0 E
Antanimbaribe, Madag. 57 C7 21 30S 44 48 E
Antarctic Pen., Antarctica 5 C18 67 0S 60 0W
Antarctica 5 E3 90 0S 0 0 E
Antelope, Zimbabwe 55 G2 21 2S 28 31 E
Antequera, Paraguay 94 A4 24 8S 57 7W
Antequera, Spain 19 D3 37 5N 4 33W
Antero, Mt., U.S.A. 83 G10 38 41N 106 15W
Anthony, Kans., U.S.A. 81 G5 37 9N 98 2W
Anthony, N. Mex., U.S.A. 83 K10 32 0N 106 36W
Anthony Lagoon, Australia 62 B2 18 0S 135 30 E
Anti Atlas, Morocco 50 C4 30 0N 8 30W
Anti-Lebanon = Ash Sharqi, Al Jabal, Lebanon 47 B5 33 40N 36 10 E
Antibes, France 18 E7 43 34N 7 6 E
Anticosti, Î. d', Canada 71 C7 49 30N 63 0W
Antigo, U.S.A. 80 C10 45 9N 89 9W
Antigonish, Canada 71 C7 45 38N 61 58W
Antigua, Canary Is. 22 F5 28 24N 14 1W
Antigua, W. Indies 89 C7 17 0N 61 50W
Antigua & Barbuda ■, W. Indies 89 C7 17 20N 61 48W
Antigua Guatemala, Guatemala 88 D1 14 34N 90 41W
Antilla, Cuba 88 B4 20 40N 75 50W
Antimony, U.S.A. 83 G8 38 7N 112 0W
Antioch, U.S.A. 84 G5 38 1N 121 48W
Antioquia, Colombia 92 B3 6 40N 75 55W
Antipodes Is., Pac. Oc. 64 M9 49 45S 178 40 E
Antler, U.S.A. 80 A4 48 59N 101 17W
Antler →, Canada 73 D8 49 8N 101 0W
Antlers, U.S.A. 81 H7 34 14N 95 37W
Antofagasta, Chile 94 A1 23 50S 70 30W
Antofagasta □, Chile 94 A2 24 0S 69 0W
Antofagasta de la Sierra, Argentina 94 B2 26 5S 67 20W
Antofalla, Argentina 94 B2 25 30S 68 5W
Antofalla, Salar de, Argentina 94 B2 25 40S 67 45W
Anton, U.S.A. 81 J3 33 49N 102 10W
Anton Chico, U.S.A. 83 J11 35 12N 105 9W
Antongila, Helodrano, Madag. 57 B8 15 30S 49 50 E
Antonibé, Madag. 57 B8 15 7S 47 24 E
Antonibé, Presqu'île d', Madag. 57 A8 14 55S 47 20 E
Antonina, Brazil 95 B6 25 26S 48 42W
Antonito, U.S.A. 83 H10 37 5N 106 0W
Antrim, U.K. 13 B5 54 43N 6 14W
Antrim □, U.K. 13 B5 54 56N 6 25W
Antrim, Mts. of, U.K. 13 A5 55 3N 6 14W
Antrim Plateau, Australia 60 C4 18 8S 128 20 E
Antsalova, Madag. 57 B7 18 40S 44 37 E
Antsirabe, Madag. 57 B8 19 55S 47 2 E
Antsiranana, Madag. 57 A8 12 25S 49 20 E
Antsohihy, Madag. 57 A8 14 50S 47 59 E
Antsohimbondrona Seranana, Madag. 57 A8 13 7S 48 48 E
Antu, China 35 C15 42 30N 128 20 E
Antwerp = Antwerpen, Belgium 15 C4 51 13N 4 25 E
Antwerp, U.S.A. 79 B9 44 12N 75 37W
Antwerpen, Belgium 15 C4 51 13N 4 25 E
Antwerpen □, Belgium 15 C4 51 15N 4 40 E
Anupgarh, India 42 E5 29 10N 73 10 E
Anuradhapura, Sri Lanka 40 Q12 8 22N 80 28 E
Anveh, Iran 45 E7 27 23N 54 11 E
Anvers = Antwerpen, Belgium 15 C4 51 13N 4 25 E
Anvers I., Antarctica 5 C17 64 30S 63 40W
Anxi, China 32 B4 40 30N 95 43 E
Anxious B., Australia 63 E1 33 24S 134 45 E
Anyang, China 34 F8 36 5N 114 21 E
Anyi, China 34 G6 35 2N 111 2 E
Anza, U.S.A. 85 M10 33 35N 116 39W
Anze, China 34 F7 36 10N 112 12 E
Anzhero-Sudzhensk, Russia 26 D9 56 10N 86 0 E
Ánzio, Italy 20 D5 41 27N 12 37 E
Aoga-Shima, Japan 31 H9 32 28N 139 46 E
Aomori, Japan 30 D10 40 45N 140 45 E
Aomori □, Japan 30 D10 40 45N 140 45 E
Aonla, India 43 E8 28 16N 79 11 E
Aosta, Italy 18 D7 45 45N 7 20 E
Apa →, S. Amer. 94 A4 22 6S 58 2W
Apache, U.S.A. 81 H5 34 54N 98 22W
Apalachee B., U.S.A. 77 L4 30 0N 84 0W
Apalachicola, U.S.A. 77 L3 29 43N 84 59W
Apalachicola →, U.S.A. 77 L3 29 43N 84 58W
Apaporis →, Colombia 92 D5 1 23S 69 25W
Aparri, Phil. 37 A6 18 22N 121 38 E
Apatity, Russia 24 A5 67 34N 33 22 E
Apatzingán, Mexico 86 D4 19 0N 102 20W
Apeldoorn, Neths. 15 B5 52 13N 5 57 E
Apennines = Appennini, Italy 20 B4 44 0N 10 0 E
Apia, W. Samoa 59 A13 13 50S 171 50W
Apiacás, Serra dos, Brazil 92 E7 9 50S 57 0W
Apizaco, Mexico 87 D5 19 26N 98 9W
Aplao, Peru 92 G4 16 0S 72 40W
Apo, Mt., Phil. 37 C7 6 53N 125 14 E
Apolakkiá, Greece 23 C9 36 5N 27 48 E
Apolakkiá, Órmos, Greece 23 C9 36 5N 27 45 E

Astara

Apolo, *Bolivia* **92 F5** 14 30S 68 30W
Aporé →, *Brazil* **93 G8** 19 27S 50 57W
Apostle Is., *U.S.A.* **80 B9** 47 0N 90 40W
Apóstoles, *Argentina* **95 B4** 28 0S 56 0W
Apostolos Andreas, C., *Cyprus* **23 D13** 35 42N 34 35 E
Apoteri, *Guyana* **92 C7** 4 2N 58 32W
Appalachian Mts., *U.S.A.* **76 G6** 38 0N 80 0W
Appennini, *Italy* **20 B4** 44 0N 10 0 E
Apple Hill, *Canada* **79 A10** 45 13N 74 46W
Apple Valley, *U.S.A.* **85 L9** 34 32N 117 14W
Appleby-in-Westmorland, *U.K.* **10 C5** 54 35N 2 29W
Appleton, *U.S.A.* **76 C1** 44 16N 88 25W
Approuague →, *Fr. Guiana* **93 C8** 4 30N 51 57W
Aprília, *Italy* **20 D5** 41 36N 12 39 E
Apucarana, *Brazil* **95 A5** 23 55S 51 33W
Apure →, *Venezuela* **92 B5** 7 37N 66 25W
Apurimac →, *Peru* **92 F4** 12 17S 73 56W
Aqaba = Al 'Aqabah, *Jordan* **47 F4** 29 31N 35 0 E
Aqaba, G. of, *Red Sea* **44 D2** 28 15N 33 20 E
'Aqabah, Khalīj al = Aqaba, G. of, *Red Sea* **44 D2** 28 15N 33 20 E
'Aqdā, *Iran* **45 C7** 32 26N 53 37 E
Aqmola, *Kazakstan* **26 D8** 51 10N 71 30 E
Aqrah, *Iraq* **44 B4** 36 46N 43 45 E
Aqtöbe, *Kazakstan* **25 D10** 50 17N 57 10 E
Aquidauana, *Brazil* **93 H7** 20 30S 55 50W
Aquiles Serdán, *Mexico* **86 B3** 28 37N 105 54W
Aquin, *Haiti* **89 C5** 18 16N 73 24W
Aquitain, Bassin, *France* **18 D3** 44 0N 0 30W
Ar Rachidiya, *Morocco* **50 B5** 31 58N 4 20W
Ar Rafid, *Syria* **47 C4** 32 57N 35 52 E
Ar Raḩḩālīyah, *Iraq* **44 C4** 32 44N 43 23 E
Ar Ramādī, *Iraq* **44 C4** 33 25N 43 20 E
Ar Ramthā, *Jordan* **47 C5** 32 34N 36 0 E
Ar Raqqah, *Syria* **44 C3** 35 59N 39 8 E
Ar Rass, *Si. Arabia* **44 E4** 25 50N 43 40 E
Ar Rifā'ī, *Iraq* **44 D5** 31 50N 46 10 E
Ar Riyāḑ, *Si. Arabia* **46 C4** 24 41N 46 42 E
Ar Ru'ays, *Qatar* **45 E6** 26 8N 51 12 E
Ar Rukhaymīyah, *Iraq* **44 D5** 29 22N 45 38 E
Ar Ruqayyidah, *Si. Arabia* **45 E6** 25 21N 49 34 E
Ar Ruşāfah, *Syria* **44 C3** 35 45N 38 49 E
Ar Ruţbah, *Iraq* **44 C4** 33 0N 40 15 E
Ara, *India* **43 G11** 25 35N 84 32 E
'Arab, Bahr el →, *Sudan* **51 G11** 9 0N 29 30 E
'Arabābād, *Iran* **45 C8** 33 2N 57 41 E
Arabia, *Asia* **28 G8** 25 0N 45 0 E
Arabian Desert = Es Sahrâ' Esh Sharqîya, *Egypt* **51 C12** 27 30N 32 30 E
Arabian Gulf = Gulf, The, *Asia* **45 E6** 27 0N 50 0 E
Arabian Sea, *Ind. Oc.* **29 H10** 16 0N 65 0 E
Aracaju, *Brazil* **93 F11** 10 55S 37 4W
Aracati, *Brazil* **93 D11** 4 30S 37 44W
Araçatuba, *Brazil* **95 A5** 21 10S 50 30W
Aracena, *Spain* **19 D2** 37 53N 6 38W
Araçuaí, *Brazil* **93 G10** 16 52S 42 4W
'Arad, *Israel* **47 D4** 31 15N 35 12 E
Arad, *Romania* **17 E11** 46 10N 21 20 E
Aradhippou, *Cyprus* **23 E12** 34 57N 33 36 E
Arafura Sea, *E. Indies* **37 F9** 9 0S 135 0 E
Aragón □, *Spain* **19 B5** 41 25N 0 40W
Aragón →, *Spain* **19 A5** 42 13N 1 44W
Araguacema, *Brazil* **93 E9** 8 50S 49 20W
Araguaia →, *Brazil* **93 E9** 5 21S 48 41W
Araguaína, *Brazil* **93 E9** 7 12S 48 12W
Araguari, *Brazil* **93 G9** 18 38S 48 11W
Araguari →, *Brazil* **93 C9** 1 15N 49 55W
Arak, *Algeria* **50 C6** 25 20N 3 45 E
Arāk, *Iran* **45 C6** 34 0N 49 40 E
Arakan Coast, *Burma* **41 K19** 19 0N 94 0 E
Arakan Yoma, *Burma* **41 K19** 20 0N 94 40 E
Araks = Aras, Rūd-e →, *Azerbaijan* **44 B5** 40 5N 48 29 E
Aral, *Kazakstan* **26 E7** 46 41N 61 45 E
Aral Sea, *Asia* **26 E7** 44 30N 60 0 E
Aral Tengizi = Aral Sea, *Asia* **26 E7** 44 30N 60 0 E
Aralsk = Aral, *Kazakstan* **26 E7** 46 41N 61 45 E
Aralskoye More = Aral Sea, *Asia* **26 E7** 44 30N 60 0 E
Aramac, *Australia* **62 C4** 22 58S 145 14 E
Arambag, *India* **43 H12** 22 53N 87 48 E
Aran I., *Ireland* **13 A3** 55 0N 8 30W
Aran Is., *Ireland* **13 C2** 53 6N 9 38W
Aranda de Duero, *Spain* **19 B4** 41 39N 3 42W
Arandān, *Iran* **44 C5** 35 23N 46 55 E
Aranjuez, *Spain* **19 B4** 40 1N 3 40W
Aranos, *Namibia* **56 C2** 24 9S 19 7 E
Aransas Pass, *U.S.A.* **81 M6** 27 55N 97 9W
Aranyaprathet, *Thailand* **38 F4** 13 41N 102 30 E
Arapahoe, *U.S.A.* **80 E5** 40 18N 99 54W
Arapey Grande →, *Uruguay* **94 C4** 30 55S 57 49W
Arapiraca, *Brazil* **93 E11** 9 45S 36 39W
Arapongas, *Brazil* **95 A5** 23 29S 51 28W
Ar'ar, *Si. Arabia* **44 D4** 30 59N 41 2 E
Araranguá, *Brazil* **95 B6** 29 0S 49 30W
Araraquara, *Brazil* **93 H9** 21 50S 48 0W
Ararás, Serra das, *Brazil* **95 B5** 25 0S 53 10W
Ararat, *Australia* **63 F3** 37 16S 143 0 E
Ararat, Mt. = Ağrı Dağı, *Turkey* **25 G7** 39 50N 44 15 E
Araria, *India* **43 F12** 26 9N 87 33 E
Araripe, Chapada do, *Brazil* **93 E11** 7 20S 40 0W
Araruama, L. de, *Brazil* **95 A7** 22 53S 42 12W
Aras, Rūd-e →, *Azerbaijan* **44 B5** 40 5N 48 29 E
Arauca, *Colombia* **92 B4** 7 0N 70 40W
Arauca →, *Venezuela* **92 B5** 7 24N 66 35W
Arauco, *Chile* **94 D1** 37 16S 73 25W
Arauco □, *Chile* **94 D1** 37 40S 73 25W
Araxá, *Brazil* **93 G9** 19 35S 46 55W
Araya, Pen. de, *Venezuela* **92 A6** 10 40N 64 0W
Arbat, *Iraq* **44 C5** 35 25N 45 35 E
Árbatax, *Italy* **20 E3** 39 56N 9 42 E
Arbil, *Iraq* **44 B5** 36 15N 44 5 E
Arborfield, *Canada* **73 C8** 53 6N 103 39W
Arborg, *Canada* **73 C9** 50 54N 97 13W
Arbroath, *U.K.* **12 E6** 56 34N 2 35W
Arbuckle, *U.S.A.* **84 F4** 39 1N 122 3W
Arcachon, *France* **18 D3** 44 40N 1 10W
Arcade, *U.S.A.* **78 D6** 42 32N 78 25W
Arcadia, *Fla., U.S.A.* **77 M5** 27 13N 81 52W
Arcadia, *La., U.S.A.* **81 J8** 32 33N 92 55W
Arcadia, *Nebr., U.S.A.* **80 E5** 41 25N 99 8W
Arcadia, *Pa., U.S.A.* **78 F6** 40 47N 78 51W
Arcadia, *Wis., U.S.A.* **80 C9** 44 15N 91 30W
Arcata, *U.S.A.* **82 F1** 40 52N 124 5W
Archangel = Arkhangelsk, *Russia* **24 B7** 64 38N 40 36 E
Archbald, *U.S.A.* **79 E9** 41 30N 75 32W
Archer →, *Australia* **62 A3** 13 28S 141 41 E
Archer B., *Australia* **62 A3** 13 20S 141 30 E
Archers Post, *Kenya* **54 B4** 0 35N 37 35 E
Arckaringa, *Australia* **63 D1** 27 56S 134 45 E
Arckaringa Cr. →, *Australia* **63 D2** 28 10S 135 22 E
Arco, *U.S.A.* **82 E7** 43 38N 113 18W
Arcola, *Canada* **73 D8** 49 40N 102 30W
Arcos de la Frontera, *Spain* **19 D3** 36 45N 5 49W
Arcot, *India* **40 N11** 12 53N 79 20 E
Arctic Bay, *Canada* **69 A11** 73 1N 85 7W
Arda →, *Bulgaria* **21 D12** 41 40N 26 30 E
Ardabīl, *Iran* **45 B6** 38 15N 48 18 E
Ardakān = Sepīdān, *Iran* **45 D7** 30 20N 52 5 E
Ardee, *Ireland* **13 C5** 53 52N 6 33W
Arden, *Canada* **78 B8** 44 43N 76 56W
Arden, *Calif., U.S.A.* **84 G5** 38 36N 121 33W
Arden, *Nev., U.S.A.* **85 J11** 36 1N 115 14W
Ardenne, *Belgium* **16 D3** 49 50N 5 5 E
Ardennes = Ardenne, *Belgium* **16 D3** 49 50N 5 5 E
Arderin, *Ireland* **13 C4** 53 2N 7 39W
Ardestān, *Iran* **45 C7** 33 20N 52 25 E
Ardivachar Pt., *U.K.* **12 D1** 57 23N 7 26W
Ardlethan, *Australia* **63 E4** 34 22S 146 53 E
Ardmore, *Australia* **62 C2** 21 39S 139 11 E
Ardmore, *Okla., U.S.A.* **81 H6** 34 10N 97 8W
Ardmore, *Pa., U.S.A.* **79 G9** 39 58N 75 18W
Ardmore, *S. Dak., U.S.A.* **80 D3** 43 1N 103 40W
Ardnamurchan, Pt. of, *U.K.* **12 E2** 56 43N 6 14W
Ardnave Pt., *U.K.* **12 F2** 55 53N 6 20W
Ardrossan, *Australia* **63 E2** 34 26S 137 53 E
Ardrossan, *U.K.* **12 F4** 55 39N 4 49W
Ards Pen., *U.K.* **13 B6** 54 33N 5 34W
Arecibo, *Puerto Rico* **89 C6** 18 29N 66 43W
Areia Branca, *Brazil* **93 E11** 5 0S 37 0W
Arena, Pt., *U.S.A.* **84 G3** 38 57N 123 44W
Arendal, *Norway* **9 G13** 58 28N 8 46 E
Arequipa, *Peru* **92 G4** 16 20S 71 30W
Arévalo, *Spain* **19 B3** 41 3N 4 43W
Arezzo, *Italy* **20 C4** 43 25N 11 53 E
Arganda, *Spain* **19 B4** 40 19N 3 26W
Argentan, *France* **18 B3** 48 45N 0 1W
Argentário, Mte., *Italy* **20 C4** 42 24N 11 9 E
Argentia, *Canada* **71 C9** 47 18N 53 58W
Argentina ■, *S. Amer.* **96 D3** 35 0S 66 0W
Argentina Is., *Antarctica* **5 C17** 66 0S 64 0W
Argentino, L., *Argentina* **96 G2** 50 10S 73 0W
Argeş →, *Romania* **17 F14** 44 5N 26 38 E
Arghandab →, *Afghan.* **42 D1** 31 30N 64 15 E
Argolikós Kólpos, *Greece* **21 F10** 37 20N 22 52 E
Árgos, *Greece* **21 F10** 37 40N 22 43 E
Argostólion, *Greece* **21 E9** 38 12N 20 33 E
Arguello, Pt., *U.S.A.* **85 L6** 34 35N 120 39W
Arguineguín, *Canary Is.* **22 G4** 27 46N 15 41W
Argun →, *Russia* **27 D13** 53 20N 121 28 E
Argus Pk., *U.S.A.* **85 K9** 35 52N 117 26W
Argyle, *U.S.A.* **80 A6** 48 20N 96 49W
Argyle, L., *Australia* **60 C4** 16 20S 128 40 E
Argyll & Bute □, *U.K.* **12 E3** 56 13N 5 28W
Århus, *Denmark* **9 H14** 56 8N 10 11 E
Ariadnoye, *Russia* **30 B7** 45 8N 134 25 E
Ariamsvlei, *Namibia* **56 D2** 28 9S 19 51 E
Arica, *Chile* **92 G4** 18 32S 70 20W
Arica, *Colombia* **92 D4** 2 0S 71 50W
Arico, *Canary Is.* **22 F3** 28 9N 16 29W
Arid, C., *Australia* **61 F3** 34 1S 123 10 E
Arida, *Japan* **31 G7** 34 5N 135 8 E
Arilla, Ákra, *Greece* **23 A3** 39 43N 19 39 E
Arima, *Trin. & Tob.* **89 D7** 10 38N 61 17W
Arinos →, *Brazil* **92 F7** 10 25S 58 20W
Ario de Rosales, *Mexico* **86 D4** 19 12N 102 0W
Aripuanã, *Brazil* **92 E6** 9 25S 60 30W
Aripuanã →, *Brazil* **92 E6** 5 7S 60 25W
Ariquemes, *Brazil* **92 E6** 9 55S 63 6W
Arisaig, *U.K.* **12 E3** 56 55N 5 51W
Aristazabal I., *Canada* **72 C3** 52 40N 129 10W
Arivaca, *U.S.A.* **83 L8** 31 37N 111 25W
Arivonimamo, *Madag.* **57 B8** 19 1S 47 11 E
Arizaro, Salar de, *Argentina* **94 A2** 24 40S 67 50W
Arizona, *Argentina* **94 D2** 35 45S 65 25W
Arizona □, *U.S.A.* **83 J8** 34 0N 112 0W
Arizpe, *Mexico* **86 A2** 30 20N 110 11W
Arjeplog, *Sweden* **8 D18** 66 3N 18 2 E
Arjona, *Colombia* **92 A3** 10 14N 75 22W
Arjuna, *Indonesia* **37 G15** 7 49S 112 34 E
Arka, *Russia* **27 C15** 60 15N 142 0 E
Arkadelphia, *U.S.A.* **81 H8** 34 7N 93 4W
Arkaig, L., *U.K.* **12 E3** 56 59N 5 10W
Arkalyk = Arqalyk, *Kazakstan* **26 D7** 50 13N 66 50 E
Arkansas □, *U.S.A.* **81 H8** 35 0N 92 30W
Arkansas →, *U.S.A.* **81 J9** 33 47N 91 4W
Arkansas City, *U.S.A.* **81 G6** 37 4N 97 2W
Arkhángelos, *Greece* **23 C10** 36 13N 28 7 E
Arkhangelsk, *Russia* **24 B7** 64 38N 40 36 E
Arklow, *Ireland* **13 D5** 52 48N 6 10W
Arkticheskiy, Mys, *Russia* **27 A10** 81 10N 95 0 E
Arlanzón →, *Spain* **19 A3** 42 3N 4 17W
Arlbergpass, *Austria* **16 E6** 47 9N 10 12 E
Arlee, *U.S.A.* **82 C6** 47 10N 114 5W
Arles, *France* **18 E6** 43 41N 4 40 E
Arlington, *S. Africa* **57 D4** 28 1S 27 53 E
Arlington, *Oreg., U.S.A.* **82 D3** 45 43N 120 12W
Arlington, *S. Dak., U.S.A.* **80 C6** 44 22N 97 8W
Arlington, *Va., U.S.A.* **76 F7** 38 53N 77 7W
Arlington, *Wash., U.S.A.* **84 B4** 48 12N 122 8W
Arlington Heights, *U.S.A.* **76 D2** 42 5N 87 59W
Arlon, *Belgium* **15 E5** 49 42N 5 49 E
Armagh, *U.K.* **13 B5** 54 21N 6 39W
Armagh □, *U.K.* **13 B5** 54 18N 6 37W
Armavir, *Russia* **25 E7** 45 2N 41 7 E
Armenia, *Colombia* **92 C3** 4 35N 75 45W
Armenia ■, *Asia* **25 F7** 40 20N 45 0 E
Armenistís, Ákra, *Greece* **23 C9** 36 8N 27 42 E
Armidale, *Australia* **63 E5** 30 30S 151 40 E
Armour, *U.S.A.* **80 D5** 43 19N 98 21W
Armstrong, *B.C., Canada* **72 C5** 50 25N 119 10W
Armstrong, *Ont., Canada* **70 B2** 50 18N 89 4W
Armstrong, *U.S.A.* **81 M6** 26 56N 97 47W
Armstrong →, *Australia* **60 C5** 16 35S 131 40 E
Arnarfjörður, *Iceland* **8 D2** 65 48N 23 40W
Arnaud →, *Canada* **69 C13** 60 0N 70 0W
Arnauti, C., *Cyprus* **23 D11** 35 6N 32 17 E
Arnett, *U.S.A.* **81 G5** 36 8N 99 46W
Arnhem, *Neths.* **15 C5** 51 58N 5 55 E
Arnhem, C., *Australia* **62 A2** 12 20S 137 30 E
Arnhem B., *Australia* **62 A2** 12 20S 136 10 E
Arnhem Land, *Australia* **62 A1** 13 10S 134 30 E
Arno →, *Italy* **20 C4** 43 41N 10 17 E
Arno Bay, *Australia* **63 E2** 33 54S 136 34 E
Arnold, *U.K.* **10 D6** 53 1N 1 7W
Arnold, *Calif., U.S.A.* **84 G6** 38 15N 120 20W
Arnold, *Nebr., U.S.A.* **80 E4** 41 26N 100 12W
Arnot, *Canada* **73 B9** 55 56N 96 41W
Arnøy, *Norway* **8 A19** 70 9N 20 40 E
Arnprior, *Canada* **70 C4** 45 26N 76 21W
Arnsberg, *Germany* **16 C5** 51 24N 8 5 E
Aroab, *Namibia* **56 D2** 26 41S 19 39 E
Arqalyk, *Kazakstan* **26 D7** 50 13N 66 50 E
Arrabury, *Australia* **63 D3** 26 45S 141 0 E
Arrah = Ara, *India* **43 G11** 25 35N 84 32 E
Arran, *U.K.* **12 F3** 55 34N 5 12W
Arrandale, *Canada* **72 C3** 54 57N 130 0W
Arras, *France* **18 A5** 50 17N 2 46 E
Arrecife, *Canary Is.* **22 F6** 28 57N 13 37W
Arrecifes, *Argentina* **94 C3** 34 6S 60 9W
Arrée, Mts. d', *France* **18 B2** 48 26N 3 55W
Arriaga, *Chiapas, Mexico* **87 D6** 16 15N 93 52W
Arriaga, *San Luis Potosí, Mexico* **86 C4** 21 55N 101 23W
Arrilalah P.O., *Australia* **62 C3** 23 43S 143 54 E
Arrino, *Australia* **61 E2** 29 30S 115 40 E
Arrow, L., *Ireland* **13 B3** 54 3N 8 19W
Arrow Rock Res., *U.S.A.* **82 E6** 43 45N 115 50W
Arrowhead, *Canada* **72 C5** 50 40N 117 55W
Arrowhead, L., *U.S.A.* **85 L9** 34 16N 117 10W
Arrowtown, *N.Z.* **59 L2** 44 57S 168 50 E
Arroyo Grande, *U.S.A.* **85 K6** 35 7N 120 35W
Ars, *Iran* **44 B5** 37 9N 47 46 E
Arsenault L., *Canada* **73 B7** 55 6N 108 32W
Arsenev, *Russia* **30 B6** 44 10N 133 15 E
Árta, *Greece* **21 E9** 39 8N 21 2 E
Artà, *Spain* **22 B10** 39 41N 3 21 E
Arteaga, *Mexico* **86 D4** 18 50N 102 20W
Artem, *Russia* **30 C6** 43 22N 132 13 E
Artemovsk, *Russia* **27 D10** 54 45N 93 35 E
Artesia = Mosomane, *Botswana* **56 C4** 24 2S 26 19 E
Artesia, *U.S.A.* **81 J2** 32 51N 104 24W
Artesia Wells, *U.S.A.* **81 L5** 28 17N 99 17W
Artesian, *U.S.A.* **80 C6** 44 1N 97 55W
Arthur →, *Australia* **62 G3** 41 2S 144 40 E
Arthur Cr. →, *Australia* **62 C2** 22 30S 136 25 E
Arthur Pt., *Australia* **62 C5** 22 7S 150 3 E
Arthur's Pass, *N.Z.* **59 K3** 42 54S 171 35 E
Arthur's Town, *Bahamas* **89 B4** 24 38N 75 42W
Artigas, *Uruguay* **94 C4** 30 20S 56 30W
Artillery L., *Canada* **73 A7** 63 9N 107 52W
Artois, *France* **18 A5** 50 20N 2 30 E
Artsyz, *Ukraine* **17 E15** 46 4N 29 26 E
Artvin, *Turkey* **25 F7** 41 14N 41 44 E
Aru, Kepulauan, *Indonesia* **37 F8** 6 0S 134 30 E
Aru Is. = Aru, Kepulauan, *Indonesia* **37 F8** 6 0S 134 30 E
Aru Meru □, *Tanzania* **54 C4** 3 20S 36 50 E
Arua, *Uganda* **54 B3** 3 1N 30 58 E
Aruanã, *Brazil* **93 F8** 14 54S 51 10W
Aruba ■, *W. Indies* **89 D6** 12 30N 70 0W
Arucas, *Canary Is.* **22 F4** 28 7N 15 32W
Arumpo, *Australia* **63 E3** 33 48S 142 55 E
Arun →, *Nepal* **43 F12** 26 55N 87 10 E
Arun →, *U.K.* **11 G7** 50 49N 0 33W
Arunachal Pradesh □, *India* **41 F19** 28 0N 95 0 E
Arusha, *Tanzania* **54 C4** 3 20S 36 40 E
Arusha □, *Tanzania* **54 C4** 4 0S 36 30 E
Arusha Chini, *Tanzania* **54 C4** 3 32S 37 20 E
Aruwimi →, *Dem. Rep. of the Congo* **54 B1** 1 13N 23 36 E
Arvada, *U.S.A.* **82 D10** 44 39N 106 8W
Árvi, *Greece* **23 E7** 34 59N 25 28 E
Arvida, *Canada* **71 C5** 48 25N 71 14W
Arvidsjaur, *Sweden* **8 D18** 65 35N 19 10 E
Arvika, *Sweden* **9 G15** 59 40N 12 36 E
Arvin, *U.S.A.* **85 K8** 35 12N 118 50W
Arxan, *China* **33 B6** 47 11N 119 57 E
Aryirádhes, *Greece* **23 B3** 39 27N 19 58 E
Aryiroúpolis, *Greece* **23 D6** 35 17N 24 20 E
Arys, *Kazakstan* **26 E7** 42 26N 68 48 E
Arzamas, *Russia* **24 C7** 55 27N 43 55 E
Aş Şadr, *U.A.E.* **45 E7** 24 40N 54 41 E
Aş Şafā, *Syria* **47 B6** 33 10N 37 0 E
'As Saffānīyah, *Si. Arabia* **45 D6** 28 5N 48 50 E
As Safīrah, *Syria* **44 B3** 36 5N 37 21 E
Aş Şahm, *Oman* **45 E8** 24 10N 56 53 E
As Sājir, *Si. Arabia* **44 E5** 25 11N 44 36 E
As Salamīyah, *Syria* **44 C3** 35 1N 37 2 E
As Salt, *Jordan* **47 C4** 32 2N 35 43 E
As Sal'w'a, *Qatar* **45 E6** 24 23N 50 50 E
As Samāwah, *Iraq* **44 D5** 31 15N 45 15 E
As Sanamayn, *Syria* **47 B5** 33 3N 36 10 E
As Sohar = Şuḩār, *Oman* **45 E8** 24 20N 56 40 E
As Sukhnah, *Syria* **44 C3** 34 52N 38 52 E
As Sulaymānīyah, *Iraq* **44 C5** 35 35N 45 29 E
As Sulaymī, *Si. Arabia* **44 E4** 26 17N 41 21 E
As Summān, *Si. Arabia* **44 E5** 25 0N 47 0 E
As Suwaydā', *Syria* **47 C5** 32 40N 36 30 E
As Suwaydā' □, *Syria* **47 C5** 32 45N 36 45 E
As Şuwayrah, *Iraq* **44 C5** 32 55N 45 0 E
Asab, *Namibia* **56 D2** 25 30S 18 0 E
Asahi-Gawa →, *Japan* **31 G6** 34 36N 133 58 E
Asahigawa, *Japan* **30 C11** 43 46N 142 22 E
Asansol, *India* **43 H12** 23 40N 87 1 E
Asbesberge, *S. Africa* **56 D3** 29 0S 23 0 E
Asbestos, *Canada* **71 C5** 45 47N 71 58W
Asbury Park, *U.S.A.* **79 F10** 40 13N 74 1W
Ascensión, *Mexico* **86 A3** 31 6N 107 59W
Ascensión, B. de la, *Mexico* **87 D7** 19 50N 87 20W
Ascension I., *Atl. Oc.* **49 G2** 8 0S 14 15W
Aschaffenburg, *Germany* **16 D5** 49 58N 9 6 E
Aschersleben, *Germany* **16 C6** 51 45N 11 29 E
Ascoli Piceno, *Italy* **20 C5** 42 51N 13 34 E
Ascope, *Peru* **92 E3** 7 46S 79 8W
Ascotán, *Chile* **94 A2** 21 45S 68 17W
Aseb, *Eritrea* **46 E3** 13 0N 42 40 E
Asela, *Ethiopia* **46 F2** 8 0N 39 0 E
Asenovgrad, *Bulgaria* **21 C11** 42 1N 24 51 E
Asgata, *Cyprus* **23 E12** 34 46N 33 15 E
Ash Fork, *U.S.A.* **83 J7** 35 13N 112 29W
Ash Grove, *U.S.A.* **81 G8** 37 19N 93 35W
Ash Shām, Bādiyat, *Asia* **28 F7** 32 0N 40 0 E
Ash Shamāl □, *Lebanon* **47 A5** 34 25N 36 0 E
Ash Shāmīyah, *Iraq* **44 D5** 31 55N 44 35 E
Ash Shāriqah, *U.A.E.* **45 E7** 25 23N 55 26 E
Ash Sharmah, *Si. Arabia* **44 D2** 28 1N 35 16 E
Ash Sharqāt, *Iraq* **44 C4** 35 27N 43 16 E
Ash Sharqi, Al Jabal, *Lebanon* **47 B5** 33 40N 36 10 E
Ash Shaţrah, *Iraq* **44 D5** 31 30N 46 10 E
Ash Shawbak, *Jordan* **44 D2** 30 32N 35 34 E
Ash Shawmari, J., *Jordan* **47 E5** 30 35N 36 35 E
Ash Shaykh, J., *Lebanon* **47 B4** 33 25N 35 50 E
Ash Shināfīyah, *Iraq* **44 D5** 31 35N 44 39 E
Ash Shu'aybah, *Si. Arabia* **44 E5** 27 53N 44 43 E
Ash Shumlūl, *Si. Arabia* **44 E5** 26 31N 47 20 E
Ash Shūr'a, *Iraq* **44 C4** 35 58N 43 13 E
Ash Shurayf, *Si. Arabia* **44 E3** 25 43N 39 14 E
Ash Shuwayfāt, *Lebanon* **47 B4** 33 45N 35 30 E
Asha, *Russia* **24 D10** 55 0N 57 16 E
Ashau, *Vietnam* **38 D6** 16 6N 107 22 E
Ashbourne, *U.K.* **10 D6** 53 2N 1 43W
Ashburn, *U.S.A.* **77 K4** 31 43N 83 39W
Ashburton, *N.Z.* **59 K3** 43 53S 171 48 E
Ashburton →, *Australia* **60 D1** 21 40S 114 56 E
Ashburton Downs, *Australia* **60 D2** 23 25S 117 4 E
Ashcroft, *Canada* **72 C4** 50 40N 121 20W
Ashdod, *Israel* **47 D3** 31 49N 34 35 E
Asheboro, *U.S.A.* **77 H6** 35 43N 79 49W
Asherton, *U.S.A.* **81 L5** 28 27N 99 46W
Asheville, *U.S.A.* **77 H4** 35 36N 82 33W
Asheweig →, *Canada* **70 B2** 54 17N 87 12W
Ashford, *Australia* **63 D5** 29 15S 151 3 E
Ashford, *U.K.* **11 F8** 51 8N 0 53 E
Ashford, *U.S.A.* **82 C2** 46 46N 122 2W
Ashgabat, *Turkmenistan* **26 F6** 38 0N 57 50 E
Ashibetsu, *Japan* **30 C11** 43 31N 142 11 E
Ashikaga, *Japan* **31 F9** 36 28N 139 29 E
Ashington, *U.K.* **10 B6** 55 11N 1 33W
Ashizuri-Zaki, *Japan* **31 H6** 32 44N 133 0 E
Ashkarkot, *Afghan.* **42 C2** 33 3N 67 58 E
Ashkhabad = Ashgabat, *Turkmenistan* **26 F6** 38 0N 57 50 E
Ashland, *Kans., U.S.A.* **81 G5** 37 11N 99 46W
Ashland, *Ky., U.S.A.* **76 F4** 38 28N 82 38W
Ashland, *Maine, U.S.A.* **71 C6** 46 38N 68 24W
Ashland, *Mont., U.S.A.* **82 D10** 45 36N 106 16W
Ashland, *Nebr., U.S.A.* **80 E6** 41 3N 96 23W
Ashland, *Ohio, U.S.A.* **78 F2** 40 52N 82 19W
Ashland, *Oreg., U.S.A.* **82 E2** 42 12N 122 43W
Ashland, *Pa., U.S.A.* **79 F8** 40 45N 76 22W
Ashland, *Va., U.S.A.* **76 G7** 37 46N 77 29W
Ashland, *Wis., U.S.A.* **80 B9** 46 35N 90 53W
Ashley, *N. Dak., U.S.A.* **80 B5** 46 2N 99 22W
Ashley, *Pa., U.S.A.* **79 E9** 41 12N 75 55W
Ashmont, *Canada* **72 C6** 54 7N 111 35W
Ashmore Reef, *Australia* **60 B3** 12 14S 123 5 E
Ashmyany, *Belarus* **9 J21** 54 26N 25 52 E
Ashqelon, *Israel* **47 D3** 31 42N 34 35 E
Ashtabula, *U.S.A.* **78 E4** 41 52N 80 47W
Ashton, *S. Africa* **56 E3** 33 50S 20 5 E
Ashton, *U.S.A.* **82 D8** 44 4N 111 27W
Ashuanipi, L., *Canada* **71 B6** 52 45N 66 15W
Asia, Kepulauan, *Indonesia* **37 D8** 1 0N 131 13 E
Āsīā Bak, *Iran* **45 C6** 35 19N 50 30 E
Asifabad, *India* **40 K11** 19 20N 79 24 E
Asinara, *Italy* **20 D3** 41 4N 8 16 E
Asinara, G. dell', *Italy* **20 D3** 41 0N 8 30 E
Asino, *Russia* **26 D9** 57 0N 86 0 E
Asipovichy, *Belarus* **17 B15** 53 19N 28 33 E
'Asīr □, *Si. Arabia* **46 D3** 18 40N 42 30 E
Asir, Ras, *Somali Rep.* **46 E5** 11 55N 51 10 E
Askersund, *Sweden* **9 G16** 58 53N 14 55 E
Askham, *S. Africa* **56 D3** 26 59S 20 47 E
Askim, *Norway* **9 G14** 59 35N 11 10 E
Askja, *Iceland* **8 D5** 65 3N 16 48W
Askøy, *Norway* **9 F11** 60 29N 5 10 E
Asmara = Asmera, *Eritrea* **46 D2** 15 19N 38 55 E
Asmera, *Eritrea* **46 D2** 15 19N 38 55 E
Åsnen, *Sweden* **9 H16** 56 37N 14 45 E
Asotin, *U.S.A.* **82 C5** 46 20N 117 3W
Aspen, *U.S.A.* **83 G10** 39 11N 106 49W
Aspermont, *U.S.A.* **81 J4** 33 8N 100 14W
Aspiring, Mt., *N.Z.* **59 L2** 44 23S 168 46 E
Asprókavos, Ákra, *Greece* **23 B4** 39 21N 20 6 E
Aspur, *India* **42 H6** 23 58N 74 7 E
Asquith, *Canada* **73 C7** 52 8N 107 13W
Assad, Bahret, *Syria* **44 C3** 36 0N 38 15 E
Assam □, *India* **41 G18** 26 0N 93 0 E
Asse, *Belgium* **15 D4** 50 24N 4 10 E
Assen, *Neths.* **15 A6** 53 0N 6 35 E
Assiniboia, *Canada* **73 D7** 49 40N 105 59W
Assiniboine →, *Canada* **73 D9** 49 53N 97 8W
Assis, *Brazil* **95 A5** 22 40S 50 20W
Assisi, *Italy* **20 C5** 43 4N 12 37 E
Assynt, L., *U.K.* **12 C3** 58 10N 5 3W
Astana = Aqmola, *Kazakstan* **26 D8** 51 10N 71 30 E
Astara, *Azerbaijan* **25 G8** 38 30N 48 50 E

Asteroúsia

Barnagar

Bairin Zuoqi, China 35 C10 43 58N 119 15 E
Bairnsdale, Australia 63 F4 37 48S 147 36 E
Baisha, China 34 G7 34 20N 112 32 E
Baitadi, Nepal 43 E9 29 35N 80 25 E
Baiyin, China 34 F3 36 45N 104 14 E
Baiyu Shan, China 34 F4 37 15N 107 30 E
Baj Baj, India 43 H13 22 30N 88 5 E
Baja, Hungary 17 E10 46 12N 18 59 E
Baja, Pta., Mexico 86 B1 29 50N 116 0W
Baja California, Mexico 86 A1 31 10N 115 12W
Baja California □, Mexico 86 B2 30 0N 115 0W
Baja California Sur □, Mexico 86 B2 25 50N 111 50W
Bajamar, Canary Is. 22 F3 28 33N 16 20W
Bajana, India 42 H4 23 7N 71 49 E
Bājgīrān, Iran 45 B8 37 36N 58 24 E
Bajimba, Mt., Australia 63 D5 29 17S 152 6 E
Bajo Nuevo, Caribbean 88 C4 15 40N 78 50W
Bajool, Australia 62 C5 23 40S 150 35 E
Bakel, Senegal 50 F3 14 56N 12 20W
Baker, Calif., U.S.A. 85 K10 35 16N 116 4W
Baker, Mont., U.S.A. 80 B2 46 22N 104 17W
Baker, Oreg., U.S.A. 82 D5 44 47N 117 50W
Baker, L., Canada 68 B10 64 0N 96 0W
Baker I., Pac. Oc. 64 G10 0 10N 176 35W
Baker L., Australia 61 E4 26 54S 126 5 E
Baker Lake, Canada 68 B10 64 20N 96 3W
Baker Mt., U.S.A. 82 B3 48 50N 121 49W
Bakers Creek, Australia 62 C4 21 13S 149 7 E
Baker's Dozen Is., Canada 70 A4 56 45N 78 45W
Bakersfield, Calif., U.S.A. 85 K8 35 23N 119 1W
Bakersfield, Vt., U.S.A. 79 B12 44 45N 72 48W
Bākhtarān, Iran 44 C5 34 23N 47 0 E
Bākhtarān □, Iran 44 C5 34 0N 46 30 E
Bakı, Azerbaijan 25 F8 40 29N 49 56 E
Bakkafjörður, Iceland 8 C6 66 2N 14 48W
Bakony, Hungary 17 E9 47 10N 17 30 E
Bakony Forest = Bakony, Hungary 17 E9 47 10N 17 30 E
Bakouma, C.A.R. 52 C4 5 40N 22 56 E
Baku = Bakı, Azerbaijan 25 F8 40 29N 49 56 E
Bakutis Coast, Antarctica 5 D15 74 0S 120 0W
Baky = Bakı, Azerbaijan 25 F8 40 29N 49 56 E
Bala, Canada 78 A5 45 1N 79 37W
Bala, U.K. 10 E4 52 54N 3 36W
Bala, L., U.K. 10 E4 52 53N 3 37W
Balabac I., Phil. 36 C5 8 0N 117 0 E
Balabac Str., E. Indies 36 C5 7 53N 117 5 E
Balabagh, Afghan. 42 B4 34 25N 70 12 E
Ba'labakk, Lebanon 47 B5 34 0N 36 10 E
Balabalangan, Kepulauan, Indonesia 36 E5 2 20S 117 30 E
Balad, Iraq 44 C5 34 1N 44 9 E
Balad Rūz, Iraq 44 C5 33 42N 45 5 E
Bālādeh, Fārs, Iran 45 D6 29 17N 51 56 E
Bālādeh, Māzandaran, Iran 45 B6 36 12N 51 48 E
Balaghat, India 40 J12 21 49N 80 12 E
Balaghat Ra., India 40 K10 18 50N 76 30 E
Balaguer, Spain 19 B6 41 50N 0 50 E
Balaklava, Australia 63 E2 34 7S 138 22 E
Balaklava, Ukraine 25 F5 44 30N 33 30 E
Balakovo, Russia 24 D8 52 4N 47 55 E
Balancán, Mexico 87 D6 17 48N 91 32W
Balashov, Russia 24 D7 51 30N 43 10 E
Balasinor, India 42 H5 22 57N 73 23 E
Balasore = Baleshwar, India 41 J15 21 35N 87 3 E
Balaton, Hungary 17 E9 46 50N 17 40 E
Balbina, Reprêsa de, Brazil 92 D7 2 0S 59 30W
Balboa, Panama 88 E4 8 57N 79 34W
Balbriggan, Ireland 13 C5 53 37N 6 11W
Balcarce, Argentina 94 D4 38 0S 58 10W
Balcarres, Canada 73 C8 50 50N 103 35W
Balchik, Bulgaria 21 C13 43 28N 28 11 E
Balclutha, N.Z. 59 M2 46 15S 169 45 E
Bald Hd., Australia 61 G2 35 6S 118 1 E
Bald I., Australia 61 F2 34 57S 118 27 E
Bald Knob, U.S.A. 81 H9 35 19N 91 34W
Baldock L., Canada 73 B9 56 33N 97 57W
Baldwin, Fla., U.S.A. 77 K4 30 18N 81 59W
Baldwin, Mich., U.S.A. 76 D3 43 54N 85 51W
Baldwinsville, U.S.A. 79 C8 43 10N 76 20W
Baldy Peak, U.S.A. 83 K9 33 54N 109 34W
Baleares, Is., Spain 22 B10 39 30N 3 0 E
Balearic Is. = Baleares, Is., Spain 22 B10 39 30N 3 0 E
Baleine = Whale →, Canada 71 A6 58 15N 67 40W
Baler, Phil. 37 A6 15 46N 121 34 E
Baleshare, U.K. 12 D1 57 31N 7 22W
Baleshwar, India 41 J15 21 35N 87 3 E
Balfate, Honduras 88 C2 15 48N 86 25W
Balfe's Creek, Australia 62 C4 20 12S 145 55 E
Balí, Greece 23 D6 35 25N 24 47 E
Bali □, Indonesia 36 F5 8 20S 115 0 E
Bali, Selat, Indonesia 37 H16 8 18S 114 25 E
Balikeşir, Turkey 25 G4 39 39N 27 53 E
Balikpapan, Indonesia 36 E5 1 10S 116 55 E
Balimbing, Phil. 37 C5 5 5N 119 58 E
Baling, Malaysia 39 K3 5 41N 100 55 E
Balipara, India 41 F18 26 50N 92 45 E
Balkan Mts. = Stara Planina, Bulgaria 21 C10 43 15N 23 0 E
Balkhash = Balqash, Kazakstan 26 E8 46 50N 74 50 E
Balkhash, Ozero = Balqash Köl, Kazakstan 26 E8 46 0N 74 50 E
Balla, Bangla. 41 G17 24 10N 91 35 E
Ballachulish, U.K. 12 E3 56 41N 5 8W
Balladonia, Australia 61 F3 32 27S 123 51 E
Ballaghaderreen, Ireland 13 C3 53 55N 8 34W
Ballarat, Australia 63 F3 37 33S 143 50 E
Ballard, L., Australia 61 E3 29 20S 120 40 E
Ballater, U.K. 12 D5 57 3N 3 3W
Ballenas, Canal de, Mexico 86 B2 29 10N 113 45W
Balleny Is., Antarctica 5 C11 66 30S 163 0 E
Ballia, India 43 G11 25 46N 84 12 E
Ballidu, Australia 61 F2 30 35S 116 45 E
Ballina, Australia 63 D5 28 50S 153 31 E
Ballina, Ireland 13 B2 54 7N 9 9W
Ballinasloe, Ireland 13 C3 53 20N 8 13W
Ballinger, U.S.A. 81 K5 31 45N 99 57W
Ballinrobe, Ireland 13 C2 53 38N 9 13W
Ballinskelligs B., Ireland 13 E1 51 48N 10 13W
Ballycastle, U.K. 13 A5 55 12N 6 15W
Ballyclare, U.K. 13 B5 54 46N 6 0W
Ballyhaunis, Ireland 13 C3 53 46N 8 46W
Ballymena, U.K. 13 B5 54 52N 6 17W
Ballymoney, U.K. 13 A5 55 5N 6 31W
Ballymote, Ireland 13 B3 54 5N 8 31W
Ballynahinch, U.K. 13 B6 54 24N 5 54W
Ballyquintin Pt., U.K. 13 B6 54 20N 5 30W
Ballyshannon, Ireland 13 B3 54 30N 8 11W
Balmaceda, Chile 96 F2 46 0S 71 50W
Balmoral, Australia 63 F3 37 15S 141 48 E
Balmorhea, U.S.A. 81 K3 30 59N 103 45W
Balonne →, Australia 63 D4 28 47S 147 56 E
Balqash, Kazakstan 26 E8 46 50N 74 50 E
Balqash Köl, Kazakstan 26 E8 46 0N 74 50 E
Balrampur, India 43 F10 27 30N 82 20 E
Balranald, Australia 63 E3 34 38S 143 33 E
Balsas, Mexico 87 D5 18 0N 99 40W
Balsas →, Mexico 86 D4 17 55N 102 10W
Balston Spa, U.S.A. 79 D11 43 0N 73 52W
Balta, Ukraine 25 E4 48 2N 29 45 E
Balta, U.S.A. 80 A4 48 10N 100 2W
Bălți, Moldova 25 E4 47 48N 27 58 E
Baltic Sea, Europe 9 H18 57 0N 19 0 E
Baltimore, Ireland 13 E2 51 29N 9 22W
Baltimore, U.S.A. 76 F7 39 17N 76 37W
Baltit, Pakistan 43 A6 36 15N 74 40 E
Baltiysk, Russia 9 J18 54 41N 19 58 E
Baluchistan □, Pakistan 40 F4 27 30N 65 0 E
Balurghat, India 43 G13 25 15N 88 44 E
Balvi, Latvia 9 H22 57 8N 27 15 E
Balya, Turkey 21 E12 39 44N 27 35 E
Bam, Iran 45 D8 29 7N 58 14 E
Bama, Nigeria 51 F8 11 33N 13 41 E
Bamako, Mali 50 F4 12 34N 7 55W
Bambari, C.A.R. 52 C4 5 40N 20 35 E
Bambaroo, Australia 62 B4 18 50S 146 10 E
Bamberg, Germany 16 D6 49 54N 10 54 E
Bamberg, U.S.A. 77 J5 33 18N 81 2W
Bambili, Dem. Rep. of the Congo 54 B2 3 40N 26 0 E
Bamfield, Canada 72 D3 48 45N 125 10W
Bāmīān □, Afghan. 40 B5 35 0N 67 0 E
Bamiancheng, China 35 C13 43 15N 124 2 E
Bampūr, Iran 45 E9 27 15N 60 21 E
Ban Ban, Laos 38 C4 19 31N 103 30 E
Ban Bang Hin, Thailand 39 H2 9 32N 98 35 E
Ban Chiang Klang, Thailand 38 C3 19 25N 100 55 E
Ban Chik, Laos 38 D4 17 15N 102 22 E
Ban Choho, Thailand 38 E4 15 2N 102 9 E
Ban Dan Lan Hoi, Thailand 38 D2 17 0N 99 35 E
Ban Don = Surat Thani, Thailand 39 H2 9 6N 99 20 E
Ban Don, Vietnam 38 F6 12 53N 107 48 E
Ban Don, Ao →, Thailand 39 H2 9 20N 99 25 E
Ban Dong, Thailand 38 C3 19 30N 100 59 E
Ban Hong, Thailand 38 C2 18 18N 98 50 E
Ban Kaeng, Thailand 38 D3 17 29N 100 7 E
Ban Kantang, Thailand 39 J2 7 25N 99 31 E
Ban Keun, Laos 38 C4 18 22N 102 35 E
Ban Khai, Thailand 38 F3 12 46N 101 18 E
Ban Kheun, Laos 38 B3 20 13N 101 7 E
Ban Khlong Kua, Thailand 39 J3 6 57N 100 8 E
Ban Khuan Mao, Thailand 39 J2 7 50N 99 37 E
Ban Ko Yai Chim, Thailand 39 G2 11 17N 99 26 E
Ban Kok, Thailand 38 D4 16 40N 103 40 E
Ban Laem, Thailand 38 F2 13 13N 99 59 E
Ban Lao Ngam, Laos 38 E6 15 28N 106 10 E
Ban Le Kathe, Thailand 38 E2 15 49N 98 53 E
Ban Mae Chedi, Thailand 38 C2 19 11N 99 31 E
Ban Mae Laeng, Thailand 38 B2 20 1N 99 17 E
Ban Mae Sariang, Thailand 38 C1 18 10N 97 56 E
Ban Mê Thuôt = Buon Ma Thuot, Vietnam 38 F7 12 40N 108 3 E
Ban Mi, Thailand 38 E3 15 3N 100 32 E
Ban Muong Mo, Laos 38 C4 19 4N 103 58 E
Ban Na Mo, Laos 38 D5 17 7N 105 40 E
Ban Na San, Thailand 39 H2 8 53N 99 52 E
Ban Na Tong, Laos 38 B3 20 56N 101 47 E
Ban Nam Bac, Laos 38 B4 20 38N 102 20 E
Ban Nam Ma, Laos 38 A3 22 2N 101 37 E
Ban Ngang, Laos 38 E6 15 59N 106 11 E
Ban Nong Bok, Laos 38 D5 17 5N 104 48 E
Ban Nong Boua, Laos 38 E6 15 40N 106 33 E
Ban Nong Pling, Thailand 38 E3 15 40N 100 10 E
Ban Pak Chan, Thailand 39 G2 10 32N 98 51 E
Ban Phai, Thailand 38 D4 16 4N 102 44 E
Ban Pong, Thailand 38 F2 13 50N 99 55 E
Ban Ron Phibun, Thailand 39 H2 8 9N 99 51 E
Ban Sanam Chai, Thailand 39 J3 7 33N 100 25 E
Ban Sangkha, Thailand 38 E4 14 37N 103 52 E
Ban Tak, Thailand 38 D2 17 2N 99 4 E
Ban Tako, Thailand 38 E4 14 5N 102 40 E
Ban Tha Dua, Thailand 38 D2 17 59N 98 39 E
Ban Tha Li, Thailand 38 D3 17 37N 101 25 E
Ban Tha Nun, Thailand 39 H2 8 12N 98 18 E
Ban Thahine, Laos 38 E5 14 12N 105 33 E
Ban Xien Kok, Laos 38 B3 20 54N 100 39 E
Ban Yen Nhan, Vietnam 38 B6 20 57N 106 2 E
Banaba, Kiribati 64 H8 0 45S 169 50 E
Bañalbufar, Spain 22 B9 39 42N 2 31 E
Banalia, Dem. Rep. of the Congo 54 B2 1 32N 25 5 E
Banam, Cambodia 39 G5 11 20N 105 17 E
Banana, Australia 62 C5 24 28S 150 8 E
Bananal, I. do, Brazil 93 F8 11 30S 50 30W
Banaras = Varanasi, India 43 G10 25 22N 83 0 E
Banas →, Gujarat, India 42 H4 23 45N 71 25 E
Banas →, Mad. P., India 43 G9 24 15N 81 30 E
Bânâs, Ras, Egypt 51 D13 23 57N 35 59 E
Banbān, Si. Arabia 44 E5 25 1N 46 35 E
Banbridge, U.K. 13 B5 54 22N 6 16W
Banbury, U.K. 11 E6 52 4N 1 20W
Banchory, U.K. 12 D6 57 3N 2 29W
Bancroft, Canada 70 C4 45 3N 77 51W
Band Bonī, Iran 45 E8 25 30N 59 33 E
Band Qīr, Iran 45 D6 31 39N 48 53 E
Banda, India 43 G9 25 30N 80 26 E
Banda, Kepulauan, Indonesia 37 E7 4 37S 129 50 E
Banda Aceh, Indonesia 36 C1 5 35N 95 20 E
Banda Banda, Mt., Australia 63 E5 31 10S 152 28 E
Banda Elat, Indonesia 37 F8 5 40S 133 5 E
Banda Is. = Banda, Kepulauan, Indonesia 37 E7 4 37S 129 50 E
Banda Sea, Indonesia 37 F8 6 0S 130 0 E
Bandai-San, Japan 30 F10 37 36N 140 4 E
Bandān, Iran 45 D9 31 23N 60 44 E
Bandanaira, Indonesia 37 E7 4 32S 129 54 E
Bandanwara, India 42 F6 26 9N 74 38 E
Bandar = Machilipatnam, India 41 L12 16 12N 81 8 E
Bandār 'Abbās, Iran 45 E8 27 15N 56 15 E
Bandar-e Anzalī, Iran 45 B6 37 30N 49 30 E
Bandar-e Bushehr = Būshehr, Iran 45 D6 28 55N 50 55 E
Bandar-e Chārak, Iran 45 E7 26 45N 54 20 E
Bandar-e Deylam, Iran 45 D6 30 5N 50 10 E
Bandar-e Khomeynı, Iran 45 D6 30 30N 49 5 E
Bandar-e Lengeh, Iran 45 E7 26 35N 54 58 E
Bandar-e Maqām, Iran 45 E7 26 56N 53 29 E
Bandar-e Ma'shur, Iran 45 D6 30 35N 49 10 E
Bandar-e Nakhīlū, Iran 45 E7 26 58N 53 30 E
Bandar-e Rīg, Iran 45 D6 29 29N 50 38 E
Bandar-e Torkeman, Iran 45 B7 37 0N 54 10 E
Bandar Maharani = Muar, Malaysia 39 L4 2 3N 102 34 E
Bandar Penggaram = Batu Pahat, Malaysia 39 M4 1 50N 102 56 E
Bandar Seri Begawan, Brunei 36 D5 4 52N 115 0 E
Bandar Sri Aman, Malaysia 36 D4 1 15N 111 32 E
Bandawe, Malawi 55 E3 11 58S 34 5 E
Bandeira, Pico da, Brazil 95 A7 20 26S 41 47W
Bandera, Argentina 94 B3 28 55S 62 20W
Bandera, U.S.A. 81 L5 29 44N 99 5W
Banderas, B. de, Mexico 86 C3 20 40N 105 30W
Bandırma, Turkey 25 F4 40 20N 28 0 E
Bandon, Ireland 13 E3 51 44N 8 44W
Bandon →, Ireland 13 E3 51 43N 8 37W
Bandula, Mozam. 55 F3 19 0S 33 7 E
Bandundu, Dem. Rep. of the Congo 52 E3 3 15S 17 22 E
Bandung, Indonesia 37 G12 6 54S 107 36 E
Bandya, Australia 61 E3 27 40S 122 5 E
Bāneh, Iran 44 C5 35 59N 45 53 E
Banes, Cuba 89 B4 21 0N 75 42W
Banff, Canada 72 C5 51 10N 115 34W
Banff, U.K. 12 D6 57 40N 2 33W
Banff Nat. Park, Canada 72 C5 51 30N 116 15W
Bang Fai →, Laos 38 D5 16 57N 104 45 E
Bang Hieng →, Laos 38 D5 16 10N 105 10 E
Bang Krathum, Thailand 38 D3 16 34N 100 18 E
Bang Lamung, Thailand 38 F3 13 3N 100 56 E
Bang Mun Nak, Thailand 38 D3 16 2N 100 23 E
Bang Pa In, Thailand 38 E3 14 14N 100 35 E
Bang Rakam, Thailand 38 D3 16 45N 100 7 E
Bang Saphan, Thailand 39 G2 11 14N 99 28 E
Bangala Dam, Zimbabwe 55 G3 21 7S 31 25 E
Bangalore, India 40 N10 12 59N 77 40 E
Bangaon, India 43 H13 23 0N 88 47 E
Bangassou, C.A.R. 52 D4 4 55N 23 7 E
Banggai, Kepulauan, Indonesia 37 E6 1 40S 123 30 E
Banggai Arch. = Banggai, Kepulauan, Indonesia 37 E6 1 40S 123 30 E
Banggi, Malaysia 36 C5 7 17N 117 12 E
Banghāzī, Libya 51 B10 32 11N 20 3 E
Bangka, Sulawesi, Indonesia 37 D7 1 50N 125 5 E
Bangka, Sumatera, Indonesia 36 E3 2 0S 105 50 E
Bangka, Selat, Indonesia 36 E3 2 30S 105 30 E
Bangkalan, Indonesia 37 G15 7 2S 112 46 E
Bangkinang, Indonesia 36 D2 0 18N 101 5 E
Bangko, Indonesia 36 E2 2 5S 102 9 E
Bangkok, Thailand 38 F3 13 45N 100 35 E
Bangladesh ■, Asia 41 H17 24 0N 90 0 E
Bangong Co, India 43 B8 35 50N 79 20 E
Bangor, Down, U.K. 13 B6 54 40N 5 40W
Bangor, Gwynedd, U.K. 10 D3 53 14N 4 8W
Bangor, Maine, U.S.A. 71 D6 44 48N 68 46W
Bangor, Pa., U.S.A. 79 F9 40 52N 75 13W
Bangued, Phil. 37 A6 17 40N 120 37 E
Bangui, C.A.R. 52 D3 4 23N 18 35 E
Banguru, Dem. Rep. of the Congo 54 B2 0 30N 27 10 E
Bangweulu, L., Zambia 55 E3 11 0S 30 0 E
Bangweulu Swamp, Zambia 55 E3 11 20S 30 15 E
Bani, Dom. Rep. 89 C5 18 16N 70 22W
Banī Sa'd, Iraq 44 C5 33 34N 44 32 E
Banihal Pass, India 43 C6 33 30N 75 12 E
Bāniyās, Syria 44 C3 35 10N 36 0 E
Banja Luka, Bos.-H. 20 B7 44 49N 17 11 E
Banjarmasin, Indonesia 36 E4 3 20S 114 35 E
Banjul, Gambia 50 F2 13 28N 16 40W
Banka Banka, Australia 62 B1 18 50S 134 0 E
Banket, Zimbabwe 55 F3 17 27S 30 19 E
Bankipore, India 43 G11 25 35N 85 10 E
Banks I., B.C., Canada 72 C3 53 20N 130 0W
Banks I., N.W.T., Canada 68 A7 73 15N 121 30W
Banks Pen., N.Z. 59 K4 43 45S 173 15 E
Banks Str., Australia 62 G4 40 40S 148 10 E
Bankura, India 43 H12 23 11N 87 18 E
Bann →, Arm., U.K. 13 B5 54 30N 6 31W
Bann →, L'derry., U.K. 13 A5 55 8N 6 41W
Bannang Sata, Thailand 39 J3 6 16N 101 16 E
Banning, U.S.A. 85 M10 33 56N 116 53W
Banningville = Bandundu, Dem. Rep. of the Congo 52 E3 3 15S 17 22 E
Bannockburn, Canada 78 B7 44 39N 77 33W
Bannockburn, U.K. 12 E5 56 5N 3 55W
Bannockburn, Zimbabwe 55 G2 20 17S 29 48 E
Bannu, Pakistan 40 C7 33 0N 70 18 E
Banská Bystrica, Slovak Rep. 17 D10 48 46N 19 14 E
Banswara, India 42 H6 23 32N 74 24 E
Bantry, Ireland 13 E2 51 41N 9 27W
Bantry B., Ireland 13 E2 51 37N 9 44W
Bantul, Indonesia 37 G14 7 55S 110 19 E
Bantva, India 42 J4 21 29N 70 12 E
Banu, Afghan. 40 B6 35 35N 69 5 E
Banyak, Kepulauan, Indonesia 36 D1 2 10N 97 10 E
Banyo, Cameroon 52 C2 6 52N 11 45 E
Banyumas, Indonesia 37 G13 7 32S 109 18 E
Banyuwangi, Indonesia 37 H16 8 13S 114 21 E
Banzare Coast, Antarctica 5 C9 68 0S 125 0 E
Banzyville = Mobayi, Dem. Rep. of the Congo 52 D4 4 15N 21 8 E
Bao Ha, Vietnam 38 A5 22 11N 104 21 E
Bao Lac, Vietnam 38 A5 22 57N 105 40 E
Bao Loc, Vietnam 39 G6 11 32N 107 48 E
Baocheng, China 34 H3 33 12N 106 56 E
Baode, China 34 E6 39 1N 111 5 E
Baodi, China 35 E9 39 38N 117 20 E
Baoding, China 34 E8 38 50N 115 28 E
Baoji, China 34 G4 34 20N 107 5 E
Baoshan, China 32 D4 25 10N 99 5 E
Baotou, China 34 D6 40 32N 110 2 E
Baoying, China 35 H10 33 17N 119 20 E
Bap, India 42 F5 27 23N 72 18 E
Bapatla, India 41 M12 15 55N 80 30 E
Bāqerābād, Iran 45 C6 33 2N 51 58 E
Ba'qūbah, Iraq 44 C5 33 45N 44 50 E
Baquedano, Chile 94 A2 23 20S 69 52W
Bar, Montenegro, Yug. 21 C8 42 8N 19 6 E
Bar, Ukraine 17 D14 49 4N 27 40 E
Bar Bigha, India 43 G11 25 21N 85 47 E
Bar Harbor, U.S.A. 71 D6 44 23N 68 13W
Bar-le-Duc, France 18 B6 48 47N 5 10 E
Barabai, Indonesia 36 E5 2 32S 115 34 E
Baraboo, U.S.A. 80 D10 43 28N 89 45W
Baracoa, Cuba 89 B5 20 20N 74 30W
Baradā →, Syria 47 B5 33 33N 36 34 E
Baradero, Argentina 94 C4 33 52S 59 29W
Baraga, U.S.A. 80 B10 46 47N 88 30W
Barahona, Dom. Rep. 89 C5 18 13N 71 7W
Barail Range, India 41 G18 25 15N 93 20 E
Barakaldo, Spain 19 A4 43 18N 2 59W
Barakhola, India 41 G18 25 0N 92 45 E
Barakot, India 43 J11 21 33N 84 59 E
Barakpur, India 43 H13 22 44N 88 30 E
Barakula, Australia 63 D5 26 30S 150 33 E
Baralaba, Australia 62 C4 24 13S 149 50 E
Baralzon L., Canada 73 B9 60 0N 98 3W
Baramula, India 43 B6 34 15N 74 20 E
Baran, India 42 G7 25 9N 76 40 E
Baranavichy, Belarus 24 D4 53 10N 26 0 E
Baranof I., U.S.A. 72 B1 57 0N 135 0W
Barapasi, Indonesia 37 E9 2 15S 137 5 E
Barasat, India 43 H13 22 46N 88 31 E
Barat Daya, Kepulauan, Indonesia 37 F7 7 30S 128 0 E
Barataria B., U.S.A. 81 L10 29 20N 89 55W
Baraut, India 42 E7 29 13N 77 7 E
Barbacena, Brazil 95 A7 21 15S 43 56W
Barbados ■, W. Indies 89 D8 13 10N 59 30W
Barbària, C. de, Spain 22 C7 38 39N 1 24 E
Barbastro, Spain 19 A6 42 2N 0 5 E
Barberton, S. Africa 57 D5 25 42S 31 2 E
Barberton, U.S.A. 78 E3 41 0N 81 39W
Barbosa, Colombia 92 B4 5 57N 73 37W
Barbourville, U.S.A. 77 G4 36 52N 83 53W
Barbuda, W. Indies 89 C7 17 30N 61 40W
Barcaldine, Australia 62 C4 23 43S 145 6 E
Barcellona Pozzo di Gotto, Italy 20 E6 38 9N 15 13 E
Barcelona, Spain 19 B7 41 21N 2 10 E
Barcelona, Venezuela 92 A6 10 10N 64 40W
Barcelos, Brazil 92 D6 1 0S 63 0W
Barcoo →, Australia 62 D3 25 30S 142 50 E
Bardaï, Chad 51 D9 21 25N 17 0 E
Bardas Blancas, Argentina 94 D2 35 49S 69 45W
Barddhaman, India 43 H12 23 14N 87 39 E
Bardejov, Slovak Rep. 17 D11 49 18N 21 15 E
Bardera, Somali Rep. 46 G3 2 20N 42 27 E
Bardīyah, Libya 51 B10 31 45N 25 5 E
Bardsey I., U.K. 10 E3 52 45N 4 47W
Bardstown, U.S.A. 76 G3 37 49N 85 28W
Bareilly, India 43 E8 28 22N 79 27 E
Barents Sea, Arctic 28 B7 73 0N 39 0 E
Barfleur, Pte. de, France 18 B3 49 42N 1 16W
Bargara, Australia 62 C5 24 50S 152 25 E
Barguzin, Russia 27 D11 53 37N 109 37 E
Barh, India 43 G11 25 29N 85 46 E
Barhaj, India 43 F10 26 18N 83 44 E
Barhi, India 43 G11 24 15N 85 25 E
Bari, India 42 F7 26 39N 77 39 E
Bari, Italy 20 D7 41 8N 16 51 E
Bari Doab, Pakistan 42 D5 30 20N 73 0 E
Bariadi □, Tanzania 54 C3 2 45S 34 40 E
Barīm, Yemen 48 E8 12 39N 43 25 E
Barinas, Venezuela 92 B4 8 36N 70 15W
Baring, C., Canada 68 B8 70 0N 117 30W
Baringo, Kenya 54 B4 0 47N 36 16 E
Baringo □, Kenya 54 B4 0 55N 36 0 E
Baringo, L., Kenya 54 B4 0 47N 36 16 E
Barisal, Bangla. 41 H17 22 45N 90 20 E
Barisan, Bukit, Indonesia 36 E2 3 30S 102 15 E
Barito →, Indonesia 36 E4 4 0S 114 50 E
Bark L., Canada 78 A7 45 27N 77 51W
Barker, U.S.A. 78 C6 43 20N 78 33W
Barkley Sound, Canada 72 D3 48 50N 125 10W
Barkly Downs, Australia 62 C2 20 30S 138 30 E
Barkly East, S. Africa 56 E4 30 58S 27 33 E
Barkly Tableland, Australia 62 B2 17 50S 136 40 E
Barkly West, S. Africa 56 D3 28 5S 24 31 E
Barkol Kazak Zizhixian, China 32 B4 43 37N 93 2 E
Barksdale, U.S.A. 81 L4 29 44N 100 2W
Bârlad, Romania 17 E14 46 15N 27 38 E
Bârlad →, Romania 17 F14 45 38N 27 32 E
Barlee, L., Australia 61 E2 29 15S 119 30 E
Barlee, Mt., Australia 61 D4 24 38S 128 13 E
Barletta, Italy 20 D7 41 19N 16 17 E
Barlovento, Canary Is. 22 F2 28 48N 17 48W
Barlow L., Canada 73 A8 62 0N 103 0W
Barmedman, Australia 63 E4 34 9S 147 21 E
Barmer, India 42 G4 25 45N 71 20 E
Barmera, Australia 63 E3 34 15S 140 28 E
Barmouth, U.K. 10 E3 52 44N 4 4W
Barnagar, India 42 H6 23 7N 75 19 E

Barnard Castle

Barnard Castle, *U.K.* **10 C6** 54 33N 1 55W
Barnato, *Australia* **63 E4** 31 38S 145 0 E
Barnaul, *Russia* **26 D9** 53 20N 83 40 E
Barnesville, *U.S.A.* **77 J3** 33 3N 84 9W
Barnet, *U.K.* **11 F7** 51 38N 0 9W
Barneveld, *Neths.* **15 B5** 52 7N 5 36 E
Barneveld, *U.S.A.* **79 C9** 43 16N 75 14W
Barngo, *Australia* **62 D4** 25 3S 147 20 E
Barnhart, *U.S.A.* **81 K4** 31 8N 101 10W
Barnsley, *U.K.* **10 D6** 53 34N 1 27W
Barnstaple, *U.K.* **11 F3** 51 5N 4 4W
Barnstaple Bay = Bideford Bay, *U.K.* **11 F3** 51 5N 4 20W
Barnsville, *U.S.A.* **80 B6** 46 43N 96 28W
Baro, *Nigeria* **50 G7** 8 35N 6 18 E
Baroda = Vadodara, *India* **42 H5** 22 20N 73 10 E
Baroda, *India* **42 G7** 25 29N 76 35 E
Baroe, *S. Africa* **56 E3** 33 13S 24 33 E
Baron Ra., *Australia* **60 D4** 23 30S 127 45 E
Barpeta, *India* **41 F17** 26 20N 91 10 E
Barques, Pt. Aux, *U.S.A.* **76 C4** 44 4N 82 58W
Barquísimeto, *Venezuela* **92 A5** 10 4N 69 19W
Barra, *Brazil* **93 F10** 11 5S 43 10W
Barra, *U.K.* **12 E1** 57 0N 7 29W
Barra, Sd. of, *U.K.* **12 D1** 57 4N 7 25W
Barra de Navidad, *Mexico* **86 D4** 19 12N 104 41W
Barra do Corda, *Brazil* **93 E9** 5 30S 45 10W
Barra do Piraí, *Brazil* **95 A7** 22 30S 43 50W
Barra Falsa, Pta. da, *Mozam.* **57 C6** 22 58S 35 37 E
Barra Hd., *U.K.* **12 E1** 56 47N 7 40W
Barra Mansa, *Brazil* **95 A7** 22 35S 44 12W
Barraba, *Australia* **63 E5** 30 21S 150 35 E
Barrackpur = Barakpur, *India* **43 H13** 22 44N 88 30 E
Barraigh = Barra, *U.K.* **12 E1** 57 0N 7 29W
Barranca, *Lima, Peru* **92 F3** 10 45S 77 50W
Barranca, *Loreto, Peru* **92 D3** 4 50S 76 50W
Barrancabermeja, *Colombia* **92 B4** 7 0N 73 50W
Barrancos, *Portugal* **19 C2** 38 10N 6 58W
Barranqueras, *Argentina* **94 B4** 27 30S 59 0W
Barranquilla, *Colombia* **92 A4** 11 0N 74 50W
Barraute, *Canada* **70 C4** 48 26N 77 38W
Barre, *Mass., U.S.A.* **79 D12** 42 25N 72 6W
Barre, *Vt., U.S.A.* **79 B12** 44 12N 72 30W
Barreal, *Argentina* **94 C2** 31 33S 69 28W
Barreiras, *Brazil* **93 F10** 12 8S 45 0W
Barreirinhas, *Brazil* **93 D10** 2 30S 42 50W
Barreiro, *Portugal* **19 C1** 38 40N 9 6W
Barren, Nosy, *Madag.* **57 B7** 18 25S 43 40 E
Barretos, *Brazil* **93 H9** 20 30S 48 35W
Barrhead, *Canada* **72 C6** 54 10N 114 24W
Barrie, *Canada* **70 D4** 44 24N 79 40W
Barrier Ra., *Australia* **63 E3** 31 0S 141 30 E
Barrière, *Canada* **72 C4** 51 12N 120 7W
Barrington, *U.S.A.* **79 E13** 41 44N 71 18W
Barrington L., *Canada* **73 B8** 56 55N 100 15W
Barrington Tops, *Australia* **63 E5** 32 6S 151 28 E
Barringun, *Australia* **63 D4** 29 1S 145 41 E
Barro do Garças, *Brazil* **93 G8** 15 54S 52 16W
Barrow, *U.S.A.* **68 A4** 71 18N 156 47W
Barrow →, *Ireland* **13 D5** 52 25N 6 58W
Barrow Creek, *Australia* **62 C1** 21 30S 133 55 E
Barrow I., *Australia* **60 D2** 20 45S 115 20 E
Barrow-in-Furness, *U.K.* **10 C4** 54 7N 3 14W
Barrow Pt., *Australia* **62 A3** 14 20S 144 40 E
Barrow Pt., *U.S.A.* **66 B4** 71 24N 156 29W
Barrow Ra., *Australia* **61 E4** 26 0S 127 40 E
Barry, *U.K.* **11 F4** 51 24N 3 16W
Barry's Bay, *Canada* **70 C4** 45 29N 77 41W
Barsat, *Pakistan* **43 A5** 36 10N 72 45 E
Barsham, *Syria* **44 C4** 35 21N 40 33 E
Barsi, *India* **40 K9** 18 10N 75 50 E
Barsoi, *India* **41 G15** 25 48N 87 57 E
Barstow, *Calif., U.S.A.* **85 L9** 34 54N 117 1W
Barstow, *Tex., U.S.A.* **81 K3** 31 28N 103 24W
Barthélemy, Col, *Vietnam* **38 C5** 19 26N 104 6 E
Bartica, *Guyana* **92 B7** 6 25N 58 40W
Bartlesville, *U.S.A.* **81 G7** 36 45N 95 59W
Bartlett, *Calif., U.S.A.* **84 J8** 36 29N 118 2W
Bartlett, *Tex., U.S.A.* **81 K6** 30 48N 97 26W
Bartlett, L., *Canada* **72 A5** 63 5N 118 20W
Bartolomeu Dias, *Mozam.* **55 G4** 21 10S 35 8 E
Barton, *Australia* **61 F5** 30 31S 132 39 E
Barton upon Humber, *U.K.* **10 D7** 53 41N 0 25W
Bartow, *U.S.A.* **77 M5** 27 54N 81 50W
Barú, Volcan, *Panama* **88 E3** 8 55N 82 35W
Barumba, *Dem. Rep. of the Congo* **54 B1** 1 3N 23 37 E
Barwani, *India* **42 H6** 22 2N 74 57 E
Barysaw, *Belarus* **24 D4** 54 17N 28 28 E
Barzān, *Iraq* **44 B5** 36 55N 44 3 E
Bāsa'idū, *Iran* **45 E7** 26 35N 55 20 E
Basal, *Pakistan* **42 C5** 33 33N 72 13 E
Basankusa, *Dem. Rep. of the Congo* **52 D3** 1 5N 19 50 E
Basarabeasca, *Moldova* **17 E15** 46 21N 28 58 E
Basawa, *Afghan.* **42 B4** 34 15N 70 50 E
Bascuñán, C., *Chile* **94 B1** 28 52S 71 35W
Basel, *Switz.* **18 C7** 47 35N 7 35 E
Bāshī, *Iran* **45 D6** 28 41N 51 4 E
Bashkir Republic = Bashkortostan □, *Russia* **24 D10** 54 0N 57 0 E
Bashkortostan □, *Russia* **24 D10** 54 0N 57 0 E
Basilan, *Phil.* **37 C6** 6 35N 122 0 E
Basilan Str., *Phil.* **37 C6** 6 50N 122 0 E
Basildon, *U.K.* **11 F8** 51 34N 0 28 E
Basim = Washim, *India* **40 J10** 20 3N 77 0 E
Basin, *U.S.A.* **82 D9** 44 23N 108 2W
Basingstoke, *U.K.* **11 F6** 51 15N 1 5W
Baskatong, Rés., *Canada* **70 C4** 46 46N 75 50W
Basle = Basel, *Switz.* **18 C7** 47 35N 7 35 E
Basoda, *India* **42 H7** 23 52N 77 54 E
Basoka, *Dem. Rep. of the Congo* **54 B1** 1 16N 23 40 E
Basque Provinces = País Vasco □, *Spain* **19 A4** 42 50N 2 45W
Basra = Al Başrah, *Iraq* **44 D5** 30 30N 47 50 E
Bass Str., *Australia* **62 F4** 39 15S 146 30 E
Bassano, *Canada* **72 C6** 50 48N 112 20W
Bassano del Grappa, *Italy* **20 B4** 45 46N 11 44 E
Bassas da India, *Ind. Oc.* **53 J7** 22 0S 39 0 E
Basse-Terre, *Guadeloupe* **89 C7** 16 0N 61 44W
Bassein, *Burma* **41 L19** 16 45N 94 30 E
Basseterre, *St. Kitts & Nevis* **89 C7** 17 17N 62 43W
Bassett, *Nebr., U.S.A.* **80 D5** 42 35N 99 32W
Bassett, *Va., U.S.A.* **77 G6** 36 46N 79 59W
Bassi, *India* **42 D7** 30 44N 76 21 E
Bastak, *Iran* **45 E7** 27 15N 54 25 E
Baştām, *Iran* **45 B7** 36 29N 55 4 E
Bastar, *India* **41 K12** 19 15N 81 40 E
Basti, *India* **43 F10** 26 52N 82 55 E
Bastia, *France* **18 E8** 42 40N 9 30 E
Bastogne, *Belgium* **15 D5** 50 1N 5 43 E
Bastrop, *U.S.A.* **81 K6** 30 7N 97 19W
Bat Yam, *Israel* **47 C3** 32 2N 34 44 E
Bata, *Eq. Guin.* **52 D1** 1 57N 9 50 E
Bataan, *Phil.* **37 B6** 14 40N 120 25 E
Batabanó, *Cuba* **88 B3** 22 40N 82 20W
Batabanó, G. de, *Cuba* **88 B3** 22 30N 82 30W
Batac, *Phil.* **37 A6** 18 3N 120 34 E
Batagai, *Russia* **27 C14** 67 38N 134 38 E
Batama, *Dem. Rep. of the Congo* **54 B2** 0 58N 26 33 E
Batamay, *Russia* **27 C13** 63 30N 129 15 E
Batang, *Indonesia* **37 G13** 6 55S 109 45 E
Batangas, *Phil.* **37 B6** 13 35N 121 10 E
Batanta, *Indonesia* **37 E8** 0 55S 130 40 E
Batatais, *Brazil* **95 A6** 20 54S 47 37W
Batavia, *U.S.A.* **78 D6** 43 0N 78 11W
Batchelor, *Australia* **60 B5** 13 4S 131 1 E
Batdambang, *Cambodia* **38 F4** 13 7N 103 12 E
Bateman's B., *Australia* **63 F5** 35 40S 150 12 E
Batemans Bay, *Australia* **63 F5** 35 44S 150 11 E
Bates Ra., *Australia* **61 E3** 27 27S 121 5 E
Batesburg, *U.S.A.* **77 J5** 33 54N 81 33W
Batesville, *Ark., U.S.A.* **81 H9** 35 46N 91 39W
Batesville, *Miss., U.S.A.* **81 H10** 34 19N 89 57W
Batesville, *Tex., U.S.A.* **81 L5** 28 58N 99 37W
Bath, *U.K.* **11 F5** 51 23N 2 22W
Bath, *Maine, U.S.A.* **71 D6** 43 55N 69 49W
Bath, *N.Y., U.S.A.* **78 D7** 42 20N 77 19W
Bath & North East Somerset □, *U.K.* **11 F5** 51 21N 2 27W
Batheay, *Cambodia* **39 G5** 11 59N 104 57 E
Bathurst = Banjul, *Gambia* **50 F2** 13 28N 16 40W
Bathurst, *Australia* **63 E4** 33 25S 149 31 E
Bathurst, *Canada* **71 C6** 47 37N 65 43W
Bathurst, *S. Africa* **56 E4** 33 30S 26 50 E
Bathurst, C., *Canada* **68 A7** 70 34N 128 0W
Bathurst B., *Australia* **62 A3** 14 16S 144 25 E
Bathurst Harb., *Australia* **62 G4** 43 15S 146 10 E
Bathurst I., *Australia* **60 B5** 11 30S 130 10 E
Bathurst I., *Canada* **66 B9** 76 0N 100 30W
Bathurst Inlet, *Canada* **68 B9** 66 50N 108 1W
Batlow, *Australia* **63 F4** 35 31S 148 9 E
Batna, *Algeria* **50 A7** 35 34N 6 15 E
Batoka, *Zambia* **55 F2** 16 45S 27 15 E
Baton Rouge, *U.S.A.* **81 K9** 30 27N 91 11W
Batong, Ko, *Thailand* **39 J2** 6 32N 99 12 E
Batopilas, *Mexico* **86 B3** 27 0N 107 45W
Batouri, *Cameroon* **52 D2** 4 30N 14 25 E
Båtsfjord, *Norway* **8 A23** 70 38N 29 39 E
Battambang = Batdambang, *Cambodia* **38 F4** 13 7N 103 12 E
Batticaloa, *Sri Lanka* **40 R12** 7 43N 81 45 E
Battipáglia, *Italy* **20 D6** 40 37N 14 58 E
Battle, *U.K.* **11 G8** 50 55N 0 30 E
Battle →, *Canada* **73 C7** 52 43N 108 15W
Battle Camp, *Australia* **62 B3** 15 20S 144 40 E
Battle Creek, *U.S.A.* **76 D3** 42 19N 85 11W
Battle Ground, *U.S.A.* **84 E4** 45 47N 122 32W
Battle Harbour, *Canada* **71 B8** 52 16N 55 35W
Battle Lake, *U.S.A.* **80 B7** 46 17N 95 43W
Battle Mountain, *U.S.A.* **82 F5** 40 38N 116 56W
Battlefields, *Zimbabwe* **55 F2** 18 37S 29 47 E
Battleford, *Canada* **73 C7** 52 45N 108 15W
Batu, Kepulauan, *Indonesia* **36 E1** 0 30S 98 25 E
Batu, Mt., *Ethiopia* **46 F2** 6 55N 39 45 E
Batu Caves, *Malaysia* **39 L3** 3 15N 101 40 E
Batu Gajah, *Malaysia* **39 K3** 4 28N 101 3 E
Batu Is. = Batu, Kepulauan, *Indonesia* **36 E1** 0 30S 98 25 E
Batu Pahat, *Malaysia* **39 M4** 1 50N 102 56 E
Batuata, *Indonesia* **37 F6** 6 12S 122 42 E
Batumi, *Georgia* **25 F7** 41 39N 41 44 E
Baturaja, *Indonesia* **36 E2** 4 11S 104 15 E
Baturité, *Brazil* **93 D11** 4 28S 38 45W
Bau, *Malaysia* **36 D4** 1 25N 110 9 E
Baubau, *Indonesia* **37 F6** 5 25S 122 38 E
Bauchi, *Nigeria* **50 F7** 10 22N 9 48 E
Baudette, *U.S.A.* **80 A7** 48 43N 94 36W
Bauer, C., *Australia* **63 E1** 32 44S 134 4 E
Bauhinia Downs, *Australia* **62 C4** 24 35S 149 18 E
Baukau, *Indonesia* **37 F7** 8 27S 126 27 E
Bauru, *Brazil* **95 A6** 22 10S 49 0W
Bauska, *Latvia* **9 H21** 56 24N 24 15 E
Bautzen, *Germany* **16 C8** 51 10N 14 26 E
Bavānāt, *Iran* **45 D7** 30 28N 53 27 E
Bavaria = Bayern □, *Germany* **16 D6** 48 50N 12 0 E
Bavi Sadri, *India* **42 G6** 24 28N 74 30 E
Bavispe →, *Mexico* **86 B3** 29 30N 109 11W
Bawdwin, *Burma* **41 H20** 23 5N 97 20 E
Bawean, *Indonesia* **36 F4** 5 46S 112 35 E
Bawku, *Ghana* **50 F5** 11 3N 0 19W
Bawlake, *Burma* **41 K20** 19 11N 97 21 E
Baxley, *U.S.A.* **77 K4** 31 47N 82 21W
Baxter Springs, *U.S.A.* **81 G7** 37 2N 94 44W
Bay Bulls, *Canada* **71 C9** 47 19N 52 50W
Bay City, *Mich., U.S.A.* **76 D4** 43 36N 83 54W
Bay City, *Oreg., U.S.A.* **82 D2** 45 31N 123 53W
Bay City, *Tex., U.S.A.* **81 L7** 28 59N 95 58W
Bay de Verde, *Canada* **71 C9** 48 5N 52 54W
Bay Minette, *U.S.A.* **77 K2** 30 53N 87 46W
Bay St. Louis, *U.S.A.* **81 K10** 30 19N 89 20W
Bay Springs, *U.S.A.* **81 K10** 31 59N 89 17W
Bay View, *N.Z.* **59 H6** 39 25S 176 50 E
Baya, *Dem. Rep. of the Congo* **55 E2** 11 53S 27 25 E
Bayamo, *Cuba* **88 B4** 20 20N 76 40W
Bayamón, *Puerto Rico* **89 C6** 18 24N 66 10W
Bayan Har Shan, *China* **32 C4** 34 0N 98 0 E
Bayan Hot = Alxa Zuoqi, *China* **34 E3** 38 50N 105 40 E
Bayan Obo, *China* **34 D5** 41 52N 109 59 E
Bayan-Ovoo, *Mongolia* **34 C4** 42 55N 106 5 E
Bayana, *India* **42 F7** 26 55N 77 18 E
Bayanaûyl, *Kazakstan* **26 D8** 50 45N 75 45 E
Bayandalay, *Mongolia* **34 C2** 43 30N 103 29 E
Bayanhongor, *Mongolia* **32 B5** 46 8N 102 43 E
Bayard, *U.S.A.* **80 E3** 41 45N 103 20W
Baybay, *Phil.* **37 B6** 10 40N 124 55 E
Bayern □, *Germany* **16 D6** 48 50N 12 0 E
Bayeux, *France* **18 B3** 49 17N 0 42W
Bayfield, *Canada* **78 C3** 43 34N 81 42W
Bayfield, *U.S.A.* **80 B9** 46 49N 90 49W
Bayındır, *Turkey* **21 E12** 38 13N 27 39 E
Baykal, Oz., *Russia* **27 D11** 53 0N 108 0 E
Baykonur = Bayqongyr, *Kazakstan* **26 E7** 47 48N 65 50 E
Baymak, *Russia* **24 D10** 52 36N 58 19 E
Baynes Mts., *Namibia* **56 B1** 17 15S 13 0 E
Bayombong, *Phil.* **37 A6** 16 30N 121 10 E
Bayonne, *France* **18 E3** 43 30N 1 28W
Bayonne, *U.S.A.* **79 F10** 40 40N 74 7W
Bayovar, *Peru* **92 E2** 5 50S 81 0W
Bayqongyr, *Kazakstan* **26 E7** 47 48N 65 50 E
Bayram-Ali = Bayramaly, *Turkmenistan* **26 F7** 37 37N 62 10 E
Bayramaly, *Turkmenistan* **26 F7** 37 37N 62 10 E
Bayramiç, *Turkey* **21 E12** 39 48N 26 36 E
Bayreuth, *Germany* **16 D6** 49 56N 11 35 E
Bayrūt, *Lebanon* **47 B4** 33 53N 35 31 E
Bayt Lahm, *West Bank* **47 D4** 31 43N 35 12 E
Baytown, *U.S.A.* **81 L7** 29 43N 94 59W
Baza, *Spain* **19 D4** 37 30N 2 47W
Bazaruto, I. do, *Mozam.* **57 C6** 21 40S 35 28 E
Bazmān, Kūh-e, *Iran* **45 D9** 28 4N 60 1 E
Beach, *U.S.A.* **80 B3** 46 58N 104 0W
Beach City, *U.S.A.* **78 F3** 40 39N 81 35W
Beachport, *Australia* **63 F3** 37 29S 140 0 E
Beachy Hd., *U.K.* **11 G8** 50 44N 0 15 E
Beacon, *Australia* **61 F2** 30 26S 117 52 E
Beacon, *U.S.A.* **79 E11** 41 30N 73 58W
Beaconia, *Canada* **73 C9** 50 25N 96 31W
Beagle, Canal, *S. Amer.* **96 H3** 55 0S 68 30W
Beagle Bay, *Australia* **60 C3** 16 58S 122 40 E
Bealanana, *Madag.* **57 A8** 14 33S 48 44 E
Beamsville, *Canada* **78 C5** 43 12N 79 28W
Bear →, *U.S.A.* **84 G5** 38 56N 121 36W
Bear I., *Ireland* **13 E2** 51 38N 9 50W
Bear L., *B.C., Canada* **72 B3** 56 10N 126 52W
Bear L., *Man., Canada* **73 B9** 55 8N 96 0W
Bear L., *U.S.A.* **82 F8** 41 59N 111 21W
Bearcreek, *U.S.A.* **82 D9** 45 11N 109 6W
Beardmore, *Canada* **70 C2** 49 36N 87 57W
Beardmore Glacier, *Antarctica* **5 E11** 84 30S 170 0 E
Beardstown, *U.S.A.* **80 F9** 40 1N 90 26W
Béarn, *France* **18 E3** 43 20N 0 30W
Bearpaw Mts., *U.S.A.* **82 B9** 48 12N 109 30W
Bearskin Lake, *Canada* **70 B1** 53 58N 91 2W
Beata, C., *Dom. Rep.* **89 C5** 17 40N 71 30W
Beata, I., *Dom. Rep.* **89 C5** 17 34N 71 31W
Beatrice, *U.S.A.* **80 E6** 40 16N 96 45W
Beatrice, *Zimbabwe* **55 F3** 18 15S 30 55 E
Beatrice, C., *Australia* **62 A2** 14 20S 136 55 E
Beatton →, *Canada* **72 B4** 56 15N 120 45W
Beatton River, *Canada* **72 B4** 57 26N 121 20W
Beatty, *U.S.A.* **84 J10** 36 54N 116 46W
Beauce, Plaine de la, *France* **18 B4** 48 10N 1 45 E
Beauceville, *Canada* **71 C5** 46 13N 70 46W
Beaudesert, *Australia* **63 D5** 27 59S 153 0 E
Beaufort, *Malaysia* **36 C5** 5 30N 115 40 E
Beaufort, *N.C., U.S.A.* **77 H7** 34 43N 76 40W
Beaufort, *S.C., U.S.A.* **77 J5** 32 26N 80 40W
Beaufort Sea, *Arctic* **66 B5** 72 0N 140 0W
Beaufort West, *S. Africa* **56 E3** 32 18S 22 36 E
Beauharnois, *Canada* **70 C5** 45 20N 73 52W
Beaulieu →, *Canada* **72 A6** 62 3N 113 11W
Beauly, *U.K.* **12 D4** 57 30N 4 28W
Beauly →, *U.K.* **12 D4** 57 29N 4 27W
Beaumaris, *U.K.* **10 D3** 53 16N 4 6W
Beaumont, *Belgium* **15 D4** 50 15N 4 14 E
Beaumont, *U.S.A.* **81 K7** 30 5N 94 6W
Beaune, *France* **18 C6** 47 2N 4 50 E
Beauraing, *Belgium* **15 D4** 50 7N 4 57 E
Beauséjour, *Canada* **73 C9** 50 5N 96 35W
Beauvais, *France* **18 B5** 49 25N 2 8 E
Beauval, *Canada* **73 B7** 55 9N 107 37W
Beaver, *Okla., U.S.A.* **81 G4** 36 49N 100 31W
Beaver, *Pa., U.S.A.* **78 F4** 40 42N 80 19W
Beaver, *Utah, U.S.A.* **83 G7** 38 17N 112 38W
Beaver →, *B.C., Canada* **72 B4** 59 52N 124 20W
Beaver →, *Ont., Canada* **70 A2** 55 55N 87 48W
Beaver →, *Sask., Canada* **73 B7** 55 26N 107 45W
Beaver City, *U.S.A.* **80 E5** 40 8N 99 50W
Beaver Dam, *U.S.A.* **80 D10** 43 28N 88 50W
Beaver Falls, *U.S.A.* **78 F4** 40 46N 80 20W
Beaver Hill L., *Canada* **73 C10** 54 5N 94 50W
Beaver I., *U.S.A.* **76 C3** 45 40N 85 33W
Beaverhill L., *Alta., Canada* **72 C6** 53 27N 112 32W
Beaverhill L., *N.W.T., Canada* **73 A8** 63 2N 104 22W
Beaverlodge, *Canada* **72 B5** 55 11N 119 29W
Beavermouth, *Canada* **72 C5** 51 32N 117 23W
Beaverstone →, *Canada* **70 B2** 54 59N 89 25W
Beaverton, *Canada* **78 B5** 44 26N 79 9W
Beaverton, *U.S.A.* **84 E4** 45 29N 122 48W
Beawar, *India* **42 F6** 26 3N 74 18 E
Bebedouro, *Brazil* **95 A6** 21 0S 48 25W
Beboa, *Madag.* **57 B7** 17 22S 44 33 E
Beccles, *U.K.* **11 E9** 52 27N 1 35 E
Bečej, *Serbia, Yug.* **21 B9** 45 36N 20 3 E
Béchar, *Algeria* **50 B5** 31 38N 2 18W
Beckley, *U.S.A.* **76 G5** 37 47N 81 11W
Bedford, *Canada* **70 C5** 45 7N 72 59W
Bedford, *S. Africa* **56 E4** 32 40S 26 10 E
Bedford, *U.K.* **11 E7** 52 8N 0 28W
Bedford, *Ind., U.S.A.* **76 F2** 38 52N 86 29W
Bedford, *Iowa, U.S.A.* **80 E7** 40 40N 94 44W
Bedford, *Ohio, U.S.A.* **78 E3** 41 23N 81 32W
Bedford, *Pa., U.S.A.* **78 F6** 40 1N 78 30W
Bedford, *Va., U.S.A.* **76 G6** 37 20N 79 31W
Bedford, C., *Australia* **62 B4** 15 14S 145 21 E
Bedford Downs, *Australia* **60 C4** 17 19S 127 20 E
Bedfordshire □, *U.K.* **11 E7** 52 4N 0 28W
Bedourie, *Australia* **62 C2** 24 30S 139 30 E
Bedum, *Neths.* **15 A6** 53 18N 6 36 E
Beech Grove, *U.S.A.* **76 F2** 39 44N 86 3W
Beechy, *Canada* **73 C7** 50 53N 107 24W
Beenleigh, *Australia* **63 D5** 27 43S 153 10 E
Be'er Menuha, *Israel* **44 D2** 30 19N 35 8 E
Be'er Sheva, *Israel* **47 D3** 31 15N 34 48 E
Beersheba = Be'er Sheva, *Israel* **47 D3** 31 15N 34 48 E
Beeston, *U.K.* **10 E6** 52 56N 1 14W
Beetaloo, *Australia* **62 B1** 17 15S 133 50 E
Beeville, *U.S.A.* **81 L6** 28 24N 97 45W
Befale, *Dem. Rep. of the Congo* **52 D4** 0 25N 20 45 E
Befandriana, *Madag.* **57 C7** 21 55S 44 0 E
Befotaka, *Madag.* **57 C8** 23 49S 47 0 E
Bega, *Australia* **63 F4** 36 41S 149 51 E
Begusarai, *India* **43 G12** 25 24N 86 9 E
Behābād, *Iran* **45 C8** 32 24N 59 47 E
Behara, *Madag.* **57 C8** 24 55S 46 20 E
Behbehān, *Iran* **45 D6** 30 30N 50 15 E
Behshahr, *Iran* **45 B7** 36 45N 53 35 E
Bei Jiang →, *China* **33 D6** 23 2N 112 58 E
Bei'an, *China* **33 B7** 48 10N 126 20 E
Beihai, *China* **33 D5** 21 28N 109 6 E
Beijing, *China* **34 E9** 39 55N 116 20 E
Beijing □, *China* **34 E9** 39 55N 116 20 E
Beilen, *Neths.* **15 B6** 52 52N 6 27 E
Beilpajah, *Australia* **63 E3** 32 54S 143 52 E
Beinn na Faoghla = Benbecula, *U.K.* **12 D1** 57 26N 7 21W
Beipiao, *China* **35 D11** 41 52N 120 32 E
Beira, *Mozam.* **55 F3** 19 50S 34 52 E
Beirut = Bayrūt, *Lebanon* **47 B4** 33 53N 35 31 E
Beitaolaizhao, *China* **35 B13** 44 58N 125 58 E
Beitbridge, *Zimbabwe* **55 G3** 22 12S 30 0 E
Beizhen, *Liaoning, China* **35 D11** 41 38N 121 54 E
Beizhen, *Shandong, China* **35 F10** 37 20N 118 2 E
Beizhengzhen, *China* **35 B12** 44 31N 123 30 E
Beja, *Portugal* **19 C2** 38 2N 7 53W
Béja, *Tunisia* **51 A7** 36 43N 9 12 E
Bejaia, *Algeria* **50 A7** 36 42N 5 2 E
Béjar, *Spain* **19 B3** 40 23N 5 46W
Bejestān, *Iran* **45 C8** 34 30N 58 5 E
Békéscsaba, *Hungary* **17 E11** 46 40N 21 5 E
Bekily, *Madag.* **57 C8** 24 13S 45 19 E
Bekok, *Malaysia* **39 L4** 2 20N 103 7 E
Bela, *India* **43 G10** 25 50N 82 0 E
Bela, *Pakistan* **42 F2** 26 12N 66 20 E
Bela Crkva, *Serbia, Yug.* **21 B9** 44 55N 21 27 E
Bela Vista, *Brazil* **94 A4** 22 12S 56 20W
Bela Vista, *Mozam.* **57 D5** 26 10S 32 44 E
Belarus ■, *Europe* **24 D4** 53 30N 27 0 E
Belau = Palau ■, *Pac. Oc.* **64 G5** 7 30N 134 30 E
Belavenona, *Madag.* **57 C8** 24 50S 47 4 E
Belawan, *Indonesia* **36 D1** 3 33N 98 32 E
Belaya →, *Russia* **24 C9** 54 40N 56 0 E
Belaya Tserkov = Bila Tserkva, *Ukraine* **25 E5** 49 45N 30 10 E
Belcher Is., *Canada* **69 C12** 56 15N 78 45W
Belden, *U.S.A.* **84 E5** 40 2N 121 17W
Belebey, *Russia* **24 D9** 54 7N 54 7 E
Belém, *Brazil* **93 D9** 1 20S 48 30W
Belén, *Argentina* **94 B2** 27 40S 67 5W
Belén, *Paraguay* **94 A4** 23 30S 57 6W
Belen, *U.S.A.* **83 J10** 34 40N 106 46W
Belet Uen, *Somali Rep.* **46 G4** 4 30N 45 5 E
Belev, *Russia* **24 D6** 53 50N 36 5 E
Belfair, *U.S.A.* **84 C4** 47 27N 122 50W
Belfast, *S. Africa* **57 D5** 25 42S 30 2 E
Belfast, *U.K.* **13 B6** 54 37N 5 56W
Belfast, *Maine, U.S.A.* **71 D6** 44 26N 69 1W
Belfast, *N.Y., U.S.A.* **78 D6** 42 21N 78 7W
Belfast L., *U.K.* **13 B6** 54 40N 5 50W
Belfield, *U.S.A.* **80 B3** 46 53N 103 12W
Belfort, *France* **18 C7** 47 38N 6 50 E
Belfry, *U.S.A.* **82 D9** 45 9N 109 1W
Belgaum, *India* **40 M9** 15 55N 74 35 E
Belgium ■, *Europe* **15 D4** 50 30N 5 0 E
Belgorod, *Russia* **25 D6** 50 35N 36 35 E
Belgorod-Dnestrovskiy = Bilhorod-Dnistrovskyy, *Ukraine* **25 E5** 46 11N 30 23 E
Belgrade = Beograd, *Serbia, Yug.* **21 B9** 44 50N 20 37 E
Belgrade, *U.S.A.* **82 D8** 45 47N 111 11W
Belhaven, *U.S.A.* **77 H7** 35 33N 76 37W
Beli Drim →, *Europe* **21 C9** 42 6N 20 25 E
Belinyu, *Indonesia* **36 E3** 1 35S 105 50 E
Beliton Is. = Belitung, *Indonesia* **36 E3** 3 10S 107 50 E
Belitung, *Indonesia* **36 E3** 3 10S 107 50 E
Belize ■, *Cent. Amer.* **87 D7** 17 0N 88 30W
Belize City, *Belize* **87 D7** 17 25N 88 0W
Belkovskiy, Ostrov, *Russia* **27 B14** 75 32N 135 44 E
Bell →, *Canada* **70 C4** 49 48N 77 38W
Bell Bay, *Australia* **62 G4** 41 6S 146 53 E
Bell I., *Canada* **71 B8** 50 46N 55 35W
Bell-Irving →, *Canada* **72 B3** 56 12N 129 5W
Bell Peninsula, *Canada* **69 B11** 63 50N 82 0W
Bell Ville, *Argentina* **94 C3** 32 40S 62 40W
Bella Bella, *Canada* **72 C3** 52 10N 128 10W
Bella Coola, *Canada* **72 C3** 52 25N 126 40W
Bella Unión, *Uruguay* **94 C4** 30 15S 57 40W
Bella Vista, *Corrientes, Argentina* **94 B4** 28 33S 59 0W
Bella Vista, *Tucuman, Argentina* **94 B2** 27 10S 65 25W
Bellaire, *U.S.A.* **78 F4** 40 1N 80 45W
Bellary, *India* **40 M10** 15 10N 76 56 E
Bellata, *Australia* **63 D4** 29 53S 149 46 E
Belle Fourche, *U.S.A.* **80 C3** 44 40N 103 51W
Belle Fourche →, *U.S.A.* **80 C3** 44 26N 102 18W
Belle Glade, *U.S.A.* **77 M5** 26 41N 80 40W
Belle-Île, *France* **18 C2** 47 20N 3 10W
Belle Isle, *Canada* **71 B8** 51 57N 55 25W
Belle Isle, Str. of, *Canada* **71 B8** 51 30N 56 30W
Belle Plaine, *Iowa, U.S.A.* **80 E8** 41 54N 92 17W
Belle Plaine, *Minn., U.S.A.* **80 C8** 44 37N 93 46W
Belledune, *Canada* **71 C6** 47 55N 65 50W

Bilyana

Bellefontaine, *U.S.A.* **76 E4** 40 22N 83 46W
Bellefonte, *U.S.A.* **78 F7** 40 55N 77 47W
Belleoram, *Canada* **71 C8** 47 31N 55 25W
Belleville, *Canada* **70 D4** 44 10N 77 23W
Belleville, *Ill., U.S.A.* **80 F10** 38 31N 89 59W
Belleville, *Kans., U.S.A.* **80 F6** 39 50N 97 38W
Belleville, *N.Y., U.S.A.* **79 C8** 43 46N 76 10W
Bellevue, *Canada* **72 D6** 49 35N 114 22W
Bellevue, *Idaho, U.S.A.* **82 E6** 43 28N 114 16W
Bellevue, *Ohio, U.S.A.* **78 E2** 41 17N 82 51W
Bellevue, *Wash., U.S.A.* **84 C4** 47 37N 122 12W
Bellin = Kangirsuk, *Canada* **69 C13** 60 0N 70 0W
Bellingen, *Australia* **63 E5** 30 25S 152 50 E
Bellingham, *U.S.A.* **84 B4** 48 46N 122 29W
Bellingshausen Sea, *Antarctica* **5 C17** 66 0S 80 0W
Bellinzona, *Switz.* **18 C8** 46 11N 9 1 E
Bello, *Colombia* **92 B3** 6 20N 75 33W
Bellows Falls, *U.S.A.* **79 C12** 43 8N 72 27W
Bellpat, *Pakistan* **42 E3** 29 0N 68 5 E
Belluno, *Italy* **20 A5** 46 9N 12 13 E
Bellville, *U.S.A.* **81 L6** 29 57N 96 15W
Bellwood, *U.S.A.* **78 F6** 40 36N 78 20W
Belmont, *Australia* **63 E5** 33 4S 151 42 E
Belmont, *Canada* **78 D3** 42 53N 81 5W
Belmont, *S. Africa* **56 D3** 29 28S 24 22 E
Belmont, *U.S.A.* **78 D6** 42 14N 78 2W
Belmonte, *Brazil* **93 G11** 16 0S 39 0W
Belmopan, *Belize* **87 D7** 17 18N 88 30W
Belmullet, *Ireland* **13 B2** 54 14N 9 58W
Belo Horizonte, *Brazil* **93 G10** 19 55S 43 56W
Belo-sur-Mer, *Madag.* **57 C7** 20 42S 44 0 E
Belo-Tsiribihina, *Madag.* **57 B7** 19 40S 44 30 E
Belogorsk, *Russia* **27 D13** 51 0N 128 20 E
Beloha, *Madag.* **57 D8** 25 10S 45 3 E
Beloit, *Kans., U.S.A.* **80 F5** 39 28N 98 6W
Beloit, *Wis., U.S.A.* **80 D10** 42 31N 89 2W
Belokorovichi, *Ukraine* **17 C15** 51 7N 28 2 E
Belomorsk, *Russia* **24 B5** 64 35N 34 54 E
Belonia, *India* **41 H17** 23 15N 91 30 E
Beloretsk, *Russia* **24 D10** 53 58N 58 24 E
Belorussia = Belarus ■, *Europe* **24 D4** 53 30N 27 0 E
Belovo, *Russia* **26 D9** 54 30N 86 0 E
Beloye, Ozero, *Russia* **24 B6** 60 10N 37 35 E
Beloye More, *Russia* **24 A6** 66 30N 38 0 E
Belozersk, *Russia* **24 B6** 60 1N 37 45 E
Beltana, *Australia* **63 E2** 30 48S 138 25 E
Belterra, *Brazil* **93 D8** 2 45S 55 0W
Belton, *S.C., U.S.A.* **77 H4** 34 31N 82 30W
Belton, *Tex., U.S.A.* **81 K6** 31 3N 97 28W
Belton Res., *U.S.A.* **81 K6** 31 8N 97 32W
Beltsy = Bălţi, *Moldova* **25 E4** 47 48N 27 58 E
Belturbet, *Ireland* **13 B4** 54 6N 7 26W
Belukha, *Russia* **26 E9** 49 50N 86 50 E
Beluran, *Malaysia* **36 C5** 5 48N 117 35 E
Belvidere, *Ill., U.S.A.* **80 D10** 42 15N 88 50W
Belvidere, *N.J., U.S.A.* **79 F9** 40 50N 75 5W
Belyando →, *Australia* **62 C4** 21 38S 146 50 E
Belyy, Ostrov, *Russia* **26 B8** 73 30N 71 0 E
Belyy Yar, *Russia* **26 D9** 58 26N 84 39 E
Belzoni, *U.S.A.* **81 J9** 33 11N 90 29W
Bemaraha, Lembalemban' i, *Madag.* **57 B7** 18 40S 44 45 E
Bemarivo, *Madag.* **57 C7** 21 45S 44 45 E
Bemarivo →, *Madag.* **57 B8** 15 27S 47 40 E
Bemavo, *Madag.* **57 C8** 21 33S 45 25 E
Bembéréke, *Benin* **50 F6** 10 11N 2 43 E
Bembesi, *Zimbabwe* **55 G2** 20 0S 28 58 E
Bembesi →, *Zimbabwe* **55 F2** 18 57S 27 47 E
Bemidji, *U.S.A.* **80 B7** 47 28N 94 53W
Ben, *Iran* **45 C6** 32 32N 50 45 E
Ben Cruachan, *U.K.* **12 E3** 56 26N 5 8W
Ben Dearg, *U.K.* **12 D4** 57 47N 4 56W
Ben Hope, *U.K.* **12 C4** 58 25N 4 36W
Ben Lawers, *U.K.* **12 E4** 56 32N 4 14W
Ben Lomond, *N.S.W., Australia* **63 E5** 30 1S 151 43 E
Ben Lomond, *Tas., Australia* **62 G4** 41 38S 147 42 E
Ben Lomond, *U.K.* **12 E4** 56 11N 4 38W
Ben Luc, *Vietnam* **39 G6** 10 39N 106 29 E
Ben Macdhui, *U.K.* **12 D5** 57 4N 3 40W
Ben Mhor, *U.K.* **12 D1** 57 15N 7 18W
Ben More, *Arg. & Bute, U.K.* **12 E2** 56 26N 6 1W
Ben More, *Stirl., U.K.* **12 E4** 56 23N 4 32W
Ben More Assynt, *U.K.* **12 C4** 58 8N 4 52W
Ben Nevis, *U.K.* **12 E3** 56 48N 5 1W
Ben Quang, *Vietnam* **38 D6** 17 3N 106 55 E
Ben Vorlich, *U.K.* **12 E4** 56 21N 4 14W
Ben Wyvis, *U.K.* **12 D4** 57 40N 4 35W
Bena, *Nigeria* **50 F7** 11 20N 5 50 E
Benagerie, *Australia* **63 E3** 31 25S 140 22 E
Benalla, *Australia* **63 F4** 36 30S 146 0 E
Benambra, Mt., *Australia* **63 F4** 36 31S 147 34 E
Benares = Varanasi, *India* **43 G10** 25 22N 83 0 E
Benavente, *Spain* **19 A3** 42 2N 5 43W
Benavides, *U.S.A.* **81 M5** 27 36N 98 25W
Benbecula, *U.K.* **12 D1** 57 26N 7 21W
Benbonyathe, *Australia* **63 E2** 30 25S 139 11 E
Bencubbin, *Australia* **61 F2** 30 48S 117 52 E
Bend, *U.S.A.* **82 D3** 44 4N 121 19W
Bender Beila, *Somali Rep.* **46 F5** 9 30N 50 48 E
Bendering, *Australia* **61 F2** 32 23S 118 18 E
Bendery = Tighina, *Moldova* **25 E4** 46 50N 29 30 E
Bendigo, *Australia* **63 F3** 36 40S 144 15 E
Benē Beraq, *Israel* **47 C3** 32 6N 34 51 E
Benenitra, *Madag.* **57 C8** 23 27S 45 5 E
Benevento, *Italy* **20 D6** 41 8N 14 45 E
Benga, *Mozam.* **55 F3** 16 11S 33 40 E
Bengal, Bay of, *Ind. Oc.* **41 M17** 15 0N 90 0 E
Bengbu, *China* **35 H9** 32 58N 117 20 E
Benghazi = Banghāzī, *Libya* **51 B10** 32 11N 20 3 E
Bengkalis, *Indonesia* **36 D2** 1 30N 102 10 E
Bengkulu, *Indonesia* **36 E2** 3 50S 102 12 E
Bengkulu □, *Indonesia* **36 E2** 3 48S 102 16 E
Bengough, *Canada* **73 D7** 49 25N 105 10W
Benguela, *Angola* **53 G2** 12 37S 13 25 E
Benguérua, I., *Mozam.* **57 C6** 21 58S 35 28 E
Beni, *Dem. Rep. of the Congo* **54 B2** 0 30N 29 27 E
Beni →, *Bolivia* **92 F5** 10 23S 65 24W
Beni Mellal, *Morocco* **50 B4** 32 21N 6 21W
Beni Suef, *Egypt* **51 C12** 29 5N 31 6 E
Beniah L., *Canada* **72 A6** 63 23N 112 17W
Benicia, *U.S.A.* **84 G4** 38 3N 122 9W
Benidorm, *Spain* **19 C5** 38 33N 0 9W
Benin ■, *Africa* **50 G6** 10 0N 2 0 E
Benin, Bight of, *W. Afr.* **50 H6** 5 0N 3 0 E
Benin City, *Nigeria* **50 G7** 6 20N 5 31 E
Benitses, *Greece* **23 A3** 39 32N 19 55 E
Benjamin Aceval, *Paraguay* **94 A4** 24 58S 57 34W
Benjamin Constant, *Brazil* **92 D4** 4 40S 70 15W
Benjamin Hill, *Mexico* **86 A2** 30 10N 111 10W
Benkelman, *U.S.A.* **80 E4** 40 3N 101 32W
Benlidi, *Australia* **62 C3** 24 35S 144 50 E
Bennett, *Canada* **72 B2** 59 56N 134 53W
Bennett, L., *Australia* **60 D5** 22 50S 131 2 E
Bennetta, Ostrov, *Russia* **27 B15** 76 21N 148 56 E
Bennettsville, *U.S.A.* **77 H6** 34 37N 79 41W
Bennington, *U.S.A.* **79 D11** 43 0N 71 55W
Benoni, *S. Africa* **57 D4** 26 11S 28 18 E
Benque Viejo, *Belize* **87 D7** 17 5N 89 8W
Benson, *U.S.A.* **83 L8** 31 58N 110 18W
Bent, *Iran* **45 E8** 26 20N 59 31 E
Benteng, *Indonesia* **37 F6** 6 10S 120 30 E
Bentinck I., *Australia* **62 B2** 17 3S 139 35 E
Bento Gonçalves, *Brazil* **95 B5** 29 10S 51 31W
Benton, *Ark., U.S.A.* **81 H8** 34 34N 92 35W
Benton, *Calif., U.S.A.* **84 H8** 37 48N 118 32W
Benton, *Ill., U.S.A.* **80 G10** 38 0N 88 55W
Benton Harbor, *U.S.A.* **76 D2** 42 6N 86 27W
Bentung, *Malaysia* **39 L3** 3 31N 101 55 E
Benue →, *Nigeria* **50 G7** 7 48N 6 46 E
Benxi, *China* **35 D12** 41 20N 123 48 E
Beo, *Indonesia* **37 D7** 4 25N 126 50 E
Beograd, *Serbia, Yug.* **21 B9** 44 50N 20 37 E
Beowawe, *U.S.A.* **82 F5** 40 35N 116 29W
Beppu, *Japan* **31 H5** 33 15N 131 30 E
Beqaa Valley = Al Biqā □, *Lebanon* **47 A5** 34 10N 36 10 E
Berati, *Albania* **21 D8** 40 43N 19 59 E
Berau, Teluk, *Indonesia* **37 E8** 2 30S 132 30 E
Berber, *Sudan* **51 E12** 18 0N 34 0 E
Berbera, *Somali Rep.* **46 E4** 10 30N 45 2 E
Berbérati, *C.A.R.* **52 D3** 4 15N 15 40 E
Berbice →, *Guyana* **92 B7** 6 20N 57 32W
Berdichev = Berdychiv, *Ukraine* **25 E4** 49 57N 28 30 E
Berdsk, *Russia* **26 D9** 54 47N 83 2 E
Berdyansk, *Ukraine* **25 E6** 46 45N 36 50 E
Berdychiv, *Ukraine* **25 E4** 49 57N 28 30 E
Berea, *U.S.A.* **76 G3** 37 34N 84 17W
Berebere, *Indonesia* **37 D7** 2 25N 128 45 E
Bereda, *Somali Rep.* **46 E5** 11 45N 51 0 E
Berehove, *Ukraine* **17 D12** 48 15N 22 35 E
Berekum, *Ghana* **50 G5** 7 29N 2 34W
Berens →, *Canada* **73 C9** 52 25N 97 2W
Berens I., *Canada* **73 C9** 52 18N 97 18W
Berens River, *Canada* **73 C9** 52 25N 97 0W
Berestechko, *Ukraine* **17 C13** 50 22N 25 5 E
Berevo, *Mahajanga, Madag.* **57 B7** 17 14S 44 17 E
Berevo, *Toliara, Madag.* **57 B7** 19 44S 44 58 E
Bereza, *Belarus* **17 B13** 52 31N 24 51 E
Berezhany, *Ukraine* **17 D13** 49 26N 24 58 E
Berezina = Byarezina →, *Belarus* **24 D5** 52 33N 30 14 E
Berezniki, *Russia* **26 D6** 59 24N 56 46 E
Berezovo, *Russia* **24 B12** 64 0N 65 0 E
Berga, *Spain* **19 A6** 42 6N 1 48 E
Bergama, *Turkey* **21 E12** 39 8N 27 11 E
Bérgamo, *Italy* **18 D8** 45 41N 9 43 E
Bergen, *Neths.* **15 B4** 52 40N 4 43 E
Bergen, *Norway* **9 F11** 60 20N 5 20 E
Bergen, *U.S.A.* **78 C7** 43 5N 77 57W
Bergen op Zoom, *Neths.* **15 C4** 51 28N 4 18 E
Bergerac, *France* **18 D4** 44 51N 0 30 E
Bergisch Gladbach, *Germany* **15 D7** 50 59N 7 8 E
Bergville, *S. Africa* **57 D4** 28 52S 29 18 E
Berhala, Selat, *Indonesia* **36 E2** 1 0S 104 15 E
Berhampore = Baharampur, *India* **43 G13** 24 2N 88 27 E
Berhampur = Brahmapur, *India* **41 K14** 19 15N 84 54 E
Bering Sea, *Pac. Oc.* **68 C1** 58 0N 171 0 E
Bering Strait, *Pac. Oc.* **68 B3** 65 30N 169 0W
Beringovskiy, *Russia* **27 C18** 63 3N 179 19 E
Berisso, *Argentina* **94 C4** 34 56S 57 50W
Berja, *Spain* **19 D4** 36 50N 2 56W
Berkeley, *U.S.A.* **84 H4** 37 52N 122 16W
Berkeley Springs, *U.S.A.* **76 F6** 39 38N 78 14W
Berkner I., *Antarctica* **5 D18** 79 30S 50 0W
Berkshire Downs, *U.K.* **11 F6** 51 33N 1 29W
Berland →, *Canada* **72 C5** 54 0N 116 50W
Berlin, *Germany* **16 B7** 52 30N 13 25 E
Berlin, *Md., U.S.A.* **76 F8** 38 20N 75 13W
Berlin, *N.H., U.S.A.* **79 B13** 44 28N 71 11W
Berlin, *Wis., U.S.A.* **76 D1** 43 58N 88 57W
Bermejo →, *Formosa, Argentina* **94 B4** 26 51S 58 23W
Bermejo →, *San Juan, Argentina* **94 C2** 32 30S 67 30W
Bermuda ■, *Atl. Oc.* **66 F13** 32 45N 65 0W
Bern, *Switz.* **18 C7** 46 57N 7 28 E
Bernado, *U.S.A.* **83 J10** 34 30N 106 53W
Bernalillo, *U.S.A.* **83 J10** 35 18N 106 33W
Bernardo de Irigoyen, *Argentina* **95 B5** 26 15S 53 40W
Bernardo O'Higgins □, *Chile* **94 C1** 34 15S 70 45W
Bernasconi, *Argentina* **94 D3** 37 55S 63 44W
Bernburg, *Germany* **16 C6** 51 47N 11 44 E
Berne = Bern, *Switz.* **18 C7** 46 57N 7 28 E
Berneray, *U.K.* **12 D1** 57 43N 7 11W
Bernier I., *Australia* **61 D1** 24 50S 113 12 E
Bernina, Piz, *Switz.* **18 C8** 46 20N 9 54 E
Beroroha, *Madag.* **57 C8** 21 40S 45 10 E
Beroun, *Czech Rep.* **16 D8** 49 57N 14 5 E
Berri, *Australia* **63 E3** 34 14S 140 35 E
Berry, *Australia* **63 E5** 34 46S 150 43 E
Berry, *France* **18 C5** 46 50N 2 0 E
Berry Is., *Bahamas* **88 A4** 25 40N 77 50W
Berryessa L., *U.S.A.* **84 G4** 38 31N 122 6W
Berryville, *U.S.A.* **81 G8** 36 22N 93 34W
Bershad, *Ukraine* **17 D15** 48 22N 29 31 E
Berthold, *U.S.A.* **80 A4** 48 19N 101 44W
Berthoud, *U.S.A.* **80 E2** 40 19N 105 5W
Bertoua, *Cameroon* **52 D2** 4 30N 13 45 E
Bertraghboy B., *Ireland* **13 C2** 53 22N 9 54W
Bertrand, *U.S.A.* **80 E5** 40 32N 99 38W
Berwick, *U.S.A.* **79 E8** 41 3N 76 14W
Berwick-upon-Tweed, *U.K.* **10 B6** 55 46N 2 0W
Berwyn Mts., *U.K.* **10 E4** 52 54N 3 26W
Besal, *Pakistan* **43 B5** 35 4N 73 56 E
Besalampy, *Madag.* **57 B7** 16 43S 44 29 E
Besançon, *France* **18 C7** 47 15N 6 2 E
Besar, *Indonesia* **36 E5** 2 40S 116 0 E
Besnard L., *Canada* **73 B7** 55 25N 106 0W
Besor, N. →, *Egypt* **47 D3** 31 28N 34 22 E
Bessarabiya, *Moldova* **17 E15** 47 0N 28 10 E
Bessarabka = Basarabeasca, *Moldova* **17 E15** 46 21N 28 58 E
Bessemer, *Ala., U.S.A.* **77 J2** 33 24N 86 58W
Bessemer, *Mich., U.S.A.* **80 B9** 46 29N 90 3W
Bet She'an, *Israel* **47 C4** 32 30N 35 30 E
Bet Shemesh, *Israel* **47 D4** 31 44N 35 0 E
Betafo, *Madag.* **57 B8** 19 50S 46 51 E
Betancuria, *Canary Is.* **22 F5** 28 25N 14 3W
Betanzos, *Spain* **19 A1** 43 15N 8 12W
Bétaré Oya, *Cameroon* **52 C2** 5 40N 14 5 E
Bethal, *S. Africa* **57 D4** 26 27S 29 28 E
Bethanien, *Namibia* **56 D2** 26 31S 17 8 E
Bethany, *U.S.A.* **80 E7** 40 16N 94 2W
Bethel, *Alaska, U.S.A.* **68 B3** 60 48N 161 45W
Bethel, *Vt., U.S.A.* **79 C12** 43 50N 72 38W
Bethel Park, *U.S.A.* **78 F4** 40 20N 80 1W
Bethlehem = Bayt Lahm, *West Bank* **47 D4** 31 43N 35 12 E
Bethlehem, *S. Africa* **57 D4** 28 14S 28 18 E
Bethlehem, *U.S.A.* **79 F9** 40 37N 75 23W
Bethulie, *S. Africa* **56 E4** 30 30S 25 59 E
Béthune, *France* **18 A5** 50 30N 2 38 E
Bethungra, *Australia* **63 E4** 34 45S 147 51 E
Betioky, *Madag.* **57 C7** 23 48S 44 20 E
Betong, *Thailand* **39 K3** 5 45N 101 5 E
Betoota, *Australia* **62 D3** 25 45S 140 42 E
Betroka, *Madag.* **57 C8** 23 16S 46 0 E
Betsiamites, *Canada* **71 C6** 48 56N 68 40W
Betsiamites →, *Canada* **71 C6** 48 56N 68 38W
Betsiboka →, *Madag.* **57 B8** 16 3S 46 36 E
Bettiah, *India* **43 F11** 26 48N 84 33 E
Betul, *India* **40 J10** 21 58N 77 59 E
Betung, *Malaysia* **36 D4** 1 24N 111 31 E
Betws-y-Coed, *U.K.* **10 D4** 53 5N 3 48W
Beulah, *U.S.A.* **80 B4** 47 16N 101 47W
Beveren, *Belgium* **15 C4** 51 12N 4 16 E
Beverley, *Australia* **61 F2** 32 9S 116 56 E
Beverley, *U.K.* **10 D7** 53 51N 0 26W
Beverly, *Mass., U.S.A.* **79 D14** 42 33N 70 53W
Beverly, *Wash., U.S.A.* **82 C4** 46 50N 119 56W
Beverly Hills, *U.S.A.* **85 L8** 34 4N 118 25W
Bexhill, *U.K.* **11 G8** 50 51N 0 29 E
Beyānlū, *Iran* **44 C5** 36 0N 47 51 E
Beyneu, *Kazakstan* **25 E10** 45 18N 55 9 E
Beypazarı, *Turkey* **25 F5** 40 10N 31 56 E
Beyşehir Gölü, *Turkey* **25 G5** 37 41N 31 33 E
Bezhitsa, *Russia* **24 D5** 53 19N 34 17 E
Béziers, *France* **18 E5** 43 20N 3 12 E
Bezwada = Vijayawada, *India* **41 L12** 16 31N 80 39 E
Bhachau, *India* **40 H7** 23 20N 70 16 E
Bhadarwah, *India* **43 C6** 32 58N 75 46 E
Bhadrakh, *India* **41 J15** 21 10N 86 30 E
Bhadravati, *India* **40 N9** 13 49N 75 40 E
Bhagalpur, *India* **43 G12** 25 10N 87 0 E
Bhakkar, *Pakistan* **42 D4** 31 40N 71 5 E
Bhakra Dam, *India* **42 D7** 31 30N 76 45 E
Bhamo, *Burma* **41 G20** 24 15N 97 15 E
Bhandara, *India* **40 J11** 21 5N 79 42 E
Bhanrer Ra., *India* **42 H8** 23 40N 79 45 E
Bharat = India ■, *Asia* **40 K11** 20 0N 78 0 E
Bharatpur, *India* **42 F7** 27 15N 77 30 E
Bhatinda, *India* **42 D6** 30 15N 74 57 E
Bhatpara, *India* **43 H13** 22 50N 88 25 E
Bhaun, *Pakistan* **42 C5** 32 55N 72 40 E
Bhaunagar = Bhavnagar, *India* **42 J5** 21 45N 72 10 E
Bhavnagar, *India* **42 J5** 21 45N 72 10 E
Bhawanipatna, *India* **41 K12** 19 55N 80 10 E
Bhera, *Pakistan* **42 C5** 32 29N 72 57 E
Bhilsa = Vidisha, *India* **42 H7** 23 28N 77 53 E
Bhilwara, *India* **42 G6** 25 25N 74 38 E
Bhima →, *India* **40 L10** 16 25N 77 17 E
Bhimavaram, *India* **41 L12** 16 30N 81 30 E
Bhimbar, *Pakistan* **43 C6** 32 59N 74 3 E
Bhind, *India* **43 F8** 26 30N 78 46 E
Bhiwandi, *India* **40 K8** 19 20N 73 0 E
Bhiwani, *India* **42 E7** 28 50N 76 9 E
Bhola, *Bangla.* **41 H17** 22 45N 90 35 E
Bhopal, *India* **42 H7** 23 20N 77 30 E
Bhubaneshwar, *India* **41 J14** 20 15N 85 50 E
Bhuj, *India* **42 H3** 23 15N 69 49 E
Bhusaval, *India* **40 J9** 21 3N 75 46 E
Bhutan ■, *Asia* **41 F17** 27 25N 90 30 E
Biafra, B. of = Bonny, Bight of, *Africa* **52 D1** 3 30N 9 20 E
Biak, *Indonesia* **37 E9** 1 10S 136 6 E
Biała Podlaska, *Poland* **17 B12** 52 4N 23 6 E
Białogard, *Poland* **16 A8** 54 2N 15 58 E
Białystok, *Poland* **17 B12** 53 10N 23 10 E
Biārjmand, *Iran* **45 B7** 36 6N 55 53 E
Biaro, *Indonesia* **37 D7** 2 5N 125 26 E
Biarritz, *France* **18 E3** 43 29N 1 33W
Bibai, *Japan* **30 C10** 43 19N 141 52 E
Bibby I., *Canada* **73 A10** 61 55N 93 0W
Biberach, *Germany* **16 D5** 48 5N 9 47 E
Biboohra, *Australia* **62 B4** 16 56S 145 25 E
Bibungwa, *Dem. Rep. of the Congo* **54 C2** 2 40S 28 15 E
Bic, *Canada* **71 C6** 48 20N 68 41W
Bicester, *U.K.* **11 F6** 51 54N 1 9W
Bickerton I., *Australia* **62 A2** 13 45S 136 10 E
Bicknell, *Ind., U.S.A.* **76 F2** 38 47N 87 19W
Bicknell, *Utah, U.S.A.* **83 G8** 38 20N 111 33W
Bida, *Nigeria* **50 G7** 9 3N 5 58 E
Bidar, *India* **40 L10** 17 55N 77 35 E
Biddeford, *U.S.A.* **71 D5** 43 30N 70 28W
Bideford, *U.K.* **11 F3** 51 1N 4 13W
Bideford Bay, *U.K.* **11 F3** 51 5N 4 20W
Bidor, *Malaysia* **39 K3** 4 6N 101 15 E
Bié, Planalto de, *Angola* **53 G3** 12 0S 16 0 E
Bieber, *U.S.A.* **82 F3** 41 7N 121 8W
Biel, *Switz.* **18 C7** 47 8N 7 14 E
Bielefeld, *Germany* **16 B5** 52 1N 8 33 E
Biella, *Italy* **18 D8** 45 34N 8 3 E
Bielsk Podlaski, *Poland* **17 B12** 52 47N 23 12 E
Bielsko-Biała, *Poland* **17 D10** 49 50N 19 2 E
Bien Hoa, *Vietnam* **39 G6** 10 57N 106 49 E
Bienfait, *Canada* **73 D8** 49 10N 102 50W
Bienne = Biel, *Switz.* **18 C7** 47 8N 7 14 E
Bienville, L., *Canada* **70 A5** 55 5N 72 40W
Biesiesfontein, *S. Africa* **56 E2** 30 57S 17 58 E
Big →, *Canada* **71 B8** 54 50N 58 55W
Big B., *Canada* **71 A7** 55 43N 60 35W
Big Bear City, *U.S.A.* **85 L10** 34 16N 116 51W
Big Bear Lake, *U.S.A.* **85 L10** 34 15N 116 56W
Big Beaver, *Canada* **73 D7** 49 10N 105 10W
Big Belt Mts., *U.S.A.* **82 C8** 46 30N 111 25W
Big Bend, *Swaziland* **57 D5** 26 50S 31 58 E
Big Bend National Park, *U.S.A.* **81 L3** 29 20N 103 5W
Big Black →, *U.S.A.* **81 K9** 32 3N 91 4W
Big Blue →, *U.S.A.* **80 F6** 39 35N 96 34W
Big Cr. →, *Canada* **72 C4** 51 42N 122 41W
Big Creek, *U.S.A.* **84 H7** 37 11N 119 14W
Big Cypress Swamp, *U.S.A.* **77 M5** 26 12N 81 10W
Big Falls, *U.S.A.* **80 A8** 48 12N 93 48W
Big Fork →, *U.S.A.* **80 A8** 48 31N 93 43W
Big Horn Mts. = Bighorn Mts., *U.S.A.* **82 D10** 44 30N 107 30W
Big Lake, *U.S.A.* **81 K4** 31 12N 101 28W
Big Moose, *U.S.A.* **79 C10** 43 49N 74 58W
Big Muddy Cr. →, *U.S.A.* **80 A2** 48 8N 104 36W
Big Pine, *U.S.A.* **84 H8** 37 10N 118 17W
Big Piney, *U.S.A.* **82 E8** 42 32N 110 7W
Big Quill L., *Canada* **73 C8** 51 55N 104 50W
Big Rapids, *U.S.A.* **76 D3** 43 42N 85 29W
Big River, *Canada* **73 C7** 53 50N 107 0W
Big Run, *U.S.A.* **78 F6** 40 57N 78 55W
Big Sable Pt., *U.S.A.* **76 C2** 44 3N 86 1W
Big Sand L., *Canada* **73 B9** 57 45N 99 45W
Big Sandy, *U.S.A.* **82 B8** 48 11N 110 7W
Big Sandy Cr. →, *U.S.A.* **80 F3** 38 7N 102 29W
Big Sioux →, *U.S.A.* **80 D6** 42 29N 96 27W
Big Spring, *U.S.A.* **81 J4** 32 15N 101 28W
Big Springs, *U.S.A.* **80 E3** 41 4N 102 5W
Big Stone City, *U.S.A.* **80 C6** 45 18N 96 28W
Big Stone Gap, *U.S.A.* **77 G4** 36 52N 82 47W
Big Stone L., *U.S.A.* **80 C6** 45 30N 96 35W
Big Sur, *U.S.A.* **84 J5** 36 15N 121 48W
Big Timber, *U.S.A.* **82 D9** 45 50N 109 57W
Big Trout L., *Canada* **70 B2** 53 40N 90 0W
Biğa, *Turkey* **21 D12** 40 13N 27 14 E
Bigadiç, *Turkey* **21 E13** 39 22N 28 7 E
Bigfork, *U.S.A.* **82 B6** 48 4N 114 4W
Biggar, *Canada* **73 C7** 52 4N 108 0W
Biggar, *U.K.* **12 F5** 55 38N 3 32W
Bigge I., *Australia* **60 B4** 14 35S 125 10 E
Biggenden, *Australia* **63 D5** 25 31S 152 4 E
Biggleswade, *U.K.* **11 E7** 52 5N 0 14W
Biggs, *U.S.A.* **84 F5** 39 25N 121 43W
Bighorn, *U.S.A.* **82 C10** 46 10N 107 27W
Bighorn →, *U.S.A.* **82 C10** 46 10N 107 28W
Bighorn Mts., *U.S.A.* **82 D10** 44 30N 107 30W
Bigstone L., *Canada* **73 C9** 53 42N 95 44W
Bigwa, *Tanzania* **54 D4** 7 10S 39 10 E
Bihać, *Bos.-H.* **16 F8** 44 49N 15 57 E
Bihar, *India* **43 G11** 25 5N 85 40 E
Bihar □, *India* **43 G12** 25 0N 86 0 E
Biharamulo, *Tanzania* **54 C3** 2 25S 31 25 E
Biharamulo □, *Tanzania* **54 C3** 2 30S 31 20 E
Bihor, Munţii, *Romania* **17 E12** 46 29N 22 47 E
Bijagós, Arquipélago dos, *Guinea-Biss.* **50 F2** 11 15N 16 10W
Bijaipur, *India* **42 F7** 26 2N 77 20 E
Bijapur, *Karnataka, India* **40 L9** 16 50N 75 55 E
Bijapur, *Mad. P., India* **41 K12** 18 50N 80 50 E
Bījār, *Iran* **44 C5** 35 52N 47 35 E
Bijeljina, *Bos.-H.* **21 B8** 44 46N 19 14 E
Bijnor, *India* **42 E8** 29 27N 78 11 E
Bikaner, *India* **42 E5** 28 2N 73 18 E
Bikapur, *India* **43 F10** 26 30N 82 7 E
Bikeqi, *China* **34 D6** 40 43N 111 20 E
Bikfayyā, *Lebanon* **47 B4** 33 55N 35 41 E
Bikin, *Russia* **27 E14** 46 50N 134 20 E
Bikin →, *Russia* **30 A7** 46 51N 134 2 E
Bikini Atoll, *Pac. Oc.* **64 F8** 12 0N 167 30 E
Bila Tserkva, *Ukraine* **25 E5** 49 45N 30 10 E
Bilara, *India* **42 F5** 26 14N 73 53 E
Bilaspur, *Mad. P., India* **43 H10** 22 2N 82 15 E
Bilaspur, *Punjab, India* **42 D7** 31 19N 76 50 E
Bilauk Taungdan, *Thailand* **38 F2** 13 0N 99 0 E
Bilbao, *Spain* **19 A4** 43 16N 2 56W
Bilbo = Bilbao, *Spain* **19 A4** 43 16N 2 56W
Bíldudalur, *Iceland* **8 D2** 65 41N 23 36W
Bílé Karpaty, *Europe* **17 D9** 49 5N 18 0 E
Bilecik, *Turkey* **25 F5** 40 5N 30 5 E
Bilhorod-Dnistrovskyy, *Ukraine* **25 E5** 46 11N 30 23 E
Bilibino, *Russia* **27 C17** 68 3N 166 20 E
Bilibiza, *Mozam.* **55 E5** 12 30S 40 20 E
Bill, *U.S.A.* **80 D2** 43 14N 105 16W
Billabalong, *Australia* **61 E2** 27 25S 115 49 E
Billiluna, *Australia* **60 C4** 19 37S 127 41 E
Billings, *U.S.A.* **82 D9** 45 47N 108 30W
Billiton Is. = Belitung, *Indonesia* **36 E3** 3 10S 107 50 E
Bilma, *Niger* **51 E8** 18 50N 13 30 E
Biloela, *Australia* **62 C5** 24 24S 150 31 E
Biloxi, *U.S.A.* **81 K10** 30 24N 88 53W
Bilpa Morea Claypan, *Australia* **62 D3** 25 0S 140 0 E
Biltine, *Chad* **51 F10** 14 40N 20 50 E
Bilyana, *Australia* **62 B4** 18 5S 145 50 E

Bima, Indonesia **37 F5** 8 22S 118 49 E
Bimini Is., Bahamas **88 A4** 25 42N 79 25W
Bin Xian, Heilongjiang, China **35 B14** 45 42N 127 32 E
Bin Xian, Shaanxi, China **34 G5** 35 2N 108 4 E
Bina-Etawah, India **42 G8** 24 13N 78 14 E
Binãb, Iran **45 B6** 36 35N 48 41 E
Binalbagan, Phil. **37 B6** 10 12N 122 50 E
Binalong, Australia **63 E4** 34 40S 148 39 E
Bīnālūd, Kūh-e, Iran **45 B8** 36 30N 58 30 E
Binatang = Bintangor, Malaysia **36 D4** 2 10N 111 40 E
Binbee, Australia **62 C4** 20 19S 147 56 E
Binche, Belgium **15 D4** 50 26N 4 10 E
Binda, Australia **63 D4** 27 52S 147 21 E
Bindle, Australia **63 D4** 27 40S 148 45 E
Bindura, Zimbabwe **55 F3** 17 18S 31 18 E
Bingara, N.S.W., Australia **63 D5** 29 52S 150 36 E
Bingara, Queens., Australia **63 D3** 28 10S 144 37 E
Bingham, U.S.A. **71 C6** 45 3N 69 53W
Bingham Canyon, U.S.A. **82 F7** 40 32N 112 9W
Binghamton, U.S.A. **79 D9** 42 6N 75 55W
Binh Dinh = An Nhon, Vietnam **38 F7** 13 55N 109 7 E
Binh Khe, Vietnam **38 F7** 13 57N 108 51 E
Binh Son, Vietnam **38 E7** 15 20N 108 40 E
Binhai, China **35 G10** 34 2N 119 49 E
Binisatua, Spain **22 B11** 39 50N 4 11 E
Binjai, Indonesia **36 D1** 3 20N 98 30 E
Binnaway, Australia **63 E4** 31 28S 149 24 E
Binongko, Indonesia **37 F6** 5 55S 123 55 E
Binscarth, Canada **73 C8** 50 37N 101 17W
Bintan, Indonesia **36 D2** 1 0N 104 0 E
Bintangor, Malaysia **36 D4** 2 10N 111 40 E
Bintulu, Malaysia **36 D4** 3 10N 113 0 E
Bintuni, Indonesia **37 E8** 2 7S 133 32 E
Binzert = Bizerte, Tunisia **51 A7** 37 15N 9 50 E
Bío Bío □, Chile **94 D1** 37 35S 72 0W
Bioko, Eq. Guin. **52 D1** 3 30N 8 40 E
Bir, India **40 K9** 19 0N 75 54 E
Bîr Abu Muḥammad, Egypt **47 F3** 29 44N 34 14 E
Bi'r ad Dabbāghāt, Jordan **47 E4** 30 26N 35 32 E
Bi'r al Butayyihāt, Jordan **47 F4** 29 47N 35 20 E
Bi'r al Mārī, Jordan **47 E4** 30 4N 35 33 E
Bi'r al Qattār, Jordan **47 F4** 29 47N 35 32 E
Bîr Beiḍa, Egypt **47 E3** 30 25N 34 29 E
Bîr el 'Abd, Egypt **47 D2** 31 2N 33 0 E
Bîr el Biarât, Egypt **47 F3** 29 30N 34 43 E
Bîr el Duweidar, Egypt **47 E1** 30 56N 32 32 E
Bîr el Garârât, Egypt **47 D2** 31 3N 33 34 E
Bîr el Heisi, Egypt **47 F3** 29 22N 34 36 E
Bîr el Jafir, Egypt **47 E1** 30 50N 32 41 E
Bîr el Mâlḥi, Egypt **47 E2** 30 38N 33 19 E
Bîr el Thamâda, Egypt **47 E2** 30 12N 33 27 E
Bîr Gebeil Ḥiṣn, Egypt **47 E2** 30 2N 33 18 E
Bi'r Ghadīr, Syria **47 A6** 34 6N 37 3 E
Bîr Ḥasana, Egypt **47 E2** 30 29N 33 46 E
Bi'r Jadīd, Iraq **44 C4** 34 1N 42 54 E
Bîr Kaseiba, Egypt **47 E2** 31 0N 33 17 E
Bîr Lahfân, Egypt **47 E2** 31 0N 33 51 E
Bîr Madkûr, Egypt **47 E1** 30 44N 32 33 E
Bir Mogreïn, Mauritania **50 C3** 25 10N 11 25W
Bi'r Muṭribah, Kuwait **44 D5** 29 54N 47 17 E
Bîr Qaṭia, Egypt **47 E1** 30 58N 32 45 E
Biratnagar, Nepal **43 F12** 26 27N 87 17 E
Birawa, Dem. Rep. of the Congo **54 C2** 2 20S 28 48 E
Birch Hills, Canada **73 C7** 52 59N 105 25W
Birch I., Canada **73 C9** 52 26N 99 54W
Birch L., N.W.T., Canada **72 A5** 62 4N 116 33W
Birch L., Ont., Canada **70 B1** 51 23N 92 18W
Birch L., U.S.A. **70 C1** 47 45N 91 51W
Birch Mts., Canada **72 B6** 57 30N 113 10W
Birch River, Canada **73 C8** 52 24N 101 6W
Birchip, Australia **63 F3** 35 56S 142 55 E
Bird, Canada **73 B10** 56 30N 94 13W
Bird City, U.S.A. **80 F4** 39 45N 101 32W
Bird I. = Aves, I. de, W. Indies **89 C7** 15 45N 63 55W
Birdsville, Australia **62 D2** 25 51S 139 20 E
Birdum, Australia **60 C5** 15 39S 133 13 E
Birein, Israel **47 E3** 30 50N 34 28 E
Bireuen, Indonesia **36 C1** 5 14N 96 39 E
Birigui, Brazil **95 A5** 21 18S 50 16W
Birkenhead, U.K. **10 D4** 53 23N 3 2W
Bîrlad = Bârlad, Romania **17 E14** 46 15N 27 38 E
Birmingham, U.K. **11 E6** 52 29N 1 52W
Birmingham, U.S.A. **77 J2** 33 31N 86 48W
Birmitrapur, India **41 H14** 22 24N 84 46 E
Birni Nkonni, Niger **50 F7** 13 55N 5 15 E
Birnin Kebbi, Nigeria **50 F6** 12 32N 4 12 E
Birobidzhan, Russia **27 E14** 48 50N 132 50 E
Birr, Ireland **13 C4** 53 6N 7 54W
Birrie →, Australia **63 D4** 29 43S 146 37 E
Birsilpur, India **42 E5** 28 11N 72 15 E
Birsk, Russia **24 C10** 55 25N 55 30 E
Birtle, Canada **73 C8** 50 30N 101 5W
Birur, India **40 N9** 13 30N 75 55 E
Biržai, Lithuania **9 H21** 56 11N 24 45 E
Birzebbugga, Malta **23 D2** 35 49N 14 32 E
Bisa, Indonesia **37 E7** 1 15S 127 28 E
Bisalpur, India **43 E8** 28 14N 79 48 E
Bisbee, U.S.A. **83 L9** 31 27N 109 55W
Biscay, B. of, Atl. Oc. **18 D1** 45 0N 2 0W
Biscayne B., U.S.A. **77 N5** 25 40N 80 12W
Biscoe Bay, Antarctica **5 D13** 77 0S 152 0W
Biscoe Is., Antarctica **5 C17** 66 0S 67 0W
Biscostasing, Canada **70 C3** 47 18N 82 9W
Bishkek, Kyrgyzstan **26 E8** 42 54N 74 46 E
Bishnupur, India **43 H12** 23 8N 87 20 E
Bisho, S. Africa **57 E4** 32 50S 27 23 E
Bishop, Calif., U.S.A. **84 H8** 37 22N 118 24W
Bishop, Tex., U.S.A. **81 M6** 27 35N 97 48W
Bishop Auckland, U.K. **10 C6** 54 39N 1 40W
Bishop's Falls, Canada **71 C9** 49 2N 55 30W
Bishop's Stortford, U.K. **11 F8** 51 52N 0 10 E
Bisina, L., Uganda **54 B3** 1 38N 33 56 E
Biskra, Algeria **50 B7** 34 50N 5 44 E
Bismarck, U.S.A. **80 B4** 46 48N 100 47W
Bismarck Arch., Papua N. G. **64 H7** 2 30S 150 0 E
Biso, Uganda **54 B3** 1 44N 31 26 E
Bison, U.S.A. **80 C3** 45 31N 102 28W
Bīsotūn, Iran **44 C5** 34 23N 47 26 E
Bissagos = Bijagós, Arquipélago dos, Guinea-Biss. **50 F2** 11 15N 16 10W
Bissau, Guinea-Biss. **50 F2** 11 45N 15 45W
Bissett, Canada **73 C9** 51 2N 95 41W
Bistcho L., Canada **72 B5** 59 45N 118 50W
Bistrița, Romania **17 E13** 47 9N 24 35 E
Bistrița →, Romania **17 E14** 46 30N 26 57 E
Biswan, India **43 F9** 27 29N 81 2 E
Bitlis, Turkey **25 G7** 38 20N 42 3 E
Bitola, Macedonia **21 D9** 41 1N 21 20 E
Bitolj = Bitola, Macedonia **21 D9** 41 1N 21 20 E
Bitter Creek, U.S.A. **82 F9** 41 33N 108 33W
Bitterfontein, S. Africa **56 E2** 31 1S 18 32 E
Bitterroot →, U.S.A. **82 C6** 46 52N 114 7W
Bitterroot Range, U.S.A. **82 D6** 46 0N 114 20W
Bitterwater, U.S.A. **84 J6** 36 23N 121 0W
Biu, Nigeria **51 F8** 10 40N 12 3 E
Biwa-Ko, Japan **31 G8** 35 15N 136 10 E
Biwabik, U.S.A. **80 B8** 47 32N 92 21W
Biyang, China **34 H7** 32 38N 113 21 E
Biysk, Russia **26 D9** 52 40N 85 0 E
Bizana, S. Africa **57 E4** 30 50S 29 52 E
Bizen, Japan **31 G7** 34 43N 134 8 E
Bizerte, Tunisia **51 A7** 37 15N 9 50 E
Bjargtangar, Iceland **8 D1** 65 30N 24 30W
Bjelovar, Croatia **20 B7** 45 56N 16 49 E
Bjørnevatn, Norway **8 B23** 69 40N 30 0 E
Black = Da →, Vietnam **38 B5** 21 15N 105 20 E
Black →, Canada **78 B5** 44 42N 79 19W
Black →, Ark., U.S.A. **81 H9** 35 38N 91 20W
Black →, N.Y., U.S.A. **79 C8** 43 59N 76 4W
Black →, Wis., U.S.A. **80 D9** 43 57N 91 22W
Black Diamond, Canada **72 C6** 50 45N 114 14W
Black Forest = Schwarzwald, Germany **16 D5** 48 30N 8 20 E
Black Hd., Ireland **13 C2** 53 9N 9 16W
Black Hills, U.S.A. **80 D3** 44 0N 103 45W
Black I., Canada **73 C9** 51 12N 96 30W
Black L., Canada **73 B7** 59 12N 105 15W
Black L., U.S.A. **76 C3** 45 28N 84 16W
Black Mesa, U.S.A. **81 G3** 36 58N 102 58W
Black Mt. = Mynydd Du, U.K. **11 F4** 51 52N 3 50W
Black Mts., U.K. **11 F4** 51 55N 3 7W
Black Range, U.S.A. **83 K10** 33 15N 107 50W
Black River, Jamaica **88 C4** 18 0N 77 50W
Black River Falls, U.S.A. **80 C9** 44 18N 90 51W
Black Sea, Eurasia **25 F6** 43 30N 35 0 E
Black Volta →, Africa **50 G5** 8 41N 1 33W
Black Warrior →, U.S.A. **77 J2** 32 32N 87 51W
Blackall, Australia **62 C4** 24 25S 145 45 E
Blackball, N.Z. **59 K3** 42 22S 171 26 E
Blackbull, Australia **62 B3** 17 55S 141 45 E
Blackburn, U.K. **10 D5** 53 45N 2 29W
Blackburn with Darwen □, U.K. **10 D5** 53 45N 2 29W
Blackduck, U.S.A. **80 B7** 47 44N 94 33W
Blackfoot, U.S.A. **82 E7** 43 11N 112 21W
Blackfoot →, U.S.A. **82 C7** 46 52N 113 53W
Blackfoot River Reservoir, U.S.A. **82 E8** 43 0N 111 43W
Blackie, Canada **72 C6** 50 36N 113 37W
Blackpool, U.K. **10 D4** 53 49N 3 3W
Blackpool □, U.K. **10 D4** 53 49N 3 3W
Blackriver, U.S.A. **78 B1** 44 46N 83 17W
Blacks Harbour, Canada **71 C6** 45 3N 66 49W
Blacksburg, U.S.A. **76 G5** 37 14N 80 25W
Blacksod B., Ireland **13 B1** 54 6N 10 0W
Blackstone, U.S.A. **76 G7** 37 4N 78 0W
Blackstone →, Canada **72 A4** 61 5N 122 55W
Blackstone Ra., Australia **61 E4** 26 0S 128 30 E
Blackville, Canada **71 C6** 46 44N 65 50W
Blackwater, Australia **62 C4** 23 35S 148 53 E
Blackwater →, Meath, Ireland **13 C4** 53 39N 6 41W
Blackwater →, Waterford, Ireland **13 D4** 52 4N 7 52W
Blackwater →, U.K. **13 B5** 54 31N 6 35W
Blackwater Cr. →, Australia **63 D3** 25 56S 144 30 E
Blackwell, U.S.A. **81 G6** 36 48N 97 17W
Blackwells Corner, U.S.A. **85 K7** 35 37N 119 47W
Blaenau Ffestiniog, U.K. **10 E4** 53 0N 3 56W
Blaenau Gwent □, U.K. **11 F4** 51 48N 3 12W
Blagodarnyy, Russia **25 E7** 45 7N 43 37 E
Blagoevgrad, Bulgaria **21 C10** 42 2N 23 5 E
Blagoveshchensk, Russia **27 D13** 50 20N 127 30 E
Blaine, U.S.A. **84 B4** 48 59N 122 45W
Blaine Lake, Canada **73 C7** 52 51N 106 52W
Blair, U.S.A. **80 E6** 41 33N 96 8W
Blair Athol, Australia **62 C4** 22 42S 147 31 E
Blair Atholl, U.K. **12 E5** 56 46N 3 50W
Blairgowrie, U.K. **12 E5** 56 35N 3 21W
Blairmore, Canada **72 D6** 49 40N 114 25W
Blairsden, U.S.A. **84 F6** 39 47N 120 37W
Blairsville, U.S.A. **78 F5** 40 26N 79 16W
Blake Pt., U.S.A. **80 A10** 48 11N 88 25W
Blakely, U.S.A. **77 K3** 31 23N 84 56W
Blanc, C., Spain **22 B9** 39 21N 2 51 E
Blanc, Mont, Alps **18 D7** 45 48N 6 50 E
Blanca, B., Argentina **96 D4** 39 10S 61 30W
Blanca Peak, U.S.A. **83 H11** 37 35N 105 29W
Blanchard, U.S.A. **81 H6** 35 8N 97 39W
Blanche, C., Australia **63 E1** 33 1S 134 9 E
Blanche, L., S. Austral., Australia **63 D2** 29 15S 139 40 E
Blanche, L., W. Austral., Australia **60 D3** 22 25S 123 17 E
Blanco, S. Africa **56 E3** 33 55S 22 23 E
Blanco, U.S.A. **81 K5** 30 6N 98 25W
Blanco →, Argentina **94 C2** 30 20S 68 42W
Blanco, C., Costa Rica **88 E2** 9 34N 85 8W
Blanco, C., U.S.A. **82 E1** 42 51N 124 34W
Blanda →, Iceland **8 D3** 65 37N 20 9W
Blandford Forum, U.K. **11 G5** 50 51N 2 9W
Blanding, U.S.A. **83 H9** 37 37N 109 29W
Blanes, Spain **19 B7** 41 40N 2 48 E
Blankenberge, Belgium **15 C3** 51 20N 3 9 E
Blanquillo, Uruguay **95 C4** 32 53S 55 37W
Blantyre, Malawi **55 F4** 15 45S 35 0 E
Blarney, Ireland **13 E3** 51 56N 8 33W
Blåvands Huk, Denmark **9 J13** 55 33N 8 4 E
Blaydon, U.K. **10 C6** 54 58N 1 42W
Blayney, Australia **63 E4** 33 32S 149 14 E
Blaze, Pt., Australia **60 B5** 12 56S 130 11 E
Blekinge, Sweden **9 H16** 56 25N 15 20 E
Blenheim, Canada **78 D3** 42 20N 82 0W
Blenheim, N.Z. **59 J4** 41 38S 173 57 E
Bletchley, U.K. **11 F7** 51 59N 0 44W
Blida, Algeria **50 A6** 36 30N 2 49 E
Bligh Sound, N.Z. **59 L1** 44 47S 167 32 E
Blind River, Canada **70 C3** 46 10N 82 58W
Blitar, Indonesia **37 H15** 8 5S 112 11 E
Block I., U.S.A. **79 E13** 41 11N 71 35W
Block Island Sd., U.S.A. **79 E13** 41 15N 71 40W
Blodgett Iceberg Tongue, Antarctica **5 C9** 66 8S 130 35 E
Bloemfontein, S. Africa **56 D4** 29 6S 26 7 E
Bloemhof, S. Africa **56 D4** 27 38S 25 32 E
Blois, France **18 C4** 47 35N 1 20 E
Blönduós, Iceland **8 D3** 65 40N 20 12W
Bloodvein →, Canada **73 C9** 51 47N 96 43W
Bloody Foreland, Ireland **13 A3** 55 10N 8 17W
Bloomer, U.S.A. **80 C9** 45 6N 91 29W
Bloomfield, Australia **62 B4** 15 56S 145 22 E
Bloomfield, Canada **78 C7** 43 59N 77 14W
Bloomfield, Iowa, U.S.A. **80 E8** 40 45N 92 25W
Bloomfield, N. Mex., U.S.A. **83 H10** 36 43N 107 59W
Bloomfield, Nebr., U.S.A. **80 D6** 42 36N 97 39W
Bloomington, Ill., U.S.A. **80 E10** 40 28N 89 0W
Bloomington, Ind., U.S.A. **76 F2** 39 10N 86 32W
Bloomington, Minn., U.S.A. **80 C8** 44 50N 93 17W
Bloomsburg, U.S.A. **79 F8** 41 0N 76 27W
Blora, Indonesia **37 G14** 6 57S 111 25 E
Blossburg, U.S.A. **78 E7** 41 41N 77 4W
Blouberg, S. Africa **57 C4** 23 8S 28 59 E
Blountstown, U.S.A. **77 K3** 30 27N 85 3W
Blue Island, U.S.A. **76 E2** 41 40N 87 40W
Blue Lake, U.S.A. **82 F2** 40 53N 123 59W
Blue Mesa Reservoir, U.S.A. **83 G10** 38 28N 107 20W
Blue Mts., Oreg., U.S.A. **82 D4** 45 15N 119 0W
Blue Mts., Pa., U.S.A. **79 F8** 40 30N 76 30W
Blue Mud B., Australia **62 A2** 13 30S 136 0 E
Blue Nile = Nîl el Azraq →, Sudan **51 E12** 15 38N 32 31 E
Blue Rapids, U.S.A. **80 F6** 39 41N 96 39W
Blue Ridge Mts., U.S.A. **77 G5** 36 30N 80 15W
Blueberry →, Canada **72 B4** 56 45N 120 49W
Bluefield, U.S.A. **76 G5** 37 15N 81 17W
Bluefields, Nic. **88 D3** 12 20N 83 50W
Bluff, Australia **62 C4** 23 35S 149 4 E
Bluff, N.Z. **59 M2** 46 37S 168 20 E
Bluff, U.S.A. **83 H9** 37 17N 109 33W
Bluff Knoll, Australia **61 F2** 34 24S 118 15 E
Bluff Pt., Australia **61 E1** 27 50S 114 5 E
Bluffton, U.S.A. **76 E3** 40 44N 85 11W
Blumenau, Brazil **95 B6** 27 0S 49 0W
Blunt, U.S.A. **80 C5** 44 31N 99 59W
Bly, U.S.A. **82 E3** 42 24N 121 3W
Blyth, Canada **78 C3** 43 44N 81 26W
Blyth, U.K. **10 B6** 55 8N 1 31W
Blythe, U.S.A. **85 M12** 33 37N 114 36W
Bo, S. Leone **50 G3** 7 55N 11 50W
Bo Duc, Vietnam **39 G6** 11 58N 106 50 E
Bo Hai, China **35 E10** 39 0N 119 0 E
Bo Xian, China **34 H8** 33 55N 115 41 E
Boa Vista, Brazil **92 C6** 2 48N 60 30W
Boaco, Nic. **88 D2** 12 29N 85 35W
Bo'ai, China **34 G7** 35 10N 113 3 E
Boardman, U.S.A. **78 E4** 41 2N 80 40W
Boatman, Australia **63 D4** 27 16S 146 55 E
Bobadah, Australia **63 E4** 32 19S 146 41 E
Bobbili, India **41 K13** 18 35N 83 30 E
Bobcaygeon, Canada **70 D4** 44 33N 78 33W
Bobo-Dioulasso, Burkina Faso **50 F5** 11 8N 4 13W
Bóbr →, Poland **16 B8** 52 4N 15 4 E
Bobraomby, Tanjon' i, Madag. **57 A8** 12 40S 49 10 E
Bobruysk = Babruysk, Belarus **24 D4** 53 10N 29 15 E
Bôca do Acre, Brazil **92 E5** 8 50S 67 27W
Boca Raton, U.S.A. **77 M5** 26 21N 80 5W
Bocas del Toro, Panama **88 E3** 9 15N 82 20W
Bochnia, Poland **17 D11** 49 58N 20 27 E
Bochum, Germany **16 C4** 51 28N 7 13 E
Bocoyna, Mexico **86 B3** 27 52N 107 35W
Bodaybo, Russia **27 D12** 57 50N 114 0 E
Boddam, U.K. **12 B7** 59 56N 1 17W
Boddington, Australia **61 F2** 32 50S 116 30 E
Bodega Bay, U.S.A. **84 G3** 38 20N 123 3W
Boden, Sweden **8 D19** 65 50N 21 42 E
Bodensee, Europe **18 C8** 47 35N 9 25 E
Bodhan, India **40 K10** 18 40N 77 44 E
Bodmin, U.K. **11 G3** 50 28N 4 43W
Bodmin Moor, U.K. **11 G3** 50 33N 4 36W
Bodø, Norway **8 C16** 67 17N 14 24 E
Bodrog →, Hungary **17 D11** 48 11N 21 22 E
Bodrum, Turkey **21 F12** 37 3N 27 30 E
Boende, Dem. Rep. of the Congo **52 E4** 0 24S 21 12 E
Boerne, U.S.A. **81 L5** 29 47N 98 44W
Bogalusa, U.S.A. **81 K10** 30 47N 89 52W
Bogan Gate, Australia **63 E4** 33 7S 147 49 E
Bogantungan, Australia **62 C4** 23 41S 147 17 E
Bogata, U.S.A. **81 J7** 33 28N 95 13W
Boggabilla, Australia **63 D5** 28 36S 150 24 E
Boggabri, Australia **63 E5** 30 45S 150 5 E
Boggeragh Mts., Ireland **13 D3** 52 2N 8 55W
Bognor Regis, U.K. **11 G7** 50 47N 0 40W
Bogo, Phil. **37 B6** 11 3N 124 0 E
Bogong, Mt., Australia **63 F4** 36 47S 147 17 E
Bogor, Indonesia **37 G12** 6 36S 106 48 E
Bogotá, Colombia **92 C4** 4 34N 74 0W
Bogotol, Russia **26 D9** 56 15N 89 50 E
Bogra, Bangla. **41 G16** 24 51N 89 22 E
Boguchany, Russia **27 D10** 58 40N 97 30 E
Bohemia Downs, Australia **60 C4** 18 53S 126 14 E
Bohemian Forest = Böhmerwald, Germany **16 D7** 49 8N 13 14 E
Bohena Cr. →, Australia **63 E4** 30 17S 149 42 E
Böhmerwald, Germany **16 D7** 49 8N 13 14 E
Bohol, Phil. **37 C6** 9 50N 124 10 E
Bohol Sea, Phil. **37 C6** 9 0N 124 0 E
Bohuslän, Sweden **9 G14** 58 25N 12 0 E
Boi, Pta. de, Brazil **95 A6** 23 55S 45 15W
Boiaçu, Brazil **92 D6** 0 27S 61 46W
Boileau, C., Australia **60 C3** 17 40S 122 7 E
Boise, U.S.A. **82 E5** 43 37N 116 13W
Boise City, U.S.A. **81 G3** 36 44N 102 31W
Boissevain, Canada **73 D8** 49 15N 100 5W
Bojador C., W. Sahara **50 C3** 26 0N 14 30W
Bojana →, Albania **21 D8** 41 52N 19 22 E
Bojnūrd, Iran **45 B8** 37 30N 57 20 E
Bojonegoro, Indonesia **37 G14** 7 11S 111 54 E
Bokhara →, Australia **63 D4** 29 55S 146 42 E
Boknafjorden, Norway **9 G11** 59 14N 5 40 E
Bokoro, Chad **51 F9** 12 25N 17 14 E
Bokpyin, Burma **39 G2** 11 18N 98 42 E
Bolan Pass, Pakistan **40 E5** 29 50N 67 20 E
Bolaños →, Mexico **86 C4** 21 14N 104 8W
Bolbec, France **18 B4** 49 30N 0 30 E
Boldājī, Iran **45 D6** 31 56N 51 3 E
Bole, China **32 B3** 45 11N 81 37 E
Bolekhiv, Ukraine **17 D12** 49 0N 23 57 E
Bolesławiec, Poland **16 C8** 51 17N 15 37 E
Bolgrad = Bolhrad, Ukraine **17 F15** 45 40N 28 32 E
Bolhrad, Ukraine **17 F15** 45 40N 28 32 E
Bolívar, Argentina **94 D3** 36 15S 60 53W
Bolivar, Mo., U.S.A. **81 G8** 37 37N 93 25W
Bolivar, Tenn., U.S.A. **81 H10** 35 12N 89 0W
Bolivia ■, S. Amer. **92 G6** 17 6S 64 0W
Bolivian Plateau, S. Amer. **90 E4** 20 0S 67 30W
Bollnäs, Sweden **9 F17** 61 21N 16 24 E
Bollon, Australia **63 D4** 28 2S 147 29 E
Bolmen, Sweden **9 H15** 56 55N 13 40 E
Bolobo, Dem. Rep. of the Congo **52 E3** 2 6S 16 20 E
Bologna, Italy **20 B4** 44 29N 11 20 E
Bologoye, Russia **24 C5** 57 55N 34 5 E
Bolonchenticul, Mexico **87 D7** 20 0N 89 49W
Boloven, Cao Nguyen, Laos **38 E6** 15 10N 106 30 E
Bolpur, India **43 H12** 23 40N 87 45 E
Bolsena, L. di, Italy **20 C4** 42 36N 11 56 E
Bolshevik, Ostrov, Russia **27 B11** 78 30N 102 0 E
Bolshezemelskaya Tundra, Russia **24 A10** 67 0N 56 0 E
Bolshoi Kavkas = Caucasus Mountains, Eurasia **25 F7** 42 50N 44 0 E
Bolshoy Anyuy →, Russia **27 C17** 68 30N 160 49 E
Bolshoy Begichev, Ostrov, Russia **27 B12** 74 20N 112 30 E
Bolshoy Lyakhovskiy, Ostrov, Russia **27 B15** 73 35N 142 0 E
Bolshoy Tyuters, Ostrov, Russia **9 G22** 59 51N 27 13 E
Bolsward, Neths. **15 A5** 53 3N 5 32 E
Bolt Head, U.K. **11 G4** 50 12N 3 48W
Bolton, Canada **78 C5** 43 54N 79 45W
Bolton, U.K. **10 D5** 53 35N 2 26W
Bolu, Turkey **25 F5** 40 45N 31 35 E
Bolungavík, Iceland **8 C2** 66 9N 23 15W
Bolvadin, Turkey **25 G5** 38 45N 31 4 E
Bolzano, Italy **20 A4** 46 31N 11 22 E
Bom Jesus da Lapa, Brazil **93 F10** 13 15S 43 25W
Boma, Dem. Rep. of the Congo **52 F2** 5 50S 13 4 E
Bomaderry, Australia **63 E5** 34 52S 150 37 E
Bombala, Australia **63 F4** 36 56S 149 15 E
Bombay = Mumbai, India **40 K8** 18 55N 72 50 E
Bomboma, Dem. Rep. of the Congo **52 D3** 2 25N 18 55 E
Bombombwa, Dem. Rep. of the Congo **54 B2** 1 40N 25 40 E
Bomili, Dem. Rep. of the Congo **54 B2** 1 45N 27 5 E
Bømlo, Norway **9 G11** 59 37N 5 13 E
Bomokandi →, Dem. Rep. of the Congo **54 B2** 3 39N 26 8 E
Bomu →, C.A.R. **52 D4** 4 40N 22 30 E
Bon, C., Tunisia **48 C5** 37 1N 11 2 E
Bon Sar Pa, Vietnam **38 F6** 12 24N 107 35 E
Bonaire, Neth. Ant. **89 D6** 12 10N 68 15W
Bonang, Australia **63 F4** 37 11S 148 41 E
Bonanza, Nic. **88 D3** 13 54N 84 35W
Bonaparte Arch., Australia **60 B3** 14 0S 124 30 E
Bonaventure, Canada **71 C6** 48 5N 65 32W
Bonavista, Canada **71 C9** 48 40N 53 5W
Bonavista, C., Canada **71 C9** 48 42N 53 5W
Bondo, Dem. Rep. of the Congo **54 B1** 3 55N 23 53 E
Bondoukou, Ivory C. **50 G5** 8 2N 2 47W
Bondowoso, Indonesia **37 G15** 7 55S 113 49 E
Bone, Teluk, Indonesia **37 E6** 4 10S 120 50 E
Bonerate, Indonesia **37 F6** 7 25S 121 5 E
Bonerate, Kepulauan, Indonesia **37 F6** 6 30S 121 10 E
Bo'ness, U.K. **12 E5** 56 1N 3 37W
Bonete, Cerro, Argentina **94 B2** 27 55S 68 40W
Bong Son = Hoai Nhon, Vietnam **38 E7** 14 28N 109 1 E
Bongor, Chad **51 F9** 10 35N 15 20 E
Bonham, U.S.A. **81 J6** 33 35N 96 11W
Bonifacio, France **18 F8** 41 24N 9 10 E
Bonin Is. = Ogasawara Gunto, Pac. Oc. **64 E6** 27 0N 142 0 E
Bonn, Germany **16 C4** 50 46N 7 6 E
Bonne Terre, U.S.A. **81 G9** 37 55N 90 33W
Bonners Ferry, U.S.A. **82 B5** 48 42N 116 19W
Bonney, L., Australia **63 F3** 37 50S 140 20 E
Bonnie Downs, Australia **62 C3** 22 7S 143 50 E
Bonnie Rock, Australia **61 F2** 30 29S 118 22 E
Bonny, Bight of, Africa **52 D1** 3 30N 9 20 E
Bonnyrigg, U.K. **12 F5** 55 53N 3 6W
Bonnyville, Canada **73 C6** 54 20N 110 45W
Bonoi, Indonesia **37 E9** 1 45S 137 41 E
Bonsall, U.S.A. **85 M9** 33 16N 117 14W

Brookmere

Bontang, *Indonesia* **36 D5** 0 10N 117 30 E
Bonthe, *S. Leone* **50 G3** 7 30N 12 33W
Bontoc, *Phil.* **37 A6** 17 7N 120 58 E
Bonython Ra., *Australia* **60 D4** 23 40S 128 45 E
Bookabie, *Australia* **61 F5** 31 50S 132 41 E
Booker, *U.S.A.* **81 G4** 36 27N 100 32W
Boolaboolka L., *Australia* **63 E3** 32 38S 143 10 E
Booligal, *Australia* **63 E3** 33 58S 144 53 E
Boonah, *Australia* **63 D5** 27 58S 152 41 E
Boone, *Iowa, U.S.A.* **80 D8** 42 4N 93 53W
Boone, *N.C., U.S.A.* **77 G5** 36 13N 81 41W
Booneville, *Ark., U.S.A.* **81 H8** 35 8N 93 55W
Booneville, *Miss., U.S.A.* **77 H1** 34 39N 88 34W
Boonville, *Calif., U.S.A.* **84 F3** 39 1N 123 22W
Boonville, *Ind., U.S.A.* **76 F2** 38 3N 87 16W
Boonville, *Mo., U.S.A.* **80 F8** 38 58N 92 44W
Boonville, *N.Y., U.S.A.* **79 C9** 43 29N 75 20W
Boorindal, *Australia* **63 E4** 30 22S 146 11 E
Boorowa, *Australia* **63 E4** 34 28S 148 44 E
Boothia, Gulf of, *Canada* **69 A11** 71 0N 90 0W
Boothia Pen., *Canada* **68 A10** 71 0N 94 0W
Bootle, *U.K.* **10 D4** 53 28N 3 1W
Booué, *Gabon* **52 E2** 0 5S 11 55 E
Boquete, *Panama* **88 E3** 8 46N 82 27W
Boquilla, Presa de la, *Mexico* **86 B3** 27 40N 105 30W
Boquillas del Carmen, *Mexico* **86 B4** 29 17N 102 53W
Bor, *Serbia, Yug.* **21 B10** 44 5N 22 7 E
Bôr, *Sudan* **51 G12** 6 10N 31 40 E
Bor Mashash, *Israel* **47 D3** 31 7N 34 50 E
Borah Peak, *U.S.A.* **82 D7** 44 8N 113 47W
Borås, *Sweden* **9 H15** 57 43N 12 56 E
Borāzjān, *Iran* **45 D6** 29 22N 51 10 E
Borba, *Brazil* **92 D7** 4 12S 59 34W
Borborema, Planalto da, *Brazil* **90 D7** 7 0S 37 0W
Bord Khūn-e Now, *Iran* **45 D6** 28 3N 51 28 E
Borda, C., *Australia* **63 F2** 35 45S 136 34 E
Bordeaux, *France* **18 D3** 44 50N 0 36W
Borden, *Australia* **61 F2** 34 3S 118 12 E
Borden, *Canada* **71 C7** 46 18N 63 47W
Bordertown, *Australia* **63 F3** 36 19S 140 45 E
Borðeyri, *Iceland* **8 D3** 65 12N 21 6W
Bordj Fly Ste. Marie, *Algeria* **50 C5** 27 19N 2 32W
Bordj-in-Eker, *Algeria* **50 D7** 24 9N 5 3 E
Bordj Omar Driss, *Algeria* **50 C7** 28 10N 6 40 E
Borehamwood, *U.K.* **11 F7** 51 40N 0 15W
Borgå = Porvoo, *Finland* **9 F21** 60 24N 25 40 E
Borgarfjörður, *Iceland* **8 D7** 65 31N 13 49W
Borgarnes, *Iceland* **8 D3** 64 32N 21 55W
Børgefjellet, *Norway* **8 D15** 65 20N 13 45 E
Borger, *Neths.* **15 B6** 52 54N 6 44 E
Borger, *U.S.A.* **81 H4** 35 39N 101 24W
Borgholm, *Sweden* **9 H17** 56 52N 16 39 E
Borikhane, *Laos* **38 C4** 18 33N 103 43 E
Borisoglebsk, *Russia* **25 D7** 51 27N 42 5 E
Borisov = Barysaw, *Belarus* **24 D4** 54 17N 28 28 E
Borja, *Peru* **92 D3** 4 20S 77 40W
Borkou, *Chad* **51 E9** 18 15N 18 50 E
Borkum, *Germany* **16 B4** 53 34N 6 40 E
Borlänge, *Sweden* **9 F16** 60 29N 15 26 E
Borley, C., *Antarctica* **5 C5** 66 15S 52 30 E
Borneo, *E. Indies* **36 D5** 1 0N 115 0 E
Bornholm, *Denmark* **9 J16** 55 10N 15 0 E
Borogontsy, *Russia* **27 C14** 62 42N 131 8 E
Boron, *U.S.A.* **85 L9** 35 0N 117 39W
Borongan, *Phil.* **37 B7** 11 37N 125 26 E
Bororen, *Australia* **62 C5** 24 13S 151 33 E
Borovichi, *Russia* **24 C5** 58 25N 33 55 E
Borrego Springs, *U.S.A.* **85 M10** 33 15N 116 23W
Borroloola, *Australia* **62 B2** 16 4S 136 17 E
Borşa, *Romania* **17 E13** 47 41N 24 50 E
Borth, *U.K.* **11 E3** 52 29N 4 2W
Borūjerd, *Iran* **45 C6** 33 55N 48 50 E
Boryslav, *Ukraine* **17 D12** 49 18N 23 28 E
Borzya, *Russia* **27 D12** 50 24N 116 31 E
Bosa, *Italy* **20 D3** 40 18N 8 30 E
Bosanska Gradiška, *Bos.-H.* **20 B7** 45 10N 17 15 E
Bosaso, *Somali Rep.* **46 E4** 11 12N 49 18 E
Boscastle, *U.K.* **11 G3** 50 41N 4 42W
Boshan, *China* **35 F9** 36 28N 117 49 E
Boshof, *S. Africa* **56 D4** 28 31S 25 13 E
Boshrūyeh, *Iran* **45 C8** 33 50N 57 30 E
Bosna →, *Bos.-H.* **21 B8** 45 4N 18 29 E
Bosna i Hercegovina = Bosnia-Herzegovina ■, *Europe* **20 B7** 44 0N 18 0 E
Bosnia-Herzegovina ■, *Europe* **20 B7** 44 0N 18 0 E
Bosnik, *Indonesia* **37 E9** 1 5S 136 10 E
Bosobolo, *Dem. Rep. of the Congo* **52 D3** 4 15N 19 50 E
Bosporus = İstanbul Boğazı, *Turkey* **25 F4** 41 10N 29 10 E
Bossangoa, *C.A.R.* **52 C3** 6 35N 17 30 E
Bossier City, *U.S.A.* **81 J8** 32 31N 93 44W
Bosso, *Niger* **51 F8** 13 43N 13 19 E
Bostānābād, *Iran* **44 B5** 37 50N 46 50 E
Bosten Hu, *China* **32 B3** 41 55N 87 40 E
Boston, *U.K.* **10 E7** 52 59N 0 2W
Boston, *U.S.A.* **79 D13** 42 22N 71 4W
Boston Bar, *Canada* **72 D4** 49 52N 121 30W
Boswell, *Canada* **72 D5** 49 28N 116 45W
Boswell, *Okla., U.S.A.* **81 H7** 34 2N 95 52W
Boswell, *Pa., U.S.A.* **78 F5** 40 10N 79 2W
Botad, *India* **42 H4** 22 15N 71 40 E
Botany B., *Australia* **63 E5** 34 0S 151 14 E
Botene, *Laos* **38 D3** 17 35N 101 12 E
Bothaville, *S. Africa* **56 D4** 27 23S 26 34 E
Bothnia, G. of, *Europe* **8 E19** 63 0N 20 15 E
Bothwell, *Australia* **62 G4** 42 20S 147 1 E
Bothwell, *Canada* **78 D3** 42 38N 81 52W
Botletle →, *Botswana* **56 C3** 20 10S 23 15 E
Botoşani, *Romania* **17 E14** 47 42N 26 41 E
Botswana ■, *Africa* **56 C3** 22 0S 24 0 E
Bottineau, *U.S.A.* **80 A4** 48 50N 100 27W
Bottrop, *Germany* **15 C6** 51 31N 6 58 E
Botucatu, *Brazil* **95 A6** 22 55S 48 30W
Botwood, *Canada* **71 C8** 49 6N 55 23W
Bouaké, *Ivory C.* **50 G4** 7 40N 5 2W
Bouar, *C.A.R.* **52 C3** 6 0N 15 40 E
Bouârfa, *Morocco* **50 B5** 32 32N 1 58W
Boucaut B., *Australia* **62 A1** 12 0S 134 25 E
Bougainville, C., *Australia* **60 B4** 13 57S 126 4 E
Bougainville Reef, *Australia* **62 B4** 15 30S 147 5 E
Bougie = Bejaia, *Algeria* **50 A7** 36 42N 5 2 E
Bougouni, *Mali* **50 F4** 11 30N 7 20W
Bouillon, *Belgium* **15 E5** 49 44N 5 3 E
Boulder, *Colo., U.S.A.* **80 E2** 40 1N 105 17W
Boulder, *Mont., U.S.A.* **82 C7** 46 14N 112 7W
Boulder City, *U.S.A.* **85 K12** 35 59N 114 50W
Boulder Creek, *U.S.A.* **84 H4** 37 7N 122 7W
Boulder Dam = Hoover Dam, *U.S.A.* **85 K12** 36 1N 114 44W
Boulia, *Australia* **62 C2** 22 52S 139 51 E
Boulogne-sur-Mer, *France* **18 A4** 50 42N 1 36 E
Boultoum, *Niger* **51 F8** 14 45N 10 25 E
Boun Neua, *Laos* **38 B3** 21 38N 101 54 E
Boun Tai, *Laos* **38 B3** 21 23N 101 58 E
Bouna, *Ivory C.* **50 G5** 9 10N 3 0W
Boundary Peak, *U.S.A.* **84 H8** 37 51N 118 21W
Boundiali, *Ivory C.* **50 G4** 9 30N 6 20W
Bountiful, *U.S.A.* **82 F8** 40 53N 111 53W
Bounty Is., *Pac. Oc.* **64 M9** 48 0S 178 30 E
Bourbonnais, *France* **18 C5** 46 28N 3 0 E
Bourem, *Mali* **50 E5** 17 0N 0 24W
Bourg-en-Bresse, *France* **18 C6** 46 13N 5 12 E
Bourg-St-Maurice, *France* **18 D7** 45 35N 6 46 E
Bourges, *France* **18 C5** 47 9N 2 25 E
Bourget, *Canada* **79 A9** 45 26N 75 9W
Bourgogne, *France* **18 C6** 47 0N 4 50 E
Bourke, *Australia* **63 E4** 30 8S 145 55 E
Bourne, *U.K.* **10 E7** 52 47N 0 22W
Bournemouth, *U.K.* **11 G6** 50 43N 1 52W
Bournemouth □, *U.K.* **11 G6** 50 43N 1 52W
Bouse, *U.S.A.* **85 M13** 33 56N 114 0W
Bouvet I. = Bouvetøya, *Antarctica* **3 G10** 54 26S 3 24 E
Bouvetøya, *Antarctica* **3 G10** 54 26S 3 24 E
Bovill, *U.S.A.* **82 C5** 46 51N 116 24W
Bow Island, *Canada* **72 D6** 49 50N 111 23W
Bowbells, *U.S.A.* **80 A3** 48 48N 102 15W
Bowdle, *U.S.A.* **80 C5** 45 27N 99 39W
Bowelling, *Australia* **61 F2** 33 25S 116 30 E
Bowen, *Australia* **62 C4** 20 0S 148 16 E
Bowen Mts., *Australia* **63 F4** 37 0S 147 50 E
Bowie, *Ariz., U.S.A.* **83 K9** 32 19N 109 29W
Bowie, *Tex., U.S.A.* **81 J6** 33 34N 97 51W
Bowkān, *Iran* **44 B5** 36 31N 46 12 E
Bowland, Forest of, *U.K.* **10 D5** 54 0N 2 30W
Bowling Green, *Ky., U.S.A.* **76 G2** 36 59N 86 27W
Bowling Green, *Ohio, U.S.A.* **76 E4** 41 23N 83 39W
Bowling Green, C., *Australia* **62 B4** 19 19S 147 25 E
Bowman, *U.S.A.* **80 B3** 46 11N 103 24W
Bowman I., *Antarctica* **5 C8** 65 0S 104 0 E
Bowmans, *Australia* **63 E2** 34 10S 138 17 E
Bowmanville, *Canada* **70 D4** 43 55N 78 41W
Bowmore, *U.K.* **12 F2** 55 45N 6 17W
Bowral, *Australia* **63 E5** 34 26S 150 27 E
Bowraville, *Australia* **63 E5** 30 37S 152 52 E
Bowron →, *Canada* **72 C4** 54 3N 121 50W
Bowser L., *Canada* **72 B3** 56 30N 129 30W
Bowsman, *Canada* **73 C8** 52 14N 101 12W
Bowwood, *Zambia* **55 F2** 17 5S 26 20 E
Boxmeer, *Neths.* **15 C5** 51 38N 5 56 E
Boxtel, *Neths.* **15 C5** 51 36N 5 20 E
Boyce, *U.S.A.* **81 K8** 31 23N 92 40W
Boyer →, *Canada* **72 B5** 58 27N 115 57W
Boyle, *Ireland* **13 C3** 53 59N 8 18W
Boyne →, *Ireland* **13 C5** 53 43N 6 15W
Boyne City, *U.S.A.* **76 C3** 45 13N 85 1W
Boynton Beach, *U.S.A.* **77 M5** 26 32N 80 4W
Boyoma, Chutes, *Dem. Rep. of the Congo* **54 B2** 0 35N 25 23 E
Boyuibe, *Bolivia* **92 G6** 20 25S 63 17W
Boyup Brook, *Australia* **61 F2** 33 50S 116 23 E
Boz Dağlan, *Turkey* **21 E13** 38 20N 28 0 E
Bozburun, *Turkey* **21 F13** 36 43N 28 4 E
Bozdoğan, *Turkey* **21 F13** 37 40N 28 17 E
Bozeman, *U.S.A.* **82 D8** 45 41N 111 2W
Bozen = Bolzano, *Italy* **20 A4** 46 31N 11 22 E
Bozoum, *C.A.R.* **52 C3** 6 25N 16 35 E
Bra, *Italy* **18 D7** 44 42N 7 51 E
Brabant □, *Belgium* **15 D4** 50 46N 4 30 E
Brabant L., *Canada* **73 B8** 55 58N 103 43W
Brač, *Croatia* **20 C7** 43 20N 16 40 E
Bracadale, L., *U.K.* **12 D2** 57 20N 6 30W
Bracciano, L. di, *Italy* **20 C5** 42 7N 12 14 E
Bracebridge, *Canada* **70 C4** 45 2N 79 19W
Brach, *Libya* **51 C8** 27 31N 14 20 E
Bräcke, *Sweden* **9 E16** 62 45N 15 26 E
Brackettville, *U.S.A.* **81 L4** 29 19N 100 25W
Bracknell, *U.K.* **11 F7** 51 25N 0 43W
Bracknell Forest □, *U.K.* **11 F7** 51 25N 0 44W
Brad, *Romania* **17 E12** 46 10N 22 50 E
Bradenton, *U.S.A.* **77 M4** 27 30N 82 34W
Bradford, *Canada* **78 B5** 44 7N 79 34W
Bradford, *U.K.* **10 D6** 53 47N 1 45W
Bradford, *Pa., U.S.A.* **78 E6** 41 58N 78 38W
Bradford, *Vt., U.S.A.* **79 C12** 43 59N 72 9W
Bradley, *Ark., U.S.A.* **81 J8** 33 6N 93 39W
Bradley, *Calif., U.S.A.* **84 K6** 35 52N 120 48W
Bradley, *S. Dak., U.S.A.* **80 C6** 45 5N 97 39W
Bradley Institute, *Zimbabwe* **55 F3** 17 7S 31 25 E
Bradore Bay, *Canada* **71 B8** 51 27N 57 18W
Bradshaw, *Australia* **60 C5** 15 21S 130 16 E
Brady, *U.S.A.* **81 K5** 31 9N 99 20W
Braemar, *Australia* **63 E2** 33 12S 139 35 E
Braemar, *U.K.* **12 D5** 57 0N 3 23W
Braeside, *Canada* **79 A8** 45 28N 76 24W
Braga, *Portugal* **19 B1** 41 35N 8 25W
Bragado, *Argentina* **94 D3** 35 2S 60 27W
Bragança, *Brazil* **93 D9** 1 0S 47 2W
Bragança, *Portugal* **19 B2** 41 48N 6 50W
Bragança Paulista, *Brazil* **95 A6** 22 55S 46 32W
Brahmanbaria, *Bangla.* **41 H17** 23 58N 91 15 E
Brahmani →, *India* **41 J15** 20 39N 86 46 E
Brahmapur, *India* **41 K14** 19 15N 84 54 E
Brahmaputra →, *India* **43 H13** 23 58N 89 50 E
Braich-y-pwll, *U.K.* **10 E3** 52 47N 4 46W
Braidwood, *Australia* **63 F4** 35 27S 149 49 E
Brăila, *Romania* **17 F14** 45 19N 27 59 E
Brainerd, *U.S.A.* **80 B7** 46 22N 94 12W
Braintree, *U.K.* **11 F8** 51 53N 0 34 E
Braintree, *U.S.A.* **79 D14** 42 13N 71 0W
Brak →, *S. Africa* **56 D3** 29 35S 22 55 E
Brakwater, *Namibia* **56 C2** 22 28S 17 3 E
Bralorne, *Canada* **72 C4** 50 50N 122 50W
Brampton, *Canada* **70 D4** 43 45N 79 45W
Brampton, *U.K.* **10 C5** 54 57N 2 44W
Bramwell, *Australia* **62 A3** 12 8S 142 37 E
Branco →, *Brazil* **92 D6** 1 20S 61 50W
Brandenburg = Neubrandenburg, *Germany* **16 B7** 53 33N 13 15 E
Brandenburg, *Germany* **16 B7** 52 25N 12 33 E
Brandenburg □, *Germany* **16 B6** 52 50N 13 0 E
Brandfort, *S. Africa* **56 D4** 28 40S 26 30 E
Brandon, *Canada* **73 D9** 49 50N 99 57W
Brandon, *U.S.A.* **79 C11** 43 48N 73 4W
Brandon B., *Ireland* **13 D1** 52 17N 10 8W
Brandon Mt., *Ireland* **13 D1** 52 15N 10 15W
Brandsen, *Argentina* **94 D4** 35 10S 58 15W
Brandvlei, *S. Africa* **56 E3** 30 25S 20 30 E
Branford, *U.S.A.* **79 E12** 41 17N 72 49W
Braniewo, *Poland* **17 A10** 54 25N 19 50 E
Bransfield Str., *Antarctica* **5 C18** 63 0S 59 0W
Branson, *Colo., U.S.A.* **81 G3** 37 1N 103 53W
Branson, *Mo., U.S.A.* **81 G8** 36 39N 93 13W
Brantford, *Canada* **70 D3** 43 10N 80 15W
Branxholme, *Australia* **63 F3** 37 52S 141 49 E
Bras d'Or, L., *Canada* **71 C7** 45 50N 60 50W
Brasil, Planalto, *Brazil* **90 E6** 18 0S 46 30W
Brasiléia, *Brazil* **92 F5** 11 0S 68 45W
Brasília, *Brazil* **93 G9** 15 47S 47 55W
Brasília Legal, *Brazil* **93 D7** 3 49S 55 36W
Braslaw, *Belarus* **9 J22** 55 38N 27 0 E
Braşov, *Romania* **17 F13** 45 38N 25 35 E
Brasschaat, *Belgium* **15 C4** 51 19N 4 27 E
Brassey, Banjaran, *Malaysia* **36 D5** 5 0N 117 15 E
Brassey Ra., *Australia* **61 E3** 25 8S 122 15 E
Brasstown Bald, *U.S.A.* **77 H4** 34 53N 83 49W
Brastad, *Sweden* **9 G14** 58 23N 11 30 E
Bratislava, *Slovak Rep.* **17 D9** 48 10N 17 7 E
Bratsk, *Russia* **27 D11** 56 10N 101 30 E
Brattleboro, *U.S.A.* **79 D12** 42 51N 72 34W
Braunau, *Austria* **16 D7** 48 15N 13 3 E
Braunschweig, *Germany* **16 B6** 52 15N 10 31 E
Braunton, *U.K.* **11 F3** 51 7N 4 10W
Bravo del Norte →, *Mexico* **86 B5** 25 57N 97 9W
Bravo del Norte, Rio → = Grande, Rio →, *U.S.A.* **81 N6** 25 58N 97 9W
Brawley, *U.S.A.* **85 N11** 32 59N 115 31W
Bray, *Ireland* **13 C5** 53 13N 6 7W
Bray, Mt., *Australia* **62 A1** 14 0S 134 30 E
Bray, Pays de, *France* **18 B4** 49 46N 1 26 E
Brazeau →, *Canada* **72 C5** 52 55N 115 14W
Brazil, *U.S.A.* **76 F2** 39 32N 87 8W
Brazil ■, *S. Amer.* **93 F9** 12 0S 50 0W
Brazilian Highlands = Brasil, Planalto, *Brazil* **90 E6** 18 0S 46 30W
Brazo Sur →, *S. Amer.* **94 B4** 25 21S 57 42W
Brazos →, *U.S.A.* **81 L7** 28 53N 95 23W
Brazzaville, *Congo* **52 E3** 4 9S 15 12 E
Brčko, *Bos.-H.* **21 B8** 44 54N 18 46 E
Breadalbane, *Australia* **62 C2** 23 50S 139 35 E
Breaden, L., *Australia* **61 E4** 25 51S 125 28 E
Breaksea Sd., *N.Z.* **59 L1** 45 35S 166 35 E
Bream B., *N.Z.* **59 F5** 35 56S 174 28 E
Bream Hd., *N.Z.* **59 F5** 35 51S 174 36 E
Breas, *Chile* **94 B1** 25 29S 70 24W
Brebes, *Indonesia* **37 G13** 6 52S 109 3 E
Brechin, *Canada* **78 B5** 44 32N 79 10W
Brechin, *U.K.* **12 E6** 56 44N 2 39W
Brecht, *Belgium* **15 C4** 51 21N 4 38 E
Breckenridge, *Colo., U.S.A.* **82 G10** 39 29N 106 3W
Breckenridge, *Minn., U.S.A.* **80 B6** 46 16N 96 35W
Breckenridge, *Tex., U.S.A.* **81 J5** 32 45N 98 54W
Breckland, *U.K.* **11 E8** 52 30N 0 40 E
Brecon, *U.K.* **11 F4** 51 57N 3 23W
Brecon Beacons, *U.K.* **11 F4** 51 53N 3 26W
Breda, *Neths.* **15 C4** 51 35N 4 45 E
Bredasdorp, *S. Africa* **56 E3** 34 33S 20 2 E
Bredbo, *Australia* **63 F4** 35 58S 149 10 E
Bree, *Belgium* **15 C5** 51 8N 5 35 E
Bregenz, *Austria* **16 E5** 47 30N 9 45 E
Breiðafjörður, *Iceland* **8 D2** 65 15N 23 15W
Brejo, *Brazil* **93 D10** 3 41S 42 47W
Bremen, *Germany* **16 B5** 53 4N 8 47 E
Bremer I., *Australia* **62 A2** 12 5S 136 45 E
Bremerhaven, *Germany* **16 B5** 53 33N 8 36 E
Bremerton, *U.S.A.* **84 C4** 47 34N 122 38W
Brenham, *U.S.A.* **81 K6** 30 10N 96 24W
Brennerpass, *Austria* **16 E6** 47 2N 11 30 E
Brent, *Canada* **70 C4** 46 2N 78 29W
Brentwood, *U.K.* **11 F8** 51 37N 0 19 E
Brentwood, *U.S.A.* **79 F11** 40 47N 73 15W
Bréscia, *Italy* **18 D9** 45 33N 10 15 E
Breskens, *Neths.* **15 C3** 51 23N 3 33 E
Breslau = Wrocław, *Poland* **17 C9** 51 5N 17 5 E
Bressanone, *Italy* **20 A4** 46 43N 11 39 E
Bressay, *U.K.* **12 A7** 60 9N 1 6W
Brest, *Belarus* **24 D3** 52 10N 23 40 E
Brest, *France* **18 B1** 48 24N 4 31W
Brest-Litovsk = Brest, *Belarus* **24 D3** 52 10N 23 40 E
Bretagne, *France* **18 B2** 48 10N 3 0W
Breton, *Canada* **72 C6** 53 7N 114 28W
Breton Sd., *U.S.A.* **81 L10** 29 35N 89 15W
Brett, C., *N.Z.* **59 F5** 35 10S 174 20 E
Brevard, *U.S.A.* **77 H4** 35 14N 82 44W
Breves, *Brazil* **93 D8** 1 40S 50 29W
Brewarrina, *Australia* **63 E4** 30 0S 146 51 E
Brewer, *U.S.A.* **71 D6** 44 48N 68 46W
Brewer, Mt., *U.S.A.* **84 J8** 36 44N 118 28W
Brewster, *N.Y., U.S.A.* **79 E11** 41 23N 73 37W
Brewster, *Wash., U.S.A.* **82 B4** 48 6N 119 47W
Brewton, *U.S.A.* **77 K2** 31 7N 87 4W
Breyten, *S. Africa* **57 D5** 26 16S 30 0 E
Brezhnev = Naberezhnyye Chelny, *Russia* **24 C9** 55 42N 52 19 E
Briançon, *France* **18 D7** 44 54N 6 39 E
Bribie I., *Australia* **63 D5** 27 0S 153 10 E
Bridgehampton, *U.S.A.* **79 F12** 40 56N 72 19W
Bridgend, *U.K.* **11 F4** 51 30N 3 34W
Bridgend □, *U.K.* **11 F4** 51 36N 3 36W
Bridgeport, *Calif., U.S.A.* **84 G7** 38 15N 119 14W
Bridgeport, *Conn., U.S.A.* **79 E11** 41 11N 73 12W
Bridgeport, *Nebr., U.S.A.* **80 E3** 41 40N 103 6W
Bridgeport, *Tex., U.S.A.* **81 J6** 33 13N 97 45W
Bridger, *U.S.A.* **82 D9** 45 18N 108 55W
Bridgeton, *U.S.A.* **76 F8** 39 26N 75 14W
Bridgetown, *Australia* **61 F2** 33 58S 116 7 E
Bridgetown, *Barbados* **89 D8** 13 5N 59 30W
Bridgetown, *Canada* **71 D6** 44 55N 65 18W
Bridgewater, *Canada* **71 D7** 44 25N 64 31W
Bridgewater, *Mass., U.S.A.* **79 E14** 41 59N 70 58W
Bridgewater, *S. Dak., U.S.A.* **80 D6** 43 33N 97 30W
Bridgewater, C., *Australia* **63 F3** 38 23S 141 23 E
Bridgnorth, *U.K.* **11 E5** 52 32N 2 25W
Bridgton, *U.S.A.* **79 B14** 44 3N 70 42W
Bridgwater, *U.K.* **11 F5** 51 8N 2 59W
Bridgwater B., *U.K.* **11 F4** 51 15N 3 15W
Bridlington, *U.K.* **10 C7** 54 5N 0 12W
Bridlington B., *U.K.* **10 C7** 54 4N 0 10W
Bridport, *Australia* **62 G4** 40 59S 147 23 E
Bridport, *U.K.* **11 G5** 50 44N 2 45W
Brig, *Switz.* **18 C7** 46 18N 7 59 E
Brigg, *U.K.* **10 D7** 53 34N 0 28W
Briggsdale, *U.S.A.* **80 E2** 40 38N 104 20W
Brigham City, *U.S.A.* **82 F7** 41 31N 112 1W
Bright, *Australia* **63 F4** 36 42S 146 56 E
Brighton, *Australia* **63 F2** 35 5S 138 30 E
Brighton, *Canada* **70 D4** 44 2N 77 44W
Brighton, *U.K.* **11 G7** 50 49N 0 7W
Brighton, *U.S.A.* **80 F2** 39 59N 104 49W
Brilliant, *Canada* **72 D5** 49 19N 117 38W
Brilliant, *U.S.A.* **78 F4** 40 15N 80 39W
Brindisi, *Italy* **21 D7** 40 39N 17 55 E
Brinkley, *U.S.A.* **81 H9** 34 53N 91 12W
Brinkworth, *Australia* **63 E2** 33 42S 138 26 E
Brinnon, *U.S.A.* **84 C4** 47 41N 122 54W
Brion, I., *Canada* **71 C7** 47 46N 61 26W
Brisbane, *Australia* **63 D5** 27 25S 153 2 E
Brisbane →, *Australia* **63 D5** 27 24S 153 9 E
Bristol, *U.K.* **11 F5** 51 26N 2 35W
Bristol, *Conn., U.S.A.* **79 E12** 41 40N 72 57W
Bristol, *Pa., U.S.A.* **79 F10** 40 6N 74 51W
Bristol, *R.I., U.S.A.* **79 E13** 41 40N 71 16W
Bristol, *S. Dak., U.S.A.* **80 C6** 45 21N 97 45W
Bristol, *Tenn., U.S.A.* **77 G4** 36 36N 82 11W
Bristol, City of □, *U.K.* **11 F5** 51 27N 2 36W
Bristol B., *U.S.A.* **68 C4** 58 0N 160 0W
Bristol Channel, *U.K.* **11 F3** 51 18N 4 30W
Bristol I., *Antarctica* **5 B1** 58 45S 28 0W
Bristol L., *U.S.A.* **83 J5** 34 23N 116 50W
Bristow, *U.S.A.* **81 H6** 35 50N 96 23W
British Columbia □, *Canada* **72 C3** 55 0N 125 15W
British Isles, *Europe* **6 E5** 54 0N 4 0W
Brits, *S. Africa* **57 D4** 25 37S 27 48 E
Britstown, *S. Africa* **56 E3** 30 37S 23 30 E
Britt, *Canada* **70 C3** 45 46N 80 34W
Brittany = Bretagne, *France* **18 B2** 48 10N 3 0W
Britton, *U.S.A.* **80 C6** 45 48N 97 45W
Brive-la-Gaillarde, *France* **18 D4** 45 10N 1 32 E
Brixen = Bressanone, *Italy* **20 A4** 46 43N 11 39 E
Brixham, *U.K.* **11 G4** 50 23N 3 31W
Brixton, *Australia* **62 C3** 23 32S 144 57 E
Brno, *Czech Rep.* **17 D9** 49 10N 16 35 E
Broad →, *U.S.A.* **77 J5** 34 1N 81 4W
Broad Arrow, *Australia* **61 F3** 30 23S 121 15 E
Broad B., *U.K.* **12 C2** 58 14N 6 18W
Broad Haven, *Ireland* **13 B2** 54 20N 9 55W
Broad Law, *U.K.* **12 F5** 55 30N 3 21W
Broad Sd., *Australia* **62 C4** 22 0S 149 45 E
Broadhurst Ra., *Australia* **60 D3** 22 30S 122 30 E
Broads, The, *U.K.* **10 E9** 52 45N 1 30 E
Broadus, *U.S.A.* **80 C2** 45 27N 105 25W
Broadview, *Canada* **73 C8** 50 22N 102 35W
Brochet, *Canada* **73 B8** 57 53N 101 40W
Brochet, L., *Canada* **73 B8** 58 36N 101 35W
Brock, *Canada* **73 C7** 51 26N 108 43W
Brocken, *Germany* **16 C6** 51 47N 10 37 E
Brockport, *U.S.A.* **78 C7** 43 13N 77 56W
Brockton, *U.S.A.* **79 D13** 42 5N 71 1W
Brockville, *Canada* **70 D4** 44 35N 75 41W
Brockway, *Mont., U.S.A.* **80 B2** 47 18N 105 45W
Brockway, *Pa., U.S.A.* **78 E6** 41 15N 78 47W
Brocton, *U.S.A.* **78 D5** 42 23N 79 26W
Brodeur Pen., *Canada* **69 A11** 72 30N 88 10W
Brodick, *U.K.* **12 F3** 55 35N 5 9W
Brodnica, *Poland* **17 B10** 53 15N 19 25 E
Brody, *Ukraine* **17 C13** 50 5N 25 10 E
Brogan, *U.S.A.* **82 D5** 44 15N 117 31W
Broken Arrow, *U.S.A.* **81 G7** 36 3N 95 48W
Broken Bow, *Nebr., U.S.A.* **80 E5** 41 24N 99 38W
Broken Bow, *Okla., U.S.A.* **81 H7** 34 2N 94 44W
Broken Hill = Kabwe, *Zambia* **55 E2** 14 30S 28 29 E
Broken Hill, *Australia* **63 E3** 31 58S 141 29 E
Bromley, *U.K.* **11 F8** 51 24N 0 2 E
Bromsgrove, *U.K.* **11 E5** 52 21N 2 2W
Brønderslev, *Denmark* **9 H13** 57 16N 9 57 E
Bronkhorstspruit, *S. Africa* **57 D4** 25 46S 28 45 E
Brønnøysund, *Norway* **8 D15** 65 28N 12 14 E
Bronte, *U.S.A.* **81 K4** 31 53N 100 18W
Bronte Park, *Australia* **62 G4** 42 8S 146 30 E
Brook Park, *U.S.A.* **78 E4** 41 24N 80 51W
Brookfield, *U.S.A.* **80 F8** 39 47N 93 4W
Brookhaven, *U.S.A.* **81 K9** 31 35N 90 26W
Brookings, *Oreg., U.S.A.* **82 E1** 42 3N 124 17W
Brookings, *S. Dak., U.S.A.* **80 C6** 44 19N 96 48W
Brooklin, *Canada* **78 C6** 43 55N 78 55W
Brooklyn Park, *U.S.A.* **80 C8** 45 6N 93 23W
Brookmere, *Canada* **72 D4** 49 52N 120 53W

Brooks

Careme

Careme = Ciremai, *Indonesia* 37 G13 6 55S 108 27 E
Carey, *Idaho, U.S.A.* 82 E7 43 19N 113 57W
Carey, *Ohio, U.S.A.* 76 E4 40 57N 83 23W
Carey, L., *Australia* 61 E3 29 0S 122 15 E
Carey L., *Canada* 73 A8 62 12N 102 55W
Carhué, *Argentina* 94 D3 37 10S 62 50W
Caria, *Turkey* 21 F13 37 20N 28 10 E
Cariacica, *Brazil* 93 H10 20 16S 40 25W
Caribbean Sea, *W. Indies* 89 D5 15 0N 75 0W
Cariboo Mts., *Canada* 72 C4 53 0N 121 0W
Caribou, *U.S.A.* 71 C6 46 52N 68 1W
Caribou —►, *Man., Canada* 73 B10 59 20N 94 44W
Caribou —►, *N.W.T., Canada* 72 A3 61 27N 125 45W
Caribou I., *Canada* 70 C2 47 22N 85 49W
Caribou Is., *Canada* 72 A6 61 55N 113 15W
Caribou L., *Man., Canada* 73 B9 59 21N 96 10W
Caribou L., *Ont., Canada* 70 B2 50 25N 89 5W
Caribou Mts., *Canada* 72 B5 59 12N 115 40W
Carichic, *Mexico* 86 B3 27 56N 107 3W
Carillo, *Mexico* 86 B4 26 50N 103 55W
Carinda, *Australia* 63 E4 30 28S 147 41 E
Carinhanha, *Brazil* 93 F10 14 15S 44 46W
Carinhanha —►, *Brazil* 93 F10 14 20S 43 47W
Carinthia □ = Kärnten □, *Austria* 16 E8 46 52N 13 30 E
Caripito, *Venezuela* 92 A6 10 8N 63 6W
Carleton Place, *Canada* 70 C4 45 8N 76 9W
Carletonville, *S. Africa* 56 D4 26 23S 27 22 E
Carlin, *U.S.A.* 82 F5 40 43N 116 7W
Carlingford L., *U.K.* 13 B5 54 3N 6 9W
Carlinville, *U.S.A.* 80 F10 39 17N 89 53W
Carlisle, *U.K.* 10 C5 54 54N 2 56W
Carlisle, *U.S.A.* 78 F7 40 12N 77 12W
Carlos Casares, *Argentina* 94 D3 35 32S 61 20W
Carlos Tejedor, *Argentina* 94 D3 35 25S 62 25W
Carlow, *Ireland* 13 D5 52 50N 6 56W
Carlow □, *Ireland* 13 D5 52 43N 6 50W
Carlsbad, *Calif., U.S.A.* 85 M9 33 10N 117 21W
Carlsbad, *N. Mex., U.S.A.* 81 J2 32 25N 104 14W
Carluke, *U.K.* 12 F5 55 45N 3 50W
Carlyle, *Canada* 73 D8 49 40N 102 20W
Carlyle, *U.S.A.* 80 F10 38 37N 89 22W
Carmacks, *Canada* 68 B6 62 5N 136 16W
Carman, *Canada* 73 D9 49 30N 98 0W
Carmangay, *Canada* 72 C6 50 10N 113 10W
Carmanville, *Canada* 71 C9 49 23N 54 19W
Carmarthen, *U.K.* 11 F3 51 52N 4 19W
Carmarthen B., *U.K.* 11 F3 51 40N 4 30W
Carmarthenshire □, *U.K.* 11 F3 51 55N 4 13W
Carmaux, *France* 18 D5 44 3N 2 10 E
Carmel, *U.S.A.* 79 E11 41 26N 73 41W
Carmel-by-the-Sea, *U.S.A.* 84 J5 36 33N 121 55W
Carmel Valley, *U.S.A.* 84 J5 36 29N 121 43W
Carmelo, *Uruguay* 94 C4 34 0S 58 20W
Carmen, *Paraguay* 95 B4 27 13S 56 12W
Carmen —►, *Mexico* 86 A3 30 42N 106 29W
Carmen, I., *Mexico* 86 B2 26 0N 111 20W
Carmen de Patagones, *Argentina* 96 E4 40 50S 63 0W
Carmensa, *Argentina* 94 D2 35 15S 67 40W
Carmi, *U.S.A.* 76 F1 38 5N 88 10W
Carmichael, *U.S.A.* 84 G5 38 38N 121 19W
Carmila, *Australia* 62 C4 21 55S 149 24 E
Carmona, *Spain* 19 D3 37 28N 5 42W
Carn Ban, *U.K.* 12 D4 57 7N 4 15W
Carn Eige, *U.K.* 12 D3 57 17N 5 8W
Carnac, *France* 18 C2 47 35N 3 6W
Carnarvon, *Queens., Australia* 62 C4 24 48S 147 45 E
Carnarvon, *W. Austral., Australia* 61 D1 24 51S 113 42 E
Carnarvon, *S. Africa* 56 E3 30 56S 22 8 E
Carnarvon Ra., *Queens., Australia* 62 D4 25 15S 148 30 E
Carnarvon Ra., *W. Austral., Australia* 61 E3 25 20S 120 45 E
Carnation, *U.S.A.* 84 C5 47 39N 121 55W
Carndonagh, *Ireland* 13 A4 55 16N 7 15W
Carnduff, *Canada* 73 D8 49 10N 101 50W
Carnegie, *U.S.A.* 78 F4 40 24N 80 5W
Carnegie, L., *Australia* 61 E3 26 5S 122 30 E
Carnic Alps = Karnische Alpen, *Europe* 16 E7 46 36N 13 0 E
Carniche Alpi = Karnische Alpen, *Europe* 16 E7 46 36N 13 0 E
Carnot, *C.A.R.* 52 D3 4 59N 15 56 E
Carnot, C., *Australia* 63 E2 34 57S 135 38 E
Carnot B., *Australia* 60 C3 17 20S 122 15 E
Carnoustie, *U.K.* 12 E6 56 30N 2 42W
Carnsore Pt., *Ireland* 13 D5 52 10N 6 22W
Caro, *U.S.A.* 76 D4 43 29N 83 24W
Carol City, *U.S.A.* 77 N5 25 56N 80 16W
Carolina, *Brazil* 93 E9 7 10S 47 30W
Carolina, *Puerto Rico* 89 C6 18 23N 65 58W
Carolina, *S. Africa* 57 D5 26 5S 30 6 E
Caroline I., *Kiribati* 65 H12 9 15S 150 3W
Caroline Is., *Pac. Oc.* 64 G7 8 0N 150 0 E
Caron, *Canada* 73 C7 50 30N 105 50W
Caroni —►, *Venezuela* 92 B6 8 21N 62 43W
Caronie = Nébrodi, Monti, *Italy* 20 F6 37 54N 14 35 E
Caroona, *Australia* 63 E5 31 24S 150 26 E
Carpathians, *Europe* 17 D11 49 30N 21 0 E
Carpaţii Meridionali, *Romania* 17 F13 45 30N 25 0 E
Carpentaria, G. of, *Australia* 62 A2 14 0S 139 0 E
Carpentaria Downs, *Australia* 62 B3 18 44S 144 20 E
Carpentras, *France* 18 D6 44 3N 5 2 E
Carpi, *Italy* 20 B4 44 47N 10 53 E
Carpinteria, *U.S.A.* 85 L7 34 24N 119 31W
Carpolac = Morea, *Australia* 63 F3 36 45S 141 18 E
Carr Boyd Ra., *Australia* 60 C4 16 15S 128 35 E
Carrabelle, *U.S.A.* 77 L3 29 51N 84 40W
Carranya, *Australia* 60 C4 19 14S 127 46 E
Carrara, *Italy* 18 D9 44 5N 10 6 E
Carrauntoohill, *Ireland* 13 D2 52 0N 9 45W
Carrick-on-Shannon, *Ireland* 13 C3 53 57N 8 5W
Carrick-on-Suir, *Ireland* 13 D4 52 21N 7 24W
Carrickfergus, *U.K.* 13 B6 54 43N 5 49W
Carrickmacross, *Ireland* 13 C5 53 59N 6 43W
Carrieton, *Australia* 63 E2 32 25S 138 31 E
Carrington, *U.S.A.* 80 B5 47 27N 99 8W
Carrizal Bajo, *Chile* 94 B1 28 5S 71 20W
Carrizalillo, *Chile* 94 B1 29 5S 71 30W
Carrizo Cr. —►, *U.S.A.* 81 G3 36 55N 103 55W
Carrizo Springs, *U.S.A.* 81 L5 28 31N 99 52W
Carrizozo, *U.S.A.* 83 K11 33 38N 105 53W
Carroll, *U.S.A.* 80 D7 42 4N 94 52W
Carrollton, *Ga., U.S.A.* 77 J3 33 35N 85 5W
Carrollton, *Ill., U.S.A.* 80 F9 39 18N 90 24W
Carrollton, *Ky., U.S.A.* 76 F3 38 41N 85 11W
Carrollton, *Mo., U.S.A.* 80 F8 39 22N 93 30W
Carrollton, *Ohio, U.S.A.* 78 F3 40 34N 81 5W
Carron —►, *U.K.* 12 D4 57 53N 4 22W
Carron, L., *U.K.* 12 D3 57 22N 5 35W
Carrot —►, *Canada* 73 C8 53 50N 101 17W
Carrot River, *Canada* 73 C8 53 17N 103 35W
Carruthers, *Canada* 73 C7 52 52N 109 16W
Carson, *Calif., U.S.A.* 85 M8 33 48N 118 17W
Carson, *N. Dak., U.S.A.* 80 B4 46 25N 101 34W
Carson —►, *U.S.A.* 84 F8 39 45N 118 40W
Carson City, *U.S.A.* 84 F7 39 10N 119 46W
Carson Sink, *U.S.A.* 82 G4 39 50N 118 25W
Cartagena, *Colombia* 92 A3 10 25N 75 33W
Cartagena, *Spain* 19 D5 37 38N 0 59W
Cartago, *Colombia* 92 C3 4 45N 75 55W
Cartago, *Costa Rica* 88 E3 9 50N 83 55W
Cartersville, *U.S.A.* 77 H3 34 10N 84 48W
Carterton, *N.Z.* 59 J5 41 2S 175 31 E
Carthage, *Ark., U.S.A.* 81 H8 34 4N 92 33W
Carthage, *Ill., U.S.A.* 80 E9 40 25N 91 8W
Carthage, *Mo., U.S.A.* 81 G7 37 11N 94 19W
Carthage, *S. Dak., U.S.A.* 80 C6 44 10N 97 43W
Carthage, *Tex., U.S.A.* 81 J7 32 9N 94 20W
Cartier I., *Australia* 60 B3 12 31S 123 29 E
Cartwright, *Canada* 71 B8 53 41N 56 58W
Caruaru, *Brazil* 93 E11 8 15S 35 55W
Carúpano, *Venezuela* 92 A6 10 39N 63 15W
Caruthersville, *U.S.A.* 81 G10 36 11N 89 39W
Carvoeiro, *Brazil* 92 D6 1 30S 61 59W
Carvoeiro, C., *Portugal* 19 C1 39 21N 9 24W
Cary, *U.S.A.* 77 H6 35 47N 78 46W
Casa Grande, *U.S.A.* 83 K8 32 53N 111 45W
Casablanca, *Chile* 94 C1 33 20S 71 25W
Casablanca, *Morocco* 50 B4 33 36N 7 36W
Casas Grandes, *Mexico* 86 A3 30 22N 108 0W
Cascade, *Idaho, U.S.A.* 82 D5 44 31N 116 2W
Cascade, *Mont., U.S.A.* 82 C8 47 16N 111 42W
Cascade Locks, *U.S.A.* 84 E5 45 40N 121 54W
Cascade Ra., *U.S.A.* 84 D5 47 0N 121 30W
Cascais, *Portugal* 19 C1 38 41N 9 25W
Cascavel, *Brazil* 95 A5 24 57S 53 28W
Cáscina, *Italy* 20 C4 43 41N 10 33 E
Caserta, *Italy* 20 D6 41 4N 14 20 E
Cashel, *Ireland* 13 D4 52 30N 7 53W
Cashmere, *U.S.A.* 82 C3 47 31N 120 28W
Cashmere Downs, *Australia* 61 E2 28 57S 119 35 E
Casiguran, *Phil.* 37 A6 16 22N 122 7 E
Casilda, *Argentina* 94 C3 33 10S 61 10W
Casino, *Australia* 63 D5 28 52S 153 3 E
Casiquiare —►, *Venezuela* 92 C5 2 1N 67 7W
Caslan, *Canada* 72 C6 54 38N 112 31W
Casma, *Peru* 92 E3 9 30S 78 20W
Casmalia, *U.S.A.* 85 L6 34 50N 120 32W
Caspe, *Spain* 19 B5 41 14N 0 1W
Casper, *U.S.A.* 82 E10 42 51N 106 19W
Caspian Depression, *Eurasia* 25 E8 47 0N 48 0 E
Caspian Sea, *Eurasia* 25 F9 43 0N 50 0 E
Cass City, *U.S.A.* 76 D4 43 36N 83 11W
Cass Lake, *U.S.A.* 80 B7 47 23N 94 37W
Casselman, *Canada* 79 A9 45 19N 75 5W
Casselton, *U.S.A.* 80 B6 46 54N 97 13W
Cassiar, *Canada* 72 B3 59 16N 129 40W
Cassiar Mts., *Canada* 72 B2 59 30N 130 30W
Cassino, *Italy* 20 D5 41 30N 13 49 E
Cassville, *U.S.A.* 81 G8 36 41N 93 52W
Castaic, *U.S.A.* 85 L8 34 30N 118 38W
Castanhal, *Brazil* 93 D9 1 18S 47 55W
Castellammare di Stábia, *Italy* 20 D6 40 42N 14 29 E
Castelli, *Argentina* 94 D4 36 7S 57 47W
Castelló de la Plana, *Spain* 19 C5 39 58N 0 3W
Castelo, *Brazil* 95 A7 20 33S 41 14W
Castelo Branco, *Portugal* 19 C2 39 50N 7 31W
Castelsarrasin, *France* 18 E4 44 2N 1 7 E
Castelvetrano, *Italy* 20 F5 37 41N 12 47 E
Casterton, *Australia* 63 F3 37 30S 141 30 E
Castilla-La Mancha □, *Spain* 19 C4 39 30N 3 30W
Castilla y Leon □, *Spain* 19 B3 42 0N 5 0W
Castillos, *Uruguay* 95 C5 34 12S 53 52W
Castle Dale, *U.S.A.* 82 G8 39 13N 111 1W
Castle Douglas, *U.K.* 12 G5 54 56N 3 56W
Castle Rock, *Colo., U.S.A.* 80 F2 39 22N 104 51W
Castle Rock, *Wash., U.S.A.* 84 D4 46 17N 122 54W
Castlebar, *Ireland* 13 C2 53 52N 9 18W
Castleblaney, *Ireland* 13 B5 54 7N 6 44W
Castlederg, *U.K.* 13 B4 54 42N 7 35W
Castleford, *U.K.* 10 D6 53 43N 1 21W
Castlegar, *Canada* 72 D5 49 20N 117 40W
Castlemaine, *Australia* 63 F3 37 2S 144 12 E
Castlepollard, *Ireland* 13 C4 53 41N 7 19W
Castlerea, *Ireland* 13 C3 53 46N 8 29W
Castlereagh —►, *Australia* 63 E4 30 12S 147 32 E
Castlereagh B., *Australia* 62 A2 12 10S 135 10 E
Castletown, *U.K.* 10 C3 54 5N 4 38W
Castletown Bearhaven, *Ireland* 13 E2 51 39N 9 55W
Castlevale, *Australia* 62 C4 24 30S 146 48 E
Castor, *Canada* 72 C6 52 15N 111 50W
Castres, *France* 18 E5 43 37N 2 13 E
Castricum, *Neths.* 15 B4 52 33N 4 40 E
Castries, *St. Lucia* 89 D7 14 2N 60 58W
Castro, *Brazil* 95 A6 24 45S 50 0W
Castro Alves, *Brazil* 93 F11 12 46S 39 33W
Castroville, *Calif., U.S.A.* 84 J5 36 46N 121 45W
Castroville, *Tex., U.S.A.* 81 L5 29 21N 98 53W
Castuera, *Spain* 19 C3 38 43N 5 37W
Casummit Lake, *Canada* 70 B1 51 29N 92 22W
Cat Ba, Dao, *Vietnam* 38 B6 20 50N 107 0 E
Cat I., *Bahamas* 89 B4 24 30N 75 30W
Cat I., *U.S.A.* 81 K10 30 14N 89 6W
Cat L., *Canada* 70 B1 51 40N 91 50W
Catacamas, *Honduras* 88 D2 14 54N 85 56W
Cataguases, *Brazil* 95 A7 21 23S 42 39W
Catahoula L., *U.S.A.* 81 K8 31 31N 92 7W
Catalão, *Brazil* 93 G9 18 10S 47 57W
Çatalca, *Turkey* 21 D13 41 8N 28 27 E
Catalina, *Canada* 71 C9 48 31N 53 4W
Catalonia = Cataluña □, *Spain* 19 B6 41 40N 1 15 E
Cataluña □, *Spain* 19 B6 41 40N 1 15 E
Catamarca, *Argentina* 94 B2 28 30S 65 50W
Catamarca □, *Argentina* 94 B2 27 0S 65 50W
Catanduanes, *Phil.* 37 B6 13 50N 124 20 E
Catanduva, *Brazil* 95 A6 21 5S 48 58W
Catánia, *Italy* 20 F6 37 30N 15 6 E
Catanzaro, *Italy* 20 E7 38 54N 16 35 E
Catarman, *Phil.* 37 B6 12 28N 124 35 E
Cateel, *Phil.* 37 C7 7 47N 126 24 E
Caterham, *U.K.* 11 F7 51 15N 0 4W
Cathcart, *S. Africa* 56 E4 32 18S 27 10 E
Cathlamet, *U.S.A.* 84 D3 46 12N 123 23W
Catlettsburg, *U.S.A.* 76 F4 38 25N 82 36W
Catoche, C., *Mexico* 87 C7 21 40N 87 8W
Catrimani, *Brazil* 92 C6 0 27N 61 41W
Catrimani —►, *Brazil* 92 C6 0 28N 61 44W
Catskill, *U.S.A.* 79 D11 42 14N 73 52W
Catskill Mts., *U.S.A.* 79 D10 42 10N 74 25W
Catt, Mt., *Australia* 62 A1 13 49S 134 23 E
Cattaraugus, *U.S.A.* 78 D6 42 22N 78 52W
Catuala, *Angola* 56 B2 16 25S 19 2 E
Catur, *Mozam.* 55 E4 13 45S 35 30 E
Catwick Is., *Vietnam* 39 H7 10 0N 109 0 E
Cauca —►, *Colombia* 92 B4 8 54N 74 28W
Caucaia, *Brazil* 93 D11 3 40S 38 35W
Caucasus Mountains, *Eurasia* 25 F7 42 50N 44 0 E
Caungula, *Angola* 52 F3 8 26S 18 38 E
Cauquenes, *Chile* 94 D1 36 0S 72 22W
Caura —►, *Venezuela* 92 B6 7 38N 64 53W
Cauresi —►, *Mozam.* 55 F3 17 8S 33 0 E
Causapscal, *Canada* 71 C6 48 19N 67 12W
Cauvery —►, *India* 40 P11 11 9N 78 52 E
Caux, Pays de, *France* 18 B4 49 38N 0 35 E
Cavalier, *U.S.A.* 80 A6 48 48N 97 37W
Cavalleria, C. de, *Spain* 22 A11 40 5N 4 5 E
Cavan, *Ireland* 13 B4 54 0N 7 22W
Cavan □, *Ireland* 13 C4 54 1N 7 16W
Cave City, *U.S.A.* 76 G3 37 8N 85 58W
Cavenagh Ra., *Australia* 61 E4 26 12S 127 55 E
Cavendish, *Australia* 63 F3 37 31S 142 2 E
Caviana, I., *Brazil* 93 C8 0 10N 50 10W
Cavite, *Phil.* 37 B6 14 29N 120 55 E
Cawndilla L., *Australia* 63 E3 32 30S 142 15 E
Cawnpore = Kanpur, *India* 43 F9 26 28N 80 20 E
Caxias, *Brazil* 93 D10 4 55S 43 20W
Caxias do Sul, *Brazil* 95 B5 29 10S 51 10W
Cay Sal Bank, *Bahamas* 88 B4 23 45N 80 0W
Cayenne, *Fr. Guiana* 93 B8 5 5N 52 18W
Cayman Brac, *Cayman Is.* 88 C4 19 43N 79 49W
Cayman Is. ■, *W. Indies* 88 C3 19 40N 80 30W
Cayo Romano, *Cuba* 88 B4 22 0N 78 0W
Cayuga, *Canada* 78 D5 42 59N 79 50W
Cayuga, *U.S.A.* 79 D8 42 54N 76 44W
Cayuga L., *U.S.A.* 79 D8 42 41N 76 41W
Cazombo, *Angola* 53 G4 11 54S 22 56 E
Ceanannus Mor, *Ireland* 13 C5 53 44N 6 53W
Ceará □, *Brazil* 93 E11 5 0S 40 0W
Ceará Mirim, *Brazil* 93 E11 5 38S 35 25W
Cebaco, I. de, *Panama* 88 E3 7 33N 81 9W
Cebollar, *Argentina* 94 B2 29 10S 66 35W
Cebu, *Phil.* 37 B6 10 18N 123 54 E
Cecil Plains, *Australia* 63 D5 27 30S 151 11 E
Cedar —►, *U.S.A.* 80 E9 41 17N 91 21W
Cedar City, *U.S.A.* 83 H7 37 41N 113 4W
Cedar Creek Reservoir, *U.S.A.* 81 J6 32 11N 96 4W
Cedar Falls, *Iowa, U.S.A.* 80 D8 42 32N 92 27W
Cedar Falls, *Wash., U.S.A.* 84 C5 47 25N 121 45W
Cedar Key, *U.S.A.* 77 L4 29 8N 83 2W
Cedar L., *Canada* 73 C9 53 10N 100 0W
Cedar Rapids, *U.S.A.* 80 E9 41 59N 91 40W
Cedartown, *U.S.A.* 77 H3 34 1N 85 15W
Cedarvale, *Canada* 72 B3 55 1N 128 22W
Cedarville, *S. Africa* 57 E4 30 23S 29 3 E
Cedarville, *U.S.A.* 82 F3 41 32N 120 10W
Cedral, *Mexico* 86 C4 23 50N 100 42W
Cedro, *Brazil* 93 E11 6 34S 39 3W
Cedros, I. de, *Mexico* 86 B1 28 10N 115 20W
Ceduna, *Australia* 63 E1 32 7S 133 46 E
Cefalù, *Italy* 20 E6 38 2N 14 1 E
Cegléd, *Hungary* 17 E10 47 11N 19 47 E
Celaya, *Mexico* 86 C4 20 31N 100 37W
Celebes = Sulawesi □, *Indonesia* 37 E6 2 0S 120 0 E
Celebes Sea, *Indonesia* 37 D6 3 0N 123 0 E
Celina, *U.S.A.* 76 E3 40 33N 84 35W
Celje, *Slovenia* 16 E8 46 16N 15 18 E
Celle, *Germany* 16 B6 52 37N 10 4 E
Cement, *U.S.A.* 81 H5 34 56N 98 8W
Center, *N. Dak., U.S.A.* 80 B4 47 7N 101 18W
Center, *Tex., U.S.A.* 81 K7 31 48N 94 11W
Centerfield, *U.S.A.* 83 G8 39 8N 111 49W
Centerville, *Calif., U.S.A.* 84 J7 36 44N 119 30W
Centerville, *Iowa, U.S.A.* 80 E8 40 44N 92 52W
Centerville, *Pa., U.S.A.* 78 F5 40 3N 79 59W
Centerville, *S. Dak., U.S.A.* 80 D6 43 7N 96 58W
Centerville, *Tenn., U.S.A.* 77 H2 35 47N 87 28W
Centerville, *Tex., U.S.A.* 81 K7 31 16N 95 59W
Central, *U.S.A.* 83 K9 32 47N 108 9W
Central □, *Kenya* 54 C4 0 30S 37 30 E
Central □, *Malawi* 55 E3 13 30S 33 30 E
Central □, *Zambia* 55 E2 14 25S 28 50 E
Central, Cordillera, *Colombia* 92 C4 5 0N 75 0W
Central, Cordillera, *Costa Rica* 88 D3 10 10N 84 5W
Central, Cordillera, *Dom. Rep.* 89 C5 19 15N 71 0W
Central African Rep. ■, *Africa* 52 C4 7 0N 20 0 E
Central City, *Ky., U.S.A.* 76 G2 37 18N 87 7W
Central City, *Nebr., U.S.A.* 80 E6 41 7N 98 0W
Central I., *Kenya* 54 B4 3 30N 36 0 E
Central Makran Range, *Pakistan* 40 F4 26 30N 64 15 E
Central Patricia, *Canada* 70 B1 51 30N 90 9W
Central Russian Uplands, *Europe* 6 E13 54 0N 36 0 E
Central Siberian Plateau, *Russia* 28 C14 65 0N 105 0 E
Centralia, *Ill., U.S.A.* 80 F10 38 32N 89 8W
Centralia, *Mo., U.S.A.* 80 F8 39 13N 92 8W
Centralia, *Wash., U.S.A.* 84 D4 46 43N 122 58W
Centreville, *Ala., U.S.A.* 77 J2 32 57N 87 8W
Centreville, *Miss., U.S.A.* 81 K9 31 5N 91 4W
Cephalonia = Kefallinía, *Greece* 21 E9 38 20N 20 30 E
Cepu, *Indonesia* 37 G14 7 9S 111 35 E
Ceram = Seram, *Indonesia* 37 E7 3 10S 129 0 E
Ceram Sea = Seram Sea, *Indonesia* 37 E7 2 30S 128 30 E
Ceredigion □, *U.K.* 11 E3 52 16N 4 15W
Ceres, *Argentina* 94 B3 29 55S 61 55W
Ceres, *S. Africa* 56 E2 33 21S 19 18 E
Ceres, *U.S.A.* 84 H6 37 35N 120 57W
Cerignola, *Italy* 20 D6 41 17N 15 53 E
Cerigo = Kíthira, *Greece* 21 F10 36 8N 23 0 E
Çerkezköy, *Turkey* 21 D12 41 17N 28 0 E
Cerralvo, I., *Mexico* 86 C3 24 20N 109 45W
Cerritos, *Mexico* 86 C4 22 27N 100 20W
Cervera, *Spain* 19 B6 41 40N 1 16 E
Cesena, *Italy* 20 B5 44 8N 12 15 E
Cēsis, *Latvia* 9 H21 57 18N 25 15 E
České Budějovice, *Czech Rep.* 16 D8 48 55N 14 25 E
Českomoravská Vrchovina, *Czech Rep.* 16 D8 49 30N 15 40 E
Çeşme, *Turkey* 21 E12 38 20N 26 23 E
Cessnock, *Australia* 63 E5 32 50S 151 21 E
Cetinje, *Montenegro, Yug.* 21 C8 42 23N 18 59 E
Cetraro, *Italy* 20 E6 39 31N 15 55 E
Ceuta, *N. Afr.* 19 E3 35 52N 5 18W
Cévennes, *France* 18 D5 44 10N 3 50 E
Ceyhan —►, *Turkey* 25 G6 36 38N 35 40 E
Ceylon = Sri Lanka ■, *Asia* 40 R12 7 30N 80 50 E
Cha-am, *Thailand* 38 F2 12 48N 99 58 E
Cha Pa, *Vietnam* 38 A4 22 20N 103 47 E
Chacabuco, *Argentina* 94 C3 34 40S 60 27W
Chachapoyas, *Peru* 92 E3 6 15S 77 50W
Chachoengsao, *Thailand* 38 F3 13 42N 101 5 E
Chachran, *Pakistan* 40 E7 28 55N 70 30 E
Chachro, *Pakistan* 42 G4 25 5N 70 15 E
Chaco □, *Argentina* 94 B3 26 30S 61 0W
Chaco □, *Paraguay* 94 B4 26 0S 60 0W
Chaco Austral, *S. Amer.* 96 B4 27 0S 61 30W
Chaco Boreal, *S. Amer.* 96 A4 22 0S 60 0W
Chaco Central, *S. Amer.* 96 A4 24 0S 61 0W
Chad ■, *Africa* 51 F8 15 0N 17 15 E
Chad, L. = Tchad, L., *Chad* 51 F8 13 30N 14 30 E
Chadan, *Russia* 27 D10 51 17N 91 35 E
Chadileuvú —►, *Argentina* 94 D2 37 46S 66 0W
Chadiza, *Zambia* 55 E3 14 45S 32 27 E
Chadron, *U.S.A.* 80 D3 42 50N 103 0W
Chadyr-Lunga = Ciadâr-Lunga, *Moldova* 17 E15 46 3N 28 51 E
Chae Hom, *Thailand* 38 C2 18 43N 99 35 E
Chaem —►, *Thailand* 38 C2 18 11N 98 38 E
Chaeryŏng, *N. Korea* 35 E13 38 24N 125 36 E
Chagai Hills, *Afghan.* 40 E3 29 30N 63 0 E
Chagda, *Russia* 27 D14 58 45N 130 38 E
Chagos Arch., *Ind. Oc.* 29 K11 6 0S 72 0 E
Chāh Ākhvor, *Iran* 45 C8 32 41N 59 40 E
Chāh Bahār, *Iran* 45 E9 25 20N 60 40 E
Chāh-e-Malek, *Iran* 45 D8 28 35N 59 7 E
Chāh Kavīr, *Iran* 45 D7 31 45N 54 52 E
Chahar Burjak, *Afghan.* 40 D3 30 15N 62 0 E
Chaibasa, *India* 41 H14 22 42N 85 49 E
Chainat, *Thailand* 38 E3 15 11N 100 8 E
Chaiya, *Thailand* 39 H2 9 23N 99 14 E
Chaj Doab, *Pakistan* 42 C5 32 15N 73 0 E
Chajari, *Argentina* 94 C4 30 42S 58 0W
Chake Chake, *Tanzania* 54 D4 5 15S 39 45 E
Chakhānsūr, *Afghan.* 40 D3 31 10N 62 0 E
Chakonipau, L., *Canada* 71 A6 56 18N 68 30W
Chakradharpur, *India* 43 H11 22 45N 85 40 E
Chakwal, *Pakistan* 42 C5 32 56N 72 53 E
Chala, *Peru* 92 G4 15 48S 74 20W
Chalchihuites, *Mexico* 86 C4 23 29N 103 53W
Chalcis = Khalkís, *Greece* 21 E10 38 27N 23 42 E
Chaleur B., *Canada* 71 C6 47 55N 65 30W
Chalfant, *U.S.A.* 84 H8 37 32N 118 21W
Chalhuanca, *Peru* 92 F4 14 15S 73 15W
Chalisgaon, *India* 40 J9 20 30N 75 10 E
Chalky Inlet, *N.Z.* 59 M1 46 3S 166 31 E
Challapata, *Bolivia* 92 G5 18 53S 66 50W
Challis, *U.S.A.* 82 D6 44 30N 114 14W
Chalna, *India* 43 H13 22 36N 89 35 E
Chalon-sur-Saône, *France* 18 C6 46 48N 4 50 E
Châlons-en-Champagne, *France* 18 B6 48 58N 4 20 E
Chalyaphum, *Thailand* 38 E4 15 48N 102 2 E
Cham, Cu Lao, *Vietnam* 38 E7 15 57N 108 30 E
Chama, *U.S.A.* 83 H10 36 54N 106 35W
Chaman, *Pakistan* 40 D5 30 58N 66 25 E
Chamba, *India* 42 C7 32 35N 76 10 E
Chamba, *Tanzania* 55 E4 11 37S 37 0 E
Chambal —►, *India* 43 F8 26 29N 79 15 E
Chamberlain, *U.S.A.* 80 D5 43 49N 99 20W
Chamberlain —►, *Australia* 60 C4 15 30S 127 54 E
Chambers, *U.S.A.* 83 J9 35 11N 109 26W
Chambersburg, *U.S.A.* 76 F7 39 56N 77 40W
Chambéry, *France* 18 D6 45 34N 5 55 E
Chambly, *Canada* 79 A11 45 27N 73 17W
Chambord, *Canada* 71 C5 48 25N 72 6W
Chamchamal, *Iraq* 44 C5 35 32N 44 50 E
Chamela, *Mexico* 86 D3 19 32N 105 5W

Chinnampo

Coronel Dorrego

Cocanada = Kakinada, *India* .... **41 L13** 16 57N 82 11 E
Cochabamba, *Bolivia* **92 G5** 17 26S 66 10W
Cochemane, *Mozam.* .... **55 F3** 17 0S 32 54 E
Cochin, *India* .... **40 Q10** 9 59N 76 22 E
Cochin China, *Vietnam* .. **39 G6** 10 30N 106 0 E
Cochise, *U.S.A.* **83 K9** 32 7N 109 55W
Cochran, *U.S.A.* **77 J4** 32 23N 83 21W
Cochrane, *Alta., Canada* . **72 C6** 51 11N 114 30W
Cochrane, *Ont., Canada* . **70 C3** 49 0N 81 0W
Cochrane, *Chile* **96 F2** 47 15S 72 33W
Cochrane →, *Canada* .. **73 B8** 59 0N 103 40W
Cochrane, L., *Chile* **96 F2** 47 10S 72 0W
Cockburn, *Australia* ..... **63 E3** 32 5S 141 0 E
Cockburn, Canal, *Chile* .. **96 G2** 54 30S 72 0W
Cockburn I., *Canada* **70 C3** 45 55N 83 22W
Cockburn Ra., *Australia* .. **60 C4** 15 46S 128 0 E
Cockermouth, *U.K.* **10 C4** 54 40N 3 22W
Cocklebiddy Motel, *Australia* .... **61 F4** 32 0S 126 3 E
Coco →, *Cent. Amer.* .. **88 D3** 15 0N 83 8W
Cocoa, *U.S.A.* **77 L5** 28 21N 80 44W
Cocobeach, *Gabon* ..... **52 D1** 0 59N 9 34 E
Cocos, I. del, *Pac. Oc.* ... **65 G19** 5 25N 87 55W
Cocos Is., *Ind. Oc.* ...... **64 J1** 12 10S 96 55 E
Cod, C., *U.S.A.* **75 B12** 42 5N 70 10W
Codajás, *Brazil* **92 D6** 3 55S 62 0W
Coderre, *Canada* **73 C7** 50 11N 106 31W
Codó, *Brazil* **93 D10** 4 30S 43 55W
Cody, *U.S.A.* **82 D9** 44 32N 109 3W
Coe Hill, *Canada* **70 D4** 44 52N 77 50W
Coelemu, *Chile* **94 D1** 36 30S 72 48W
Coen, *Australia* .... **62 A3** 13 52S 143 12 E
Cœur d'Alene, *U.S.A.* ... **82 C5** 47 45N 116 51W
Cœur d'Alene L., *U.S.A.* .. **82 C5** 47 32N 116 48W
Coevorden, *Neths.* ...... **15 B6** 52 40N 6 44 E
Cofete, *Canary Is.* **22 F5** 28 6N 14 23W
Coffeyville, *U.S.A.* **81 G7** 37 2N 95 37W
Coffin B., *Australia* ...... **63 E2** 34 38S 135 28 E
Coffin Bay Peninsula, *Australia* .... **63 E2** 34 32S 135 15 E
Coffs Harbour, *Australia* . **63 E5** 30 16S 153 5 E
Cognac, *France* **18 D3** 45 41N 0 20W
Cohagen, *U.S.A.* **82 C10** 47 3N 106 37W
Cohoes, *U.S.A.* **79 D11** 42 46N 73 42W
Cohuna, *Australia* ...... **63 F3** 35 45S 144 15 E
Coiba, I., *Panama* **88 E3** 7 30N 81 40W
Coig →, *Argentina* **96 G3** 51 0S 69 10W
Coigeach, Rubha, *U.K.* ... **12 C3** 58 6N 5 26W
Coihaique, *Chile* **96 F2** 45 30S 71 45W
Coimbatore, *India* ...... **40 P10** 11 2N 76 59 E
Coimbra, *Brazil* **92 G7** 19 55S 57 48W
Coimbra, *Portugal* **19 B1** 40 15N 8 27W
Coín, *Spain* **19 D3** 36 40N 4 48W
Coipasa, Salar de, *Bolivia* **92 G5** 19 26S 68 9W
Cojimies, *Ecuador* **92 C3** 0 20N 80 0W
Cojutepequé, *El Salv.* **88 D2** 13 41N 88 54W
Cokeville, *U.S.A.* **82 E8** 42 5N 110 57W
Colac, *Australia* .... **63 F3** 38 21S 143 35 E
Colatina, *Brazil* **93 G10** 19 32S 40 37W
Colbeck, C., *Antarctica* ... **5 D13** 77 6S 157 48W
Colbinabbin, *Australia* ... **63 F3** 36 38S 144 48 E
Colborne, *Canada* **78 C7** 44 0N 77 53W
Colby, *U.S.A.* **80 F4** 39 24N 101 3W
Colchagua □, *Chile* **94 C1** 34 30S 71 0W
Colchester, *U.K.* .... **11 F8** 51 54N 0 55 E
Coldstream, *U.K.* **12 F6** 55 39N 2 15W
Coldwater, *Canada* **78 B5** 44 42N 79 40W
Coldwater, *U.S.A.* **81 G5** 37 16N 99 20W
Colebrook, *Australia* .... **62 G4** 42 31S 147 21 E
Colebrook, *U.S.A.* **79 B13** 44 54N 71 30W
Coleman, *Canada* **72 D6** 49 40N 114 30W
Coleman, *U.S.A.* **81 K5** 31 50N 99 26W
Coleman →, *Australia* . **62 B3** 15 6S 141 38 E
Colenso, *S. Africa* ...... **57 D4** 28 44S 29 50 E
Coleraine, *Australia* ..... **63 F3** 37 36S 141 40 E
Coleraine, *U.K.* **13 A5** 55 8N 6 41W
Coleridge, L., *N.Z.* ...... **59 K3** 43 17S 171 30 E
Colesberg, *S. Africa* ..... **56 E4** 30 45S 25 5 E
Coleville, *U.S.A.* **84 G7** 38 34N 119 30W
Colfax, *Calif., U.S.A.* **84 F6** 39 6N 120 57W
Colfax, *La., U.S.A.* **81 K8** 31 31N 92 42W
Colfax, *Wash., U.S.A.* ... **82 C5** 46 53N 117 22W
Colhué Huapi, L., *Argentina* **96 F3** 45 30S 69 0W
Coligny, *S. Africa* .... **57 D4** 26 17S 26 15 E
Colima, *Mexico* **86 D4** 19 14N 103 43W
Colima □, *Mexico* **86 D4** 19 10N 103 40W
Colima, Nevado de, *Mexico* **86 D4** 19 35N 103 45W
Colina, *Chile* **94 C1** 33 13S 70 45W
Coll, *U.K.* **12 E2** 56 39N 6 34W
Collaguasi, *Chile* **94 A2** 21 5S 68 45W
Collarenebri, *Australia* ... **63 D4** 29 33S 148 34 E
Collbran, *U.S.A.* **83 G10** 39 14N 107 58W
Colleen Bawn, *Zimbabwe* **55 G2** 21 0S 29 12 E
College Park, *U.S.A.* **77 J3** 33 40N 84 27W
College Station, *U.S.A.* .. **81 K6** 30 37N 96 21W
Collette, *Canada* **71 C6** 46 40N 65 30W
Collie, *Australia* .... **61 F2** 33 22S 116 8 E
Collier B., *Australia* ..... **60 C3** 16 10S 124 15 E
Collier Ra., *Australia* .... **60 D2** 24 45S 119 10 E
Collina, Passo di, *Italy* ... **20 B4** 44 2N 10 56 E
Collingwood, *Canada* **78 B4** 44 29N 80 13W
Collingwood, *N.Z.* ...... **59 J4** 40 41S 172 40 E
Collins, *Canada* **70 B2** 50 17N 89 27W
Collinsville, *Australia* .... **62 C4** 20 30S 147 56 E
Collipulli, *Chile* **94 D1** 37 55S 72 30W
Collooney, *Ireland* **13 B3** 54 11N 8 29W
Colmar, *France* .... **18 B7** 48 5N 7 20 E
Colo →, *Australia* ..... **63 E5** 33 25S 150 52 E
Cologne = Köln, *Germany* **16 C4** 50 56N 6 57 E
Colom, I., *Spain* .... **22 B11** 39 58N 4 16 E
Coloma, *U.S.A.* **84 G6** 38 48N 120 53W
Colomb-Béchar = Béchar, *Algeria* **50 B5** 31 38N 2 18W
Colombia ■, *S. Amer.* ... **92 C4** 3 45N 73 0W
Colombian Basin, *S. Amer.* **66 H12** 14 0N 76 0W
Colombo, *Sri Lanka* ..... **40 R11** 6 56N 79 58 E
Colome, *U.S.A.* **80 D5** 43 16N 99 43W
Colón, *Argentina* **94 C4** 32 12S 58 10W
Colón, *Cuba* **88 B3** 22 42N 80 54W
Colón, *Panama* **88 E4** 9 20N 79 54W
Colona, *Australia* .... **61 F5** 31 38S 132 4 E
Colonia de San Jordi, *Spain* .... **22 B9** 39 19N 2 59 E
Colonia del Sacramento, *Uruguay* **94 C4** 34 25S 57 50W
Colonia Dora, *Argentina* . **94 B3** 28 34S 62 59W
Colonial Heights, *U.S.A.* . **76 G7** 37 15N 77 25W
Colonsay, *Canada* **73 C7** 51 59N 105 52W
Colonsay, *U.K.* **12 E2** 56 5N 6 12W
Colorado □, *U.S.A.* **83 G10** 39 30N 105 30W
Colorado →, *Argentina* . **96 D4** 39 50S 62 8W
Colorado →, *N. Amer.* . **83 L6** 31 45N 114 40W
Colorado →, *U.S.A.* **81 L7** 28 36N 95 59W
Colorado City, *U.S.A.* ... **81 J4** 32 24N 100 52W
Colorado Desert, *U.S.A.* . **74 D3** 34 20N 116 0W
Colorado Plateau, *U.S.A.* **83 H8** 37 0N 111 0W
Colorado River Aqueduct, *U.S.A.* **85 L12** 34 17N 114 10W
Colorado Springs, *U.S.A.* **80 F2** 38 50N 104 49W
Colotlán, *Mexico* **86 C4** 22 6N 103 16W
Colton, *N.Y., U.S.A.* **79 B10** 44 33N 74 56W
Colton, *Wash., U.S.A.* ... **82 C5** 46 34N 117 8W
Columbia, *La., U.S.A.* ... **81 J8** 32 6N 92 5W
Columbia, *Miss., U.S.A.* . **81 K10** 31 15N 89 50W
Columbia, *Mo., U.S.A.* ... **80 F8** 38 57N 92 20W
Columbia, *Pa., U.S.A.* ... **79 F8** 40 2N 76 30W
Columbia, *S.C., U.S.A.* ... **77 J5** 34 0N 81 2W
Columbia, *Tenn., U.S.A.* . **77 H2** 35 37N 87 2W
Columbia →, *U.S.A.* ... **82 C1** 46 15N 124 5W
Columbia, District of □, *U.S.A.* **76 F7** 38 55N 77 0W
Columbia, Mt., *Canada* .. **72 C5** 52 8N 117 20W
Columbia Basin, *U.S.A.* .. **82 C4** 46 45N 119 5W
Columbia Falls, *U.S.A.* .. **82 B6** 48 23N 114 11W
Columbia Heights, *U.S.A.* **80 C8** 45 3N 93 15W
Columbiana, *U.S.A.* **78 F4** 40 53N 80 42W
Columbretes, Is., *Spain* .. **19 C6** 39 50N 0 50 E
Columbus, *Ga., U.S.A.* ... **77 J3** 32 28N 84 59W
Columbus, *Ind., U.S.A.* .. **76 F3** 39 13N 85 55W
Columbus, *Kans., U.S.A.* . **81 G7** 37 10N 94 50W
Columbus, *Miss., U.S.A.* . **77 J1** 33 30N 88 25W
Columbus, *Mont., U.S.A.* . **82 D9** 45 38N 109 15W
Columbus, *N. Dak., U.S.A.* **80 A3** 48 54N 102 47W
Columbus, *N. Mex., U.S.A.* **83 L10** 31 50N 107 38W
Columbus, *Nebr., U.S.A.* . **80 E6** 41 26N 97 22W
Columbus, *Ohio, U.S.A.* . **76 F4** 39 58N 83 0W
Columbus, *Tex., U.S.A.* .. **81 L6** 29 42N 96 33W
Columbus, *Wis., U.S.A.* .. **80 D10** 43 21N 89 1W
Colusa, *U.S.A.* **84 F4** 39 13N 122 1W
Colville, *U.S.A.* **82 B5** 48 33N 117 54W
Colville →, *U.S.A.* **68 A4** 70 25N 150 30W
Colville, C., *N.Z.* .... **59 G5** 36 29S 175 21 E
Colwyn Bay, *U.K.* **10 D4** 53 18N 3 44W
Comácchio, *Italy* .... **20 B5** 44 42N 12 11 E
Comalcalco, *Mexico* **87 D6** 18 16N 93 13W
Comallo, *Argentina* **96 E2** 41 0S 70 5W
Comanche, *Okla., U.S.A.* . **81 H6** 34 22N 97 58W
Comanche, *Tex., U.S.A.* .. **81 K5** 31 54N 98 36W
Comayagua, *Honduras* ... **88 D2** 14 25N 87 37W
Combahee →, *U.S.A.* ... **77 J5** 32 30N 80 31W
Comber, *Canada* **78 D2** 42 14N 82 33W
Comber, *U.K.* **13 B6** 54 33N 5 45W
Comblain-au-Pont, *Belgium* .... **15 D5** 50 29N 5 35 E
Comeragh Mts., *Ireland* . **13 D4** 52 18N 7 34W
Comet, *Australia* .... **62 C4** 23 36S 148 38 E
Comilla, *Bangla.* .... **41 H17** 23 28N 91 10 E
Comino, *Malta* .... **23 C1** 36 2N 14 20 E
Comino, C., *Italy* .... **20 D3** 40 32N 9 49 E
Comitán, *Mexico* **87 D6** 16 18N 92 9W
Commerce, *Ga., U.S.A.* .. **77 H4** 34 12N 83 28W
Commerce, *Tex., U.S.A.* . **81 J7** 33 15N 95 54W
Committee B., *Canada* ... **69 B11** 68 30N 86 30W
Commonwealth B., *Antarctica* .... **5 C10** 67 0S 144 0 E
Commoron Cr. →, *Australia* .... **63 D5** 28 22S 150 8 E
Communism Pk. = Kommunizma, Pik, *Tajikistan* .... **26 F8** 39 0N 72 2 E
Como, *Italy* .... **18 D8** 45 47N 9 5 E
Como, L. di, *Italy* .... **18 D8** 46 0N 9 11 E
Comodoro Rivadavia, *Argentina* **96 F3** 45 50S 67 40W
Comorin, C., *India* ...... **40 Q10** 8 3N 77 40 E
Comoro Is. = Comoros ■, *Ind. Oc.* .... **49 H8** 12 10S 44 15 E
Comoros ■, *Ind. Oc.* .... **49 H8** 12 10S 44 15 E
Comox, *Canada* **72 D4** 49 42N 124 55W
Compiègne, *France* ..... **18 B5** 49 24N 2 50 E
Compostela, *Mexico* **86 C4** 21 15N 104 53W
Comprida, I., *Brazil* **95 A6** 24 50S 47 42W
Compton, *U.S.A.* **85 M8** 33 54N 118 13W
Compton Downs, *Australia* **63 E4** 30 28S 146 30 E
Comrat, *Moldova* .... **17 E15** 46 18N 28 40 E
Con Cuong, *Vietnam* .... **38 C5** 19 2N 104 54 E
Con Son, *Vietnam* ...... **39 H6** 8 41N 106 37 E
Conakry, *Guinea* **50 G3** 9 29N 13 49W
Conara Junction, *Australia* **62 G4** 41 50S 147 26 E
Concarneau, *France* **18 C2** 47 52N 3 56W
Conceição, *Mozam.* ..... **55 F4** 18 47S 36 7 E
Conceição da Barra, *Brazil* **93 G11** 18 35S 39 45W
Conceição do Araguaia, *Brazil* **93 E9** 8 0S 49 2W
Concepción, *Argentina* .. **94 B2** 27 20S 65 35W
Concepción, *Chile* **94 D1** 36 50S 73 0W
Concepción, *Mexico* **87 D6** 18 15N 90 5W
Concepción, *Paraguay* ... **94 A4** 23 22S 57 26W
Concepción □, *Chile* **94 D1** 37 0S 72 30W
Concepción →, *Mexico* . **86 A2** 30 32N 113 2W
Concepción, Est. de, *Chile* **96 G2** 50 30S 74 55W
Concepción, L., *Bolivia* .. **92 G6** 17 20S 61 20W
Concepción, Punta, *Mexico* **86 B2** 26 55N 111 59W
Concepción del Oro, *Mexico* **86 C4** 24 40N 101 30W
Concepción del Uruguay, *Argentina* **94 C4** 32 35S 58 20W
Conception, Pt., *U.S.A.* .. **85 L6** 34 27N 120 28W
Conception B., *Namibia* . **56 C1** 23 55S 14 22 E
Conception I., *Bahamas* . **89 B4** 23 52N 75 9W
Concession, *Zimbabwe* .. **55 F3** 17 27S 30 56 E
Conchas Dam, *U.S.A.* ... **81 H2** 35 22N 104 11W
Conche, *Canada* **71 B8** 50 55N 55 58W
Concho, *U.S.A.* **83 J9** 34 28N 109 36W
Concho →, *U.S.A.* **81 K5** 31 34N 99 43W
Conchos →, *Chihuahua, Mexico* **86 B4** 29 32N 105 0W
Conchos →, *Tamaulipas, Mexico* **87 B5** 25 9N 98 35W
Concord, *Calif., U.S.A.* ... **84 H4** 37 59N 122 2W
Concord, *N.C., U.S.A.* ... **77 H5** 35 25N 80 35W
Concord, *N.H., U.S.A.* ... **79 C13** 43 12N 71 32W
Concordia, *Argentina* ... **94 C4** 31 20S 58 2W
Concórdia, *Brazil* **92 D5** 4 36S 66 36W
Concordia, *Mexico* **86 C3** 23 18N 106 2W
Concordia, *U.S.A.* **80 F6** 39 34N 97 40W
Concrete, *U.S.A.* **82 B3** 48 32N 121 45W
Condamine, *Australia* ... **63 D5** 26 56S 150 9 E
Conde, *U.S.A.* **80 C5** 45 9N 98 6W
Condeúba, *Brazil* **93 F10** 14 52S 42 0W
Condobolin, *Australia* ... **63 E4** 33 4S 147 6 E
Condon, *U.S.A.* **82 D3** 45 14N 120 11W
Conegliano, *Italy* .... **20 B5** 45 53N 12 18 E
Conejera, I. = Conills, I. des, *Spain* .... **22 B9** 39 11N 2 58 E
Conejos, *Mexico* **86 B4** 26 14N 103 53W
Confuso →, *Paraguay* .. **94 B4** 25 9S 57 34W
Congleton, *U.K.* **10 D5** 53 10N 2 13W
Congo (Kinshasa) = Congo, Dem. Rep. of the ■, *Africa* .... **52 E4** 3 0S 23 0 E
Congo ■, *Africa* .... **52 E3** 1 0S 16 0 E
Congo →, *Africa* .... **52 F2** 6 4S 12 24 E
Congo, Dem. Rep. of the ■, *Africa* .... **52 E4** 3 0S 23 0 E
Congo Basin, *Africa* ..... **48 G6** 0 10S 24 30 E
Congonhas, *Brazil* **95 A7** 20 30S 43 52W
Congress, *U.S.A.* **83 J7** 34 9N 112 51W
Conills, I. des, *Spain* .... **22 B9** 39 11N 2 58 E
Coniston, *Canada* **70 C3** 46 29N 80 51W
Conjeeveram = Kanchipuram, *India* ... **40 N11** 12 52N 79 45 E
Conjuboy, *Australia* ..... **62 B3** 18 35S 144 35 E
Conklin, *Canada* **73 B6** 55 38N 111 5W
Conlea, *Australia* .... **63 E3** 30 7S 144 35 E
Conn, L., *Ireland* **13 B2** 54 3N 9 15W
Connacht □, *Ireland* **13 C2** 53 43N 9 12W
Conneaut, *U.S.A.* **78 E4** 41 57N 80 34W
Connecticut □, *U.S.A.* ... **79 E12** 41 30N 72 45W
Connecticut →, *U.S.A.* . **79 E12** 41 16N 72 20W
Connell, *U.S.A.* **82 C4** 46 40N 118 52W
Connellsville, *U.S.A.* **78 F5** 40 1N 79 35W
Connemara, *Ireland* **13 C2** 53 29N 9 45W
Connemaugh →, *U.S.A.* **78 F5** 40 28N 79 19W
Connersville, *U.S.A.* **76 F3** 39 39N 85 8W
Connors Ra., *Australia* .. **62 C4** 21 40S 149 10 E
Conoble, *Australia* ...... **63 E3** 32 55S 144 33 E
Conquest, *Canada* **73 C7** 51 32N 107 14W
Conrad, *U.S.A.* **82 B8** 48 10N 111 57W
Conran, C., *Australia* .... **63 F4** 37 49S 148 44 E
Conroe, *U.S.A.* **81 K7** 30 19N 95 27W
Conselheiro Lafaiete, *Brazil* **95 A7** 20 40S 43 48W
Consett, *U.K.* **10 C6** 54 51N 1 50W
Consort, *Canada* **73 C6** 52 1N 110 46W
Constance = Konstanz, *Germany* .... **16 E5** 47 40N 9 10 E
Constance, L. = Bodensee, *Europe* .... **18 C8** 47 35N 9 25 E
Constanța, *Romania* .... **17 F15** 44 14N 28 38 E
Constantine, *Algeria* .... **50 A7** 36 25N 6 42 E
Constitución, *Chile* **94 D1** 35 20S 72 30W
Constitución, *Uruguay* ... **94 C4** 31 0S 57 50W
Consul, *Canada* **73 D7** 49 20N 109 30W
Contact, *U.S.A.* **82 F6** 41 46N 114 45W
Contai, *India* .... **43 J12** 21 54N 87 46 E
Contamana, *Peru* **92 E4** 7 19S 74 55W
Contas →, *Brazil* **93 F11** 14 17S 39 1W
Contoocook, *U.S.A.* **79 C13** 43 13N 71 45W
Contra Costa, *Mozam.* ... **57 D5** 25 9S 33 30 E
Conway = Conwy, *U.K.* . **10 D4** 53 17N 3 50W
Conway = Conwy →, *U.K.* **10 D4** 53 17N 3 50W
Conway, *Ark., U.S.A.* **81 H8** 35 5N 92 26W
Conway, *N.H., U.S.A.* ... **79 C13** 43 59N 71 7W
Conway, *S.C., U.S.A.* **77 J6** 33 51N 79 3W
Conway, L., *Australia* ... **63 D2** 28 17S 135 35 E
Conwy, *U.K.* **10 D4** 53 17N 3 50W
Conwy □, *U.K.* **10 D4** 53 10N 3 44W
Conwy →, *U.K.* **10 D4** 53 17N 3 50W
Coober Pedy, *Australia* .. **63 D1** 29 1S 134 43 E
Cooch Behar = Koch Bihar, *India* .... **41 F16** 26 22N 89 29 E
Coodardy, *Australia* ..... **61 E2** 27 15S 117 39 E
Cook, *Australia* .... **61 F5** 30 37S 130 25 E
Cook, *U.S.A.* **80 B8** 47 49N 92 39W
Cook, B., *Chile* **96 H3** 55 10S 70 0W
Cook, Mt., *N.Z.* .... **59 K3** 43 36S 170 9 E
Cook Inlet, *U.S.A.* **68 C4** 60 0N 152 0W
Cook Is., *Pac. Oc.* **65 J12** 17 0S 160 0W
Cook Strait, *N.Z.* .... **59 J5** 41 15S 174 29 E
Cookeville, *U.S.A.* **77 G3** 36 10N 85 30W
Cookhouse, *S. Africa* .... **56 E4** 32 44S 25 47 E
Cookshire, *Canada* **79 A13** 45 25N 71 38W
Cookstown, *U.K.* **13 B5** 54 39N 6 45W
Cooksville, *Canada* **78 C5** 43 36N 79 35W
Cooktown, *Australia* .... **62 B4** 15 30S 145 16 E
Coolabah, *Australia* ..... **63 E4** 31 1S 146 43 E
Cooladdi, *Australia* ..... **63 D4** 26 37S 145 23 E
Coolah, *Australia* .... **63 E4** 31 48S 149 41 E
Coolamon, *Australia* .... **63 E4** 34 46S 147 8 E
Coolangatta, *Australia* ... **63 D5** 28 11S 153 29 E
Coolgardie, *Australia* .... **61 F3** 30 55S 121 8 E
Coolibah, *Australia* ..... **60 C5** 15 33S 130 56 E
Coolidge, *U.S.A.* **83 K8** 32 59N 111 31W
Coolidge Dam, *U.S.A.* ... **83 K8** 33 0N 110 20W
Cooma, *Australia* .... **63 F4** 36 12S 149 8 E
Coon Rapids, *U.S.A.* **80 C8** 45 9N 93 19W
Coonabarabran, *Australia* **63 E4** 31 14S 149 18 E
Coonamble, *Australia* ... **63 E4** 30 56S 148 27 E
Coonana, *Australia* ..... **61 F3** 31 0S 123 0 E
Coondapoor, *India* ...... **40 N9** 13 42N 74 40 E
Coongie, *Australia* ...... **63 D3** 27 9S 140 8 E
Coongoola, *Australia* .... **63 D4** 27 43S 145 51 E
Cooninie, L., *Australia* ... **63 D2** 26 4S 139 59 E
Cooper, *U.S.A.* **81 J7** 33 23N 95 42W
Cooper →, *U.S.A.* **77 J6** 32 50N 79 56W
Cooper Cr. →, *Australia* **63 D2** 28 29S 137 46 E
Cooperstown, *N. Dak., U.S.A.* **80 B5** 47 27N 98 8W
Cooperstown, *N.Y., U.S.A.* **79 D10** 42 42N 74 56W
Coorabie, *Australia* ..... **61 F5** 31 54S 132 18 E
Coorabulka, *Australia* ... **62 C3** 23 41S 140 20 E
Coorow, *Australia* ...... **61 E2** 29 53S 116 2 E
Cooroy, *Australia* .... **63 D5** 26 22S 152 54 E
Coos Bay, *U.S.A.* **82 E1** 43 22N 124 13W
Cootamundra, *Australia* . **63 E4** 34 36S 148 1 E
Cootehill, *Ireland* **13 B4** 54 4N 7 5W
Cooyar, *Australia* .... **63 D5** 26 59S 151 51 E
Cooyeana, *Australia* .... **62 C2** 24 29S 138 45 E
Copahue Paso, *Argentina* **94 D1** 37 49S 71 8W
Copainalá, *Mexico* **87 D6** 17 8N 93 11W
Copán, *Honduras* **88 D2** 14 50N 89 9W
Cope, *U.S.A.* **80 F3** 39 40N 102 51W
Copenhagen = København, *Denmark* . **9 J15** 55 41N 12 34 E
Copiapó, *Chile* **94 B1** 27 30S 70 20W
Copiapó →, *Chile* **94 B1** 27 19S 70 56W
Copley, *Australia* .... **63 E2** 30 36S 138 26 E
Copp L., *Canada* **72 A6** 60 14N 114 40W
Coppename →, *Surinam* **93 B7** 5 48N 55 55W
Copper Cliff, *Canada* **70 C3** 46 28N 81 4W
Copper Harbor, *U.S.A.* .. **76 B2** 47 28N 87 53W
Copper Queen, *Zimbabwe* **55 F2** 17 29S 29 18 E
Copperbelt □, *Zambia* ... **55 E2** 13 15S 27 30 E
Coppermine = Kugluktuk, *Canada* **68 B8** 67 50N 115 5W
Coppermine →, *Canada* **68 B8** 67 49N 116 4W
Copperopolis, *U.S.A.* **84 H6** 37 58N 120 38W
Coquet →, *U.K.* **10 B6** 55 20N 1 32W
Coquilhatville = Mbandaka, *Dem. Rep. of the Congo* **52 D3** 0 1N 18 18 E
Coquille, *U.S.A.* **82 E1** 43 11N 124 11W
Coquimbo, *Chile* **94 C1** 30 0S 71 20W
Coquimbo □, *Chile* **94 C1** 31 0S 71 0W
Corabia, *Romania* ...... **17 G13** 43 48N 24 30 E
Coracora, *Peru* **92 G4** 15 5S 73 45W
Coral Gables, *U.S.A.* **77 N5** 25 45N 80 16W
Coral Sea, *Pac. Oc.* ...... **64 J7** 15 0S 150 0 E
Coral Springs, *U.S.A.* ... **77 M5** 26 16N 80 13W
Coraopolis, *U.S.A.* **78 F4** 40 31N 80 10W
Corato, *Italy* .... **20 D7** 41 9N 16 25 E
Corbin, *U.S.A.* **76 G3** 36 57N 84 6W
Corby, *U.K.* **11 E7** 52 30N 0 41W
Corcaigh = Cork, *Ireland* **13 E3** 51 54N 8 29W
Corcoran, *U.S.A.* **84 J7** 36 6N 119 33W
Corcubión, *Spain* **19 A1** 42 56N 9 12W
Cordele, *U.S.A.* **77 K4** 31 58N 83 47W
Cordell, *U.S.A.* **81 H5** 35 17N 98 59W
Córdoba, *Argentina* **94 C3** 31 20S 64 10W
Córdoba, *Mexico* **87 D5** 18 50N 97 0W
Córdoba, *Spain* **19 D3** 37 50N 4 50W
Córdoba □, *Argentina* ... **94 C3** 31 22S 64 15W
Córdoba, Sierra de, *Argentina* **94 C3** 31 10S 64 25W
Cordova, *Ala., U.S.A.* **77 J2** 33 46N 87 11W
Cordova, *Alaska, U.S.A.* . **68 B5** 60 33N 145 45W
Corella →, *Australia* ... **62 B3** 19 34S 140 47 E
Corfield, *Australia* ...... **62 C3** 21 40S 143 21 E
Corfu, Str of, *Greece* .... **23 A4** 39 34N 20 0 E
Coria, *Spain* **19 C2** 39 58N 6 33W
Corigliano Cálabro, *Italy* . **20 E7** 39 36N 16 31 E
Coringa Is., *Australia* .... **62 B4** 16 58S 149 58 E
Corinna, *Australia* ...... **62 G4** 41 35S 145 10 E
Corinth = Kórinthos, *Greece* .... **21 F10** 37 56N 22 55 E
Corinth, *Miss., U.S.A.* ... **77 H1** 34 56N 88 31W
Corinth, *N.Y., U.S.A.* **79 C11** 43 15N 73 49W
Corinth, G. of = Korinthiakós Kólpos, *Greece* .... **21 E10** 38 16N 22 30 E
Corinto, *Brazil* **93 G10** 18 20S 44 30W
Corinto, *Nic.* **88 D2** 12 30N 87 10W
Cork, *Ireland* **13 E3** 51 54N 8 29W
Cork □, *Ireland* **13 E3** 51 57N 8 40W
Cork Harbour, *Ireland* ... **13 E3** 51 47N 8 16W
Çorlu, *Turkey* .... **21 D12** 41 11N 27 49 E
Cormack L., *Canada* **72 A4** 60 56N 121 37W
Cormorant, *Canada* **73 C8** 54 14N 100 35W
Cormorant L., *Canada* ... **73 C8** 54 15N 100 50W
Corn Is. = Maíz, Is. del, *Nic.* **88 D3** 12 15N 83 4W
Cornélio Procópio, *Brazil* **95 A5** 23 7S 50 40W
Cornell, *U.S.A.* **80 C9** 45 10N 91 9W
Corner Brook, *Canada* ... **71 C8** 48 57N 57 58W
Cornești, *Moldova* ...... **17 E15** 47 21N 28 1 E
Corning, *Ark., U.S.A.* **81 G9** 36 25N 90 35W
Corning, *Calif., U.S.A.* ... **82 G2** 39 56N 122 11W
Corning, *Iowa, U.S.A.* ... **80 E7** 40 59N 94 44W
Corning, *N.Y., U.S.A.* **78 D7** 42 9N 77 3W
Cornwall, *Canada* **70 C5** 45 2N 74 44W
Cornwall □, *U.K.* **11 G3** 50 26N 4 40W
Corny Pt., *Australia* ..... **63 E2** 34 55S 137 0 E
Coro, *Venezuela* **92 A5** 11 25N 69 41W
Coroatá, *Brazil* **93 D10** 4 8S 44 0W
Corocoro, *Bolivia* **92 G5** 17 15S 68 28W
Coroico, *Bolivia* **92 G5** 16 0S 67 50W
Coromandel, *N.Z.* .... **59 G5** 36 45S 175 31 E
Coromandel Coast, *India* **40 N12** 12 30N 81 0 E
Corona, *Australia* .... **63 E3** 31 16S 141 24 E
Corona, *Calif., U.S.A.* ... **85 M9** 33 53N 117 34W
Corona, *N. Mex., U.S.A.* . **83 J11** 34 15N 105 36W
Coronado, *U.S.A.* **85 N9** 32 41N 117 11W
Coronado, B. de, *Costa Rica* **88 E3** 9 0N 83 40W
Coronados, Is. los, *U.S.A.* **85 N9** 32 25N 117 15W
Coronation, *Canada* **72 C6** 52 5N 111 27W
Coronation Gulf, *Canada* **68 B9** 68 25N 110 0W
Coronation I., *Antarctica* . **5 C18** 60 45S 46 0W
Coronation I., *U.S.A.* **72 B2** 55 52N 134 20W
Coronation Is., *Australia* . **60 B3** 14 57S 124 55 E
Coronda, *Argentina* **94 C3** 31 58S 60 56W
Coronel, *Chile* **94 D1** 37 0S 73 10W
Coronel Bogado, *Paraguay* **94 B4** 27 11S 56 18W
Coronel Dorrego, *Argentina* **94 D3** 38 40S 61 10W

Coronel Oviedo

Coronel Oviedo, Paraguay 94 B4 25 24S 56 30W
Coronel Pringles, Argentina 94 D3 38 0S 61 30W
Coronel Suárez, Argentina 94 D3 37 30S 61 52W
Coronel Vidal, Argentina 94 D4 37 28S 57 45W
Coropuna, Nevado, Peru 92 G4 15 30S 72 41W
Corowa, Australia 63 F4 35 58S 146 21 E
Corozal, Belize 87 D7 18 23N 88 23W
Corpus, Argentina 95 B4 27 10S 55 30W
Corpus Christi, U.S.A. 81 M6 27 47N 97 24W
Corpus Christi, L., U.S.A. 81 L6 28 2N 97 52W
Corralejo, Canary Is. 22 F6 28 43N 13 53W
Corraun Pen., Ireland 13 C2 53 54N 9 54W
Correntes, C. das, Mozam. 57 C6 24 6S 35 34 E
Corrib, L., Ireland 13 C2 53 27N 9 16W
Corrientes, Argentina 94 B4 27 30S 58 45W
Corrientes □, Argentina 94 B4 28 0S 57 0W
Corrientes →, Argentina 94 C4 30 42S 59 38W
Corrientes →, Peru 92 D4 3 43S 74 35W
Corrientes, C., Colombia 92 B3 5 30N 77 34W
Corrientes, C., Cuba 88 B3 21 43N 84 30W
Corrientes, C., Mexico 86 C3 20 25N 105 42W
Corrigan, U.S.A. 81 K7 31 0N 94 52W
Corrigin, Australia 61 F2 32 20S 117 53 E
Corry, U.S.A. 78 E5 41 55N 79 39W
Corse, France 18 F8 42 0N 9 0 E
Corse, C., France 18 E8 43 1N 9 25 E
Corsica = Corse, France 18 F8 42 0N 9 0 E
Corsicana, U.S.A. 81 J6 32 6N 96 28W
Corte, France 18 E8 42 19N 9 11 E
Cortez, U.S.A. 83 H9 37 21N 108 35W
Cortland, U.S.A. 79 D8 42 36N 76 11W
Çorum, Turkey 25 F5 40 30N 34 57 E
Corumbá, Brazil 92 G7 19 0S 57 30W
Corunna = A Coruña, Spain 19 A1 43 20N 8 25W
Corvallis, U.S.A. 82 D2 44 34N 123 16W
Corvette, L. de la, Canada 70 B5 53 25N 74 3W
Corydon, U.S.A. 80 E8 40 46N 93 19W
Cosalá, Mexico 86 C3 24 28N 106 40W
Cosamaloapan, Mexico 87 D5 18 23N 95 50W
Cosenza, Italy 20 E7 39 18N 16 15 E
Coshocton, U.S.A. 78 F3 40 16N 81 51W
Cosmo Newberry, Australia 61 E3 28 0S 122 54 E
Coso Junction, U.S.A. 85 J9 36 3N 117 57W
Coso Pk., U.S.A. 85 J9 36 13N 117 44W
Cosquín, Argentina 94 C3 31 15S 64 30W
Costa Blanca, Spain 19 C5 38 25N 0 10W
Costa Brava, Spain 19 B7 41 30N 3 0 E
Costa del Sol, Spain 19 D3 36 30N 4 30W
Costa Dorada, Spain 19 B6 41 12N 1 15 E
Costa Mesa, U.S.A. 85 M9 33 38N 117 55W
Costa Rica ■, Cent. Amer. 88 E3 10 0N 84 0W
Costilla, U.S.A. 83 H11 36 59N 105 32W
Cosumnes →, U.S.A. 84 G5 38 16N 121 26W
Cotabato, Phil. 37 C6 7 14N 124 15 E
Cotagaita, Bolivia 94 A2 20 45S 65 40W
Côte d'Azur, France 18 E7 43 25N 7 10 E
Côte-d'Ivoire = Ivory Coast ■, Africa 50 G4 7 30N 5 0W
Coteau des Prairies, U.S.A. 80 C6 45 20N 97 50W
Coteau du Missouri, U.S.A. 80 B4 47 0N 100 0W
Coteau Landing, Canada 79 A10 45 15N 74 13W
Cotentin, France 18 B3 49 15N 1 30W
Cotillo, Canary Is. 22 F5 28 41N 14 1W
Cotonou, Benin 50 G6 6 20N 2 25 E
Cotopaxi, Ecuador 92 D3 0 40S 78 30W
Cotswold Hills, U.K. 11 F5 51 42N 2 10W
Cottage Grove, U.S.A. 82 E2 43 48N 123 3W
Cottbus, Germany 16 C8 51 45N 14 20 E
Cottonwood, U.S.A. 83 J7 34 45N 112 1W
Cotulla, U.S.A. 81 L5 28 26N 99 14W
Coudersport, U.S.A. 78 E6 41 46N 78 1W
Couedic, C. du, Australia 63 F2 36 5S 136 40 E
Coulee City, U.S.A. 82 C4 47 37N 119 17W
Coulman I., Antarctica 5 D11 73 35S 170 0 E
Coulonge →, Canada 70 C4 45 52N 76 46W
Coulterville, U.S.A. 84 H6 37 43N 120 12W
Council, U.S.A. 82 D5 44 44N 116 26W
Council Bluffs, U.S.A. 80 E7 41 16N 95 52W
Council Grove, U.S.A. 80 F6 38 40N 96 29W
Coupeville, U.S.A. 84 B4 48 13N 122 41W
Courantyne →, S. Amer. 92 B7 5 55N 57 5W
Courcelles, Belgium 15 D4 50 28N 4 22 E
Courtenay, Canada 72 D4 49 45N 125 0W
Courtland, U.S.A. 84 G5 38 20N 121 34W
Courtrai = Kortrijk, Belgium 15 D3 50 50N 3 17 E
Courtright, Canada 78 D2 42 49N 82 28W
Coushatta, U.S.A. 81 J8 32 1N 93 21W
Coutts, Canada 72 D6 49 0N 111 57W
Couvin, Belgium 15 D4 50 3N 4 29 E
Coventry, U.K. 11 E6 52 25N 1 28W
Coventry L., Canada 73 A7 61 15N 106 15W
Covilhã, Portugal 19 B2 40 17N 7 31W
Covington, Ga., U.S.A. 77 J4 33 36N 83 51W
Covington, Ky., U.S.A. 76 F3 39 5N 84 31W
Covington, Okla., U.S.A. 81 G6 36 18N 97 35W
Covington, Tenn., U.S.A. 81 H10 35 34N 89 39W
Cowal, L., Australia 63 E4 33 40S 147 25 E
Cowan, Canada 73 C8 52 5N 100 45W
Cowan, L., Australia 61 F3 31 45S 121 45 E
Cowan L., Canada 73 C7 54 0N 107 15W
Cowangie, Australia 63 F3 35 12S 141 26 E
Cowansville, Canada 79 A12 45 14N 72 46W
Cowarie, Australia 63 D2 27 45S 138 15 E
Cowcowing Lakes, Australia 61 F2 30 55S 117 20 E
Cowdenbeath, U.K. 12 E5 56 7N 3 21W
Cowell, Australia 63 E2 33 39S 136 56 E
Cowes, U.K. 11 G6 50 45N 1 18W
Cowlitz →, U.S.A. 84 D4 46 6N 122 55W
Cowra, Australia 63 E4 33 49S 148 42 E
Coxilha Grande, Brazil 95 B5 28 18S 51 30W
Coxim, Brazil 93 G8 18 30S 54 55W
Cox's Bazar, Bangla. 41 J17 21 26N 91 59 E
Cox's Cove, Canada 71 C8 49 7N 58 5W
Coyame, Mexico 86 B3 29 28N 105 6W
Coyote Wells, U.S.A. 85 N11 32 44N 115 58W
Coyuca de Benítez, Mexico 87 D4 17 1N 100 8W
Coyuca de Catalan, Mexico 86 D4 18 18N 100 41W
Cozad, U.S.A. 80 E5 40 52N 99 59W
Cozumel, Mexico 87 C7 20 31N 86 55W
Cozumel, I. de, Mexico 87 C7 20 30N 86 40W
Craboon, Australia 63 E4 32 3S 149 30 E
Cracow = Kraków, Poland 17 C10 50 4N 19 57 E
Cracow, Australia 63 D5 25 17S 150 17 E
Cradock, S. Africa 56 E4 32 8S 25 36 E
Craig, Alaska, U.S.A. 72 B2 55 29N 133 9W
Craig, Colo., U.S.A. 82 F10 40 31N 107 33W
Craigavon, U.K. 13 B5 54 27N 6 23W
Craigmore, Zimbabwe 55 G3 20 28S 32 50 E
Crailsheim, Germany 16 D6 49 8N 10 5 E
Craiova, Romania 17 F12 44 21N 23 48 E
Cramsie, Australia 62 C3 23 20S 144 15 E
Cranberry Portage, Canada 73 C8 54 35N 101 23W
Cranbrook, Tas., Australia 62 G4 42 0S 148 5 E
Cranbrook, W. Austral., Australia 61 F2 34 18S 117 33 E
Cranbrook, Canada 72 D5 49 30N 115 46W
Crandon, U.S.A. 80 C10 45 34N 88 54W
Crane, Oreg., U.S.A. 82 E4 43 25N 118 35W
Crane, Tex., U.S.A. 81 K3 31 24N 102 21W
Cranston, U.S.A. 79 E13 41 47N 71 26W
Crater L., U.S.A. 82 E2 42 56N 122 6W
Crateús, Brazil 93 E10 5 10S 40 39W
Crato, Brazil 93 E11 7 10S 39 25W
Crawford, U.S.A. 80 D3 42 41N 103 25W
Crawfordsville, U.S.A. 76 E2 40 2N 86 54W
Crawley, U.K. 11 F7 51 7N 0 11W
Crazy Mts., U.S.A. 82 C8 46 12N 110 20W
Crean L., Canada 73 C7 54 5N 106 9W
Crediton, Canada 78 C3 43 17N 81 33W
Credo, Australia 61 F3 30 28S 120 45 E
Cree →, Canada 73 B7 58 57N 105 47W
Cree →, U.K. 12 G4 54 55N 4 25W
Cree L., Canada 73 B7 57 30N 106 30W
Creede, U.S.A. 83 H10 37 51N 106 56W
Creel, Mexico 86 B3 27 45N 107 38W
Creighton, U.S.A. 80 D6 42 28N 97 54W
Crema, Italy 18 D8 45 22N 9 41 E
Cremona, Italy 18 D9 45 7N 10 2 E
Cres, Croatia 16 F8 44 58N 14 25 E
Cresbard, U.S.A. 80 C5 45 10N 98 57W
Crescent, Okla., U.S.A. 81 H6 35 57N 97 36W
Crescent, Oreg., U.S.A. 82 E3 43 28N 121 42W
Crescent City, U.S.A. 82 F1 41 45N 124 12W
Crespo, Argentina 94 C3 32 2S 60 19W
Cressy, Australia 63 F3 38 2S 143 40 E
Crested Butte, U.S.A. 83 G10 38 52N 106 59W
Crestline, Calif., U.S.A. 85 L9 34 14N 117 18W
Crestline, Ohio, U.S.A. 78 F2 40 47N 82 44W
Creston, Canada 72 D5 49 10N 116 31W
Creston, Calif., U.S.A. 84 K6 35 32N 120 33W
Creston, Iowa, U.S.A. 80 E7 41 4N 94 22W
Creston, Wash., U.S.A. 82 C4 47 46N 118 31W
Crestview, Calif., U.S.A. 84 H8 37 46N 118 58W
Crestview, Fla., U.S.A. 77 K2 30 46N 86 34W
Crete = Kríti, Greece 23 D7 35 15N 25 0 E
Crete, U.S.A. 80 E6 40 38N 96 58W
Créteil, France 18 B5 48 47N 2 28 E
Creus, C. de, Spain 19 A7 42 20N 3 19 E
Creuse →, France 18 C4 47 0N 0 34 E
Crewe, U.K. 10 D5 53 6N 2 26W
Crewkerne, U.K. 11 G5 50 53N 2 48W
Criciúma, Brazil 95 B6 28 40S 49 23W
Crieff, U.K. 12 E5 56 22N 3 50W
Crimean Pen. = Krymskyy Pivostriv, Ukraine 25 F5 45 0N 34 0 E
Crişul Alb →, Romania 17 E11 46 42N 21 17 E
Crişul Negru →, Romania 17 E11 46 42N 21 16 E
Crna →, Macedonia 21 D9 41 33N 21 59 E
Crna Gora = Montenegro □, Yugoslavia 21 C8 42 40N 19 20 E
Crna Gora, Macedonia 21 C9 42 10N 21 30 E
Crna Reka = Crna →, Macedonia 21 D9 41 33N 21 59 E
Croagh Patrick, Ireland 13 C2 53 46N 9 40W
Croatia ■, Europe 16 F9 45 20N 16 0 E
Crocker, Banjaran, Malaysia 36 C5 5 40N 116 30 E
Crockett, U.S.A. 81 K7 31 19N 95 27W
Crocodile = Krokodil →, Mozam. 57 D5 25 14S 32 18 E
Crocodile Is., Australia 62 A1 12 3S 134 58 E
Crohy Hd., Ireland 13 B3 54 55N 8 26W
Croix, L. La, Canada 70 C1 48 20N 92 15W
Croker, C., Australia 60 B5 10 58S 132 35 E
Croker I., Australia 60 B5 11 12S 132 32 E
Cromarty, Canada 73 B10 58 3N 94 9W
Cromarty, U.K. 12 D4 57 40N 4 2W
Cromer, U.K. 10 E9 52 56N 1 17 E
Cromwell, N.Z. 59 L2 45 3S 169 14 E
Cronulla, Australia 63 E5 34 3S 151 8 E
Crook, U.K. 10 C6 54 43N 1 45W
Crooked →, Canada 72 C4 54 50N 122 54W
Crooked →, U.S.A. 82 D3 44 32N 121 16W
Crooked I., Bahamas 89 B5 22 50N 74 10W
Crooked Island Passage, Bahamas 89 B5 23 0N 74 30W
Crookston, Minn., U.S.A. 80 B6 47 47N 96 37W
Crookston, Nebr., U.S.A. 80 D4 42 56N 100 45W
Crooksville, U.S.A. 76 F4 39 46N 82 6W
Crookwell, Australia 63 E4 34 28S 149 24 E
Crosby, U.K. 10 D4 53 30N 3 3W
Crosby, Minn., U.S.A. 80 B8 46 29N 93 58W
Crosby, N. Dak., U.S.A. 73 D8 48 55N 103 18W
Crosby, Pa., U.S.A. 78 E6 41 45N 78 23W
Crosbyton, U.S.A. 81 J4 33 40N 101 14W
Cross City, U.S.A. 77 L4 29 38N 83 7W
Cross Fell, U.K. 10 C5 54 43N 2 28W
Cross L., Canada 73 C9 54 45N 97 30W
Cross Plains, U.S.A. 81 J5 32 8N 99 11W
Cross Sound, U.S.A. 68 C6 58 0N 135 0W
Crossett, U.S.A. 81 J9 33 8N 91 58W
Crossfield, Canada 72 C6 51 25N 114 0W
Crosshaven, Ireland 13 E3 51 47N 8 17W
Croton-on-Hudson, U.S.A. 79 E11 41 12N 73 55W
Crotone, Italy 20 E7 39 5N 17 8 E
Crow →, Canada 72 B4 59 41N 124 20W
Crow Agency, U.S.A. 82 D10 45 36N 107 28W
Crow Hd., Ireland 13 E1 51 35N 10 9W
Crowell, U.S.A. 81 J5 33 59N 99 43W
Crowley, U.S.A. 81 K8 30 13N 92 22W
Crowley, L., U.S.A. 84 H8 37 35N 118 42W
Crown Point, U.S.A. 76 E2 41 25N 87 22W
Crows Landing, U.S.A. 84 H5 37 23N 121 6W
Crows Nest, Australia 63 D5 27 16S 152 4 E
Crowsnest Pass, Canada 72 D6 49 40N 114 40W
Croydon, Australia 62 B3 18 13S 142 14 E
Croydon, U.K. 11 F7 51 22N 0 5W
Crozet Is., Ind. Oc. 3 G12 46 27S 52 0 E
Cruz, C., Cuba 88 C4 19 50N 77 50W
Cruz Alta, Brazil 95 B5 28 45S 53 40W
Cruz del Eje, Argentina 94 C3 30 45S 64 50W
Cruzeiro, Brazil 95 A7 22 33S 45 0W
Cruzeiro do Oeste, Brazil 95 A5 23 46S 53 4W
Cruzeiro do Sul, Brazil 92 E4 7 35S 72 35W
Cry L., Canada 72 B3 58 45N 129 0W
Crystal Bay, U.S.A. 84 F7 39 15N 120 0W
Crystal Brook, Australia 63 E2 33 21S 138 12 E
Crystal City, Mo., U.S.A. 80 F9 38 13N 90 23W
Crystal City, Tex., U.S.A. 81 L5 28 41N 99 50W
Crystal Falls, U.S.A. 76 B1 46 5N 88 20W
Crystal River, U.S.A. 77 L4 28 54N 82 35W
Crystal Springs, U.S.A. 81 K9 31 59N 90 21W
Csongrád, Hungary 17 E11 46 43N 20 12 E
Cu Lao Hon, Vietnam 39 G7 10 54N 108 18 E
Cua Rao, Vietnam 38 C5 19 16N 104 27 E
Cuácua →, Mozam. 55 F4 17 54S 37 0 E
Cuamato, Angola 56 B2 17 2S 15 7 E
Cuamba, Mozam. 55 E4 14 45S 36 22 E
Cuando →, Angola 53 H4 17 30S 23 15 E
Cuando Cubango □, Angola 56 B3 16 25S 20 0 E
Cuangar, Angola 56 B2 17 36S 18 39 E
Cuanza →, Angola 48 G5 9 2S 13 30 E
Cuarto →, Argentina 94 C3 33 25S 63 2W
Cuatrociénegas, Mexico 86 B4 26 59N 102 5W
Cuauhtémoc, Mexico 86 B3 28 25N 106 52W
Cuba, N. Mex., U.S.A. 83 J10 36 1N 107 4W
Cuba, N.Y., U.S.A. 78 D6 42 13N 78 17W
Cuba ■, W. Indies 88 B4 22 0N 79 0W
Cuballing, Australia 61 F2 32 50S 117 10 E
Cubango →, Africa 56 B3 18 50S 22 25 E
Cuchumatanes, Sierra de los, Guatemala 88 C1 15 35N 91 25W
Cuckfield, U.K. 11 F7 51 1N 0 8W
Cucuí, Brazil 92 C5 1 12N 66 50W
Cucurpe, Mexico 86 A2 30 20N 110 43W
Cúcuta, Colombia 92 B4 7 54N 72 31W
Cuddalore, India 40 P11 11 46N 79 45 E
Cuddapah, India 40 M11 14 30N 78 47 E
Cuddapan, L., Australia 62 D3 25 45S 141 26 E
Cudgewa, Australia 63 F4 36 10S 147 42 E
Cue, Australia 61 E2 27 25S 117 54 E
Cuenca, Ecuador 92 D3 2 50S 79 9W
Cuenca, Spain 19 B4 40 5N 2 10W
Cuenca, Serranía de, Spain 19 C5 39 55N 1 50W
Cuernavaca, Mexico 87 D5 18 55N 99 15W
Cuero, U.S.A. 81 L6 29 6N 97 17W
Cuervo, U.S.A. 81 H2 35 2N 104 25W
Cuevas del Almanzora, Spain 19 D5 37 18N 1 58W
Cuevo, Bolivia 92 H6 20 15S 63 30W
Cuiabá, Brazil 93 G7 15 30S 56 0W
Cuiabá →, Brazil 93 G7 17 5S 56 36W
Cuijk, Neths. 15 C5 51 44N 5 50 E
Cuilco, Guatemala 88 C1 15 24N 91 58W
Cuillin Hills, U.K. 12 D2 57 13N 6 15W
Cuillin Sd., U.K. 12 D2 57 4N 6 20W
Cuito →, Angola 56 B3 18 1S 20 48 E
Cuitzeo, L. de, Mexico 86 D4 19 55N 101 5W
Cukai, Malaysia 39 K4 4 13N 103 25 E
Culbertson, U.S.A. 80 A2 48 9N 104 31W
Culcairn, Australia 63 F4 35 41S 147 3 E
Culgoa →, Australia 63 D4 29 56S 146 20 E
Culiacán, Mexico 86 C3 24 50N 107 23W
Culiacán →, Mexico 86 C3 24 30N 107 42W
Culion, Phil. 37 B6 11 54N 119 58 E
Cullarin Ra., Australia 63 E4 34 30S 149 30 E
Cullen, U.K. 12 D6 57 42N 2 49W
Cullen Pt., Australia 62 A3 11 57S 141 54 E
Cullera, Spain 19 C5 39 9N 0 17W
Cullman, U.S.A. 77 H2 34 11N 86 51W
Culpeper, U.S.A. 76 F7 38 30N 78 0W
Culuene →, Brazil 93 F8 12 56S 52 51W
Culver, Pt., Australia 61 F3 32 54S 124 43 E
Culverden, N.Z. 59 K4 42 47S 172 49 E
Cumaná, Venezuela 92 A6 10 30N 64 5W
Cumberland, Canada 72 D4 49 40N 125 0W
Cumberland, Md., U.S.A. 76 F6 39 39N 78 46W
Cumberland, Wis., U.S.A. 80 C8 45 32N 92 1W
Cumberland →, U.S.A. 77 G2 36 15N 87 0W
Cumberland I., U.S.A. 77 K5 30 50N 81 25W
Cumberland Is., Australia 62 C4 20 35S 149 10 E
Cumberland L., Canada 73 C8 54 3N 102 18W
Cumberland Pen., Canada 69 B13 67 0N 64 0W
Cumberland Plateau, U.S.A. 77 H3 36 0N 85 0W
Cumberland Sd., Canada 69 B13 65 30N 66 0W
Cumbernauld, U.K. 12 F5 55 57N 3 58W
Cumborah, Australia 63 D4 29 40S 147 45 E
Cumbria □, U.K. 10 C5 54 42N 2 52W
Cumbrian Mts., U.K. 10 C5 54 30N 3 0W
Cumbum, India 40 M11 15 40N 79 10 E
Cuminá →, Brazil 93 D7 1 30S 56 0W
Cummings Mt., U.S.A. 85 K8 35 2N 118 34W
Cummins, Australia 63 E2 34 16S 135 43 E
Cumnock, Australia 63 E4 32 59S 148 46 E
Cumnock, U.K. 12 F4 55 28N 4 17W
Cumpas, Mexico 86 B3 30 0N 109 48W
Cumplida, Pta., Canary Is. 22 F2 28 50N 17 48W
Cunco, Chile 96 D2 38 55S 72 2W
Cuncumén, Chile 94 C1 31 53S 70 38W
Cundeelee, Australia 61 F3 30 43S 123 26 E
Cunderdin, Australia 61 F2 31 37S 117 12 E
Cunene →, Angola 56 B1 17 20S 11 50 E
Cúneo, Italy 18 D7 44 23N 7 32 E
Cunillera, I. = Sa Conillera, Spain 22 C7 38 59N 1 13 E
Cunnamulla, Australia 63 D4 28 2S 145 38 E
Cupar, Canada 73 C8 50 57N 104 10W
Cupar, U.K. 12 E5 56 19N 3 1W
Cupica, G. de, Colombia 92 B3 6 25N 77 30W
Curaçao, Neth. Ant. 89 D6 12 10N 69 0W
Curanilahue, Chile 94 D1 37 29S 73 28W
Curaray →, Peru 92 D4 2 20S 74 5W
Curepto, Chile 94 D1 35 8S 72 1W
Curiapo, Venezuela 92 B6 8 33N 61 5W
Curicó, Chile 94 C1 34 55S 71 20W
Curicó □, Chile 94 C1 34 50S 71 15W
Curitiba, Brazil 95 B6 25 20S 49 10W
Currabubula, Australia 63 E5 31 16S 150 44 E
Currais Novos, Brazil 93 E11 6 13S 36 30W
Curralinho, Brazil 93 D9 1 45S 49 46W
Currant, U.S.A. 82 G6 38 51N 115 32W
Curraweena, Australia 63 E4 30 47S 145 54 E
Currawilla, Australia 62 D3 25 10S 141 20 E
Current →, U.S.A. 81 G9 36 15N 90 55W
Currie, Australia 62 F3 39 56S 143 53 E
Currie, U.S.A. 82 F6 40 16N 114 45W
Currituck Sd., U.S.A. 77 G8 36 20N 75 52W
Curtea de Argeş, Romania 17 F13 45 12N 24 42 E
Curtis, U.S.A. 80 E4 40 38N 100 31W
Curtis Group, Australia 62 F4 39 30S 146 37 E
Curtis I., Australia 62 C5 23 35S 151 10 E
Curuápanema →, Brazil 93 D7 2 25S 55 2W
Curuçá, Brazil 93 D9 0 43S 47 50W
Curuguaty, Paraguay 95 A4 24 31S 55 42W
Çürüksu Çayi →, Turkey 25 G4 37 27N 27 11 E
Curup, Indonesia 36 E2 4 26S 102 13 E
Cururupu, Brazil 93 D10 1 50S 44 50W
Curuzú Cuatiá, Argentina 94 B4 29 50S 58 5W
Curvelo, Brazil 93 G10 18 45S 44 27W
Cushing, U.S.A. 81 H6 35 59N 96 46W
Cushing, Mt., Canada 72 B3 57 35N 126 57W
Cusihuiriáchic, Mexico 86 B3 28 10N 106 50W
Custer, U.S.A. 80 D3 43 46N 103 36W
Cut Bank, U.S.A. 82 B7 48 38N 112 20W
Cuthbert, U.S.A. 77 K3 31 46N 84 48W
Cutler, U.S.A. 84 J7 36 31N 119 17W
Cuttaburra →, Australia 63 D3 29 43S 144 22 E
Cuttack, India 41 J14 20 25N 85 57 E
Cuvier, C., Australia 61 D1 23 14S 113 22 E
Cuvier I., N.Z. 59 G5 36 27S 175 50 E
Cuxhaven, Germany 16 B5 53 51N 8 41 E
Cuyahoga Falls, U.S.A. 78 E3 41 8N 81 29W
Cuyo, Phil. 37 B6 10 50N 121 5 E
Cuyuni →, Guyana 92 B7 6 23N 58 41W
Cuzco, Bolivia 92 H5 20 0S 66 50W
Cuzco, Peru 92 F4 13 32S 72 0W
Cwmbran, U.K. 11 F4 51 39N 3 2W
Cyangugu, Rwanda 54 C2 2 29S 28 54 E
Cyclades = Kikládhes, Greece 21 F11 37 0N 24 30 E
Cygnet, Australia 62 G4 43 8S 147 1 E
Cynthiana, U.S.A. 76 F3 38 23N 84 18W
Cypress Hills, Canada 73 D7 49 40N 109 30W
Cyprus ■, Asia 23 E12 35 0N 33 0 E
Cyrenaica, Libya 51 C10 27 0N 23 0 E
Czar, Canada 73 C6 52 27N 110 50W
Czech Rep. ■, Europe 16 D8 50 0N 15 0 E
Częstochowa, Poland 17 C10 50 49N 19 7 E

D

Da →, Vietnam 38 B5 21 15N 105 20 E
Da Hinggan Ling, China 33 B7 48 0N 121 0 E
Da Lat, Vietnam 39 G7 11 56N 108 25 E
Da Nang, Vietnam 38 D7 16 4N 108 13 E
Da Qaidam, China 32 C4 37 50N 95 15 E
Da Yunhe →, China 35 G11 34 25N 120 5 E
Da'an, China 35 B13 45 30N 124 7 E
Daba Shan, China 33 C5 32 0N 109 0 E
Dabhoi, India 42 H5 22 10N 73 20 E
Dabo = Pasirkuning, Indonesia 36 E2 0 30S 104 33 E
Dabola, Guinea 50 F3 10 50N 11 5W
Dabung, Malaysia 39 K4 5 23N 102 1 E
Dacca = Dhaka, Bangla. 43 H14 23 43N 90 26 E
Dacca = Dhaka □, Bangla. 43 G14 24 25N 90 25 E
Dachau, Germany 16 D6 48 15N 11 26 E
Dadanawa, Guyana 92 C7 2 50N 59 30W
Dade City, U.S.A. 77 L4 28 22N 82 11W
Dadra & Nagar Haveli □, India 40 J8 20 5N 73 0 E
Dadri = Charkhi Dadri, India 42 E7 28 37N 76 17 E
Dadu, Pakistan 42 F2 26 45N 67 45 E
Daet, Phil. 37 B6 14 2N 122 55 E
Dagana, Senegal 50 E2 16 30N 15 35W
Dagestan □, Russia 25 F8 42 30N 47 0 E
Daggett, U.S.A. 85 L10 34 52N 116 52W
Daghestan Republic = Dagestan □, Russia 25 F8 42 30N 47 0 E
Dagö = Hiiumaa, Estonia 24 C3 58 50N 22 45 E
Dagu, China 35 E9 38 59N 117 40 E
Dagupan, Phil. 37 A6 16 3N 120 20 E
Dahlak Kebir, Eritrea 46 D3 15 50N 40 10 E
Dahlonega, U.S.A. 77 H4 34 32N 83 59W
Dahod, India 42 H6 22 50N 74 15 E
Dahomey = Benin ■, Africa 50 G6 10 0N 2 0 E
Dai Hao, Vietnam 38 C6 18 1N 106 25 E
Dai-Sen, Japan 31 G6 35 22N 133 32 E
Dai Xian, China 34 E7 39 4N 112 58 E
Daicheng, China 34 E9 38 42N 116 38 E
Daingean, Ireland 13 C4 53 18N 7 17W
Daintree, Australia 62 B4 16 20S 145 20 E
Daiō-Misaki, Japan 31 G8 34 15N 136 45 E
Daisetsu-Zan, Japan 30 C11 43 30N 142 57 E
Dajarra, Australia 62 C2 21 42S 139 30 E
Dak Dam, Cambodia 38 F6 12 20N 107 21 E
Dak Nhe, Vietnam 38 E6 15 28N 107 48 E
Dak Pek, Vietnam 38 E6 15 4N 107 44 E
Dak Song, Vietnam 38 F6 12 19N 107 35 E
Dak Sui, Vietnam 38 E6 14 55N 107 43 E
Dakar, Senegal 50 F2 14 34N 17 29W
Dakhla, W. Sahara 50 D2 23 50N 15 53W

Derwent

Dakhla, El Wâhât el-, *Egypt* **51 C11** 25 30N 28 50 E
Dakhovskaya, *Russia* **25 F7** 44 13N 40 13 E
Dakor, *India* **42 H5** 22 45N 73 11 E
Dakota City, *U.S.A.* **80 D6** 42 25N 96 25W
Đakovica, *Serbia, Yug.* **21 C9** 42 22N 20 26 E
Dalachi, *China* **34 F3** 36 48N 105 0 E
Dalai Nur, *China* **34 C9** 43 20N 116 45 E
Dālakī, *Iran* **45 D6** 29 26N 51 17 E
Dalälven, *Sweden* **9 F17** 60 12N 16 43 E
Dalaman →, *Turkey* **21 F13** 36 41N 28 43 E
Dalandzadgad, *Mongolia* **34 C3** 43 27N 104 30 E
Dalarna, *Sweden* **9 F16** 61 0N 14 0 E
Dālbandīn, *Pakistan* **40 E4** 29 0N 64 23 E
Dalbeattie, *U.K.* **12 G5** 54 56N 3 50W
Dalby, *Australia* **63 D5** 27 10S 151 17 E
Dalgān, *Iran* **45 E8** 27 31N 59 19 E
Dalhart, *U.S.A.* **81 G3** 36 4N 102 31W
Dalhousie, *Canada* **71 C6** 48 5N 66 26W
Dalhousie, *India* **42 C6** 32 38N 75 58 E
Dali, *Shaanxi, China* **34 G5** 34 48N 109 58 E
Dali, *Yunnan, China* **32 D5** 25 40N 100 10 E
Dalian, *China* **35 E11** 38 50N 121 40 E
Daliang Shan, *China* **32 D5** 28 0N 102 45 E
Daling He →, *China* **35 D11** 40 55N 121 40 E
Dāliyat el Karmel, *Israel* **47 C4** 32 43N 35 2 E
Dalkeith, *U.K.* **12 F5** 55 54N 3 4W
Dall I., *U.S.A.* **72 C2** 54 59N 133 25W
Dallarnil, *Australia* **63 D5** 25 19S 152 2 E
Dallas, *Oreg., U.S.A.* **82 D2** 44 55N 123 19W
Dallas, *Tex., U.S.A.* **81 J6** 32 47N 96 49W
Dalmacija, *Croatia* **20 C7** 43 20N 17 0 E
Dalmatia = Dalmacija, *Croatia* **20 C7** 43 20N 17 0 E
Dalmellington, *U.K.* **12 F4** 55 19N 4 23W
Dalnegorsk, *Russia* **30 B7** 44 32N 135 33 E
Dalnerechensk, *Russia* **30 B6** 45 50N 133 40 E
Daloa, *Ivory C.* **50 G4** 7 0N 6 30W
Dalry, *U.K.* **12 F4** 55 42N 4 43W
Dalsland, *Sweden* **9 G14** 58 50N 12 15 E
Daltenganj, *India* **43 H11** 24 0N 84 4 E
Dalton, *Canada* **70 C3** 48 11N 84 1W
Dalton, *Ga., U.S.A.* **77 H3** 34 46N 84 58W
Dalton, *Mass., U.S.A.* **79 D11** 42 28N 73 11W
Dalton, *Nebr., U.S.A.* **80 E3** 41 25N 102 58W
Dalton Iceberg Tongue, *Antarctica* **5 C9** 66 15S 121 30 E
Dalton-in-Furness, *U.K.* **10 C4** 54 10N 3 11W
Dalvík, *Iceland* **8 D4** 65 58N 18 32W
Daly →, *Australia* **60 B5** 13 35S 130 19 E
Daly City, *U.S.A.* **84 H4** 37 42N 122 28W
Daly L., *Canada* **73 B7** 56 32N 105 39W
Daly Waters, *Australia* **62 B1** 16 15S 133 24 E
Dam Doi, *Vietnam* **39 H5** 8 50N 105 12 E
Dam Ha, *Vietnam* **38 B6** 21 21N 107 36 E
Daman, *India* **40 J8** 20 25N 72 57 E
Dāmaneh, *Iran* **45 C6** 33 1N 50 29 E
Damanhûr, *Egypt* **51 B12** 31 0N 30 30 E
Damanzhuang, *China* **34 E9** 38 5N 116 35 E
Damar, *Indonesia* **37 F7** 7 7S 128 40 E
Damaraland, *Namibia* **56 C2** 20 0S 15 0 E
Damascus = Dimashq, *Syria* **47 B5** 33 30N 36 18 E
Damāvand, *Iran* **45 C7** 35 47N 52 0 E
Damāvand, Qolleh-ye, *Iran* **45 C7** 35 56N 52 10 E
Damba, *Angola* **52 F3** 6 44S 15 20 E
Dâmboviţa →, *Romania* **17 F14** 44 12N 26 26 E
Dame Marie, *Haiti* **89 C5** 18 36N 74 26W
Dāmghān, *Iran* **45 B7** 36 10N 54 17 E
Damiel, *Spain* **19 C4** 39 4N 3 37W
Damietta = Dumyât, *Egypt* **51 B12** 31 24N 31 48 E
Daming, *China* **34 F8** 36 15N 115 6 E
Damīr Qābū, *Syria* **44 B4** 36 58N 41 51 E
Dammam = Ad Dammām, *Si. Arabia* **45 E6** 26 20N 50 5 E
Damodar →, *India* **43 H12** 23 17N 87 35 E
Damoh, *India* **43 H8** 23 50N 79 28 E
Dampier, *Australia* **60 D2** 20 41S 116 42 E
Dampier, Selat, *Indonesia* **37 E8** 0 40S 131 0 E
Dampier Arch., *Australia* **60 D2** 20 38S 116 32 E
Damrei, Chuor Phnum, *Cambodia* **39 G4** 11 30N 103 0 E
Dan Xian, *China* **38 C7** 19 31N 109 33 E
Dana, *Indonesia* **37 F6** 11 0S 122 52 E
Dana, L., *Canada* **70 B4** 50 53N 77 20W
Dana, Mt., *U.S.A.* **84 H7** 37 54N 119 12W
Danbury, *U.S.A.* **79 E11** 41 24N 73 28W
Danby L., *U.S.A.* **83 J6** 34 13N 115 5W
Dand, *Afghan.* **42 D1** 31 28N 65 32 E
Dandaragan, *Australia* **61 F2** 30 40S 115 40 E
Dandeldhura, *Nepal* **43 E9** 29 20N 80 35 E
Dandeli, *India* **40 M9** 15 5N 74 30 E
Dandenong, *Australia* **63 F4** 38 0S 145 15 E
Dandong, *China* **35 D13** 40 10N 124 20 E
Danfeng, *China* **34 H6** 33 45N 110 25 E
Danforth, *U.S.A.* **71 C6** 45 40N 67 52W
Danger Is. = Pukapuka, *Cook Is.* **65 J11** 10 53S 165 49W
Danger Pt., *S. Africa* **56 E2** 34 40S 19 17 E
Dangla Shan = Tanggula Shan, *China* **32 C4** 32 40N 92 10 E
Dangrek, Phnom, *Thailand* **38 E5** 14 15N 105 0 E
Dangriga, *Belize* **87 D7** 17 0N 88 13W
Dangshan, *China* **34 G9** 34 27N 116 22 E
Daniel, *U.S.A.* **82 E8** 42 52N 110 4W
Daniel's Harbour, *Canada* **71 B8** 50 13N 57 35W
Danielskuil, *S. Africa* **56 D3** 28 11S 23 33 E
Danielson, *U.S.A.* **79 E13** 41 48N 71 53W
Danilov, *Russia* **24 C7** 58 16N 40 13 E
Daning, *China* **34 F6** 36 28N 110 45 E
Danissa, *Kenya* **54 B5** 3 15N 40 58 E
Dankhar Gompa, *India* **40 C11** 32 10N 78 10 E
Danlí, *Honduras* **88 D2** 14 4N 86 35W
Dannemora, *U.S.A.* **79 B11** 44 43N 73 44W
Dannevirke, *N.Z.* **59 J6** 40 12S 176 8 E
Dannhauser, *S. Africa* **57 D5** 28 0S 30 3 E
Dansville, *U.S.A.* **78 D7** 42 34N 77 42W
Dantan, *India* **43 J12** 21 57N 87 20 E
Dante, *Somali Rep.* **46 E5** 10 25N 51 16 E
Danube = Dunărea →, *Europe* **17 F15** 45 20N 29 40 E
Danvers, *U.S.A.* **79 D14** 42 34N 70 56W
Danville, *Ill., U.S.A.* **76 E2** 40 8N 87 37W
Danville, *Ky., U.S.A.* **76 G3** 37 39N 84 46W
Danville, *Va., U.S.A.* **77 G6** 36 36N 79 23W
Danzig = Gdańsk, *Poland* **17 A10** 54 22N 18 40 E
Daqing Shan, *China* **34 D6** 40 40N 111 0 E
Dar Banda, *Africa* **48 F6** 8 0N 23 0 E
Dar el Beida = Casablanca, *Morocco* **50 B4** 33 36N 7 36W
Dar es Salaam, *Tanzania* **54 D4** 6 50S 39 12 E
Dar Mazār, *Iran* **45 D8** 29 14N 57 20 E
Dar'ā, *Syria* **47 C5** 32 36N 36 7 E
Dar'ā □, *Syria* **47 C5** 32 55N 36 10 E
Dārāb, *Iran* **45 D7** 28 50N 54 30 E
Daraj, *Libya* **51 B8** 30 10N 10 28 E
Dārān, *Iran* **45 C6** 32 59N 50 24 E
Dārayyā, *Syria* **47 B5** 33 28N 36 15 E
Darband, *Pakistan* **42 B5** 34 20N 72 50 E
Darband, Kūh-e, *Iran* **45 D8** 31 34N 57 8 E
Darbhanga, *India* **43 F11** 26 15N 85 55 E
Darby, *U.S.A.* **82 C6** 46 1N 114 11W
Dardanelle, *Ark., U.S.A.* **81 H8** 35 13N 93 9W
Dardanelle, *Calif., U.S.A.* **84 G7** 38 20N 119 50W
Dardanelles = Çanakkale Boğazı, *Turkey* **25 F4** 40 17N 26 32 E
Dārestān, *Iran* **45 D8** 29 9N 58 42 E
Dârfûr, *Sudan* **51 F10** 13 40N 24 0 E
Dargai, *Pakistan* **42 B4** 34 25N 71 55 E
Dargan Ata, *Uzbekistan* **26 E7** 40 29N 62 10 E
Dargaville, *N.Z.* **59 F4** 35 57S 173 52 E
Darhan, *Mongolia* **32 B5** 49 37N 106 21 E
Darhan Muminggan Lianheqi, *China* **34 D6** 41 40N 110 28 E
Darıca, *Turkey* **21 D13** 40 45N 29 23 E
Darién, G. del, *Colombia* **92 B3** 9 0N 77 0W
Dariganga, *Mongolia* **34 B7** 45 21N 113 45 E
Darjeeling = Darjiling, *India* **43 F13** 27 3N 88 18 E
Darjiling, *India* **43 F13** 27 3N 88 18 E
Dark Cove, *Canada* **71 C9** 48 47N 54 13W
Darkan, *Australia* **61 F2** 33 20S 116 43 E
Darkhazīneh, *Iran* **45 D6** 31 54N 48 39 E
Darkot Pass, *Pakistan* **43 A5** 36 45N 73 26 E
Darling →, *Australia* **63 E3** 34 4S 141 54 E
Darling Downs, *Australia* **63 D5** 27 30S 150 30 E
Darling Ra., *Australia* **61 F2** 32 30S 116 0 E
Darlington, *U.K.* **10 C6** 54 32N 1 33W
Darlington, *S.C., U.S.A.* **77 H6** 34 18N 79 52W
Darlington, *Wis., U.S.A.* **80 D9** 42 41N 90 7W
Darlington □, *U.K.* **10 C6** 54 32N 1 33W
Darlington, L., *S. Africa* **56 E4** 33 10S 25 9 E
Darlot, L., *Australia* **61 E3** 27 48S 121 35 E
Darłowo, *Poland* **16 A9** 54 25N 16 25 E
Darmstadt, *Germany* **16 D5** 49 51N 8 39 E
Darnah, *Libya* **51 B10** 32 45N 22 45 E
Darnall, *S. Africa* **57 D5** 29 23S 31 18 E
Darnley, C., *Antarctica* **5 C6** 68 0S 69 0 E
Darnley B., *Canada* **68 B7** 69 30N 123 30W
Darr, *Australia* **62 C3** 23 13S 144 7 E
Darr →, *Australia* **62 C3** 23 39S 143 50 E
Darrington, *U.S.A.* **82 B3** 48 15N 121 36W
Dart →, *U.K.* **11 G4** 50 24N 3 39W
Dart, C., *Antarctica* **5 D14** 73 6S 126 20W
Dartford, *U.K.* **11 F8** 51 26N 0 13 E
Dartmoor, *U.K.* **11 G4** 50 38N 3 57W
Dartmouth, *Australia* **62 C3** 23 31S 144 44 E
Dartmouth, *Canada* **71 D7** 44 40N 63 30W
Dartmouth, *U.K.* **11 G4** 50 21N 3 36W
Dartmouth, L., *Australia* **63 D4** 26 4S 145 18 E
Dartuch, C., *Spain* **22 B10** 39 55N 3 49 E
Darvaza, *Turkmenistan* **26 E6** 40 11N 58 24 E
Darvel, Teluk = Lahad Datu, Teluk, *Malaysia* **37 D5** 4 50N 118 20 E
Darwen, *U.K.* **10 D5** 53 42N 2 29W
Darwha, *India* **40 J10** 20 15N 77 45 E
Darwin, *Australia* **60 B5** 12 25S 130 51 E
Darwin, *U.S.A.* **85 J9** 36 15N 117 35W
Darwin River, *Australia* **60 B5** 12 50S 130 58 E
Daryoi Amu = Amudarya →, *Uzbekistan* **26 E6** 43 58N 59 34 E
Dās, *U.A.E.* **45 E7** 25 20N 53 30 E
Dashetai, *China* **34 D5** 41 0N 109 5 E
Dashhowuz, *Turkmenistan* **26 E6** 41 49N 59 58 E
Dasht, *Iran* **45 B8** 37 17N 56 7 E
Dasht →, *Pakistan* **40 G2** 25 10N 61 40 E
Dasht-e Mārgow, *Afghan.* **40 D3** 30 40N 62 30 E
Dasht-i-Nawar, *Afghan.* **42 C3** 33 52N 68 0 E
Daska, *Pakistan* **42 C6** 32 20N 74 20 E
Datça, *Turkey* **21 F12** 36 46N 27 40 E
Datia, *India* **43 G8** 25 39N 78 27 E
Datong, *China* **34 D7** 40 6N 113 18 E
Datu, Tanjung, *Indonesia* **36 D3** 2 5N 109 39 E
Datu Piang, *Phil.* **37 C6** 7 2N 124 30 E
Daugava →, *Latvia* **24 C3** 57 4N 24 3 E
Daugavpils, *Latvia* **24 C4** 55 53N 26 32 E
Daulpur, *India* **42 F7** 26 45N 77 59 E
Dauphin, *Canada* **73 C8** 51 9N 100 5W
Dauphin I., *U.S.A.* **77 K1** 30 15N 88 11W
Dauphin L., *Canada* **73 C9** 51 20N 99 45W
Dauphiné, *France* **18 D6** 45 15N 5 25 E
Dausa, *India* **42 F7** 26 52N 76 20 E
Davangere, *India* **40 M9** 14 25N 75 55 E
Davao, *Phil.* **37 C7** 7 0N 125 40 E
Davao, G. of, *Phil.* **37 C7** 6 30N 125 48 E
Dāvar Panāh, *Iran* **45 E9** 27 25N 62 15 E
Davenport, *Calif., U.S.A.* **84 H4** 37 1N 122 12W
Davenport, *Iowa, U.S.A.* **80 E9** 41 32N 90 35W
Davenport, *Wash., U.S.A.* **82 C4** 47 39N 118 9W
Davenport Downs, *Australia* **62 C3** 24 8S 141 7 E
Davenport Ra., *Australia* **62 C1** 20 28S 134 0 E
Daventry, *U.K.* **11 E6** 52 16N 1 10W
David, *Panama* **88 E3** 8 30N 82 30W
David City, *U.S.A.* **80 E6** 41 15N 97 8W
David Gorodok = Davyd Haradok, *Belarus* **17 B14** 52 4N 27 8 E
Davidson, *Canada* **73 C7** 51 16N 105 59W
Davis, *U.S.A.* **84 G5** 38 33N 121 44W
Davis Dam, *U.S.A.* **85 K12** 35 11N 114 34W
Davis Inlet, *Canada* **71 A7** 55 50N 60 59W
Davis Mts., *U.S.A.* **81 K2** 30 50N 103 55W
Davis Sea, *Antarctica* **5 C7** 66 0S 92 0 E
Davis Str., *N. Amer.* **69 B14** 65 0N 58 0W
Davos, *Switz.* **18 C8** 46 48N 9 49 E
Davy L., *Canada* **73 B7** 58 53N 108 18W
Davyd Haradok, *Belarus* **17 B14** 52 4N 27 8 E
Dawei, *Burma* **38 E2** 14 2N 98 12 E
Dawes Ra., *Australia* **62 C5** 24 40S 150 40 E
Dawlish, *U.K.* **11 G4** 50 35N 3 28W
Dawros Hd., *Ireland* **13 B3** 54 50N 8 33W
Dawson, *Canada* **68 B6** 64 10N 139 30W
Dawson, *Ga., U.S.A.* **77 K3** 31 46N 84 27W
Dawson, *N. Dak., U.S.A.* **80 B5** 46 52N 99 45W
Dawson, I., *Chile* **96 G2** 53 50S 70 50W
Dawson Creek, *Canada* **72 B4** 55 45N 120 15W
Dawson Inlet, *Canada* **73 A10** 61 50N 93 25W
Dawson Ra., *Australia* **62 C4** 24 30S 149 48 E
Dax, *France* **18 E3** 43 44N 1 3W
Daxian, *China* **32 C5** 31 15N 107 23 E
Daxindian, *China* **35 F11** 37 30N 120 50 E
Daxinggou, *China* **35 C15** 43 25N 129 40 E
Daxue Shan, *China* **32 C5** 30 30N 101 30 E
Daylesford, *Australia* **63 F3** 37 21S 144 9 E
Dayr az Zawr, *Syria* **44 C4** 35 20N 40 5 E
Daysland, *Canada* **72 C6** 52 50N 112 20W
Dayton, *Nev., U.S.A.* **84 F7** 39 14N 119 36W
Dayton, *Ohio, U.S.A.* **76 F3** 39 45N 84 12W
Dayton, *Pa., U.S.A.* **78 F5** 40 53N 79 15W
Dayton, *Tenn., U.S.A.* **77 H3** 35 30N 85 1W
Dayton, *Wash., U.S.A.* **82 C4** 46 19N 117 59W
Daytona Beach, *U.S.A.* **77 L5** 29 13N 81 1W
Dayville, *U.S.A.* **82 D4** 44 28N 119 32W
De Aar, *S. Africa* **56 E3** 30 39S 24 0 E
De Funiak Springs, *U.S.A.* **77 K2** 30 43N 86 7W
De Grey, *Australia* **60 D2** 20 12S 119 12 E
De Grey →, *Australia* **60 D2** 20 12S 119 13 E
De Haan, *Belgium* **15 C3** 51 16N 3 2 E
De Kalb, *U.S.A.* **80 E10** 41 56N 88 46W
De Land, *U.S.A.* **77 L5** 29 2N 81 18W
De Leon, *U.S.A.* **81 J5** 32 7N 98 32W
De Panne, *Belgium* **15 C2** 51 6N 2 34 E
De Pere, *U.S.A.* **76 C1** 44 27N 88 4W
De Queen, *U.S.A.* **81 H7** 34 2N 94 21W
De Quincy, *U.S.A.* **81 K8** 30 27N 93 26W
De Ridder, *U.S.A.* **81 K8** 30 51N 93 17W
De Smet, *U.S.A.* **80 C6** 44 23N 97 33W
De Soto, *U.S.A.* **80 F9** 38 8N 90 34W
De Tour Village, *U.S.A.* **76 C4** 46 0N 83 56W
De Witt, *U.S.A.* **81 H9** 34 18N 91 20W
Dead Sea, *Asia* **47 D4** 31 30N 35 30 E
Deadwood, *U.S.A.* **80 C3** 44 23N 103 44W
Deadwood L., *Canada* **72 B3** 59 10N 128 30W
Deakin, *Australia* **61 F4** 30 46S 128 58 E
Deal, *U.K.* **11 F9** 51 13N 1 25 E
Deal I., *Australia* **62 F4** 39 30S 147 20 E
Dealesville, *S. Africa* **56 D4** 28 41S 25 44 E
Dean, Forest of, *U.K.* **11 F5** 51 45N 2 33W
Deán Funes, *Argentina* **94 C3** 30 20S 64 20W
Dearborn, *U.S.A.* **70 D3** 42 19N 83 11W
Dease →, *Canada* **72 B3** 59 56N 128 32W
Dease L., *Canada* **72 B2** 58 40N 130 5W
Dease Lake, *Canada* **72 B2** 58 25N 130 6W
Death Valley, *U.S.A.* **85 J10** 36 15N 116 50W
Death Valley Junction, *U.S.A.* **85 J10** 36 20N 116 25W
Death Valley National Monument, *U.S.A.* **85 J10** 36 45N 117 15W
Debar, *Macedonia* **21 D9** 41 31N 20 30 E
Debden, *Canada* **73 C7** 53 30N 106 50W
Dębica, *Poland* **17 C11** 50 2N 21 25 E
Debolt, *Canada* **72 B5** 55 12N 118 1W
Deborah East, L., *Australia* **61 F2** 30 45S 119 0 E
Deborah West, L., *Australia* **61 F2** 30 45S 118 50 E
Debre Markos, *Ethiopia* **46 E2** 10 20N 37 40 E
Debre Tabor, *Ethiopia* **46 E2** 11 50N 38 26 E
Debrecen, *Hungary* **17 E11** 47 33N 21 42 E
Decatur, *Ala., U.S.A.* **77 H2** 34 36N 86 59W
Decatur, *Ga., U.S.A.* **77 J3** 33 47N 84 18W
Decatur, *Ill., U.S.A.* **80 F10** 39 51N 88 57W
Decatur, *Ind., U.S.A.* **76 E3** 40 50N 84 56W
Decatur, *Tex., U.S.A.* **81 J6** 33 14N 97 35W
Deccan, *India* **40 L11** 18 0N 79 0 E
Deception L., *Canada* **73 B8** 56 33N 104 13W
Děčín, *Czech Rep.* **16 C8** 50 47N 14 12 E
Deckerville, *U.S.A.* **78 C2** 43 32N 82 44W
Decorah, *U.S.A.* **80 D9** 43 18N 91 48W
Dedéagach = Alexandroúpolis, *Greece* **21 D11** 40 50N 25 54 E
Dedham, *U.S.A.* **79 D13** 42 15N 71 10W
Dedza, *Malawi* **55 E3** 14 20S 34 20 E
Dee →, *Aberds., U.K.* **12 D6** 57 9N 2 5W
Dee →, *Dumf. & Gall., U.K.* **12 G4** 54 51N 4 3W
Dee →, *Wales, U.K.* **10 D4** 53 22N 3 17W
Deep B., *Canada* **72 A5** 61 15N 116 35W
Deep Well, *Australia* **62 C1** 24 20S 134 0 E
Deepwater, *Australia* **63 D5** 29 25S 151 51 E
Deer →, *Canada* **73 B10** 58 23N 94 13W
Deer Lake, *Nfld., Canada* **71 C8** 49 11N 57 27W
Deer Lake, *Ont., Canada* **73 C10** 52 36N 94 20W
Deer Lodge, *U.S.A.* **82 C7** 46 24N 112 44W
Deer Park, *U.S.A.* **82 C5** 47 57N 117 28W
Deer River, *U.S.A.* **80 B8** 47 20N 93 48W
Deeral, *Australia* **62 B4** 17 14S 145 55 E
Deerdepoort, *S. Africa* **56 C4** 24 37S 26 27 E
Deferiet, *U.S.A.* **79 B9** 44 2N 75 41W
Defiance, *U.S.A.* **76 E3** 41 17N 84 22W
Deggendorf, *Germany* **16 D7** 48 50N 12 57 E
Deh Bīd, *Iran* **45 D7** 30 39N 53 11 E
Deh-e Shīr, *Iran* **45 D7** 31 29N 53 45 E
Dehaj, *Iran* **45 D7** 30 42N 54 53 E
Dehdez, *Iran* **45 D6** 31 43N 50 17 E
Dehestān, *Iran* **45 D7** 28 30N 55 35 E
Dehgolān, *Iran* **44 C5** 35 17N 47 25 E
Dehi Titan, *Afghan.* **40 C3** 33 45N 63 50 E
Dehibat, *Tunisia* **51 B8** 32 0N 10 47 E
Dehlorān, *Iran* **44 C5** 32 41N 47 16 E
Dehnow-e Kūhestān, *Iran* **45 E8** 27 58N 58 32 E
Dehra Dun, *India* **42 D8** 30 20N 78 4 E
Dehri, *India* **43 G11** 24 50N 84 15 E
Dehui, *China* **35 B13** 44 30N 125 40 E
Deinze, *Belgium* **15 D3** 50 59N 3 32 E
Dej, *Romania* **17 E12** 47 10N 23 52 E
Dekese, *Dem. Rep. of the Congo* **52 E4** 3 24S 21 24 E
Del Mar, *U.S.A.* **85 N9** 32 58N 117 16W
Del Norte, *U.S.A.* **83 H10** 37 41N 106 21W
Del Rio, *U.S.A.* **81 L4** 29 22N 100 54W
Delano, *U.S.A.* **85 K7** 35 46N 119 15W
Delareyville, *S. Africa* **56 D4** 26 41S 25 26 E
Delavan, *U.S.A.* **80 D10** 42 38N 88 39W
Delaware, *U.S.A.* **76 E4** 40 18N 83 4W
Delaware □, *U.S.A.* **76 F8** 39 0N 75 20W
Delaware →, *U.S.A.* **76 F8** 39 15N 75 20W
Delaware B., *U.S.A.* **75 C12** 39 0N 75 10W
Delegate, *Australia* **63 F4** 37 4S 148 56 E
Delft, *Neths.* **15 B4** 52 1N 4 22 E
Delfzijl, *Neths.* **15 A6** 53 20N 6 55 E
Delgado, C., *Mozam.* **55 E5** 10 45S 40 40 E
Delgerhet, *Mongolia* **34 B6** 45 50N 110 30 E
Delgo, *Sudan* **51 D12** 20 6N 30 40 E
Delhi, *Canada* **78 D4** 42 51N 80 30W
Delhi, *India* **42 E7** 28 38N 77 17 E
Delhi, *U.S.A.* **79 D10** 42 17N 74 55W
Delia, *Canada* **72 C6** 51 38N 112 23W
Delice →, *Turkey* **25 G5** 39 45N 34 15 E
Delicias, *Mexico* **86 B3** 28 10N 105 30W
Delījān, *Iran* **45 C6** 33 59N 50 40 E
Déline, *Canada* **68 B7** 65 10N 123 30W
Dell City, *U.S.A.* **83 L11** 31 56N 105 12W
Dell Rapids, *U.S.A.* **80 D6** 43 50N 96 43W
Delmar, *U.S.A.* **79 D11** 42 37N 73 47W
Delmenhorst, *Germany* **16 B5** 53 3N 8 37 E
Delong, Ostrova, *Russia* **27 B15** 76 40N 149 20 E
Deloraine, *Australia* **62 G4** 41 30S 146 40 E
Deloraine, *Canada* **73 D8** 49 15N 100 29W
Delphi, *U.S.A.* **76 E2** 40 36N 86 41W
Delphos, *U.S.A.* **76 E3** 40 51N 84 21W
Delportshoop, *S. Africa* **56 D3** 28 22S 24 20 E
Delray Beach, *U.S.A.* **77 M5** 26 28N 80 4W
Delta, *Colo., U.S.A.* **83 G9** 38 44N 108 4W
Delta, *Utah, U.S.A.* **82 G7** 39 21N 112 35W
Delungra, *Australia* **63 D5** 29 39S 150 51 E
Delvinë, *Albania* **21 E9** 39 59N 20 6 E
Demanda, Sierra de la, *Spain* **19 A4** 42 15N 3 0W
Demavand = Damāvand, *Iran* **45 C7** 35 47N 52 0 E
Dembia, *Dem. Rep. of the Congo* **54 B2** 3 33N 25 48 E
Dembidolo, *Ethiopia* **46 F1** 8 34N 34 50 E
Demer →, *Belgium* **15 D4** 50 57N 4 42 E
Deming, *N. Mex., U.S.A.* **83 K10** 32 16N 107 46W
Deming, *Wash., U.S.A.* **84 B4** 48 50N 122 13W
Demini →, *Brazil* **92 D6** 0 46S 62 56W
Demirci, *Turkey* **21 E13** 39 2N 28 38 E
Demirköy, *Turkey* **21 D12** 41 49N 27 45 E
Demopolis, *U.S.A.* **77 J2** 32 31N 87 50W
Den Burg, *Neths.* **15 A4** 53 3N 4 47 E
Den Chai, *Thailand* **38 D3** 17 59N 100 4 E
Den Haag = 's-Gravenhage, *Neths.* **15 B4** 52 7N 4 17 E
Den Helder, *Neths.* **15 B4** 52 57N 4 45 E
Den Oever, *Neths.* **15 B5** 52 56N 5 2 E
Denair, *U.S.A.* **84 H6** 37 32N 120 48W
Denau, *Uzbekistan* **26 F7** 38 16N 67 54 E
Denbigh, *U.K.* **10 D4** 53 12N 3 25W
Denbighshire □, *U.K.* **10 D4** 53 8N 3 22W
Dendang, *Indonesia* **36 E3** 3 7S 107 56 E
Dendermonde, *Belgium* **15 C4** 51 2N 4 5 E
Dengfeng, *China* **34 G7** 34 25N 113 2 E
Dengkou, *China* **34 D4** 40 18N 106 55 E
Denham, *Australia* **61 E1** 25 56S 113 31 E
Denham Ra., *Australia* **62 C4** 21 55S 147 46 E
Denham Sd., *Australia* **61 E1** 25 45S 113 15 E
Denia, *Spain* **19 C6** 38 49N 0 8 E
Denial B., *Australia* **63 E1** 32 14S 133 32 E
Deniliquin, *Australia* **63 F3** 35 30S 144 58 E
Denison, *Iowa, U.S.A.* **80 E7** 42 1N 95 21W
Denison, *Tex., U.S.A.* **81 J6** 33 45N 96 33W
Denison Plains, *Australia* **60 C4** 18 35S 128 0 E
Denizli, *Turkey* **25 G4** 37 42N 29 2 E
Denman Glacier, *Antarctica* **5 C7** 66 45S 99 25 E
Denmark, *Australia* **61 F2** 34 59S 117 25 E
Denmark ■, *Europe* **9 J13** 55 45N 10 0 E
Denmark Str., *Atl. Oc.* **66 C17** 66 0N 30 0W
Dennison, *U.S.A.* **78 F3** 40 24N 81 19W
Denny, *U.K.* **12 E5** 56 1N 3 55W
Denpasar, *Indonesia* **36 F5** 8 45S 115 14 E
Denton, *Mont., U.S.A.* **82 C9** 47 19N 109 57W
Denton, *Tex., U.S.A.* **81 J6** 33 13N 97 8W
D'Entrecasteaux, Pt., *Australia* **61 F2** 34 50S 115 57 E
Denver, *U.S.A.* **80 F2** 39 44N 104 59W
Denver City, *U.S.A.* **81 J3** 32 58N 102 50W
Deoband, *India* **42 E7** 29 42N 77 43 E
Deoghar, *India* **43 G12** 24 30N 86 42 E
Deolali, *India* **40 K8** 19 58N 73 50 E
Deoli = Devli, *India* **42 G6** 25 50N 75 20 E
Deoria, *India* **43 F10** 26 31N 83 48 E
Deosai Mts., *Pakistan* **43 B6** 35 40N 75 0 E
Deping, *China* **35 F9** 37 25N 116 58 E
Deposit, *U.S.A.* **79 D9** 42 4N 75 25W
Depot Springs, *Australia* **61 E3** 27 55S 120 3 E
Deputatskiy, *Russia* **27 C14** 69 18N 139 54 E
Dera Ghazi Khan, *Pakistan* **42 D4** 30 5N 70 43 E
Dera Ismail Khan, *Pakistan* **42 D4** 31 50N 70 50 E
Derbent, *Russia* **25 F8** 42 5N 48 15 E
Derby, *Australia* **60 C3** 17 18S 123 38 E
Derby, *U.K.* **10 E6** 52 56N 1 28W
Derby, *Conn., U.S.A.* **79 E11** 41 19N 73 5W
Derby, *N.Y., U.S.A.* **78 D6** 42 41N 78 58W
Derby City □, *U.K.* **10 E6** 52 56N 1 28W
Derbyshire □, *U.K.* **10 D6** 53 11N 1 38W
Derg →, *U.K.* **13 B4** 54 44N 7 26W
Derg, L., *Ireland* **13 D3** 53 0N 8 20W
Dergaon, *India* **41 F19** 26 45N 94 0 E
Dernieres, Isles, *U.S.A.* **81 L9** 29 2N 90 50W
Derry = Londonderry, *U.K.* **13 B4** 55 0N 7 20W
Derry = Londonderry □, *U.K.* **13 B4** 55 0N 7 20W
Derryveagh Mts., *Ireland* **13 B3** 54 56N 8 11W
Derwent, *Canada* **73 C6** 53 41N 110 58W
Derwent →, *Cumb., U.K.* **10 C4** 54 39N 3 33W

Derwent

Derwent →, Derby, U.K. 10 E6 52 57N 1 28W
Derwent →, N. Yorks., U.K. 10 D7 53 45N 0 58W
Derwent Water, U.K. 10 C4 54 35N 3 9W
Des Moines, Iowa, U.S.A. 80 E8 41 35N 93 37W
Des Moines, N. Mex., U.S.A. 81 G3 36 46N 103 50W
Des Moines →, U.S.A. 80 E9 40 23N 91 25W
Desaguadero →, Argentina 94 C2 34 30S 66 46W
Desaguadero →, Bolivia 92 G5 16 35S 69 5W
Descanso, Pta., Mexico 85 N9 32 21N 117 3W
Deschaillons, Canada 71 C5 46 32N 72 7W
Descharme →, Canada 73 B7 56 51N 109 13W
Deschutes →, U.S.A. 82 D3 45 38N 120 55W
Dese, Ethiopia 46 E2 11 5N 39 40 E
Deseado →, Argentina 96 F3 47 45S 65 54W
Desert Center, U.S.A. 85 M11 33 43N 115 24W
Desert Hot Springs, U.S.A. 85 M10 33 58N 116 30W
Désirade, I., Guadeloupe 89 C7 16 18N 61 3W
Deskenatlata L., Canada 72 A6 60 55N 112 3W
Desna →, Ukraine 24 D5 50 33N 30 32 E
Desolación, I., Chile 96 G2 53 0S 74 0W
Despeñaperros, Paso, Spain 19 C4 38 24N 3 30W
Dessau, Germany 16 C7 51 51N 12 14 E
Dessye = Dese, Ethiopia 46 E2 11 5N 39 40 E
D'Estrees B., Australia 63 F2 35 55S 137 45 E
Desuri, India 42 G5 25 18N 73 35 E
Det Udom, Thailand 38 E5 14 54N 105 5 E
Dete, Zimbabwe 55 F2 18 38S 26 50 E
Detmold, Germany 16 C5 51 56N 8 52 E
Detour, Pt., U.S.A. 76 C2 45 40N 86 40W
Detroit, Mich., U.S.A. 75 B10 42 20N 83 3W
Detroit, Tex., U.S.A. 81 J7 33 40N 95 16W
Detroit Lakes, U.S.A. 80 B7 46 49N 95 51W
Deurne, Neths. 15 C5 51 27N 5 49 E
Deutsche Bucht, Germany 16 A5 54 15N 8 0 E
Deva, Romania 17 F12 45 53N 22 55 E
Devakottai, India 40 Q11 9 55N 78 45 E
Devaprayag, India 43 D8 30 13N 78 35 E
Deventer, Neths. 15 B6 52 15N 6 10 E
Deveron →, U.K. 12 D6 57 41N 2 32W
Devgadh Bariya, India 42 H5 22 40N 73 55 E
Devils Den, U.S.A. 84 K7 35 46N 119 58W
Devils Lake, U.S.A. 80 A5 48 7N 98 52W
Devils Paw, Canada 72 B2 58 47N 134 0W
Devizes, U.K. 11 F6 51 22N 1 58W
Devli, India 42 G6 25 50N 75 20 E
Devon, Canada 72 C6 53 24N 113 44W
Devon □, U.K. 11 G4 50 50N 3 40W
Devon I., Canada 66 B11 75 10N 85 0W
Devonport, Australia 62 G4 41 10S 146 22 E
Devonport, N.Z. 59 G5 36 49S 174 49 E
Dewas, India 42 H7 22 59N 76 3 E
Dewetsdorp, S. Africa 56 D4 29 33S 26 39 E
Dexter, Mo., U.S.A. 81 G10 36 48N 89 57W
Dexter, N. Mex., U.S.A. 81 J2 33 12N 104 22W
Dey-Dey, L., Australia 61 E5 29 12S 131 4 E
Deyhük, Iran 45 C8 33 15N 57 30 E
Deyyer, Iran 45 E6 27 55N 51 55 E
Dezadeash L., Canada 72 A1 60 28N 136 58W
Dezfūl, Iran 45 C6 32 20N 48 30 E
Dezhneva, Mys, Russia 27 C19 66 5N 169 40W
Dezhou, China 34 F9 37 26N 116 18 E
Dháfni, Greece 23 D7 35 13N 25 3 E
Dhahiriya = Az̧ Z̧āhirīyah, West Bank 47 D3 31 25N 34 58 E
Dhahran = Az̧ Z̧ahrān, Si. Arabia 45 E6 26 10N 50 7 E
Dhaka, Bangla. 43 H14 23 43N 90 26 E
Dhaka □, Bangla. 43 G14 24 25N 90 25 E
Dhali, Cyprus 23 D12 35 1N 33 25 E
Dhampur, India 43 E8 29 19N 78 33 E
Dhamtari, India 41 J12 20 42N 81 35 E
Dhanbad, India 43 H12 23 50N 86 30 E
Dhangarhi, Nepal 41 E12 28 55N 80 40 E
Dhankuta, Nepal 43 F12 26 55N 87 40 E
Dhar, India 42 H6 22 35N 75 26 E
Dharampur, India 42 H6 22 13N 75 18 E
Dharamsala = Dharmsala, India 42 C7 32 16N 76 23 E
Dharmapuri, India 40 N11 12 10N 78 10 E
Dharmsala, India 42 C7 32 16N 76 23 E
Dharwad, India 40 M9 15 22N 75 15 E
Dhaulagiri, Nepal 43 E10 28 39N 83 28 E
Dhebar, L., India 42 G6 24 10N 74 0 E
Dheftera, Cyprus 23 D12 35 5N 33 16 E
Dhenkanal, India 41 J14 20 45N 85 35 E
Dherinia, Cyprus 23 D12 35 3N 33 57 E
Dhiarrizos →, Cyprus 23 E11 34 41N 32 34 E
Dhībān, Jordan 47 D4 31 30N 35 46 E
Dhíkti Óros, Greece 23 D7 35 8N 25 30 E
Dhírfis = Dhírfis Óros, Greece 21 E10 38 40N 23 54 E
Dhírfis Óros, Greece 21 E10 38 40N 23 54 E
Dhodhekánisos, Greece 21 F12 36 35N 27 0 E
Dholka, India 42 H5 22 44N 72 29 E
Dhoraji, India 42 J4 21 45N 70 37 E
Dhráhstis, Ákra, Greece 23 A3 39 48N 19 40 E
Dhrangadhra, India 42 H4 22 59N 71 31 E
Dhrápanon, Ákra, Greece 23 D6 35 28N 24 14 E
Dhrol, India 42 H4 22 33N 70 25 E
Dhuburi, India 41 F16 26 2N 89 59 E
Dhule, India 40 J9 20 58N 74 50 E
Di Linh, Vietnam 39 G7 11 35N 108 4 E
Di Linh, Cao Nguyen, Vietnam 39 G7 11 30N 108 0 E
Día, Greece 23 D7 35 28N 25 14 E
Diablo, Mt., U.S.A. 84 H5 37 53N 121 56W
Diablo Range, U.S.A. 84 J5 37 20N 121 25W
Diafarabé, Mali 50 F5 14 9N 4 57W
Diamante, Argentina 94 C3 32 5S 60 40W
Diamante →, Argentina 94 C2 34 30S 66 46W
Diamantina, Brazil 93 G10 18 17S 43 40W
Diamantina →, Australia 63 D2 26 45S 139 10 E
Diamantino, Brazil 93 F7 14 30S 56 30W
Diamond Bar, U.S.A. 85 L9 34 1N 117 48W
Diamond Harbour, India 43 H13 22 11N 88 14 E
Diamond Is., Australia 62 B5 17 25S 151 5 E
Diamond Mts., U.S.A. 82 G6 39 50N 115 30W
Diamond Springs, U.S.A. 84 G6 38 42N 120 49W
Diamondville, U.S.A. 82 F8 41 47N 110 32W
Dībā, Oman 45 E8 25 45N 56 16 E
Dibaya-Lubue, Dem. Rep. of the Congo 52 E3 4 12S 19 54 E
Dibete, Botswana 56 C4 23 45S 26 32 E
Dibrugarh, India 41 F19 27 29N 94 55 E
Dickinson, U.S.A. 80 B3 46 53N 102 47W
Dickson = Dikson, Russia 26 B9 73 40N 80 5 E
Dickson, U.S.A. 77 G2 36 5N 87 23W
Dickson City, U.S.A. 79 E9 41 29N 75 40W
Didiéni, Mali 50 F4 13 53N 8 6W
Didsbury, Canada 72 C6 51 35N 114 10W
Didwana, India 42 F6 27 23N 74 36 E
Diefenbaker L., Canada 73 C7 51 0N 106 55W
Diego de Almagro, Chile 96 B2 26 23S 70 3W
Diego Garcia, Ind. Oc. 3 E13 7 50S 72 50 E
Diekirch, Lux. 15 E6 49 52N 6 10 E
Dien Ban, Vietnam 38 E7 15 53N 108 16 E
Dien Bien, Vietnam 38 B4 21 20N 103 0 E
Dien Khanh, Vietnam 39 F7 12 15N 109 6 E
Dieppe, France 18 B4 49 54N 1 4 E
Dierks, U.S.A. 81 H8 34 7N 94 1W
Diest, Belgium 15 D5 50 58N 5 4 E
Differdange, Lux. 15 E5 49 31N 5 54 E
Dig, India 42 F7 27 28N 77 20 E
Digba, Dem. Rep. of the Congo 54 B2 4 25N 25 48 E
Digby, Canada 71 D6 44 38N 65 50W
Digges, Canada 73 B10 58 40N 94 0W
Dighinala, Bangla. 41 H18 23 15N 92 5 E
Dighton, U.S.A. 80 F4 38 29N 100 28W
Digne-les-Bains, France 18 D7 44 5N 6 12 E
Digos, Phil. 37 C7 6 45N 125 20 E
Digranes, Iceland 8 C6 66 4N 14 44W
Digul →, Indonesia 37 F9 7 7S 138 42 E
Dihang →, India 41 F19 27 48N 95 30 E
Dīhōk, Iraq 44 B3 36 50N 43 1 E
Dijlah, Nahr →, Asia 44 D5 31 0N 47 25 E
Dijon, France 18 C6 47 20N 5 3 E
Dikomu di Kai, Botswana 56 C3 24 58S 24 36 E
Diksmuide, Belgium 15 C2 51 2N 2 52 E
Dikson, Russia 26 B9 73 40N 80 5 E
Dili, Indonesia 37 F7 8 39S 125 34 E
Dilley, U.S.A. 81 L5 28 40N 99 10W
Dillingham, U.S.A. 68 C4 59 3N 158 28W
Dillon, Canada 73 B7 55 56N 108 35W
Dillon, Mont., U.S.A. 82 D7 45 13N 112 38W
Dillon, S.C., U.S.A. 77 H6 34 25N 79 22W
Dillon →, Canada 73 B7 55 56N 108 56W
Dilolo, Dem. Rep. of the Congo 52 G4 10 28S 22 18 E
Dilston, Australia 62 G4 41 22S 147 10 E
Dimas, Mexico 86 C3 23 43N 106 47W
Dimashq, Syria 47 B5 33 30N 36 18 E
Dimashq □, Syria 47 B5 33 30N 36 30 E
Dimbaza, S. Africa 57 E4 32 50S 27 14 E
Dimboola, Australia 63 F3 36 28S 142 7 E
Dîmboviţa = Dâmboviţa →, Romania 17 F14 44 12N 26 26 E
Dimbulah, Australia 62 B4 17 8S 145 4 E
Dimitrovgrad, Bulgaria 21 C11 42 5N 25 35 E
Dimitrovgrad, Russia 24 D8 54 14N 49 39 E
Dimitrovo = Pernik, Bulgaria 21 C10 42 35N 23 2 E
Dimmitt, U.S.A. 81 H3 34 33N 102 19W
Dimona, Israel 47 D4 31 2N 35 1 E
Dinagat, Phil. 37 B7 10 10N 125 40 E
Dinajpur, Bangla. 41 G16 25 33N 88 43 E
Dinan, France 18 B2 48 28N 2 2W
Dīnān Āb, Iran 45 C8 32 4N 56 49 E
Dinant, Belgium 15 D4 50 16N 4 55 E
Dinapur, India 43 G11 25 38N 85 5 E
Dīnār, Kūh-e, Iran 45 D6 30 42N 51 46 E
Dinara Planina, Croatia 20 C7 44 0N 16 30 E
Dinard, France 18 B2 48 38N 2 6W
Dinaric Alps = Dinara Planina, Croatia 20 C7 44 0N 16 30 E
Dindigul, India 40 P11 10 25N 78 0 E
Ding Xian, China 34 E8 38 30N 114 59 E
Dingbian, China 34 F4 37 35N 107 32 E
Dingle, Ireland 13 D1 52 9N 10 17W
Dingle B., Ireland 13 D1 52 3N 10 20W
Dingmans Ferry, U.S.A. 79 E10 41 13N 74 55W
Dingo, Australia 62 C4 23 38S 149 19 E
Dingtao, China 34 G8 35 5N 115 35 E
Dingwall, U.K. 12 D4 57 36N 4 26W
Dingxi, China 34 G3 35 30N 104 33 E
Dingxiang, China 34 E7 38 30N 112 58 E
Dinh, Mui, Vietnam 39 G7 11 22N 109 1 E
Dinh Lap, Vietnam 38 B6 21 33N 107 6 E
Dinokwe, Botswana 56 C4 23 29S 26 37 E
Dinosaur National Monument, U.S.A. 82 F9 40 30N 108 45W
Dinuba, U.S.A. 84 J7 36 32N 119 23W
Diplo, Pakistan 42 G3 24 35N 69 35 E
Dipolog, Phil. 37 C6 8 36N 123 20 E
Dir, Pakistan 40 B7 35 8N 71 59 E
Dire Dawa, Ethiopia 46 F3 9 35N 41 45 E
Diriamba, Nic. 88 D2 11 51N 86 19W
Dirk Hartog I., Australia 61 E1 25 50S 113 5 E
Dirranbandi, Australia 63 D4 28 33S 148 17 E
Disa, India 42 G5 24 18N 72 10 E
Disappointment, C., U.S.A. 82 C2 46 18N 124 5W
Disappointment, L., Australia 60 D3 23 20S 122 40 E
Disaster B., Australia 63 F4 37 15S 149 58 E
Discovery B., Australia 63 F3 38 10S 140 40 E
Disko, Greenland 66 C14 69 45N 53 30W
Diss, U.K. 11 E9 52 23N 1 7 E
Disteghil Sar, Pakistan 43 A6 36 20N 75 12 E
Distrito Federal □, Brazil 93 G9 15 45S 47 45W
Diu, India 42 J4 20 45N 70 58 E
Dīvāndarreh, Iran 44 C5 35 55N 47 2 E
Divide, U.S.A. 82 D7 45 45N 112 45W
Dividing Ra., Australia 61 E2 27 45S 116 0 E
Divinópolis, Brazil 93 H10 20 10S 44 54W
Divnoye, Russia 25 E7 45 55N 43 21 E
Dīwāl Kol, Afghan. 42 B2 34 23N 67 52 E
Dixie Mt., U.S.A. 84 F6 39 55N 120 16W
Dixon, Calif., U.S.A. 84 G5 38 27N 121 49W
Dixon, Ill., U.S.A. 80 E10 41 50N 89 29W
Dixon, Mont., U.S.A. 82 C6 47 19N 114 19W
Dixon, N. Mex., U.S.A. 83 H11 36 12N 105 53W
Dixon Entrance, U.S.A. 72 C2 54 30N 132 0W
Dixonville, Canada 72 B5 56 32N 117 40W
Diyarbakır, Turkey 25 G7 37 55N 40 18 E
Djakarta = Jakarta, Indonesia 37 G12 6 9S 106 49 E
Djamba, Angola 56 B1 16 45S 13 58 E
Djambala, Congo 52 E2 2 32S 14 30 E
Djanet, Algeria 50 D7 24 35N 9 32 E
Djawa = Jawa, Indonesia 37 G14 7 0S 110 0 E
Djelfa, Algeria 50 B6 34 40N 3 15 E
Djema, C.A.R. 54 A2 6 3N 25 15 E
Djerba, I. de, Tunisia 51 B8 33 50N 10 48 E
Djerid, Chott, Tunisia 50 B7 33 42N 8 30 E
Djibouti, Djibouti 46 E3 11 30N 43 5 E
Djibouti ■, Africa 46 E3 12 0N 43 0 E
Djolu, Dem. Rep. of the Congo 52 D4 0 35N 22 5 E
Djoum, Cameroon 52 D2 2 41N 12 35 E
Djourab, Erg du, Chad 51 E9 16 40N 18 50 E
Djugu, Dem. Rep. of the Congo 54 B3 1 55N 30 35 E
Djúpivogur, Iceland 8 D6 64 39N 14 17W
Dmitriya Lapteva, Proliv, Russia 27 B15 73 0N 140 0 E
Dnepr → = Dnipro →, Ukraine 25 E5 46 30N 32 18 E
Dneprodzerzhinsk = Dniprodzerzhynsk, Ukraine 25 E5 48 32N 34 37 E
Dnepropetrovsk = Dnipropetrovsk, Ukraine 25 E6 48 30N 35 0 E
Dnestr → = Dnister →, Europe 25 E5 46 18N 30 17 E
Dnestrovski = Belgorod, Russia 25 D6 50 35N 36 35 E
Dnieper = Dnipro →, Ukraine 25 E5 46 30N 32 18 E
Dniester = Dnister →, Europe 25 E5 46 18N 30 17 E
Dnipro →, Ukraine 25 E5 46 30N 32 18 E
Dniprodzerzhynsk, Ukraine 25 E5 48 32N 34 37 E
Dnipropetrovsk, Ukraine 25 E6 48 30N 35 0 E
Dnister →, Europe 25 E5 46 18N 30 17 E
Dnistrovskyy Lyman, Ukraine 17 E16 46 15N 30 17 E
Dnyapro = Dnipro →, Ukraine 25 E5 46 30N 32 18 E
Doan Hung, Vietnam 38 B5 21 30N 105 10 E
Doba, Chad 51 G9 8 40N 16 50 E
Dobbyn, Australia 62 B3 19 44S 140 2 E
Dobele, Latvia 9 H20 56 37N 23 16 E
Doberai, Jazirah, Indonesia 37 E8 1 25S 133 0 E
Doblas, Argentina 94 D3 37 5S 64 0W
Dobo, Indonesia 37 F8 5 45S 134 15 E
Doboj, Bos.-H. 21 B8 44 46N 18 4 E
Dobreta-Turnu Severin, Romania 17 F12 44 39N 22 41 E
Dobrich, Bulgaria 21 C12 43 37N 27 49 E
Dobruja, Europe 17 F15 44 30N 28 15 E
Dobrush, Belarus 17 B16 52 25N 31 22 E
Doc, Mui, Vietnam 38 D6 17 58N 106 30 E
Doda, India 43 C6 33 10N 75 34 E
Dodecanese = Dhodhekánisos, Greece 21 F12 36 35N 27 0 E
Dodge Center, U.S.A. 80 C8 44 2N 92 52W
Dodge City, U.S.A. 81 G5 37 45N 100 1W
Dodge L., Canada 73 B7 59 50N 105 36W
Dodgeville, U.S.A. 80 D9 42 58N 90 8W
Dodoma, Tanzania 54 D4 6 8S 35 45 E
Dodoma □, Tanzania 54 D4 6 0S 36 0 E
Dodsland, Canada 73 C7 51 50N 108 45W
Dodson, U.S.A. 82 B9 48 24N 108 15W
Doesburg, Neths. 15 B6 52 1N 6 9 E
Doetinchem, Neths. 15 C6 51 59N 6 18 E
Dog Creek, Canada 72 C4 51 35N 122 14W
Dog L., Man., Canada 73 C9 51 2N 98 31W
Dog L., Ont., Canada 70 C2 48 48N 89 30W
Dogi, Afghan. 40 C3 32 20N 62 50 E
Dogran, Pakistan 42 D5 31 48N 73 35 E
Doha = Ad Dawhah, Qatar 45 E6 25 15N 51 35 E
Dohazari, Bangla. 41 H18 22 10N 92 5 E
Doi, Indonesia 37 D7 2 14N 127 49 E
Doi Luang, Thailand 38 C3 18 30N 101 0 E
Doi Saket, Thailand 38 C2 18 52N 99 9 E
Doig →, Canada 72 B4 56 25N 120 40W
Dois Irmãos, Sa., Brazil 93 E10 9 0S 42 30W
Dokkum, Neths. 15 A5 53 20N 5 59 E
Dokri, Pakistan 42 F3 27 25N 68 7 E
Dolak, Pulau, Indonesia 37 F9 8 0S 138 30 E
Doland, U.S.A. 80 C5 44 54N 98 6W
Dolbeau, Canada 71 C5 48 53N 72 18W
Dole, France 18 C6 47 7N 5 31 E
Dolgellau, U.K. 10 E4 52 45N 3 53W
Dolgelley = Dolgellau, U.K. 10 E4 52 45N 3 53W
Dollard, Neths. 15 A7 53 20N 7 10 E
Dolomites = Dolomiti, Italy 20 A4 46 23N 11 51 E
Dolomiti, Italy 20 A4 46 23N 11 51 E
Dolores, Argentina 94 D4 36 20S 57 40W
Dolores, Uruguay 94 C4 33 34S 58 15W
Dolores, U.S.A. 83 H9 37 28N 108 30W
Dolores →, U.S.A. 83 G9 38 49N 109 17W
Dolphin, C., Falk. Is. 96 G5 51 10S 59 0W
Dolphin and Union Str., Canada 68 B8 69 5N 114 45W
Dom Pedrito, Brazil 95 C5 31 0S 54 40W
Domasi, Malawi 55 F4 15 15S 35 22 E
Dombarovskiy, Russia 26 D6 50 46N 59 32 E
Dombås, Norway 9 E13 62 4N 9 8 E
Domel I. = Letsôk-aw Kyun, Burma 39 G2 11 30N 98 25 E
Domeyko, Chile 94 B1 29 0S 71 0W
Domeyko, Cordillera, Chile 94 A2 24 30S 69 0W
Dominador, Chile 94 A2 24 21S 69 20W
Dominica ■, W. Indies 89 C7 15 20N 61 20W
Dominica Passage, W. Indies 89 C7 15 10N 61 20W
Dominican Rep. ■, W. Indies 89 C5 19 0N 70 30W
Domodóssola, Italy 18 C8 46 7N 8 17 E
Domville, Mt., Australia 63 D5 28 1S 151 15 E
Don →, Russia 25 E6 47 4N 39 18 E
Don →, Aberds., U.K. 12 D6 57 11N 2 5W
Don →, S. Yorks., U.K. 10 D7 53 41N 0 52W
Don, C., Australia 60 B5 11 18S 131 46 E
Don Benito, Spain 19 C3 38 53N 5 51W
Don Martín, Presa de, Mexico 86 B4 27 30N 100 50W
Dona Ana = Nhamaabué, Mozam. 55 F4 17 25S 35 5 E
Donaghadee, U.K. 13 B6 54 39N 5 33W
Donald, Australia 63 F3 36 23S 143 0 E
Donalda, Canada 72 C6 52 35N 112 34W
Donaldsonville, U.S.A. 81 K9 30 6N 90 59W
Donalsonville, U.S.A. 77 K3 31 3N 84 53W
Donau = Dunărea →, Europe 17 F15 45 20N 29 40 E
Donau →, Austria 15 D3 48 10N 17 0 E
Donauwörth, Germany 16 D6 48 43N 10 47 E
Doncaster, U.K. 10 D6 53 32N 1 6W
Dondo, Mozam. 55 F3 19 33S 34 46 E
Dondo, Teluk, Indonesia 37 D6 0 50N 120 30 E
Dondra Head, Sri Lanka 40 S12 5 55N 80 40 E
Donegal, Ireland 13 B3 54 39N 8 5W
Donegal □, Ireland 13 B4 54 53N 8 0W
Donegal B., Ireland 13 B3 54 31N 8 49W
Donets →, Russia 25 E7 47 33N 40 55 E
Donetsk, Ukraine 25 E6 48 0N 37 45 E
Dong Ba Thin, Vietnam 39 F7 12 8N 109 13 E
Dong Dang, Vietnam 38 B6 21 54N 106 42 E
Dong Giam, Vietnam 38 C5 19 25N 105 31 E
Dong Ha, Vietnam 38 D6 16 55N 107 8 E
Dong Hene, Laos 38 D5 16 40N 105 18 E
Dong Hoi, Vietnam 38 D6 17 29N 106 36 E
Dong Khe, Vietnam 38 A6 22 26N 106 27 E
Dong Ujimqin Qi, China 34 B9 45 32N 116 55 E
Dong Van, Vietnam 38 A5 23 16N 105 22 E
Dong Xoai, Vietnam 39 G6 11 32N 106 55 E
Dongara, Australia 61 E1 29 14S 114 57 E
Dongbei, China 35 D13 45 0N 125 0 E
Dongchuan, China 32 D5 26 8N 103 1 E
Dongfang, China 38 C7 18 50N 108 33 E
Dongfeng, China 35 C13 42 40N 125 34 E
Donggala, Indonesia 37 E5 0 30S 119 40 E
Donggou, China 35 E13 39 52N 124 10 E
Dongguang, China 34 F9 37 50N 116 30 E
Dongjingcheng, China 35 B15 44 5N 129 10 E
Dongning, China 35 B16 44 2N 131 5 E
Dongola, Sudan 51 E12 19 9N 30 22 E
Dongping, China 34 G9 35 55N 116 20 E
Dongsheng, China 34 E6 39 50N 110 0 E
Dongtai, China 35 H11 32 51N 120 21 E
Dongting Hu, China 33 D6 29 18N 112 45 E
Donington, C., Australia 63 E2 34 45S 136 0 E
Doniphan, U.S.A. 81 G9 36 37N 90 50W
Dønna, Norway 8 C15 66 6N 12 30 E
Donna, U.S.A. 81 M5 26 9N 98 4W
Donnaconna, Canada 71 C5 46 41N 71 41W
Donnelly's Crossing, N.Z. 59 F4 35 42S 173 38 E
Donnybrook, Australia 61 F2 33 34S 115 48 E
Donnybrook, S. Africa 57 D4 29 59S 29 48 E
Donora, U.S.A. 78 F5 40 11N 79 52W
Donor's Hill, Australia 62 B3 18 42S 140 33 E
Donostia = Donostia-San Sebastián, Spain 19 A5 43 17N 1 58W
Donostia-San Sebastián, Spain 19 A5 43 17N 1 58W
Doon →, U.K. 12 F4 55 27N 4 39W
Dora, L., Australia 60 D3 22 0S 123 0 E
Dora Báltea →, Italy 18 D8 45 11N 8 3 E
Doran L., Canada 73 A7 61 13N 108 6W
Dorchester, U.K. 11 G5 50 42N 2 27W
Dorchester, C., Canada 69 B12 65 27N 77 27W
Dordogne →, France 18 D3 45 2N 0 36W
Dordrecht, Neths. 15 C4 51 48N 4 39 E
Dordrecht, S. Africa 56 E4 31 20S 27 3 E
Doré L., Canada 73 C7 54 46N 107 17W
Doré Lake, Canada 73 C7 54 38N 107 36W
Dori, Burkina Faso 50 F5 14 3N 0 2W
Doring →, S. Africa 56 E2 31 54S 18 39 E
Doringbos, S. Africa 56 E2 31 59S 19 16 E
Dorion, Canada 70 C5 45 23N 74 3W
Dornbirn, Austria 16 E5 47 25N 9 45 E
Dornie, U.K. 12 D3 57 17N 5 31W
Dornoch, U.K. 12 D4 57 53N 4 2W
Dornoch Firth, U.K. 12 D4 57 51N 4 4W
Dornogovĭ □, Mongolia 34 C6 44 0N 110 0 E
Dorohoi, Romania 17 E14 47 56N 26 23 E
Döröö Nuur, Mongolia 32 B4 48 0N 93 0 E
Dorr, Iran 45 C6 33 17N 50 38 E
Dorre I., Australia 61 E1 25 13S 113 12 E
Dorrigo, Australia 63 E5 30 20S 152 44 E
Dorris, U.S.A. 82 F3 41 58N 121 55W
Dorset, Canada 78 A6 45 14N 78 54W
Dorset, U.S.A. 78 E4 41 4N 80 40W
Dorset □, U.K. 11 G5 50 45N 2 26W
Dortmund, Germany 16 C4 51 30N 7 28 E
Doruma, Dem. Rep. of the Congo 54 B2 4 42N 27 33 E
Dorūneh, Iran 45 C8 35 10N 57 18 E
Dos Bahías, C., Argentina 96 E3 44 58S 65 32W
Dos Hermanas, Spain 19 D3 37 16N 5 55W
Dos Palos, U.S.A. 84 J6 36 59N 120 37W
Dosso, Niger 50 F6 13 0N 3 13 E
Dothan, U.S.A. 77 K3 31 13N 85 24W
Doty, U.S.A. 84 D3 46 38N 123 17W
Douai, France 18 A5 50 21N 3 4 E
Douala, Cameroon 52 D1 4 0N 9 45 E
Douarnenez, France 18 B1 48 6N 4 21W
Double Island Pt., Australia 63 D5 25 56S 153 11 E
Doubs →, France 18 C6 46 53N 5 1 E
Doubtful Sd., N.Z. 59 L1 45 20S 166 49 E
Doubtless B., N.Z. 59 F4 34 55S 173 26 E
Douglas, S. Africa 56 D3 29 4S 23 46 E
Douglas, U.K. 10 C3 54 10N 4 28W
Douglas, Alaska, U.S.A. 72 B2 58 17N 134 24W
Douglas, Ariz., U.S.A. 83 L9 31 21N 109 33W
Douglas, Ga., U.S.A. 77 K4 31 31N 82 51W
Douglas, Wyo., U.S.A. 80 D2 42 45N 105 24W
Douglastown, Canada 71 C7 48 46N 64 24W
Douglasville, U.S.A. 77 J3 33 45N 84 45W

Greenland

Godwin Austen = K2, *Pakistan* .... **43 B7** 35 58N 76 32 E
Goeie Hoop, Kaap die = Good Hope, C. of, *S. Africa* .... **56 E2** 34 24S 18 30 E
Goéland, L. au, *Canada* .. **70 C4** 49 50N 76 48W
Goeree, *Neths.* .... **15 C3** 51 50N 4 0 E
Goes, *Neths.* .... **15 C3** 51 30N 3 55 E
Gogama, *Canada* **70 C3** 47 35N 81 43W
Gogango, *Australia* ..... **62 C5** 23 40S 150 2 E
Gogebic, L., *U.S.A.* **80 B10** 46 30N 89 35W
Gogra = Ghaghara →, *India* .... **43 G11** 25 45N 84 40 E
Goiânia, *Brazil* **93 G9** 16 43S 49 20W
Goiás, *Brazil* **93 G8** 15 55S 50 10W
Goiás □, *Brazil* **93 F9** 12 10S 48 0W
Goio-Ere, *Brazil* **95 A5** 24 12S 53 1W
Gojō, *Japan* .... **31 G7** 34 21N 135 42 E
Gojra, *Pakistan* .... **42 D5** 31 10N 72 40 E
Gokarannath, *India* ..... **43 F9** 27 57N 80 39 E
Gökçeada, *Turkey* ..... **21 D11** 40 10N 25 50 E
Gökova Körfezi, *Turkey* .. **21 F12** 36 55N 27 50 E
Gokteik, *Burma* .... **41 H20** 22 26N 97 0 E
Gokurt, *Pakistan* .... **42 E2** 29 40N 67 26 E
Gola, *India* .... **43 E9** 28 3N 80 32 E
Golakganj, *India* .... **43 F13** 26 8N 89 52 E
Golan Heights = Hagolan, *Syria* .... **47 C4** 33 0N 35 45 E
Golāshkerd, *Iran* .... **45 E8** 27 59N 57 16 E
Golconda, *U.S.A.* **82 F5** 40 58N 117 30W
Gold Beach, *U.S.A.* **82 E1** 42 25N 124 25W
Gold Coast, *Australia* .... **63 D5** 28 0S 153 25 E
Gold Coast, *W. Afr.* **48 F3** 4 0N 1 40W
Gold Hill, *U.S.A.* **82 E2** 42 26N 123 3W
Golden, *Canada* **72 C5** 51 20N 116 59W
Golden, *U.S.A.* **80 F2** 39 42N 105 15W
Golden B., *N.Z.* .... **59 J4** 40 40S 172 50 E
Golden Gate, *U.S.A.* **82 H2** 37 54N 122 30W
Golden Hinde, *Canada* .. **72 D3** 49 40N 125 44W
Golden Lake, *Canada* .. **78 A7** 45 34N 77 21W
Golden Prairie, *Canada* .. **73 C7** 50 13N 109 37W
Golden Vale, *Ireland* **13 D3** 52 33N 8 17W
Goldendale, *U.S.A.* **82 D3** 45 49N 120 50W
Goldfield, *U.S.A.* **83 H5** 37 42N 117 14W
Goldfields, *Canada* **73 B7** 59 28N 108 29W
Goldsand L., *Canada* **73 B8** 57 2N 101 8W
Goldsboro, *U.S.A.* **77 H7** 35 23N 77 59W
Goldsmith, *U.S.A.* **81 K3** 31 59N 102 37W
Goldsworthy, *Australia* .. **60 D2** 20 21S 119 30 E
Goldthwaite, *U.S.A.* **81 K5** 31 27N 98 34W
Goleniów, *Poland* ..... **16 B8** 53 35N 14 50 E
Golestānak, *Iran* ..... **45 D7** 30 36N 54 14 E
Goleta, *U.S.A.* **85 L7** 34 27N 119 50W
Golfito, *Costa Rica* **88 E3** 8 41N 83 5W
Golfo Aranci, *Italy* ..... **20 D3** 40 59N 9 38 E
Goliad, *U.S.A.* **81 L6** 28 40N 97 23W
Golpāyegān, *Iran* ..... **45 C6** 33 27N 50 18 E
Golra, *Pakistan* .... **42 C5** 33 37N 72 56 E
Golspie, *U.K.* **12 D5** 57 58N 3 59W
Goma, *Dem. Rep. of the Congo* **54 C2** 1 37S 29 10 E
Gomati →, *India* ..... **43 G10** 25 32N 83 11 E
Gombari, *Dem. Rep. of the Congo* **54 B2** 2 45N 29 3 E
Gombe →, *Tanzania* ... **54 C3** 4 38S 31 40 E
Gomel = Homyel, *Belarus* **24 D5** 52 28N 31 0 E
Gomera, *Canary Is.* **22 F2** 28 7N 17 14W
Gómez Palacio, *Mexico* .. **86 B4** 25 40N 104 0W
Gomīshān, *Iran* .... **45 B7** 37 4N 54 6 E
Gomogomo, *Indonesia* .. **37 F8** 6 39S 134 43 E
Gomoh, *India* .... **41 H15** 23 52N 86 10 E
Gompa = Ganta, *Liberia* . **50 G4** 7 15N 8 59W
Gonābād, *Iran* .... **45 C8** 34 15N 58 45 E
Gonaïves, *Haiti* **89 C5** 19 20N 72 42W
Gonâve, G. de la, *Haiti* .. **89 C5** 19 29N 72 42W
Gonâve, I. de la, *Haiti* .. **89 C5** 18 45N 73 0W
Gonbad-e Kāvūs, *Iran* ... **45 B7** 37 20N 55 25 E
Gonda, *India* .... **43 F9** 27 9N 81 58 E
Gondal, *India* .... **42 J4** 21 58N 70 52 E
Gonder, *Ethiopia* .... **46 E2** 12 39N 37 30 E
Gondia, *India* .... **40 J12** 21 23N 80 10 E
Gondola, *Mozam.* ..... **55 F3** 19 10S 33 37 E
Gönen, *Turkey* .... **21 D12** 40 6N 27 39 E
Gonghe, *China* .... **32 C5** 36 18N 100 32 E
Gongolgon, *Australia* ... **63 E4** 30 21S 146 54 E
Gonzales, *Calif., U.S.A.* .. **84 J5** 36 30N 121 26W
Gonzales, *Tex., U.S.A.* ... **81 L6** 29 30N 97 27W
González Chaves, *Argentina* **94 D3** 38 2S 60 5W
Good Hope, C. of, *S. Africa* .... **56 E2** 34 24S 18 30 E
Gooderham, *Canada* **70 D4** 44 54N 78 21W
Goodeve, *Canada* **73 C8** 51 4N 103 10W
Gooding, *U.S.A.* **82 E6** 42 56N 114 43W
Goodland, *U.S.A.* **80 F4** 39 21N 101 43W
Goodnight, *U.S.A.* **81 H4** 35 2N 101 11W
Goodooga, *Australia* ... **63 D4** 29 3S 147 28 E
Goodsoil, *Canada* **73 C7** 54 24N 109 13W
Goodsprings, *U.S.A.* **83 J6** 35 50N 115 26W
Goole, *U.K.* **10 D7** 53 42N 0 53W
Goolgowi, *Australia* ..... **63 E4** 33 58S 145 41 E
Goomalling, *Australia* ... **61 F2** 31 15S 116 49 E
Goombalie, *Australia* ... **63 D4** 29 59S 145 26 E
Goonda, *Mozam.* ..... **55 F3** 19 48S 33 57 E
Goondiwindi, *Australia* .. **63 D5** 28 30S 150 21 E
Goongarrie, L., *Australia* . **61 F3** 30 3S 121 9 E
Goonyella, *Australia* ... **62 C4** 21 47S 147 58 E
Gooray, *Australia* ..... **63 D5** 28 25S 150 2 E
Goose →, *Canada* **71 B7** 53 20N 60 35W
Goose L., *U.S.A.* **82 F3** 41 56N 120 26W
Gop, *India* .... **40 H6** 22 5N 69 50 E
Gopalganj, *India* .... **43 F11** 26 28N 84 30 E
Göppingen, *Germany* ... **16 D5** 48 42N 9 39 E
Gorakhpur, *India* ..... **43 F10** 26 47N 83 23 E
Goražde, *Bos.-H.* .... **21 C8** 43 38N 18 58 E
Gorda, *U.S.A.* **84 K5** 35 53N 121 26W
Gorda, Pta., *Canary Is.* .. **22 F2** 28 45N 18 0W
Gorda, Pta., *Nic.* **88 D3** 14 20N 83 10W
Gordan B., *Australia* .... **60 B5** 11 35S 130 10 E
Gordon, *U.S.A.* **80 D3** 42 48N 102 12W
Gordon →, *Australia* ... **62 G4** 42 27S 145 30 E
Gordon Downs, *Australia* **60 C4** 18 48S 128 33 E
Gordon L., *Alta., Canada* . **73 B6** 56 30N 110 25W
Gordon L., *N.W.T., Canada* **72 A6** 63 5N 113 11W
Gordonvale, *Australia* ... **62 B4** 17 5S 145 50 E
Gore, *Australia* .... **63 D5** 28 17S 151 30 E
Gore, *Ethiopia* .... **46 F2** 8 12N 35 32 E
Gore, *N.Z.* .... **59 M2** 46 5S 168 58 E
Gore Bay, *Canada* **70 C3** 45 57N 82 28W
Gorey, *Ireland* **13 D5** 52 41N 6 18W
Gorg, *Iran* .... **45 D8** 29 29N 59 43 E
Gorgān, *Iran* .... **45 B7** 36 50N 54 29 E
Gorgona, I., *Colombia* ... **92 C3** 3 0N 78 10W
Gorham, *U.S.A.* **79 B13** 44 23N 71 10W
Gorinchem, *Neths.* ..... **15 C4** 51 50N 4 59 E
Gorízia, *Italy* .... **20 B5** 45 56N 13 37 E
Gorki = Nizhniy Novgorod, *Russia* ..... **24 C7** 56 20N 44 0 E
Gorkiy = Nizhniy Novgorod, *Russia* ..... **24 C7** 56 20N 44 0 E
Gorkovskoye Vdkhr., *Russia* .... **24 C7** 57 2N 43 4 E
Görlitz, *Germany* ..... **16 C8** 51 9N 14 58 E
Gorlovka = Horlivka, *Ukraine* .... **25 E6** 48 19N 38 5 E
Gorman, *Calif., U.S.A.* ... **85 L8** 34 47N 118 51W
Gorman, *Tex., U.S.A.* ... **81 J5** 32 12N 98 41W
Gorna Dzhumayo = Blagoevgrad, *Bulgaria* . **21 C10** 42 2N 23 5 E
Gorna Oryakhovitsa, *Bulgaria* .... **21 C11** 43 7N 25 40 E
Gorno-Altay □, *Russia* .. **26 D9** 51 0N 86 0 E
Gorno-Altaysk, *Russia* ... **26 D9** 51 50N 86 5 E
Gornyatski, *Russia* ..... **24 A11** 67 32N 64 3 E
Gornyi, *Russia* .... **30 B6** 44 57N 133 59 E
Gorodenka = Horodenka, *Ukraine* .... **17 D13** 48 41N 25 29 E
Gorodok = Horodok, *Ukraine* .... **17 D12** 49 46N 23 32 E
Gorokhov = Horokhiv, *Ukraine* .... **17 C13** 50 30N 24 45 E
Goromonzi, *Zimbabwe* .. **55 F3** 17 52S 31 22 E
Gorongose →, *Mozam.* . **57 C5** 20 30S 34 40 E
Gorongoza, *Mozam.* .... **55 F3** 18 44S 34 2 E
Gorongoza, Sa. da, *Mozam.* .... **55 F3** 18 27S 34 2 E
Gorontalo, *Indonesia* ... **37 D6** 0 35N 123 5 E
Gort, *Ireland* **13 C3** 53 3N 8 49W
Gortis, *Greece* .... **23 D6** 35 4N 24 58 E
Gorzów Wielkopolski, *Poland* .... **16 B8** 52 43N 15 15 E
Gosford, *Australia* ..... **63 E5** 33 23S 151 18 E
Goshen, *Calif., U.S.A.* ... **84 J7** 36 21N 119 25W
Goshen, *Ind., U.S.A.* **76 E3** 41 35N 85 50W
Goshen, *N.Y., U.S.A.* ... **79 E10** 41 24N 74 20W
Goshogawara, *Japan* ... **30 D10** 40 48N 140 27 E
Goslar, *Germany* .... **16 C6** 51 54N 10 25 E
Gospič, *Croatia* .... **16 F8** 44 35N 15 23 E
Gosport, *U.K.* **11 G6** 50 48N 1 9W
Gosse →, *Australia* ... **62 B1** 19 32S 134 37 E
Göta älv →, *Sweden* ... **9 H14** 57 42N 11 54 E
Göta kanal, *Sweden* ... **9 G16** 58 30N 15 58 E
Götaland, *Sweden* ..... **9 G15** 57 30N 14 30 E
Göteborg, *Sweden* ..... **9 H14** 57 43N 11 59 E
Gotha, *Germany* .... **16 C6** 50 56N 10 42 E
Gothenburg = Göteborg, *Sweden* .... **9 H14** 57 43N 11 59 E
Gothenburg, *U.S.A.* **80 E4** 40 56N 100 10W
Gotland, *Sweden* .... **9 H18** 57 30N 18 33 E
Gotska Sandön, *Sweden* . **9 G18** 58 24N 19 15 E
Gōtsu, *Japan* .... **31 G6** 35 0N 132 14 E
Göttingen, *Germany* ..... **16 C5** 51 31N 9 55 E
Gottwaldov = Zlín, *Czech Rep.* .... **17 D9** 49 14N 17 40 E
Goubangzi, *China* ..... **35 D11** 41 20N 121 52 E
Gouda, *Neths.* .... **15 B4** 52 1N 4 42 E
Goúdhoura, Ákra, *Greece* **23 E8** 34 59N 26 6 E
Gough I., *Atl. Oc.* **2 G9** 40 10S 9 45W
Gouin, Rés., *Canada* **70 C5** 48 35N 74 40W
Goulburn, *Australia* ..... **63 E4** 34 44S 149 44 E
Goulburn Is., *Australia* .. **62 A1** 11 40S 133 20 E
Gourits →, *S. Africa* ... **56 E3** 34 21S 21 52 E
Goúrnais, *Greece* ..... **23 D7** 35 19N 25 16 E
Gourock Ra., *Australia* ... **63 F4** 36 0S 149 25 E
Gouverneur, *U.S.A.* **79 B9** 44 20N 75 28W
Gouviá, *Greece* .... **23 A3** 39 39N 19 50 E
Govan, *Canada* **73 C8** 51 20N 105 0W
Governador Valadares, *Brazil* **93 G10** 18 15S 41 57W
Governor's Harbour, *Bahamas* **88 A4** 25 10N 76 14W
Gowan Ra., *Australia* .... **62 D4** 25 0S 145 0 E
Gowanda, *U.S.A.* **78 D6** 42 28N 78 56W
Gowd-e Zirreh, *Afghan.* . **40 E3** 29 45N 62 0 E
Gower, *U.K.* **11 F3** 51 35N 4 10W
Gowna, L., *Ireland* **13 C4** 53 51N 7 34W
Goya, *Argentina* **94 B4** 29 10S 59 10W
Goyder Lagoon, *Australia* **63 D2** 27 3S 138 58 E
Goyllarisquisga, *Peru* ... **92 F3** 10 31S 76 24W
Goz Beïda, *Chad* .... **51 F10** 12 10N 21 20 E
Gozo, *Malta* .... **23 C1** 36 3N 14 13 E
Graaff-Reinet, *S. Africa* .. **56 E3** 32 13S 24 32 E
Gračac, *Croatia* .... **16 F8** 44 18N 15 57 E
Grace, *U.S.A.* **82 E8** 42 35N 111 44W
Graceville, *U.S.A.* **80 C6** 45 34N 96 26W
Gracias a Dios, C., *Honduras* **88 D3** 15 0N 83 10W
Graciosa, I., *Canary Is.* .. **22 E6** 29 15N 13 32W
Grado, *Spain* **19 A2** 43 23N 6 4W
Gradule, *Australia* ..... **63 D4** 28 32S 149 15 E
Grady, *U.S.A.* **81 H3** 34 49N 103 19W
Grafham Water, *U.K.* **11 E7** 52 19N 0 18W
Grafton, *Australia* ..... **63 D5** 29 38S 152 58 E
Grafton, *U.S.A.* **80 A6** 48 25N 97 25W
Graham, *Canada* **70 C1** 49 20N 90 30W
Graham, *N.C., U.S.A.* **77 G6** 36 5N 79 25W
Graham, *Tex., U.S.A.* **81 J5** 33 6N 98 35W
Graham →, *Canada* **72 B4** 56 31N 122 17W
Graham, Mt., *U.S.A.* **83 K9** 32 42N 109 52W
Graham Bell, Ostrov = Greem-Bell, Ostrov, *Russia* .... **26 A7** 81 0N 62 0 E
Graham I., *Canada* **72 C2** 53 40N 132 30W
Graham Land, *Antarctica* **5 C17** 65 0S 64 0W
Grahamdale, *Canada* **73 C9** 51 23N 98 30W
Grahamstown, *S. Africa* . **56 E4** 33 19S 26 31 E
Grain Coast, *W. Afr.* **48 F2** 4 20N 10 0W
Grajaú, *Brazil* **93 E9** 5 50S 46 4W
Grajaú →, *Brazil* **93 D10** 3 41S 44 48W
Grampian Highlands = Grampian Mts., *U.K.* .. **12 E5** 56 50N 4 0W
Grampian Mts., *U.K.* **12 E5** 56 50N 4 0W
Gran Canaria, *Canary Is.* . **22 G4** 27 55N 15 35W
Gran Chaco, *S. Amer.* ... **94 B3** 25 0S 61 0W
Gran Paradiso, *Italy* ..... **18 D7** 45 33N 7 17 E
Gran Sasso d'Itália, *Italy* . **20 C5** 42 27N 13 42 E
Granada, *Nic.* **88 D2** 11 58N 86 0W
Granada, *Spain* **19 D4** 37 10N 3 35W
Granada, *U.S.A.* **81 F3** 38 4N 102 19W
Granadilla de Abona, *Canary Is.* **22 F3** 28 7N 16 33W
Granard, *Ireland* **13 C4** 53 47N 7 30W
Granbury, *U.S.A.* **81 J6** 32 27N 97 47W
Granby, *Canada* **70 C5** 45 25N 72 45W
Grand →, *Mo., U.S.A.* ... **80 F8** 39 23N 93 7W
Grand →, *S. Dak., U.S.A.* **80 C4** 45 40N 100 45W
Grand Bahama, *Bahamas* **88 A4** 26 40N 78 30W
Grand Bank, *Canada* **71 C8** 47 6N 55 48W
Grand Bassam, *Ivory C.* . **50 G5** 5 10N 3 49W
Grand-Bourg, *Guadeloupe* **89 C7** 15 53N 61 19W
Grand Canal = Yun Ho →, *China* .... **35 E9** 39 10N 117 10 E
Grand Canyon, *U.S.A.* ... **83 H7** 36 3N 112 9W
Grand Canyon National Park, *U.S.A.* **83 H7** 36 15N 112 30W
Grand Cayman, *Cayman Is.* **88 C3** 19 20N 81 20W
Grand Coulee, *U.S.A.* **82 C4** 47 57N 119 0W
Grand Coulee Dam, *U.S.A.* **82 C4** 47 57N 118 59W
Grand Falls, *Canada* **71 C8** 48 56N 55 40W
Grand Forks, *Canada* **72 D5** 49 0N 118 30W
Grand Forks, *U.S.A.* **80 B6** 47 55N 97 3W
Grand Haven, *U.S.A.* **76 D2** 43 4N 86 13W
Grand I., *U.S.A.* **76 B2** 46 31N 86 40W
Grand Island, *U.S.A.* **80 E5** 40 55N 98 21W
Grand Isle, *U.S.A.* **81 L10** 29 14N 90 0W
Grand Junction, *U.S.A.* .. **83 G9** 39 4N 108 33W
Grand L., *N.B., Canada* .. **71 C6** 45 57N 66 7W
Grand L., *Nfld., Canada* .. **71 C8** 49 0N 57 30W
Grand L., *Nfld., Canada* .. **71 B7** 53 40N 60 30W
Grand L., *U.S.A.* **81 L8** 29 55N 92 47W
Grand Lac Victoria, *Canada* **70 C4** 47 35N 77 35W
Grand Lake, *U.S.A.* **82 F11** 40 15N 105 49W
Grand Manan I., *Canada* . **71 D6** 44 45N 66 52W
Grand Marais, *Canada* .. **80 B9** 47 45N 90 25W
Grand Marais, *U.S.A.* ... **76 B3** 46 40N 85 59W
Grand-Mère, *Canada* **70 C5** 46 36N 72 40W
Grand Portage, *U.S.A.* ... **70 C2** 47 58N 89 41W
Grand Prairie, *U.S.A.* ... **81 J6** 32 47N 97 0W
Grand Rapids, *Canada* .. **73 C9** 53 12N 99 19W
Grand Rapids, *Mich., U.S.A.* **76 D2** 42 58N 85 40W
Grand Rapids, *Minn., U.S.A.* **80 B8** 47 14N 93 31W
Grand St-Bernard, Col du, *Europe* .... **18 D7** 45 50N 7 10 E
Grand Teton, *U.S.A.* **82 E8** 43 54N 111 50W
Grand Union Canal, *U.K.* **11 E7** 52 7N 0 53W
Grand Valley, *U.S.A.* **82 G9** 39 27N 108 3W
Grand View, *Canada* **73 C8** 51 10N 100 42W
Grande →, *Jujuy, Argentina* **94 A2** 24 20S 65 2W
Grande →, *Mendoza, Argentina* **94 D2** 36 52S 69 45W
Grande →, *Bolivia* **92 G6** 15 51S 64 39W
Grande →, *Bahia, Brazil* **93 F10** 11 30S 44 30W
Grande →, *Minas Gerais, Brazil* **93 H8** 20 6S 51 4W
Grande, B., *Argentina* ... **96 G3** 50 30S 68 20W
Grande, Rio →, *U.S.A.* .. **81 N6** 25 58N 97 9W
Grande Baie, *Canada* **71 C5** 48 19N 70 52W
Grande Baleine, R. de la →, *Canada* **70 A4** 55 16N 77 47W
Grande Cache, *Canada* .. **72 C5** 53 53N 119 8W
Grande de Santiago →, *Mexico* **86 C3** 21 36N 105 26W
Grande-Entrée, *Canada* .. **71 C7** 47 30N 61 40W
Grande Prairie, *Canada* .. **72 B5** 55 10N 118 50W
Grande-Rivière, *Canada* . **71 C7** 48 26N 64 30W
Grande-Vallée, *Canada* .. **71 C6** 49 14N 65 8W
Grandes-Bergeronnes, *Canada* **71 C6** 48 16N 69 35W
Grandfalls, *U.S.A.* **81 K3** 31 20N 102 51W
Grandoe Mines, *Canada* . **72 B3** 56 29N 129 54W
Grandview, *U.S.A.* **82 C4** 46 15N 119 54W
Graneros, *Chile* **94 C1** 34 5S 70 45W
Grangemouth, *U.K.* **12 E5** 56 1N 3 42W
Granger, *Wash., U.S.A.* .. **82 C3** 46 21N 120 11W
Granger, *Wyo., U.S.A.* ... **82 F9** 41 35N 109 58W
Grangeville, *U.S.A.* **82 D5** 45 56N 116 7W
Granite City, *U.S.A.* **80 F9** 38 42N 90 9W
Granite Falls, *U.S.A.* ... **80 C7** 44 49N 95 33W
Granite Mt., *U.S.A.* **85 M10** 33 5N 116 28W
Granite Peak, *Australia* .. **61 E3** 25 40S 121 20 E
Granite Peak, *U.S.A.* ... **82 D9** 45 10N 109 48W
Granity, *N.Z.* .... **59 J3** 41 39S 171 51 E
Granja, *Brazil* **93 D10** 3 7S 40 50W
Granollers, *Spain* ..... **19 B7** 41 39N 2 18 E
Grant, *U.S.A.* **80 E4** 40 53N 101 42W
Grant, Mt., *U.S.A.* **82 G4** 38 34N 118 48W
Grant City, *U.S.A.* **80 E7** 40 29N 94 25W
Grant I., *Australia* ..... **60 B5** 11 10S 132 52 E
Grant Range, *U.S.A.* **83 G6** 38 30N 115 25W
Grantham, *U.K.* **10 E7** 52 55N 0 38W
Grantown-on-Spey, *U.K.* . **12 D5** 57 20N 3 36W
Grants, *U.S.A.* **83 J10** 35 9N 107 52W
Grants Pass, *U.S.A.* **82 E2** 42 26N 123 19W
Grantsburg, *U.S.A.* **80 C8** 45 47N 92 41W
Grantsville, *U.S.A.* **82 F7** 40 36N 112 28W
Granville, *France* **18 B3** 48 50N 1 35W
Granville, *N. Dak., U.S.A.* **80 A4** 48 16N 100 47W
Granville, *N.Y., U.S.A.* ... **76 D9** 43 24N 73 16W
Granville L., *Canada* **73 B8** 56 18N 100 30W
Grapeland, *U.S.A.* **81 K7** 31 30N 95 29W
Graskop, *S. Africa* ..... **57 C5** 24 56S 30 49 E
Grass →, *Canada* **73 B9** 56 3N 96 33W
Grass Range, *U.S.A.* **82 C9** 47 0N 109 0W
Grass River Prov. Park, *Canada* **73 C8** 54 40N 100 50W
Grass Valley, *Calif., U.S.A.* **84 F6** 39 13N 121 4W
Grass Valley, *Oreg., U.S.A.* **82 D3** 45 22N 120 47W
Grasse, *France* .... **18 E7** 43 38N 6 56 E
Grassmere, *Australia* .... **63 E3** 31 24S 142 38 E
Graulhet, *France* ..... **18 E4** 43 45N 1 59 E
Gravelbourg, *Canada* **73 D7** 49 50N 106 35W
's-Gravenhage, *Neths.* ... **15 B4** 52 7N 4 17 E
Gravenhurst, *Canada* **78 B5** 44 52N 79 20W
Gravesend, *Australia* .... **63 D5** 29 35S 150 20 E
Gravesend, *U.K.* .... **11 F8** 51 26N 0 22 E
Gravois, Pointe-à-, *Haiti* . **89 C5** 18 15N 73 56W
Grayling, *U.S.A.* **76 C3** 44 40N 84 43W
Grayling →, *Canada* **72 B4** 59 21N 125 0W
Grays Harbor, *U.S.A.* **82 C1** 46 59N 124 1W
Grays L., *U.S.A.* **82 E8** 43 4N 111 26W
Grays River, *U.S.A.* **84 D3** 46 21N 123 37W
Grayson, *Canada* **73 C8** 50 45N 102 40W
Graz, *Austria* .... **16 E8** 47 4N 15 27 E
Greasy L., *Canada* **72 A4** 62 55N 122 12W
Great Abaco I., *Bahamas* **88 A4** 26 25N 77 10W
Great Artesian Basin, *Australia* .... **62 C3** 23 0S 144 0 E
Great Australian Bight, *Australia* .... **61 F5** 33 30S 130 0 E
Great Bahama Bank, *Bahamas* **88 B4** 23 15N 78 0W
Great Barrier I., *N.Z.* .... **59 G5** 36 11S 175 25 E
Great Barrier Reef, *Australia* .... **62 B4** 18 0S 146 50 E
Great Barrington, *U.S.A.* . **79 D11** 42 12N 73 22W
Great Basin, *U.S.A.* **82 G5** 40 0N 117 0W
Great Bear →, *Canada* .. **68 B7** 65 0N 124 0W
Great Bear L., *Canada* .. **68 B8** 65 30N 120 0W
Great Belt = Store Bælt, *Denmark* .... **9 J14** 55 20N 11 0 E
Great Bend, *Kans., U.S.A.* **80 F5** 38 22N 98 46W
Great Bend, *Pa., U.S.A.* .. **79 E9** 41 58N 75 45W
Great Blasket I., *Ireland* .. **13 D1** 52 6N 10 32W
Great Britain, *Europe* **6 E5** 54 0N 2 15W
Great Central, *Canada* ... **72 D3** 49 20N 125 10W
Great Dividing Ra., *Australia* .... **62 C4** 23 0S 146 0 E
Great Driffield = Driffield, *U.K.* **10 C7** 54 0N 0 26W
Great Exuma I., *Bahamas* **88 B4** 23 30N 75 50W
Great Falls, *Canada* **73 C9** 50 27N 96 1W
Great Falls, *U.S.A.* **82 C8** 47 30N 111 17W
Great Fish = Groot Vis →, *S. Africa* ..... **56 E4** 33 28S 27 5 E
Great Guana Cay, *Bahamas* **88 B4** 24 0N 76 20W
Great Harbour Deep, *Canada* **71 B8** 50 25N 56 32W
Great I., *Canada* **73 B9** 58 53N 96 35W
Great Inagua I., *Bahamas* **89 B5** 21 0N 73 20W
Great Indian Desert = Thar Desert, *India* ..... **42 F5** 28 0N 72 0 E
Great Karoo, *S. Africa* ... **56 E3** 31 55S 21 0 E
Great Lake, *Australia* ... **62 G4** 41 50S 146 40 E
Great Malvern, *U.K.* **11 E5** 52 7N 2 18W
Great Ormes Head, *U.K.* . **10 D4** 53 20N 3 52W
Great Ouse →, *U.K.* ..... **10 E8** 52 48N 0 21 E
Great Palm I., *Australia* .. **62 B4** 18 45S 146 40 E
Great Plains, *N. Amer.* .. **74 A6** 47 0N 105 0W
Great Ruaha →, *Tanzania* **54 D4** 7 56S 37 52 E
Great Saint Bernard Pass = Grand St-Bernard, Col du, *Europe* .... **18 D7** 45 50N 7 10 E
Great Salt L., *U.S.A.* **82 F7** 41 15N 112 40W
Great Salt Lake Desert, *U.S.A.* **82 F7** 40 50N 113 30W
Great Salt Plains L., *U.S.A.* **81 G5** 36 45N 98 8W
Great Sandy Desert, *Australia* .... **60 D3** 21 0S 124 0 E
Great Sangi = Sangihe, Pulau, *Indonesia* ..... **37 D7** 3 45N 125 30 E
Great Skellig, *Ireland* **13 E1** 51 47N 10 33W
Great Slave L., *Canada* .. **72 A5** 61 23N 115 38W
Great Smoky Mts. Nat. Park, *U.S.A.* **77 H4** 35 40N 83 40W
Great Stour = Stour →, *U.K.* .... **11 F9** 51 18N 1 22 E
Great Victoria Desert, *Australia* .... **61 E4** 29 30S 126 30 E
Great Wall, *China* ..... **34 E5** 38 30N 109 30 E
Great Whernside, *U.K.* .. **10 C6** 54 10N 1 58W
Great Yarmouth, *U.K.* ... **11 E9** 52 37N 1 44 E
Greater Antilles, *W. Indies* **89 C5** 17 40N 74 0W
Greater London □, *U.K.* . **11 F7** 51 31N 0 6W
Greater Manchester □, *U.K.* **10 D5** 53 30N 2 15W
Greater Sunda Is., *Indonesia* .... **36 F4** 7 0S 112 0 E
Greco, C., *Cyprus* ..... **23 E13** 34 57N 34 5 E
Gredos, Sierra de, *Spain* . **19 B3** 40 20N 5 0W
Greece, *U.S.A.* **78 C7** 43 13N 77 41W
Greece ■, *Europe* ..... **21 E9** 40 0N 23 0 E
Greeley, *Colo., U.S.A.* ... **80 E2** 40 25N 104 42W
Greeley, *Nebr., U.S.A.* ... **80 E5** 41 33N 98 32W
Greem-Bell, Ostrov, *Russia* **26 A7** 81 0N 62 0 E
Green →, *Ky., U.S.A.* ... **76 G2** 37 54N 87 30W
Green →, *Utah, U.S.A.* .. **83 G9** 38 11N 109 53W
Green B., *U.S.A.* **76 C2** 45 0N 87 30W
Green Bay, *U.S.A.* **76 C2** 44 31N 88 0W
Green C., *Australia* ..... **63 F5** 37 13S 150 1 E
Green Cove Springs, *U.S.A.* **77 L5** 29 59N 81 42W
Green River, *U.S.A.* **83 G8** 38 59N 110 10W
Greenbank, *U.S.A.* **84 B4** 48 6N 122 34W
Greenbush, *Mich., U.S.A.* **78 B1** 44 35N 83 19W
Greenbush, *Minn., U.S.A.* **80 A6** 48 42N 96 11W
Greencastle, *U.S.A.* **76 F2** 39 38N 86 52W
Greene, *U.S.A.* **79 D9** 42 20N 75 46W
Greenfield, *Calif., U.S.A.* . **84 J5** 36 19N 121 15W
Greenfield, *Calif., U.S.A.* . **85 K8** 35 15N 119 0W
Greenfield, *Ind., U.S.A.* .. **76 F3** 39 47N 85 46W
Greenfield, *Iowa, U.S.A.* . **80 E7** 41 18N 94 28W
Greenfield, *Mass., U.S.A.* **79 D12** 42 35N 72 36W
Greenfield, *Mo., U.S.A.* .. **81 G8** 37 25N 93 51W
Greenfield Park, *Canada* . **79 A11** 45 29N 73 29W
Greenland ■, *N. Amer.* .. **66 C15** 66 0N 45 0W

Greenock

Greenock, U.K. 12 F4 55 57N 4 46W
Greenore, Ireland 13 B5 54 2N 6 8W
Greenore Pt., Ireland 13 D5 52 14N 6 19W
Greenough →, Australia 61 E1 28 51S 114 38 E
Greenport, U.S.A. 79 E12 41 6N 72 22W
Greensboro, Ga., U.S.A. 77 J4 33 35N 83 11W
Greensboro, N.C., U.S.A. 77 G6 36 4N 79 48W
Greensburg, Ind., U.S.A. 76 F3 39 20N 85 29W
Greensburg, Kans., U.S.A. 81 G5 37 36N 99 18W
Greensburg, Pa., U.S.A. 78 F5 40 18N 79 33W
Greenstone Pt., U.K. 12 D3 57 55N 5 37W
Greenville, Ala., U.S.A. 77 K2 31 50N 86 38W
Greenville, Calif., U.S.A. 84 E6 40 8N 120 57W
Greenville, Ill., U.S.A. 80 F10 38 53N 89 25W
Greenville, Maine, U.S.A. 71 C6 45 28N 69 35W
Greenville, Mich., U.S.A. 76 D3 43 11N 85 15W
Greenville, Miss., U.S.A. 81 J9 33 24N 91 4W
Greenville, N.C., U.S.A. 77 H7 35 37N 77 23W
Greenville, Ohio, U.S.A. 76 E3 40 6N 84 38W
Greenville, Pa., U.S.A. 78 E4 41 24N 80 23W
Greenville, S.C., U.S.A. 77 H4 34 51N 82 24W
Greenville, Tenn., U.S.A. 77 G4 36 13N 82 51W
Greenville, Tex., U.S.A. 81 J6 33 8N 96 7W
Greenwater Lake Prov. Park, Canada 73 C8 52 32N 103 30W
Greenwich, U.K. 11 F8 51 29N 0 1 E
Greenwich, Conn., U.S.A. 79 E11 41 2N 73 38W
Greenwich, N.Y., U.S.A. 79 C11 43 5N 73 30W
Greenwich, Ohio, U.S.A. 78 E2 41 2N 82 31W
Greenwood, Canada 72 D5 49 10N 118 40W
Greenwood, Miss., U.S.A. 81 J9 33 31N 90 11W
Greenwood, S.C., U.S.A. 77 H4 34 12N 82 10W
Greenwood, Mt., Australia 60 B5 13 48S 130 4 E
Gregory, U.S.A. 80 D5 43 14N 99 20W
Gregory →, Australia 62 B2 17 53S 139 17 E
Gregory, L., S. Austral., Australia 63 D2 28 55S 139 0 E
Gregory, L., W. Austral., Australia 61 E2 25 38S 119 58 E
Gregory Downs, Australia 62 B2 18 35S 138 45 E
Gregory L., Australia 60 D4 20 0S 127 40 E
Gregory Ra., Queens., Australia 62 B3 19 30S 143 40 E
Gregory Ra., W. Austral., Australia 60 D3 21 20S 121 12 E
Greifswald, Germany 16 A7 54 5N 13 23 E
Greiz, Germany 16 C7 50 39N 12 10 E
Gremikha, Russia 24 A6 67 59N 39 47 E
Grenå, Denmark 9 H14 56 25N 10 53 E
Grenada, U.S.A. 81 J10 33 47N 89 49W
Grenada ■, W. Indies 89 D7 12 10N 61 40W
Grenadines, W. Indies 89 D7 12 40N 61 20W
Grenen, Denmark 9 H14 57 44N 10 40 E
Grenfell, Australia 63 E4 33 52S 148 8 E
Grenfell, Canada 73 C8 50 30N 102 56W
Grenoble, France 18 D6 45 12N 5 42 E
Grenora, U.S.A. 80 A3 48 37N 103 56W
Grenville, C., Australia 62 A3 12 0S 143 13 E
Grenville Chan., Canada 72 C3 53 40N 129 46W
Gresham, U.S.A. 84 E4 45 30N 122 26W
Gresik, Indonesia 37 G15 7 13S 112 38 E
Gretna, U.K. 12 F5 55 0N 3 3W
Grevenmacher, Lux. 15 E6 49 41N 6 26 E
Grey →, N.Z. 59 K3 42 27S 171 12 E
Grey, C., Australia 62 A2 13 0S 136 35 E
Grey Ra., Australia 63 D3 27 0S 143 30 E
Grey Res., Canada 71 C8 48 20N 56 30W
Greybull, U.S.A. 82 D9 44 30N 108 3W
Greymouth, N.Z. 59 K3 42 29S 171 13 E
Greystones, Ireland 13 C5 53 9N 6 5W
Greytown, N.Z. 59 J5 41 5S 175 29 E
Greytown, S. Africa 57 D5 29 1S 30 36 E
Gribbell I., Canada 72 C3 53 23N 129 0W
Gridley, U.S.A. 84 F5 39 22N 121 42W
Griekwastad, S. Africa 56 D3 28 49S 23 15 E
Griffin, U.S.A. 77 J3 33 15N 84 16W
Griffith, Australia 63 E4 34 18S 146 2 E
Grimaylov = Hrymayliv, Ukraine 17 D14 49 20N 26 5 E
Grimes, U.S.A. 84 F5 39 4N 121 54W
Grimsay, U.K. 12 D1 57 29N 7 14W
Grimsby, Canada 78 C5 43 12N 79 34W
Grimsby, U.K. 10 D7 53 34N 0 5W
Grímsey, Iceland 8 C5 66 33N 17 58W
Grimshaw, Canada 72 B5 56 10N 117 40W
Grimstad, Norway 9 G13 58 20N 8 35 E
Grinnell, U.S.A. 80 E8 41 45N 92 43W
Gris-Nez, C., France 18 A4 50 52N 1 35 E
Groais I., Canada 71 B8 50 55N 55 35W
Groblersdal, S. Africa 57 D4 25 15S 29 25 E
Grodno = Hrodna, Belarus 24 D3 53 42N 23 52 E
Grodzyanka = Hrodzyanka, Belarus 17 B15 53 31N 28 42 E
Groesbeck, U.S.A. 81 K6 30 48N 96 31W
Grójec, Poland 17 C11 51 50N 20 58 E
Grong, Norway 8 D15 64 25N 12 8 E
Groningen, Neths. 15 A6 53 15N 6 35 E
Groningen □, Neths. 15 A6 53 16N 6 40 E
Groom, U.S.A. 81 H4 35 12N 101 6W
Groot →, S. Africa 56 E3 33 45S 24 36 E
Groot Berg →, S. Africa 56 E2 32 47S 18 8 E
Groot-Brakrivier, S. Africa 56 E3 34 2S 22 18 E
Groot-Kei →, S. Africa 57 E4 32 41S 28 22 E
Groot Vis →, S. Africa 56 E4 33 28S 27 5 E
Groote Eylandt, Australia 62 A2 14 0S 136 40 E
Grootfontein, Namibia 56 B2 19 31S 18 6 E
Grootlaagte →, Africa 56 C3 20 55S 21 27 E
Grootvloer, S. Africa 56 E3 30 0S 20 40 E
Gros C., Canada 72 A6 61 59N 113 32W
Grossa, Pta., Spain 22 B8 39 6N 1 36 E
Grosser Arber, Germany 16 D7 49 6N 13 8 E
Grosseto, Italy 20 C4 42 46N 11 8 E
Grossglockner, Austria 16 E7 47 5N 12 40 E
Groswater B., Canada 71 B8 54 20N 57 40W
Groton, Conn., U.S.A. 79 E12 41 21N 72 5W
Groton, S. Dak., U.S.A. 80 C5 45 27N 98 6W
Grouard Mission, Canada 72 B5 55 33N 116 9W
Groundhog →, Canada 70 C3 48 45N 82 58W
Grouse Creek, U.S.A. 82 F7 41 42N 113 53W
Grouw, Neths. 15 A5 53 5N 5 51 E
Grove City, U.S.A. 78 E4 41 10N 80 5W
Groveland, U.S.A. 84 H6 37 50N 120 14W
Grover City, U.S.A. 85 K6 35 7N 120 37W
Groveton, N.H., U.S.A. 79 B13 44 36N 71 31W
Groveton, Tex., U.S.A. 81 K7 31 4N 95 8W
Groznyy, Russia 25 F8 43 20N 45 45 E
Grudziądz, Poland 17 B10 53 30N 18 47 E
Gruinard B., U.K. 12 D3 57 56N 5 35W
Grundy Center, U.S.A. 80 D8 42 22N 92 47W
Gruver, U.S.A. 81 G4 36 16N 101 24W
Gryazi, Russia 24 D6 52 30N 39 58 E
Gryazovets, Russia 26 D5 58 50N 40 10 E
Gua, India 41 H14 22 18N 85 20 E
Gua Musang, Malaysia 39 K3 4 53N 101 58 E
Guacanayabo, G. de, Cuba 88 B4 20 40N 77 20W
Guachípas →, Argentina 94 B2 25 40S 65 30W
Guadalajara, Mexico 86 C4 20 40N 103 20W
Guadalajara, Spain 19 B4 40 37N 3 12W
Guadalcanal, Solomon Is. 64 H8 9 32S 160 12 E
Guadales, Argentina 94 C2 34 30S 67 55W
Guadalete →, Spain 19 D2 36 35N 6 13W
Guadalquivir →, Spain 19 D2 36 47N 6 22W
Guadalupe = Guadeloupe ■, W. Indies 89 C7 16 20N 61 40W
Guadalupe, Mexico 85 N10 32 4N 116 32W
Guadalupe, U.S.A. 85 L6 34 59N 120 33W
Guadalupe →, Mexico 85 N10 32 6N 116 51W
Guadalupe →, U.S.A. 81 L6 28 27N 96 47W
Guadalupe, Sierra de, Spain 19 C3 39 28N 5 30W
Guadalupe Bravos, Mexico 86 A3 31 20N 106 10W
Guadalupe I., Pac. Oc. 66 G8 29 0N 118 50W
Guadalupe Peak, U.S.A. 83 L11 31 50N 104 52W
Guadalupe y Calvo, Mexico 86 B3 26 6N 106 58W
Guadarrama, Sierra de, Spain 19 B4 41 0N 4 0W
Guadeloupe ■, W. Indies 89 C7 16 20N 61 40W
Guadeloupe Passage, W. Indies 89 C7 16 50N 62 15W
Guadiana →, Portugal 19 D2 37 14N 7 22W
Guadix, Spain 19 D4 37 18N 3 11W
Guafo, Boca del, Chile 96 E2 43 35S 74 0W
Guainía →, Colombia 92 C5 2 1N 67 7W
Guaíra, Brazil 95 A5 24 5S 54 10W
Guaitecas, Is., Chile 96 E2 44 0S 74 30W
Guajará-Mirim, Brazil 92 F5 10 50S 65 20W
Guajira, Pen. de la, Colombia 92 A4 12 0N 72 0W
Gualán, Guatemala 88 C2 15 8N 89 22W
Gualeguay, Argentina 94 C4 33 10S 59 14W
Gualeguaychú, Argentina 94 C4 33 3S 59 31W
Guam ■, Pac. Oc. 64 F6 13 27N 144 45 E
Guaminí, Argentina 94 D3 37 1S 62 28W
Guamúchil, Mexico 86 B3 25 25N 108 3W
Guanabacoa, Cuba 88 B3 23 8N 82 18W
Guanacaste, Cordillera del, Costa Rica 88 D2 10 40N 85 4W
Guanaceví, Mexico 86 B3 25 40N 106 0W
Guanahani = San Salvador, Bahamas 89 B5 24 0N 74 40W
Guanajay, Cuba 88 B3 22 56N 82 42W
Guanajuato, Mexico 86 C4 21 0N 101 20W
Guanajuato □, Mexico 86 C4 20 40N 101 20W
Guandacol, Argentina 94 B2 29 30S 68 40W
Guane, Cuba 88 B3 22 10N 84 7W
Guangdong □, China 33 D6 23 0N 113 0 E
Guangling, China 34 E8 39 47N 114 22 E
Guangrao, China 35 F10 37 5N 118 25 E
Guangwu, China 34 F3 37 48N 105 57 E
Guangxi Zhuangzu Zizhiqu □, China 33 D5 24 0N 109 0 E
Guangzhou, China 33 D6 23 5N 113 10 E
Guanipa →, Venezuela 92 B6 9 56N 62 26W
Guannan, China 35 G10 34 8N 119 21 E
Guantánamo, Cuba 89 B4 20 10N 75 14W
Guantao, China 34 F8 36 42N 115 25 E
Guanyun, China 35 G10 34 20N 119 18 E
Guápiles, Costa Rica 88 D3 10 10N 83 46W
Guaporé →, Brazil 92 F5 11 55S 65 4W
Guaqui, Bolivia 92 G5 16 41S 68 54W
Guarapari, Brazil 95 A7 20 40S 40 30W
Guarapuava, Brazil 95 B5 25 20S 51 30W
Guaratinguetá, Brazil 95 A6 22 49S 45 9W
Guaratuba, Brazil 95 B6 25 53S 48 38W
Guarda, Portugal 19 B2 40 32N 7 20W
Guardafui, C. = Asir, Ras, Somali Rep. 46 E5 11 55N 51 10 E
Guaria □, Paraguay 94 B4 25 45S 56 30W
Guárico □, Venezuela 92 B5 8 40N 66 35W
Guarujá, Brazil 95 A6 24 2S 46 25W
Guarus, Brazil 95 A7 21 44S 41 20W
Guasave, Mexico 86 B3 25 34N 108 27W
Guasdualito, Venezuela 92 B4 7 15N 70 44W
Guatemala, Guatemala 88 D1 14 40N 90 22W
Guatemala ■, Cent. Amer. 88 C1 15 40N 90 30W
Guaviare →, Colombia 92 C5 4 3N 67 44W
Guaxupé, Brazil 95 A6 21 10S 47 5W
Guayama, Puerto Rico 89 C6 17 59N 66 7W
Guayaquil, Ecuador 92 D3 2 15S 79 52W
Guayaquil, G. de, Ecuador 92 D2 3 10S 81 0W
Guaymas, Mexico 86 B2 27 59N 110 54W
Guba, Dem. Rep. of the Congo 55 E2 10 38S 26 27 E
Gudbrandsdalen, Norway 9 F14 61 33N 10 10 E
Guddu Barrage, Pakistan 40 E6 28 30N 69 50 E
Gudivada, India 41 L12 16 30N 81 3 E
Gudur, India 40 M11 14 12N 79 55 E
Guecho = Getxo, Spain 19 A4 43 21N 2 59W
Guelph, Canada 70 D3 43 35N 80 20W
Guéret, France 18 C4 46 11N 1 51 E
Guerneville, U.S.A. 84 G4 38 30N 123 0W
Guernica = Gernika-Lumo, Spain 19 A4 43 19N 2 40W
Guernsey, U.K. 11 H5 49 26N 2 35W
Guernsey, U.S.A. 80 D2 42 19N 104 45W
Guerrero □, Mexico 87 D5 17 30N 100 0W
Gueydan, U.S.A. 81 K8 30 2N 92 31W
Gügher, Iran 45 D8 29 28N 56 27 E
Guia, Canary Is. 22 F4 28 8N 15 38W
Guia de Isora, Canary Is. 22 F3 28 12N 16 46W
Guia Lopes da Laguna, Brazil 95 A4 21 26S 56 7W
Guiana, S. Amer. 90 C4 5 10N 60 40W
Guidónia-Montecélio, Italy 20 C5 42 1N 12 45 E
Guijá, Mozam. 57 C5 24 27S 33 0 E
Guildford, U.K. 11 F7 51 14N 0 34W
Guilford, U.S.A. 71 C6 45 10N 69 23W
Guilin, China 33 D6 25 18N 110 15 E
Güimar, Canary Is. 22 F3 28 18N 16 24W
Guimarães, Portugal 19 B1 41 28N 8 24W
Guimaras, Phil. 37 B6 10 35N 122 37 E
Guinda, U.S.A. 84 G4 38 50N 122 12W
Guinea, Africa 48 F4 8 0N 8 0 E
Guinea ■, W. Afr. 50 F3 10 20N 11 30W
Guinea, Gulf of, Atl. Oc. 48 F4 3 0N 2 30 E
Guinea-Bissau ■, Africa 50 F3 12 0N 15 0W
Güines, Cuba 88 B3 22 50N 82 0W
Guingamp, France 18 B2 48 34N 3 10W
Güiria, Venezuela 92 A6 10 32N 62 18W
Guiuan, Phil. 37 B7 11 5N 125 55 E
Guiyang, China 32 D5 26 32N 106 40 E
Guizhou □, China 32 D5 27 0N 107 0 E
Gujarat □, India 42 H4 23 20N 71 0 E
Gujranwala, Pakistan 42 C6 32 10N 74 12 E
Gujrat, Pakistan 42 C6 32 40N 74 2 E
Gulbarga, India 40 L10 17 20N 76 50 E
Gulbene, Latvia 9 H22 57 8N 26 52 E
Gulf, The, Asia 45 E6 27 0N 50 0 E
Gulfport, U.S.A. 81 K10 30 22N 89 6W
Gulgong, Australia 63 E4 32 20S 149 49 E
Gulistan, Pakistan 42 D2 30 30N 66 35 E
Gull Lake, Canada 73 C7 50 10N 108 29W
Güllük, Turkey 21 F12 37 14N 27 35 E
Gulmarg, India 43 B6 34 3N 74 25 E
Gulshad, Kazakstan 26 E8 46 45N 74 25 E
Gulu, Uganda 54 B3 2 48N 32 17 E
Gulwe, Tanzania 54 D4 6 30S 36 25 E
Gum Lake, Australia 63 E3 32 42S 143 9 E
Gumal →, Pakistan 42 D4 31 40N 71 50 E
Gumbaz, Pakistan 42 D3 30 2N 69 0 E
Gumlu, Australia 62 B4 19 53S 147 41 E
Gumma □, Japan 31 F9 36 30N 138 20 E
Gumzai, Indonesia 37 F8 5 28S 134 42 E
Guna, India 42 G7 24 40N 77 19 E
Gundagai, Australia 63 F4 35 3S 148 6 E
Gunisao →, Canada 73 C9 53 56N 97 53W
Gunisao L., Canada 73 C9 53 33N 96 15W
Gunnedah, Australia 63 E5 30 59S 150 15 E
Gunningbar Cr. →, Australia 63 E4 31 14S 147 6 E
Gunnison, Colo., U.S.A. 83 G10 38 33N 106 56W
Gunnison, Utah, U.S.A. 82 G8 39 9N 111 49W
Gunnison →, U.S.A. 83 G9 39 4N 108 35W
Gunpowder, Australia 62 B2 19 42S 139 22 E
Guntakal, India 40 M10 15 11N 77 27 E
Guntersville, U.S.A. 77 H2 34 21N 86 18W
Guntong, Malaysia 39 K3 4 36N 101 3 E
Guntur, India 41 L12 16 23N 80 30 E
Gunungapi, Indonesia 37 F7 6 45S 126 30 E
Gunungsitoli, Indonesia 36 D1 1 15N 97 30 E
Gunza, Angola 52 G2 10 50S 13 50 E
Guo He →, China 35 H9 32 59N 117 10 E
Guoyang, China 34 H9 33 32N 116 12 E
Gupis, Pakistan 43 A5 36 15N 73 20 E
Gurdaspur, India 42 C6 32 5N 75 31 E
Gurdon, U.S.A. 81 J8 33 55N 93 9W
Gurgaon, India 42 E7 28 27N 77 1 E
Gurgueia →, Brazil 93 E10 6 50S 43 24W
Gurha, India 42 G4 25 12N 71 39 E
Guri, Embalse de, Venezuela 92 B6 7 50N 62 52W
Gurkha, Nepal 43 E11 28 5N 84 40 E
Gurley, Australia 63 D4 29 45S 149 48 E
Gurué, Mozam. 55 F4 15 25S 36 58 E
Gurun, Malaysia 39 K3 5 49N 100 27 E
Gurupá, Brazil 93 D8 1 25S 51 35W
Gurupá, I. Grande de, Brazil 93 D8 1 25S 51 45W
Gurupi, Brazil 93 F9 11 43S 49 4W
Gurupi →, Brazil 93 D9 1 13S 46 6W
Guryev = Atyraū, Kazakstan 25 E9 47 5N 52 0 E
Gusau, Nigeria 50 F7 12 12N 6 40 E
Gusev, Russia 9 J20 54 35N 22 10 E
Gushan, China 35 E12 39 50N 123 35 E
Gushgy, Turkmenistan 26 F7 35 20N 62 18 E
Gusinoozersk, Russia 27 D11 51 16N 106 27 E
Gustine, U.S.A. 84 H6 37 16N 121 0W
Güstrow, Germany 16 B7 53 47N 12 10 E
Gütersloh, Germany 16 C5 51 54N 8 24 E
Gutha, Australia 61 E2 28 58S 115 55 E
Guthalongra, Australia 62 B4 19 52S 147 50 E
Guthrie, U.S.A. 81 H6 35 53N 97 25W
Guttenberg, U.S.A. 80 D9 42 47N 91 6W
Guyana ■, S. Amer. 92 C7 5 0N 59 0W
Guyane française = French Guiana ■, S. Amer. 93 C8 4 0N 53 0W
Guyang, China 34 D6 41 0N 110 5 E
Guyenne, France 18 D4 44 30N 0 40 E
Guymon, U.S.A. 81 G4 36 41N 101 29W
Guyra, Australia 63 E5 30 15S 151 40 E
Guyuan, Hebei, China 34 D8 41 37N 115 40 E
Guyuan, Ningxia Huizu, China 34 G4 36 0N 106 20 E
Guzhen, China 35 H9 33 22N 117 18 E
Guzmán, L. de, Mexico 86 A3 31 25N 107 25W
Gvardeysk, Russia 9 J19 54 39N 21 5 E
Gwa, Burma 41 L19 17 36N 94 34 E
Gwaai, Zimbabwe 55 F2 19 15S 27 45 E
Gwabegar, Australia 63 E4 30 31S 149 0 E
Gwādar, Pakistan 40 G3 25 10N 62 18 E
Gwalia, Australia 61 E3 28 54S 121 20 E
Gwalior, India 42 F8 26 12N 78 10 E
Gwanda, Zimbabwe 55 G2 20 55S 29 0 E
Gwane, Dem. Rep. of the Congo 54 B2 4 45N 25 48 E
Gweebarra B., Ireland 13 B3 54 51N 8 23W
Gweedore, Ireland 13 A3 55 3N 8 13W
Gweru, Zimbabwe 55 F2 19 28S 29 45 E
Gwinn, U.S.A. 76 B2 46 19N 87 27W
Gwydir →, Australia 63 D4 29 27S 149 48 E
Gwynedd □, U.K. 10 E3 52 52N 4 10W
Gyandzha = Gäncä, Azerbaijan 25 F8 40 45N 46 20 E
Gyaring Hu, China 32 C4 34 50N 97 40 E
Gydanskiy Poluostrov, Russia 26 C8 70 0N 78 0 E
Gympie, Australia 63 D5 26 11S 152 38 E
Gyöngyös, Hungary 17 E10 47 48N 19 56 E
Győr, Hungary 17 E9 47 41N 17 40 E
Gypsum Pt., Canada 72 A6 61 53N 114 35W
Gypsumville, Canada 73 C9 51 45N 98 40W
Gyula, Hungary 17 E11 46 38N 21 17 E
Gyumri, Armenia 25 F7 40 47N 43 50 E
Gyzylarbat, Turkmenistan 26 F6 39 4N 56 23 E

H

Ha 'Arava →, Israel 47 E4 30 50N 35 20 E
Ha Coi, Vietnam 38 B6 21 26N 107 46 E
Ha Dong, Vietnam 38 B5 20 58N 105 46 E
Ha Giang, Vietnam 38 A5 22 50N 104 59 E
Ha Tien, Vietnam 39 G5 10 23N 104 29 E
Ha Tinh, Vietnam 38 C5 18 20N 105 54 E
Ha Trung, Vietnam 38 C5 19 58N 105 50 E
Haaksbergen, Neths. 15 B6 52 9N 6 45 E
Haapsalu, Estonia 9 G20 58 56N 23 30 E
Haarlem, Neths. 15 B4 52 23N 4 39 E
Haast →, N.Z. 59 K2 43 50S 169 2 E
Haast Bluff, Australia 60 D5 23 22S 132 0 E
Hab Nadi Chauki, Pakistan 42 G2 25 0N 66 50 E
Habaswein, Kenya 54 B4 1 2N 39 30 E
Habay, Canada 72 B5 58 50N 118 44W
Ḩabbānīyah, Iraq 44 C4 33 17N 43 29 E
Haboro, Japan 30 B10 44 22N 141 42 E
Hachijō-Jima, Japan 31 H9 33 5N 139 45 E
Hachinohe, Japan 30 D10 40 30N 141 29 E
Hachiōji, Japan 31 G9 35 40N 139 20 E
Hachŏn, N. Korea 35 D15 41 29N 129 2 E
Hackensack, U.S.A. 79 F10 40 53N 74 3W
Hadali, Pakistan 42 C5 32 16N 72 11 E
Hadarba, Ras, Sudan 51 D13 22 4N 36 51 E
Hadarom □, Israel 47 E4 31 0N 35 0 E
Haden, Australia 63 D5 27 13S 151 54 E
Hadera, Israel 47 C3 32 27N 34 55 E
Hadera, N. →, Israel 47 C3 32 28N 34 52 E
Haderslev, Denmark 9 J13 55 15N 9 30 E
Hadhramaut = Ḩaḑramawt, Yemen 46 D4 15 30N 49 30 E
Hadong, S. Korea 35 G14 35 5N 127 44 E
Ḩaḑramawt, Yemen 46 D4 15 30N 49 30 E
Ḩadrānīyah, Iraq 44 C4 35 38N 43 14 E
Hadrian's Wall, U.K. 10 B5 55 0N 2 30W
Haeju, N. Korea 35 E13 38 3N 125 45 E
Haenam, S. Korea 35 G14 34 34N 126 35 E
Haerhpin = Harbin, China 35 B14 45 48N 126 40 E
Hafar al Bāţin, Si. Arabia 44 D5 28 32N 45 52 E
Ḩafīrat al 'Aydā, Si. Arabia 44 E3 26 26N 39 12 E
Hafizabad, Pakistan 42 C5 32 5N 73 40 E
Haflong, India 41 G18 25 10N 93 5 E
Hafnarfjörður, Iceland 8 D3 64 4N 21 57W
Hafun, Ras, Somali Rep. 46 E5 10 29N 51 30 E
Hagalil, Israel 47 C4 32 53N 35 18 E
Hagen, Germany 16 C4 51 21N 7 27 E
Hagerman, U.S.A. 81 J2 33 7N 104 20W
Hagerstown, U.S.A. 76 F7 39 39N 77 43W
Hagfors, Sweden 9 F15 60 3N 13 45 E
Hagi, Japan 31 G5 34 30N 131 22 E
Hagolan, Syria 47 C4 33 0N 35 45 E
Hagondange, France 18 B7 49 16N 6 11 E
Hags Hd., Ireland 13 D2 52 57N 9 28W
Hague, C. de la, France 18 B3 49 44N 1 56W
Hague, The = 's-Gravenhage, Neths. 15 B4 52 7N 4 17 E
Haguenau, France 18 B7 48 49N 7 47 E
Hai □, Tanzania 54 C4 3 10S 37 10 E
Hai Duong, Vietnam 38 B6 20 56N 106 19 E
Haicheng, China 35 D12 40 50N 122 45 E
Haidar Khel, Afghan. 42 C3 33 58N 68 38 E
Haifa = Ḥefa, Israel 47 C4 32 46N 35 0 E
Haig, Australia 61 F4 30 55S 126 10 E
Haikou, China 33 D6 20 1N 110 16 E
Ḩā'il, Si. Arabia 44 E4 27 28N 41 45 E
Hailar, China 33 B6 49 10N 119 38 E
Hailey, U.S.A. 82 E6 43 31N 114 19W
Haileybury, Canada 70 C4 47 30N 79 38W
Hailin, China 35 B15 44 37N 129 30 E
Hailong, China 35 C13 42 32N 125 40 E
Hailuoto, Finland 8 D21 65 3N 24 45 E
Hainan □, China 33 E5 19 0N 109 30 E
Hainaut □, Belgium 15 D4 50 30N 4 0 E
Haines, U.S.A. 82 D5 44 55N 117 56W
Haines City, U.S.A. 77 L5 28 7N 81 38W
Haines Junction, Canada 72 A1 60 45N 137 30W
Haiphong, Vietnam 32 D5 20 47N 106 41 E
Haiti ■, W. Indies 89 C5 19 0N 72 30W
Haiya, Sudan 51 E13 18 20N 36 21 E
Haiyang, China 35 F11 36 47N 121 9 E
Haiyuan, China 34 F3 36 35N 105 52 E
Haizhou, China 35 G10 34 37N 119 7 E
Haizhou Wan, China 35 G10 34 50N 119 20 E
Hajdúböszörmény, Hungary 17 E11 47 40N 21 30 E
Hajipur, India 43 G11 25 45N 85 13 E
Ḩājjī Muḩsin, Iraq 44 C5 32 35N 45 29 E
Ḩājjīābād, Eşfahan, Iran 45 C7 33 41N 54 50 E
Ḩājjīābād, Hormozgān, Iran 45 D7 28 19N 55 55 E
Hajnówka, Poland 17 B12 52 47N 23 35 E
Hakansson, Mts., Dem. Rep. of the Congo 55 D2 8 40S 25 45 E
Hakken-Zan, Japan 31 G7 34 10N 135 54 E
Hakodate, Japan 30 D10 41 45N 140 44 E
Haku-San, Japan 31 F8 36 9N 136 46 E
Hakui, Japan 31 F8 36 53N 136 47 E
Hala, Pakistan 40 G6 25 43N 68 20 E
Ḩalab, Syria 44 B3 36 10N 37 15 E
Ḩalabjah, Iraq 44 C5 35 10N 45 58 E
Halaib, Sudan 51 D13 22 12N 36 30 E
Hālat 'Ammār, Si. Arabia 44 D3 29 10N 36 4 E
Halbā, Lebanon 47 A5 34 34N 36 6 E
Halberstadt, Germany 16 C6 51 54N 11 3 E
Halcombe, N.Z. 59 J5 40 8S 175 30 E
Halcon, Phil. 37 B6 13 0N 121 30 E
Halden, Norway 9 G14 59 9N 11 23 E

Helmand

Haldia, *India* 41 H16 22 5N 88 3 E
Haldwani, *India* 43 E8 29 31N 79 30 E
Hale →, *Australia* 62 C2 24 56S 135 53 E
Haleakala Crater, *U.S.A.* 74 H16 20 43N 156 16W
Halesowen, *U.K.* 11 E5 52 27N 2 3W
Haleyville, *U.S.A.* 77 H2 34 14N 87 37W
Halfway →, *Canada* 72 B4 56 12N 121 32W
Haliburton, *Canada* 70 C4 45 3N 78 30W
Halifax, *Australia* 62 B4 18 32S 146 22 E
Halifax, *Canada* 71 D7 44 38N 63 35W
Halifax, *U.K.* 10 D6 53 43N 1 52W
Halifax B., *Australia* 62 B4 18 50S 147 0 E
Halifax I., *Namibia* 56 D2 26 38S 15 4 E
Halīl →, *Iran* 45 E8 27 40N 58 30 E
Halkirk, *U.K.* 12 C5 58 30N 3 29W
Hall Pt., *Australia* 60 C3 15 40S 124 23 E
Halland, *Sweden* 9 H15 57 8N 12 47 E
Halle, *Belgium* 15 D4 50 44N 4 13 E
Halle, *Germany* 16 C6 51 30N 11 56 E
Hällefors, *Sweden* 9 G16 59 47N 14 31 E
Hallett, *Australia* 63 E2 33 25S 138 55 E
Hallettsville, *U.S.A.* 81 L6 29 27N 96 57W
Halliday, *U.S.A.* 80 B3 47 21N 102 20W
Halliday L., *Canada* 73 A7 61 21N 108 56W
Hallim, *S. Korea* 35 H14 33 24N 126 15 E
Hallingdalselvi →, *Norway* 9 F13 60 23N 9 35 E
Hallock, *U.S.A.* 73 D9 48 47N 96 57W
Halls Creek, *Australia* 60 C4 18 16S 127 38 E
Hallsberg, *Sweden* 9 G16 59 5N 15 7 E
Hallstead, *U.S.A.* 79 E9 41 58N 75 45W
Halmahera, *Indonesia* 37 D7 0 40N 128 0 E
Halmstad, *Sweden* 9 H15 56 41N 12 52 E
Hälsingborg = Helsingborg, *Sweden* 9 H15 56 3N 12 42 E
Hälsingland, *Sweden* 9 F16 61 40N 16 5 E
Halstad, *U.S.A.* 80 B6 47 21N 96 50W
Halstead, *U.K.* 11 F8 51 57N 0 40 E
Halti, *Finland* 8 B19 69 17N 21 18 E
Halton □, *U.K.* 10 D5 53 22N 2 45W
Haltwhistle, *U.K.* 10 C5 54 58N 2 26W
Halul, *Qatar* 45 E7 25 40N 52 40 E
Ḩalvān, *Iran* 45 C8 33 57N 56 15 E
Ham Tan, *Vietnam* 39 G6 10 40N 107 45 E
Ham Yen, *Vietnam* 38 A5 22 4N 105 3 E
Hamab, *Namibia* 56 D2 28 7S 19 16 E
Hamada, *Japan* 31 G6 34 56N 132 4 E
Hamadān, *Iran* 45 C6 34 52N 48 32 E
Hamadān □, *Iran* 45 C6 35 0N 49 0 E
Hamāh, *Syria* 44 C3 35 5N 36 40 E
Hamamatsu, *Japan* 31 G8 34 45N 137 45 E
Hamar, *Norway* 9 F14 60 48N 11 7 E
Hambantota, *Sri Lanka* 40 R12 6 10N 81 10 E
Hamber Prov. Park, *Canada* 72 C5 52 20N 118 0W
Hamburg, *Germany* 16 B5 53 33N 9 59 E
Hamburg, *Ark., U.S.A.* 81 J9 33 14N 91 48W
Hamburg, *Iowa, U.S.A.* 80 E7 40 36N 95 39W
Hamburg, *N.Y., U.S.A.* 78 D6 42 43N 78 50W
Hamburg, *Pa., U.S.A.* 79 F9 40 33N 75 59W
Ḩamd, W. al →, *Si. Arabia* 44 E3 24 55N 36 20 E
Hamden, *U.S.A.* 79 E12 41 23N 72 54W
Häme, *Finland* 9 F20 61 38N 25 10 E
Hämeenlinna, *Finland* 9 F21 61 0N 24 28 E
Hamelin Pool, *Australia* 61 E1 26 22S 114 20 E
Hameln, *Germany* 16 B5 52 6N 9 21 E
Hamerkaz □, *Israel* 47 C3 32 15N 34 55 E
Hamersley Ra., *Australia* 60 D2 22 0S 117 45 E
Hamhung, *N. Korea* 35 E14 39 54N 127 30 E
Hami, *China* 32 B4 42 55N 93 25 E
Hamilton, *Australia* 63 F3 37 45S 142 2 E
Hamilton, *Canada* 70 D4 43 15N 79 50W
Hamilton, *N.Z.* 59 G5 37 47S 175 19 E
Hamilton, *U.K.* 12 F4 55 46N 4 2W
Hamilton, *Mo., U.S.A.* 80 F8 39 45N 93 59W
Hamilton, *Mont., U.S.A.* 82 C6 46 15N 114 10W
Hamilton, *N.Y., U.S.A.* 79 D9 42 50N 75 33W
Hamilton, *Ohio, U.S.A.* 76 F3 39 24N 84 34W
Hamilton, *Tex., U.S.A.* 81 K5 31 42N 98 7W
Hamilton →, *Australia* 62 C2 23 30S 139 47 E
Hamilton City, *U.S.A.* 84 F4 39 45N 122 1W
Hamilton Hotel, *Australia* 62 C3 22 45S 140 40 E
Hamilton Inlet, *Canada* 71 B8 54 0N 57 30W
Hamina, *Finland* 9 F22 60 34N 27 12 E
Hamiota, *Canada* 73 C8 50 11N 100 38W
Hamlet, *U.S.A.* 77 H6 34 53N 79 42W
Hamley Bridge, *Australia* 63 E2 34 17S 138 35 E
Hamlin = Hameln, *Germany* 16 B5 52 6N 9 21 E
Hamlin, *N.Y., U.S.A.* 78 C7 43 17N 77 55W
Hamlin, *Tex., U.S.A.* 81 J4 32 53N 100 8W
Hamm, *Germany* 16 C4 51 40N 7 50 E
Hammerfest, *Norway* 8 A20 70 39N 23 41 E
Hammond, *Ind., U.S.A.* 76 E2 41 38N 87 30W
Hammond, *La., U.S.A.* 81 K9 30 30N 90 28W
Hammonton, *U.S.A.* 76 F8 39 39N 74 48W
Hampden, *N.Z.* 59 L3 45 18S 170 50 E
Hampshire □, *U.K.* 11 F6 51 7N 1 23W
Hampshire Downs, *U.K.* 11 F6 51 15N 1 10W
Hampton, *Ark., U.S.A.* 81 J8 33 32N 92 28W
Hampton, *Iowa, U.S.A.* 80 D8 42 45N 93 13W
Hampton, *N.H., U.S.A.* 79 D14 42 57N 70 50W
Hampton, *S.C., U.S.A.* 77 J5 32 52N 81 7W
Hampton, *Va., U.S.A.* 76 G7 37 2N 76 21W
Hampton Tableland, *Australia* 61 F4 32 0S 127 0 E
Hamyang, *S. Korea* 35 G14 35 32N 127 42 E
Han Pijesak, *Bos.-H.* 21 B8 44 5N 18 57 E
Hana, *U.S.A.* 74 H17 20 45N 155 59W
Hanak, *Si. Arabia* 44 E3 25 32N 37 0 E
Hanamaki, *Japan* 30 E10 39 23N 141 7 E
Hanang, *Tanzania* 54 C4 4 30S 35 25 E
Hanau, *Germany* 16 C5 50 7N 8 56 E
Hanbogd, *Mongolia* 34 C4 43 11N 107 10 E
Hancheng, *China* 34 G6 35 31N 110 25 E
Hancock, *Mich., U.S.A.* 80 B10 47 8N 88 35W
Hancock, *Minn., U.S.A.* 80 C7 45 30N 95 48W
Hancock, *N.Y., U.S.A.* 79 E9 41 57N 75 17W
Handa, *Japan* 31 G8 34 53N 136 55 E
Handan, *China* 34 F8 36 35N 114 28 E
Handeni, *Tanzania* 54 D4 5 25S 38 2 E
Handeni □, *Tanzania* 54 D4 5 30S 38 0 E
Handwara, *India* 43 B6 34 21N 74 20 E
Hanegev, *Israel* 47 E4 30 50N 35 0 E
Haney, *Canada* 72 D4 49 12N 122 40W
Hanford, *U.S.A.* 84 J7 36 20N 119 39W
Hang Chat, *Thailand* 38 C2 18 20N 99 21 E
Hang Dong, *Thailand* 38 C2 18 41N 98 55 E
Hangang →, *S. Korea* 35 F14 37 50N 126 30 E
Hangayn Nuruu, *Mongolia* 32 B4 47 30N 99 0 E
Hangchou = Hangzhou, *China* 33 C7 30 18N 120 11 E
Hanggin Houqi, *China* 34 D4 40 58N 107 4 E
Hanggin Qi, *China* 34 E5 39 52N 108 50 E
Hangu, *China* 35 E9 39 18N 117 53 E
Hangzhou, *China* 33 C7 30 18N 120 11 E
Hangzhou Wan, *China* 33 C7 30 15N 120 45 E
Hanhongor, *Mongolia* 34 C3 43 55N 104 28 E
Hanīdh, *Si. Arabia* 45 E6 26 35N 48 38 E
Ḩanīsh, *Yemen* 46 E3 13 45N 42 46 E
Hankinson, *U.S.A.* 80 B6 46 4N 96 54W
Hanko, *Finland* 9 G20 59 50N 22 57 E
Hanksville, *U.S.A.* 83 G8 38 22N 110 43W
Hanle, *India* 43 C8 32 42N 79 4 E
Hanmer Springs, *N.Z.* 59 K4 42 32S 172 50 E
Hann →, *Australia* 60 C4 17 26S 126 17 E
Hann, Mt., *Australia* 60 C4 15 45S 126 0 E
Hanna, *Canada* 72 C6 51 40N 111 54W
Hannaford, *U.S.A.* 80 B5 47 19N 98 11W
Hannah, *U.S.A.* 80 A5 48 58N 98 42W
Hannah B., *Canada* 70 B4 51 40N 80 0W
Hannibal, *U.S.A.* 80 F9 39 42N 91 22W
Hannover, *Germany* 16 B5 52 22N 9 46 E
Hanoi, *Vietnam* 32 D5 21 5N 105 55 E
Hanover = Hannover, *Germany* 16 B5 52 22N 9 46 E
Hanover, *Canada* 78 B3 44 9N 81 2W
Hanover, *S. Africa* 56 E3 31 4S 24 29 E
Hanover, *N.H., U.S.A.* 79 C12 43 42N 72 17W
Hanover, *Ohio, U.S.A.* 78 F2 40 4N 82 16W
Hanover, *Pa., U.S.A.* 76 F7 39 48N 76 59W
Hanover, I., *Chile* 96 G2 51 0S 74 50W
Hansi, *India* 42 E6 29 10N 75 57 E
Hanson, L., *Australia* 63 E2 31 0S 136 15 E
Hantsavichy, *Belarus* 17 B14 52 49N 26 30 E
Hanzhong, *China* 34 H4 33 10N 107 1 E
Hanzhuang, *China* 35 G9 34 33N 117 23 E
Haora, *India* 43 H13 22 37N 88 20 E
Haparanda, *Sweden* 8 D21 65 52N 24 8 E
Happy, *U.S.A.* 81 H4 34 45N 101 52W
Happy Camp, *U.S.A.* 82 F2 41 48N 123 23W
Happy Valley-Goose Bay, *Canada* 71 B7 53 15N 60 20W
Hapsu, *N. Korea* 35 D15 41 13N 128 51 E
Hapur, *India* 42 E7 28 45N 77 45 E
Ḩaql, *Si. Arabia* 47 F3 29 10N 34 58 E
Har, *Indonesia* 37 F8 5 16S 133 14 E
Har-Ayrag, *Mongolia* 34 B5 45 47N 109 16 E
Har Hu, *China* 32 C4 38 20N 97 38 E
Har Us Nuur, *Mongolia* 32 B4 48 0N 92 0 E
Har Yehuda, *Israel* 47 D3 31 35N 34 57 E
Ḩaraḑ, *Si. Arabia* 46 C4 24 22N 49 0 E
Haranomachi, *Japan* 30 F10 37 38N 140 58 E
Harare, *Zimbabwe* 55 F3 17 43S 31 2 E
Harbin, *China* 35 B14 45 48N 126 40 E
Harbor Beach, *U.S.A.* 76 D4 43 51N 82 39W
Harbor Springs, *U.S.A.* 76 C3 45 26N 85 0W
Harbour Breton, *Canada* 71 C8 47 29N 55 50W
Harbour Grace, *Canada* 71 C9 47 40N 53 22W
Harda, *India* 42 H7 22 27N 77 5 E
Hardangerfjorden, *Norway* 9 F12 60 5N 6 0 E
Hardangervidda, *Norway* 9 F12 60 7N 7 20 E
Hardap Dam, *Namibia* 56 C2 24 32S 17 50 E
Hardenberg, *Neths.* 15 B6 52 34N 6 37 E
Harderwijk, *Neths.* 15 B5 52 21N 5 38 E
Hardey →, *Australia* 60 D2 22 45S 116 8 E
Hardin, *U.S.A.* 82 D10 45 44N 107 37W
Harding, *S. Africa* 57 E4 30 35S 29 55 E
Harding Ra., *Australia* 60 C3 16 17S 124 55 E
Hardisty, *Canada* 72 C6 52 40N 111 18W
Hardman, *U.S.A.* 82 D4 45 10N 119 41W
Hardoi, *India* 43 F9 27 26N 80 6 E
Hardwar = Haridwar, *India* 42 E8 29 58N 78 9 E
Hardwick, *U.S.A.* 79 B12 44 30N 72 22W
Hardy, *U.S.A.* 81 G9 36 19N 91 29W
Hardy, Pen., *Chile* 96 H3 55 30S 68 20W
Hare B., *Canada* 71 B8 51 15N 55 45W
Hareid, *Norway* 9 E12 62 22N 6 1 E
Harer, *Ethiopia* 46 F3 9 20N 42 8 E
Hargeisa, *Somali Rep.* 46 F3 9 30N 44 2 E
Hari →, *Indonesia* 36 E2 1 16S 104 5 E
Haria, *Canary Is.* 22 E6 29 8N 13 32W
Haridwar, *India* 42 E8 29 58N 78 9 E
Haringhata →, *Bangla.* 41 J16 22 0N 89 58 E
Harīrūd →, *Asia* 40 A2 37 24N 60 38 E
Härjedalen, *Sweden* 9 E15 62 22N 13 5 E
Harlan, *Iowa, U.S.A.* 80 E7 41 39N 95 19W
Harlan, *Ky., U.S.A.* 77 G4 36 51N 83 19W
Harlech, *U.K.* 10 E3 52 52N 4 6W
Harlem, *U.S.A.* 82 B9 48 32N 108 47W
Harlingen, *Neths.* 15 A5 53 11N 5 25 E
Harlingen, *U.S.A.* 81 M6 26 12N 97 42W
Harlow, *U.K.* 11 F8 51 46N 0 8 E
Harlowton, *U.S.A.* 82 C9 46 26N 109 50W
Harney Basin, *U.S.A.* 82 E4 43 30N 119 0W
Harney L., *U.S.A.* 82 E4 43 14N 119 8W
Harney Peak, *U.S.A.* 80 D3 43 52N 103 32W
Härnösand, *Sweden* 9 E17 62 38N 17 55 E
Haroldswick, *U.K.* 12 A8 60 48N 0 50W
Harp L., *Canada* 71 A7 55 5N 61 50W
Harrand, *Pakistan* 42 E4 29 28N 70 3 E
Harriman, *U.S.A.* 77 H3 35 56N 84 33W
Harrington Harbour, *Canada* 71 B8 50 31N 59 30W
Harris, *U.K.* 12 D2 57 50N 6 55W
Harris, Sd. of, *U.K.* 12 D1 57 44N 7 6W
Harris L., *Australia* 63 E2 31 10S 135 10 E
Harrisburg, *Ill., U.S.A.* 81 G10 37 44N 88 32W
Harrisburg, *Nebr., U.S.A.* 80 E3 41 33N 103 44W
Harrisburg, *Oreg., U.S.A.* 82 D2 44 16N 123 10W
Harrisburg, *Pa., U.S.A.* 78 F8 40 16N 76 53W
Harrismith, *S. Africa* 57 D4 28 15S 29 8 E
Harrison, *Ark., U.S.A.* 81 G8 36 14N 93 7W
Harrison, *Idaho, U.S.A.* 82 C5 47 27N 116 47W
Harrison, *Nebr., U.S.A.* 80 D3 42 41N 103 53W
Harrison, C., *Canada* 71 B8 54 55N 57 55W
Harrison L., *Canada* 72 D4 49 33N 121 50W
Harrisonburg, *U.S.A.* 76 F6 38 27N 78 52W
Harrisonville, *U.S.A.* 80 F7 38 39N 94 21W
Harriston, *Canada* 70 D3 43 57N 80 53W
Harrisville, *U.S.A.* 78 B1 44 39N 83 17W
Harrogate, *U.K.* 10 C6 54 0N 1 33W
Harrow, *U.K.* 11 F7 51 35N 0 21W
Harsīn, *Iran* 44 C5 34 18N 47 33 E
Harstad, *Norway* 8 B17 68 48N 16 30 E
Hart, *U.S.A.* 76 D2 43 42N 86 22W
Hart, L., *Australia* 63 E2 31 10S 136 25 E
Hartbees →, *S. Africa* 56 D3 28 45S 20 32 E
Hartford, *Conn., U.S.A.* 79 E12 41 46N 72 41W
Hartford, *Ky., U.S.A.* 76 G2 37 27N 86 55W
Hartford, *S. Dak., U.S.A.* 80 D6 43 38N 96 57W
Hartford, *Wis., U.S.A.* 80 D10 43 19N 88 22W
Hartford City, *U.S.A.* 76 E3 40 27N 85 22W
Hartland, *Canada* 71 C6 46 20N 67 32W
Hartland Pt., *U.K.* 11 F3 51 1N 4 32W
Hartlepool, *U.K.* 10 C6 54 42N 1 13W
Hartlepool □, *U.K.* 10 C6 54 42N 1 17W
Hartley Bay, *Canada* 72 C3 53 25N 129 15W
Hartmannberge, *Namibia* 56 B1 17 0S 13 0 E
Hartney, *Canada* 73 D8 49 30N 100 35W
Harts →, *S. Africa* 56 D3 28 24S 24 17 E
Hartselle, *U.S.A.* 77 H2 34 27N 86 56W
Hartshorne, *U.S.A.* 81 H7 34 51N 95 34W
Hartsville, *U.S.A.* 77 H5 34 23N 80 4W
Hartwell, *U.S.A.* 77 H4 34 21N 82 56W
Harunabad, *Pakistan* 42 E5 29 35N 73 8 E
Harvand, *Iran* 45 D7 28 25N 55 43 E
Harvey, *Australia* 61 F2 33 5S 115 54 E
Harvey, *Ill., U.S.A.* 76 E2 41 36N 87 50W
Harvey, *N. Dak., U.S.A.* 80 B5 47 47N 99 56W
Harwich, *U.K.* 11 F9 51 56N 1 17 E
Haryana □, *India* 42 E7 29 0N 76 10 E
Haryn →, *Belarus* 17 B14 52 7N 27 17 E
Harz, *Germany* 16 C6 51 38N 10 44 E
Hasan Kīādeh, *Iran* 45 B6 37 24N 49 58 E
Ḩasanābād, *Iran* 45 C7 32 8N 52 44 E
Hasanpur, *India* 42 E8 28 43N 78 17 E
Hashimoto, *Japan* 31 G7 34 19N 135 37 E
Hashtjerd, *Iran* 45 C6 35 52N 50 40 E
Haskell, *Okla., U.S.A.* 81 H7 35 50N 95 40W
Haskell, *Tex., U.S.A.* 81 J5 33 10N 99 44W
Haslemere, *U.K.* 11 F7 51 5N 0 43W
Hasselt, *Belgium* 15 D5 50 56N 5 21 E
Hassi Messaoud, *Algeria* 50 B7 31 51N 6 1 E
Hässleholm, *Sweden* 9 H15 56 10N 13 46 E
Hastings, *N.Z.* 59 H6 39 39S 176 52 E
Hastings, *U.K.* 11 G8 50 51N 0 35 E
Hastings, *Mich., U.S.A.* 76 D3 42 39N 85 17W
Hastings, *Minn., U.S.A.* 80 C8 44 44N 92 51W
Hastings, *Nebr., U.S.A.* 80 E5 40 35N 98 23W
Hastings Ra., *Australia* 63 E5 31 15S 152 14 E
Hat Yai, *Thailand* 39 J3 7 1N 100 27 E
Hatanbulag, *Mongolia* 34 C5 43 8N 109 5 E
Hatay = Antalya, *Turkey* 25 G5 36 52N 30 45 E
Hatch, *U.S.A.* 83 K10 32 40N 107 9W
Hatches Creek, *Australia* 62 C2 20 56S 135 12 E
Hatchet L., *Canada* 73 B8 58 36N 103 40W
Hateruma-Shima, *Japan* 31 M1 24 3N 123 47 E
Hatfield P.O., *Australia* 63 E3 33 54S 143 49 E
Hatgal, *Mongolia* 32 A5 50 26N 100 9 E
Hathras, *India* 42 F8 27 36N 78 6 E
Hatia, *Bangla.* 41 H17 22 30N 91 5 E
Hato Mayor, *Dom. Rep.* 89 C6 18 46N 69 15W
Hattah, *Australia* 63 E3 34 48S 142 17 E
Hatteras, C., *U.S.A.* 77 H8 35 14N 75 32W
Hattiesburg, *U.S.A.* 81 K10 31 20N 89 17W
Hatvan, *Hungary* 17 E10 47 40N 19 45 E
Hau Duc, *Vietnam* 38 E7 15 20N 108 13 E
Haugesund, *Norway* 9 G11 59 23N 5 13 E
Haukipudas, *Finland* 8 D21 65 12N 25 20 E
Haultain →, *Canada* 73 B7 55 51N 106 46W
Hauraki G., *N.Z.* 59 G5 36 35S 175 5 E
Haut Atlas, *Morocco* 50 B4 32 30N 5 0W
Haut-Zaïre □, *Dem. Rep. of the Congo* 54 B2 2 20N 26 0 E
Hauterive, *Canada* 71 C6 49 10N 68 16W
Hautes Fagnes = Hohe Venn, *Belgium* 15 D6 50 30N 6 5 E
Hauts Plateaux, *Algeria* 48 C4 35 0N 1 0 E
Havana = La Habana, *Cuba* 88 B3 23 8N 82 22W
Havana, *U.S.A.* 80 E9 40 18N 90 4W
Havant, *U.K.* 11 G7 50 51N 0 58W
Havasu, L., *U.S.A.* 85 L12 34 18N 114 28W
Havel →, *Germany* 16 B7 52 50N 12 3 E
Havelian, *Pakistan* 42 B5 34 2N 73 10 E
Havelock, *N.B., Canada* 71 C6 46 2N 65 24W
Havelock, *Ont., Canada* 70 D4 44 26N 77 53W
Havelock, *N.Z.* 59 J4 41 17S 173 48 E
Haverfordwest, *U.K.* 11 F3 51 48N 4 58W
Haverhill, *U.S.A.* 79 D13 42 47N 71 5W
Haverstraw, *U.S.A.* 79 E11 41 12N 73 58W
Havířov, *Czech.* 17 D10 49 46N 18 20 E
Havlíčkův Brod, *Czech Rep.* 16 D8 49 36N 15 33 E
Havre, *U.S.A.* 82 B9 48 33N 109 41W
Havre-Aubert, *Canada* 71 C7 47 12N 61 56W
Havre-St.-Pierre, *Canada* 71 B7 50 18N 63 33W
Haw →, *U.S.A.* 77 H6 35 36N 79 3W
Hawaii □, *U.S.A.* 74 H16 19 30N 156 30W
Hawaii I., *Pac. Oc.* 74 J17 20 0N 155 0W
Hawaiian Is., *Pac. Oc.* 74 H17 20 30N 156 0W
Hawaiian Ridge, *Pac. Oc.* 65 E11 24 0N 165 0W
Hawarden, *Canada* 73 C7 51 25N 106 36W
Hawarden, *U.S.A.* 80 D6 43 0N 96 29W
Hawea, L., *N.Z.* 59 L2 44 28S 169 19 E
Hawera, *N.Z.* 59 H5 39 35S 174 19 E
Hawick, *U.K.* 12 F6 55 26N 2 47W
Hawk Junction, *Canada* 70 C3 48 5N 84 38W
Hawke B., *N.Z.* 59 H6 39 25S 177 20 E
Hawker, *Australia* 63 E2 31 59S 138 22 E
Hawkesbury, *Canada* 70 C5 45 37N 74 37W
Hawkesbury I., *Canada* 72 C3 53 37N 129 3W
Hawkesbury Pt., *Australia* 62 A1 11 55S 134 5 E
Hawkinsville, *U.S.A.* 77 J4 32 17N 83 28W
Hawkwood, *Australia* 63 D5 25 45S 150 50 E
Hawley, *U.S.A.* 80 B6 46 53N 96 19W
Hawrān, *Syria* 44 C3 32 45N 36 15 E
Hawsh Mūssá, *Lebanon* 47 B4 33 45N 35 55 E
Hawthorne, *U.S.A.* 82 G4 38 32N 118 38W
Haxtun, *U.S.A.* 80 E3 40 39N 102 38W
Hay, *Australia* 63 E3 34 30S 144 51 E
Hay →, *Australia* 62 C2 24 50S 138 0 E
Hay →, *Canada* 72 A5 60 50N 116 26W
Hay, C., *Australia* 60 B4 14 5S 129 29 E
Hay L., *Canada* 72 B5 58 50N 118 50W
Hay Lakes, *Canada* 72 C6 53 12N 113 2W
Hay-on-Wye, *U.K.* 11 E4 52 5N 3 8W
Hay River, *Canada* 72 A5 60 51N 115 44W
Hay Springs, *U.S.A.* 80 D3 42 41N 102 41W
Haya = Tehoru, *Indonesia* 37 E7 3 19S 129 37 E
Hayachine-San, *Japan* 30 E10 39 34N 141 29 E
Hayden, *Ariz., U.S.A.* 83 K8 33 0N 110 47W
Hayden, *Colo., U.S.A.* 82 F10 40 30N 107 16W
Haydon, *Australia* 62 B3 18 0S 141 30 E
Hayes, *U.S.A.* 80 C4 44 23N 101 1W
Hayes →, *Canada* 73 B10 57 3N 92 12W
Hayle, *U.K.* 11 G2 50 11N 5 26W
Hayling I., *U.K.* 11 G7 50 48N 0 59W
Haynesville, *U.S.A.* 81 J8 32 58N 93 8W
Hayrabolu, *Turkey* 21 D12 41 12N 27 5 E
Hays, *Canada* 72 C6 50 6N 111 48W
Hays, *U.S.A.* 80 F5 38 53N 99 20W
Haysyn, *Ukraine* 17 D15 48 57N 29 25 E
Hayvoron, *Ukraine* 17 D15 48 22N 29 52 E
Hayward, *Calif., U.S.A.* 84 H4 37 40N 122 5W
Hayward, *Wis., U.S.A.* 80 B9 46 1N 91 29W
Haywards Heath, *U.K.* 11 G7 51 0N 0 5W
Hazafon □, *Israel* 47 C4 32 40N 35 20 E
Hazarām, Kūh-e, *Iran* 45 D8 29 30N 57 18 E
Hazard, *U.S.A.* 76 G4 37 15N 83 12W
Hazaribag, *India* 43 H11 23 58N 85 26 E
Hazaribag Road, *India* 43 G11 24 12N 85 57 E
Hazelton, *Canada* 72 B3 55 20N 127 42W
Hazelton, *U.S.A.* 80 B4 46 29N 100 17W
Hazen, *N. Dak., U.S.A.* 80 B4 47 18N 101 38W
Hazen, *Nev., U.S.A.* 82 G4 39 34N 119 3W
Hazlehurst, *Ga., U.S.A.* 77 K4 31 52N 82 36W
Hazlehurst, *Miss., U.S.A.* 81 K9 31 52N 90 24W
Hazleton, *U.S.A.* 79 F9 40 57N 75 59W
Hazlett, L., *Australia* 60 D4 21 30S 128 48 E
Head of Bight, *Australia* 61 F5 31 30S 131 25 E
Headlands, *Zimbabwe* 55 F3 18 15S 32 2 E
Healdsburg, *U.S.A.* 84 G4 38 37N 122 52W
Healdton, *U.S.A.* 81 H6 34 14N 97 29W
Healesville, *Australia* 63 F4 37 35S 145 30 E
Heard I., *Ind. Oc.* 3 G13 53 0S 74 0 E
Hearne, *U.S.A.* 81 K6 30 53N 96 36W
Hearne B., *Canada* 73 A9 60 10N 99 10W
Hearne L., *Canada* 72 A6 62 20N 113 10W
Hearst, *Canada* 70 C3 49 40N 83 41W
Heart →, *U.S.A.* 80 B4 46 46N 100 50W
Heart's Content, *Canada* 71 C9 47 54N 53 27W
Heath Pt., *Canada* 71 C7 49 8N 61 40W
Heath Steele, *Canada* 71 C6 47 17N 66 5W
Heavener, *U.S.A.* 81 H7 34 53N 94 36W
Hebbronville, *U.S.A.* 81 M5 27 18N 98 41W
Hebei □, *China* 34 E9 39 0N 116 0 E
Hebel, *Australia* 63 D4 28 58S 147 47 E
Heber, *U.S.A.* 85 N11 32 44N 115 32W
Heber Springs, *U.S.A.* 81 H9 35 30N 92 2W
Hebert, *Canada* 73 C7 50 30N 107 10W
Hebgen L., *U.S.A.* 82 D8 44 52N 111 20W
Hebi, *China* 34 G8 35 57N 114 7 E
Hebrides, *U.K.* 6 D4 57 30N 7 0W
Hebron = Al Khalīl, *West Bank* 47 D4 31 32N 35 6 E
Hebron, *Canada* 69 C13 58 5N 62 30W
Hebron, *N. Dak., U.S.A.* 80 B3 46 54N 102 3W
Hebron, *Nebr., U.S.A.* 80 E6 40 10N 97 35W
Hecate Str., *Canada* 72 C2 53 10N 130 30W
Hechi, *China* 32 D5 24 40N 108 2 E
Hechuan, *China* 32 C5 30 2N 106 12 E
Hecla, *U.S.A.* 80 C5 45 53N 98 9W
Hecla I., *Canada* 73 C9 51 10N 96 43W
Hede, *Sweden* 9 E15 62 23N 13 30 E
Hedemora, *Sweden* 9 F16 60 18N 15 58 E
Hedley, *U.S.A.* 81 H4 34 52N 100 39W
Heerde, *Neths.* 15 B6 52 24N 6 2 E
Heerenveen, *Neths.* 15 B5 52 57N 5 55 E
Heerhugowaard, *Neths.* 15 B4 52 40N 4 51 E
Heerlen, *Neths.* 18 A6 50 55N 5 58 E
Hefa, *Israel* 47 C4 32 46N 35 0 E
Hefa □, *Israel* 47 C4 32 40N 35 0 E
Hefei, *China* 33 C6 31 52N 117 18 E
Hegang, *China* 33 B8 47 20N 130 19 E
Heichengzhen, *China* 34 F4 36 24N 106 3 E
Heidelberg, *Germany* 16 D5 49 24N 8 42 E
Heidelberg, *S. Africa* 56 E3 34 6S 20 59 E
Heilbron, *S. Africa* 57 D4 27 16S 27 59 E
Heilbronn, *Germany* 16 D5 49 9N 9 13 E
Heilongjiang □, *China* 35 A14 48 0N 126 0 E
Heilunkiang = Heilongjiang □, *China* 35 A14 48 0N 126 0 E
Heimaey, *Iceland* 8 E3 63 26N 20 17W
Heinola, *Finland* 9 F22 61 13N 26 2 E
Heinze Is., *Burma* 41 M20 14 25N 97 45 E
Heishan, *China* 35 D12 41 40N 122 5 E
Heishui, *China* 35 C10 42 8N 119 30 E
Hejaz = Ḩijāz □, *Si. Arabia* 46 C3 24 0N 40 0 E
Hejian, *China* 34 E9 38 25N 116 5 E
Hejin, *China* 34 G6 35 35N 110 42 E
Hekla, *Iceland* 8 E4 63 56N 19 35W
Hekou, *Gansu, China* 34 F2 36 10N 103 28 E
Hekou, *Yunnan, China* 32 D5 22 30N 103 59 E
Helan Shan, *China* 34 E3 38 30N 105 55 E
Helena, *Ark., U.S.A.* 81 H9 34 32N 90 36W
Helena, *Mont., U.S.A.* 82 C7 46 36N 112 2W
Helendale, *U.S.A.* 85 L9 34 44N 117 19W
Helensburgh, *U.K.* 12 E4 56 1N 4 43W
Helensville, *N.Z.* 59 G5 36 41S 174 29 E
Helgeland, *Norway* 8 C15 66 7N 13 29 E
Helgoland, *Germany* 16 A4 54 10N 7 53 E
Heligoland = Helgoland, *Germany* 16 A4 54 10N 7 53 E
Heligoland B. = Deutsche Bucht, *Germany* 16 A5 54 15N 8 0 E
Hella, *Iceland* 8 E3 63 50N 20 24W
Hellevoetsluis, *Neths.* 15 C4 51 50N 4 8 E
Hellín, *Spain* 19 C5 38 31N 1 40W
Helmand □, *Afghan.* 40 D4 31 20N 64 0 E

Helmand

Helmand →, *Afghan.* **40 D2** 31 12N 61 34 E
Helmond, *Neths.* **15 C5** 51 29N 5 41 E
Helmsdale, *U.K.* **12 C5** 58 7N 3 39W
Helmsdale →, *U.K.* **12 C5** 58 7N 3 40W
Helong, *China* **35 C15** 42 40N 129 0 E
Helper, *U.S.A.* **82 G8** 39 41N 110 51W
Helsingborg, *Sweden* **9 H15** 56 3N 12 42 E
Helsingfors = Helsinki, *Finland* **9 F21** 60 15N 25 3 E
Helsingør, *Denmark* **9 H15** 56 2N 12 35 E
Helsinki, *Finland* **9 F21** 60 15N 25 3 E
Helston, *U.K.* **11 G2** 50 6N 5 17W
Helvellyn, *U.K.* **10 C4** 54 32N 3 1W
Hemel Hempstead, *U.K.* **11 F7** 51 44N 0 28W
Hemet, *U.S.A.* **85 M10** 33 45N 116 58W
Hemingford, *U.S.A.* **80 D3** 42 19N 103 4W
Hemphill, *U.S.A.* **81 K8** 31 20N 93 51W
Hempstead, *U.S.A.* **81 K6** 30 6N 96 5W
Hemse, *Sweden* **9 H18** 57 15N 18 22 E
Henan □, *China* **34 H8** 34 0N 114 0 E
Henares →, *Spain* **19 B4** 40 24N 3 30W
Henashi-Misaki, *Japan* **30 D9** 40 37N 139 51 E
Henderson, *Argentina* **94 D3** 36 18S 61 43W
Henderson, *Ky., U.S.A.* **76 G2** 37 50N 87 35W
Henderson, *N.C., U.S.A.* **77 G6** 36 20N 78 25W
Henderson, *Nev., U.S.A.* **85 J12** 36 2N 114 59W
Henderson, *Tenn., U.S.A.* **77 H1** 35 26N 88 38W
Henderson, *Tex., U.S.A.* **81 J7** 32 9N 94 48W
Hendersonville, *U.S.A.* **77 H4** 35 19N 82 28W
Hendījān, *Iran* **45 D6** 30 14N 49 43 E
Hendon, *Australia* **63 D5** 28 5S 151 50 E
Hengcheng, *China* **34 E4** 38 18N 106 28 E
Hengdaohezi, *China* **35 B15** 44 52N 129 0 E
Hengelo, *Neths.* **15 B6** 52 16N 6 48 E
Hengshan, *China* **34 F5** 37 58N 109 5 E
Hengshui, *China* **34 F8** 37 41N 115 40 E
Hengyang, *China* **33 D6** 26 52N 112 33 E
Henlopen, C., *U.S.A.* **76 F8** 38 48N 75 6W
Hennenman, *S. Africa* **56 D4** 27 59S 27 1 E
Hennessey, *U.S.A.* **81 G6** 36 6N 97 54W
Henrietta, *U.S.A.* **81 J5** 33 49N 98 12W
Henrietta, Ostrov = Genriyetty, Ostrov, *Russia* **27 B16** 77 6N 156 30 E
Henrietta Maria, C., *Canada* **70 A3** 55 9N 82 20W
Henry, *U.S.A.* **80 E10** 41 7N 89 22W
Henryetta, *U.S.A.* **81 H7** 35 27N 95 59W
Hensall, *Canada* **78 C3** 43 26N 81 30W
Hentiyn Nuruu, *Mongolia* **33 B5** 48 30N 108 30 E
Henty, *Australia* **63 F4** 35 30S 147 0 E
Henzada, *Burma* **41 L19** 17 38N 95 26 E
Heppner, *U.S.A.* **82 D4** 45 21N 119 33W
Hepworth, *Canada* **78 B3** 44 37N 81 9W
Hequ, *China* **34 E6** 39 20N 111 15 E
Héraðsflói, *Iceland* **8 D6** 65 42N 14 12W
Héraðsvötn →, *Iceland* **8 D4** 65 45N 19 25W
Herald Cays, *Australia* **62 B4** 16 58S 149 9 E
Herāt, *Afghan.* **40 B3** 34 20N 62 7 E
Herāt □, *Afghan.* **40 B3** 35 0N 62 0 E
Herbert →, *Australia* **62 B4** 18 31S 146 17 E
Herbert Downs, *Australia* **62 C2** 23 7S 139 9 E
Herberton, *Australia* **62 B4** 17 20S 145 25 E
Herceg-Novi, *Montenegro, Yug.* **21 C8** 42 30N 18 33 E
Herðubreið, *Iceland* **8 D5** 65 11N 16 21W
Hereford, *U.K.* **11 E5** 52 4N 2 43W
Hereford, *U.S.A.* **81 H3** 34 49N 102 24W
Herefordshire □, *U.K.* **11 E5** 52 8N 2 40W
Herentals, *Belgium* **15 C4** 51 12N 4 51 E
Herford, *Germany* **16 B5** 52 7N 8 39 E
Herington, *U.S.A.* **80 F6** 38 40N 96 57W
Herkimer, *U.S.A.* **79 D10** 43 0N 74 59W
Herlong, *U.S.A.* **84 E6** 40 8N 120 8W
Herm, *U.K.* **11 H5** 49 30N 2 28W
Herman, *U.S.A.* **80 C6** 45 49N 96 9W
Hermann, *U.S.A.* **80 F9** 38 42N 91 27W
Hermannsburg Mission, *Australia* **60 D5** 23 57S 132 45 E
Hermanus, *S. Africa* **56 E2** 34 27S 19 12 E
Hermidale, *Australia* **63 E4** 31 30S 146 42 E
Hermiston, *U.S.A.* **82 D4** 45 51N 119 17W
Hermitage, *N.Z.* **59 K3** 43 44S 170 5 E
Hermite, I., *Chile* **96 H3** 55 50S 68 0W
Hermon, Mt. = Ash Shaykh, J., *Lebanon* **47 B4** 33 25N 35 50 E
Hermosillo, *Mexico* **86 B2** 29 10N 111 0W
Hernád →, *Hungary* **17 D11** 47 56N 21 8 E
Hernandarias, *Paraguay* **95 B5** 25 20S 54 40W
Hernandez, *U.S.A.* **84 J6** 36 24N 120 46W
Hernando, *Argentina* **94 C3** 32 28S 63 40W
Hernando, *U.S.A.* **81 H10** 34 50N 90 0W
Herne, *Germany* **15 C7** 51 32N 7 14 E
Herne Bay, *U.K.* **11 F9** 51 21N 1 8 E
Herning, *Denmark* **9 H13** 56 8N 8 58 E
Heroica = Caborca, *Mexico* **86 A2** 30 40N 112 10W
Heroica Nogales = Nogales, *Mexico* **86 A2** 31 20N 110 56W
Heron Bay, *Canada* **70 C2** 48 40N 86 25W
Herradura, Pta. de la, *Canary Is.* **22 F5** 28 26N 14 8W
Herreid, *U.S.A.* **80 C4** 45 50N 100 4W
Herrick, *Australia* **62 G4** 41 5S 147 55 E
Herrin, *U.S.A.* **81 G10** 37 48N 89 2W
Hersonissos, *Greece* **23 D7** 35 18N 25 22 E
Herstal, *Belgium* **15 D5** 50 40N 5 38 E
Hertford, *U.K.* **11 F7** 51 48N 0 4W
Hertfordshire □, *U.K.* **11 F7** 51 51N 0 5W
's-Hertogenbosch, *Neths.* **15 C5** 51 42N 5 17 E
Hertzogville, *S. Africa* **56 D4** 28 9S 25 30 E
Herzliyya, *Israel* **47 C3** 32 10N 34 50 E
Ḥeşār, *Fārs, Iran* **45 D6** 29 52N 50 16 E
Ḥeşār, *Markazī, Iran* **45 C6** 35 50N 49 12 E
Heshui, *China* **34 G5** 36 0N 108 0 E
Heshun, *China* **34 F7** 37 22N 113 32 E
Hesperia, *U.S.A.* **85 L9** 34 25N 117 18W
Hesse = Hessen □, *Germany* **16 C5** 50 30N 9 0 E
Hessen □, *Germany* **16 C5** 50 30N 9 0 E
Hetch Hetchy Aqueduct, *U.S.A.* **84 H5** 37 29N 122 19W
Hettinger, *U.S.A.* **80 C3** 46 0N 102 42W
Hexham, *U.K.* **10 C5** 54 58N 2 4W
Hexigten Qi, *China* **35 C9** 43 18N 117 30 E
Ḥeydarābād, *Iran* **45 D7** 30 33N 55 38 E
Heyfield, *Australia* **63 F4** 37 59S 146 47 E
Heysham, *U.K.* **10 C5** 54 3N 2 53W
Heywood, *Australia* **63 F3** 38 8S 141 37 E
Heze, *China* **34 G8** 35 14N 115 20 E
Hi Vista, *U.S.A.* **85 L9** 34 45N 117 46W
Hialeah, *U.S.A.* **77 N5** 25 50N 80 17W
Hiawatha, *Kans., U.S.A.* **80 F7** 39 51N 95 32W
Hiawatha, *Utah, U.S.A.* **82 G8** 39 29N 111 1W
Hibbing, *U.S.A.* **80 B8** 47 25N 92 56W
Hibbs B., *Australia* **62 G4** 42 35S 145 15 E
Hibernia Reef, *Australia* **60 B3** 12 0S 123 23 E
Hickory, *U.S.A.* **77 H5** 35 44N 81 21W
Hicks, Pt., *Australia* **63 F4** 37 49S 149 17 E
Hicksville, *U.S.A.* **79 F11** 40 46N 73 32W
Hida-Gawa →, *Japan* **31 G8** 35 26N 137 3 E
Hida-Sammyaku, *Japan* **31 F8** 36 30N 137 40 E
Hidaka-Sammyaku, *Japan* **30 C11** 42 35N 142 45 E
Hidalgo, *Mexico* **87 C5** 24 15N 99 26W
Hidalgo □, *Mexico* **87 C5** 20 30N 99 10W
Hidalgo, Presa M., *Mexico* **86 B3** 26 30N 108 35W
Hidalgo, Pta. del, *Canary Is.* **22 F3** 28 33N 16 19W
Hidalgo del Parral, *Mexico* **86 B3** 26 58N 105 40W
Hierro, *Canary Is.* **22 G1** 27 44N 18 0W
Higashiajima-San, *Japan* **30 F10** 37 40N 140 10 E
Higashiōsaka, *Japan* **31 G7** 34 40N 135 37 E
Higgins, *U.S.A.* **81 G4** 36 7N 100 2W
Higgins Corner, *U.S.A.* **84 F5** 39 2N 121 5W
Higginsville, *Australia* **61 F3** 31 42S 121 38 E
High Atlas = Haut Atlas, *Morocco* **50 B4** 32 30N 5 0W
High I., *Canada* **71 A7** 56 40N 61 10W
High Island, *U.S.A.* **81 L7** 29 34N 94 24W
High Level, *Canada* **72 B5** 58 31N 117 8W
High Point, *U.S.A.* **77 H6** 35 57N 80 0W
High Prairie, *Canada* **72 B5** 55 30N 116 30W
High River, *Canada* **72 C6** 50 30N 113 50W
High Springs, *U.S.A.* **77 L4** 29 50N 82 36W
High Tatra = Tatry, *Slovak Rep.* **17 D11** 49 20N 20 0 E
High Veld, *Africa* **48 J6** 27 0S 27 0 E
High Wycombe, *U.K.* **11 F7** 51 37N 0 45W
Highbury, *Australia* **62 B3** 16 25S 143 9 E
Highland □, *U.K.* **12 D4** 57 17N 4 21W
Highland Park, *U.S.A.* **76 D2** 42 11N 87 48W
Highmore, *U.S.A.* **80 C5** 44 31N 99 27W
Highrock L., *Canada* **73 B7** 57 5N 105 32W
Higüey, *Dom. Rep.* **89 C6** 18 37N 68 42W
Hiiumaa, *Estonia* **24 C3** 58 50N 22 45 E
Ḥijāz □, *Si. Arabia* **46 C3** 24 0N 40 0 E
Hijo = Tagum, *Phil.* **37 C7** 7 33N 125 53 E
Hikari, *Japan* **31 H5** 33 58N 131 58 E
Hiko, *U.S.A.* **84 H11** 37 32N 115 14W
Hikone, *Japan* **31 G8** 35 15N 136 10 E
Hikurangi, *N.Z.* **59 F5** 35 36S 174 17 E
Hikurangi, Mt., *N.Z.* **59 H6** 38 21S 176 52 E
Hildesheim, *Germany* **16 B5** 52 9N 9 56 E
Hill →, *Australia* **61 F2** 30 23S 115 3 E
Hill City, *Idaho, U.S.A.* **82 E6** 43 18N 115 3W
Hill City, *Kans., U.S.A.* **80 F5** 39 22N 99 51W
Hill City, *Minn., U.S.A.* **80 B8** 46 59N 93 36W
Hill City, *S. Dak., U.S.A.* **80 D3** 43 56N 103 35W
Hill Island L., *Canada* **73 A7** 60 30N 109 50W
Hillcrest Center, *U.S.A.* **85 K8** 35 23N 118 57W
Hillegom, *Neths.* **15 B4** 52 18N 4 35 E
Hillerød, *Denmark* **9 J15** 55 56N 12 19 E
Hillman, *U.S.A.* **76 C4** 45 4N 83 54W
Hillmond, *Canada* **73 C7** 53 26N 109 41W
Hillsboro, *Kans., U.S.A.* **80 F6** 38 21N 97 12W
Hillsboro, *N. Dak., U.S.A.* **80 B6** 47 26N 97 3W
Hillsboro, *N.H., U.S.A.* **79 C13** 43 7N 71 54W
Hillsboro, *N. Mex., U.S.A.* **83 K10** 32 55N 107 34W
Hillsboro, *Oreg., U.S.A.* **84 E4** 45 31N 122 59W
Hillsboro, *Tex., U.S.A.* **81 J6** 32 1N 97 8W
Hillsborough, *Grenada* **89 D7** 12 28N 61 28W
Hillsdale, *Mich., U.S.A.* **76 E3** 41 56N 84 38W
Hillsdale, *N.Y., U.S.A.* **79 D11** 42 11N 73 30W
Hillside, *Australia* **60 D2** 21 45S 119 23 E
Hillsport, *Canada* **70 C2** 49 27N 85 34W
Hillston, *Australia* **63 E4** 33 30S 145 31 E
Hilo, *U.S.A.* **74 J17** 19 44N 155 5W
Hilton, *U.S.A.* **78 C7** 43 17N 77 48W
Hilversum, *Neths.* **15 B5** 52 14N 5 10 E
Himachal Pradesh □, *India* **42 D7** 31 30N 77 0 E
Himalaya, *Asia* **43 E11** 29 0N 84 0 E
Himatnagar, *India* **40 H8** 23 37N 72 57 E
Himeji, *Japan* **31 G7** 34 50N 134 40 E
Himi, *Japan* **31 F8** 36 50N 136 55 E
Ḥimş, *Syria* **47 A5** 34 40N 36 45 E
Ḥims □, *Syria* **47 A6** 34 30N 37 0 E
Hinche, *Haiti* **89 C5** 19 9N 72 1W
Hinchinbrook I., *Australia* **62 B4** 18 20S 146 15 E
Hinckley, *U.K.* **11 E6** 52 33N 1 22W
Hinckley, *U.S.A.* **82 G7** 39 20N 112 40W
Hindaun, *India* **42 F7** 26 44N 77 5 E
Hindmarsh, L., *Australia* **63 F3** 36 5S 141 55 E
Hindu Bagh, *Pakistan* **42 D2** 30 56N 67 50 E
Hindu Kush, *Asia* **40 B7** 36 0N 71 0 E
Hindubagh, *Pakistan* **40 D5** 30 56N 67 57 E
Hindupur, *India* **40 N10** 13 49N 77 32 E
Hines Creek, *Canada* **72 B5** 56 20N 118 40W
Hinganghat, *India* **40 J11** 20 30N 78 52 E
Hingham, *U.S.A.* **82 B8** 48 33N 110 25W
Hingoli, *India* **40 K10** 19 41N 77 15 E
Hinna = Imi, *Ethiopia* **46 F3** 6 28N 42 10 E
Hinnøya, *Norway* **8 B16** 68 35N 15 50 E
Hinojosa del Duque, *Spain* **19 C3** 38 30N 5 9W
Hinsdale, *U.S.A.* **82 B10** 48 24N 107 5W
Hinton, *Canada* **72 C5** 53 26N 117 34W
Hinton, *U.S.A.* **76 G5** 37 40N 80 54W
Hirado, *Japan* **31 H4** 33 22N 129 33 E
Hirakud Dam, *India* **41 J13** 21 32N 83 45 E
Hiratsuka, *Japan* **31 G9** 35 19N 139 21 E
Hiroo, *Japan* **30 C11** 42 17N 143 19 E
Hirosaki, *Japan* **30 D10** 40 34N 140 28 E
Hiroshima, *Japan* **31 G6** 34 24N 132 30 E
Hiroshima □, *Japan* **31 G6** 34 50N 133 0 E
Hisar, *India* **42 E6** 29 12N 75 45 E
Hisb →, *Iraq* **44 D5** 31 45N 44 17 E
Ḥismá, *Si. Arabia* **44 D3** 28 30N 36 0 E
Hispaniola, *W. Indies* **89 C5** 19 0N 71 0W
Hīt, *Iraq* **44 C4** 33 38N 42 49 E
Hita, *Japan* **31 H5** 33 20N 130 58 E
Hitachi, *Japan* **31 F10** 36 36N 140 39 E
Hitchin, *U.K.* **11 F7** 51 58N 0 16W
Hitoyoshi, *Japan* **31 H5** 32 13N 130 45 E
Hitra, *Norway* **8 E13** 63 30N 8 45 E
Ḫiyyon, N. →, *Israel* **47 E4** 30 25N 35 10 E
Hjalmar L., *Canada* **73 A7** 61 33N 109 25W
Hjälmaren, *Sweden* **9 G16** 59 18N 15 40 E
Hjørring, *Denmark* **9 H13** 57 29N 9 59 E
Hluhluwe, *S. Africa* **57 D5** 28 1S 32 15 E
Hlyboka, *Ukraine* **17 D13** 48 5N 25 56 E
Ho Chi Minh City = Phanh Bho Ho Chi Minh, *Vietnam* **39 G6** 10 58N 106 40 E
Ho Thuong, *Vietnam* **38 C5** 19 32N 105 48 E
Hoa Binh, *Vietnam* **38 B5** 20 50N 105 20 E
Hoa Da, *Vietnam* **39 G7** 11 16N 108 40 E
Hoa Hiep, *Vietnam* **39 G5** 11 34N 105 51 E
Hoai Nhon, *Vietnam* **38 E7** 14 28N 109 1 E
Hoang Lien Son, *Vietnam* **38 A4** 22 0N 104 0 E
Hobart, *Australia* **62 G4** 42 50S 147 21 E
Hobart, *U.S.A.* **81 H5** 35 1N 99 6W
Hobbs, *U.S.A.* **81 J3** 32 42N 103 8W
Hobbs Coast, *Antarctica* **5 D14** 74 50S 131 0W
Hoboken, *U.S.A.* **79 F10** 40 45N 74 4W
Hobro, *Denmark* **9 H13** 56 39N 9 46 E
Hoburgen, *Sweden* **9 H18** 56 55N 18 7 E
Hodaka-Dake, *Japan* **31 F8** 36 17N 137 39 E
Hodgson, *Canada* **73 C9** 51 13N 97 36W
Hódmezővásárhely, *Hungary* **17 E11** 46 28N 20 22 E
Hodna, Chott el, *Algeria* **50 A6** 35 26N 4 43 E
Hodonín, *Czech Rep.* **17 D9** 48 50N 17 10 E
Hoeamdong, *N. Korea* **35 C16** 42 30N 130 16 E
Hoek van Holland, *Neths.* **15 C4** 52 0N 4 7 E
Hoengsŏng, *S. Korea* **35 F14** 37 29N 127 59 E
Hoeryong, *N. Korea* **35 C15** 42 30N 129 45 E
Hoeyang, *N. Korea* **35 E14** 38 43N 127 36 E
Hof, *Germany* **16 C6** 50 19N 11 55 E
Hofmeyr, *S. Africa* **56 E4** 31 39S 25 50 E
Höfn, *Iceland* **8 D6** 64 15N 15 13W
Hofors, *Sweden* **9 F17** 60 31N 16 15 E
Hofsjökull, *Iceland* **8 D4** 64 49N 18 48W
Hōfu, *Japan* **31 G5** 34 3N 131 34 E
Hogan Group, *Australia* **62 F4** 39 13S 147 1 E
Hogansville, *U.S.A.* **77 J3** 33 10N 84 55W
Hogeland, *U.S.A.* **82 B9** 48 51N 108 40W
Hoggar = Ahaggar, *Algeria* **50 D7** 23 0N 6 30 E
Hogsty Reef, *Bahamas* **89 B5** 21 41N 73 48W
Hoh →, *U.S.A.* **84 C2** 47 45N 124 29W
Hohe Venn, *Belgium* **15 D6** 50 30N 6 5 E
Hohenwald, *U.S.A.* **77 H2** 35 33N 87 33W
Hohhot, *China* **34 D6** 40 52N 111 40 E
Hóhlakas, *Greece* **23 D9** 35 57N 27 53 E
Hoi An, *Vietnam* **38 E7** 15 30N 108 19 E
Hoi Xuan, *Vietnam* **38 B5** 20 25N 105 9 E
Hoisington, *U.S.A.* **80 F5** 38 31N 98 47W
Hōjō, *Japan* **31 H6** 33 58N 132 46 E
Hokianga Harbour, *N.Z.* **59 F4** 35 31S 173 22 E
Hokitika, *N.Z.* **59 K3** 42 42S 171 0 E
Hokkaidō □, *Japan* **30 C11** 43 30N 143 0 E
Holbrook, *Australia* **63 F4** 35 42S 147 18 E
Holbrook, *U.S.A.* **83 J8** 34 54N 110 10W
Holden, *Canada* **72 C6** 53 13N 112 11W
Holden, *U.S.A.* **82 G7** 39 6N 112 16W
Holdenville, *U.S.A.* **81 H6** 35 5N 96 24W
Holdfast, *Canada* **73 C7** 50 58N 105 25W
Holdrege, *U.S.A.* **80 E5** 40 26N 99 23W
Holguín, *Cuba* **88 B4** 20 50N 76 20W
Hollams Bird I., *Namibia* **56 C1** 24 40S 14 30 E
Holland, *U.S.A.* **76 D2** 42 47N 86 7W
Hollandia = Jayapura, *Indonesia* **37 E10** 2 28S 140 38 E
Hollidaysburg, *U.S.A.* **78 F6** 40 26N 78 24W
Hollis, *U.S.A.* **81 H5** 34 41N 99 55W
Hollister, *Calif., U.S.A.* **84 J5** 36 51N 121 24W
Hollister, *Idaho, U.S.A.* **82 E6** 42 21N 114 35W
Holly, *U.S.A.* **80 F3** 38 3N 102 7W
Holly Hill, *U.S.A.* **77 L5** 29 16N 81 3W
Holly Springs, *U.S.A.* **81 H10** 34 46N 89 27W
Hollywood, *Calif., U.S.A.* **83 J4** 34 7N 118 25W
Hollywood, *Fla., U.S.A.* **77 N5** 26 1N 80 9W
Holman, *Canada* **68 A8** 70 42N 117 41W
Hólmavík, *Iceland* **8 D3** 65 42N 21 40W
Holmes Reefs, *Australia* **62 B4** 16 27S 148 0 E
Holmsund, *Sweden* **8 E19** 63 41N 20 20 E
Holroyd →, *Australia* **62 A3** 14 10S 141 36 E
Holstebro, *Denmark* **9 H13** 56 22N 8 37 E
Holsworthy, *U.K.* **11 G3** 50 48N 4 22W
Holton, *Canada* **71 B8** 54 31N 57 12W
Holton, *U.S.A.* **80 F7** 39 28N 95 44W
Holtville, *U.S.A.* **85 N11** 32 49N 115 23W
Holwerd, *Neths.* **15 A5** 53 22N 5 54 E
Holy I., *Angl., U.K.* **10 D3** 53 17N 4 37W
Holy I., *Northumb., U.K.* **10 B6** 55 40N 1 47W
Holyhead, *U.K.* **10 D3** 53 18N 4 38W
Holyoke, *Colo., U.S.A.* **80 E3** 40 35N 102 18W
Holyoke, *Mass., U.S.A.* **79 D12** 42 12N 72 37W
Holyrood, *Canada* **71 C9** 47 27N 53 8W
Homa Bay, *Kenya* **54 C3** 0 36S 34 30 E
Homa Bay □, *Kenya* **54 C3** 0 50S 34 30 E
Homalin, *Burma* **41 G19** 24 55N 95 0 E
Homand, *Iran* **45 C8** 32 28N 59 37 E
Hombori, *Mali* **50 E5** 15 20N 1 38W
Home B., *Canada* **69 B13** 68 40N 67 10W
Home Hill, *Australia* **62 B4** 19 43S 147 25 E
Homedale, *U.S.A.* **82 E5** 43 37N 116 56W
Homer, *Alaska, U.S.A.* **68 C4** 59 39N 151 33W
Homer, *La., U.S.A.* **81 J8** 32 48N 93 4W
Homestead, *Australia* **62 C4** 20 20S 145 40 E
Homestead, *Fla., U.S.A.* **77 N5** 25 28N 80 29W
Homestead, *Oreg., U.S.A.* **82 D5** 45 2N 116 51W
Homewood, *U.S.A.* **84 F6** 39 4N 120 8W
Hominy, *U.S.A.* **81 G6** 36 25N 96 24W
Homoine, *Mozam.* **57 C6** 23 55S 35 8 E
Homs = Ḥimş, *Syria* **47 A5** 34 40N 36 45 E
Homyel, *Belarus* **24 D5** 52 28N 31 0 E
Hon Chong, *Vietnam* **39 G5** 10 25N 104 30 E
Hon Me, *Vietnam* **38 C5** 19 23N 105 56 E
Honan = Henan □, *China* **34 H8** 34 0N 114 0 E
Honbetsu, *Japan* **30 C11** 43 7N 143 37 E
Honcut, *U.S.A.* **84 F5** 39 20N 121 32W
Hondeklipbaai, *S. Africa* **56 E2** 30 19S 17 17 E
Hondo, *Japan* **31 H5** 32 27N 130 12 E
Hondo, *U.S.A.* **81 L5** 29 21N 99 9W
Hondo →, *Belize* **87 D7** 18 25N 88 21W
Honduras ■, *Cent. Amer.* **88 D2** 14 40N 86 30W
Honduras, G. de, *Caribbean* **88 C2** 16 50N 87 0W
Hønefoss, *Norway* **9 F14** 60 10N 10 18 E
Honesdale, *U.S.A.* **79 E9** 41 34N 75 16W
Honey L., *U.S.A.* **84 E6** 40 15N 120 19W
Honfleur, *France* **18 B4** 49 25N 0 13 E
Hong →, *Vietnam* **32 D5** 22 0N 104 0 E
Hong Gai, *Vietnam* **38 B6** 20 57N 107 5 E
Hong He →, *China* **34 H8** 32 25N 115 35 E
Hong Kong, *China* **33 D6** 22 11N 114 14 E
Hongchŏn, *S. Korea* **35 F14** 37 44N 127 53 E
Hongjiang, *China* **33 D5** 27 7N 109 59 E
Hongliu He →, *China* **34 F5** 38 0N 109 50 E
Hongor, *Mongolia* **34 B7** 45 45N 112 50 E
Hongsa, *Laos* **38 C3** 19 43N 101 20 E
Hongshui He →, *China* **33 D5** 23 48N 109 30 E
Hongsŏng, *S. Korea* **35 F14** 36 37N 126 38 E
Hongtong, *China* **34 F6** 36 16N 111 40 E
Honguedo, Détroit d', *Canada* **71 C7** 49 15N 64 0W
Hongwon, *N. Korea* **35 E14** 40 0N 127 56 E
Hongze Hu, *China* **35 H10** 33 15N 118 35 E
Honiara, *Solomon Is.* **64 H7** 9 27S 159 57 E
Honiton, *U.K.* **11 G4** 50 47N 3 11W
Honjō, *Japan* **30 E10** 39 23N 140 3 E
Honningsvåg, *Norway* **8 A21** 70 59N 25 59 E
Honolulu, *U.S.A.* **74 H16** 21 19N 157 52W
Honshū, *Japan* **31 G9** 36 0N 138 0 E
Hood, Mt., *U.S.A.* **82 D3** 45 23N 121 42W
Hood, Pt., *Australia* **61 F2** 34 23S 119 34 E
Hood River, *U.S.A.* **82 D3** 45 43N 121 31W
Hoodsport, *U.S.A.* **84 C3** 47 24N 123 9W
Hoogeveen, *Neths.* **15 B6** 52 44N 6 28 E
Hoogezand-Sappemeer, *Neths.* **15 A6** 53 9N 6 45 E
Hooghly → = Hugli →, *India* **43 J13** 21 56N 88 4 E
Hooghly-Chinsura = Chunchura, *India* **43 H13** 22 53N 88 27 E
Hook Hd., *Ireland* **13 D5** 52 7N 6 56W
Hook I., *Australia* **62 C4** 20 4S 149 0 E
Hook of Holland = Hoek van Holland, *Neths.* **15 C4** 52 0N 4 7 E
Hooker, *U.S.A.* **81 G4** 36 52N 101 13W
Hooker Creek, *Australia* **60 C5** 18 23S 130 38 E
Hoopeston, *U.S.A.* **76 E2** 40 28N 87 40W
Hoopstad, *S. Africa* **56 D4** 27 50S 25 55 E
Hoorn, *Neths.* **15 B5** 52 38N 5 4 E
Hoover Dam, *U.S.A.* **85 K12** 36 1N 114 44W
Hooversville, *U.S.A.* **78 F6** 40 9N 78 55W
Hop Bottom, *U.S.A.* **79 E9** 41 42N 75 46W
Hope, *Canada* **72 D4** 49 25N 121 25W
Hope, *Ariz., U.S.A.* **85 M13** 33 43N 113 42W
Hope, *Ark., U.S.A.* **81 J8** 33 40N 93 36W
Hope, *N. Dak., U.S.A.* **80 B6** 47 19N 97 43W
Hope, L., *Australia* **63 D2** 28 24S 139 18 E
Hope Town, *Bahamas* **88 A4** 26 35N 76 57W
Hopedale, *Canada* **71 A7** 55 28N 60 13W
Hopefield, *S. Africa* **56 E2** 33 3S 18 22 E
Hopei = Hebei □, *China* **34 E9** 39 0N 116 0 E
Hopelchén, *Mexico* **87 D7** 19 46N 89 50W
Hopetoun, *Vic., Australia* **63 F3** 35 42S 142 22 E
Hopetoun, *W. Austral., Australia* **61 F3** 33 57S 120 7 E
Hopetown, *S. Africa* **56 D3** 29 34S 24 3 E
Hopkins, *U.S.A.* **80 E7** 40 33N 94 49W
Hopkins, L., *Australia* **60 D4** 24 15S 128 35 E
Hopkinsville, *U.S.A.* **77 G2** 36 52N 87 29W
Hopland, *U.S.A.* **84 G3** 38 58N 123 7W
Hoquiam, *U.S.A.* **84 D3** 46 59N 123 53W
Horden Hills, *Australia* **60 D5** 20 15S 130 0 E
Horinger, *China* **34 D6** 40 28N 111 48 E
Horlick Mts., *Antarctica* **5 E15** 84 0S 102 0W
Horlivka, *Ukraine* **25 E6** 48 19N 38 5 E
Hormoz, *Iran* **45 E7** 27 35N 55 0 E
Hormoz, Jaz. ye, *Iran* **45 E8** 27 8N 56 28 E
Hormuz, Str. of, *The Gulf* **45 E8** 26 30N 56 30 E
Horn, *Austria* **16 D8** 48 39N 15 40 E
Horn, *Iceland* **8 C2** 66 28N 22 28W
Horn →, *Canada* **72 A5** 61 30N 118 1W
Horn, Cape = Hornos, C. de, *Chile* **96 H3** 55 50S 67 30W
Horn Head, *Ireland* **13 A3** 55 14N 8 0W
Horn I., *Australia* **62 A3** 10 37S 142 17 E
Horn I., *U.S.A.* **77 K1** 30 14N 88 39W
Horn Mts., *Canada* **72 A5** 62 15N 119 15W
Hornavan, *Sweden* **8 C17** 66 15N 17 30 E
Hornbeck, *U.S.A.* **81 K8** 31 20N 93 24W
Hornbrook, *U.S.A.* **82 F2** 41 55N 122 33W
Horncastle, *U.K.* **10 D7** 53 13N 0 7W
Hornell, *U.S.A.* **78 D7** 42 20N 77 40W
Hornell L., *Canada* **72 A5** 62 20N 119 25W
Hornepayne, *Canada* **70 C3** 49 14N 84 48W
Hornitos, *U.S.A.* **84 H6** 37 30N 120 14W
Hornos, C. de, *Chile* **96 H3** 55 50S 67 30W
Hornsby, *Australia* **63 E5** 33 42S 151 2 E
Hornsea, *U.K.* **10 D7** 53 55N 0 11W
Horobetsu, *Japan* **30 C10** 42 24N 141 6 E
Horodenka, *Ukraine* **17 D13** 48 41N 25 29 E
Horodok, *Khmelnytskyy, Ukraine* **17 D14** 49 10N 26 34 E
Horodok, *Lviv, Ukraine* **17 D12** 49 46N 23 32 E
Horokhiv, *Ukraine* **17 C13** 50 30N 24 45 E
Horqin Youyi Qianqi, *China* **35 A12** 46 5N 122 3 E
Horqueta, *Paraguay* **94 A4** 23 15S 56 55W
Horse Creek, *U.S.A.* **80 E3** 41 57N 105 10W
Horse Is., *Canada* **71 B8** 50 15N 55 50W
Horsefly L., *Canada* **72 C4** 52 25N 121 0W
Horsens, *Denmark* **9 J13** 55 52N 9 51 E
Horsham, *Australia* **63 F3** 36 44S 142 13 E
Horsham, *U.K.* **11 F7** 51 4N 0 20W
Horten, *Norway* **9 G14** 59 25N 10 32 E
Horton, *U.S.A.* **80 F7** 39 40N 95 32W
Horton →, *Canada* **68 B7** 69 56N 126 52W
Horwood, L., *Canada* **70 C3** 48 5N 82 20W

Imlay

Hose, Gunung-Gunung, Malaysia 36 D4 2 5N 114 6 E
Ḥoseynābād, Khuzestān, Iran 45 C6 32 45N 48 20 E
Ḥoseynābād, Kordestān, Iran 44 C5 35 33N 47 8 E
Hoshangabad, India 42 H7 22 45N 77 45 E
Hoshiarpur, India 42 D6 31 30N 75 58 E
Hosmer, U.S.A. 80 C5 45 34N 99 28W
Hospet, India 40 M10 15 15N 76 20 E
Hoste, I., Chile 96 H3 55 0S 69 0W
Hot, Thailand 38 C2 18 8N 98 29 E
Hot Creek Range, U.S.A. 82 G6 38 40N 116 20W
Hot Springs, Ark., U.S.A. 81 H8 34 31N 93 3W
Hot Springs, S. Dak., U.S.A. 80 D3 43 26N 103 29W
Hotagen, Sweden 8 E16 63 50N 14 30 E
Hotan, China 32 C2 37 25N 79 55 E
Hotazel, S. Africa 56 D3 27 17S 22 58 E
Hotchkiss, U.S.A. 83 G10 38 48N 107 43W
Hotham, C., Australia 60 B5 12 2S 131 18 E
Hoting, Sweden 8 D17 64 8N 16 15 E
Hotte, Massif de la, Haiti 89 C5 18 30N 73 45W
Hottentotsbaai, Namibia 56 D1 26 8S 14 59 E
Houck, U.S.A. 83 J9 35 20N 109 10W
Houei Sai, Laos 38 B3 20 18N 100 26 E
Houffalize, Belgium 15 D5 50 8N 5 48 E
Houghton, U.S.A. 80 B10 47 7N 88 34W
Houghton L., U.S.A. 76 C3 44 21N 84 44W
Houhora Heads, N.Z. 59 F4 34 49S 173 9 E
Houlton, U.S.A. 71 C6 46 8N 67 51W
Houma, U.S.A. 81 L9 29 36N 90 43W
Houston, Canada 72 C3 54 25N 126 39W
Houston, Mo., U.S.A. 81 G9 37 22N 91 58W
Houston, Tex., U.S.A. 81 L7 29 46N 95 22W
Houtman Abrolhos, Australia 61 E1 28 43S 113 48 E
Hovd, Mongolia 32 B4 48 2N 91 37 E
Hove, U.K. 11 G7 50 50N 0 10W
Hoveyzeh, Iran 45 D6 31 27N 48 4 E
Hövsgöl, Mongolia 34 C5 43 37N 109 39 E
Hövsgöl Nuur, Mongolia 32 A5 51 0N 100 30 E
Howard, Australia 63 D5 25 16S 152 32 E
Howard, Kans., U.S.A. 81 G6 37 28N 96 16W
Howard, Pa., U.S.A. 78 F7 41 1N 77 40W
Howard, S. Dak., U.S.A. 80 C6 44 1N 97 32W
Howard I., Australia 62 A2 12 10S 135 24 E
Howard L., Canada 73 A7 62 15N 105 57W
Howe, U.S.A. 82 E7 43 48N 113 0W
Howe, C., Australia 63 F5 37 30S 150 0 E
Howell, U.S.A. 76 D4 42 36N 83 56W
Howick, Canada 79 A11 45 11N 73 51W
Howick, S. Africa 57 D5 29 28S 30 14 E
Howick Group, Australia 62 A4 14 20S 145 30 E
Howitt, L., Australia 63 D2 27 40S 138 40 E
Howland I., Pac. Oc. 64 G10 0 48N 176 38W
Howley, Canada 71 C8 49 12N 57 2W
Howrah = Haora, India 43 H13 22 37N 88 20 E
Howth Hd., Ireland 13 C5 53 22N 6 3W
Höxter, Germany 16 C5 51 46N 9 22 E
Hoy, U.K. 12 C5 58 50N 3 15W
Høyanger, Norway 9 F12 61 13N 6 4 E
Hoyerswerda, Germany 16 C8 51 26N 14 14 E
Hoylake, U.K. 10 D4 53 24N 3 10W
Hpungan Pass, Burma 41 F20 27 30N 96 55 E
Hradec Králové, Czech Rep. 16 C8 50 15N 15 50 E
Hrodna, Belarus 24 D3 53 42N 23 52 E
Hrodzyanka, Belarus 17 B15 53 31N 28 42 E
Hron →, Slovak Rep. 17 E10 47 49N 18 45 E
Hrvatska = Croatia ■, Europe 16 F9 45 20N 16 0 E
Hrymayliv, Ukraine 17 D14 49 20N 26 5 E
Hsenwi, Burma 41 H20 23 22N 97 55 E
Hsiamen = Xiamen, China 33 D6 24 25N 118 4 E
Hsian = Xi'an, China 34 G5 34 15N 109 0 E
Hsinchu, Taiwan 33 D7 24 48N 120 58 E
Hsinhailien = Lianyungang, China 35 G10 34 40N 119 11 E
Hsüchou = Xuzhou, China 35 G9 34 18N 117 10 E
Hu Xian, China 34 G5 34 8N 108 42 E
Hua Hin, Thailand 38 F2 12 34N 99 58 E
Hua Xian, Henan, China 34 G8 35 30N 114 30 E
Hua Xian, Shaanxi, China 34 G5 34 30N 109 48 E
Huachinera, Mexico 86 A3 30 9N 108 55W
Huacho, Peru 92 F3 11 10S 77 35W
Huade, China 34 D7 41 55N 113 59 E
Huadian, China 35 C14 43 0N 126 40 E
Huai He →, China 33 C6 33 0N 118 30 E
Huai Yot, Thailand 39 J2 7 45N 99 37 E
Huai'an, Hebei, China 34 D8 40 30N 114 20 E
Huai'an, Jiangsu, China 35 H10 33 30N 119 10 E
Huaibei, China 34 G9 34 0N 116 48 E
Huaide, China 35 C13 43 30N 124 40 E
Huaidezhen, China 35 C13 43 48N 124 50 E
Huainan, China 33 C6 32 38N 116 58 E
Huairen, China 34 E7 39 48N 113 20 E
Huairou, China 34 D9 40 20N 116 35 E
Huaiyang, China 34 H8 33 40N 114 52 E
Huaiyuan, China 35 H9 32 55N 117 10 E
Huajianzi, China 35 D13 41 23N 125 20 E
Huajuapan de Leon, Mexico 87 D5 17 50N 97 48W
Hualapai Peak, U.S.A. 83 J7 35 5N 113 54W
Huallaga →, Peru 92 E3 5 15S 75 30W
Huambo, Angola 53 G3 12 42S 15 54 E
Huan Jiang →, China 34 G5 34 28N 109 0 E
Huan Xian, China 34 F4 36 33N 107 7 E
Huancabamba, Peru 92 E3 5 10S 79 15W
Huancane, Peru 92 G5 15 10S 69 44W
Huancavelica, Peru 92 F3 12 50S 75 5W
Huancayo, Peru 92 F3 12 5S 75 12W
Huanchaca, Bolivia 92 H5 20 15S 66 40W
Huang Hai = Yellow Sea, China 35 G12 35 0N 123 0 E
Huang He →, China 35 F10 37 55N 118 50 E
Huang Xian, China 35 F11 37 38N 120 30 E
Huangling, China 34 G5 35 34N 109 15 E
Huanglong, China 34 G5 35 30N 109 59 E
Huangshi, China 33 C6 30 10N 115 3 E
Huangsongdian, China 35 C14 43 45N 127 25 E
Huantai, China 35 F9 36 58N 117 56 E
Huánuco, Peru 92 E3 9 55S 76 15W
Huaraz, Peru 92 E3 9 30S 77 32W
Huarmey, Peru 92 F3 10 5S 78 5W
Huascarán, Peru 92 E3 9 8S 77 36W
Huasco, Chile 94 B1 28 30S 71 15W
Huasco →, Chile 94 B1 28 27S 71 13W
Huasna, U.S.A. 85 K6 35 6N 120 24W
Huatabampo, Mexico 86 B3 26 50N 109 50W
Huauchinango, Mexico 87 C5 20 11N 98 3W
Huautla de Jiménez, Mexico 87 D5 18 8N 96 51W
Huay Namota, Mexico 86 C4 21 56N 104 30W
Huayin, China 34 G6 34 35N 110 5 E
Hubbard, U.S.A. 81 K6 31 51N 96 48W
Hubbart Pt., Canada 73 B10 59 21N 94 41W
Hubei □, China 33 C6 31 0N 112 0 E
Hubli-Dharwad = Dharwad, India 40 M9 15 22N 75 15 E
Huchang, N. Korea 35 D14 41 25N 127 2 E
Hucknall, U.K. 10 D6 53 3N 1 13W
Huddersfield, U.K. 10 D6 53 39N 1 47W
Hudiksvall, Sweden 9 F17 61 43N 17 10 E
Hudson, Canada 73 C10 50 6N 92 9W
Hudson, Mass., U.S.A. 79 D13 42 23N 71 34W
Hudson, Mich., U.S.A. 76 E3 41 51N 84 21W
Hudson, N.Y., U.S.A. 79 D11 42 15N 73 46W
Hudson, Wis., U.S.A. 80 C8 44 58N 92 45W
Hudson, Wyo., U.S.A. 82 E9 42 54N 108 35W
Hudson →, U.S.A. 79 F10 40 42N 74 2W
Hudson Bay, N.W.T., Canada 69 C11 60 0N 86 0W
Hudson Bay, Sask., Canada 73 C8 52 51N 102 23W
Hudson Falls, U.S.A. 79 C11 43 18N 73 35W
Hudson Mts., Antarctica 5 D16 74 32S 99 20W
Hudson Str., Canada 69 B13 62 0N 70 0W
Hudson's Hope, Canada 72 B4 56 0N 121 54W
Hue, Vietnam 38 D6 16 30N 107 35 E
Huehuetenango, Guatemala 88 C1 15 20N 91 28W
Huejúcar, Mexico 86 C4 22 21N 103 13W
Huelva, Spain 19 D2 37 18N 6 57W
Huentelauquén, Chile 94 C1 31 38S 71 33W
Huerta, Sa. de la, Argentina 94 C2 31 10S 67 30W
Huesca, Spain 19 A5 42 8N 0 25W
Huetamo, Mexico 86 D4 18 36N 100 54W
Hugh →, Australia 62 D1 25 1S 134 1 E
Hughenden, Australia 62 C3 20 52S 144 10 E
Hughes, Australia 61 F4 30 42S 129 31 E
Hugli →, India 43 J13 21 56N 88 4 E
Hugo, U.S.A. 80 F3 39 8N 103 28W
Hugoton, U.S.A. 81 G4 37 11N 101 21W
Hui Xian, Gansu, China 34 H4 33 50N 106 4 E
Hui Xian, Henan, China 34 G7 35 27N 113 12 E
Hui'anbu, China 34 F4 37 28N 106 38 E
Huichapán, Mexico 87 C5 20 24N 99 40W
Huifa He →, China 35 C14 43 0N 127 50 E
Huila, Nevado del, Colombia 92 C3 3 0N 76 0W
Huimin, China 35 F9 37 27N 117 28 E
Huinan, China 35 C14 42 40N 126 2 E
Huinca Renancó, Argentina 94 C3 34 51S 64 22W
Huining, China 34 G3 35 38N 105 0 E
Huinong, China 34 E4 39 5N 106 35 E
Huiting, China 34 G9 34 5N 116 5 E
Huixtla, Mexico 87 D6 15 9N 92 28W
Huize, China 32 D5 26 24N 103 15 E
Hukawng Valley, Burma 41 F20 26 30N 96 30 E
Hukuntsi, Botswana 56 C3 23 58S 21 45 E
Ḥulayfā', Si. Arabia 44 E4 25 58N 40 45 E
Huld, Mongolia 34 B3 45 5N 105 30 E
Hulin He →, China 35 B12 45 0N 122 10 E
Hull = Kingston upon Hull, U.K. 10 D7 53 45N 0 21W
Hull, Canada 70 C4 45 25N 75 44W
Hull →, U.K. 10 D7 53 44N 0 20W
Hulst, Neths. 15 C4 51 17N 4 2 E
Hulun Nur, China 33 B6 49 0N 117 30 E
Humahuaca, Argentina 94 A2 23 10S 65 25W
Humaitá, Brazil 92 E6 7 35S 63 1W
Humaitá, Paraguay 94 B4 27 2S 58 31W
Humansdorp, S. Africa 56 E3 34 2S 24 46 E
Humbe, Angola 56 B1 16 40S 14 55 E
Humber →, U.K. 10 D7 53 42N 0 27W
Humbert River, Australia 60 C5 16 30S 130 45 E
Humble, U.S.A. 81 L8 29 59N 93 18W
Humboldt, Canada 73 C7 52 15N 105 9W
Humboldt, Iowa, U.S.A. 80 D7 42 44N 94 13W
Humboldt, Tenn., U.S.A. 81 H10 35 50N 88 55W
Humboldt →, U.S.A. 82 F4 39 59N 118 36W
Hume, U.S.A. 84 J8 36 48N 118 54W
Hume, L., Australia 63 F4 36 0S 147 5 E
Humenné, Slovak Rep. 17 D11 48 55N 21 50 E
Humphreys, Mt., U.S.A. 84 H8 37 17N 118 40W
Humphreys Peak, U.S.A. 83 J8 35 21N 111 41W
Humptulips, U.S.A. 84 C3 47 14N 123 57W
Hūn, Libya 51 C9 29 2N 16 0 E
Hun Jiang →, China 35 D13 40 50N 125 38 E
Húnaflói, Iceland 8 D3 65 50N 20 50W
Hunan □, China 33 D6 27 30N 112 0 E
Hunchun, China 35 C16 42 52N 130 28 E
Hundred Mile House, Canada 72 C4 51 38N 121 18W
Hunedoara, Romania 17 F12 45 40N 22 50 E
Hung Yen, Vietnam 38 B6 20 39N 106 4 E
Hungary ■, Europe 17 E10 47 20N 19 20 E
Hungary, Plain of, Europe 6 F10 47 0N 20 0 E
Hungerford, Australia 63 D3 28 58S 144 24 E
Hŭngnam, N. Korea 35 E14 39 49N 127 45 E
Hunsberge, Namibia 56 D2 27 45S 17 12 E
Hunsrück, Germany 16 D4 49 56N 7 27 E
Hunstanton, U.K. 10 E8 52 56N 0 29 E
Hunter, N. Dak., U.S.A. 80 B6 47 12N 97 13W
Hunter, N.Y., U.S.A. 79 D10 42 13N 74 13W
Hunter I., Australia 62 G3 40 30S 144 45 E
Hunter I., Canada 72 C3 51 55N 128 0W
Hunter Ra., Australia 63 E5 32 45S 150 15 E
Hunters Road, Zimbabwe 55 F2 19 9S 29 49 E
Hunterville, N.Z. 59 H5 39 56S 175 35 E
Huntingburg, U.S.A. 76 F2 38 18N 86 57W
Huntingdon, Canada 70 C5 45 6N 74 10W
Huntingdon, U.K. 11 E7 52 20N 0 11W
Huntingdon, U.S.A. 78 F6 40 30N 78 1W
Huntington, Ind., U.S.A. 76 E3 40 53N 85 30W
Huntington, N.Y., U.S.A. 79 F11 40 52N 73 26W
Huntington, Oreg., U.S.A. 82 D5 44 21N 117 16W
Huntington, Utah, U.S.A. 82 G8 39 20N 110 58W
Huntington, W. Va., U.S.A. 76 F4 38 25N 82 27W
Huntington Beach, U.S.A. 85 M9 33 40N 118 5W
Huntington Park, U.S.A. 83 K4 33 58N 118 15W
Huntly, N.Z. 59 G5 37 34S 175 11 E
Huntly, U.K. 12 D6 57 27N 2 47W
Huntsville, Canada 70 C4 45 20N 79 14W
Huntsville, Ala., U.S.A. 77 H2 34 44N 86 35W
Huntsville, Tex., U.S.A. 81 K7 30 43N 95 33W
Hunyani →, Zimbabwe 55 F3 15 57S 30 39 E
Hunyuan, China 34 E7 39 42N 113 42 E
Hunza →, India 43 B6 35 54N 74 20 E
Huo Xian, China 34 F6 36 36N 111 42 E
Huong Hoa, Vietnam 38 D6 16 37N 106 45 E
Huong Khe, Vietnam 38 C5 18 13N 105 41 E
Huonville, Australia 62 G4 43 0S 147 5 E
Hupeh = Hubei □, China 33 C6 31 0N 112 0 E
Ḥūr, Iran 45 D8 30 50N 57 7 E
Hure Qi, China 35 C11 42 45N 121 45 E
Hurley, N. Mex., U.S.A. 83 K9 32 42N 108 8W
Hurley, Wis., U.S.A. 80 B9 46 27N 90 11W
Huron, Calif., U.S.A. 84 J6 36 12N 120 6W
Huron, Ohio, U.S.A. 78 E2 41 24N 82 33W
Huron, S. Dak., U.S.A. 80 C5 44 22N 98 13W
Huron, L., U.S.A. 78 B2 44 30N 82 40W
Hurricane, U.S.A. 83 H7 37 11N 113 17W
Hurunui →, N.Z. 59 K4 42 54S 173 18 E
Húsavík, Iceland 8 C5 66 3N 17 21W
Huşi, Romania 17 E15 46 41N 28 7 E
Huskvarna, Sweden 9 H16 57 47N 14 15 E
Hussar, Canada 72 C6 51 3N 112 41W
Hustadvika, Norway 8 E12 63 0N 7 0 E
Hutchinson, Kans., U.S.A. 81 F6 38 5N 97 56W
Hutchinson, Minn., U.S.A. 80 C7 44 54N 94 22W
Huttig, U.S.A. 81 J8 33 2N 92 11W
Hutton, Mt., Australia 63 D4 25 51S 148 20 E
Huy, Belgium 15 D5 50 31N 5 15 E
Hvammstangi, Iceland 8 D3 65 24N 20 57W
Hvar, Croatia 20 C7 43 11N 16 28 E
Hvítá →, Iceland 8 D3 64 30N 21 58W
Hwachon-chosuji, S. Korea 35 E14 38 5N 127 50 E
Hwang Ho = Huang He →, China 35 F10 37 55N 118 50 E
Hwange, Zimbabwe 55 F2 18 18S 26 30 E
Hwange Nat. Park, Zimbabwe 56 B4 19 0S 26 30 E
Hyannis, U.S.A. 80 E4 42 0N 101 46W
Hyargas Nuur, Mongolia 32 B4 49 0N 93 0 E
Hyden, Australia 61 F2 32 24S 118 53 E
Hyderabad, India 40 L11 17 22N 78 29 E
Hyderabad, Pakistan 42 G3 25 23N 68 24 E
Hyères, France 18 E7 43 8N 6 9 E
Hyères, Îs. d', France 18 E7 43 0N 6 20 E
Hyesan, N. Korea 35 D15 41 20N 128 10 E
Hyland →, Canada 72 B3 59 52N 128 12W
Hymia, India 43 C8 33 40N 78 2 E
Hyndman Peak, U.S.A. 82 E6 43 45N 114 8W
Hyōgo □, Japan 31 G7 35 15N 134 50 E
Hyrum, U.S.A. 82 F8 41 38N 111 51W
Hysham, U.S.A. 82 C10 46 18N 107 14W
Hythe, U.K. 11 F9 51 4N 1 5 E
Hyūga, Japan 31 H5 32 25N 131 35 E
Hyvinge = Hyvinkää, Finland 9 F21 60 38N 24 50 E
Hyvinkää, Finland 9 F21 60 38N 24 50 E

I

I-n-Gall, Niger 50 E7 16 51N 7 1 E
Iaco →, Brazil 92 E5 9 3S 68 34W
Iakora, Madag. 57 C8 23 6S 46 40 E
Ialomiţa →, Romania 17 F14 44 42N 27 51 E
Iaşi, Romania 25 E4 47 10N 27 40 E
Iba, Phil. 37 A6 15 22N 120 0 E
Ibadan, Nigeria 50 G6 7 22N 3 58 E
Ibagué, Colombia 92 C3 4 20N 75 20W
Ibar →, Serbia, Yug. 21 C9 43 43N 20 45 E
Ibaraki □, Japan 31 F10 36 10N 140 10 E
Ibarra, Ecuador 92 C3 0 21N 78 7W
Ibembo, Dem. Rep. of the Congo 54 B1 2 35N 23 35 E
Ibera, L., Argentina 94 B4 28 30S 57 9W
Iberian Peninsula, Europe 6 H5 40 0N 5 0W
Iberville, Canada 70 C5 45 19N 73 17W
Iberville, Lac d', Canada 70 A5 55 55N 73 15W
Ibiá, Brazil 93 G9 19 30S 46 30W
Ibicuy, Argentina 94 C4 33 55S 59 10W
Ibioapaba, Sa. da, Brazil 93 D10 4 0S 41 30W
Ibiza = Eivissa, Spain 22 C7 38 54N 1 26 E
Ibo, Mozam. 55 E5 12 22S 40 40 E
Ibonma, Indonesia 37 E8 3 29S 133 31 E
Ibotirama, Brazil 93 F10 12 13S 43 12W
Ibrāhīm →, Lebanon 47 A4 34 4N 35 38 E
Ibu, Indonesia 37 D7 1 35N 127 33 E
Ibusuki, Japan 31 J5 31 12N 130 40 E
Ica, Peru 92 F3 14 0S 75 48W
Iça →, Brazil 92 D5 2 55S 67 58W
Içana, Brazil 92 C5 0 21N 67 19W
Içana →, Brazil 92 C5 0 26N 67 19W
İçel = Mersin, Turkey 25 G5 36 51N 34 36 E
Iceland ■, Europe 8 D4 64 45N 19 0W
Ich'ang = Yichang, China 33 C6 30 40N 111 20 E
Ichchapuram, India 41 K14 19 10N 84 40 E
Ichihara, Japan 31 G10 35 28N 140 5 E
Ichikawa, Japan 31 G9 35 44N 139 55 E
Ichilo →, Bolivia 92 G6 15 57S 64 50W
Ichinohe, Japan 30 D10 40 13N 141 17 E
Ichinomiya, Japan 31 G8 35 18N 136 48 E
Ichinoseki, Japan 30 E10 38 55N 141 8 E
Ichŏn, S. Korea 35 F14 37 17N 127 27 E
Icod, Canary Is. 22 F3 28 22N 16 43W
Icy Str., U.S.A. 72 B1 58 20N 135 30W
Ida Grove, U.S.A. 80 D7 42 21N 95 28W
Ida Valley, Australia 61 E3 28 42S 120 29 E
Idabel, U.S.A. 81 J7 33 54N 94 50W
Idaho □, U.S.A. 82 D7 45 0N 115 0W
Idaho City, U.S.A. 82 E6 43 50N 115 50W
Idaho Falls, U.S.A. 82 E7 43 30N 112 2W
Idaho Springs, U.S.A. 82 G11 39 45N 105 31W
Idar-Oberstein, Germany 16 D4 49 43N 7 16 E
Idfû, Egypt 51 D12 24 55N 32 49 E
Ídhi Óros, Greece 23 D6 35 15N 24 45 E
Idi, Indonesia 36 C1 5 2N 97 37 E
Idiofa, Dem. Rep. of the Congo 52 E3 4 55S 19 42 E
Idlib, Syria 44 C3 35 55N 36 36 E
Idria, U.S.A. 84 J6 36 25N 120 41W
Idutywa, S. Africa 57 E4 32 8S 28 18 E
Ieper, Belgium 15 D2 50 51N 2 53 E
Ierápetra, Greece 23 E7 35 1N 25 44 E
Iesi, Italy 20 C5 43 31N 13 14 E
'Ifāl, W. al →, Si. Arabia 44 D2 28 7N 35 3 E
Ifanadiana, Madag. 57 C8 21 19S 47 39 E
Ife, Nigeria 50 G6 7 30N 4 31 E
Iffley, Australia 62 B3 18 53S 141 12 E
Ifni, Morocco 50 C3 29 29N 10 12W
Iforas, Adrar des, Mali 50 E6 19 40N 1 40 E
Ifould, L., Australia 61 F5 30 52S 132 6 E
Iganga, Uganda 54 B3 0 37N 33 28 E
Igarapava, Brazil 93 H9 20 3S 47 47W
Igarka, Russia 26 C9 67 30N 86 33 E
Igatimi, Paraguay 95 A4 24 5S 55 40W
Iggesund, Sweden 9 F17 61 39N 17 10 E
Iglésias, Italy 20 E3 39 19N 8 32 E
Igloolik, Canada 69 B11 69 20N 81 49W
Ignace, Canada 70 C1 49 30N 91 40W
İğneada Burnu, Turkey 21 D13 41 53N 28 2 E
Igoumenítsa, Greece 21 E9 39 32N 20 18 E
Iguaçu →, Brazil 95 B5 25 36S 54 36W
Iguaçu, Cat. del, Brazil 95 B5 25 41S 54 26W
Iguaçu Falls = Iguaçu, Cat. del, Brazil 95 B5 25 41S 54 26W
Iguala, Mexico 87 D5 18 20N 99 40W
Igualada, Spain 19 B6 41 37N 1 37 E
Iguassu = Iguaçu →, Brazil 95 B5 25 36S 54 36W
Iguatu, Brazil 93 E11 6 20S 39 18W
Igunga □, Tanzania 54 C3 4 20S 33 45 E
Iharana, Madag. 57 A9 13 25S 50 0 E
Iheya-Shima, Japan 31 L3 27 4N 127 58 E
Ihosy, Madag. 57 C8 22 24S 46 8 E
Ihotry, L., Madag. 57 C7 21 56S 43 41 E
Ii, Finland 8 D21 65 19N 25 22 E
Ii-Shima, Japan 31 L3 26 43N 127 47 E
Iida, Japan 31 G8 35 35N 137 50 E
Iijoki →, Finland 8 D21 65 20N 25 20 E
Iisalmi, Finland 8 E22 63 32N 27 10 E
Iiyama, Japan 31 F9 36 51N 138 22 E
Iizuka, Japan 31 H5 33 38N 130 42 E
Ijebu-Ode, Nigeria 50 G6 6 47N 3 58 E
IJmuiden, Neths. 15 B4 52 28N 4 35 E
IJssel →, Neths. 15 B5 52 35N 5 50 E
IJsselmeer, Neths. 15 B5 52 45N 5 20 E
Ijuí →, Brazil 95 B4 27 58S 55 20W
Ikaría, Greece 21 F12 37 35N 26 10 E
Ikeda, Japan 31 G6 34 1N 133 48 E
Ikela, Dem. Rep. of the Congo 52 E4 1 6S 23 6 E
Iki, Japan 31 H4 33 45N 129 42 E
Ikimba L., Tanzania 54 C3 1 30S 31 20 E
Ikopa →, Madag. 57 B8 16 45S 46 40 E
Ikungu, Tanzania 54 C3 1 33S 33 42 E
Ilagan, Phil. 37 A6 17 7N 121 53 E
Īlām, Iran 44 C5 33 36N 46 36 E
Ilam, Nepal 43 F12 26 58N 87 58 E
Ilanskiy, Russia 27 D10 56 14N 96 3 E
Iława, Poland 17 B10 53 36N 19 34 E
Ilbilbie, Australia 62 C4 21 45S 149 20 E
Ile-à-la-Crosse, Canada 73 B7 55 27N 107 53W
Ile-à-la-Crosse, Lac, Canada 73 B7 55 40N 107 45W
Île-de-France □, France 18 B5 49 0N 2 20 E
Ilebo, Dem. Rep. of the Congo 52 E4 4 17S 20 55 E
Ileje □, Tanzania 55 D3 9 30S 33 25 E
Ilek, Russia 26 D6 51 32N 53 21 E
Ilek →, Russia 24 D9 51 30N 53 22 E
Ilford, Canada 73 B9 56 4N 95 35W
Ilfracombe, Australia 62 C3 23 30S 144 30 E
Ilfracombe, U.K. 11 F3 51 12N 4 8W
Ilhéus, Brazil 93 F11 14 49S 39 2W
Ili →, Kazakstan 26 E8 45 53N 77 10 E
Iliff, U.S.A. 80 E3 40 45N 103 4W
Iligan, Phil. 37 C6 8 12N 124 13 E
Ilion, U.S.A. 79 D9 43 1N 75 2W
Ilkeston, U.K. 10 E6 52 58N 1 19W
Ilkley, U.K. 10 D6 53 56N 1 48W
Illampu = Ancohuma, Nevada, Bolivia 92 G5 16 0S 68 50W
Illana B., Phil. 37 C6 7 35N 123 45 E
Illapel, Chile 94 C1 32 0S 71 10W
Iller →, Germany 16 D6 48 23N 9 58 E
Illetas, Spain 22 B9 39 32N 2 35 E
Illimani, Bolivia 92 G5 16 30S 67 50W
Illinois □, U.S.A. 75 B9 40 15N 89 30W
Illinois →, U.S.A. 75 C8 38 58N 90 28W
Illium = Troy, Turkey 21 E12 39 57N 26 12 E
Ilmajoki, Finland 9 E20 62 44N 22 34 E
Ilmen, Ozero, Russia 24 C5 58 15N 31 10 E
Ilo, Peru 92 G4 17 40S 71 20W
Iloilo, Phil. 37 B6 10 45N 122 33 E
Ilorin, Nigeria 50 G6 8 30N 4 35 E
Ilwaco, U.S.A. 84 D2 46 19N 124 3W
Ilwaki, Indonesia 37 F7 7 55S 126 30 E
Imabari, Japan 31 G6 34 4N 133 0 E
Imaloto →, Madag. 57 C8 23 27S 45 13 E
Imandra, Ozero, Russia 24 A5 67 30N 33 0 E
Imari, Japan 31 H4 33 15N 129 52 E
Imbler, U.S.A. 82 D5 45 28N 117 58W
imeni 26 Bakinskikh Komissarov = Neftçala, Azerbaijan 25 G8 39 19N 49 12 E
imeni 26 Bakinskikh Komissarov, Turkmenistan 25 G9 39 22N 54 10 E
Imeri, Serra, Brazil 92 C5 0 50N 65 25W
Imerimandroso, Madag. 57 B8 17 26S 48 35 E
Imi, Ethiopia 46 F3 6 28N 42 10 E
Imlay, U.S.A. 82 F4 40 40N 118 9W

Keokuk

Kaolack, Senegal 50 F2 14 5N 16 8W
Kaoshan, China 35 B13 44 38N 124 50 E
Kapadvanj, India 42 H5 23 5N 73 0 E
Kapan, Armenia 25 G8 39 18N 46 27 E
Kapanga, Dem. Rep. of the Congo 52 F4 8 30S 22 40 E
Kapchagai = Qapshaghay, Kazakstan 26 E8 43 51N 77 14 E
Kapela = Velika Kapela, Croatia 16 F8 45 10N 15 5 E
Kapema, Dem. Rep. of the Congo 55 E2 10 45S 28 22 E
Kapfenberg, Austria 16 E8 47 26N 15 18 E
Kapiri Mposhi, Zambia 55 E2 13 59S 28 43 E
Kapiskau →, Canada 70 B3 52 47N 81 55W
Kapit, Malaysia 36 D4 2 0N 112 55 E
Kapiti I., N.Z. 59 J5 40 50S 174 56 E
Kapoe, Thailand 39 H2 9 34N 98 32 E
Kapoeta, Sudan 51 H12 4 50N 33 35 E
Kaposvár, Hungary 17 E9 46 25N 17 47 E
Kapowsin, U.S.A. 84 D4 46 59N 122 13W
Kapps, Namibia 56 C2 22 32S 17 18 E
Kapsan, N. Korea 35 D15 41 4N 128 19 E
Kapsukas = Marijampolė, Lithuania 9 J20 54 33N 23 19 E
Kapuas →, Indonesia 36 E3 0 25S 109 20 E
Kapuas Hulu, Pegunungan, Malaysia 36 D4 1 30N 113 30 E
Kapuas Hulu Ra. = Kapuas Hulu, Pegunungan, Malaysia 36 D4 1 30N 113 30 E
Kapulo, Dem. Rep. of the Congo 55 D2 8 18S 29 15 E
Kapunda, Australia 63 E2 34 20S 138 56 E
Kapuni, N.Z. 59 H5 39 29S 174 8 E
Kapurthala, India 42 D6 31 23N 75 25 E
Kapuskasing, Canada 70 C3 49 25N 82 30W
Kapuskasing →, Canada 70 C3 49 49N 82 0W
Kaputar, Australia 63 E5 30 15S 150 10 E
Kaputir, Kenya 54 B4 2 5N 35 28 E
Kara, Russia 26 C7 69 10N 65 0 E
Kara Bogaz Gol, Zaliv = Garabogazköl Aylagy, Turkmenistan 25 F9 41 0N 53 30 E
Kara Kalpak Republic □ = Karakalpakstan □, Uzbekistan 26 E6 43 0N 58 0 E
Kara Kum, Turkmenistan 26 F7 39 30N 60 0 E
Kara Sea, Russia 26 B8 75 0N 70 0 E
Karabiğa, Turkey 21 D12 40 23N 27 17 E
Karaburun, Turkey 21 E12 38 41N 26 28 E
Karabutak = Qarabutaq, Kazakstan 26 E7 49 59N 60 14 E
Karacabey, Turkey 21 D13 40 12N 28 21 E
Karacasu, Turkey 21 F13 37 43N 28 35 E
Karachi, Pakistan 42 G2 24 53N 67 0 E
Karad, India 40 L9 17 15N 74 10 E
Karaganda = Qaraghandy, Kazakstan 26 E8 49 50N 73 10 E
Karagayly, Kazakstan 26 E8 49 26N 76 0 E
Karaginskiy, Ostrov, Russia 27 D17 58 45N 164 0 E
Karagiye, Vpadina, Kazakstan 25 F9 43 27N 51 45 E
Karagiye Depression = Karagiye, Vpadina, Kazakstan 25 F9 43 27N 51 45 E
Karagwe □, Tanzania 54 C3 2 0S 31 0 E
Karaikal, India 40 P11 10 59N 79 50 E
Karaikkudi, India 40 P11 10 5N 78 45 E
Karaj, Iran 45 C6 35 48N 51 0 E
Karak, Malaysia 39 L4 3 25N 102 2 E
Karakalpakstan □, Uzbekistan 26 E6 43 0N 58 0 E
Karakelong, Indonesia 37 D7 4 35N 126 50 E
Karakitang, Indonesia 37 D7 3 14N 125 28 E
Karaklis = Vanadzor, Armenia 25 F7 40 48N 44 30 E
Karakoram Pass, Pakistan 43 B7 35 33N 77 50 E
Karakoram Ra., Pakistan 43 B7 35 30N 77 0 E
Karalon, Russia 27 D12 57 5N 115 50 E
Karaman, Turkey 25 G5 37 14N 33 13 E
Karamay, China 32 B3 45 30N 84 58 E
Karambu, Indonesia 36 E5 3 53S 116 6 E
Karamea Bight, N.Z. 59 J3 41 22S 171 40 E
Karamsad, India 42 H5 22 35N 72 50 E
Karand, Iran 44 C5 34 16N 46 15 E
Karanganyar, Indonesia 37 G13 7 38S 109 37 E
Karasburg, Namibia 56 D2 28 0S 18 44 E
Karasino, Russia 26 C9 66 50N 86 50 E
Karasjok, Norway 8 B21 69 27N 25 30 E
Karasuk, Russia 26 D8 53 44N 78 2 E
Karasuyama, Japan 31 F10 36 39N 140 9 E
Karatau = Qarataū, Kazakstan 26 E8 43 10N 70 28 E
Karatau, Khrebet, Kazakstan 26 E7 43 30N 69 30 E
Karauli, India 42 F7 26 30N 77 4 E
Karavostasi, Cyprus 23 D11 35 8N 32 50 E
Karawang, Indonesia 37 G12 6 30S 107 15 E
Karawanken, Europe 16 E8 46 30N 14 40 E
Karazhal, Kazakstan 26 E8 48 2N 70 49 E
Karbalā, Iraq 44 C5 32 36N 44 3 E
Karcag, Hungary 17 E11 47 19N 20 57 E
Karcha →, Pakistan 43 B7 34 45N 76 10 E
Kardhítsa, Greece 21 E9 39 23N 21 54 E
Kärdla, Estonia 9 G20 58 50N 22 40 E
Kareeberge, S. Africa 56 E3 30 59S 21 50 E
Karelia □, Russia 24 A5 65 30N 32 30 E
Karelian Republic □ = Karelia □, Russia 24 A5 65 30N 32 30 E
Kārevāndar, Iran 45 E9 27 53N 60 44 E
Kargasok, Russia 26 D9 59 3N 80 53 E
Kargat, Russia 26 D9 55 10N 80 15 E
Kargil, India 43 B7 34 32N 76 12 E
Kargopol, Russia 24 B6 61 30N 38 58 E
Karīān, Iran 45 E8 26 57N 57 14 E
Kariba, Zimbabwe 55 F2 16 28S 28 50 E
Kariba, L., Zimbabwe 55 F2 16 40S 28 25 E
Kariba Dam, Zimbabwe 55 F2 16 30S 28 35 E
Kariba Gorge, Zambia 55 F2 16 30S 28 50 E
Karibib, Namibia 56 C2 22 0S 15 56 E
Karimata, Kepulauan, Indonesia 36 E3 1 25S 109 0 E
Karimata, Selat, Indonesia 36 E3 2 0S 108 40 E
Karimata Is. = Karimata, Kepulauan, Indonesia 36 E3 1 25S 109 0 E
Karimnagar, India 40 K11 18 26N 79 10 E
Karimunjawa, Kepulauan, Indonesia 36 F4 5 50S 110 30 E
Karin, Somali Rep. 46 E4 10 50N 45 52 E
Karīt, Iran 45 C8 33 29N 56 55 E
Kariya, Japan 31 G8 34 58N 137 1 E
Karkaralinsk = Qarqaraly, Kazakstan 26 E8 49 26N 75 30 E
Karkinitska Zatoka, Ukraine 25 E5 45 56N 33 0 E
Karkinitskiy Zaliv = Karkinitska Zatoka, Ukraine 25 E5 45 56N 33 0 E
Karl-Marx-Stadt = Chemnitz, Germany 16 C7 50 51N 12 54 E
Karlovac, Croatia 16 F8 45 31N 15 36 E
Karlovo, Bulgaria 21 C11 42 38N 24 47 E
Karlovy Vary, Czech Rep. 16 C7 50 13N 12 51 E
Karlsbad = Karlovy Vary, Czech Rep. 16 C7 50 13N 12 51 E
Karlsborg, Sweden 9 G16 58 33N 14 33 E
Karlshamn, Sweden 9 H16 56 10N 14 51 E
Karlskoga, Sweden 9 G16 59 28N 14 33 E
Karlskrona, Sweden 9 H16 56 10N 15 35 E
Karlsruhe, Germany 16 D5 49 0N 8 23 E
Karlstad, Sweden 9 G15 59 23N 13 30 E
Karlstad, U.S.A. 80 A6 48 35N 96 31W
Karnal, India 42 E7 29 42N 77 2 E
Karnali →, Nepal 43 E9 28 45N 81 16 E
Karnaphuli Res., Bangla. 41 H18 22 40N 92 20 E
Karnataka □, India 40 N10 13 15N 77 0 E
Karnes City, U.S.A. 81 L6 28 53N 97 54W
Karnische Alpen, Europe 16 E7 46 36N 13 0 E
Kärnten □, Austria 16 E8 46 52N 13 30 E
Karoi, Zimbabwe 55 F2 16 48S 29 45 E
Karonga, Malawi 55 D3 9 57S 33 55 E
Karoonda, Australia 63 F2 35 1S 139 59 E
Karora, Sudan 51 E13 17 44N 38 15 E
Karpasia □, Cyprus 23 D13 35 32N 34 15 E
Karpinsk, Russia 24 C11 59 45N 60 1 E
Karpogory, Russia 24 B7 64 0N 44 27 E
Karpuz Burnu = Apostolos Andreas, C., Cyprus 23 D13 35 42N 34 35 E
Kars, Turkey 25 F7 40 40N 43 5 E
Karsakpay, Kazakstan 26 E7 47 55N 66 40 E
Karshi = Qarshi, Uzbekistan 26 F7 38 53N 65 48 E
Karsiyang, India 43 F13 26 56N 88 18 E
Karsun, Russia 24 D8 54 14N 46 57 E
Kartaly, Russia 26 D7 53 3N 60 40 E
Kartapur, India 42 D6 31 27N 75 32 E
Karthaus, U.S.A. 78 E6 41 8N 78 9W
Karufa, Indonesia 37 E8 3 50S 133 20 E
Karumba, Australia 62 B3 17 31S 140 50 E
Karumo, Tanzania 54 C3 2 25S 32 50 E
Karumwa, Tanzania 54 C3 3 12S 32 38 E
Karungu, Kenya 54 C3 0 50S 34 10 E
Karviná, Czech Rep. 17 D10 49 53N 18 31 E
Karwar, India 40 M9 14 55N 74 13 E
Karwi, India 43 G9 25 12N 80 57 E
Kasache, Malawi 55 E3 13 25S 34 20 E
Kasai →, Dem. Rep. of the Congo 52 E3 3 30S 16 10 E
Kasai Oriental □, Dem. Rep. of the Congo 54 D1 5 0S 24 30 E
Kasaji, Dem. Rep. of the Congo 55 E1 10 25S 23 27 E
Kasama, Zambia 55 E3 10 16S 31 9 E
Kasan-dong, N. Korea 35 D14 41 18N 126 55 E
Kasane, Namibia 56 B3 17 34S 24 50 E
Kasanga, Tanzania 55 D3 8 30S 31 10 E
Kasaragod, India 40 N9 12 30N 74 58 E
Kasba L., Canada 73 A8 60 20N 102 10W
Kāseh Garān, Iran 44 C5 34 5N 46 2 E
Kasempa, Zambia 55 E2 13 30S 25 44 E
Kasenga, Dem. Rep. of the Congo 55 E2 10 20S 28 45 E
Kasese, Uganda 54 B3 0 13N 30 3 E
Kasewa, Zambia 55 E2 14 28S 28 53 E
Kasganj, India 43 F8 27 48N 78 42 E
Kashabowie, Canada 70 C1 48 40N 90 26W
Kāshān, Iran 45 C6 34 5N 51 30 E
Kashi, China 32 C2 39 30N 76 2 E
Kashimbo, Dem. Rep. of the Congo 55 E2 11 12S 26 19 E
Kashipur, India 43 E8 29 15N 79 0 E
Kashiwazaki, Japan 31 F9 37 22N 138 33 E
Kashk-e Kohneh, Afghan. 40 B3 34 55N 62 30 E
Kāshmar, Iran 45 C8 35 16N 58 26 E
Kashmir, Asia 43 C7 34 0N 76 0 E
Kashmor, Pakistan 42 E3 28 28N 69 32 E
Kashun Noerh = Gaxun Nur, China 32 B5 42 22N 100 30 E
Kasimov, Russia 24 D7 54 55N 41 20 E
Kasinge, Dem. Rep. of the Congo 54 D2 6 15S 26 58 E
Kasiruta, Indonesia 37 E7 0 25S 127 12 E
Kaskaskia →, U.S.A. 80 G10 37 58N 89 57W
Kaskattama →, Canada 73 B10 57 3N 90 4W
Kaskinen, Finland 9 E19 62 22N 21 15 E
Kaslo, Canada 72 D5 49 55N 116 55W
Kasmere L., Canada 73 B8 59 34N 101 10W
Kasongo, Dem. Rep. of the Congo 54 C2 4 30S 26 33 E
Kasongo Lunda, Dem. Rep. of the Congo 52 F3 6 35S 16 49 E
Kásos, Greece 21 G12 35 20N 26 55 E
Kassalâ, Sudan 51 E13 15 30N 36 0 E
Kassel, Germany 16 C5 51 18N 9 26 E
Kassiópi, Greece 23 A3 39 48N 19 53 E
Kastamonu, Turkey 25 F5 41 25N 33 43 E
Kastélli, Greece 23 D5 35 29N 23 38 E
Kastéllion, Greece 23 D7 35 12N 25 20 E
Kasterlee, Belgium 15 C4 51 15N 4 59 E
Kastoria, Greece 21 D9 40 30N 21 19 E
Kasulu, Tanzania 54 C3 4 37S 30 5 E
Kasulu □, Tanzania 54 C3 4 37S 30 5 E
Kasumi, Japan 31 G7 35 38N 134 38 E
Kasungu, Malawi 55 E3 13 0S 33 29 E
Kasur, Pakistan 42 D6 31 5N 74 25 E
Kataba, Zambia 55 F2 16 5S 25 10 E
Katako Kombe, Dem. Rep. of the Congo 54 C1 3 25S 24 20 E
Katale, Tanzania 54 C3 4 52S 31 7 E
Katamatite, Australia 63 F4 36 6S 145 41 E
Katanda, Kivu, Dem. Rep. of the Congo 54 C2 0 55S 29 21 E
Katanda, Shaba, Dem. Rep. of the Congo 54 D1 7 52S 24 13 E
Katanga = Shaba □, Dem. Rep. of the Congo 54 D2 8 0S 25 0 E
Katangi, India 40 J11 21 56N 79 50 E
Katavi Swamp, Tanzania 54 D3 6 50S 31 10 E
Katerini, Greece 21 D10 40 18N 22 37 E
Katha, Burma 41 G20 24 10N 96 30 E
Katherine, Australia 60 B5 14 27S 132 20 E
Kathiawar, India 42 H4 22 20N 71 0 E
Kathikas, Cyprus 23 E11 34 55N 32 25 E
Katihar, India 43 G12 25 34N 87 36 E
Katima Mulilo, Zambia 56 B3 17 28S 24 13 E
Katimbira, Malawi 55 E3 12 40S 34 0 E
Katingan = Mendawai →, Indonesia 36 E4 3 30S 113 0 E
Katiola, Ivory C. 50 G4 8 10N 5 10W
Katmandu, Nepal 43 F11 27 45N 85 20 E
Káto Arkhánai, Greece 23 D7 35 15N 25 10 E
Káto Khorió, Greece 23 D7 35 3N 25 47 E
Kato Pyrgos, Cyprus 23 D11 35 11N 32 41 E
Katompe, Dem. Rep. of the Congo 54 D2 6 2S 26 23 E
Katonga →, Uganda 54 B3 0 34N 31 50 E
Katoomba, Australia 63 E5 33 41S 150 19 E
Katowice, Poland 17 C10 50 17N 19 5 E
Katrine, L., U.K. 12 E4 56 15N 4 30W
Katrineholm, Sweden 9 G17 59 9N 16 12 E
Katsepe, Madag. 57 B8 15 45S 46 15 E
Katsina, Nigeria 50 F7 13 0N 7 32 E
Katsumoto, Japan 31 H4 33 51N 129 42 E
Katsuura, Japan 31 G10 35 10N 140 20 E
Katsuyama, Japan 31 F8 36 3N 136 30 E
Kattaviá, Greece 23 D9 35 57N 27 46 E
Kattegat, Denmark 9 H14 56 40N 11 20 E
Katumba, Dem. Rep. of the Congo 54 D2 7 40S 25 17 E
Katungu, Kenya 54 C5 2 55S 40 3 E
Katwa, India 43 H13 23 30N 88 5 E
Katwijk, Neths. 15 B4 52 12N 4 24 E
Kauai, U.S.A. 74 H15 22 3N 159 30W
Kauai Channel, U.S.A. 74 H15 21 45N 158 50W
Kaufman, U.S.A. 81 J6 32 35N 96 19W
Kauhajoki, Finland 9 E20 62 25N 22 10 E
Kaukauna, U.S.A. 76 C1 44 17N 88 17W
Kaukauveld, Namibia 56 C3 20 0S 20 15 E
Kaunas, Lithuania 24 D3 54 54N 23 54 E
Kautokeino, Norway 8 B20 69 0N 23 4 E
Kavacha, Russia 27 C17 60 16N 169 51 E
Kavalerovo, Russia 30 B7 44 15N 135 4 E
Kavali, India 40 M12 14 55N 80 1 E
Kavála, Greece 21 D11 40 57N 24 28 E
Kavār, Iran 45 D7 29 11N 52 44 E
Kavos, Greece 23 B4 39 23N 20 3 E
Kaw, Fr. Guiana 93 C8 4 30N 52 15W
Kawagama L., Canada 78 A6 45 18N 78 45W
Kawagoe, Japan 31 G9 35 55N 139 29 E
Kawaguchi, Japan 31 G9 35 52N 139 45 E
Kawaihae, U.S.A. 74 H17 20 3N 155 50W
Kawambwa, Zambia 55 D2 9 48S 29 3 E
Kawanoe, Japan 31 G6 34 1N 133 34 E
Kawardha, India 43 J9 22 0N 81 17 E
Kawasaki, Japan 31 G9 35 35N 139 42 E
Kawasi, Indonesia 37 E7 1 38S 127 28 E
Kawene, Canada 70 C1 48 45N 91 15W
Kawerau, N.Z. 59 H6 38 7S 176 42 E
Kawhia Harbour, N.Z. 59 H5 38 5S 174 51 E
Kawio, Kepulauan, Indonesia 37 D7 4 30N 125 30 E
Kawnro, Burma 41 H21 22 48N 99 8 E
Kawthaung, Burma 39 H2 10 5N 98 36 E
Kawthoolei = Kawthule □, Burma 41 L20 18 0N 97 30 E
Kawthule □, Burma 41 L20 18 0N 97 30 E
Kaya, Burkina Faso 50 F5 13 4N 1 10W
Kayah □, Burma 41 K20 19 15N 97 15 E
Kayan →, Indonesia 36 D5 2 55N 117 35 E
Kaycee, U.S.A. 82 E10 43 43N 106 38W
Kayeli, Indonesia 37 E7 3 20S 127 10 E
Kayenta, U.S.A. 83 H8 36 44N 110 15W
Kayes, Mali 50 F3 14 25N 11 30W
Kayoa, Indonesia 37 D7 0 1N 127 28 E
Kayomba, Zambia 55 E1 13 11S 24 2 E
Kayrunnera, Australia 63 E3 30 40S 142 30 E
Kayseri, Turkey 25 G6 38 45N 35 30 E
Kaysville, U.S.A. 82 F8 41 2N 111 56W
Kazachye, Russia 27 B14 70 52N 135 58 E
Kazakstan ■, Asia 26 E8 50 0N 70 0 E
Kazan, Russia 24 C8 55 50N 49 10 E
Kazan-Rettō, Pac. Oc. 64 E6 25 0N 141 0 E
Kazanlŭk, Bulgaria 21 C11 42 38N 25 20 E
Kazatin = Kozyatyn, Ukraine 17 D15 49 45N 28 50 E
Kāzerūn, Iran 45 D6 29 38N 51 40 E
Kazuno, Japan 30 D10 40 10N 140 45 E
Kazym →, Russia 26 C7 63 54N 65 50 E
Keady, U.K. 13 B5 54 15N 6 42W
Keams Canyon, U.S.A. 83 J8 35 49N 110 12W
Kearney, U.S.A. 80 E5 40 42N 99 5W
Keban, Turkey 25 G6 38 50N 38 50 E
Kebnekaise, Sweden 8 C18 67 53N 18 33 E
Kebri Dehar, Ethiopia 46 F3 6 45N 44 17 E
Kebumen, Indonesia 37 G13 7 42S 109 40 E
Kechika →, Canada 72 B3 59 41N 127 12W
Kecskemét, Hungary 17 E10 46 57N 19 42 E
Kedainiai, Lithuania 9 J21 55 15N 24 2 E
Kedgwick, Canada 71 C6 47 40N 67 20W
Kédhros Óros, Greece 23 D6 35 11N 24 37 E
Kedia Hill, Botswana 56 C3 21 28S 24 37 E
Kediri, Indonesia 37 G15 7 51S 112 1 E
Keeler, U.S.A. 84 J9 36 29N 117 52W
Keeley L., Canada 73 C7 54 54N 108 8W
Keeling Is. = Cocos Is., Ind. Oc. 64 J1 12 10S 96 55 E
Keene, Calif., U.S.A. 85 K8 35 13N 118 33W
Keene, N.H., U.S.A. 79 D12 42 56N 72 17W
Keeper Hill, Ireland 13 D3 52 45N 8 16W
Keer-Weer, C., Australia 62 A3 14 0S 141 32 E
Keeseville, U.S.A. 79 B11 44 29N 73 30W
Keetmanshoop, Namibia 56 D2 26 35S 18 8 E
Keewatin, U.S.A. 80 B8 47 24N 93 5W
Keewatin □, Canada 73 A10 63 20N 95 0W
Keewatin →, Canada 73 B8 56 29N 100 46W
Kefallinía, Greece 21 E9 38 20N 20 30 E
Kefamenanu, Indonesia 37 F6 9 28S 124 29 E
Keffi, Nigeria 50 G7 8 55N 7 43 E
Keflavík, Iceland 8 D2 64 2N 22 35W
Keg River, Canada 72 B5 57 54N 117 55W
Kegaska, Canada 71 B7 50 9N 61 18W
Keighley, U.K. 10 D6 53 52N 1 54W
Keila, Estonia 9 G21 59 18N 24 25 E
Keimoes, S. Africa 56 D3 28 41S 20 59 E
Keitele, Finland 8 E22 63 10N 26 20 E
Keith, Australia 63 F3 36 6S 140 20 E
Keith, U.K. 12 D6 57 32N 2 57W
Kekri, India 42 G6 26 0N 75 10 E
Kelan, China 34 E6 38 43N 111 31 E
Kelang, Malaysia 39 L3 3 2N 101 26 E
Kelantan →, Malaysia 39 J4 6 13N 102 14 E
Keller, U.S.A. 82 B4 48 5N 118 41W
Kellerberrin, Australia 61 F2 31 36S 117 38 E
Kelleys I., U.S.A. 78 E2 41 36N 82 42W
Kellogg, U.S.A. 82 C5 47 32N 116 7W
Kells = Ceanannus Mor, Ireland 13 C5 53 44N 6 53W
Kelokedhara, Cyprus 23 E11 34 48N 32 39 E
Kelowna, Canada 72 D5 49 50N 119 25W
Kelsey Bay, Canada 72 C3 50 25N 126 0W
Kelseyville, U.S.A. 84 G4 38 59N 122 50W
Kelso, N.Z. 59 L2 45 54S 169 15 E
Kelso, U.K. 12 F6 55 36N 2 26W
Kelso, U.S.A. 84 D4 46 9N 122 54W
Keluang, Malaysia 39 L4 2 3N 103 18 E
Kelvington, Canada 73 C8 52 10N 103 30W
Kem, Russia 24 B5 65 0N 34 38 E
Kem →, Russia 24 B5 64 57N 34 41 E
Kema, Indonesia 37 D7 1 22N 125 8 E
Kemano, Canada 72 C3 53 35N 128 0W
Kemasik, Malaysia 39 K4 4 25N 103 27 E
Kemerovo, Russia 26 D9 55 20N 86 5 E
Kemi, Finland 8 D21 65 44N 24 34 E
Kemi älv = Kemijoki →, Finland 8 D21 65 47N 24 32 E
Kemijärvi, Finland 8 C22 66 43N 27 22 E
Kemijoki →, Finland 8 D21 65 47N 24 32 E
Kemmerer, U.S.A. 82 F8 41 48N 110 32W
Kemmuna = Comino, Malta 23 C1 36 2N 14 20 E
Kemp, L., U.S.A. 81 J5 33 46N 99 9W
Kemp Land, Antarctica 5 C5 69 0S 55 0 E
Kempsey, Australia 63 E5 31 1S 152 50 E
Kempt, L., Canada 70 C5 47 25N 74 22W
Kempten, Germany 16 E6 47 45N 10 17 E
Kemptville, Canada 70 D4 45 0N 75 38W
Kendal, Indonesia 37 G14 6 56S 110 14 E
Kendal, U.K. 10 C5 54 20N 2 44W
Kendall, Australia 63 E5 31 35S 152 44 E
Kendall →, Australia 62 A3 14 4S 141 35 E
Kendallville, U.S.A. 76 E3 41 27N 85 16W
Kendari, Indonesia 37 E6 3 50S 122 30 E
Kendawangan, Indonesia 36 E4 2 32S 110 17 E
Kendenup, Australia 61 F2 34 30S 117 38 E
Kendrapara, India 41 J15 20 35N 86 30 E
Kendrew, S. Africa 56 E3 32 32S 24 30 E
Kendrick, U.S.A. 82 C5 46 37N 116 39W
Kene Thao, Laos 38 D3 17 44N 101 10 E
Kenedy, U.S.A. 81 L6 28 49N 97 51W
Kenema, S. Leone 50 G3 7 50N 11 14W
Keng Kok, Laos 38 D5 16 26N 105 12 E
Keng Tawng, Burma 41 J21 20 45N 98 18 E
Keng Tung, Burma 41 J21 21 0N 99 30 E
Kengeja, Tanzania 54 D4 5 26S 39 45 E
Kenhardt, S. Africa 56 D3 29 19S 21 12 E
Kenitra, Morocco 50 B4 34 15N 6 40W
Kenli, China 35 F10 37 30N 118 20 E
Kenmare, Ireland 13 E2 51 53N 9 36W
Kenmare, U.S.A. 80 A3 48 41N 102 5W
Kenmare River, Ireland 13 E2 51 48N 9 51W
Kennebec, U.S.A. 80 D5 43 54N 99 52W
Kennedy, Zimbabwe 55 F2 18 52S 27 10 E
Kennedy Ra., Australia 61 D2 24 45S 115 10 E
Kennedy Taungdeik, Burma 41 H18 23 15N 93 45 E
Kenner, U.S.A. 81 L9 29 59N 90 15W
Kennet →, U.K. 11 F7 51 27N 0 57W
Kenneth Ra., Australia 60 D2 23 50S 117 8 E
Kennett, U.S.A. 81 G9 36 14N 90 3W
Kennewick, U.S.A. 82 C4 46 12N 119 7W
Kénogami, Canada 71 C5 48 25N 71 15W
Kenogami →, Canada 70 B3 51 6N 84 28W
Kenora, Canada 73 D10 49 47N 94 29W
Kenosha, U.S.A. 76 D2 42 35N 87 49W
Kensington, Canada 71 C7 46 28N 63 34W
Kensington, U.S.A. 80 F5 39 46N 99 2W
Kensington Downs, Australia 62 C3 22 31S 144 19 E
Kent, Ohio, U.S.A. 78 E3 41 9N 81 22W
Kent, Oreg., U.S.A. 82 D3 45 12N 120 42W
Kent, Tex., U.S.A. 81 K2 31 4N 104 13W
Kent, Wash., U.S.A. 84 C4 47 23N 122 14W
Kent □, U.K. 11 F8 51 12N 0 40 E
Kent Group, Australia 62 F4 39 30S 147 20 E
Kent Pen., Canada 68 B9 68 30N 107 0W
Kentau, Kazakstan 26 E7 43 32N 68 36 E
Kentland, U.S.A. 76 E2 40 46N 87 27W
Kenton, U.S.A. 76 E4 40 39N 83 37W
Kentucky □, U.S.A. 76 G3 37 0N 84 0W
Kentucky →, U.S.A. 76 F3 38 41N 85 11W
Kentucky L., U.S.A. 77 G2 37 1N 88 16W
Kentville, Canada 71 C7 45 6N 64 29W
Kentwood, U.S.A. 81 K9 30 56N 90 31W
Kenya ■, Africa 54 B4 1 0N 38 0 E
Kenya, Mt., Kenya 54 C4 0 10S 37 18 E
Keo Neua, Deo, Vietnam 38 C5 18 23N 105 10 E
Keokuk, U.S.A. 80 E9 40 24N 91 24W

Kep, *Cambodia* **39 G5** 10 29N 104 19 E
Kep, *Vietnam* **38 B6** 21 24N 106 16 E
Kepi, *Indonesia* **37 F9** 6 32S 139 19 E
Kerala □, *India* **40 P10** 11 0N 76 15 E
Kerama-Rettō, *Japan* **31 L3** 26 5N 127 15 E
Keran, *Pakistan* **43 B5** 34 35N 73 59 E
Kerang, *Australia* **63 F3** 35 40S 143 55 E
Keraudren, C., *Australia* **60 C2** 19 58S 119 45 E
Kerava, *Finland* **9 F21** 60 25N 25 5 E
Kerch, *Ukraine* **25 E6** 45 20N 36 20 E
Kerguelen, *Ind. Oc.* **3 G13** 49 15S 69 10 E
Kericho, *Kenya* **54 C4** 0 22S 35 15 E
Kericho □, *Kenya* **54 C4** 0 30S 35 15 E
Kerinci, *Indonesia* **36 E2** 1 40S 101 15 E
Kerki, *Turkmenistan* **26 F7** 37 50N 65 12 E
Kerkrade, *Neths.* **15 D6** 50 53N 6 4 E
Kermadec Is., *Pac. Oc.* **64 L10** 30 0S 178 15W
Kermadec Trench, *Pac. Oc.* **64 L10** 30 30S 176 0W
Kermān, *Iran* **45 D8** 30 15N 57 1 E
Kerman, *U.S.A.* **84 J6** 36 43N 120 4W
Kermān □, *Iran* **45 D8** 30 0N 57 0 E
Kermānshāh = Bākhtarān, *Iran* **44 C5** 34 23N 47 0 E
Kermit, *U.S.A.* **81 K3** 31 52N 103 6W
Kern →, *U.S.A.* **85 K7** 35 16N 119 18W
Kernville, *U.S.A.* **85 K8** 35 45N 118 26W
Keroh, *Malaysia* **39 K3** 5 43N 101 1 E
Kerrera, *U.K.* **12 E3** 56 24N 5 33W
Kerrobert, *Canada* **73 C7** 51 56N 109 8W
Kerrville, *U.S.A.* **81 K5** 30 3N 99 8W
Kerry □, *Ireland* **13 D2** 52 7N 9 35W
Kerry Hd., *Ireland* **13 D2** 52 25N 9 56W
Kerulen →, *Asia* **33 B6** 48 48N 117 0 E
Kerzaz, *Algeria* **50 C5** 29 29N 1 37W
Kesagami →, *Canada* **70 B4** 51 40N 79 45W
Kesagami L., *Canada* **70 B3** 50 23N 80 15W
Keşan, *Turkey* **21 D12** 40 49N 26 38 E
Kesennuma, *Japan* **30 E10** 38 54N 141 35 E
Keshit, *Iran* **45 D8** 29 43N 58 17 E
Kestell, *S. Africa* **57 D4** 28 17S 28 42 E
Kestenga, *Russia* **24 A5** 65 50N 31 45 E
Keswick, *U.K.* **10 C4** 54 36N 3 8W
Ket →, *Russia* **26 D9** 58 55N 81 32 E
Ketapang, *Indonesia* **36 E4** 1 55S 110 0 E
Ketchikan, *U.S.A.* **68 C6** 55 21N 131 39W
Ketchum, *U.S.A.* **82 E6** 43 41N 114 22W
Keti Bandar, *Pakistan* **42 G2** 24 8N 67 27 E
Ketri, *India* **42 E6** 28 1N 75 50 E
Kętrzyn, *Poland* **17 A11** 54 7N 21 22 E
Kettering, *U.K.* **11 E7** 52 24N 0 43W
Kettering, *U.S.A.* **76 F3** 39 41N 84 10W
Kettle →, *Canada* **73 B11** 56 40N 89 34W
Kettle Falls, *U.S.A.* **82 B4** 48 37N 118 3W
Kettleman City, *U.S.A.* **84 J7** 36 1N 119 58W
Keuruu, *Finland* **9 E21** 62 16N 24 41 E
Kevin, *U.S.A.* **82 B8** 48 45N 111 58W
Kewanee, *U.S.A.* **80 E10** 41 14N 89 56W
Kewaunee, *U.S.A.* **76 C2** 44 27N 87 31W
Keweenaw B., *U.S.A.* **76 B1** 47 0N 88 15W
Keweenaw Pen., *U.S.A.* **76 B2** 47 30N 88 0W
Keweenaw Pt., *U.S.A.* **76 B2** 47 25N 87 43W
Key Harbour, *Canada* **70 C3** 45 50N 80 45W
Key West, *U.S.A.* **75 F10** 24 33N 81 48W
Keynsham, *U.K.* **11 F5** 51 24N 2 29W
Keyser, *U.S.A.* **76 F6** 39 26N 78 59W
Keystone, *U.S.A.* **80 D3** 43 54N 103 25W
Kezhma, *Russia* **27 D11** 58 59N 101 9 E
Khabarovsk, *Russia* **27 E14** 48 30N 135 5 E
Khabr, *Iran* **45 D8** 28 51N 56 22 E
Khābūr →, *Syria* **44 C4** 35 17N 40 35 E
Khachrod, *India* **42 H6** 23 25N 75 20 E
Khadro, *Pakistan* **42 F3** 26 11N 68 50 E
Khadzhilyangar, *India* **43 B8** 35 45N 79 20 E
Khagaria, *India* **43 G12** 25 30N 86 32 E
Khaipur, *Bahawalpur, Pakistan* **42 E5** 29 34N 72 17 E
Khaipur, *Hyderabad, Pakistan* **42 F3** 27 32N 68 49 E
Khair, *India* **42 F7** 27 57N 77 46 E
Khairabad, *India* **43 F9** 27 33N 80 47 E
Khairagarh, *India* **43 J9** 21 27N 81 2 E
Khairpur, *Pakistan* **40 F6** 27 32N 68 49 E
Khakassia □, *Russia* **26 D9** 53 0N 90 0 E
Khakhea, *Botswana* **56 C3** 24 48S 23 22 E
Khalafābād, *Iran* **45 D6** 30 54N 49 24 E
Khalilabad, *India* **43 F10** 26 48N 83 5 E
Khalīlī, *Iran* **45 E7** 27 38N 53 17 E
Khalkhāl, *Iran* **45 B6** 37 37N 48 32 E
Khalkís, *Greece* **21 E10** 38 27N 23 42 E
Khalmer-Sede = Tazovskiy, *Russia* **26 C8** 67 30N 78 44 E
Khalmer Yu, *Russia* **24 A12** 67 58N 65 1 E
Khalturin, *Russia* **24 C8** 58 40N 48 50 E
Khalūf, *Oman* **46 C6** 20 30N 58 13 E
Kham Keut, *Laos* **38 C5** 18 15N 104 43 E
Khamas Country, *Botswana* **56 C4** 21 45S 26 30 E
Khambhaliya, *India* **42 H3** 22 14N 69 41 E
Khambhat, *India* **42 H5** 22 23N 72 33 E
Khambhat, G. of, *India* **42 J5** 20 45N 72 30 E
Khamīr, *Iran* **45 E7** 26 57N 55 36 E
Khamir, *Yemen* **46 D3** 16 2N 44 0 E
Khamsa, *Egypt* **47 E1** 30 27N 32 23 E
Khān Abū Shāmat, *Syria* **47 B5** 33 39N 36 53 E
Khān Azād, *Iraq* **44 C5** 33 7N 44 22 E
Khān Mujiddah, *Iraq* **44 C4** 32 21N 43 48 E
Khān Shaykhūn, *Syria* **44 C3** 35 26N 36 38 E
Khān Yūnis, *Gaza Strip* **47 D3** 31 21N 34 18 E
Khānaqīn, *Iraq* **44 C5** 34 23N 45 25 E
Khānbāghī, *Iran* **45 B7** 36 10N 55 25 E
Khandwa, *India* **40 J10** 21 49N 76 22 E
Khandyga, *Russia* **27 C14** 62 42N 135 35 E
Khāneh, *Iran* **44 B5** 36 41N 45 8 E
Khanewal, *Pakistan* **42 D4** 30 20N 71 55 E
Khanh Duong, *Vietnam* **38 F7** 12 44N 108 44 E
Khaniá, *Greece* **23 D6** 35 30N 24 4 E
Khaniá □, *Greece* **23 D6** 35 30N 24 0 E
Khaníon, Kólpos, *Greece* **23 D5** 35 33N 23 55 E
Khanka, L., *Asia* **30 B6** 45 0N 132 24 E
Khankendy = Xankändi, *Azerbaijan* **25 G8** 39 52N 46 49 E
Khanna, *India* **42 D7** 30 42N 76 16 E
Khanpur, *Pakistan* **42 E4** 28 42N 70 35 E
Khanty-Mansiysk, *Russia* **26 C7** 61 0N 69 0 E
Khapalu, *Pakistan* **43 B7** 35 10N 76 20 E
Khapcheranga, *Russia* **27 E12** 49 42N 112 24 E
Kharagpur, *India* **43 H12** 22 20N 87 25 E
Khárakas, *Greece* **23 D7** 35 1N 25 7 E
Kharan Kalat, *Pakistan* **40 E4** 28 34N 65 21 E
Kharānaq, *Iran* **45 C7** 32 20N 54 45 E
Kharda, *India* **40 K9** 18 40N 75 34 E
Khardung La, *India* **43 B7** 34 20N 77 43 E
Khârga, El Wâhât el, *Egypt* **51 C12** 25 10N 30 35 E
Khargon, *India* **40 J9** 21 45N 75 40 E
Khārk, Jazireh, *Iran* **45 D6** 29 15N 50 28 E
Kharkiv, *Ukraine* **25 E6** 49 58N 36 20 E
Kharkov = Kharkiv, *Ukraine* **25 E6** 49 58N 36 20 E
Kharovsk, *Russia* **24 C7** 59 56N 40 13 E
Kharta, *Turkey* **21 D13** 40 55N 29 7 E
Khartoum = El Khartûm, *Sudan* **51 E12** 15 31N 32 35 E
Khasan, *Russia* **30 C5** 42 25N 130 40 E
Khāsh, *Iran* **40 E2** 28 15N 61 15 E
Khashm el Girba, *Sudan* **51 F13** 14 59N 35 58 E
Khaskovo, *Bulgaria* **21 D11** 41 56N 25 30 E
Khatanga, *Russia* **27 B11** 72 0N 102 20 E
Khatanga →, *Russia* **27 B11** 72 55N 106 0 E
Khatauli, *India* **42 E7** 29 17N 77 43 E
Khātūnābād, *Iran* **45 C6** 35 30N 51 40 E
Khatyrka, *Russia* **27 C18** 62 3N 175 15 E
Khaybar, Harrat, *Si. Arabia* **44 E4** 25 45N 40 0 E
Khāzimiyah, *Iraq* **44 C4** 34 46N 43 37 E
Khe Bo, *Vietnam* **38 C5** 19 8N 104 41 E
Khe Long, *Vietnam* **38 B5** 21 29N 104 46 E
Khed Brahma, *India* **40 G8** 24 7N 73 5 E
Khekra, *India* **42 E7** 28 52N 77 20 E
Khemarak Phouminville, *Cambodia* **39 G4** 11 37N 102 59 E
Khemmarat, *Thailand* **38 D5** 16 10N 105 15 E
Khenāmān, *Iran* **45 D8** 30 27N 56 29 E
Khenchela, *Algeria* **50 A7** 35 28N 7 11 E
Kherson, *Ukraine* **25 E5** 46 35N 32 35 E
Khersónisos Akrotíri, *Greece* **23 D6** 35 30N 24 10 E
Kheta →, *Russia* **27 B11** 71 54N 102 6 E
Khilok, *Russia* **27 D12** 51 30N 110 45 E
Khiuma = Hiiumaa, *Estonia* **24 C3** 58 50N 22 45 E
Khiva, *Uzbekistan* **26 E7** 41 30N 60 18 E
Khīyāv, *Iran* **44 B5** 38 30N 47 45 E
Khlong Khlung, *Thailand* **38 D2** 16 12N 99 43 E
Khmelnik, *Ukraine* **17 D14** 49 33N 27 58 E
Khmelnitskiy = Khmelnytskyy, *Ukraine* **25 E4** 49 23N 27 0 E
Khmelnytskyy, *Ukraine* **25 E4** 49 23N 27 0 E
Khmer Rep. = Cambodia ■, *Asia* **38 F5** 12 15N 105 0 E
Khoai, Hon, *Vietnam* **39 H5** 8 26N 104 50 E
Khodoriv, *Ukraine* **17 D13** 49 24N 24 19 E
Khodzent = Khudzhand, *Tajikistan* **26 E7** 40 17N 69 37 E
Khojak Pass, *Afghan.* **40 D5** 30 55N 66 30 E
Khok Kloi, *Thailand* **39 H2** 8 17N 98 19 E
Khok Pho, *Thailand* **39 J3** 6 43N 101 6 E
Kholm, *Russia* **24 C5** 57 10N 31 15 E
Kholmsk, *Russia* **27 E15** 47 40N 142 5 E
Khomas Hochland, *Namibia* **56 C2** 22 40S 16 0 E
Khomeyn, *Iran* **45 C6** 33 40N 50 7 E
Khon Kaen, *Thailand* **38 D4** 16 30N 102 47 E
Khong →, *Cambodia* **38 F5** 13 32N 105 58 E
Khong Sedone, *Laos* **38 E5** 15 34N 105 49 E
Khonuu, *Russia* **27 C15** 66 30N 143 12 E
Khóra Sfakíon, *Greece* **23 D6** 35 15N 24 9 E
Khorāsān □, *Iran* **45 C8** 34 0N 58 0 E
Khorat = Nakhon Ratchasima, *Thailand* **38 E4** 14 59N 102 12 E
Khorat, Cao Nguyen, *Thailand* **38 E4** 15 30N 102 50 E
Khorixas, *Namibia* **56 C1** 20 16S 14 59 E
Khorramābād, *Khorāsān, Iran* **45 C8** 35 6N 57 57 E
Khorramābād, *Lorestān, Iran* **45 C6** 33 30N 48 25 E
Khorrāmshahr, *Iran* **45 D6** 30 29N 48 15 E
Khorugh, *Tajikistan* **26 F8** 37 30N 71 36 E
Khosravī, *Iran* **45 D6** 30 48N 51 28 E
Khosrowābād, *Khuzestān, Iran* **45 D6** 30 10N 48 25 E
Khosrowābād, *Kordestān, Iran* **44 C5** 35 31N 47 38 E
Khosūyeh, *Iran* **45 D7** 28 32N 54 26 E
Khotyn, *Ukraine* **17 D14** 48 31N 26 27 E
Khouribga, *Morocco* **50 B4** 32 58N 6 57W
Khowai, *Bangla.* **41 G17** 24 5N 91 40 E
Khoyniki, *Belarus* **17 C15** 51 54N 29 55 E
Khrysokhou B., *Cyprus* **23 D11** 35 6N 32 25 E
Khu Khan, *Thailand* **38 E5** 14 42N 104 12 E
Khudzhand, *Tajikistan* **26 E7** 40 17N 69 37 E
Khuff, *Si. Arabia* **44 E5** 24 55N 44 53 E
Khūgīānī, *Afghan.* **42 D1** 31 28N 65 14 E
Khulna, *Bangla.* **41 H16** 22 45N 89 34 E
Khulna □, *Bangla.* **41 H16** 22 25N 89 35 E
Khumago, *Botswana* **56 C3** 20 26S 24 32 E
Khūnsorkh, *Iran* **45 E8** 27 9N 56 7 E
Khūr, *Iran* **45 C8** 32 55N 58 18 E
Khurai, *India* **42 G8** 24 3N 78 23 E
Khurayş, *Si. Arabia* **45 E6** 25 6N 48 2 E
Khurīyā Murīyā, Jazā 'ir, *Oman* **46 D6** 17 30N 55 58 E
Khurja, *India* **42 E7** 28 15N 77 58 E
Khūsf, *Iran* **45 C8** 32 46N 58 53 E
Khush, *Afghan.* **40 C3** 32 55N 62 10 E
Khushab, *Pakistan* **42 C5** 32 20N 72 20 E
Khust, *Ukraine* **17 D12** 48 10N 23 18 E
Khuzdar, *Pakistan* **42 F2** 27 52N 66 30 E
Khūzestān □, *Iran* **45 D6** 31 0N 49 0 E
Khvājeh, *Iran* **44 B5** 38 9N 46 35 E
Khvānsār, *Iran* **45 D7** 29 56N 54 8 E
Khvor, *Iran* **45 C7** 33 45N 55 0 E
Khvorgū, *Iran* **45 E8** 27 34N 56 27 E
Khvormūj, *Iran* **45 D6** 28 40N 51 30 E
Khvoy, *Iran* **44 B5** 38 35N 45 0 E
Khyber Pass, *Afghan.* **42 B4** 34 10N 71 8 E
Kiabukwa, *Dem. Rep. of the Congo* **55 D1** 8 40S 24 48 E
Kiama, *Australia* **63 E5** 34 40S 150 50 E
Kiamba, *Phil.* **37 C6** 6 2N 124 46 E
Kiambi, *Dem. Rep. of the Congo* **54 D2** 7 15S 28 0 E
Kiambu, *Kenya* **54 C4** 1 8S 36 50 E
Kiangsi = Jiangxi □, *China* **33 D6** 27 30N 116 0 E
Kiangsu = Jiangsu □, *China* **35 H11** 33 0N 120 0 E
Kibanga Port, *Uganda* **54 B3** 0 10N 32 58 E
Kibara, *Tanzania* **54 C3** 2 8S 33 30 E
Kibare, Mts., *Dem. Rep. of the Congo* **54 D2** 8 25S 27 10 E
Kibombo, *Dem. Rep. of the Congo* **54 C2** 3 57S 25 53 E
Kibondo, *Tanzania* **54 C3** 3 35S 30 45 E
Kibondo □, *Tanzania* **54 C3** 4 0S 30 55 E
Kibumbu, *Burundi* **54 C2** 3 32S 29 45 E
Kibungo, *Rwanda* **54 C3** 2 10S 30 32 E
Kibuye, *Burundi* **54 C2** 3 39S 29 59 E
Kibuye, *Rwanda* **54 C2** 2 3S 29 21 E
Kibwesa, *Tanzania* **54 D2** 6 30S 29 58 E
Kibwezi, *Kenya* **54 C4** 2 27S 37 57 E
Kicking Horse Pass, *Canada* **72 C5** 51 28N 116 16W
Kidal, *Mali* **50 E6** 18 26N 1 22 E
Kidderminster, *U.K.* **11 E5** 52 24N 2 15W
Kidete, *Tanzania* **54 D4** 6 25S 37 17 E
Kidnappers, C., *N.Z.* **59 H6** 39 38S 177 5 E
Kidsgrove, *U.K.* **10 D5** 53 5N 2 14W
Kidston, *Australia* **62 B3** 18 52S 144 8 E
Kidugallo, *Tanzania* **54 D4** 6 49S 38 15 E
Kiel, *Germany* **16 A6** 54 19N 10 8 E
Kiel Canal = Nord-Ostsee-Kanal →, *Germany* **16 A5** 54 12N 9 32 E
Kielce, *Poland* **17 C11** 50 52N 20 42 E
Kielder Water, *U.K.* **10 B5** 55 11N 2 31W
Kieler Bucht, *Germany* **16 A6** 54 35N 10 25 E
Kien Binh, *Vietnam* **39 H5** 9 55N 105 19 E
Kien Tan, *Vietnam* **39 G5** 10 7N 105 17 E
Kienge, *Dem. Rep. of the Congo* **55 E2** 10 30S 27 30 E
Kiev = Kyyiv, *Ukraine* **25 D5** 50 30N 30 28 E
Kiffa, *Mauritania* **50 E3** 16 37N 11 24W
Kifrī, *Iraq* **44 C5** 34 45N 45 0 E
Kigali, *Rwanda* **54 C3** 1 59S 30 4 E
Kigarama, *Tanzania* **54 C3** 1 1S 31 50 E
Kigoma □, *Tanzania* **54 D3** 5 0S 30 0 E
Kigoma-Ujiji, *Tanzania* **54 C2** 4 55S 29 36 E
Kigomasha, Ras, *Tanzania* **54 C4** 4 58S 38 58 E
Kihee, *Australia* **63 D3** 27 23S 142 37 E
Kihnu, *Estonia* **9 G21** 58 9N 24 1 E
Kii-Sanchi, *Japan* **31 G8** 34 20N 136 0 E
Kii-Suidō, *Japan* **31 H7** 33 40N 134 45 E
Kikaiga-Shima, *Japan* **31 K4** 28 19N 129 59 E
Kikinda, *Serbia, Yug.* **21 B9** 45 50N 20 30 E
Kikládhes, *Greece* **21 F11** 37 0N 24 30 E
Kikwit, *Dem. Rep. of the Congo* **52 F3** 5 0S 18 45 E
Kilauea Crater, *U.S.A.* **74 J17** 19 25N 155 17W
Kilbrannan Sd., *U.K.* **12 F3** 55 37N 5 26W
Kilchu, *N. Korea* **35 D15** 40 57N 129 25 E
Kilcoy, *Australia* **63 D5** 26 59S 152 30 E
Kildare, *Ireland* **13 C5** 53 9N 6 55W
Kildare □, *Ireland* **13 C5** 53 10N 6 50W
Kilfinnane, *Ireland* **13 D3** 52 21N 8 28W
Kilgore, *U.S.A.* **81 J7** 32 23N 94 53W
Kilifi, *Kenya* **54 C4** 3 40S 39 48 E
Kilifi □, *Kenya* **54 C4** 3 30S 39 40 E
Kilimanjaro, *Tanzania* **54 C4** 3 7S 37 20 E
Kilimanjaro □, *Tanzania* **54 C4** 4 0S 38 0 E
Kilindini, *Kenya* **54 C4** 4 4S 39 40 E
Kiliya, *Ukraine* **17 F15** 45 28N 29 16 E
Kilkee, *Ireland* **13 D2** 52 41N 9 39W
Kilkeel, *U.K.* **13 B5** 54 4N 6 0W
Kilkenny, *Ireland* **13 D4** 52 39N 7 15W
Kilkenny □, *Ireland* **13 D4** 52 35N 7 15W
Kilkieran B., *Ireland* **13 C2** 53 20N 9 41W
Kilkís, *Greece* **21 D10** 40 58N 22 57 E
Killala, *Ireland* **13 B2** 54 13N 9 12W
Killala B., *Ireland* **13 B2** 54 16N 9 8W
Killaloe, *Ireland* **13 D3** 52 48N 8 28W
Killaloe Sta., *Canada* **78 A7** 45 33N 77 25W
Killam, *Canada* **72 C6** 52 47N 111 51W
Killarney, *Australia* **63 D5** 28 20S 152 18 E
Killarney, *Canada* **70 C3** 45 55N 81 30W
Killarney, *Ireland* **13 D2** 52 4N 9 30W
Killary Harbour, *Ireland* **13 C2** 53 38N 9 52W
Killdeer, *Canada* **73 D7** 49 6N 106 22W
Killdeer, *U.S.A.* **80 B3** 47 26N 102 48W
Killeen, *U.S.A.* **81 K6** 31 7N 97 44W
Killin, *U.K.* **12 E4** 56 28N 4 19W
Killíni, *Greece* **21 F10** 37 54N 22 25 E
Killorglin, *Ireland* **13 D2** 52 6N 9 47W
Killybegs, *Ireland* **13 B3** 54 38N 8 26W
Kilmarnock, *U.K.* **12 F4** 55 37N 4 29W
Kilmore, *Australia* **63 F3** 37 25S 144 53 E
Kilondo, *Tanzania* **55 D3** 9 45S 34 20 E
Kilosa, *Tanzania* **54 D4** 6 48S 37 0 E
Kilosa □, *Tanzania* **54 D4** 6 48S 37 0 E
Kilrush, *Ireland* **13 D2** 52 38N 9 29W
Kilwa □, *Tanzania* **55 D4** 9 0S 39 0 E
Kilwa Kisiwani, *Tanzania* **55 D4** 8 58S 39 32 E
Kilwa Kivinje, *Tanzania* **55 D4** 8 45S 39 25 E
Kilwa Masoko, *Tanzania* **55 D4** 8 55S 39 30 E
Kilwinning, *U.K.* **12 F4** 55 39N 4 43W
Kim, *U.S.A.* **81 G3** 37 15N 103 21W
Kimaam, *Indonesia* **37 F9** 7 58S 138 53 E
Kimamba, *Tanzania* **54 D4** 6 45S 37 10 E
Kimba, *Australia* **63 E2** 33 8S 136 23 E
Kimball, *Nebr., U.S.A.* **80 E3** 41 14N 103 40W
Kimball, *S. Dak., U.S.A.* **80 D5** 43 45N 98 57W
Kimberley, *Canada* **72 D5** 49 40N 115 59W
Kimberley, *S. Africa* **56 D3** 28 43S 24 46 E
Kimberley Downs, *Australia* **60 C3** 17 24S 124 22 E
Kimberly, *U.S.A.* **82 E6** 42 32N 114 22W
Kimchaek, *N. Korea* **35 D15** 40 40N 129 10 E
Kimchŏn, *S. Korea* **35 F15** 36 11N 128 4 E
Kimje, *S. Korea* **35 G14** 35 48N 126 45 E
Kimmirut, *Canada* **69 B13** 62 50N 69 50W
Kimry, *Russia* **24 C6** 56 55N 37 15 E
Kimsquit, *Canada* **72 C3** 52 45N 126 57W
Kinabalu, Gunong, *Malaysia* **36 C5** 6 3N 116 14 E
Kinaskan L., *Canada* **72 B2** 57 38N 130 8W
Kinbasket L., *Canada* **72 C5** 52 0N 118 10W
Kincaid, *Canada* **73 D7** 49 40N 107 0W
Kincardine, *Canada* **70 D3** 44 10N 81 40W
Kinda, *Dem. Rep. of the Congo* **55 D2** 9 18S 25 4 E
Kinder Scout, *U.K.* **10 D6** 53 24N 1 52W
Kindersley, *Canada* **73 C7** 51 30N 109 10W
Kindia, *Guinea* **50 F3** 10 0N 12 52W
Kindu, *Dem. Rep. of the Congo* **54 C2** 2 55S 25 50 E
Kineshma, *Russia* **24 C7** 57 30N 42 5 E
Kinesi, *Tanzania* **54 C3** 1 25S 33 50 E
King, L., *Australia* **61 F2** 33 10S 119 35 E
King, Mt., *Australia* **62 D4** 25 10S 147 30 E
King City, *U.S.A.* **84 J5** 36 13N 121 8W
King Cr. →, *Australia* **62 C2** 24 35S 139 30 E
King Edward →, *Australia* **60 B4** 14 14S 126 35 E
King George B., *Falk. Is.* **96 G4** 51 30S 60 30W
King George I., *Antarctica* **5 C18** 60 0S 60 0W
King George Is., *Canada* **69 C11** 57 20N 80 30W
King I. = Kadan Kyun, *Burma* **38 F2** 12 30N 98 20 E
King I., *Australia* **62 F3** 39 50S 144 0 E
King I., *Canada* **72 C3** 52 10N 127 40W
King Leopold Ranges, *Australia* **60 C4** 17 30S 125 45 E
King Sd., *Australia* **60 C3** 16 50S 123 20 E
King William I., *Canada* **68 B10** 69 10N 97 25W
King William's Town, *S. Africa* **56 E4** 32 51S 27 22 E
Kingaroy, *Australia* **63 D5** 26 32S 151 51 E
Kingfisher, *U.S.A.* **81 H6** 35 52N 97 56W
Kingirbān, *Iraq* **44 C5** 34 40N 44 54 E
Kingisepp = Kuressaare, *Estonia* **9 G20** 58 15N 22 30 E
Kingman, *Ariz., U.S.A.* **85 K12** 35 12N 114 4W
Kingman, *Kans., U.S.A.* **81 G5** 37 39N 98 7W
Kingoonya, *Australia* **63 E2** 30 55S 135 19 E
Kings →, *U.S.A.* **84 J7** 36 3N 119 50W
Kings Canyon National Park, *U.S.A.* **84 J8** 36 50N 118 40W
King's Lynn, *U.K.* **10 E8** 52 45N 0 24 E
Kings Mountain, *U.S.A.* **77 H5** 35 15N 81 20W
King's Peak, *U.S.A.* **82 F8** 40 46N 110 27W
Kingsbridge, *U.K.* **11 G4** 50 17N 3 47W
Kingsburg, *U.S.A.* **84 J7** 36 31N 119 33W
Kingscote, *Australia* **63 F2** 35 40S 137 38 E
Kingscourt, *Ireland* **13 C5** 53 55N 6 48W
Kingsley, *U.S.A.* **80 D7** 42 35N 95 58W
Kingsport, *U.S.A.* **77 G4** 36 33N 82 33W
Kingston, *Canada* **70 D4** 44 14N 76 30W
Kingston, *Jamaica* **88 C4** 18 0N 76 50W
Kingston, *N.Z.* **59 L2** 45 20S 168 43 E
Kingston, *N.Y., U.S.A.* **79 E11** 41 56N 73 59W
Kingston, *Pa., U.S.A.* **79 E9** 41 16N 75 54W
Kingston, *R.I., U.S.A.* **79 E13** 41 29N 71 30W
Kingston Pk., *U.S.A.* **85 K11** 35 45N 115 54W
Kingston South East, *Australia* **63 F2** 36 51S 139 55 E
Kingston upon Hull, *U.K.* **10 D7** 53 45N 0 21W
Kingston upon Hull □, *U.K.* **10 D7** 53 45N 0 21W
Kingston-upon-Thames, *U.K.* **11 F7** 51 24N 0 17W
Kingstown, *St. Vincent* **89 D7** 13 10N 61 10W
Kingstree, *U.S.A.* **77 J6** 33 40N 79 50W
Kingsville, *Canada* **70 D3** 42 2N 82 45W
Kingsville, *U.S.A.* **81 M6** 27 31N 97 52W
Kingussie, *U.K.* **12 D4** 57 6N 4 2W
Kınık, *Turkey* **21 E12** 39 6N 27 24 E
Kinistino, *Canada* **73 C7** 52 57N 105 2W
Kinkala, *Congo* **52 E2** 4 18S 14 49 E
Kinki □, *Japan* **31 H8** 33 45N 136 0 E
Kinleith, *N.Z.* **59 H5** 38 20S 175 56 E
Kinmount, *Canada* **78 B6** 44 48N 78 45W
Kinna, *Sweden* **9 H15** 57 32N 12 42 E
Kinnaird, *Canada* **72 D5** 49 17N 117 39W
Kinnairds Hd., *U.K.* **12 D6** 57 43N 2 1W
Kinnarodden, *Norway* **6 A11** 71 8N 27 40 E
Kino, *Mexico* **86 B2** 28 45N 111 59W
Kinoje →, *Canada* **70 B3** 52 8N 81 25W
Kinomoto, *Japan* **31 G8** 35 30N 136 13 E
Kinoni, *Uganda* **54 C3** 0 41S 30 28 E
Kinross, *U.K.* **12 E5** 56 13N 3 25W
Kinsale, *Ireland* **13 E3** 51 42N 8 31W
Kinsale, Old Hd. of, *Ireland* **13 E3** 51 37N 8 33W
Kinsha = Chang Jiang →, *China* **33 C7** 31 48N 121 10 E
Kinshasa, *Dem. Rep. of the Congo* **52 E3** 4 20S 15 15 E
Kinsley, *U.S.A.* **81 G5** 37 55N 99 25W
Kinston, *U.S.A.* **77 H7** 35 16N 77 35W
Kintore Ra., *Australia* **60 D4** 23 15S 128 47 E
Kintyre, *U.K.* **12 F3** 55 30N 5 35W
Kintyre, Mull of, *U.K.* **12 F3** 55 17N 5 47W
Kinushseo →, *Canada* **70 A3** 55 15N 83 45W
Kinuso, *Canada* **72 B5** 55 20N 115 25W
Kinyangiri, *Tanzania* **54 C3** 4 25S 34 37 E
Kinzua, *U.S.A.* **78 E6** 41 52N 78 58W
Kinzua Dam, *U.S.A.* **78 E6** 41 53N 79 0W
Kiosk, *Canada* **70 C4** 46 6N 78 53W
Kiowa, *Kans., U.S.A.* **81 G5** 37 1N 98 29W
Kiowa, *Okla., U.S.A.* **81 H7** 34 43N 95 54W
Kipahigan L., *Canada* **73 B8** 55 20N 101 55W
Kipanga, *Tanzania* **54 D4** 6 15S 35 20 E
Kiparissía, *Greece* **21 F9** 37 15N 21 40 E
Kiparissiakós Kólpos, *Greece* **21 F9** 37 25N 21 25 E
Kipembawe, *Tanzania* **54 D3** 7 38S 33 27 E
Kipengere Ra., *Tanzania* **55 D3** 9 12S 34 15 E
Kipili, *Tanzania* **54 D3** 7 28S 30 32 E
Kipini, *Kenya* **54 C5** 2 30S 40 32 E
Kipling, *Canada* **73 C8** 50 6N 102 38W
Kippure, *Ireland* **13 C5** 53 11N 6 21W
Kipushi, *Dem. Rep. of the Congo* **55 E2** 11 48S 27 12 E
Kiratpur, *India* **42 E8** 29 32N 78 12 E

K'oshih

Kirensk, Russia 27 D11 57 50N 107 55 E
Kirgella Rocks, Australia 61 F3 30 5S 122 50 E
Kirghizia = Kyrgyzstan ■, Asia 26 E8 42 0N 75 0 E
Kirghizstan = Kyrgyzstan ■, Asia 26 E8 42 0N 75 0 E
Kirgiziya Steppe, Eurasia 25 E10 50 0N 55 0 E
Kiribati ■, Pac. Oc. 64 H10 5 0S 180 0 E
Kırıkkale, Turkey 25 G5 39 51N 33 32 E
Kirillov, Russia 24 C6 59 49N 38 24 E
Kirin = Jilin, China 35 C14 43 44N 126 30 E
Kiritimati, Kiribati 65 G12 1 58N 157 27W
Kirkby, U.K. 10 D5 53 30N 2 54W
Kirkby Lonsdale, U.K. 10 C5 54 12N 2 36W
Kirkcaldy, U.K. 12 E5 56 7N 3 9W
Kirkcudbright, U.K. 12 G4 54 50N 4 2W
Kirkee, India 40 K8 18 34N 73 56 E
Kirkenes, Norway 8 B23 69 40N 30 5 E
Kirkjubæjarklaustur, Iceland 8 E4 63 47N 18 4W
Kirkkonummi, Finland 9 F21 60 8N 24 26 E
Kirkland, U.S.A. 83 J7 34 25N 112 43W
Kirkland Lake, Canada 70 C3 48 9N 80 2W
Kırklareli, Turkey 21 D12 41 44N 27 15 E
Kirksville, U.S.A. 80 E8 40 12N 92 35W
Kirkūk, Iraq 44 C5 35 30N 44 21 E
Kirkwall, U.K. 12 C6 58 59N 2 58W
Kirkwood, S. Africa 56 E4 33 22S 25 15 E
Kirov, Russia 24 C8 58 35N 49 40 E
Kirovabad = Gäncä, Azerbaijan 25 F8 40 45N 46 20 E
Kirovakan = Vanadzor, Armenia 25 F7 40 48N 44 30 E
Kirovograd = Kirovohrad, Ukraine 25 E5 48 35N 32 20 E
Kirovohrad, Ukraine 25 E5 48 35N 32 20 E
Kirovsk = Babadayhan, Turkmenistan 26 F7 37 42N 60 23 E
Kirovsk, Russia 24 A5 67 32N 33 41 E
Kirovskiy, Kamchatka, Russia 27 D16 54 27N 155 42 E
Kirovskiy, Primorsk, Russia 30 B6 45 7N 133 30 E
Kirriemuir, U.K. 12 E5 56 41N 3 1W
Kirsanov, Russia 24 D7 52 35N 42 40 E
Kırşehir, Turkey 25 G5 39 14N 34 5 E
Kirthar Range, Pakistan 42 F2 27 0N 67 0 E
Kiruna, Sweden 8 C19 67 52N 20 15 E
Kirundu, Dem. Rep. of the Congo 54 C2 0 50S 25 35 E
Kirup, Australia 61 F2 33 40S 115 50 E
Kiryū, Japan 31 F9 36 24N 139 20 E
Kisaga, Tanzania 54 C3 4 30S 34 23 E
Kisalaya, Nic. 88 D3 14 40N 84 3W
Kisámou, Kólpos, Greece 23 D5 35 30N 23 38 E
Kisanga, Dem. Rep. of the Congo 54 B2 2 30N 26 35 E
Kisangani, Dem. Rep. of the Congo 54 B2 0 35N 25 15 E
Kisar, Indonesia 37 F7 8 5S 127 10 E
Kisarawe, Tanzania 54 D4 6 53S 39 0 E
Kisarawe □, Tanzania 54 D4 7 3S 39 0 E
Kisarazu, Japan 31 G9 35 23N 139 55 E
Kishanganga ➝, Pakistan 43 B5 34 18N 73 28 E
Kishanganj, India 43 F13 26 3N 88 14 E
Kishangarh, India 42 F4 27 50N 70 30 E
Kishinev = Chişinău, Moldova 25 E4 47 2N 28 50 E
Kishiwada, Japan 31 G7 34 28N 135 22 E
Kishtwar, India 43 C6 33 20N 75 48 E
Kisii, Kenya 54 C3 0 40S 34 45 E
Kisii □, Kenya 54 C3 0 40S 34 45 E
Kisiju, Tanzania 54 D4 7 23S 39 19 E
Kisizi, Uganda 54 C2 1 0S 29 58 E
Kiskatinaw ➝, Canada 72 B4 56 8N 120 10W
Kiskittogisu L., Canada 73 C9 54 13N 98 20W
Kiskőrös, Hungary 17 E10 46 37N 19 20 E
Kiskunfélegyháza, Hungary 17 E10 46 42N 19 53 E
Kiskunhalas, Hungary 17 E10 46 28N 19 37 E
Kislovodsk, Russia 25 F7 43 50N 42 45 E
Kismayu = Chisimaio, Somali Rep. 49 G8 0 22S 42 32 E
Kiso-Gawa ➝, Japan 31 G8 35 20N 136 45 E
Kiso-Sammyaku, Japan 31 G8 35 45N 137 45 E
Kisofukushima, Japan 31 G8 35 52N 137 43 E
Kisoro, Uganda 54 C2 1 17S 29 48 E
Kissidougou, Guinea 50 G3 9 5N 10 5W
Kissimmee, U.S.A. 77 L5 28 18N 81 24W
Kissimmee ➝, U.S.A. 77 M5 27 9N 80 52W
Kississing L., Canada 73 B8 55 10N 101 20W
Kissónerga, Cyprus 23 E11 34 49N 32 24 E
Kisumu, Kenya 54 C3 0 3S 34 45 E
Kiswani, Tanzania 54 C4 4 5S 37 57 E
Kiswere, Tanzania 55 D4 9 27S 39 30 E
Kit Carson, U.S.A. 80 F3 38 46N 102 48W
Kita, Mali 50 F4 13 5N 9 25W
Kitaibaraki, Japan 31 F10 36 50N 140 45 E
Kitakami, Japan 30 E10 39 20N 141 10 E
Kitakami-Gawa ➝, Japan 30 E10 38 25N 141 19 E
Kitakami-Sammyaku, Japan 30 E10 39 30N 141 30 E
Kitakata, Japan 30 F9 37 39N 139 52 E
Kitakyūshū, Japan 31 H5 33 50N 130 50 E
Kitale, Kenya 54 B4 1 0N 35 0 E
Kitami, Japan 30 C11 43 48N 143 54 E
Kitami-Sammyaku, Japan 30 B11 44 22N 142 43 E
Kitangiri, L., Tanzania 54 C3 4 5S 34 20 E
Kitaya, Tanzania 55 E5 10 38S 40 8 E
Kitchener, Australia 61 F3 30 55S 124 8 E
Kitchener, Canada 70 D3 43 27N 80 29W
Kitega = Gitega, Burundi 54 C2 3 26S 29 56 E
Kitengo, Dem. Rep. of the Congo 54 D1 7 26S 24 8 E
Kiteto □, Tanzania 54 D4 5 0S 37 0 E
Kitgum, Uganda 54 B3 3 17N 32 52 E
Kíthira, Greece 21 F10 36 8N 23 0 E
Kíthnos, Greece 21 F11 37 26N 24 27 E
Kiti, Cyprus 23 E12 34 50N 33 34 E
Kiti, C., Cyprus 23 E12 34 48N 33 36 E
Kitimat, Canada 72 C3 54 3N 128 38W
Kitinen ➝, Finland 8 C22 67 14N 27 27 E
Kitsuki, Japan 31 H5 33 25N 131 37 E
Kittakittaooloo, L., Australia 63 D2 28 3S 138 14 E
Kittanning, U.S.A. 78 F5 40 49N 79 31W
Kittatinny Mts., U.S.A. 79 F10 41 0N 75 0W
Kittery, U.S.A. 77 D10 43 5N 70 45W
Kittilä, Finland 8 C21 67 40N 24 51 E
Kitui, Kenya 54 C4 1 17S 38 0 E
Kitui □, Kenya 54 C4 1 30S 38 25 E
Kitwe, Zambia 55 E2 12 54S 28 13 E
Kivarli, India 42 G5 24 33N 72 46 E
Kivertsi, Ukraine 17 C13 50 50N 25 28 E
Kividhes, Cyprus 23 E11 34 46N 32 51 E
Kivu □, Dem. Rep. of the Congo 54 C2 3 10S 27 0 E
Kivu, L., Dem. Rep. of the Congo 54 C2 1 48S 29 0 E
Kiyev = Kyyiv, Ukraine 25 D5 50 30N 30 28 E
Kiyevskoye Vdkhr. = Kyyivske Vdskh., Ukraine 25 D5 51 0N 30 25 E
Kizel, Russia 24 C10 59 3N 57 40 E
Kiziguru, Rwanda 54 C3 1 46S 30 23 E
Kızıl Irmak ➝, Turkey 25 F6 41 44N 35 58 E
Kizil Jilga, India 43 B8 35 26N 78 50 E
Kizimkazi, Tanzania 54 D4 6 28S 39 30 E
Kizlyar, Russia 25 F8 43 51N 46 40 E
Kizyl-Arvat = Gyzylarbat, Turkmenistan 26 F6 39 4N 56 23 E
Kjölur, Iceland 8 D4 64 50N 19 25W
Kladno, Czech Rep. 16 C8 50 10N 14 7 E
Klaeng, Thailand 38 F3 12 47N 101 39 E
Klagenfurt, Austria 16 E8 46 38N 14 20 E
Klaipeda, Lithuania 24 C3 55 43N 21 10 E
Klaksvík, Færoe Is. 8 E9 62 14N 6 35W
Klamath ➝, U.S.A. 82 F1 41 33N 124 5W
Klamath Falls, U.S.A. 82 E3 42 13N 121 46W
Klamath Mts., U.S.A. 82 F2 41 20N 123 0W
Klappan ➝, Canada 72 B3 58 0N 129 43W
Klarälven ➝, Sweden 9 G15 59 23N 13 32 E
Klatovy, Czech Rep. 16 D7 49 23N 13 18 E
Klawer, S. Africa 56 E2 31 44S 18 36 E
Klawock, U.S.A. 72 B2 55 33N 133 6W
Klazienaveen, Neths. 15 B6 52 44N 7 0 E
Kleena Kleene, Canada 72 C4 52 0N 124 59W
Klein, U.S.A. 82 C9 46 24N 108 33W
Klein-Karas, Namibia 56 D2 27 33S 18 7 E
Klerksdorp, S. Africa 56 D4 26 53S 26 38 E
Kletsk = Klyetsk, Belarus 17 B14 53 5N 26 45 E
Kletskiy, Russia 26 E5 49 16N 43 11 E
Klickitat, U.S.A. 82 D3 45 49N 121 9W
Klickitat ➝, U.S.A. 84 E5 45 42N 121 17W
Klidhes, Cyprus 23 D13 35 42N 34 36 E
Klinaklini ➝, Canada 72 C3 51 21N 125 40W
Klipdale, S. Africa 56 E2 34 19S 19 57 E
Klipplaat, S. Africa 56 E3 33 1S 24 22 E
Kłodzko, Poland 17 C9 50 28N 16 38 E
Klouto, Togo 50 G6 6 57N 0 44 E
Kluane L., Canada 68 B6 61 15N 138 40W
Kluczbork, Poland 17 C10 50 58N 18 12 E
Klyetsk, Belarus 17 B14 53 5N 26 45 E
Klyuchevskaya, Gora, Russia 27 D17 55 50N 160 30 E
Knaresborough, U.K. 10 C6 54 1N 1 28W
Knee L., Man., Canada 73 B10 55 3N 94 45W
Knee L., Sask., Canada 73 B7 55 51N 107 0W
Knight Inlet, Canada 72 C3 50 45N 125 40W
Knighton, U.K. 11 E4 52 21N 3 3W
Knights Ferry, U.S.A. 84 H6 37 50N 120 40W
Knights Landing, U.S.A. 84 G5 38 48N 121 43W
Knob, C., Australia 61 F2 34 32S 119 16 E
Knock, Ireland 13 C3 53 48N 8 55W
Knockmealdown Mts., Ireland 13 D4 52 14N 7 56W
Knokke-Heist, Belgium 15 C3 51 21N 3 17 E
Knossós, Greece 23 D7 35 16N 25 10 E
Knox, U.S.A. 76 E2 41 18N 86 37W
Knox, C., Canada 72 C2 54 11N 133 5W
Knox City, U.S.A. 81 J5 33 25N 99 49W
Knox Coast, Antarctica 5 C8 66 30S 108 0 E
Knoxville, Iowa, U.S.A. 80 E8 41 19N 93 6W
Knoxville, Tenn., U.S.A. 77 H4 35 58N 83 55W
Knysna, S. Africa 56 E3 34 2S 23 2 E
Ko Kha, Thailand 38 C2 18 11N 99 24 E
Koartac = Quaqtaq, Canada 69 B13 60 55N 69 40W
Koba, Indonesia 37 F8 6 37S 134 37 E
Kobarid, Slovenia 16 E7 46 15N 13 30 E
Kobayashi, Japan 31 J5 31 56N 130 59 E
Kobdo = Hovd, Mongolia 32 B4 48 2N 91 37 E
Kōbe, Japan 31 G7 34 45N 135 10 E
København, Denmark 9 J15 55 41N 12 34 E
Kōbi-Sho, Japan 31 M1 25 56N 123 41 E
Koblenz, Germany 16 C4 50 21N 7 36 E
Kobryn, Belarus 17 B13 52 15N 24 22 E
Kocaeli, Turkey 25 F4 40 45N 29 50 E
Kočani, Macedonia 21 D10 41 55N 22 25 E
Koch Bihar, India 41 F16 26 22N 89 29 E
Kochang, S. Korea 35 G14 35 41N 127 55 E
Kochas, India 43 G10 25 15N 83 56 E
Kōchi, Japan 31 H6 33 30N 133 35 E
Kōchi □, Japan 31 H6 33 40N 133 30 E
Kochiu = Gejiu, China 32 D5 23 20N 103 10 E
Kodiak, U.S.A. 68 C4 57 47N 152 24W
Kodiak I., U.S.A. 68 C4 57 30N 152 45W
Kodinar, India 42 J4 20 46N 70 46 E
Koes, Namibia 56 D2 26 0S 19 15 E
Koffiefontein, S. Africa 56 D4 29 30S 25 0 E
Kofiau, Indonesia 37 E7 1 11S 129 50 E
Koforidua, Ghana 50 G5 6 3N 0 17W
Kōfu, Japan 31 G9 35 40N 138 30 E
Koga, Japan 31 F9 36 11N 139 43 E
Kogaluk ➝, Canada 71 A7 56 12N 61 44W
Kogan, Australia 63 D5 27 2S 150 40 E
Køge, Denmark 9 J15 55 27N 12 11 E
Koh-i-Bābā, Afghan. 40 B5 34 30N 67 0 E
Koh-i-Khurd, Afghan. 42 C1 33 30N 65 59 E
Kohat, Pakistan 42 C4 33 40N 71 29 E
Kohima, India 41 G19 25 35N 94 10 E
Kohkīlūyeh va Būyer Aḥmadi □, Iran 45 D6 31 30N 50 30 E
Kohler Ra., Antarctica 5 D15 77 0S 110 0W
Kohtla-Järve, Estonia 9 G22 59 20N 27 20 E
Koillismaa, Finland 8 D23 65 44N 28 36 E
Koin-dong, N. Korea 35 D14 40 28N 126 18 E
Kojō, N. Korea 35 E14 38 58N 127 58 E
Kojonup, Australia 61 F2 33 48S 117 10 E
Kojūr, Iran 45 B6 36 23N 51 43 E
Kokand = Qŭqon, Uzbekistan 26 E8 40 30N 70 57 E
Kokanee Glacier Prov. Park, Canada 72 D5 49 47N 117 10W
Kokas, Indonesia 37 E8 2 42S 132 26 E
Kokchetav = Kökshetaū, Kazakstan 26 D7 53 20N 69 25 E
Kokemäenjoki ➝, Finland 9 F19 61 32N 21 44 E
Kokkola, Finland 8 E20 63 50N 23 8 E
Koko Kyunzu, Burma 41 M18 14 10N 93 25 E
Kokomo, U.S.A. 76 E2 40 29N 86 8W
Koksan, N. Korea 35 E14 38 46N 126 40 E
Kökshetaū, Kazakstan 26 D7 53 20N 69 25 E
Koksoak ➝, Canada 69 C13 58 30N 68 10W
Kokstad, S. Africa 57 E4 30 32S 29 29 E
Kokubu, Japan 31 J5 31 44N 130 46 E
Kola, Indonesia 37 F8 5 35S 134 30 E
Kola, Russia 24 A5 68 45N 33 8 E
Kola Pen. = Kolskiy Poluostrov, Russia 24 A6 67 30N 38 0 E
Kolahoi, India 43 B6 34 12N 75 22 E
Kolaka, Indonesia 37 E6 4 3S 121 46 E
Kolar, India 40 N11 13 12N 78 15 E
Kolar Gold Fields, India 40 N11 12 58N 78 16 E
Kolari, Finland 8 C20 67 20N 23 48 E
Kolayat, India 40 F8 27 50N 72 50 E
Kolchugino = Leninsk-Kuznetskiy, Russia 26 D9 54 44N 86 10 E
Kolding, Denmark 9 J13 55 30N 9 29 E
Kolepom = Dolak, Pulau, Indonesia 37 F9 8 0S 138 30 E
Kolguyev, Ostrov, Russia 24 A8 69 20N 48 30 E
Kolhapur, India 40 L9 16 43N 74 15 E
Kolín, Czech Rep. 16 C8 50 2N 15 9 E
Kolkas rags, Latvia 9 H20 57 46N 22 37 E
Kollum, Neths. 15 A6 53 17N 6 10 E
Kolmanskop, Namibia 56 D2 26 45S 15 14 E
Köln, Germany 16 C4 50 56N 6 57 E
Koło, Poland 17 B10 52 14N 18 40 E
Kołobrzeg, Poland 16 A8 54 10N 15 35 E
Kolomna, Russia 24 C6 55 8N 38 45 E
Kolomyya, Ukraine 25 E4 48 31N 25 2 E
Kolonodale, Indonesia 37 E6 2 3S 121 25 E
Kolosib, India 41 G18 24 15N 92 45 E
Kolpashevo, Russia 26 D9 58 20N 83 5 E
Kolpino, Russia 24 C5 59 44N 30 39 E
Kolskiy Poluostrov, Russia 24 A6 67 30N 38 0 E
Kolskiy Zaliv, Russia 24 A5 69 23N 34 0 E
Kolwezi, Dem. Rep. of the Congo 55 E2 10 40S 25 25 E
Kolyma ➝, Russia 27 C17 69 30N 161 0 E
Kolymskoye Nagorye, Russia 27 C16 63 0N 157 0 E
Komandorskiye Is. = Komandorskiye Ostrova, Russia 27 D17 55 0N 167 0 E
Komandorskiye Ostrova, Russia 27 D17 55 0N 167 0 E
Komárno, Slovak Rep. 17 E10 47 49N 18 5 E
Komatipoort, S. Africa 57 D5 25 25S 31 55 E
Komatou Yialou, Cyprus 23 D13 35 25N 34 8 E
Komatsu, Japan 31 F8 36 25N 136 30 E
Komatsujima, Japan 31 H7 34 0N 134 35 E
Komi □, Russia 24 B10 64 0N 55 0 E
Kommunarsk = Alchevsk, Ukraine 25 E6 48 30N 38 45 E
Kommunizma, Pik, Tajikistan 26 F8 39 0N 72 2 E
Komodo, Indonesia 37 F5 8 37S 119 20 E
Komoran, Pulau, Indonesia 37 F9 8 18S 138 45 E
Komoro, Japan 31 F9 36 19N 138 26 E
Komotini, Greece 21 D11 41 9N 25 26 E
Kompasberg, S. Africa 56 E3 31 45S 24 32 E
Kompong Bang, Cambodia 39 F5 12 24N 104 40 E
Kompong Cham, Cambodia 39 G5 12 0N 105 30 E
Kompong Chhnang = Kampang Chhnang, Cambodia 39 F5 12 20N 104 35 E
Kompong Chikreng, Cambodia 38 F5 13 5N 104 18 E
Kompong Kleang, Cambodia 38 F5 13 6N 104 8 E
Kompong Luong, Cambodia 39 G5 11 49N 104 48 E
Kompong Pranak, Cambodia 38 F5 13 35N 104 55 E
Kompong Som = Kampong Saom, Cambodia 39 G4 10 38N 103 30 E
Kompong Som, Chhung = Kampong Saom, Chaak, Cambodia 39 G4 10 50N 103 32 E
Kompong Speu, Cambodia 39 G5 11 26N 104 32 E
Kompong Sralao, Cambodia 38 E5 14 5N 105 46 E
Kompong Thom, Cambodia 38 F5 12 35N 104 51 E
Kompong Trabeck, Cambodia 38 F5 13 6N 105 14 E
Kompong Trabeck, Cambodia 39 G5 11 9N 105 28 E
Kompong Trach, Cambodia 39 G5 11 25N 105 48 E
Kompong Tralach, Cambodia 39 G5 11 54N 104 47 E
Komrat = Comrat, Moldova 17 E15 46 18N 28 40 E
Komsberg, S. Africa 56 E3 32 40S 20 45 E
Komsomolets, Ostrov, Russia 27 A10 80 30N 95 0 E
Komsomolsk, Russia 27 D14 50 30N 137 0 E
Kon Tum, Vietnam 38 E7 14 24N 108 0 E
Kon Tum, Plateau du, Vietnam 38 E7 14 30N 108 30 E
Konarhá □, Afghan. 40 B7 35 30N 71 3 E
Konārī, Iran 45 D6 28 13N 51 36 E
Konawa, U.S.A. 81 H6 34 58N 96 45W
Konch, India 43 G8 26 0N 79 10 E
Konde, Tanzania 54 C4 4 57S 39 45 E
Kondinin, Australia 61 F2 32 34S 118 8 E
Kondoa, Tanzania 54 C4 4 55S 35 50 E
Kondoa □, Tanzania 54 D4 5 0S 36 0 E
Kondókali, Greece 23 A3 39 38N 19 51 E
Kondopaga, Russia 24 B5 62 12N 34 17 E
Kondratyevo, Russia 27 D10 57 22N 98 15 E
Köneürgench, Turkmenistan 26 E6 42 19N 59 10 E
Konevo, Russia 24 B6 62 8N 39 20 E
Kong, Ivory C. 50 G5 8 54N 4 36W
Kong ➝ = Khong ➝, Cambodia 38 F5 13 32N 105 58 E
Kong, Koh, Cambodia 39 G4 11 20N 103 0 E
Kongju, S. Korea 35 F14 36 30N 127 0 E
Konglu, Burma 41 F20 27 13N 97 57 E
Kongolo, Kasai Or., Dem. Rep. of the Congo 54 D1 5 26S 24 49 E
Kongolo, Shaba, Dem. Rep. of the Congo 54 D2 5 22S 27 0 E
Kongsberg, Norway 9 G13 59 39N 9 39 E
Kongsvinger, Norway 9 F15 60 12N 12 2 E
Kongwa, Tanzania 54 D4 6 11S 36 26 E
Koni, Dem. Rep. of the Congo 55 E2 10 40S 27 11 E
Koni, Mts., Dem. Rep. of the Congo 55 E2 10 36S 27 10 E
Königsberg = Kaliningrad, Russia 24 D3 54 42N 20 32 E
Konin, Poland 17 B10 52 12N 18 15 E
Konjic, Bos.-H. 21 C7 43 42N 17 58 E
Konkiep, Namibia 56 D2 26 49S 17 15 E
Konosha, Russia 24 B7 61 0N 40 5 E
Kōnosu, Japan 31 F9 36 3N 139 31 E
Konotop, Ukraine 25 D5 51 12N 33 7 E
Końskie, Poland 17 C11 51 15N 20 23 E
Konstanz, Germany 16 E5 47 40N 9 10 E
Kont, Iran 45 E9 26 55N 61 50 E
Kontagora, Nigeria 50 F7 10 23N 5 27 E
Konya, Turkey 25 G5 37 52N 32 35 E
Konza, Kenya 54 C4 1 45S 37 7 E
Kookynie, Australia 61 E3 29 17S 121 22 E
Kooline, Australia 60 D2 22 57S 116 20 E
Kooloonong, Australia 63 E3 34 48S 143 10 E
Koolyanobbing, Australia 61 F2 30 48S 119 36 E
Koondrook, Australia 63 F3 35 33S 144 8 E
Koonibba, Australia 63 E1 31 54S 133 25 E
Koorawatha, Australia 63 E4 34 2S 148 33 E
Koorda, Australia 61 F2 30 48S 117 35 E
Kooskia, U.S.A. 82 C6 46 9N 115 59W
Kootenai ➝, Canada 82 B5 49 15N 117 39W
Kootenay L., Canada 72 D5 49 45N 116 50W
Kootenay Nat. Park, Canada 72 C5 51 0N 116 0W
Kootjieskolk, S. Africa 56 E3 31 15S 20 21 E
Kopaonik, Serbia, Yug. 21 C9 43 10N 20 50 E
Kópavogur, Iceland 8 D3 64 6N 21 55W
Koper, Slovenia 16 F7 45 31N 13 44 E
Kopervik, Norway 9 G11 59 17N 5 17 E
Kopi, Australia 63 E2 33 24S 135 40 E
Köping, Sweden 9 G17 59 31N 16 3 E
Koppeh Dāgh, Asia 45 B8 38 0N 58 0 E
Koppies, S. Africa 57 D4 27 20S 27 30 E
Koprivnica, Croatia 20 A7 46 12N 16 45 E
Kopychyntsi, Ukraine 17 D13 49 7N 25 58 E
Korab, Macedonia 21 D9 41 44N 20 40 E
Korakiána, Greece 23 A3 39 42N 19 45 E
Korba, India 43 H10 22 20N 82 45 E
Korbu, G., Malaysia 39 K3 4 41N 101 18 E
Korça, Albania 21 D9 40 37N 20 50 E
Korce = Korça, Albania 21 D9 40 37N 20 50 E
Korčula, Croatia 20 C7 42 56N 16 57 E
Kord Kūy, Iran 45 B7 36 48N 54 7 E
Kord Sheykh, Iran 45 D7 28 31N 52 53 E
Kordestān □, Iran 44 C5 36 0N 47 0 E
Kordofân, Sudan 51 F11 13 0N 29 0 E
Korea, North ■, Asia 35 E14 40 0N 127 0 E
Korea, South ■, Asia 35 G15 36 0N 128 0 E
Korea Bay, Korea 35 E13 39 0N 124 0 E
Korea Strait, Asia 35 H15 34 0N 129 30 E
Korets, Ukraine 17 C14 50 40N 27 5 E
Korhogo, Ivory C. 50 G4 9 29N 5 28W
Korinthiakós Kólpos, Greece 21 E10 38 16N 22 30 E
Kórinthos, Greece 21 F10 37 56N 22 55 E
Korissa, Límni, Greece 23 B3 39 27N 19 53 E
Kōriyama, Japan 30 F10 37 24N 140 23 E
Korla, China 32 B3 41 45N 86 4 E
Kormakiti, C., Cyprus 23 D11 35 23N 32 56 E
Korneshty = Cornești, Moldova 17 E15 47 21N 28 1 E
Koro, Fiji 59 C8 17 19S 179 23 E
Koro, Ivory C. 50 G4 8 32N 7 30W
Koro Sea, Fiji 59 C9 17 30S 179 45W
Korogwe, Tanzania 54 D4 5 5S 38 25 E
Korogwe □, Tanzania 54 D4 5 0S 38 20 E
Koroit, Australia 63 F3 38 18S 142 24 E
Koror, Pac. Oc. 37 C8 7 20N 134 28 E
Körös ➝, Hungary 17 E11 46 43N 20 12 E
Korosten, Ukraine 17 C15 50 54N 28 36 E
Korostyshev, Ukraine 17 C15 50 19N 29 4 E
Korraraika, Helodranon' i, Madag. 57 B7 17 45S 43 57 E
Korsakov, Russia 27 E15 46 36N 142 42 E
Korshunovo, Russia 27 D12 58 37N 110 10 E
Korsør, Denmark 9 J14 55 20N 11 9 E
Kortrijk, Belgium 15 D3 50 50N 3 17 E
Korwai, India 42 G8 24 7N 78 5 E
Koryakskoye Nagorye, Russia 27 C18 61 0N 171 0 E
Koryŏng, S. Korea 35 G15 35 44N 128 15 E
Koschagyl, Kazakstan 25 E9 46 40N 54 0 E
Kościan, Poland 17 B9 52 5N 16 40 E
Kosciusko, U.S.A. 81 J10 33 4N 89 35W
Kosciusko I., U.S.A. 72 B2 56 0N 133 40W
Kosciuszko, Mt., Australia 63 F4 36 27S 148 16 E
Kosha, Sudan 51 D12 20 50N 30 30 E
K'oshih = Kashi, China 32 C2 39 30N 76 2 E

Lopatina, Gora

Lille Bælt, Denmark 9 J13 55 20N 9 45 E
Lillehammer, Norway 9 F14 61 8N 10 30 E
Lillesand, Norway 9 G13 58 15N 8 23 E
Lillian Point, Mt., Australia 61 E4 27 40S 126 6 E
Lillooet →, Canada 72 D4 49 15N 121 57W
Lilongwe, Malawi 55 E3 14 0S 33 48 E
Liloy, Phil. 37 C6 8 4N 122 39 E
Lim →, Bos.-H. 21 C8 43 45N 19 15 E
Lima, Indonesia 37 E7 3 37S 128 4 E
Lima, Peru 92 F3 12 0S 77 0W
Lima, Mont., U.S.A. 82 D7 44 38N 112 36W
Lima, Ohio, U.S.A. 76 E3 40 44N 84 6W
Lima →, Portugal 19 B1 41 41N 8 50W
Limages, Canada 79 A9 45 20N 75 16W
Limassol, Cyprus 23 E12 34 42N 33 1 E
Limavady, U.K. 13 A5 55 3N 6 56W
Limay →, Argentina 96 D3 39 0S 68 0W
Limay Mahuida, Argentina 94 D2 37 10S 66 45W
Limbang, Brunei 36 D5 4 42N 115 6 E
Limbaži, Latvia 9 H21 57 31N 24 42 E
Limbdi, India 42 H4 22 34N 71 51 E
Limbe, Cameroon 52 D1 4 1N 9 10 E
Limbri, Australia 63 E5 31 3S 151 5 E
Limbunya, Australia 60 C4 17 14S 129 50 E
Limburg, Germany 16 C5 50 22N 8 4 E
Limburg □, Belgium 15 C5 51 2N 5 25 E
Limburg □, Neths. 15 C5 51 20N 5 55 E
Limeira, Brazil 95 A6 22 35S 47 28W
Limerick, Ireland 13 D3 52 40N 8 37W
Limerick □, Ireland 13 D3 52 30N 8 50W
Limestone, U.S.A. 78 D6 42 2N 78 38W
Limestone →, Canada 73 B10 56 31N 94 7W
Limfjorden, Denmark 9 H13 56 55N 9 0 E
Limia = Lima →, Portugal 19 B1 41 41N 8 50W
Limingen, Norway 8 D15 64 48N 13 35 E
Limmen Bight, Australia 62 A2 14 40S 135 35 E
Limmen Bight →, Australia 62 B2 15 7S 135 44 E
Límnos, Greece 21 E11 39 50N 25 5 E
Limoges, France 18 D4 45 50N 1 15 E
Limón, Costa Rica 88 E3 10 0N 83 2W
Limon, U.S.A. 80 F3 39 16N 103 41W
Limousin, France 18 D4 45 30N 1 30 E
Limoux, France 18 E5 43 4N 2 12 E
Limpopo →, Africa 57 D5 25 5S 33 30 E
Limuru, Kenya 54 C4 1 2S 36 35 E
Lin Xian, China 34 F6 37 57N 110 58 E
Linares, Chile 94 D1 35 50S 71 40W
Linares, Mexico 87 C5 24 50N 99 40W
Linares, Spain 19 C4 38 10N 3 40W
Linares □, Chile 94 D1 36 0S 71 0W
Lincheng, China 34 F8 37 25N 114 30 E
Lincoln, Argentina 94 C3 34 55S 61 30W
Lincoln, N.Z. 59 K4 43 38S 172 30 E
Lincoln, U.K. 10 D7 53 14N 0 32W
Lincoln, Calif., U.S.A. 84 G5 38 54N 121 17W
Lincoln, Ill., U.S.A. 80 E10 40 9N 89 22W
Lincoln, Kans., U.S.A. 80 F5 39 3N 98 9W
Lincoln, Maine, U.S.A. 71 C6 45 22N 68 30W
Lincoln, N.H., U.S.A. 79 B13 44 3N 71 40W
Lincoln, N. Mex., U.S.A. 83 K11 33 30N 105 23W
Lincoln, Nebr., U.S.A. 80 E6 40 49N 96 41W
Lincolnshire □, U.K. 10 D7 53 14N 0 32W
Lincolnshire Wolds, U.K. 10 D7 53 26N 0 13W
Lincolnton, U.S.A. 77 H5 35 29N 81 16W
Lind, U.S.A. 82 C4 46 58N 118 37W
Linda, U.S.A. 84 F5 39 8N 121 34W
Linden, Guyana 92 B7 6 0N 58 10W
Linden, Calif., U.S.A. 84 G5 38 1N 121 5W
Linden, Tex., U.S.A. 81 J7 33 1N 94 22W
Lindenhurst, U.S.A. 79 F11 40 41N 73 23W
Lindesnes, Norway 9 H12 57 58N 7 3 E
Líndhos, Greece 23 C10 36 6N 28 4 E
Líndhos, Ákra, Greece 23 C10 36 4N 28 10 E
Lindi, Tanzania 55 D4 9 58S 39 38 E
Lindi □, Tanzania 55 D4 9 40S 38 30 E
Lindi →, Dem. Rep. of the Congo 54 B2 0 33N 25 5 E
Lindsay, Canada 70 D4 44 22N 78 43W
Lindsay, Calif., U.S.A. 84 J7 36 12N 119 5W
Lindsay, Okla., U.S.A. 81 H6 34 50N 97 38W
Lindsborg, U.S.A. 80 F6 38 35N 97 40W
Linfen, China 34 F6 36 3N 111 30 E
Ling Xian, China 34 F9 37 22N 116 30 E
Lingao, China 38 C7 19 56N 109 42 E
Lingayen, Phil. 37 A6 16 1N 120 14 E
Lingayen G., Phil. 37 A6 16 10N 120 15 E
Lingbi, China 35 H9 33 33N 117 33 E
Lingchuan, China 34 G7 35 45N 113 12 E
Lingen, Germany 16 B4 52 31N 7 19 E
Lingga, Indonesia 36 E2 0 12S 104 37 E
Lingga, Kepulauan, Indonesia 36 E2 0 10S 104 30 E
Lingga Arch. = Lingga, Kepulauan, Indonesia 36 E2 0 10S 104 30 E
Lingle, U.S.A. 80 D2 42 8N 104 21W
Lingqiu, China 34 E8 39 28N 114 22 E
Lingshi, China 34 F6 36 48N 111 48 E
Lingshou, China 34 E8 38 20N 114 20 E
Lingshui, China 38 C8 18 27N 110 0 E
Lingtai, China 34 G4 35 0N 107 40 E
Linguère, Senegal 50 E2 15 25N 15 5W
Lingwu, China 34 E4 38 6N 106 20 E
Lingyuan, China 35 D10 41 10N 119 15 E
Linhai, China 33 D7 28 50N 121 8 E
Linhares, Brazil 93 G10 19 25S 40 4W
Linhe, China 34 D4 40 48N 107 20 E
Linjiang, China 35 D14 41 50N 127 0 E
Linköping, Sweden 9 G16 58 28N 15 36 E
Linkou, China 35 B16 45 15N 130 18 E
Linnhe, L., U.K. 12 E3 56 36N 5 25W
Linosa, I., Medit. S. 20 G5 35 51N 12 50 E
Linqi, China 34 G7 35 45N 113 52 E
Linqing, China 34 F8 36 50N 115 42 E
Linqu, China 35 F10 36 25N 118 30 E
Linru, China 34 G7 34 11N 112 52 E
Lins, Brazil 95 A6 21 40S 49 44W
Lintao, China 34 G2 35 18N 103 52 E
Lintlaw, Canada 73 C8 52 4N 103 14W
Linton, Canada 71 C5 47 15N 72 16W
Linton, Ind., U.S.A. 76 F2 39 2N 87 10W
Linton, N. Dak., U.S.A. 80 B4 46 16N 100 14W
Lintong, China 34 G5 34 20N 109 10 E
Linville, Australia 63 D5 26 50S 152 11 E
Linwood, Canada 78 C4 43 35N 80 43W
Linxi, China 35 C10 43 36N 118 2 E
Linxia, China 32 C5 35 36N 103 10 E
Linyanti →, Africa 56 B4 17 50S 25 5 E
Linyi, China 35 G10 35 5N 118 21 E
Linz, Austria 16 D8 48 18N 14 18 E
Linzhenzhen, China 34 F5 36 30N 109 59 E
Linzi, China 35 F10 36 50N 118 20 E
Lion, G. du, France 18 E6 43 10N 4 0 E
Lionárisso, Cyprus 23 D13 35 28N 34 8 E
Lions, G. of = Lion, G. du, France 18 E6 43 10N 4 0 E
Lion's Den, Zimbabwe 55 F3 17 15S 30 5 E
Lion's Head, Canada 70 D3 44 58N 81 15W
Lipa, Phil. 37 B6 13 57N 121 10 E
Lipali, Mozam. 55 F4 15 50S 35 50 E
Lípari, Italy 20 E6 38 26N 14 58 E
Lípari, Is. = Eólie, Ís., Italy 20 E6 38 30N 14 57 E
Lipcani, Moldova 17 D14 48 14N 26 48 E
Lipetsk, Russia 24 D6 52 37N 39 35 E
Lipkany = Lipcani, Moldova 17 D14 48 14N 26 48 E
Lipovcy Manzovka, Russia 30 B6 44 12N 132 26 E
Lipovets, Ukraine 17 D15 49 12N 29 1 E
Lippe →, Germany 16 C4 51 39N 6 36 E
Lipscomb, U.S.A. 81 G4 36 14N 100 16W
Liptrap C., Australia 63 F4 38 50S 145 55 E
Lira, Uganda 54 B3 2 17N 32 57 E
Liria = Lliria, Spain 19 C5 39 37N 0 35W
Lisala, Dem. Rep. of the Congo 52 D4 2 12N 21 38 E
Lisboa, Portugal 19 C1 38 42N 9 10W
Lisbon = Lisboa, Portugal 19 C1 38 42N 9 10W
Lisbon, N. Dak., U.S.A. 80 B6 46 27N 97 41W
Lisbon, N.H., U.S.A. 79 B13 44 13N 71 55W
Lisbon, Ohio, U.S.A. 78 F4 40 46N 80 46W
Lisburn, U.K. 13 B5 54 31N 6 3W
Liscannor B., Ireland 13 D2 52 55N 9 24W
Lishi, China 34 F6 37 31N 111 8 E
Lishu, China 35 C13 43 20N 124 18 E
Lisianski I., Pac. Oc. 64 E10 26 2N 174 0W
Lisichansk = Lysychansk, Ukraine 25 E6 48 55N 38 30 E
Lisieux, France 18 B4 49 10N 0 12 E
Liski, Russia 25 D6 51 3N 39 30 E
Lismore, Australia 63 D5 28 44S 153 21 E
Lismore, Ireland 13 D4 52 8N 7 55W
Lista, Norway 9 G12 58 7N 6 39 E
Lister, Mt., Antarctica 5 D11 78 0S 162 0 E
Liston, Australia 63 D5 28 39S 152 6 E
Listowel, Canada 70 D3 43 44N 80 58W
Listowel, Ireland 13 D2 52 27N 9 29W
Litani →, Lebanon 47 B4 33 20N 35 15 E
Litchfield, Calif., U.S.A. 84 E6 40 24N 120 23W
Litchfield, Conn., U.S.A. 79 E11 41 45N 73 11W
Litchfield, Ill., U.S.A. 80 F10 39 11N 89 39W
Litchfield, Minn., U.S.A. 80 C7 45 8N 94 32W
Lithgow, Australia 63 E5 33 25S 150 8 E
Líthinon, Ákra, Greece 23 E6 34 55N 24 44 E
Lithuania ■, Europe 24 C3 55 30N 24 0 E
Litoměřice, Czech Rep. 16 C8 50 33N 14 10 E
Little Abaco I., Bahamas 88 A4 26 50N 77 30W
Little Barrier I., N.Z. 59 G5 36 12S 175 8 E
Little Belt Mts., U.S.A. 82 C8 46 40N 110 45W
Little Blue →, U.S.A. 80 F6 39 42N 96 41W
Little Cadotte →, Canada 72 B5 56 41N 117 6W
Little Cayman, I., Cayman Is. 88 C3 19 41N 80 3W
Little Churchill →, Canada 73 B9 57 30N 95 22W
Little Colorado →, U.S.A. 83 H8 36 12N 111 48W
Little Current, Canada 70 C3 45 55N 82 0W
Little Current →, Canada 70 B3 50 57N 84 36W
Little Falls, Minn., U.S.A. 80 C7 45 59N 94 22W
Little Falls, N.Y., U.S.A. 79 C10 43 3N 74 51W
Little Fork →, U.S.A. 80 A8 48 31N 93 35W
Little Grand Rapids, Canada 73 C9 52 0N 95 29W
Little Humboldt →, U.S.A. 82 F5 41 1N 117 43W
Little Inagua I., Bahamas 89 B5 21 40N 73 50W
Little Karoo, S. Africa 56 E3 33 45S 21 0 E
Little Lake, U.S.A. 85 K9 35 56N 117 55W
Little Laut Is. = Laut Kecil, Kepulauan, Indonesia 36 E5 4 45S 115 40 E
Little Minch, U.K. 12 D2 57 35N 6 45W
Little Missouri →, U.S.A. 80 B3 47 36N 102 25W
Little Ouse →, U.K. 11 E9 52 22N 1 12 E
Little Rann, India 42 H4 23 25N 71 25 E
Little Red →, U.S.A. 81 H9 35 11N 91 27W
Little River, N.Z. 59 K4 43 45S 172 49 E
Little Rock, U.S.A. 81 H8 34 45N 92 17W
Little Ruaha →, Tanzania 54 D4 7 57S 37 53 E
Little Sable Pt., U.S.A. 76 D2 43 38N 86 33W
Little Sioux →, U.S.A. 80 E6 41 48N 96 4W
Little Smoky →, Canada 72 C5 54 44N 117 11W
Little Snake →, U.S.A. 82 F9 40 27N 108 26W
Little Valley, U.S.A. 78 D6 42 15N 78 48W
Little Wabash →, U.S.A. 76 G1 37 55N 88 5W
Littlefield, U.S.A. 81 J3 33 55N 102 20W
Littlefork, U.S.A. 80 A8 48 24N 93 34W
Littlehampton, U.K. 11 G7 50 49N 0 32W
Littleton, U.S.A. 79 B13 44 18N 71 46W
Liu He →, China 35 D11 40 55N 121 35 E
Liuba, China 34 H4 33 38N 106 55 E
Liugou, China 35 D10 40 57N 118 15 E
Liuhe, China 35 C13 42 17N 125 43 E
Liukang Tenggaja = Sabalana, Kepulauan, Indonesia 37 F5 6 45S 118 50 E
Liuli, Tanzania 55 E3 11 3S 34 38 E
Liuwa Plain, Zambia 53 G4 14 20S 22 30 E
Liuzhou, China 33 D5 24 22N 109 22 E
Liuzhuang, China 35 H11 33 12N 120 18 E
Livadhia, Cyprus 23 E12 34 57N 33 38 E
Live Oak, Calif., U.S.A. 84 F5 39 17N 121 40W
Live Oak, Fla., U.S.A. 77 K4 30 18N 82 59W
Liveras, Cyprus 23 D11 35 23N 32 57 E
Liveringa, Australia 60 C3 18 3S 124 10 E
Livermore, U.S.A. 84 H5 37 41N 121 47W
Livermore, Mt., U.S.A. 81 K2 30 38N 104 11W
Liverpool, Australia 63 E5 33 54S 150 58 E
Liverpool, Canada 71 D7 44 5N 64 41W
Liverpool, U.K. 10 D4 53 25N 3 0W
Liverpool Bay, U.K. 10 D4 53 30N 3 20W
Liverpool Plains, Australia 63 E5 31 15S 150 15 E
Liverpool Ra., Australia 63 E5 31 50S 150 30 E
Livingston, Guatemala 88 C2 15 50N 88 50W
Livingston, U.K. 12 F5 55 54N 3 30W
Livingston, Calif., U.S.A. 84 H6 37 23N 120 43W
Livingston, Mont., U.S.A. 82 D8 45 40N 110 34W
Livingston, Tex., U.S.A. 81 K7 30 43N 94 56W
Livingstone, Zambia 55 F2 17 46S 25 52 E
Livingstone Mts., Tanzania 55 D3 9 40S 34 20 E
Livingstonia, Malawi 55 E3 10 38S 34 5 E
Livny, Russia 24 D6 52 30N 37 30 E
Livonia, U.S.A. 76 D4 42 23N 83 23W
Livorno, Italy 20 C4 43 33N 10 19 E
Livramento, Brazil 95 C4 30 55S 55 30W
Liwale, Tanzania 55 D4 9 48S 37 58 E
Liwale □, Tanzania 55 D4 9 0S 38 0 E
Lizard I., Australia 62 A4 14 42S 145 30 E
Lizard Pt., U.K. 11 H2 49 57N 5 13W
Ljubljana, Slovenia 16 E8 46 4N 14 33 E
Ljungan →, Sweden 9 E17 62 18N 17 23 E
Ljungby, Sweden 9 H15 56 49N 13 55 E
Ljusdal, Sweden 9 F17 61 46N 16 3 E
Ljusnan →, Sweden 9 F17 61 12N 17 8 E
Ljusne, Sweden 9 F17 61 13N 17 7 E
Llancanelo, Salina, Argentina 94 D2 35 40S 69 8W
Llandeilo, U.K. 11 F4 51 53N 3 59W
Llandovery, U.K. 11 F4 51 59N 3 48W
Llandrindod Wells, U.K. 11 E4 52 14N 3 22W
Llandudno, U.K. 10 D4 53 19N 3 50W
Llanelli, U.K. 11 F3 51 41N 4 10W
Llanes, Spain 19 A3 43 25N 4 50W
Llangollen, U.K. 10 E4 52 58N 3 11W
Llanidloes, U.K. 11 E4 52 27N 3 31W
Llano, U.S.A. 81 K5 30 45N 98 41W
Llano →, U.S.A. 81 K5 30 39N 98 26W
Llano Estacado, U.S.A. 81 J3 33 30N 103 0W
Llanos, S. Amer. 92 C4 5 0N 71 35W
Llanquihue, L., Chile 96 E1 41 10S 75 50W
Llanwrtyd Wells, U.K. 11 E4 52 7N 3 38W
Llebetx, C., Spain 22 B9 39 33N 2 18 E
Lleida, Spain 19 B6 41 37N 0 39 E
Llentrisca, C., Spain 22 C7 38 52N 1 15 E
Llera, Mexico 87 C5 23 19N 99 1W
Lleyn Peninsula, U.K. 10 E3 52 51N 4 36W
Llico, Chile 94 C1 34 46S 72 5W
Lliria, Spain 19 C5 39 37N 0 35W
Llobregat →, Spain 19 B7 41 19N 2 9 E
Lloret de Mar, Spain 19 B7 41 41N 2 53 E
Lloyd B., Australia 62 A3 12 45S 143 27 E
Lloyd L., Canada 73 B7 57 22N 108 57W
Lloydminster, Canada 73 C7 53 17N 110 0W
Llucmajor, Spain 22 B9 39 29N 2 53 E
Llullaillaco, Volcán, S. Amer. 94 A2 24 43S 68 30W
Lo →, Vietnam 38 B5 21 18N 105 25 E
Loa, U.S.A. 83 G8 38 24N 111 39W
Loa →, Chile 94 A1 21 26S 70 41W
Lobatse, Botswana 56 D4 25 12S 25 40 E
Lobería, Argentina 94 D4 38 10S 58 40W
Lobito, Angola 53 G2 12 18S 13 35 E
Lobos, Argentina 94 D4 35 10S 59 0W
Lobos, I., Mexico 86 B2 27 15N 110 30W
Lobos, I. de, Canary Is. 22 F6 28 45N 13 50W
Loc Binh, Vietnam 38 B6 21 46N 106 54 E
Loc Ninh, Vietnam 39 G6 11 50N 106 34 E
Locarno, Switz. 18 C8 46 10N 8 47 E
Loch Baghasdail = Lochboisdale, U.K. 12 D1 57 9N 7 20W
Loch Garman = Wexford, Ireland 13 D5 52 20N 6 28W
Loch Nam Madadh = Lochmaddy, U.K. 12 D1 57 36N 7 10W
Lochaber, U.K. 12 E3 56 59N 5 1W
Locharbriggs, U.K. 12 F5 55 7N 3 35W
Lochboisdale, U.K. 12 D1 57 9N 7 20W
Lochem, Neths. 15 B6 52 9N 6 26 E
Loches, France 18 C4 47 7N 1 0 E
Lochgilphead, U.K. 12 E3 56 2N 5 26W
Lochinver, U.K. 12 C3 58 9N 5 14W
Lochmaddy, U.K. 12 D1 57 36N 7 10W
Lochnagar, Australia 62 C4 23 33S 145 38 E
Lochnagar, U.K. 12 E5 56 57N 3 15W
Lochy, L., U.K. 12 E4 57 0N 4 53W
Lock, Australia 63 E2 33 34S 135 46 E
Lock Haven, U.S.A. 78 E7 41 8N 77 28W
Lockeford, U.S.A. 84 G5 38 10N 121 9W
Lockeport, Canada 71 D6 43 47N 65 4W
Lockerbie, U.K. 12 F5 55 7N 3 21W
Lockhart, U.S.A. 81 L6 29 53N 97 40W
Lockhart, L., Australia 61 F2 33 15S 119 3 E
Lockney, U.S.A. 81 H4 34 7N 101 27W
Lockport, U.S.A. 78 C6 43 10N 78 42W
Lod, Israel 47 D3 31 57N 34 54 E
Lodeinoye Pole, Russia 24 B5 60 44N 33 33 E
Lodge Grass, U.S.A. 82 D10 45 19N 107 22W
Lodgepole, U.S.A. 80 E3 41 9N 102 38W
Lodgepole Cr. →, U.S.A. 80 E2 41 20N 104 30W
Lodhran, Pakistan 42 E4 29 32N 71 30 E
Lodi, Italy 18 D8 45 19N 9 30 E
Lodi, U.S.A. 84 G5 38 8N 121 16W
Lodja, Dem. Rep. of the Congo 54 C1 3 30S 23 23 E
Lodwar, Kenya 54 B4 3 10N 35 40 E
Łódź, Poland 17 C10 51 45N 19 27 E
Loei, Thailand 38 D3 17 29N 101 35 E
Loengo, Dem. Rep. of the Congo 54 C2 4 48S 26 30 E
Loeriesfontein, S. Africa 56 E2 31 0S 19 26 E
Lofoten, Norway 8 B15 68 30N 14 0 E
Logan, Kans., U.S.A. 80 F5 39 40N 99 34W
Logan, Ohio, U.S.A. 76 F4 39 32N 82 25W
Logan, Utah, U.S.A. 82 F8 41 44N 111 50W
Logan, W. Va., U.S.A. 76 G5 37 51N 81 59W
Logan, Mt., Canada 68 B5 60 31N 140 22W
Logan Pass, U.S.A. 72 D6 48 41N 113 44W
Logandale, U.S.A. 85 J12 36 36N 114 29W
Logansport, Ind., U.S.A. 76 E2 40 45N 86 22W
Logansport, La., U.S.A. 81 K8 31 58N 94 0W
Logone →, Chad 51 F9 12 6N 15 2 E
Logroño, Spain 19 A4 42 28N 2 27W
Lohardaga, India 43 H11 23 27N 84 45 E
Lohja, Finland 9 F21 60 12N 24 5 E
Loi-kaw, Burma 41 K20 19 40N 97 17 E
Loimaa, Finland 9 F20 60 50N 23 5 E
Loir →, France 18 C3 47 33N 0 32W
Loire →, France 18 C2 47 16N 2 10W
Loja, Ecuador 92 D3 3 59S 79 16W
Loja, Spain 19 D3 37 10N 4 10W
Loji = Kawasi, Indonesia 37 E7 1 38S 127 28 E
Lokandu, Dem. Rep. of the Congo 54 C2 2 30S 25 45 E
Lokeren, Belgium 15 C3 51 6N 3 59 E
Lokichokio, Kenya 54 B3 4 19N 34 13 E
Lokitaung, Kenya 54 B4 4 12N 35 48 E
Lokkan tekojärvi, Finland 8 C22 67 55N 27 35 E
Lokoja, Nigeria 50 G7 7 47N 6 45 E
Lola, Mt., U.S.A. 84 F6 39 26N 120 22W
Loliondo, Tanzania 54 C4 2 2S 35 39 E
Lolland, Denmark 9 J14 54 45N 11 30 E
Lolo, U.S.A. 82 C6 46 45N 114 5W
Lom, Bulgaria 21 C10 43 48N 23 12 E
Lom Kao, Thailand 38 D3 16 53N 101 14 E
Lom Sak, Thailand 38 D3 16 47N 101 15 E
Loma, U.S.A. 82 C8 47 56N 110 30W
Loma Linda, U.S.A. 85 L9 34 3N 117 16W
Lomami →, Dem. Rep. of the Congo 54 B1 0 46N 24 16 E
Lomas de Zamóra, Argentina 94 C4 34 45S 58 25W
Lombadina, Australia 60 C3 16 31S 122 54 E
Lombárdia □, Italy 18 D8 45 40N 9 30 E
Lombardy = Lombárdia □, Italy 18 D8 45 40N 9 30 E
Lomblen, Indonesia 37 F6 8 30S 123 32 E
Lombok, Indonesia 36 F5 8 45S 116 30 E
Lomé, Togo 50 G6 6 9N 1 20 E
Lomela, Dem. Rep. of the Congo 52 E4 2 19S 23 15 E
Lomela →, Dem. Rep. of the Congo 52 E4 0 15S 20 40 E
Lometa, U.S.A. 81 K5 31 13N 98 24W
Lommel, Belgium 15 C5 51 14N 5 19 E
Lomond, Canada 72 C6 50 24N 112 36W
Lomond, L., U.K. 12 E4 56 8N 4 38W
Lomphat, Cambodia 38 F6 13 30N 106 59 E
Lompobatang, Indonesia 37 F5 5 24S 119 56 E
Lompoc, U.S.A. 85 L6 34 38N 120 28W
Łomża, Poland 17 B12 53 10N 22 2 E
Loncoche, Chile 96 D2 39 20S 72 50W
Londa, India 40 M9 15 30N 74 30 E
Londiani, Kenya 54 C4 0 10S 35 33 E
London, Canada 70 D3 42 59N 81 15W
London, U.K. 11 F7 51 30N 0 3W
London, Ky., U.S.A. 76 G3 37 8N 84 5W
London, Ohio, U.S.A. 76 F4 39 53N 83 27W
London, Greater □, U.K. 11 F7 51 36N 0 5W
Londonderry, U.K. 13 B4 55 0N 7 20W
Londonderry □, U.K. 13 B4 55 0N 7 20W
Londonderry, C., Australia 60 B4 13 45S 126 55 E
Londonderry, I., Chile 96 H2 55 0S 71 0W
Londres, Argentina 96 B3 27 43S 67 7W
Londrina, Brazil 95 A5 23 18S 51 10W
Lone Pine, U.S.A. 84 J8 36 36N 118 4W
Long Beach, Calif., U.S.A. 85 M8 33 47N 118 11W
Long Beach, N.Y., U.S.A. 79 F11 40 35N 73 39W
Long Beach, Wash., U.S.A. 84 D2 46 21N 124 3W
Long Branch, U.S.A. 79 F11 40 18N 74 0W
Long Creek, U.S.A. 82 D4 44 43N 119 6W
Long Eaton, U.K. 10 E6 52 53N 1 15W
Long I., Australia 62 C4 22 8S 149 53 E
Long I., Bahamas 89 B4 23 20N 75 10W
Long I., Ireland 13 E2 51 30N 9 34W
Long I., U.S.A. 79 F11 40 45N 73 30W
Long Island Sd., U.S.A. 79 E12 41 10N 73 0W
Long L., Canada 70 C2 49 30N 86 50W
Long Lake, U.S.A. 79 C10 43 58N 74 25W
Long Pine, U.S.A. 80 D5 42 32N 99 42W
Long Point B., Canada 78 D4 42 40N 80 10W
Long Pt., Nfld., Canada 71 C8 48 47N 58 46W
Long Pt., Ont., Canada 78 D4 42 35N 80 2W
Long Range Mts., Canada 71 C8 49 30N 57 30W
Long Reef, Australia 60 B4 14 1S 125 48 E
Long Thanh, Vietnam 39 G6 10 47N 106 57 E
Long Xian, China 34 G4 34 55N 106 55 E
Long Xuyen, Vietnam 39 G5 10 19N 105 28 E
Longbenton, U.K. 10 B6 55 1N 1 31W
Longde, China 34 G4 35 30N 106 20 E
Longford, Australia 62 G4 41 32S 147 3 E
Longford, Ireland 13 C4 53 43N 7 49W
Longford □, Ireland 13 C4 53 42N 7 45W
Longguan, China 34 D8 40 45N 115 30 E
Longhua, China 35 D9 41 18N 117 45 E
Longido, Tanzania 54 C4 2 43S 36 42 E
Longiram, Indonesia 36 E5 0 5S 115 45 E
Longkou, China 35 F11 37 40N 120 18 E
Longlac, Canada 70 C2 49 45N 86 25W
Longmont, U.S.A. 80 E2 40 10N 105 6W
Longnawan, Indonesia 36 D4 1 51N 114 55 E
Longreach, Australia 62 C3 23 28S 144 14 E
Longton, Australia 62 C4 20 58S 145 55 E
Longueuil, Canada 79 A11 45 32N 73 28W
Longview, Canada 72 C6 50 32N 114 10W
Longview, Tex., U.S.A. 81 J7 32 30N 94 44W
Longview, Wash., U.S.A. 84 D4 46 8N 122 57W
Longxi, China 34 G3 34 53N 104 40 E
Lonoke, U.S.A. 81 H9 34 47N 91 54W
Lonquimay, Chile 96 D2 38 26S 71 14W
Lons-le-Saunier, France 18 C6 46 40N 5 31 E
Looe, U.K. 11 G3 50 22N 4 28W
Lookout, C., Canada 70 A3 55 18N 83 56W
Lookout, C., U.S.A. 77 H7 34 35N 76 32W
Loolmalasin, Tanzania 54 C4 3 0S 35 53 E
Loon →, Alta., Canada 72 B5 57 8N 115 3W
Loon →, Man., Canada 73 B8 55 53N 101 59W
Loon Lake, Canada 73 C7 54 2N 109 10W
Loongana, Australia 61 F4 30 52S 127 5 E
Loop Hd., Ireland 13 D2 52 34N 9 56W
Lop Buri, Thailand 38 E3 14 48N 100 37 E
Lop Nor = Lop Nur, China 32 B4 40 20N 90 10 E
Lop Nur, China 32 B4 40 20N 90 10 E
Lopatina, Gora, Russia 27 D15 50 47N 143 10 E

Malyn

McGehee, U.S.A. 81 J9 33 38N 91 24W
McGill, U.S.A. 82 G6 39 23N 114 47W
Macgillycuddy's Reeks, Ireland 13 E2 51 58N 9 45W
MacGregor, Canada 73 D9 49 57N 98 48W
McGregor, U.S.A. 80 D9 43 1N 91 11W
McGregor →, Canada 72 B4 55 10N 122 0W
McGregor Ra., Australia 63 D3 27 0S 142 45 E
Mach, Pakistan 40 E5 29 50N 67 20 E
Māch Kowr, Iran 45 E9 25 48N 61 28 E
Machado = Jiparaná →, Brazil 92 E6 8 3S 62 52W
Machagai, Argentina 94 B3 26 56S 60 2W
Machakos, Kenya 54 C4 1 30S 37 15 E
Machakos □, Kenya 54 C4 1 30S 37 15 E
Machala, Ecuador 92 D3 3 20S 79 57W
Machanga, Mozam. 57 C6 20 59S 35 0 E
Machattie, L., Australia 62 C2 24 50S 139 48 E
Machava, Mozam. 57 D5 25 54S 32 28 E
Machece, Mozam. 55 F4 19 15S 35 32 E
Machias, U.S.A. 71 D6 44 43N 67 28W
Machichi →, Canada 73 B10 57 3N 92 6W
Machico, Madeira 22 D3 32 43N 16 44W
Machilipatnam, India 41 L12 16 12N 81 8 E
Machiques, Venezuela 92 A4 10 4N 72 34W
Machupicchu, Peru 92 F4 13 8S 72 30W
Machynlleth, U.K. 11 E4 52 35N 3 50W
McIlwraith Ra., Australia 62 A3 13 50S 143 20 E
McIntosh, U.S.A. 80 C4 45 55N 101 21W
McIntosh L., Canada 73 B8 55 45N 105 0W
Macintosh Ra., Australia 61 E4 27 39S 125 32 E
Macintyre →, Australia 63 D5 28 37S 150 47 E
Mackay, Australia 62 C4 21 8S 149 11 E
Mackay, U.S.A. 82 E7 43 55N 113 37W
MacKay →, Canada 72 B6 57 10N 111 38W
Mackay, L., Australia 60 D4 22 30S 129 0 E
McKay Ra., Australia 60 D3 23 0S 122 30 E
McKeesport, U.S.A. 78 F5 40 21N 79 52W
McKenna, U.S.A. 84 D4 46 56N 122 33W
Mackenzie, Canada 72 B4 55 20N 123 5W
McKenzie, U.S.A. 77 G1 36 8N 88 31W
Mackenzie →, Australia 62 C4 23 38S 149 46 E
Mackenzie →, Canada 68 B6 69 10N 134 20W
McKenzie →, U.S.A. 82 D2 44 7N 123 6W
Mackenzie City = Linden, Guyana 92 B7 6 0N 58 10W
Mackenzie Highway, Canada 72 B5 58 0N 117 15W
Mackenzie Mts., Canada 68 B7 64 0N 130 0W
Mackinaw City, U.S.A. 76 C3 45 47N 84 44W
McKinlay, Australia 62 C3 21 16S 141 18 E
McKinlay →, Australia 62 C3 20 50S 141 28 E
McKinley, Mt., U.S.A. 68 B4 63 4N 151 0W
McKinney, U.S.A. 81 J6 33 12N 96 37W
Mackinnon Road, Kenya 54 C4 3 40S 39 1 E
Macksville, Australia 63 E5 30 40S 152 56 E
McLaughlin, U.S.A. 80 C4 45 49N 100 49W
Maclean, Australia 63 D5 29 26S 153 16 E
McLean, U.S.A. 81 H4 35 14N 100 36W
McLeansboro, U.S.A. 80 F10 38 6N 88 32W
Maclear, S. Africa 57 E4 31 2S 28 23 E
Macleay →, Australia 63 E5 30 56S 153 0 E
McLennan, Canada 72 B5 55 42N 116 50W
MacLeod, B., Canada 73 A7 62 53N 110 0W
McLeod, L., Australia 61 D1 24 9S 113 47 E
MacLeod Lake, Canada 72 C4 54 58N 123 0W
McLoughlin, Mt., U.S.A. 82 E2 42 27N 122 19W
McLure, Canada 72 C4 51 2N 120 13W
McMechen, U.S.A. 78 G4 39 57N 80 44W
McMillan, L., U.S.A. 81 J2 32 36N 104 21W
McMinnville, Oreg., U.S.A. 82 D2 45 13N 123 12W
McMinnville, Tenn., U.S.A. 77 H3 35 41N 85 46W
McMorran, Canada 73 C7 51 19N 108 42W
McMurdo Sd., Antarctica 5 D11 77 0S 170 0 E
McMurray = Fort McMurray, Canada 72 B6 56 44N 111 7W
McMurray, U.S.A. 84 B4 48 19N 122 14W
McNary, U.S.A. 83 J9 34 4N 109 51W
MacNutt, Canada 73 C8 51 5N 101 36W
Macodoene, Mozam. 57 C6 23 32S 35 5 E
Macomb, U.S.A. 80 E9 40 27N 90 40W
Mâcon, France 18 C6 46 19N 4 50 E
Macon, Ga., U.S.A. 77 J4 32 51N 83 38W
Macon, Miss., U.S.A. 77 J1 33 7N 88 34W
Macon, Mo., U.S.A. 80 F8 39 44N 92 28W
Macossa, Mozam. 55 F3 17 55S 33 56 E
Macoun L., Canada 73 B8 56 32N 103 40W
Macovane, Mozam. 57 C6 21 30S 35 2 E
McPherson, U.S.A. 80 F6 38 22N 97 40W
McPherson Pk., U.S.A. 85 L7 34 53N 119 53W
McPherson Ra., Australia 63 D5 28 15S 153 15 E
Macquarie Harbour, Australia 62 G4 42 15S 145 23 E
Macquarie Is., Pac. Oc. 64 N7 54 36S 158 55 E
MacRobertson Land, Antarctica 5 D6 71 0S 64 0 E
Macroom, Ireland 13 E3 51 54N 8 57W
Macroy, Australia 60 D2 20 53S 118 2 E
MacTier, Canada 78 A5 45 9N 79 46W
Macubela, Mozam. 55 F4 16 53S 37 49 E
Macuiza, Mozam. 55 F3 18 7S 34 29 E
Macusani, Peru 92 F4 14 4S 70 29W
Macuse, Mozam. 55 F4 17 45S 37 10 E
Macuspana, Mexico 87 D6 17 46N 92 36W
Macusse, Angola 56 B3 17 48S 20 23 E
McVille, U.S.A. 80 B5 47 46N 98 11W
Madadeni, S. Africa 57 D5 27 43S 30 3 E
Madagascar ■, Africa 57 C8 20 0S 47 0 E
Madā'in Sālih, Si. Arabia 44 E3 26 46N 37 57 E
Madama, Niger 51 D8 22 0N 13 40 E
Madame I., Canada 71 C7 45 30N 60 58W
Madaripur, Bangla. 41 H17 23 19N 90 15 E
Madauk, Burma 41 L20 17 56N 96 52 E
Madawaska, Canada 78 A7 45 30N 78 0W
Madawaska →, Canada 78 A8 45 27N 76 21W
Madaya, Burma 41 H20 22 12N 96 10 E
Maddalena, Italy 20 D3 41 16N 9 23 E
Madeira, Atl. Oc. 22 D3 32 50N 17 0W
Madeira →, Brazil 92 D7 3 22S 58 45W
Madeleine, Is. de la, Canada 71 C7 47 30N 61 40W
Madera, U.S.A. 84 J6 36 57N 120 3W
Madha, India 40 L9 18 0N 75 30 E
Madhubani, India 43 F12 26 21N 86 7 E
Madhya Pradesh □, India 42 J8 22 50N 78 0 E
Madidi →, Bolivia 92 F5 12 32S 66 52W
Madikeri, India 40 N9 12 30N 75 45 E
Madill, U.S.A. 81 H6 34 6N 96 46W
Madimba, Dem. Rep. of the Congo 52 E3 4 58S 15 5 E
Ma'din, Syria 44 C3 35 45N 39 36 E
Madingou, Congo 52 E2 4 10S 13 33 E
Madirovalo, Madag. 57 B8 16 26S 46 32 E
Madison, Calif., U.S.A. 84 G5 38 41N 121 59W
Madison, Fla., U.S.A. 77 K4 30 28N 83 25W
Madison, Ind., U.S.A. 76 F3 38 44N 85 23W
Madison, Nebr., U.S.A. 80 E6 41 50N 97 27W
Madison, Ohio, U.S.A. 78 E3 41 46N 81 3W
Madison, S. Dak., U.S.A. 80 D6 44 0N 97 7W
Madison, Wis., U.S.A. 80 D10 43 4N 89 24W
Madison →, U.S.A. 82 D8 45 56N 111 31W
Madisonville, Ky., U.S.A. 76 G2 37 20N 87 30W
Madisonville, Tex., U.S.A. 81 K7 30 57N 95 55W
Madista, Botswana 56 C4 21 15S 25 6 E
Madiun, Indonesia 37 G14 7 38S 111 32 E
Madona, Latvia 9 H22 56 53N 26 5 E
Madras = Chennai, India 40 N12 13 8N 80 19 E
Madras = Tamil Nadu □, India 40 P10 11 0N 77 0 E
Madras, U.S.A. 82 D3 44 38N 121 8W
Madre, L., Mexico 87 C5 25 0N 97 30W
Madre, Laguna, U.S.A. 81 M6 27 0N 97 30W
Madre, Sierra, Phil. 37 A6 17 0N 122 0 E
Madre de Dios →, Bolivia 92 F5 10 59S 66 8W
Madre de Dios, I., Chile 96 G1 50 20S 75 10W
Madre del Sur, Sierra, Mexico 87 D5 17 30N 100 0W
Madre Occidental, Sierra, Mexico 86 B3 27 0N 107 0W
Madre Oriental, Sierra, Mexico 86 C5 25 0N 100 0W
Madri, India 42 G5 24 16N 73 32 E
Madrid, Spain 19 B4 40 25N 3 45W
Madura, Selat, Indonesia 37 G15 7 30S 113 20 E
Madura Motel, Australia 61 F4 31 55S 127 0 E
Madurai, India 40 Q11 9 55N 78 10 E
Madurantakam, India 40 N11 12 30N 79 50 E
Mae Chan, Thailand 38 B2 20 9N 99 52 E
Mae Hong Son, Thailand 38 C2 19 16N 97 56 E
Mae Khlong →, Thailand 38 F3 13 24N 100 0 E
Mae Phrik, Thailand 38 D2 17 27N 99 7 E
Mae Ramat, Thailand 38 D2 16 58N 98 31 E
Mae Rim, Thailand 38 C2 18 54N 98 57 E
Mae Sot, Thailand 38 D2 16 43N 98 34 E
Mae Suai, Thailand 38 C2 19 39N 99 33 E
Mae Tha, Thailand 38 C2 18 28N 99 8 E
Maebashi, Japan 31 F9 36 24N 139 4 E
Maesteg, U.K. 11 F4 51 36N 3 40W
Maestra, Sierra, Cuba 88 B4 20 15N 77 0W
Maestrazgo, El, Spain 19 B5 40 30N 0 25W
Maevatanana, Madag. 57 B8 16 56S 46 49 E
Mafeking = Mafikeng, S. Africa 56 D4 25 50S 25 38 E
Mafeking, Canada 73 C8 52 40N 101 10W
Mafeteng, Lesotho 56 D4 29 51S 27 15 E
Maffra, Australia 63 F4 37 53S 146 58 E
Mafia I., Tanzania 54 D4 7 45S 39 50 E
Mafikeng, S. Africa 56 D4 25 50S 25 38 E
Mafra, Brazil 95 B6 26 10S 49 55W
Mafra, Portugal 19 C1 38 55N 9 20W
Mafungabusi Plateau, Zimbabwe 55 F2 18 30S 29 8 E
Magadan, Russia 27 D16 59 38N 150 50 E
Magadi, Kenya 54 C4 1 54S 36 19 E
Magadi, L., Kenya 54 C4 1 54S 36 19 E
Magaliesburg, S. Africa 57 D4 26 0S 27 32 E
Magallanes, Estrecho de, Chile 96 G2 52 30S 75 0W
Magangué, Colombia 92 B4 9 14N 74 45W
Magdalen Is. = Madeleine, Is. de la, Canada 71 C7 47 30N 61 40W
Magdalena, Argentina 94 D4 35 5S 57 30W
Magdalena, Bolivia 92 F6 13 13S 63 57W
Magdalena, Mexico 86 A2 30 50N 112 0W
Magdalena, U.S.A. 83 J10 34 7N 107 15W
Magdalena →, Colombia 92 A4 11 6N 74 51W
Magdalena →, Mexico 86 A2 30 40N 112 25W
Magdalena, B., Mexico 86 C2 24 30N 112 10W
Magdalena, Llano de la, Mexico 86 C2 25 0N 111 30W
Magdeburg, Germany 16 B6 52 7N 11 38 E
Magdelaine Cays, Australia 62 B5 16 33S 150 18 E
Magee, U.S.A. 81 K10 31 52N 89 44W
Magelang, Indonesia 37 G14 7 29S 110 13 E
Magellan's Str. = Magallanes, Estrecho de, Chile 96 G2 52 30S 75 0W
Magenta, L., Australia 61 F2 33 30S 119 2 E
Magerøya, Norway 8 A21 71 3N 25 40 E
Maggiore, L., Italy 18 D8 45 57N 8 39 E
Magherafelt, U.K. 13 B5 54 45N 6 37W
Magistralnyy, Russia 27 D11 56 16N 107 36 E
Magnetic Pole (South) = South Magnetic Pole, Antarctica 5 C9 64 8S 138 8 E
Magnitogorsk, Russia 24 D10 53 27N 59 4 E
Magnolia, Ark., U.S.A. 81 J8 33 16N 93 14W
Magnolia, Miss., U.S.A. 81 K9 31 9N 90 28W
Magog, Canada 71 C5 45 18N 72 9W
Magoro, Uganda 54 B3 1 45N 34 12 E
Magosa = Famagusta, Cyprus 23 D12 35 8N 33 55 E
Magouládhes, Greece 23 A3 39 45N 19 42 E
Magoye, Zambia 55 F2 16 1S 27 30 E
Magpie L., Canada 71 B7 51 0N 64 41W
Magrath, Canada 72 D6 49 25N 112 50W
Magu □, Tanzania 54 C3 2 31S 33 28 E
Maguarinho, C., Brazil 93 D9 0 15S 48 30W
Mağusa = Famagusta, Cyprus 23 D12 35 8N 33 55 E
Maguse L., Canada 73 A9 61 40N 95 10W
Maguse Pt., Canada 73 A10 61 20N 93 50W
Magwe, Burma 41 J19 20 10N 95 0 E
Maha Sarakham, Thailand 38 D4 16 12N 103 16 E
Mahābād, Iran 44 B5 36 50N 45 45 E
Mahabharat Lekh, Nepal 43 E10 28 30N 82 0 E
Mahabo, Madag. 57 C7 20 23S 44 40 E
Mahadeo Hills, India 42 H8 22 20N 78 30 E
Mahagi, Dem. Rep. of the Congo 54 B3 2 20N 31 0 E
Mahajamba →, Madag. 57 B8 15 33S 47 8 E
Mahajamba, Helodranon' i, Madag. 57 B8 15 24S 47 5 E
Mahajan, India 42 E5 28 48N 73 56 E
Mahajanga, Madag. 57 B8 15 40S 46 25 E
Mahajanga □, Madag. 57 B8 17 0S 47 0 E
Mahajilo →, Madag. 57 B8 19 42S 45 22 E
Mahakam →, Indonesia 36 E5 0 35S 117 17 E
Mahalapye, Botswana 56 C4 23 1S 26 51 E
Maḩallāt, Iran 45 C6 33 55N 50 30 E
Māhān, Iran 45 D8 30 5N 57 18 E
Mahanadi →, India 41 J15 20 20N 86 25 E
Mahanoro, Madag. 57 B8 19 54S 48 48 E
Mahanoy City, U.S.A. 79 F8 40 49N 76 9W
Maharashtra □, India 40 J9 20 30N 75 30 E
Mahari Mts., Tanzania 54 D3 6 20S 30 0 E
Mahasham, W. →, Egypt 47 E3 30 15N 34 10 E
Mahasolo, Madag. 57 B8 19 7S 46 22 E
Mahattat ash Shīdīyah, Jordan 47 F4 29 55N 35 55 E
Mahattat 'Unayzah, Jordan 47 E4 30 30N 35 47 E
Mahaxay, Laos 38 D5 17 22N 105 12 E
Mahbubnagar, India 40 L10 16 45N 77 59 E
Maḩḑah, Oman 45 E7 24 24N 55 59 E
Mahdia, Tunisia 51 A8 35 28N 11 0 E
Mahe, India 43 C8 33 10N 78 32 E
Mahenge, Tanzania 55 D4 8 45S 36 41 E
Maheno, N.Z. 59 L3 45 10S 170 50 E
Mahesana, India 42 H5 23 39N 72 26 E
Mahia Pen., N.Z. 59 H6 39 9S 177 55 E
Mahilyow, Belarus 24 D5 53 55N 30 18 E
Mahmud Kot, Pakistan 42 D4 30 16N 71 0 E
Mahnomen, U.S.A. 80 B7 47 19N 95 58W
Mahoba, India 43 G8 25 15N 79 55 E
Mahón = Maó, Spain 22 B11 39 53N 4 16 E
Mahone Bay, Canada 71 D7 44 30N 64 20W
Mai-Ndombe, L., Dem. Rep. of the Congo 52 E3 2 0S 18 20 E
Mai-Sai, Thailand 38 B2 20 20N 99 55 E
Maicurú →, Brazil 93 D8 2 14S 54 17W
Maidan Khula, Afghan. 42 C3 33 36N 69 50 E
Maidenhead, U.K. 11 F7 51 31N 0 42W
Maidstone, Canada 73 C7 53 5N 109 20W
Maidstone, U.K. 11 F8 51 16N 0 32 E
Maiduguri, Nigeria 51 F8 12 0N 13 20 E
Maijdi, Bangla. 41 H17 22 48N 91 10 E
Maikala Ra., India 41 J12 22 0N 81 0 E
Mailsi, Pakistan 42 E5 29 48N 72 15 E
Main →, Germany 16 C5 50 0N 8 18 E
Main →, U.K. 13 B5 54 48N 6 18W
Main Centre, Canada 73 C7 50 35N 107 21W
Maine, France 18 C3 48 20N 0 15W
Maine □, U.S.A. 71 C6 45 20N 69 0W
Maine →, Ireland 13 D2 52 9N 9 45W
Maingkwan, Burma 41 F20 26 15N 96 37 E
Mainit, L., Phil. 37 C7 9 31N 125 30 E
Mainland, Orkney, U.K. 12 C5 58 59N 3 8W
Mainland, Shet., U.K. 12 A7 60 15N 1 22W
Mainpuri, India 43 F8 27 18N 79 4 E
Maintirano, Madag. 57 B7 18 3S 44 1 E
Mainz, Germany 16 C5 50 1N 8 14 E
Maipú, Argentina 94 D4 36 52S 57 50W
Maiquetía, Venezuela 92 A5 10 36N 66 57W
Mairabari, India 41 F18 26 30N 92 22 E
Maisí, Cuba 89 B5 20 17N 74 9W
Maisí, Pta. de, Cuba 89 B5 20 10N 74 10W
Maitland, N.S.W., Australia 63 E5 32 33S 151 36 E
Maitland, S. Austral., Australia 63 E2 34 23S 137 40 E
Maitland →, Canada 78 C3 43 45N 81 43W
Maiz, Is. del, Nic. 88 D3 12 15N 83 4W
Maizuru, Japan 31 G7 35 25N 135 22 E
Majalengka, Indonesia 37 G13 6 50S 108 13 E
Majene, Indonesia 37 E5 3 38S 118 57 E
Major, Canada 73 C7 51 52N 109 37W
Majorca = Mallorca, Spain 22 B10 39 30N 3 0 E
Makale, Indonesia 37 E5 3 6S 119 51 E
Makamba, Burundi 54 C2 4 8S 29 49 E
Makarikari = Makgadikgadi Salt Pans, Botswana 56 C4 20 40S 25 45 E
Makarovo, Russia 27 D11 57 40N 107 45 E
Makasar = Ujung Pandang, Indonesia 37 F5 5 10S 119 20 E
Makasar, Selat, Indonesia 37 E5 1 0S 118 20 E
Makasar, Str. of = Makasar, Selat, Indonesia 37 E5 1 0S 118 20 E
Makat, Kazakstan 25 E9 47 39N 53 19 E
Makedhonía □, Greece 21 D10 40 39N 22 0 E
Makedonija = Macedonia ■, Europe 21 D9 41 53N 21 40 E
Makena, U.S.A. 74 H16 20 39N 156 27W
Makeyevka = Makiyivka, Ukraine 25 E6 48 0N 38 0 E
Makgadikgadi Salt Pans, Botswana 56 C4 20 40S 25 45 E
Makhachkala, Russia 25 F8 43 0N 47 30 E
Makhmūr, Iraq 44 C4 35 46N 43 35 E
Makian, Indonesia 37 D7 0 20N 127 20 E
Makindu, Kenya 54 C4 2 18S 37 50 E
Makinsk, Kazakstan 26 D8 52 37N 70 26 E
Makiyivka, Ukraine 25 E6 48 0N 38 0 E
Makkah, Si. Arabia 46 C2 21 30N 39 54 E
Makkovik, Canada 71 A8 55 10N 59 10W
Makó, Hungary 17 E11 46 14N 20 33 E
Makokou, Gabon 52 D2 0 40N 12 50 E
Makongo, Dem. Rep. of the Congo 54 B2 3 25N 26 17 E
Makoro, Dem. Rep. of the Congo 54 B2 3 10N 29 59 E
Makrai, India 40 H10 22 2N 77 0 E
Makran Coast Range, Pakistan 40 G4 25 40N 64 0 E
Makrana, India 42 F6 27 2N 74 46 E
Makriyialos, Greece 23 D7 35 2N 25 59 E
Mākū, Iran 44 B5 39 15N 44 31 E
Makunda, Botswana 56 C3 22 30S 20 7 E
Makurazaki, Japan 31 J5 31 15N 130 20 E
Makurdi, Nigeria 50 G7 7 43N 8 35 E
Makūyeh, Iran 45 D7 28 7N 53 9 E
Makwassie, S. Africa 56 D4 27 17S 26 0 E
Mal B., Ireland 13 D2 52 50N 9 30W
Mala, Pta., Panama 88 E3 7 28N 80 2W
Malabar Coast, India 40 P9 11 0N 75 0 E
Malabo = Rey Malabo, Eq. Guin. 52 D1 3 45N 8 50 E
Malacca, Str. of, Indonesia 39 L3 3 0N 101 0 E
Malad City, U.S.A. 82 E7 42 12N 112 15W
Maladzyechna, Belarus 17 A14 54 20N 26 50 E
Málaga, Spain 19 D3 36 43N 4 23W
Malaga, U.S.A. 81 J2 32 14N 104 4W
Malagarasi, Tanzania 54 D3 5 5S 30 50 E
Malagarasi →, Tanzania 54 D2 5 12S 29 47 E
Malahide, Ireland 13 C5 53 26N 6 9W
Malaimbandy, Madag. 57 C8 20 20S 45 36 E
Malakâl, Sudan 51 G12 9 33N 31 40 E
Malakand, Pakistan 42 B4 34 40N 71 55 E
Malakoff, U.S.A. 81 J7 32 10N 96 1W
Malang, Indonesia 37 G15 7 59S 112 45 E
Malangen, Norway 8 B18 69 24N 18 37 E
Malanje, Angola 52 F3 9 36S 16 17 E
Mälaren, Sweden 9 G17 59 30N 17 10 E
Malargüe, Argentina 94 D2 35 32S 69 30W
Malartic, Canada 70 C4 48 9N 78 9W
Malaryta, Belarus 17 C13 51 50N 24 3 E
Malatya, Turkey 25 G6 38 25N 38 20 E
Malawi ■, Africa 55 E3 11 55S 34 0 E
Malawi, L. = Nyasa, L., Africa 55 E3 12 30S 34 30 E
Malay Pen., Asia 39 J3 7 25N 100 0 E
Malaybalay, Phil. 37 C7 8 5N 125 7 E
Malāyer, Iran 45 C6 34 19N 48 51 E
Malaysia ■, Asia 36 D4 5 0N 110 0 E
Malazgirt, Turkey 25 G7 39 10N 42 33 E
Malbon, Australia 62 C3 21 5S 140 17 E
Malbooma, Australia 63 E1 30 41S 134 11 E
Malbork, Poland 17 B10 54 3N 19 1 E
Malcolm, Australia 61 E3 28 51S 121 25 E
Malcolm, Pt., Australia 61 F3 33 48S 123 45 E
Maldegem, Belgium 15 C3 51 14N 3 26 E
Malden, Mass., U.S.A. 79 D13 42 26N 71 4W
Malden, Mo., U.S.A. 81 G10 36 34N 89 57W
Malden I., Kiribati 65 H12 4 3S 155 1W
Maldives ■, Ind. Oc. 29 J11 5 0N 73 0 E
Maldonado, Uruguay 95 C5 34 59S 55 0W
Maldonado, Punta, Mexico 87 D5 16 19N 98 35W
Malé Karpaty, Slovak Rep. 17 D9 48 30N 17 20 E
Maléa, Ákra, Greece 21 F10 36 28N 23 7 E
Malegaon, India 40 J9 20 30N 74 38 E
Malei, Mozam. 55 F4 17 12S 36 58 E
Malek Kandī, Iran 44 B5 37 9N 46 6 E
Malela, Dem. Rep. of the Congo 54 C2 4 22S 26 8 E
Malema, Mozam. 55 E4 14 57S 37 20 E
Maleme, Greece 23 D5 35 31N 23 49 E
Malerkotla, India 42 D6 30 32N 75 58 E
Máles, Greece 23 D7 35 6N 25 35 E
Malgomaj, Sweden 8 D17 64 40N 16 30 E
Malha, Sudan 51 E11 15 8N 25 10 E
Malheur →, U.S.A. 82 D5 44 4N 116 59W
Malheur L., U.S.A. 82 E4 43 20N 118 48W
Mali ■, Africa 50 E5 17 0N 3 0W
Mali →, Burma 41 G20 25 40N 97 40 E
Mali Kyun, Burma 38 F2 13 0N 98 20 E
Malibu, U.S.A. 85 L8 34 2N 118 41W
Maliku, Indonesia 37 E6 0 39S 123 16 E
Malili, Indonesia 37 E6 2 42S 121 6 E
Malimba, Mts., Dem. Rep. of the Congo 54 D2 7 30S 29 30 E
Malin Hd., Ireland 13 A4 55 23N 7 23W
Malin Pen., Ireland 13 A4 55 20N 7 17W
Malindi, Kenya 54 C5 3 12S 40 5 E
Malines = Mechelen, Belgium 15 C4 51 2N 4 29 E
Malino, Indonesia 37 D6 1 0N 121 0 E
Malinyi, Tanzania 55 D4 8 56S 36 0 E
Malita, Phil. 37 C7 6 19N 125 39 E
Malkara, Turkey 21 D12 40 53N 26 53 E
Mallacoota, Australia 63 F4 37 40S 149 40 E
Mallacoota Inlet, Australia 63 F4 37 34S 149 40 E
Mallaig, U.K. 12 D3 57 0N 5 50W
Mallawan, India 43 F9 27 4N 80 12 E
Mallawi, Egypt 51 C12 27 44N 30 44 E
Mállia, Greece 23 D7 35 17N 25 32 E
Mallión, Kólpos, Greece 23 D7 35 19N 25 27 E
Mallorca, Spain 22 B10 39 30N 3 0 E
Mallorytown, Canada 79 B9 44 29N 75 53W
Mallow, Ireland 13 D3 52 8N 8 39W
Malmberget, Sweden 8 C19 67 11N 20 40 E
Malmédy, Belgium 15 D6 50 25N 6 2 E
Malmesbury, S. Africa 56 E2 33 28S 18 41 E
Malmö, Sweden 9 J15 55 36N 12 59 E
Malolos, Phil. 37 B6 14 50N 120 49 E
Malombe L., Malawi 55 E4 14 40S 35 15 E
Malone, U.S.A. 79 B10 44 51N 74 18W
Måløy, Norway 9 F11 61 57N 5 6 E
Malozemelskaya Tundra, Russia 24 A9 67 0N 50 0 E
Malpaso, Canary Is. 22 G1 27 43N 18 3W
Malpelo, Colombia 92 C2 4 3N 81 35W
Malta, Idaho, U.S.A. 82 E7 42 18N 113 22W
Malta, Mont., U.S.A. 82 B10 48 21N 107 52W
Malta ■, Europe 23 D2 35 50N 14 30 E
Maltahöhe, Namibia 56 C2 24 55S 17 0 E
Malton, Canada 78 C5 43 42N 79 38W
Malton, U.K. 10 C7 54 8N 0 49W
Maluku, Indonesia 37 E7 1 0S 127 0 E
Maluku □, Indonesia 37 E7 3 0S 128 0 E
Maluku Sea = Molucca Sea, Indonesia 37 E6 2 0S 124 0 E
Malvan, India 40 L8 16 2N 73 30 E
Malvern, U.S.A. 81 H8 34 22N 92 49W
Malvern Hills, U.K. 11 E5 52 0N 2 19W
Malvinas, Is. = Falkland Is. □, Atl. Oc. 96 G5 51 30S 59 0W
Malya, Tanzania 54 C3 3 5S 33 38 E
Malyn, Ukraine 17 C15 50 46N 29 3 E

Melchor Ocampo

Melchor Ocampo, *Mexico* **86 C4** 24 52N 101 40W
Mélèzes →, *Canada* **69 C12** 57 30N 71 0W
Melfort, *Canada* **73 C8** 52 50N 104 37W
Melfort, *Zimbabwe* **55 F3** 18 0S 31 25 E
Melhus, *Norway* **8 E14** 63 17N 10 18 E
Melilla, *N. Afr.* **19 E4** 35 21N 2 57W
Melipilla, *Chile* **94 C1** 33 42S 71 15W
Mélissa, Ákra, *Greece* **23 D6** 35 6N 24 33 E
Melita, *Canada* **73 D8** 49 15N 101 0W
Melitopol, *Ukraine* **25 E6** 46 50N 35 22 E
Melk, *Austria* **16 D8** 48 13N 15 20 E
Mellansel, *Sweden* **8 E18** 63 25N 18 17 E
Mellen, *U.S.A.* **80 B9** 46 20N 90 40W
Mellerud, *Sweden* **9 G15** 58 41N 12 28 E
Mellette, *U.S.A.* **80 C5** 45 9N 98 30W
Mellieha, *Malta* **23 D1** 35 57N 14 21 E
Melo, *Uruguay* **95 C5** 32 20S 54 10W
Melolo, *Indonesia* **37 F6** 9 53S 120 40 E
Melouprey, *Cambodia* **38 F5** 13 48N 105 16 E
Melrose, *N.S.W., Australia* **63 E4** 32 42S 146 57 E
Melrose, *W. Austral., Australia* **61 E3** 27 50S 121 15 E
Melrose, *U.K.* **12 F6** 55 36N 2 43W
Melrose, *U.S.A.* **81 H3** 34 26N 103 38W
Melstone, *U.S.A.* **82 C10** 46 36N 107 52W
Melton Mowbray, *U.K.* **10 E7** 52 47N 0 54W
Melun, *France* **18 B5** 48 32N 2 39 E
Melville, *Canada* **73 C8** 50 55N 102 50W
Melville, C., *Australia* **62 A3** 14 11S 144 30 E
Melville, L., *Canada* **71 B8** 53 30N 60 0W
Melville B., *Australia* **62 A2** 12 0S 136 45 E
Melville I., *Australia* **60 B5** 11 30S 131 0 E
Melville I., *Canada* **66 B8** 75 30N 112 0W
Melville Pen., *Canada* **69 B11** 68 0N 84 0W
Melvin →, *Canada* **72 B5** 59 11N 117 31W
Memba, *Mozam.* **55 E5** 14 11S 40 30 E
Memboro, *Indonesia* **37 F5** 9 30S 119 30 E
Memel = Klaipeda, *Lithuania* **24 C3** 55 43N 21 10 E
Memel, *S. Africa* **57 D4** 27 38S 29 36 E
Memmingen, *Germany* **16 E6** 47 58N 10 10 E
Mempawah, *Indonesia* **36 D3** 0 30N 109 5 E
Memphis, *Tenn., U.S.A.* **81 H10** 35 8N 90 3W
Memphis, *Tex., U.S.A.* **81 H4** 34 44N 100 33W
Mena, *U.S.A.* **81 H7** 34 35N 94 15W
Menai Strait, *U.K.* **10 D3** 53 11N 4 13W
Ménaka, *Mali* **50 E6** 15 59N 2 18 E
Menan = Chao Phraya →, *Thailand* **38 F3** 13 32N 100 36 E
Menarandra →, *Madag.* **57 D7** 25 17S 44 30 E
Menard, *U.S.A.* **81 K5** 30 55N 99 47W
Menasha, *U.S.A.* **76 C1** 44 13N 88 26W
Mendawai →, *Indonesia* **36 E4** 3 30S 113 0 E
Mende, *France* **18 D5** 44 31N 3 30 E
Mendez, *Mexico* **87 B5** 25 7N 98 34W
Mendhar, *India* **43 C6** 33 35N 74 10 E
Mendip Hills, *U.K.* **11 F5** 51 17N 2 40W
Mendocino, *U.S.A.* **82 G2** 39 19N 123 48W
Mendocino, C., *U.S.A.* **82 F1** 40 26N 124 25W
Mendota, *Calif., U.S.A.* **84 J6** 36 45N 120 23W
Mendota, *Ill., U.S.A.* **80 E10** 41 33N 89 7W
Mendoza, *Argentina* **94 C2** 32 50S 68 52W
Mendoza □, *Argentina* **94 C2** 33 0S 69 0W
Mene Grande, *Venezuela* **92 B4** 9 49N 70 56W
Menemen, *Turkey* **21 E12** 38 34N 27 3 E
Menen, *Belgium* **15 D3** 50 47N 3 7 E
Menggala, *Indonesia* **36 E3** 4 30S 105 15 E
Mengjin, *China* **34 G7** 34 55N 112 45 E
Mengyin, *China* **35 G9** 35 40N 117 58 E
Mengzi, *China* **32 D5** 23 20N 103 22 E
Menihek L., *Canada* **71 B6** 54 0N 67 0W
Menin = Menen, *Belgium* **15 D3** 50 47N 3 7 E
Menindee, *Australia* **63 E3** 32 20S 142 25 E
Menindee L., *Australia* **63 E3** 32 20S 142 25 E
Meningie, *Australia* **63 F2** 35 50S 139 18 E
Menlo Park, *U.S.A.* **84 H4** 37 27N 122 12W
Menominee, *U.S.A.* **76 C2** 45 6N 87 37W
Menominee →, *U.S.A.* **76 C2** 45 6N 87 36W
Menomonie, *U.S.A.* **80 C9** 44 53N 91 55W
Menongue, *Angola* **53 G3** 14 48S 17 52 E
Menorca, *Spain* **22 B11** 40 0N 4 0 E
Mentakab, *Malaysia* **39 L4** 3 29N 102 21 E
Mentawai, Kepulauan, *Indonesia* **36 E1** 2 0S 99 0 E
Menton, *France* **18 E7** 43 50N 7 29 E
Mentor, *U.S.A.* **78 E3** 41 40N 81 21W
Menzelinsk, *Russia* **24 C9** 55 47N 53 11 E
Menzies, *Australia* **61 E3** 29 40S 121 2 E
Me'ona, *Israel* **47 B4** 33 1N 35 15 E
Meoqui, *Mexico* **86 B3** 28 17N 105 29W
Mepaco, *Mozam.* **55 F3** 15 57S 30 48 E
Meppel, *Neths.* **15 B6** 52 42N 6 12 E
Mer Rouge, *U.S.A.* **81 J9** 32 47N 91 48W
Merabéllou, Kólpos, *Greece* **23 D7** 35 10N 25 50 E
Meramangye, L., *Australia* **61 E5** 28 25S 132 13 E
Meran = Merano, *Italy* **20 A4** 46 40N 11 9 E
Merano, *Italy* **20 A4** 46 40N 11 9 E
Merauke, *Indonesia* **37 F10** 8 29S 140 24 E
Merbein, *Australia* **63 E3** 34 10S 142 2 E
Merca, *Somali Rep.* **46 G3** 1 48N 44 50 E
Merced, *U.S.A.* **84 H6** 37 18N 120 29W
Merced Pk., *U.S.A.* **84 H7** 37 36N 119 24W
Mercedes, *Buenos Aires, Argentina* **94 C4** 34 40S 59 30W
Mercedes, *Corrientes, Argentina* **94 B4** 29 10S 58 5W
Mercedes, *San Luis, Argentina* **94 C2** 33 40S 65 21W
Mercedes, *Uruguay* **94 C4** 33 12S 58 0W
Merceditas, *Chile* **94 B1** 28 20S 70 35W
Mercer, *N.Z.* **59 G5** 37 16S 175 5 E
Mercer, *U.S.A.* **78 E4** 41 14N 80 15W
Mercury, *U.S.A.* **85 J11** 36 40N 115 58W
Mercy C., *Canada* **69 B13** 65 0N 63 30W
Mere, *U.K.* **11 F5** 51 6N 2 16W
Meredith, C., *Falk. Is.* **96 G4** 52 15S 60 40W
Meredith, L., *U.S.A.* **81 H4** 35 43N 101 33W
Mergui, *Burma* **38 F2** 12 26N 98 34 E
Mergui Arch. = Myeik Kyunzu, *Burma* **39 G1** 11 30N 97 30 E
Mérida, *Mexico* **87 C7** 20 58N 89 37W
Mérida, *Spain* **19 C2** 38 55N 6 25W
Mérida, *Venezuela* **92 B4** 8 24N 71 8W
Mérida, Cord. de, *Venezuela* **90 C3** 9 0N 71 0W
Meriden, *U.K.* **11 E6** 52 26N 1 38W
Meriden, *U.S.A.* **79 E12** 41 32N 72 48W
Meridian, *Calif., U.S.A.* **84 F5** 39 9N 121 55W
Meridian, *Idaho, U.S.A.* **82 E5** 43 37N 116 24W
Meridian, *Miss., U.S.A.* **77 J1** 32 22N 88 42W
Meridian, *Tex., U.S.A.* **81 K6** 31 56N 97 39W
Meriruma, *Brazil* **93 C8** 1 15N 54 50W
Merkel, *U.S.A.* **81 J5** 32 28N 100 1W
Mermaid Reef, *Australia* **60 C2** 17 6S 119 36 E
Merredin, *Australia* **61 F2** 31 28S 118 18 E
Merrick, *U.K.* **12 F4** 55 8N 4 28W
Merrickville, *Canada* **79 B9** 44 55N 75 50W
Merrill, *Oreg., U.S.A.* **82 E3** 42 1N 121 36W
Merrill, *Wis., U.S.A.* **80 C10** 45 11N 89 41W
Merriman, *U.S.A.* **80 D4** 42 55N 101 42W
Merritt, *Canada* **72 C4** 50 10N 120 45W
Merriwa, *Australia* **63 E5** 32 6S 150 22 E
Merriwagga, *Australia* **63 E4** 33 47S 145 43 E
Merry I., *Canada* **70 A4** 55 29N 77 31W
Merrygoen, *Australia* **63 E4** 31 51S 149 12 E
Merryville, *U.S.A.* **81 K8** 30 45N 93 33W
Mersch, *Lux.* **15 E6** 49 44N 6 7 E
Mersea I., *U.K.* **11 F8** 51 47N 0 58 E
Merseburg, *Germany* **16 C6** 51 22N 11 59 E
Mersey →, *U.K.* **10 D4** 53 25N 3 1W
Merseyside □, *U.K.* **10 D4** 53 31N 3 2W
Mersin, *Turkey* **25 G5** 36 51N 34 36 E
Mersing, *Malaysia* **39 L4** 2 25N 103 50 E
Merta, *India* **42 F6** 26 39N 74 4 E
Merthyr Tydfil, *U.K.* **11 F4** 51 45N 3 22W
Merthyr Tydfil □, *U.K.* **11 F4** 51 46N 3 21W
Mértola, *Portugal* **19 D2** 37 40N 7 40W
Mertzon, *U.S.A.* **81 K4** 31 16N 100 49W
Meru, *Kenya* **54 B4** 0 3N 37 40 E
Meru, *Tanzania* **54 C4** 3 15S 36 46 E
Meru □, *Kenya* **54 B4** 0 3N 37 46 E
Mesa, *U.S.A.* **83 K8** 33 25N 111 50W
Mesanagrós, *Greece* **23 C9** 36 1N 27 49 E
Mesaoría □, *Cyprus* **23 D12** 35 12N 33 14 E
Mesarás, Kólpos, *Greece* **23 D6** 35 6N 24 47 E
Mesgouez, L., *Canada* **70 B5** 51 20N 75 0W
Meshed = Mashhad, *Iran* **45 B8** 36 20N 59 35 E
Meshoppen, *U.S.A.* **79 E8** 41 36N 76 3W
Mesick, *U.S.A.* **76 C3** 44 24N 85 43W
Mesilinka →, *Canada* **72 B4** 56 6N 124 30W
Mesilla, *U.S.A.* **83 K10** 32 16N 106 48W
Mesolóngion, *Greece* **21 E9** 38 21N 21 28 E
Mesopotamia = Al Jazirah, *Iraq* **44 C5** 33 30N 44 0 E
Mesquite, *U.S.A.* **83 H6** 36 47N 114 6W
Mess Cr. →, *Canada* **72 B2** 57 55N 131 14W
Messalo →, *Mozam.* **55 E4** 12 25S 39 15 E
Messina, *Italy* **20 E6** 38 11N 15 34 E
Messina, *S. Africa* **57 C5** 22 20S 30 5 E
Messina, Str. di, *Italy* **20 F6** 38 15N 15 35 E
Messíni, *Greece* **21 F10** 37 4N 22 1 E
Messiniakós Kólpos, *Greece* **21 F10** 36 45N 22 5 E
Messonghi, *Greece* **23 B3** 39 29N 19 56 E
Mesta →, *Bulgaria* **21 D11** 40 54N 24 49 E
Meta →, *S. Amer.* **92 B5** 6 12N 67 28W
Metairie, *U.S.A.* **81 L9** 29 58N 90 10W
Metaline Falls, *U.S.A.* **82 B5** 48 52N 117 22W
Metán, *Argentina* **94 B3** 25 30S 65 0W
Metangula, *Mozam.* **55 E3** 12 40S 34 50 E
Metengobalame, *Mozam.* **55 E3** 14 49S 34 30 E
Methven, *N.Z.* **59 K3** 43 38S 171 40 E
Methy L., *Canada* **73 B7** 56 28N 109 30W
Metil, *Mozam.* **55 F4** 16 24S 39 0 E
Metlakatla, *U.S.A.* **72 B2** 55 8N 131 35W
Metropolis, *U.S.A.* **81 G10** 37 9N 88 44W
Mettur Dam, *India* **40 P10** 11 45N 77 45 E
Metz, *France* **18 B7** 49 8N 6 10 E
Meulaboh, *Indonesia* **36 D1** 4 11N 96 3 E
Meureudu, *Indonesia* **36 C1** 5 19N 96 10 E
Meuse →, *Europe* **18 A6** 50 45N 5 41 E
Mexia, *U.S.A.* **81 K6** 31 41N 96 29W
Mexiana, I., *Brazil* **93 D9** 0 0 49 30W
Mexicali, *Mexico* **86 A1** 32 40N 115 30W
Mexican Plateau, *Mexico* **66 G9** 25 0N 104 0W
México, *Mexico* **87 D5** 19 20N 99 10W
Mexico, *Maine, U.S.A.* **79 B14** 44 34N 70 33W
Mexico, *Mo., U.S.A.* **80 F9** 39 10N 91 53W
México □, *Mexico* **86 D5** 19 20N 99 10W
Mexico ■, *Cent. Amer.* **86 C4** 25 0N 105 0W
Mexico, G. of, *Cent. Amer.* **87 C7** 25 0N 90 0W
Meymaneh, *Afghan.* **40 B4** 35 53N 64 38 E
Mezen, *Russia* **24 A7** 65 50N 44 20 E
Mezen →, *Russia* **24 A7** 65 44N 44 22 E
Mézenc, Mt., *France* **18 D6** 44 54N 4 11 E
Mezőkövesd, *Hungary* **17 E11** 47 49N 20 35 E
Mezőtúr, *Hungary* **17 E11** 47 1N 20 41 E
Mezquital, *Mexico* **86 C4** 23 29N 104 23W
Mgeta, *Tanzania* **55 D4** 8 22S 36 6 E
Mhlaba Hills, *Zimbabwe* **55 F3** 18 30S 30 30 E
Mhow, *India* **42 H6** 22 33N 75 50 E
Miahuatlán, *Mexico* **87 D5** 16 21N 96 36W
Miallo, *Australia* **62 B4** 16 28S 145 22 E
Miami, *Ariz., U.S.A.* **83 K8** 33 24N 110 52W
Miami, *Fla., U.S.A.* **77 N5** 25 47N 80 11W
Miami, *Tex., U.S.A.* **81 H4** 35 42N 100 38W
Miami →, *U.S.A.* **76 F3** 39 20N 84 40W
Miami Beach, *U.S.A.* **77 N5** 25 47N 80 8W
Mian Xian, *China* **34 H4** 33 10N 106 32 E
Mianchi, *China* **34 G6** 34 48N 111 48 E
Mīāndowāb, *Iran* **44 B5** 37 0N 46 5 E
Miandrivazo, *Madag.* **57 B8** 19 31S 45 29 E
Mīāneh, *Iran* **44 B5** 37 30N 47 40 E
Mianwali, *Pakistan* **42 C4** 32 38N 71 28 E
Miarinarivo, *Madag.* **57 B8** 18 57S 46 55 E
Miass, *Russia* **24 D11** 54 59N 60 6 E
Michalovce, *Slovak Rep.* **17 D11** 48 47N 21 58 E
Michigan □, *U.S.A.* **76 C3** 44 0N 85 0W
Michigan, L., *U.S.A.* **76 D2** 44 0N 87 0W
Michigan City, *U.S.A.* **76 E2** 41 43N 86 54W
Michikamau L., *Canada* **71 B7** 54 20N 63 10W
Michipicoten, *Canada* **70 C3** 47 55N 84 55W
Michipicoten I., *Canada* **70 C2** 47 40N 85 40W
Michoacan □, *Mexico* **86 D4** 19 0N 102 0W
Michurin, *Bulgaria* **21 C12** 42 9N 27 51 E
Michurinsk, *Russia* **24 D7** 52 58N 40 27 E
Miclere, *Australia* **62 C4** 22 34S 147 32 E
Mico, Pta., *Nic.* **88 D3** 12 0N 83 30W
Micronesia, Federated States of ■, *Pac. Oc.* **64 G7** 9 0N 150 0 E
Midai, *Indonesia* **39 L6** 3 0N 107 47 E
Midale, *Canada* **73 D8** 49 25N 103 20W
Middelburg, *Neths.* **15 C3** 51 30N 3 36 E
Middelburg, *Eastern Cape, S. Africa* **56 E4** 31 30S 25 0 E
Middelburg, *Mpumalanga, S. Africa* **57 D4** 25 49S 29 28 E
Middelwit, *S. Africa* **56 C4** 24 51S 27 3 E
Middle Alkali L., *U.S.A.* **82 F3** 41 27N 120 5W
Middle Fork Feather →, *U.S.A.* **84 F5** 38 33N 121 30W
Middle I., *Australia* **61 F3** 34 6S 123 11 E
Middle Loup →, *U.S.A.* **80 E5** 41 17N 98 24W
Middleboro, *U.S.A.* **79 E14** 41 54N 70 55W
Middleburg, *N.Y., U.S.A.* **79 D10** 42 36N 74 20W
Middleburg, *Pa., U.S.A.* **78 F7** 40 47N 77 3W
Middlebury, *U.S.A.* **79 B11** 44 1N 73 10W
Middleport, *U.S.A.* **76 F4** 39 0N 82 3W
Middlesboro, *U.S.A.* **77 G4** 36 36N 83 43W
Middlesbrough, *U.K.* **10 C6** 54 35N 1 13W
Middlesbrough □, *U.K.* **10 C6** 54 28N 1 13W
Middlesex, *Belize* **88 C2** 17 2N 88 31W
Middlesex, *U.S.A.* **79 F10** 40 36N 74 30W
Middleton, *Australia* **62 C3** 22 22S 141 32 E
Middleton, *Canada* **71 D6** 44 57N 65 4W
Middletown, *U.K.* **13 B5** 54 17N 6 51W
Middletown, *Calif., U.S.A.* **84 G4** 38 45N 122 37W
Middletown, *Conn., U.S.A.* **79 E12** 41 34N 72 39W
Middletown, *N.Y., U.S.A.* **79 E10** 41 27N 74 25W
Middletown, *Ohio, U.S.A.* **76 F3** 39 31N 84 24W
Middletown, *Pa., U.S.A.* **79 F8** 40 12N 76 44W
Midhurst, *U.K.* **11 G7** 50 59N 0 44W
Midi, Canal du →, *France* **18 E4** 43 45N 1 21 E
Midland, *Canada* **70 D4** 44 45N 79 50W
Midland, *Calif., U.S.A.* **85 M12** 33 52N 114 48W
Midland, *Mich., U.S.A.* **76 D3** 43 37N 84 14W
Midland, *Pa., U.S.A.* **78 F4** 40 39N 80 27W
Midland, *Tex., U.S.A.* **81 K3** 32 0N 102 3W
Midlands □, *Zimbabwe* **55 F2** 19 40S 29 0 E
Midleton, *Ireland* **13 E3** 51 55N 8 10W
Midlothian, *U.S.A.* **81 J6** 32 30N 97 0W
Midlothian □, *U.K.* **12 F5** 55 51N 3 5W
Midongy, Tangorombohitr' i, *Madag.* **57 C8** 23 30S 47 0 E
Midongy Atsimo, *Madag.* **57 C8** 23 35S 47 1 E
Midway Is., *Pac. Oc.* **64 E10** 28 13N 177 22W
Midway Wells, *U.S.A.* **85 N11** 32 41N 115 7W
Midwest, *U.S.A.* **75 B9** 42 0N 90 0W
Midwest, *Wyo., U.S.A.* **82 E10** 43 25N 106 16W
Midwest City, *U.S.A.* **81 H6** 35 27N 97 24W
Midzŏr, *Bulgaria* **21 C10** 43 24N 22 40 E
Mie □, *Japan* **31 G8** 34 30N 136 10 E
Międzychód, *Poland* **16 B8** 52 35N 15 53 E
Międzyrzec Podlaski, *Poland* **17 C12** 51 58N 22 45 E
Mielec, *Poland* **17 C11** 50 15N 21 25 E
Mienga, *Angola* **56 B2** 17 12S 19 48 E
Miercurea-Ciuc, *Romania* **17 E13** 46 21N 25 48 E
Mieres, *Spain* **19 A3** 43 18N 5 48W
Mifflintown, *U.S.A.* **78 F7** 40 34N 77 24W
Mifraz Hefa, *Israel* **47 C4** 32 52N 35 0 E
Miguel Alemán, Presa, *Mexico* **87 D5** 18 15N 96 40W
Mihara, *Japan* **31 G6** 34 24N 133 5 E
Mikese, *Tanzania* **54 D4** 6 48S 37 55 E
Mikhaylovgrad = Montana, *Bulgaria* **21 C10** 43 27N 23 16 E
Mikkeli, *Finland* **9 F22** 61 43N 27 15 E
Mikkwa →, *Canada* **72 B6** 58 25N 114 46W
Mikumi, *Tanzania* **54 D4** 7 26S 37 0 E
Mikun, *Russia* **24 B9** 62 20N 50 0 E
Milaca, *U.S.A.* **80 C8** 45 45N 93 39W
Milagro, *Ecuador* **92 D3** 2 11S 79 36W
Milan = Milano, *Italy* **18 D8** 45 28N 9 12 E
Milan, *Mo., U.S.A.* **80 E8** 40 12N 93 7W
Milan, *Tenn., U.S.A.* **77 H1** 35 55N 88 46W
Milang, *Australia* **63 E2** 32 2S 139 10 E
Milange, *Mozam.* **55 F4** 16 3S 35 45 E
Milano, *Italy* **18 D8** 45 28N 9 12 E
Milâs, *Turkey* **25 G4** 37 20N 27 50 E
Mílatos, *Greece* **23 D7** 35 18N 25 34 E
Milazzo, *Italy* **20 E6** 38 13N 15 15 E
Milbank, *U.S.A.* **80 C6** 45 13N 96 38W
Milden, *Canada* **73 C7** 51 29N 107 32W
Mildenhall, *U.K.* **11 E8** 52 21N 0 32 E
Mildmay, *Canada* **78 B3** 44 3N 81 7W
Mildura, *Australia* **63 E3** 34 13S 142 9 E
Miles, *Australia* **63 D5** 26 40S 150 9 E
Miles, *U.S.A.* **81 K4** 31 36N 100 11W
Miles City, *U.S.A.* **80 B2** 46 25N 105 51W
Milestone, *Canada* **73 D8** 49 59N 104 31W
Miletus, *Turkey* **21 F12** 37 30N 27 18 E
Mileura, *Australia* **61 E2** 26 22S 117 20 E
Milford, *Calif., U.S.A.* **84 E6** 40 10N 120 22W
Milford, *Conn., U.S.A.* **79 E11** 41 14N 73 3W
Milford, *Del., U.S.A.* **76 F8** 38 55N 75 26W
Milford, *Mass., U.S.A.* **79 D13** 42 8N 71 31W
Milford, *Pa., U.S.A.* **79 E10** 41 19N 74 48W
Milford, *Utah, U.S.A.* **83 G7** 38 24N 113 1W
Milford Haven, *U.K.* **11 F2** 51 42N 5 7W
Milford Sd., *N.Z.* **59 L1** 44 41S 167 47 E
Milgun, *Australia* **61 D2** 24 56S 118 18 E
Milh, Bahr al, *Iraq* **44 C4** 32 40N 43 35 E
Miling, *Australia* **61 F2** 30 30S 116 17 E
Milk →, *U.S.A.* **82 B10** 48 4N 106 19W
Milk River, *Canada* **72 D6** 49 10N 112 5W
Mill City, *U.S.A.* **82 D2** 44 45N 122 29W
Mill I., *Antarctica* **5 C8** 66 0S 101 30 E
Mill Valley, *U.S.A.* **84 H4** 37 54N 122 32W
Millau, *France* **18 D5** 44 8N 3 4 E
Millbridge, *Canada* **78 B7** 44 41N 77 36W
Millbrook, *Canada* **78 B6** 44 10N 78 29W
Mille Lacs, L. des, *Canada* **70 C1** 48 45N 90 35W
Mille Lacs L., *U.S.A.* **80 B8** 46 15N 93 39W
Milledgeville, *U.S.A.* **77 J4** 33 5N 83 14W
Millen, *U.S.A.* **77 J5** 32 48N 81 57W
Miller, *U.S.A.* **80 C5** 44 31N 98 59W
Millersburg, *Ohio, U.S.A.* **78 F3** 40 33N 81 55W
Millersburg, *Pa., U.S.A.* **78 F8** 40 32N 76 58W
Millerton, *U.S.A.* **79 E11** 41 57N 73 31W
Millerton L., *U.S.A.* **84 J7** 37 1N 119 41W
Millicent, *Australia* **63 F3** 37 34S 140 21 E
Millinocket, *U.S.A.* **71 C6** 45 39N 68 43W
Millmerran, *Australia* **63 D5** 27 53S 151 16 E
Millom, *U.K.* **10 C4** 54 13N 3 16W
Mills L., *Canada* **72 A5** 61 30N 118 20W
Millsboro, *U.S.A.* **78 G5** 40 0N 80 0W
Milltown Malbay, *Ireland* **13 D2** 52 52N 9 24W
Millville, *U.S.A.* **76 F8** 39 24N 75 2W
Millwood L., *U.S.A.* **81 J8** 33 42N 93 58W
Milne →, *Australia* **62 C2** 21 10S 137 33 E
Milnor, *U.S.A.* **80 B6** 46 16N 97 27W
Milo, *Canada* **72 C6** 50 34N 112 53W
Mílos, *Greece* **21 F11** 36 44N 24 25 E
Milparinka P.O., *Australia* **63 D3** 29 46S 141 57 E
Milton, *Canada* **78 C5** 43 31N 79 53W
Milton, *N.Z.* **59 M2** 46 7S 169 59 E
Milton, *Calif., U.S.A.* **84 G6** 38 3N 120 51W
Milton, *Fla., U.S.A.* **77 K2** 30 38N 87 3W
Milton, *Pa., U.S.A.* **78 F8** 41 1N 76 51W
Milton-Freewater, *U.S.A.* **82 D4** 45 56N 118 23W
Milton Keynes, *U.K.* **11 E7** 52 1N 0 44W
Milton Keynes □, *U.K.* **11 E7** 52 1N 0 44W
Milverton, *Canada* **78 C4** 43 34N 80 55W
Milwaukee, *U.S.A.* **76 D2** 43 2N 87 55W
Milwaukee Deep, *Atl. Oc.* **89 C6** 19 50N 68 0W
Milwaukie, *U.S.A.* **84 E4** 45 27N 122 38W
Min Jiang →, *Fujian, China* **33 D6** 26 0N 119 35 E
Min Jiang →, *Sichuan, China* **32 D5** 28 45N 104 40 E
Min Xian, *China* **34 G3** 34 25N 104 5 E
Mina, *U.S.A.* **83 G4** 38 24N 118 7W
Mina Pirquitas, *Argentina* **94 A2** 22 40S 66 30W
Mīnā Su'ud, *Si. Arabia* **45 D6** 28 45N 48 28 E
Mīnā'al Aḥmadī, *Kuwait* **45 D6** 29 5N 48 10 E
Mīnāb, *Iran* **45 E8** 27 10N 57 1 E
Minago →, *Canada* **73 C9** 54 33N 98 59W
Minaki, *Canada* **73 D10** 49 59N 94 40W
Minamata, *Japan* **31 H5** 32 10N 130 30 E
Minami-Tori-Shima, *Pac. Oc.* **64 E7** 24 0N 153 45 E
Minas, *Uruguay* **95 C4** 34 20S 55 10W
Minas, Sierra de las, *Guatemala* **88 C2** 15 9N 89 31W
Minas Basin, *Canada* **71 C7** 45 20N 64 12W
Minas Gerais □, *Brazil* **93 G9** 18 50S 46 0W
Minatitlán, *Mexico* **87 D6** 17 59N 94 31W
Minbu, *Burma* **41 J19** 20 10N 94 52 E
Mindanao, *Phil.* **37 C7** 8 0N 125 0 E
Mindanao Sea = Bohol Sea, *Phil.* **37 C6** 9 0N 124 0 E
Mindanao Trench, *Pac. Oc.* **37 B7** 12 0N 126 6 E
Minden, *Canada* **78 B6** 44 55N 78 43W
Minden, *Germany* **16 B5** 52 17N 8 55 E
Minden, *La., U.S.A.* **81 J8** 32 37N 93 17W
Minden, *Nev., U.S.A.* **84 G7** 38 57N 119 46W
Mindiptana, *Indonesia* **37 F10** 5 55S 140 22 E
Mindoro, *Phil.* **37 B6** 13 0N 121 0 E
Mindoro Str., *Phil.* **37 B6** 12 30N 120 30 E
Mine, *Japan* **31 G5** 34 12N 131 7 E
Minehead, *U.K.* **11 F4** 51 12N 3 29W
Mineola, *U.S.A.* **81 J7** 32 40N 95 29W
Mineral King, *U.S.A.* **84 J8** 36 27N 118 36W
Mineral Wells, *U.S.A.* **81 J5** 32 48N 98 7W
Minersville, *Pa., U.S.A.* **79 F8** 40 41N 76 16W
Minersville, *Utah, U.S.A.* **83 G7** 38 13N 112 56W
Minerva, *U.S.A.* **78 F3** 40 44N 81 6W
Minetto, *U.S.A.* **79 C8** 43 24N 76 28W
Mingäçevir Su Anban, *Azerbaijan* **25 F8** 40 57N 46 50 E
Mingan, *Canada* **71 B7** 50 20N 64 0W
Mingechaurskoye Vdkhr. = Mingäçevir Su Anban, *Azerbaijan* **25 F8** 40 57N 46 50 E
Mingela, *Australia* **62 B4** 19 52S 146 38 E
Mingenew, *Australia* **61 E2** 29 12S 115 21 E
Mingera Cr. →, *Australia* **62 C2** 20 38S 137 45 E
Mingin, *Burma* **41 H19** 22 50N 94 30 E
Mingt'iehkaitafan = Mintaka Pass, *Pakistan* **43 A6** 37 0N 74 58 E
Mingyuegue, *China* **35 C15** 43 2N 128 50 E
Minho = Miño →, *Spain* **19 A2** 41 52N 8 40W
Minho, *Portugal* **19 B1** 41 25N 8 20W
Minidoka, *U.S.A.* **82 E7** 42 45N 113 29W
Minigwal, L., *Australia* **61 E3** 29 31S 123 14 E
Minilya, *Australia* **61 D1** 23 55S 114 0 E
Minilya →, *Australia* **61 D1** 23 45S 114 0 E
Minipi, L., *Canada* **71 B7** 52 25N 60 45W
Mink L., *Canada* **72 A5** 61 54N 117 40W
Minna, *Nigeria* **50 G7** 9 37N 6 30 E
Minneapolis, *Kans., U.S.A.* **80 F6** 39 8N 97 42W
Minneapolis, *Minn., U.S.A.* **80 C8** 44 59N 93 16W
Minnedosa, *Canada* **73 C9** 50 14N 99 50W
Minnesota □, *U.S.A.* **80 B8** 46 0N 94 15W
Minnie Creek, *Australia* **61 D2** 24 3S 115 42 E
Minnipa, *Australia* **63 E2** 32 51S 135 9 E
Minnitaki L., *Canada* **70 C1** 49 57N 92 10W
Mino, *Japan* **31 G8** 35 32N 136 55 E
Miño →, *Spain* **19 A2** 41 52N 8 40W
Minorca = Menorca, *Spain* **22 B11** 40 0N 4 0 E
Minore, *Australia* **63 E4** 32 14S 148 27 E
Minot, *U.S.A.* **80 A4** 48 14N 101 18W
Minqin, *China* **34 E2** 38 38N 103 20 E
Minsk, *Belarus* **24 D4** 53 52N 27 30 E
Mińsk Mazowiecki, *Poland* **17 B11** 52 10N 21 33 E
Mintaka Pass, *Pakistan* **43 A6** 37 0N 74 58 E
Minton, *Canada* **73 D8** 49 10N 104 35W
Minturn, *U.S.A.* **82 G10** 39 35N 106 26W
Minusinsk, *Russia* **27 D10** 53 43N 91 20 E
Minutang, *India* **41 E20** 28 15N 96 30 E
Mīr Kūh, *Iran* **45 E8** 26 22N 58 55 E
Mīr Shahdād, *Iran* **45 E8** 26 15N 58 29 E
Mira, *Italy* **20 B5** 45 26N 12 8 E
Mira por vos Cay, *Bahamas* **89 B5** 22 9N 74 30W
Miraj, *India* **40 L9** 16 50N 74 45 E
Miram Shah, *Pakistan* **42 C4** 33 0N 70 2 E
Miramar, *Argentina* **94 D4** 38 15S 57 50W

Moores Res.

Miramar, *Mozam.* 57 C6 23 50S 35 35 E
Miramichi B., *Canada* 71 C7 47 15N 65 0W
Miranda, *Brazil* 93 H7 20 10S 56 15W
Miranda →, *Brazil* 92 G7 19 25S 57 20W
Miranda de Ebro, *Spain* 19 A4 42 41N 2 57W
Miranda do Douro, *Portugal* 19 B2 41 30N 6 16W
Mirando City, *U.S.A.* 81 M5 27 26N 99 0W
Mirandópolis, *Brazil* 95 A5 21 9S 51 6W
Mirango, *Malawi* 55 E3 13 32S 34 58 E
Mirani, *Australia* 62 C4 21 9S 148 53 E
Mirassol, *Brazil* 95 A6 20 46S 49 28W
Mirbāţ, *Oman* 46 D5 17 0N 54 45 E
Miri, *Malaysia* 36 D4 4 23N 113 59 E
Miriam Vale, *Australia* 62 C5 24 20S 151 33 E
Mirim, L., *S. Amer.* 95 C5 32 45S 52 50W
Mirnyy, *Russia* 27 C12 62 33N 113 53 E
Mirond L., *Canada* 73 B8 55 6N 102 47W
Mirpur, *Pakistan* 43 C5 33 32N 73 56 E
Mirpur Bibiwari, *Pakistan* 42 E2 28 33N 67 44 E
Mirpur Khas, *Pakistan* 42 G3 25 30N 69 0 E
Mirpur Sakro, *Pakistan* 42 G2 24 33N 67 41 E
Mirror, *Canada* 72 C6 52 30N 113 7W
Miryang, *S. Korea* 35 G15 35 31N 128 44 E
Mirzapur, *India* 43 G10 25 10N 82 34 E
Mirzapur-cum-Vindhyachal = Mirzapur, *India* 43 G10 25 10N 82 34 E
Misantla, *Mexico* 87 D5 19 56N 96 50W
Misawa, *Japan* 30 D10 40 41N 141 24 E
Miscou I., *Canada* 71 C7 47 57N 64 31W
Mish'āb, Ra'as al, *Si. Arabia* 45 D6 28 15N 48 43 E
Mishan, *China* 33 B8 45 37N 131 48 E
Mishawaka, *U.S.A.* 76 E2 41 40N 86 11W
Mishima, *Japan* 31 G9 35 10N 138 52 E
Misión, *Mexico* 85 N10 32 6N 116 53W
Misiones □, *Argentina* 95 B5 27 0S 55 0W
Misiones □, *Paraguay* 94 B4 27 0S 56 0W
Miskah, *Si. Arabia* 44 E4 24 49N 42 56 E
Miskitos, Cayos, *Nic.* 88 D3 14 26N 82 50W
Miskolc, *Hungary* 17 D11 48 7N 20 50 E
Misoke, *Dem. Rep. of the Congo* 54 C2 0 42S 28 2 E
Misool, *Indonesia* 37 E8 1 52S 130 10 E
Misrātah, *Libya* 51 B9 32 24N 15 3 E
Missanabie, *Canada* 70 C3 48 20N 84 6W
Missinaibi →, *Canada* 70 B3 50 43N 81 29W
Missinaibi L., *Canada* 70 C3 48 23N 83 40W
Mission, *S. Dak., U.S.A.* 80 D4 43 18N 100 39W
Mission, *Tex., U.S.A.* 81 M5 26 13N 98 20W
Mission City, *Canada* 72 D4 49 10N 122 15W
Mission Viejo, *U.S.A.* 85 M9 33 36N 117 40W
Missisa L., *Canada* 70 B2 52 20N 85 7W
Mississagi →, *Canada* 70 C3 46 15N 83 9W
Mississippi □, *U.S.A.* 81 J10 33 0N 90 0W
Mississippi →, *U.S.A.* 81 L10 29 9N 89 15W
Mississippi L., *Canada* 79 A8 45 5N 76 10W
Mississippi River Delta, *U.S.A.* 81 L9 29 10N 89 15W
Mississippi Sd., *U.S.A.* 81 K10 30 20N 89 0W
Missoula, *U.S.A.* 82 C7 46 52N 114 1W
Missouri □, *U.S.A.* 80 F8 38 25N 92 30W
Missouri →, *U.S.A.* 80 F9 38 49N 90 7W
Missouri Valley, *U.S.A.* 80 E7 41 34N 95 53W
Mist, *U.S.A.* 84 E3 45 59N 123 15W
Mistake B., *Canada* 73 A10 62 8N 93 0W
Mistassini →, *Canada* 71 C5 48 42N 72 20W
Mistassini L., *Canada* 70 B5 51 0N 73 30W
Mistastin L., *Canada* 71 A7 55 57N 63 20W
Mistatim, *Canada* 73 C8 52 52N 103 22W
Misty L., *Canada* 73 B8 58 53N 101 40W
Misurata = Misrātah, *Libya* 51 B9 32 24N 15 3 E
Mitchell, *Australia* 63 D4 26 29S 147 58 E
Mitchell, *Canada* 78 C3 43 28N 81 12W
Mitchell, *Ind., U.S.A.* 76 F2 38 44N 86 28W
Mitchell, *Nebr., U.S.A.* 80 E3 41 57N 103 49W
Mitchell, *Oreg., U.S.A.* 82 D3 44 34N 120 9W
Mitchell, *S. Dak., U.S.A.* 80 D6 43 43N 98 2W
Mitchell →, *Australia* 62 B3 15 12S 141 35 E
Mitchell, Mt., *U.S.A.* 77 H4 35 46N 82 16W
Mitchell Ranges, *Australia* 62 A2 12 49S 135 36 E
Mitchelstown, *Ireland* 13 D3 52 15N 8 16W
Mitha Tiwana, *Pakistan* 42 C5 32 13N 72 6 E
Mitilini, *Greece* 21 E12 39 6N 26 35 E
Mito, *Japan* 31 F10 36 20N 140 30 E
Mitrovica = Kosovska Mitrovica, *Serbia, Yug.* 21 C9 42 54N 20 52 E
Mitsinjo, *Madag.* 57 B8 16 1S 45 52 E
Mitsiwa, *Eritrea* 46 D2 15 35N 39 25 E
Mitsukaidō, *Japan* 31 F9 36 1N 139 59 E
Mittagong, *Australia* 63 E5 34 28S 150 29 E
Mitú, *Colombia* 92 C4 1 8N 70 3W
Mitumba, *Tanzania* 54 D3 7 8S 31 2 E
Mitumba, *Dem. Rep. of the Congo* 54 D2 7 0S 27 30 E
Mitwaba, *Dem. Rep. of the Congo* 55 D2 8 2S 27 17 E
Mityana, *Uganda* 54 B3 0 23N 32 2 E
Mixteco →, *Mexico* 87 D5 18 11N 98 30W
Miyagi □, *Japan* 30 E10 38 15N 140 45 E
Miyah, W. el →, *Syria* 44 C3 34 44N 39 57 E
Miyake-Jima, *Japan* 31 G9 34 5N 139 30 E
Miyako, *Japan* 30 E10 39 40N 141 59 E
Miyako-Jima, *Japan* 31 M2 24 45N 125 20 E
Miyako-Rettō, *Japan* 31 M2 24 24N 125 0 E
Miyakonojō, *Japan* 31 J5 31 40N 131 5 E
Miyanoura-Dake, *Japan* 31 J5 30 20N 130 31 E
Miyazaki, *Japan* 31 J5 31 56N 131 30 E
Miyazaki □, *Japan* 31 H5 32 30N 131 30 E
Miyazu, *Japan* 31 G7 35 35N 135 10 E
Miyet, Bahr el = Dead Sea, *Asia* 47 D4 31 30N 35 30 E
Miyoshi, *Japan* 31 G6 34 48N 132 51 E
Miyun, *China* 34 D9 40 28N 116 50 E
Miyun Shuiku, *China* 35 D9 40 30N 117 0 E
Mizdah, *Libya* 51 B8 31 30N 13 0 E
Mizen Hd., *Cork, Ireland* 13 E2 51 27N 9 50W
Mizen Hd., *Wick., Ireland* 13 D5 52 51N 6 4W
Mizhi, *China* 34 F6 37 47N 110 12 E
Mizoram □, *India* 41 H18 23 30N 92 40 E
Mizpe Ramon, *Israel* 47 E3 30 34N 34 49 E
Mizusawa, *Japan* 30 E10 39 8N 141 8 E
Mjölby, *Sweden* 9 G16 58 20N 15 10 E
Mjøsa, *Norway* 9 F14 60 40N 11 0 E
Mkata, *Tanzania* 54 D4 5 45S 38 20 E
Mkokotoni, *Tanzania* 54 D4 5 55S 39 15 E
Mkomazi, *Tanzania* 54 C4 4 40S 38 7 E
Mkomazi →, *S. Africa* 57 E5 30 12S 30 50 E
Mkulwe, *Tanzania* 55 D3 8 37S 32 20 E
Mkumbi, Ras, *Tanzania* 54 D4 7 38S 39 55 E
Mkushi, *Zambia* 55 E2 14 25S 29 15 E
Mkushi River, *Zambia* 55 E2 13 32S 29 45 E
Mkuze, *S. Africa* 57 D5 27 10S 32 0 E
Mladá Boleslav, *Czech Rep.* 16 C8 50 27N 14 53 E
Mlala Hills, *Tanzania* 54 D3 6 50S 31 40 E
Mlange = Mulanje, *Malawi* 55 F4 16 2S 35 33 E
Mława, *Poland* 17 B11 53 9N 20 25 E
Mljet, *Croatia* 20 C7 42 43N 17 30 E
Mmabatho, *S. Africa* 56 D4 25 49S 25 30 E
Mo i Rana, *Norway* 8 C16 66 20N 14 7 E
Moa, *Indonesia* 37 F7 8 0S 128 0 E
Moab, *U.S.A.* 83 G9 38 35N 109 33W
Moala, *Fiji* 59 D8 18 36S 179 53 E
Moalie Park, *Australia* 63 D3 29 42S 143 3 E
Moate, *Ireland* 13 C4 53 24N 7 44W
Moba, *Dem. Rep. of the Congo* 54 D2 7 0S 29 48 E
Mobārakābād, *Iran* 45 D7 28 24N 53 20 E
Mobārakīyeh, *Iran* 45 C6 32 23N 51 37 E
Mobaye, *C.A.R.* 52 D4 4 25N 21 5 E
Mobayi, *Dem. Rep. of the Congo* 52 D4 4 15N 21 8 E
Moberly, *U.S.A.* 80 F8 39 25N 92 26W
Moberly →, *Canada* 72 B4 56 12N 120 55W
Mobile, *U.S.A.* 77 K1 30 41N 88 3W
Mobile B., *U.S.A.* 77 K2 30 30N 88 0W
Mobridge, *U.S.A.* 80 C4 45 32N 100 26W
Mobutu Sese Seko, L. = Albert L., *Africa* 54 B3 1 30N 31 0 E
Moc Chau, *Vietnam* 38 B5 20 50N 104 38 E
Moc Hoa, *Vietnam* 39 G5 10 46N 105 56 E
Mocabe Kasari, *Dem. Rep. of the Congo* 55 D2 9 58S 26 12 E
Moçambique, *Mozam.* 55 F5 15 3S 40 42 E
Moçâmedes = Namibe, *Angola* 53 H2 15 7S 12 11 E
Mochudi, *Botswana* 56 C4 24 27S 26 7 E
Mocimboa da Praia, *Mozam.* 55 E5 11 25S 40 20 E
Moclips, *U.S.A.* 84 C2 47 14N 124 13W
Mocoa, *Colombia* 92 C3 1 7N 76 35W
Mococa, *Brazil* 95 A6 21 28S 47 0W
Mocorito, *Mexico* 86 B3 25 30N 107 53W
Moctezuma, *Mexico* 86 B3 29 50N 109 0W
Moctezuma →, *Mexico* 87 C5 21 59N 98 34W
Mocuba, *Mozam.* 55 F4 16 54S 36 57 E
Mocúzari, Presa, *Mexico* 86 B3 27 10N 109 10W
Modane, *France* 18 D7 45 12N 6 40 E
Modasa, *India* 42 H5 23 30N 73 21 E
Modder →, *S. Africa* 56 D3 29 2S 24 37 E
Modderrivier, *S. Africa* 56 D3 29 2S 24 38 E
Módena, *Italy* 20 B4 44 40N 10 55 E
Modena, *U.S.A.* 83 H7 37 48N 113 56W
Modesto, *U.S.A.* 84 H6 37 39N 121 0W
Módica, *Italy* 20 F6 36 52N 14 46 E
Moe, *Australia* 63 F4 38 12S 146 19 E
Moebase, *Mozam.* 55 F4 17 3S 38 41 E
Moengo, *Surinam* 93 B8 5 45N 54 20W
Moffat, *U.K.* 12 F5 55 21N 3 27W
Moga, *India* 42 D6 30 48N 75 8 E
Mogadishu = Muqdisho, *Somali Rep.* 46 G4 2 2N 45 25 E
Mogador = Essaouira, *Morocco* 50 B4 31 32N 9 42W
Mogalakwena →, *S. Africa* 57 C4 22 38S 28 40 E
Mogami →, *Japan* 30 E10 38 45N 140 0 E
Mogán, *Canary Is.* 22 G4 27 53N 15 43W
Mogaung, *Burma* 41 G20 25 20N 97 0 E
Mogi das Cruzes, *Brazil* 95 A6 23 31S 46 11W
Mogi-Guaçu →, *Brazil* 95 A6 20 53S 48 10W
Mogi-Mirim, *Brazil* 95 A6 22 29S 47 0W
Mogilev = Mahilyow, *Belarus* 24 D5 53 55N 30 18 E
Mogilev-Podolskiy = Mohyliv-Podilskyy, *Ukraine* 25 E4 48 26N 27 48 E
Mogincual, *Mozam.* 55 F5 15 35S 40 25 E
Mogocha, *Russia* 27 D12 53 40N 119 50 E
Mogok, *Burma* 41 H20 23 0N 96 40 E
Mogumber, *Australia* 61 F2 31 2S 116 3 E
Mohács, *Hungary* 17 F10 45 58N 18 41 E
Mohales Hoek, *Lesotho* 56 E4 30 7S 27 26 E
Mohall, *U.S.A.* 80 A4 48 46N 101 31W
Moḩammadābād, *Iran* 45 B8 37 52N 59 5 E
Mohave, L., *U.S.A.* 85 K12 35 12N 114 34W
Mohawk →, *U.S.A.* 79 D11 42 47N 73 41W
Mohoro, *Tanzania* 54 D4 8 6S 39 8 E
Mohyliv-Podilskyy, *Ukraine* 25 E4 48 26N 27 48 E
Moidart, L., *U.K.* 12 E3 56 47N 5 52W
Moíres, *Greece* 23 D6 35 4N 24 56 E
Moisaküla, *Estonia* 9 G21 58 3N 25 12 E
Moisie, *Canada* 71 B6 50 12N 66 1W
Moisie →, *Canada* 71 B6 50 14N 66 5W
Mojave, *U.S.A.* 85 K8 35 3N 118 10W
Mojave Desert, *U.S.A.* 85 L10 35 0N 116 30W
Mojo, *Bolivia* 94 A2 21 48S 65 33W
Mojokerto, *Indonesia* 37 G15 7 28S 112 26 E
Mokai, *N.Z.* 59 H5 38 32S 175 56 E
Mokambo, *Dem. Rep. of the Congo* 55 E2 12 25S 28 20 E
Mokameh, *India* 43 G11 25 24N 85 55 E
Mokelumne →, *U.S.A.* 84 G5 38 13N 121 28W
Mokelumne Hill, *U.S.A.* 84 G6 38 18N 120 43W
Mokhós, *Greece* 23 D7 35 16N 25 27 E
Mokhotlong, *Lesotho* 57 D4 29 22S 29 2 E
Mokokchung, *India* 41 F19 26 15N 94 30 E
Mokpo, *S. Korea* 35 G14 34 50N 126 25 E
Mokra Gora, *Serbia, Yug.* 21 C9 42 50N 20 30 E
Mol, *Belgium* 15 C5 51 11N 5 5 E
Molchanovo, *Russia* 26 D9 57 40N 83 50 E
Mold, *U.K.* 10 D4 53 9N 3 8W
Moldavia = Moldova ■, *Europe* 25 E4 47 0N 28 0 E
Molde, *Norway* 8 E12 62 45N 7 9 E
Moldova ■, *Europe* 25 E4 47 0N 28 0 E
Moldoveana, Vf., *Romania* 17 F13 45 36N 24 45 E
Mole →, *U.K.* 11 F7 51 24N 0 21W
Molepolole, *Botswana* 56 C4 24 28S 25 28 E
Molfetta, *Italy* 20 D7 41 12N 16 36 E
Moline, *U.S.A.* 80 E9 41 30N 90 31W
Molinos, *Argentina* 94 B2 25 28S 66 15W
Moliro, *Dem. Rep. of the Congo* 54 D3 8 12S 30 30 E
Mollahat, *Bangla.* 43 H13 22 56N 89 48 E
Mollendo, *Peru* 92 G4 17 0S 72 0W
Mollerin, L., *Australia* 61 F2 30 30S 117 35 E
Molodechno = Maladzyechna, *Belarus* 17 A14 54 20N 26 50 E
Molokai, *U.S.A.* 74 H16 21 8N 157 0W
Molong, *Australia* 63 E4 33 5S 148 54 E
Molopo →, *Africa* 56 D3 27 30S 20 13 E
Molotov = Perm, *Russia* 24 C10 58 0N 56 10 E
Molson L., *Canada* 73 C9 54 22N 96 40W
Molteno, *S. Africa* 56 E4 31 22S 26 22 E
Molu, *Indonesia* 37 F8 6 45S 131 40 E
Molucca Sea, *Indonesia* 37 E6 2 0S 124 0 E
Moluccas = Maluku, *Indonesia* 37 E7 1 0S 127 0 E
Moma, *Dem. Rep. of the Congo* 54 C1 1 35S 23 52 E
Moma, *Mozam.* 55 F4 16 47S 39 4 E
Mombasa, *Kenya* 54 C4 4 2S 39 43 E
Mombetsu, *Japan* 30 B11 44 21N 143 22 E
Momchilgrad, *Bulgaria* 21 D11 41 33N 25 23 E
Momi, *Dem. Rep. of the Congo* 54 C2 1 42S 27 0 E
Mompós, *Colombia* 92 B4 9 14N 74 26W
Møn, *Denmark* 9 J15 54 57N 12 20 E
Mon →, *Burma* 41 J19 20 25N 94 30 E
Mona, Canal de la, *W. Indies* 89 C6 18 30N 67 45W
Mona, Isla, *Puerto Rico* 89 C6 18 5N 67 54W
Mona, Pta., *Costa Rica* 88 E3 9 37N 82 36W
Monaco ■, *Europe* 18 E7 43 46N 7 23 E
Monadhliath Mts., *U.K.* 12 D4 57 10N 4 4W
Monaghan, *Ireland* 13 B5 54 15N 6 57W
Monaghan □, *Ireland* 13 B5 54 11N 6 56W
Monahans, *U.S.A.* 81 K3 31 36N 102 54W
Monapo, *Mozam.* 55 E5 14 56S 40 19 E
Monar, L., *U.K.* 12 D3 57 26N 5 8W
Monarch Mt., *Canada* 72 C3 51 55N 125 57W
Monasterevin, *Ireland* 13 C4 53 8N 7 4W
Monastir = Bitola, *Macedonia* 21 D9 41 1N 21 20 E
Moncayo, Sierra del, *Spain* 19 B5 41 48N 1 50W
Monchegorsk, *Russia* 24 A5 67 54N 32 58 E
Mönchengladbach, *Germany* 16 C4 51 11N 6 27 E
Monchique, *Portugal* 19 D1 37 19N 8 38W
Monclova, *Mexico* 86 B4 26 50N 101 30W
Moncton, *Canada* 71 C7 46 7N 64 51W
Mondego →, *Portugal* 19 B1 40 9N 8 52W
Mondeodo, *Indonesia* 37 E6 3 34S 122 9 E
Mondovì, *Italy* 18 D7 44 23N 7 49 E
Mondovi, *U.S.A.* 80 C9 44 34N 91 40W
Mondrain I., *Australia* 61 F3 34 9S 122 14 E
Monduli □, *Tanzania* 54 C4 3 0S 36 0 E
Monessen, *U.S.A.* 78 F5 40 9N 79 54W
Monett, *U.S.A.* 81 G8 36 55N 93 55W
Moneymore, *U.K.* 13 B5 54 41N 6 40W
Monforte de Lemos, *Spain* 19 A2 42 31N 7 33W
Mong Hsu, *Burma* 41 J21 21 54N 98 30 E
Mong Kung, *Burma* 41 J20 21 35N 97 35 E
Mong Nai, *Burma* 41 J20 20 32N 97 46 E
Mong Pawk, *Burma* 41 H21 22 4N 99 16 E
Mong Ton, *Burma* 41 J21 20 17N 98 45 E
Mong Wa, *Burma* 41 J22 21 26N 100 27 E
Mong Yai, *Burma* 41 H21 22 21N 98 3 E
Mongalla, *Sudan* 51 G12 5 8N 31 42 E
Mongers, L., *Australia* 61 E2 29 25S 117 5 E
Monghyr = Munger, *India* 43 G12 25 23N 86 30 E
Mongibello = Etna, *Italy* 20 F6 37 50N 14 55 E
Mongo, *Chad* 51 F9 12 14N 18 43 E
Mongolia ■, *Asia* 27 E10 47 0N 103 0 E
Mongu, *Zambia* 53 H4 15 16S 23 12 E
Mônguá, *Angola* 56 B2 16 43S 15 20 E
Monifieth, *U.K.* 12 E6 56 30N 2 48W
Monkey Bay, *Malawi* 55 E4 14 7S 35 1 E
Monkey River, *Belize* 87 D7 16 22N 88 29W
Monkira, *Australia* 62 C3 24 46S 140 30 E
Monkoto, *Dem. Rep. of the Congo* 52 E4 1 38S 20 35 E
Monmouth, *U.K.* 11 F5 51 48N 2 42W
Monmouth, *U.S.A.* 80 E9 40 55N 90 39W
Monmouthshire □, *U.K.* 11 F5 51 48N 2 54W
Mono L., *U.S.A.* 84 H7 38 1N 119 1W
Monolith, *U.S.A.* 85 K8 35 7N 118 22W
Monólithos, *Greece* 23 C9 36 7N 27 45 E
Monongahela, *U.S.A.* 78 F5 40 12N 79 56W
Monópoli, *Italy* 20 D7 40 57N 17 18 E
Monroe, *Ga., U.S.A.* 77 J4 33 47N 83 43W
Monroe, *La., U.S.A.* 81 J8 32 30N 92 7W
Monroe, *Mich., U.S.A.* 76 E4 41 55N 83 24W
Monroe, *N.C., U.S.A.* 77 H5 34 59N 80 33W
Monroe, *N.Y., U.S.A.* 79 E10 41 20N 74 11W
Monroe, *Utah, U.S.A.* 83 G7 38 38N 112 7W
Monroe, *Wash., U.S.A.* 84 C5 47 51N 121 58W
Monroe, *Wis., U.S.A.* 80 D10 42 36N 89 38W
Monroe City, *U.S.A.* 80 F9 39 39N 91 44W
Monroeville, *Ala., U.S.A.* 77 K2 31 31N 87 20W
Monroeville, *Pa., U.S.A.* 78 F5 40 26N 79 45W
Monrovia, *Liberia* 50 G3 6 18N 10 47W
Mons, *Belgium* 15 D3 50 27N 3 58 E
Monse, *Indonesia* 37 E6 4 0S 123 10 E
Mont-de-Marsan, *France* 18 E3 43 54N 0 31W
Mont-Joli, *Canada* 71 C6 48 37N 68 10W
Mont-Laurier, *Canada* 70 C4 46 35N 75 30W
Mont-St.-Michel, Le = Le Mont-St.-Michel, *France* 18 B3 48 40N 1 30W
Mont Tremblant Prov. Park, *Canada* 70 C5 46 30N 74 30W
Montagu, *S. Africa* 56 E3 33 45S 20 8 E
Montagu I., *Antarctica* 5 B1 58 25S 26 20W
Montague, *Canada* 71 C7 46 10N 62 39W
Montague, *U.S.A.* 82 F2 41 44N 122 32W
Montague, I., *Mexico* 86 A2 31 40N 114 56W
Montague Ra., *Australia* 61 E2 27 15S 119 30 E
Montague Sd., *Australia* 60 B4 14 28S 125 20 E
Montalbán, *Spain* 19 B5 40 50N 0 45W
Montalvo, *U.S.A.* 85 L7 34 15N 119 12W
Montana, *Bulgaria* 21 C10 43 27N 23 16 E
Montaña, *Peru* 92 E4 6 0S 73 0W
Montana □, *U.S.A.* 82 C9 47 0N 110 0W
Montaña Clara, I., *Canary Is.* 22 E6 29 17N 13 33W
Montargis, *France* 18 C5 47 59N 2 43 E
Montauban, *France* 18 D4 44 2N 1 21 E
Montauk, *U.S.A.* 79 E13 41 3N 71 57W
Montauk Pt., *U.S.A.* 79 E13 41 4N 71 52W
Montbéliard, *France* 18 C7 47 31N 6 48 E
Montceau-les-Mines, *France* 18 C6 46 40N 4 23 E
Montclair, *U.S.A.* 79 F10 40 49N 74 13W
Monte Albán, *Mexico* 87 D5 17 2N 96 45W
Monte Alegre, *Brazil* 93 D8 2 0S 54 0W
Monte Azul, *Brazil* 93 G10 15 9S 42 53W
Monte Bello Is., *Australia* 60 D2 20 30S 115 45 E
Monte-Carlo, *Monaco* 18 E7 43 46N 7 23 E
Monte Caseros, *Argentina* 94 C4 30 10S 57 50W
Monte Comán, *Argentina* 94 C2 34 40S 67 53W
Monte Cristi, *Dom. Rep.* 89 C5 19 52N 71 39W
Monte Lindo →, *Paraguay* 94 A4 23 56S 57 12W
Monte Quemado, *Argentina* 94 B3 25 53S 62 41W
Monte Rio, *U.S.A.* 84 G4 38 28N 123 0W
Monte Santu, C. di, *Italy* 20 D3 40 5N 9 44 E
Monte Vista, *U.S.A.* 83 H10 37 35N 106 9W
Monteagudo, *Argentina* 95 B5 27 14S 54 8W
Montebello, *Canada* 70 C5 45 40N 74 55W
Montecito, *U.S.A.* 85 L7 34 26N 119 40W
Montecristo, *Italy* 20 C4 42 20N 10 19 E
Montego Bay, *Jamaica* 88 C4 18 30N 78 0W
Montejinnie, *Australia* 60 C5 16 40S 131 38 E
Montélimar, *France* 18 D6 44 33N 4 45 E
Montello, *U.S.A.* 80 D10 43 48N 89 20W
Montemorelos, *Mexico* 87 B5 25 11N 99 42W
Montenegro, *Brazil* 95 B5 29 39S 51 29W
Montenegro □, *Yugoslavia* 21 C8 42 40N 19 20 E
Montepuez, *Mozam.* 55 E4 13 8S 38 59 E
Montepuez →, *Mozam.* 55 E5 12 32S 40 27 E
Monterey, *U.S.A.* 84 J5 36 37N 121 55W
Monterey B., *U.S.A.* 84 J5 36 45N 122 0W
Montería, *Colombia* 92 B3 8 46N 75 53W
Monteros, *Argentina* 94 B2 27 11S 65 30W
Monterrey, *Mexico* 86 B4 25 40N 100 30W
Montes Claros, *Brazil* 93 G10 16 30S 43 50W
Montesano, *U.S.A.* 84 D3 46 59N 123 36W
Montesilvano, *Italy* 20 C6 42 29N 14 8 E
Montevideo, *Uruguay* 95 C4 34 50S 56 11W
Montevideo, *U.S.A.* 80 C7 44 57N 95 43W
Montezuma, *U.S.A.* 80 E8 41 35N 92 32W
Montgomery = Sahiwal, *Pakistan* 42 D5 30 45N 73 8 E
Montgomery, *U.K.* 11 E4 52 34N 3 8W
Montgomery, *Ala., U.S.A.* 77 J2 32 23N 86 19W
Montgomery, *W. Va., U.S.A.* 76 F5 38 11N 81 19W
Monticello, *Ark., U.S.A.* 81 J9 33 38N 91 47W
Monticello, *Fla., U.S.A.* 77 K4 30 33N 83 52W
Monticello, *Ind., U.S.A.* 76 E2 40 45N 86 46W
Monticello, *Iowa, U.S.A.* 80 D9 42 15N 91 12W
Monticello, *Ky., U.S.A.* 77 G3 36 50N 84 51W
Monticello, *Minn., U.S.A.* 80 C8 45 18N 93 48W
Monticello, *Miss., U.S.A.* 81 K9 31 33N 90 7W
Monticello, *N.Y., U.S.A.* 79 E10 41 39N 74 42W
Monticello, *Utah, U.S.A.* 83 H9 37 52N 109 21W
Montijo, *Portugal* 19 C1 38 41N 8 54W
Montilla, *Spain* 19 D3 37 36N 4 40W
Montluçon, *France* 18 C5 46 22N 2 36 E
Montmagny, *Canada* 71 C5 46 58N 70 34W
Montmartre, *Canada* 73 C8 50 14N 103 27W
Montmorency, *Canada* 71 C5 46 53N 71 11W
Montmorillon, *France* 18 C4 46 26N 0 50 E
Monto, *Australia* 62 C5 24 52S 151 6 E
Montoro, *Spain* 19 C3 38 1N 4 27W
Montour Falls, *U.S.A.* 78 D8 42 21N 76 51W
Montpelier, *Idaho, U.S.A.* 82 E8 42 19N 111 18W
Montpelier, *Ohio, U.S.A.* 76 E3 41 35N 84 37W
Montpelier, *Vt., U.S.A.* 79 B12 44 16N 72 35W
Montpellier, *France* 18 E5 43 37N 3 52 E
Montréal, *Canada* 70 C5 45 31N 73 34W
Montreal L., *Canada* 73 C7 54 20N 105 45W
Montreal Lake, *Canada* 73 C7 54 3N 105 46W
Montreux, *Switz.* 18 C7 46 26N 6 55 E
Montrose, *U.K.* 12 E6 56 44N 2 27W
Montrose, *Colo., U.S.A.* 83 G10 38 29N 107 53W
Montrose, *Pa., U.S.A.* 79 E9 41 50N 75 53W
Monts, Pte. des, *Canada* 71 C6 49 20N 67 12W
Montserrat ■, *W. Indies* 89 C7 16 40N 62 10W
Montuiri, *Spain* 22 B9 39 34N 2 59 E
Monywa, *Burma* 41 H19 22 7N 95 11 E
Monza, *Italy* 18 D8 45 35N 9 16 E
Monze, *Zambia* 55 F2 16 17S 27 29 E
Monze, C., *Pakistan* 42 G2 24 47N 66 37 E
Monzón, *Spain* 19 B6 41 52N 0 10 E
Mooi River, *S. Africa* 57 D4 29 13S 29 50 E
Moolawatana, *Australia* 63 D2 29 55S 139 45 E
Mooliabeenee, *Australia* 61 F2 31 20S 116 2 E
Mooloogool, *Australia* 61 E2 26 2S 119 5 E
Moomin Cr. →, *Australia* 63 D4 29 44S 149 20 E
Moonah →, *Australia* 62 C2 22 3S 138 33 E
Moonbeam, *Canada* 70 C3 49 20N 82 10W
Moonda, L., *Australia* 62 D3 25 52S 140 25 E
Moonie, *Australia* 63 D5 27 46S 150 20 E
Moonie →, *Australia* 63 D4 29 19S 148 43 E
Moonta, *Australia* 63 E2 34 6S 137 32 E
Moora, *Australia* 61 F2 30 37S 115 58 E
Mooraberree, *Australia* 62 D3 25 13S 140 54 E
Moorarie, *Australia* 61 E2 25 56S 117 35 E
Moorcroft, *U.S.A.* 80 C2 44 16N 104 57W
Moore →, *Australia* 61 F2 31 22S 115 30 E
Moore, L., *Australia* 61 E2 29 50S 117 35 E
Moore Reefs, *Australia* 62 B4 16 0S 149 5 E
Moorefield, *U.S.A.* 76 F6 39 5N 78 59W
Moores Res., *U.S.A.* 79 B13 44 45N 71 50W

Mooresville

Mooresville, *U.S.A.* **77 H5** 35 35N 80 48W
Moorfoot Hills, *U.K.* **12 F5** 55 44N 3 8W
Moorhead, *U.S.A.* **80 B6** 46 53N 96 45W
Mooroopna, *Australia* ... **63 F4** 36 25S 145 22 E
Moorpark, *U.S.A.* **85 L8** 34 17N 118 53W
Moorreesburg, *S. Africa* . **56 E2** 33 6S 18 38 E
Moose →, *Canada* **70 B3** 51 20N 80 25W
Moose Factory, *Canada* . **70 B3** 51 16N 80 32W
Moose I., *Canada* **73 C9** 51 42N 97 10W
Moose Jaw, *Canada* **73 C7** 50 24N 105 30W
Moose Jaw →, *Canada* . **73 C7** 50 34N 105 18W
Moose Lake, *Canada* **73 C8** 53 43N 100 20W
Moose Lake, *U.S.A.* **80 B8** 46 27N 92 46W
Moose Mountain Cr. →, *Canada* **73 D8** 49 13N 102 12W
Moose Mountain Prov. Park, *Canada* **73 D8** 49 48N 102 25W
Moose River, *Canada* ... **70 B3** 50 48N 81 17W
Moosehead L., *U.S.A.* ... **71 C6** 45 38N 69 40W
Moosomin, *Canada* **73 C8** 50 9N 101 40W
Moosonee, *Canada* **70 B3** 51 17N 80 39W
Moosup, *U.S.A.* **79 E13** 41 43N 71 53W
Mopeia Velha, *Mozam.* .. **55 F4** 17 30S 35 40 E
Mopipi, *Botswana* ...... **56 C3** 21 6S 24 55 E
Mopoi, *C.A.R.* .... **54 A2** 5 6N 26 54 E
Mopti, *Mali* **50 F5** 14 30N 4 0W
Moquegua, *Peru* **92 G4** 17 15S 70 46W
Mora, *Sweden* .... **9 F16** 61 2N 14 38 E
Mora, *Minn., U.S.A.* **80 C8** 45 53N 93 18W
Mora, *N. Mex., U.S.A.* ... **83 J11** 35 58N 105 20W
Moradabad, *India* ...... **43 E8** 28 50N 78 50 E
Morafenobe, *Madag.* .... **57 B7** 17 50S 44 53 E
Moramanga, *Madag.* .... **57 B8** 18 56S 48 12 E
Moran, *Kans., U.S.A.* **81 G7** 37 55N 95 10W
Moran, *Wyo., U.S.A.* **82 E8** 43 53N 110 37W
Moranbah, *Australia* .... **62 C4** 22 1S 148 6 E
Morant Cays, *Jamaica* ... **88 C4** 17 22N 76 0W
Morant Pt., *Jamaica* **88 C4** 17 55N 76 12W
Morar, L., *U.K.* **12 E3** 56 57N 5 40W
Moratuwa, *Sri Lanka* .... **40 R11** 6 45N 79 55 E
Morava →, *Serbia, Yug.* **21 B9** 44 36N 21 4 E
Morava →, *Slovak Rep.* **17 D9** 48 10N 16 59 E
Moravia, *U.S.A.* **80 E8** 40 53N 92 49W
Moravian Hts. = Českomoravská Vrchovina, *Czech Rep.* . **16 D8** 49 30N 15 40 E
Morawa, *Australia* ...... **61 E2** 29 13S 116 0 E
Morawhanna, *Guyana* ... **92 B7** 8 30N 59 40W
Moray □, *U.K.* **12 D5** 57 31N 3 18W
Moray Firth, *U.K.* **12 D5** 57 40N 3 52W
Morbi, *India* .... **42 H4** 22 50N 70 42 E
Morden, *Canada* **73 D9** 49 15N 98 10W
Mordovian Republic □ = Mordvinia □, *Russia* .. **24 D7** 54 20N 44 30 E
Mordvinia □, *Russia* .... **24 D7** 54 20N 44 30 E
Morea, *Australia* ...... **63 F3** 36 45S 141 18 E
Morea, *Greece* .... **6 H10** 37 45N 22 10 E
Moreau →, *U.S.A.* **80 C4** 45 18N 100 43W
Morecambe, *U.K.* **10 C5** 54 5N 2 52W
Morecambe B., *U.K.* **10 C5** 54 7N 3 0W
Moree, *Australia* ...... **63 D4** 29 28S 149 54 E
Morehead, *U.S.A.* **76 F4** 38 11N 83 26W
Morehead City, *U.S.A.* .. **77 H7** 34 43N 76 43W
Morelia, *Mexico* **86 D4** 19 42N 101 7W
Morella, *Australia* ..... **62 C3** 23 0S 143 52 E
Morella, *Spain* **19 B5** 40 35N 0 5W
Morelos, *Mexico* **86 B3** 26 42N 107 40W
Morelos □, *Mexico* **87 D5** 18 40N 99 10W
Morena, Sierra, *Spain* ... **19 C3** 38 20N 4 0W
Morenci, *U.S.A.* **83 K9** 33 5N 109 22W
Moreno Valley, *U.S.A.* ... **85 M10** 33 56N 116 58W
Moresby I., *Canada* **72 C2** 52 30N 131 40W
Moreton, *Australia* ..... **62 A3** 12 22S 142 40 E
Moreton I., *Australia* ... **63 D5** 27 10S 153 25 E
Morey, *Spain* .... **22 B10** 39 44N 3 20 E
Morgan, *Australia* ...... **63 E2** 34 2S 139 35 E
Morgan, *U.S.A.* **82 F8** 41 2N 111 41W
Morgan City, *U.S.A.* **81 L9** 29 42N 91 12W
Morgan Hill, *U.S.A.* **84 H5** 37 8N 121 39W
Morganfield, *U.S.A.* **76 G2** 37 41N 87 55W
Morganton, *U.S.A.* **77 H5** 35 45N 81 41W
Morgantown, *U.S.A.* **76 F6** 39 38N 79 57W
Morgenzon, *S. Africa* ... **57 D4** 26 45S 29 36 E
Morghak, *Iran* .... **45 D8** 29 7N 57 54 E
Morice L., *Canada* **72 C3** 53 50N 127 40W
Morinville, *Canada* **72 C6** 53 49N 113 41W
Morioka, *Japan* .... **30 E10** 39 45N 141 8 E
Moris, *Mexico* **86 B3** 28 8N 108 32W
Morlaix, *France* **18 B2** 48 36N 3 52W
Mornington, *Vic., Australia* **63 F4** 38 15S 145 5 E
Mornington, *W. Austral., Australia* .... **60 C4** 17 31S 126 6 E
Mornington, I., *Chile* **96 F1** 49 50S 75 30W
Mornington I., *Australia* . **62 B2** 16 30S 139 30 E
Moro G., *Phil.* .... **37 C6** 6 30N 123 0 E
Morocco ■, *N. Afr.* **50 B4** 32 0N 5 50W
Morogoro, *Tanzania* .... **54 D4** 6 50S 37 40 E
Morogoro □, *Tanzania* .. **54 D4** 8 0S 37 0 E
Moroleón, *Mexico* **86 C4** 20 8N 101 32W
Morombe, *Madag.* ...... **57 C7** 21 45S 43 22 E
Moron, *Argentina* **94 C4** 34 39S 58 37W
Morón, *Cuba* **88 B4** 22 8N 78 39W
Morón de la Frontera, *Spain* **19 D3** 37 6N 5 28W
Morona →, *Peru* **92 D3** 4 40S 77 10W
Morondava, *Madag.* .... **57 C7** 20 17S 44 17 E
Morongo Valley, *U.S.A.* . **85 L10** 34 3N 116 37W
Morotai, *Indonesia* ..... **37 D7** 2 10N 128 30 E
Moroto, *Uganda* .... **54 B3** 2 28N 34 42 E
Moroto Summit, *Kenya* .. **54 B3** 2 30N 34 43 E
Morpeth, *U.K.* **10 B6** 55 10N 1 41W
Morphou, *Cyprus* ...... **23 D11** 35 12N 32 59 E
Morphou Bay, *Cyprus* ... **23 D11** 35 15N 32 50 E
Morrilton, *U.S.A.* **81 H8** 35 9N 92 44W
Morrinsville, *N.Z.* ...... **59 G5** 37 40S 175 32 E
Morris, *Canada* **73 D9** 49 25N 97 22W
Morris, *Ill., U.S.A.* **76 E1** 41 22N 88 26W
Morris, *Minn., U.S.A.* **80 C7** 45 35N 95 55W
Morris, Mt., *Australia* ... **61 E5** 26 9S 131 4 E
Morrisburg, *Canada* **70 D4** 44 55N 75 7W
Morrison, *U.S.A.* **80 E10** 41 49N 89 58W
Morristown, *Ariz., U.S.A.* **83 K7** 33 51N 112 37W
Morristown, *N.J., U.S.A.* . **79 F10** 40 48N 74 29W
Morristown, *S. Dak., U.S.A.* **80 C4** 45 56N 101 43W
Morristown, *Tenn., U.S.A.* **77 G4** 36 13N 83 18W
Morro, Pta., *Chile* **94 B1** 27 6S 71 0W
Morro Bay, *U.S.A.* **84 K6** 35 22N 120 51W
Morro del Jable, *Canary Is.* **22 F5** 28 3N 14 23W
Morro Jable, Pta. de, *Canary Is.* **22 F5** 28 2N 14 20W
Morrosquillo, G. de, *Colombia* **88 E4** 9 35N 75 40W
Morrumbene, *Mozam.* ... **57 C6** 23 31S 35 16 E
Morshansk, *Russia* ..... **24 D7** 53 28N 41 50 E
Morteros, *Argentina* **94 C3** 30 50S 62 0W
Mortlake, *Australia* .... **63 F3** 38 5S 142 50 E
Morton, *Tex., U.S.A.* **81 J3** 33 44N 102 46W
Morton, *Wash., U.S.A.* .. **84 D4** 46 34N 122 17W
Morundah, *Australia* .... **63 E4** 34 57S 146 19 E
Moruya, *Australia* ...... **63 F5** 35 58S 150 3 E
Morvan, *France* .... **18 C6** 47 5N 4 3 E
Morven, *Australia* ...... **63 D4** 26 22S 147 5 E
Morvern, *U.K.* **12 E3** 56 38N 5 44W
Morwell, *Australia* ..... **63 F4** 38 10S 146 22 E
Morzhovets, Ostrov, *Russia* .... **24 A7** 66 44N 42 35 E
Moscos Is. = Maungmagan Is., *Burma* **41 N20** 14 0N 97 30 E
Moscow = Moskva, *Russia* .... **24 C6** 55 45N 37 35 E
Moscow, *U.S.A.* **82 C5** 46 44N 117 0W
Mosel →, *Europe* ...... **18 A7** 50 22N 7 36 E
Moselle = Mosel →, *Europe* .... **18 A7** 50 22N 7 36 E
Moses Lake, *U.S.A.* **82 C4** 47 8N 119 17W
Mosgiel, *N.Z.* .... **59 L3** 45 53S 170 21 E
Moshi, *Tanzania* .... **54 C4** 3 22S 37 18 E
Moshi □, *Tanzania* ..... **54 C4** 3 22S 37 18 E
Moshupa, *Botswana* .... **56 C4** 24 46S 25 29 E
Mosjøen, *Norway* ...... **8 D15** 65 51N 13 12 E
Moskenesøya, *Norway* .. **8 C15** 67 58N 13 0 E
Moskenstraumen, *Norway* **8 C15** 67 47N 12 45 E
Moskva, *Russia* .... **24 C6** 55 45N 37 35 E
Moskva →, *Russia* ..... **24 C6** 55 5N 38 51 E
Mosomane, *Botswana* ... **56 C4** 24 2S 26 19 E
Moson-magyaróvár, *Hungary* .... **17 E9** 47 52N 17 18 E
Mosquera, *Colombia* **92 C3** 2 35N 78 24W
Mosquero, *U.S.A.* **81 H3** 35 47N 103 58W
Mosquitia, *Honduras* **88 C3** 15 20N 84 10W
Mosquitos, G. de los, *Panama* **88 E3** 9 15N 81 10W
Moss, *Norway* .... **9 G14** 59 27N 10 40 E
Moss Vale, *Australia* .... **63 E5** 34 32S 150 25 E
Mossbank, *Canada* **73 D7** 49 56N 105 56W
Mossburn, *N.Z.* .... **59 L2** 45 41S 168 15 E
Mosselbaai, *S. Africa* ... **56 E3** 34 11S 22 8 E
Mossendjo, *Congo* ...... **52 E2** 2 55S 12 42 E
Mossgiel, *Australia* ..... **63 E3** 33 15S 144 5 E
Mossman, *Australia* .... **62 B4** 16 21S 145 15 E
Mossoró, *Brazil* **93 E11** 5 10S 37 15W
Mossuril, *Mozam.* ...... **55 E5** 14 58S 40 42 E
Mossy →, *Canada* **73 C8** 54 5N 102 58W
Most, *Czech Rep.* ...... **16 C7** 50 31N 13 38 E
Mosta, *Malta* .... **23 D1** 35 54N 14 24 E
Moşţafáābād, *Iran* ...... **45 C7** 33 39N 54 53 E
Mostaganem, *Algeria* ... **50 A6** 35 54N 0 5 E
Mostar, *Bos.-H.* .... **21 C7** 43 22N 17 50 E
Mostardas, *Brazil* **95 C5** 31 2S 50 51W
Mostiska = Mostyska, *Ukraine* .... **17 D12** 49 48N 23 4 E
Mosty = Masty, *Belarus* . **17 B13** 53 27N 24 38 E
Mostyska, *Ukraine* ..... **17 D12** 49 48N 23 4 E
Mosul = Al Mawşil, *Iraq* . **44 B4** 36 15N 43 5 E
Mosulpo, *S. Korea* ..... **35 H14** 33 20N 126 17 E
Motagua →, *Guatemala* **88 C2** 15 44N 88 14W
Motala, *Sweden* .... **9 G16** 58 32N 15 1 E
Motherwell, *U.K.* **12 F5** 55 47N 3 58W
Motihari, *India* .... **43 F11** 26 30N 84 55 E
Motozintla de Mendoza, *Mexico* **87 D6** 15 21N 92 14W
Motril, *Spain* **19 D4** 36 31N 3 37W
Mott, *U.S.A.* **80 B3** 46 23N 102 20W
Motueka, *N.Z.* .... **59 J4** 41 7S 173 1 E
Motueka →, *N.Z.* ...... **59 J4** 41 5S 173 1 E
Motul, *Mexico* **87 C7** 21 0N 89 20W
Mouchalagane →, *Canada* **71 B6** 50 56N 68 41W
Moúdhros, *Greece* ..... **21 E11** 39 50N 25 18 E
Mouila, *Gabon* .... **52 E2** 1 50S 11 0 E
Moulamein, *Australia* ... **63 F3** 35 3S 144 1 E
Moulianá, *Greece* ...... **23 D7** 35 10N 25 59 E
Moulins, *France* .... **18 C5** 46 35N 3 19 E
Moulmein, *Burma* ...... **41 L20** 16 30N 97 40 E
Moulton, *U.S.A.* **81 L6** 29 35N 97 9W
Moultrie, *U.S.A.* **77 K4** 31 11N 83 47W
Moultrie, L., *U.S.A.* **77 J5** 33 20N 80 5W
Mound City, *Mo., U.S.A.* . **80 E7** 40 7N 95 14W
Mound City, *S. Dak., U.S.A.* **80 C4** 45 44N 100 4W
Moundou, *Chad* .... **51 G9** 8 40N 16 10 E
Moundsville, *U.S.A.* **78 G4** 39 55N 80 44W
Moung, *Cambodia* ..... **38 F4** 12 46N 103 27 E
Mount Airy, *U.S.A.* **77 G5** 36 31N 80 37W
Mount Albert, *Canada* ... **78 B5** 44 8N 79 19W
Mount Amherst, *Australia* **60 C4** 18 24S 126 58 E
Mount Angel, *U.S.A.* **82 D2** 45 4N 122 48W
Mount Augustus, *Australia* **60 D2** 24 20S 116 56 E
Mount Barker, *S. Austral., Australia* .... **63 F2** 35 5S 138 52 E
Mount Barker, *W. Austral., Australia* .... **61 F2** 34 38S 117 40 E
Mount Carmel, *U.S.A.* ... **76 F2** 38 25N 87 46W
Mount Clemens, *U.S.A.* .. **78 D2** 42 35N 82 53W
Mount Coolon, *Australia* . **62 C4** 21 25S 147 25 E
Mount Darwin, *Zimbabwe* **55 F3** 16 47S 31 38 E
Mount Desert I., *U.S.A.* .. **71 D6** 44 21N 68 20W
Mount Dora, *U.S.A.* **77 L5** 28 48N 81 38W
Mount Douglas, *Australia* **62 C4** 21 35S 146 50 E
Mount Eba, *Australia* ... **63 E2** 30 11S 135 40 E
Mount Edgecumbe, *U.S.A.* **72 B1** 57 3N 135 21W
Mount Elizabeth, *Australia* **60 C4** 16 0S 125 50 E
Mount Fletcher, *S. Africa* **57 E4** 30 40S 28 30 E
Mount Forest, *Canada* ... **70 D3** 43 59N 80 43W
Mount Gambier, *Australia* **63 F3** 37 50S 140 46 E
Mount Garnet, *Australia* . **62 B4** 17 37S 145 6 E
Mount Hope, *N.S.W., Australia* .... **63 E4** 32 51S 145 51 E
Mount Hope, *S. Austral., Australia* .... **63 E2** 34 7S 135 23 E
Mount Hope, *U.S.A.* **76 G5** 37 54N 81 10W
Mount Horeb, *U.S.A.* **80 D10** 43 1N 89 44W
Mount Howitt, *Australia* . **63 D3** 26 31S 142 16 E
Mount Isa, *Australia* .... **62 C2** 20 42S 139 26 E
Mount Keith, *Australia* .. **61 E3** 27 15S 120 30 E
Mount Laguna, *U.S.A.* ... **85 N10** 32 52N 116 25W
Mount Larcom, *Australia* **62 C5** 23 48S 150 59 E
Mount Lofty Ra., *Australia* **63 E2** 34 35S 139 5 E
Mount Magnet, *Australia* **61 E2** 28 2S 117 47 E
Mount Margaret, *Australia* **63 D3** 26 54S 143 21 E
Mount Maunganui, *N.Z.* . **59 G6** 37 40S 176 14 E
Mount Molloy, *Australia* . **62 B4** 16 42S 145 20 E
Mount Monger, *Australia* **61 F3** 31 0S 122 0 E
Mount Morgan, *Australia* **62 C5** 23 40S 150 25 E
Mount Morris, *U.S.A.* ... **78 D7** 42 44N 77 52W
Mount Mulligan, *Australia* **62 B3** 16 45S 144 47 E
Mount Narryer, *Australia* **61 E2** 26 30S 115 55 E
Mount Oxide Mine, *Australia* .... **62 B2** 19 30S 139 29 E
Mount Pearl, *Canada* **71 C9** 47 31N 52 47W
Mount Perry, *Australia* .. **63 D5** 25 13S 151 42 E
Mount Phillips, *Australia* . **60 D2** 24 25S 116 15 E
Mount Pleasant, *Iowa, U.S.A.* **80 E9** 40 58N 91 33W
Mount Pleasant, *Mich., U.S.A.* **76 D3** 43 36N 84 46W
Mount Pleasant, *Pa., U.S.A.* **78 F5** 40 9N 79 33W
Mount Pleasant, *S.C., U.S.A.* **77 J6** 32 47N 79 52W
Mount Pleasant, *Tenn., U.S.A.* **77 H2** 35 32N 87 12W
Mount Pleasant, *Tex., U.S.A.* **81 J7** 33 9N 94 58W
Mount Pleasant, *Utah, U.S.A.* **82 G8** 39 33N 111 27W
Mount Pocono, *U.S.A.* ... **79 E9** 41 7N 75 22W
Mount Rainier National Park, *U.S.A.* **84 D5** 46 55N 121 50W
Mount Revelstoke Nat. Park, *Canada* **72 C5** 51 5N 118 30W
Mount Robson Prov. Park, *Canada* **72 C5** 53 0N 119 0W
Mount Sandiman, *Australia* .... **61 D2** 24 25S 115 30 E
Mount Shasta, *U.S.A.* ... **82 F2** 41 19N 122 19W
Mount Signal, *U.S.A.* ... **85 N11** 32 39N 115 37W
Mount Sterling, *Ill., U.S.A.* **80 F9** 39 59N 90 45W
Mount Sterling, *Ky., U.S.A.* **76 F4** 38 4N 83 56W
Mount Surprise, *Australia* **62 B3** 18 10S 144 17 E
Mount Union, *U.S.A.* **78 F7** 40 23N 77 53W
Mount Vernon, *Australia* . **60 D2** 24 9S 118 2 E
Mount Vernon, *Ind., U.S.A.* **80 F10** 38 17N 88 57W
Mount Vernon, *N.Y., U.S.A.* **79 F11** 40 55N 73 50W
Mount Vernon, *Ohio, U.S.A.* **78 F2** 40 23N 82 29W
Mount Vernon, *Wash., U.S.A.* **84 B4** 48 25N 122 20W
Mountain Ash, *U.K.* **11 F4** 51 40N 3 23W
Mountain Center, *U.S.A.* . **85 M10** 33 42N 116 44W
Mountain City, *Nev., U.S.A.* **82 F6** 41 50N 115 58W
Mountain City, *Tenn., U.S.A.* **77 G5** 36 29N 81 48W
Mountain Grove, *U.S.A.* . **81 G8** 37 8N 92 16W
Mountain Home, *Ark., U.S.A.* **81 G8** 36 20N 92 23W
Mountain Home, *Idaho, U.S.A.* **82 E6** 43 8N 115 41W
Mountain Iron, *U.S.A.* ... **80 B8** 47 32N 92 37W
Mountain Park, *Canada* . **72 C5** 52 50N 117 15W
Mountain Pass, *U.S.A.* .. **85 K11** 35 29N 115 35W
Mountain View, *Ark., U.S.A.* **81 H8** 35 52N 92 7W
Mountain View, *Calif., U.S.A.* **84 H4** 37 23N 122 5W
Mountainair, *U.S.A.* **83 J10** 34 31N 106 15W
Mountmellick, *Ireland* ... **13 C4** 53 7N 7 20W
Mountrath, *Ireland* **13 D4** 53 0N 7 28W
Moura, *Australia* .... **62 C4** 24 35S 149 58 E
Moura, *Brazil* **92 D6** 1 32S 61 38W
Moura, *Portugal* **19 C2** 38 7N 7 30W
Mourdi, Dépression du, *Chad* .... **51 E10** 18 10N 23 0 E
Mourilyan, *Australia* .... **62 B4** 17 35S 146 3 E
Mourne →, *U.K.* **13 B4** 54 52N 7 26W
Mourne Mts., *U.K.* **13 B5** 54 10N 6 0W
Mourniaí, *Greece* ...... **23 D6** 35 29N 24 1 E
Mournies = Mourniaí, *Greece* .... **23 D6** 35 29N 24 1 E
Mouscron, *Belgium* ..... **15 D3** 50 45N 3 12 E
Moussoro, *Chad* .... **51 F9** 13 41N 16 35 E
Moutohara, *N.Z.* .... **59 H6** 38 27S 177 32 E
Moutong, *Indonesia* .... **37 D6** 0 28N 121 13 E
Movas, *Mexico* **86 B3** 28 10N 109 25W
Moville, *Ireland* **13 A4** 55 11N 7 3W
Moy →, *Ireland* **13 B2** 54 8N 9 8W
Moyale, *Kenya* .... **54 B4** 3 30N 39 0 E
Moyen Atlas, *Morocco* .. **50 B4** 33 0N 5 0W
Moyo, *Indonesia* .... **36 F5** 8 10S 117 40 E
Moyobamba, *Peru* **92 E3** 6 0S 77 0W
Moyyero →, *Russia* .... **27 C11** 68 44N 103 42 E
Moyynty, *Kazakstan* .... **26 E8** 47 10N 73 18 E
Mozambique = Moçambique, *Mozam.* ... **55 F5** 15 3S 40 42 E
Mozambique ■, *Africa* ... **55 F4** 19 0S 35 0 E
Mozambique Chan., *Africa* **57 B7** 17 30S 42 30 E
Mozdok, *Russia* .... **25 F7** 43 45N 44 48 E
Mozdūrān, *Iran* .... **45 B9** 36 9N 60 35 E
Mozhnābād, *Iran* .... **45 C9** 34 7N 60 6 E
Mozyr = Mazyr, *Belarus* . **24 D4** 51 59N 29 15 E
Mpanda, *Tanzania* ..... **54 D3** 6 23S 31 1 E
Mpanda □, *Tanzania* .... **54 D3** 6 23S 31 40 E
Mpika, *Zambia* .... **55 E3** 11 51S 31 25 E
Mpulungu, *Zambia* ..... **55 D3** 8 51S 31 5 E
Mpumalanga, *S. Africa* .. **57 D5** 29 50S 30 33 E
Mpumalanga □, *S. Africa* **57 B5** 26 0S 30 0 E
Mpwapwa, *Tanzania* .... **54 D4** 6 23S 36 30 E
Mpwapwa □, *Tanzania* .. **54 D4** 6 30S 36 20 E
Msambansovu, *Zimbabwe* **55 F3** 15 50S 30 3 E
Msoro, *Zambia* .... **55 E3** 13 35S 31 50 E
Mstislavl = Mstsislaw, *Belarus* .... **17 A16** 54 0N 31 50 E
Mstsislaw, *Belarus* ...... **17 A16** 54 0N 31 50 E
Mtama, *Tanzania* .... **55 E4** 10 17S 39 21 E
Mtilikwe →, *Zimbabwe* . **55 G3** 21 9S 31 30 E
Mtubatuba, *S. Africa* .... **57 D5** 28 30S 32 8 E
Mtwara-Mikindani, *Tanzania* .... **55 E5** 10 20S 40 20 E
Mu Gia, Deo, *Vietnam* ... **38 D5** 17 40N 105 47 E
Mu Us Shamo, *China* ... **34 E5** 39 0N 109 0 E
Muang Chiang Rai, *Thailand* .... **38 C2** 19 52N 99 50 E
Muang Khong, *Laos* .... **38 E5** 14 7N 105 51 E
Muang Lamphun, *Thailand* .... **38 C2** 18 40N 99 2 E
Muang Pak Beng, *Laos* .. **38 C3** 19 54N 101 8 E
Muar, *Malaysia* .... **39 L4** 2 3N 102 34 E
Muarabungo, *Indonesia* . **36 E2** 1 28S 102 52 E
Muaraenim, *Indonesia* .. **36 E2** 3 40S 103 50 E
Muarajuloi, *Indonesia* ... **36 E4** 0 12S 114 3 E
Muarakaman, *Indonesia* . **36 E5** 0 2S 116 45 E
Muaratebo, *Indonesia* ... **36 E2** 1 30S 102 26 E
Muaratembesi, *Indonesia* **36 E2** 1 42S 103 8 E
Muaratewe, *Indonesia* ... **36 E4** 0 58S 114 52 E
Mubarakpur, *India* ...... **43 F10** 26 6N 83 18 E
Mubarraz = Al Mubarraz, *Si. Arabia* .... **45 E6** 25 30N 49 40 E
Mubende, *Uganda* ...... **54 B3** 0 33N 31 22 E
Mubi, *Nigeria* .... **51 F8** 10 18N 13 16 E
Mubur, Pulau, *Indonesia* . **39 L6** 3 20N 106 12 E
Mucajaí →, *Brazil* **92 C6** 2 25N 60 52W
Muchachos, Roque de los, *Canary Is.* **22 F2** 28 44N 17 52W
Muchinga Mts., *Zambia* . **55 E3** 11 30S 31 30 E
Muck, *U.K.* **12 E2** 56 50N 6 15W
Muckadilla, *Australia* .... **63 D4** 26 35S 148 23 E
Mucuri, *Brazil* **93 G11** 18 0S 39 36W
Mucusso, *Angola* .... **56 B3** 18 1S 21 25 E
Muda, *Canary Is.* **22 F6** 28 34N 13 57W
Mudan Jiang →, *China* . **35 A15** 46 20N 129 30 E
Mudanjiang, *China* ..... **35 B15** 44 38N 129 30 E
Mudanya, *Turkey* .... **21 D13** 40 25N 28 50 E
Muddy Cr. →, *U.S.A.* ... **83 H8** 38 24N 110 42W
Mudgee, *Australia* ...... **63 E4** 32 32S 149 31 E
Mudjatik →, *Canada* **73 B7** 56 1N 107 36W
Muecate, *Mozam.* ...... **55 E4** 14 55S 39 40 E
Mueda, *Mozam.* .... **55 E4** 11 36S 39 28 E
Mueller Ra., *Australia* ... **60 C4** 18 18S 126 46 E
Muende, *Mozam.* .... **55 E3** 14 28S 33 0 E
Muerto, Mar, *Mexico* **87 D6** 16 10N 94 10W
Mufindi □, *Tanzania* .... **55 D4** 8 30S 35 20 E
Mufulira, *Zambia* .... **55 E2** 12 32S 28 15 E
Mufumbiro Range, *Africa* **54 C2** 1 25S 29 30 E
Mughayrā', *Si. Arabia* ... **44 D3** 29 17N 37 41 E
Mugi, *Japan* .... **31 H7** 33 40N 134 25 E
Mugila, Mts., *Dem. Rep. of the Congo* **54 D2** 7 0S 28 50 E
Muğla, *Turkey* .... **25 G4** 37 15N 28 22 E
Mugu, *Nepal* .... **43 E10** 29 45N 82 30 E
Muhammad Qol, *Sudan* . **51 D13** 20 53N 37 9 E
Muhammadabad, *India* .. **43 F10** 26 4N 83 25 E
Muhesi →, *Tanzania* .... **54 D4** 7 0S 35 20 E
Muheza □, *Tanzania* .... **54 D4** 5 0S 39 0 E
Mühlhausen, *Germany* ... **16 C6** 51 12N 10 27 E
Mühlig Hofmann fjell, *Antarctica* .... **5 D3** 72 30S 5 0 E
Muhos, *Finland* .... **8 D22** 64 47N 25 59 E
Muhu, *Estonia* .... **9 G20** 58 36N 23 11 E
Muhutwe, *Tanzania* ..... **54 C3** 1 35S 31 45 E
Muikamachi, *Japan* ..... **31 F9** 37 15N 138 50 E
Muine Bheag, *Ireland* ... **13 D5** 52 42N 6 58W
Muir, L., *Australia* ...... **61 F2** 34 30S 116 40 E
Mukacheve, *Ukraine* .... **17 D12** 48 27N 22 45 E
Mukachevo = Mukacheve, *Ukraine* .... **17 D12** 48 27N 22 45 E
Mukah, *Malaysia* .... **36 D4** 2 55N 112 5 E
Mukdahan, *Thailand* .... **38 D5** 16 32N 104 43 E
Mukden = Shenyang, *China* .... **35 D12** 41 48N 123 27 E
Mukhtuya = Lensk, *Russia* **27 C12** 60 48N 114 55 E
Mukinbudin, *Australia* ... **61 F2** 30 55S 118 5 E
Mukishi, *Dem. Rep. of the Congo* **55 D1** 8 30S 24 44 E
Mukomuko, *Indonesia* ... **36 E2** 2 30S 101 10 E
Mukomwenze, *Dem. Rep. of the Congo* **54 D2** 6 49S 27 15 E
Muktsar, *India* .... **42 D6** 30 30N 74 30 E
Mukur, *Afghan.* .... **42 C2** 32 50N 67 42 E
Mukutawa →, *Canada* .. **73 C9** 53 10N 97 24W
Mukwela, *Zambia* ...... **55 F2** 17 0S 26 40 E
Mula, *Spain* **19 C5** 38 3N 1 33W
Mulange, *Dem. Rep. of the Congo* **54 C2** 3 40S 27 10 E
Mulanje, *Malawi* .... **55 F4** 16 2S 35 33 E
Mulchén, *Chile* **94 D1** 37 45S 72 20W
Mulde →, *Germany* ..... **16 C7** 51 53N 12 15 E
Mule Creek, *U.S.A.* **80 D2** 43 19N 104 8W
Muleba, *Tanzania* ...... **54 C3** 1 50S 31 37 E
Muleba □, *Tanzania* .... **54 C3** 2 0S 31 30 E
Muleshoe, *U.S.A.* **81 H3** 34 13N 102 43W
Mulgathing, *Australia* ... **63 E1** 30 15S 134 8 E
Mulgrave, *Canada* **71 C7** 45 38N 61 31W
Mulhacén, *Spain* **19 D4** 37 4N 3 20W
Mülheim, *Germany* ..... **33 C6** 51 25N 6 54 E
Mulhouse, *France* ...... **18 C7** 47 40N 7 20 E
Muling, *China* .... **35 B16** 44 35N 130 10 E
Mull, *U.K.* **12 E3** 56 25N 5 56W
Mull, Sound of, *U.K.* **12 E3** 56 30N 5 50W
Mullaittivu, *Sri Lanka* ... **40 Q12** 9 15N 80 49 E
Mullen, *U.S.A.* **80 D4** 42 3N 101 1W
Mullengudgery, *Australia* **63 E4** 31 43S 147 23 E
Mullens, *U.S.A.* **76 G5** 37 35N 81 23W
Muller, Pegunungan, *Indonesia* .... **36 D4** 0 30N 113 30 E
Mullet Pen., *Ireland* **13 B1** 54 13N 10 2W
Mullewa, *Australia* ..... **61 E2** 28 29S 115 30 E

Nanam

Mulligan →, Australia 62 D2 25 0S 139 0 E
Mullin, U.S.A. 81 K5 31 33N 98 40W
Mullingar, Ireland 13 C4 53 31N 7 21W
Mullins, U.S.A. 77 H6 34 12N 79 15W
Mullumbimby, Australia 63 D5 28 30S 153 30 E
Mulobezi, Zambia 55 F2 16 45S 25 7 E
Mulroy B., Ireland 13 A4 55 15N 7 46W
Multan, Pakistan 42 D4 30 15N 71 36 E
Mulumbe, Mts.,
Dem. Rep. of the Congo 55 D2 8 40S 27 30 E
Mulungushi Dam, Zambia 55 E2 14 48S 28 48 E
Mulvane, U.S.A. 81 G6 37 29N 97 15W
Mulwala, Australia 63 F4 35 59S 146 0 E
Mumbai, India 40 K8 18 55N 72 50 E
Mumbwa, Zambia 55 F2 15 0S 27 0 E
Mun →, Thailand 38 E5 15 19N 105 30 E
Muna, Indonesia 37 F6 5 0S 122 30 E
Munamagi, Estonia 9 H22 57 43N 27 4 E
München, Germany 16 D6 48 8N 11 34 E
Munchen-Gladbach =
Mönchengladbach,
Germany 16 C4 51 11N 6 27 E
Muncho Lake, Canada 72 B3 59 0N 125 50W
Munchŏn, N. Korea 35 E14 39 14N 127 19 E
Muncie, U.S.A. 76 E3 40 12N 85 23W
Muncoonie, L., Australia 62 D2 25 12S 138 40 E
Mundare, Canada 72 C6 53 35N 112 20W
Munday, U.S.A. 81 J5 33 27N 99 38W
Münden, Germany 16 C5 51 25N 9 38 E
Mundiwindi, Australia 60 D3 23 47S 120 9 E
Mundo Novo, Brazil 93 F10 11 50S 40 29W
Mundra, India 42 H3 22 54N 69 48 E
Mundrabilla, Australia 61 F4 31 52S 127 51 E
Mungallala, Australia 63 D4 26 28S 147 34 E
Mungallala Cr. →,
Australia 63 D4 28 53S 147 5 E
Mungana, Australia 62 B3 17 8S 144 27 E
Mungaoli, India 42 G8 24 24N 78 7 E
Mungari, Mozam. 55 F3 17 12S 33 30 E
Mungbere,
Dem. Rep. of the Congo 54 B2 2 36N 28 28 E
Munger, India 43 G12 25 23N 86 30 E
Mungindi, Australia 63 D4 28 58S 149 1 E
Munich = München,
Germany 16 D6 48 8N 11 34 E
Munising, U.S.A. 76 B2 46 25N 86 40W
Munku-Sardyk, Russia 27 D11 51 45N 100 20 E
Muñoz Gamero, Pen.,
Chile 96 G2 52 30S 73 5W
Munroe L., Canada 73 B9 59 13N 98 35W
Munsan, S. Korea 35 F14 37 51N 126 48 E
Münster, Germany 16 C4 51 58N 7 37 E
Munster □, Ireland 13 D3 52 18N 8 44W
Muntadgin, Australia 61 F2 31 45S 118 33 E
Muntok, Indonesia 36 E3 2 5S 105 10 E
Munyama, Zambia 55 F2 16 5S 28 31 E
Muong Beng, Laos 38 B3 20 23N 101 46 E
Muong Boum, Vietnam 38 A4 22 24N 102 49 E
Muong Et, Laos 38 B5 20 49N 104 1 E
Muong Hai, Laos 38 B3 21 3N 101 49 E
Muong Hiem, Laos 38 B4 20 5N 103 22 E
Muong Houn, Laos 38 B3 20 8N 101 23 E
Muong Hung, Vietnam 38 B4 20 56N 103 53 E
Muong Kau, Laos 38 E5 15 6N 105 47 E
Muong Khao, Laos 38 C4 19 38N 103 32 E
Muong Khoua, Laos 38 B4 21 5N 102 31 E
Muong Liep, Laos 38 C3 18 29N 101 40 E
Muong May, Laos 38 E6 14 49N 106 56 E
Muong Ngeun, Laos 38 B3 20 36N 101 3 E
Muong Ngoi, Laos 38 B4 20 43N 102 41 E
Muong Nhie, Vietnam 38 A4 22 12N 102 28 E
Muong Nong, Laos 38 D6 16 22N 106 30 E
Muong Ou Tay, Laos 38 A3 22 7N 101 48 E
Muong Oua, Laos 38 C3 18 18N 101 20 E
Muong Peun, Laos 38 B4 20 13N 103 52 E
Muong Phalane, Laos 38 D5 16 39N 105 34 E
Muong Phieng, Laos 38 C3 19 6N 101 32 E
Muong Phine, Laos 38 D6 16 32N 106 2 E
Muong Sai, Laos 38 B3 20 42N 101 59 E
Muong Saiapoun, Laos 38 C3 18 24N 101 31 E
Muong Sen, Vietnam 38 C5 19 24N 104 8 E
Muong Sing, Laos 38 B3 21 11N 101 9 E
Muong Son, Laos 38 B4 20 27N 103 19 E
Muong Soui, Laos 38 C4 19 33N 102 52 E
Muong Va, Laos 38 B4 21 53N 102 19 E
Muong Xia, Vietnam 38 B5 20 19N 104 50 E
Muonio, Finland 8 C20 67 57N 23 40 E
Muonionjoki →, Finland 8 C20 67 11N 23 34 E
Muping, China 35 F11 37 22N 121 36 E
Muqdisho, Somali Rep. 46 G4 2 2N 45 25 E
Mur →, Austria 17 E9 46 18N 16 52 E
Murakami, Japan 30 E9 38 14N 139 29 E
Murallón, Cerro, Chile 96 F2 49 48S 73 30W
Muranda, Rwanda 54 C2 1 52S 29 20 E
Murang'a, Kenya 54 C4 0 45S 37 9 E
Murashi, Russia 24 C8 59 30N 49 0 E
Muratlı, Turkey 21 D12 41 10N 27 29 E
Murayama, Japan 30 E10 38 30N 140 25 E
Murban, U.A.E. 45 F7 23 50N 53 45 E
Murchison →, Australia 61 E1 27 45S 114 0 E
Murchison, Mt., Antarctica 5 D11 73 0S 168 0 E
Murchison Falls, Uganda 54 B3 2 15N 31 30 E
Murchison House,
Australia 61 E1 27 39S 114 14 E
Murchison Ra., Australia 62 C1 20 0S 134 10 E
Murchison Rapids, Malawi 55 F3 15 55S 34 35 E
Murcia, Spain 19 D5 38 5N 1 10W
Murcia □, Spain 19 D5 37 50N 1 30W
Murdo, U.S.A. 80 D4 43 53N 100 43W
Murdoch Pt., Australia 62 A3 14 37S 144 55 E
Mureş →, Romania 17 E11 46 15N 20 13 E
Mureşul = Mureş →,
Romania 17 E11 46 15N 20 13 E
Murfreesboro, U.S.A. 77 H2 35 51N 86 24W
Murgab = Murghob,
Tajikistan 26 F8 38 10N 74 2 E
Murghob, Tajikistan 26 F8 38 10N 74 2 E
Murgon, Australia 63 D5 26 15S 151 54 E
Murgoo, Australia 61 E2 27 24S 116 28 E
Muria, Indonesia 37 G14 6 36S 110 53 E
Muriaé, Brazil 95 A7 21 8S 42 23W
Muriel Mine, Zimbabwe 55 F3 17 14S 30 40 E
Müritz, Germany 16 B7 53 25N 12 42 E
Murka, Kenya 54 C4 3 27S 38 0 E
Murmansk, Russia 24 A5 68 57N 33 10 E
Muro, Spain 22 B10 39 44N 3 3 E
Murom, Russia 24 C7 55 35N 42 3 E
Muroran, Japan 30 C10 42 25N 141 0 E
Muroto, Japan 31 H7 33 18N 134 9 E
Muroto-Misaki, Japan 31 H7 33 15N 134 10 E
Murphy, U.S.A. 82 E5 43 13N 116 33W
Murphys, U.S.A. 84 G6 38 8N 120 28W
Murphysboro, U.S.A. 81 G10 37 46N 89 20W
Murray, Ky., U.S.A. 77 G1 36 37N 88 19W
Murray, Utah, U.S.A. 82 F8 40 40N 111 53W
Murray →, Australia 63 F2 35 20S 139 22 E
Murray →, Canada 72 B4 56 11N 120 45W
Murray, L., U.S.A. 77 H5 34 3N 81 13W
Murray Bridge, Australia 63 F2 35 6S 139 14 E
Murray Downs, Australia 62 C1 21 4S 134 40 E
Murray Harbour, Canada 71 C7 46 0N 62 28W
Murraysburg, S. Africa 56 E3 31 58S 23 47 E
Murree, Pakistan 42 C5 33 56N 73 28 E
Murrieta, U.S.A. 85 M9 33 33N 117 13W
Murrin Murrin, Australia 61 E3 28 58S 121 33 E
Murrumbidgee →,
Australia 63 E3 34 43S 143 12 E
Murrumburrah, Australia 63 E4 34 32S 148 22 E
Murrurundi, Australia 63 E5 31 42S 150 51 E
Murshidabad, India 43 G13 24 11N 88 19 E
Murtle L., Canada 72 C5 52 8N 119 38W
Murtoa, Australia 63 F3 36 35S 142 28 E
Murungu, Tanzania 54 C3 4 12S 31 10 E
Murwara, India 43 H9 23 46N 80 28 E
Murwillumbah, Australia 63 D5 28 18S 153 27 E
Mürzzuschlag, Austria 16 E8 47 36N 15 41 E
Muş, Turkey 25 G7 38 45N 41 30 E
Mûsa, Gebel, Egypt 51 C12 28 33N 33 59 E
Musa Khel, Pakistan 42 D3 30 59N 69 52 E
Mūsá Qal'eh, Afghan. 40 C4 32 20N 64 50 E
Musaffargarh, Pakistan 40 D7 30 10N 71 10 E
Musala, Bulgaria 21 C10 42 13N 23 37 E
Musala, Indonesia 36 D1 1 41N 98 28 E
Musan, N. Korea 35 C15 42 12N 129 12 E
Musangu,
Dem. Rep. of the Congo 55 E1 10 28S 23 55 E
Musasa, Tanzania 54 C3 3 25S 31 30 E
Musay'id, Qatar 45 E6 25 0N 51 33 E
Muscat = Masqat, Oman 46 C6 23 37N 58 36 E
Muscat & Oman =
Oman ■, Asia 46 C6 23 0N 58 0 E
Muscatine, U.S.A. 80 E9 41 25N 91 3W
Musgrave, Australia 62 A3 14 47S 143 30 E
Musgrave Ranges,
Australia 61 E5 26 0S 132 0 E
Mushie,
Dem. Rep. of the Congo 52 E3 2 56S 16 55 E
Musi →, Indonesia 36 E2 2 20S 104 56 E
Muskeg →, Canada 72 A4 60 20N 123 20W
Muskegon, U.S.A. 76 D2 43 14N 86 16W
Muskegon →, U.S.A. 76 D2 43 14N 86 21W
Muskegon Heights, U.S.A. 76 D2 43 12N 86 16W
Muskogee, U.S.A. 81 H7 35 45N 95 22W
Muskwa →, Canada 72 B4 58 47N 122 48W
Muslimiyah, Syria 44 B3 36 19N 37 12 E
Musofu, Zambia 55 E2 13 30S 29 0 E
Musoma, Tanzania 54 C3 1 30S 33 48 E
Musoma □, Tanzania 54 C3 1 50S 34 30 E
Musquaro, L., Canada 71 B7 50 38N 61 5W
Musquodoboit Harbour,
Canada 71 D7 44 50N 63 9W
Musselburgh, U.K. 12 F5 55 57N 3 2W
Musselshell →, U.S.A. 82 C10 47 21N 107 57W
Mussoorie, India 42 D8 30 27N 78 6 E
Mussuco, Angola 56 B2 17 2S 19 3 E
Mustafakemalpaşa, Turkey 21 D13 40 2N 28 24 E
Mustang, Nepal 43 E10 29 10N 83 55 E
Musters, L., Argentina 96 F3 45 20S 69 25W
Musudan, N. Korea 35 D15 40 50N 129 43 E
Muswellbrook, Australia 63 E5 32 16S 150 56 E
Mût, Egypt 51 C11 25 28N 28 58 E
Mutanda, Mozam. 57 C5 21 0S 33 34 E
Mutanda, Zambia 55 E2 12 24S 26 13 E
Mutare, Zimbabwe 55 F3 18 58S 32 38 E
Muting, Indonesia 37 F10 7 23S 140 20 E
Mutoray, Russia 27 C11 60 56N 101 0 E
Mutshatsha,
Dem. Rep. of the Congo 55 E1 10 35S 24 20 E
Mutsu, Japan 30 D10 41 5N 140 55 E
Mutsu-Wan, Japan 30 D10 41 5N 140 55 E
Muttaburra, Australia 62 C3 22 38S 144 29 E
Mutton I., Ireland 13 D2 52 49N 9 32W
Mutuáli, Mozam. 55 E4 14 55S 37 0 E
Muweilih, Egypt 47 E3 30 42N 34 19 E
Muy Muy, Nic. 88 D2 12 39N 85 36W
Muyinga, Burundi 54 C3 3 14S 30 33 E
Muynak, Uzbekistan 26 E6 43 44N 59 10 E
Muzaffarabad, Pakistan 43 B5 34 25N 73 30 E
Muzaffargarh, Pakistan 42 D4 30 5N 71 14 E
Muzaffarnagar, India 42 E7 29 26N 77 40 E
Muzaffarpur, India 43 F11 26 7N 85 23 E
Muzhi, Russia 26 C7 65 25N 64 40 E
Muzon, C., U.S.A. 72 C2 54 40N 132 42W
Mvuma, Zimbabwe 55 F3 19 16S 30 30 E
Mvurwi, Zimbabwe 55 F3 17 0S 30 57 E
Mwadui, Tanzania 54 C3 3 26S 33 32 E
Mwambo, Tanzania 55 E5 10 30S 40 22 E
Mwandi, Zambia 55 F1 17 30S 24 51 E
Mwanza,
Dem. Rep. of the Congo 54 D2 7 55S 26 43 E
Mwanza, Tanzania 54 C3 2 30S 32 58 E
Mwanza, Zambia 55 F1 16 58S 24 28 E
Mwanza □, Tanzania 54 C3 2 0S 33 0 E
Mwaya, Tanzania 55 D3 9 32S 33 55 E
Mweelrea, Ireland 13 C2 53 39N 9 49W
Mweka,
Dem. Rep. of the Congo 52 E4 4 50S 21 34 E
Mwenezi, Zimbabwe 55 G3 21 15S 30 48 E
Mwenezi →, Mozam. 55 G3 22 40S 31 50 E
Mwenga,
Dem. Rep. of the Congo 54 C2 3 1S 28 28 E
Mweru, L., Zambia 55 D2 9 0S 28 40 E
Mweza Range, Zimbabwe 55 G3 21 0S 30 0 E
Mwilambwe,
Dem. Rep. of the Congo 54 D2 8 7S 25 5 E
Mwimbi, Tanzania 55 D3 8 38S 31 39 E
Mwinilunga, Zambia 55 E1 11 43S 24 25 E
My Tho, Vietnam 39 G6 10 29N 106 23 E
Myajlar, India 42 F4 26 15N 70 20 E
Myanaung, Burma 41 K19 18 18N 95 22 E
Myanmar = Burma ■,
Asia 41 J20 21 0N 96 30 E
Myaungmya, Burma 41 L19 16 30N 94 40 E
Mycenæ, Greece 21 F10 37 39N 22 52 E
Myeik Kyunzu, Burma 39 G1 11 30N 97 30 E
Myerstown, U.S.A. 79 F8 40 22N 76 19W
Myingyan, Burma 41 J19 21 30N 95 20 E
Myitkyina, Burma 41 G20 25 24N 97 26 E
Mykines, Færoe Is. 8 E9 62 7N 7 35W
Mykolayiv, Ukraine 25 E5 46 58N 32 0 E
Mymensingh, Bangla. 41 G17 24 45N 90 24 E
Mynydd Du, U.K. 11 F4 51 52N 3 50W
Mýrdalsjökull, Iceland 8 E4 63 40N 19 6W
Myroodah, Australia 60 C3 18 7S 124 16 E
Myrtle Beach, U.S.A. 77 J6 33 42N 78 53W
Myrtle Creek, U.S.A. 82 E2 43 1N 123 17W
Myrtle Point, U.S.A. 82 E1 43 4N 124 8W
Myrtou, Cyprus 23 D12 35 18N 33 4 E
Mysia, Turkey 21 E12 39 50N 27 0 E
Mysore = Karnataka □,
India 40 N10 13 15N 77 0 E
Mysore, India 40 N10 12 17N 76 41 E
Mystic, U.S.A. 79 E13 41 21N 71 58W
Myszków, Poland 17 C10 50 45N 19 22 E
Mytishchi, Russia 24 C6 55 50N 37 50 E
Myton, U.S.A. 82 F8 40 12N 110 4W
Mývatn, Iceland 8 D5 65 36N 17 0W
Mzimba, Malawi 55 E3 11 55S 33 39 E
Mzimkulu →, S. Africa 57 E5 30 44S 30 28 E
Mzimvubu →, S. Africa 57 E4 31 38S 29 33 E
Mzuzu, Malawi 55 E3 11 30S 33 55 E

N

Na Hearadh = Harris, U.K. 12 D2 57 50N 6 55W
Na Noi, Thailand 38 C3 18 19N 100 43 E
Na Phao, Laos 38 D5 17 35N 105 44 E
Na Sam, Vietnam 38 A6 22 3N 106 37 E
Na San, Vietnam 38 B5 21 12N 104 2 E
Naab →, Germany 16 D6 49 1N 12 2 E
Naantali, Finland 9 F19 60 29N 22 2 E
Naas, Ireland 13 C5 53 12N 6 40W
Nababiep, S. Africa 56 D2 29 36S 17 46 E
Nabadwip = Navadwip,
India 43 H13 23 34N 88 20 E
Nabari, Japan 31 G8 34 37N 136 5 E
Nabawa, Australia 61 E1 28 30S 114 48 E
Nabberu, L., Australia 61 E3 25 50S 120 30 E
Naberezhnyye Chelny,
Russia 24 C9 55 42N 52 19 E
Nabeul, Tunisia 51 A8 36 30N 10 44 E
Nabha, India 42 D7 30 26N 76 14 E
Nabīd, Iran 45 D8 29 40N 57 38 E
Nabire, Indonesia 37 E9 3 15S 135 26 E
Nabisar, Pakistan 42 G3 25 8N 69 40 E
Nabisipi →, Canada 71 B7 50 14N 62 13W
Nabiswera, Uganda 54 B3 1 27N 32 15 E
Nablus = Nābulus,
West Bank 47 C4 32 14N 35 15 E
Naboomspruit, S. Africa 57 C4 24 32S 28 40 E
Nābulus, West Bank 47 C4 32 14N 35 15 E
Nacala, Mozam. 55 E5 14 31S 40 34 E
Nacala-Velha, Mozam. 55 E5 14 32S 40 34 E
Nacaome, Honduras 88 D2 13 31N 87 30W
Nacaroa, Mozam. 55 E4 14 22S 39 56 E
Naches, U.S.A. 82 C3 46 44N 120 42W
Naches →, U.S.A. 84 D6 46 38N 120 31W
Nachingwea, Tanzania 55 E4 10 23S 38 49 E
Nachingwea □, Tanzania 55 E4 10 30S 38 30 E
Nachna, India 42 F4 27 34N 71 41 E
Nacimiento Reservoir,
U.S.A. 84 K6 35 46N 120 53W
Nackara, Australia 63 E2 32 48S 139 12 E
Naco, Mexico 86 A3 31 20N 109 56W
Naco, U.S.A. 83 L9 31 20N 109 57W
Nacogdoches, U.S.A. 81 K7 31 36N 94 39W
Nácori Chico, Mexico 86 B3 29 39N 109 1W
Nacozari, Mexico 86 A3 30 24N 109 39W
Nadiad, India 42 H5 22 41N 72 56 E
Nadur, Malta 23 C1 36 2N 14 17 E
Nadūshan, Iran 45 C7 32 2N 53 35 E
Nadvirna, Ukraine 17 D13 48 37N 24 30 E
Nadvoitsy, Russia 24 B5 63 52N 34 14 E
Nadvornaya = Nadvirna,
Ukraine 17 D13 48 37N 24 30 E
Nadym, Russia 26 C8 65 35N 72 42 E
Nadym →, Russia 26 C8 66 12N 72 0 E
Nærbø, Norway 9 G11 58 40N 5 39 E
Næstved, Denmark 9 J14 55 13N 11 44 E
Naftshahr, Iran 44 C5 34 0N 45 30 E
Nafud Desert = An Nafūd,
Si. Arabia 44 D4 28 15N 41 0 E
Naga, Phil. 37 B6 13 38N 123 15 E
Nagagami →, Canada 70 C3 49 40N 84 40W
Nagahama, Japan 31 G8 35 23N 136 16 E
Nagai, Japan 30 E10 38 6N 140 2 E
Nagaland □, India 41 G19 26 0N 94 30 E
Nagano, Japan 31 F9 36 40N 138 10 E
Nagano □, Japan 31 F9 36 15N 138 0 E
Nagaoka, Japan 31 F9 37 27N 138 51 E
Nagappattinam, India 40 P11 10 46N 79 51 E
Nagar Parkar, Pakistan 42 G4 24 28N 70 46 E
Nagasaki, Japan 31 H4 32 47N 129 50 E
Nagasaki □, Japan 31 H4 32 50N 129 40 E
Nagato, Japan 31 G5 34 19N 131 5 E
Nagaur, India 42 F5 27 15N 73 45 E
Nagercoil, India 40 Q10 8 12N 77 26 E
Nagina, India 43 E8 29 30N 78 30 E
Nagineh, Iran 45 C8 34 20N 57 15 E
Nagir, Pakistan 43 A6 36 12N 74 42 E
Nagoorin, Australia 62 C5 24 17S 151 15 E
Nagornyy, Russia 27 D13 55 58N 124 57 E
Nagoya, Japan 31 G8 35 10N 136 50 E
Nagpur, India 40 J11 21 8N 79 10 E
Nagua, Dom. Rep. 89 C6 19 23N 69 50W
Nagykanizsa, Hungary 17 E9 46 28N 17 0 E
Nagykőrös, Hungary 17 E10 47 5N 19 48 E
Naha, Japan 31 L3 26 13N 127 42 E
Nahanni Butte, Canada 72 A4 61 2N 123 31W
Nahanni Nat. Park, Canada 72 A4 61 15N 125 0W
Nahariyya, Israel 44 C2 33 1N 35 5 E
Nahāvand, Iran 45 C6 34 10N 48 22 E
Nahlin, Canada 72 B2 58 55N 131 38W
Naicá, Mexico 86 B3 27 53N 105 31W
Naicam, Canada 73 C8 52 30N 104 30W
Nain, Canada 71 A7 56 34N 61 40W
Nā'īn, Iran 45 C7 32 54N 53 0 E
Naini Tal, India 43 E8 29 30N 79 30 E
Nainpur, India 40 H12 22 30N 80 10 E
Nairn, U.K. 12 D5 57 35N 3 53W
Nairobi, Kenya 54 C4 1 17S 36 48 E
Naissaar, Estonia 9 G21 59 34N 24 29 E
Naivasha, Kenya 54 C4 0 40S 36 30 E
Naivasha, L., Kenya 54 C4 0 48S 36 20 E
Najafābād, Iran 45 C6 32 40N 51 15 E
Najibabad, India 42 E8 29 40N 78 20 E
Najin, N. Korea 35 C16 42 12N 130 15 E
Najmah, Si. Arabia 45 E6 26 42N 50 6 E
Naju, S. Korea 35 G14 35 3N 126 43 E
Nakadōri-Shima, Japan 31 H4 32 57N 129 4 E
Nakalagba,
Dem. Rep. of the Congo 54 B2 2 50N 27 58 E
Nakaminato, Japan 31 F10 36 21N 140 36 E
Nakamura, Japan 31 H6 32 59N 132 56 E
Nakano, Japan 31 F9 36 45N 138 22 E
Nakano-Shima, Japan 31 K4 29 51N 129 52 E
Nakashibetsu, Japan 30 C12 43 33N 144 59 E
Nakfa, Eritrea 46 D2 16 40N 38 32 E
Nakhichevan = Naxçıvan,
Azerbaijan 25 G8 39 12N 45 15 E
Nakhichevan Republic □
= Naxçıvan □,
Azerbaijan 25 G8 39 25N 45 26 E
Nakhl, Egypt 47 F2 29 55N 33 43 E
Nakhl-e Taqī, Iran 45 E7 27 28N 52 36 E
Nakhodka, Russia 30 C6 42 53N 132 54 E
Nakhon Nayok, Thailand 38 E3 14 12N 101 13 E
Nakhon Pathom, Thailand 38 F3 13 49N 100 3 E
Nakhon Phanom, Thailand 38 D5 17 23N 104 43 E
Nakhon Ratchasima,
Thailand 38 E4 14 59N 102 12 E
Nakhon Sawan, Thailand 38 E3 15 35N 100 10 E
Nakhon Si Thammarat,
Thailand 39 H3 8 29N 100 0 E
Nakhon Thai, Thailand 38 D3 17 5N 100 44 E
Nakina, B.C., Canada 72 B2 59 12N 132 52W
Nakina, Ont., Canada 70 B2 50 10N 86 40W
Nakodar, India 42 D6 31 8N 75 31 E
Nakskov, Denmark 9 J14 54 50N 11 8 E
Naktong →, S. Korea 35 G15 35 7N 128 57 E
Nakuru, Kenya 54 C4 0 15S 36 4 E
Nakuru □, Kenya 54 C4 0 15S 35 5 E
Nakuru, L., Kenya 54 C4 0 23S 36 5 E
Nakusp, Canada 72 C5 50 20N 117 45W
Nal →, Pakistan 42 G1 25 20N 65 30 E
Nalchik, Russia 25 F7 43 30N 43 33 E
Nalgonda, India 40 L11 17 6N 79 15 E
Nalhati, India 43 G12 24 17N 87 52 E
Nallamalai Hills, India 40 M11 15 30N 78 50 E
Nam Can, Vietnam 39 H5 8 46N 104 59 E
Nam Co, China 32 C4 30 30N 90 45 E
Nam Dinh, Vietnam 38 B6 20 25N 106 5 E
Nam Du, Hon, Vietnam 39 H5 9 41N 104 21 E
Nam Ngum Dam, Laos 38 C4 18 35N 102 34 E
Nam-Phan = Cochin
China, Vietnam 39 G6 10 30N 106 0 E
Nam Phong, Thailand 38 D4 16 42N 102 52 E
Nam Tha, Laos 38 B3 20 58N 101 30 E
Nam Tok, Thailand 38 E2 14 21N 99 4 E
Namacunde, Angola 56 B2 17 18S 15 50 E
Namacurra, Mozam. 57 B6 17 30S 36 50 E
Namak, Daryācheh-ye,
Iran 45 C7 34 30N 52 0 E
Namak, Kavir-e, Iran 45 C8 34 30N 57 30 E
Namaland, Namibia 56 C2 26 0S 17 0 E
Namangan, Uzbekistan 26 E8 41 0N 71 40 E
Namapa, Mozam. 55 E4 13 43S 39 50 E
Namaqualand, S. Africa 56 E2 30 0S 17 25 E
Namasagali, Uganda 54 B3 1 2N 33 0 E
Namber, Indonesia 37 E8 1 2S 134 49 E
Nambour, Australia 63 D5 26 32S 152 58 E
Nambucca Heads,
Australia 63 E5 30 37S 153 0 E
Namcha Barwa, China 32 D4 29 40N 95 10 E
Namche Bazar, Nepal 43 F12 27 51N 86 47 E
Namchonjŏm, N. Korea 35 E14 38 15N 126 26 E
Namecunda, Mozam. 55 E4 14 54S 37 37 E
Nameponda, Mozam. 55 F4 15 50S 39 50 E
Nametil, Mozam. 55 F4 15 40S 39 21 E
Namew L., Canada 73 C8 54 14N 101 56W
Namib Desert =
Namibwoestyn, Namibia 56 C2 22 30S 15 0 E
Namibe, Angola 53 H2 15 7S 12 11 E
Namibe □, Angola 56 B1 16 35S 12 30 E
Namibia ■, Africa 56 C2 22 0S 18 9 E
Namibwoestyn, Namibia 56 C2 22 30S 15 0 E
Namlea, Indonesia 37 E7 3 18S 127 5 E
Namoi →, Australia 63 E4 30 12S 149 30 E
Nampa, U.S.A. 82 E5 43 34N 116 34W
Nampo, N. Korea 35 E13 38 52N 125 10 E
Nampō-Shotō, Japan 31 J10 32 0N 140 0 E
Nampula, Mozam. 55 F4 15 6S 39 15 E
Namrole, Indonesia 37 E7 3 46S 126 46 E
Namse Shankou, China 41 E13 30 0N 82 25 E
Namsen →, Norway 8 D14 64 28N 11 37 E
Namsos, Norway 8 D14 64 29N 11 30 E
Namtsy, Russia 27 C13 62 43N 129 37 E
Namtu, Burma 41 H20 23 5N 97 28 E
Namtumbo, Tanzania 55 E4 10 30S 36 4 E
Namu, Canada 72 C3 51 52N 127 50W
Namur, Belgium 15 D4 50 27N 4 52 E
Namur □, Belgium 15 D4 50 17N 5 0 E
Namutoni, Namibia 56 B2 18 49S 16 55 E
Namwala, Zambia 55 F2 15 44S 26 30 E
Namwŏn, S. Korea 35 G14 35 23N 127 23 E
Nan, Thailand 38 C3 18 48N 100 46 E
Nan →, Thailand 38 E3 15 42N 100 9 E
Nanaimo, Canada 72 D4 49 10N 124 0W
Nanam, N. Korea 35 D15 41 44N 129 40 E

Nanango

Nanango, *Australia* **63 D5** 26 40S 152 0 E
Nanao, *Japan* **31 F8** 37 0N 137 0 E
Nanchang, *China* **33 D6** 28 42N 115 55 E
Nanching = Nanjing, *China* **33 C6** 32 2N 118 47 E
Nanchong, *China* **32 C5** 30 43N 106 2 E
Nancy, *France* **18 B7** 48 42N 6 12 E
Nanda Devi, *India* **43 D8** 30 23N 79 59 E
Nandan, *Japan* **31 G7** 34 10N 134 42 E
Nanded, *India* **40 K10** 19 10N 77 20 E
Nandewar Ra., *Australia* **63 E5** 30 15S 150 35 E
Nandi, *Fiji* **59 C7** 17 42S 177 20 E
Nandi □, *Kenya* **54 B4** 0 15N 35 0 E
Nandurbar, *India* **40 J9** 21 20N 74 15 E
Nandyal, *India* **40 M11** 15 30N 78 30 E
Nanga, *Australia* **61 E1** 26 7S 113 45 E
Nanga-Eboko, *Cameroon* **52 D2** 4 41N 12 22 E
Nanga Parbat, *Pakistan* **43 B6** 35 10N 74 35 E
Nangade, *Mozam.* **55 E4** 11 5S 39 36 E
Nangapinoh, *Indonesia* **36 E4** 0 20S 111 44 E
Nangarhár □, *Afghan.* **40 B7** 34 20N 70 0 E
Nangatayap, *Indonesia* **36 E4** 1 32S 110 34 E
Nangeya Mts., *Uganda* **54 B3** 3 30N 33 30 E
Nangong, *China* **34 F8** 37 23N 115 22 E
Nanhuang, *China* **35 F11** 36 58N 121 48 E
Nanjeko, *Zambia* **55 F1** 15 31S 23 30 E
Nanjing, *China* **33 C6** 32 2N 118 47 E
Nanjirinji, *Tanzania* **55 D4** 9 41S 39 5 E
Nankana Sahib, *Pakistan* **42 D5** 31 27N 73 38 E
Nanking = Nanjing, *China* **33 C6** 32 2N 118 47 E
Nankoku, *Japan* **31 H6** 33 39N 133 44 E
Nanning, *China* **32 D5** 22 48N 108 20 E
Nannup, *Australia* **61 F2** 33 59S 115 48 E
Nanpara, *India* **43 F9** 27 52N 81 33 E
Nanpi, *China* **34 E9** 38 2N 116 45 E
Nanping, *China* **33 D6** 26 38N 118 10 E
Nanripe, *Mozam.* **55 E4** 13 52S 38 52 E
Nansei-Shotō = Ryūkyū-rettō, *Japan* **31 M3** 26 0N 126 0 E
Nansio, *Tanzania* **54 C3** 2 3S 33 4 E
Nantes, *France* **18 C3** 47 12N 1 33W
Nanticoke, *U.S.A.* **79 E8** 41 12N 76 0W
Nanton, *Canada* **72 C6** 50 21N 113 46W
Nantong, *China* **33 C7** 32 1N 120 52 E
Nantucket I., *U.S.A.* **66 E12** 41 16N 70 5W
Nantwich, *U.K.* **10 D5** 53 4N 2 31W
Nanuque, *Brazil* **93 G10** 17 50S 40 21W
Nanusa, Kepulauan, *Indonesia* **37 D7** 4 45N 127 1 E
Nanutarra, *Australia* **60 D2** 22 32S 115 30 E
Nanyang, *China* **34 H7** 33 11N 112 30 E
Nanyuan, *China* **34 E9** 39 44N 116 22 E
Nanyuki, *Kenya* **54 B4** 0 2N 37 4 E
Nao, C. de la, *Spain* **19 C6** 38 44N 0 14 E
Naococane L., *Canada* **71 B5** 52 50N 70 45W
Naoetsu, *Japan* **31 F9** 37 12N 138 10 E
Napa, *U.S.A.* **84 G4** 38 18N 122 17W
Napa →, *U.S.A.* **84 G4** 38 10N 122 19W
Napanee, *Canada* **70 D4** 44 15N 77 0W
Napanoch, *U.S.A.* **79 E10** 41 44N 74 22W
Nape, *Laos* **38 C5** 18 18N 105 6 E
Nape Pass = Keo Neua, Deo, *Vietnam* **38 C5** 18 23N 105 10 E
Napier, *N.Z.* **59 H6** 39 30S 176 56 E
Napier Broome B., *Australia* **60 B4** 14 2S 126 37 E
Napier Downs, *Australia* **60 C3** 17 11S 124 36 E
Napier Pen., *Australia* **62 A2** 12 4S 135 43 E
Naples = Nápoli, *Italy* **20 D6** 40 50N 14 15 E
Naples, *U.S.A.* **77 M5** 26 8N 81 48W
Napo →, *Peru* **92 D4** 3 20S 72 40W
Napoleon, *N. Dak., U.S.A.* **80 B5** 46 30N 99 46W
Napoleon, *Ohio, U.S.A.* **76 E3** 41 23N 84 8W
Nápoli, *Italy* **20 D6** 40 50N 14 15 E
Napopo, *Dem. Rep. of the Congo* **54 B2** 4 15N 28 0 E
Nappa Merrie, *Australia* **63 D3** 27 36S 141 7 E
Naqqāsh, *Iran* **45 C6** 35 40N 49 6 E
Nara, *Japan* **31 G7** 34 40N 135 49 E
Nara, *Mali* **50 E4** 15 10N 7 20W
Nara □, *Japan* **31 G8** 34 30N 136 0 E
Nara Canal, *Pakistan* **42 G3** 24 30N 69 20 E
Nara Visa, *U.S.A.* **81 H3** 35 37N 103 6W
Naracoorte, *Australia* **63 F3** 36 58S 140 45 E
Naradhan, *Australia* **63 E4** 33 34S 146 17 E
Narasapur, *India* **41 L12** 16 26N 81 40 E
Narathiwat, *Thailand* **39 J3** 6 30N 101 48 E
Narayanganj, *Bangla.* **41 H17** 23 40N 90 33 E
Narayanpet, *India* **40 L10** 16 45N 77 30 E
Narbonne, *France* **18 E5** 43 11N 3 0 E
Nardīn, *Iran* **45 B7** 37 3N 55 59 E
Nardò, *Italy* **21 D8** 40 11N 18 2 E
Narembeen, *Australia* **61 F2** 32 7S 118 24 E
Nares Str., *Arctic* **66 A13** 80 0N 70 0W
Naretha, *Australia* **61 F3** 31 0S 124 45 E
Narew →, *Poland* **17 B11** 52 26N 20 41 E
Nari →, *Pakistan* **42 F2** 28 0N 67 40 E
Narin, *Afghan.* **40 A6** 36 5N 69 0 E
Narindra, Helodranon' i, *Madag.* **57 A8** 14 55S 47 30 E
Narita, *Japan* **31 G10** 35 47N 140 19 E
Narmada →, *India* **42 J5** 21 38N 72 36 E
Narmland, *Sweden* **9 F15** 60 0N 13 30 E
Narnaul, *India* **42 E7** 28 5N 76 11 E
Narodnaya, *Russia* **24 A10** 65 5N 59 58 E
Narok, *Kenya* **54 C4** 1 55S 35 52 E
Narok □, *Kenya* **54 C4** 1 20S 36 30 E
Narooma, *Australia* **63 F5** 36 14S 150 4 E
Narowal, *Pakistan* **42 C6** 32 6N 74 52 E
Narrabri, *Australia* **63 E4** 30 19S 149 46 E
Narran →, *Australia* **63 D4** 28 37S 148 12 E
Narrandera, *Australia* **63 E4** 34 42S 146 31 E
Narraway →, *Canada* **72 B5** 55 44N 119 55W
Narrogin, *Australia* **61 F2** 32 58S 117 14 E
Narromine, *Australia* **63 E4** 32 12S 148 12 E
Narsimhapur, *India* **43 H8** 22 54N 79 14 E
Naruto, *Japan* **31 G7** 34 11N 134 37 E
Narva, *Estonia* **24 C4** 59 23N 28 12 E
Narva →, *Russia* **9 G22** 59 27N 28 2 E
Narvik, *Norway* **8 B17** 68 28N 17 26 E
Narwana, *India* **42 E7** 29 39N 76 6 E
Naryan-Mar, *Russia* **24 A9** 67 42N 53 12 E
Naryilco, *Australia* **63 D3** 28 37S 141 53 E
Narym, *Russia* **26 D9** 59 0N 81 30 E
Naryn, *Kyrgyzstan* **26 E8** 41 26N 75 58 E
Nasa, *Norway* **8 C16** 66 29N 15 23 E
Naseby, *N.Z.* **59 L3** 45 1S 170 10 E
Naselle, *U.S.A.* **84 D3** 46 22N 123 49W
Naser, Buheirat en, *Egypt* **51 D12** 23 0N 32 30 E
Nashua, *Iowa, U.S.A.* **80 D8** 42 57N 92 32W
Nashua, *Mont., U.S.A.* **82 B10** 48 8N 106 22W
Nashua, *N.H., U.S.A.* **79 D13** 42 45N 71 28W
Nashville, *Ark., U.S.A.* **81 J8** 33 57N 93 51W
Nashville, *Ga., U.S.A.* **77 K4** 31 12N 83 15W
Nashville, *Tenn., U.S.A.* **77 G2** 36 10N 86 47W
Nasik, *India* **40 K8** 19 58N 73 50 E
Nasirabad, *India* **42 F6** 26 15N 74 45 E
Naskaupi →, *Canada* **71 B7** 53 47N 60 51W
Naṣriān-e Pā'īn, *Iran* **44 C5** 32 52N 46 52 E
Nass →, *Canada* **72 C3** 55 0N 129 40W
Nassau, *Bahamas* **88 A4** 25 5N 77 20W
Nassau, *U.S.A.* **79 D11** 42 31N 73 37W
Nassau, B., *Chile* **96 H3** 55 20S 68 0W
Nasser, L. = Naser, Buheirat en, *Egypt* **51 D12** 23 0N 32 30 E
Nässjö, *Sweden* **9 H16** 57 39N 14 42 E
Nat Kyizin, *Burma* **41 M20** 14 57N 97 59 E
Nata, *Botswana* **56 C4** 20 12S 26 12 E
Natal, *Brazil* **93 E11** 5 47S 35 13W
Natal, *Canada* **72 D6** 49 43N 114 51W
Natal, *Indonesia* **36 D1** 0 35N 99 7 E
Naṭanz, *Iran* **45 C6** 33 30N 51 55 E
Natashquan, *Canada* **71 B7** 50 14N 61 46W
Natashquan →, *Canada* **71 B7** 50 7N 61 50W
Natchez, *U.S.A.* **81 K9** 31 34N 91 24W
Natchitoches, *U.S.A.* **81 K8** 31 46N 93 5W
Nathalia, *Australia* **63 F4** 36 1S 145 13 E
Nathdwara, *India* **42 G5** 24 55N 73 50 E
Nati, Pta., *Spain* **22 A10** 40 3N 3 50 E
Natimuk, *Australia* **63 F3** 36 42S 142 0 E
Nation →, *Canada* **72 B4** 55 30N 123 32W
National City, *U.S.A.* **85 N9** 32 41N 117 6W
Natitingou, *Benin* **50 F6** 10 20N 1 26 E
Natividad, I., *Mexico* **86 B1** 27 50N 115 10W
Natoma, *U.S.A.* **80 F5** 39 11N 99 2W
Natron, L., *Tanzania* **54 C4** 2 20S 36 0 E
Natrona Heights, *U.S.A.* **78 F5** 40 37N 79 44W
Natuna Besar, Kepulauan, *Indonesia* **39 L7** 4 0N 108 15 E
Natuna Is. = Natuna Besar, Kepulauan, *Indonesia* **39 L7** 4 0N 108 15 E
Natuna Selatan, Kepulauan, *Indonesia* **39 L7** 2 45N 109 0 E
Natural Bridge, *U.S.A.* **79 B9** 44 5N 75 30W
Naturaliste, C., *Australia* **62 G4** 40 50S 148 15 E
Nau Qala, *Afghan.* **42 B3** 34 5N 68 5 E
Naubinway, *U.S.A.* **70 C2** 46 6N 85 27W
Naugatuck, *U.S.A.* **79 E11** 41 30N 73 3W
Naumburg, *Germany* **16 C6** 51 9N 11 47 E
Nā'ūr at Tunayb, *Jordan* **47 D4** 31 48N 35 57 E
Nauru ■, *Pac. Oc.* **64 H8** 1 0S 166 0 E
Naushahra = Nowshera, *Pakistan* **40 C8** 34 0N 72 0 E
Nauta, *Peru* **92 D4** 4 31S 73 35W
Nautanwa, *India* **41 F13** 27 20N 83 25 E
Nautla, *Mexico* **87 C5** 20 20N 96 50W
Nava, *Mexico* **86 B4** 28 25N 100 46W
Navadwip, *India* **43 H13** 23 34N 88 20 E
Navahrudak, *Belarus* **17 B13** 53 40N 25 50 E
Navajo Reservoir, *U.S.A.* **83 H10** 36 48N 107 36W
Navalmoral de la Mata, *Spain* **19 C3** 39 52N 5 33W
Navan = An Uaimh, *Ireland* **13 C5** 53 39N 6 41W
Navarino, I., *Chile* **96 H3** 55 0S 67 40W
Navarra □, *Spain* **19 A5** 42 40N 1 40W
Navarre, *U.S.A.* **78 F3** 40 43N 81 31W
Navarro →, *U.S.A.* **84 F3** 39 11N 123 45W
Navasota, *U.S.A.* **81 K6** 30 23N 96 5W
Navassa, *W. Indies* **89 C5** 18 30N 75 0W
Naver →, *U.K.* **12 C4** 58 32N 4 14W
Navidad, *Chile* **94 C1** 33 57S 71 50W
Năvodari, *Romania* **17 F15** 44 19N 28 36 E
Navoi = Nawoiy, *Uzbekistan* **26 E7** 40 9N 65 22 E
Navojoa, *Mexico* **86 B3** 27 0N 109 30W
Navolato, *Mexico* **86 C3** 24 47N 107 42W
Návpaktos, *Greece* **21 E9** 38 24N 21 50 E
Návplion, *Greece* **21 F10** 37 33N 22 50 E
Navsari, *India* **40 J8** 20 57N 72 59 E
Nawa Kot, *Pakistan* **42 E4** 28 21N 71 24 E
Nawabganj, *Ut. P., India* **43 F9** 26 56N 81 14 E
Nawabganj, *Ut. P., India* **43 E8** 28 32N 79 40 E
Nawabshah, *Pakistan* **42 F3** 26 15N 68 25 E
Nawada, *India* **43 G11** 24 50N 85 33 E
Nawakot, *Nepal* **43 F11** 27 55N 85 10 E
Nawalgarh, *India* **42 F6** 27 50N 75 15 E
Nawanshahr, *India* **43 C6** 32 33N 74 48 E
Nawoiy, *Uzbekistan* **26 E7** 40 9N 65 22 E
Naxçıvan, *Azerbaijan* **25 G8** 39 12N 45 15 E
Naxçıvan □, *Azerbaijan* **25 G8** 39 25N 45 26 E
Nāy Band, *Iran* **45 E7** 27 20N 52 40 E
Nayakhan, *Russia* **27 C16** 61 56N 159 0 E
Nayarit □, *Mexico* **86 C4** 22 0N 105 0W
Nayoro, *Japan* **30 B11** 44 21N 142 28 E
Nayyāl, W. →, *Si. Arabia* **44 D3** 28 35N 39 4 E
Nazareth = Naẓerat, *Israel* **47 C4** 32 42N 35 17 E
Nazas, *Mexico* **86 B4** 25 10N 104 6W
Nazas →, *Mexico* **86 B4** 25 35N 103 25W
Nazca, *Peru* **92 F4** 14 50S 74 57W
Naze, The, *U.K.* **11 F9** 51 53N 1 18 E
Naẓerat, *Israel* **47 C4** 32 42N 35 17 E
Nāzīk, *Iran* **44 B5** 39 1N 45 4 E
Nazilli, *Turkey* **21 F13** 37 55N 28 15 E
Nazir Hat, *Bangla.* **41 H17** 22 35N 91 49 E
Nazko, *Canada* **72 C4** 53 1N 123 37W
Nazko →, *Canada* **72 C4** 53 7N 123 34W
Nchanga, *Zambia* **55 E2** 12 30S 27 49 E
Ncheu, *Malawi* **55 E3** 14 50S 34 47 E
Ndala, *Tanzania* **54 C3** 4 45S 33 15 E
Ndalatando, *Angola* **52 F2** 9 12S 14 48 E
Ndareda, *Tanzania* **54 C4** 4 12S 35 30 E
Ndélé, *C.A.R.* **52 C4** 8 25N 20 36 E
Ndjamena, *Chad* **51 F8** 12 10N 14 59 E
Ndola, *Zambia* **55 E2** 13 0S 28 34 E
Ndoto Mts., *Kenya* **54 B4** 2 0N 37 0 E
Nduguti, *Tanzania* **54 C3** 4 18S 34 41 E
Neagh, Lough, *U.K.* **13 B5** 54 37N 6 25W
Neah Bay, *U.S.A.* **84 B2** 48 22N 124 37W
Neale, L., *Australia* **60 D5** 24 15S 130 0 E
Neápolis, *Greece* **23 D7** 35 15N 25 37 E
Near Is., *U.S.A.* **68 C1** 52 30N 174 0 E
Neath, *U.K.* **11 F4** 51 39N 3 48W
Neath Port Talbot □, *U.K.* **11 F4** 51 42N 3 45W
Nebine Cr. →, *Australia* **63 D4** 29 27S 146 56 E
Nebitdag, *Turkmenistan* **25 G9** 39 30N 54 22 E
Nebraska □, *U.S.A.* **80 E5** 41 30N 99 30W
Nebraska City, *U.S.A.* **80 E7** 40 41N 95 52W
Nébrodi, Monti, *Italy* **20 F6** 37 54N 14 35 E
Necedah, *U.S.A.* **80 C9** 44 2N 90 4W
Nechako →, *Canada* **72 C4** 53 30N 122 44W
Neches →, *U.S.A.* **81 L8** 29 58N 93 51W
Neckar →, *Germany* **16 D5** 49 27N 8 29 E
Necochea, *Argentina* **94 D4** 38 30S 58 50W
Needles, *U.S.A.* **85 L12** 34 51N 114 37W
Needles, The, *U.K.* **11 G6** 50 39N 1 35W
Ñeembucú □, *Paraguay* **94 B4** 27 0S 58 0W
Neemuch = Nimach, *India* **42 G6** 24 30N 74 56 E
Neenah, *U.S.A.* **76 C1** 44 11N 88 28W
Neepawa, *Canada* **73 C9** 50 15N 99 30W
Neftçala, *Azerbaijan* **25 G8** 39 19N 49 12 E
Neftyannyye Kamni, *Azerbaijan* **25 F9** 40 20N 50 55 E
Nefyn, *U.K.* **10 E3** 52 56N 4 31W
Negapatam = Nagappattinam, *India* **40 P11** 10 46N 79 51 E
Negaunee, *U.S.A.* **76 B2** 46 30N 87 36W
Negele, *Ethiopia* **46 F2** 5 20N 39 36 E
Negev Desert = Hanegev, *Israel* **47 E4** 30 50N 35 0 E
Negombo, *Sri Lanka* **40 R11** 7 12N 79 50 E
Negotin, *Serbia, Yug.* **21 B10** 44 16N 22 37 E
Negra, Pta., *Peru* **92 E2** 6 6S 81 10W
Negrais, C. = Maudin Sun, *Burma* **41 M19** 16 0N 94 30 E
Negro →, *Argentina* **96 E4** 41 2S 62 47W
Negro →, *Brazil* **90 D4** 3 0S 60 0W
Negro →, *Uruguay* **95 C4** 33 24S 58 22W
Negros, *Phil.* **37 C6** 9 30N 122 40 E
Nehalem →, *U.S.A.* **84 E3** 45 40N 123 56W
Nehāvand, *Iran* **45 C6** 35 56N 49 31 E
Nehbandān, *Iran* **45 D9** 31 35N 60 5 E
Nei Monggol Zizhiqu □, *China* **34 D7** 42 0N 112 0 E
Neidpath, *Canada* **73 C7** 50 12N 107 20W
Neihart, *U.S.A.* **82 C8** 47 0N 110 44W
Neijiang, *China* **32 D5** 29 35N 104 55 E
Neilton, *U.S.A.* **82 C2** 47 25N 123 53W
Neiqiu, *China* **34 F8** 37 15N 114 30 E
Neiva, *Colombia* **92 C3** 2 56N 75 18W
Neixiang, *China* **34 H6** 33 10N 111 52 E
Nejanilini L., *Canada* **73 B9** 59 33N 97 48W
Nekā, *Iran* **45 B7** 36 39N 53 19 E
Nekemte, *Ethiopia* **46 F2** 9 4N 36 30 E
Neksø, *Denmark* **9 J16** 55 4N 15 8 E
Nelia, *Australia* **62 C3** 20 39S 142 12 E
Neligh, *U.S.A.* **80 D5** 42 8N 98 2W
Nelkan, *Russia* **27 D14** 57 40N 136 4 E
Nellore, *India* **40 M11** 14 27N 79 59 E
Nelson, *Canada* **72 D5** 49 30N 117 20W
Nelson, *N.Z.* **59 J4** 41 18S 173 16 E
Nelson, *U.K.* **10 D5** 53 50N 2 13W
Nelson, *U.S.A.* **83 J7** 35 31N 113 19W
Nelson →, *Canada* **73 C9** 54 33N 98 2W
Nelson, C., *Australia* **63 F3** 38 26S 141 32 E
Nelson, Estrecho, *Chile* **96 G2** 51 30S 75 0W
Nelson Forks, *Canada* **72 B4** 59 30N 124 0W
Nelson House, *Canada* **73 B9** 55 47N 98 51W
Nelson L., *Canada* **73 B8** 55 48N 100 7W
Nelspoort, *S. Africa* **56 E3** 32 7S 23 0 E
Nelspruit, *S. Africa* **57 D5** 25 29S 30 59 E
Néma, *Mauritania* **50 E4** 16 40N 7 15W
Neman, *Russia* **9 J20** 55 2N 22 2 E
Neman →, *Lithuania* **24 C3** 55 25N 21 10 E
Nemeiben L., *Canada* **73 B7** 55 20N 105 20W
Nemunas = Neman →, *Lithuania* **24 C3** 55 25N 21 10 E
Nemuro, *Japan* **30 C12** 43 20N 145 35 E
Nemuro-Kaikyō, *Japan* **30 C12** 43 30N 145 30 E
Nen Jiang →, *China* **35 B13** 45 28N 124 30 E
Nenagh, *Ireland* **13 D3** 52 52N 8 11W
Nenasi, *Malaysia* **39 L4** 3 9N 103 23 E
Nene →, *U.K.* **11 E8** 52 49N 0 11 E
Nenjiang, *China* **33 B7** 49 10N 125 10 E
Neno, *Malawi* **55 F3** 15 25S 34 40 E
Neodesha, *U.S.A.* **81 G7** 37 25N 95 41W
Neosho, *U.S.A.* **81 G7** 36 52N 94 22W
Neosho →, *U.S.A.* **81 H7** 36 48N 95 18W
Nepal ■, *Asia* **43 F11** 28 0N 84 30 E
Nepalganj, *Nepal* **43 E9** 28 5N 81 40 E
Nephi, *U.S.A.* **82 G8** 39 43N 111 50W
Nephin, *Ireland* **13 B2** 54 1N 9 22W
Neptune, *U.S.A.* **79 F10** 40 13N 74 2W
Nerchinsk, *Russia* **27 D12** 52 0N 116 39 E
Néret L., *Canada* **71 B5** 54 45N 70 44W
Neretva →, *Croatia* **21 C7** 43 1N 17 27 E
Neringa, *Lithuania* **9 J19** 55 20N 21 5 E
Ness, L., *U.K.* **12 D4** 57 15N 4 32W
Nesterov, *Poland* **17 C12** 50 4N 23 58 E
Nesvizh = Nyasvizh, *Belarus* **17 B14** 53 14N 26 38 E
Netanya, *Israel* **47 C3** 32 20N 34 51 E
Nete →, *Belgium* **15 C4** 51 7N 4 14 E
Netherdale, *Australia* **62 C4** 21 10S 148 33 E
Netherlands ■, *Europe* **15 C5** 52 0N 5 30 E
Netherlands Antilles ■, *W. Indies* **92 A5** 12 15N 69 0W
Nettilling L., *Canada* **69 B12** 66 30N 71 0W
Netzahualcoyotl, Presa, *Mexico* **87 D6** 17 10N 93 30W
Neubrandenburg, *Germany* **16 B7** 53 33N 13 15 E
Neuchâtel, *Switz.* **18 C7** 47 0N 6 55 E
Neuchâtel, Lac de, *Switz.* **18 C7** 46 53N 6 50 E
Neufchâteau, *Belgium* **15 E5** 49 50N 5 25 E
Neumünster, *Germany* **16 A5** 54 4N 9 58 E
Neunkirchen, *Germany* **16 D4** 49 20N 7 9 E
Neuquén, *Argentina* **96 D3** 38 55S 68 0W
Neuquén □, *Argentina* **94 D2** 38 0S 69 50W
Neuruppin, *Germany* **16 B7** 52 55N 12 48 E
Neuse →, *U.S.A.* **77 H7** 35 6N 76 29W
Neusiedler See, *Austria* **17 E9** 47 50N 16 47 E
Neustrelitz, *Germany* **16 B7** 53 21N 13 4 E
Neva →, *Russia* **24 C5** 59 50N 30 30 E
Nevada, *U.S.A.* **81 G7** 37 51N 94 22W
Nevada □, *U.S.A.* **82 G5** 39 0N 117 0W
Nevada, Sierra, *Spain* **19 D4** 37 3N 3 15W
Nevada, Sierra, *U.S.A.* **82 G3** 39 0N 120 30W
Nevada City, *U.S.A.* **84 F6** 39 16N 121 1W
Nevado, Cerro, *Argentina* **94 D2** 35 30S 68 32W
Nevers, *France* **18 C5** 47 0N 3 9 E
Nevertire, *Australia* **63 E4** 31 50S 147 44 E
Neville, *Canada* **73 D7** 49 58N 107 39W
Nevinnomyssk, *Russia* **25 F7** 44 40N 42 0 E
Nevis, *W. Indies* **89 C7** 17 0N 62 30W
Nevyansk, *Russia* **24 C11** 57 30N 60 13 E
New Albany, *Ind., U.S.A.* **76 F3** 38 18N 85 49W
New Albany, *Miss., U.S.A.* **81 H10** 34 29N 89 0W
New Albany, *Pa., U.S.A.* **79 E8** 41 36N 76 27W
New Amsterdam, *Guyana* **92 B7** 6 15N 57 36W
New Angledool, *Australia* **63 D4** 29 5S 147 55 E
New Bedford, *U.S.A.* **79 E14** 41 38N 70 56W
New Bern, *U.S.A.* **77 H7** 35 7N 77 3W
New Bethlehem, *U.S.A.* **78 F5** 41 0N 79 20W
New Bloomfield, *U.S.A.* **78 F7** 40 25N 77 11W
New Boston, *U.S.A.* **81 J7** 33 28N 94 25W
New Braunfels, *U.S.A.* **81 L5** 29 42N 98 8W
New Brighton, *N.Z.* **59 K4** 43 29S 172 43 E
New Brighton, *U.S.A.* **78 F4** 40 42N 80 19W
New Britain, *Papua N. G.* **64 H7** 5 50S 150 20 E
New Britain, *U.S.A.* **79 E12** 41 40N 72 47W
New Brunswick, *U.S.A.* **79 F10** 40 30N 74 27W
New Brunswick □, *Canada* **71 C6** 46 50N 66 30W
New Caledonia ■, *Pac. Oc.* **64 K8** 21 0S 165 0 E
New Castle, *Ind., U.S.A.* **76 F3** 39 55N 85 22W
New Castle, *Pa., U.S.A.* **78 F4** 41 0N 80 21W
New City, *U.S.A.* **79 E11** 41 9N 73 59W
New Cumberland, *U.S.A.* **78 F4** 40 30N 80 36W
New Cuyama, *U.S.A.* **85 L7** 34 57N 119 38W
New Delhi, *India* **42 E7** 28 37N 77 13 E
New Denver, *Canada* **72 D5** 50 0N 117 25W
New Don Pedro Reservoir, *U.S.A.* **84 H6** 37 43N 120 24W
New England, *U.S.A.* **80 B3** 46 32N 102 52W
New England Ra., *Australia* **63 E5** 30 20S 151 45 E
New Forest, *U.K.* **11 G6** 50 53N 1 34W
New Galloway, *U.K.* **12 F4** 55 5N 4 9W
New Glasgow, *Canada* **71 C7** 45 35N 62 36W
New Guinea, *Oceania* **64 H5** 4 0S 136 0 E
New Hamburg, *Canada* **78 C4** 43 23N 80 42W
New Hampshire □, *U.S.A.* **79 C13** 44 0N 71 30W
New Hampton, *U.S.A.* **80 D8** 43 3N 92 19W
New Hanover, *S. Africa* **57 D5** 29 22S 30 31 E
New Haven, *Conn., U.S.A.* **79 E12** 41 18N 72 55W
New Haven, *Mich., U.S.A.* **78 D2** 42 44N 82 48W
New Hazelton, *Canada* **72 B3** 55 20N 127 30W
New Hebrides = Vanuatu ■, *Pac. Oc.* **64 J8** 15 0S 168 0 E
New Iberia, *U.S.A.* **81 K9** 30 1N 91 49W
New Ireland, *Papua N. G.* **64 H7** 3 20S 151 50 E
New Jersey □, *U.S.A.* **79 F10** 40 0N 74 30W
New Kensington, *U.S.A.* **78 F5** 40 34N 79 46W
New Lexington, *U.S.A.* **76 F4** 39 43N 82 13W
New Liskeard, *Canada* **70 C4** 47 31N 79 41W
New London, *Conn., U.S.A.* **79 E12** 41 22N 72 6W
New London, *Minn., U.S.A.* **80 C7** 45 18N 94 56W
New London, *Ohio, U.S.A.* **78 E2** 41 5N 82 24W
New London, *Wis., U.S.A.* **80 C10** 44 23N 88 45W
New Madrid, *U.S.A.* **81 G10** 36 36N 89 32W
New Meadows, *U.S.A.* **82 D5** 44 58N 116 18W
New Melones L., *U.S.A.* **84 H6** 37 57N 120 31W
New Mexico □, *U.S.A.* **83 J10** 34 30N 106 0W
New Milford, *Conn., U.S.A.* **79 E11** 41 35N 73 25W
New Milford, *Pa., U.S.A.* **79 E9** 41 52N 75 44W
New Norcia, *Australia* **61 F2** 30 57S 116 13 E
New Norfolk, *Australia* **62 G4** 42 46S 147 2 E
New Orleans, *U.S.A.* **81 L9** 29 58N 90 4W
New Philadelphia, *U.S.A.* **78 F3** 40 30N 81 27W
New Plymouth, *N.Z.* **59 H5** 39 4S 174 5 E
New Plymouth, *U.S.A.* **82 E5** 43 58N 116 49W
New Providence, *Bahamas* **88 A4** 25 25N 78 35W
New Quay, *U.K.* **11 E3** 52 13N 4 21W
New Radnor, *U.K.* **11 E4** 52 15N 3 9W
New Richmond, *U.S.A.* **80 C8** 45 7N 92 32W
New Roads, *U.S.A.* **81 K9** 30 42N 91 26W
New Rochelle, *U.S.A.* **79 F11** 40 55N 73 47W
New Rockford, *U.S.A.* **80 B5** 47 41N 99 8W
New Romney, *U.K.* **11 G8** 50 59N 0 57 E
New Ross, *Ireland* **13 D5** 52 23N 6 57W
New Salem, *U.S.A.* **80 B4** 46 51N 101 25W
New Scone, *U.K.* **12 E5** 56 25N 3 24W
New Siberian I. = Novaya Sibir, Ostrov, *Russia* **27 B16** 75 10N 150 0 E
New Siberian Is. = Novosibirskiye Ostrova, *Russia* **27 B15** 75 0N 142 0 E
New Smyrna Beach, *U.S.A.* **77 L5** 29 1N 80 56W
New South Wales □, *Australia* **63 E4** 33 0S 146 0 E
New Springs, *Australia* **61 E3** 25 49S 120 1 E
New Town, *U.S.A.* **80 B3** 47 59N 102 30W
New Tredegar, *U.K.* **11 F4** 51 44N 3 16W
New Ulm, *U.S.A.* **80 C7** 44 19N 94 28W
New Waterford, *Canada* **71 C7** 46 13N 60 4W
New Westminster, *Canada* **72 D4** 49 13N 122 55W
New York □, *U.S.A.* **79 D9** 43 0N 75 0W
New York City, *U.S.A.* **79 F11** 40 45N 74 0W
New Zealand ■, *Oceania* **59 J6** 40 0S 176 0 E
Newala, *Tanzania* **55 E4** 10 58S 39 18 E
Newala □, *Tanzania* **55 E4** 10 46S 39 20 E
Newark, *Del., U.S.A.* **76 F8** 39 41N 75 46W
Newark, *N.J., U.S.A.* **79 F10** 40 44N 74 10W
Newark, *N.Y., U.S.A.* **78 C7** 43 3N 77 6W
Newark, *Ohio, U.S.A.* **78 F2** 40 3N 82 24W
Newark-on-Trent, *U.K.* **10 D7** 53 5N 0 48W
Newaygo, *U.S.A.* **76 D3** 43 25N 85 48W
Newberg, *U.S.A.* **82 D2** 45 18N 122 58W
Newberry, *Mich., U.S.A.* **76 B3** 46 21N 85 30W

North Rhine Westphalia

Newberry, *S.C., U.S.A.* **77 H5** 34 17N 81 37W
Newberry Springs, *U.S.A.* **85 L10** 34 50N 116 41W
Newbridge = Droichead Nua, *Ireland* **13 C5** 53 11N 6 48W
Newbrook, *Canada* **72 C6** 54 24N 112 57W
Newburgh, *U.S.A.* **79 E10** 41 30N 74 1W
Newbury, *U.K.* **11 F6** 51 24N 1 20W
Newbury, *U.S.A.* **79 B12** 43 19N 72 3W
Newburyport, *U.S.A.* **79 D14** 42 49N 70 53W
Newcastle, *Australia* **63 E5** 33 0S 151 46 E
Newcastle, *Canada* **71 C6** 47 1N 65 38W
Newcastle, *S. Africa* **57 D4** 27 45S 29 58 E
Newcastle, *U.K.* **13 B6** 54 13N 5 54W
Newcastle, *Calif., U.S.A.* **84 G5** 38 53N 121 8W
Newcastle, *Wyo., U.S.A.* **80 D2** 43 50N 104 11W
Newcastle Emlyn, *U.K.* **11 E3** 52 2N 4 28W
Newcastle Ra., *Australia* **60 C5** 15 45S 130 15 E
Newcastle-under-Lyme, *U.K.* **10 D5** 53 1N 2 14W
Newcastle-upon-Tyne, *U.K.* **10 C6** 54 58N 1 36W
Newcastle Waters, *Australia* **62 B1** 17 30S 133 28 E
Newcastle West, *Ireland* **13 D2** 52 27N 9 3W
Newdegate, *Australia* **61 F2** 33 6S 119 0 E
Newell, *U.S.A.* **80 C3** 44 43N 103 25W
Newfoundland □, *Canada* **71 B8** 53 0N 58 0W
Newfoundland I., *N. Amer.* **66 E14** 49 0N 55 0W
Newhalem, *U.S.A.* **72 D4** 48 40N 121 15W
Newhall, *U.S.A.* **85 L8** 34 23N 118 32W
Newhaven, *U.K.* **11 G8** 50 47N 0 3 E
Newkirk, *U.S.A.* **81 G6** 36 53N 97 3W
Newlyn, *U.K.* **11 G2** 50 6N 5 34W
Newman, *Australia* **60 D2** 23 18S 119 45 E
Newman, *U.S.A.* **84 H5** 37 19N 121 1W
Newmarket, *Canada* **78 B5** 44 3N 79 28W
Newmarket, *Ireland* **13 D2** 52 13N 9 0W
Newmarket, *U.K.* **11 E8** 52 15N 0 25 E
Newmarket, *U.S.A.* **79 C14** 43 5N 70 56W
Newnan, *U.S.A.* **77 J3** 33 23N 84 48W
Newport, *Ireland* **13 C2** 53 53N 9 33W
Newport, *I. of W., U.K.* **11 G6** 50 42N 1 17W
Newport, *Newp., U.K.* **11 F5** 51 35N 3 0W
Newport, *Ark., U.S.A.* **81 H9** 35 37N 91 16W
Newport, *Ky., U.S.A.* **76 F3** 39 5N 84 30W
Newport, *N.H., U.S.A.* **79 C12** 43 22N 72 10W
Newport, *Oreg., U.S.A.* **82 D1** 44 39N 124 3W
Newport, *Pa., U.S.A.* **78 F7** 40 29N 77 8W
Newport, *R.I., U.S.A.* **79 E13** 41 29N 71 19W
Newport, *Tenn., U.S.A.* **77 H4** 35 58N 83 11W
Newport, *Vt., U.S.A.* **79 B12** 44 56N 72 13W
Newport, *Wash., U.S.A.* **82 B5** 48 11N 117 3W
Newport □, *U.K.* **11 F4** 51 33N 3 1W
Newport Beach, *U.S.A.* **85 M9** 33 37N 117 56W
Newport News, *U.S.A.* **76 G7** 36 59N 76 25W
Newport Pagnell, *U.K.* **11 E7** 52 5N 0 43W
Newquay, *U.K.* **11 G2** 50 25N 5 6W
Newry, *U.K.* **13 B5** 54 11N 6 21W
Newton, *Iowa, U.S.A.* **80 E8** 41 42N 93 3W
Newton, *Mass., U.S.A.* **79 D13** 42 21N 71 12W
Newton, *Miss., U.S.A.* **81 J10** 32 19N 89 10W
Newton, *N.C., U.S.A.* **77 H5** 35 40N 81 13W
Newton, *N.J., U.S.A.* **79 E10** 41 3N 74 45W
Newton, *Tex., U.S.A.* **81 K8** 30 51N 93 46W
Newton Abbot, *U.K.* **11 G4** 50 32N 3 37W
Newton Aycliffe, *U.K.* **10 C6** 54 37N 1 34W
Newton Boyd, *Australia* **63 D5** 29 45S 152 16 E
Newton Stewart, *U.K.* **12 G4** 54 57N 4 30W
Newtonmore, *U.K.* **12 D4** 57 4N 4 8W
Newtown, *U.K.* **11 E4** 52 31N 3 19W
Newtownabbey, *U.K.* **13 B6** 54 40N 5 56W
Newtownards, *U.K.* **13 B6** 54 36N 5 42W
Newtownbarry = Bunclody, *Ireland* **13 D5** 52 39N 6 40W
Newtownstewart, *U.K.* **13 B4** 54 43N 7 23W
Newville, *U.S.A.* **78 F7** 40 10N 77 24W
Neya, *Russia* **24 C7** 58 21N 43 49 E
Neyrīz, *Iran* **45 D7** 29 15N 54 19 E
Neyshābūr, *Iran* **45 B8** 36 10N 58 50 E
Nezhin = Nizhyn, *Ukraine* **25 D5** 51 5N 31 55 E
Nezperce, *U.S.A.* **82 C5** 46 14N 116 14W
Ngabang, *Indonesia* **36 D3** 0 23N 109 55 E
Ngabordamlu, Tanjung, *Indonesia* **37 F8** 6 56S 134 11 E
Ngami Depression, *Botswana* **56 C3** 20 30S 22 46 E
Ngamo, *Zimbabwe* **55 F2** 19 3S 27 32 E
Nganglong Kangri, *China* **41 C12** 33 0N 81 0 E
Ngao, *Thailand* **38 C2** 18 46N 99 59 E
Ngaoundéré, *Cameroon* **52 C2** 7 15N 13 35 E
Ngapara, *N.Z.* **59 L3** 44 57S 170 46 E
Ngara, *Tanzania* **54 C3** 2 29S 30 40 E
Ngara □, *Tanzania* **54 C3** 2 29S 30 40 E
Ngawi, *Indonesia* **37 G14** 7 24S 111 26 E
Nghia Lo, *Vietnam* **38 B5** 21 33N 104 28 E
Ngoma, *Malawi* **55 E3** 13 8S 33 45 E
Ngomahura, *Zimbabwe* **55 G3** 20 26S 30 43 E
Ngomba, *Tanzania* **55 D3** 8 20S 32 53 E
Ngoring Hu, *China* **32 C4** 34 55N 97 5 E
Ngorongoro, *Tanzania* **54 C4** 3 11S 35 32 E
Ngozi, *Burundi* **54 C2** 2 54S 29 50 E
Ngudu, *Tanzania* **54 C3** 2 58S 33 25 E
Nguigmi, *Niger* **51 F8** 14 20N 13 20 E
Ngukurr, *Australia* **62 A1** 14 44S 134 44 E
Ngunga, *Tanzania* **54 C3** 3 37S 33 37 E
Nguru, *Nigeria* **51 F8** 12 56N 10 29 E
Nguru Mts., *Tanzania* **54 D4** 6 0S 37 30 E
Nguyen Binh, *Vietnam* **38 A5** 22 39N 105 56 E
Nha Trang, *Vietnam* **39 F7** 12 16N 109 10 E
Nhacoongo, *Mozam.* **57 C6** 24 18S 35 14 E
Nhamaabué, *Mozam.* **55 F4** 17 25S 35 5 E
Nhamundá →, *Brazil* **93 D7** 2 12S 56 41W
Nhangutazi, L., *Mozam.* **57 C5** 24 0S 34 30 E
Nhill, *Australia* **63 F3** 36 18S 141 40 E
Nho Quan, *Vietnam* **38 B5** 20 18N 105 45 E
Nhulunbuy, *Australia* **62 A2** 12 10S 137 20 E
Nia-nia, *Dem. Rep. of the Congo* **54 B2** 1 30N 27 40 E
Niagara, *U.S.A.* **76 C2** 45 45N 88 0W
Niagara Falls, *Canada* **70 D4** 43 7N 79 5W
Niagara Falls, *U.S.A.* **78 C6** 43 5N 79 4W
Niagara-on-the-Lake, *Canada* **78 C5** 43 15N 79 4W
Niah, *Malaysia* **36 D4** 3 58N 113 46 E
Niamey, *Niger* **50 F6** 13 27N 2 6 E
Niangara, *Dem. Rep. of the Congo* **54 B2** 3 42N 27 50 E
Nias, *Indonesia* **36 D1** 1 0N 97 30 E
Niassa □, *Mozam.* **55 E4** 13 30S 36 0 E
Nicaragua ■, *Cent. Amer.* **88 D2** 11 40N 85 30W
Nicaragua, L. de, *Nic.* **88 D2** 12 0N 85 30W
Nicastro, *Italy* **20 E7** 38 59N 16 19 E
Nice, *France* **18 E7** 43 42N 7 14 E
Niceville, *U.S.A.* **77 K2** 30 31N 86 30W
Nichinan, *Japan* **31 J5** 31 38N 131 23 E
Nicholás, Canal, *W. Indies* **88 B3** 23 30N 80 5W
Nicholasville, *U.S.A.* **76 G3** 37 53N 84 34W
Nichols, *U.S.A.* **79 D8** 42 1N 76 22W
Nicholson, *Australia* **60 C4** 18 2S 128 54 E
Nicholson, *U.S.A.* **79 E9** 41 37N 75 47W
Nicholson →, *Australia* **62 B2** 17 31S 139 36 E
Nicholson Ra., *Australia* **61 E2** 27 15S 116 45 E
Nicobar Is., *Ind. Oc.* **28 J13** 9 0N 93 0 E
Nicola, *Canada* **72 C4** 50 12N 120 40W
Nicolet, *Canada* **70 C5** 46 17N 72 35W
Nicolls Town, *Bahamas* **88 A4** 25 8N 78 0W
Nicosia, *Cyprus* **23 D12** 35 10N 33 25 E
Nicoya, *Costa Rica* **88 D2** 10 9N 85 27W
Nicoya, G. de, *Costa Rica* **88 E3** 10 0N 85 0W
Nicoya, Pen. de, *Costa Rica* **88 E2** 9 45N 85 40W
Nidd →, *U.K.* **10 D6** 53 59N 1 23W
Niedersachsen □, *Germany* **16 B5** 52 50N 9 0 E
Niekerkshoop, *S. Africa* **56 D3** 29 19S 22 51 E
Niemba, *Dem. Rep. of the Congo* **54 D2** 5 58S 28 24 E
Niemen = Neman →, *Lithuania* **24 C3** 55 25N 21 10 E
Nienburg, *Germany* **16 B5** 52 39N 9 13 E
Nieu Bethesda, *S. Africa* **56 E3** 31 51S 24 34 E
Nieuw Amsterdam, *Surinam* **93 B7** 5 53N 55 5W
Nieuw Nickerie, *Surinam* **93 B7** 6 0N 56 59W
Nieuwoudtville, *S. Africa* **56 E2** 31 23S 19 7 E
Nieuwpoort, *Belgium* **15 C2** 51 8N 2 45 E
Nieves, Pico de las, *Canary Is.* **22 G4** 27 57N 15 35W
Niğde, *Turkey* **25 G5** 37 58N 34 40 E
Nigel, *S. Africa* **57 D4** 26 27S 28 25 E
Niger ■, *W. Afr.* **50 E7** 17 30N 10 0 E
Niger →, *W. Afr.* **50 G7** 5 33N 6 33 E
Nigeria ■, *W. Afr.* **50 G7** 8 30N 8 0 E
Nightcaps, *N.Z.* **59 L2** 45 57S 168 2 E
Nihtaur, *India* **43 E8** 29 20N 78 23 E
Nii-Jima, *Japan* **31 G9** 34 20N 139 15 E
Niigata, *Japan* **30 F9** 37 58N 139 0 E
Niigata □, *Japan* **31 F9** 37 15N 138 45 E
Niihama, *Japan* **31 H6** 33 55N 133 16 E
Niihau, *U.S.A.* **74 H14** 21 54N 160 9W
Niimi, *Japan* **31 G6** 34 59N 133 28 E
Niitsu, *Japan* **30 F9** 37 48N 139 7 E
Nijil, *Jordan* **47 E4** 30 32N 35 33 E
Nijkerk, *Neths.* **15 B5** 52 13N 5 30 E
Nijmegen, *Neths.* **15 C5** 51 50N 5 52 E
Nijverdal, *Neths.* **15 B6** 52 22N 6 28 E
Nīk Pey, *Iran* **45 B6** 36 50N 48 10 E
Nikiniki, *Indonesia* **37 F6** 9 49S 124 30 E
Nikkō, *Japan* **31 F9** 36 45N 139 35 E
Nikolayev = Mykolayiv, *Ukraine* **25 E5** 46 58N 32 0 E
Nikolayevsk, *Russia* **25 E8** 50 0N 45 35 E
Nikolayevsk-na-Amur, *Russia* **27 D15** 53 8N 140 44 E
Nikolskoye, *Russia* **27 D17** 55 12N 166 0 E
Nikopol, *Ukraine* **25 E5** 47 35N 34 25 E
Nīkshahr, *Iran* **45 E9** 26 15N 60 10 E
Nikšić, *Montenegro, Yug.* **21 C8** 42 50N 18 57 E
Nîl, Nahr en →, *Africa* **51 B12** 30 10N 31 6 E
Nîl el Abyad →, *Sudan* **51 E12** 15 38N 32 31 E
Nîl el Azraq →, *Sudan* **51 E12** 15 38N 32 31 E
Niland, *U.S.A.* **85 M11** 33 14N 115 31W
Nile = Nîl, Nahr en →, *Africa* **51 B12** 30 10N 31 6 E
Niles, *U.S.A.* **78 E4** 41 11N 80 46W
Nimach, *India* **42 G6** 24 30N 74 56 E
Nimbahera, *India* **42 G6** 24 37N 74 45 E
Nîmes, *France* **18 E6** 43 50N 4 23 E
Nimfaíon, Ákra = Pínnes, Ákra, *Greece* **21 D11** 40 5N 24 20 E
Nimmitabel, *Australia* **63 F4** 36 29S 149 15 E
Nīnawá, *Iraq* **44 B4** 36 25N 43 10 E
Nindigully, *Australia* **63 D4** 28 21S 148 50 E
Ninemile, *U.S.A.* **72 B2** 56 0N 130 7W
Nineveh = Nīnawá, *Iraq* **44 B4** 36 25N 43 10 E
Ning Xian, *China* **34 G4** 35 30N 107 58 E
Ningaloo, *Australia* **60 D1** 22 41S 113 41 E
Ning'an, *China* **35 B15** 44 22N 129 20 E
Ningbo, *China* **33 D7** 29 51N 121 28 E
Ningcheng, *China* **35 D10** 41 32N 119 53 E
Ningjin, *China* **34 F8** 37 35N 114 57 E
Ningjing Shan, *China* **32 D4** 30 0N 98 20 E
Ningling, *China* **34 G8** 34 25N 115 22 E
Ningpo = Ningbo, *China* **33 D7** 29 51N 121 28 E
Ningqiang, *China* **34 H4** 32 47N 106 15 E
Ningshan, *China* **34 H5** 33 21N 108 21 E
Ningsia Hui A.R. = Ningxia Huizu Zizhiqu □, *China* **34 F4** 38 0N 106 0 E
Ningwu, *China* **34 E7** 39 0N 112 18 E
Ningxia Huizu Zizhiqu □, *China* **34 F4** 38 0N 106 0 E
Ningyang, *China* **34 G9** 35 47N 116 45 E
Ninh Binh, *Vietnam* **38 B5** 20 15N 105 55 E
Ninh Giang, *Vietnam* **38 B6** 20 44N 106 24 E
Ninh Hoa, *Vietnam* **38 F7** 12 30N 109 7 E
Ninh Ma, *Vietnam* **38 F7** 12 48N 109 21 E
Ninove, *Belgium* **15 D4** 50 51N 4 2 E
Nioaque, *Brazil* **95 A4** 21 5S 55 50W
Niobrara, *U.S.A.* **80 D6** 42 45N 98 2W
Niobrara →, *U.S.A.* **80 D6** 42 46N 98 3W
Nioro du Sahel, *Mali* **50 E4** 15 15N 9 30W
Niort, *France* **18 C3** 46 19N 0 29W
Nipawin, *Canada* **73 C8** 53 20N 104 0W
Nipawin Prov. Park, *Canada* **73 C8** 54 0N 104 37W
Nipigon, *Canada* **70 C2** 49 0N 88 17W
Nipigon, L., *Canada* **70 C2** 49 50N 88 30W
Nipin →, *Canada* **73 B7** 55 46N 108 35W
Nipishish L., *Canada* **71 B7** 54 12N 60 45W
Nipissing L., *Canada* **70 C4** 46 20N 80 0W
Nipomo, *U.S.A.* **85 K6** 35 3N 120 29W
Nipton, *U.S.A.* **85 K11** 35 28N 115 16W
Niquelândia, *Brazil* **93 F9** 14 33S 48 23W
Nīr, *Iran* **44 B5** 38 2N 47 59 E
Nirasaki, *Japan* **31 G9** 35 42N 138 27 E
Nirmal, *India* **40 K11** 19 3N 78 20 E
Nirmali, *India* **43 F12** 26 20N 86 35 E
Niš, *Serbia, Yug.* **21 C9** 43 19N 21 58 E
Nişāb, *Si. Arabia* **44 D5** 29 11N 44 43 E
Nişāb, *Yemen* **46 E4** 14 25N 46 29 E
Nishinomiya, *Japan* **31 G7** 34 45N 135 20 E
Nishino'omote, *Japan* **31 J5** 30 43N 130 59 E
Nishiwaki, *Japan* **31 G7** 34 59N 134 58 E
Niskibi →, *Canada* **70 A2** 56 29N 88 9W
Nisqually →, *U.S.A.* **84 C4** 47 6N 122 42W
Nissáki, *Greece* **23 A3** 39 43N 19 52 E
Nissum Bredning, *Denmark* **9 H13** 56 40N 8 20 E
Nistru = Dnister →, *Europe* **25 E5** 46 18N 30 17 E
Nisutlin →, *Canada* **72 A2** 60 14N 132 34W
Nitchequon, *Canada* **71 B5** 53 10N 70 58W
Niterói, *Brazil* **95 A7** 22 52S 43 0W
Nith →, *U.K.* **12 F5** 55 14N 3 33W
Nitra, *Slovak Rep.* **17 D10** 48 19N 18 4 E
Nitra →, *Slovak Rep.* **17 E10** 47 46N 18 10 E
Niuafo'ou, *Tonga* **59 B11** 15 30S 175 58W
Niue, *Cook Is.* **65 J11** 19 2S 169 54W
Niut, *Indonesia* **36 D4** 0 55N 110 6 E
Niuzhuang, *China* **35 D12** 40 58N 122 28 E
Nivala, *Finland* **8 E21** 63 56N 24 57 E
Nivelles, *Belgium* **15 D4** 50 35N 4 20 E
Nivernais, *France* **18 C5** 47 15N 3 30 E
Nixon, *U.S.A.* **81 L6** 29 16N 97 46W
Nizamabad, *India* **40 K11** 18 45N 78 7 E
Nizamghat, *India* **41 E19** 28 20N 95 45 E
Nizhne Kolymsk, *Russia* **27 C17** 68 34N 160 55 E
Nizhnekamsk, *Russia* **24 C9** 55 38N 51 49 E
Nizhneudinsk, *Russia* **27 D10** 54 54N 99 3 E
Nizhnevartovsk, *Russia* **26 C8** 60 56N 76 38 E
Nizhniy Novgorod, *Russia* **24 C7** 56 20N 44 0 E
Nizhniy Tagil, *Russia* **24 C10** 57 55N 59 57 E
Nizhyn, *Ukraine* **25 D5** 51 5N 31 55 E
Nízké Tatry, *Slovak Rep.* **17 D10** 48 55N 19 30 E
Njakwa, *Malawi* **55 E3** 11 1S 33 56 E
Njanji, *Zambia* **55 E3** 14 25S 31 46 E
Njinjo, *Tanzania* **55 D4** 8 48S 38 54 E
Njombe, *Tanzania* **55 D3** 9 20S 34 50 E
Njombe □, *Tanzania* **55 D3** 9 20S 34 49 E
Njombe →, *Tanzania* **54 D4** 6 56S 35 6 E
Nkana, *Zambia* **55 E2** 12 50S 28 8 E
Nkayi, *Zimbabwe* **55 F2** 19 41S 29 20 E
Nkhotakota, *Malawi* **55 E3** 12 56S 34 15 E
Nkongsamba, *Cameroon* **52 D1** 4 55N 9 55 E
Nkurenkuru, *Namibia* **56 B2** 17 42S 18 32 E
Nmai →, *Burma* **41 G20** 25 30N 97 25 E
Noakhali = Maijdi, *Bangla.* **41 H17** 22 48N 91 10 E
Nobel, *Canada* **78 A4** 45 25N 80 6W
Nobeoka, *Japan* **31 H5** 32 36N 131 41 E
Noblesville, *U.S.A.* **76 E3** 40 3N 86 1W
Nocera Inferiore, *Italy* **20 D6** 40 44N 14 38 E
Nockatunga, *Australia* **63 D3** 27 42S 142 42 E
Nocona, *U.S.A.* **81 J6** 33 47N 97 44W
Noda, *Japan* **31 G9** 35 56N 139 52 E
Noel, *U.S.A.* **81 G7** 36 33N 94 29W
Nogales, *Mexico* **86 A2** 31 20N 110 56W
Nogales, *U.S.A.* **83 L8** 31 20N 110 56W
Nōgata, *Japan* **31 H5** 33 48N 130 44 E
Noggerup, *Australia* **61 F2** 33 32S 116 5 E
Noginsk, *Russia* **27 C10** 64 30N 90 50 E
Nogoa →, *Australia* **62 C4** 23 40S 147 55 E
Nogoyá, *Argentina* **94 C4** 32 24S 59 48W
Nohar, *India* **42 E6** 29 11N 74 49 E
Noire, Mts., *France* **18 B2** 48 7N 3 28W
Noirmoutier, Î. de, *France* **18 C2** 46 58N 2 10W
Nojane, *Botswana* **56 C3** 23 15S 20 14 E
Nojima-Zaki, *Japan* **31 G9** 34 54N 139 53 E
Nok Kundi, *Pakistan* **40 E3** 28 50N 62 45 E
Nokaneng, *Botswana* **56 B3** 19 40S 22 17 E
Nokia, *Finland* **9 F20** 61 30N 23 30 E
Nokomis, *Canada* **73 C8** 51 35N 105 0W
Nokomis L., *Canada* **73 B8** 57 0N 103 0W
Nola, *C.A.R.* **52 D3** 3 35N 16 4 E
Noma Omuramba →, *Namibia* **56 B3** 18 52S 20 53 E
Noman L., *Canada* **73 A7** 62 15N 108 55W
Nombre de Dios, *Panama* **88 E4** 9 34N 79 28W
Nome, *U.S.A.* **68 B3** 64 30N 165 25W
Nomo-Zaki, *Japan* **31 H4** 32 35N 129 44 E
Nonacho L., *Canada* **73 A7** 61 42N 109 40W
Nonda, *Australia* **62 C3** 20 40S 142 28 E
Nong Chang, *Thailand* **38 E2** 15 23N 99 51 E
Nong Het, *Laos* **38 C4** 19 29N 103 59 E
Nong Khai, *Thailand* **38 D4** 17 50N 102 46 E
Nong'an, *China* **35 B13** 44 25N 125 5 E
Nongoma, *S. Africa* **57 D5** 27 58S 31 35 E
Nonoava, *Mexico* **86 B3** 27 28N 106 44W
Nonthaburi, *Thailand* **38 F3** 13 51N 100 34 E
Noonamah, *Australia* **60 B5** 12 40S 131 4 E
Noonan, *U.S.A.* **80 A3** 48 54N 103 1W
Noondoo, *Australia* **63 D4** 28 35S 148 30 E
Noonkanbah, *Australia* **60 C3** 18 30S 124 50 E
Noord Brabant □, *Neths.* **15 C5** 51 40N 5 0 E
Noord Holland □, *Neths.* **15 B4** 52 30N 4 45 E
Noordbeveland, *Neths.* **15 C3** 51 35N 3 50 E
Noordoostpolder, *Neths.* **15 B5** 52 45N 5 45 E
Noordwijk, *Neths.* **15 B4** 52 14N 4 26 E
Nootka, *Canada* **72 D3** 49 38N 126 38W
Nootka I., *Canada* **72 D3** 49 32N 126 42W
Noranda = Rouyn-Noranda, *Canada* **70 C4** 48 20N 79 0W
Norco, *U.S.A.* **85 M9** 33 56N 117 33W
Nord-Ostsee-Kanal →, *Germany* **16 A5** 54 12N 9 32 E
Nordegg, *Canada* **72 C5** 52 29N 116 5W
Norderney, *Germany* **16 B4** 53 42N 7 9 E
Norderstedt, *Germany* **16 B5** 53 42N 10 1 E
Nordfjord, *Norway* **9 F11** 61 55N 5 30 E
Nordfriesische Inseln, *Germany* **16 A5** 54 40N 8 20 E
Nordhausen, *Germany* **16 C6** 51 30N 10 47 E
Norðoyar, *Færoe Is.* **8 E9** 62 17N 6 35W
Nordkapp, *Norway* **8 A21** 71 10N 25 50 E
Nordkinn = Kinnarodden, *Norway* **6 A11** 71 8N 27 40 E
Nordkinn-halvøya, *Norway* **8 A22** 70 55N 27 40 E
Nordrhein-Westfalen □, *Germany* **16 C4** 51 45N 7 30 E
Nordvik, *Russia* **27 B12** 74 2N 111 32 E
Nore →, *Ireland* **13 D4** 52 25N 6 58W
Norembega, *Canada* **70 C3** 48 59N 80 43W
Norfolk, *Nebr., U.S.A.* **80 D6** 42 2N 97 25W
Norfolk, *Va., U.S.A.* **76 G7** 36 51N 76 17W
Norfolk □, *U.K.* **11 E8** 52 39N 0 54 E
Norfolk I., *Pac. Oc.* **64 K8** 28 58S 168 3 E
Norfork Res., *U.S.A.* **81 G8** 36 13N 92 15W
Norilsk, *Russia* **27 C9** 69 20N 88 6 E
Norley, *Australia* **63 D3** 27 45S 143 48 E
Norma, Mt., *Australia* **62 C3** 20 55S 140 42 E
Normal, *U.S.A.* **80 E10** 40 31N 88 59W
Norman, *U.S.A.* **81 H6** 35 13N 97 26W
Norman →, *Australia* **62 B3** 19 18S 141 51 E
Norman Wells, *Canada* **68 B7** 65 17N 126 51W
Normanby →, *Australia* **62 A3** 14 23S 144 10 E
Normandie, *France* **18 B4** 48 45N 0 10 E
Normandin, *Canada* **70 C5** 48 49N 72 31W
Normandy = Normandie, *France* **18 B4** 48 45N 0 10 E
Normanhurst, Mt., *Australia* **61 E3** 25 4S 122 30 E
Normanton, *Australia* **62 B3** 17 40S 141 10 E
Norquay, *Canada* **73 C8** 51 53N 102 5W
Norquinco, *Argentina* **96 E2** 41 51S 70 55W
Norrbotten □, *Sweden* **8 C19** 66 30N 22 30 E
Norris, *U.S.A.* **82 D8** 45 34N 111 41W
Norristown, *U.S.A.* **79 F9** 40 7N 75 21W
Norrköping, *Sweden* **9 G17** 58 37N 16 11 E
Norrland, *Sweden* **9 E16** 62 15N 15 45 E
Norrtälje, *Sweden* **9 G18** 59 46N 18 42 E
Norseman, *Australia* **61 F3** 32 8S 121 43 E
Norsk, *Russia* **27 D14** 52 30N 130 5 E
Norte, Pta. del, *Canary Is.* **22 G2** 27 51N 17 57W
Norte, Serra do, *Brazil* **92 F7** 11 20S 59 0W
North Adams, *U.S.A.* **79 D11** 42 42N 73 7W
North Ayrshire □, *U.K.* **12 F4** 55 45N 4 44W
North Battleford, *Canada* **73 C7** 52 50N 108 17W
North Bay, *Canada* **70 C4** 46 20N 79 30W
North Belcher Is., *Canada* **70 A4** 56 50N 79 50W
North Bend, *Canada* **72 D4** 49 50N 121 27W
North Bend, *Oreg., U.S.A.* **82 E1** 43 24N 124 14W
North Bend, *Pa., U.S.A.* **78 E7** 41 20N 77 42W
North Bend, *Wash., U.S.A.* **84 C5** 47 30N 121 47W
North Berwick, *U.K.* **12 E6** 56 4N 2 42W
North Berwick, *U.S.A.* **79 C14** 43 18N 70 44W
North C., *Canada* **71 C7** 47 2N 60 20W
North C., *N.Z.* **59 F4** 34 23S 173 4 E
North Canadian →, *U.S.A.* **81 H7** 35 16N 95 31W
North Cape = Nordkapp, *Norway* **8 A21** 71 10N 25 50 E
North Caribou L., *Canada* **70 B1** 52 50N 90 40W
North Carolina □, *U.S.A.* **77 H6** 35 30N 80 0W
North Channel, *Canada* **70 C3** 46 0N 83 0W
North Channel, *U.K.* **12 F3** 55 13N 5 52W
North Charleston, *U.S.A.* **77 J6** 32 53N 79 58W
North Chicago, *U.S.A.* **76 D2** 42 19N 87 51W
North Dakota □, *U.S.A.* **80 B5** 47 30N 100 15W
North Dandalup, *Australia* **61 F2** 32 30S 115 57 E
North Downs, *U.K.* **11 F8** 51 19N 0 21 E
North East, *U.S.A.* **78 D5** 42 13N 79 50W
North East Frontier Agency = Arunachal Pradesh □, *India* **41 F19** 28 0N 95 0 E
North East Lincolnshire □, *U.K.* **10 D7** 53 34N 0 2W
North East Providence Chan., *W. Indies* **88 A4** 26 0N 76 0W
North Eastern □, *Kenya* **54 B5** 1 30N 40 0 E
North Esk →, *U.K.* **12 E6** 56 46N 2 24W
North European Plain, *Europe* **6 E10** 55 0N 25 0 E
North Foreland, *U.K.* **11 F9** 51 22N 1 28 E
North Fork, *U.S.A.* **84 H7** 37 14N 119 21W
North Fork American →, *U.S.A.* **84 G5** 38 57N 120 59W
North Fork Feather →, *U.S.A.* **84 F5** 38 33N 121 30W
North Frisian Is. = Nordfriesische Inseln, *Germany* **16 A5** 54 40N 8 20 E
North Henik L., *Canada* **73 A9** 61 45N 97 40W
North Highlands, *U.S.A.* **84 G5** 38 40N 121 23W
North Horr, *Kenya* **54 B4** 3 20N 37 8 E
North I., *Kenya* **54 B4** 4 5N 36 5 E
North I., *N.Z.* **59 H5** 38 0S 175 0 E
North Kingsville, *U.S.A.* **78 E4** 41 54N 80 42W
North Knife →, *Canada* **73 B10** 58 53N 94 45W
North Koel →, *India* **43 G10** 24 45N 83 50 E
North Korea ■, *Asia* **35 E14** 40 0N 127 0 E
North Lakhimpur, *India* **41 F19** 27 14N 94 7 E
North Lanarkshire □, *U.K.* **12 F5** 55 52N 3 56W
North Las Vegas, *U.S.A.* **85 J11** 36 12N 115 7W
North Lincolnshire □, *U.K.* **10 D7** 53 36N 0 30W
North Little Rock, *U.S.A.* **81 H8** 34 45N 92 16W
North Loup →, *U.S.A.* **80 E5** 41 17N 98 24W
North Minch, *U.K.* **12 C3** 58 5N 5 55W
North Nahanni →, *Canada* **72 A4** 62 15N 123 20W
North Olmsted, *U.S.A.* **78 E3** 41 25N 81 56W
North Ossetia □, *Russia* **25 F7** 43 30N 44 30 E
North Pagai, I. = Pagai Utara, Pulau, *Indonesia* **36 E2** 2 35S 100 0 E
North Palisade, *U.S.A.* **84 H8** 37 6N 118 31W
North Platte, *U.S.A.* **80 E4** 41 8N 100 46W
North Platte →, *U.S.A.* **80 E4** 41 7N 100 42W
North Portal, *Canada* **73 D8** 49 0N 102 33W
North Powder, *U.S.A.* **82 D5** 45 2N 117 55W
North Pt., *Canada* **71 C7** 47 5N 64 0W
North Rhine Westphalia □ = Nordrhein-Westfalen □, *Germany* **16 C4** 51 45N 7 30 E

North Ronaldsay

North Ronaldsay, U.K. **12 B6** 59 22N 2 26W
North Saskatchewan →, Canada **73 C7** 53 15N 105 5W
North Sea, Europe **6 D6** 56 0N 4 0 E
North Somerset □, U.K. **11 F5** 51 24N 2 45W
North Sporades = Vóriai Sporádhes, Greece **21 E10** 39 15N 23 30 E
North Sydney, Canada **71 C7** 46 12N 60 15W
North Taranaki Bight, N.Z. **59 H5** 38 50S 174 15 E
North Thompson →, Canada **72 C4** 50 40N 120 20W
North Tonawanda, U.S.A. **78 C6** 43 2N 78 53W
North Troy, U.S.A. **79 B12** 45 0N 72 24W
North Truchas Pk., U.S.A. **83 J11** 36 0N 105 30W
North Twin I., Canada **70 B4** 53 20N 80 0W
North Tyne →, U.K. **10 B5** 55 0N 2 8W
North Uist, U.K. **12 D1** 57 40N 7 15W
North Vancouver, Canada **72 D4** 49 25N 123 3W
North Vernon, U.S.A. **76 F3** 39 0N 85 38W
North Wabasca L., Canada **72 B6** 56 0N 113 55W
North Walsham, U.K. **10 E9** 52 50N 1 22 E
North-West □, S. Africa **56 D4** 27 0S 25 0 E
North West C., Australia **60 D1** 21 45S 114 9 E
North West Christmas I. Ridge, Pac. Oc. **65 G11** 6 30N 165 0W
North West Frontier □, Pakistan **42 C4** 34 0N 72 0 E
North West Highlands, U.K. **12 D4** 57 33N 4 58W
North West Providence Channel, W. Indies **88 A4** 26 0N 78 0W
North West River, Canada **71 B7** 53 30N 60 10W
North Western □, Zambia **55 E2** 13 30S 25 30 E
North York Moors, U.K. **10 C7** 54 23N 0 53W
North Yorkshire □, U.K. **10 C6** 54 15N 1 25W
Northallerton, U.K. **10 C6** 54 20N 1 26W
Northam, S. Africa **56 C4** 24 56S 27 18 E
Northampton, Australia **61 E1** 28 27S 114 33 E
Northampton, U.K. **11 E7** 52 15N 0 53W
Northampton, Mass., U.S.A. **79 D12** 42 19N 72 38W
Northampton, Pa., U.S.A. **79 F9** 40 41N 75 30W
Northampton Downs, Australia **62 C4** 24 35S 145 48 E
Northamptonshire □, U.K. **11 E7** 52 16N 0 55W
Northbridge, U.S.A. **79 D13** 42 9N 71 39W
Northcliffe, Australia **61 F2** 34 39S 116 7 E
Northern □, Malawi **55 E3** 11 0S 34 0 E
Northern □, Uganda **54 B3** 3 5N 32 30 E
Northern □, Zambia **55 E3** 10 30S 31 0 E
Northern Cape □, S. Africa **56 D3** 30 0S 20 0 E
Northern Circars, India **41 L13** 17 30N 82 30 E
Northern Indian L., Canada **73 B9** 57 20N 97 20W
Northern Ireland □, U.K. **13 B5** 54 45N 7 0W
Northern Light, L., Canada **70 C1** 48 15N 90 39W
Northern Marianas ■, Pac. Oc. **64 F6** 17 0N 145 0 E
Northern Territory □, Australia **60 D5** 20 0S 133 0 E
Northern Transvaal □, S. Africa **57 C4** 24 0S 29 0 E
Northfield, U.S.A. **80 C8** 44 27N 93 9W
Northland □, N.Z. **59 F4** 35 30S 173 30 E
Northome, U.S.A. **80 B7** 47 52N 94 17W
Northport, Ala., U.S.A. **77 J2** 33 14N 87 35W
Northport, Mich., U.S.A. **76 C3** 45 8N 85 37W
Northport, Wash., U.S.A. **82 B5** 48 55N 117 48W
Northumberland □, U.K. **10 B6** 55 12N 2 0W
Northumberland, C., Australia **63 F3** 38 5S 140 40 E
Northumberland Is., Australia **62 C4** 21 30S 149 50 E
Northumberland Str., Canada **71 C7** 46 20N 64 0W
Northwest Territories □, Canada **68 B9** 67 0N 110 0W
Northwood, Iowa, U.S.A. **80 D8** 43 27N 93 13W
Northwood, N. Dak., U.S.A. **80 B6** 47 44N 97 34W
Norton, U.S.A. **80 F5** 39 50N 99 53W
Norton, Zimbabwe **55 F3** 17 52S 30 40 E
Norton Sd., U.S.A. **68 B3** 63 50N 164 0W
Norwalk, Calif., U.S.A. **85 M8** 33 54N 118 5W
Norwalk, Conn., U.S.A. **79 E11** 41 7N 73 22W
Norwalk, Ohio, U.S.A. **78 E2** 41 15N 82 37W
Norway, U.S.A. **76 C2** 45 47N 87 55W
Norway ■, Europe **8 E14** 63 0N 11 0 E
Norway House, Canada **73 C9** 53 59N 97 50W
Norwegian Sea, Atl. Oc. **6 B6** 66 0N 1 0 E
Norwich, Canada **78 D4** 42 59N 80 36W
Norwich, U.K. **11 E9** 52 38N 1 18 E
Norwich, Conn., U.S.A. **79 E12** 41 31N 72 5W
Norwich, N.Y., U.S.A. **79 D9** 42 32N 75 32W
Norwood, Canada **78 B7** 44 23N 77 59W
Noshiro, Japan **30 D10** 40 12N 140 0 E
Noss Hd., U.K. **12 C5** 58 28N 3 3W
Nossob →, S. Africa **56 D3** 26 55S 20 45 E
Nosy Be, Madag. **53 G9** 13 25S 48 15 E
Nosy Boraha, Madag. **57 B8** 16 50S 49 55 E
Nosy Varika, Madag. **57 C8** 20 35S 48 32 E
Noteć →, Poland **16 B8** 52 44N 15 26 E
Notigi Dam, Canada **73 B9** 56 40N 99 10W
Notikewin →, Canada **72 B5** 57 2N 117 38W
Notodden, Norway **9 G13** 59 35N 9 17 E
Notre-Dame, Canada **71 C7** 46 18N 64 46W
Notre Dame B., Canada **71 C8** 49 45N 55 30W
Notre Dame de Koartac = Quaqtaq, Canada **69 B13** 60 55N 69 40W
Notre Dame d'Ivugivic = Ivujivik, Canada **69 B12** 62 24N 77 55W
Nottaway →, Canada **70 B4** 51 22N 78 55W
Nottingham, U.K. **10 E6** 52 58N 1 10W
Nottingham, City of □, U.K. **10 E6** 52 58N 1 10W
Nottinghamshire □, U.K. **10 D6** 53 10N 1 3W
Nottoway →, U.S.A. **76 G7** 36 33N 76 55W
Notwane →, Botswana **56 C4** 23 35S 26 58 E
Nouâdhibou, Mauritania **50 D2** 20 54N 17 0W
Nouâdhibou, Ras, Mauritania **50 D2** 20 50N 17 0W
Nouakchott, Mauritania **50 E2** 18 9N 15 58W
Nouméa, N. Cal. **64 K8** 22 17S 166 30 E
Noupoort, S. Africa **56 E3** 31 10S 24 57 E
Nouveau Comptoir = Wemindji, Canada **70 B4** 53 0N 78 49W
Nouvelle-Calédonie = New Caledonia ■, Pac. Oc. **64 K8** 21 0S 165 0 E
Nova Casa Nova, Brazil **93 E10** 9 25S 41 5W
Nova Esperança, Brazil **95 A5** 23 8S 52 24W
Nova Friburgo, Brazil **95 A7** 22 16S 42 30W
Nova Gaia = Cambundi-Catembo, Angola **52 G3** 10 10S 17 35 E
Nova Iguaçu, Brazil **95 A7** 22 45S 43 28W
Nova Iorque, Brazil **93 E10** 7 0S 44 5W
Nova Lima, Brazil **95 A7** 19 59S 43 51W
Nova Lisboa = Huambo, Angola **53 G3** 12 42S 15 54 E
Nova Lusitânia, Mozam. **55 F3** 19 50S 34 34 E
Nova Mambone, Mozam. **57 C6** 21 0S 35 3 E
Nova Scotia □, Canada **71 C7** 45 10N 63 0W
Nova Sofala, Mozam. **57 C5** 20 7S 34 42 E
Nova Venécia, Brazil **93 G10** 18 45S 40 24W
Nova Zagora, Bulgaria **21 C11** 42 32N 26 1 E
Novara, Italy **18 D8** 45 28N 8 38 E
Novato, U.S.A. **84 G4** 38 6N 122 35W
Novaya Ladoga, Russia **24 B5** 60 7N 32 16 E
Novaya Lyalya, Russia **26 D7** 59 4N 60 45 E
Novaya Sibir, Ostrov, Russia **27 B16** 75 10N 150 0 E
Novaya Zemlya, Russia **26 B6** 75 0N 56 0 E
Nové Zámky, Slovak Rep. **17 D10** 48 2N 18 8 E
Novgorod, Russia **24 C5** 58 30N 31 25 E
Novgorod-Severskiy = Novhorod-Siverskyy, Ukraine **24 D5** 52 2N 33 10 E
Novhorod-Siverskyy, Ukraine **24 D5** 52 2N 33 10 E
Novi Lígure, Italy **18 D8** 44 46N 8 47 E
Novi Pazar, Serbia, Yug. **21 C9** 43 12N 20 28 E
Novi Sad, Serbia, Yug. **21 B8** 45 18N 19 52 E
Nôvo Hamburgo, Brazil **95 B5** 29 37S 51 7W
Novo Mesto, Slovenia **20 B6** 45 47N 15 12 E
Novo Remanso, Brazil **93 E10** 9 41S 42 4W
Novoataysk, Russia **26 D9** 53 30N 84 0 E
Novocherkassk, Russia **25 E7** 47 27N 40 15 E
Novogrudok = Navahrudak, Belarus **17 B13** 53 40N 25 50 E
Novohrad-Volynskyy, Ukraine **17 C14** 50 34N 27 35 E
Novokachalinsk, Russia **30 B6** 45 5N 132 0 E
Novokazalinsk = Zhangaqazaly, Kazakstan **26 E7** 45 48N 62 6 E
Novokuybyshevsk, Russia **24 D8** 53 7N 49 58 E
Novokuznetsk, Russia **26 D9** 53 45N 87 10 E
Novomoskovsk, Russia **24 D6** 54 5N 38 15 E
Novorossiysk, Russia **25 F6** 44 43N 37 46 E
Novorybnoye, Russia **27 B11** 72 50N 105 50 E
Novoselytsya, Ukraine **17 D14** 48 14N 26 15 E
Novoshakhtinsk, Russia **25 E6** 47 46N 39 58 E
Novosibirsk, Russia **26 D9** 55 0N 83 5 E
Novosibirskiye Ostrova, Russia **27 B15** 75 0N 142 0 E
Novotroitsk, Russia **26 D6** 51 10N 58 15 E
Novouzensk, Russia **25 D8** 50 32N 48 17 E
Novovolynsk, Ukraine **17 C13** 50 45N 24 4 E
Novska, Croatia **20 B7** 45 19N 17 0 E
Novyy Port, Russia **26 C8** 67 40N 72 30 E
Now Shahr, Iran **45 B6** 36 40N 51 30 E
Nowa Sól, Poland **16 C8** 51 48N 15 44 E
Nowbarān, Iran **45 C6** 35 8N 49 42 E
Nowghāb, Iran **45 C8** 33 53N 59 4 E
Nowgong, India **41 F18** 26 20N 92 50 E
Nowra, Australia **63 E5** 34 53S 150 35 E
Nowshera, Pakistan **40 C8** 34 0N 72 0 E
Nowy Sącz, Poland **17 D11** 49 40N 20 41 E
Nowy Targ, Poland **17 D11** 49 29N 20 2 E
Nowy Tomyśl, Poland **16 B9** 52 19N 16 10 E
Noxen, U.S.A. **79 E8** 41 25N 76 4W
Noxon, U.S.A. **82 C6** 48 0N 115 43W
Noyes I., U.S.A. **72 B2** 55 30N 133 40W
Noyon, France **18 B5** 49 34N 2 59 E
Noyon, Mongolia **34 C2** 43 2N 102 4 E
Nsanje, Malawi **55 F4** 16 55S 35 12 E
Nsomba, Zambia **55 E2** 10 45S 29 51 E
Nu Jiang →, China **32 D4** 29 58N 97 25 E
Nu Shan, China **32 D4** 26 0N 99 20 E
Nubia, Africa **48 D7** 21 0N 32 0 E
Nubian Desert = Nûbîya, Es Sahrâ en, Sudan **51 D12** 21 30N 33 30 E
Nûbîya, Es Sahrâ en, Sudan **51 D12** 21 30N 33 30 E
Ñuble □, Chile **94 D1** 37 0S 72 0W
Nuboai, Indonesia **37 E9** 2 10S 136 30 E
Nubra →, India **43 B7** 34 35N 77 35 E
Nueces →, U.S.A. **81 M6** 27 51N 97 30W
Nueltin L., Canada **73 A9** 60 30N 99 30W
Nueva Asunción □, Paraguay **94 A3** 21 0S 61 0W
Nueva Gerona, Cuba **88 B3** 21 53N 82 49W
Nueva Palmira, Uruguay **94 C4** 33 52S 58 20W
Nueva Rosita, Mexico **86 B4** 28 0N 101 11W
Nueva San Salvador, El Salv. **88 D2** 13 40N 89 18W
Nuéve de Julio, Argentina **94 D3** 35 30S 61 0W
Nuevitas, Cuba **88 B4** 21 30N 77 20W
Nuevo, G., Argentina **96 E4** 43 0S 64 30W
Nuevo Guerrero, Mexico **87 B5** 26 34N 99 15W
Nuevo Laredo, Mexico **87 B5** 27 30N 99 30W
Nuevo León □, Mexico **86 C5** 25 0N 100 0W
Nuevo Rocafuerte, Ecuador **92 D3** 0 55S 75 27W
Nugget Pt., N.Z. **59 M2** 46 27S 169 50 E
Nuhaka, N.Z. **59 H6** 39 3S 177 45 E
Nukey Bluff, Australia **63 E2** 32 26S 135 29 E
Nuku'alofa, Tonga **59 E12** 21 10S 174 0W
Nukus, Uzbekistan **26 E6** 42 27N 59 41 E
Nullagine →, Australia **60 D3** 21 20S 120 20 E
Nullarbor, Australia **61 F5** 31 28S 130 55 E
Nullarbor Plain, Australia **61 F4** 31 10S 129 0 E
Numalla, L., Australia **63 D3** 28 43S 144 20 E
Numan, Nigeria **51 G8** 9 29N 12 3 E
Numata, Japan **31 F9** 36 45N 139 4 E
Numazu, Japan **31 G9** 35 7N 138 51 E
Numbulwar, Australia **62 A2** 14 15S 135 45 E
Numfoor, Indonesia **37 E8** 1 0S 134 50 E
Numurkah, Australia **63 F4** 36 5S 145 26 E
Nunaksaluk I., Canada **71 A7** 55 49N 60 20W
Nunavut □, Canada **69 B11** 66 0N 85 0W
Nungo, Mozam. **55 E4** 13 23S 37 43 E
Nungwe, Tanzania **54 C3** 2 48S 32 2 E
Nunivak I., U.S.A. **68 C3** 60 10N 166 30W
Nunkun, India **43 C7** 33 57N 76 2 E
Núoro, Italy **20 D3** 40 20N 9 20 E
Nūrābād, Iran **45 E8** 27 47N 57 12 E
Nuremberg = Nürnberg, Germany **16 D6** 49 27N 11 3 E
Nuri, Mexico **86 B3** 28 2N 109 22W
Nurina, Australia **61 F4** 30 56S 126 33 E
Nuriootpa, Australia **63 E2** 34 27S 139 0 E
Nurmes, Finland **8 E23** 63 33N 29 10 E
Nürnberg, Germany **16 D6** 49 27N 11 3 E
Nurran, L. = Terewah, L., Australia **63 D4** 29 52S 147 35 E
Nurrari Lakes, Australia **61 E5** 29 1S 130 5 E
Nusa Barung, Indonesia **37 H15** 8 30S 113 30 E
Nusa Kambangan, Indonesia **37 G13** 7 40S 108 10 E
Nusa Tenggara Barat □, Indonesia **36 F5** 8 50S 117 30 E
Nusa Tenggara Timur □, Indonesia **37 F6** 9 30S 122 0 E
Nusaybin, Turkey **25 G7** 37 3N 41 10 E
Nushki, Pakistan **42 E2** 29 35N 66 0 E
Nutwood Downs, Australia **62 B1** 15 49S 134 10 E
Nuuk, Greenland **69 B14** 64 10N 51 35W
Nuwakot, Nepal **43 E10** 28 10N 83 55 E
Nuweveldberge, S. Africa **56 E3** 32 10S 21 45 E
Nuyts, C., Australia **61 F5** 32 2S 132 21 E
Nuyts Arch., Australia **63 E1** 32 35S 133 20 E
Nxau-Nxau, Botswana **56 B3** 18 57S 21 4 E
Nyack, U.S.A. **79 E11** 41 5N 73 55W
Nyah West, Australia **63 F3** 35 16S 143 21 E
Nyahanga, Tanzania **54 C3** 2 20S 33 37 E
Nyahua, Tanzania **54 D3** 5 25S 33 23 E
Nyahururu, Kenya **54 B4** 0 2N 36 27 E
Nyainqentanglha Shan, China **32 D4** 30 0N 90 0 E
Nyakanazi, Tanzania **54 C3** 3 2S 31 10 E
Nyâlâ, Sudan **51 F10** 12 2N 24 58 E
Nyamandhlovu, Zimbabwe **55 F2** 19 55S 28 16 E
Nyambiti, Tanzania **54 C3** 2 48S 33 27 E
Nyamwaga, Tanzania **54 C3** 1 27S 34 33 E
Nyandekwa, Tanzania **54 C3** 3 57S 32 32 E
Nyandoma, Russia **24 B7** 61 40N 40 12 E
Nyangana, Namibia **56 B3** 18 0S 20 40 E
Nyanguge, Tanzania **54 C3** 2 30S 33 12 E
Nyanza, Rwanda **54 C2** 2 20S 29 42 E
Nyanza □, Kenya **54 C3** 0 10S 34 15 E
Nyanza-Lac, Burundi **54 C2** 4 21S 29 36 E
Nyarling →, Canada **72 A6** 60 41N 113 23W
Nyasa, L., Africa **55 E3** 12 30S 34 30 E
Nyasvizh, Belarus **17 B14** 53 14N 26 38 E
Nyazepetrovsk, Russia **24 C10** 56 3N 59 36 E
Nyazura, Zimbabwe **55 F3** 18 40S 32 16 E
Nyazwidzi →, Zimbabwe **55 G3** 20 0S 31 17 E
Nybro, Sweden **9 H16** 56 44N 15 55 E
Nyda, Russia **26 C8** 66 40N 72 58 E
Nyeri, Kenya **54 C4** 0 23S 36 56 E
Nyíregyháza, Hungary **17 E11** 47 58N 21 47 E
Nykøbing, Storstrøm, Denmark **9 J14** 54 56N 11 52 E
Nykøbing, Vestsjælland, Denmark **9 J14** 55 55N 11 40 E
Nykøbing, Viborg, Denmark **9 H13** 56 48N 8 51 E
Nyköping, Sweden **9 G17** 58 45N 17 1 E
Nylstroom, S. Africa **57 C4** 24 42S 28 22 E
Nymagee, Australia **63 E4** 32 7S 146 20 E
Nynäshamn, Sweden **9 G17** 58 54N 17 57 E
Nyngan, Australia **63 E4** 31 30S 147 8 E
Nyoman = Neman →, Lithuania **24 C3** 55 25N 21 10 E
Nysa, Poland **17 C9** 50 30N 17 22 E
Nysa →, Europe **16 B8** 52 4N 14 46 E
Nyssa, U.S.A. **82 E5** 43 53N 117 0W
Nyunzu, Dem. Rep. of the Congo **54 D2** 5 57S 27 58 E
Nyurba, Russia **27 C12** 63 17N 118 28 E
Nzega, Tanzania **54 C3** 4 10S 33 12 E
Nzega □, Tanzania **54 C3** 4 10S 33 10 E
N'zérékoré, Guinea **50 G4** 7 49N 8 48W
Nzeto, Angola **52 F2** 7 10S 12 52 E
Nzilo, Chutes de, Dem. Rep. of the Congo **55 E2** 10 18S 25 27 E
Nzubuka, Tanzania **54 C3** 4 45S 32 50 E

O

Ō-Shima, Nagasaki, Japan **31 G4** 34 29N 129 33 E
Ō-Shima, Shizuoka, Japan **31 G9** 34 44N 139 24 E
Oa, Mull of, U.K. **12 F2** 55 35N 6 20W
Oacoma, U.S.A. **80 D5** 43 48N 99 24W
Oahe, L., U.S.A. **80 C4** 44 27N 100 24W
Oahe Dam, U.S.A. **80 C4** 44 27N 100 24W
Oahu, U.S.A. **74 H16** 21 28N 157 58W
Oak Creek, U.S.A. **82 F10** 40 16N 106 57W
Oak Harbor, U.S.A. **84 B4** 48 18N 122 39W
Oak Hill, U.S.A. **76 G5** 37 59N 81 9W
Oak Park, U.S.A. **76 E2** 41 53N 87 47W
Oak Ridge, U.S.A. **77 G3** 36 1N 84 16W
Oak View, U.S.A. **85 L7** 34 24N 119 18W
Oakan-Dake, Japan **30 C12** 43 27N 144 10 E
Oakbank, Australia **63 E3** 33 4S 140 33 E
Oakdale, Calif., U.S.A. **84 H6** 37 46N 120 51W
Oakdale, La., U.S.A. **81 K8** 30 49N 92 40W
Oakes, U.S.A. **80 B5** 46 8N 98 6W
Oakesdale, U.S.A. **82 C5** 47 8N 117 15W
Oakey, Australia **63 D5** 27 25S 151 43 E
Oakham, U.K. **11 E7** 52 40N 0 43W
Oakhurst, U.S.A. **84 H7** 37 19N 119 40W
Oakland, Calif., U.S.A. **84 H4** 37 49N 122 16W
Oakland, Oreg., U.S.A. **82 E2** 43 25N 123 18W
Oakland City, U.S.A. **76 F2** 38 20N 87 21W
Oakley, Idaho, U.S.A. **82 E7** 42 15N 113 53W
Oakley, Kans., U.S.A. **80 F4** 39 8N 100 51W
Oakover →, Australia **60 D3** 21 0S 120 40 E
Oakridge, U.S.A. **82 E2** 43 45N 122 28W
Oakville, U.S.A. **84 D3** 46 51N 123 14W
Oamaru, N.Z. **59 L3** 45 5S 170 59 E
Oasis, Calif., U.S.A. **85 M10** 33 28N 116 6W
Oasis, Nev., U.S.A. **84 H9** 37 29N 117 55W
Oates Land, Antarctica **5 C11** 69 0S 160 0 E
Oatman, U.S.A. **85 K12** 35 1N 114 19W
Oaxaca, Mexico **87 D5** 17 2N 96 40W
Oaxaca □, Mexico **87 D5** 17 0N 97 0W
Ob →, Russia **26 C7** 66 45N 69 30 E
Oba, Canada **70 C3** 49 4N 84 7W
Obama, Japan **31 G7** 35 30N 135 45 E
Oban, U.K. **12 E3** 56 25N 5 29W
Obbia, Somali Rep. **46 F4** 5 25N 48 30 E
Obed, Canada **72 C5** 53 30N 117 10W
Obera, Argentina **95 B4** 27 21S 55 2W
Oberhausen, Germany **16 C4** 51 28N 6 51 E
Oberlin, Kans., U.S.A. **80 F4** 39 49N 100 32W
Oberlin, La., U.S.A. **81 K8** 30 37N 92 46W
Oberlin, Ohio, U.S.A. **78 E2** 41 18N 82 13W
Oberon, Australia **63 E4** 33 45S 149 52 E
Obi, Kepulauan, Indonesia **37 E7** 1 23S 127 45 E
Obi Is. = Obi, Kepulauan, Indonesia **37 E7** 1 23S 127 45 E
Óbidos, Brazil **93 D7** 1 50S 55 30W
Obihiro, Japan **30 C11** 42 56N 143 12 E
Obilatu, Indonesia **37 E7** 1 25S 127 20 E
Obluchye, Russia **27 E14** 49 1N 131 4 E
Obo, C.A.R. **54 A2** 5 20N 26 32 E
Oboa, Mt., Uganda **54 B3** 1 45N 34 45 E
Oboyan, Russia **26 D4** 51 15N 36 21 E
Obozerskaya = Obozerskiy, Russia **26 C5** 63 34N 40 21 E
Obozerskiy, Russia **26 C5** 63 34N 40 21 E
Observatory Inlet, Canada **72 B3** 55 10N 129 54W
Obshchi Syrt, Russia **6 E16** 52 0N 53 0 E
Obskaya Guba, Russia **26 C8** 69 0N 73 0 E
Obuasi, Ghana **50 G5** 6 17N 1 40W
Ocala, U.S.A. **77 L4** 29 11N 82 8W
Ocampo, Mexico **86 B3** 28 9N 108 24W
Ocaña, Spain **19 C4** 39 55N 3 30W
Oconomowoc, U.S.A. **80 D10** 43 7N 88 30W
Ocate, U.S.A. **81 G2** 36 11N 105 3W
Occidental, Cordillera, Colombia **92 C3** 5 0N 76 0W
Ocean City, N.J., U.S.A. **76 F8** 39 17N 74 35W
Ocean City, Wash., U.S.A. **84 C2** 47 4N 124 10W
Ocean I. = Banaba, Kiribati **64 H8** 0 45S 169 50 E
Ocean Park, U.S.A. **84 D2** 46 30N 124 3W
Oceano, U.S.A. **85 K6** 35 6N 120 37W
Oceanport, U.S.A. **79 F10** 40 19N 74 3W
Oceanside, U.S.A. **85 M9** 33 12N 117 23W
Ochil Hills, U.K. **12 E5** 56 14N 3 40W
Ochre River, Canada **73 C9** 51 4N 99 47W
Ocilla, U.S.A. **77 K4** 31 36N 83 15W
Ocmulgee →, U.S.A. **77 K4** 31 58N 82 33W
Ocniţa, Moldova **17 D14** 48 25N 27 30 E
Oconee →, U.S.A. **77 K4** 31 58N 82 33W
Oconto, U.S.A. **76 C2** 44 53N 87 52W
Oconto Falls, U.S.A. **76 C1** 44 52N 88 9W
Ocosingo, Mexico **87 D6** 17 10N 92 15W
Ocotal, Nic. **88 D2** 13 41N 86 31W
Ocotlán, Mexico **86 C4** 20 21N 102 42W
Octave, U.S.A. **83 J7** 34 10N 112 43W
Ōda, Japan **31 G6** 35 11N 132 30 E
Ódáðahraun, Iceland **8 D5** 65 5N 17 0W
Odate, Japan **30 D10** 40 16N 140 34 E
Odawara, Japan **31 G9** 35 20N 139 6 E
Odda, Norway **9 F12** 60 3N 6 35 E
Odei →, Canada **73 B9** 56 6N 96 54W
Ödemiş, Turkey **21 E13** 38 15N 28 0 E
Odendaalsrus, S. Africa **56 D4** 27 48S 26 45 E
Odense, Denmark **9 J14** 55 22N 10 23 E
Oder →, Europe **16 B8** 53 33N 14 38 E
Odesa, Ukraine **25 E5** 46 30N 30 45 E
Odessa = Odesa, Ukraine **25 E5** 46 30N 30 45 E
Odessa, Canada **79 B8** 44 17N 76 43W
Odessa, Tex., U.S.A. **81 K3** 31 52N 102 23W
Odessa, Wash., U.S.A. **82 C4** 47 20N 118 41W
Odiakwe, Botswana **56 C4** 20 12S 25 17 E
Odienné, Ivory C. **50 G4** 9 30N 7 34W
Odintsovo, Russia **24 C6** 55 39N 37 15 E
O'Donnell, U.S.A. **81 J4** 32 58N 101 50W
Odorheiu Secuiesc, Romania **17 E13** 46 21N 25 21 E
Odra = Oder →, Europe **16 B8** 53 33N 14 38 E
Odzi, Zimbabwe **57 B5** 19 0S 32 20 E
Oeiras, Brazil **93 E10** 7 0S 42 8W
Oelrichs, U.S.A. **80 D3** 43 11N 103 14W
Oelwein, U.S.A. **80 D9** 42 41N 91 55W
Oenpelli, Australia **60 B5** 12 20S 133 4 E
Ofanto →, Italy **20 D7** 41 22N 16 13 E
Offa, Nigeria **50 G6** 8 13N 4 42 E
Offaly □, Ireland **13 C4** 53 15N 7 30W
Offenbach, Germany **16 C5** 50 6N 8 44 E
Offenburg, Germany **16 D4** 48 28N 7 56 E
Ofotfjorden, Norway **8 B17** 68 27N 17 0 E
Ōfunato, Japan **30 E10** 39 4N 141 43 E
Oga, Japan **30 E9** 39 55N 139 50 E
Oga-Hantō, Japan **30 E9** 39 58N 139 47 E
Ogahalla, Canada **70 B2** 50 6N 85 51W
Ōgaki, Japan **31 G8** 35 21N 136 37 E
Ogallala, U.S.A. **80 E4** 41 8N 101 43W
Ogasawara Gunto, Pac. Oc. **64 E6** 27 0N 142 0 E
Ogbomosho, Nigeria **50 G6** 8 1N 4 11 E
Ogden, Iowa, U.S.A. **80 D8** 42 2N 94 2W
Ogden, Utah, U.S.A. **82 F7** 41 13N 111 58W
Ogdensburg, U.S.A. **79 B9** 44 42N 75 30W
Ogeechee →, U.S.A. **77 K5** 31 50N 81 3W
Ogilby, U.S.A. **85 N12** 32 49N 114 50W
Oglio →, Italy **20 B4** 45 2N 10 39 E
Ogmore, Australia **62 C4** 22 37S 149 35 E
Ogoki →, Canada **70 B2** 51 38N 85 57W
Ogoki L., Canada **70 B2** 50 50N 87 10W
Ogoki Res., Canada **70 B2** 50 45N 88 15W
Ogooué →, Gabon **52 E1** 1 0S 9 0 E

Óssa, Óros

Ogowe = Ogooué →, *Gabon* **52 E1** 1 0S 9 0 E
Ogre, *Latvia* **9 H21** 56 49N 24 36 E
Ohai, *N.Z.* **59 L2** 45 55S 168 0 E
Ohakune, *N.Z.* **59 H5** 39 24S 175 24 E
Ohata, *Japan* **30 D10** 41 24N 141 10 E
Ohau, L., *N.Z.* **59 L2** 44 15S 169 53 E
Ohio □, *U.S.A.* **76 E3** 40 15N 82 45W
Ohio →, *U.S.A.* **76 G1** 36 59N 89 8W
Ohře →, *Czech Rep.* **16 C8** 50 30N 14 10 E
Ohrid, *Macedonia* **21 D9** 41 8N 20 52 E
Ohridsko Jezero, *Macedonia* **21 D9** 41 8N 20 52 E
Ohrigstad, *S. Africa* **57 C5** 24 39S 30 36 E
Oiapoque, *Brazil* **93 C8** 3 50N 51 50W
Oikou, *China* **35 E9** 38 35N 117 42 E
Oil City, *U.S.A.* **78 E5** 41 26N 79 42W
Oildale, *U.S.A.* **85 K7** 35 25N 119 1W
Oise →, *France* **18 B5** 49 0N 2 4 E
Ōita, *Japan* **31 H5** 33 14N 131 36 E
Ōita □, *Japan* **31 H5** 33 15N 131 30 E
Oiticica, *Brazil* **93 E10** 5 3S 41 5W
Ojai, *U.S.A.* **85 L7** 34 27N 119 15W
Ojinaga, *Mexico* **86 B4** 29 34N 104 25W
Ojiya, *Japan* **31 F9** 37 18N 138 48 E
Ojos del Salado, Cerro, *Argentina* **94 B2** 27 0S 68 40W
Oka →, *Russia* **26 D5** 56 20N 43 59 E
Okaba, *Indonesia* **37 F9** 8 6S 139 42 E
Okahandja, *Namibia* **56 C2** 22 0S 16 59 E
Okahukura, *N.Z.* **59 H5** 38 48S 175 14 E
Okanagan L., *Canada* **72 D5** 50 0N 119 30W
Okanogan, *U.S.A.* **82 B4** 48 22N 119 35W
Okanogan →, *U.S.A.* **82 B4** 48 6N 119 44W
Okaputa, *Namibia* **56 C2** 20 5S 17 0 E
Okara, *Pakistan* **42 D5** 30 50N 73 31 E
Okarito, *N.Z.* **59 K3** 43 15S 170 9 E
Okaukuejo, *Namibia* **56 B2** 19 10S 16 0 E
Okavango Swamps, *Botswana* **56 B3** 18 45S 22 45 E
Okaya, *Japan* **31 F9** 36 5N 138 10 E
Okayama, *Japan* **31 G6** 34 40N 133 54 E
Okayama □, *Japan* **31 G6** 35 0N 133 50 E
Okazaki, *Japan* **31 G8** 34 57N 137 10 E
Okeechobee, *U.S.A.* **77 M5** 27 15N 80 50W
Okeechobee, L., *U.S.A.* **77 M5** 27 0N 80 50W
Okefenokee Swamp, *U.S.A.* **77 K4** 30 40N 82 20W
Okehampton, *U.K.* **11 G4** 50 44N 4 0W
Okha, *Russia* **27 D15** 53 40N 143 0 E
Okhotsk, *Russia* **27 D15** 59 20N 143 10 E
Okhotsk, Sea of, *Asia* **27 D15** 55 0N 145 0 E
Okhotskiy Perevoz, *Russia* **27 C14** 61 52N 135 35 E
Oki-Shotō, *Japan* **31 F6** 36 5N 133 15 E
Okiep, *S. Africa* **56 D2** 29 39S 17 53 E
Okinawa □, *Japan* **31 L4** 26 40N 128 0 E
Okinawa-Guntō, *Japan* **31 L4** 26 40N 128 0 E
Okinawa-Jima, *Japan* **31 L4** 26 32N 128 0 E
Okino-erabu-Shima, *Japan* **31 L4** 27 21N 128 33 E
Oklahoma □, *U.S.A.* **81 H6** 35 20N 97 30W
Oklahoma City, *U.S.A.* **81 H6** 35 30N 97 30W
Okmulgee, *U.S.A.* **81 H7** 35 37N 95 58W
Oknitsa = Ocniţa, *Moldova* **17 D14** 48 25N 27 30 E
Okolo, *Uganda* **54 B3** 2 37N 31 8 E
Okolona, *U.S.A.* **81 J10** 34 0N 88 45W
Oksibil, *Indonesia* **37 E10** 4 59S 140 35 E
Oksovskiy, *Russia* **24 B6** 62 33N 39 57 E
Oktabrsk = Oktyabrsk, *Kazakstan* **25 E10** 49 28N 57 25 E
Oktyabrsk, *Kazakstan* **25 E10** 49 28N 57 25 E
Oktyabrskiy = Aktsyabrski, *Belarus* **17 B15** 52 38N 28 53 E
Oktyabrskiy, *Russia* **24 D9** 54 28N 53 28 E
Oktyabrskoy Revolyutsii, Ostrov, *Russia* **27 B10** 79 30N 97 0 E
Okuru, *N.Z.* **59 K2** 43 55S 168 55 E
Okushiri-Tō, *Japan* **30 C9** 42 15N 139 30 E
Okwa →, *Botswana* **56 C3** 22 30S 23 0 E
Ola, *U.S.A.* **81 H8** 35 2N 93 13W
Ólafsfjörður, *Iceland* **8 C4** 66 4N 18 39W
Ólafsvík, *Iceland* **8 D2** 64 53N 23 43W
Olancha, *U.S.A.* **85 J8** 36 17N 118 1W
Olancha Pk., *U.S.A.* **85 J8** 36 15N 118 7W
Olanchito, *Honduras* **88 C2** 15 30N 86 30W
Öland, *Sweden* **9 H17** 56 45N 16 38 E
Olary, *Australia* **63 E3** 32 18S 140 19 E
Olascoaga, *Argentina* **94 D3** 35 15S 60 39W
Olathe, *U.S.A.* **80 F7** 38 53N 94 49W
Olavarría, *Argentina* **94 D3** 36 55S 60 20W
Oława, *Poland* **17 C9** 50 57N 17 20 E
Ólbia, *Italy* **20 D3** 40 55N 9 31 E
Old Bahama Chan. = Bahama, Canal Viejo de, *W. Indies* **88 B4** 22 10N 77 30W
Old Baldy Pk. = San Antonio, Mt., *U.S.A.* **85 L9** 34 17N 117 38W
Old Cork, *Australia* **62 C3** 22 57S 141 52 E
Old Crow, *Canada* **68 B6** 67 30N 139 55W
Old Dale, *U.S.A.* **85 L11** 34 8N 115 47W
Old Forge, *N.Y., U.S.A.* **79 C10** 43 43N 74 58W
Old Forge, *Pa., U.S.A.* **79 E9** 41 22N 75 45W
Old Fort →, *Canada* **73 B6** 58 36N 110 24W
Old Shinyanga, *Tanzania* **54 C3** 3 33S 33 27 E
Old Speck Mt., *U.S.A.* **79 B14** 44 34N 70 57W
Old Town, *U.S.A.* **71 D6** 44 56N 68 39W
Old Wives L., *Canada* **73 C7** 50 5N 106 0W
Oldbury, *U.K.* **11 F5** 51 38N 2 33W
Oldcastle, *Ireland* **13 C4** 53 46N 7 10W
Oldeani, *Tanzania* **54 C4** 3 22S 35 35 E
Oldenburg, *Germany* **16 B5** 53 9N 8 13 E
Oldenzaal, *Neths.* **15 B6** 52 19N 6 53 E
Oldham, *U.K.* **10 D5** 53 33N 2 7W
Oldman →, *Canada* **72 D6** 49 57N 111 42W
Oldmeldrum, *U.K.* **12 D6** 57 20N 2 19W
Olds, *Canada* **72 C6** 51 50N 114 10W
Olean, *U.S.A.* **78 D6** 42 5N 78 26W
Olekma →, *Russia* **27 C13** 60 22N 120 42 E
Olekminsk, *Russia* **27 C13** 60 25N 120 30 E
Oleksandriya, *Ukraine* **17 C14** 50 37N 26 19 E
Olema, *U.S.A.* **84 G4** 38 3N 122 47W
Olenegorsk, *Russia* **24 A5** 68 9N 33 18 E
Olenek, *Russia* **27 C12** 68 28N 112 18 E
Olenek →, *Russia* **27 B13** 73 0N 120 10 E
Oléron, Î. d', *France* **18 D3** 45 55N 1 15W
Oleśnica, *Poland* **17 C9** 51 13N 17 22 E
Olevsk, *Ukraine* **17 C14** 51 12N 27 39 E
Olga, *Russia* **27 E14** 43 50N 135 14 E
Olga, L., *Canada* **70 C4** 49 47N 77 15W
Olga, Mt., *Australia* **61 E5** 25 20S 130 50 E
Olhão, *Portugal* **19 D2** 37 3N 7 48W
Olifants →, *Africa* **57 C5** 23 57S 31 58 E
Olifantshoek, *S. Africa* **56 D3** 27 57S 22 42 E
Ólimbos, Óros, *Greece* **21 D10** 40 6N 22 23 E
Olímpia, *Brazil* **95 A6** 20 44S 48 54W
Olinda, *Brazil* **93 E12** 8 1S 34 51W
Oliva, *Argentina* **94 C3** 32 0S 63 38W
Olivehurst, *U.S.A.* **84 F5** 39 6N 121 34W
Olivenza, *Spain* **19 C2** 38 41N 7 9W
Oliver, *Canada* **72 D5** 49 13N 119 37W
Oliver L., *Canada* **73 B8** 56 56N 103 22W
Ollagüe, *Chile* **94 A2** 21 15S 68 10W
Olney, *Ill., U.S.A.* **76 F1** 38 44N 88 5W
Olney, *Tex., U.S.A.* **81 J5** 33 22N 98 45W
Olomane →, *Canada* **71 B7** 50 14N 60 37W
Olomouc, *Czech Rep.* **17 D9** 49 38N 17 12 E
Olonets, *Russia* **24 B5** 61 0N 32 54 E
Olongapo, *Phil.* **37 B6** 14 50N 120 18 E
Olot, *Spain* **19 A7** 42 11N 2 30 E
Olovyannaya, *Russia* **27 D12** 50 58N 115 35 E
Oloy →, *Russia* **27 C16** 66 29N 159 29 E
Olsztyn, *Poland* **17 B11** 53 48N 20 29 E
Olt →, *Romania* **17 G13** 43 43N 24 51 E
Olteniţa, *Romania* **17 F14** 44 7N 26 42 E
Olton, *U.S.A.* **81 H3** 34 11N 102 8W
Olymbos, *Cyprus* **23 D12** 35 21N 33 45 E
Olympia, *Greece* **21 F9** 37 39N 21 39 E
Olympia, *U.S.A.* **84 D4** 47 3N 122 53W
Olympic Mts., *U.S.A.* **84 C3** 47 55N 123 45W
Olympic Nat. Park, *U.S.A.* **84 C3** 47 48N 123 30W
Olympus, *Cyprus* **23 E11** 34 56N 32 52 E
Olympus, Mt. = Ólimbos, Óros, *Greece* **21 D10** 40 6N 22 23 E
Olympus, Mt. = Uludağ, *Turkey* **21 D13** 40 4N 29 13 E
Olympus, Mt., *U.S.A.* **84 C3** 47 48N 123 43W
Olyphant, *U.S.A.* **79 E9** 41 27N 75 36W
Om →, *Russia* **26 D8** 54 59N 73 22 E
Om Koi, *Thailand* **38 D2** 17 48N 98 22 E
Ōma, *Japan* **30 D10** 41 45N 141 5 E
Ōmachi, *Japan* **31 F8** 36 30N 137 50 E
Omae-Zaki, *Japan* **31 G9** 34 36N 138 14 E
Ōmagari, *Japan* **30 E10** 39 27N 140 29 E
Omagh, *U.K.* **13 B4** 54 36N 7 19W
Omagh □, *U.K.* **13 B4** 54 35N 7 15W
Omaha, *U.S.A.* **80 E7** 41 17N 95 58W
Omak, *U.S.A.* **82 B4** 48 25N 119 31W
Omalos, *Greece* **23 D5** 35 19N 23 55 E
Oman ■, *Asia* **46 C6** 23 0N 58 0 E
Oman, G. of, *Asia* **45 E8** 24 30N 58 30 E
Omaruru, *Namibia* **56 C2** 21 26S 16 0 E
Omaruru →, *Namibia* **56 C1** 22 7S 14 15 E
Omate, *Peru* **92 G4** 16 45S 71 0W
Ombai, Selat, *Indonesia* **37 F6** 8 30S 124 50 E
Omboué, *Gabon* **52 E1** 1 35S 9 15 E
Ombrone →, *Italy* **20 C4** 42 42N 11 5 E
Omdurmân, *Sudan* **51 E12** 15 40N 32 28 E
Omeonga, *Dem. Rep. of the Congo* **54 C1** 3 40S 24 22 E
Ometepe, I. de, *Nic.* **88 D2** 11 32N 85 35W
Ometepec, *Mexico* **87 D5** 16 39N 98 23W
Ominato, *Japan* **30 D10** 41 17N 141 10 E
Omineca →, *Canada* **72 B4** 56 3N 124 16W
Omitara, *Namibia* **56 C2** 22 16S 18 2 E
Ōmiya, *Japan* **31 G9** 35 54N 139 38 E
Ommen, *Neths.* **15 B6** 52 31N 6 26 E
Ömnögovĭ □, *Mongolia* **34 C3** 43 15N 104 0 E
Omo →, *Ethiopia* **46 F2** 6 25N 36 10 E
Omodhos, *Cyprus* **23 E11** 34 51N 32 48 E
Omolon →, *Russia* **27 C16** 68 42N 158 36 E
Omono-Gawa →, *Japan* **30 E10** 39 46N 140 3 E
Omsk, *Russia* **26 D8** 55 0N 73 12 E
Omsukchan, *Russia* **27 C16** 62 32N 155 48 E
Ōmu, *Japan* **30 B11** 44 34N 142 58 E
Omul, Vf., *Romania* **17 F13** 45 27N 25 29 E
Ōmura, *Japan* **31 H4** 32 56N 129 57 E
Omuramba Omatako →, *Namibia* **53 H4** 17 45S 20 25 E
Ōmuta, *Japan* **31 H5** 33 5N 130 26 E
Onaga, *U.S.A.* **80 F6** 39 29N 96 10W
Onalaska, *U.S.A.* **80 D9** 43 53N 91 14W
Onamia, *U.S.A.* **80 B8** 46 4N 93 40W
Onancock, *U.S.A.* **76 G8** 37 43N 75 45W
Onang, *Indonesia* **37 E5** 3 2S 118 49 E
Onaping L., *Canada* **70 C3** 47 3N 81 30W
Onavas, *Mexico* **86 B3** 28 28N 109 30W
Onawa, *U.S.A.* **80 D6** 42 2N 96 6W
Onaway, *U.S.A.* **76 C3** 45 21N 84 14W
Oncócua, *Angola* **56 B1** 16 30S 13 25 E
Onda, *Spain* **19 C5** 39 55N 0 17W
Ondaejin, *N. Korea* **35 D15** 41 34N 129 40 E
Ondangua, *Namibia* **56 B2** 17 57S 16 4 E
Ondjiva, *Angola* **56 B2** 16 48S 15 50 E
Öndörshil, *Mongolia* **34 B5** 45 13N 108 5 E
Öndverðarnes, *Iceland* **8 D1** 64 52N 24 0W
Onega, *Russia* **24 B6** 64 0N 38 10 E
Onega →, *Russia* **24 B6** 63 58N 38 2 E
Onega, G. of = Onezhskaya Guba, *Russia* **24 B6** 64 24N 36 38 E
Onega, L. = Onezhskoye Ozero, *Russia* **24 B6** 61 44N 35 22 E
Onehunga, *N.Z.* **59 G5** 36 55S 174 48 E
Oneida, *U.S.A.* **79 C9** 43 6N 75 39W
Oneida L., *U.S.A.* **79 C9** 43 12N 75 54W
O'Neill, *U.S.A.* **80 D5** 42 27N 98 39W
Onekotan, Ostrov, *Russia* **27 E16** 49 25N 154 45 E
Onema, *Dem. Rep. of the Congo* **54 C1** 4 35S 24 30 E
Oneonta, *Ala., U.S.A.* **77 J2** 33 57N 86 28W
Oneonta, *N.Y., U.S.A.* **79 D9** 42 27N 75 4W
Oneşti, *Romania* **17 E14** 46 15N 26 45 E
Onezhskaya Guba, *Russia* **24 B6** 64 24N 36 38 E
Onezhskoye Ozero, *Russia* **24 B6** 61 44N 35 22 E
Ongarue, *N.Z.* **59 H5** 38 42S 175 19 E
Ongerup, *Australia* **61 F2** 33 58S 118 28 E
Ongjin, *N. Korea* **35 F13** 37 56N 125 21 E
Ongkharak, *Thailand* **38 E3** 14 8N 101 1 E
Ongniud Qi, *China* **35 C10** 43 0N 118 38 E
Ongoka, *Dem. Rep. of the Congo* **54 C2** 1 20S 26 0 E
Ongole, *India* **40 M12** 15 33N 80 2 E
Ongon, *Mongolia* **34 B7** 45 41N 113 5 E
Onida, *U.S.A.* **80 C4** 44 42N 100 4W
Onilahy →, *Madag.* **57 C7** 23 34S 43 45 E
Onitsha, *Nigeria* **50 G7** 6 6N 6 42 E
Onoda, *Japan* **31 G5** 34 2N 131 25 E
Onpyŏng-ni, *S. Korea* **35 H14** 33 25N 126 55 E
Onslow, *Australia* **60 D2** 21 40S 115 12 E
Onslow B., *U.S.A.* **77 H7** 34 20N 77 15W
Ontake-San, *Japan* **31 G8** 35 53N 137 29 E
Ontario, *Calif., U.S.A.* **85 L9** 34 4N 117 39W
Ontario, *Oreg., U.S.A.* **82 D5** 44 2N 116 58W
Ontario □, *Canada* **70 B2** 48 0N 83 0W
Ontario, L., *U.S.A.* **70 D4** 43 20N 78 0W
Ontonagon, *U.S.A.* **80 B10** 46 52N 89 19W
Onyx, *U.S.A.* **85 K8** 35 41N 118 14W
Oodnadatta, *Australia* **63 D2** 27 33S 135 30 E
Ooldea, *Australia* **61 F5** 30 27S 131 50 E
Oombulgurri, *Australia* **60 C4** 15 15S 127 45 E
Oona River, *Canada* **72 C2** 53 57N 130 16W
Oorindi, *Australia* **62 C3** 20 40S 141 1 E
Oost-Vlaanderen □, *Belgium* **15 C3** 51 5N 3 50 E
Oostende, *Belgium* **15 C2** 51 15N 2 54 E
Oosterhout, *Neths.* **15 C4** 51 39N 4 47 E
Oosterschelde, *Neths.* **15 C4** 51 33N 4 0 E
Oosterwolde, *Neths.* **15 B6** 53 0N 6 17 E
Ootacamund = Udagamandalam, *India* **40 P10** 11 30N 76 44 E
Ootsa L., *Canada* **72 C3** 53 50N 126 2W
Opala, *Dem. Rep. of the Congo* **54 C1** 0 40S 24 20 E
Opanake, *Sri Lanka* **40 R12** 6 35N 80 40 E
Opasatika, *Canada* **70 C3** 49 30N 82 50W
Opasquia, *Canada* **73 C10** 53 16N 93 34W
Opava, *Czech Rep.* **17 D9** 49 57N 17 58 E
Opelousas, *U.S.A.* **81 K8** 30 32N 92 5W
Opémisca, L., *Canada* **70 C5** 49 56N 74 52W
Opheim, *U.S.A.* **82 B10** 48 51N 106 24W
Ophthalmia Ra., *Australia* **60 D2** 23 15S 119 30 E
Opinaca →, *Canada* **70 B4** 52 15N 78 2W
Opinaca L., *Canada* **70 B4** 52 39N 76 20W
Opiskotish, L., *Canada* **71 B6** 53 10N 67 50W
Opole, *Poland* **17 C9** 50 42N 17 58 E
Oporto = Porto, *Portugal* **19 B1** 41 8N 8 40W
Opotiki, *N.Z.* **59 H6** 38 1S 177 19 E
Opp, *U.S.A.* **77 K2** 31 17N 86 16W
Oppdal, *Norway* **9 E13** 62 35N 9 41 E
Opua, *N.Z.* **59 F5** 35 19S 174 9 E
Opunake, *N.Z.* **59 H4** 39 26S 173 52 E
Ora, *Cyprus* **23 E12** 34 51N 33 12 E
Ora Banda, *Australia* **61 F3** 30 20S 121 0 E
Oracle, *U.S.A.* **83 K8** 32 37N 110 46W
Oradea, *Romania* **17 E11** 47 2N 21 58 E
Öræfajökull, *Iceland* **8 D5** 64 2N 16 39W
Orai, *India* **43 G8** 25 58N 79 30 E
Oral = Zhayyq →, *Kazakstan* **25 E9** 47 0N 51 48 E
Oral, *Kazakstan* **24 D9** 51 20N 51 20 E
Oran, *Algeria* **50 A5** 35 45N 0 39W
Oran, *Argentina* **94 A3** 23 10S 64 20W
Orange, *Australia* **63 E4** 33 15S 149 7 E
Orange, *France* **18 D6** 44 8N 4 47 E
Orange, *Calif., U.S.A.* **85 M9** 33 47N 117 51W
Orange, *Mass., U.S.A.* **79 D12** 42 35N 72 19W
Orange, *Tex., U.S.A.* **81 K8** 30 6N 93 44W
Orange, *Va., U.S.A.* **76 F6** 38 15N 78 7W
Orange →, *S. Africa* **56 D2** 28 41S 16 28 E
Orange, C., *Brazil* **93 C8** 4 20N 51 30W
Orange Cove, *U.S.A.* **84 J7** 36 38N 119 19W
Orange Free State □ = Free State □, *S. Africa* **56 D4** 28 30S 27 0 E
Orange Grove, *U.S.A.* **81 M6** 27 58N 97 56W
Orange Walk, *Belize* **87 D7** 18 6N 88 33W
Orangeburg, *U.S.A.* **77 J5** 33 30N 80 52W
Orangeville, *Canada* **70 D3** 43 55N 80 5W
Oranienburg, *Germany* **16 B7** 52 45N 13 14 E
Oranje = Orange →, *S. Africa* **56 D2** 28 41S 16 28 E
Oranje Vrystaat □ = Free State □, *S. Africa* **56 D4** 28 30S 27 0 E
Oranjemund, *Namibia* **56 D2** 28 38S 16 29 E
Oranjerivier, *S. Africa* **56 D3** 29 40S 24 12 E
Oras, *Phil.* **37 B7** 12 9N 125 28 E
Oraşul Stalin = Braşov, *Romania* **17 F13** 45 38N 25 35 E
Orbetello, *Italy* **20 C4** 42 27N 11 13 E
Orbost, *Australia* **63 F4** 37 40S 148 29 E
Orchila, I., *Venezuela* **92 A5** 11 48N 66 10W
Orcutt, *U.S.A.* **85 L6** 34 52N 120 27W
Ord →, *Australia* **60 C4** 15 33S 128 15 E
Ord, Mt., *Australia* **60 C4** 17 20S 125 34 E
Orderville, *U.S.A.* **83 H7** 37 17N 112 38W
Ordos = Mu Us Shamo, *China* **34 E5** 39 0N 109 0 E
Ordway, *U.S.A.* **80 F3** 38 13N 103 46W
Ordzhonikidze = Vladikavkaz, *Russia* **25 F7** 43 0N 44 35 E
Ore, *Dem. Rep. of the Congo* **54 B2** 3 17N 29 30 E
Ore Mts. = Erzgebirge, *Germany* **16 C7** 50 27N 12 55 E
Örebro, *Sweden* **9 G16** 59 20N 15 18 E
Oregon, *U.S.A.* **80 D10** 42 1N 89 20W
Oregon □, *U.S.A.* **82 E3** 44 0N 121 0W
Oregon City, *U.S.A.* **84 E4** 45 21N 122 36W
Orekhovo-Zuyevo, *Russia* **24 C6** 55 50N 38 55 E
Orel, *Russia* **24 D6** 52 57N 36 3 E
Orem, *U.S.A.* **82 F8** 40 19N 111 42W
Ören, *Turkey* **21 F12** 37 3N 27 57 E
Orenburg, *Russia* **24 D10** 51 45N 55 6 E
Orense = Ourense, *Spain* **19 A2** 42 19N 7 55W
Orepuki, *N.Z.* **59 M1** 46 19S 167 46 E
Orestiás, *Greece* **21 D12** 41 30N 26 33 E
Orford Ness, *U.K.* **11 E9** 52 5N 1 35 E
Organos, Pta. de los, *Canary Is.* **22 F2** 28 12N 17 17W
Orgaz, *Spain* **19 C4** 39 39N 3 53W
Orgeyev = Orhei, *Moldova* **17 E15** 47 24N 28 50 E
Orhaneli, *Turkey* **21 E13** 39 54N 28 59 E
Orhangazi, *Turkey* **21 D13** 40 29N 29 18 E
Orhei, *Moldova* **17 E15** 47 24N 28 50 E
Orhon Gol →, *Mongolia* **32 A5** 50 21N 106 0 E
Orient, *Australia* **63 D3** 28 7S 142 50 E
Oriental, Cordillera, *Colombia* **92 B4** 6 0N 73 0W
Oriente, *Argentina* **94 D3** 38 44S 60 37W
Orihuela, *Spain* **19 C5** 38 7N 0 55W
Orinoco →, *Venezuela* **92 B6** 9 15N 61 30W
Orissa □, *India* **41 K14** 20 0N 84 0 E
Orissaare, *Estonia* **9 G20** 58 34N 23 5 E
Oristano, *Italy* **20 E3** 39 54N 8 36 E
Oristano, G. di, *Italy* **20 E3** 39 50N 8 29 E
Orizaba, *Mexico* **87 D5** 18 51N 97 6W
Orkanger, *Norway* **8 E13** 63 18N 9 52 E
Orkla →, *Norway* **8 E13** 63 18N 9 51 E
Orkney, *S. Africa* **56 D4** 26 58S 26 40 E
Orkney □, *U.K.* **12 B5** 59 2N 3 13W
Orkney Is., *U.K.* **12 B6** 59 0N 3 0W
Orland, *U.S.A.* **84 F4** 39 45N 122 12W
Orlando, *U.S.A.* **77 L5** 28 33N 81 23W
Orléanais, *France* **18 C5** 48 0N 2 0 E
Orléans, *France* **18 C4** 47 54N 1 52 E
Orleans, *U.S.A.* **79 B12** 44 49N 72 12W
Orléans, I. d', *Canada* **71 C5** 46 54N 70 58W
Ormara, *Pakistan* **40 G4** 25 16N 64 33 E
Ormoc, *Phil.* **37 B6** 11 0N 124 37 E
Ormond, *N.Z.* **59 H6** 38 33S 177 56 E
Ormond Beach, *U.S.A.* **77 L5** 29 17N 81 3W
Ormskirk, *U.K.* **10 D5** 53 35N 2 54W
Ormstown, *Canada* **79 A11** 45 8N 74 0W
Örnsköldsvik, *Sweden* **8 E18** 63 17N 18 40 E
Oro, *N. Korea* **35 D14** 40 1N 127 27 E
Oro →, *Mexico* **86 B3** 25 35N 105 2W
Oro Grande, *U.S.A.* **85 L9** 34 36N 117 20W
Orocué, *Colombia* **92 C4** 4 48N 71 20W
Orogrande, *U.S.A.* **83 K10** 32 24N 106 5W
Orol Dengizi = Aral Sea, *Asia* **26 E7** 44 30N 60 0 E
Oromocto, *Canada* **71 C6** 45 54N 66 29W
Orono, *Canada* **78 C6** 43 59N 78 37W
Oronsay, *U.K.* **12 E2** 56 1N 6 15W
Oroqen Zizhiqi, *China* **33 A7** 50 34N 123 43 E
Oroquieta, *Phil.* **37 C6** 8 32N 123 44 E
Orosháza, *Hungary* **17 E11** 46 32N 20 42 E
Orotukan, *Russia* **27 C16** 62 16N 151 42 E
Oroville, *Calif., U.S.A.* **84 F5** 39 31N 121 33W
Oroville, *Wash., U.S.A.* **82 B4** 48 56N 119 26W
Oroville, L., *U.S.A.* **84 F5** 39 33N 121 29W
Orroroo, *Australia* **63 E2** 32 43S 138 38 E
Orrville, *U.S.A.* **78 F3** 40 50N 81 46W
Orsha, *Belarus* **24 D5** 54 30N 30 25 E
Orsk, *Russia* **24 D10** 51 12N 58 34 E
Orşova, *Romania* **17 F12** 44 41N 22 25 E
Ortaca, *Turkey* **21 F13** 36 49N 28 45 E
Ortegal, C., *Spain* **19 A2** 43 43N 7 52W
Orthez, *France* **18 E3** 43 29N 0 48W
Ortigueira, *Spain* **19 A2** 43 40N 7 50W
Orting, *U.S.A.* **84 C4** 47 6N 122 12W
Ortles, *Italy* **18 C9** 46 31N 10 33 E
Ortón →, *Bolivia* **92 F5** 10 50S 67 0W
Orūmīyeh, *Iran* **44 B5** 37 40N 45 0 E
Orūmīyeh, Daryācheh-ye, *Iran* **44 B5** 37 50N 45 30 E
Oruro, *Bolivia* **92 G5** 18 0S 67 9W
Orust, *Sweden* **9 G14** 58 10N 11 40 E
Oruzgān □, *Afghan.* **40 C5** 33 30N 66 0 E
Orvieto, *Italy* **20 C5** 42 43N 12 7 E
Orwell, *U.S.A.* **78 E4** 41 32N 80 52W
Orwell →, *U.K.* **11 F9** 51 59N 1 18 E
Oryakhovo, *Bulgaria* **21 C10** 43 40N 23 57 E
Osa, *Russia* **24 C10** 57 17N 55 26 E
Osa, Pen. de, *Costa Rica* **88 E3** 8 0N 84 0W
Osage, *Iowa, U.S.A.* **80 D8** 43 17N 92 49W
Osage, *Wyo., U.S.A.* **80 D2** 43 59N 104 25W
Osage →, *U.S.A.* **80 F9** 38 35N 91 57W
Osage City, *U.S.A.* **80 F7** 38 38N 95 50W
Ōsaka, *Japan* **31 G7** 34 40N 135 30 E
Osan, *S. Korea* **35 F14** 37 11N 127 4 E
Osawatomie, *U.S.A.* **80 F7** 38 31N 94 57W
Osborne, *U.S.A.* **80 F5** 39 26N 98 42W
Osceola, *Ark., U.S.A.* **81 H10** 35 42N 89 58W
Osceola, *Iowa, U.S.A.* **80 E8** 41 2N 93 46W
Oscoda, *U.S.A.* **78 B1** 44 26N 83 20W
Ösel = Saaremaa, *Estonia* **24 C3** 58 30N 22 30 E
Osh, *Kyrgyzstan* **26 E8** 40 37N 72 49 E
Oshawa, *Canada* **70 D4** 43 50N 78 50W
Oshkosh, *Nebr., U.S.A.* **80 E3** 41 24N 102 21W
Oshkosh, *Wis., U.S.A.* **80 C10** 44 1N 88 33W
Oshmyany = Ashmyany, *Belarus* **9 J21** 54 26N 25 52 E
Oshnovīyeh, *Iran* **44 B5** 37 2N 45 6 E
Oshogbo, *Nigeria* **50 G6** 7 48N 4 37 E
Oshtorīnān, *Iran* **45 C6** 34 1N 48 38 E
Oshwe, *Dem. Rep. of the Congo* **52 E3** 3 25S 19 28 E
Osijek, *Croatia* **21 B8** 45 34N 18 41 E
Osipenko = Berdyansk, *Ukraine* **25 E6** 46 45N 36 50 E
Osipovichi = Asipovichy, *Belarus* **17 B15** 53 19N 28 33 E
Osizweni, *S. Africa* **57 D5** 27 49S 30 7 E
Oskaloosa, *U.S.A.* **80 E8** 41 18N 92 39W
Oskarshamn, *Sweden* **9 H17** 57 15N 16 27 E
Oskélanéo, *Canada* **70 C4** 48 5N 75 15W
Öskemen, *Kazakstan* **26 E9** 50 0N 82 36 E
Oslo, *Norway* **9 G14** 59 55N 10 45 E
Oslofjorden, *Norway* **9 G14** 59 20N 10 35 E
Osmanabad, *India* **40 K10** 18 5N 76 10 E
Osmaniye, *Turkey* **25 G6** 37 5N 36 10 E
Osnabrück, *Germany* **16 B5** 52 17N 8 3 E
Osorio, *Brazil* **95 B5** 29 53S 50 17W
Osorno, *Chile* **96 E2** 40 25S 73 0W
Osoyoos, *Canada* **72 D5** 49 0N 119 30W
Osøyro, *Norway* **9 F11** 60 9N 5 30 E
Ospika →, *Canada* **72 B4** 56 20N 124 0W
Osprey Reef, *Australia* **62 A4** 13 52S 146 36 E
Oss, *Neths.* **15 C5** 51 46N 5 32 E
Óssa, Mt., *Australia* **62 G4** 41 52S 146 3 E
Óssa, Óros, *Greece* **21 E10** 39 47N 22 42 E

Ossabaw I.

Ossabaw I., *U.S.A.* 77 K5 31 50N 81 5W
Ossining, *U.S.A.* 79 E11 41 10N 73 55W
Ossipee, *U.S.A.* 79 C13 43 41N 71 7W
Ossokmanuan L., *Canada* 71 B7 53 25N 65 0W
Ossora, *Russia* 27 D17 59 20N 163 13 E
Ostend = Oostende, *Belgium* 15 C2 51 15N 2 54 E
Oster, *Ukraine* 17 C16 50 57N 30 53 E
Österdalälven, *Sweden* 9 F16 61 30N 13 45 E
Østerdalen, *Norway* 9 F14 61 40N 10 50 E
Östersund, *Sweden* 8 E16 63 10N 14 38 E
Ostfriesische Inseln, *Germany* 16 B4 53 42N 7 0 E
Ostrava, *Czech Rep.* 17 D10 49 51N 18 18 E
Ostróda, *Poland* 17 B10 53 42N 19 58 E
Ostroh, *Ukraine* 17 C14 50 20N 26 30 E
Ostrołęka, *Poland* 17 B11 53 4N 21 32 E
Ostrów Mazowiecka, *Poland* 17 B11 52 50N 21 51 E
Ostrów Wielkopolski, *Poland* 17 C9 51 36N 17 44 E
Ostrowiec-Świętokrzyski, *Poland* 17 C11 50 55N 21 22 E
Ostuni, *Italy* 21 D7 40 44N 17 35 E
Ōsumi-Kaikyō, *Japan* 31 J5 30 55N 131 0 E
Ōsumi-Shotō, *Japan* 31 J5 30 30N 130 0 E
Osuna, *Spain* 19 D3 37 14N 5 8W
Oswego, *U.S.A.* 79 C8 43 27N 76 31W
Oswestry, *U.K.* 10 E4 52 52N 3 3W
Oświęcim, *Poland* 17 C10 50 2N 19 11 E
Otago □, *N.Z.* 59 L2 45 15S 170 0 E
Otago Harbour, *N.Z.* 59 L3 45 47S 170 42 E
Ōtake, *Japan* 31 G6 34 12N 132 13 E
Otaki, *N.Z.* 59 J5 40 45S 175 10 E
Otaru, *Japan* 30 C10 43 10N 141 0 E
Otaru-Wan = Ishikari-Wan, *Japan* 30 C10 43 25N 141 1 E
Otavalo, *Ecuador* 92 C3 0 13N 78 20W
Otavi, *Namibia* 56 B2 19 40S 17 24 E
Otchinjau, *Angola* 56 B1 16 30S 13 56 E
Othello, *U.S.A.* 82 C4 46 50N 119 10W
Otira Gorge, *N.Z.* 59 K3 42 53S 171 33 E
Otis, *U.S.A.* 80 E3 40 9N 102 58W
Otjiwarongo, *Namibia* 56 C2 20 30S 16 33 E
Otoineppu, *Japan* 30 B11 44 44N 142 16 E
Otorohanga, *N.Z.* 59 H5 38 12S 175 14 E
Otoskwin →, *Canada* 70 B2 52 13N 88 6W
Otosquen, *Canada* 73 C8 53 17N 102 1W
Otra →, *Norway* 9 G13 58 9N 8 1 E
Otranto, *Italy* 21 D8 40 9N 18 28 E
Otranto, C. d', *Italy* 21 D8 40 7N 18 30 E
Otranto, Str. of, *Italy* 21 D8 40 15N 18 40 E
Otse, *S. Africa* 56 D4 25 2S 25 45 E
Ōtsu, *Japan* 31 G7 35 0N 135 50 E
Ōtsuki, *Japan* 31 G9 35 36N 138 57 E
Ottawa = Outaouais →, *Canada* 70 C5 45 27N 74 8W
Ottawa, *Canada* 70 C4 45 27N 75 42W
Ottawa, *Ill., U.S.A.* 80 E10 41 21N 88 51W
Ottawa, *Kans., U.S.A.* 80 F7 38 37N 95 16W
Ottawa Is., *Canada* 69 C11 59 35N 80 10W
Otter L., *Canada* 73 B8 55 35N 104 39W
Otter Rapids, *Ont., Canada* 70 B3 50 11N 81 39W
Otter Rapids, *Sask., Canada* 73 B8 55 38N 104 44W
Otterville, *Canada* 78 D4 42 55N 80 36W
Ottery St. Mary, *U.K.* 11 G4 50 44N 3 17W
Otto Beit Bridge, *Zimbabwe* 55 F2 15 59S 28 56 E
Ottosdal, *S. Africa* 56 D4 26 46S 25 59 E
Ottumwa, *U.S.A.* 80 E8 41 1N 92 25W
Oturkpo, *Nigeria* 50 G7 7 16N 8 8 E
Otway, B., *Chile* 96 G2 53 30S 74 0W
Otway, C., *Australia* 63 F3 38 52S 143 30 E
Otwock, *Poland* 17 B11 52 5N 21 20 E
Ou →, *Laos* 38 B4 20 4N 102 13 E
Ou Neua, *Laos* 38 A3 22 18N 101 48 E
Ou-Sammyaku, *Japan* 30 E10 39 20N 140 35 E
Ouachita →, *U.S.A.* 81 K9 31 38N 91 49W
Ouachita, L., *U.S.A.* 81 H8 34 34N 93 12W
Ouachita Mts., *U.S.A.* 81 H7 34 40N 94 25W
Ouagadougou, *Burkina Faso* 50 F5 12 25N 1 30W
Ouahran = Oran, *Algeria* 50 A5 35 45N 0 39W
Ouallene, *Algeria* 50 D6 24 41N 1 11 E
Ouargla, *Algeria* 50 B7 31 59N 5 16 E
Ouarzazate, *Morocco* 50 B4 30 55N 6 50W
Oubangi →, *Dem. Rep. of the Congo* 52 E3 0 30S 17 50 E
Ouddorp, *Neths.* 15 C3 51 50N 3 57 E
Oude Rijn →, *Neths.* 15 B4 52 12N 4 24 E
Oudenaarde, *Belgium* 15 D3 50 50N 3 37 E
Oudtshoorn, *S. Africa* 56 E3 33 35S 22 14 E
Ouessant, Î. d', *France* 18 B1 48 28N 5 6W
Ouesso, *Congo* 52 D3 1 37N 16 5 E
Ouest, Pte., *Canada* 71 C7 49 52N 64 40W
Ouezzane, *Morocco* 50 B4 34 51N 5 35W
Oughterard, *Ireland* 13 C2 53 26N 9 18W
Oujda, *Morocco* 50 B5 34 41N 1 55W
Oulainen, *Finland* 8 D21 64 17N 24 47 E
Oulu, *Finland* 8 D21 65 1N 25 29 E
Oulujärvi, *Finland* 8 D22 64 25N 27 15 E
Oulujoki →, *Finland* 8 D21 65 1N 25 30 E
Oum Chalouba, *Chad* 51 E10 15 48N 20 46 E
Oum Hadjer, *Chad* 51 F9 13 18N 19 41 E
Ounasjoki →, *Finland* 8 C21 66 31N 25 40 E
Ounguati, *Namibia* 56 C2 22 0S 15 46 E
Ounianga Sérir, *Chad* 51 E10 18 54N 20 51 E
Our →, *Lux.* 15 E6 49 55N 6 5 E
Ouray, *U.S.A.* 83 G10 38 1N 107 40W
Ourense, *Spain* 19 A2 42 19N 7 55W
Ouricuri, *Brazil* 93 E10 7 53S 40 5W
Ourinhos, *Brazil* 95 A6 23 0S 49 54W
Ouro Fino, *Brazil* 95 A6 22 16S 46 25W
Ouro Prêto, *Brazil* 95 A7 20 20S 43 30W
Ourthe →, *Belgium* 15 D5 50 29N 5 35 E
Ouse, *Australia* 62 G4 42 38S 146 42 E
Ouse →, *E. Susx., U.K.* 11 G8 50 47N 0 4 E
Ouse →, *N. Yorks., U.K.* 10 D7 53 44N 0 55W
Outaouais →, *Canada* 70 C5 45 27N 74 8W
Outardes →, *Canada* 71 C6 49 24N 69 30W
Outer Hebrides, *U.K.* 12 D1 57 30N 7 40W
Outer I., *Canada* 71 B8 51 10N 58 35W
Outjo, *Namibia* 56 C2 20 5S 16 7 E
Outlook, *Canada* 73 C7 51 30N 107 0W
Outlook, *U.S.A.* 80 A2 48 53N 104 47W
Outokumpu, *Finland* 8 E23 62 43N 29 1 E
Ouyen, *Australia* 63 F3 35 1S 142 22 E
Ovalau, *Fiji* 59 C8 17 40S 178 48 E
Ovalle, *Chile* 94 C1 30 33S 71 18W
Ovamboland, *Namibia* 56 B2 18 30S 16 0 E
Overflakkee, *Neths.* 15 C4 51 44N 4 10 E
Overijssel □, *Neths.* 15 B6 52 25N 6 35 E
Overland Park, *U.S.A.* 80 F7 38 55N 94 50W
Overton, *U.S.A.* 85 J12 36 33N 114 27W
Övertorneå, *Sweden* 8 C20 66 23N 23 38 E
Ovid, *U.S.A.* 80 E3 40 58N 102 23W
Oviedo, *Spain* 19 A3 43 25N 5 50W
Oviši, *Latvia* 9 H19 57 33N 21 44 E
Övör Hangay □, *Mongolia* 34 B2 45 0N 102 30 E
Øvre Årdal, *Norway* 9 F12 61 19N 7 48 E
Ovruch, *Ukraine* 17 C15 51 25N 28 45 E
Owaka, *N.Z.* 59 M2 46 27S 169 40 E
Owambo = Ovamboland, *Namibia* 56 B2 18 30S 16 0 E
Owase, *Japan* 31 G8 34 7N 136 12 E
Owatonna, *U.S.A.* 80 C8 44 5N 93 14W
Owbeh, *Afghan.* 40 B3 34 28N 63 10 E
Owego, *U.S.A.* 79 D8 42 6N 76 16W
Owen Falls Dam, *Uganda* 54 B3 0 30N 33 5 E
Owen Sound, *Canada* 70 D3 44 35N 80 55W
Owens →, *U.S.A.* 84 J9 36 32N 117 59W
Owens L., *U.S.A.* 85 J9 36 26N 117 57W
Owensboro, *U.S.A.* 76 G2 37 46N 87 7W
Owensville, *U.S.A.* 80 F9 38 21N 91 30W
Owl →, *Canada* 73 B10 57 51N 92 44W
Owo, *Nigeria* 50 G7 7 10N 5 39 E
Owosso, *U.S.A.* 76 D3 43 0N 84 10W
Owyhee, *U.S.A.* 82 F5 41 57N 116 6W
Owyhee →, *U.S.A.* 82 E5 43 49N 117 2W
Owyhee, L., *U.S.A.* 82 E5 43 38N 117 14W
Ox Mts. = Slieve Gamph, *Ireland* 13 B3 54 6N 9 0W
Öxarfjörður, *Iceland* 8 C5 66 15N 16 45W
Oxelösund, *Sweden* 9 G17 58 43N 17 5 E
Oxford, *N.Z.* 59 K4 43 18S 172 11 E
Oxford, *U.K.* 11 F6 51 46N 1 15W
Oxford, *Miss., U.S.A.* 81 H10 34 22N 89 31W
Oxford, *N.C., U.S.A.* 77 G6 36 19N 78 35W
Oxford, *Ohio, U.S.A.* 76 F3 39 31N 84 45W
Oxford L., *Canada* 73 C9 54 51N 95 37W
Oxfordshire □, *U.K.* 11 F6 51 48N 1 16W
Oxley, *Australia* 63 E3 34 11S 144 6 E
Oxnard, *U.S.A.* 85 L7 34 12N 119 11W
Oxus = Amudarya →, *Uzbekistan* 26 E6 43 58N 59 34 E
Oya, *Malaysia* 36 D4 2 55N 111 55 E
Oyama, *Japan* 31 F9 36 18N 139 48 E
Oyem, *Gabon* 52 D2 1 34N 11 31 E
Oyen, *Canada* 73 C6 51 22N 110 28W
Oykel →, *U.K.* 12 D4 57 56N 4 26W
Oymyakon, *Russia* 27 C15 63 25N 142 44 E
Oyo, *Nigeria* 50 G6 7 46N 3 56 E
Oyster Bay, *U.S.A.* 79 F11 40 52N 73 32W
Ōyūbari, *Japan* 30 C11 43 1N 142 5 E
Ozamiz, *Phil.* 37 C6 8 15N 123 50 E
Ozark, *Ala., U.S.A.* 77 K3 31 28N 85 39W
Ozark, *Ark., U.S.A.* 81 H8 35 29N 93 50W
Ozark, *Mo., U.S.A.* 81 G8 37 1N 93 12W
Ozark Plateau, *U.S.A.* 81 G9 37 20N 91 40W
Ozarks, L. of the, *U.S.A.* 80 F8 38 12N 92 38W
Ózd, *Hungary* 17 D11 48 14N 20 15 E
Ozette L., *U.S.A.* 84 B2 48 6N 124 38W
Ozona, *U.S.A.* 81 K4 30 43N 101 12W
Ozuluama, *Mexico* 87 C5 21 40N 97 50W

P

Pa-an, *Burma* 41 L20 16 51N 97 40 E
Pa Mong Dam, *Thailand* 38 D4 18 0N 102 22 E
Paarl, *S. Africa* 56 E2 33 45S 18 56 E
Paauilo, *U.S.A.* 74 H17 20 2N 155 22W
Pab Hills, *Pakistan* 42 F2 26 30N 66 45 E
Pabbay, *U.K.* 12 D1 57 46N 7 14W
Pabianice, *Poland* 17 C10 51 40N 19 20 E
Pabna, *Bangla.* 41 G16 24 1N 89 18 E
Pabo, *Uganda* 54 B3 3 1N 32 10 E
Pacaja →, *Brazil* 93 D8 1 56S 50 50W
Pacaraima, Sierra, *Venezuela* 90 C4 4 0N 62 30W
Pacasmayo, *Peru* 92 E3 7 20S 79 35W
Pachhar, *India* 42 G7 24 40N 77 42 E
Pachitea →, *Peru* 92 E4 8 46S 74 33W
Pachpadra, *India* 40 G8 25 58N 72 10 E
Pachuca, *Mexico* 87 C5 20 10N 98 40W
Pacific, *Canada* 72 C3 54 48N 128 28W
Pacific-Antarctic Ridge, *Pac. Oc.* 65 M16 43 0S 115 0W
Pacific Grove, *U.S.A.* 84 J5 36 38N 121 56W
Pacific Ocean, *Pac. Oc.* 65 G14 10 0N 140 0W
Pacifica, *U.S.A.* 84 H4 37 36N 122 30W
Pacitan, *Indonesia* 37 H14 8 12S 111 7 E
Packwood, *U.S.A.* 84 D5 46 36N 121 40W
Padaido, Kepulauan, *Indonesia* 37 E9 1 5S 138 0 E
Padang, *Indonesia* 36 E2 1 0S 100 20 E
Padang Endau, *Malaysia* 39 L4 2 40N 103 38 E
Padangpanjang, *Indonesia* 36 E2 0 40S 100 20 E
Padangsidempuan, *Indonesia* 36 D1 1 30N 99 15 E
Paddockwood, *Canada* 73 C7 53 30N 105 30W
Paderborn, *Germany* 16 C5 51 42N 8 45 E
Pádova, *Italy* 20 B4 45 25N 11 53 E
Padra, *India* 42 H5 22 15N 73 7 E
Padrauna, *India* 43 F10 26 54N 83 59 E
Padre I., *U.S.A.* 81 M6 27 10N 97 25W
Padstow, *U.K.* 11 G3 50 33N 4 58W
Padua = Pádova, *Italy* 20 B4 45 25N 11 53 E
Paducah, *Ky., U.S.A.* 76 G1 37 5N 88 37W
Paducah, *Tex., U.S.A.* 81 H4 34 1N 100 18W
Paengnyong-do, *S. Korea* 35 F13 37 57N 124 40 E
Paeroa, *N.Z.* 59 G5 37 23S 175 41 E
Pafúri, *Mozam.* 57 C5 22 28S 31 17 E
Pag, *Croatia* 16 F8 44 25N 15 3 E
Pagadian, *Phil.* 37 C6 7 55N 123 30 E
Pagai Selatan, Pulau, *Indonesia* 36 E2 3 0S 100 15 E
Pagai Utara, Pulau, *Indonesia* 36 E2 2 35S 100 0 E
Pagalu = Annobón, *Atl. Oc.* 49 G4 1 25S 5 36 E
Pagastikós Kólpos, *Greece* 21 E10 39 15N 23 0 E
Pagatan, *Indonesia* 36 E5 3 33S 115 59 E
Page, *Ariz., U.S.A.* 83 H8 36 57N 111 27W
Page, *N. Dak., U.S.A.* 80 B6 47 10N 97 34W
Pago Pago, *Amer. Samoa* 59 B13 14 16S 170 43W
Pagosa Springs, *U.S.A.* 83 H10 37 16N 107 1W
Pagwa River, *Canada* 70 B2 50 2N 85 14W
Pahala, *U.S.A.* 74 J17 19 12N 155 29W
Pahang →, *Malaysia* 39 L4 3 30N 103 9 E
Pahiatua, *N.Z.* 59 J5 40 27S 175 50 E
Pahokee, *U.S.A.* 77 M5 26 50N 80 40W
Pahrump, *U.S.A.* 85 J11 36 12N 115 59W
Pahute Mesa, *U.S.A.* 84 H10 37 20N 116 45W
Pai, *Thailand* 38 C2 19 19N 98 27 E
Paia, *U.S.A.* 74 H16 20 54N 156 22W
Paicines, *U.S.A.* 84 J5 36 44N 121 17W
Paide, *Estonia* 9 G21 58 57N 25 31 E
Paignton, *U.K.* 11 G4 50 26N 3 35W
Päijänne, *Finland* 9 F21 61 30N 25 30 E
Pailin, *Cambodia* 38 F4 12 46N 102 36 E
Painan, *Indonesia* 36 E2 1 21S 100 34 E
Painesville, *U.S.A.* 78 E3 41 43N 81 15W
Paint Hills = Wemindji, *Canada* 70 B4 53 0N 78 49W
Paint L., *Canada* 73 B9 55 28N 97 57W
Paint Rock, *U.S.A.* 81 K5 31 31N 99 55W
Painted Desert, *U.S.A.* 83 J8 36 0N 111 0W
Paintsville, *U.S.A.* 76 G4 37 49N 82 48W
País Vasco □, *Spain* 19 A4 42 50N 2 45W
Paisley, *Canada* 78 B3 44 18N 81 16W
Paisley, *U.K.* 12 F4 55 50N 4 25W
Paisley, *U.S.A.* 82 E3 42 42N 120 32W
Paita, *Peru* 92 E2 5 11S 81 9W
Pajares, Puerto de, *Spain* 19 A3 42 58N 5 46W
Pak Lay, *Laos* 38 C3 18 15N 101 27 E
Pak Phanang, *Thailand* 39 H3 8 21N 100 12 E
Pak Sane, *Laos* 38 C4 18 22N 103 39 E
Pak Song, *Laos* 38 E6 15 11N 106 14 E
Pak Suong, *Laos* 38 C4 19 58N 102 15 E
Pákhnes, *Greece* 23 D6 35 16N 24 4 E
Pakistan ■, *Asia* 42 E4 30 0N 70 0 E
Pakkading, *Laos* 38 C4 18 19N 103 59 E
Pakokku, *Burma* 41 J19 21 20N 95 0 E
Pakpattan, *Pakistan* 42 D5 30 25N 73 27 E
Paktīā □, *Afghan.* 40 C6 33 0N 69 15 E
Pakwach, *Uganda* 54 B3 2 28N 31 27 E
Pakxe, *Laos* 38 E5 15 5N 105 52 E
Pala, *Chad* 51 G9 9 25N 15 5 E
Pala, *Dem. Rep. of the Congo* 54 D2 6 45S 29 30 E
Pala, *U.S.A.* 85 M9 33 22N 117 5W
Palabek, *Uganda* 54 B3 3 22N 32 33 E
Palacios, *U.S.A.* 81 L6 28 42N 96 13W
Palagruža, *Croatia* 20 C7 42 24N 16 15 E
Palaiókastron, *Greece* 23 D8 35 12N 26 15 E
Palaiokhóra, *Greece* 23 D5 35 16N 23 39 E
Palam, *India* 40 K10 19 0N 77 0 E
Palampur, *India* 42 C7 32 10N 76 30 E
Palana, *Australia* 62 F4 39 45S 147 55 E
Palana, *Russia* 27 D16 59 10N 159 59 E
Palanan, *Phil.* 37 A6 17 8N 122 29 E
Palanan Pt., *Phil.* 37 A6 17 17N 122 30 E
Palandri, *Pakistan* 43 C5 33 42N 73 40 E
Palanga, *Lithuania* 9 J19 55 58N 21 3 E
Palangkaraya, *Indonesia* 36 E4 2 16S 113 56 E
Palani Hills, *India* 40 P10 10 14N 77 33 E
Palanpur, *India* 42 G5 24 10N 72 25 E
Palapye, *Botswana* 56 C4 22 30S 27 7 E
Palas, *Pakistan* 43 B5 35 4N 73 14 E
Palatka, *Russia* 27 C16 60 6N 150 54 E
Palatka, *U.S.A.* 77 L5 29 39N 81 38W
Palau ■, *Pac. Oc.* 64 G5 7 30N 134 30 E
Palauk, *Burma* 38 F2 13 10N 98 40 E
Palawan, *Phil.* 36 C5 9 30N 118 30 E
Palayankottai, *India* 40 Q10 8 45N 77 45 E
Paldiski, *Estonia* 9 G21 59 23N 24 9 E
Paleleh, *Indonesia* 37 D6 1 10N 121 50 E
Palembang, *Indonesia* 36 E2 3 0S 104 50 E
Palencia, *Spain* 19 A3 42 1N 4 34W
Paleokastrítsa, *Greece* 23 A3 39 40N 19 41 E
Paleometokho, *Cyprus* 23 D12 35 7N 33 11 E
Palermo, *Italy* 20 E5 38 7N 13 22 E
Palermo, *U.S.A.* 82 G3 39 26N 121 33W
Palestina, *Chile* 96 A3 23 50S 69 47W
Palestine, *Asia* 47 D4 32 0N 35 0 E
Palestine, *U.S.A.* 81 K7 31 46N 95 38W
Paletwa, *Burma* 41 J18 21 10N 92 50 E
Palghat, *India* 40 P10 10 46N 76 42 E
Palgrave, Mt., *Australia* 60 D2 23 22S 115 58 E
Pali, *India* 42 G5 25 50N 73 20 E
Palioúrion, Ákra, *Greece* 21 E10 39 57N 23 45 E
Palisade, *U.S.A.* 80 E4 40 21N 101 7W
Paliseul, *Belgium* 15 E5 49 54N 5 8 E
Palitana, *India* 42 J4 21 32N 71 49 E
Palizada, *Mexico* 87 D6 18 18N 92 8W
Palk Bay, *Asia* 40 Q11 9 30N 79 15 E
Palk Strait, *Asia* 40 Q11 10 0N 79 45 E
Palkānah, *Iraq* 44 C5 35 49N 44 26 E
Palla Road = Dinokwe, *Botswana* 56 C4 23 29S 26 37 E
Pallanza = Verbánia, *Italy* 18 D8 45 56N 8 33 E
Pallisa, *Uganda* 54 B3 1 12N 33 43 E
Pallu, *India* 42 E6 28 59N 74 14 E
Palm Bay, *U.S.A.* 77 L5 28 2N 80 35W
Palm Beach, *U.S.A.* 77 M6 26 43N 80 2W
Palm Desert, *U.S.A.* 85 M10 33 43N 116 22W
Palm Is., *Australia* 62 B4 18 40S 146 35 E
Palm Springs, *U.S.A.* 85 M10 33 50N 116 33W
Palma, *Mozam.* 55 E5 10 46S 40 29 E
Palma, B. de, *Spain* 22 B9 39 30N 2 39 E
Palma de Mallorca, *Spain* 22 B9 39 35N 2 39 E
Palma Soriano, *Cuba* 88 B4 20 15N 76 0W
Palmares, *Brazil* 93 E11 8 41S 35 28W
Palmas, *Brazil* 95 B5 26 29S 52 0W
Palmas, C., *Liberia* 50 H4 4 27N 7 46W
Pálmas, G. di, *Italy* 20 E3 39 0N 8 30 E
Palmdale, *U.S.A.* 85 L8 34 35N 118 7W
Palmeira dos Índios, *Brazil* 93 E11 9 25S 36 37W
Palmer, *U.S.A.* 68 B5 61 36N 149 7W
Palmer →, *Australia* 62 B3 16 0S 142 26 E
Palmer Arch., *Antarctica* 5 C17 64 15S 65 0W
Palmer Lake, *U.S.A.* 80 F2 39 7N 104 55W
Palmer Land, *Antarctica* 5 D18 73 0S 63 0W
Palmerston, *Canada* 78 C4 43 50N 80 51W
Palmerston, *N.Z.* 59 L3 45 29S 170 43 E
Palmerston North, *N.Z.* 59 J5 40 21S 175 39 E
Palmerton, *U.S.A.* 79 F9 40 48N 75 37W
Palmetto, *U.S.A.* 77 M4 27 31N 82 34W
Palmi, *Italy* 20 E6 38 21N 15 51 E
Palmira, *Argentina* 94 C2 32 59S 68 34W
Palmira, *Colombia* 92 C3 3 32N 76 16W
Palmyra = Tudmur, *Syria* 44 C3 34 36N 38 15 E
Palmyra, *Mo., U.S.A.* 80 F9 39 48N 91 32W
Palmyra, *N.Y., U.S.A.* 78 C7 43 5N 77 18W
Palmyra Is., *Pac. Oc.* 65 G11 5 52N 162 5W
Palo Alto, *U.S.A.* 84 H4 37 27N 122 10W
Palo Verde, *U.S.A.* 85 M12 33 26N 114 44W
Palopo, *Indonesia* 37 E6 3 0S 120 16 E
Palos, C. de, *Spain* 19 D5 37 38N 0 40W
Palos Verdes, *U.S.A.* 85 M8 33 48N 118 23W
Palos Verdes, Pt., *U.S.A.* 85 M8 33 43N 118 26W
Palouse, *U.S.A.* 82 C5 46 55N 117 4W
Palparara, *Australia* 62 C3 24 47S 141 28 E
Palu, *Indonesia* 37 E5 1 0S 119 52 E
Palu, *Turkey* 25 G7 38 45N 40 0 E
Palwal, *India* 42 E7 28 8N 77 19 E
Pamanukan, *Indonesia* 37 G12 6 16S 107 49 E
Pamiers, *France* 18 E4 43 7N 1 39 E
Pamir, *Tajikistan* 26 F8 37 40N 73 0 E
Pamlico →, *U.S.A.* 77 H7 35 20N 76 28W
Pamlico Sd., *U.S.A.* 77 H8 35 20N 76 0W
Pampa, *U.S.A.* 81 H4 35 32N 100 58W
Pampa de las Salinas, *Argentina* 94 C2 32 1S 66 58W
Pampanua, *Indonesia* 37 E6 4 16S 120 8 E
Pampas, *Argentina* 94 D3 35 0S 63 0W
Pampas, *Peru* 92 F4 12 20S 74 50W
Pamplona, *Colombia* 92 B4 7 23N 72 39W
Pamplona, *Spain* 19 A5 42 48N 1 38W
Pampoenpoort, *S. Africa* 56 E3 31 3S 22 40 E
Pana, *U.S.A.* 80 F10 39 23N 89 5W
Panaca, *U.S.A.* 83 H6 37 47N 114 23W
Panaitan, *Indonesia* 37 G11 6 36S 105 12 E
Panaji, *India* 40 M8 15 25N 73 50 E
Panamá, *Panama* 88 E4 9 0N 79 25W
Panama ■, *Cent. Amer.* 88 E4 8 48N 79 55W
Panamá, G. de, *Panama* 88 E4 8 4N 79 20W
Panama Canal, *Panama* 88 E4 9 10N 79 37W
Panama City, *U.S.A.* 77 K3 30 10N 85 40W
Panamint Range, *U.S.A.* 85 J9 36 20N 117 20W
Panamint Springs, *U.S.A.* 85 J9 36 20N 117 28W
Panão, *Peru* 92 E3 9 55S 75 55W
Panare, *Thailand* 39 J3 6 51N 101 30 E
Panay, *Phil.* 37 B6 11 10N 122 30 E
Panay, G., *Phil.* 37 B6 11 0N 122 30 E
Pancake Range, *U.S.A.* 83 G6 38 30N 115 50W
Pančevo, *Serbia, Yug.* 21 B9 44 52N 20 41 E
Pandan, *Phil.* 37 B6 11 45N 122 10 E
Pandegelang, *Indonesia* 37 G12 6 25S 106 5 E
Pandharpur, *India* 40 L9 17 41N 75 20 E
Pando, *Uruguay* 95 C4 34 44S 56 0W
Pando, L. = Hope, L., *Australia* 63 D2 28 24S 139 18 E
Pandokrátor, *Greece* 23 A3 39 45N 19 50 E
Pandora, *Costa Rica* 88 E3 9 43N 83 3W
Panevėžys, *Lithuania* 24 C3 55 42N 24 25 E
Panfilov, *Kazakstan* 26 E9 44 10N 80 0 E
Pang-Long, *Burma* 41 H21 23 11N 98 45 E
Pang-Yang, *Burma* 41 H21 22 7N 98 48 E
Panga, *Dem. Rep. of the Congo* 54 B2 1 52N 26 18 E
Pangalanes, Canal des, *Madag.* 57 C8 22 48S 47 50 E
Pangani, *Tanzania* 54 D4 5 25S 38 58 E
Pangani □, *Tanzania* 54 D4 5 25S 39 0 E
Pangani →, *Tanzania* 54 D4 5 26S 38 58 E
Pangfou = Bengbu, *China* 35 H9 32 58N 117 20 E
Pangil, *Dem. Rep. of the Congo* 54 C2 3 10S 26 35 E
Pangkah, Tanjung, *Indonesia* 37 G15 6 51S 112 33 E
Pangkajene, *Indonesia* 37 E5 4 46S 119 34 E
Pangkalanbrandan, *Indonesia* 36 D1 4 1N 98 20 E
Pangkalanbuun, *Indonesia* 36 E4 2 41S 111 37 E
Pangkalpinang, *Indonesia* 36 E3 2 0S 106 0 E
Pangnirtung, *Canada* 69 B13 66 8N 65 54W
Panguitch, *U.S.A.* 83 H7 37 50N 112 26W
Pangutaran Group, *Phil.* 37 C6 6 18N 120 34 E
Panhandle, *U.S.A.* 81 H4 35 21N 101 23W
Pani Mines, *India* 42 H5 22 29N 73 50 E
Pania-Mutombo, *Dem. Rep. of the Congo* 54 D1 5 11S 23 51 E
Panipat, *India* 42 E7 29 25N 77 2 E
Panjal Range, *India* 42 C7 32 30N 76 50 E
Panjgur, *Pakistan* 40 F4 27 0N 64 5 E
Panjim = Panaji, *India* 40 M8 15 25N 73 50 E
Panjinad Barrage, *Pakistan* 40 E7 29 22N 71 15 E
Panjwai, *Afghan.* 42 D1 31 26N 65 27 E
Panmunjŏm, *N. Korea* 35 F14 37 59N 126 38 E
Panna, *India* 43 G9 24 40N 80 15 E
Panna Hills, *India* 43 G9 24 40N 81 15 E
Pano Lefkara, *Cyprus* 23 E12 34 53N 33 20 E
Pano Panayia, *Cyprus* 23 E11 34 55N 32 38 E
Panorama, *Brazil* 95 A5 21 21S 51 51W
Pánormon, *Greece* 23 D6 35 25N 24 41 E
Panshan, *China* 35 D12 41 3N 122 2 E
Panshi, *China* 35 C14 42 58N 126 5 E
Pantanal, *Brazil* 92 H7 17 30S 57 40W
Pantar, *Indonesia* 37 F6 8 28S 124 10 E
Pante Macassar, *Indonesia* 37 F6 9 30S 123 58 E
Pantelleria, *Italy* 20 F4 36 50N 11 57 E
Pánuco, *Mexico* 87 C5 22 0N 98 15W
Paola, *Malta* 23 D2 35 52N 14 30 E
Paola, *U.S.A.* 80 F7 38 35N 94 53W
Paonia, *U.S.A.* 83 G10 38 52N 107 36W
Paoting = Baoding, *China* 34 E8 38 50N 115 28 E
Paot'ou = Baotou, *China* 34 D6 40 32N 110 2 E

Perdu, Mt.

Paoua, C.A.R. 52 C3 7 9N 16 20 E
Pápa, Hungary 17 E9 47 22N 17 30 E
Papa Stour, U.K. 12 A7 60 20N 1 42W
Papa Westray, U.K. 12 B6 59 20N 2 55W
Papagayo →, Mexico 87 D5 16 36N 99 43W
Papagayo, G. de, Costa Rica 88 D2 10 30N 85 50W
Papakura, N.Z. 59 G5 37 4S 174 59 E
Papantla, Mexico 87 C5 20 30N 97 30W
Papar, Malaysia 36 C5 5 45N 116 0 E
Paphos, Cyprus 23 E11 34 46N 32 25 E
Papien Chiang = Da →, Vietnam 38 B5 21 15N 105 20 E
Papigochic →, Mexico 86 B3 29 9N 109 40W
Paposo, Chile 94 B1 25 0S 70 30W
Papoutsa, Cyprus 23 E12 34 54N 33 4 E
Papua New Guinea ■, Oceania 64 H6 8 0S 145 0 E
Papudo, Chile 94 C1 32 29S 71 27W
Papun, Burma 41 K20 18 2N 97 30 E
Papunya, Australia 60 D5 23 15S 131 54 E
Pará = Belém, Brazil 93 D9 1 20S 48 30W
Paraburdoo, Australia 60 D2 23 14S 117 32 E
Paracatu, Brazil 93 G9 17 10S 46 50W
Paracel Is., S. China Sea 36 A4 15 50N 112 0 E
Parachilna, Australia 63 E2 31 10S 138 21 E
Parachinar, Pakistan 42 C4 33 55N 70 5 E
Paradhísi, Greece 23 C10 36 18N 28 7 E
Paradip, India 41 J15 20 15N 86 35 E
Paradise, Calif., U.S.A. 84 F5 39 46N 121 37W
Paradise, Mont., U.S.A. 82 C6 47 23N 114 48W
Paradise, Nev., U.S.A. 85 J11 36 9N 115 10W
Paradise →, Canada 71 B8 53 27N 57 19W
Paradise Valley, U.S.A. 82 F5 41 30N 117 32W
Parado, Indonesia 37 F5 8 42S 118 30 E
Paragould, U.S.A. 81 G9 36 3N 90 29W
Paragua →, Venezuela 92 B6 6 55N 62 55W
Paraguaçu →, Brazil 93 F11 12 45S 38 54W
Paraguaçu Paulista, Brazil 95 A5 22 22S 50 35W
Paraguaná, Pen. de, Venezuela 92 A5 12 0N 70 0W
Paraguarí, Paraguay 94 B4 25 36S 57 0W
Paraguarí □, Paraguay 94 B4 26 0S 57 10W
Paraguay ■, S. Amer. 94 A4 23 0S 57 0W
Paraguay →, Paraguay 94 B4 27 18S 58 38W
Paraíba = João Pessoa, Brazil 93 E12 7 10S 34 52W
Paraíba □, Brazil 93 E11 7 0S 36 0W
Paraíba do Sul →, Brazil 95 A7 21 37S 41 3W
Parainen, Finland 9 F20 60 18N 22 18 E
Paraiso, Mexico 87 D6 18 24N 93 14W
Parak, Iran 45 E7 27 38N 52 25 E
Parakou, Benin 50 G6 9 25N 2 40 E
Paralimni, Cyprus 23 D12 35 2N 33 58 E
Paramaribo, Surinam 93 B7 5 50N 55 10W
Paramushir, Ostrov, Russia 27 D16 50 24N 156 0 E
Paran →, Israel 47 E4 30 20N 35 10 E
Paraná, Argentina 94 C3 31 45S 60 30W
Paranã, Brazil 93 F9 12 30S 47 48W
Paraná □, Brazil 95 A5 24 30S 51 0W
Paraná →, Argentina 94 C4 33 43S 59 15W
Paranaguá, Brazil 95 B6 25 30S 48 30W
Paranaíba, Brazil 93 G8 19 40S 51 11W
Paranaíba →, Brazil 93 H8 20 6S 51 4W
Paranapanema →, Brazil 95 A5 22 40S 53 9W
Paranapiacaba, Serra do, Brazil 95 A6 24 31S 48 35W
Paranavaí, Brazil 95 A5 23 4S 52 56W
Parang, Jolo, Phil. 37 C6 5 55N 120 54 E
Parang, Mindanao, Phil. 37 C6 7 23N 124 16 E
Parângul Mare, Vf., Romania 17 F12 45 20N 23 37 E
Paratoo, Australia 63 E2 32 42S 139 20 E
Parattah, Australia 62 G4 42 22S 147 23 E
Parbati →, India 42 G7 25 50N 76 30 E
Parbhani, India 40 K10 19 8N 76 52 E
Parchim, Germany 16 B6 53 26N 11 52 E
Pardes Hanna-Karkur, Israel 47 C3 32 28N 34 57 E
Pardo →, Bahia, Brazil 93 G11 15 40S 39 0W
Pardo →, Mato Grosso, Brazil 95 A5 21 46S 52 9W
Pardubice, Czech Rep. 16 C8 50 3N 15 45 E
Pare, Indonesia 37 G15 7 43S 112 12 E
Pare □, Tanzania 54 C4 4 10S 38 0 E
Pare Mts., Tanzania 54 C4 4 0S 37 45 E
Parecis, Serra dos, Brazil 92 F7 13 0S 60 0W
Pareh, Iran 44 B5 38 52N 45 42 E
Paren, Russia 27 C17 62 30N 163 15 E
Parent, Canada 70 C5 47 55N 74 35W
Parent, L., Canada 70 C4 48 31N 77 1W
Parepare, Indonesia 37 E5 4 0S 119 40 E
Párga, Greece 21 E9 39 15N 20 29 E
Pargo, Pta. do, Madeira 22 D2 32 49N 17 17W
Parguba, Russia 24 B5 62 20N 34 27 E
Pariaguán, Venezuela 92 B6 8 51N 64 34W
Paricutín, Cerro, Mexico 86 D4 19 28N 102 15W
Parigi, Indonesia 37 E6 0 50S 120 5 E
Parika, Guyana 92 B7 6 50N 58 20W
Parima, Serra, Brazil 92 C6 2 30N 64 0W
Parinari, Peru 92 D4 4 35S 74 25W
Pariñas, Pta., S. Amer. 90 D2 4 30S 82 0W
Parintins, Brazil 93 D7 2 40S 56 50W
Pariparit Kyun, Burma 41 M18 14 55N 93 45 E
Paris, Canada 70 D3 43 12N 80 25W
Paris, France 18 B5 48 50N 2 20 E
Paris, Idaho, U.S.A. 82 E8 42 14N 111 24W
Paris, Ky., U.S.A. 76 F3 38 13N 84 15W
Paris, Tenn., U.S.A. 77 G1 36 18N 88 19W
Paris, Tex., U.S.A. 81 J7 33 40N 95 33W
Parish, U.S.A. 79 C8 43 25N 76 8W
Park, U.S.A. 84 B4 48 45N 122 18W
Park City, U.S.A. 82 F8 40 39N 111 30W
Park Falls, U.S.A. 80 C9 45 56N 90 27W
Park Range, U.S.A. 82 G10 40 0N 106 30W
Park Rapids, U.S.A. 80 B7 46 55N 95 4W
Park River, U.S.A. 80 A6 48 24N 97 45W
Park Rynie, S. Africa 57 E5 30 25S 30 45 E
Parkā Bandar, Iran 45 E8 25 55N 59 35 E
Parkano, Finland 9 E20 62 1N 23 0 E
Parker, Ariz., U.S.A. 85 L12 34 9N 114 17W
Parker, S. Dak., U.S.A. 80 D6 43 24N 97 8W
Parker Dam, U.S.A. 85 L12 34 18N 114 8W
Parkersburg, U.S.A. 76 F5 39 16N 81 34W
Parkerview, Canada 73 C8 51 21N 103 18W
Parkes, Australia 63 E4 33 9S 148 11 E
Parkfield, U.S.A. 84 K6 35 54N 120 26W
Parkland, U.S.A. 84 C4 47 9N 122 26W
Parkside, Canada 73 C7 53 10N 106 33W
Parkston, U.S.A. 80 D6 43 24N 97 59W
Parksville, Canada 72 D4 49 20N 124 21W
Parla, Spain 19 B4 40 14N 3 46W
Parma, Italy 18 D9 44 48N 10 20 E
Parma, Idaho, U.S.A. 82 E5 43 47N 116 57W
Parma, Ohio, U.S.A. 78 E3 41 23N 81 43W
Parnaguá, Brazil 93 F10 10 10S 44 38W
Parnaíba →, Brazil 93 D10 3 0S 41 50W
Parnassós, Greece 21 E10 38 35N 22 30 E
Pärnu, Estonia 24 C3 58 28N 24 33 E
Paroo →, Australia 63 E3 31 28S 143 32 E
Parowan, U.S.A. 83 H7 37 51N 112 50W
Parral, Chile 94 D1 36 10S 71 52W
Parramatta, Australia 63 E5 33 48S 151 1 E
Parras, Mexico 86 B4 25 30N 102 20W
Parrett →, U.K. 11 F4 51 12N 3 1W
Parris I., U.S.A. 77 J5 32 20N 80 41W
Parrsboro, Canada 71 C7 45 30N 64 25W
Parry Is., Canada 66 B8 77 0N 110 0W
Parry Sound, Canada 70 C4 45 20N 80 0W
Parshall, U.S.A. 80 B3 47 57N 102 8W
Parsnip →, Canada 72 B4 55 10N 123 2W
Parsons, U.S.A. 81 G7 37 20N 95 16W
Parsons Ra., Australia 62 A2 13 30S 135 15 E
Partinico, Italy 20 E5 38 3N 13 7 E
Paru →, Brazil 93 D8 1 33S 52 38W
Parvān □, Afghan. 40 B6 35 0N 69 0 E
Parvatipuram, India 41 K13 18 50N 83 25 E
Parys, S. Africa 56 D4 26 52S 27 29 E
Pasadena, Calif., U.S.A. 85 L8 34 9N 118 9W
Pasadena, Tex., U.S.A. 81 L7 29 43N 95 13W
Pasaje →, Argentina 94 B3 25 39S 63 56W
Pascagoula, U.S.A. 81 K10 30 21N 88 33W
Pascagoula →, U.S.A. 81 K10 30 23N 88 37W
Paşcani, Romania 17 E14 47 14N 26 45 E
Pasco, U.S.A. 82 C4 46 14N 119 6W
Pasco, Cerro de, Peru 92 F3 10 45S 76 10W
Pascua, I. de, Pac. Oc. 65 K17 27 0S 109 0W
Pasfield L., Canada 73 B7 58 24N 105 20W
Pashiwari, Pakistan 43 B6 34 40N 75 10 E
Pashmakli = Smolyan, Bulgaria 21 D11 41 36N 24 38 E
Pasir Mas, Malaysia 39 J4 6 2N 102 8 E
Pasirian, Indonesia 37 H15 8 13S 113 8 E
Pasirkuning, Indonesia 36 E2 0 30S 104 33 E
Paskūh, Iran 45 E9 27 34N 61 39 E
Pasley, C., Australia 61 F3 33 52S 123 35 E
Pašman, Croatia 16 G8 43 58N 15 20 E
Pasni, Pakistan 40 G3 25 15N 63 27 E
Paso Cantinela, Mexico 85 N11 32 33N 115 47W
Paso de Indios, Argentina 96 E3 43 55S 69 0W
Paso de los Libres, Argentina 94 B4 29 44S 57 10W
Paso de los Toros, Uruguay 94 C4 32 45S 56 30W
Paso Robles, U.S.A. 83 J3 35 38N 120 41W
Paspébiac, Canada 71 C6 48 3N 65 17W
Pasrur, Pakistan 42 C6 32 16N 74 43 E
Passage West, Ireland 13 E3 51 52N 8 21W
Passaic, U.S.A. 79 F10 40 51N 74 7W
Passau, Germany 16 D7 48 34N 13 28 E
Passero, C., Italy 20 F6 36 41N 15 10 E
Passo Fundo, Brazil 95 B5 28 10S 52 20W
Passos, Brazil 93 H9 20 45S 46 37W
Pastavy, Belarus 9 J22 55 4N 26 50 E
Pastaza →, Peru 92 D3 4 50S 76 52W
Pasto, Colombia 92 C3 1 13N 77 17W
Pasuruan, Indonesia 37 G15 7 40S 112 44 E
Patagonia, Argentina 96 F3 45 0S 69 0W
Patagonia, U.S.A. 83 L8 31 33N 110 45W
Patambar, Iran 45 D9 29 45N 60 17 E
Patan, India 40 H8 23 54N 72 14 E
Patan, Maharashtra, India 42 H5 23 54N 72 14 E
Patan, Nepal 41 F14 27 40N 85 20 E
Patani, Indonesia 37 D7 0 20N 128 50 E
Pataudi, India 42 E7 28 18N 76 48 E
Patchewollock, Australia 63 F3 35 22S 142 12 E
Patchogue, U.S.A. 79 F11 40 46N 73 1W
Patea, N.Z. 59 H5 39 45S 174 30 E
Patensie, S. Africa 56 E3 33 46S 24 49 E
Paternò, Italy 20 F6 37 34N 14 54 E
Pateros, U.S.A. 82 B4 48 3N 119 54W
Paterson, U.S.A. 79 F10 40 55N 74 11W
Paterson Ra., Australia 60 D3 21 45S 122 10 E
Pathankot, India 42 C6 32 18N 75 45 E
Pathfinder Reservoir, U.S.A. 82 E10 42 28N 106 51W
Pathiu, Thailand 39 G2 10 42N 99 19 E
Pathum Thani, Thailand 38 E3 14 1N 100 32 E
Pati, Indonesia 37 G14 6 45S 111 1 E
Patía →, Colombia 92 C3 2 13N 78 40W
Patiala, India 42 D7 30 23N 76 26 E
Patkai Bum, India 41 F19 27 0N 95 30 E
Patna, India 43 G11 25 35N 85 12 E
Pato Branco, Brazil 95 B5 26 13S 52 40W
Patonga, Uganda 54 B3 2 45N 33 15 E
Patos, Brazil 93 E11 6 55S 37 16W
Patos, L. dos, Brazil 95 C5 31 20S 51 0W
Patos de Minas, Brazil 93 G9 18 35S 46 32W
Patquía, Argentina 94 C2 30 2S 66 55W
Pátrai, Greece 21 E9 38 14N 21 47 E
Pátraikós Kólpos, Greece 21 E9 38 17N 21 30 E
Patras = Pátrai, Greece 21 E9 38 14N 21 47 E
Patrocínio, Brazil 93 G9 18 57S 47 0W
Patta, Kenya 54 C5 2 10S 41 0 E
Pattani, Thailand 39 J3 6 48N 101 15 E
Patten, U.S.A. 71 C6 46 0N 68 38W
Patterson, Calif., U.S.A. 84 H5 37 28N 121 8W
Patterson, La., U.S.A. 81 L9 29 42N 91 18W
Patterson, Mt., U.S.A. 84 G7 38 29N 119 20W
Patti, India 42 D6 31 17N 74 54 E
Pattoki, Pakistan 42 D5 31 5N 73 52 E
Patton, U.S.A. 78 F6 40 38N 78 39W
Patuakhali, Bangla. 41 H17 22 20N 90 25 E
Patuca →, Honduras 88 C3 15 50N 84 18W
Patuca, Punta, Honduras 88 C3 15 49N 84 14W
Pátzcuaro, Mexico 86 D4 19 30N 101 40W
Pau, France 18 E3 43 19N 0 25W
Pauk, Burma 41 J19 21 27N 94 30 E
Paul I., Canada 71 A7 56 30N 61 20W
Paulis = Isiro, Dem. Rep. of the Congo 54 B2 2 53N 27 40 E
Paulistana, Brazil 93 E10 8 9S 41 9W
Paullina, U.S.A. 80 D7 42 59N 95 41W
Paulo Afonso, Brazil 93 E11 9 21S 38 15W
Paulpietersburg, S. Africa 57 D5 27 23S 30 50 E
Pauls Valley, U.S.A. 81 H6 34 44N 97 13W
Pauma Valley, U.S.A. 85 M10 33 16N 116 58W
Pāveh, Iran 44 C5 35 3N 46 22 E
Pavia, Italy 18 D8 45 7N 9 8 E
Pāvilosta, Latvia 9 H19 56 53N 21 14 E
Pavlodar, Kazakstan 26 D8 52 33N 77 0 E
Pavlograd = Pavlohrad, Ukraine 25 E6 48 30N 35 52 E
Pavlohrad, Ukraine 25 E6 48 30N 35 52 E
Pavlovo, Russia 24 C7 55 58N 43 5 E
Pavlovsk, Russia 25 D7 50 26N 40 5 E
Pawhuska, U.S.A. 81 G6 36 40N 96 20W
Pawling, U.S.A. 79 E11 41 34N 73 36W
Pawnee, U.S.A. 81 G6 36 20N 96 48W
Pawnee City, U.S.A. 80 E6 40 7N 96 9W
Pawtucket, U.S.A. 79 E13 41 53N 71 23W
Paximádhia, Greece 23 E6 35 0N 24 35 E
Paxoí, Greece 21 E9 39 14N 20 12 E
Paxton, Ill., U.S.A. 76 E1 40 27N 88 6W
Paxton, Nebr., U.S.A. 80 E4 41 7N 101 21W
Payakumbuh, Indonesia 36 E2 0 20S 100 35 E
Payette, U.S.A. 82 D5 44 5N 116 56W
Payne Bay = Kangirsuk, Canada 69 C13 60 0N 70 0W
Paynes Find, Australia 61 E2 29 15S 117 42 E
Paynesville, U.S.A. 80 C7 45 23N 94 43W
Paysandú, Uruguay 94 C4 32 19S 58 8W
Payson, Ariz., U.S.A. 83 J8 34 14N 111 20W
Payson, Utah, U.S.A. 82 F8 40 3N 111 44W
Paz →, Guatemala 88 D1 13 44N 90 10W
Paz, B. la, Mexico 86 C2 24 15N 110 25W
Pāzanān, Iran 45 D6 30 35N 49 59 E
Pazardzhik, Bulgaria 21 C11 42 12N 24 20 E
Pe Ell, U.S.A. 84 D3 46 34N 123 18W
Peabody, U.S.A. 79 D14 42 31N 70 56W
Peace →, Canada 72 B6 59 0N 111 25W
Peace Point, Canada 72 B6 59 7N 112 27W
Peace River, Canada 72 B5 56 15N 117 18W
Peach Springs, U.S.A. 83 J7 35 32N 113 25W
Peak, The = Kinder Scout, U.K. 10 D6 53 24N 1 52W
Peak Downs, Australia 62 C4 22 55S 148 5 E
Peak Downs Mine, Australia 62 C4 22 17S 148 11 E
Peak Hill, N.S.W., Australia 63 E4 32 47S 148 11 E
Peak Hill, W. Austral., Australia 61 E2 25 35S 118 43 E
Peak Ra., Australia 62 C4 22 50S 148 20 E
Peake, Australia 63 F2 35 25S 139 55 E
Peake Cr. →, Australia 63 D2 28 2S 136 7 E
Peale, Mt., U.S.A. 83 G9 38 26N 109 14W
Pearblossom, U.S.A. 85 L9 34 30N 117 55W
Pearl →, U.S.A. 81 K10 30 11N 89 32W
Pearl City, U.S.A. 74 H16 21 24N 157 59W
Pearsall, U.S.A. 81 L5 28 54N 99 6W
Pearse I., Canada 72 C2 54 52N 130 14W
Pease →, U.S.A. 81 H5 34 12N 99 2W
Pebane, Mozam. 55 F4 17 10S 38 8 E
Pebas, Peru 92 D4 3 10S 71 46W
Pebble Beach, U.S.A. 84 J5 36 34N 121 57W
Peć, Serbia, Yug. 21 C9 42 40N 20 17 E
Pechenga, Russia 24 A5 69 29N 31 4 E
Pechenizhyn, Ukraine 17 D13 48 30N 24 48 E
Pechiguera, Pta., Canary Is. 22 F6 28 51N 13 53W
Pechora →, Russia 24 A9 68 13N 54 15 E
Pechorskaya Guba, Russia 24 A9 68 40N 54 0 E
Pečory, Russia 9 H22 57 48N 27 40 E
Pecos, U.S.A. 81 K3 31 26N 103 30W
Pecos →, U.S.A. 81 L3 29 42N 101 22W
Pécs, Hungary 17 E10 46 5N 18 15 E
Pedder, L., Australia 62 G4 42 55S 146 10 E
Peddie, S. Africa 57 E4 33 14S 27 7 E
Pedernales, Dom. Rep. 89 C5 18 2N 71 44W
Pedieos →, Cyprus 23 D12 35 10N 33 54 E
Pedirka, Australia 63 D2 26 40S 135 14 E
Pedra Azul, Brazil 93 G10 16 2S 41 17W
Pedreiras, Brazil 93 D10 4 32S 44 40W
Pedro Afonso, Brazil 93 E9 9 0S 48 10W
Pedro Cays, Jamaica 88 C4 17 5N 77 48W
Pedro de Valdivia, Chile 94 A2 22 55S 69 38W
Pedro Juan Caballero, Paraguay 95 A4 22 30S 55 40W
Peebinga, Australia 63 E3 34 52S 140 57 E
Peebles, U.K. 12 F5 55 40N 3 11W
Peekskill, U.S.A. 79 E11 41 17N 73 55W
Peel, U.K. 10 C3 54 13N 4 40W
Peel →, Australia 63 E5 30 50S 150 29 E
Peel →, Canada 68 B6 67 0N 135 0W
Peera Peera Poolanna L., Australia 63 D2 26 30S 138 0 E
Peers, Canada 72 C5 53 40N 116 0W
Pegasus Bay, N.Z. 59 K4 43 20S 173 10 E
Pegu, Burma 41 L20 17 20N 96 29 E
Pegu Yoma, Burma 41 K20 19 0N 96 0 E
Pehuajó, Argentina 94 D3 35 45S 62 0W
Pei Xian, China 34 G9 34 44N 116 55 E
Peine, Chile 94 A2 23 45S 68 8W
Peine, Germany 16 B6 52 19N 10 14 E
Peip'ing = Beijing, China 34 E9 39 55N 116 20 E
Peipus, L. = Chudskoye, Oz., Russia 24 C4 58 13N 27 30 E
Peixe, Brazil 93 F9 12 0S 48 40W
Peixe →, Brazil 93 H8 21 31S 51 58W
Pekalongan, Indonesia 37 G13 6 53S 109 40 E
Pekan, Malaysia 39 L4 3 30N 103 25 E
Pekanbaru, Indonesia 36 D2 0 30N 101 15 E
Pekin, U.S.A. 80 E10 40 35N 89 40W
Peking = Beijing, China 34 E9 39 55N 116 20 E
Pelabuhan Kelang, Malaysia 39 L3 3 0N 101 23 E
Pelabuhan Ratu, Teluk, Indonesia 37 G12 7 5S 106 30 E
Pelabuhanratu, Indonesia 37 G12 7 0S 106 32 E
Pelagie, Is., Italy 20 G5 35 39N 12 33 E
Pelaihari, Indonesia 36 E4 3 55S 114 45 E
Peleaga, Vf., Romania 17 F12 45 22N 22 55 E
Pelée, Mt., Martinique 89 D7 14 48N 61 10W
Pelee, Pt., Canada 70 D3 41 54N 82 31W
Pelee I., Canada 70 D3 41 47N 82 40W
Pelekech, Kenya 54 B4 3 52N 35 8 E
Peleng, Indonesia 37 E6 1 20S 123 30 E
Pelham, U.S.A. 77 K3 31 8N 84 9W
Pelican L., Canada 73 C8 52 28N 100 20W
Pelican Narrows, Canada 73 B8 55 10N 102 56W
Pelican Rapids, Canada 73 C8 52 45N 100 42W
Pelješac, Croatia 20 C7 42 55N 17 25 E
Pelkosenniemi, Finland 8 C22 67 6N 27 28 E
Pella, S. Africa 56 D2 29 1S 19 6 E
Pella, U.S.A. 80 E8 41 25N 92 55W
Pello, Finland 8 C21 66 47N 23 59 E
Pelly →, Canada 68 B6 62 47N 137 19W
Pelly Bay, Canada 69 B11 68 38N 89 50W
Peloponnese = Pelopónnisos □, Greece 21 F10 37 10N 22 0 E
Pelopónnisos □, Greece 21 F10 37 10N 22 0 E
Pelorus Sd., N.Z. 59 J4 40 59S 173 59 E
Pelotas, Brazil 95 C5 31 42S 52 23W
Pelvoux, Massif du, France 18 D7 44 52N 6 20 E
Pemalang, Indonesia 37 G13 6 53S 109 23 E
Pematangsiantar, Indonesia 36 D1 2 57N 99 5 E
Pemba, Mozam. 55 E5 12 58S 40 30 E
Pemba, Zambia 55 F2 16 30S 27 28 E
Pemba Channel, Tanzania 54 D4 5 0S 39 37 E
Pemba I., Tanzania 54 D4 5 0S 39 45 E
Pemberton, Australia 61 F2 34 30S 116 0 E
Pemberton, Canada 72 C4 50 25N 122 50W
Pembina, U.S.A. 80 A6 48 58N 97 15W
Pembina →, U.S.A. 73 D9 48 58N 97 14W
Pembine, U.S.A. 76 C2 45 38N 87 59W
Pembroke, Canada 70 C4 45 50N 77 7W
Pembroke, U.K. 11 F3 51 41N 4 55W
Pembroke, U.S.A. 77 J5 32 8N 81 37W
Pembrokeshire □, U.K. 11 F3 51 52N 4 56W
Pen-y-Ghent, U.K. 10 C5 54 10N 2 14W
Penang = Pinang, Malaysia 39 K3 5 25N 100 15 E
Penápolis, Brazil 95 A6 21 30S 50 0W
Peñarroya-Pueblonuevo, Spain 19 C3 38 19N 5 16W
Penarth, U.K. 11 F4 51 26N 3 11W
Peñas, C. de, Spain 19 A3 43 42N 5 52W
Penas, G. de, Chile 96 F2 47 0S 75 0W
Peñas del Chache, Canary Is. 22 E6 29 6N 13 33W
Pench'i = Benxi, China 35 D12 41 20N 123 48 E
Pend Oreille →, U.S.A. 82 B5 49 4N 117 37W
Pend Oreille, L., U.S.A. 82 C5 48 10N 116 21W
Pendembu, S. Leone 50 G3 9 7N 11 14W
Pender B., Australia 60 C3 16 45S 122 42 E
Pendleton, Calif., U.S.A. 85 M9 33 16N 117 23W
Pendleton, Oreg., U.S.A. 82 D4 45 40N 118 47W
Penedo, Brazil 93 F11 10 15S 36 36W
Penetanguishene, Canada 70 D4 44 50N 79 55W
Pengalengan, Indonesia 37 G12 7 9S 107 30 E
Penge, Kasai Or., Dem. Rep. of the Congo 54 D1 5 30S 24 33 E
Penge, Kivu, Dem. Rep. of the Congo 54 C2 4 27S 28 25 E
Penglai, China 35 F11 37 48N 120 42 E
Penguin, Australia 62 G4 41 8S 146 6 E
Penhalonga, Zimbabwe 55 F3 18 52S 32 40 E
Peniche, Portugal 19 C1 39 19N 9 22W
Penicuik, U.K. 12 F5 55 50N 3 13W
Penida, Indonesia 36 F5 8 45S 115 30 E
Peninsular Malaysia □, Malaysia 39 L4 4 0N 102 0 E
Penitente, Serra dos, Brazil 93 E9 8 45S 46 20W
Penkridge, U.K. 10 E5 52 44N 2 6W
Penmarch, Pte. de, France 18 C1 47 48N 4 22W
Penn Hills, U.S.A. 78 F5 40 28N 79 52W
Penn Yan, U.S.A. 78 D7 42 40N 77 3W
Pennant, Canada 73 C7 50 32N 108 14W
Penner →, India 40 M12 14 35N 80 10 E
Pennines, U.K. 10 C5 54 45N 2 27W
Pennington, U.S.A. 84 F5 39 15N 121 47W
Pennsylvania □, U.S.A. 76 E7 40 45N 77 30W
Penny, Canada 72 C4 53 51N 121 20W
Penola, Australia 63 F3 37 25S 140 48 E
Penong, Australia 61 F5 31 56S 133 1 E
Penonomé, Panama 88 E3 8 31N 80 21W
Penrith, Australia 63 E5 33 43S 150 38 E
Penrith, U.K. 10 C5 54 40N 2 45W
Penryn, U.K. 11 G2 50 9N 5 7W
Pensacola, U.S.A. 77 K2 30 25N 87 13W
Pensacola Mts., Antarctica 5 E1 84 0S 40 0W
Pense, Canada 73 C8 50 25N 104 59W
Penshurst, Australia 63 F3 37 49S 142 20 E
Penticton, Canada 72 D5 49 30N 119 38W
Pentland, Australia 62 C4 20 32S 145 25 E
Pentland Firth, U.K. 12 C5 58 43N 3 10W
Pentland Hills, U.K. 12 F5 55 48N 3 25W
Penylan L., Canada 73 A7 61 50N 106 20W
Penza, Russia 24 D8 53 15N 45 5 E
Penzance, U.K. 11 G2 50 7N 5 33W
Penzhino, Russia 27 C17 63 30N 167 55 E
Penzhinskaya Guba, Russia 27 C17 61 30N 163 0 E
Peoria, Ariz., U.S.A. 83 K7 33 35N 112 14W
Peoria, Ill., U.S.A. 80 E10 40 42N 89 36W
Pera Hd., Australia 62 A3 12 55S 141 37 E
Perabumulih, Indonesia 36 E2 3 27S 104 15 E
Perak →, Malaysia 39 K3 4 0N 100 50 E
Pérama, Kérkira, Greece 23 A3 39 34N 19 54 E
Pérama, Kríti, Greece 23 D6 35 20N 24 40 E
Peräpohjola, Finland 8 C22 66 16N 26 10 E
Percé, Canada 71 C7 48 31N 64 13W
Perche, Collines du, France 18 B4 48 30N 0 40 E
Percival Lakes, Australia 60 D4 21 25S 125 0 E
Percy Is., Australia 62 C5 21 39S 150 16 E
Perdido, Mte., Spain 19 A6 42 40N 0 5 E
Perdu, Mt. = Perdido, Mte., Spain 19 A6 42 40N 0 5 E

Sado, Japan 30 F9 38 0N 138 25 E
Sadon, Burma 41 G20 25 28N 97 55 E
Sæby, Denmark 9 H14 57 21N 10 30 E
Saegerstown, U.S.A. 78 E4 41 43N 80 9W
Şafājah, Si. Arabia 44 E3 26 25N 39 0 E
Säffle, Sweden 9 G15 59 8N 12 55 E
Safford, U.S.A. 83 K9 32 50N 109 43W
Saffron Walden, U.K. 11 E8 52 1N 0 16 E
Safi, Morocco 50 B4 32 18N 9 20W
Şafīābād, Iran 45 B8 36 45N 57 58 E
Safīd Dasht, Iran 45 C6 33 27N 48 11 E
Safīd Kūh, Afghan. 40 B3 34 45N 63 0 E
Safwān, Iraq 44 D5 30 7N 47 43 E
Sag Harbor, U.S.A. 79 F12 41 0N 72 18W
Saga, Japan 31 H5 33 15N 130 16 E
Saga □, Japan 31 H5 33 15N 130 20 E
Sagae, Japan 30 E10 38 22N 140 17 E
Sagar, India 40 M9 14 14N 75 6 E
Sagara, L., Tanzania 54 D3 5 20S 31 0 E
Saginaw, U.S.A. 76 D4 43 26N 83 56W
Saginaw B., U.S.A. 76 D4 43 50N 83 40W
Saglouc = Salluit, Canada 69 B12 62 14N 75 38W
Sagŏ-ri, S. Korea 35 G14 35 25N 126 49 E
Sagua la Grande, Cuba 88 B3 22 50N 80 10W
Saguache, U.S.A. 83 G10 38 5N 106 8W
Saguenay →, Canada 71 C5 48 22N 71 0W
Sagunt, Spain 19 C5 39 42N 0 18W
Sagunto = Sagunt, Spain 19 C5 39 42N 0 18W
Sahagún, Spain 19 A3 42 18N 5 2W
Saḩam al Jawlān, Syria 47 C4 32 45N 35 55 E
Sahand, Kūh-e, Iran 44 B5 37 44N 46 27 E
Sahara, Africa 50 D6 23 0N 5 0 E
Saharan Atlas = Saharien, Atlas, Algeria 50 B6 33 30N 1 0 E
Saharanpur, India 42 E7 29 58N 77 33 E
Saharien, Atlas, Algeria 50 B6 33 30N 1 0 E
Sahasinaka, Madag. 57 C8 21 49S 47 49 E
Sahaswan, India 43 E8 28 5N 78 45 E
Sahibganj, India 43 G12 25 12N 87 40 E
Sāḩilīyah, Iraq 44 C4 33 43N 42 42 E
Sahiwal, Pakistan 42 D5 30 45N 73 8 E
Şaḩneh, Iran 44 C5 34 29N 47 41 E
Sahtaneh →, Canada 72 B4 59 2N 122 28W
Sahuaripa, Mexico 86 B3 29 0N 109 13W
Sahuarita, U.S.A. 83 L8 31 57N 110 58W
Sahuayo, Mexico 86 C4 20 4N 102 43W
Sai Buri, Thailand 39 J3 6 43N 101 45 E
Sa'id Bundas, Sudan 51 G10 8 24N 24 48 E
Sa'īdābād, Kermān, Iran 45 D7 29 30N 55 45 E
Sa'īdābād, Semnān, Iran 45 B7 36 8N 54 11 E
Sa'īdīyeh, Iran 45 B6 36 20N 48 55 E
Saidpur, Bangla. 41 G16 25 48N 89 0 E
Saidu, Pakistan 43 B5 34 43N 72 24 E
Saigon = Phanh Bho Ho Chi Minh, Vietnam 39 G6 10 58N 106 40 E
Saijō, Japan 31 H6 33 55N 133 11 E
Saikhoa Ghat, India 41 F19 27 50N 95 40 E
Saiki, Japan 31 H5 32 58N 131 51 E
Sailolof, Indonesia 37 E8 1 7S 130 46 E
Saimaa, Finland 9 F23 61 15N 28 15 E
Şa'in Dezh, Iran 44 B5 36 40N 46 25 E
St. Abb's Head, U.K. 12 F6 55 55N 2 8W
St. Alban's, Canada 71 C8 47 51N 55 50W
St. Albans, U.K. 11 F7 51 45N 0 19W
St. Albans, Vt., U.S.A. 79 B11 44 49N 73 5W
St. Albans, W. Va., U.S.A. 76 F5 38 23N 81 50W
St. Alban's Head, U.K. 11 G5 50 34N 2 4W
St. Albert, Canada 72 C6 53 37N 113 32W
St. Andrew's, Canada 71 C8 47 45N 59 15W
St. Andrews, U.K. 12 E6 56 20N 2 47W
St-Anicet, Canada 79 A10 45 8N 74 22W
St. Ann B., Canada 71 C7 46 22N 60 25W
St. Ann's Bay, Jamaica 88 C4 18 26N 77 15W
St. Anthony, Canada 71 B8 51 22N 55 35W
St. Anthony, U.S.A. 82 E8 43 58N 111 41W
St. Arnaud, Australia 63 F3 36 40S 143 16 E
St. Arthur, Canada 71 C6 47 33N 67 46W
St-Augustin-Saguenay, Canada 71 B8 51 13N 58 38W
St. Augustine, U.S.A. 77 L5 29 54N 81 19W
St. Austell, U.K. 11 G3 50 20N 4 47W
St-Barthélemy, W. Indies 89 C7 17 50N 62 50W
St. Bees Hd., U.K. 10 C4 54 31N 3 38W
St. Boniface, Canada 73 D9 49 53N 97 5W
St. Bride's, Canada 71 C9 46 56N 54 10W
St. Brides B., U.K. 11 F2 51 49N 5 9W
St-Brieuc, France 18 B2 48 30N 2 46W
St. Catharines, Canada 70 D4 43 10N 79 15W
St. Catherines I., U.S.A. 77 K5 31 40N 81 10W
St. Catherine's Pt., U.K. 11 G6 50 34N 1 18W
St-Chamond, France 18 D6 45 28N 4 31 E
St. Charles, Ill., U.S.A. 76 E1 41 54N 88 19W
St. Charles, Mo., U.S.A. 80 F9 38 47N 90 29W
St. Christopher = St. Kitts, W. Indies 89 C7 17 20N 62 40W
St. Christopher-Nevis ■ = St. Kitts & Nevis ■, W. Indies 89 C7 17 20N 62 40W
St. Clair, Mich., U.S.A. 78 D2 42 50N 82 30W
St. Clair, Pa., U.S.A. 79 F8 40 43N 76 12W
St. Clair, L., Canada 70 D3 42 30N 82 45W
St. Clairsville, U.S.A. 78 F4 40 5N 80 54W
St. Claude, Canada 73 D9 49 40N 98 20W
St. Cloud, Fla., U.S.A. 77 L5 28 15N 81 17W
St. Cloud, Minn., U.S.A. 80 C7 45 34N 94 10W
St-Coeur de Marie, Canada 71 C5 48 39N 71 43W
St. Cricq, C., Australia 61 E1 25 17S 113 6 E
St. Croix, Virgin Is. 89 C7 17 45N 64 45W
St. Croix →, U.S.A. 80 C8 44 45N 92 48W
St. Croix Falls, U.S.A. 80 C8 45 24N 92 38W
St. David's, Canada 71 C8 48 12N 58 52W
St. David's, U.K. 11 F2 51 53N 5 16W
St. David's Head, U.K. 11 F2 51 54N 5 19W
St-Denis, France 18 B5 48 56N 2 22 E
St-Dizier, France 18 B6 48 38N 4 56 E
St. Elias, Mt., U.S.A. 68 B5 60 18N 140 56W
St. Elias Mts., Canada 72 A1 60 33N 139 28W
St-Étienne, France 18 D6 45 27N 4 22 E
St. Eugène, Canada 79 A10 45 30N 74 28W
St. Eustatius, W. Indies 89 C7 17 20N 63 0W
St-Félicien, Canada 70 C5 48 40N 72 25W
St-Flour, France 18 D5 45 2N 3 6 E
St. Francis, U.S.A. 80 F4 39 47N 101 48W
St. Francis →, U.S.A. 81 H9 34 38N 90 36W
St. Francis, C., S. Africa 56 E3 34 14S 24 49 E
St. Francisville, U.S.A. 81 K9 30 47N 91 23W
St-François, L., Canada 79 A10 45 10N 74 22W
St-Gabriel-de-Brandon, Canada 70 C5 46 17N 73 24W
St. Gallen = Sankt Gallen, Switz. 18 C8 47 26N 9 22 E
St-Gaudens, France 18 E4 43 6N 0 44 E
St. George, Australia 63 D4 28 1S 148 30 E
St. George, Canada 71 C6 45 11N 66 50W
St. George, S.C., U.S.A. 77 J5 33 11N 80 35W
St. George, Utah, U.S.A. 83 H7 37 6N 113 35W
St. George, C., Canada 71 C8 48 30N 59 16W
St. George, C., U.S.A. 77 L3 29 40N 85 5W
St. George Ra., Australia 60 C4 18 40S 125 0 E
St. George's, Canada 71 C8 48 26N 58 31W
St-Georges, Canada 71 C5 46 8N 70 40W
St. George's, Grenada 89 D7 12 5N 61 43W
St. George's B., Canada 71 C8 48 24N 58 53W
St. Georges Basin, Australia 60 C4 15 23S 125 2 E
St. George's Channel, Europe 13 E6 52 0N 6 0W
St. Georges Hd., Australia 63 F5 35 12S 150 42 E
St. Gotthard P. = San Gottardo, P. del, Switz. 18 C8 46 33N 8 33 E
St. Helena, U.S.A. 82 G2 38 30N 122 28W
St. Helena ■, Atl. Oc. 49 H3 15 55S 5 44W
St. Helena, Mt., U.S.A. 84 G4 38 40N 122 36W
St. Helena B., S. Africa 56 E2 32 40S 18 10 E
St. Helens, Australia 62 G4 41 20S 148 15 E
St. Helens, U.K. 10 D5 53 27N 2 44W
St. Helens, U.S.A. 84 E4 45 52N 122 48W
St. Helens, Mt., U.S.A. 84 D4 46 12N 122 12W
St. Helier, U.K. 11 H5 49 10N 2 7W
St-Hubert, Belgium 15 D5 50 2N 5 23 E
St-Hyacinthe, Canada 70 C5 45 40N 72 58W
St. Ignace, U.S.A. 76 C3 45 52N 84 44W
St. Ignace I., Canada 70 C2 48 45N 88 0W
St. Ignatius, U.S.A. 82 C6 47 19N 114 6W
St. Ives, U.K. 11 G2 50 12N 5 30W
St. James, U.S.A. 80 D7 43 59N 94 38W
St-Jean, Canada 70 C5 45 20N 73 20W
St-Jean →, Canada 71 B7 50 17N 64 20W
St-Jean, L., Canada 71 C5 48 40N 72 0W
St. Jean Baptiste, Canada 73 D9 49 15N 97 20W
St-Jean-Port-Joli, Canada 71 C5 47 15N 70 13W
St-Jérôme, Qué., Canada 70 C5 45 47N 74 0W
St-Jérôme, Qué., Canada 71 C5 48 26N 71 53W
St. John, Canada 71 C6 45 20N 66 8W
St. John, Kans., U.S.A. 81 G5 38 0N 98 46W
St. John, N. Dak., U.S.A. 80 A5 48 57N 99 43W
St. John →, U.S.A. 71 C6 45 12N 66 5W
St. John, C., Canada 71 C8 50 0N 55 32W
St. John's, Antigua 89 C7 17 6N 61 51W
St. John's, Canada 71 C9 47 35N 52 40W
St. Johns, Ariz., U.S.A. 83 J9 34 30N 109 22W
St. Johns, Mich., U.S.A. 76 D3 43 0N 84 33W
St. Johns →, U.S.A. 77 K5 30 24N 81 24W
St. John's Pt., Ireland 13 B3 54 34N 8 27W
St. Johnsbury, U.S.A. 79 B12 44 25N 72 1W
St. Johnsville, U.S.A. 79 D10 43 0N 74 43W
St. Joseph, La., U.S.A. 81 K9 31 55N 91 14W
St. Joseph, Mich., U.S.A. 76 D2 42 6N 86 29W
St. Joseph, Mo., U.S.A. 80 F7 39 46N 94 50W
St. Joseph →, U.S.A. 76 D2 42 7N 86 29W
St. Joseph, I., Canada 70 C3 46 12N 83 58W
St. Joseph, L., Canada 70 B1 51 10N 90 35W
St-Jovite, Canada 70 C5 46 8N 74 38W
St. Kilda, N.Z. 59 L3 45 53S 170 31 E
St. Kitts, W. Indies 89 C7 17 20N 62 40W
St. Kitts & Nevis ■, W. Indies 89 C7 17 20N 62 40W
St. Laurent, Canada 73 C9 50 25N 97 58W
St. Lawrence, Australia 62 C4 22 16S 149 31 E
St. Lawrence, Canada 71 C8 46 54N 55 23W
St. Lawrence →, Canada 71 C6 49 30N 66 0W
St. Lawrence, Gulf of, Canada 71 C7 48 25N 62 0W
St. Lawrence I., U.S.A. 68 B3 63 30N 170 30W
St. Leonard, Canada 71 C6 47 12N 67 58W
St. Lewis →, Canada 71 B8 52 26N 56 11W
St-Lô, France 18 B3 49 7N 1 5W
St-Louis, Senegal 50 E2 16 8N 16 27W
St. Louis, Mich., U.S.A. 76 D3 43 25N 84 36W
St. Louis, Mo., U.S.A. 80 F9 38 37N 90 12W
St. Louis →, U.S.A. 80 B8 47 15N 92 45W
St. Lucia ■, W. Indies 89 D7 14 0N 60 50W
St. Lucia, L., S. Africa 57 D5 28 5S 32 30 E
St. Lucia Channel, W. Indies 89 D7 14 15N 61 0W
St. Lunaire-Griquet, Canada 71 B8 51 31N 55 28W
St. Maarten, W. Indies 89 C7 18 0N 63 5W
St. Magnus B., U.K. 12 A7 60 25N 1 35W
St-Malo, France 18 B2 48 39N 2 1W
St-Marc, Haiti 89 C5 19 10N 72 41W
St. Maries, U.S.A. 82 C5 47 19N 116 35W
St-Martin, W. Indies 89 C7 18 0N 63 0W
St. Martin, L., Canada 73 C9 51 40N 98 30W
St. Martins, Canada 71 C6 45 22N 65 34W
St. Martinville, U.S.A. 81 K9 30 7N 91 50W
St. Mary Pk., Australia 63 E2 31 32S 138 34 E
St. Marys, Australia 62 G4 41 35S 148 11 E
St. Marys, Canada 78 C3 43 20N 81 10W
St. Mary's, Corn., U.K. 11 H1 49 55N 6 18W
St. Mary's, Orkney, U.K. 12 C6 58 54N 2 54W
St. Marys, U.S.A. 78 E6 41 26N 78 34W
St. Mary's, C., Canada 71 C9 46 50N 54 12W
St. Mary's B., Canada 71 C9 46 50N 53 50W
St. Marys Bay, Canada 71 D6 44 25N 66 10W
St-Mathieu, Pte., France 18 B1 48 20N 4 45W
St. Matthews, I. = Zadetkyi Kyun, Burma 39 H2 10 0N 98 25 E
St-Maurice →, Canada 70 C5 46 21N 72 31W
St-Nazaire, France 18 C2 47 17N 2 12W
St. Neots, U.K. 11 E7 52 14N 0 15W
St-Niklaas, Belgium 15 C4 51 10N 4 8 E
St-Omer, France 18 A5 50 45N 2 15 E
St-Pacome, Canada 71 C6 47 24N 69 58W
St-Pamphile, Canada 71 C6 46 58N 69 48W
St. Pascal, Canada 71 C6 47 32N 69 48W
St. Paul, Canada 72 C6 54 0N 111 17W
St. Paul, Minn., U.S.A. 80 C8 44 57N 93 6W
St. Paul, Nebr., U.S.A. 80 E5 41 13N 98 27W
St. Paul, I., Ind. Oc. 3 F13 38 55S 77 34 E
St. Paul I., Canada 71 C7 47 12N 60 9W
St. Peter, U.S.A. 80 C8 44 20N 93 57W
St. Peter Port, U.K. 11 H5 49 26N 2 33W
St. Peters, N.S., Canada 71 C7 45 40N 60 53W
St. Peters, P.E.I., Canada 71 C7 46 25N 62 35W
St. Petersburg = Sankt-Peterburg, Russia 24 C5 59 55N 30 20 E
St. Petersburg, U.S.A. 77 M4 27 46N 82 39W
St-Pierre, St- P. & M. 71 C8 46 46N 56 12W
St-Pierre, L., Canada 70 C5 46 12N 72 52W
St-Pierre et Miquelon □, St- P. & M. 71 C8 46 55N 56 10W
St-Quentin, France 18 B5 49 50N 3 16 E
St. Regis, U.S.A. 82 C6 47 18N 115 6W
St. Sebastien, Tanjon' i, Madag. 57 A8 12 26S 48 44 E
St-Siméon, Canada 71 C6 47 51N 69 54W
St. Stephen, Canada 71 C6 45 16N 67 17W
St. Thomas, Canada 70 D3 42 45N 81 10W
St. Thomas I., Virgin Is. 89 C7 18 20N 64 55W
St-Tite, Canada 70 C5 46 45N 72 34W
St-Tropez, France 18 E7 43 17N 6 38 E
St. Troud = St. Truiden, Belgium 15 D5 50 48N 5 10 E
St. Truiden, Belgium 15 D5 50 48N 5 10 E
St. Vincent, W. Indies 89 D7 13 10N 61 10W
St. Vincent, G., Australia 63 F2 35 0S 138 0 E
St. Vincent & the Grenadines ■, W. Indies 89 D7 13 0N 61 10W
St. Vincent Passage, W. Indies 89 D7 13 30N 61 0W
St-Vith, Belgium 15 D6 50 17N 6 9 E
Ste-Agathe-des-Monts, Canada 70 C5 46 3N 74 17W
Ste-Anne de Beaupré, Canada 71 C5 47 2N 70 58W
Ste-Anne-des-Monts, Canada 71 C6 49 8N 66 30W
Ste. Genevieve, U.S.A. 80 G9 37 59N 90 2W
Ste-Marguerite →, Canada 71 B6 50 9N 66 36W
Ste-Marie, Martinique 89 D7 14 48N 61 1W
Ste-Marie de la Madeleine, Canada 71 C5 46 26N 71 0W
Ste-Rose, Guadeloupe 89 C7 16 20N 61 45W
Ste. Rose du Lac, Canada 73 C9 51 4N 99 30W
Saintes, France 18 D3 45 45N 0 37W
Saintes, I. des, Guadeloupe 89 C7 15 50N 61 35W
Saintfield, U.K. 13 B6 54 28N 5 49W
Saintonge, France 18 D3 45 40N 0 50W
Saipan, Pac. Oc. 64 F6 15 12N 145 45 E
Sairang, India 41 H18 23 50N 92 45 E
Sairecábur, Cerro, Bolivia 94 A2 22 43S 67 54W
Saitama □, Japan 31 F9 36 25N 139 30 E
Sajama, Bolivia 92 G5 18 7S 69 0W
Sajószentpéter, Hungary 17 D11 48 12N 20 44 E
Sajum, India 43 C8 33 20N 79 0 E
Sak →, S. Africa 56 E3 30 52S 20 25 E
Sakai, Japan 31 G7 34 30N 135 30 E
Sakaide, Japan 31 G6 34 15N 133 50 E
Sakaiminato, Japan 31 G6 35 38N 133 11 E
Sakākah, Si. Arabia 44 D4 30 0N 40 8 E
Sakakawea, L., U.S.A. 80 B4 47 30N 101 25W
Sakami, L., Canada 70 B4 53 15N 77 0W
Sakania, Dem. Rep. of the Congo 55 E2 12 43S 28 30 E
Sakarya = Adapazan, Turkey 25 F5 40 48N 30 25 E
Sakarya →, Turkey 25 F5 41 7N 30 39 E
Sakashima-Guntō, Japan 31 M2 24 46N 124 0 E
Sakata, Japan 30 E9 38 55N 139 50 E
Sakchu, N. Korea 35 D13 40 23N 125 2 E
Sakeny →, Madag. 57 C8 20 0S 45 25 E
Sakha □, Russia 27 C14 66 0N 130 0 E
Sakhalin, Russia 27 D15 51 0N 143 0 E
Sakhalinskiy Zaliv, Russia 27 D15 54 0N 141 0 E
Šakiai, Lithuania 9 J20 54 59N 23 2 E
Sakon Nakhon, Thailand 38 D5 17 10N 104 9 E
Sakrand, Pakistan 42 F3 26 10N 68 15 E
Sakrivier, S. Africa 56 E3 30 54S 20 28 E
Sakuma, Japan 31 G8 35 3N 137 49 E
Sakurai, Japan 31 G7 34 30N 135 51 E
Sala, Sweden 9 G17 59 58N 16 35 E
Sala Consilina, Italy 20 D6 40 23N 15 36 E
Sala-y-Gómez, Pac. Oc. 65 K17 26 28S 105 28W
Salaberry-de-Valleyfield, Canada 70 C5 45 15N 74 8W
Saladas, Argentina 94 B4 28 15S 58 40W
Saladillo, Argentina 94 D4 35 40S 59 55W
Salado →, Buenos Aires, Argentina 94 D4 35 44S 57 22W
Salado →, La Pampa, Argentina 96 D3 37 30S 67 0W
Salado →, Santa Fe, Argentina 94 C3 31 40S 60 41W
Salado →, Mexico 86 B5 26 52N 99 19W
Salaga, Ghana 50 G5 8 31N 0 31W
Sālah, Syria 47 C5 32 40N 36 45 E
Sálakhos, Greece 23 C9 36 17N 27 57 E
Salālah, Oman 46 D5 16 56N 53 59 E
Salamanca, Chile 94 C1 31 46S 70 59W
Salamanca, Spain 19 B3 40 58N 5 39W
Salamanca, U.S.A. 78 D6 42 10N 78 43W
Salāmatābād, Iran 44 C5 35 39N 47 50 E
Salamis, Cyprus 23 D12 35 11N 33 54 E
Salar de Atacama, Chile 94 A2 23 30S 68 25W
Salar de Uyuni, Bolivia 92 H5 20 30S 67 45W
Salatiga, Indonesia 37 G14 7 19S 110 30 E
Salavat, Russia 24 D10 53 21N 55 55 E
Salaverry, Peru 92 E3 8 15S 79 0W
Salawati, Indonesia 37 E8 1 7S 130 52 E
Salayar, Indonesia 37 F6 6 7S 120 30 E
Salcombe, U.K. 11 G4 50 14N 3 47W
Saldanha, S. Africa 56 E2 33 0S 17 58 E
Saldanha B., S. Africa 56 E2 33 6S 18 0 E
Saldus, Latvia 9 H20 56 38N 22 30 E
Sale, Australia 63 F4 38 6S 147 6 E
Salé, Morocco 50 B4 34 3N 6 48W
Sale, U.K. 10 D5 53 26N 2 19W
Salekhard, Russia 24 A12 66 30N 66 35 E
Salem, India 40 P11 11 40N 78 11 E
Salem, Ind., U.S.A. 76 F2 38 36N 86 6W
Salem, Mass., U.S.A. 79 D14 42 31N 70 53W
Salem, Mo., U.S.A. 81 G9 37 39N 91 32W
Salem, N.J., U.S.A. 76 F8 39 34N 75 28W
Salem, Ohio, U.S.A. 78 F4 40 54N 80 52W
Salem, Oreg., U.S.A. 82 D2 44 56N 123 2W
Salem, S. Dak., U.S.A. 80 D6 43 44N 97 23W
Salem, Va., U.S.A. 76 G5 37 18N 80 3W
Salerno, Italy 20 D6 40 41N 14 47 E
Salford, U.K. 10 D5 53 30N 2 18W
Salgótarján, Hungary 17 D10 48 5N 19 47 E
Salgueiro, Brazil 93 E11 8 4S 39 6W
Salida, U.S.A. 74 C5 38 32N 106 0W
Salihli, Turkey 21 E13 38 28N 28 8 E
Salihorsk, Belarus 17 B14 52 51N 27 27 E
Salima, Malawi 53 G6 13 47S 34 28 E
Salina, Italy 20 E6 38 34N 14 50 E
Salina, U.S.A. 80 F6 38 50N 97 37W
Salina Cruz, Mexico 87 D5 16 10N 95 10W
Salinas, Brazil 93 G10 16 10S 42 10W
Salinas, Chile 94 A2 23 31S 69 29W
Salinas, Ecuador 92 D2 2 10S 80 58W
Salinas, U.S.A. 84 J5 36 40N 121 39W
Salinas →, Guatemala 87 D6 16 28N 90 31W
Salinas →, U.S.A. 84 J5 36 45N 121 48W
Salinas, B. de, Nic. 88 D2 11 4N 85 45W
Salinas, Pampa de las, Argentina 94 C2 31 58S 66 42W
Salinas Ambargasta, Argentina 94 B3 29 0S 65 0W
Salinas de Hidalgo, Mexico 86 C4 22 30N 101 40W
Salinas Grandes, Argentina 94 C3 30 0S 65 0W
Saline →, Ark., U.S.A. 81 J8 33 10N 92 8W
Saline →, Kans., U.S.A. 80 F6 38 52N 97 30W
Salines, Spain 22 B10 39 21N 3 3 E
Salines, C. de ses, Spain 22 B10 39 16N 3 4 E
Salinópolis, Brazil 93 D9 0 40S 47 20W
Salisbury = Harare, Zimbabwe 55 F3 17 43S 31 2 E
Salisbury, Australia 63 E2 34 46S 138 40 E
Salisbury, U.K. 11 F6 51 4N 1 47W
Salisbury, Md., U.S.A. 76 F8 38 22N 75 36W
Salisbury, N.C., U.S.A. 77 H5 35 40N 80 29W
Salisbury Plain, U.K. 11 F6 51 14N 1 55W
Şalkhad, Syria 47 C5 32 29N 36 43 E
Salla, Finland 8 C23 66 50N 28 49 E
Sallisaw, U.S.A. 81 H7 35 28N 94 47W
Salluit, Canada 69 B12 62 14N 75 38W
Salmās, Iran 44 B5 38 11N 44 47 E
Salmo, Canada 72 D5 49 10N 117 20W
Salmon, U.S.A. 82 D7 45 11N 113 54W
Salmon →, Canada 72 C4 54 3N 122 40W
Salmon →, U.S.A. 82 D5 45 51N 116 47W
Salmon Arm, Canada 72 C5 50 40N 119 15W
Salmon Falls, U.S.A. 82 E6 42 48N 114 59W
Salmon Gums, Australia 61 F3 32 59S 121 38 E
Salmon Res., Canada 71 C8 48 5N 56 0W
Salmon River Mts., U.S.A. 82 D6 45 0N 114 30W
Salo, Finland 9 F20 60 22N 23 10 E
Salome, U.S.A. 85 M13 33 47N 113 37W
Salon-de-Provence, France 18 E6 43 39N 5 6 E
Salonica = Thessaloníki, Greece 21 D10 40 38N 22 58 E
Salonta, Romania 17 E11 46 49N 21 42 E
Salpausselkä, Finland 9 F22 61 0N 27 0 E
Salsacate, Argentina 94 C2 31 20S 65 5W
Salsk, Russia 25 E7 46 28N 41 30 E
Salso →, Italy 20 F5 37 6N 13 57 E
Salt →, Canada 72 B6 60 0N 112 25W
Salt →, U.S.A. 83 K7 33 23N 112 19W
Salt Creek, Australia 63 F2 36 8S 139 38 E
Salt Fork Arkansas →, U.S.A. 81 G6 36 36N 97 3W
Salt Lake City, U.S.A. 82 F8 40 45N 111 53W
Salt Range, Pakistan 42 C5 32 30N 72 25 E
Salta, Argentina 94 A2 24 57S 65 25W
Salta □, Argentina 94 A2 24 48S 65 30W
Saltash, U.K. 11 G3 50 24N 4 14W
Saltburn by the Sea, U.K. 10 C7 54 35N 0 58W
Saltcoats, U.K. 12 F4 55 38N 4 47W
Saltee Is., Ireland 13 D5 52 7N 6 37W
Saltfjellet, Norway 8 C16 66 40N 15 15 E
Saltfjorden, Norway 8 C16 67 15N 14 10 E
Saltillo, Mexico 86 B4 25 25N 101 0W
Salto, Argentina 94 C3 34 20S 60 15W
Salto, Uruguay 94 C4 31 27S 57 50W
Salto →, Italy 20 C5 42 26N 12 25 E
Salto del Guaíra, Paraguay 96 A6 24 3S 54 17W
Salton City, U.S.A. 85 M11 33 29N 115 51W
Salton Sea, U.S.A. 85 M11 33 15N 115 45W
Saltville, U.S.A. 76 G5 36 53N 81 46W
Saluda →, U.S.A. 77 J5 34 1N 81 4W
Salûm, Egypt 51 B11 31 31N 25 7 E
Salur, India 41 K13 18 27N 83 18 E
Salvador, Brazil 93 F11 13 0S 38 30W
Salvador, Canada 73 C7 52 10N 109 32W
Salvador, L., U.S.A. 81 L9 29 43N 90 15W
Salween →, Burma 41 L20 16 31N 97 37 E
Salyan, Azerbaijan 25 G8 39 33N 48 59 E
Salyersville, U.S.A. 76 G4 37 45N 83 4W
Salzach →, Austria 16 D7 48 12N 12 56 E
Salzburg, Austria 16 E7 47 48N 13 2 E
Salzgitter, Germany 16 B6 52 9N 10 19 E
Salzwedel, Germany 16 B6 52 52N 11 10 E
Sam Neua, Laos 38 B5 20 29N 104 5 E
Sam Ngao, Thailand 38 D2 17 18N 99 0 E
Sam Rayburn Reservoir, U.S.A. 81 K7 31 4N 94 5W
Sam Son, Vietnam 38 C5 19 44N 105 54 E
Sam Teu, Laos 38 C5 19 59N 104 38 E
Sama de Langreo = Langreo, Spain 19 A3 43 18N 5 40W
Samagaltay, Russia 27 D10 50 36N 95 3 E

159

161

Szombathely

Storm Lake, U.S.A. 80 D7 42 39N 95 13W
Stormberge, S. Africa 56 E4 31 16S 26 17 E
Stormsrivier, S. Africa 56 E3 33 59S 23 52 E
Stornoway, U.K. 12 C2 58 13N 6 23W
Storozhinets = Storozhynets, Ukraine 17 D13 48 14N 25 45 E
Storozhynets, Ukraine 17 D13 48 14N 25 45 E
Storsjön, Sweden 8 E16 63 9N 14 30 E
Storuman, Sweden 8 D17 65 5N 17 10 E
Storuman, sjö, Sweden 8 D17 65 13N 16 50 E
Stoughton, Canada 73 D8 49 40N 103 0W
Stour →, Dorset, U.K. 11 G6 50 43N 1 47W
Stour →, Kent, U.K. 11 F9 51 18N 1 22 E
Stour →, Suffolk, U.K. 11 F9 51 57N 1 4 E
Stourbridge, U.K. 11 E5 52 28N 2 8W
Stout, L., Canada 73 C10 52 0N 94 40W
Stove Pipe Wells Village, U.S.A. 85 J9 36 35N 117 11W
Stowbtsy, Belarus 17 B14 53 30N 26 43 E
Stowmarket, U.K. 11 E9 52 12N 1 0 E
Strabane, U.K. 13 B4 54 50N 7 27W
Strahan, Australia 62 G4 42 9S 145 20 E
Stralsund, Germany 16 A7 54 18N 13 4 E
Strand, S. Africa 56 E2 34 9S 18 48 E
Stranda, Møre og Romsdal, Norway 9 E12 62 19N 6 58 E
Stranda, Nord-Trøndelag, Norway 8 E14 63 33N 10 14 E
Strangford L., U.K. 13 B6 54 30N 5 37W
Strangsville, U.S.A. 78 E3 41 19N 81 50W
Stranraer, U.K. 12 G3 54 54N 5 1W
Strasbourg, Canada 73 C8 51 4N 104 55W
Strasbourg, France 18 B7 48 35N 7 42 E
Strasburg, U.S.A. 80 B4 46 8N 100 10W
Stratford, Canada 70 D3 43 23N 81 0W
Stratford, N.Z. 59 H5 39 20S 174 19 E
Stratford, Calif., U.S.A. 84 J7 36 11N 119 49W
Stratford, Conn., U.S.A. 79 E11 41 12N 73 8W
Stratford, Tex., U.S.A. 81 G3 36 20N 102 4W
Stratford-upon-Avon, U.K. 11 E6 52 12N 1 42W
Strath Spey, U.K. 12 D5 57 9N 3 49W
Strathalbyn, Australia 63 F2 35 13S 138 53 E
Strathaven, U.K. 12 F4 55 40N 4 5W
Strathcona Prov. Park, Canada 72 D3 49 38N 125 40W
Strathmore, Australia 62 B3 17 50S 142 35 E
Strathmore, Canada 72 C6 51 5N 113 18W
Strathmore, U.K. 12 E5 56 37N 3 7W
Strathmore, U.S.A. 84 J7 36 9N 119 4W
Strathnaver, Canada 72 C4 53 20N 122 33W
Strathpeffer, U.K. 12 D4 57 35N 4 32W
Strathroy, Canada 70 D3 42 58N 81 38W
Strathy Pt., U.K. 12 C4 58 36N 4 1W
Stratton, U.S.A. 80 F3 39 19N 102 36W
Straubing, Germany 16 D7 48 52N 12 34 E
Straumnes, Iceland 8 C2 66 26N 23 8W
Strawberry Reservoir, U.S.A. 82 F8 40 8N 111 9W
Strawn, U.S.A. 81 J5 32 33N 98 30W
Streaky B., Australia 63 E1 32 48S 134 13 E
Streaky Bay, Australia 63 E1 32 51S 134 18 E
Streator, U.S.A. 80 E10 41 8N 88 50W
Streeter, U.S.A. 80 B5 46 39N 99 21W
Streetsville, Canada 78 C5 43 35N 79 42W
Strelka, Russia 27 D10 58 5N 93 3 E
Streng →, Cambodia 38 F4 13 12N 103 37 E
Streymoy, Færoe Is. 8 E9 62 8N 7 5W
Strezhevoy, Russia 26 C8 60 42N 77 34 E
Strimón →, Greece 21 D10 40 46N 23 51 E
Strimonikós Kólpos, Greece 21 D11 40 33N 24 0 E
Stroma, U.K. 12 C5 58 41N 3 7W
Strómboli, Italy 20 E6 38 47N 15 13 E
Stromeferry, U.K. 12 D3 57 21N 5 33W
Stromness, U.K. 12 C5 58 58N 3 17W
Stromsburg, U.S.A. 80 E6 41 7N 97 36W
Strömstad, Sweden 9 G14 58 56N 11 10 E
Strömsund, Sweden 8 E16 63 51N 15 33 E
Stronsay, U.K. 12 B6 59 7N 2 35W
Stroud, U.K. 11 F5 51 45N 2 13W
Stroud Road, Australia 63 E5 32 18S 151 57 E
Stroudsburg, U.S.A. 79 F9 40 59N 75 12W
Stroumbi, Cyprus 23 E11 34 53N 32 29 E
Struer, Denmark 9 H13 56 30N 8 35 E
Strumica, Macedonia 21 D10 41 28N 22 41 E
Struthers, Canada 70 C2 48 41N 85 51W
Struthers, U.S.A. 78 E4 41 4N 80 39W
Stryker, U.S.A. 82 B6 48 41N 114 46W
Stryy, Ukraine 17 D12 49 16N 23 48 E
Strzelecki Cr. →, Australia 63 D2 29 37S 139 59 E
Stuart, Fla., U.S.A. 77 M5 27 12N 80 15W
Stuart, Nebr., U.S.A. 80 D5 42 36N 99 8W
Stuart →, Canada 72 C4 54 0N 123 35W
Stuart Bluff Ra., Australia 60 D5 22 50S 131 52 E
Stuart L., Canada 72 C4 54 30N 124 30W
Stuart Ra., Australia 63 D1 29 10S 134 56 E
Stull, L., Canada 70 B1 54 24N 92 34W
Stung Treng = Stoeng Treng, Cambodia 38 F5 13 31N 105 58 E
Stupart →, Canada 73 B10 56 0N 93 25W
Sturgeon B., Canada 73 C9 52 0N 97 50W
Sturgeon Bay, U.S.A. 76 C2 44 50N 87 23W
Sturgeon Falls, Canada 70 C4 46 25N 79 57W
Sturgeon L., Alta., Canada 72 B5 55 6N 117 32W
Sturgeon L., Ont., Canada 70 C1 50 0N 90 45W
Sturgeon L., Ont., Canada 78 B6 44 28N 78 43W
Sturgis, Mich., U.S.A. 76 E3 41 48N 85 25W
Sturgis, S. Dak., U.S.A. 80 C3 44 25N 103 31W
Sturt Cr. →, Australia 60 C4 19 8S 127 50 E
Sturt Creek, Australia 60 C4 19 12S 128 8 E
Stutterheim, S. Africa 56 E4 32 33S 27 28 E
Stuttgart, Germany 16 D5 48 48N 9 11 E
Stuttgart, U.S.A. 81 H9 34 30N 91 33W
Stuyvesant, U.S.A. 79 D11 42 23N 73 45W
Stykkishólmur, Iceland 8 D2 65 2N 22 40W
Styria = Steiermark □, Austria 16 E8 47 26N 15 0 E
Su Xian, China 34 H9 33 41N 116 59 E
Suakin, Sudan 51 E13 19 8N 37 20 E
Suan, N. Korea 35 E14 38 42N 126 22 E
Suaqui, Mexico 86 B3 29 12N 109 41W
Subang, Indonesia 37 G12 6 34S 107 45 E
Subansiri →, India 41 F18 26 48N 93 50 E
Subayhah, Si. Arabia 44 D3 30 2N 38 50 E
Subi, Indonesia 39 L7 2 58N 108 50 E
Subotica, Serbia, Yug. 21 A8 46 6N 19 39 E
Success, Canada 73 C7 50 28N 108 6W
Suceava, Romania 17 E14 47 38N 26 16 E
Suchan, Russia 30 C6 43 8N 133 9 E
Suchitoto, El Salv. 88 D2 13 56N 89 0W
Suchou = Suzhou, China 33 C7 31 19N 120 38 E
Süchow = Xuzhou, China 35 G9 34 18N 117 10 E
Suck →, Ireland 13 C3 53 17N 8 3W
Sucre, Bolivia 92 G5 19 0S 65 15W
Sucuriú →, Brazil 93 H8 20 47S 51 38W
Sud, Pte., Canada 71 C7 49 3N 62 14W
Sud-Ouest, Pte. du, Canada 71 C7 49 23N 63 36W
Sudan, U.S.A. 81 H3 34 4N 102 32W
Sudan ■, Africa 51 E11 15 0N 30 0 E
Sudbury, Canada 70 C3 46 30N 81 0W
Sudbury, U.K. 11 E8 52 2N 0 45 E
Sûdd, Sudan 51 G12 8 20N 30 0 E
Sudeten Mts. = Sudety, Europe 17 C9 50 20N 16 45 E
Sudety, Europe 17 C9 50 20N 16 45 E
Suðuroy, Færoe Is. 8 F9 61 32N 6 50W
Sudi, Tanzania 55 E4 10 11S 39 57 E
Sudirman, Pegunungan, Indonesia 37 E9 4 30S 137 0 E
Sueca, Spain 19 C5 39 12N 0 21W
Suez = El Suweis, Egypt 51 C12 29 58N 32 31 E
Suez, G. of = Suweis, Khalîg el, Egypt 51 C12 28 40N 33 0 E
Suffield, Canada 73 C6 50 12N 111 10W
Suffolk, U.S.A. 76 G7 36 44N 76 35W
Suffolk □, U.K. 11 E9 52 16N 1 0 E
Sugar City, U.S.A. 80 F3 38 14N 103 40W
Sugluk = Salluit, Canada 69 B12 62 14N 75 38W
Şuḩār, Oman 45 E8 24 20N 56 40 E
Sühbaatar □, Mongolia 34 B8 45 30N 114 0 E
Suhl, Germany 16 C6 50 36N 10 42 E
Sui Xian, China 34 G8 34 25N 115 2 E
Suide, China 34 F6 37 30N 110 12 E
Suifenhe, China 35 B16 44 25N 131 10 E
Suihua, China 33 B7 46 32N 126 55 E
Suining, China 35 H9 33 56N 117 58 E
Suiping, China 34 H7 33 10N 113 59 E
Suir →, Ireland 13 D4 52 16N 7 9W
Suiyang, China 35 B16 44 30N 130 56 E
Suizhong, China 35 D11 40 21N 120 20 E
Sujangarh, India 42 F6 27 42N 74 31 E
Sukabumi, Indonesia 37 G12 6 56S 106 50 E
Sukadana, Indonesia 36 E4 1 10S 110 0 E
Sukagawa, Japan 31 F10 37 17N 140 23 E
Sukaraja, Indonesia 36 E4 2 28S 110 25 E
Sukarnapura = Jayapura, Indonesia 37 E10 2 28S 140 38 E
Sukchŏn, N. Korea 35 E13 39 22N 125 35 E
Sukhona →, Russia 24 C6 61 15N 46 39 E
Sukhothai, Thailand 38 D2 17 1N 99 49 E
Sukhumi = Sokhumi, Georgia 25 F7 43 0N 41 0 E
Sukkur, Pakistan 42 F3 27 42N 68 54 E
Sukkur Barrage, Pakistan 42 F3 27 40N 68 50 E
Sukumo, Japan 31 H6 32 56N 132 44 E
Sukunka →, Canada 72 B4 55 45N 121 15W
Sula, Kepulauan, Indonesia 37 E7 1 45S 125 0 E
Sulaco →, Honduras 88 C2 15 2N 87 44W
Sulaiman Range, Pakistan 42 D3 30 30N 69 50 E
Sūlār, Iran 45 D6 31 53N 51 54 E
Sulawesi □, Indonesia 37 E6 2 0S 120 0 E
Sulawesi Sea = Celebes Sea, Indonesia 37 D6 3 0N 123 0 E
Sulima, S. Leone 50 G3 6 58N 11 32W
Sulina, Romania 17 F15 45 10N 29 40 E
Sulitjelma, Norway 8 C17 67 9N 16 3 E
Sullana, Peru 92 D2 4 52S 80 39W
Sullivan, Ill., U.S.A. 80 F10 39 36N 88 37W
Sullivan, Ind., U.S.A. 76 F2 39 6N 87 24W
Sullivan, Mo., U.S.A. 80 F9 38 13N 91 10W
Sullivan Bay, Canada 72 C3 50 55N 126 50W
Sullivan I. = Lambi Kyun, Burma 39 G2 10 50N 98 20 E
Sulphur, La., U.S.A. 81 K8 30 14N 93 23W
Sulphur, Okla., U.S.A. 81 H6 34 31N 96 58W
Sulphur Pt., Canada 72 A6 60 56N 114 48W
Sulphur Springs, U.S.A. 81 J7 33 8N 95 36W
Sulphur Springs Draw →, U.S.A. 81 J4 32 12N 101 36W
Sultan, Canada 70 C3 47 36N 82 47W
Sultan, U.S.A. 84 C5 47 52N 121 49W
Sultanpur, India 43 F10 26 18N 82 4 E
Sultsa, Russia 24 B8 63 27N 46 2 E
Sulu Arch., Phil. 37 C6 6 0N 121 0 E
Sulu Sea, E. Indies 37 C6 8 0N 120 0 E
Suluq, Libya 51 B10 31 44N 20 14 E
Sulzberger Ice Shelf, Antarctica 5 D10 78 0S 150 0 E
Sumalata, Indonesia 37 D6 1 0N 122 31 E
Sumampa, Argentina 94 B3 29 25S 63 29W
Sumatera □, Indonesia 36 D2 0 40N 100 20 E
Sumatra = Sumatera □, Indonesia 36 D2 0 40N 100 20 E
Sumatra, U.S.A. 82 C10 46 37N 107 33W
Sumba, Indonesia 37 F5 9 45S 119 35 E
Sumba, Selat, Indonesia 37 F5 9 0S 118 40 E
Sumbawa, Indonesia 36 F5 8 26S 117 30 E
Sumbawa Besar, Indonesia 36 F5 8 30S 117 26 E
Sumbawanga □, Tanzania 54 D3 8 0S 31 30 E
Sumbe, Angola 52 G2 11 10S 13 48 E
Sumburgh Hd., U.K. 12 B7 59 52N 1 17W
Sumdo, India 43 B8 35 6N 78 41 E
Sumedang, Indonesia 37 G12 6 52S 107 55 E
Šumen = Shumen, Bulgaria 21 C12 43 18N 26 55 E
Sumenep, Indonesia 37 G15 7 1S 113 52 E
Sumgait = Sumqayıt, Azerbaijan 25 F8 40 34N 49 38 E
Summer L., U.S.A. 82 E3 42 50N 120 45W
Summerland, Canada 72 D5 49 32N 119 41W
Summerside, Canada 71 C7 46 24N 63 47W
Summerville, Ga., U.S.A. 77 H3 34 29N 85 21W
Summerville, S.C., U.S.A. 77 J5 33 1N 80 11W
Summit Lake, Canada 72 C4 54 20N 122 40W
Summit Peak, U.S.A. 83 H10 37 21N 106 42W
Sumner, Iowa, U.S.A. 80 D8 42 51N 92 6W
Sumner, Wash., U.S.A. 84 C4 47 12N 122 14W
Sumoto, Japan 31 G7 34 21N 134 54 E
Šumperk, Czech Rep. 17 D9 49 59N 16 59 E
Sumqayıt, Azerbaijan 25 F8 40 34N 49 38 E
Sumter, U.S.A. 77 J5 33 55N 80 21W
Sumy, Ukraine 25 D5 50 57N 34 50 E
Sun City, Ariz., U.S.A. 83 K7 33 36N 112 17W
Sun City, Calif., U.S.A. 85 M9 33 42N 117 11W
Sunagawa, Japan 30 C10 43 29N 141 55 E
Sunan, N. Korea 35 E13 39 15N 125 40 E
Sunart, L., U.K. 12 E3 56 42N 5 43W
Sunburst, U.S.A. 82 B8 48 53N 111 55W
Sunbury, Australia 63 F3 37 35S 144 44 E
Sunbury, U.S.A. 79 F8 40 52N 76 48W
Sunchales, Argentina 94 C3 30 58S 61 35W
Suncho Corral, Argentina 94 B3 27 55S 63 27W
Sunchon, S. Korea 35 G14 34 52N 127 31 E
Suncook, U.S.A. 79 C13 43 8N 71 27W
Sunda, Selat, Indonesia 36 F3 6 20S 105 30 E
Sunda Is., Indonesia 64 H2 5 0S 105 0 E
Sunda Str. = Sunda, Selat, Indonesia 36 F3 6 20S 105 30 E
Sundance, U.S.A. 80 C2 44 24N 104 23W
Sundarbans, The, Asia 41 J16 22 0N 89 0 E
Sundargarh, India 41 H14 22 4N 84 5 E
Sundays = Sondags →, S. Africa 56 E4 33 44S 25 51 E
Sunderland, Canada 78 B5 44 16N 79 4W
Sunderland, U.K. 10 C6 54 55N 1 23W
Sundre, Canada 72 C6 51 49N 114 38W
Sundridge, Canada 70 C4 45 45N 79 25W
Sundsvall, Sweden 9 E17 62 23N 17 17 E
Sung Hei, Vietnam 39 G6 10 20N 106 2 E
Sungai Kolok, Thailand 39 J3 6 2N 101 58 E
Sungai Lembing, Malaysia 39 L4 3 55N 103 3 E
Sungai Petani, Malaysia 39 K3 5 37N 100 30 E
Sungaigerong, Indonesia 36 E2 2 59S 104 52 E
Sungailiat, Indonesia 36 E3 1 51S 106 8 E
Sungaipenuh, Indonesia 36 E2 2 1S 101 20 E
Sungari = Songhua Jiang →, China 33 B8 47 45N 132 30 E
Songhua Chiang = Songhua Jiang →, China 33 B8 47 45N 132 30 E
Sunndalsøra, Norway 9 E13 62 40N 8 33 E
Sunnyside, Utah, U.S.A. 82 G8 39 34N 110 23W
Sunnyside, Wash., U.S.A. 82 C3 46 20N 120 0W
Sunnyvale, U.S.A. 84 H4 37 23N 122 2W
Sunray, U.S.A. 81 G4 36 1N 101 49W
Suntar, Russia 27 C12 62 15N 117 30 E
Suomenselkä, Finland 8 E21 62 52N 24 0 E
Suomussalmi, Finland 8 D23 64 54N 29 10 E
Suoyarvi, Russia 24 B5 62 3N 32 20 E
Supai, U.S.A. 83 H7 36 15N 112 41W
Supaul, India 43 F12 26 10N 86 40 E
Superior, Ariz., U.S.A. 83 K8 33 18N 111 6W
Superior, Mont., U.S.A. 82 C6 47 12N 114 53W
Superior, Nebr., U.S.A. 80 E5 40 1N 98 4W
Superior, Wis., U.S.A. 80 B8 46 44N 92 6W
Superior, L., U.S.A. 70 C2 47 0N 87 0W
Suphan Buri, Thailand 38 E3 14 14N 100 10 E
Supiori, Indonesia 37 E9 1 0S 136 0 E
Supung Shuiku, China 35 D13 40 35N 124 50 E
Sūq Suwayq, Si. Arabia 44 E3 24 23N 38 27 E
Suqian, China 35 H10 33 54N 118 8 E
Sūr, Lebanon 47 B4 33 19N 35 16 E
Sur, Pt., U.S.A. 84 J5 36 18N 121 54W
Sura →, Russia 24 C8 56 6N 46 0 E
Surab, Pakistan 42 E2 28 25N 66 15 E
Surabaja = Surabaya, Indonesia 37 G15 7 17S 112 45 E
Surabaya, Indonesia 37 G15 7 17S 112 45 E
Surakarta, Indonesia 37 G14 7 35S 110 48 E
Surat, Australia 63 D4 27 10S 149 6 E
Surat, India 40 J8 21 12N 72 55 E
Surat Thani, Thailand 39 H2 9 6N 99 20 E
Suratgarh, India 42 E5 29 18N 73 55 E
Surendranagar, India 42 H4 22 45N 71 40 E
Surf, U.S.A. 85 L6 34 41N 120 36W
Surgut, Russia 26 C8 61 14N 73 20 E
Suriapet, India 40 L11 17 10N 79 40 E
Surigao, Phil. 37 C7 9 47N 125 29 E
Surin, Thailand 38 E4 14 50N 103 34 E
Surin Nua, Ko, Thailand 39 H1 9 30N 97 55 E
Surinam ■, S. Amer. 93 C7 4 0N 56 0W
Suriname = Surinam ■, S. Amer. 93 C7 4 0N 56 0W
Suriname →, Surinam 93 B7 5 50N 55 15W
Sūrmaq, Iran 45 D7 31 3N 52 48 E
Surprise L., Canada 72 B2 59 40N 133 15W
Surrey □, U.K. 11 F7 51 15N 0 31W
Surt, Libya 51 B9 31 11N 16 39 E
Surt, Khalīj, Libya 51 B9 31 40N 18 30 E
Surtsey, Iceland 8 E3 63 20N 20 30W
Suruga-Wan, Japan 31 G9 34 45N 138 30 E
Susaki, Japan 31 H6 33 22N 133 17 E
Sūsangerd, Iran 45 D6 31 35N 48 6 E
Susanville, U.S.A. 82 F3 40 25N 120 39W
Susquehanna →, U.S.A. 79 G8 39 33N 76 5W
Susquehanna Depot, U.S.A. 79 E9 41 57N 75 36W
Susques, Argentina 94 A2 23 35S 66 25W
Sussex, Canada 71 C6 45 45N 65 37W
Sussex, U.S.A. 79 E10 41 13N 74 37W
Sussex, E. □, U.K. 11 G8 51 0N 0 20 E
Sussex, W. □, U.K. 11 G7 51 0N 0 30W
Sustut →, Canada 72 B3 56 20N 127 30W
Susuman, Russia 27 C15 62 47N 148 10 E
Susunu, Indonesia 37 E8 3 20S 133 25 E
Susurluk, Turkey 21 E13 39 54N 28 8 E
Sutherland, S. Africa 56 E3 32 24S 20 40 E
Sutherland, U.S.A. 80 E4 41 10N 101 8W
Sutherland Falls, N.Z. 59 L1 44 48S 167 46 E
Sutherlin, U.S.A. 82 E2 43 23N 123 19W
Sutlej →, Pakistan 42 E4 29 23N 71 3 E
Sutter, U.S.A. 84 F5 39 10N 121 45W
Sutter Creek, U.S.A. 84 G6 38 24N 120 48W
Sutton, Canada 79 A12 45 6N 72 37W
Sutton, U.S.A. 80 E6 40 36N 97 52W
Sutton →, Canada 70 A3 55 15N 83 45W
Sutton Coldfield, U.K. 11 E6 52 35N 1 49W
Sutton in Ashfield, U.K. 10 D6 53 8N 1 16W
Suttor →, Australia 62 C4 21 36S 147 2 E
Suttsu, Japan 30 C10 42 48N 140 14 E
Suva, Fiji 59 D8 18 6S 178 30 E
Suva Planina, Serbia, Yug. 21 C10 43 10N 22 5 E
Suvorov Is. = Suwarrow Is., Cook Is. 65 J11 15 0S 163 0W
Suwałki, Poland 17 A12 54 8N 22 59 E
Suwannaphum, Thailand 38 E4 15 33N 103 47 E
Suwannee →, U.S.A. 77 L4 29 17N 83 10W
Suwanose-Jima, Japan 31 K4 29 38N 129 43 E
Suwarrow Is., Cook Is. 65 J11 15 0S 163 0W
Suwayq aş Şuqban, Iraq 44 D5 31 32N 46 7 E
Suweis, Khalîg el, Egypt 51 C12 28 40N 33 0 E
Suwŏn, S. Korea 35 F14 37 17N 127 1 E
Suzdal, Russia 24 C7 56 29N 40 26 E
Suzhou, China 33 C7 31 19N 120 38 E
Suzu, Japan 31 F8 37 25N 137 17 E
Suzu-Misaki, Japan 31 F8 37 31N 137 21 E
Suzuka, Japan 31 G8 34 55N 136 36 E
Svalbard, Arctic 3 A10 78 0N 17 0 E
Svappavaara, Sweden 8 C19 67 40N 21 3 E
Svartisen, Norway 8 C15 66 40N 13 50 E
Svay Chek, Cambodia 38 F4 13 48N 102 58 E
Svay Rieng, Cambodia 39 G5 11 5N 105 48 E
Svealand □, Sweden 9 G16 60 20N 15 0 E
Sveg, Sweden 9 E16 62 2N 14 21 E
Svendborg, Denmark 9 J14 55 4N 10 35 E
Sverdlovsk = Yekaterinburg, Russia 24 C11 56 50N 60 30 E
Sverdrup Is., Canada 66 B10 79 0N 97 0W
Svetlaya, Russia 30 A9 46 33N 138 18 E
Svetlogorsk = Svyetlahorsk, Belarus 17 B15 52 38N 29 46 E
Svir →, Russia 24 B5 60 30N 32 48 E
Svishtov, Bulgaria 21 C11 43 36N 25 23 E
Svislach, Belarus 17 B13 53 3N 24 2 E
Svobodnyy, Russia 27 D13 51 20N 128 0 E
Svolvær, Norway 8 B16 68 15N 14 34 E
Svyetlahorsk, Belarus 17 B15 52 38N 29 46 E
Swabian Alps = Schwäbische Alb, Germany 16 D5 48 20N 9 30 E
Swainsboro, U.S.A. 77 J4 32 36N 82 20W
Swakopmund, Namibia 56 C1 22 37S 14 30 E
Swale →, U.K. 10 C6 54 5N 1 20W
Swan Hill, Australia 63 F3 35 20S 143 33 E
Swan Hills, Canada 72 C5 54 42N 115 24W
Swan Is., W. Indies 88 C3 17 22N 83 57W
Swan L., Canada 73 C8 52 30N 100 40W
Swan River, Canada 73 C8 52 10N 101 16W
Swanage, U.K. 11 G6 50 36N 1 58W
Swansea, Australia 63 E5 33 3S 151 35 E
Swansea, U.K. 11 F4 51 37N 3 57W
Swansea □, U.K. 11 F3 51 38N 4 3W
Swar →, Pakistan 43 B5 34 40N 72 5 E
Swartberge, S. Africa 56 E3 33 20S 22 0 E
Swartmodder, S. Africa 56 D3 28 1S 20 32 E
Swartruggens, S. Africa 56 D4 25 39S 26 42 E
Swastika, Canada 70 C3 48 7N 80 6W
Swatow = Shantou, China 33 D6 23 18N 116 40 E
Swaziland ■, Africa 57 D5 26 30S 31 30 E
Sweden ■, Europe 9 G16 57 0N 15 0 E
Sweet Home, U.S.A. 82 D2 44 24N 122 44W
Sweetwater, Nev., U.S.A. 84 G7 38 27N 119 9W
Sweetwater, Tex., U.S.A. 81 J4 32 28N 100 25W
Sweetwater →, U.S.A. 82 E10 42 31N 107 2W
Swellendam, S. Africa 56 E3 34 1S 20 26 E
Świdnica, Poland 17 C9 50 50N 16 30 E
Świdnik, Poland 17 C12 51 13N 22 39 E
Świebodzin, Poland 16 B8 52 15N 15 31 E
Świecie, Poland 17 B10 53 25N 18 30 E
Swift Current, Canada 73 C7 50 20N 107 45W
Swiftcurrent →, Canada 73 C7 50 38N 107 44W
Swilly, L., Ireland 13 A4 55 12N 7 33W
Swindle, I., Canada 72 C3 52 30N 128 35W
Swindon, U.K. 11 F6 51 34N 1 46W
Swindon □, U.K. 11 F6 51 34N 1 46W
Swinemünde = Świnoujście, Poland 16 B8 53 54N 14 16 E
Swinford, Ireland 13 C3 53 57N 8 58W
Świnoujście, Poland 16 B8 53 54N 14 16 E
Switzerland ■, Europe 18 C8 46 30N 8 0 E
Swords, Ireland 13 C5 53 28N 6 13W
Sydney, Australia 63 E5 33 53S 151 10 E
Sydney, Canada 71 C7 46 7N 60 7W
Sydney Mines, Canada 71 C7 46 18N 60 15W
Sydra, G. of = Surt, Khalīj, Libya 51 B9 31 40N 18 30 E
Syktyvkar, Russia 24 B9 61 45N 50 40 E
Sylacauga, U.S.A. 77 J2 33 10N 86 15W
Sylarna, Sweden 8 E15 63 2N 12 13 E
Sylhet, Bangla. 41 G17 24 54N 91 52 E
Sylt, Germany 16 A5 54 54N 8 22 E
Sylvan Lake, Canada 72 C6 52 20N 114 3W
Sylvania, U.S.A. 77 J5 32 45N 81 38W
Sylvester, U.S.A. 77 K4 31 32N 83 50W
Sym, Russia 26 C9 60 20N 88 18 E
Symón, Mexico 86 C4 24 42N 102 35W
Synnott Ra., Australia 60 C4 16 30S 125 20 E
Syracuse, Kans., U.S.A. 81 G4 37 59N 101 45W
Syracuse, N.Y., U.S.A. 79 C8 43 3N 76 9W
Syrdarya →, Kazakstan 26 E7 46 3N 61 0 E
Syria ■, Asia 44 C3 35 0N 38 0 E
Syrian Desert = Ash Shām, Bādiyat, Asia 28 F7 32 0N 40 0 E
Syzran, Russia 24 D8 53 12N 48 30 E
Szczecin, Poland 16 B8 53 27N 14 27 E
Szczecinek, Poland 17 B9 53 43N 16 41 E
Szczeciński, Zalew = Stettiner Haff, Germany 16 B8 53 47N 14 15 E
Szczytno, Poland 17 B11 53 33N 21 0 E
Szechwan = Sichuan □, China 32 C5 30 30N 103 0 E
Szeged, Hungary 17 E11 46 16N 20 10 E
Székesfehérvár, Hungary 17 E10 47 15N 18 25 E
Szekszárd, Hungary 17 E10 46 22N 18 42 E
Szentes, Hungary 17 E11 46 39N 20 21 E
Szolnok, Hungary 17 E11 47 10N 20 15 E
Szombathely, Hungary 17 E9 47 14N 16 38 E

T

Vilagarcía de Arousa

V

Vaal →, S. Africa 56 D3 29 4S 23 38 E
Vaal Dam, S. Africa 57 D4 27 0S 28 14 E
Vaalwater, S. Africa 57 C4 24 15S 28 8 E
Vaasa, Finland 8 E19 63 6N 21 38 E
Vác, Hungary 17 E10 47 49N 19 10 E
Vacaria, Brazil 95 B5 28 31S 50 52W
Vacaville, U.S.A. 84 G5 38 21N 121 59W
Vach → = Vakh →, Russia 26 C8 60 45N 76 45 E
Vache, Î. à, Haiti 89 C5 18 2N 73 35W
Vadnagar, India 42 H5 23 47N 72 40 E
Vadodara, India 42 H5 22 20N 73 10 E
Vadsø, Norway 8 A23 70 3N 29 50 E
Vaduz, Liech. 18 C8 47 8N 9 31 E
Værøy, Norway 8 C15 67 40N 12 40 E
Vágar, Færoe Is. 8 E9 62 5N 7 15W
Vågsfjorden, Norway 8 B17 68 50N 16 50 E
Váh →, Slovak Rep. 17 D9 47 43N 18 7 E
Vahsel B., Antarctica 5 D1 75 0S 35 0W
Váï, Greece 23 D8 35 15N 26 18 E
Vaigach, Russia 26 B6 70 10N 59 0 E
Vakh →, Russia 26 C8 60 45N 76 45 E
Val-d'Or, Canada 70 C4 48 7N 77 47W
Val Marie, Canada 73 D7 49 15N 107 45W
Valahia, Romania 17 F13 44 35N 25 0 E
Valandovo, Macedonia 21 D10 41 19N 22 34 E
Valcheta, Argentina 96 E3 40 40S 66 8W
Valdayskaya Vozvyshennost, Russia 24 C5 57 0N 33 30 E
Valdepeñas, Spain 19 C4 38 43N 3 25W
Valdés, Pen., Argentina 96 E4 42 30S 63 45W
Valdez, U.S.A. 68 B5 61 7N 146 16W
Valdivia, Chile 96 D2 39 50S 73 14W
Valdosta, U.S.A. 77 K4 30 50N 83 17W
Valdres, Norway 9 F13 61 5N 9 5 E
Vale, U.S.A. 82 E5 43 59N 117 15W
Vale of Glamorgan □, U.K. 11 F4 51 28N 3 25W
Valença, Brazil 93 F11 13 20S 39 5W
Valença do Piauí, Brazil 93 E10 6 20S 41 45W
Valence, France 18 D6 44 57N 4 54 E
Valencia, Spain 19 C5 39 27N 0 23W
Valencia, Venezuela 92 A5 10 11N 68 0W
Valencia □, Spain 19 C5 39 20N 0 40W
Valencia, G. de, Spain 19 C6 39 30N 0 20 E
Valencia de Alcántara, Spain 19 C2 39 25N 7 14W
Valencia I., Ireland 13 E1 51 54N 10 22W
Valenciennes, France 18 A5 50 20N 3 34 E
Valentim, Sa. do, Brazil 93 E10 6 0S 43 30W
Valentin, Russia 30 C7 43 8N 134 17 E
Valentine, Nebr., U.S.A. 80 D4 42 52N 100 33W
Valentine, Tex., U.S.A. 81 K2 30 35N 104 30W
Valera, Venezuela 92 B4 9 19N 70 37W
Valga, Estonia 9 H22 57 47N 26 2 E
Valier, U.S.A. 82 B7 48 18N 112 16W
Valjevo, Serbia, Yug. 21 B8 44 18N 19 53 E
Valka, Latvia 9 H21 57 42N 25 57 E
Valkeakoski, Finland 9 F20 61 16N 24 2 E
Valkenswaard, Neths. 15 C5 51 21N 5 29 E
Vall de Uxó = La Vall d'Uixó, Spain 19 C5 39 49N 0 15W
Valladolid, Mexico 87 C7 20 40N 88 11W
Valladolid, Spain 19 B3 41 38N 4 43W
Valldemossa, Spain 22 B9 39 43N 2 37 E
Valle de la Pascua, Venezuela 92 B5 9 13N 66 0W
Valle de las Palmas, Mexico 85 N10 32 20N 116 43W
Valle de Santiago, Mexico 86 C4 20 25N 101 15W
Valle de Suchil, Mexico 86 C4 23 38N 103 55W
Valle de Zaragoza, Mexico 86 B3 27 28N 105 49W
Valle Fértil, Sierra del, Argentina 94 C2 30 20S 68 0W
Valle Hermoso, Mexico 87 B5 25 35N 97 40W
Valledupar, Colombia 92 A4 10 29N 73 15W
Vallehermoso, Canary Is. 22 F2 28 10N 17 15W
Vallejo, U.S.A. 84 G4 38 7N 122 14W
Vallenar, Chile 94 B1 28 30S 70 50W
Valletta, Malta 23 D2 35 54N 14 31 E
Valley Center, U.S.A. 85 M9 33 13N 117 2W
Valley City, U.S.A. 80 B6 46 55N 98 0W
Valley Falls, U.S.A. 82 E3 42 29N 120 17W
Valley Springs, U.S.A. 84 G6 38 12N 120 50W
Valley Wells, U.S.A. 85 K11 35 27N 115 46W
Valleyview, Canada 72 B5 55 5N 117 17W
Vallimanca, Arroyo, Argentina 94 D4 35 40S 59 10W
Valls, Spain 19 B6 41 18N 1 15 E
Valmiera, Latvia 9 H21 57 37N 25 29 E
Valognes, France 18 B3 49 30N 1 28W
Valona = Vlóra, Albania 21 D8 40 32N 19 28 E
Valozhyn, Belarus 17 A14 54 3N 26 30 E
Valparaíso, Chile 94 C1 33 2S 71 40W
Valparaíso, Mexico 86 C4 22 50N 103 32W
Valparaiso, U.S.A. 76 E2 41 28N 87 4W
Valparaíso □, Chile 94 C1 33 2S 71 40W
Vals →, S. Africa 56 D4 27 23S 26 30 E
Vals, Tanjung, Indonesia 37 F9 8 26S 137 25 E
Valsad, India 40 J8 20 40N 72 58 E
Valverde, Canary Is. 22 G2 27 48N 17 55W
Valverde del Camino, Spain 19 D2 37 35N 6 47W
Vammala, Finland 9 F20 61 20N 22 54 E
Vámos, Greece 23 D6 35 24N 24 13 E
Van, Turkey 25 G7 38 30N 43 20 E
Van, L. = Van Gölü, Turkey 25 G7 38 30N 43 0 E
Van Alstyne, U.S.A. 81 J6 33 25N 96 35W
Van Blommestein Meer, Surinam 93 C7 4 45N 55 5W
Van Bruyssel, Canada 71 C5 47 56N 72 9W
Van Buren, Canada 71 C6 47 10N 67 55W
Van Buren, Ark., U.S.A. 81 H7 35 26N 94 21W
Van Buren, Maine, U.S.A. 77 B11 47 10N 67 58W
Van Buren, Mo., U.S.A. 81 G9 37 0N 91 1W
Van Canh, Vietnam 38 F7 13 37N 109 0 E
Van Diemen, C., N. Terr., Australia 60 B5 11 9S 130 24 E
Van Diemen, C., Queens., Australia 62 B2 16 30S 139 46 E
Van Diemen G., Australia 60 B5 11 45S 132 0 E
Van Gölü, Turkey 25 G7 38 30N 43 0 E
Van Horn, U.S.A. 81 K2 31 3N 104 50W
Van Ninh, Vietnam 38 F7 12 42N 109 14 E
Van Rees, Pegunungan, Indonesia 37 E9 2 35S 138 15 E
Van Tassell, U.S.A. 80 D2 42 40N 104 5W
Van Wert, U.S.A. 76 E3 40 52N 84 35W
Van Yen, Vietnam 38 B5 21 4N 104 42 E
Vanadzor, Armenia 25 F7 40 48N 44 30 E
Vanavara, Russia 27 C11 60 22N 102 16 E
Vancouver, Canada 72 D4 49 15N 123 10W
Vancouver, U.S.A. 84 E4 45 38N 122 40W
Vancouver, C., Australia 61 G2 35 2S 118 11 E
Vancouver I., Canada 72 D3 49 50N 126 0W
Vandalia, Ill., U.S.A. 80 F10 38 58N 89 6W
Vandalia, Mo., U.S.A. 80 F9 39 19N 91 29W
Vandenburg, U.S.A. 85 L6 34 35N 120 33W
Vanderbijlpark, S. Africa 57 D4 26 42S 27 54 E
Vandergrift, U.S.A. 78 F5 40 36N 79 34W
Vanderhoof, Canada 72 C4 54 0N 124 0W
Vanderkloof Dam, S. Africa 56 E3 30 4S 24 40 E
Vanderlin I., Australia 62 B2 15 44S 137 2 E
Vandyke, Australia 62 C4 24 10S 147 51 E
Vänern, Sweden 9 G15 58 47N 13 30 E
Vänersborg, Sweden 9 G15 58 26N 12 19 E
Vang Vieng, Laos 38 C4 18 58N 102 32 E
Vanga, Kenya 54 C4 4 35S 39 12 E
Vangaindrano, Madag. 57 C8 23 21S 47 36 E
Vanguard, Canada 73 D7 49 55N 107 20W
Vanier, Canada 70 C4 45 27N 75 40W
Vanino, Russia 27 E15 48 50N 140 5 E
Vankleek Hill, Canada 70 C5 45 32N 74 40W
Vanna, Norway 8 A18 70 6N 19 50 E
Vännäs, Sweden 8 E18 63 58N 19 48 E
Vannes, France 18 C2 47 40N 2 47W
Vanrhynsdorp, S. Africa 56 E2 31 36S 18 44 E
Vanrook, Australia 62 B3 16 57S 141 57 E
Vansbro, Sweden 9 F16 60 32N 14 15 E
Vansittart B., Australia 60 B4 14 3S 126 17 E
Vantaa, Finland 9 F21 60 18N 24 58 E
Vanthli, India 42 J4 21 28N 70 25 E
Vanua Levu, Fiji 59 C8 16 33S 179 15 E
Vanua Mbalavu, Fiji 59 C9 17 40S 178 57W
Vanuatu ■, Pac. Oc. 64 J8 15 0S 168 0 E
Vanwyksvlei, S. Africa 56 E3 30 18S 21 49 E
Vanzylsrus, S. Africa 56 D3 26 52S 22 4 E
Vapnyarka, Ukraine 17 D15 48 32N 28 45 E
Varanasi, India 43 G10 25 22N 83 0 E
Varanger-halvøya, Norway 8 A23 70 25N 29 30 E
Varangerfjorden, Norway 8 A23 70 3N 29 25 E
Varaždin, Croatia 16 E9 46 20N 16 20 E
Varberg, Sweden 9 H15 57 6N 12 20 E
Vardar = Axiós →, Greece 21 D10 40 57N 22 35 E
Varde, Denmark 9 J13 55 38N 8 29 E
Vardø, Norway 8 A24 70 23N 31 5 E
Varella, Mui, Vietnam 38 F7 12 54N 109 26 E
Varėna, Lithuania 9 J21 54 12N 24 30 E
Varese, Italy 18 D8 45 48N 8 50 E
Varginha, Brazil 95 A6 21 33S 45 25W
Variadero, U.S.A. 81 H2 35 43N 104 17W
Varillas, Chile 94 A1 24 0S 70 10W
Varkaus, Finland 9 E22 62 19N 27 50 E
Varna, Bulgaria 21 C12 43 13N 27 56 E
Värnamo, Sweden 9 H16 57 10N 14 3 E
Vars, Canada 79 A9 45 21N 75 21W
Varzaneh, Iran 45 C7 32 25N 52 40 E
Vasa Barris →, Brazil 93 F11 11 10S 37 10W
Vascongadas = País Vasco □, Spain 19 A4 42 50N 2 45W
Vasht = Khāsh, Iran 40 E2 28 15N 61 15 E
Vasilevichi, Belarus 17 B15 52 15N 29 50 E
Vasilkov = Vasylkiv, Ukraine 17 C16 50 7N 30 15 E
Vaslui, Romania 17 E14 46 38N 27 42 E
Vassar, Canada 73 D9 49 10N 95 55W
Vassar, U.S.A. 76 D4 43 22N 83 35W
Västerås, Sweden 9 G17 59 37N 16 38 E
Västerbotten, Sweden 8 D18 64 36N 20 4 E
Västerdalälven →, Sweden 9 F16 60 30N 14 7 E
Västervik, Sweden 9 H17 57 43N 16 33 E
Västmanland, Sweden 9 G16 59 45N 16 20 E
Vasto, Italy 20 C6 42 8N 14 40 E
Vasylkiv, Ukraine 17 C16 50 7N 30 15 E
Vatersay, U.K. 12 E1 56 55N 7 32W
Vatican City ■, Europe 20 D5 41 54N 12 27 E
Vatili, Cyprus 23 D12 35 6N 33 40 E
Vatnajökull, Iceland 8 D5 64 30N 16 48W
Vatoa, Fiji 59 D9 19 50S 178 13W
Vatólakkos, Greece 23 D5 35 27N 23 53 E
Vatoloha, Madag. 57 B8 17 52S 47 48 E
Vatomandry, Madag. 57 B8 19 20S 48 59 E
Vatra-Dornei, Romania 17 E13 47 22N 25 22 E
Vättern, Sweden 9 G16 58 25N 14 30 E
Vaughn, Mont., U.S.A. 82 C8 47 33N 111 33W
Vaughn, N. Mex., U.S.A. 83 J11 34 36N 105 13W
Vaupés = Uaupés →, Brazil 92 C5 0 2N 67 16W
Vaupes □, Colombia 92 C4 1 0N 71 0W
Vauxhall, Canada 72 C6 50 5N 112 9W
Vava'u, Tonga 59 D12 18 36S 174 0W
Vawkavysk, Belarus 17 B13 53 9N 24 30 E
Växjö, Sweden 9 H16 56 52N 14 50 E
Vaygach, Ostrov, Russia 26 C7 70 0N 60 0 E
Váyia, Ákra, Greece 23 C10 36 15N 28 11 E
Vechte →, Neths. 15 B6 52 34N 6 6 E
Vedea →, Romania 17 G13 43 42N 25 41 E
Vedia, Argentina 94 C3 34 30S 61 31W
Veendam, Neths. 15 A6 53 5N 6 52 E
Veenendaal, Neths. 15 B5 52 2N 5 34 E
Vefsna →, Norway 8 D15 65 48N 13 10 E
Vega, Norway 8 D14 65 40N 11 55 E
Vega, U.S.A. 81 H3 35 15N 102 26W
Vegreville, Canada 72 C6 53 30N 112 5W
Vejer de la Frontera, Spain 19 D3 36 15N 5 59W
Vejle, Denmark 9 J13 55 43N 9 30 E
Velas, C., Costa Rica 88 D2 10 21N 85 52W
Velasco, Sierra de, Argentina 94 B2 29 20S 67 10W
Velddrif, S. Africa 56 E2 32 42S 18 11 E
Velebit Planina, Croatia 16 F8 44 50N 15 20 E
Veles, Macedonia 21 D9 41 46N 21 47 E
Vélez-Málaga, Spain 19 D3 36 48N 4 5W
Vélez Rubio, Spain 19 D4 37 41N 2 5W
Velhas →, Brazil 93 G10 17 13S 44 49W
Velika Kapela, Croatia 16 F8 45 10N 15 5 E
Velikaya →, Russia 24 C4 57 48N 28 10 E
Velikaya Kema, Russia 30 B8 45 30N 137 12 E
Veliki Ustyug, Russia 24 B8 60 47N 46 20 E
Velikiye Luki, Russia 24 C5 56 25N 30 32 E
Veliko Tŭrnovo, Bulgaria 21 C11 43 5N 25 41 E
Velikonda Range, India 40 M11 14 45N 79 10 E
Velletri, Italy 20 D5 41 41N 12 47 E
Vellore, India 40 N11 12 57N 79 10 E
Velsk, Russia 24 B7 61 10N 42 5 E
Velva, U.S.A. 80 A4 48 4N 100 56W
Venado Tuerto, Argentina 94 C3 33 50S 62 0W
Vendée □, France 18 C3 46 50N 1 35W
Vendôme, France 18 C4 47 47N 1 3 E
Venézia, Italy 20 B5 45 27N 12 21 E
Venézia, G. di, Italy 20 B5 45 15N 13 0 E
Venezuela ■, S. Amer. 92 B5 8 0N 66 0W
Venezuela, G. de, Venezuela 92 A4 11 30N 71 0W
Vengurla, India 40 M8 15 53N 73 45 E
Venice = Venézia, Italy 20 B5 45 27N 12 21 E
Venkatapuram, India 41 K12 18 20N 80 30 E
Venlo, Neths. 15 C6 51 22N 6 11 E
Vennesla, Norway 9 G12 58 15N 7 59 E
Venray, Neths. 15 C6 51 31N 6 0 E
Ventana, Punta de la, Mexico 86 C3 24 4N 109 48W
Ventana, Sa. de la, Argentina 94 D3 38 0S 62 30W
Ventersburg, S. Africa 56 D4 28 7S 27 9 E
Venterstad, S. Africa 56 E4 30 47S 25 48 E
Ventnor, U.K. 11 G6 50 36N 1 12W
Ventotène, Italy 20 D5 40 47N 13 25 E
Ventoux, Mt., France 18 D6 44 10N 5 17 E
Ventspils, Latvia 24 C3 57 25N 21 32 E
Ventuarí →, Venezuela 92 C5 3 58N 67 2W
Ventucopa, U.S.A. 85 L7 34 50N 119 29W
Ventura, U.S.A. 85 L7 34 17N 119 18W
Venus B., Australia 63 F4 38 40S 145 42 E
Vera, Argentina 94 B3 29 30S 60 20W
Vera, Spain 19 D5 37 15N 1 51W
Veracruz, Mexico 87 D5 19 10N 96 10W
Veracruz □, Mexico 87 D5 19 0N 96 15W
Veraval, India 42 J4 20 53N 70 27 E
Verbánia, Italy 18 D8 45 56N 8 33 E
Vercelli, Italy 18 D8 45 19N 8 25 E
Verdalsøra, Norway 8 E14 63 48N 11 30 E
Verde →, Goiás, Brazil 93 G8 18 1S 50 14W
Verde →, Mato Grosso do Sul, Brazil 93 H8 21 25S 52 20W
Verde →, Chihuahua, Mexico 86 B3 26 29N 107 58W
Verde →, Oaxaca, Mexico 87 D5 15 59N 97 50W
Verde →, Veracruz, Mexico 86 C4 21 10N 102 50W
Verde →, Paraguay 94 A4 23 9S 57 37W
Verde, Cay, Bahamas 88 B4 23 0N 75 5W
Verden, Germany 16 B5 52 55N 9 14 E
Verdi, U.S.A. 84 F7 39 31N 119 59W
Verdigre, U.S.A. 80 D6 42 36N 98 2W
Verdun, France 18 B6 49 9N 5 24 E
Vereeniging, S. Africa 57 D4 26 38S 27 57 E
Vérendrye, Parc Prov. de la, Canada 70 C4 47 20N 76 40W
Verga, C., Guinea 50 F3 10 30N 14 10W
Vergemont, Australia 62 C3 23 33S 143 1 E
Vergemont Cr. →, Australia 62 C3 24 16S 143 16 E
Vergennes, U.S.A. 79 B11 44 10N 73 15W
Verín, Spain 19 B2 41 57N 7 27W
Verkhnevilyuysk, Russia 27 C13 63 27N 120 18 E
Verkhniy Baskunchak, Russia 25 E8 48 14N 46 44 E
Verkhoyansk, Russia 27 C14 67 35N 133 25 E
Verkhoyansk Ra. = Verkhoyanskiy Khrebet, Russia 27 C13 66 0N 129 0 E
Verkhoyanskiy Khrebet, Russia 27 C13 66 0N 129 0 E
Verlo, Canada 73 C7 50 19N 108 35W
Vermilion, Canada 73 C6 53 20N 110 50W
Vermilion →, Alta., Canada 73 C6 53 22N 110 51W
Vermilion →, Qué., Canada 70 C5 47 38N 72 56W
Vermilion, B., U.S.A. 81 L9 29 45N 91 55W
Vermilion Bay, Canada 73 D10 49 51N 93 34W
Vermilion Chutes, Canada 72 B6 58 22N 114 51W
Vermilion L., U.S.A. 80 B8 47 53N 92 26W
Vermillion, U.S.A. 80 D6 42 47N 96 56W
Vermont □, U.S.A. 79 C12 44 0N 73 0W
Vernal, U.S.A. 82 F9 40 27N 109 32W
Vernalis, U.S.A. 84 H5 37 36N 121 17W
Verner, Canada 70 C3 46 25N 80 8W
Verneukpan, S. Africa 56 E3 30 0S 21 0 E
Vernon, Canada 72 C5 50 20N 119 15W
Vernon, U.S.A. 81 H5 34 9N 99 17W
Vernonia, U.S.A. 84 E3 45 52N 123 11W
Vero Beach, U.S.A. 77 M5 27 38N 80 24W
Véroia, Greece 21 D10 40 34N 22 12 E
Verona, Italy 20 B4 45 27N 10 59 E
Versailles, France 18 B5 48 48N 2 8 E
Vert, C., Senegal 50 F2 14 45N 17 30W
Verulam, S. Africa 57 D5 29 38S 31 2 E
Verviers, Belgium 15 D5 50 37N 5 52 E
Veselovskoye Vdkhr., Russia 25 E7 46 58N 41 25 E
Vesoul, France 18 C7 47 40N 6 11 E
Vesterålen, Norway 8 B16 68 45N 15 0 E
Vestfjorden, Norway 8 C15 67 55N 14 0 E
Vestmannaeyjar, Iceland 8 E3 63 27N 20 15W
Vestvågøy, Norway 8 B15 68 18N 13 50 E
Vesuvio, Italy 20 D6 40 49N 14 26 E
Vesuvius, Mt. = Vesuvio, Italy 20 D6 40 49N 14 26 E
Veszprém, Hungary 17 E9 47 8N 17 57 E
Vetlanda, Sweden 9 H16 57 24N 15 3 E
Vettore, Mte., Italy 20 C5 42 49N 13 16 E
Veurne, Belgium 15 C2 51 5N 2 40 E
Veys, Iran 45 D6 31 30N 49 0 E
Vezhen, Bulgaria 21 C11 42 50N 24 20 E
Vi Thanh, Vietnam 39 H5 9 42N 105 26 E
Viacha, Bolivia 92 G5 16 39S 68 18W
Viamão, Brazil 95 C5 30 5S 51 0W
Viana, Brazil 93 D10 3 13S 44 55W
Viana do Alentejo, Portugal 19 C2 38 17N 7 59W
Viana do Castelo, Portugal 19 B1 41 42N 8 50W
Vianden, Lux. 15 E6 49 56N 6 12 E
Vianópolis, Brazil 93 G9 16 40S 48 35W
Viaréggio, Italy 20 C4 43 52N 10 14 E
Vibank, Canada 73 C8 50 20N 103 56W
Vibo Valéntia, Italy 20 E7 38 40N 16 6 E
Viborg, Denmark 9 H13 56 27N 9 23 E
Vic, Spain 19 B7 41 58N 2 19 E
Vicenza, Italy 20 B4 45 33N 11 33 E
Vich = Vic, Spain 19 B7 41 58N 2 19 E
Vichada →, Colombia 92 C5 4 55N 67 50W
Vichy, France 18 C5 46 9N 3 26 E
Vicksburg, Ariz., U.S.A. 85 M13 33 45N 113 45W
Vicksburg, Mich., U.S.A. 76 D3 42 7N 85 32W
Vicksburg, Miss., U.S.A. 81 J9 32 21N 90 53W
Victor, India 42 J4 21 0N 71 30 E
Victor, Colo., U.S.A. 80 F2 38 43N 105 9W
Victor, N.Y., U.S.A. 78 D7 42 58N 77 24W
Victor Harbor, Australia 63 F2 35 30S 138 37 E
Victoria = Labuan, Malaysia 36 C5 5 20N 115 14 E
Victoria, Argentina 94 C3 32 40S 60 10W
Victoria, Canada 72 D4 48 30N 123 25W
Victoria, Malta 23 C1 36 2N 14 14 E
Victoria, Kans., U.S.A. 80 F5 38 52N 99 9W
Victoria, Tex., U.S.A. 81 L6 28 48N 97 0W
Victoria □, Australia 63 F3 37 0S 144 0 E
Victoria →, Australia 60 C4 15 10S 129 40 E
Victoria, Grand L., Canada 70 C4 47 31N 77 30W
Victoria, L., Africa 54 C3 1 0S 33 0 E
Victoria, L., Australia 63 E3 33 57S 141 15 E
Victoria Beach, Canada 73 C9 50 40N 96 35W
Victoria de Durango = Durango, Mexico 86 C4 24 3N 104 39W
Victoria de las Tunas, Cuba 88 B4 20 58N 76 59W
Victoria Falls, Zimbabwe 55 F2 17 58S 25 52 E
Victoria Harbour, Canada 70 D4 44 45N 79 45W
Victoria I., Canada 68 A8 71 0N 111 0W
Victoria Ld., Antarctica 5 D11 75 0S 160 0 E
Victoria Nile →, Uganda 54 B3 2 14N 31 26 E
Victoria Res., Canada 71 C8 48 20N 57 27W
Victoria River Downs, Australia 60 C5 16 25S 131 0 E
Victoria Taungdeik, Burma 41 J18 21 15N 93 55 E
Victoria West, S. Africa 56 E3 31 25S 23 4 E
Victoriaville, Canada 71 C5 46 4N 71 56W
Victorica, Argentina 94 D2 36 20S 65 30W
Victorville, U.S.A. 85 L9 34 32N 117 18W
Vicuña, Chile 94 C1 30 0S 70 50W
Vicuña Mackenna, Argentina 94 C3 33 53S 64 25W
Vidal, U.S.A. 85 L12 34 7N 114 31W
Vidal Junction, U.S.A. 85 L12 34 11N 114 34W
Vidalia, U.S.A. 77 J4 32 13N 82 25W
Vídho, Greece 23 A3 39 38N 19 55 E
Vidin, Bulgaria 21 C10 43 59N 22 50 E
Vidisha, India 42 H7 23 28N 77 53 E
Vidzy, Belarus 9 J22 55 23N 26 37 E
Viedma, Argentina 96 E4 40 50S 63 0W
Viedma, L., Argentina 96 F2 49 30S 72 30W
Vielsalm, Belgium 15 D5 50 17N 5 54 E
Vieng Pou Kha, Laos 38 B3 20 41N 101 4 E
Vienna = Wien, Austria 16 D9 48 12N 16 22 E
Vienna, U.S.A. 81 G10 37 25N 88 54W
Vienne, France 18 D6 45 31N 4 53 E
Vienne →, France 18 C4 47 13N 0 5 E
Vientiane, Laos 38 D4 17 58N 102 36 E
Vientos, Paso de los, Caribbean 89 C5 20 0N 74 0W
Vierzon, France 18 C5 47 13N 2 5 E
Vietnam ■, Asia 38 C6 19 0N 106 0 E
Vigan, Phil. 37 A6 17 35N 120 28 E
Vigévano, Italy 18 D8 45 19N 8 51 E
Vigia, Brazil 93 D9 0 50S 48 5W
Vigía Chico, Mexico 87 D7 19 46N 87 35W
Víglas, Ákra, Greece 23 D9 35 54N 27 51 E
Vigo, Spain 19 A1 42 12N 8 41W
Vijayawada, India 41 L12 16 31N 80 39 E
Vík, Iceland 8 E4 63 25N 19 1W
Vikeke, Indonesia 37 F7 8 52S 126 23 E
Viking, Canada 72 C6 53 7N 111 50W
Vikna, Norway 8 D14 64 55N 10 58 E
Vila da Maganja, Mozam. 55 F4 17 18S 37 30 E
Vila de João Belo = Xai-Xai, Mozam. 57 D5 25 6S 33 31 E
Vila do Bispo, Portugal 19 D1 37 5N 8 53W
Vila do Chibuto, Mozam. 57 C5 24 40S 33 33 E
Vila Franca de Xira, Portugal 19 C1 38 57N 8 59W
Vila Gamito, Mozam. 55 E3 14 12S 33 0 E
Vila Gomes da Costa, Mozam. 57 C5 24 20S 33 37 E
Vila Machado, Mozam. 55 F3 19 15S 34 14 E
Vila Mouzinho, Mozam. 55 E3 14 48S 34 25 E
Vila Nova de Gaia, Portugal 19 B1 41 8N 8 37W
Vila Real, Portugal 19 B2 41 17N 7 48W
Vila-real de los Infantes, Spain 19 C5 39 55N 0 3W
Vila Real de Santo António, Portugal 19 D2 37 10N 7 28W
Vila Vasco da Gama, Mozam. 55 E3 14 54S 32 14 E
Vila Velha, Brazil 95 A7 20 20S 40 17W
Vilagarcía de Arousa, Spain 19 A1 42 34N 8 46W

Vilaine

Vilaine →, *France* 18 C2 47 30N 2 27W
Vilanandro, Tanjona, *Madag.* 57 B7 16 11S 44 27 E
Vilanculos, *Mozam.* 57 C6 22 1S 35 17 E
Vilanova i la Geltrú, *Spain* 19 B6 41 13N 1 40 E
Vileyka, *Belarus* 17 A14 54 30N 26 53 E
Vilhelmina, *Sweden* 8 D17 64 35N 16 39 E
Vilhena, *Brazil* 92 F6 12 40S 60 5W
Viliga, *Russia* 27 C16 61 36N 156 56 E
Viliya →, *Lithuania* 9 J21 55 8N 24 16 E
Viljandi, *Estonia* 9 G21 58 28N 25 30 E
Vilkitskogo, Proliv, *Russia* 27 B11 78 0N 103 0 E
Vilkovo = Vylkove, *Ukraine* 17 F15 45 28N 29 32 E
Villa Abecia, *Bolivia* 94 A2 21 0S 68 18W
Villa Ahumada, *Mexico* 86 A3 30 38N 106 30W
Villa Ana, *Argentina* 94 B4 28 28S 59 40W
Villa Ángela, *Argentina* 94 B3 27 34S 60 45W
Villa Bella, *Bolivia* 92 F5 10 25S 65 22W
Villa Bens = Tarfaya, *Morocco* 50 C3 27 55N 12 55W
Villa Cañás, *Argentina* 94 C3 34 0S 61 35W
Villa Carlos, *Spain* 22 B11 39 53N 4 17 E
Villa Cisneros = Dakhla, *W. Sahara* 50 D2 23 50N 15 53W
Villa Colón, *Argentina* 94 C2 31 38S 68 20W
Villa Constitución, *Argentina* 94 C3 33 15S 60 20W
Villa de María, *Argentina* 94 B3 29 55S 63 43W
Villa Dolores, *Argentina* 94 C2 31 58S 65 15W
Villa Frontera, *Mexico* 86 B4 26 56N 101 27W
Villa Guillermina, *Argentina* 94 B4 28 15S 59 29W
Villa Hayes, *Paraguay* 94 B4 25 5S 57 20W
Villa Iris, *Argentina* 94 D3 38 12S 63 12W
Villa Juárez, *Mexico* 86 B4 27 37N 100 44W
Villa María, *Argentina* 94 C3 32 20S 63 10W
Villa Mazán, *Argentina* 94 B2 28 40S 66 30W
Villa Montes, *Bolivia* 94 A3 21 10S 63 30W
Villa Ocampo, *Argentina* 94 B4 28 30S 59 20W
Villa Ocampo, *Mexico* 86 B3 26 29N 105 30W
Villa Ojo de Agua, *Argentina* 94 B3 29 30S 63 44W
Villa San José, *Argentina* 94 C4 32 12S 58 15W
Villa San Martín, *Argentina* 94 B3 28 15S 64 9W
Villa Unión, *Mexico* 86 C3 23 12N 106 14W
Villacarrillo, *Spain* 19 C4 38 7N 3 3W
Villach, *Austria* 16 E7 46 37N 13 51 E
Villafranca de los Caballeros, *Spain* 22 B10 39 34N 3 25 E
Villagrán, *Mexico* 87 C5 24 29N 99 29W
Villaguay, *Argentina* 94 C4 32 0S 59 0W
Villahermosa, *Mexico* 87 D6 17 59N 92 55W
Villajoyosa, *Spain* 19 C5 38 30N 0 12W
Villalba, *Spain* 19 A2 43 26N 7 40W
Villanueva, *U.S.A.* 83 J11 35 16N 105 22W
Villanueva de la Serena, *Spain* 19 C3 38 59N 5 50W
Villanueva y Geltrú = Vilanova i la Geltrú, *Spain* 19 B6 41 13N 1 40 E
Villarreal = Vila-real de los Infantes, *Spain* 19 C5 39 55N 0 3W
Villarrica, *Chile* 96 D2 39 15S 72 15W
Villarrica, *Paraguay* 94 B4 25 40S 56 30W
Villarrobledo, *Spain* 19 C4 39 18N 2 36W
Villavicencio, *Argentina* 94 C2 32 28S 69 0W
Villavicencio, *Colombia* 92 C4 4 9N 73 37W
Villaviciosa, *Spain* 19 A3 43 32N 5 27W
Villazón, *Bolivia* 94 A2 22 0S 65 35W
Ville-Marie, *Canada* 70 C4 47 20N 79 30W
Ville Platte, *U.S.A.* 81 K8 30 41N 92 17W
Villena, *Spain* 19 C5 38 39N 0 52W
Villeneuve-d'Ascq, *France* 18 A5 50 38N 3 9 E
Villeneuve-sur-Lot, *France* 18 D4 44 24N 0 42 E
Villiers, *S. Africa* 57 D4 27 2S 28 36 E
Villingen-Schwenningen, *Germany* 16 D5 48 3N 8 26 E
Villisca, *U.S.A.* 80 E7 40 56N 94 59W
Vilna, *Canada* 72 C6 54 7N 111 55W
Vilnius, *Lithuania* 24 D4 54 38N 25 19 E
Vilvoorde, *Belgium* 15 D4 50 56N 4 26 E
Vilyuy →, *Russia* 27 C13 64 24N 126 26 E
Vilyuysk, *Russia* 27 C13 63 40N 121 35 E
Viña del Mar, *Chile* 94 C1 33 0S 71 30W
Vinarós, *Spain* 19 B6 40 30N 0 27 E
Vincennes, *U.S.A.* 76 F2 38 41N 87 32W
Vincent, *U.S.A.* 85 L8 34 33N 118 11W
Vinchina, *Argentina* 94 B2 28 45S 68 15W
Vindelälven →, *Sweden* 8 E18 63 55N 19 50 E
Vindeln, *Sweden* 8 D18 64 12N 19 43 E
Vindhya Ra., *India* 42 H7 22 50N 77 0 E
Vineland, *U.S.A.* 76 F8 39 29N 75 2W
Vinh, *Vietnam* 38 C5 18 45N 105 38 E
Vinh Linh, *Vietnam* 38 D6 17 4N 107 2 E
Vinh Long, *Vietnam* 39 G5 10 16N 105 57 E
Vinh Yen, *Vietnam* 38 B5 21 21N 105 35 E
Vinita, *U.S.A.* 81 G7 36 39N 95 9W
Vinkovci, *Croatia* 21 B8 45 19N 18 48 E
Vinnitsa = Vinnytsya, *Ukraine* 25 E4 49 15N 28 30 E
Vinnytsya, *Ukraine* 25 E4 49 15N 28 30 E
Vinton, *Calif., U.S.A.* 84 F6 39 48N 120 10W
Vinton, *Iowa, U.S.A.* 80 D8 42 10N 92 1W
Vinton, *La., U.S.A.* 81 K8 30 11N 93 35W
Virac, *Phil.* 37 B6 13 30N 124 20 E
Virachei, *Cambodia* 38 F6 13 59N 106 49 E
Virago Sd., *Canada* 72 C2 54 0N 132 30W
Viramgam, *India* 42 H5 23 5N 72 0 E
Virden, *Canada* 73 D8 49 50N 100 56W
Vire, *France* 18 B3 48 50N 0 53W
Vírgenes, C., *Argentina* 96 G3 52 19S 68 21W
Virgin →, *Canada* 73 B7 57 2N 108 17W
Virgin →, *U.S.A.* 83 H6 36 28N 114 21W
Virgin Gorda, *Virgin Is.* 89 C7 18 30N 64 26W
Virgin Is. (British) ■, *W. Indies* 89 C7 18 30N 64 30W
Virgin Is. (U.S.) ■, *W. Indies* 89 C7 18 20N 65 0W
Virginia, *S. Africa* 56 D4 28 8S 26 55 E
Virginia, *U.S.A.* 80 B8 47 31N 92 32W
Virginia □, *U.S.A.* 76 G7 37 30N 78 45W
Virginia Beach, *U.S.A.* 76 G8 36 51N 75 59W
Virginia City, *Mont., U.S.A.* 82 D8 45 18N 111 56W
Virginia City, *Nev., U.S.A.* 84 F7 39 19N 119 39W
Virginia Falls, *Canada* 72 A3 61 38N 125 42W
Virginiatown, *Canada* 70 C4 48 9N 79 36W
Viroqua, *U.S.A.* 80 D9 43 34N 90 53W
Virovitica, *Croatia* 20 B7 45 51N 17 21 E
Virton, *Belgium* 15 E5 49 35N 5 32 E
Virudunagar, *India* 40 Q10 9 30N 77 58 E
Vis, *Croatia* 20 C7 43 4N 16 10 E
Visalia, *U.S.A.* 84 J7 36 20N 119 18W
Visayan Sea, *Phil.* 37 B6 11 30N 123 30 E
Visby, *Sweden* 9 H18 57 37N 18 18 E
Viscount Melville Sd., *Canada* 66 B9 74 10N 108 0W
Visé, *Belgium* 15 D5 50 44N 5 41 E
Višegrad, *Bos.-H.* 21 C8 43 47N 19 17 E
Viseu, *Brazil* 93 D9 1 10S 46 5W
Viseu, *Portugal* 19 B2 40 40N 7 55W
Vishakhapatnam, *India* 41 L13 17 45N 83 20 E
Visnagar, *India* 42 H5 23 45N 72 32 E
Viso, Mte., *Italy* 18 D7 44 38N 7 5 E
Visokoi I., *Antarctica* 5 B1 56 43S 27 15W
Vista, *U.S.A.* 85 M9 33 12N 117 14W
Vistula = Wisła →, *Poland* 17 A10 54 22N 18 55 E
Vitebsk = Vitsyebsk, *Belarus* 24 C5 55 10N 30 15 E
Viterbo, *Italy* 20 C5 42 25N 12 6 E
Viti Levu, *Fiji* 59 C7 17 30S 177 30 E
Vitigudino, *Spain* 19 B2 41 1N 6 26W
Vitim, *Russia* 27 D12 59 28N 112 35 E
Vitim →, *Russia* 27 D12 59 26N 112 34 E
Vitória, *Brazil* 93 H10 20 20S 40 22W
Vitória da Conquista, *Brazil* 93 F10 14 51S 40 51W
Vitória de São Antão, *Brazil* 93 E11 8 10S 35 20W
Vitoria-Gasteiz, *Spain* 19 A4 42 50N 2 41W
Vitsyebsk, *Belarus* 24 C5 55 10N 30 15 E
Vittória, *Italy* 20 F6 36 57N 14 32 E
Vittório Véneto, *Italy* 20 B5 45 59N 12 18 E
Viveiro, *Spain* 19 A2 43 39N 7 38W
Vizcaíno, Desierto de, *Mexico* 86 B2 27 40N 113 50W
Vizcaíno, Sierra, *Mexico* 86 B2 27 30N 114 0W
Vize, *Turkey* 21 D12 41 34N 27 45 E
Vizianagaram, *India* 41 K13 18 6N 83 30 E
Vjosa →, *Albania* 21 D8 40 37N 19 24 E
Vlaardingen, *Neths.* 15 C4 51 55N 4 21 E
Vladikavkaz, *Russia* 25 F7 43 0N 44 35 E
Vladimir, *Russia* 24 C7 56 15N 40 30 E
Vladimir Volynskiy = Volodymyr-Volynskyy, *Ukraine* 17 C13 50 50N 24 18 E
Vladivostok, *Russia* 30 C5 43 10N 131 53 E
Vlieland, *Neths.* 15 A4 53 16N 4 55 E
Vlissingen, *Neths.* 15 C3 51 26N 3 34 E
Vlóra, *Albania* 21 D8 40 32N 19 28 E
Vltava →, *Czech Rep.* 16 D8 50 21N 14 30 E
Vo Dat, *Vietnam* 39 G6 11 9N 107 31 E
Voe, *U.K.* 12 A7 60 21N 1 16W
Vogelkop = Doberai, Jazirah, *Indonesia* 37 E8 1 25S 133 0 E
Vogelsberg, *Germany* 16 C5 50 31N 9 12 E
Voghera, *Italy* 18 D8 44 59N 9 1 E
Vohibinany, *Madag.* 57 B8 18 49S 49 4 E
Vohimarina = Iharana, *Madag.* 57 A9 13 25S 50 0 E
Vohimena, Tanjon' i, *Madag.* 57 D8 25 36S 45 8 E
Vohipeno, *Madag.* 57 C8 22 22S 47 51 E
Voi, *Kenya* 54 C4 3 25S 38 32 E
Voiron, *France* 18 D6 45 22N 5 35 E
Voisey B., *Canada* 71 A7 56 15N 61 50W
Vojmsjön, *Sweden* 8 D17 64 55N 16 40 E
Vojvodina □, *Serbia, Yug.* 21 B9 45 20N 20 0 E
Volborg, *U.S.A.* 80 C2 45 51N 105 41W
Volcano Is. = Kazan-Rettō, *Pac. Oc.* 64 E6 25 0N 141 0 E
Volda, *Norway* 9 E12 62 9N 6 5 E
Volga →, *Russia* 25 E8 46 0N 48 30 E
Volga Hts. = Privolzhskaya Vozvyshennost, *Russia* 25 D8 51 0N 46 0 E
Volgodonsk, *Russia* 25 E7 47 33N 42 5 E
Volgograd, *Russia* 25 E7 48 40N 44 25 E
Volgogradskoye Vdkhr., *Russia* 25 E8 50 0N 45 20 E
Volkhov →, *Russia* 24 B5 60 8N 32 20 E
Volkovysk = Vawkavysk, *Belarus* 17 B13 53 9N 24 30 E
Volksrust, *S. Africa* 57 D4 27 24S 29 53 E
Volochanka, *Russia* 27 B10 71 0N 94 28 E
Volodymyr-Volynskyy, *Ukraine* 17 C13 50 50N 24 18 E
Vologda, *Russia* 24 C6 59 10N 39 45 E
Vólos, *Greece* 21 E10 39 24N 22 59 E
Volovets, *Ukraine* 17 D12 48 43N 23 11 E
Volozhin = Valozhyn, *Belarus* 17 A14 54 3N 26 30 E
Volsk, *Russia* 24 D8 52 5N 47 22 E
Volta →, *Ghana* 48 F4 5 46N 0 41 E
Volta, L., *Ghana* 50 G6 7 30N 0 0 E
Volta Redonda, *Brazil* 95 A7 22 31S 44 5W
Voltaire, C., *Australia* 60 B4 14 16S 125 35 E
Volterra, *Italy* 20 C4 43 24N 10 51 E
Volturno →, *Italy* 20 D5 41 1N 13 55 E
Volvo, *Australia* 63 E3 31 41S 143 57 E
Volzhskiy, *Russia* 25 E7 48 56N 44 46 E
Vondrozo, *Madag.* 57 C8 22 49S 47 20 E
Vopnafjörður, *Iceland* 8 D6 65 45N 14 50W
Vóriai Sporádhes, *Greece* 21 E10 39 15N 23 30 E
Vorkuta, *Russia* 24 A11 67 48N 64 20 E
Vormsi, *Estonia* 9 G20 59 1N 23 13 E
Voronezh, *Russia* 24 D6 51 40N 39 10 E
Voroshilovgrad = Luhansk, *Ukraine* 25 E6 48 38N 39 15 E
Voroshilovsk = Alchevsk, *Ukraine* 25 E6 48 30N 38 45 E
Võrts Järv, *Estonia* 9 G22 58 16N 26 3 E
Võru, *Estonia* 9 H22 57 48N 26 54 E
Vosges, *France* 18 B7 48 20N 7 10 E
Voss, *Norway* 9 F12 60 38N 6 26 E
Vostok I., *Kiribati* 65 J12 10 5S 152 23W
Votkinsk, *Russia* 24 C9 57 0N 53 55 E
Votkinskoye Vdkhr., *Russia* 24 C10 57 22N 55 12 E
Vouga →, *Portugal* 19 B1 40 41N 8 40W
Voúxa, Ákra, *Greece* 23 D5 35 37N 23 32 E
Vozhe Ozero, *Russia* 24 B6 60 45N 39 0 E
Voznesensk, *Ukraine* 25 E5 47 35N 31 21 E
Voznesenye, *Russia* 24 B6 61 0N 35 28 E
Vrangelya, Ostrov, *Russia* 27 B19 71 0N 180 0 E
Vranje, *Serbia, Yug.* 21 C9 42 34N 21 54 E
Vratsa, *Bulgaria* 21 C10 43 15N 23 30 E
Vrbas →, *Bos.-H.* 20 B7 45 8N 17 29 E
Vrede, *S. Africa* 57 D4 27 24S 29 6 E
Vredefort, *S. Africa* 56 D4 27 0S 27 22 E
Vredenburg, *S. Africa* 56 E2 32 56S 18 0 E
Vredendal, *S. Africa* 56 E2 31 41S 18 35 E
Vrindavan, *India* 42 F7 27 37N 77 40 E
Vríses, *Greece* 23 D6 35 23N 24 13 E
Vršac, *Serbia, Yug.* 21 B9 45 8N 21 20 E
Vryburg, *S. Africa* 56 D3 26 55S 24 45 E
Vryheid, *S. Africa* 57 D5 27 45S 30 47 E
Vu Liet, *Vietnam* 38 C5 18 43N 105 23 E
Vukovar, *Croatia* 21 B8 45 21N 18 59 E
Vulcan, *Canada* 72 C6 50 25N 113 15W
Vulcan, *Romania* 17 F12 45 23N 23 17 E
Vulcan, *U.S.A.* 76 C2 45 47N 87 53W
Vulcaneşti, *Moldova* 17 F15 45 41N 28 18 E
Vulcano, *Italy* 20 E6 38 24N 14 58 E
Vulkaneshty = Vulcaneşti, *Moldova* 17 F15 45 41N 28 18 E
Vunduzi →, *Mozam.* 55 F3 18 56S 34 1 E
Vung Tau, *Vietnam* 39 G6 10 21N 107 4 E
Vyatka = Kirov, *Russia* 24 C8 58 35N 49 40 E
Vyatka →, *Russia* 24 C9 55 37N 51 28 E
Vyatskiye Polyany, *Russia* 24 C9 56 14N 51 5 E
Vyazemskiy, *Russia* 27 E14 47 32N 134 45 E
Vyazma, *Russia* 24 C5 55 10N 34 15 E
Vyborg, *Russia* 24 B4 60 43N 28 47 E
Vychegda →, *Russia* 24 B8 61 18N 46 36 E
Vychodné Beskydy, *Europe* 17 D11 49 20N 22 0 E
Vyg-ozero, *Russia* 24 B5 63 47N 34 29 E
Vylkove, *Ukraine* 17 F15 45 28N 29 32 E
Vynohradiv, *Ukraine* 17 D12 48 9N 23 2 E
Vyrnwy, L., *U.K.* 10 E4 52 48N 3 31W
Vyshniy Volochek, *Russia* 24 C5 57 30N 34 30 E
Vyshzha = imeni 26 Bakinskikh Komissarov, *Turkmenistan* 25 G9 39 22N 54 10 E
Vyškov, *Czech Rep.* 17 D9 49 17N 17 0 E
Vytegra, *Russia* 24 B6 61 0N 36 27 E

W

W.A.C. Bennett Dam, *Canada* 72 B4 56 2N 122 6W
Waal →, *Neths.* 15 C5 51 37N 5 0 E
Waalwijk, *Neths.* 15 C5 51 42N 5 4 E
Wabakimi L., *Canada* 70 B2 50 38N 89 45W
Wabana, *Canada* 71 C9 47 40N 53 0W
Wabasca, *Canada* 72 B6 55 57N 113 56W
Wabash, *U.S.A.* 76 E3 40 48N 85 49W
Wabash →, *U.S.A.* 76 G1 37 48N 88 2W
Wabeno, *U.S.A.* 76 C1 45 26N 88 39W
Wabigoon L., *Canada* 73 D10 49 44N 92 44W
Wabowden, *Canada* 73 C9 54 55N 98 38W
Wabuk Pt., *Canada* 70 A2 55 20N 85 5W
Wabush, *Canada* 71 B6 52 55N 66 52W
Wabuska, *U.S.A.* 82 G4 39 9N 119 11W
Waco, *U.S.A.* 81 K6 31 33N 97 9W
Waconichi, L., *Canada* 70 B5 50 8N 74 0W
Wad, *Pakistan* 42 F2 27 22N 66 23 E
Wad Hamid, *Sudan* 51 E12 16 30N 32 45 E
Wâd Medanî, *Sudan* 51 F12 14 28N 33 30 E
Wadai, *Africa* 48 E5 12 0N 19 0 E
Wadayama, *Japan* 31 G7 35 19N 134 52 E
Waddeneilanden, *Neths.* 15 A5 53 20N 5 10 E
Waddenzee, *Neths.* 15 A5 53 6N 5 10 E
Wadderin Hill, *Australia* 61 F2 32 0S 118 25 E
Waddington, *U.S.A.* 79 B9 44 52N 75 12W
Waddington, Mt., *Canada* 72 C3 51 23N 125 15W
Waddy Pt., *Australia* 63 C5 24 58S 153 21 E
Wadebridge, *U.K.* 11 G3 50 31N 4 51W
Wadena, *Canada* 73 C8 51 57N 103 47W
Wadena, *U.S.A.* 80 B7 46 26N 95 8W
Wadesboro, *U.S.A.* 77 H5 34 58N 80 5W
Wadhams, *Canada* 72 C3 51 30N 127 30W
Wādī as Sīr, *Jordan* 47 D4 31 56N 35 49 E
Wadi Halfa, *Sudan* 51 D12 21 53N 31 19 E
Wadsworth, *U.S.A.* 82 G4 39 38N 119 17W
Waegwan, *S. Korea* 35 G15 35 59N 128 23 E
Wafrah, *Si. Arabia* 44 D5 28 33N 47 56 E
Wageningen, *Neths.* 15 C5 51 58N 5 40 E
Wager B., *Canada* 69 B11 65 26N 88 40W
Wagga Wagga, *Australia* 63 F4 35 7S 147 24 E
Waghete, *Indonesia* 37 E9 4 10S 135 50 E
Wagin, *Australia* 61 F2 33 17S 117 25 E
Wagon Mound, *U.S.A.* 81 G2 36 1N 104 42W
Wagoner, *U.S.A.* 81 H7 35 58N 95 22W
Wah, *Pakistan* 42 C5 33 45N 72 40 E
Wahai, *Indonesia* 37 E7 2 48S 129 35 E
Wahiawa, *U.S.A.* 74 H15 21 30N 158 2W
Wâḥid, *Egypt* 47 E1 30 48N 32 21 E
Wahnai, *Afghan.* 42 C1 32 40N 65 50 E
Wahoo, *U.S.A.* 80 E6 41 13N 96 37W
Wahpeton, *U.S.A.* 80 B6 46 16N 96 36W
Wai, Koh, *Cambodia* 39 H4 9 55N 102 55 E
Waiau →, *N.Z.* 59 K4 42 47S 173 22 E
Waibeem, *Indonesia* 37 E8 0 30S 132 59 E
Waigeo, *Indonesia* 37 E8 0 20S 130 40 E
Waihi, *N.Z.* 59 G5 37 23S 175 52 E
Waihou →, *N.Z.* 59 G5 37 15S 175 40 E
Waika, *Dem. Rep. of the Congo* 54 C2 2 22S 25 42 E
Waikabubak, *Indonesia* 37 F5 9 45S 119 25 E
Waikari, *N.Z.* 59 K4 42 58S 172 41 E
Waikato →, *N.Z.* 59 G5 37 23S 174 43 E
Waikerie, *Australia* 63 E3 34 9S 140 0 E
Waikokopu, *N.Z.* 59 H6 39 3S 177 52 E
Waikouaiti, *N.Z.* 59 L3 45 36S 170 41 E
Waimakariri →, *N.Z.* 59 K4 43 24S 172 42 E
Waimate, *N.Z.* 59 L3 44 45S 171 3 E
Wainganga →, *India* 40 K11 18 50N 79 55 E
Waingapu, *Indonesia* 37 F6 9 35S 120 11 E
Waini →, *Guyana* 92 B7 8 20N 59 50W
Wainwright, *Canada* 73 C6 52 50N 110 50W
Waiouru, *N.Z.* 59 H5 39 28S 175 41 E
Waipara, *N.Z.* 59 K4 43 3S 172 46 E
Waipawa, *N.Z.* 59 H6 39 56S 176 38 E
Waipiro, *N.Z.* 59 H7 38 2S 178 22 E
Waipu, *N.Z.* 59 F5 35 59S 174 29 E
Waipukurau, *N.Z.* 59 J6 40 1S 176 33 E
Wairakei, *N.Z.* 59 H6 38 37S 176 6 E
Wairarapa, L., *N.Z.* 59 J5 41 14S 175 15 E
Wairoa, *N.Z.* 59 H6 39 3S 177 25 E
Waitaki →, *N.Z.* 59 L3 44 56S 171 7 E
Waitara, *N.Z.* 59 H5 38 59S 174 15 E
Waitsburg, *U.S.A.* 82 C5 46 16N 118 9W
Waiuku, *N.Z.* 59 G5 37 15S 174 45 E
Wajima, *Japan* 31 F8 37 30N 137 0 E
Wajir, *Kenya* 54 B5 1 42N 40 5 E
Wajir □, *Kenya* 54 B5 1 42N 40 20 E
Wakasa, *Japan* 31 G7 35 20N 134 24 E
Wakasa-Wan, *Japan* 31 G7 35 40N 135 30 E
Wakatipu, L., *N.Z.* 59 L2 45 5S 168 33 E
Wakaw, *Canada* 73 C7 52 39N 105 44W
Wakayama, *Japan* 31 G7 34 15N 135 15 E
Wakayama-ken □, *Japan* 31 H7 33 50N 135 30 E
Wake Forest, *U.S.A.* 77 H6 35 59N 78 30W
Wake I., *Pac. Oc.* 64 F8 19 18N 166 36 E
Wakefield, *N.Z.* 59 J4 41 24S 173 5 E
Wakefield, *U.K.* 10 D6 53 41N 1 29W
Wakefield, *Mass., U.S.A.* 79 D13 42 30N 71 4W
Wakefield, *Mich., U.S.A.* 80 B10 46 29N 89 56W
Wakema, *Burma* 41 L19 16 30N 95 11 E
Wakkanai, *Japan* 30 B10 45 28N 141 35 E
Wakkerstroom, *S. Africa* 57 D5 27 24S 30 10 E
Wakool, *Australia* 63 F3 35 28S 144 23 E
Wakool →, *Australia* 63 F3 35 5S 143 33 E
Wakre, *Indonesia* 37 E8 0 19S 131 5 E
Wakuach L., *Canada* 71 A6 55 34N 67 32W
Walamba, *Zambia* 55 E2 13 30S 28 42 E
Wałbrzych, *Poland* 16 C9 50 45N 16 18 E
Walbury Hill, *U.K.* 11 F6 51 21N 1 28W
Walcha, *Australia* 63 E5 30 55S 151 31 E
Walcheren, *Neths.* 15 C3 51 30N 3 35 E
Walcott, *U.S.A.* 82 F10 41 46N 106 51W
Wałcz, *Poland* 16 B9 53 17N 16 27 E
Waldburg Ra., *Australia* 60 D2 24 40S 117 35 E
Walden, *Colo., U.S.A.* 82 F10 40 44N 106 17W
Walden, *N.Y., U.S.A.* 79 E10 41 34N 74 11W
Waldport, *U.S.A.* 82 D1 44 26N 124 4W
Waldron, *U.S.A.* 81 H7 34 54N 94 5W
Wales □, *U.K.* 11 E3 52 19N 4 43W
Walgett, *Australia* 63 E4 30 0S 148 5 E
Walgreen Coast, *Antarctica* 5 D15 75 15S 105 0W
Walhalla, *Australia* 63 F4 37 56S 146 29 E
Walhalla, *U.S.A.* 73 D9 48 55N 97 55W
Walker, *U.S.A.* 80 B7 47 6N 94 35W
Walker L., *Man., Canada* 73 C9 54 42N 95 57W
Walker L., *Qué., Canada* 71 B6 50 20N 67 11W
Walker L., *U.S.A.* 82 G4 38 42N 118 43W
Walkerston, *Australia* 62 C4 21 11S 149 8 E
Walkerton, *Canada* 78 B3 44 10N 81 10W
Wall, *U.S.A.* 80 D3 44 0N 102 8W
Walla Walla, *U.S.A.* 82 C4 46 4N 118 20W
Wallabadah, *Australia* 62 B3 17 57S 142 15 E
Wallace, *Idaho, U.S.A.* 82 C6 47 28N 115 56W
Wallace, *N.C., U.S.A.* 77 H7 34 44N 77 59W
Wallace, *Nebr., U.S.A.* 80 E4 40 50N 101 10W
Wallaceburg, *Canada* 70 D3 42 34N 82 23W
Wallachia = Valahia, *Romania* 17 F13 44 35N 25 0 E
Wallal, *Australia* 63 D4 26 32S 146 7 E
Wallal Downs, *Australia* 60 C3 19 47S 120 40 E
Wallambin, L., *Australia* 61 F2 30 57S 117 35 E
Wallaroo, *Australia* 63 E2 33 56S 137 39 E
Wallerawang, *Australia* 63 E5 33 25S 150 4 E
Wallhallow, *Australia* 62 B2 17 50S 135 50 E
Wallingford, *U.S.A.* 79 E12 41 27N 72 50W
Wallis & Futuna, Is., *Pac. Oc.* 64 J10 13 18S 176 10W
Wallowa, *U.S.A.* 82 D5 45 34N 117 32W
Wallowa Mts., *U.S.A.* 82 D5 45 20N 117 30W
Walls, *U.K.* 12 A7 60 14N 1 33W
Wallsend, *Australia* 63 E5 32 55S 151 40 E
Wallula, *U.S.A.* 82 C4 46 5N 118 54W
Wallumbilla, *Australia* 63 D4 26 33S 149 9 E
Walmsley, L., *Canada* 73 A7 63 25N 108 36W
Walney, I. of, *U.K.* 10 C4 54 6N 3 15W
Walnut Creek, *U.S.A.* 84 H4 37 54N 122 4W
Walnut Ridge, *U.S.A.* 81 G9 36 4N 90 57W
Walsall, *U.K.* 11 E6 52 35N 1 58W
Walsenburg, *U.S.A.* 81 G2 37 38N 104 47W
Walsh, *U.S.A.* 81 G3 37 23N 102 17W
Walsh →, *Australia* 62 B3 16 31S 143 42 E
Walsh P.O., *Australia* 62 B3 16 40S 144 0 E
Walterboro, *U.S.A.* 77 J5 32 55N 80 40W
Walters, *U.S.A.* 81 H5 34 22N 98 19W
Waltham, *U.S.A.* 79 D13 42 23N 71 14W
Waltham Station, *Canada* 70 C4 45 57N 76 57W
Waltman, *U.S.A.* 82 E10 43 4N 107 12W
Walton, *U.S.A.* 79 D9 42 10N 75 8W
Walton-on-the-Naze, *U.K.* 11 F9 51 51N 1 17 E
Walvis Bay, *Namibia* 56 C1 23 0S 14 28 E
Walvisbaai = Walvis Bay, *Namibia* 56 C1 23 0S 14 28 E
Wamba, *Dem. Rep. of the Congo* 54 B2 2 10N 27 57 E
Wamba, *Kenya* 54 B4 0 58N 37 19 E
Wamego, *U.S.A.* 80 F6 39 12N 96 18W
Wamena, *Indonesia* 37 E9 4 4S 138 57 E
Wamulan, *Indonesia* 37 E7 3 27S 126 7 E
Wan Xian, *China* 34 E8 38 47N 115 7 E
Wana, *Pakistan* 42 C3 32 20N 69 32 E
Wanaaring, *Australia* 63 D3 29 38S 144 9 E
Wanaka, *N.Z.* 59 L2 44 42S 169 9 E
Wanaka L., *N.Z.* 59 L2 44 33S 169 7 E

Westmeath

Wanapitei L., Canada ... 70 C3 46 45N 80 40W
Wanbi, Australia .... 63 E3 34 46S 140 17 E
Wandarrie, Australia .... 61 E2 27 50S 117 52 E
Wanderer, Zimbabwe ... 55 F3 19 36S 30 1 E
Wandoan, Australia ..... 63 D4 26 5S 149 55 E
Wanfu, China .... 35 D12 40 8N 122 38 E
Wang →, Thailand .... 38 D2 17 8N 99 2 E
Wang Noi, Thailand ..... 38 E3 14 13N 100 44 E
Wang Saphung, Thailand 38 D3 17 18N 101 46 E
Wang Thong, Thailand .. 38 D3 16 50N 100 26 E
Wanga, Dem. Rep. of the Congo 54 B2 2 58N 29 12 E
Wangal, Indonesia ...... 37 F8 6 8S 134 9 E
Wanganella, Australia ... 63 F3 35 6S 144 49 E
Wanganui, N.Z. .... 59 H5 39 56S 175 3 E
Wangaratta, Australia ... 63 F4 36 21S 146 19 E
Wangary, Australia ...... 63 E2 34 35S 135 29 E
Wangdu, China .... 34 E8 38 40N 115 7 E
Wangerooge, Germany .. 16 B4 53 47N 7 54 E
Wangi, Kenya .... 54 C5 1 58S 40 58 E
Wangiwangi, Indonesia .. 37 F6 5 22S 123 37 E
Wangqing, China .... 35 C15 43 12N 129 42 E
Wankaner, India .... 42 H4 22 35N 71 0 E
Wanless, Canada 73 C8 54 11N 101 21W
Wanning, Taiwan .... 38 C8 23 15N 121 17 E
Wanon Niwat, Thailand .. 38 D4 17 38N 103 46 E
Wanquan, China .... 34 D8 40 50N 114 40 E
Wanrong, China .... 34 G6 35 25N 110 50 E
Wantage, U.K. 11 F6 51 35N 1 25W
Wanxian, China .... 33 C5 30 42N 108 20 E
Wapakoneta, U.S.A. 76 E3 40 34N 84 12W
Wapato, U.S.A. 82 C3 46 27N 120 25W
Wapawekka L., Canada ... 73 C8 54 55N 104 40W
Wapikopa L., Canada 70 B2 52 56N 87 53W
Wappingers Falls, U.S.A. 79 E11 41 36N 73 55W
Wapsipinicon →, U.S.A. 80 E9 41 44N 90 19W
Warangal, India .... 40 L11 17 58N 79 35 E
Waratah, Australia ...... 62 G4 41 30S 145 30 E
Waratah B., Australia ... 63 F4 38 54S 146 5 E
Warburton, Vic., Australia 63 F4 37 47S 145 42 E
Warburton, W. Austral., Australia .... 61 E4 26 8S 126 35 E
Warburton Ra., Australia 61 E4 25 55S 126 28 E
Ward, N.Z. .... 59 J5 41 49S 174 11 E
Ward →, Australia ..... 63 D4 26 28S 146 6 E
Ward Cove, U.S.A. 72 B2 55 25N 132 43W
Ward Mt., U.S.A. 84 H8 37 12N 118 54W
Warden, S. Africa ...... 57 D4 27 50S 29 0 E
Wardha, India .... 40 J11 20 45N 78 39 E
Wardha →, India ...... 40 K11 19 57N 79 11 E
Wardlow, Canada 72 C6 50 56N 111 31W
Ware, Canada 72 B3 57 26N 125 41W
Ware, U.S.A. 79 D12 42 16N 72 14W
Waregem, Belgium ..... 15 D3 50 53N 3 27 E
Wareham, U.S.A. 79 E14 41 46N 70 43W
Waremme, Belgium ..... 15 D5 50 43N 5 15 E
Warialda, Australia ..... 63 D5 29 29S 150 33 E
Wariap, Indonesia ...... 37 E8 1 30S 134 5 E
Warin Chamrap, Thailand 38 E5 15 12N 104 53 E
Warkopi, Indonesia ..... 37 E8 1 12S 134 9 E
Warm Springs, U.S.A. ... 83 G5 38 10N 116 20W
Warman, Canada 73 C7 52 19N 106 30W
Warmbad, Namibia ..... 56 D2 28 25S 18 42 E
Warmbad, S. Africa ..... 57 C4 24 51S 28 19 E
Warminster, U.K. 11 F5 51 12N 2 10W
Warnambool Downs, Australia .... 62 C3 22 48S 142 52 E
Warner, Canada 72 D6 49 17N 112 12W
Warner Mts., U.S.A. 82 F3 41 40N 120 15W
Warner Robins, U.S.A. ... 77 J4 32 37N 83 36W
Waroona, Australia ..... 61 F2 32 50S 115 58 E
Warracknabeal, Australia 63 F3 36 9S 142 26 E
Warragul, Australia ..... 63 F4 38 10S 145 58 E
Warrawagine, Australia .. 60 D3 20 51S 120 42 E
Warrego →, Australia .. 63 E4 30 24S 145 21 E
Warrego Ra., Australia .. 62 C4 24 58S 146 0 E
Warren, Australia ...... 63 E4 31 42S 147 51 E
Warren, Ark., U.S.A. 81 J8 33 37N 92 4W
Warren, Mich., U.S.A. ... 76 D4 42 30N 83 0W
Warren, Minn., U.S.A. ... 80 A6 48 12N 96 46W
Warren, Ohio, U.S.A. 78 E4 41 14N 80 49W
Warren, Pa., U.S.A. 78 E5 41 51N 79 9W
Warrenpoint, U.K. 13 B5 54 6N 6 15W
Warrensburg, U.S.A. 80 F8 38 46N 93 44W
Warrenton, S. Africa .... 56 D3 28 9S 24 47 E
Warrenton, U.S.A. 84 D3 46 10N 123 56W
Warrenville, Australia ... 63 D4 25 48S 147 22 E
Warri, Nigeria .... 50 G7 5 30N 5 41 E
Warrina, Australia ...... 63 D2 28 12S 135 50 E
Warrington, U.K. 10 D5 53 24N 2 35W
Warrington, U.S.A. 77 K2 30 23N 87 17W
Warrington □, U.K. 10 D5 53 24N 2 35W
Warrnambool, Australia . 63 F3 38 25S 142 30 E
Warroad, U.S.A. 80 A7 48 54N 95 19W
Warsa, Indonesia .... 37 E9 0 47S 135 55 E
Warsaw = Warszawa, Poland .... 17 B11 52 13N 21 0 E
Warsaw, Ind., U.S.A. 76 E3 41 14N 85 51W
Warsaw, N.Y., U.S.A. 78 D6 42 45N 78 8W
Warsaw, Ohio, U.S.A. 78 F3 40 20N 82 0W
Warszawa, Poland ...... 17 B11 52 13N 21 0 E
Warta →, Poland ...... 16 B8 52 35N 14 39 E
Warthe = Warta →, Poland .... 16 B8 52 35N 14 39 E
Waru, Indonesia .... 37 E8 3 30S 130 36 E
Warwick, Australia ...... 63 D5 28 10S 152 1 E
Warwick, U.K. 11 E6 52 18N 1 35W
Warwick, U.S.A. 79 E13 41 42N 71 28W
Warwickshire □, U.K. ... 11 E6 52 14N 1 38W
Wasaga Beach, Canada .. 78 B4 44 31N 80 1W
Wasatch Ra., U.S.A. 82 F8 40 30N 111 15W
Wasbank, S. Africa ..... 57 D5 28 15S 30 9 E
Wasco, Calif., U.S.A. 85 K7 35 36N 119 20W
Wasco, Oreg., U.S.A. 82 D3 45 36N 120 42W
Waseca, U.S.A. 80 C8 44 5N 93 30W
Wasekamio L., Canada .. 73 B7 56 45N 108 45W
Wash, The, U.K. .... 10 E8 52 58N 0 20 E
Washago, Canada 78 B5 44 45N 79 20W
Washburn, N. Dak., U.S.A. 80 B4 47 17N 101 2W
Washburn, Wis., U.S.A. .. 80 B9 46 40N 90 54W
Washim, India .... 40 J10 20 3N 77 0 E
Washington, U.K. 10 C6 54 55N 1 30W
Washington, D.C., U.S.A. 76 F7 38 54N 77 2W
Washington, Ga., U.S.A. . 77 J4 33 44N 82 44W
Washington, Ind., U.S.A. . 76 F2 38 40N 87 10W
Washington, Iowa, U.S.A. 80 E9 41 18N 91 42W
Washington, Mo., U.S.A. 80 F9 38 33N 91 1W
Washington, N.C., U.S.A. 77 H7 35 33N 77 3W
Washington, N.J., U.S.A. 79 F10 40 46N 74 59W
Washington, Pa., U.S.A. . 78 F4 40 10N 80 15W
Washington, Utah, U.S.A. 83 H7 37 8N 113 31W
Washington □, U.S.A. ... 82 C3 47 30N 120 30W
Washington, Mt., U.S.A. . 79 B13 44 16N 71 18W
Washington I., U.S.A. ... 76 C2 45 23N 86 54W
Washougal, U.S.A. 84 E4 45 35N 122 21W
Wasian, Indonesia ...... 37 E8 1 47S 133 19 E
Wasior, Indonesia ...... 37 E8 2 43S 134 30 E
Waskaganish, Canada ... 70 B4 51 30N 78 40W
Waskaiowaka, L., Canada 73 B9 56 33N 96 23W
Waskesiu Lake, Canada .. 73 C7 53 55N 106 5W
Wasserkuppe, Germany . 16 C5 50 29N 9 55 E
Waswanipi, Canada 70 C4 49 40N 76 29W
Waswanipi, L., Canada .. 70 C4 49 35N 76 40W
Watampone, Indonesia .. 37 E6 4 29S 120 25 E
Water Park Pt., Australia . 62 C5 22 56S 150 47 E
Water Valley, U.S.A. 81 H10 34 10N 89 38W
Waterberge, S. Africa ... 57 C4 24 10S 28 0 E
Waterbury, Conn., U.S.A. 79 E11 41 33N 73 3W
Waterbury, Vt., U.S.A. ... 79 B12 44 20N 72 46W
Waterbury L., Canada ... 73 B8 58 10N 104 22W
Waterdown, Canada 78 C5 43 20N 79 53W
Waterford, Canada 78 D4 42 56N 80 17W
Waterford, Ireland 13 D4 52 15N 7 8W
Waterford, U.S.A. 84 H6 37 38N 120 46W
Waterford □, Ireland 13 D4 52 10N 7 40W
Waterford Harbour, Ireland 13 D5 52 8N 6 58W
Waterhen L., Man., Canada 73 C9 52 10N 99 40W
Waterhen L., Sask., Canada 73 C7 54 28N 108 25W
Waterloo, Belgium ...... 15 D4 50 43N 4 25 E
Waterloo, Ont., Canada .. 70 D3 43 30N 80 32W
Waterloo, Qué., Canada . 79 A12 45 22N 72 32W
Waterloo, Ill., U.S.A. 80 F9 38 20N 90 9W
Waterloo, Iowa, U.S.A. .. 80 D8 42 30N 92 21W
Waterloo, N.Y., U.S.A. .. 78 D8 42 54N 76 52W
Watersmeet, U.S.A. 80 B10 46 16N 89 11W
Waterton-Glacier International Peace Park, U.S.A. 82 B7 48 45N 115 0W
Watertown, Conn., U.S.A. 79 E11 41 36N 73 7W
Watertown, N.Y., U.S.A. . 79 C9 43 59N 75 55W
Watertown, S. Dak., U.S.A. 80 C6 44 54N 97 7W
Watertown, Wis., U.S.A. . 80 D10 43 12N 88 43W
Waterval-Boven, S. Africa 57 D5 25 40S 30 18 E
Waterville, Canada 79 A13 45 16N 71 54W
Waterville, Maine, U.S.A. 71 D6 44 33N 69 38W
Waterville, N.Y., U.S.A. . 79 D9 42 56N 75 23W
Waterville, Pa., U.S.A. .. 78 E7 41 19N 77 21W
Waterville, Wash., U.S.A. 82 C3 47 39N 120 4W
Watervliet, U.S.A. 79 D11 42 44N 73 42W
Wates, Indonesia .... 37 G14 7 51S 110 10 E
Watford, Canada 78 D3 42 57N 81 53W
Watford, U.K. 11 F7 51 40N 0 24W
Watford City, U.S.A. 80 B3 47 48N 103 17W
Wathaman →, Canada .. 73 B8 57 16N 102 59W
Watheroo, Australia ..... 61 F2 30 15S 116 0 E
Wating, China .... 34 G4 35 40N 106 38 E
Watkins Glen, U.S.A. 78 D8 42 23N 76 52W
Watling I. = San Salvador, Bahamas 89 B5 24 0N 74 40W
Watonga, U.S.A. 81 H5 35 51N 98 25W
Watrous, Canada 73 C7 51 40N 105 25W
Watrous, U.S.A. 81 H2 35 48N 104 59W
Watsa, Dem. Rep. of the Congo 54 B2 3 4N 29 30 E
Watseka, U.S.A. 76 E2 40 47N 87 44W
Watson, Australia ...... 61 F5 30 29S 131 31 E
Watson, Canada 73 C8 52 10N 104 30W
Watson Lake, Canada ... 72 A3 60 6N 128 49W
Watsonville, U.S.A. 84 J5 36 55N 121 45W
Wattiwarriganna Cr. →, Australia .... 63 D2 28 57S 136 10 E
Watuata = Batuata, Indonesia .... 37 F6 6 12S 122 42 E
Watubela, Kepulauan, Indonesia .... 37 E8 4 28S 131 35 E
Watubela Is. = Watubela, Kepulauan, Indonesia . 37 E8 4 28S 131 35 E
Wau, Sudan .... 49 F6 7 45N 28 1 E
Waubamik, Canada 78 A4 45 27N 80 1W
Waubay, U.S.A. 80 C6 45 20N 97 18W
Waubra, Australia ...... 63 F3 37 21S 143 39 E
Wauchope, Australia .... 63 E5 31 28S 152 45 E
Wauchula, U.S.A. 77 M5 27 33N 81 49W
Waugh, Canada 73 D9 49 40N 95 11W
Waukarlycarly, L., Australia .... 60 D3 21 18S 121 56 E
Waukegan, U.S.A. 76 D2 42 22N 87 50W
Waukesha, U.S.A. 76 D1 43 1N 88 14W
Waukon, U.S.A. 80 D9 43 16N 91 29W
Wauneta, U.S.A. 80 E4 40 25N 101 23W
Waupaca, U.S.A. 80 C10 44 21N 89 5W
Waupun, U.S.A. 80 D10 43 38N 88 44W
Waurika, U.S.A. 81 H6 34 10N 98 0W
Wausau, U.S.A. 80 C10 44 58N 89 38W
Wautoma, U.S.A. 80 C10 44 4N 89 18W
Wauwatosa, U.S.A. 76 D2 43 3N 88 0W
Wave Hill, Australia ..... 60 C5 17 32S 131 0 E
Waveney →, U.K. ...... 11 E9 52 35N 1 39 E
Waverley, N.Z. .... 59 H5 39 46S 174 37 E
Waverly, Iowa, U.S.A. ... 80 D8 42 44N 92 29W
Waverly, N.Y., U.S.A. 79 E8 42 1N 76 32W
Wavre, Belgium .... 15 D4 50 43N 4 38 E
Wâw, Sudan .... 51 G11 7 45N 28 1 E
Wāw al Kabīr, Libya ..... 51 C9 25 20N 16 43 E
Wawa, Canada 70 C3 47 59N 84 47W
Wawanesa, Canada 73 D9 49 36N 99 40W
Wawona, U.S.A. 84 H7 37 32N 119 39W
Waxahachie, U.S.A. 81 J6 32 24N 96 51W
Way, L., Australia ...... 61 E3 26 45S 120 16 E
Wayatinah, Australia .... 62 G4 42 19S 146 27 E
Waycross, U.S.A. 77 K4 31 13N 82 21W
Wayne, Nebr., U.S.A. ... 80 D6 42 14N 97 1W
Wayne, W. Va., U.S.A. ... 76 F4 38 13N 82 27W
Waynesboro, Ga., U.S.A. 77 J4 33 6N 82 1W
Waynesboro, Miss., U.S.A. 77 K1 31 40N 88 39W
Waynesboro, Pa., U.S.A. . 76 F7 39 45N 77 35W
Waynesboro, Va., U.S.A. . 76 F6 38 4N 78 53W
Waynesburg, U.S.A. 76 F5 39 54N 80 11W
Waynesville, U.S.A. 77 H4 35 28N 82 58W
Waynoka, U.S.A. 81 G5 36 35N 98 53W
Wazirabad, Pakistan .... 42 C6 32 30N 74 8 E
We, Indonesia .... 36 C1 5 51N 95 18 E
Weald, The, U.K. .... 11 F8 51 4N 0 20 E
Wear →, U.K. 10 C6 54 55N 1 23W
Weatherford, Okla., U.S.A. 81 H5 35 32N 98 43W
Weatherford, Tex., U.S.A. 81 J6 32 46N 97 48W
Weaverville, U.S.A. 82 F2 40 44N 122 56W
Webb City, U.S.A. 81 G7 37 9N 94 28W
Webster, Mass., U.S.A. .. 79 D13 42 3N 71 53W
Webster, N.Y., U.S.A. .. 78 C7 43 13N 77 26W
Webster, S. Dak., U.S.A. . 80 C6 45 20N 97 31W
Webster, Wis., U.S.A. ... 80 C8 45 53N 92 22W
Webster City, U.S.A. ... 80 D8 42 28N 93 49W
Webster Green, U.S.A. .. 80 F9 38 38N 90 20W
Webster Springs, U.S.A. . 76 F5 38 29N 80 25W
Weda, Indonesia .... 37 D7 0 21N 127 50 E
Weda, Teluk, Indonesia . 37 D7 0 30N 127 50 E
Weddell I., Falk. Is. 96 G4 51 50S 61 0W
Weddell Sea, Antarctica . 5 D1 72 30S 40 0W
Wedderburn, Australia .. 63 F3 36 26S 143 33 E
Wedgeport, Canada 71 D6 43 44N 65 59W
Wedza, Zimbabwe ...... 55 F3 18 40S 31 33 E
Wee Waa, Australia ..... 63 E4 30 11S 149 26 E
Weed, U.S.A. 82 F2 41 25N 122 23W
Weed Heights, U.S.A. ... 84 G7 38 59N 119 13W
Weedsport, U.S.A. 79 C8 43 3N 76 35W
Weedville, U.S.A. 78 E6 41 17N 78 30W
Weemelah, Australia .... 63 D4 29 2S 149 15 E
Weenen, S. Africa ...... 57 D5 28 48S 30 7 E
Weert, Neths. .... 15 C5 51 15N 5 43 E
Wei He →, Hebei, China 34 F8 36 10N 115 45 E
Wei He →, Shaanxi, China .... 34 G6 34 38N 110 15 E
Weichang, China .... 35 D9 41 58N 117 49 E
Weichuan, China .... 34 G7 34 20N 113 59 E
Weiden, Germany ...... 16 D7 49 41N 12 10 E
Weifang, China .... 35 F10 36 44N 119 7 E
Weihai, China .... 35 F12 37 30N 122 6 E
Weimar, Germany ...... 16 C6 50 58N 11 19 E
Weinan, China .... 34 G5 34 31N 109 29 E
Weipa, Australia .... 62 A3 12 40S 141 50 E
Weir →, Australia ..... 63 D4 28 20S 149 50 E
Weir →, Canada 73 B10 56 54N 93 21W
Weir River, Canada 73 B10 56 49N 94 6W
Weirton, U.S.A. 78 F4 40 24N 80 35W
Weiser, U.S.A. 82 D5 44 10N 117 0W
Weishan, China .... 35 G9 34 47N 117 5 E
Weiyuan, China .... 34 G3 35 7N 104 10 E
Wejherowo, Poland ..... 17 A10 54 35N 18 12 E
Wekusko L., Canada 73 C9 54 40N 99 50W
Welbourn Hill, Australia . 63 D1 27 21S 134 6 E
Welch, U.S.A. 76 G5 37 26N 81 35W
Welkom, S. Africa ...... 56 D4 28 0S 26 46 E
Welland, Canada 70 D4 43 0N 79 15W
Welland →, U.K. 11 E7 52 51N 0 5W
Wellesley Is., Australia .. 62 B2 16 42S 139 30 E
Wellingborough, U.K. ... 11 E7 52 19N 0 41W
Wellington, Australia ... 63 E4 32 35S 148 59 E
Wellington, Canada 70 D4 43 57N 77 20W
Wellington, N.Z. .... 59 J5 41 19S 174 46 E
Wellington, S. Africa .... 56 E2 33 38S 19 1 E
Wellington, Somst., U.K. . 11 G4 50 58N 3 13W
Wellington, Telford & Wrekin, U.K. 11 E5 52 42N 2 30W
Wellington, Colo., U.S.A. 80 E2 40 42N 105 0W
Wellington, Kans., U.S.A. 81 G6 37 16N 97 24W
Wellington, Nev., U.S.A. . 84 G7 38 45N 119 23W
Wellington, Ohio, U.S.A. . 78 E2 41 10N 82 13W
Wellington, Tex., U.S.A. . 81 H4 34 51N 100 13W
Wellington, I., Chile 96 F2 49 30S 75 0W
Wellington, L., Australia . 63 F4 38 6S 147 20 E
Wells, U.K. 11 F5 51 13N 2 39W
Wells, Maine, U.S.A. 79 C14 43 20N 70 35W
Wells, Minn., U.S.A. 80 D8 43 45N 93 44W
Wells, Nev., U.S.A. 82 F6 41 7N 114 58W
Wells, L., Australia ..... 61 E3 26 44S 123 15 E
Wells Gray Prov. Park, Canada 72 C4 52 30N 120 15W
Wells-next-the-Sea, U.K. . 10 E8 52 57N 0 51 E
Wells River, U.S.A. 79 B12 44 9N 72 4W
Wellsboro, U.S.A. 78 E7 41 45N 77 18W
Wellsburg, U.S.A. 78 F4 40 16N 80 37W
Wellsville, Mo., U.S.A. .. 80 F9 39 4N 91 34W
Wellsville, N.Y., U.S.A. . 78 D7 42 7N 77 57W
Wellsville, Ohio, U.S.A. . 78 F4 40 36N 80 39W
Wellsville, Utah, U.S.A. . 82 F8 41 38N 111 56W
Wellton, U.S.A. 83 K6 32 40N 114 8W
Wels, Austria .... 16 D8 48 9N 14 1 E
Welshpool, U.K. 11 E4 52 39N 3 8W
Welwyn Garden City, U.K. 11 F7 51 48N 0 12W
Wem, U.K. 10 E5 52 52N 2 44W
Wembere →, Tanzania . 54 C3 4 10S 34 15 E
Wemindji, Canada 70 B4 53 0N 78 49W
Wen Xian, Gansu, China . 34 H3 32 43N 104 36 E
Wen Xian, Henan, China . 34 G7 34 55N 113 5 E
Wenatchee, U.S.A. 82 C3 47 25N 120 19W
Wenchang, China ...... 38 C8 19 38N 110 42 E
Wenchi, Ghana 50 G5 7 46N 2 8W
Wenchow = Wenzhou, China .... 33 D7 28 0N 120 38 E
Wendell, U.S.A. 82 E6 42 47N 114 42W
Wenden, U.S.A. 85 M13 33 49N 113 33W
Wendeng, China .... 35 F12 37 15N 122 5 E
Wendesi, Indonesia ..... 37 E8 2 30S 134 17 E
Wendover, U.S.A. 82 F6 40 44N 114 2W
Wenlock →, Australia .. 62 A3 12 2S 141 55 E
Wenshan, China .... 32 D5 23 20N 104 18 E
Wenshang, China ...... 34 G9 35 45N 116 30 E
Wenshui, China .... 34 F7 37 26N 112 1 E
Wensleydale, U.K. 10 C6 54 17N 2 0W
Wensu, China .... 32 B3 41 15N 80 10 E
Wensum →, U.K. ...... 10 E8 52 40N 1 15 E
Wentworth, Australia ... 63 E3 34 2S 141 54 E
Wenut, Indonesia .... 37 E8 3 11S 133 19 E
Wenxi, China .... 34 G6 35 20N 111 10 E
Wenzhou, China .... 33 D7 28 0N 120 38 E
Weott, U.S.A. 82 F2 40 20N 123 55W
Wepener, S. Africa ..... 56 D4 29 42S 27 3 E
Werda, Botswana .... 56 D3 25 24S 23 15 E
Weri, Indonesia .... 37 E8 3 10S 132 38 E
Werra →, Germany .... 16 C5 51 24N 9 39 E
Werribee, Australia ..... 63 F3 37 54S 144 40 E
Werrimull, Australia .... 63 E3 34 25S 141 38 E
Werris Creek, Australia .. 63 E5 31 18S 150 38 E
Weser →, Germany .... 16 B5 53 36N 8 28 E
Wesiri, Indonesia .... 37 F7 7 30S 126 30 E
Wesley Vale, U.S.A. 83 J10 35 3N 106 2W
Wesleyville, Canada 71 C9 49 8N 53 36W
Wesleyville, U.S.A. 78 D4 42 9N 80 0W
Wessel, C., Australia ... 62 A2 10 59S 136 46 E
Wessel Is., Australia .... 62 A2 11 10S 136 45 E
Wessington, U.S.A. 80 C5 44 27N 98 42W
Wessington Springs, U.S.A. 80 C5 44 5N 98 34W
West, U.S.A. 81 K6 31 48N 97 6W
West Allis, U.S.A. 76 D1 43 1N 88 0W
West B., U.S.A. 81 L10 29 3N 89 22W
West Baines →, Australia 60 C4 15 38S 129 59 E
West Bank □, Asia ...... 47 C4 32 6N 35 13 E
West Bend, U.S.A. 76 D1 43 25N 88 11W
West Bengal □, India ... 43 H13 23 0N 88 0 E
West Berkshire □, U.K. .. 11 F6 51 25N 1 17W
West Beskids = Západné Beskydy, Europe ...... 17 D10 49 30N 19 0 E
West Branch, U.S.A. 76 C3 44 17N 84 14W
West Bromwich, U.K. ... 11 E6 52 32N 1 59W
West Burra, U.K. 12 A7 60 5N 1 21W
West Cape Howe, Australia .... 61 G2 35 8S 117 36 E
West Chazy, U.S.A. 79 B11 44 49N 73 28W
West Chester, U.S.A. 76 F8 39 58N 75 36W
West Columbia, U.S.A. .. 81 L7 29 9N 95 39W
West Covina, U.S.A. 85 L9 34 4N 117 54W
West Des Moines, U.S.A. 80 E8 41 35N 93 43W
West Dunbartonshire □, U.K. 12 F4 55 59N 4 30W
West End, Bahamas 88 A4 26 41N 78 58W
West Falkland, Falk. Is. .. 96 G5 51 40S 60 0W
West Fjord = Vestfjorden, Norway .... 8 C15 67 55N 14 0 E
West Frankfort, U.S.A. ... 80 G10 37 54N 88 55W
West Hartford, U.S.A. ... 79 E12 41 45N 72 44W
West Haven, U.S.A. 79 E12 41 17N 72 57W
West Helena, U.S.A. 81 H9 34 33N 90 38W
West Ice Shelf, Antarctica 5 C7 67 0S 85 0 E
West Indies, Cent. Amer. 89 D7 15 0N 65 0W
West Lorne, Canada 78 D3 42 36N 81 36W
West Lothian □, U.K. 12 F5 55 54N 3 36W
West Lunga →, Zambia 55 E1 13 6S 24 39 E
West Memphis, U.S.A. ... 81 H9 35 9N 90 11W
West Midlands □, U.K. .. 11 E6 52 26N 2 0W
West Mifflin, U.S.A. 78 F5 40 22N 79 52W
West Monroe, U.S.A. 81 J8 32 31N 92 9W
West Newton, U.S.A. 78 F5 40 14N 79 46W
West Nicholson, Zimbabwe .... 55 G2 21 2S 29 20 E
West Palm Beach, U.S.A. 77 M5 26 43N 80 3W
West Plains, U.S.A. 81 G9 36 44N 91 51W
West Point, Ga., U.S.A. .. 77 J3 32 53N 85 11W
West Point, Miss., U.S.A. 77 J1 33 36N 88 39W
West Point, Nebr., U.S.A. 80 E6 41 51N 96 43W
West Point, Va., U.S.A. .. 76 G7 37 32N 76 48W
West Pokot □, Kenya .... 54 B4 1 30N 35 15 E
West Pt. = Ouest, Pte., Canada 71 C7 49 52N 64 40W
West Pt., Australia ..... 63 F2 35 1S 135 56 E
West Road →, Canada . 72 C4 53 18N 122 53W
West Rutland, U.S.A. 79 C11 43 38N 73 5W
West Schelde = Westerschelde →, Neths. .... 15 C3 51 25N 3 25 E
West Seneca, U.S.A. 78 D6 42 51N 78 48W
West Siberian Plain, Russia .... 28 C11 62 0N 75 0 E
West Sussex □, U.K. 11 G7 50 55N 0 30W
West-Terschelling, Neths. 15 A5 53 22N 5 13 E
West Valley City, U.S.A. . 82 F8 40 42N 111 57W
West Virginia □, U.S.A. .. 76 F5 38 45N 80 30W
West-Vlaanderen □, Belgium .... 15 D2 51 0N 3 0 E
West Walker →, U.S.A. . 84 G7 38 54N 119 9W
West Wyalong, Australia 63 E4 33 56S 147 10 E
West Yellowstone, U.S.A. 82 D8 44 40N 111 6W
West Yorkshire □, U.K. .. 10 D6 53 45N 1 40W
Westall Pt., Australia ... 63 E1 32 55S 134 4 E
Westbrook, Maine, U.S.A. 77 D10 43 41N 70 22W
Westbrook, Tex., U.S.A. . 81 J4 32 21N 101 1W
Westbury, Australia ..... 62 G4 41 30S 146 51 E
Westby, U.S.A. 80 A2 48 52N 104 3W
Westend, U.S.A. 85 K9 35 42N 117 24W
Westerland, Germany .... 9 J13 54 54N 8 17 E
Western □, Kenya ...... 54 B3 0 30N 34 30 E
Western □, Uganda ..... 54 B3 1 45N 31 30 E
Western □, Zambia ..... 55 F1 15 15S 24 30 E
Western Australia □, Australia .... 61 E2 25 0S 118 0 E
Western Cape □, S. Africa 56 E3 34 0S 20 0 E
Western Dvina = Daugava →, Latvia .. 24 C3 57 4N 24 3 E
Western Ghats, India .... 40 N9 14 0N 75 0 E
Western Isles □, U.K. ... 12 D1 57 30N 7 10W
Western Sahara ■, Africa 50 D3 25 0N 13 0W
Western Samoa ■, Pac. Oc. 59 B13 14 0S 172 0W
Westernport, U.S.A. 76 F6 39 29N 79 3W
Westerschelde →, Neths. 15 C3 51 25N 3 25 E
Westerwald, Germany ... 16 C4 50 38N 7 56 E
Westfield, Mass., U.S.A. . 79 D12 42 7N 72 45W
Westfield, N.Y., U.S.A. .. 78 D5 42 20N 79 35W
Westfield, Pa., U.S.A. ... 78 E7 41 55N 77 32W
Westhill, U.K. 12 D6 57 9N 2 19W
Westhope, U.S.A. 80 A4 48 55N 101 1W
Westland Bight, N.Z. .... 59 K3 42 55S 170 5 E
Westlock, Canada 72 C6 54 9N 113 55W
Westmeath □, Ireland ... 13 C4 53 33N 7 34W

Westminster

Westminster, *U.S.A.* **76 F7** 39 34N 76 59W
Westmorland, *U.S.A.* **83 K6** 33 2N 115 37W
Weston, *Oreg., U.S.A.* **82 D4** 45 49N 118 26W
Weston, *W. Va., U.S.A.* **76 F5** 39 2N 80 28W
Weston I., *Canada* **70 B4** 52 33N 79 36W
Weston-super-Mare, *U.K.* **11 F5** 51 21N 2 58W
Westport, *Canada* **79 B8** 44 40N 76 25W
Westport, *Ireland* **13 C2** 53 48N 9 31W
Westport, *N.Z.* **59 J3** 41 46S 171 37 E
Westport, *Oreg., U.S.A.* **84 D3** 46 8N 123 23W
Westport, *Wash., U.S.A.* **82 C1** 46 53N 124 6W
Westray, *Canada* **73 C8** 53 36N 101 24W
Westray, *U.K.* **12 B5** 59 18N 3 0W
Westree, *Canada* **70 C3** 47 26N 81 34W
Westville, *Calif., U.S.A.* **84 F6** 39 8N 120 42W
Westville, *Ill., U.S.A.* **76 E2** 40 2N 87 38W
Westville, *Okla., U.S.A.* **81 H7** 35 58N 94 40W
Westwood, *U.S.A.* **82 F3** 40 18N 121 0W
Wetar, *Indonesia* **37 F7** 7 30S 126 30 E
Wetaskiwin, *Canada* **72 C6** 52 55N 113 24W
Wetherby, *U.K.* **10 D6** 53 56N 1 23W
Wethersfield, *U.S.A.* **79 E12** 41 42N 72 40W
Wetteren, *Belgium* **15 D3** 51 0N 3 53 E
Wetzlar, *Germany* **16 C5** 50 32N 8 31 E
Wewoka, *U.S.A.* **81 H6** 35 9N 96 30W
Wexford, *Ireland* **13 D5** 52 20N 6 28W
Wexford □, *Ireland* **13 D5** 52 20N 6 25W
Wexford Harbour, *Ireland* **13 D5** 52 20N 6 25W
Weyburn, *Canada* **73 D8** 49 40N 103 50W
Weyburn L., *Canada* **72 A5** 63 0N 117 59W
Weymouth, *Canada* **71 D6** 44 30N 66 1W
Weymouth, *U.K.* **11 G5** 50 37N 2 28W
Weymouth, *U.S.A.* **79 D14** 42 13N 70 58W
Weymouth, C., *Australia* **62 A3** 12 37S 143 27 E
Wha Ti, *Canada* **68 B8** 63 8N 117 16W
Whakatane, *N.Z.* **59 G6** 37 57S 177 1 E
Whale →, *Canada* **71 A6** 58 15N 67 40W
Whale Cove, *Canada* **73 A10** 62 11N 92 36W
Whales, B. of, *Antarctica* **5 D12** 78 0S 165 0W
Whalsay, *U.K.* **12 A8** 60 22N 0 59W
Whangamomona, *N.Z.* **59 H5** 39 8S 174 44 E
Whangarei, *N.Z.* **59 F5** 35 43S 174 21 E
Whangarei Harb., *N.Z.* **59 F5** 35 45S 174 28 E
Wharfe →, *U.K.* **10 D6** 53 51N 1 9W
Wharfedale, *U.K.* **10 C5** 54 6N 2 1W
Wharton, *N.J., U.S.A.* **79 F10** 40 54N 74 35W
Wharton, *Pa., U.S.A.* **78 E6** 41 31N 78 1W
Wharton, *Tex., U.S.A.* **81 L6** 29 19N 96 6W
Wheatland, *Calif., U.S.A.* **84 F5** 39 1N 121 25W
Wheatland, *Wyo., U.S.A.* **80 D2** 42 3N 104 58W
Wheatley, *Canada* **78 D2** 42 6N 82 27W
Wheaton, *U.S.A.* **80 C6** 45 48N 96 30W
Wheelbarrow Pk., *U.S.A.* **84 H10** 37 26N 116 5W
Wheeler, *Oreg., U.S.A.* **82 D2** 45 41N 123 53W
Wheeler, *Tex., U.S.A.* **81 H4** 35 27N 100 16W
Wheeler →, *Canada* **73 B7** 57 25N 105 30W
Wheeler Pk., *N. Mex., U.S.A.* **83 H11** 36 34N 105 25W
Wheeler Pk., *Nev., U.S.A.* **83 G6** 38 57N 114 15W
Wheeler Ridge, *U.S.A.* **85 L8** 35 0N 118 57W
Wheeling, *U.S.A.* **78 F4** 40 4N 80 43W
Whernside, *U.K.* **10 C5** 54 14N 2 24W
Whidbey I., *U.S.A.* **72 D4** 48 12N 122 17W
Whiskey Gap, *Canada* **72 D6** 49 0N 113 3W
Whiskey Jack L., *Canada* **73 B8** 58 23N 101 55W
Whistleduck Cr. →, *Australia* **62 C2** 20 15S 135 18 E
Whitby, *Canada* **78 C6** 43 52N 78 56W
Whitby, *U.K.* **10 C7** 54 29N 0 37W
White →, *Ark., U.S.A.* **81 J9** 33 57N 91 5W
White →, *Ind., U.S.A.* **76 F2** 38 25N 87 45W
White →, *S. Dak., U.S.A.* **80 D5** 43 42N 99 27W
White →, *Utah, U.S.A.* **82 F9** 40 4N 109 41W
White →, *Wash., U.S.A.* **84 C4** 47 12N 122 15W
White, L., *Australia* **60 D4** 21 9S 128 56 E
White B., *Canada* **71 C8** 50 0N 56 35W
White Bear Res., *Canada* **71 C8** 48 10N 57 5W
White Bird, *U.S.A.* **82 D5** 45 46N 116 18W
White Butte, *U.S.A.* **80 B3** 46 23N 103 18W
White City, *U.S.A.* **80 F6** 38 48N 96 44W
White Cliffs, *Australia* **63 E3** 30 50S 143 10 E
White Deer, *U.S.A.* **81 H4** 35 26N 101 10W
White Hall, *U.S.A.* **80 F9** 39 26N 90 24W
White Haven, *U.S.A.* **79 E9** 41 4N 75 47W
White Horse, Vale of, *U.K.* **11 F6** 51 37N 1 30W
White I., *N.Z.* **59 G6** 37 30S 177 13 E
White L., *Canada* **79 A8** 45 18N 76 31W
White L., *U.S.A.* **81 L8** 29 44N 92 30W
White Mts., *Calif., U.S.A.* **84 H8** 37 30N 118 15W
White Mts., *N.H., U.S.A.* **75 B12** 44 15N 71 15W
White Nile = Nîl el Abyad →, *Sudan* **51 E12** 15 38N 32 31 E
White Otter L., *Canada* **70 C1** 49 5N 91 55W
White Pass, *Canada* **72 B1** 59 40N 135 3W
White Pass, *U.S.A.* **84 D5** 46 38N 121 24W
White Plains, *U.S.A.* **79 E11** 41 2N 73 46W
White River, *Canada* **70 C2** 48 35N 85 20W
White River, *S. Africa* **57 D5** 25 20S 31 0 E
White River, *U.S.A.* **80 D4** 43 34N 100 45W
White Russia = Belarus ■, *Europe* **24 D4** 53 30N 27 0 E
White Sea = Beloye More, *Russia* **24 A6** 66 30N 38 0 E
White Sulphur Springs, *Mont., U.S.A.* **82 C8** 46 33N 110 54W
White Sulphur Springs, *W. Va., U.S.A.* **76 G5** 37 48N 80 18W
White Swan, *U.S.A.* **84 D6** 46 23N 120 44W
Whitecliffs, *N.Z.* **59 K3** 43 26S 171 55 E
Whitecourt, *Canada* **72 C5** 54 10N 115 45W
Whiteface, *U.S.A.* **81 J3** 33 36N 102 37W
Whitefield, *U.S.A.* **79 B13** 44 23N 71 37W
Whitefish, *U.S.A.* **82 B6** 48 25N 114 20W
Whitefish L., *Canada* **73 A7** 62 41N 106 48W
Whitefish Point, *U.S.A.* **76 B3** 46 45N 84 59W
Whitegull, L., *Canada* **71 A7** 55 27N 64 17W
Whitehall, *Mich., U.S.A.* **76 D2** 43 24N 86 21W
Whitehall, *Mont., U.S.A.* **82 D7** 45 52N 112 6W
Whitehall, *N.Y., U.S.A.* **79 C11** 43 33N 73 24W
Whitehall, *Wis., U.S.A.* **80 C9** 44 22N 91 19W
Whitehaven, *U.K.* **10 C4** 54 33N 3 35W
Whitehorse, *Canada* **72 A1** 60 43N 135 3W
Whitemark, *Australia* **62 G4** 40 7S 148 3 E
Whitemouth, *Canada* **73 D9** 49 57N 95 58W
Whitesboro, *N.Y., U.S.A.* **79 C9** 43 7N 75 18W
Whitesboro, *Tex., U.S.A.* **81 J6** 33 39N 96 54W
Whiteshell Prov. Park, *Canada* **73 D9** 50 0N 95 40W
Whitetail, *U.S.A.* **80 A2** 48 54N 105 10W
Whiteville, *U.S.A.* **77 H6** 34 20N 78 42W
Whitewater, *U.S.A.* **76 D1** 42 50N 88 44W
Whitewater Baldy, *U.S.A.* **83 K9** 33 20N 108 39W
Whitewater L., *Canada* **70 B2** 50 50N 89 10W
Whitewood, *Australia* **62 C3** 21 28S 143 30 E
Whitewood, *Canada* **73 C8** 50 20N 102 20W
Whitfield, *Australia* **63 F4** 36 42S 146 24 E
Whithorn, *U.K.* **12 G4** 54 44N 4 26W
Whitianga, *N.Z.* **59 G5** 36 47S 175 41 E
Whitman, *U.S.A.* **79 D14** 42 5N 70 56W
Whitmire, *U.S.A.* **77 H5** 34 30N 81 37W
Whitney, *Canada* **78 A6** 45 31N 78 14W
Whitney, Mt., *U.S.A.* **84 J8** 36 35N 118 18W
Whitney Point, *U.S.A.* **79 D9** 42 20N 75 58W
Whitstable, *U.K.* **11 F9** 51 21N 1 3 E
Whitsunday I., *Australia* **62 C4** 20 15S 149 4 E
Whittier, *U.S.A.* **85 M8** 33 58N 118 3W
Whittlesea, *Australia* **63 F4** 37 27S 145 9 E
Whitwell, *U.S.A.* **77 H3** 35 12N 85 31W
Wholdaia L., *Canada* **73 A8** 60 43N 104 20W
Whyalla, *Australia* **63 E2** 33 2S 137 30 E
Whyjonta, *Australia* **63 D3** 29 41S 142 28 E
Wiarton, *Canada* **78 B3** 44 40N 81 10W
Wiay, *U.K.* **12 D1** 57 24N 7 13W
Wibaux, *U.S.A.* **80 B2** 46 59N 104 11W
Wichian Buri, *Thailand* **38 E3** 15 39N 101 7 E
Wichita, *U.S.A.* **81 G6** 37 42N 97 20W
Wichita Falls, *U.S.A.* **81 J5** 33 54N 98 30W
Wick, *U.K.* **12 C5** 58 26N 3 5W
Wickenburg, *U.S.A.* **83 K7** 33 58N 112 44W
Wickepin, *Australia* **61 F2** 32 50S 117 30 E
Wickham, C., *Australia* **62 F3** 39 35S 143 57 E
Wickliffe, *U.S.A.* **78 E3** 41 36N 81 28W
Wicklow, *Ireland* **13 D5** 52 59N 6 3W
Wicklow □, *Ireland* **13 D5** 52 57N 6 25W
Wicklow Hd., *Ireland* **13 D6** 52 58N 6 0W
Wicklow Mts., *Ireland* **13 C5** 52 58N 6 26W
Widgiemooltha, *Australia* **61 F3** 31 30S 121 34 E
Widnes, *U.K.* **10 D5** 53 23N 2 45W
Wieluń, *Poland* **17 C10** 51 15N 18 34 E
Wien, *Austria* **16 D9** 48 12N 16 22 E
Wiener Neustadt, *Austria* **16 E9** 47 49N 16 16 E
Wiesbaden, *Germany* **16 C5** 50 4N 8 14 E
Wigan, *U.K.* **10 D5** 53 33N 2 38W
Wiggins, *Colo., U.S.A.* **80 E2** 40 14N 104 4W
Wiggins, *Miss., U.S.A.* **81 K10** 30 51N 89 8W
Wight, I. of □, *U.K.* **11 G6** 50 40N 1 20W
Wigston, *U.K.* **11 E6** 52 35N 1 6W
Wigton, *U.K.* **10 C4** 54 50N 3 10W
Wigtown, *U.K.* **12 G4** 54 53N 4 27W
Wigtown B., *U.K.* **12 G4** 54 46N 4 15W
Wilber, *U.S.A.* **80 E6** 40 29N 96 58W
Wilberforce, *Canada* **78 A6** 45 2N 78 13W
Wilberforce, C., *Australia* **62 A2** 11 54S 136 35 E
Wilburton, *U.S.A.* **81 H7** 34 55N 95 19W
Wilcannia, *Australia* **63 E3** 31 30S 143 26 E
Wilcox, *U.S.A.* **78 E6** 41 35N 78 41W
Wildrose, *Calif., U.S.A.* **85 J9** 36 14N 117 11W
Wildrose, *N. Dak., U.S.A.* **80 A3** 48 38N 103 11W
Wildspitze, *Austria* **16 E6** 46 53N 10 53 E
Wildwood, *U.S.A.* **76 F8** 38 59N 74 50W
Wilge →, *S. Africa* **57 D4** 27 3S 28 20 E
Wilhelm II Coast, *Antarctica* **5 C7** 68 0S 90 0 E
Wilhelmshaven, *Germany* **16 B5** 53 31N 8 7 E
Wilhelmstal, *Namibia* **56 C2** 21 58S 16 21 E
Wilkes-Barre, *U.S.A.* **79 E9** 41 15N 75 53W
Wilkesboro, *U.S.A.* **77 G5** 36 9N 81 10W
Wilkie, *Canada* **73 C7** 52 27N 108 42W
Wilkinsburg, *U.S.A.* **78 F5** 40 26N 79 53W
Wilkinson Lakes, *Australia* **61 E5** 29 40S 132 39 E
Willamina, *U.S.A.* **82 D2** 45 5N 123 29W
Willandra Billabong Creek →, *Australia* **63 E4** 33 22S 145 52 E
Willapa B., *U.S.A.* **82 C2** 46 40N 124 0W
Willapa Hills, *U.S.A.* **84 D3** 46 35N 123 25W
Willard, *N. Mex., U.S.A.* **83 J10** 34 36N 106 2W
Willard, *Utah, U.S.A.* **82 F7** 41 25N 112 2W
Willcox, *U.S.A.* **83 K9** 32 15N 109 50W
Willemstad, *Neth. Ant.* **89 D6** 12 5N 69 0W
Willeroo, *Australia* **60 C5** 15 14S 131 37 E
William →, *Canada* **73 B7** 59 8N 109 19W
William Creek, *Australia* **63 D2** 28 58S 136 22 E
Williambury, *Australia* **61 D2** 23 45S 115 12 E
Williams, *Australia* **61 F2** 33 2S 116 52 E
Williams, *Ariz., U.S.A.* **83 J7** 35 15N 112 11W
Williams, *Calif., U.S.A.* **84 F4** 39 9N 122 9W
Williams Lake, *Canada* **72 C4** 52 10N 122 10W
Williamsburg, *Ky., U.S.A.* **77 G3** 36 44N 84 10W
Williamsburg, *Pa., U.S.A.* **78 F6** 40 28N 78 12W
Williamsburg, *Va., U.S.A.* **76 G7** 37 17N 76 44W
Williamson, *N.Y., U.S.A.* **78 C7** 43 14N 77 11W
Williamson, *W. Va., U.S.A.* **76 G4** 37 41N 82 17W
Williamsport, *U.S.A.* **78 E7** 41 15N 77 0W
Williamston, *U.S.A.* **77 H7** 35 51N 77 4W
Williamstown, *Australia* **63 F3** 37 51S 144 52 E
Williamstown, *Mass., U.S.A.* **79 D11** 42 41N 73 12W
Williamstown, *N.Y., U.S.A.* **79 C9** 43 26N 75 53W
Williamsville, *U.S.A.* **81 G9** 36 58N 90 33W
Willimantic, *U.S.A.* **79 E12** 41 43N 72 13W
Willis Group, *Australia* **62 B5** 16 18S 150 0 E
Williston, *S. Africa* **56 E3** 31 20S 20 53 E
Williston, *Fla., U.S.A.* **77 L4** 29 23N 82 27W
Williston, *N. Dak., U.S.A.* **80 A3** 48 9N 103 37W
Williston L., *Canada* **72 B4** 56 0N 124 0W
Willits, *U.S.A.* **82 G2** 39 25N 123 21W
Willmar, *U.S.A.* **80 C7** 45 7N 95 3W
Willoughby, *U.S.A.* **78 E3** 41 39N 81 24W
Willow Bunch, *Canada* **73 D7** 49 20N 105 35W
Willow L., *Canada* **72 A5** 62 10N 119 8W
Willow Lake, *U.S.A.* **80 C6** 44 38N 97 38W
Willow Springs, *U.S.A.* **81 G9** 37 0N 91 58W
Willow Wall, The, *China* **35 C12** 42 10N 122 0 E
Willowlake →, *Canada* **72 A4** 62 42N 123 8W
Willowmore, *S. Africa* **56 E3** 33 15S 23 30 E
Willows, *Australia* **62 C4** 23 39S 147 25 E
Willows, *U.S.A.* **84 F4** 39 31N 122 12W
Willowvale = Gatyana, *S. Africa* **57 E4** 32 16S 28 31 E
Wills, L., *Australia* **60 D4** 21 25S 128 51 E
Wills Cr. →, *Australia* **62 C3** 22 43S 140 2 E
Wills Point, *U.S.A.* **81 J7** 32 43N 96 1W
Willunga, *Australia* **63 F2** 35 15S 138 30 E
Wilmette, *U.S.A.* **76 D2** 42 5N 87 42W
Wilmington, *Australia* **63 E2** 32 39S 138 7 E
Wilmington, *Del., U.S.A.* **76 F8** 39 45N 75 33W
Wilmington, *Ill., U.S.A.* **76 E1** 41 18N 88 9W
Wilmington, *N.C., U.S.A.* **77 H7** 34 14N 77 55W
Wilmington, *Ohio, U.S.A.* **76 F4** 39 27N 83 50W
Wilmslow, *U.K.* **10 D5** 53 19N 2 13W
Wilpena Cr. →, *Australia* **63 E2** 31 25S 139 29 E
Wilsall, *U.S.A.* **82 D8** 45 59N 110 38W
Wilson, *U.S.A.* **77 H7** 35 44N 77 55W
Wilson →, *Queens., Australia* **63 D3** 27 38S 141 24 E
Wilson →, *W. Austral., Australia* **60 C4** 16 48S 128 16 E
Wilson Bluff, *Australia* **61 F4** 31 41S 129 0 E
Wilsons Promontory, *Australia* **63 F4** 38 55S 146 25 E
Wilton, *U.S.A.* **80 B4** 47 10N 100 47W
Wilton →, *Australia* **62 A1** 14 45S 134 33 E
Wiltshire □, *U.K.* **11 F6** 51 18N 1 53W
Wiltz, *Lux.* **15 E5** 49 57N 5 55 E
Wiluna, *Australia* **61 E3** 26 36S 120 14 E
Wimborne Minster, *U.K.* **11 G6** 50 48N 1 59W
Wimmera →, *Australia* **63 F3** 36 8S 141 56 E
Winam G., *Kenya* **54 C3** 0 20S 34 15 E
Winburg, *S. Africa* **56 D4** 28 30S 27 2 E
Winchendon, *U.S.A.* **79 D12** 42 41N 72 3W
Winchester, *U.K.* **11 F6** 51 4N 1 18W
Winchester, *Conn., U.S.A.* **79 E11** 41 53N 73 9W
Winchester, *Idaho, U.S.A.* **82 C5** 46 14N 116 38W
Winchester, *Ind., U.S.A.* **76 E3** 40 10N 84 59W
Winchester, *Ky., U.S.A.* **76 G3** 38 0N 84 11W
Winchester, *N.H., U.S.A.* **79 D12** 42 46N 72 23W
Winchester, *Nev., U.S.A.* **85 J11** 36 6N 115 10W
Winchester, *Tenn., U.S.A.* **77 H2** 35 11N 86 7W
Winchester, *Va., U.S.A.* **76 F6** 39 11N 78 10W
Wind →, *U.S.A.* **82 E9** 43 12N 108 12W
Wind River Range, *U.S.A.* **82 E9** 43 0N 109 30W
Windau = Ventspils, *Latvia* **24 C3** 57 25N 21 32 E
Windber, *U.S.A.* **78 F6** 40 14N 78 50W
Windermere, *U.K.* **10 C5** 54 23N 2 55W
Windfall, *Canada* **72 C5** 54 12N 116 13W
Windflower L., *Canada* **72 A5** 62 52N 118 30W
Windhoek, *Namibia* **56 C2** 22 35S 17 4 E
Windom, *U.S.A.* **80 D7** 43 52N 95 7W
Windorah, *Australia* **62 D3** 25 24S 142 36 E
Window Rock, *U.S.A.* **83 J9** 35 41N 109 3W
Windrush →, *U.K.* **11 F6** 51 43N 1 24W
Windsor, *Australia* **63 E5** 33 37S 150 50 E
Windsor, *N.S., Canada* **71 D7** 44 59N 64 5W
Windsor, *Nfld., Canada* **71 C8** 48 57N 55 40W
Windsor, *Ont., Canada* **70 D3** 42 18N 83 0W
Windsor, *U.K.* **11 F7** 51 29N 0 36W
Windsor, *Colo., U.S.A.* **80 E2** 40 29N 104 54W
Windsor, *Conn., U.S.A.* **79 E12** 41 50N 72 39W
Windsor, *Mo., U.S.A.* **80 F8** 38 32N 93 31W
Windsor, *N.Y., U.S.A.* **79 D9** 42 5N 75 37W
Windsor, *Vt., U.S.A.* **79 C12** 43 29N 72 24W
Windsor & Maidenhead □, *U.K.* **11 F7** 51 29N 0 40W
Windsorton, *S. Africa* **56 D3** 28 16S 24 44 E
Windward Is., *W. Indies* **89 D7** 13 0N 61 0W
Windward Passage = Vientos, Paso de los, *Caribbean* **89 C5** 20 0N 74 0W
Windy L., *Canada* **73 A8** 60 20N 100 2W
Winefred L., *Canada* **73 B6** 55 30N 110 30W
Winfield, *U.S.A.* **81 G6** 37 15N 96 59W
Wingate Mts., *Australia* **60 B5** 14 25S 130 40 E
Wingen, *Australia* **63 E5** 31 54S 150 54 E
Wingham, *Australia* **63 E5** 31 48S 152 22 E
Wingham, *Canada* **70 D3** 43 55N 81 20W
Winifred, *U.S.A.* **82 C9** 47 34N 109 23W
Winisk, *Canada* **70 A2** 55 20N 85 15W
Winisk →, *Canada* **70 A2** 55 17N 85 5W
Winisk L., *Canada* **70 B2** 52 55N 87 22W
Wink, *U.S.A.* **81 K3** 31 45N 103 9W
Winkler, *Canada* **73 D9** 49 10N 97 56W
Winlock, *U.S.A.* **84 D4** 46 30N 122 56W
Winnebago, *U.S.A.* **80 D7** 43 46N 94 10W
Winnebago, L., *U.S.A.* **76 D1** 44 0N 88 26W
Winnecke Cr. →, *Australia* **60 C5** 18 35S 131 34 E
Winnemucca, *U.S.A.* **82 F5** 40 58N 117 44W
Winnemucca L., *U.S.A.* **82 F4** 40 7N 119 21W
Winner, *U.S.A.* **80 D5** 43 22N 99 52W
Winnett, *U.S.A.* **82 C9** 47 0N 108 21W
Winnfield, *U.S.A.* **81 K8** 31 56N 92 38W
Winnibigoshish, L., *U.S.A.* **80 B7** 47 27N 94 13W
Winning, *Australia* **60 D1** 23 9S 114 30 E
Winnipeg, *Canada* **73 D9** 49 54N 97 9W
Winnipeg →, *Canada* **73 C9** 50 38N 96 19W
Winnipeg, L., *Canada* **73 C9** 52 0N 97 0W
Winnipeg Beach, *Canada* **73 C9** 50 30N 96 58W
Winnipegosis, *Canada* **73 C9** 51 39N 99 55W
Winnipegosis L., *Canada* **73 C9** 52 30N 100 0W
Winnipesaukee, L., *U.S.A.* **79 C13** 43 38N 71 21W
Winnsboro, *La., U.S.A.* **81 J9** 32 10N 91 43W
Winnsboro, *S.C., U.S.A.* **77 H5** 34 23N 81 5W
Winnsboro, *Tex., U.S.A.* **81 J7** 32 58N 95 17W
Winokapau, L., *Canada* **71 B7** 53 15N 62 50W
Winona, *Minn., U.S.A.* **80 C9** 44 3N 91 39W
Winona, *Miss., U.S.A.* **81 J10** 33 29N 89 44W
Winooski, *U.S.A.* **79 B11** 44 29N 73 11W
Winschoten, *Neths.* **15 A7** 53 9N 7 3 E
Winsford, *U.K.* **10 D5** 53 12N 2 31W
Winslow, *Ariz., U.S.A.* **83 J8** 35 2N 110 42W
Winslow, *Wash., U.S.A.* **84 C4** 47 38N 122 31W
Winsted, *U.S.A.* **79 E11** 41 55N 73 4W
Winston-Salem, *U.S.A.* **77 G5** 36 6N 80 15W
Winter Garden, *U.S.A.* **77 L5** 28 34N 81 35W
Winter Haven, *U.S.A.* **77 M5** 28 1N 81 44W
Winter Park, *U.S.A.* **77 L5** 28 36N 81 20W
Winterhaven, *U.S.A.* **85 N12** 32 47N 114 39W
Winters, *Calif., U.S.A.* **84 G5** 38 32N 121 58W
Winters, *Tex., U.S.A.* **81 K5** 31 58N 99 58W
Winterset, *U.S.A.* **80 E8** 41 20N 94 1W
Wintersville, *U.S.A.* **78 F4** 40 23N 80 42W
Winterswijk, *Neths.* **15 C6** 51 58N 6 43 E
Winterthur, *Switz.* **18 C8** 47 30N 8 44 E
Winthrop, *Minn., U.S.A.* **80 C7** 44 32N 94 22W
Winthrop, *Wash., U.S.A.* **82 B3** 48 28N 120 10W
Winton, *Australia* **62 C3** 22 24S 143 3 E
Winton, *N.Z.* **59 M2** 46 8S 168 20 E
Winton, *U.S.A.* **77 G7** 36 24N 76 56W
Wirrulla, *Australia* **63 E1** 32 24S 134 31 E
Wisbech, *U.K.* **11 E8** 52 41N 0 9 E
Wisconsin □, *U.S.A.* **80 C10** 44 45N 89 30W
Wisconsin →, *U.S.A.* **80 D9** 43 0N 91 15W
Wisconsin Dells, *U.S.A.* **80 D10** 43 38N 89 46W
Wisconsin Rapids, *U.S.A.* **80 C10** 44 23N 89 49W
Wisdom, *U.S.A.* **82 D7** 45 37N 113 27W
Wishaw, *U.K.* **12 F5** 55 46N 3 54W
Wishek, *U.S.A.* **80 B5** 46 16N 99 33W
Wisła →, *Poland* **17 A10** 54 22N 18 55 E
Wismar, *Germany* **16 B6** 53 54N 11 29 E
Wisner, *U.S.A.* **80 E6** 41 59N 96 55W
Witbank, *S. Africa* **57 D4** 25 51S 29 14 E
Witdraai, *S. Africa* **56 D3** 26 58S 20 48 E
Witham, *U.K.* **11 F8** 51 48N 0 40 E
Witham →, *U.K.* **10 E7** 52 59N 0 2W
Withernsea, *U.K.* **10 D8** 53 44N 0 1 E
Witney, *U.K.* **11 F6** 51 48N 1 28W
Witnossob →, *Namibia* **56 D3** 26 55S 20 37 E
Wittenberge, *Germany* **16 B6** 53 0N 11 45 E
Wittenoom, *Australia* **60 D2** 22 15S 118 20 E
Wkra →, *Poland* **17 B11** 52 27N 20 44 E
Wlingi, *Indonesia* **37 H15** 8 5S 112 25 E
Włocławek, *Poland* **17 B10** 52 40N 19 3 E
Włodawa, *Poland* **17 C12** 51 33N 23 31 E
Woburn, *U.S.A.* **79 D13** 42 29N 71 9W
Wodian, *China* **34 H7** 32 50N 112 35 E
Wodonga, *Australia* **63 F4** 36 5S 146 50 E
Wokam, *Indonesia* **37 F8** 5 45S 134 28 E
Woking, *U.K.* **11 F7** 51 19N 0 34W
Wokingham □, *U.K.* **11 F7** 51 25N 0 51W
Wolf →, *Canada* **72 A2** 60 17N 132 33W
Wolf Creek, *U.S.A.* **82 C7** 47 0N 112 4W
Wolf L., *Canada* **72 A2** 60 24N 131 40W
Wolf Point, *U.S.A.* **80 A2** 48 5N 105 39W
Wolfe I., *Canada* **70 D4** 44 7N 76 20W
Wolfsberg, *Austria* **16 E8** 46 50N 14 52 E
Wolfsburg, *Germany* **16 B6** 52 25N 10 48 E
Wolin, *Poland* **16 B8** 53 50N 14 37 E
Wollaston, Is., *Chile* **96 H3** 55 40S 67 30W
Wollaston L., *Canada* **73 B8** 58 7N 103 10W
Wollaston Pen., *Canada* **68 B8** 69 30N 115 0W
Wollogorang, *Australia* **62 B2** 17 13S 137 57 E
Wollongong, *Australia* **63 E5** 34 25S 150 54 E
Wolmaransstad, *S. Africa* **56 D4** 27 12S 25 59 E
Wolseley, *Australia* **63 F3** 36 23S 140 54 E
Wolseley, *Canada* **73 C8** 50 25N 103 15W
Wolseley, *S. Africa* **56 E2** 33 26S 19 7 E
Wolstenholme, C., *Canada* **66 C12** 62 35N 77 30W
Wolvega, *Neths.* **15 B6** 52 52N 6 0 E
Wolverhampton, *U.K.* **11 E5** 52 35N 2 7W
Wonarah, *Australia* **62 B2** 19 55S 136 20 E
Wondai, *Australia* **63 D5** 26 20S 151 49 E
Wongalarroo L., *Australia* **63 E3** 31 32S 144 0 E
Wongan Hills, *Australia* **61 F2** 30 51S 116 37 E
Wongawol, *Australia* **61 E3** 26 5S 121 55 E
Wŏnju, *S. Korea* **35 F14** 37 22N 127 58 E
Wonosari, *Indonesia* **37 G14** 7 58S 110 36 E
Wŏnsan, *N. Korea* **35 E14** 39 11N 127 27 E
Wonthaggi, *Australia* **63 F4** 38 37S 145 37 E
Woocalla, *Australia* **63 E2** 31 42S 137 12 E
Wood Buffalo Nat. Park, *Canada* **72 B6** 59 0N 113 41W
Wood Is., *Australia* **60 C3** 16 24S 123 19 E
Wood L., *Canada* **73 B8** 55 17N 103 17W
Wood Lake, *U.S.A.* **80 D4** 42 38N 100 14W
Woodah I., *Australia* **62 A2** 13 27S 136 10 E
Woodanilling, *Australia* **61 F2** 33 31S 117 24 E
Woodbridge, *Canada* **78 C5** 43 47N 79 36W
Woodbridge, *U.K.* **11 E9** 52 6N 1 20 E
Woodburn, *Australia* **63 D5** 29 6S 153 23 E
Woodenbong, *Australia* **63 D5** 28 24S 152 39 E
Woodend, *Australia* **63 F3** 37 20S 144 33 E
Woodfords, *U.S.A.* **84 G7** 38 47N 119 50W
Woodgreen, *Australia* **62 C1** 22 26S 134 12 E
Woodlake, *U.S.A.* **84 J7** 36 25N 119 6W
Woodland, *U.S.A.* **84 G5** 38 41N 121 46W
Woodlands, *Australia* **60 D2** 24 46S 118 8 E
Woodpecker, *Canada* **72 C4** 53 30N 122 40W
Woodridge, *Canada* **73 D9** 49 20N 96 9W
Woodroffe, Mt., *Australia* **61 E5** 26 20S 131 45 E
Woodruff, *Ariz., U.S.A.* **83 J8** 34 51N 110 1W
Woodruff, *Utah, U.S.A.* **82 F8** 41 31N 111 10W
Woods, L., *Australia* **62 B1** 17 50S 133 30 E
Woods, L., *Canada* **71 B6** 54 30N 65 13W
Woods, L. of the, *Canada* **73 D10** 49 15N 94 45W
Woodstock, *Queens., Australia* **62 B4** 19 35S 146 50 E
Woodstock, *W. Austral., Australia* **60 D2** 21 41S 118 57 E
Woodstock, *N.B., Canada* **71 C6** 46 11N 67 37W
Woodstock, *Ont., Canada* **70 D3** 43 10N 80 45W
Woodstock, *U.K.* **11 F6** 51 51N 1 20W
Woodstock, *Ill., U.S.A.* **80 D10** 42 19N 88 27W
Woodstock, *Vt., U.S.A.* **79 C12** 43 37N 72 31W
Woodsville, *U.S.A.* **79 B13** 44 9N 72 2W
Woodville, *N.Z.* **59 J5** 40 20S 175 53 E
Woodville, *U.S.A.* **81 K7** 30 47N 94 25W
Woodward, *U.S.A.* **81 G5** 36 26N 99 24W
Woody, *U.S.A.* **85 K8** 35 42N 118 50W
Woolamai, C., *Australia* **63 F4** 38 30S 145 23 E
Wooler, *U.K.* **10 B5** 55 33N 2 1W
Woolgoolga, *Australia* **63 E5** 30 6S 153 11 E
Woombye, *Australia* **63 D5** 26 40S 152 55 E
Woomera, *Australia* **63 E2** 31 5S 136 50 E
Woonsocket, *R.I., U.S.A.* **79 E13** 42 0N 71 31W
Woonsocket, *S. Dak., U.S.A.* **80 C5** 44 3N 98 17W
Wooramel, *Australia* **61 E1** 25 45S 114 17 E
Wooramel →, *Australia* **61 E1** 25 47S 114 10 E
Wooroloo, *Australia* **61 F2** 31 48S 116 18 E
Wooster, *U.S.A.* **78 F3** 40 48N 81 56W

Z

World: Regions in the News

Maps show the situation in June 1998

FORMER YUGOSLAVIA

0 50 100 150 200 km

- ·—··—·· International boundaries
- ·——·——· Republic boundaries
- ·———·——· Province boundaries
- ■ Capital cities
- ——— Dayton Peace Agreement Boundary
- ☐ Muslim-Croat Federation
- ☐ Bosnian Serb Republic

THE BREAK-UP OF YUGOSLAVIA

The former country of Yugoslavia comprised six republics. In 1991 Slovenia and Croatia declared independence. Bosnia-Herzegovina followed in 1992 and Macedonia in 1993. Yugoslavia now comprises the remaining two republics, Serbia and Montenegro.

YUGOSLAVIA
Population: 10,881,000 (Serb 62.6%, Albanian 16.5%, Montenegrin 5%, Hungarian 3.3%, Muslim 3.2%)

Serbia Population: 6,060,000 (Serb 87.7%, excluding the former autonomous provinces of Kosovo and Vojvodina)

Kosovo Population: 1,989,050 (Albanian 81.6%, Serb 9.9%)
Vojvodina Population: 2,131,900 (Serb 56.8%, Hungarian 16.9%)

Montenegro Population: 700,050 (Montenegrin 61.9%, Muslim 14.6%, Albanian 7%)

CROATIA
Population: 4,850,000 (Croat 78.1%, Serb 12.2%)

SLOVENIA
Population: 2,000,000 (Slovene 88%)

MACEDONIA (F. Y. R. O. M.)
Population: 2,150,000 (Macedonian 64%, Albanian 21.7%, Turkish 5%)

BOSNIA-HERZEGOVINA
Population: 3,600,000 (Muslim 49%, Serb 31.2%, Croat 17.2%)

TAIWAN

0 50 100 150 200 km

- ☐ Territory of People's Republic of China
- ☐ Territory of Republic of China (Taiwan)

SOUTH CHINA SEA

0 250 500 km

- ▲ Philippine terr.
- ▼ Vietnamese terr.
- ■ Chinese terr.
- ● Taiwanese terr.
- —·— Philippine claim
- ——— Vietnamese claim
- —·—·— Chinese claim
- ······· Malaysian claim

THE CAUCASUS

0 100 200 km

- ·—··—·· International boundaries
- ·——·——· Republic boundaries

Georgia, Armenia and Azerbaijan achieved independence in 1991. Abkhazia, Ajaria and South Ossetia seek independence from Georgia. Chechenia has been trying to break away from Russia since 1991, but Russia has resisted with military force. Hostility also continues between Armenia and Azerbaijan over the enclave of Nagorno-Karabakh.

COUNTRIES AND REPUBLICS OF THE CAUCASUS REGION

RUSSIAN REPUBLICS IN THE NEWS

North Ossetia (Alania) Population: 695,000 (Ossetian 53%, Russian 29%, Chechen 5.2%, Armenian 1.9%)

Chechenia Population: 1,308,000 (Chechen and Ingush 70.7%, Russian 23.1%, Armenian 1.2%)

Ingushetia (Split from Chechenia in June 1993) Population: 250,000

GEORGIA
Population: 5,450,000 (Georgian 70.1%, Armenian 8.1%, Russian 6.3%, Azerbaijani 5.7%, Ossetian 3%, Greek 2%, Abkhazian 2%)

Abkhazia Population: 537,500 (Georgian 45.7%, Abkhazian 17.8%, Armenian 14.6%, Russian 14.3%)

Ajaria Population: 382,000 (Georgian 82.8%, Russian 7.7%, Armenian 4%)

ARMENIA
Population: 3,800,000 (Armenian 93%, Azerbaijani 3%)

Nagorno-Karabakh Population: 192,400 (Armenian 76.9%, Azerbaijani 21.5%)

AZERBAIJAN
Population: 7,650,000 (Azerbaijani 83%, Russian 6%, Armenian 6%, Lezgin 2%)

Naxçivan Population: 300,400

ISRAEL
Population: 5,900,000 (inc. East Jerusalem and Jewish settlers in the areas under Israeli administration. (Jewish 82%, Arab Muslim 13.8%, Arab Christian 2.5%, Druze 1.7%)

West Bank
Population: 1,122,900 (Palestinian Arabs 97% [of whom Arab Muslim 85%, Jewish 7%, Christian 8%])

Gaza Strip
Population: 748,400 (Arab Muslim 98%)

JORDAN
Population: 5,600,000 (Arab 99% [of whom about 50% are Palestinian Arab])

- ·—··—·· 1949 Armistice Line
- ·——·——· 1974 Cease-fire Lines
- ● Efrata Main Jewish settlements in the West Bank and Gaza Strip
- ■ Halhul Main Palestinian Arab towns in the West Bank and Gaza Strip
- ■ 'Amman Capital cities

THE NEAR EAST

0 25 50 km

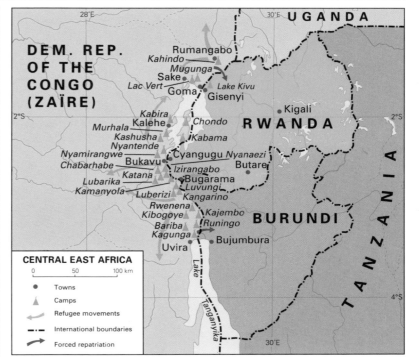

CENTRAL EAST AFRICA

0 50 100 km

- ● Towns
- ▲ Camps
- ⬅ Refugee movements
- ·—··—·· International boundaries
- ➡ Forced repatriation

KEY TO WORLD MAP PAGES

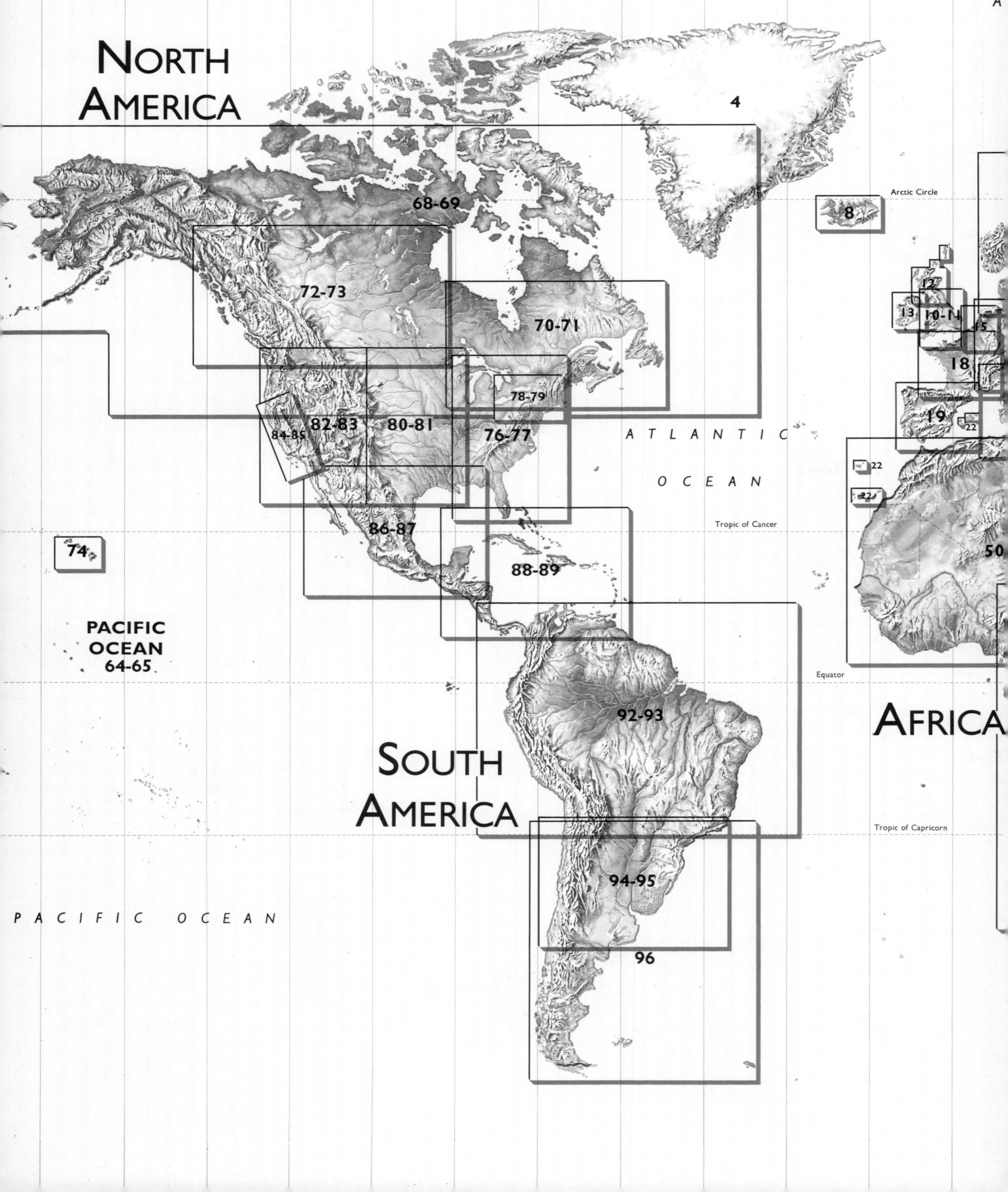

NORTH AMERICA

4

Arctic Circle

8

68-69

12

13 **10-14** **5**

72-73

70-71

18

78-79

19

ATLANTIC

22

82-83 **80-81** **76-77**

22

84-85

OCEAN

22

Tropic of Cancer

50

74

86-87

PACIFIC
OCEAN
64-65

88-89

Equator

AFRICA

92-93

SOUTH

AMERICA

Tropic of Capricorn

94-95

PACIFIC OCEAN

96